House of Representatives

HOUSE OF REPRESENTATIVES.—Situated in the left wing of the Capitol, as you approach from the east of it. Here Congress meets and at times it becomes quite a busy place.

A COMPILATION

OF THE

MESSAGES AND PAPERS

OF THE

PRESIDENTS

Prepared Under the Direction of the Joint Committee
on Printing, of the House and Senate,
Pursuant to an Act of the Fifty-Second Congress
of the United States

(With Additions and Encyclopedic Index
by Private Enterprise)

VOLUME VIII

PUBLISHED BY

BUREAU OF NATIONAL LITERATURE

1913

Prefatory Note

This volume comprises the Garfield-Arthur term of four years and the first term of Cleveland. The period covered is from March 4, 1881, to March 4, 1889. The death of President Garfield at the hand of an assassin early in his Administration created a vacancy in the office of the Chief Executive, and for the fourth time in our history the Vice-President succeeded to that office. The intense excitement throughout the land brought about by the tragic death of the President, and the succession of the Vice-President, caused no dangerous strain upon our institutions, and once more proof was given, if, indeed, further evidence was required, that our Government was strong enough to quietly and peacefully endure a sudden change of rulers and of administration, no matter how distressing and odious the cause.

During the Administration of President Arthur a treaty between the United States and the Republic of Nicaragua was signed, providing for an interoceanic canal across the territory of that State. An able and learned discussion of this proposition will be found among his papers. This treaty was pending when he retired from office, and was promptly withdrawn by President Cleveland. The act to regulate and improve the civil service of the United States was approved by President Arthur, and he put into operation rules and regulations wide in their scope and far-reaching for the enforcement of the measure. In his papers will be found frequent and interesting discussions of this question. His vetoes of "An act to execute certain treaty stipulations relating to Chinese" and of "An act making appropriations for the construction, repair, and preservation of certain works on rivers and harbors, and for other purposes," are interesting and effective papers.

The latter half of the period comprised in this volume, as already stated, covers the Administration of Cleveland. His accession to the Presidency marked the return of the Democratic party to power. No

Democrat who had been chosen by his party had held the office since the retirement of Buchanan, in 1861. President Cleveland's papers fill 558 pages of this volume, occupying more space than any other Chief Magistrate, Andrew Johnson being next with 457 pages. At an early date after Mr. Cleveland's inauguration he became involved in an important and rather acrimonious discussion with the Senate on the subject of suspensions from office. The Senate demanded of him and of the heads of some of the Executive Departments the reasons for the suspension of certain officials and the papers and correspondence incident thereto. In an exhaustive and interesting paper he declined to comply with the demand. His annual message of December, 1887, was devoted exclusively to a discussion of the tariff. It is conceded by all to be an able document, and is the only instance where a President in his annual message made reference to only one question. His vetoes are more numerous than those of any other Chief Executive, amounting within the four years to over three hundred, or more than twice the number in the aggregate of all his predecessors. These vetoes relate to almost all subjects of legislation, but mainly to pension cases and bills providing for the erection of public buildings throughout the country.

JAMES D. RICHARDSON.

NOTE.

The pages of "The Messages and Papers of the Presidents" have been renumbered from page one to the end, and the division into volumes has been altered. This plan is required by the addition of new matter and the desirability of keeping the volumes as nearly uniform in size as possible.

ILLUSTRATIONS IN VOLUME EIGHT

The United States provided a proper tribunal for the trial of claims founded upon Mexican grants. This claim was there tried, and if fraud affected the judgment it is not, I think, chargeable to the Government; the contest was chiefly between rival claimants. In this state of the case it would seem that if the United States consents to open the litigation and to wipe out all judicial findings and decrees a less exacting measure of damages than that proposed in the bill should be agreed on.

It is not my purpose, as I have intimated, to express the opinion that Mr. McGarrahan is entitled to no relief. It seems to me, however, clear that he is not entitled to the relief given by this bill, and that it does not adequately protect the interests of the United States.

BENJ. HARRISON.

EXECUTIVE MANSION, *August 3, 1892.*

To the Senate:

I return herewith without my approval the bill (S. 1111) entitled "An act to amend the act of Congress approved March 3, 1887, entitled 'An act to provide for the bringing of suits against the Government of the United States.'"

If I may judge from the very limited discussion of this measure in Congress, the sweeping effects of it upon the administration of the public lands could hardly have been fully realized. From the beginning of the Government the administration of the public lands and the issuing of patents under the land laws have been an Executive function.

The jurisdiction of the courts as to contesting claims for patents has awaited the action of the General Land Office. Land offices have been established and maintained in all the districts where public lands were found, located with reference to the convenience of the settlers, and the proceedings have been informal and inexpensive. It is true that at times, by an administration of the Land Office unfriendly toward the settlers, unnecessary delays involving much hardship have intervened in the issuing of patents, but such is not the case now. The work of the Land Office within the last three years has been so efficient and so friendly to the *bona fide* settler that the large accumulation of cases there has been swept away, and the office, as I am informed by the Secretary of the Interior, is now engaged upon current business.

It seems to me that a transfer in whole or in part of this business to the courts, some of whose dockets are already loaded with cases, can not tend to expedition, while it is very manifest that, by reason of the greater formality in the taking and presentation of evidence which would be required in court and of the long distances which settlers would have to traverse in order to attend court, the costs in such cases would be enormously increased.

It is proposed by this bill to give what is called concurrent jurisdiction to the district courts of the United States and to the Court of Claims to hear and determine all claims for land patents under any law or grant of the United States. Whether concurrent with each other or with each other and the Land Office is not clear.

It is quite doubtful under the rulings of the Supreme Court whether the courts now provided by law for the Territories are "district courts of the United States" within the meaning of this bill. The effect of this legislation would, if they were held not to be such, be that as to all suits relating to lands in the Territories of New Mexico, Arizona, Utah, and Oklahoma no other forum is provided than the Court of Claims at Washington. In this state of the case a settler, or one who has taken a mineral claim in any of these Territories, would be subject to be brought to the city of Washington for the trial of his case.

In view of the fact that all recent legislation of Congress has been in the direction of subdividing judicial districts and of bringing the United States courts nearer to the litigants, I can only attribute to oversight the passage of this bill, which in my opinion would burden the homesteader and preemptor whose claim is contested, whether by another individual or by any corporation, by compelling him to appear at Washington and to conduct with the formality and expense incident to court proceedings the defense of his title. But even in the case of land contests arising in the States where district courts exist the plaintiff, it will be observed, by this act is given the option to sue in those courts or to bring his adversary to Washington to litigate the claim. Why should he have this advantage, one that is not given so far as I know in any other law fixing the forum of litigation between individuals? Not only is this true, but the Court of Claims was established for the trial of cases between individuals and corporations on the one side and the United States on the other, and so far as I now recall wholly for the trial of money claims.

There are no adequate provisions of law, if any at all, for conducting suits between individuals contesting private rights. The court has one bailiff and one messenger, no marshal, and is not provided, I think, either with the machinery or with the appropriation to send its processes to the most distant parts of the country. Yet it is apparent that under this bill the real issue would frequently be between rival claimants, and not between either and the United States. This court, too, is already burdened with business since the reference to it of the Indian depredation claims, the French spoliation claims, etc., and it certainly can not be thought that a more speedy settlement of land claims could be there obtained than is now given.

Again, the bill is so indefinite in its provisions that it can not be told, I think, what function, if any, remains to be discharged by the General Land Office. It was said in answer to an interrogatory when the bill was under consideration that it did not affect claims pending in the Land Office; and yet it seems to me that its effect is to allow any contestant in the Land Office at any stage of the proceedings there to transfer the whole controversy to the courts. He may take his chances of success in the Land Office, and if at any time he becomes apprehensive of an adverse decision he may begin *de novo* in the courts.

If it was intended to preserve the jurisdiction of the Land Office and to hold cases there until a judgment had been reached, the bill should have so provided, for it is capable of, and indeed seems to me compels, the construction that either party may forsake the Land Office at any stage of a contest. I am quite inclined to believe that if provision were made, as in section 1063 of the Revised Statutes, relating to claims in other departments, for the transfer to a proper court, under proper regulations, of certain contest cases involving questions affecting large classes of claims, it would be a relief to the Land Office and would tend to a more speedy adjustment of land titles in such cases, a result which would be in the interest of all our people.

Nothing is more disadvantageous to a community, its progress and peace, than unsettled land titles. This bill, however, as I have said, is so radical and seems to me to be so indefinite in its provisions that I can not give it my approval.

BENJ. HARRISON.

PROCLAMATIONS.

By the President of the United States of America.

A PROCLAMATION.

Whereas, pursuant to section 3 of the act of Congress approved October 1, 1890, entitled "An act to reduce the revenue and equalize duties on imports, and for other purposes," the Secretary of State of the United States of America communicated to the Government of Salvador the action of the Congress of the United States of America, with a view to secure reciprocal trade, in declaring the articles enumerated in said section 3 to be exempt from duty upon their importation into the United States of America; and

Whereas the envoy extraordinary and minister plenipotentiary of Salvador at Washington has communicated to the Secretary of State the fact that, in reciprocity for the admission into the United States of America free of all duty of the articles enumerated in section 3 of said act, the Government of Salvador will by due legal enactment, as a provisional measure and until a more complete arrangement may be negotiated and put in operation, admit free of all duty, from and after February 1, 1892, into all the established ports of entry of Salvador the articles or merchandise named in the following schedule, provided that the same be the product or manufacture of the United States:

SCHEDULE OF PRODUCTS AND MANUFACTURES WHICH THE REPUBLIC OF SALVA-
DOR WILL ADMIT FREE OF ALL CUSTOMS, MUNICIPAL, AND ANY OTHER KIND
OF DUTY.

1. Animals for breeding purposes.
2. Corn, rice, barley, and rye.
3. Beans.
4. Hay and straw for forage.
5. Fruits, fresh.
6. Preparations of flour in biscuits, crackers not sweetened, macaroni, vermicelli, and tallarin.
7. Coal, mineral.
8. Roman cement.
9. Hydraulic lime.
10. Bricks, fire bricks, and crucibles for melting.
11. Marble, dressed, for furniture, statues, fountains, gravestones, and building purposes.
12. Tar, vegetable and mineral.
13. Guano and other fertilizers, natural or artificial.
14. Plows and all other agricultural tools and implements.
15. Machinery of all kinds, including sewing machines, and separate or extra parts for the same.
16. Materials of all kinds for the construction and equipment of railroads.
17. Materials of all kinds for the construction and operation of telegraphic and telephonic lines.
18. Materials of all kinds for lighting by electricity and gas.
19. Materials of all kinds for the construction of wharves.
20. Apparatus for distilling liquors.
21. Wood of all kinds for building, in trunks or pieces, beams, rafters, planks, boards, shingles, or flooring.
22. Wooden staves, heads, and hoops, and barrels and boxes for packing, mounted or in pieces.
23. Houses of wood or iron, complete or in parts.
24. Wagons, carts, and carriages of all kinds.
25. Barrels, casks, and tanks of iron for water.
26. Tubes of iron and all other accessories necessary for water supply.
27. Wire, barbed, and staples for fences.
28. Plates of iron for building purposes.
29. Mineral ores.
30. Kettles of iron for making salt.
31. Kettles of iron for making sugar.
32. Molds for making sugar.
33. Guys for mining purposes.
34. Furnaces and instruments for assaying metals.
35. Scientific instruments.
36. Models of machinery and buildings.
37. Boats, lighters, tackle, anchors, chains, girtlines, sails, and all other articles for vessels, to be used in the ports, lakes, and rivers of the Republic.
38. Printing materials, including presses, type, ink, and all other accessories.
39. Printed books, pamphlets, and newspapers, bound or unbound, maps, photographs, printed music, and paper for music.
40. Paper for printing newspapers.
41. Quicksilver.
42. Loadstones.
43. Hops.

44. Sulphate of quinine.
45. Gold and silver in bars, dust, or coin.
46. Samples of merchandise the duties on which do not exceed $1.

It is understood that the packages or coverings in which the articles named in the foregoing schedule are imported shall be free of duty if they are usual and proper for the purpose.

And that the Government of Salvador has further stipulated that the laws and regulations adopted to protect its revenue and prevent fraud in the declarations and proof that the articles named in the foregoing sched-ule are the product or manufacture of the United States of America shall impose no additional charges on the importer nor undue restrictions on the articles imported; and

Whereas the Secretary of State has, by my direction, given assurance to the envoy extraordinary and minister plenipotentiary of Salvador at Washington that this action of the Government of Salvador in granting freedom of duties to the products and manufactures of the United States of America on their importation into Salvador and in stipulating for a more complete reciprocity arrangement is accepted as a due reciprocity for the action of Congress as set forth in section 3 of said act:

Now, therefore, be it known that I, Benjamin Harrison, President of the United States of America, have caused the above-stated modifications of the tariff laws of Salvador to be made public for the information of the citizens of the United States of America.

In testimony whereof I have hereunto set my hand and caused the seal of the United States to be affixed.

[SEAL.]   Done at the city of Washington, this 31st day of December, 1891, and of the Independence of the United States of America the one hundred and sixteenth.

By the President: BENJ. HARRISON.

JAMES G. BLAINE, *Secretary of State.*

BY THE PRESIDENT OF THE UNITED STATES OF AMERICA.

A PROCLAMATION.

Whereas it is provided by section 24 of the act of Congress approved March 3, 1891, entitled "An act to repeal timber-culture laws, and for other purposes"—

That the President of the United States may from time to time set apart and reserve in any State or Territory having public land bearing forests, in any part of the public lands wholly or in part covered with timber or undergrowth, whether of commercial value or not, as public reservations; and the President shall by public proclamation declare the establishment of such reservation and the limits thereof.

And whereas the public lands in the Territory of New Mexico within the limits hereinafter described are in part covered with timber, and it appears that the public good would be promoted by setting apart and reserving said lands as a public reservation:

Now, therefore, I, Benjamin Harrison, President of the United States,

by virtue of the power in me vested by section 24 of the aforesaid act of Congress, do hereby make known and proclaim that there is hereby reserved from entry or settlement and set apart as a public reservation all those certain tracts, pieces, or parcels of land lying and being situate in the Territory of New Mexico and particularly described as follows, to wit:

Commencing at the standard corner to township seventeen (17) north, ranges thirteen (13) and fourteen (14) east (New Mexico principal base and meridian) on the fourth (4th) standard parallel north; thence northerly along the range line between ranges thirteen (13) and fourteen (14) east to the closing corner between ranges thirteen (13) and fourteen (14) east on the fifth (5th) standard parallel north; thence along said fifth (5th) standard parallel to the southeast corner of township twenty-one (21) north, range thirteen (13) east; thence north six (6) miles; thence west twelve (12) miles; thence due south to the fifth (5th) standard parallel; thence westerly on said fifth (5th) standard parallel to a point due north of the northwest corner of township seventeen (17) north, range eleven (11) east; thence south to the fourth (4th) standard parallel; thence westerly on said fourth (4th) standard parallel north seven and sixty-two one-hundredths (7.62) chains to the northwest corner of township sixteen (16) north, range eleven (11) east; thence southerly on the range line between townships sixteen (16) north, ranges ten (10) and eleven (11) east, three (3) miles and three and forty-three hundredths (3.43) chains to the corner to sections thirteen (13), eighteen (18), nineteen (19), and twenty-four (24) on said range line; thence easterly along the section lines to the range line between ranges eleven (11) and twelve (12) east; thence northerly three (3) miles and three (3) chains to the fourth (4th) standard parallel north; thence easterly on said fourth (4th) standard parallel eight (8) and fifty-hundredths (8.50) chains to the standard corner to township seventeen (17) north, ranges eleven (11) and twelve (12) east; thence northerly on the range line to the southwest corner of township eighteen (18) north, range twelve (12) east; thence easterly on the township line six (6) miles one and six-hundredths (1.06) chains to the southeast corner of township eighteen (18) north, range twelve (12) east; thence south six (6) miles to the fourth (4th) standard parallel north; thence east along said fourth (4th) standard parallel to the place of beginning.

Excepting from the force and effect of this proclamation all land which may have been prior to the date hereof embraced in any valid Spanish or Mexican grant or in any legal entry or covered by any lawful filing duly made in the proper United States land office, and all mining claims duly located and held according to the laws of the United States and rules and regulations not in conflict therewith.

Provided, That this exception shall not continue to apply to any particular tract of land unless the entryman or claimant continues to comply with the law under which the entry, filing, or location was made.

Warning is hereby expressly given to all persons not to enter or make settlement upon the tract of land reserved by this proclamation.

In witness whereof I have hereunto set my hand and caused the seal of the United States to be affixed.

[SEAL.] Done at the city of Washington, this 11th day of January, A. D. 1892, and of the Independence of the United States the one hundred and sixteenth. BENJ. HARRISON.

By the President:

JAMES G. BLAINE, *Secretary of State.*

BY THE PRESIDENT OF THE UNITED STATES OF AMERICA.

A PROCLAMATION.

Whereas, pursuant to section 3 of the act of Congress approved October 1, 1890, entitled "An act to reduce the revenue and equalize duties on imports, and for other purposes," the attention of the Government of Great Britain was called to the action of the Congress of the United States of America, with a view to secure reciprocal trade, in declaring the articles enumerated in said section 3 to be exempt from duty upon their importation into the United States of America; and

Whereas the envoy extraordinary and minister plenipotentiary of Great Britain at Washington has communicated to the Secretary of State the fact that, in view of the act of Congress above cited, the Government of Great Britain has by due legal enactment authorized the admission, from and after February 1, 1892, of the articles in merchandise named in the following schedules, on the terms stated therein, into the British colonies of Trinidad (which includes Tobago), Barbados, the Leeward Islands (consisting of the islands of Antigua, Montserrat, St. Christopher, Nevis, Dominica, with their respective dependencies, and the Virgin Islands), the Windward Islands (consisting of St. Lucia, St. Vincent, and their dependencies, but exclusive of Grenada and its dependencies), and into the colony of British Guiana on and after April 1, 1892:

TABLE NO. 1.—APPLICABLE TO BRITISH GUIANA, TRINIDAD AND TOBAGO, BARBADOS, THE LEEWARD ISLANDS, AND THE WINDWARD ISLANDS EXCEPTING THE ISLAND OF GRENADA.

SCHEDULE A.

Articles to be admitted free of all customs duty and any other national, colonial, or municipal charges:

1. Animals, alive, to include only asses, sheep, goats, hogs, and poultry, and horses for breeding.
2. Beef, including tongues, smoked and dried.
3. Beef and pork preserved in cans.
4. Belting for machinery, of leather, canvas, or india rubber.
5. Boats and lighters.
6. Books,* bound or unbound, pamphlets, newspapers, and printed matter in all languages.
7. Bones and horns.
8. Bottles of glass or stone ware.
9. Bran, middlings, and shorts.

* The importation of books is subject to the provisions of copyright laws.

10. Bridges of iron or wood, or of both combined.

11. Brooms, brushes, and whisks of broom straw.

12. Candles, tallow.

13. Carts, wagons, cars, and barrows, with or without springs, for ordinary roads and agricultural use, not including vehicles of pleasure.

14. Clocks, mantel or wall.

15. Copper, bronze, zinc, and lead articles, plain and nickel plated, for industrial and domestic uses and for building.

16. Cotton seed and its products.

17. Crucibles and melting pots of all kinds.

18. Eggs.

19. Fertilizers of all kinds, natural and artificial.

20. Fish, fresh or on ice, and salmon and oysters in cans.

21. Fishing apparatus of all kinds.

22. Fruits and vegetables, fresh and dried, when not canned, tinned, or bottled.

23. Gas fixtures and pipes.

24. Gold and silver coin of the United States, and bullion.

25. Hay and straw for forage.

26. Houses of wood, complete.

27. Ice.

28. India-rubber and gutta-percha goods, including waterproof clothing made wholly or in part thereof.

29. Implements, utensils, and tools for agriculture, exclusive of cutlasses and forks

30. Lamps and lanterns.

31. Lime of all kinds.

32. Locomotives, railway rolling stock, rails, railway ties, and all materials an appliances for railways and tramways.

33. Marble or alabaster, in the rough or squared, worked or carved, for buildin purposes or monuments.

34. Medicinal extracts and preparations of all kinds, including proprietary or pat ent medicines, but exclusive of quinine or preparations of quinine, opium, gange, and bhang.

35. Paper of all kinds for printing.

36. Paper of wood or straw for wrapping and packing, including surface coated o glazed.

37. Photographic apparatus and chemicals.

38. Printers' ink, all colors.

39. Printing presses, types, rules, spaces, and all accessories for printing.

40. Quicksilver.

41. Resin, tar, pitch, and turpentine.

42. Salt.

43. Sewing machines and all parts and accessories thereof.

44. Shipbuilding materials and accessories of all kinds, when used in the construc tion, equipment, or repair of vessels or boats of any kind, except rope and cordage of all kinds, including wire rope.

45. Starch of Indian corn or maize.

46. Steam and power engines, and machines, machinery, and apparatus, whethe stationary or portable, worked by power or by hand, for agriculture, irrigation, min ing, the arts and industries of all kinds, and all necessary parts and appliances for the erection or repair thereof or the communication of motive power thereto.

47. Steam boilers and steam pipes.

48. Sulphur.

49. Tan bark of all kinds, whole or ground.

50. Telegraph wire, telegraphic, telephonic, and electrical apparatus and appli ances of all kinds for communication or illumination.

51. Trees, plants, vines, and seeds and grains of all kinds, for propagation o cultivation.

52. Varnish, not containing spirits.
53. Wall papers.
54. Watches when not cased in gold or silver, and watch movements uncased.
55. Water pipes of all classes, materials, and dimensions.
56. Wire for fences, the hooks, staples, nails, and the like appliances for fastening the same.
57. Yeast cake and baking powders.
58. Zinc, tin, and lead, in sheets, asbestus, and tar paper, for roofing.

It is understood that the packages or coverings in which the articles named in the foregoing schedule are imported shall be free of duty if they are usual and proper for the purpose.

SCHEDULE B.

Articles to be admitted at 50 per cent reduction of the duty designated in the respective customs tariff now in force in each of said colonies:

1. Bacon and bacon hams.
2. Boots and shoes made wholly or in part of leather.
3. Bread and biscuit.
4. Cheese.
5. Lard and its compounds.
6. Mules.
7. Oleomargarine.
8. Shooks and staves.

SCHEDULE C.

Articles to be admitted at 25 per cent reduction of the duty designated in the respective customs tariff now in force in each of said colonies:

1. Beef, salted or pickled.
2. Corn or maize.
3. Corn meal.
4. Flour of wheat.
5. Lumber of pitch pine, in rough or prepared for buildings.
6. Petroleum and its products, crude or refined.
7. Pork, salted or pickled.
8. Wheat.

It is understood that No. 4 of this schedule shall not apply to the colony of Trinidad, but it is stipulated that the duty on flour in said colony shall not exceed 75 cents per barrel.

And that the Government of Great Britain has by due legal enactment authorized the admission, from and after February 1, 1892, of the articles or merchandise named in the following schedules, on the terms stated therein, into the British colony of Jamaica and its dependencies:

TABLE NO. 2.—APPLICABLE TO THE COLONY OF JAMAICA AND ITS DEPENDENCIES.

SCHEDULE A.

Articles to be admitted free of all customs duty and any other national, colonial, or municipal charges:

1. Animals, alive, and poultry.
2. Beef, including tongues, smoked and dried.
3. Beef and pork preserved in cans.
4. Belting for machinery, of leather, canvas, or india rubber.
5. Boats and lighters.
6. Books,* bound or unbound, pamphlets, newspapers, and printed matter in all languages.
7. Bones and horns.

*The importation of books is subject to the provisions of copyright laws.

8. Bottles of glass or stone ware.

9. Bran, middlings, and shorts.

10. Bridges of iron or wood, or of both combined.

11. Brooms, brushes, and whisks of broom straw.

12. Candles, tallow.

13. Carts, wagons, cars, and barrows, with or without springs, for ordinary roads and agricultural use, not including vehicles of pleasure.

14. Coal and coke.

15. Clocks, mantel or wall.

16. Cotton seed and its products, to include meal, meal cake, oil, and cottolene.

17. Crucibles and melting pots of all kinds.

18. Drawings, paintings, engravings, lithographs, and photographs

19. Eggs.

20. Fertilizers of all kinds, natural and artificial.

21. Fish, fresh or on ice, and oysters in cans.

22. Fishing apparatus of all kinds.

23. Fruits and vegetables, fresh and dried, when not canned, tinned, or bottled.

24. Gas fixtures and pipes.

25. Gold and silver coin of the United States, and bullion.

26. Hay and straw for forage.

27. Houses of wood, complete.

28. Ice.

29. India-rubber and gutta-percha goods, including waterproof clothing made wholly or in part thereof.

30. Implements, utensils, and tools for agriculture, exclusive of cutlasses and forks.

31. Iron, galvanized.

32. Iron for roofing.

33. Lamps and lanterns, not exceeding 10 shillings each in value.

34. Lime of all kinds.

35. Locomotives, railway rolling stock, rails, railway ties, and all materials and appliances for railways and tramways.

36. Marble or alabaster, in the rough or squared, worked or carved, for building purposes or monuments.

37. Paper of all kinds for printing.

38. Paper of wood or straw for wrapping and packing, including surface coated or glazed.

39. Photographic apparatus and chemicals.

40. Printers' ink, all colors.

41. Printing presses, types, rules, spaces, and all accessories for printing.

42. Proprietary or patent medicines, recommended by their proprietors as calculated to cure disease or alleviate pain in the human subject.

43. Quicksilver.

44. Resin, tar, pitch, and turpentine.

45. Sewing machines and all parts and accessories thereof.

46. Shipbuilding materials and accessories of all kinds, when used in the construction, equipment, or repair of vessels or boats of any kind, except rope and cordage of all kinds, including wire rope, and subject to specific regulations to avoid abuse in the importation.

47. Shooks and staves.

48. Starch of Indian corn or maize.

49. Steam and power engines, and machines, machinery, and apparatus, whether stationary or portable, worked by power or by hand, for agriculture, irrigation, mining, the arts and industries of all kinds, and all necessary parts and appliances for the erection or repair thereof or the communication of motive power thereto.

50. Steam boilers and steam pipes.
51. Sugar, refined.
52. Sulphur.
53. Tallow and animal greases.
54. Tan bark of all kinds, whole or ground.
55. Telegraph wire, telegraphic, telephonic, and electrical apparatus and appliances of all kinds for communication or illumination.
56. Trees, plants, vines, and seeds and grains of all kinds for propagation or cultivation.
57. Varnish, not containing spirits.
58. Wall papers.
59. Watches when not cased in gold or silver, and watch movements uncased.
60. Water pipes of all classes, materials, and dimensions.
61. Wire for fences, with the hooks, staples, nails, and the like appliances for fastening the same.
62. Yeast cake and baking powders.
63. Zinc, tin, and lead, in sheets, asbestus, and tar paper, for roofing.

It is understood that the packages or coverings in which the articles named in the foregoing schedule are imported shall be free of duty if they are usual and proper for the purpose.

SCHEDULE B.

Articles to be admitted at 50 per cent reduction of the duty designated in the customs tariff now in force:
1. Bacon and bacon hams.
2. Bread and biscuit.
3. Butter.
4. Cheese.
5. Lard and its compounds.

Lumber of pitch pine, in rough or prepared for buildings, to be reduced to 9 shillings per 1,000 feet.

SCHEDULE C.

Articles to be admitted at 25 per cent reduction of the duty designated in the customs tariff now in force:
1. Beef, salted or pickled.
2. Corn and maize.
3. Corn meal.
4. Oats.
5. Petroleum and its products, crude or refined.
6. Pork, salted or pickled.
7. Wheat.

And whereas the Secretary of State has, by my direction, given the assurance to the envoy extraordinary and minister plenipotentiary of Great Britain at Washington that this action of the Government of Great Britain in granting remissions and alterations of duties in the British colonies above mentioned is accepted as a due reciprocity for the action of Congress as set forth in section 3 of said act:

Now, therefore, be it known that I, Benjamin Harrison, President of the United States of America, have caused the above-stated modifications of the tariff laws of the aforesaid British colonies to be made public for the information of the citizens of the United States of America.

In testimony whereof I have hereunto set my hand and caused the seal of the United States to be affixed.

[SEAL.]   Done at the city of Washington, this 1st day of February, 1892, and of the Independence of the United States of America the one hundred and sixteenth.

BENJ. HARRISON.

By the President:

JAMES G. BLAINE, *Secretary of State.*

BY THE PRESIDENT OF THE UNITED STATES OF AMERICA.

A PROCLAMATION.

Whereas, pursuant to section 3 of the act of Congress approved October 1, 1890, entitled "An act to reduce the revenue and equalize duties on imports and for other purposes," the attention of the Government of the German Empire was called to the action of the Congress of the United States of America, with a view to secure reciprocal trade, in declaring the articles enumerated in said section 3 to be exempt from duty upon their importation into the United States of America; and

Whereas the chargé d'affaires of the German Empire at Washington has communicated to the special plenipotentiary of the United States the fact that, in view of the act of Congress above cited, the German Imperial Government has by due legal enactment authorized the admission, from and after February 1, 1892, into the German Empire of the articles or merchandise the product of the United States of America named in the following schedule, on the terms stated therein:

Schedules of articles to be admitted into Germany.

Articles.	Rate of duty per 100 kilograms.
	Marks.
1. Bran; malted germs..	Free.
2. Flax, raw, dried, broken, or hatcheled; also refuse portions...........	Free.
3. Wheat..	3.50
4. Rye	3.50
5. Oats...	2.80
6. Buckwheat...	2.00
7. Pulse...	1.50
8. Other kinds of grain not specially mentioned	1.00
9. Barley..	2.00
10. Rape seed, turnip seed, poppy, sesame, peanuts, and other oleaginous products not specially mentioned.................................	2.00
11. Maize (Indian corn)..	1.60
12. Malt (malted barley)..	3.60
13. Anise, coriander, fennel, and caraway seed........................	3.00
14. Agricultural productions not otherwise designated.................	Free.
15. Horsehair, raw, hatcheled, boiled, dyed, also laid in the form of tresses and spun; bristles; raw bed feathers...............................	Free.

Schedules of articles to be admitted into Germany—Continued.

Articles.	Rate of duty per 100 kilograms.
	Marks.
16. Bed feathers, cleaned and prepared..........................	Free.
17. Hides and skins, raw (green, salted, limed, dried), and stripped of the hair for the manufacture of leather..............	Free.
18. Charcoal	Free.
19. Bark of wood and tan bark...............................	Free.
20. Lumber and timber:	
(*a*) Raw or merely roughhewn with ax or saw, with or without bark; oaken barrel staves....................	0. 20
(*b*) Marked in the direction of the longitudinal axis, or prepared or cut otherwise than by roughhewing; barrel staves not included under (*a*); unpeeled osiers and hoops; hubs, fellies, and spokes..	0. 30
(*c*) Sawed in the direction of the longitudinal axis; unplaned boards; sawed cantle woods and other articles sawn or hewn	0. 80
21. Wood in cut veneering; unglued, unstained parts of floors............	5. 00
22. Hops; also hop meal....................................	*14. 00
23. Butter; also artificial butter...............................	17. 00
24. Meat, slaughtered, fresh, with the exception of pork..............	15. 00
25. Pork, slaughtered, fresh, and dressed meat, with the exception of bacon, fresh or prepared	17. 00
26. Game of all kinds (not alive)............................	20. 00
27. Cheese, except Strecchino, Gorgonzola, and Parmesan................	20. 00
28. Fruit, seeds, berries, leaves, flowers, mushrooms, vegetables, dried, baked, pulverized, only boiled down or salted—all these products so far as they are not included under other numbers of the tariff; juices of fruits, berries, and turnips, preserved without sugar, to be eaten; dry nuts..............................	4. 00
29. Mill products of grain and pulse, to wit, ground or shelled grains, peeled barley, groats, grits, flour, common cakes (bakers' products)..	7. 30
30. Residue, solid, from the manufacture of fat oils, also ground..........	Free.
31. Goose grease and other greasy fats, such as oleomargarine, sperfett (a mixture of stearic fats with oil), beef marrow.....................	10. 00
32. Live animals and animal products not mentioned elsewhere; also beehives with live bees	Free.
33. Horses (remarks).......................................each..	20. 00
(*a*) Horses up to 2 years old ....do...	10. 00
(*b*) Colts following their dams.............................	Free.
34. Bulls and cows...	9. 00
35. Oxen..	25. 50
36. Calves less than 6 weeks old...............................	3. 00
37. Hogs	5. 00
38. Pigs weighing less than 10 kilograms........................	1. 00
39. Sheep..	1. 00
40. Lambs	0. 50
41. Wool, including animal hair not mentioned elsewhere, as well as stuffs made thereof:	
(*a*) Wool, raw, dyed, ground; also hair, raw, hatcheled, boiled, dyed; also curled...	Free.

* Gross.

And whereas the special plenipotentiary of the United States has, by my direction, given assurance to the chargé d'affaires of the German Empire at Washington that this action of the Government of the German Empire in granting exemption of duties to the products and manufactures of the United States of America on their importation into Germany is accepted as a due reciprocity for the action of Congress as set forth in section 3 of said act:

Now, therefore, be it known that I, Benjamin Harrison, President of the United States of America, have caused the above-stated modifications of the tariff laws of the German Empire to be made public for the information of the citizens of the United States of America.

In testimony whereof I have hereunto set my hand and caused the seal of the United States to be affixed.

[SEAL.]   Done at the city of Washington, this 1st day of February, 1892, and of the Independence of the United States of America the one hundred and sixteenth.

BENJ. HARRISON.

By the President:

JAMES G. BLAINE,
    Secretary of State.

BY THE PRESIDENT OF THE UNITED STATES OF AMERICA.

A PROCLAMATION.

Whereas it is provided by section 24 of the act of Congress approved March 3, 1891, entitled "An act to repeal timber-culture laws, and for other purposes"—

That the President of the United States may from time to time set apart and reserve in any State or Territory having public land bearing forests, in any part of the public lands wholly or in part covered with timber or undergrowth, whether of commercial value or not, as public reservations; and the President shall by public proclamation declare the establishment of such reservations and the limits thereof.

And whereas the public lands in the State of Colorado within the limits hereafter described are in part covered with timber, and it appears that the public good would be promoted by setting apart and reserving said lands as a public reservation:

Now, therefore, I, Benjamin Harrison, President of the United States, by virtue of the power in me vested by section 24 of the aforesaid act of Congress, do hereby make known and proclaim that there is hereby reserved from entry or settlement and set apart as a public reservation all those certain tracts, pieces, or parcels of land lying and being situate in the State of Colorado and particularly described as follows, to wit:

Commencing at the northeast corner of section four (4), township eleven (11) north, range sixty-seven (67) west of the sixth (6th) principal meridian; thence proceeding westerly along the township line between townships ten (10) and eleven (11) south to the northwest corner of section six (6), township eleven (11) south, range sixty-eight (68) west; thence southerly along the range line between ranges sixty-eight (68) and sixty-nine (69) west to the southwest corner of section eighteen (18), township thirteen (13) south, range sixty-eight (68) west; thence westerly along the section line to the northwest corner of section nineteen (19), township thirteen (13) south, range sixty-nine (69) west; thence southerly along the range line between ranges sixty-nine (69) and seventy (70) west to the southwest corner of section thirty-one (31), township thirteen (13) south, range sixty-nine (69) west; thence east along the township line between townships thirteen (13) and fourteen (14) south to the half-section corner on said township line of section two (2), township fourteen (14) south, range sixty-nine (69) west; thence southerly through the middle of sections two (2), eleven (11), and fourteen (14) to a point in the middle of the north line of section twenty-three (23) of said township and range; thence easterly along said northern section line to the northeast corner of said section; thence southerly between sections twenty-three (23) and twenty-four (24) to the middle of the east line of section twenty-three (23); thence easterly through the middle of section twenty-four (24) to the middle of the east line of said section twenty-four (24), township fourteen (14) south, range sixty-nine (69) west; thence southerly along the range line between ranges sixty-eight (68) and sixty-nine (69) west to the southwest corner of section thirty-one (31), township fifteen (15) south, range sixty-eight (68) west; thence east along the township line between townships fifteen (15) and sixteen (16) south to the southeast corner of section thirty-four (34), township fifteen (15) south, range sixty-seven (67) west; thence northerly along the section line to the northeast corner of the southeast quarter of section twenty-two (22), township fifteen (15) south, range sixty-seven (67) west; thence westerly to the northwest corner of the southeast quarter of section twenty-one (21) of said last-named township and range; thence southerly to the southwest corner of the southeast quarter of section twenty-eight (28) of said township and range; thence westerly along the section line to the corner common to sections twenty-five (25), thirty-one (31), and thirty-six (36) of said township and range; thence northerly on the section line to the corner common to sections one (1), six (6), and twelve (12) of said township and range; thence easterly along the section line to the corner common to sections five (5), six (6), and eight (8); thence southerly along the section line to the southwest corner of section eight (8) of said township and range; thence easterly along the section line to the corner common to sections ten (10), eleven (11), and fourteen (14) of said township and range; thence northerly along the section line to the northeast corner of section three (3); thence westerly to the northwest corner of section three (3) of said township and range; thence northerly along the section line to the corner common to sections sixteen (16), twenty-one (21), twenty-two (22), and fifteen (15), township fourteen (14) south, range sixty-seven (67) west; thence westerly along the section line to the northwest corner of section nineteen (19) of said township and range; thence northerly along the range line between ranges sixty-seven (67) and sixty-eight (68) to the northeast corner of section one (1), township fourteen (14) south, range sixty-eight (68) west; thence easterly along the township line between townships thirteen (13) and fourteen (14) south to the southeast corner of section thirty-three (33) of township thirteen (13) south, range sixty-seven (67) west; thence northerly along the section line to the place of beginning.

Excepting from the force and effect of this proclamation all surveyed land which may have been prior to the date hereof embraced in any legal entry or covered by any lawful filing duly made in the proper United States land office, all unsurveyed lands on which valid settlement has been made under any law of the United States, and all mining claims duly located and held according to the laws of the United States and rules and regulations not in conflict therewith.

Provided, That this exception shall not continue to apply to any particular tract of land unless the entryman, settler, or claimant continues to comply with the law under which the entry, filing, settlement, or location was made.

Warning is hereby expressly given to all persons not to enter or make settlement upon the tract of land reserved by this proclamation.

In witness whereof I have hereunto set my hand and caused the seal of the United States to be affixed.

[SEAL.]　　Done at the city of Washington, this 11th day of February, A. D. 1892, and of the Independence of the United States the one hundred and sixteenth.　　　　BENJ. HARRISON.

By the President:
　　JAMES G. BLAINE,
　　　　Secretary of State.

BY THE PRESIDENT OF THE UNITED STATES OF AMERICA.

A PROCLAMATION.

The following provisions of the laws of the United States are hereby published for the information of all concerned:

Section 1956, Revised Statutes, chapter 3, Title XXIII, enacts that—

No person shall kill any otter, mink, marten, sable, or fur seal, or other fur-bearing animal within the limits of Alaska Territory or in the waters thereof; and every person guilty thereof shall for each offense be fined not less than $200 nor more than $1,000, or imprisoned not more than six months, or both; and all vessels, their tackle, apparel, furniture, and cargo, found engaged in violation of this section shall be forfeited; but the Secretary of the Treasury shall have power to authorize the killing of any such mink, marten, sable, or other fur-bearing animal, except fur seals, under such regulations as he may prescribe; and it shall be the duty of the Secretary to prevent the killing of any fur seal and to provide for the execution of the provisions of this section until it is otherwise provided by law, nor shall he grant any special privileges under this section.

Section 3 of the act entitled "An act to provide for the protection of the salmon fisheries of Alaska," approved March 2, 1889, provides that--

SEC. 3. That section 1956 of the Revised Statutes of the United States is hereby declared to include and apply to all the dominion of the United States in the waters of Bering Sea; and it shall be the duty of the President at a timely season in each year to issue his proclamation, and cause the same to be published for one month at least in one newspaper (if any such there be) published at each United States port of entry on the Pacific coast, warning all persons against entering said waters for the purpose of violating the provisions of said section; and he shall also cause one or more vessels of the United States to diligently cruise said waters and arrest all persons and seize all vessels found to be or to have been engaged in any violation of the laws of the United States therein.

Now, therefore, I, Benjamin Harrison, President of the United States, pursuant to the above-recited statutes, hereby warn all persons against entering the waters of Bering Sea within the dominion of the United States for the purpose of violating the provisions of said section 1956, Revised Statutes; and I hereby proclaim that all persons found to be or to have been engaged in any violation of the laws of the United States in said waters will be arrested and punished as above provided, and that all vessels so employed, their tackle, apparel, furniture, and cargoes, will be seized and forfeited.

In testimony whereof I have hereunto set my hand and caused the seal of the United States to be affixed.

[SEAL.] Done at the city of Washington, this 15th day of February, 1892, and of the Independence of the United States the one hundred and sixteenth.

BENJ. HARRISON.

By the President:

JAMES G. BLAINE,
Secretary of State.

BY THE PRESIDENT OF THE UNITED STATES OF AMERICA.

A PROCLAMATION.

Whereas, pursuant to section 3 of the act of Congress approved October 1, 1890, entitled "An act to reduce the revenue and equalize duties on imports, and for other purposes," the Secretary of State of the United States of America communicated to the Government of Nicaragua the action of the Congress of the United States of America, with a view to secure reciprocal trade, in declaring the articles enumerated in said section 3 to be exempt from duty upon their importation into the United States of America; and

Whereas the envoy extraordinary and minister plenipotentiary of Nicaragua at Washington has communicated to the Secretary of State the fact that, in reciprocity for the admission into the United States of America free of all duty of the articles enumerated in section 3 of said act, the

Government of Nicaragua will by due legal enactment admit free of all duty, from and after April 15, 1892, into all the ports of entry of Nicaragua the articles or merchandise named in the following schedule, provided that the same be the product of the United States:

SCHEDULE OF ARTICLES WHICH THE REPUBLIC OF NICARAGUA WILL ADMIT FREE OF ALL KIND OF DUTY.

1. Animals, live.
2. Barley, Indian corn, wheat, oats, rye, and rice.
3. Seeds of all kinds for agriculture and horticulture.
4. Live plants of all kinds.
5. Corn meal.
6. Starch.
7. Beans, potatoes, and all other vegetables, fresh or dried.
8. Fruits, fresh or dried.
9. Hay, bran, and straw for forage.
10. Cotton-seed oil and all other products of said seed.
11. Tar, resin, and turpentine.
12. Asphalt, crude or manufactured in blocks.
13. Quicksilver for mining purposes.
14. Coal, mineral or animal.
15. Fertilizers for land.
16. Lime and cement.
17. Wood and lumber, in the rough or prepared for building purposes.
18. Houses of wood or iron.
19. Marble, in the rough or dressed, for fountains, gravestones, and building purposes.
20. Tools and implements for agricultural and horticultural purposes.
21. Wagons, carts, and handcarts.
22. Iron and steel, in rails for railroads and other similar uses, and structural iron and steel for bridges and building purposes.
23. Wire, for fences, with or without barbs, clamps, posts, clips, and other accessories of wire, not less than 3 lines in diameter.
24. Machinery of all kinds for agricultural purposes, arts, and trades, and parts of such machinery.
25. Motors of steam or animal power.
26. Forgers, water pumps of metal, pump hose, sledge hammers, drills for mining purposes, iron piping with its keys and faucets, crucibles for melting metals, iron water tanks, and lightning rods.
27. Roofs of galvanized iron, gutters, ridging, clamps, and screws for the same.
28. Printing materials.
29. Books, pamphlets, and other printed matter, and ruled paper for printed music, printing paper in sheets not less than 29 by 20 inches.
30. Geographical maps or charts and celestial and terrestrial spheres or globes.
31. Surgical and mathematical instruments.
32. Stones and fire bricks for smelting furnaces.
33. Vessels and boats of all kinds, fitted together or in parts.
34. Gold and silver in bullion, bars, or coin.

It is understood that the packages or coverings in which the articles named in the foregoing schedule are imported shall be free of duty if they are usual and proper for the purpose.

And that the Government of Nicaragua has further stipulated that the laws and regulations adopted to protect its revenue and prevent fraud in the declarations and proof that the articles named in the foregoing schedule are the product of the United States of America shall impose no undue restrictions on the importer nor additional charges on the articles imported; and

Whereas the Secretary of State has, by my direction, given assurance to the envoy extraordinary and minister plenipotentiary of Nicaragua at Washington that this action of the Government of Nicaragua in granting freedom of duties to the products of the United States of America on their importation into Nicaragua is accepted as a due reciprocity for the action of Congress as set forth in section 3 of said act:

Now, therefore, be it known that I, Benjamin Harrison, President of the United States of America, have caused the above-stated modifications of the tariff laws of Nicaragua to be made public for the information of the citizens of the United States of America.

In testimony whereof I have hereunto set my hand and caused the seal of the United States to be affixed.

[SEAL.] Done at the city of Washington, this 12th day of March, 1892, and of the Independence of the United States of America the one hundred and sixteenth.

BENJ. HARRISON.

By the President:
WILLIAM F. WHARTON,
Acting Secretary of State.

BY THE PRESIDENT OF THE UNITED STATES OF AMERICA.

A PROCLAMATION.

Whereas in section 3 of an act passed by the Congress of the United States entitled "An act to reduce the revenue and equalize duties on imports, and for other purposes," approved October 1, 1890, it was provided as follows:

That with a view to secure reciprocal trade with countries producing the following articles, and for this purpose, on and after the 1st day of January, 1892, whenever and so often as the President shall be satisfied that the government of any country producing and exporting sugars, molasses, coffee, tea, and hides, raw and uncured, or any of such articles, imposes duties or other exactions upon the agricultural or other products of the United States which, in view of the free introduction of such sugar, molasses, coffee, tea, and hides into the United States, he may deem to be reciprocally unequal and unreasonable, he shall have the power and it shall be his duty to suspend, by proclamation to that effect, the provisions of this act relating to the free introduction of such sugar, molasses, coffee, tea, and hides the production of such country for such time as he shall deem just; and in such case and during such suspension duties shall be levied, collected, and paid upon sugar, molasses, coffee, tea, and hides the product of or exported from such designated country—

the duties hereinafter set forth; and

Whereas it has been established to my satisfaction and I find the fact

4908

to be that the Government of Colombia does impose duties or other exactions upon the agricultural and other products of the United States which, in view of the free introduction of such sugars, molasses, coffee, tea, and hides into the United States, in accordance with the provisions of said act, I deem to be reciprocally unequal and unreasonable:

Now, therefore, I, Benjamin Harrison, President of the United States of America, by virtue of the authority vested in me by section 3 of said act, by which it is made my duty to take action, do hereby declare and proclaim that the provisions of said act relating to the free introduction of sugars, molasses, coffee, tea, and hides the production of Colombia shall be suspended from and after this 15th day of March, 1892, and until such time as said unequal and unreasonable duties and exactions are removed by Colombia and public notice of that fact given by the President of the United States; and I do hereby proclaim that on and after this 15th day of March, 1892, there will be levied, collected, and paid upon sugars, molasses, coffee, tea, and hides the product of or exported from Colombia during such suspension duties as provided by said act, as follows:

All sugars not above No. 13 Dutch standard in color shall pay duty on their polariscopic tests as follows, namely:

All sugars not above No. 13 Dutch standard in color, all tank bottoms, sirups of cane juice or of beet juice, melada, concentrated melada, concrete and concentrated molasses, testing by the polariscope not above 75°, seven-tenths of 1 cent per pound, and for every additional degree or fraction of a degree shown by the polariscopic test two-hundredths of 1 cent per pound additional.

All sugars above No. 13 Dutch standard in color shall be classified by the Dutch standard of color and pay duty as follows, namely:

All sugars above No. 13 and not above No. 16 Dutch standard of color, $1\frac{3}{8}$ cents per pound.

All sugars above No. 16 and not above No. 20 Dutch standard of color, $1\frac{5}{8}$ cents per pound.

All sugars above No. 20 Dutch standard of color, 2 cents per pound.

Molasses testing above 56°, 4 cents per gallon.

Sugar drainings and sugar sweepings shall be subject to duty either as molasses or sugar, as the case may be, according to polariscopic test.

On coffee, 3 cents per pound.

On tea, 10 cents per pound.

Hides, raw or uncured, whether dry, salted, or pickled; Angora-goat skins, raw, without the wool, unmanufactured; asses' skins, raw or unmanufactured, and skins, except sheepskins, with the wool on, $1\frac{1}{2}$ cents per pound.

In witness whereof I have hereunto set my hand and caused the seal of the United States to be affixed.

[SEAL.]   Done at the city of Washington, this 15th day of March, 1892, and of the Independence of the United States of America the one hundred and sixteenth.

BENJ. HARRISON.

By the President:
    WILLIAM F. WHARTON,
        Acting Secretary of State.

By the President of the United States of America.

A PROCLAMATION.

Whereas in section 3 of an act passed by the Congress of the United States entitled "An act to reduce the revenue and equalize duties on imports, and for other purposes," approved October 1, 1890, it was provided as follows:

That with a view to secure reciprocal trade with countries producing the following articles, and for this purpose, on and after the 1st day of January, 1892, whenever and so often as the President shall be satisfied that the government of any country producing and exporting sugars, molasses, coffee, tea, and hides, raw and uncured, or any of such articles, imposes duties or other exactions upon the agricultural or other products of the United States which, in view of the free introduction of such sugar, molasses, coffee, tea, and hides into the United States, he may deem to be reciprocally unequal and unreasonable, he shall have the power and it shall be his duty to suspend, by proclamation to that effect, the provisions of this act relating to the free introduction of such sugar, molasses, coffee, tea, and hides the production of such country for such time as he shall deem just; and in such case and during such suspension duties shall be levied, collected, and paid upon sugar, molasses, coffee, tea, and hides the product of or exported from such designated country—

the duties hereinafter set forth; and

Whereas it has been established to my satisfaction and I find the fact to be that the Government of Hayti does impose duties or other exactions upon the agricultural and other products of the United States which, in view of the free introduction of such sugars, molasses, coffee, tea, and hides into the United States, in accordance with the provisions of said act, I deem to be reciprocally unequal and unreasonable:

Now, therefore, I, Benjamin Harrison, President of the United States of America, by virtue of the authority vested in me by section 3 of said act, by which it is made my duty to take action, do hereby declare and proclaim that the provisions of said act relating to the free introduction of sugars, molasses, coffee, tea, and hides the production of Hayti shall be suspended from and after this 15th day of March, 1892, and until such time as said unequal and unreasonable duties and exactions are removed by Hayti and public notice of that fact given by the President of the United States; and I do hereby proclaim that on and after this 15th day of March, 1892, there will be levied, collected, and paid upon sugars, molasses, coffee, tea, and hides the product of or exported from Hayti during such suspension duties as provided by said act, as follows:

All sugars not above No. 13 Dutch standard in color shall pay duty on their polariscopic tests as follows, namely :

All sugars not above No. 13 Dutch standard in color, all tank bottoms, sirups of cane juice or of beet juice, melada, concentrated melada, concrete and concentrated molasses, testing by the polariscope not above 75°, seven-tenths of 1 cent per pound and for every additional degree or fraction of a degree shown by the polariscopic test two-hundredths of 1 cent per pound additional.

All sugars above No. 13 Dutch standard in color shall be classified by the Dutch standard of color and pay duty as follows, namely:

All sugar above No. 13 and not above No. 16 Dutch standard of color, 1⅜ cents per pound.

All sugar above No. 16 and not above No. 20 Dutch standard of color, 1⅝ cents per pound.

All sugars above No. 20 Dutch standard of color, 2 cents per pound.

Molasses testing above 56°, 4 cents per gallon.

Sugar drainings and sugar sweepings shall be subject to duty either as molasses or sugar, as the case may be, according to polariscopic test.

On coffee, 3 cents per pound.

On tea, 10 cents per pound.

Hides, raw or uncured, whether dry, salted, or pickled; Angora-goat skins, raw, without the wool, unmanufactured; asses' skins, raw or unmanufactured, and skins, except sheepskins, with the wool on, 1½ cents per pound.

In witness whereof I have hereunto set my hand and caused the seal of the United States to be affixed.

[SEAL.]   Done at the city of Washington, this 15th day of March, 1892, and of the Independence of the United States of America the one hundred and sixteenth.

BENJ. HARRISON.

By the President:

WILLIAM F. WHARTON,
Acting Secretary of State.

BY THE PRESIDENT OF THE UNITED STATES OF AMERICA.

A PROCLAMATION.

Whereas in section 3 of an act passed by the Congress of the United States entitled "An act to reduce the revenue and equalize duties on imports, and for other purposes," approved October 1, 1890, it was provided as follows:

That with a view to secure reciprocal trade with countries producing the following articles, and for this purpose, on and after the 1st day of January, 1892, whenever and so often as the President shall be satisfied that the government of any country producing and exporting sugars, molasses, coffee, tea, and hides, raw and uncured, or any of such articles, imposes duties or other exactions upon the agricultural or other products of the United States which, in view of the free introduction of such sugar, molasses, coffee, tea, and hides into the United States, he may deem to be reciprocally unequal and unreasonable, he shall have the power and it shall be his duty to suspend, by proclamation to that effect, the provisions of this act relating to the free introduction of such sugar, molasses, coffee, tea, and hides the production of such country for such time as he shall deem just; and in such case and during such suspension duties shall be levied, collected, and paid upon sugar, molasses, coffee, tea, and hides the product of or exported from such designated country—

the duties hereinafter set forth; and

Whereas it has been established to my satisfaction and I find the fact to be that the Government of Venezuela does impose duties or other exactions upon the agricultural and other products of the United States which, in view of the free introduction of such sugars, molasses, coffee, tea, and hides into the United States, in accordance with the provisions of said act, I deem to be reciprocally unequal and unreasonable:

Now, therefore, I, Benjamin Harrison, President of the United States of America, by virtue of the authority vested in me by section 3 of said act, by which it is made my duty to take action, do hereby declare and proclaim that the provisions of said act relating to the free introduction of sugars, molasses, coffee, tea, and hides the production of Venezuela shall be suspended from and after this 15th day of March, 1892, and until such time as said unequal and unreasonable duties and exactions are removed by Venezuela and public notice of that fact given by the President of the United States; and I do hereby proclaim that on and after this 15th day of March, 1892, there will be levied, collected, and paid upon sugars, molasses, coffee, tea, and hides the product of or exported from Venezuela during such suspension duties as provided by said act, as follows:

All sugars not above No. 13 Dutch standard in color shall pay duty on their polariscopic tests as follows, namely:

All sugars not above No. 13 Dutch standard in color, all tank bottoms, sirups of cane juice or of beet juice, melada, concentrated melada, concrete and concentrated molasses, testing by the polariscope not above 75°, seven-tenths of 1 cent per pound, and for every additional degree or fraction of a degree shown by the polariscopic test two-hundredths of 1 cent per pound additional.

All sugars above No. 13 Dutch standard in color shall be classified by the Dutch standard of color and pay duty as follows, namely:

All sugar above No. 13 and not above No. 16 Dutch standard of color, 1⅜ cents per pound.

All sugar above No. 16 and not above No. 20 Dutch standard of color, 1⅝ cents per pound.

All sugars above No. 20 Dutch standard of color, 2 cents per pound.

Molasses testing above 56°, 4 cents per gallon.

Sugar drainings and sugar sweepings shall be subject to duty either as molasses or sugar, as the case may be, according to polariscopic test.

On coffee, 3 cents per pound.

On tea, 10 cents per pound.

Hides, raw or uncured, whether dry, salted, or pickled; Angora-goat skins, raw, without the wool, unmanufactured; asses' skins, raw or unmanufactured, and skins, except sheepskins, with the wool on, 1½ cents per pound.

In witness whereof I have hereunto set my hand and caused the seal of the United States to be affixed.

[SEAL.] Done at the city of Washington, this 15th day of March, 1892, and of the Independence of the United States of America the one hundred and sixteenth.

BENJ. HARRISON.

By the President:
WILLIAM F. WHARTON,
Acting Secretary of State.

BY THE PRESIDENT OF THE UNITED STATES OF AMERICA.

A PROCLAMATION.

Whereas it is provided by section 24 of an act approved March 3 1891, entitled "An act to repeal timber-culture laws, and for other pur poses"—

That the President of the United States may from time to time set apart and reserve in any State or Territory having public land bearing forests, in any part of the public lands wholly or in part covered with timber or undergrowth, whether of commercial value or not, as public reservations; and the President shall by public proclamation declare the establishment of such reservations and the limits thereof.

And whereas the lands hereinafter described are public and forest bearing, and on the 11th day of February last I issued a proclamation * intended to reserve the same as authorized in said act; but as some question has arisen as to the boundaries proclaimed being sufficiently definite to cover the lands intended to be reserved:

Now, therefore, I, Benjamin Harrison, President of the United States, for the purpose of removing any doubt and making the boundaries of said reservation more definite, by virtue of the power in me vested by said act, do hereby issue this my second proclamation and hereby set apart, reserve, and establish as a public reservation all that tract of land situate in the State of Colorado embraced within the following boundary:

Beginning at the northeast corner of section four (4), township eleven (11) south, range sixty-seven (67) west of the sixth (6th) principal meridian; thence westerly along the second (2d) correction line south between townships ten (10) and eleven (11) south to the northwest corner of section six (6), township eleven (11) south, range sixty-eight (68) west; thence southerly along the range line between ranges sixty-eight (68) and sixty-nine (69) west to the southwest corner of section eighteen (18), township thirteen (13) south, range sixty-eight (68) west; thence westerly along the section line between sections thirteen (13) and twenty-four (24), fourteen (14) and twenty-three (23), fifteen (15) and twenty-two (22), sixteen (16) and twenty-one (21), seventeen (17) and twenty (20), and eighteen (18) and nineteen (19) to the northwest corner of section nineteen (19), township thirteen (13) south, range sixty-nine (69) west; thence southerly along the range line between ranges sixty-nine (69) and seventy (70) west to the southwest corner of section thirty-one (31) of said township; thence easterly along the township line between townships thirteen (13) and fourteen (14) south to the quarter-section corner on said township line between section thirty-five (35), township thirteen (13) south, range sixty-nine (69) west, and section two (2), township fourteen (14) south, range sixty-nine (69) west; thence southerly through the middle of sections two (2), eleven (11), and fourteen (14), township fourteen (14) south, range sixty-nine (69) west, to the

*See pp. 5695-5697.

quarter-section corner on the section line between sections fourteen (14) and twenty-three (23) of said township and range; thence easterly along said section line to the northeast corner of section twenty-three (23) of said township and range; thence southerly along the section line to the quarter-section corner on said line between sections twenty-three (23) and twenty-four (24) of said township and range; thence easterly through the middle of section twenty-four (24) to the quarter-section corner on the range line between section nineteen (19), township fourteen (14) south, range sixty-eight (68) west, and section twenty-four (24), township fourteen (14) south, range sixty-nine (69) west; thence southerly along said range line to the southwest corner of section thirty-one (31), township fifteen (15) south, range sixty-eight (68) west; thence easterly along the third (3d) correction line south between townships fifteen (15) and sixteen (16) south to the southeast corner of section thirty-four (34), township fifteen (15) south, range sixty-seven (67) west; thence northerly along the section line between sections thirty-four (34) and thirty-five (35), twenty-six (26) and twenty-seven (27), to the point for the quarter-section corner on the section line between sections twenty-two (22) and twenty-three (23), township fifteen (15) south, range sixty-seven (67) west; thence westerly to a point for the legal center of section twenty-one (21) of said township and range; thence southerly to the southwest corner of the southeast quarter of section twenty-eight (28) of said township and range; thence westerly along the section line between sections twenty-eight (28) and thirty-three (33), twenty-nine (29) and thirty-two (32), thirty (30) and thirty-one (31), to the northwest corner of section thirty-one (31) of said township and range; thence northerly on the range line between ranges sixty-seven (67) and sixty-eight (68) west to the southwest corner of section six (6) of said township and range; thence easterly along the section line to the southeast corner of section six (6) of said township and range; thence southerly along the section line to the southwest corner of section eight (8) of said township and range; thence easterly along the section line to the southeast corner of section ten (10) of said township and range; thence northerly along the section line between sections ten (10) and eleven (11), two (2) and three (3), township fifteen (15) south, range sixty-seven (67) west, to the northeast corner of section three (3) of said township and range; thence westerly along the township line between townships fourteen (14) and fifteen (15) south to the northwest corner of section three (3), township fifteen (15) south, range sixty-seven (67) west; thence northerly along the section line between sections thirty-three (33) and thirty-four (34), twenty-seven (27) and twenty-eight (28), twenty-one (21) and twenty-two (22), to the northeast corner of section twenty-one (21), township fourteen (14) south, range sixty-seven (67) west; thence westerly along the section line between sections sixteen (16) and twenty-one (21), seventeen (17) and twenty (20), eighteen (18) and nineteen

(19), to the northwest corner of section nineteen (19) of said township and range; thence northerly along the range line between ranges sixty-seven (67) and sixty-eight (68) west to the northeast corner of section one (1), township fourteen (14) south, range sixty-eight (68) west; thence easterly along the township line between townships thirteen (13) and fourteen (14) south to the southeast corner of section thirty-three (33), township thirteen (13) south, range sixty-seven (67) west; thence northerly along the section line between sections thirty-three (33) and thirty-four (34), twenty-seven (27) and twenty-eight (28), twenty-one (21) and twenty-two (22), fifteen (15) and sixteen (16), nine (9) and ten (10), and three (3) and four (4) of townships thirteen (13), twelve (12), and eleven (11) south, range sixty-seven (67) west, to the place of beginning.

Excepting from the force and effect of this proclamation all lands which may have been prior to the date hereof embraced in any legal entry or covered by any lawful filing duly of record in the proper United States land office, or upon which any valid settlement has been made pursuant to law and the statutory period within which to make entry or filing of record has not expired, and all mining claims duly located and held according to the laws of the United States and rules and regulations not in conflict therewith.

Provided, That this exception shall not continue to apply to any particular tract of land unless the entryman, settler, or claimant continues to comply with the law under which the entry, filing, settlement, or location was made.

Warning is hereby expressly given to all persons not to enter or make settlement upon the tract of land reserved by this proclamation.

In witness whereof I have hereunto set my hand and caused the seal of the United States to be affixed.

[SEAL.]   Done at the city of Washington, this 18th day of March, A. D. 1892, and of the Independence of the United States the one hundred and sixteenth.

BENJ. HARRISON.

By the President:

WILLIAM F. WHARTON,
    Acting Secretary of State.

BY THE PRESIDENT OF THE UNITED STATES OF AMERICA.

A PROCLAMATION.

Whereas by the third article of the treaty between the United States of America and the Sisseton and Wahpeton bands of Dakota or Sioux Indians concluded February 19, 1867, proclaimed May 2, 1867 (15 U. S. Statutes at Large, p. 505), the United States set apart and reserved for certain of said Indians certain lands, particularly described, being situated partly in North Dakota and partly in South Dakota and known as the Lake Traverse Reservation; and

Whereas by agreement made with said Indians residing on said reservation dated December 12, 1889, they conveyed, as set forth in article 1 thereof, to the United States all their title and interest in and to all the unallotted lands within the limits of the reservation set apart as aforesaid remaining after the allotments shall have been made, which are provided for in article 4 of the agreement, as follows:

That there shall be allotted to each individual member of the bands of Indians parties hereto a sufficient quantity, which, with the lands heretofore allotted, shall make in each case 160 acres, and in case no allotment has been made to any individual member of said bands, then an allotment of 160 acres shall be made to such individual.

And whereas it is provided in article 2 of said agreement—

That the cession, sale, relinquishment, and conveyance of the lands described in article 1 of this agreement shall not take effect and be in force until the sum of $342,778.37, together with the sum of $18,400, shall have been paid to said bands of Indians, as set forth and stipulated in article 3 of this agreement.

And whereas it is provided in the act of Congress approved March 3, 1891 (26 U. S. Statutes at Large, pp. 1036–1038), section 30, accepting and ratifying the agreement with said Indians—

That the lands by said agreement ceded, sold, relinquished, and conveyed to the United States shall immediately, upon the payment to the parties entitled thereto of their share of the funds made immediately available by this act, and upon the completion of the allotments as provided for in said agreement, be subject only to entry and settlement under the homestead and town-site laws of the United States, excepting the sixteenth and thirty-sixth sections of said lands, which shall be reserved for common-school purposes and be subject to the laws of the State wherein located: *Provided*, That patents shall not issue until the settler or entryman shall have paid to the United States the sum of $2.50 per acre for the land taken up by such homesteader, and the title to the lands so entered shall remain in the United States until said money is duly paid by such entryman or his legal representatives, or his widow, who shall have the right to pay the money and complete the entry of her deceased husband in her own name and shall receive a patent for the same.

And whereas payment as required by said act has been made by the United States; and

Whereas allotments as provided for in said agreement, as now appears by the records of the Department of the Interior, will have been made, approved, and completed and all other terms and considerations required will have been complied with on the day and hour hereinafter fixed for opening said lands to settlement:

Now, therefore, I, Benjamin Harrison, President of the United States, do hereby declare and make known that all of the lands embraced in said reservation, saving and excepting the lands reserved for and allotted to said Indians and the lands reserved for other purposes in pursuance of the provisions of said agreement and the said act of Congress ratifying the same and other the laws relating thereto, will, at and after the hour of 12 o'clock noon (central standard time) on the 15th day of April, A. D. 1892, and not before, be opened to settlement under the terms of and subject to all the terms and conditions, limitations, reservations, and restrictions contained in said agreements, the statutes above specified, and the laws of the United States applicable thereto.

The lands to be opened for settlement are for greater convenience particularly described in the accompanying schedule, entitled "Schedule of lands within the Lake Traverse Reservation opened to settlement by proclamation of the President dated April 11, 1892," and which schedule is made a part hereof.

Warning, moreover, is hereby given that until said lands are opened to settlement as herein provided all persons save said Indians are forbidden to enter upon and occupy the same or any part thereof.

And further notice is hereby given that it has been duly ordered that the lands mentioned and included in this proclamation shall be, and the same are, attached to the Fargo and Watertown land districts, in said States, as follows:

1. All that portion of the Lake Traverse Reservation commencing at the northwest corner of said reservation; thence south 12° 2' west, following the west boundary of the reservation, to the new seventh standard parallel, or boundary line between the States of North and South Dakota; thence east, following the new seventh standard parallel to its intersection with the north boundary of said Indian reservation; thence northwesterly with said boundary to the place of beginning, is attached to the Fargo land district, the office of which is now located at Fargo, N. Dak.

2. All that portion of the Lake Traverse Reservation commencing at a point where the new seventh standard parallel intersects the west boundary of said reservation; thence southerly along the west boundary of said reservation to its extreme southern limit; thence northerly along the east boundary of said reservation to Lake Traverse; thence north with said lake to the northeast corner of the Lake Traverse Indian Reservation; thence westerly with the north boundary of said reservation to its intersection with the new seventh standard parallel, or boundary line between the States of North and South Dakota; thence with the new seventh standard parallel to the place of beginning, is attached to the Watertown land district, the office of which is now located at Watertown, S. Dak.

In witness whereof I have hereunto set my hand and caused the seal of the United States to be affixed.

[SEAL.]   Done at the city of Washington, this 11th day of April, A. D. 1892, and of the Independence of the United States the one hundred and sixteenth.

                                            BENJ. HARRISON.

By the President:

JAMES G. BLAINE,
        Secretary of State.

By the President of the United States of America.

A PROCLAMATION.

Whereas by a written agreement made on the ——— day of October, 1890, the Cheyenne and Arapahoe tribes of Indians ceded, conveyed, transferred, relinquished, and surrendered all their claim, title, and interest in and to the lands described in article 2 of said agreement as follows, to wit:

Commencing at a point where the Washita River crosses the ninety-eighth degree of west longitude, as surveyed in the years 1858 and 1871; thence north on a line with said ninety-eighth degree to the point where it is crossed by the Red Fork of the Arkansas (sometimes called the Cimarron River); thence up said river, in the middle of the main channel thereof, to the north boundary of the country ceded to the United States by the treaty of June 14, 1866, with the Creek Nation of Indians; thence west on said north boundary and the north boundary of the country ceded to the United States by the treaty of March 21, 1866, with the Seminole Indians to the one hundredth degree of west longitude; thence south on the line of said one hundredth degree to the point where it strikes the North Fork of the Red River; thence down said North Fork of the Red River to a point where it strikes the north line of the Kiowa and Comanche Reservation; thence east along said boundary to a point where it strikes the Washita River; thence down said Washita River, in the middle of the main channel thereof, to the place of beginning; and all other lands or tracts of country in the Indian Territory to which they have or may set up or allege any right, title, interest, or claim whatsoever.

Provided, That every member of said tribes shall have an allotment of 160 acres of land, as in said agreement provided, to be selected within the tract of country so ceded, except land in any part of said reservation now used or occupied for military, agency, school, school-farm, religious, or other public uses, or in sections 16 or 36 in each Congressional township, except, in cases where any Cheyenne or Arapahoe Indian has heretofore made improvements upon and now uses and occupies a part of said sections 16 and 36, such Indian may make his or her selection within the boundaries so prescribed so as to include his or her improvements; and except in that part of the lands by said agreement ceded, now occupied and claimed by the Wichita and affiliated bands of Indians described as follows, to wit:

Commencing at a point in the middle of the main channel of the Washita River where the ninety-eighth meridian of west longitude crosses the same; thence up the middle of the main channel of the said river to the line of 98° 40′ west longitude; thence up said line of 98° 40′ due north to the middle of the main channel of the main Canadian River; thence down the middle of the main Canadian River to where it crosses the ninety-eighth meridian; thence due south to the place of beginning.

And provided, That said sections 16 and 36 in each Congressional township in said reservation shall not become subject to homestead entry, but shall be held by the United States and finally sold for public-school purposes; and that when the allotments of lands shall have been selected and taken by the members of the Cheyenne and Arapahoe tribes as aforesaid and approved by the Secretary of the Interior the title thereto shall be held in trust for the allottees, respectively, for the period of twenty-five years in the manner and to the extent provided for in the act of Congress approved February 8, 1887 (24 U. S. Statutes at Large, p. 388); and .

Whereas it is provided in the act of Congress accepting, ratifying, and confirming the said agreement with the Cheyenne and Arapahoe Indians, approved March 3, 1891 (26 U. S. Statutes at Large, pp. 989–1044), section 16—

That whenever any of the lands acquired by either of the * * * foregoing agreements respecting lands in the Indian or Oklahoma Territory shall by operation of law or proclamation of the President of the United States be opened to settlement they shall be disposed of to actual settlers only, under the provisions of the homestead and town-site laws, except section 2301 of the Revised Statutes of the United States, which shall not apply: *Provided, however*, That each settler on said lands shall before making a final proof and receiving a certificate of entry pay to the United States for the land so taken by him, in addition to the fees provided by law, and within five years from the date of the first original entry, the sum of $1.50 per acre, one-half of which shall be paid within two years; but the rights of honorably discharged Union soldiers and sailors as defined and described in sections 2304 and 2305 of the Revised Statutes of the United States shall not be abridged except as to the sum to be paid as aforesaid; and all the lands in Oklahoma are hereby declared to be agricultural lands, and proof of their nonmineral character shall not be required as a condition precedent to final entry.

And whereas allotments of land in severalty to said Cheyenne and Arapahoe Indians have been made and approved in accordance with law and the provisions of the before-mentioned agreement with them; and

Whereas the lands acquired by the said agreement hereinbefore mentioned have been divided into counties by the Secretary of the Interior, as required by said last-mentioned act of Congress, before the same shall be opened to settlement, and lands have been reserved for county-seat purposes as therein required, as follows, to wit:

For County C, the south one-half of section 19, township 16 north, range 11 west; for County D, the north one-half of section 13, township 18 north, range 17 west; for County E, the south one-half of section 15, township 17 north, range 22 west; for County F, the south one-half of section 8, township 13 north, range 23 west; for County G, the north one-half of section 25, township 13 north, range 17 west; for County H, the south one-half of section 13, township 9 north, range 16 west; and

Whereas it is provided by act of Congress for temporary government of Oklahoma, approved May 2, 1890, section 23 (26 U. S. Statutes at Large, p. 92), that there shall be reserved public highways 4 rods wide between each section of land in said Territory, the section lines being the center of said highways; but no deduction shall be made where cash payments are provided for in the amount to be paid for each quarter section of land by reason of such reservation; and

Whereas all the terms, conditions, and considerations required by said

THE *MAINE* A FEW DAYS AFTER THE EXPLOSION

THE WRECK OF THE *MAINE*

"The *Maine* was sent to Havana, Cuba, in January, 1898, on a peaceful mission. She was received by the Spanish forts and naval vessels in the harbor with the courtesies usually extended to visiting warships of a friendly power. Her anchorage was selected by the Spanish authorities. On the night of February 15, 1898, the *Maine* was destroyed by a submarine mine (6277). It was believed that the Spaniards, who at the time were very much incensed at the interest Americans were taking in the Cuban insurrection, had maliciously destroyed the vessel and crew. Two officers and 258 sailors and marines lost their lives by the explosion (6296). An investigation failed to place the responsibility for the catastrophe, and Spain hastened to send a message of regret at what she called an incident. The blowing up of the *Maine* was among the causes of the war with Spain, begun soon afterwards."

Quoted from the article, "Maine, The," in the encyclopedic index (volume eleven). The numerals in the body of the article refer to pages on which President McKinley, in his official history of the Spanish-American War, refers to the subject.

agreement made with said tribes of Indians and by the laws relating thereto precedent to opening said lands to settlement have been, as I hereby declare, complied with:

Now, therefore, I, Benjamin Harrison, President of the United States, by virtue of the power in me vested by the statutes hereinbefore mentioned, also an act of Congress entitled "An act making appropriations for the current and contingent expenses of the Indian Department and for fulfilling treaty stipulations with various Indian tribes for the year ending June 30, 1892, and for other purposes," approved March 3, 1891, and by other of the laws of the United States, and by said agreement, do hereby declare and make known that all of said lands hereinbefore described acquired from the Cheyenne and Arapahoe Indians by the agreement aforesaid, saving and excepting the lands allotted to the Indians as in said agreement provided, excepting also the lands hereinbefore described as occupied and claimed by the Wichita and affiliated bands of Indians, or otherwise reserved in pursuance of the provisions of said agreement and the said act of Congress ratifying the same, and other the laws relating thereto, will at the hour of 12 o'clock noon (central standard time), Tuesday, the 19th day of the present month of April, and not before, be opened to settlement under the terms of and subject to all the conditions, limitations, reservations, and restrictions contained in said agreement, the statutes above specified, and the laws of the United States applicable thereto.

The lands to be so opened to settlement are for greater convenience particularly described in the accompanying schedule, entitled "Schedule of lands within the Cheyenne and Arapahoe Indian Reservation, Oklahoma Territory, opened to settlement by proclamation of the President."

Each entry shall be in square form as nearly as applicable; and no other lands in the Territory of Oklahoma are opened to settlement under this proclamation, the agreement with the said Cheyenne and Arapahoe Indians, or the act ratifying the same.

Notice, moreover, is hereby given that it is by law enacted that until said lands are opened to settlement by proclamation no person shall be permitted to enter upon and occupy the same, and no person violating this provision shall be permitted to enter any of said lands or acquire any right thereto, and that the officers of the United States will be required to enforce this provision.

And further notice is hereby given that it has been duly ordered that the lands mentioned and included in this proclamation shall be, and the same are, attached to the Western land district, office at Kingfisher, and the Oklahoma land district, office at Oklahoma City, in said Territory of Oklahoma, as follows:

1. All of said lands lying north of the township line between townships 13 and 14 north are attached to the Western land district, the office of which is at Kingfisher, in said Territory.

2. All of said lands lying south of the township line between townships 13 and 14 north are attached to the Oklahoma land district. the office of which is at Oklahoma City, in the said Territory.

In witness whereof I have hereunto set my hand and caused the seal of the United States to be affixed.

[SEAL.]   Done at the city of Washington, this 12th day of April, A. D. 1892, and of the Independence of the United States the one hundred and sixteenth.   BENJ. HARRISON.

By the President:

JAMES G. BLAINE, *Secretary of State.*

BY THE PRESIDENT OF THE UNITED STATES OF AMERICA.

A PROCLAMATION.

Whereas it is provided by section 13 of the act of Congress of March 3, 1891, entitled "An act to amend Title LX, chapter 3, of the Revised Statutes of the United States, relating to copyrights," that said act "shall only apply to a citizen or subject of a foreign state or nation when such foreign state or nation permits to citizens of the United States of America the benefit of copyright on substantially the same basis as its own citizens, or when such foreign state or nation is a party to an international agreement which provides for reciprocity in the granting of copyright, by the terms of which agreement the United States of America may at its pleasure become a party to such agreement;" and

Whereas it is also provided by said section that "the existence of either of the conditions aforesaid shall be determined by the President of the United States by proclamation made from time to time as the purposes of this act may require;" and

Whereas in virtue of said section 13 of the aforesaid act of Congress a copyright agreement was signed at Washington on January 15, 1892, in the English and German languages, by the representatives of the United States of America and the German Empire, a true copy of the English version of which agreement is, word for word, as follows:

The President of the United States of America and His Majesty the German Emperor, King of Prussia, in the name of the German Empire, being actuated by the desire to extend to their subjects and citizens the full benefit of the legal provisions in force in both countries in regard to copyright, have to this end decided to conclude an agreement and have appointed as their plenipotentiaries:

The President of the United States of America, James G. Blaine, Secretary of State of the United States;

His Majesty the German Emperor, King of Prussia, Alfons Mumm von Schwarzenstein, his chargé d'affaires near the Government of the United States of America, who, being duly authorized, have concluded the following agreement, subject to due ratification:

ARTICLE I. Citizens of the United States of America shall enjoy in the German Empire the protection of copyright as regards works of literature and art, as well as photographs, against illegal reproduction, on the same basis on which such protection is granted to subjects of the Empire.

ART. II. The United States Government engages in return that the President of the United States shall, in pursuance of section 13 of the act of Congress of March 3, 1891, issue the proclamation therein provided for in regard to the extension of the provisions of that act to German subjects as soon as the Secretary of State shall have been officially notified that the present agreement has received the necessary legislative sanction in the German Empire.

ART. III. This agreement shall be ratified and the ratifications shall be exchanged at Washington as soon as possible.

The agreement shall go into operation at the expiration of three weeks from the date of the exchange of its ratifications, and shall be applicable only to works not published at the time when it shall have gone into operation. It shall remain in force until the expiration of three months from the day on which notice of a desire for the cessation of its effects shall have been given by one of the contracting parties.

Done in duplicate in the English and German languages, at the city of Washington, this 15th day of January, 1892.

JAMES G. BLAINE. [SEAL.]
A. v. MUMM. [SEAL.]

And whereas the official notification contemplated by Article II of the said agreement has been received by this Government:

Now, therefore, I, Benjamin Harrison, President of the United States of America, do declare and proclaim that the first of the conditions specified in section 13 of the act of March 3, 1891, is now fulfilled in respect to the subjects of the German Empire.

In testimony whereof I have hereunto set my hand and caused the seal of the United States to be affixed.

[SEAL.] Done at the city of Washington, the 15th day of April, 1892, and of the Independence of the United States the one hundred and sixteenth.

BENJ. HARRISON.

By the President:
JAMES G. BLAINE, *Secretary of State.*

BY THE PRESIDENT OF THE UNITED STATES OF AMERICA.

A PROCLAMATION.

Whereas, pursuant to section 3 of the act of Congress approved October 1, 1890, entitled "An act to reduce the revenue and equalize duties on imports, and for other purposes," the Secretary of State of the United States of America communicated to the Government of Honduras the action of the Congress of the United States of America, with a view to secure reciprocal trade, in declaring the articles enumerated in said section 3 to be exempt from duty upon their importation into the United States of America; and

Whereas the consul-general of Honduras at New York has communicated to the Secretary of State the fact that, in reciprocity for the admission into the United States of America free of all duty of the articles enumerated in section 3 of said act, the Government of Honduras will by due legal enactment, as a provisional measure and until a more complete arrangement may be negotiated and put in operation, admit free of all duty, from and after May 25, 1892, into all the established ports of entry of Honduras the articles or merchandise named in the following schedule, provided that the same be the product or manufacture of the United States:

SCHEDULE OF PRODUCTS AND MANUFACTURES FROM THE UNITED STATES WHICH THE REPUBLIC OF HONDURAS WILL ADMIT FREE OF ALL CUSTOMS, MUNICIPAL, AND ANY OTHER KIND OF DUTY.

1. Animals for breeding purposes.
2. Corn, rice, barley, and rye.
3. Beans.
4. Hay and straw for forage.
5. Fruits, fresh.
6. Preparations of flour in biscuits, crackers not sweetened, macaroni, vermicelli, and tallarin.
7. Coal, mineral.
8. Roman cement.
9. Hydraulic lime.
10. Bricks, fire bricks, and crucibles for melting.
11. Marble, dressed, for furniture, statues, fountains, gravestones, and building purposes.
12. Tar, vegetable and mineral.
13. Guano and other fertilizers, natural or artificial.
14. Plows and all other agricultural tools and implements.
15. Machinery of all kinds, including sewing machines, and separate or extra parts of the same.
16. Materials of all kinds for the construction and equipment of railroads.
17. Materials of all kinds for the construction and operation of telegraphic and telephonic lines.
18. Materials of all kinds for lighting by electricity and gas.
19. Materials of all kinds for the construction of wharves.
20. Apparatus for distilling liquors.
21. Wood of all kinds for building, in trunks or pieces, beams, rafters, planks, boards, shingles, or flooring.
22. Wooden staves, heads, and hoops, and barrels and boxes for packing, mounted or in pieces.
23. Houses of wood or iron, complete or in parts.
24. Wagons, carts, and carriages of all kinds.
25. Barrels, casks, and tanks of iron for water.
26. Tubes of iron and all other accessories necessary for water supply.
27. Wire, barbed, and staples for fences.
28. Plates of iron for building purposes.
29. Mineral ores.
30. Kettles of iron for making salt.
31. Sugar boilers.
32. Molds for sugar.
33. Guys for mining purposes.
34. Furnaces and instruments for assaying metals.
35. Scientific instruments.
36 Models of machinery and buildings.
37. Boats, lighters, tackle, anchors, chains, girtlines, sails, and all other articles for vessels, to be used in the ports, lakes, and rivers of the Republic.

38. Printing materials, including presses, type, ink, and all other accessories.

39. Printed books, pamphlets, and newspapers, bound or unbound, maps, photographs, printed music, and paper for music.

40. Paper for printing newspapers.

41. Quicksilver.

42. Loadstones.

43. Hops.

44. Sulphate of quinine.

45. Gold and silver in bars, dust, or coin.

46. Samples of merchandise the duties on which do not exceed $1.

It is understood that the packages or coverings in which the articles named in the foregoing schedule are imported shall be free of duty if they are usual and proper for the purpose.

And that the Government of Honduras has further stipulated that the laws and regulations adopted to protect its revenue and prevent fraud in the declarations and proof that the articles named in the foregoing schedule are the product or manufacture of the United States of America shall impose no additional charges on the importer nor undue restrictions on the articles imported; and

Whereas the Secretary of State has, by my direction, given assurance to the consul-general of Honduras at New York that this action of the Government of Honduras in granting freedom of duties to the products and manufactures of the United States of America on their importation into Honduras and in stipulating for a more complete reciprocity arrangement is accepted as a due reciprocity for the action of Congress as set forth in section 3 of said act:

Now, therefore, be it known that I, Benjamin Harrison, President of the United States of America, have caused the above-stated modifications of the tariff laws of Honduras to be made public for the information of the citizens of the United States of America.

In testimony whereof I have hereunto set my hand and caused the seal of the United States to be affixed.

[SEAL.]   Done at the city of Washington, this 30th day of April, 1892, and of the Independence of the United States of America the one hundred and sixteenth.

BENJ. HARRISON.

By the President:

JAMES G. BLAINE, *Secretary of State.*

BY THE PRESIDENT OF THE UNITED STATES OF AMERICA.

A PROCLAMATION.

Whereas, pursuant to section 3 of the act of Congress approved October 1, 1890, entitled "An act to reduce the revenue and equalize duties on imports, and for other purposes," the Secretary of State of the United States of America communicated to the Government of Guatemala the action of the Congress of the United States of America, with a view to secure reciprocal trade, in declaring the articles enumerated in said section 3 to be exempt from duty upon their importation into the United States of America; and

Whereas the envoy extraordinary and minister plenipotentiary of Guatemala at Washington has communicated to the Secretary of State the fact that, in reciprocity for the admission into the United States of America free of all duty of the articles enumerated in section 3 of said act, the Government of Guatemala will by due legal enactment of the National Congress of that Republic admit free of all duty, from and after the 30th day after the passage of the said act by the Congress of Guatemala, into all the established ports of entry of that Republic the articles or merchandise named in the following schedule, provided that the same be the product or manufacture of the United States:

SCHEDULE OF ARTICLES THE PRODUCT OR MANUFACTURE OF THE UNITED STATES
TO BE ADMITTED INTO GUATEMALA FREE OF ALL CUSTOMS DUTIES AND OF ANY
NATIONAL OR MUNICIPAL DUES AND NATIONAL PORT CHARGES.

1. Live animals.
2. Barley, corn or maize, and rye.
3. Corn meal.
4. Potatoes, pease, and beans.
5. Fresh vegetables.
6. Rice.
7. Hay and straw for forage.
8. Tar, pitch, resin, turpentine, and asphalt.
9. Cotton-seed oil and other products of said seed.
10. Quicksilver.
11. Mineral coal.
12. Guano and other fertilizers.
13. Lumber and timber, in the rough or prepared for building purposes.
14. Houses of wood or iron, complete or in parts.
15. Fire bricks, lime, cement, shingles, and tiles of clay or glass for roofing and construction of buildings.
16. Marble in slabs, columns, cornices, door and window frames, and fountains, and dressed or undressed marble for buildings.
17. Piping of clay, glazed or unglazed, for aqueducts and sewers.
18. Wire, plain or barbed, for fences, with hooks and staples for same.
19. Printed books, bound or unbound; printed music; maps, charts, and globes.
20. Materials for the construction and equipment of railways.
21. Materials for electrical illumination.
22. Materials expressly for the construction of wharves.
23. Anchors and hoisting tackle.
24. Railings of cast or wrought iron.
25. Balconies of cast or wrought iron.
26. Window blinds of wood or metal.
27. Iron fireplaces or stoves.
28. Machinery, including steam machinery for agriculture and mining, and separate parts of the same.
29. Gold and silver, in bullion, dust, or coin.

It is understood that the packages or coverings in which the articles named in the foregoing schedule are imported shall enter free of duty if they are usual and proper for the purpose.

And whereas the Government of Guatemala has further stipulated that the laws and regulations adopted to protect its revenue and prevent fraud in the declarations and proof that the articles named in the foregoing schedule are the product or manufacture of the United States of America shall impose no undue restrictions on the importer and no additional charges on the articles imported; and

Whereas the Secretary of State has, by my direction, given assurance to the envoy extraordinary and minister plenipotentiary of Guatemala at Washington that this action of the Government of Guatemala in granting freedom of duties to the products and manufactures of the United States of America on their importation into Guatemala, is accepted as a due reciprocity for the action of Congress as set forth in section 3 of said act; and

Whereas the diplomatic representative of the United States of America at the city of Guatemala has been advised by the Government of Guatemala of the passage on April 30, 1892, of an act by the National Congress of that Republic approving the commercial arrangement concluded between the Governments of the two Republics and of the issue of a decree admitting, on and after the 30th day of May, 1892, the articles mentioned in the above schedule being the product or manufacture of the United States of America into the ports of Guatemala free of all duties whatsoever:

Now, therefore, be it known that I, Benjamin Harrison, President of the United States of America, have caused the above-stated modifications of the tariff laws of Guatemala to be made public for the information of the citizens of the United States of America.

In testimony whereof I have hereunto set my hand and caused the seal of the United States to be affixed.

[SEAL.] Done at the city of Washington, this 18th day of May, 1892, and of the Independence of the United States of America the one hundred and sixteenth. BENJ. HARRISON.

By the President:
    JAMES G. BLAINE,
        Secretary of State.

BY THE PRESIDENT OF THE UNITED STATES OF AMERICA.

A PROCLAMATION.

Whereas, pursuant to section 3 of the act of Congress approved October 1, 1890, entitled "An act to reduce the revenue and equalize duties on imports, and for other purposes," the attention of the Government of Austria-Hungary was called to the action of the Congress of the United States of America, with a view to secure reciprocal trade, in declaring the articles enumerated in said section 3 to be exempt from duty upon their importation into the United States of America; and

Whereas the minister plenipotentiary of Austria-Hungary at Washington has communicated to the Secretary of State the fact that, in view of the act of Congress above cited, the Government of Austria-Hungary has by due legal enactment authorized the admission, from and after May 25, 1892, into Austria-Hungary of all the articles of merchandise the product of the United States of America named in the commercial treaties which Austria-Hungary has celebrated with Germany and other nations on the terms stated in said treaties; and

Whereas the Secretary of State has, by my direction, given assurance to the minister plenipotentiary of Austria-Hungary at Washington that this action of the Government of Austria-Hungary in granting exemption of duties to the products and manufactures of the United States of America on their importation into Austria-Hungary is accepted as a due reciprocity for the action of Congress as set forth in section 3 of said act:

Now, therefore, be it known that I, Benjamin Harrison, President of the United States of America, have caused the above-stated modifications of the tariff laws of Austria-Hungary to be made public for the information of the citizens of the United States of America.

In testimony whereof I have hereunto set my hand and caused the seal of the United States to be affixed.

[SEAL.]   Done at the city of Washington, this 26th day of May, 1892, and of the Independence of the United States of America the one hundred and sixteenth.

BENJ. HARRISON.

By the President:

WILLIAM F. WHARTON, *Acting Secretary of State.*

BY THE PRESIDENT OF THE UNITED STATES OF AMERICA.

A PROCLAMATION.

Whereas it is provided by section 24 of the act of Congress approved March 3, 1891, entitled "An act to repeal timber-culture laws, and for other purposes"—

That the President of the United States may from time to time set apart and reserve in any State or Territory having public land bearing forests, in any part of the public lands wholly or in part covered with timber or undergrowth, whether of commercial value or not, as public reservations; and the President shall by public proclamation declare the establishment of such reservations and the limits thereof.

And whereas the public lands in the State of Oregon within the limits hereinafter described are in part covered with timber, and it appears that the public good would be promoted by setting apart and reserving said lands as a public reservation:

Now, therefore, I, Benjamin Harrison, President of the United States,

by virtue of the power in me vested by section 24 of the aforesaid act of Congress, do hereby make known and proclaim that there is hereby reserved from entry or settlement and set apart as a public reservation all those certain tracts, pieces, or parcels of land lying and being situate in the State of Oregon and particularly described as follows, to wit:

Beginning at the northwest corner of section six (6), township one (1) south, range six (f) east, Willamette meridian; thence easterly on the base line between townships one (1) north and one (1) south to the southwest corner of section thirty-two (32), township one (1) north, range six (6) east; thence northerly on the section line between sections thirty-one (31) and thirty-two (32) to the northwest corner of section thirty-two (32); thence easterly on the section line between sections twenty-nine (29) and thirty-two (32) to the northeast corner of section thirty-two (32); thence northerly on the section line between sections twenty-eight (28) and twenty-nine (29) to the northwest corner of section twenty-eight (28); thence easterly on the section line between sections twenty-one (21) and twenty-eight (28) to the northeast corner of section twenty-eight (28); thence northerly on the section line between sections twenty-one (21) and twenty-two (22) to the northwest corner of section twenty-two (22); thence easterly on the section line between sections fifteen (15) and twenty-two (22) and fourteen (14) and twenty-three (23) to the northeast corner of section twenty-three (23); thence northerly along the section line between sections thirteen (13) and fourteen (14) and eleven (11) and twelve (12) to the northwest corner of section twelve (12); thence easterly on the section line between sections one (1) and twelve (12) to the northeast corner of section twelve (12); thence northerly on the eastern boundary of section one (1) to the northeast corner of section one (1), all of said sections being in township one (1) north, range six (6) east; thence easterly to a point for the northeast corner of township one (1) north, range seven (7) east; thence southerly to a point for the southeast corner of section one (1), township one (1) north, range seven (7) east; thence easterly to a point for the northeast corner of section eight (8), township one (1) north, range eight (8) east; thence southerly to a point for the northeast corner of section thirty-two (32) of said township and range; thence easterly to a point for the northeast corner of section thirty-three (33) of said township and range; thence southerly to the southeast corner of section thirty-three (33) of said township and range; thence westerly along the base line to the northwest corner of section four (4), township one (1) south, range eight (8) east; thence southerly on the section line between sections four (4) and five (5) and eight (8) and nine (9) to the southeast corner of section eight (8); thence easterly along the section line between sections nine (9) and sixteen (16) to a point for the northeast corner of section sixteen (16); thence southerly along the section line between sections fifteen (15) and sixteen (16) to the southeast corner of section sixteen (16); thence easterly along the section line between sections fifteen (15) and twenty-two to the northeast corner of section twenty-two (22); thence southerly between sections twenty-two (22), twenty-three (23), twenty-six (26), twenty-seven (27), thirty-four (34), and thirty-five (35) to the southeast corner of section thirty-four (34); thence easterly along the southern boundary line of sections thirty-five (35) and thirty-six (36) to the southeast corner of section thirty-six (36), all of said sections being in township one (1) south, range eight (8) east; thence southerly to a point for the southeast corner of township two (2) south, range eight (8) east; thence westerly to the southeast corner of township two (2) south, range seven (7) east; thence northerly along the eastern boundary line of sections thirty-six (36), twenty-five (25), twenty-four (24), and thirteen (13), township two (2) south, range seven (7) east, to the southeast corner of section twelve (12) of said township and range; thence westerly along the section line between sections twelve (12) and thirteen (13), eleven (11) and fourteen (14), ten (10) and fifteen (15), nine (9) and sixteen (16), eight (8) and seventeen (17), and seven (7) and eighteen (18), township two (2) south, range seven (7) east, and sections twelve (12) and thirteen (13), eleven (11) and fourteen (14), ten (10) and fifteen (15), nine (9) and sixteen (16), eight (8) and seventeen (17), and seven (7) and eighteen (18), township two (2) south, range six (6) east, to the southwest corner of section seven (7) of said township and range; thence northerly along the western boundary of section seven (7) to the northwest corner of said section, township two (2) south, range six (6) east; thence westerly on the section line between sections one (1) and twelve (12), two (2) and eleven (11), three (3) and ten (10), and four (4) and nine (9) to the southwest corner of section four (4), township two (2) south, range five (5) east; thence northerly on the section line between sections four (4) and five (5) to the northwest corner of section four (4) in said township and range; thence easterly on the township line between townships one (1) and two (2) south, range five (5) east, to the southwest corner of section thirty-five (35), township one (1) south, range five (5) east; thence northerly on the section line between sections thirty-four (34), thirty-five (35), twenty-six (26), twenty-seven (27), twenty-two (22), and twenty-three (23) to the northwest corner of section twenty-three (23) of said township and range; thence easterly on the section line between sections fourteen (14) and twenty-three (23), thirteen (13) and twenty-four (24), to the northeast corner of section twenty-four (24) of said township and range; thence northerly along the range line between ranges five (5) and six (6) east to the place of beginning.

Excepting from the force and effect of this proclamation all lands which may have been prior to the date hereof embraced in any legal entry or covered by any lawful filing duly of record in the proper United States land office, or upon which any valid settlement has been made pursuant to law and the statutory period within which to make entry or filing of record has not expired, and all mining claims duly located and held according to the laws of the United States and rules and regulations not in conflict therewith.

Provided, That this exception shall not continue to apply to any particular tract of land unless the entryman, settler, or claimant continues to comply with the law under which the entry, filing, settlement, or location was made.

Warning is hereby expressly given to all persons not to enter or make settlement upon the tract of land reserved by this proclamation.

In witness whereof I have hereunto set my hand and caused the seal of the United States to be affixed.

[SEAL.]   Done at the city of Washington, this 17th day of June, A. D. 1892, and of the Independence of the United States the one hundred and sixteenth.

BENJ. HARRISON.

By the President:

WILLIAM F. WHARTON,
Acting Secretary of State.

BY THE PRESIDENT OF THE UNITED STATES OF AMERICA.

A PROCLAMATION.

Whereas it is provided by section 24 of the act of Congress approved March 3, 1891, entitled "An act to repeal timber-culture laws, and for other purposes"—

That the President of the United States may from time to time set apart and reserve in any State or Territory having public land bearing forests, in any part of the public lands wholly or in part covered with timber or undergrowth, whether of commercial value or not, as public reservations; and the President shall by public proclamation declare the establishment of such reservations and the limits thereof.

And whereas the public lands in the State of Colorado within the limits hereinafter described are in part covered with timber, and it appears that the public good would be promoted by setting apart and reserving said lands as a public reservation:

Now, therefore, I, Benjamin Harrison, President of the United States, by virtue of the power in me vested by section 24 of the aforesaid act of Congress, do hereby make known and proclaim that there is hereby reserved from entry or settlement and set apart as a public reservation all those certain tracts, pieces, or parcels of land lying and being situate in the State of Colorado and particularly described as follows, to wit:

Township ten (10) south of ranges sixty-eight (68), sixty-nine (69), and seventy (70) west; township nine (9) south of ranges sixty-eight (68) and sixty-nine (69) west; township eight (8) south of range sixty-nine (69) west, and so much of township ten (10) south of range seventy-one (71) west, township nine (9) south of range seventy (70) west, township eight (8) south of range seventy (70) west, and township seven (7 south of range sixty-nine (69) west as lie to the eastward of the South Platte River.

Excepting from the force and effect of this proclamation all lands which may have been prior to the date hereof embraced in any legal entry or covered by any lawful filing duly of record in the proper United States land office, or upon which any valid settlement has been made pursuant to law and the statutory period within which to make entry or filing of record has not expired, and all mining claims duly located and held according to the laws of the United States and rules and regulations not in conflict therewith.

Provided, That this exception shall not continue to apply .o any particular tract of land unless the entryman, settler, or claimant continues to comply with the law under which the entry, filing, settlement, or location was made.

Warning is hereby expressly given to all persons not to enter or make settlement upon the tract of land reserved by this proclamation.

In witness whereof I have hereunto set my hand and caused the seal of the United States to be affixed.

[SEAL.] Done at the city of Washington, this 23d day of June, A. D. 1892, and of the Independence of the United States the one hundred and sixteenth.

BENJ. HARRISON.

By the President:

WILLIAM F. WHARTON,

Acting Secretary of State.

BY THE PRESIDENT OF THE UNITED STATES OF AMERICA.

A PROCLAMATION.

To whom it may concern:

Whereas the governor of the State of Idaho has represented to me that within said State there exist an insurrection and condition of domestic violence and resistance to the laws to meet and overcome which the resources at his command are unequal; and

Whereas he has further represented that the legislature of said State is not now in session and can not be promptly convened; and

Whereas by reason of said conditions the said governor, as chief executive of the State, has called upon me, as Chief Executive of the Government of the United States, for assistance in repressing said violence and restoring and maintaining the peace:

Now, therefore, I, Benjamin Harrison, President of the United States, by virtue of section 4, Article IV, of the Constitution of the United States and of the laws of Congress enacted in pursuance thereof, do hereby command all persons engaged in said insurrection and in resistance to the laws to immediately disperse and retire peaceably to their respective abodes.

In witness whereof I have hereunto set my hand and caused the seal of the United States to be affixed.

[SEAL.]   Done at the city of Washington, this 15th day of July, A. D. 1892, and of the Independence of the United States the one hundred and seventeenth.

                           BENJ. HARRISON.

By the President:

    JOHN W. FOSTER, *Secretary of State.*

BY THE PRESIDENT OF THE UNITED STATES OF AMERICA.

A PROCLAMATION.

Whereas by a joint resolution approved June 29, 1892, it was resolved by the Senate and House of Representatives of the United States of America in Congress assembled—

That the President of the United States be authorized and directed to issue a proclamation recommending to the people the observance in all their localities of the four hundredth anniversary of the discovery of America, on the 21st of October, 1892, by public demonstrations and by suitable exercises in their schools and other places of assembly.

Now, therefore, I, Benjamin Harrison, President of the United States of America, in pursuance of the aforesaid joint resolution, do hereby appoint Friday, October 21, 1892, the four hundredth anniversary of the discovery of America by Columbus, as a general holiday for the people of the United States. On that day let the people, so far as possible, cease from toil and devote themselves to such exercises as may best express honor to the discoverer and their appreciation of the great achievements of the four completed centuries of American life.

Columbus stood in his age as the pioneer of progress and enlightenment. The system of universal education is in our age the most prominent and salutary feature of the spirit of enlightenment, and it is peculiarly appropriate that the schools be made by the people the center of the day's demonstration. Let the national flag float over every schoolhouse in the country and the exercises be such as shall impress upon our youth the patriotic duties of American citizenship.

In the churches and in the other places of assembly of the people let there be expressions of gratitude to Divine Providence for the devout faith of the discoverer and for the divine care and guidance which has directed our history and so abundantly blessed our people.

In testimony whereof I have hereunto set my hand and caused the seal of the United States to be affixed.

[SEAL.]   Done at the city of Washington, this 21st day of July, A. D. 1892, and of the Independence of the United States the one hundred and seventeenth.

                           BENJ. HARRISON.

By the President:

    JOHN W. FOSTER, *Secretary of State.*

BY THE PRESIDENT OF THE UNITED STATES OF AMERICA.

A PROCLAMATION.

Whereas by reason of unlawful obstructions, combinations, and assemblages of persons it has become impracticable, in my judgment, to enforce by the ordinary course of judicial proceedings the laws of the United States within the State and district of Wyoming, the United States marshal, after repeated efforts, being unable by his ordinary deputies or by any civil posse which he is able to obtain to execute the process of the United States courts:

Now, therefore, be it known that I, Benjamin Harrison, President of the United States, do hereby command all persons engaged in such resistance to the laws and the process of the courts of the United States to cease such opposition and resistance and to disperse and retire peaceably to their respective abodes on or before Wednesday, the 3d day of August next.

In witness whereof I have hereunto set my hand and caused the seal of the United States to be affixed.

[SEAL.]   Done at the city of Washington, this 30th day of July, A. D. 1892, and of the Independence of the United States the one hundred and seventeenth.

                                                BENJ. HARRISON.

By the President:

  JOHN W. FOSTER,
      Secretary of State.

BY THE PRESIDENT OF THE UNITED STATES OF AMERICA.

A PROCLAMATION.

Whereas by an act of Congress approved July 26, 1892, entitled "An act to enforce reciprocal commercial relations between the United States and Canada, and for other purposes," it is provided—

That with a view of securing reciprocal advantages for the citizens, ports, and vessels of the United States, on and after the 1st day of August, 1892, whenever and so often as the President shall be satisfied that the passage through any canal or lock connected with the navigation of the St. Lawrence River, the Great Lakes, or the waterways connecting the same of any vessels of the United States, or of cargoes or passengers in transit to any port of the United States, is prohibited or is made difficult or burdensome by the imposition of tolls or otherwise which, in view of the free passage through the St. Marys Falls Canal now permitted to vessels of all nations, he shall deem to be reciprocally unjust and unreasonable, he shall have the power, and it shall be his duty, to suspend, by proclamation to that effect, for such time and to such extent (including absolute prohibition) as he shall deem just, the right of free passage through the St. Marys Falls Canal so far as it relates to vessels owned by the subjects of the government so discriminating against the citizens, ports, or vessels of the United States or to any cargoes, portions of cargoes or passengers in transit to the ports of the government making such discrimination. whether carried in vessels of the United States or of other nations.

In such case and during such suspension tolls shall be levied, collected, and paid as follows, to wit: Upon freight of whatever kind or description not to exceed $2 per ton, upon passengers not to exceed $5 each, as shall be from time to time determined by the President: *Provided*, That no tolls shall be charged or collected upon freight or passengers carried to and landed at Ogdensburg, or any port west of Ogdensburg and south of a line drawn from the northern boundary of the State of New York through the St. Lawrence River, the Great Lakes, and their connecting channels to the northern boundary of the State of Minnesota.

SEC. 2. All tolls so charged shall be collected under such regulations as shall be prescribed by the Secretary of the Treasury, who may require the master of each vessel to furnish a sworn statement of the amount and kind of cargo and the number of passengers carried and the destination of the same, and such proof of the actual delivery of such cargo or passengers at some port or place within the limits above named as he shall deem satisfactory; and until such proof is furnished such freight and passengers may be considered to have been landed at some port or place outside of those limits, and the amount of tolls which would have accrued if they had been so delivered shall constitute a lien, which may be enforced against the vessel in default wherever and whenever found in the waters of the United States.

And whereas the government of the Dominion of Canada imposes a toll amounting to about 20 cents per ton on all freight passing through the Welland Canal in transit to a port of the United States, and also a further toll on all vessels of the United States and on all passengers in transit to a port of the United States, all of which tolls are without rebate; and

Whereas the government of the Dominion of Canada, in accordance with an order in council of April 4, 1892, refunds 18 cents per ton of the 20-cent toll at the Welland Canal on wheat, Indian corn, pease, barley, rye, oats, flaxseed, and buckwheat upon condition that they are originally shipped for and carried to Montreal or some port east of Montreal for export, and that if transshipped at an intermediate point such transshipment is made within the Dominion of Canada, but allows no such nor any other rebate on said products when shipped to a port of the United States or when carried to Montreal for export if transshipped within the United States; and

Whereas the government of the Dominion of Canada by said system of rebate and otherwise discriminates against the citizens of the United States in the use of said Welland Canal, in violation of the provisions of Article XXVII of the treaty of Washington concluded May 8, 1871; and

Whereas said Welland Canal is connected with the navigation of the Great Lakes, and I am satisfied that the passage through it of cargoes in transit to ports of the United States is made difficult and burdensome by said discriminating system of rebate and otherwise and is reciprocally unjust and unreasonable:

Now, therefore, I, Benjamin Harrison, President of the United States of America, by virtue of the power to that end conferred upon me by said act of Congress approved July 26, 1892, do hereby direct that from and after September 1, 1892, until further notice a toll of 20 cents per ton be levied, collected, and paid on all freight of whatever kind or description passing through the St. Marys Falls Canal in transit to any port of the Dominion of Canada, whether carried in vessels of the United States or of other nations; and to that extent I do hereby suspend from and after said date the right of free passage through said St. Marys Falls Canal of any and all cargoes or portions of cargoes in transit to Canadian ports.

In testimony whereof I have hereunto set my hand and caused the seal of the United States to be affixed.

[SEAL.]   Done at the city of Washington, this 18th day of August, A. D. 1892, and of the Independence of the United States of America the one hundred and seventeenth.

BENJ. HARRISON.

By the President:

JOHN W. FOSTER,
Secretary of State.

BY THE PRESIDENT OF THE UNITED STATES OF AMERICA.

A PROCLAMATION.

Whereas by a written agreement made on the 8th day of December, 1890, the Crow tribe of Indians, in the State of Montana, agreed to dispose of and sell to the United States, for certain considerations in said agreement specified, all that portion of the Crow Indian Reservation in the State of Montana lying west and south of the following lines, to wit:

Beginning in the mid-channel of the Yellowstone River at a point which is the northwest corner of section No. 36, township No. 2 north of range 27 east of the principal meridian of Montana; thence running in a southwesterly direction, following the top of the natural divide between the waters flowing into the Yellowstone and Clarks Fork rivers upon the west and those flowing into Pryor Creek and West Pryor Creek on the east, to the base of West Pryor Mountain; thence due south and up the north slope of said Pryor Mountain on a true meridian line to a point 15 miles due north from the established line between Montana and Wyoming; thence in a due easterly course on a parallel of latitude to a point where it intersects the mid-channel of the Big Horn River; thence following up the mid-channel of said river to a point where it crosses the Montana and Wyoming State line.

And whereas it is stipulated in the eleventh clause or section of said agreement that all lands upon that portion of the reservation by said agreement ceded which prior to the date thereof had been allotted in severalty to Indians of the Crow tribe shall be retained and enjoyed by them; and

Whereas it is provided in the twelfth clause or section of said agreement that, in accordance with the provisions of article 6 of the treaty of May 7, A. D. 1868, said cession of lands shall not be construed to deprive without his or her consent any individual Indian of the Crow tribe of his or her right to any tract of land selected by him or her in conformity with said treaty or as provided by the agreement approved by Congress April 11, A. D. 1882; and

Whereas it is further provided in said twelfth clause or section that in ratifying said agreement the Congress of the United States shall cause all such lands to be surveyed and certificates duly issued for the same to said Indians, as provided in the treaty of May 7, 1868, before said ceded portion of the reservation shall be opened for settlement; and

Whereas by the thirteenth clause or section of said agreement of December 8, 1890, it is made a condition of said agreement that it shall not be binding upon either party until ratified by the Congress of the United States, and when so ratified that said cession of lands so acquired by the United States shall not be opened for settlement until the boundary lines set forth and described in said agreement have been surveyed and definitely marked by suitable permanent monuments, erected every half mile wherever practicable, along the entire length of said boundary line; and

Whereas said agreement was duly ratified and confirmed by the thirty-first section of the act of Congress approved March 3, 1891; and

Whereas it is provided in section 34 of said act of March 3, 1891—

That whenever any of the lands acquired by the agreement with said Crow Indians hereby ratified and confirmed shall by operation of law or the proclamation of the President of the United States be open to settlement, they shall, except mineral lands, be disposed of to actual settlers only under the provisions of the homestead laws, except section 2301 of the Revised Statutes, which shall not apply: *Provided, however*, That each settler under and in accordance with the provisions of said homestead laws shall before receiving a patent for his homestead pay to the United States for the land so taken by him, in addition to the fees provided by law, and within five years from the date of the first original entry, the sum of $1.50 for each acre thereof, one-half of which shall be paid within two years; and any person otherwise qualified who has attempted to but for any cause failed to secure a title in fee to a homestead under existing law, or who made entry under what is known as the commuted provision of the homestead law, shall be qualified to make a homestead entry upon any of said lands in conformity with the provisions of this section; that any person who may be entitled to the privilege of selecting land in severalty under the provisions of article 6 of the treaty of May 7, 1868, with the Crow Indians, and which provisions were continued in force by the agreement with said Indians ratified and confirmed by the act of Congress approved April 11, 1882, or any other act or treaty, shall have the right for a period of sixty days to make such selections in any part of the territory by said agreement ceded, and such locations are hereby confirmed: *Provided further*, That all white persons who located upon said Crow Reservation by reason of an erroneous survey of the boundary and were afterwards allowed to file upon their location in the United States land office shall have thirty days in which to renew their filings, and their locations are hereby confirmed; and that in all cases where claims were located under the mining laws of the United States, and such location was made prior to December 1, 1890, by a locator qualified therefor who believed that he or she was so locating on lands outside the Crow Indian Reservation, such locator shall be allowed thirty days within which to relocate the said mining claims so theretofore located by them within the limits of the ceded portion of said Crow Indian Reservation, and upon such relocation such proceedings shall be had as are conformable to law and in accordance with the provisions of this act.

And whereas the boundary lines of said ceded lands have been duly surveyed and marked as stipulated in the thirteenth clause or section of said agreement; and

Whereas a written agreement was concluded with said Crow Indians on the 27th day of August, 1892, under and by virtue of the following clause in the Indian appropriation act of Congress approved July 13, 1892, to wit:

* * * To enable the Secretary of the Interior, in his discretion, to appoint a commission to negotiate with the Crow Indians of Montana for a modification of the agreement concluded with said Indians December 8, 1890, and ratified by Congress March 3, 1891, and to pay the necessary and actual expenses of said commissioners: *Provided*, That no such modification shall be valid unless assented to by a majority of the male adult members of the Crow tribe of Indians and be approved by the Secretary of the Interior.

Which said agreement was assented to by a majority of the male adult members of the Crow tribe of Indians, as attested by their signatures thereto, and has been duly approved by the Secretary of the Interior; and

Whereas it is stipulated and agreed in the first clause or section of said agreement of August 27, 1892, that the persons named in a schedule attached to and made a part of said agreement, marked ''Schedule A,'' include all the members of said Crow tribe who are entitled to the benefits of the eleventh section of said agreement of December 8, 1890, and that each of said persons is entitled to the land therein described as his selection in full satisfaction of his claim under said section; and that the persons named in a schedule attached to and made a part of said agreement of August 27, 1892, marked ''Schedule B,'' include all the members of said tribe who are entitled to the benefits of the twelfth section of said agreement of December 8, 1890, and of the proviso of the thirty-fourth section of the act of Congress approved March 3, 1891, extending the privilege of making selections on the ceded lands for a period of sixty days, and that each of the said persons therein named is entitled to retain the tract of land theretofore selected by him within the limits of the tract of land therein described as containing his selection of his claim under the said section (or the said proviso); and

Whereas it is stipulated and agreed by the second clause or section of said agreement of August 27, 1892, that all lands ceded by said agreement may be opened to settlement, upon the approval of the said agreement, by proclamation of the President:

Provided, That all lands within the ceded tract selected or set apart for the use of individual Indians and described in the aforesaid Schedules ''A'' and ''B'' shall be exempt from cession and shall remain a part of the Crow Indian Reservation, and shall continue under the exclusive control of the Interior Department until they shall have been surveyed and certificates or patents issued therefor as provided in the agreement of December 8, 1890, or until relinquished or surrendered by the Indian or Indians claiming the same: *Provided further*, That such lands shall be described as set forth in Schedules ''A'' and ''B,'' and shall be exempted from settlement in the proclamation of the President opening the ceded lands, and that where lands so set apart are not described by legal subdivisions then the township or section or tract of land within whose limits such Indians' selections are located shall not be opened to settlement until the Indian allotments therein contained shall have been surveyed and proper evidence of title issued therefor.

Now, therefore, I, Benjamin Harrison, President of the United States, by virtue of the power in me vested by the agreements and statutes hereinbefore mentioned and by other the laws of the United States, do hereby declare and make known that all of the lands within that portion of the Crow Indian Reservation in Montana ceded to the United States by the said agreement of December 8, 1890, and hereinbefore described, except those hereinafter mentioned and described, are open to settlement under the terms of and subject to all the conditions, limitations, reservations, and restrictions contained in the thirty-fourth section of the act of Congress approved March 3, 1891, and hereinbefore quoted, and other laws applicable thereto.

The lands exempted from the operation of this proclamation, being those embraced in Schedules "A" and "B" attached to the agreement of August 27, 1892, are described as follows:

1.—SURVEYED LANDS.

IN TOWNSHIP 1 NORTH, RANGE 26 EAST.

Fractional section 24; the north half, the east half of southeast quarter, and west half of southwest quarter of fractional section 25; fractional section 26; lot 5 of fractional section 34; the north half of northeast quarter and the northeast quarter of northwest quarter of section 35; and the northeast quarter of northeast quarter of section 36.

IN TOWNSHIP 1 NORTH, RANGE 27 EAST.

Fractional section 7; lots 1, 2, 3, 4, 5, and 6, the southwest quarter of northeast quarter, the southeast quarter, and the south half of the southwest quarter of fractional section 8; the south half of northwest quarter of section 9; the north half of the northwest quarter and the southwest quarter of the northwest quarter of section 17; fractional section 18; the north half and the southwest quarter of section 19.

IN TOWNSHIP 3 SOUTH, RANGE 24 EAST.

The north half of the southwest quarter of section 3; the southeast quarter of the northeast quarter and lots 2, 3, and 4 of section 4; fractional section 5; the southeast quarter and the south half of the southwest quarter of section 6; section 7; west half of section 8; the east half of the northwest quarter and the southwest quarter of the northwest quarter of section 17; lots 1, 2, 3, 4, 5, and 6, the northeast quarter of the northeast quarter, the south half of the northeast quarter, and the southeast quarter of the northwest quarter and the south half of section 18; lots 1, 3, 4, and 5 and the east half of southwest quarter, section 19; and lots 1, 2, 3, and 4 in section 30.

IN TOWNSHIP 4 SOUTH, RANGE 23 EAST.

Lots 4, 5, 6, 7, 8, 9, and 13, the south half of northwest quarter, the southeast quarter of southeast quarter, and the northeast quarter of the southwest quarter, section 1; section 2; the north half, the southeast quarter, and the north half of southwest quarter, section 3; section 4; the east half and the southwest quarter of section 8; the north half and the southwest quarter of section 9; the east half and the southwest quarter of section 11; section 12; the north half, the south half of the southeast quarter, the east half of the southwest quarter, and lots 1, 2, and 3 of section 13; the north half, the southeast quarter, and the south half of the southwest quarter of section 14; the north half of section 17; the north half, the east half of the southeast quarter, and the north half of the southwest quarter of section 18; the northwest quarter of section 19; the east half and the northwest quarter of section 20; the south half of the northwest quarter of section 22; all of section 23 except the northwest quarter of northwest quarter; section 24; lots 2 and 3 in section 25; the north half of northeast quarter, the northwest quarter, the north half of the southwest quarter, and lots 1, 2, 5, 6, 7, and 8 of section 26; the south half of the southeast quarter of section 27; the northwest quarter of section 33; the fractional east half and the southwest quarter of section 34; lots 2, 3, 4, 5, 6, 7, 9, and 10 of section 35.

IN TOWNSHIP 5 SOUTH OF RANGE 23 EAST.

Lot 5 and southwest quarter of northwest quarter of section 2; lots 1, 2, 6, 7, 8, 9, 12, and 14 and southeast quarter of southeast quarter of section 3; the fractional east half, the south half of northwest quarter, and the southwest quarter of section 4; the south half of the northeast quarter and the north half of the southeast quarter of section 7; the south half of the north half and the south half of section 8; lots 1, 2, 3, 4, 6, 7, and 8 and the west half of section 9; lots 1, 2, 3, and 4, the west half of the northeast quarter, and the south half of section 10; the northwest quarter of section 15; section 16; the east half of the northeast quarter and the south half of section 17; the northwest quarter of the northeast quarter, the southeast quarter of the southeast quarter, the west half, and lots 1, 2, 4, and 5, section 20; the southwest quarter of section 21; the west half of southwest quarter, section 26; the south half of section 27; the west half of the northeast quarter, the northwest quarter, and the south half of section 28; lots 1, 2, 3, 4, 6, and 7, the northwest quarter, the south half of the southeast quarter, and the west half of the southwest quarter of section 29; the northeast quarter of northeast quarter, the northeast quarter of the southeast quarter, and the south half of the southeast quarter of section 30; the northeast quarter, the northeast quarter of the northwest quarter, and the southeast quarter of section 31; lots 3, 4, 5, 6, 9, and 10, the southwest quarter of the southeast quarter, and the southwest quarter of section 32; lot 1, the north half of the northeast quarter, and the northwest quarter of section 33; and the west half of the northeast quarter and the northwest quarter of section 34.

2.—UNSURVEYED LANDS WHICH WHEN SURVEYED WILL BE DESCRIBED AS FOLLOWS:

IN TOWNSHIP 1 NORTH OF RANGE 15 EAST.

The southwest quarter of the northwest quarter, the northwest quarter of the southwest quarter, and the south half of the southwest quarter of section 27; the southeast quarter of the northeast quarter and the east half of the southeast quarter of section 28; the east half of the northeast quarter of section 33; the north half, the north half of the southeast quarter, and the northeast quarter of the southwest quarter of section 34; the south half of the north half and the south half of section 35; and the southwest quarter of the northwest quarter, the southeast quarter, the north half of the southwest quarter, and the southwest quarter of the southwest quarter of section 36.

IN TOWNSHIP 1 NORTH, RANGE 16 EAST.

The southwest quarter of the southwest quarter of section 31.

IN TOWNSHIP 1 SOUTH OF RANGE 15 EAST.

The north half of the north half and the southeast quarter of the northeast quarter of section 1.

IN TOWNSHIP 1 SOUTH OF RANGE 16 EAST.

The north half of the northeast quarter and the southwest quarter of the northwest quarter of section 6, and the southeast quarter of the northeast quarter of section 24.

IN TOWNSHIP 1 SOUTH OF RANGE 18 EAST.

The southeast quarter of the southwest quarter of section 27; the northwest quarter of the southeast quarter and the south half of the southeast quarter of section 28; the north half of the northeast quarter of section 33; and the northeast quarter and the east half of the northwest quarter of section 34.

IN TOWNSHIP 1 SOUTH OF RANGE 17 EAST.

The east half of the northeast quarter, the east half of the northwest quarter, the southwest quarter of the northwest quarter, the northwest quarter of the southeast quarter, and the northeast quarter of the southwest quarter of section 19; the south half of the southeast quarter and the southeast quarter of the southwest quarter of section 28; and the north half of the northeast quarter and the northeast quarter of the northwest quarter of section 33.

IN TOWNSHIP 1 SOUTH OF RANGE 25 EAST.

The northeast quarter of the southeast quarter, the south half of the southeast quarter, and the southeast quarter of the southwest quarter of section 25, and the northeast quarter of the northwest quarter and the west half of section 36.

IN TOWNSHIP 1 SOUTH OF RANGE 26 EAST.

The south half of the southeast quarter of section 19; the southeast quarter, the northeast quarter of the southwest quarter, and the south half of the southwest quarter of section 20; the west half of the southwest quarter of section 21; the west half of the northwest quarter of section 28; the north half and the northwest quarter of the southwest quarter of section 29; the north half of the northeast quarter, the southeast quarter of the northeast quarter, the southwest quarter of the northwest quarter, the north half of the southeast quarter, and the southwest quarter of section 30.

IN TOWNSHIP 2 SOUTH OF RANGE 13 EAST.

The southwest quarter of the northwest quarter and the northwest quarter of the southwest quarter of section 27; the southeast quarter of the northeast quarter and the east half of the southeast quarter of section 28; and the east half, the east half of the northwest quarter, the northeast quarter of the southeast quarter, and the northeast quarter of the southwest quarter of section 33.

IN TOWNSHIP 2 SOUTH OF RANGE 18 EAST.

The southeast quarter and the east half of the southwest quarter of section 1

IN TOWNSHIP 2 SOUTH OF RANGE 20 EAST.

The east half, the east half of the northwest quarter, the southwest quarter of the northwest quarter, and the north half of the southwest quarter of section 28; the northeast quarter and the north half of the southeast quarter of section 29; the south half of the northeast quarter, the north half of the southeast quarter, and the southeast quarter of the southeast quarter of section 34; the south half of the north half and the south half of section 35; and the southwest quarter of the northwest quarter, the northwest quarter of the southeast quarter, the south half of the southeast quarter, and the southwest quarter of section 36.

IN TOWNSHIP 2 SOUTH OF RANGE 21 EAST.

The west half of the northeast quarter, the northwest quarter of the southeast quarter, the east half of the west half, and the southwest quarter of the southwest quarter of section 32.

IN TOWNSHIP 2 SOUTH OF RANGE 24 EAST.

The northeast quarter of the southeast quarter and the south half of the southeast quarter of section 21; the northeast quarter, the north half of the southeast quarter, and the southwest quarter of section 22; the west half of the northwest quarter of section 27; the northeast quarter of section 28; and the northeast quarter, the southeast quarter of the northwest quarter, the north half of the southeast quarter, and the southwest quarter of section 29.

IN TOWNSHIP 3 SOUTH OF RANGE 18 EAST.

The west half of section 14; the west half of the northeast quarter and the east half of the northwest quarter of section 23; the southwest quarter of the northeast quarter, the southeast quarter of the northwest quarter, the northwest quarter of the southeast quarter, and the northeast quarter of the southwest quarter of section 31; the northeast quarter, the south half of the northwest quarter, and the north half of the southwest quarter of section 32; the south half of the northeast quarter and the southeast quarter of section 33; the southwest quarter of the northeast quarter and the south half of the northwest quarter, the west half of the southeast quarter, and the southwest quarter of section 34; the south half of section 35; and the southeast quarter of the northeast quarter and the southeast quarter of section 36.

IN TOWNSHIP 3 SOUTH OF RANGE 19 EAST.

The northeast quarter, the north half of the southeast quarter, the southwest quarter of the southeast quarter, and the east half of the southwest quarter of section 12; the northwest quarter of section 29; the east half of the northeast quarter, the southwest quarter of the northeast quarter, the southeast quarter of the northwest quarter, and the south half of section 30; and the southwest quarter of the northwest quarter and the west half of the southwest quarter of section 31.

IN TOWNSHIP 3 SOUTH OF RANGE 20 EAST.

The northeast quarter, the north half of the northwest quarter, the southeast quarter of the northwest quarter, and the northeast quarter of the southeast quarter of section 1; the north half of the northeast quarter and the northeast quarter of the northwest quarter of section 2; the north half of the northwest quarter, the southwest quarter of the northwest quarter, and the west half of the southwest quarter of section 5; the southeast quarter of the northeast quarter, the southeast quarter, and the southeast quarter of the southwest quarter of section 6; and the west half of the northeast quarter and the northwest quarter of section 7.

IN TOWNSHIP 3 SOUTH OF RANGE 21 EAST.

The northwest quarter of the southwest quarter and the south half of the southwest quarter of section 5; the east half of the southeast quarter and the west half of section 6; the northeast quarter of the northeast quarter of section 7; and the north half of the northwest quarter of section 8.

IN TOWNSHIP 3 SOUTH OF RANGE 23 EAST.

The southeast quarter of the northeast quarter and the east half of the southeast quarter of section 12; the east half of section 13; the southeast quarter of the southeast quarter of section 23; the southeast quarter of the northeast quarter, the east half of the southeast quarter, and the southwest quarter of the southwest quarter of section 24; the east half of the east half, the west half of the northwest quarter, and the southwest quarter of section 25; the northeast quarter of the southeast quarter and the south half of the southeast quarter of section 26; the south half of the south half of section 34; the northeast quarter, the north half of the southeast quarter, the southwest quarter of the southeast quarter, and the south half of the southwest quarter of section 35; and the northwest quarter of section 36.

IN TOWNSHIP 4 SOUTH OF RANGE 18 EAST.

The northwest quarter of the northeast quarter and the north half of the northwest quarter of section 3; the north half of the northeast quarter of section 4; the southeast quarter of the southwest quarter of section 13; the west half of the northeast quarter, the east half of the northwest quarter, the southeast quarter, and the northeast quarter of the southwest quarter of section 24; the northeast quarter, the north half of the southeast quarter, the southwest quarter of the southeast quarter, and the southwest quarter of section 25; the south half of the southeast quarter of section 29; the northwest quarter of the northeast quarter and the northeast quarter of the northwest quarter of section 32; the northeast quarter of the northeast quarter, the northwest quarter, the northeast quarter of the southeast quarter, and the south half of the southeast quarter of section 35; and the west half of the northeast quarter, the northwest quarter, and the northwest quarter of the southwest quarter of section 36

IN TOWNSHIP 6 SOUTH OF RANGE 18 EAST.

The east half of the southeast quarter and the southwest quarter of the southeast quarter of section 20, and the west half of the northeast quarter, the northeast quarter of the northwest quarter, and the south half of the northwest quarter of section 29.

IN TOWNSHIP 6 SOUTH OF RANGE 19 EAST.

The northeast quarter, the east half of the northwest quarter, the southwest quarter of the northwest quarter, the north half of the southeast quarter, and the northwest quarter of the southwest quarter of section 15; the southeast quarter of the northwest quarter and the northeast quarter of the southwest quarter of section 16; the south half of the northeast quarter and the north half of the southeast quarter of section 19; and the south half of the northwest quarter and the north half of the southwest quarter of section 20.

IN TOWNSHIP 6 SOUTH OF RANGE 23 EAST.

The north half of the northwest quarter and the north half of the southeast quarter of section 5; the south half of the southeast quarter of section 8; section 17; and the west half of the northwest quarter of section 16.

3.—TOWNSHIPS, SECTIONS, OR TRACTS OF LAND WITHIN WHICH INDIAN SELECTIONS ARE LOCATED.

TRACT I.

Beginning at a point in the mid-channel of the Yellowstone River 1½ miles below the mouth of the Clarks Fork River; thence running in a southwesterly direction along a line parallel to and 1½ miles distant from the mid-channel of the Clarks Fork River to the south line of township 2 south of range 24 east; thence west along said township line to the mid-channel of the Clarks Fork River; thence northeast along the mid-channel of the Clarks Fork River to the mid-channel of the Yellowstone River; thence northeast along the mid-channel of said river to the point of beginning.

TRACT 2.

All that part of township 2 south of range 24 east lying south of the Yellowstone River and west of the Clarks Fork River.

TRACT 3.

Sections 29, 31, and 32, township 5 south of range 21 east; sections 5, 6, 7, 8, 17, and 18, township 6 south of range 21 east; and sections 1, 2, 11, 12, 13, and 14, township 6 south of range 20 east.

TRACT 4.

Beginning at a point in the mid-channel of the Yellowstone River opposite the mouth of Duck Creek; thence running in a southwesterly direction along the mid-channel of the Yellowstone River to a point 1½ miles below the mouth of the Clarks Fork River; thence in a southwesterly direction along a line parallel to and 1½ miles distant from the mid-channel of the said Clarks Fork River to a point 1½ miles due south of the mid-channel of the said Yellowstone River; thence running in a northeasterly direction along a line parallel to and 1½ miles distant from the mid-channel of the Yellowstone River to the mid-channel of Duck Creek; thence in a northerly direction along the mid-channel of Duck Creek to the point of beginning.

TRACT 5.

All that part of townships 2 and 3 south of range 23 lying south of the mid-channel of the Yellowstone River and north of a line running parallel thereto and 1½ miles distant therefrom.

TRACT 6.

Beginning in the mid-channel of the main or West Fork of Red Lodge Creek at the point where it intersects the line known as the line of the Blake survey, and which was formerly supposed to be the south boundary of the Crow Indian Reserve; thence running due east along the lines of said Blake survey for a distance of 1 mile; thence running northeasterly along a line parallel to and 1 mile from the mid-channel of the said West Fork of said Red Lodge Creek for a distance of 10 miles; thence due west to the mid-channel of the said West Fork of said Red Lodge Creek; thence southwesterly along the mid-channel of the said West Fork of said creek to the place of beginning.

TRACT 7.

Townships 4 south of ranges 21 and 22 east.

TRACT 8.

All that part of the east half of township 1 south of range 26 east lying south of the Yellowstone River, and all that part of the west half of township 1 south of range 27 east lying south of the Yellowstone River.

TRACT 9.

Section 14, township 3 south of range 19 east.

TRACT 10.

Beginning in the mid-channel of the main or West Fork of Red Lodge Creek at the point where it intersects the line known as the line of the Blake survey, and which was formerly supposed to be the south boundary of the Crow Indian Reserve; thence running due east along the line of said Blake survey for a distance of 1 mile; thence running northeasterly along a line parallel to and 1 mile from the mid-channel of the said West Fork of said Red Lodge Creek for a distance of 10 miles; thence due west to the mid-channel of the said West Fork of said Red Lodge Creek; thence southwesterly along the mid-channel of the said West Fork of said Red Lodge Creek to the place of beginning.

In witness whereof I have hereunto set my hand and caused the seal of the United States to be affixed.

[SEAL.]   Done at the city of Washington, this 15th day of October, A. D. 1892, and of the Independence of the United States the one hundred and seventeenth.   BENJ. HARRISON.

By the President:

JOHN W. FOSTER, *Secretary of State.*

BY THE PRESIDENT OF THE UNITED STATES OF AMERICA.

A PROCLAMATION.

Whereas it is provided by section 13 of the act of Congress of March 3, 1891, entitled "An act to amend Title LX, chapter 3, of the Revised Statutes of the United States, relating to copyrights," that said act "shall only apply to a citizen or subject of a foreign state or nation when such foreign state or nation permits to citizens of the United States of America the benefit of copyright on substantially the same basis as its own citizens, or when such foreign state or nation is a party to an international agreement which provides for reciprocity in the granting of copyright, by the terms of which agreement the United States of America may at its pleasure become a party to such agreement;" and

Whereas it is also provided by said section that "the existence of either of the conditions aforesaid shall be determined by the President of the United States by proclamation made from time to time as the purposes of this act may require;" and

Whereas satisfactory official assurances have been given that in Italy the law permits to citizens of the United States the benefit of copyright on substantially the same basis as to the subjects of Italy:

Now, therefore, I, Benjamin Harrison, President of the United States of America, do declare and proclaim that the first of the conditions specified in section 13 of the act of March 3, 1891, now exists and is fulfilled in respect to the subjects of Italy.

In testimony whereof I have hereunto set my hand and caused the seal of the United States to be affixed.

[SEAL.]   Done at the city of Washington, this 31st day of October, 1892, and of the Independence of the United States the one hundred and seventeenth.   BENJ. HARRISON.

By the President:

JOHN W. FOSTER, *Secretary of State.*

BY THE PRESIDENT OF THE UNITED STATES OF AMERICA.

A PROCLAMATION.

The gifts of God to our people during the past year have been so abundant and so special that the spirit of devout thanksgiving awaits not a call, but only the appointment of a day when it may have a common expression. He has stayed the pestilence at our door; He has given us more love for the free civil institutions in the creation of which His directing providence was so conspicuous; He has awakened a deeper reverence for law; He has widened our philanthropy by a call to succor the distress in other lands; He has blessed our schools and is bringing forward a patriotic and God-fearing generation to execute His great and benevolent designs for our country; He has given us great increase in material wealth and a wide diffusion of contentment and comfort in the homes of our people; He has given His grace to the sorrowing.

Wherefore, I, Benjamin Harrison, President of the United States, do call upon all our people to observe, as we have been wont, Thursday, the 24th day of this month of November, as a day of thanksgiving to God for His mercies and of supplication for His continued care and grace.

In testimony whereof I have hereunto set my hand and caused the seal of the United States to be affixed.

[SEAL.]   Done at the city of Washington, this 4th day of November, 1892, and of the Independence of the United States the one hundred and seventeenth.

BENJ. HARRISON.

By the President:

JOHN W. FOSTER,
        Secretary of State.

EXECUTIVE ORDERS.

AMENDMENT OF CIVIL-SERVICE RULES.

JANUARY 20, 1892.

Special Departmental Rule No. 1 is hereby amended by adding at the end of paragraph 10 the following: ''and elevator conductors;'' so that as amended the paragraph will read:

In all the Departments: Bookbinders and elevator conductors.

BENJ. HARRISON.

AMENDMENT OF CIVIL-SERVICE RULES.

UNITED STATES CIVIL SERVICE COMMISSION,
Washington, D. C., January 12, 1892.

The PRESIDENT.

SIR: We have the honor to recommend that Executive orders heretofore issued designating the places to be filled by noncompetitive examination under clause (*d*) of section 2 of General Rule III be amended so as to include among those places, in all the Departments where authorized by law and employed, ''captains of the watch'' and ''lieutenants of the watch.'' The captains and lieutenants of the watch in the Treasury Department and the captain of the watch in the Post-Office Department are now included in this category, and the object of this recommendation is to place all the Departments on the same footing with respect to these places.

The occasion for the recommendation at this time is the receipt by this Commission of a request from the Secretary of the Interior for a noncompetitive examination of a person named by him for appointment as captain of the watch in the Interior Department.

The place is now subject to competitive examination, but the Commission sees no good reason why one rule should not apply to all the Departments; hence this recommendation.

If you approve the recommendation, your indorsement of approval on this letter and its return to the Commission is requested. As it is not a change of rule, it does not require to go to the Department of State for record.

We have the honor to be, your obedient servants,

CHAS. LYMAN,
HUGH S. THOMPSON,
Commissioners.

EXECUTIVE MANSION, *January 25, 1892.*

The within recommendation is approved.

BENJ HARRISON.

AMENDMENTS OF CIVIL-SERVICE RULES.

FEBRUARY 23, 1892.

Indian Rule VI is hereby amended by inserting after the word "appointment" the following: "from one agency to another;" so that as amended the rule will read:

Subject to the conditions stated in Rule IV, transfers may be made after absolute appointment from one agency to another, from one school to another, and from one district to another, under such regulations as the Commissioner of Indian Affairs, with the approval of the Secretary of the Interior, may prescribe.

Indian Rule IV, section 1, clause (*b*), is hereby amended by inserting after the word "averages" the following: "who have not been three times certified;" so that as amended the clause will read:

If fitness for the vacant place is tested by competitive examination, the Commission shall certify from the proper register of the district in which the vacancy exists the names of the three eligibles thereon, of the sex called for, having the highest averages, who have not been three times certified: *Provided,* That the eligibles upon any register who have been allowed preference under section 1754 of the Revised Statutes shall be certified, according to their grade, before all other eligibles thereon: *And provided further,* That if the vacancy is in the grade of matron or teacher, and the wife of the superintendent of the school in which the vacancy exists is an eligible, she may be given preference in certification if the appointing officer so requests.

Section 5 of the same rule is also hereby amended by inserting after the word "vacancy" the following: "in any agency or;" so that as amended the clause will read:

In case of the sudden occurrence of a vacancy in any agency or in any school during a school term which the public interest requires to be immediately filled the

Commissioner of Indian Affairs is authorized, in his discretion, to provide for the temporary filling of the same until a regular appointment can be made under the provisions of sections 1, 2, and 3 of this rule, and when such regular appointment is made the temporary appointment shall terminate. All temporary appointments made under this authority and their termination shall at once be reported to the Commission.

BENJ. HARRISON.

EXECUTIVE MANSION,
Washington, D. C., May 5, 1892.

In the exercise of the authority vested in the President by the seventeen hundred and fifty-third section of the Revised Statutes—

It is ordered, That the office of the United States Commission of Fish and Fisheries be, and the same is hereby, classified as a part of the classified departmental service and for the purpose of applying the civil-service rules thereto the officers, clerks, and other employees of said Commission are hereby arranged in the following classes, viz:

Class A.—All persons receiving an annual salary of less than $720, or a compensation at the rate of less than $720 per annum.

Class B.—All persons receiving an annual salary of $720 or more, or a compensation at the rate of $720 or more, but less than $840 per annum.

Class C.—All persons receiving an annual salary of $840 or more, or a compensation at the rate of $840 or more, but less than $900 per annum.

Class D.—All persons receiving an annual salary of $900 or more, or a compensation at the rate of $900 or more, but less than $1,000 per annum.

Class E.—All persons receiving an annual salary of $1,000 or more, or a compensation at the rate of $1,000 or more, but less than $1,200 per annum.

Class 1.—All persons receiving an annual salary of $1,200 or more, or a compensation at the rate of $1,200 or more, but less than $1,400 per annum.

Class 2.—All persons receiving an annual salary of $1,400 or more, or a compensation at the rate of $1,400 or more, but less than $1,600 per annum.

Class 3.—All persons receiving an annual salary of $1,600 or more, or a compensation at the rate of $1,600 or more, but less than $1,800 per annum.

Class 4.—All persons receiving an annual salary of $1,800 or more, or a compensation at the rate of $1,800 or more, but less than $2,000 per annum.

Class 5.—All persons receiving an annual salary of $2,000 or more, or a compensation at the rate of $2,000 per annum.

Provided, That no person who may be appointed to an office by and with the advice and consent of the Senate, and that no person who may be employed merely as a messenger, laborer, workman, or watchman, shall be considered as within this classification, and no person so employed shall be assigned to the duties of a classified place.

Provided further, That no person shall be admitted to any place not excepted from examination by the civil-service rules in any of the classes above designated until he or she shall have passed an appropriate examination under the United States Civil Service Commission and his or her eligibility has been certified to by said Commission.

BENJ. HARRISON

CIVIL SERVICE.—AMENDMENT OF EXECUTIVE ORDERS.

MAY 7, 1892.

Executive orders heretofore issued declaring the places subject to noncompetitive examination under clause (*d*) of section 2 of General Rule III are hereby amended so as to include among said places the following:

In the Commission of Fish and Fisheries: Fish culturists and machinists.

BENJ. HARRISON.

AMENDMENT OF CIVIL-SERVICE RULES.

MAY 7, 1892.

Special Departmental Rule No. 1 is hereby amended so as to include among the places excepted from examination therein the following:

In the Commission of Fish and Fisheries: Ichthyologist and editor, one scientific assistant, captains, officers, ships writers and crews on vessels of the Commission, and pilots.

BENJ. HARRISON.

SEPTEMBER 16, 1892.

In order that the members of the Grand Army of the Republic employed in the public service in the city of Washington may have the opportunity of joining in the parade arranged for Tuesday, the 20th of September instant, and that all others may unite with the citizens of the District of Columbia in showing honor to the Union soldiers and sailors to be gathered in the national capital on that occasion—

It is hereby ordered, That the several Executive Departments and the Public Printing Office be closed on that day.

By the President:

BENJ. HARRISON.

AMENDMENT OF CIVIL-SERVICE RULES.

EXECUTIVE MANSION, *September 23, 1892.*

Departmental Rule X, Customs Rule VII, Postal Rule VII, and Indian Rule VII are hereby amended by inserting in the proviso of each of said rules, after the word "therefrom," the words "or the widow of any such person," and after the word "he" the words "or she;" so that as amended the proviso of each of said rules will read:

Provided, That certification may be made, subject to the other conditions of this rule, for the reinstatement of any person who served in the military or naval service in the late War of the Rebellion and was honorably discharged therefrom, or the widow of any such person, without regard to the length of time he or she has been separated from the service.

BENJ. HARRISON.

FOURTH ANNUAL MESSAGE.

EXECUTIVE MANSION, *December 6, 1892.*

To the Senate and House of Representatives:

In submitting my annual message to Congress I have great satisfaction in being able to say that the general conditions affecting the commercial and industrial interests of the United States are in the highest degree favorable. A comparison of the existing conditions with those of the most favored period in the history of the country will, I believe, show that so high a degree of prosperity and so general a diffusion of the comforts of life were never before enjoyed by our people.

The total wealth of the country in 1860 was $16,159,616,068. In 1890 it amounted to $62,610,000,000, an increase of 287 per cent.

The total mileage of railways in the United States in 1860 was 30,626. In 1890 it was 167,741, an increase of 448 per cent; and it is estimated that there will be about 4,000 miles of track added by the close of the year 1892.

The official returns of the Eleventh Census and those of the Tenth Census for seventy-five leading cities furnish the basis for the following comparisons:

In 1880 the capital invested in manufacturing was $1,232,839,670.

In 1890 the capital invested in manufacturing was $2,900,735,884.

In 1880 the number of employees was 1,301,388.

In 1890 the number of employees was 2,251,134.

In 1880 the wages earned were $501,965,778.

In 1890 the wages earned were $1,221,170,454.

In 1880 the value of the product was $2,711,579,899.

In 1890 the value of the product was $4,860,286,837.

I am informed by the Superintendent of the Census that the omission of certain industries in 1880 which were included in 1890 accounts in part for the remarkable increase thus shown, but after making full allowance for differences of method and deducting the returns for all industries not included in the census of 1880 there remain in the reports from these seventy-five cities an increase in the capital employed of $1,522,-745,604, in the value of the product of $2,024,236,166, in wages earned of $677,943,929, and in the number of wage earners employed of 856,029. The wage earnings not only show an increased aggregate, but an increase per capita from $386 in 1880 to $547 in 1890, or 41.71 per cent.

The new industrial plants established since October 6, 1890, and up to October 22, 1892, as partially reported in the American Economist, number 345, and the extension of existing plants 108; the new capital invested amounts to $40,449,050, and the number of additional employees to 37,285.

The Textile World for July, 1892, states that during the first six months of the present calendar year 135 new factories were built, of which 40 are cotton mills, 48 knitting mills, 26 woolen mills, 15 silk mills, 4 plush mills, and 2 linen mills. Of the 40 cotton mills 21 have been built in the Southern States. Mr. A. B. Shepperson, of the New York Cotton Exchange, estimates the number of working spindles in the United States on September 1, 1892, at 15,200,000, an increase of 660,000 over the year 1891. The consumption of cotton by American mills in 1891 was 2,396,-000 bales, and in 1892 2,584,000 bales, an increase of 188,000 bales. From the year 1869 to 1892, inclusive, there has been an increase in the consumption of cotton in Europe of 92 per cent, while during the same period the increased consumption in the United States has been about 150 per cent.

The report of Ira Ayer, special agent of the Treasury Department, shows that at the date of September 30, 1892, there were 32 companies manufacturing tin and terne plate in the United States and 14 companies building new works for such manufacture. The estimated investment in buildings and plants at the close of the fiscal year June 30, 1893, if existing conditions were to be continued, was $5,000,000 and the estimated rate of production 200,000,000 pounds per annum. The actual production for the quarter ending September 30, 1892, was 10,952,725 pounds.

The report of Labor Commissioner Peck, of New York, shows that during the year 1891, in about 6,000 manufacturing establishments in that State embraced within the special inquiry made by him, and representing 67 different industries, there was a net increase over the year 1890 of $31,315,130.68 in the value of the product and of $6,377,925.09 in the amount of wages paid. The report of the commissioner of labor for the State of Massachusetts shows that 3,745 industries in that State paid $129,416,248 in wages during the year 1891, against $126,030,303 in 1890, an increase of $3,335,945, and that there was an increase of $9,932,490 in the amount of capital and of 7,346 in the number of persons employed in the same period.

During the last six months of the year 1891 and the first six months of 1892 the total production of pig iron was 9,710,819 tons, as against

9,202,703 tons in the year 1890, which was the largest annual production ever attained. For the same twelve months of 1891-92 the production of Bessemer ingots was 3,878,581 tons, an increase of 189,710 gross tons over the previously unprecedented yearly production of 3,688,871 gross tons in 1890. The production of Bessemer steel rails for the first six months of 1892 was 772,436 gross tons, as against 702,080 gross tons during the last six months of the year 1891.

The total value of our foreign trade (exports and imports of merchandise) during the last fiscal year was $1,857,680,610, an increase of $128,-283,604 over the previous fiscal year. The average annual value of our imports and exports of merchandise for the ten fiscal years prior to 1891 was $1,457,322,019. It will be observed that our foreign trade for 1892 exceeded this annual average value by $400,358,591, an increase of 27.47 per cent. The significance and value of this increase are shown by the fact that the excess in the trade of 1892 over 1891 was wholly in the value of exports, for there was a decrease in the value of imports of $17,513,754.

The value of our exports during the fiscal year 1892 reached the highest figure in the history of the Government, amounting to $1,030,278,148, exceeding by $145,797,338 the exports of 1891 and exceeding the value of the imports by $202,875,686. A comparison of the value of our exports for 1892 with the annual average for the ten years prior to 1891 shows an excess of $265,142,651, or of 34.65 per cent. The value of our imports of merchandise for 1892, which was $829,402,462, also exceeded the annual average value of the ten years prior to 1891 by $135,-215,940. During the fiscal year 1892 the value of imports free of duty amounted to $457,999,658, the largest aggregate in the history of our commerce. The value of the imports of merchandise entered free of duty in 1892 was 55.35 per cent of the total value of imports, as compared with 43.35 per cent in 1891 and 33.66 per cent in 1890.

In our coastwise trade a most encouraging development is in progress, there having been in the last four years an increase of 16 per cent. In internal commerce the statistics show that no such period of prosperity has ever before existed. The freight carried in the coastwise trade of the Great Lakes in 1890 aggregated 28,295,959 tons. On the Mississippi, Missouri, and Ohio rivers and tributaries in the same year the traffic aggregated 29,405,046 tons, and the total vessel tonnage passing through the Detroit River during that year was 21,684,000 tons. The vessel tonnage entered and cleared in the foreign trade of London during 1890 amounted to 13,480,767 tons, and of Liverpool 10,941,800 tons, a total for these two great shipping ports of 24,422,568 tons, only slightly in excess of the vessel tonnage passing through the Detroit River. And it should be said that the season for the Detroit River was but 228 days, while of course in London and Liverpool the season was for the entire year. The vessel tonnage passing through the St. Marys Canal for the fiscal year

1892 amounted to 9,828,874 tons, and the freight tonnage of the Detroit River is estimated for that year at 25,000,000 tons, against 23,209,619 tons in 1891. The aggregate traffic on our railroads for the year 1891 amounted to 704,398,609 tons of freight, compared with 691,344,437 tons in 1890, an increase of 13,054,172 tons.

Another indication of the general prosperity of the country is found in the fact that the number of depositors in savings banks increased from 693,870 in 1860 to 4,258,893 in 1890, an increase of 513 per cent, and the amount of deposits from $149,277,504 in 1860 to $1,524,844,506 in 1890, an increase of 921 per cent. In 1891 the amount of deposits in savings banks was $1,623,079,749. It is estimated that 90 per cent of these deposits represent the savings of wage earners. The bank clearances for nine months ending September 30, 1891, amounted to $41,049,390,808. For the same months in 1892 they amounted to $45,189,601,947, an excess for the nine months of $4,140,211,139.

There never has been a time in our history when work was so abundant or when wages were as high, whether measured by the currency in which they are paid or by their power to supply the necessaries and comforts of life. It is true that the market prices of cotton and wheat have been low. It is one of the unfavorable incidents of agriculture that the farmer can not produce upon orders. He must sow and reap in ignorance of the aggregate production of the year, and is peculiarly subject to the depreciation which follows overproduction. But while the fact I have stated is true as to the crops mentioned, the general average of prices has been such as to give to agriculture a fair participation in the general prosperity. The value of our total farm products has increased from $1,363,-646,866 in 1860 to $4,500,000,000 in 1891, as estimated by statisticians, an increase of 230 per cent. The number of hogs January 1, 1891, was 50,625,106 and their value $210,193,925; on January 1, 1892, the number was 52,398,019 and the value $241,031,415. On January 1, 1891, the number of cattle was 36,875,648 and the value $544,127,908; on January 1, 1892, the number was 37,651,239 and the value $570,749,155.

If any are discontented with their state here, if any believe that wages or prices, the returns for honest toil, are inadequate, they should not fail to remember that there is no other country in the world where the conditions that seem to them hard would not be accepted as highly prosperous. The English agriculturist would be glad to exchange the returns of his labor for those of the American farmer and the Manchester workmen their wages for those of their fellows at Fall River.

I believe that the protective system, which has now for something more than thirty years continuously prevailed in our legislation, has been a mighty instrument for the development of our national wealth and a most powerful agency in protecting the homes of our workingmen from the invasion of want. I have felt a most solicitous interest to preserve to our working people rates of wages that would not only give daily bread, but supply a comfortable margin for those home attractions and family comforts and enjoyments without which life is neither hopeful nor sweet. They are American citizens—a part of the great people for whom our Constitution and Government were framed and instituted—and it can not be a perversion of that Constitution to so legislate as to preserve in their homes the comfort, independence, loyalty, and sense of interest in the Government which are essential to good citizenship in peace, and which will bring this stalwart throng, as in 1861, to the defense of the flag when it is assailed.

It is not my purpose to renew here the argument in favor of a protective tariff. The result of the recent election must be accepted as having introduced a new policy. We must assume that the present tariff, constructed upon the lines of protection, is to be repealed and that there is to be substituted for it a tariff law constructed solely with reference to revenue; that no duty is to be higher because the increase will keep open an American mill or keep up the wages of an American workman, but that in every case such a rate of duty is to be imposed as will bring to the Treasury of the United States the largest returns of revenue. The contention has not been between schedules, but between principles, and it would be offensive to suggest that the prevailing party will not carry into legislation the principles advocated by it and the pledges given to the people. The tariff bills passed by the House of Representatives at the last session were, as I suppose, even in the opinion of their promoters, inadequate, and justified only by the fact that the Senate and House of Representatives were not in accord and that a general revision could not therefore be undertaken.

I recommend that the whole subject of tariff revision be left to the incoming Congress. It is matter of regret that this work must be delayed for at least three months, for the threat of great tariff changes introduces so much uncertainty that an amount, not easily estimated, of business inaction and of diminished production will necessarily result. It is possible also that this uncertainty may result in decreased revenues from customs duties, for our merchants will make cautious orders for foreign goods in view of the prospect of tariff reductions and the uncertainty as to when they will take effect. Those who have advocated a protective tariff can well afford to have their disastrous forecasts of a change of policy disappointed. If a system of customs duties can be framed that will set the idle wheels and looms of Europe in motion and crowd our warehouses with foreign-made goods and at the same time keep our own mills busy; that will give us an increased participation in the "markets of the world" of greater value than the home market we surrender; that will give increased work to foreign workmen upon products to be consumed by our people without diminishing the amount of work to be done here; that will enable the American manufacturer to pay to his workmen from 50 to 100 per cent more in wages than is paid in the foreign mill, and yet to compete in our market and in foreign markets with the foreign producer; that will further reduce the cost of articles of wear and food without reducing the wages of those who produce them; that can be celebrated, after its effects have been realized, as its expectation has been in European as well as in American cities, the authors and promoters of it will be entitled to the highest praise. We have had in our history several experiences of the contrasted effects of a revenue and of a protective tariff, but this generation has not felt them, and the experience of one generation is not highly instructive to the next. The friends of the protective system with undiminished confidence in the principles they have advocated will await the results of the new experiment.

The strained and too often disturbed relations existing between the employees and the employers in our great manufacturing establishments have not been favorable to a calm consideration by the wage earner of the effect upon wages of the protective system. The facts that his wages were the highest paid in like callings in the world and that a maintenance of this rate of wages in the absence of protective duties upon the product of his labor was impossible were obscured by the passion evoked by these contests. He may now be able to review the question in the light of his personal experience under the operation of a tariff for revenue only. If that experience shall demonstrate that present rates of wages are thereby maintained or increased, either absolutely or in their purchasing power, and that the aggregate volume of work to be done in this country is increased or even maintained, so that there are more or as many days' work in a year, at as good or better wages, for the American workmen as has been the case under the protective system, everyone will rejoice. A general process of wage reduction can not be contemplated by any patriotic citizen without the gravest apprehension. It may be, indeed I believe is, possible for the American manufacturer to compete successfully with his foreign rival in many branches of production without the defense of protective duties if the pay rolls are equalized; but the conflict that stands between the producer and that result and the distress of our working people when it is attained are not pleasant to contemplate. The Society of the Unemployed, now holding its frequent and threatening parades in the streets of foreign cities, should not be allowed to acquire an American domicile.

The reports of the heads of the several Executive Departments, which are herewith submitted, have very naturally included a résumé of the whole work of the Administration with the transactions of the last fiscal year. The attention not only of Congress but of the country is again invited to the methods of administration which have been pursued and to the results which have been attained. Public revenues amounting to $1,414,079,292.28 have been collected and disbursed without loss from misappropriation, without a single defalcation of such importance as to attract the public attention, and at a diminished per cent of cost for collection.   The public business has been transacted not only with fidelity, but progressively and with a view to giving to the people in the fullest possible degree the benefits of a service established and maintained for their protection and comfort.

Our relations with other nations are now undisturbed by any serious controversy.   The complicated and threatening differences with Germany and England relating to Samoan affairs, with England in relation to the seal fisheries in the Bering Sea, and with Chile growing out of the *Baltimore* affair have been adjusted.

There have been negotiated and concluded, under section 3 of the tariff law, commercial agreements relating to reciprocal trade with the following countries: Brazil, Dominican Republic, Spain for Cuba and Puerto Rico, Guatemala, Salvador, the German Empire, Great Britain for certain West Indian colonies and British Guiana, Nicaragua, Honduras, and Austria-Hungary.*

Of these, those with Guatemala, Salvador, the German Empire, Great Britain, Nicaragua, Honduras, and Austria-Hungary have been concluded since my last annual message.   Under these trade arrangements a free or favored admission has been secured in every case for an important list of American products.   Especial care has been taken to secure markets for farm products, in order to relieve that great underlying industry of the depression which the lack of an adequate foreign market for our surplus often brings.   An opening has also been made for manufactured products that will undoubtedly, if this policy is maintained, greatly augment our export trade.   The full benefits of these arrangements can not be realized instantly.   New lines of trade are to be opened.   The commercial traveler must survey the field.   The manufacturer must adapt his goods to the new markets and facilities for exchange must be established.   This work has been well begun, our merchants and manufacturers having entered the new fields with courage and enterprise.   In the case of food products, and especially with Cuba, the trade did not need to wait, and the immediate results have been most gratifying.   If this policy and these trade arrangements can be continued in force and aided by the establishment of American steamship lines, I do not doubt that we shall within a short period secure fully one-third of the total trade of the countries of Central and South America, which now amounts to about $600,-000,000 annually.   In 1885 we had only 8 per cent of this trade.

The following statistics show the increase in our trade with the countries with which we have reciprocal trade agreements from the date when such agreements went into effect up to September 30, 1892, the increase being in some almost wholly and in others in an important degree the result of these agreements:

The domestic exports to Germany and Austria-Hungary have in-

* See pp. 5576–5577, 5587–5590, 5583–5587, 5716–5718, 5684–5686, 5693–5695, 5688–5693, 5698–5700, 5714–5716, 5718–5719.

creased in value from $47,673,756 to $57,993,064, an increase of $10,-319,308, or 21.63 per cent. With American countries the value of our exports has increased from $44,160,285 to $54,613,598, an increase of $10,453,313, or 23.67 per cent. The total increase in the value of exports to all the countries with which we have reciprocity agreements has been $20,772,621. This increase is chiefly in wheat, flour, meat, and dairy products and in manufactures of iron and steel and lumber. There has been a large increase in the value of imports from all these countries since the commercial agreements went into effect, amounting to $74,294,525, but it has been entirely in imports from the American countries, consisting mostly of sugar, coffee, india rubber, and crude drugs. The alarmed attention of our European competitors for the South American market has been attracted to this new American policy and to our acquisition and their loss of South American trade.

A treaty providing for the arbitration of the dispute between Great Britain and the United States as to the killing of seals in the Bering Sea was concluded on the 29th of February last. This treaty was accompanied by an agreement prohibiting pelagic sealing pending the arbitration, and a vigorous effort was made during this season to drive out all poaching sealers from the Bering Sea. Six naval vessels, three revenue cutters, and one vessel from the Fish Commission, all under the command of Commander Evans, of the Navy, were sent into the sea, which was systematically patrolled. Some seizures were made, and it is believed that the catch in the Bering Sea by poachers amounted to less than 500 seals. It is true, however, that in the North Pacific, while the seal herds were on their way to the passes between the Aleutian Islands, a very large number, probably 35,000, were taken. The existing statutes of the United States do not restrain our citizens from taking seals in the Pacific Ocean, and perhaps should not unless the prohibition can be extended to the citizens of other nations. I recommend that power be given to the President by proclamation to prohibit the taking of seals in the North Pacific by American vessels in case, either as the result of the findings of the Tribunal of Arbitration or otherwise, the restraints can be applied to the vessels of all countries. The case of the United States for the Tribunal of Arbitration has been prepared with great care and industry by the Hon. John W. Foster, and the counsel who represent this Government express confidence that a result substantially establishing our claims and preserving this great industry for the benefit of all nations will be attained.

During the past year a suggestion was received through the British minister that the Canadian government would like to confer as to the possibility of enlarging upon terms of mutual advantage the commercial exchanges of Canada and of the United States, and a conference was held at Washington, with Mr. Blaine acting for this Government and the British minister at this capital and three members of the Dominion cabinet acting as commissioners on the part of Great Britain. The conference developed the fact that the Canadian government was only prepared to offer to the United States in exchange for the concessions asked the admission of natural products. The statement was frankly made that favored rates could not be given to the United States as against the mother country. This admission, which was foreseen, necessarily terminated the conference upon this question. The benefits of an exchange of natural products would be almost wholly with the people of Canada. Some other topics of interest were considered in the conference, and have resulted in the making of a convention for examining the Alaskan boundary and the waters of Passamaquoddy Bay adjacent to Eastport, Me., and in the initiation of an arrangement for the protection of fish life in the coterminous and neighboring waters of our northern border.

The controversy as to tolls upon the Welland Canal, which was presented to Congress at the last session by special message,* having failed of adjustment, I felt constrained to exercise the authority conferred by the act of July 26, 1892, and to proclaim a suspension of the free use of St. Marys Falls Canal to cargoes in transit to ports in Canada.† The Secretary of the Treasury established such tolls as were thought to be equivalent to the exactions unjustly levied upon our commerce in the Canadian canals.

If, as we must suppose, the political relations of Canada and the disposition of the Canadian government are to remain unchanged, a somewhat radical revision of our trade relations should, I think, be made. Our relations must continue to be intimate, and they should be friendly. I regret to say, however, that in many of the controversies, notably those as to the fisheries on the Atlantic, the sealing interests on the Pacific, and the canal tolls, our negotiations with Great Britain have continuously been thwarted or retarded by unreasonable and unfriendly objections and protests from Canada. In the matter of the canal tolls our treaty rights were flagrantly disregarded. It is hardly too much to say that the Canadian Pacific and other railway lines which parallel our northern boundary are sustained by commerce having either its origin or terminus, or both, in the United States. Canadian railroads compete with those of the United States for our traffic, and without the restraints of our interstate-commerce act. Their cars pass almost without detention into and out of our territory.

The Canadian Pacific Railway brought into the United States from China and Japan via British Columbia during the year ended June 30, 1892, 23,239,689 pounds of freight, and it carried from the United States, to be shipped to China and Japan via British Columbia, 24,068,346 pounds of freight. There were also shipped from the United States over this road from Eastern ports of the United States to our Pacific ports during the same year 13,912,073 pounds of freight, and there were received over this road at the United States Eastern ports from ports on the Pacific

Coast 13,293,315 pounds of freight.   Mr. Joseph Nimmo, jr., former chief
of the Bureau of Statistics, when before the Senate Select Committee on
Relations with Canada, April 26, 1890, said that "the value of goods thus
transported between different points in the United States across Canadian
territory probably amounts to $100,000,000 a year."

There is no disposition on the part of the people or Government of the
United States to interfere in the smallest degree with the political relations of Canada.   That question is wholly with her own people.   It is
time for us, however, to consider whether, if the present state of things
and trend of things is to continue, our interchanges upon lines of land
transportation should not be put upon a different basis and our entire
independence of Canadian canals and of the St. Lawrence as an outlet to
the sea secured by the construction of an American canal around the Falls
of Niagara and the opening of ship communication between the Great
Lakes and one of our own seaports.   We should not hesitate to avail
ourselves of our great natural trade advantages.   We should withdraw
the support which is given to the railroads and steamship lines of Canada
by a traffic that properly belongs to us and no longer furnish the earnings which lighten the otherwise crushing weight of the enormous public subsidies that have been given to them.   The subject of the power of
the Treasury to deal with this matter without further legislation has been
under consideration, but circumstances have postponed a conclusion.   It
is probable that a consideration of the propriety of a modification or abrogation of the article of the treaty of Washington relating to the transit
of goods in bond is involved in any complete solution of the question.

Congress at the last session was kept advised of the progress of the
serious and for a time threatening difference between the United States
and Chile.   It gives me now great gratification to report that the Chilean
Government in a most friendly and honorable spirit has tendered and
paid as an indemnity to the families of the sailors of the *Baltimore* who
were killed and to those who were injured in the outbreak in the city of
Valparaiso the sum of $75,000.   This has been accepted not only as an
indemnity for a wrong done, but as a most gratifying evidence that the
Government of Chile rightly appreciates the disposition of this Government to act in a spirit of the most absolute fairness and friendliness in
our intercourse with that brave people.   A further and conclusive evidence of the mutual respect and confidence now existing is furnished by
the fact that a convention submitting to arbitration the mutual claims
of the citizens of the respective Governments has been agreed upon.
Some of these claims have been pending for many years and have been
the occasion of much unsatisfactory diplomatic correspondence.

I have endeavored in every way to assure our sister Republics of Central and South America that the United States Government and its people
have only the most friendly disposition toward them all.   We do not covet
their territory.   We have no disposition to be oppressive or exacting in

our dealings with any of them, even the weakest. Our interests and our hopes for them all lie in the direction of stable governments by their people and of the largest development of their great commercial resources. The mutual benefits of enlarged commercial exchanges and of a more familiar and friendly intercourse between our peoples we do desire, and in this have sought their friendly cooperation.

I have believed, however, while holding these sentiments in the greatest sincerity, that we must insist upon a just responsibility for any injuries inflicted upon our official representatives or upon our citizens. This insistence, kindly and justly but firmly made, will, I believe, promote peace and mutual respect.

Our relations with Hawaii have been such as to attract an increased interest, and must continue to do so. I deem it of great importance that the projected submarine cable, a survey for which has been made, should be promoted. Both for naval and commercial uses we should have quick communication with Honolulu. We should before this have availed ourselves of the concession made many years ago to this Government for a harbor and naval station at Pearl River. Many evidences of the friendliness of the Hawaiian Government have been given in the past, and it is gratifying to believe that the advantage and necessity of a continuance of very close relations is appreciated.

The friendly act of this Government in expressing to the Government of Italy its reprobation and abhorrence of the lynching of Italian subjects in New Orleans by the payment of 125,000 francs, or $24,330.90, was accepted by the King of Italy with every manifestation of gracious appreciation, and the incident has been highly promotive of mutual respect and good will.

In consequence of the action of the French Government in proclaiming a protectorate over certain tribal districts of the west coast of Africa eastward of the San Pedro River, which has long been regarded as the southeastern boundary of Liberia, I have felt constrained to make protest against this encroachment upon the territory of a Republic which was founded by citizens of the United States and toward which this country has for many years held the intimate relation of a friendly counselor.

The recent disturbances of the public peace by lawless foreign marauders on the Mexican frontier have afforded this Government an opportunity to testify its good will for Mexico and its earnest purpose to fulfill the obligations of international friendship by pursuing and dispersing the evil doers. The work of relocating the boundary of the treaty of Guadalupe Hidalgo westward from El Paso is progressing favorably.

Our intercourse with Spain continues on a friendly footing. I regret, however, not to be able to report as yet the adjustment of the claims of the American missionaries arising from the disorders at Ponape, in the Caroline Islands, but I anticipate a satisfactory adjustment in view of renewed and urgent representations to the Government at Madrid.

The treatment of the religious and educational establishments of American citizens in Turkey has of late called for a more than usual share of attention. A tendency to curtail the toleration which has so beneficially prevailed is discernible and has called forth the earnest remonstrance of this Government. Harassing regulations in regard to schools and churches have been attempted in certain localities, but not without due protest and the assertion of the inherent and conventional rights of our countrymen. Violations of domicile and search of the persons and effects of citizens of the United States by apparently irresponsible officials in the Asiatic *vilayets* have from time to time been reported. An aggravated instance of injury to the property of an American missionary at Bourdour, in the Province of Konia, called forth an urgent claim for reparation, which I am pleased to say was promptly heeded by the Government of the Porte. Interference with the trading ventures of our citizens in Asia Minor is also reported, and the lack of consular representation in that region is a serious drawback to instant and effective protection. I can not believe that these incidents represent a settled policy, and shall not cease to urge the adoption of proper remedies.

International copyright has been extended to Italy by proclamation* in conformity with the act of March 3, 1891, upon assurance being given that Italian law permits to citizens of the United States the benefit of copyright on substantially the same basis as to subjects of Italy. By a special convention proclaimed January 15, 1892, reciprocal provisions of copyright have been applied between the United States and Germany. Negotiations are in progress with other countries to the same end.

I repeat with great earnestness the recommendation which I have made in several previous messages that prompt and adequate support be given to the American company engaged in the construction of the Nicaragua ship canal. It is impossible to overstate the value from every standpoint of this great enterprise, and I hope that there may be time, even in this Congress, to give to it an impetus that will insure the early completion of the canal and secure to the United States its proper relation to it when completed.

The Congress has been already advised that the invitations of this Government for the assembling of an international monetary conference to consider the question of an enlarged use of silver were accepted by the nations to which they were addressed. The conference assembled at Brussels on the 22d of November, and has entered upon the consideration of this great question. I have not doubted, and have taken occasion to express that belief as well in the invitations issued for this conference as in my public messages, that the free coinage of silver upon an agreed international ratio would greatly promote the interests of our people and equally those of other nations. It is too early to predict what results may be accomplished by the conference. If any temporary check or delay

*See p. 5736.

intervenes, I believe that very soon commercial conditions will compel the now reluctant governments to unite with us in this movement to secure the enlargement of the volume of coined money needed for the transaction of the business of the world.

The report of the Secretary of the Treasury will attract especial interest in view of the many misleading statements that have been made as to the state of the public revenues. Three preliminary facts should not only be stated but emphasized before looking into details: First, that the public debt has been reduced since March 4, 1889, $259,074,200, and the annual interest charge $11,684,469; second, that there have been paid out for pensions during this Administration up to November 1, 1892, $432,564,178.70, an excess of $114,466,386.09 over the sum expended during the period from March 1, 1885, to March 1, 1889; and, third, that under the existing tariff up to December 1 about $93,000,000 of revenue which would have been collected upon imported sugars if the duty had been maintained has gone into the pockets of the people, and not into the public Treasury, as before. If there are any who still think that the surplus should have been kept out of circulation by hoarding it in the Treasury, or deposited in favored banks without interest while the Government continued to pay to these very banks interest upon the bonds deposited as security for the deposits, or who think that the extended pension legislation was a public robbery, or that the duties upon sugar should have been maintained, I am content to leave the argument where it now rests while we wait to see whether these criticisms will take the form of legislation.

The revenues for the fiscal year ending June 30, 1892, from all sources were $425,868,260.22, and the expenditures for all purposes were $415,-953,806.56, leaving a balance of $9,914,453.66. There were paid during the year upon the public debt $40,570,467.98. The surplus in the Treasury and the bank redemption fund passed by the act of July 14, 1890, to the general fund furnished in large part the cash available and used for the payments made upon the public debt. Compared with the year 1891, our receipts from customs duties fell off $42,069,241.08, while our receipts from internal revenue increased $8,284,823.13, leaving the net loss of revenue from these principal sources $33,784,417.95. The net loss of revenue from all sources was $32,675,972.81.

The revenues, estimated and actual, for the fiscal year ending June 30, 1893, are placed by the Secretary at $463,336,350.44, and the expenditures at $461,336,350.44, showing a surplus of receipts over expenditures of $2,000,000. The cash balance in the Treasury at the end of the fiscal year it is estimated will be $20,992,377.03. So far as these figures are based upon estimates of receipts and expenditures for the remaining months of the current fiscal year, there are not only the usual elements of uncertainty, but some added elements. New revenue legislation, or even the expectation of it, may seriously reduce the public revenues during the period of uncertainty and during the process of business adjustment to the new conditions when they become known. But the Secretary has very wisely refrained from guessing as to the effect of possible changes in our revenue laws, since the scope of those changes and the time of their taking effect can not in any degree be forecast or foretold by him. His estimates must be based upon existing laws and upon a continuance of existing business conditions, except so far as these conditions may be affected by causes other than new legislation.

The estimated receipts for the fiscal year ending June 30, 1894, are $490,121,365.38, and the estimated appropriations $457,261,335.33, leaving an estimated surplus of receipts over expenditures of $32,860,-030.05. This does not include any payment to the sinking fund. In the recommendation of the Secretary that the sinking-fund law be repealed I concur. The redemption of bonds since the passage of the law to June 30, 1892, has already exceeded the requirements by the sum of $990,510,681.49. The retirement of bonds in the future before maturity should be a matter of convenience, not of compulsion. We should not collect revenue for that purpose, but only use any casual surplus. To the balance of $32,860,030.05 of receipts over expenditures for the year 1894 should be added the estimated surplus at the beginning of the year, $20,992,377.03, and from this aggregate there must be deducted, as stated by the Secretary, about $44,000,000 of estimated unexpended appropriations.

The public confidence in the purpose and ability of the Government to maintain the parity of all of our money issues, whether coin or paper, must remain unshaken. The demand for gold in Europe and the consequent calls upon us are in a considerable degree the result of the efforts of some of the European Governments to increase their gold reserves, and these efforts should be met by appropriate legislation on our part. The conditions that have created this drain of the Treasury gold are in an important degree political, and not commercial. In view of the fact that a general revision of our revenue laws in the near future seems to be probable, it would be better that any changes should be a part of that revision rather than of a temporary nature.

During the last fiscal year the Secretary purchased under the act of July 14, 1890, 54,355,748 ounces of silver and issued in payment therefor $51,106,608 in notes. The total purchases since the passage of the act have been 120,479,981 ounces and the aggregate of notes issued $116,-783,590. The average price paid for silver during the year was 94 cents per ounce, the highest price being $1.02¾ July 1, 1891, and the lowest 83 cents March 21, 1892. In view of the fact that the monetary conference is now sitting and that no conclusion has yet been reached, I withhold any recommendation as to legislation upon this subject.

The report of the Secretary of War brings again to the attention of Congress some important suggestions as to the reorganization of the infantry and artillery arms of the service, which his predecessors have before urgently presented. Our Army is small, but its organization should all the more be put upon the most approved modern basis. The conditions upon what we have called the "frontier" have heretofore required the maintenance of many small posts, but now the policy of concentration is obviously the right one. The new posts should have the proper strategic relations to the only "frontiers" we now have—those of the seacoast and of our northern and part of our southern boundary. I do not think that any question of advantage to localities or to States should determine the location of the new posts. The reorganization and enlargement of the Bureau of Military Information which the Secretary has effected is a work the usefulness of which will become every year more apparent. The work of building heavy guns and the construction of coast defenses has been well begun and should be carried on without check.

The report of the Attorney-General is by law submitted directly to Congress, but I can not refrain from saying that he has conducted the increasing work of the Department of Justice with great professional skill. He has in several directions secured from the courts decisions giving increased protection to the officers of the United States and bringing some classes of crime that escaped local cognizance and punishment into the tribunals of the United States, where they could be tried with impartiality.

The numerous applications for Executive clemency presented in behalf of persons convicted in United States courts and given penitentiary sentences have called my attention to a fact referred to by the Attorney-General in his report, namely, that a time allowance for good behavior for such prisoners is prescribed by the Federal statutes only where the State in which the penitentiary is located has made no such provision. Prisoners are given the benefit of the provisions of the State law regulating the penitentiary to which they may be sent. These are various, some perhaps too liberal and some perhaps too illiberal. The result is that a sentence for five years means one thing if the prisoner is sent to one State for confinement and quite a different thing if he is sent to another. I recommend that a uniform credit for good behavior be prescribed by Congress.

I have before expressed my concurrence in the recommendation of the Attorney-General that degrees of murder should be recognized in the Federal statutes, as they are, I believe, in all the States. These grades are founded on correct distinctions in crime. The recognition of them would enable the courts to exercise some discretion in apportioning punishment and would greatly relieve the Executive of what is coming to be a very heavy burden—the examination of these cases on application for commutation.

The aggregate of claims pending against the Government in the Court of Claims is enormous. Claims to the amount of nearly $400,000,000 for the taking of or injury to the property of persons claiming to be loyal during the war are now before that court for examination. When to these are added the Indian depredation claims and the French spoliation claims, an aggregate is reached that is indeed startling. In the defense of all these cases the Government is at great disadvantage. The claimants have preserved their evidence, whereas the agents of the Government are sent into the field to rummage for what they can find. This difficulty is peculiarly great where the fact to be established is the disloyalty of the claimant during the war. If this great threat against our revenues is to have no other check, certainly Congress should supply the Department of Justice with appropriations sufficiently liberal to secure the best legal talent in the defense of these claims and to pursue its vague search for evidence effectively.

The report of the Postmaster-General shows a most gratifying increase and a most efficient and progressive management of the great business of that Department. The remarkable increase in revenues, in the number of post-offices, and in the miles of mail carriage furnishes further evidence of the high state of prosperity which our people are enjoying. New offices mean new hamlets and towns, new routes mean the extension of our border settlements, and increased revenues mean an active commerce. The Postmaster-General reviews the whole period of his administration of the office and brings some of his statistics down to the month of November last. The postal revenues have increased during the last year nearly $5,000,000. The deficit for the year ending June 30, 1892, is $848,341 less than the deficiency of the preceding year. The deficiency of the present fiscal year it is estimated will be reduced to $1,552,423, which will not only be extinguished during the next fiscal year but a surplus of nearly $1,000,000 should then be shown. In these calculations the payments to be made under the contracts for ocean mail service have not been included. There have been added 1,590 new mail routes during the year, with a mileage of 8,563 miles, and the total number of new miles of mail trips added during the year is nearly 17,000,000. The number of miles of mail journeys added during the last four years is about 76,000,000, this addition being 21,000,000 miles more than were in operation in the whole country in 1861.

The number of post-offices has been increased by 2,790 during the year, and during the past four years, and up to October 29 last, the total increase in the number of offices has been nearly 9,000. The number of free-delivery offices has been nearly doubled in the last four years, and the number of money-order offices more than doubled within that time.

For the three years ending June 30, 1892, the postal revenue amounted to $197,744,359, which was an increase of $52,263,150 over the revenue for the three years ending June 30, 1888, the increase during the last three years being more than three and a half times as great as the increase during the three years ending June 30, 1888.   No such increase as that shown for these three years has ever previously appeared in the revenues of the Department.   The Postmaster-General has extended to the post-offices in the larger cities the merit system of promotion introduced by my direction into the Departments here, and it has resulted there, as in the Departments, in a larger volume of work and that better done.

Ever since our merchant marine was driven from the sea by the rebel cruisers during the War of the Rebellion the United States has been pay-ing an enormous annual tribute to foreign countries in the shape of freight and passage moneys.   Our grain and meats have been taken at our own docks and our large imports there laid down by foreign shipmasters.   An increasing torrent of American travel to Europe has contributed a vast sum annually to the dividends of foreign shipowners.   The balance of trade shown by the books of our custom-houses has been very largely reduced and in many years altogether extinguished by this constant drain.   In the year 1892 only 12.3 per cent of our imports were brought in American vessels.   These great foreign steamships maintained by our traffic are many of them under contracts with their respective Govern-ments by which in time of war they will become a part of their armed naval establishments.   Profiting by our commerce in peace, they will become the most formidable destroyers of our commerce in time of war. I have felt, and have before expressed the feeling, that this condition of things was both intolerable and disgraceful.   A wholesome change of pol-icy, and one having in it much promise, as it seems to me, was begun by the law of March 3, 1891.   Under this law contracts have been made by the Postmaster-General for eleven mail routes.   The expenditure involved by these contracts for the next fiscal year approximates $954,-123.33.   As one of the results already reached sixteen American steam-ships, of an aggregate tonnage of 57,400 tons, costing $7,400,000, have been built or contracted to be built in American shipyards.

The estimated tonnage of all steamships required under existing con-tracts is 165,802, and when the full service required by these contracts is established there will be forty-one mail steamers under the American flag, with the probability of further necessary additions in the Brazilian and Argentine service.   The contracts recently let for transatlantic serv-ice will result in the construction of five ships of 10,000 tons each, cost-ing $9,000,000 to $10,000,000, and will add, with the *City of New York* and *City of Paris*, to which the Treasury Department was authorized by legislation at the last session to give American registry, seven of the swiftest vessels upon the sea to our naval reserve.   The contracts made with the lines sailing to Central and South American ports have increased the frequency and shortened the time of the trips, added new ports of call, and sustained some lines that otherwise would almost certainly have been withdrawn.   The service to Buenos Ayres is the first to the Argen-tine Republic under the American flag.   The service to Southampton,

Boulogne, and Antwerp is also new, and is to be begun with the steamships *City of New York* and *City of Paris* in February next.

I earnestly urge the continuance of the policy inaugurated by this legislation, and that the appropriations required to meet the obligations of the Government under the contracts may be made promptly, so that the lines that have entered into these engagements may not be embarrassed. We have had, by reason of connections with the transcontinental railway lines constructed through our own territory, some advantages in the ocean trade of the Pacific that we did not possess on the Atlantic. The construction of the Canadian Pacific Railway and the establishment under large subventions from Canada and England of fast steamship service from Vancouver with Japan and China seriously threaten our shipping interests in the Pacific. This line of English steamers receives, as is stated by the Commissioner of Navigation, a direct subsidy of $400,000 annually, or $30,767 per trip for thirteen voyages, in addition to some further aid from the Admiralty in connection with contracts under which the vessels may be used for naval purposes. The competing American Pacific mail line under the act of March 3, 1891, receives only $6,389 per round trip.

Efforts have been making within the last year, as I am informed, to establish under similar conditions a line between Vancouver and some Australian port, with a view of seizing there a trade in which we have had a large interest. The Commissioner of Navigation states that a very large per cent of our imports from Asia are now brought to us by English steamships and their connecting railways in Canada. With a view of promoting this trade, especially in tea, Canada has imposed a discriminating duty of 10 per cent upon tea and coffee brought into the Dominion from the United States. If this unequal contest between American lines without subsidy, or with diminished subsidies, and the English Canadian line to which I have referred is to continue, I think we should at least see that the facilities for customs entry and transportation across our territory are not such as to make the Canadian route a favored one, and that the discrimination as to duties to which I have referred is met by a like discrimination as to the importation of these articles from Canada.

No subject, I think, more nearly touches the pride, the power, and the prosperity of our country than this of the development of our merchant marine upon the sea. If we could enter into conference with other competitors and all would agree to withhold government aid, we could perhaps take our chances with the rest; but our great competitors have established and maintained their lines by government subsidies until they now have practically excluded us from participation. In my opinion no choice is left to us but to pursue, moderately at least, the same lines.

The report of the Secretary of the Navy exhibits great progress in the construction of our new Navy. When the present Secretary entered upon his duties, only 3 modern steel vessels were in commission. The vessels since put in commission and to be put in commission during the winter will make a total of 19 during his administration of the Department. During the current year 10 war vessels and 3 navy tugs have been launched, and during the four years 25 vessels will have been launched. Two other large ships and a torpedo boat are under contract and the work upon them well advanced, and the 4 monitors are awaiting only the arrival of their armor, which has been unexpectedly delayed, or they would have been before this in commission.

Contracts have been let during this Administration, under the appropriations for the increase of the Navy, including new vessels and their appurtenances, to the amount of $35,000,000, and there has been expended during the same period for labor at navy-yards upon similar work $8,000,000 without the smallest scandal or charge of fraud or partiality. The enthusiasm and interest of our naval officers, both of the staff and line, have been greatly kindled. They have responded magnificently to the confidence of Congress and have demonstrated to the world an unexcelled capacity in construction, in ordnance, and in everything involved in the building, equipping, and sailing of great war ships.

At the beginning of Secretary Tracy's administration several difficult problems remained to be grappled with and solved before the efficiency in action of our ships could be secured. It is believed that as the result of new processes in the construction of armor plate our later ships will be clothed with defensive plates of higher resisting power than are found on any war vessels afloat. We were without torpedoes. Tests have been made to ascertain the relative efficiency of different constructions, a torpedo has been adopted, and the work of construction is now being carried on successfully. We were without armor-piercing shells and without a shop instructed and equipped for the construction of them. We are now making what is believed to be a projectile superior to any before in use. A smokeless powder has been developed and a slow-burning powder for guns of large caliber. A high explosive capable of use in shells fired from service guns has been found, and the manufacture of gun cotton has been developed so that the question of supply is no longer in doubt.

The development of a naval militia, which has been organized in eight States and brought into cordial and cooperative relations with the Navy, is another important achievement. There are now enlisted in these organizations 1,800 men, and they are likely to be greatly extended. I recommend such legislation and appropriations as will encourage and develop this movement. The recommendations of the Secretary will, I do not doubt, receive the friendly consideration of Congress, for he has enjoyed, as he has deserved, the confidence of all those interested in the development of our Navy, without any division upon partisan lines. I earnestly express the hope that a work which has made such noble progress may not now be stayed. The wholesome influence for peace and the increased sense of security which our citizens domiciled in other lands feel when these magnificent ships under the American flag appear is already most gratefully apparent. The ships from our Navy which will appear in the great naval parade next April in the harbor of New York will be a convincing demonstration to the world that the United States is again a naval power.

The work of the Interior Department, always very burdensome, has been larger than ever before during the administration of Secretary Noble. The disability-pension law, the taking of the Eleventh Census, the opening of vast areas of Indian lands to settlement, the organization of Oklahoma, and the negotiations for the cession of Indian lands furnish some of the particulars of the increased work, and the results achieved testify to the ability, fidelity, and industry of the head of the Department and his efficient assistants.

Several important agreements for the cession of Indian lands negotiated by the commission appointed under the act of March 2, 1889, are awaiting the action of Congress. Perhaps the most important of these is that for the cession of the Cherokee Strip. This region has been the source of great vexation to the executive department and of great friction and unrest between the settlers who desire to occupy it and the Indians who assert title. The agreement which has been made by the commission is perhaps the most satisfactory that could have been reached. It will be noticed that it is conditioned upon its ratification by Congress before March 4, 1893. The Secretary of the Interior, who has given the subject very careful thought, recommends the ratification of the agreement, and I am inclined to follow his recommendation. Certain it is that some action by which this controversy shall be brought to an end and these lands opened to settlement is urgent.

The form of government provided by Congress on May 17, 1884, for Alaska was in its frame and purpose temporary. The increase of population and the development of some important mining and commercial interests make it imperative that the law should be revised and better provision made for the arrest and punishment of criminals.

The report of the Secretary shows a very gratifying state of facts as to the condition of the General Land Office. The work of issuing agricultural patents, which seemed to be hopelessly in arrear when the present Secretary undertook the duties of his office, has been so expedited that the bureau is now upon current business. The relief thus afforded to honest and worthy settlers upon the public lands by giving to them an assured title to their entries has been of incalculable benefit in developing the new States and the Territories.

The Court of Private Land Claims, established by Congress for the promotion of this policy of speedily settling contested land titles, is making satisfactory progress in its work, and when the work is completed a great impetus will be given to the development of those regions where unsettled claims under Mexican grants have so long exercised their repressive influence. When to these results are added the enormous cessions of Indian lands which have been opened to settlement, aggregating during this Administration nearly 26,000,000 acres, and the agreements negotiated and now pending in Congress for ratification by which about 10,000,000 additional acres will be opened to settlement, it will be seen how much has been accomplished.

The work in the Indian Bureau in the execution of the policy of recent legislation has been largely directed to two chief purposes: First, the allotment of lands in severalty to the Indians and the cession to the United States of the surplus lands, and, secondly, to the work of educating the Indian for his own protection in his closer contact with the white man and for the intelligent exercise of his new citizenship. Allotments have been made and patents issued to 5,900 Indians under the present Secretary and Commissioner, and 7,600 additional allotments have been made for which patents are now in process of preparation. The school attendance of Indian children has been increased during that time over 13 per cent, the enrollment for 1892 being nearly 20,000. A uniform system of school text-books and of study has been adopted and the work in these national schools brought as near as may be to the basis of the free common schools of the States. These schools can be transferred and merged into the common-school systems of the States when the Indian has fully assumed his new relation to the organized civil community in which he resides and the new States are able to assume the burden. I have several times been called upon to remove Indian agents appointed by me, and have done so promptly upon every sustained complaint of unfitness or misconduct. I believe, however, that the Indian service at the agencies has been improved and is now administered on the whole with a good degree of efficiency. If any legislation is possible by which the selection of Indian agents can be wholly removed from all partisan suggestions or considerations, I am sure it would be a great relief to the Executive and a great benefit to the service. The appropriation for the subsistence of the Cheyenne and Arapahoe Indians made at the last session of Congress was inadequate. This smaller appropriation was estimated for by the Commissioner upon the theory that the large fund belonging to the tribe in the public Treasury could be and ought to be used for their support. In view, however, of the pending depredation claims against this fund and other considerations, the Secretary of the Interior on the 12th of April last submitted a supplemental estimate for $50,000. This appropriation was not made, as it should have been, and the oversight ought to be remedied at the earliest possible date.

In a special message to this Congress at the last session * I stated the reasons why I had not approved the deed for the release to the United

*See pp. 5664-5669.

States by the Choctaws and Chickasaws of the lands formerly embraced in the Cheyenne and Arapahoe Reservation and remaining after allotments to that tribe. A resolution of the Senate expressing the opinion of that body that notwithstanding the facts stated in my special message the deed should be approved and the money, $2,991,450, paid over was presented to me May 10, 1892. My special message was intended to call the attention of Congress to the subject, and in view of the fact that it is conceded that the appropriation proceeded upon a false basis as to the amount of lands to be paid for and is by $50,000 in excess of the amount they are entitled to (even if their claim to the land is given full recognition at the rate agreed upon), I have not felt willing to approve the deed, and shall not do so, at least until both Houses of Congress have acted upon the subject. It has been informally proposed by the claimants to release this sum of $50,000, but I have no power to demand or accept such a release, and such an agreement would be without consideration and void.

I desire further to call the attention of Congress to the fact that the recent agreement concluded with the Kiowas and Comanches relates to lands which were a part of the "leased district," and to which the claim of the Choctaws and Chickasaws is precisely that recognized by Congress in the legislation I have referred to. The surplus lands to which this claim would attach in the Kiowa and Comanche Reservation is 2,500,000 acres, and at the same rate the Government will be called upon to pay to the Choctaws and Chickasaws for these lands $3,125,000. This sum will be further augmented, especially if the title of the Indians to the tract now Greer County, Tex., is established. The duty devolved upon me in this connection was simply to pass upon the form of the deed; but as in my opinion the facts mentioned in my special message were not adequately brought to the attention of Congress in connection with the legislation, I have felt that I would not be justified in acting without some new expression of the legislative will.

The report of the Commissioner of Pensions, to which extended notice is given by the Secretary of the Interior in his report, will attract great attention. Judged by the aggregate amount of work done, the last year has been the greatest in the history of the office. I believe that the organization of the office is efficient and that the work has been done with fidelity. The passage of what is known as the disability bill has, as was foreseen, very largely increased the annual disbursements to the disabled veterans of the Civil War. The estimate for this fiscal year was $144,956,000, and that amount was appropriated. A deficiency amounting to $10,508,621 must be provided for at this session. The estimate for pensions for the fiscal year ending June 30, 1894, is $165,000,000. The Commissioner of Pensions believes that if the present legislation and methods are maintained and further additions to the pension laws are not made the maximum expenditure for pensions will be reached June 30, 1894, and will be at the highest point $188,000,000 per annum.

I adhere to the views expressed in previous messages that the care of the disabled soldiers of the War of the Rebellion is a matter of national concern and duty. Perhaps no emotion cools sooner than that of gratitude, but I can not believe that this process has yet reached a point with our people that would sustain the policy of remitting the care of these disabled veterans to the inadequate agencies provided by local laws. The parade on the 20th of September last upon the streets of this capital of 60,000 of the surviving Union veterans of the War of the Rebellion was a most touching and thrilling episode, and the rich and gracious welcome extended to them by the District of Columbia and the applause that greeted their progress from tens of thousands of people from all the States did much to revive the glorious recollections of the Grand Review when these men and many thousand others now in their graves were welcomed with grateful joy as victors in a struggle in which the national unity, honor, and wealth were all at issue.

In my last annual message I called attention to the fact that some legislative action was necessary in order to protect the interests of the Government in its relations with the Union Pacific Railway. The Commissioner of Railroads has submitted a very full report, giving exact information as to the debt, the liens upon the company's property, and its resources. We must deal with the question as we find it and take that course which will under existing conditions best secure the interests of the United States. I recommended in my last annual message that a commission be appointed to deal with this question, and I renew that recommendation and suggest that the commission be given full power.

The report of the Secretary of Agriculture contains not only a most interesting statement of the progressive and valuable work done under the administration of Secretary Rusk, but many suggestions for the enlarged usefulness of this important Department. In the successful efforts to break down the restrictions to the free introduction of our meat products in the countries of Europe the Secretary has been untiring from the first, stimulating and aiding all other Government officers at home and abroad whose official duties enabled them to participate in the work. The total trade in hog products with Europe in May, 1892, amounted to 82,000,000 pounds, against 46,900,000 in the same month of 1891; in June, 1892, the export aggregated 85,700,000 pounds, against 46,500,000 pounds in the same month of the previous year; in July there was an increase of 41 per cent and in August of 55 per cent over the corresponding months of 1891. Over 40,000,000 pounds of inspected pork have been exported since the law was put into operation, and a comparison of the four months of May, June, July, and August, 1892, with the same months of 1891 shows an increase in the number of pounds of our export of pork products of 62 per cent and an increase in value of 66½ per cent. The exports of dressed beef increased from 137,900,000 pounds in 1889 to 220,500,000 pounds in 1892, or about 60 per cent. During the past year there have been exported 394,607 head of live cattle, as against 205,786 exported in 1889. This increased exportation has been largely promoted by the inspection authorized by law and the faithful efforts of the Secretary and his efficient subordinates to make that inspection thorough and to carefully exclude from all cargoes diseased or suspected cattle. The requirement of the English regulations that live cattle arriving from the United States must be slaughtered at the docks had its origin in the claim that pleuro-pneumonia existed among American cattle and that the existence of the disease could only certainly be determined by a *post mortem* inspection.

The Department of Agriculture has labored with great energy and faithfulness to extirpate this disease, and on the 26th day of September last a public announcement was made by the Secretary that the disease no longer existed anywhere within the United States. He is entirely satisfied after the most searching inquiry that this statement was justified, and that by a continuance of the inspection and quarantine now required of cattle brought into this country the disease can be prevented from again getting any foothold. The value to the cattle industry of the United States of this achievement can hardly be estimated. We can not, perhaps, at once insist that this evidence shall be accepted as satisfactory by other countries; but if the present exemption from the disease is maintained and the inspection of our cattle arriving at foreign ports, in which our own veterinarians participate, confirms it, we may justly expect that the requirement that our cattle shall be slaughtered at the docks will be revoked, as the sanitary restrictions upon our pork products have been. If our cattle can be taken alive to the interior, the trade will be enormously increased.

Agricultural products constituted 78.1 per cent of our unprecedented exports for the fiscal year which closed June 30, 1892, the total exports being $1,030,278,030 and the value of the agricultural products $793,717,676, which exceeds by more than $150,000,000 the shipment of agricultural products in any previous year.

An interesting and a promising work for the benefit of the American farmer has been begun through agents of the Agricultural Department in Europe, and consists in efforts to introduce the various products of Indian corn as articles of human food. The high price of rye offered a favorable opportunity for the experiment in Germany of combining corn meal with rye to produce a cheaper bread. A fair degree of success has been attained, and some mills for grinding corn for food have been introduced. The Secretary is of the opinion that this new use of the products of corn has already stimulated exportations, and that if diligently prosecuted large and important markets can presently be opened for this great American product.

The suggestions of the Secretary for an enlargement of the work of the Department are commended to your favorable consideration. It may, I think, be said without challenge that in no corresponding period has so much been done as during the last four years for the benefit of American agriculture.

The subject of quarantine regulations, inspection, and control was brought suddenly to my attention by the arrival at our ports in August last of vessels infected with cholera. Quarantine regulations should be uniform at all our ports. Under the Constitution they are plainly within the exclusive Federal jurisdiction when and so far as Congress shall legislate. In my opinion the whole subject should be taken into national control and adequate power given to the Executive to protect our people against plague invasions. On the 1st of September last I approved regulations establishing a twenty-day quarantine for all vessels bringing immigrants from foreign ports. This order will be continued in force. Some loss and suffering have resulted to passengers, but a due care for the homes of our people justifies in such cases the utmost precaution. There is danger that with the coming of spring cholera will again appear, and a liberal appropriation should be made at this session to enable our quarantine and port officers to exclude the deadly plague.

But the most careful and stringent quarantine regulations may not be sufficient absolutely to exclude the disease. The progress of medical and sanitary science has been such, however, that if approved precautions are taken at once to put all of our cities and towns in the best sanitary condition, and provision is made for isolating any sporadic cases and for a thorough disinfection, an epidemic can, I am sure, be avoided. This work appertains to the local authorities, and the responsibility and the penalty will be appalling if it is neglected or unduly delayed.

We are peculiarly subject in our great ports to the spread of infectious diseases by reason of the fact that unrestricted immigration brings to us out of European cities, in the overcrowded steerages of great steamships, a large number of persons whose surroundings make them the easy victims of the plague. This consideration, as well as those affecting the political, moral, and industrial interests of our country, leads me to renew the suggestion that admission to our country and to the high privileges of its citizenship should be more restricted and more careful. We have, I think, a right and owe a duty to our own people, and especially to our working people, not only to keep out the vicious, the ignorant, the civil disturber, the pauper, and the contract laborer, but to check the too great flow of immigration now coming by further limitations.

The report of the World's Columbian Exposition has not yet been submitted. That of the board of management of the Government exhibit has been received and is herewith transmitted. The work of construction and of preparation for the opening of the exposition in May next has progressed most satisfactorily and upon a scale of liberality and magnificence that will worthily sustain the honor of the United States.

The District of Columbia is left by a decision of the supreme court of the District without any law regulating the liquor traffic. An old statute of the legislature of the District relating to the licensing of various vocations has hitherto been treated by the Commissioners as giving them power to grant or refuse licenses to sell intoxicating liquors and as subjecting those who sold without licenses to penalties; but in May last the supreme court of the District held against this view of the powers of the Commissioners. It is of urgent importance, therefore, that Congress should supply, either by direct enactment or by conferring discretionary powers upon the Commissioners, proper limitations and restraints upon the liquor traffic in the District. The District has suffered in its reputation by many crimes of violence, a large per cent of them resulting from drunkenness and the liquor traffic. The capital of the nation should be freed from this reproach by the enactment of stringent restrictions and limitations upon the traffic.

In renewing the recommendation which I have made in three preceding annual messages that Congress should legislate for the protection of railroad employees against the dangers incident to the old and inadequate methods of braking and coupling which are still in use upon freight trains, I do so with the hope that this Congress may take action upon the subject. Statistics furnished by the Interstate Commerce Commission show that during the year ending June 30, 1891, there were forty-seven different styles of car couplers reported to be in use, and that during the same period there were 2,660 employees killed and 26,140 injured. Nearly 16 per cent of the deaths occurred in the coupling and uncoupling of cars and over 36 per cent of the injuries had the same origin.

The Civil Service Commission ask for an increased appropriation for needed clerical assistance, which I think should be given. I extended the classified service March 1, 1892, to include physicians, superintendents, assistant superintendents, school-teachers, and matrons in the Indian service, and have had under consideration the subject of some further extensions, but have not as yet fully determined the lines upon which extensions can most properly and usefully be made.

I have in each of the three annual messages which it has been my duty to submit to Congress called attention to the evils and dangers connected with our election methods and practices as they are related to the choice of officers of the National Government. In my last annual message I endeavored to invoke serious attention to the evils of unfair apportionments for Congress. I can not close this message without again calling attention to these grave and threatening evils. I had hoped that it was possible to secure a nonpartisan inquiry by means of a commission into evils the existence of which is known to all, and that out of this might grow legislation from which all thought of partisan advantage should be eliminated and only the higher thought appear of maintaining the freedom and purity of the ballot and the equality of the elector, without the guaranty of which the Government could never have been formed and without the continuance of which it can not continue to exist in peace and prosperity.

It is time that mutual charges of unfairness and fraud between the great parties should cease and that the sincerity of those who profess a desire for pure and honest elections should be brought to the test of their willingness to free our legislation and our election methods from every-thing that tends to impair the public confidence in the announced result. The necessity for an inquiry and for legislation by Congress upon this subject is emphasized by the fact that the tendency of the legislation in some States in recent years has in some important particulars been away from and not toward free and fair elections and equal apportionments. Is it not time that we should come together upon the high plane of patriotism while we devise methods that shall secure the right of every man qualified by law to cast a free ballot and give to every such ballot an equal value in choosing our public officers and in directing the policy of the Government?

Lawlessness is not less such, but more, where it usurps the functions of the peace officer and of the courts. The frequent lynching of colored people accused of crime is without the excuse, which has sometimes been urged by mobs for a failure to pursue the appointed methods for the punishment of crime, that the accused have an undue influence over courts and juries. Such acts are a reproach to the community where they occur, and so far as they can be made the subject of Federal juris-diction the strongest repressive legislation is demanded. A public senti-ment that will sustain the officers of the law in resisting mobs and in protecting accused persons in their custody should be promoted by every possible means. The officer who gives his life in the brave discharge of this duty is worthy of special honor. No lesson needs to be so urgently impressed upon our people as this, that no worthy end or cause can be promoted by lawlessness.

This exhibit of the work of the Executive Departments is submitted to Congress and to the public in the hope that there will be found in it a due sense of responsibility and an earnest purpose to maintain the national honor and to promote the happiness and prosperity of all our people, and this brief exhibit of the growth and prosperity of the country will give us a level from which to note the increase or decadence that new legislative policies may bring to us. There is no reason why the national influence, power, and prosperity should not observe the same rates of in-crease that have characterized the past thirty years. We carry the great impulse and increase of these years into the future. There is no reason why in many lines of production we should not surpass all other nations, as we have already done in some. There are no near frontiers to our possible development. Retrogression would be a crime.

BENJ. HARRISON.

SPECIAL MESSAGES.

EXECUTIVE MANSION, *December 7, 1892.*

To the Senate:

In response to the resolution of the Senate of April 11, 1892, requesting information in regard to the agreement between the United States and Great Britain of 1817 concerning the naval forces to be maintained by the two Governments on the Great Lakes, I transmit herewith a report of the Secretary of State and accompanying papers, giving all the information existing in that Department in regard to the agreement in question.

BENJ. HARRISON.

EXECUTIVE MANSION, *January 4, 1893.*

To the Senate and House of Representatives:

I transmit herewith, for the consideration of Congress, a communication of the 23d of December, 1892, from the Secretary of the Interior, accompanied by an agreement concluded by and between the Cherokee Commission and the Comanche, Kiowa, and Apache tribes of Indians in the Territory of Oklahoma, for the cession of certain lands and for other purposes.

BENJ. HARRISON.

EXECUTIVE MANSION, *January 4, 1893.*

To the Senate and House of Representatives:

I transmit herewith, for the consideration of Congress, a communication of the 23d of December, 1892, from the Secretary of the Interior, accompanied by an agreement concluded by and between the Cherokee Commission and the Pawnee tribe of Indians in the Territory of Oklahoma, for the cession of certain lands and for other purposes.

BENJ. HARRISON.

EXECUTIVE MANSION,
Washington, January 7, 1893.

To the Senate:

In response to the resolution of the Senate of January 6, 1893, calling on the Secretary of State for information whether the provisions of Senate bill No. 3513, absolutely suspending immigration for the period of one year, are in conflict with any treaties now existing between the United States and any foreign countries, I transmit herewith a report from the Secretary of State, giving the information called for.

BENJ. HARRISON.

EXECUTIVE MANSION,
Washington, January 11, 1893.

To the Senate:

In response to the resolutions of the Senate dated December 20, 1892, and January 5, 1893, respectively, I transmit herewith a report from the Secretary of State of the 10th instant, accompanying the reports of Mr. Walter T. Griffin, United States commercial agent at Limoges, France, and Mr. W. H. Edwards, United States consul-general at Berlin, Germany, which were called for by the aforesaid resolutions.

BENJ. HARRISON.

EXECUTIVE MANSION, *January 13, 1893.*

To the Senate and House of Representatives:

I transmit herewith, for your information, a letter from the Secretary of State, inclosing the annual report of the Bureau of American Republics for the year ending June 30, 1892.

BENJ. HARRISON.

EXECUTIVE MANSION,
Washington, January 25, 1893.

To the Senate of the United States:

In response to the resolution of the Senate of the 21st instant, relating to the alleged killing of Frank B. Riley, a sailor of the United States steamship *Newark*, in Genoa, Italy, I transmit herewith a report on the subject from the Secretary of State.

BENJ. HARRISON.

EXECUTIVE MANSION, *January 26, 1893.*

To the Senate and House of Representatives:

I transmit herewith, for the information of Congress, the third regular report of the World's Columbian Commission and the report of the president of the board of lady managers, with the accompanying papers.

BENJ. HARRISON.

EXECUTIVE MANSION, *January 31, 1893.*

To the Senate of the United States:

In compliance with a resolution of the Senate, the House of Representatives concurring, I return herewith the bill (S. 2625) entitled "An act to provide for the punishment of offenses on the high seas."

BENJ. HARRISON.

EXECUTIVE MANSION, *February 2, 1893.*

To the Senate and House of Representatives:

On the 23d of July last the following resolution of the House of Representatives was communicated to me:

Resolved, That the President be requested to inform the House, if not incompatible with the public interests, what regulations are now in force concerning the transportation of imported merchandise in bond or duty paid, and products or manufactures of the United States, from one port in the United States, over Canadian territory, to another port therein, under the provisions of section 3006 of the Revised Statutes; whether further legislation thereon is necessary or advisable, and especially whether a careful inspection of such merchandise should not be had at the frontiers of the United States upon the departure and arrival of such merchandise, and whether the interests of the United States do not require that each car containing such merchandise while in Canadian territory be in the custody and under the surveillance of an inspector of the customs department, the cost of such surveillance to be paid by the foreign carrier transporting such merchandise.

The resolution is limited in its scope to the subject of the transit of merchandise from one port in the United States, through Canadian territory, to another port in the United States, under the provisions of section 3006 of the Revised Statutes; but I have concluded that a review of our treaty obligations, if any, and of our legislation upon the whole subject of the transit of goods from, to, or through Canada is desirable, and therefore address this message to the Congress.

It should be known before new legislation is proposed whether the United States is under any treaty obligations which affect this subject growing out of the provisions of Article XXIX of the treaty of Washington. That article is as follows:

It is agreed that for the term of years mentioned in Article XXXIII of this treaty goods, wares, or merchandise arriving at the ports of New York, Boston, and Portland, and any other ports in the United States which have been or may from time to time be specially designated by the President of the United States, and destined for Her Britannic Majesty's possessions in North America, may be entered at the proper custom-house and conveyed in transit, without the payment of duties, through the territory of the United States, under such rules, regulations, and conditions for the protection of the revenue as the Government of the United States may from time to time prescribe; and under like rules, regulations, and conditions goods, wares, or merchandise may be conveyed in transit, without the payment of duties, from such possessions through the territory of the United States for export from the said ports of the United States.

It is further agreed that for the like period goods, wares, or merchandise arriving at any of the ports of Her Britannic Majesty's possessions in North America and destined for the United States may be entered at the proper custom-house and conveyed in transit, without the payment of duties, through the said possessions under such rules and regulations and conditions for the protection of the revenue as the governments of the said possessions may from time to time prescribe; and under like rules, regulations, and conditions goods, wares, or merchandise may be conveyed in transit, without payment of duties, from the United States through the said possessions to other places in the United States, or for export from ports in the said possessions.

It will be noticed that provision is here made—

First. For the transit in bond, without the payment of duties, of goods arriving at specified ports of the United States, and at others to be designated by the President, destined for Canada.

Second. For the transit from Canada to ports of the United States, without the payment of duties, of merchandise for export.

Third. For the transit of merchandise arriving at Canadian ports, destined for the United States, through Canadian territory to the United States, without the payment of duties to the Dominion government.

Fourth. For the transit of merchandise from the United States to Canadian ports for export without the payment of duties.

Fifth. For the transit of merchandise, without the payment of duties, from the United States, through Canada, to other places in the United States.

The first and second of these provisions were concessions by the United States and were made subject to "such rules, regulations, and conditions for the protection of the revenue as the Government of the United States may from time to time prescribe." The third, fourth, and fifth provisions of the articles are concessions on the part of the Dominion of Canada and are made subject to "such rules and regulations and conditions for the protection of the revenue as the governments of the said possessions may from time to time prescribe." The first and second and the third and fourth of these provisions are reciprocal in their nature. The fifth, which provides for the transit of merchandise from one point in the United States, through Canada, to another point in the United States, is not met by a reciprocal provision for the passage of Canadian goods from one point in Canada to another point in Canada through the United States. If this article of the treaty is in force, the obligations assumed by the United States should be fully and honorably observed until such time as this Government shall free itself from them by methods provided in the treaty or recognized by international law. It is, however, no part of the obligation resting upon the United States under the treaty that it will use the concessions made to it by Canada. This Government would undoubtedly meet its full duty by yielding in an ample manner the concessions made by it to Canada. There could be no just cause of complaint by Great Britain or Canada if the compensating concession to the United States should not be exercised. We have not stipulated in the treaty that we will permit merchandise to be moved through Canadian territory from one point of the United States to another at the will of the shipper. The stipulation is on the part of Canada that it will permit such merchandise to enter its territory from the United States, to pass through it, and to return to the United States without the exaction of duties and without other burdens than such as may be necessary to protect its revenues.

The questions whether we shall continue to allow merchandise to pass from one point in the United States, through Canadian territory, to another point in the United States, and, if so, to what exactions and examinations it shall be subjected on reentering our territory, are wholly within the power of Congress without reference to the question whether Article XXIX is or is not in force.

The treaty of Washington embraced a number of absolutely independent subjects. Its purpose, as recited, was "to provide for an amicable settlement of all causes of difference between the two countries." It provided for four distinct arbitrations of unsettled questions, including the Alabama claims, for a temporary settlement of the questions growing out of the fisheries, and for various arrangements affecting commerce and intercourse between the United States and the British North American possessions. Some of its provisions were made terminable by methods pointed out in the treaty. Articles I to XVII, inclusive, provide for the settlement of the Alabama claims and of the claims of British subjects against the United States, and have been fully executed. Articles XVIII to XXV, inclusive, relate to the subject of the fisheries, and provide for a joint commission to determine what indemnity should be paid to Great Britain for the fishing privileges conceded. These articles have been terminated by the notice provided for in the treaty.

Article XXVI provides for the free navigation of the St. Lawrence, Yukon, Porcupine, and Stikine rivers. Article XXVII provides for the equal use of certain frontier canals and waterways, and contains no provision for termination upon notice. Article XXVIII opens Lake Michigan to the commerce of British subjects under proper regulations, and contains a provision for its abrogation, to which reference will presently be made. Article XXX provides for certain privileges of transshipment on the Lakes and northern waterways, and contains the same provision as Article XXIX as to the method by which it may be terminated. Article XXXI provides for the nonimposition of a Canadian export duty on lumber cut in certain districts in Maine and floated to the sea by the St. Johns River, and contains no limitation as to time and no provision for its abrogation. Article XXXII extended to Newfoundland in the event of proper legislation by that Province the fishery provisions of Articles XVIII to XXV, and was of course abrogated with those articles. Article XXXIII, which provides a method for the abrogation of certain articles of the treaty, I will presently quote at length. The remaining articles of the treaty, namely XXXV to XLII, provide for the arbitration of the dispute as to the Vancouver Island and De Haro Channel boundary, and have been fully executed. Articles XVIII, XIX, XXI, XXVIII, XXIX, and XXX each contains a provision limiting their life to "the term of years mentioned in Article XXXIII of this treaty." The articles between XVIII and XXX, inclusive, which do not contain this provision, are those that provide for an arbitration of the fishery question, which were of course terminable by the completion of the arbitration; Article XXVI, relating to the navigation of the St. Lawrence and other rivers, and Article XXVII, relating to the use of the canals. The question whether Article XXIX is still in force depends, so far as the construction of the treaty goes, upon the meaning of the words "the term of years mentioned in Article XXXIII." That article is as follows:

> The foregoing Articles XVIII to XXV, inclusive, and Article XXX of this treaty shall take effect as soon as the laws required to carry them into operation shall have been passed by the Imperial Parliament of Great Britain, by the parliament of Canada, and by the legislature of Prince Edwards Island on the one hand and by the Congress of the United States on the other. Such assent having been given, the said articles shall remain in force for the period of ten years from the date at which they may come into operation, and, further, until the expiration of two years after either of the high contracting parties shall have given notice to the other of its wish to terminate the same; each of the high contracting parties being at liberty to give such notice to the other at the end of the said period of ten years or at any time afterwards.

The question of construction here presented is whether the reference to "the term of years mentioned in Article XXXIII" is to be construed as limiting the continuance of Article XXIX to the duration of Articles XVIII to XXV and XXX in such a way that the abrogation of those articles necessarily carried with it the other articles of the treaty which contained the reference to Article XXXIII already quoted, or whether the reference to this "term of years" in Articles XXVIII and XXIX was intended to provide a method of abrogation after ten years from the time of their taking effect, viz, a notice of two years of an intention to abrogate. The language of the treaty, considered alone, might support the conclusion that Article XXXIII was intended to provide a uniform method of abrogation for certain other articles. It will be noticed that the treaty does not expressly call for legislation to put Article XXIX into operation. Senator Edmunds, in the discussion in the Senate of the joint resolution terminating the fisheries article, took the view that no legislation was necessary. It seems to me, however, that such legislation was necessary, and Congress acted upon this view in the law of 1873, to which reference will presently be made. An examination of the discussion between the plenipotentiaries who framed the treaty furnishes this entry, which President Cleveland thought to be conclusive of the intention of the plenipotentiaries, viz:

> The transit question was discussed, and it was agreed that any settlement that might be made should include a reciprocal arrangement in that respect for the period for which the fishery articles should be in force.

On March 1, 1873, Congress passed an act entitled "An act to carry into effect the provisions of the treaty between the United States and Great Britain signed in the city of Washington the 8th day of May, 1871, relating to the fisheries." The act consisted of five sections, the first and second of which provided for carrying into effect the provisions of the treaty "relating to the fisheries." The fourth section provided for carrying into effect section 30 of the treaty. These three sections furnished the legislation contemplated by Article **XXXIII** of the treaty to carry into effect Articles **XVIII** to **XXV** and **XXX**. The act, however, went further, as will be seen by an examination of section 3, which is as follows:

That from the date of the President's proclamation authorized by the first section of this act, and so long as the Articles **XVIII** to **XXV**, inclusive, and Article **XXX** of said treaty shall remain in force, according to the terms and conditions of Article **XXXIII** of said treaty, all goods, wares, or merchandise arriving at the ports of New York, Boston, and Portland, and any other ports in the United States which have been or may from time to time be specially designated by the President of the United States, and destined for Her Britannic Majesty's possessions in North America, may be entered at the proper custom-house and conveyed in transit, without the payment of duties, through the territory of the United States, under such rules, regulations, and conditions for the protection of the revenue as the Secretary of the Treasury may from time to time prescribe; and under like rules, regulations, and conditions goods, wares, or merchandise may be conveyed in transit, without the payment of duties, from such possessions through the territory of the United States, for export from the said ports of the United States.

It will be noticed that provision is here made for carrying into effect the two provisions of Article **XXIX** which I have already characterized as the concessions on the part of the United States, namely, the passage duty free from certain designated ports of the United States to Canada of imported goods, and the passage duty free to ports of the United States of Canadian goods for export. Section 3 of the law of 1873, which I have quoted, however, contains a legislative construction of Article **XXIX** of the treaty in the limitation that the provisions therein contained as to the transit of goods should continue in force only so long as Articles **XVIII** to **XXV**, inclusive, and **XXX** of the treaty should remain in force.

On March 3, 1883, Congress passed a joint resolution entitled as follows: "Joint resolution providing for the termination of articles numbered **XVIII** to **XXV**, inclusive, and article numbered **XXX** of the treaty between the United States of America and Her Britannic Majesty concluded at Washington May 8, 1871."

The resolution provided for the giving of notice of the abrogation of the articles of the treaty named in the title, and of no others. Section 3 contained the following provision:

And the act of Congress approved March 1, A. D. 1873, entitled * * * so far as it relates to the articles of said treaty so to be terminated, shall be and stand repealed and be of no force on and after the time of the expiration of said two years.

An examination of the debates at the time of the passage of this joint resolution very clearly shows that Congress made an attempt to save Article **XXIX** of the treaty and section 3 of the act of 1873. In the Senate on the 21st of February, 1883, the resolution being under consideration, several Senators, including Mr. Edmunds, the chairman of the Judiciary Committee, expressed the opinion that Article **XXIX** would not be affected by the abrogation of Articles **XVIII** to **XXV** and **XXX**, and an amendment was made to the resolution with a view to leave section 3 of the act of 1873 in force. The same view was taken in the debates in the House.

The subject again came before Congress in connection with the consideration of a bill (S. 3173) to "authorize the President of the United States to protect and defend the rights of American fishing vessels, American fishermen, American trading and other vessels in certain cases, and for other purposes."

In the course of the debate upon the bill in the Senate January 24, 1887, and in the House February 23 following, the prevailing opinion was, though not without some dissent, that Article XXIX was still in force.

On the 6th of July, 1887, in response to an inquiry by the Secretary of the Treasury, Mr. Bayard wrote a letter, a copy of which accompanies this message, in which he expresses the opinion that Article XXIX of the treaty was unaffected by the abrogation of the fisheries articles and was still in force. In August, 1888, however, Mr. Cleveland, in a message to Congress, expresses his opinion of the question in the following language:

In any event, and whether the law of 1873 construes the treaty or governs it, section 29 of such treaty, I have no doubt, terminated with the proceedings taken by our Government to terminate Articles XVIII to XXV, inclusive, and Article XXX of the treaty. * * *

If by any language used in the joint resolution it was intended to relieve section 3 of the act of 1873, embodying Article XXIX of the treaty, from its own limitations, or to save the article itself, I am entirely satisfied that the intention miscarried.

I have asked the opinion of the Attorney-General upon this question, and his answer accompanies this message. He is of the opinion that Article XXIX has been abrogated.

It should be added that the United States has continuously, through the Treasury Department, conducted our trade intercourse with Canada as if Article XXIX of the treaty and section 3 of the act of 1873 remained in force, and that Canada has continued to yield in practice the concessions made by her in that article. No change in our Treasury methods was made following Mr. Cleveland's message from which I have quoted. I am inclined to think that, using the aids which the protocol and the nearly contemporaneous legislation by Congress in the act of 1873 furnish in construing the treaty, the better opinion is that Article XXIX of the treaty is no longer operative. The enactment of section 3 of the act of 1873 was a clear declaration that legislation was necessary to put Article XXIX of the treaty into operation, and that under the treaty our obligation to provide such legislation terminated whenever Articles XVIII to XXV and XXX should be abrogated. This legislation was accepted by Great Britain as a compliance with our obligations under the treaty. No objection was made that our statute treated Article XXIX as having force only so long as the other articles named were in force.

But the question whether Article XXIX is in force has less practical

THE WRECK OF THE *MAINE*, JUNE, 1911

THE RAISING OF THE *MAINE*

After considering proposals from many engineers, the Government decided to leave the task of recovering the *Maine* to the Engineers of the United States Army. Under their direction caissons were sunk in the harbor, as shown in the illustration, so as to enclose the wreck. The water within was then gradually pumped out. The danger was that the pressure of water on the outside of the caissons might destroy the protecting ring, and demolish all that had been constructed and wipe out the lives of the workmen. The plan, however, worked well, and enough has been seen of the hulk to prove that she was destroyed by two explosions, the first being that of some mine or projectile, and the second, that of the *Maine's* own magazine.

See the encyclopedic index (volume eleven) article, "Maine, The," and also President McKinley's account of the catastrophe on page 6277.

importance than has been supposed, for it does not, if in force, place any restraints upon the United States as to the method of dealing with imported merchandise destined for the United States arriving at a Canadian port for transportation to the United States, or of merchandise passing through Canadian territory from one place in the United States to another. It would be no infraction either of the letter or of the spirit of the treaty if we should stop, unload, and carefully inspect every vehicle arriving at our border with such merchandise; nor, on the other hand, would Canada violate her obligations under the treaty by a like treatment of merchandise imported through the port of New York on its arrival in Canada. Neither Government has placed itself under any restraint as to merchandise intended for the use of its own people when such merchandise comes within its own territory. The question, therefore, as to how we shall deal with merchandise imported by our own people through a Canadian port and with merchandise passing from one place in the United States to another through Canadian territory is wholly one of domestic policy and law.

I turn now to consider the legislation of Congress upon this subject, upon which, as it seems to me, the duties of the Treasury and the rights of our people as to those phases of the transportation question to which I have just alluded wholly depend. Sections 3005 and 3006 of the Revised Statutes, which are taken from the act of July 28, 1866, entitled "An act to protect the revenue, and for other purposes" (14 U. S. Statutes at Large, p. 328), are as follows:

SEC. 3005. All merchandise arriving at the ports of New York, Boston, Portland in Maine, or any other port specially designated by the Secretary of the Treasury, and destined for places in the adjacent British Provinces, or arriving at the port of [*Point Isabel*] [Brownsville] in Texas, or any other port specially designated by the Secretary of the Treasury, and destined for places in the Republic of Mexico, may be entered at the custom-house and conveyed in transit through the territory of the United States without the payment of duties, under such regulations as the Secretary of the Treasury may prescribe.

SEC. 3006. Imported merchandise in bond, or duty paid, and products or manufactures of the United States, may, with the consent of the proper authorities of the British Provinces or Republic of Mexico, be transported from one port in the United States to another port therein, over the territory of such Provinces or Republic, by such routes and under such rules, regulations, and conditions as the Secretary of the Treasury may prescribe; and the merchandise so transported shall, upon arrival in the United States from such Provinces or Republic, be treated in regard to the liability to or exemption from duty or tax as if the transportation had taken place entirely within the limits of the United States.

Section 3102 of the Revised Statutes is also related to this subject, and is as follows:

To avoid the inspection at the first port of arrival, the owner, agent, master, or conductor of any such vessel, car, or other vehicle, or owner, agent, or other person having charge of any such merchandise, baggage, effects, or other articles, may apply to any officer of the United States duly authorized to act in the premises to seal or close the same, under and according to the regulations hereinafter authorized, previous to their importation into the United States, which officer shall seal or close the same accordingly; whereupon the same may proceed to their port of destination without further inspection. Every such vessel, car, or other vehicle shall proceed without unnecessary delay to the port of its destination, as named in the manifest of its cargo, freight, or contents, and be there inspected. Nothing contained in this section shall be construed to exempt such vessel, car, or vehicle, or its contents, from such examination as may be necessary and proper to prevent frauds upon the revenue and violations of this title.

It will be noticed that section 3005 does not provide for the transit of merchandise through our territory from Canada to ports of the United States for export, nor have I been able to find any other law now in force that does provide for such transit. It would seem, therefore, that as to this concession made by the United States in Article XXIX of the treaty, legislation to put it into force was necessary, and that there is no such legislation unless section 3 of the act of 1873 was saved by the amendment to the joint resolution abrogating the fisheries articles and Article XXX, limiting the repeal to so much of said act as "relates to the articles of said treaty so to be terminated." The joint resolution certainly did not repeal section 3, and if that section has ceased to be operative it is by virtue of the limitation contained in the section itself. I think it did expire by its own express limitation.

The question has presented itself whether section 3 of the act of 1873 (U. S. Revised Statutes, sec. 2866) repealed by implication that section of the act of July, 1866, which is now section 3005 of the Revised Statutes; but I am of the opinion that the last-named section was not repealed. Section 3 of the act of 1873 was expressly intended to carry into effect a treaty obligation and was limited as to time. It contained no express repeal of the act of 1866, and while its provisions were broader than the last-named act, they were not inconsistent, save in the provision that while the act of 1873 was in force the additional ports in the United States at which Canadian goods might be received were to be designated by the President, whereas under the act of 1866 the designation was by the Secretary of the Treasury. The last-named act related also to inter-course with Mexico, and I think was unaffected by the act of 1873.

It will be seen that the law permits merchandise arriving at the ports of New York, Boston, Portland in Maine, and at other ports specially designated by the Secretary of the Treasury, for places in the adjacent British Provinces, to be entered at the custom-house of the port where it is landed and conveyed through the territory of the United States without the payment of duty, under regulations to be prescribed by the Secretary of the Treasury. As these goods come immediately and fully under the inspection of our customs officers at the principal ports, are entered there and remain until they cross our border into Canada fully under our supervision, there is little or no danger involved to our revenue. The regulations prescribed by the Treasury for conducting this traffic seem to me to be adequate.

As to merchandise imported into the United States from a contiguous foreign country, it is provided by section 3102 that the inspection at the first port of arrival in the United States may be avoided if the vehicle in which the same arrives has been sealed or closed by some officer of the United States duly authorized at some point in the contiguous country. When the act of closing or sealing conformably to the regulations of the Treasury has been effected, the car or other vehicle may proceed without unnecessary delay to the port of its destination, as named in the manifest of its cargo, freight, or contents, and be there inspected. This privilege, however, is subject to such examination at the point of entry to the United States as may be necessary to prevent fraud. It is important to be noticed that the merchandise to which this section refers is described in section 3100 as merchandise, etc., "imported into the United States from any contiguous foreign country."

A practice has grown up, and a traffic of considerable dimensions under it, of allowing merchandise from China and Japan, purchased and imported from those countries by our own citizens and landed at ports in the Dominion of Canada, to be there loaded into cars, which, being sealed by an officer of the United States or some one supposed to represent him, are forwarded through the territory of Canada, across the entire continent, and allowed to cross our frontier without other inspection than an examination of the seals. The real fact is that the American consul can not and does not either compare the manifest with the contents of the cars or attach the seals. The agents of the transportation companies are furnished by the consul with the seals and place them upon the cars. The practice of sealing such merchandise, notwithstanding it has been allowed by the Treasury for some years, I think is unauthorized. Such merchandise is not imported from a "contiguous country," but from China and Japan.

It has never become subject to the Canadian revenue laws as an importation from Japan to Canada, but by force of the treaty or by the courtesy of that government has been treated as subject to the revenue laws of the United States from the time of landing at the Canadian port. Our Treasury seal has been placed upon it; Canada only gives it passage. It is no more an importation from Canada than is a train load of wheat that starts from Detroit and is transported through Canada to another port of the United States. Section 3102 was enacted in 1864, two years before sections 3005 and 3006, and could not have had reference to the later methods of importing merchandise through one country to the other.

The practice to which I have referred not only equalizes the advantages of Canadian seaports with our own in the importation of goods for our domestic consumption, but makes the Canadian ports favored ports of entry. The detentions under this system at the Canadian ports are less than when the merchandise is landed at a port of the United States to be forwarded in bond to another port therein. Full effect should be given to section 3102 as to merchandise imported into the United States from Canada, so far as the appropriations enable the Treasury to provide the officers to do the work of closing and sealing. It will, however, be required that all this kind of work be done, and carefully done, by an officer of the United States, and that the duty shall in no case be delegated to the employees of the transportation companies. The considerations that it is quite doubtful whether a fraud committed in Canada by one of our agents upon our revenue would be punishable in our courts, and that such a fraud committed by anyone else certainly would not be, and that even if such acts are made penal by our statutes the criminal would be secure against extradition, seem to me to be conclusive against the policy of attempting to maintain such revenue agents in Canadian territory.

I come now to discuss another element of this international traffic, namely, the transportation of merchandise from one "port" in the United States to another "port" therein over the territory of Canada. This traffic is enormous in its dimensions, and very great interests have grown up in the United States in connection with it. Section 3006 authorizes this traffic, subject to "such rules, regulations, and conditions as the Secretary of the Treasury may prescribe;" but the important limitation is from "port" to "port." Section 3007 of the Revised Statutes, which exempts sealed cars from certain fees, preserves the terms of the preceding section—from "port" to "port." It seems to me that sections 3006 and 3007 contemplate the delivery of the sealed cars at a "port" of the United States, there to be examined by a revenue officer and their contents verified; but in practice the car, if the seal is found at the border to be intact, is passed to places not "ports" and is opened and unloaded by the consignee, no officer being present. The bill or manifest accompanying the merchandise and the unbroken seal on the car may furnish *prima facie* evidence that the amount and kind of merchandise named in the manifest and said to be contained in the car came from a port in the United States, but certainly it was not intended that the merchandise should go to the owner without an official ascertainment of the correspondence between the bill and the actual contents of the car.

I pass at this point any discussion of the question whether as a national policy this traffic should be promoted. It is enough to say that as the law stands it is authorized between "ports" of the United States, and that the rules, regulations, and conditions to be prescribed by the Secretary of the Treasury must not, in view of this declaration of the legislative will, be further restrictive of the traffic than may reasonably be necessary to protect the revenues of the United States. In determining whether further regulations are reasonably necessary to prevent frauds against our revenue it is not conclusive, at least, to say that frauds against the revenue under the existing system have not been discovered. The question is, Are the regulations such as to provide proper safeguards against fraud, or are they such as to make fraud easy to those who have the disposition to commit it? If all cars carrying this merchandise are carefully and honestly inspected at the point of lading and are securely closed during the transit, the revenue would be secure, for the proper lading of these cars is not subject to duty. Frauds can only be perpetrated by introducing products not subject to free entry. In practice the seals and locks provided by the Treasury Department do not give security that these cars, in the long transit in which they are free from observation by officers of the revenue, may not be opened and dutiable merchandise added.

The duplication of the seals used, composed of wire and lead, is easy, and the opening of locks scarcely less so. If, however, the cars, when they arrive in the United States, either at the point where our boundary is crossed or at some other port of the United States, were subject to the inspection of a revenue officer before the delivery to the consignee or owner, the manifest could be verified. The inspection, however, is now limited to an examination of the lock or seal. The car is not weighed or opened to verify its contents. I do not think this is an adequate protection against the surreptitious introduction into the cars, while on foreign territory, of dutiable articles. It will be seen by the letter of the Secretary of the Treasury that grain the product of the United States is now largely transported in American vessels to Canadian lake ports, and after being there placed in elevators is sent east in cars sealed by agents of the Treasury.

No observation is taken of this grain until its arrival in Canada, where only the amount and grade are noted by a Treasury agent, and a like amount in grade and quantity (though it may be not the identical grain) is by such agent billed and sealed in cars for carriage to the United States. I do not find any statute authorizing this practice. Section 3006, which authorizes this interstate trade through Canada, is limited to merchandise passing from "port" to "port" of the United States, and plainly means that such merchandise shall be taken up by our revenue officers at a "port" of the United States as a starting point.

The following are the conclusions at which I have arrived:

First. That Article XXIX of the treaty of Washington has been abrogated.

Second. That even if this article were in force there is no law in force to execute it.

Third. That when in force the treaty imposed no obligation upon the United States to use the concessions as to transit made by Canada, and no limitation upon the powers of the United States in dealing with merchandise imported for the use of our citizens through Canadian ports or passing from one place in the United States to another through Canada, upon the arrival of such merchandise at our border.

Fourth. That therefore, treaty or no treaty, the question of sealing cars containing such merchandise and the treatment of such sealed cars when they cross our border is and always has been one to be settled by our laws, according to our convenience and our interests as we may see them.

Fifth. That the law authorizing the sealing of cars in Canada containing foreign merchandise imported from a contiguous country does not apply to merchandise imported by our own people from countries not contiguous and carried through Canada for delivery to such owners.

Sixth. That the law did not contemplate the passing of sealed cars to any place not a "port," nor the delivery of such cars to the owner or consignee, to be opened by him without the supervision of a revenue officer.

Seventh. That such a practice is inconsistent with the safety of the revenue.

The statutes relating to the transportation of merchandise between the United States and the British possessions should be the subject of revision. The Treasury regulations have given to these laws a construction and a scope that I do not think was contemplated by Congress. A policy adapted to the new conditions, growing in part out of the construction of the Canadian Pacific Railroad, should be declared, and the business placed upon a basis more just to our people and to our transportation companies.

If we continue the policy of supervising rates and requiring that they shall be equal and reasonable upon the railroads of the United States, we can not in fairness at the same time give these unusual facilities for competition to Canadian roads that are free to pursue the practices as to cut rates and favored rates that we condemn and punish if practiced by our own railroads.

I regret that circumstances prevented an earlier examination by me of these questions, but submit now these views in the hope that they may lead to a revision of the laws upon a safer and juster basis.

I transmit herewith the correspondence between the Secretary of the Treasury and the Attorney-General upon some phases of this question.

BENJ. HARRISON.

EXECUTIVE MANSION, *February 6, 1893.*

To the Senate and House of Representatives:

I transmit herewith, for the consideration of Congress, a communication from the Secretary of the Interior, dated 4th instant, accompanied by an agreement concluded by and between the Turtle Mountain Indians and the commission appointed under the provisions of the Indian appropriation act of July 13, 1892, to negotiate with the Turtle Mountain band of Chippewa Indians in North Dakota for the cession and relinquishment to the United States of whatever right or interest they have in and to any and all lands in said State to which they claim title, and for their removal to and settlement upon lands to be hereafter selected and determined upon by the Secretary of the Interior upon the recommendation of the proposed commissioners, subject to the approval of Congress.

BENJ. HARRISON.

EXECUTIVE MANSION,
Washington, February 6, 1893.

To the Senate:

I transmit herewith, as desired by the resolution of the Senate of the 4th instant, a report from the Secretary of State of the 6th instant, with its accompanying correspondence, in relation to the draft of an uncompleted treaty with Hawaii made in 1854.

BENJ. HARRISON.

EXECUTIVE MANSION,
Washington, D. C., February 8, 1893.

To the Senate and House of Representatives:

I transmit herewith the eighth annual report of the Commissioner of Labor. This report relates to industrial education in the United States and foreign countries.

BENJ. HARRISON.

EXECUTIVE MANSION,
Washington, D. C., February 14, 1893.

To the Senate and House of Representatives:

I transmit herewith a special report of the Commissioner of Labor relating to compulsory insurance of workingmen in Germany and other countries.

BENJ. HARRISON.

EXECUTIVE MANSION, *February 14, 1893.*

To the Senate and House of Representatives:

I transmit herewith a communication of the 13th instant from the Secretary of the Interior, transmitting copy of reports of Lieutenants Brown, Gurovits, and Suplee, United States Army, who were charged with the duty of inspecting the Navajo country, so that the Interior Department could be advised as to the practicability of restraining the Navajoes within their present reservations and of furnishing irrigation and water for their flocks, together with report of the Commissioner of Indian Affairs upon the matter with draft of an item of appropriation to carry the same into effect.

BENJ. HARRISON.

EXECUTIVE MANSION,
Washington, February 15, 1893.

To the Senate:

I transmit herewith, with a view to its ratification, a treaty of annexation concluded on the 14th day of February, 1893, between John W. Foster, Secretary of State, who was duly empowered to act in that behalf on the part of the United States, and Lorin A. Thurston, W. R. Castle, W. C. Wilder, C. L. Carter, and Joseph Marsden, the commissioners on the part of the Government of the Hawaiian Islands. The provisional treaty, it will be observed, does not attempt to deal in detail with the questions that grow out of the annexation of the Hawaiian Islands to the United States. The commissioners representing the Hawaiian Government have consented to leave to the future and to the just and benevolent purposes of the United States the adjustment of all such questions.

I do not deem it necessary to discuss at any length the conditions which have resulted in this decisive action. It has been the policy of the Administration not only to respect but to encourage the continuance of an independent government in the Hawaiian Islands so long as it afforded suitable guaranties for the protection of life and property and maintained a stability and strength that gave adequate security against the domination of any other power. The moral support of this Government has continually manifested itself in the most friendly diplomatic relations and in many acts of courtesy to the Hawaiian rulers.

The overthrow of the monarchy was not in any way promoted by this Government, but had its origin in what seems to have been a reactionary and revolutionary policy on the part of Queen Liliuokalani, which put in serious peril not only the large and preponderating interests of the United States in the islands, but all foreign interests, and, indeed, the decent administration of civil affairs and the peace of the islands. It is quite evident that the monarchy had become effete and the Queen's Government so weak and inadequate as to be the prey of designing and unscrupulous persons. The restoration of Queen Liliuokalani to her throne is undesirable, if not impossible, and unless actively supported by the United States would be accompanied by serious disaster and the disorganization of all business interests. The influence and interest of the United States in the islands must be increased and not diminished.

Only two courses are now open—one the establishment of a protectorate by the United States, and the other annexation full and complete. I think the latter course, which has been adopted in the treaty, will be highly promotive of the best interests of the Hawaiian people, and is the only one that will adequately secure the interests of the United States. These interests are not wholly selfish. It is essential that none of the other great powers shall secure these islands. Such a possession would not consist with our safety and with the peace of the world. This view of the situation is so apparent and conclusive that no protest has been heard from any government against proceedings looking to annexation. Every foreign representative at Honolulu promptly acknowledged the Provisional Government, and I think there is a general concurrence in the opinion that the deposed Queen ought not to be restored.

Prompt action upon this treaty is very desirable. If it meets the approval of the Senate, peace and good order will be secured in the islands under existing laws until such time as Congress can provide by legislation a permanent form of government for the islands. This legislation should be, and I do not doubt will be, not only just to the natives and all other residents and citizens of the islands, but should be characterized by great liberality and a high regard to the rights of all people and of all foreigners domiciled there. The correspondence which accompanies the treaty will put the Senate in possession of all the facts known to the Executive.

BENJ. HARRISON.

EXECUTIVE MANSION,
Washington, February 16, 1893.

To the Senate:

I transmit herewith a letter from the Secretary of State of the 15th instant, covering a report, with accompanying correspondence, respecting relations between the United States and the Hawaiian Islands from September, 1820, to January, 1893.

BENJ. HARRISON.

EXECUTIVE MANSION,
Washington, February 20, 1893.

To the Senate of the United States:

I transmit herewith a report submitted by the Acting Secretary of State in response to the resolution of the Senate of February 2 last, relating to the building of the Ozama River bridge at Santo Domingo City by American citizens.

BENJ. HARRISON.

EXECUTIVE MANSION,
Washington, February 21, 1893.

To the Senate and House of Representatives:

I transmit herewith a communication of the Secretary of State, transmitting the official report of the American delegates to the International Monetary Conference convened at Brussels on November 22, 1892, with its accompaniments.

BENJ. HARRISON.

EXECUTIVE MANSION, *February 25, 1893.*

To the Senate of the United States:

In compliance with a resolution of the Senate, the House of Representatives concurring, I return herewith the bill (S. 3811) entitled "An

act to amend an act entitled 'An act to grant to the Mobile and Dau
phin Island Railroad and Harbor Company the right to trestle across the
shoal water between Cedar Point and Dauphin Island,' approved September 26, 1890.''

BENJ. HARRISON.

EXECUTIVE MANSION,
Washington, February 27, 1893.

To the Senate and House of Representatives:

I herewith transmit, for the information of Congress, a communication from the Acting Secretary of State, forwarding certain bulletins of
the Bureau of the American Republics.

BENJ. HARRISON.

EXECUTIVE MANSION,
Washington, D. C., March 1, 1893.

To the Senate and House of Representatives:

I transmit herewith the fifth special report of the Commissioner of
Labor. The report relates to the so-called ''Gothenburg system'' of regulating the liquor traffic, the system prevailing in Norway and Sweden.

BENJ. HARRISON.

VETO MESSAGE.

EXECUTIVE MANSION, *February 27, 1893.*

To the House of Representatives:

I return herewith without my approval an act (H. R. 9612) entitled
''An act to prescribe the number of district attorneys and marshals in
the judicial districts of the State of Alabama.''

Under the present law there is a district attorney for the southern district of Alabama, a district attorney for the northern and middle districts,
a marshal for the northern district, and a marshal for the southern and
middle districts.

An examination of the records of the Attorney-General's office as to
the amount of business in the courts in these districts leads me to believe
that two districts would provide amply for the disposition of all public
and private cases. The law creates two new officers, whose aggregate
compensation may be $12,000 per annum, without, it seems to me, a jus-
tifying necessity. But the most serious objection to the legislation is
that it creates at once upon the taking effect of the law the offices of district attorney and marshal for each of the three districts, and the effect,
it seems to me, must be to abolish the offices as they now exist.

No provision is made for a continued discharge of the duties of marshal and district attorney by the present incumbents. A serious question would be raised as to whether these officers were not at once legislated out of office and vacancies created. As these vacancies could not be filled immediately, the business of the courts would seriously suffer. The law should at least have contained a provision for the continued discharge of their duties by the incumbents until the new officers were appointed and qualified.

BENJ. HARRISON.

PROCLAMATIONS.

By the President of the United States of America.

A PROCLAMATION.

Whereas it is provided by section 24 of the act of Congress approved March 3, 1891, entitled "An act to repeal timber-culture laws, and for other purposes"—

That the President of the United States may from time to time set apart and reserve in any State or Territory having public land bearing forests, in any part of the public lands wholly or in part covered with timber or undergrowth, whether of commercial value or not, as public reservations; and the President shall by public proclamation declare the establishment of such reservations and the limits thereof.

And whereas it is made to appear, by petition and otherwise, that the interests of the public and the welfare of the people of the State of Colorado will be materially benefited and subserved by the reservation of the public and forest lands hereinafter described:

Now, therefore, I, Benjamin Harrison, President of the United States, by virtue of the power in me vested by said act, do hereby set apart, reserve, and establish as a public reservation all that tract of land in the State of Colorado embraced in the following boundary and description, to wit:

Beginning at the confluence of the North Fork of the South Platte River with the South Platte River; thence up the middle of the channel of the North Fork of the South Platte River to the range line between township seven (7) south, ranges seventy-four (74) and seventy-five (75) west of the sixth (6th) principal meridian; thence northerly on said range line to the northeast corner of township seven (7) south, range seventy-five (75) west; thence westerly on the township line between townships six (6) and seven (7) south to the northwest corner of township seven (7) south, range seventy-six (76) west; thence southerly on the range line between ranges seventy-six (76) and seventy-seven (77) west to the northeast corner of section thirteen (13), township seven (7) south, range

seventy-seven (77) west; thence westerly on the section line between sections twelve (12) and thirteen (13) to the northwest corner of section
thirteen (13) of said township and range; thence southerly on the section
line between sections thirteen (13) and fourteen (14), twenty-three (23)
and twenty-four (24), and twenty-five (25) and twenty-six (26) to the
northeast corner of section thirty-five (35) of said township and range;
thence westerly on the section line between sections twenty-six (26) and
thirty-five (35) and twenty-seven (27) and thirty-four (34) to the northwest corner of section thirty-four (34) of said township and range; thence
southerly on the section line between sections thirty-three (33) and thirty-
four (34) of said township and range and sections three (3) and four (4),
nine (9) and ten (10), and fifteen (15) and sixteen (16), township eight (8)
south, range seventy-seven (77) west, to the northeast corner of section
twenty-one (21) of said last-named township and range; thence westerly
on the section line between sections sixteen (16) and twenty-one (21),
seventeen (17) and twenty (20), and eighteen (18) and nineteen (19) to
the northwest corner of section nineteen (19) of said township and range;
thence southerly on the range line between ranges seventy-seven (77) and
seventy-eight (78) west to the northeast corner of section thirteen (13),
township nine (9) south, range seventy-eight (78) west; thence westerly
on the section line between sections twelve (12) and thirteen (13) and
eleven (11) and fourteen (14) to the northwest corner of section fourteen
(14) of said township and range; thence southerly on the section line between sections fourteen (14) and fifteen (15) to the southwest corner of
said section fourteen (14); thence westerly on the section line between
sections fifteen (15) and twenty-two (22) and sixteen (16) and twenty-one
(21) to the northwest corner of section twenty-one (21) of said township
and range; thence southerly on the section line between sections twenty
(20) and twenty-one (21) and twenty-eight (28) and twenty-nine (29) to
the southwest corner of section twenty-eight (28) of said township and
range; thence easterly on the section line between sections twenty-eight
(28) and thirty-three (33) to the southeast corner of said section twenty-
eight (28); thence southerly on the section line between sections thirty-
three (33) and thirty-four (34) of said township and range and sections
three (3) and four (4), nine (9) and ten (10), and fifteen (15) and sixteen
(16), township ten (10) south, range seventy-eight (78) west, to the northeast corner of section twenty-one (21) of said last-named township and
range; thence westerly on the section line between sections sixteen (16)
and twenty-one (21), seventeen (17) and twenty (20), and eighteen (18)
and nineteen (19) to the northwest corner of section nineteen (19) of said
township and range; thence southerly on the range line between ranges
seventy-eight (78) and seventy-nine (79) west to the southwest corner of
township ten (10) south, range seventy-eight (78) west; thence westerly
on the second (2d) correction line south to the northwest corner of section one (1), township eleven (11) south, range seventy-nine (79) west;

thence southerly on the section line between sections one (1) and two (2), eleven (11) and twelve (12), thirteen (13) and fourteen (14), twenty-three (23) and twenty-four (24), twenty-five (25) and twenty-six (26), and thirty-five (35) and thirty-six (36) of said township and range and sections one (1) and two (2), eleven (11) and twelve (12), and thirteen (13) and fourteen (14), township twelve (12) south, range seventy-nine (79) west, to the southwest corner of section thirteen (13) of said last-named township and range; thence easterly on the section line between sections thirteen (13) and twenty-four (24) of said township and range and sections eighteen (18) and nineteen (19), seventeen (17) and twenty (20), sixteen (16) and twenty-one (21), and fifteen (15) and twenty-two (22), township twelve (12) south, range seventy-eight (78) west, to the quarter-section corner between said sections fifteen (15) and twenty-two (22); thence southerly through the middle of sections twenty-two (22), twenty-seven (27), and thirty-four (34) to the quarter-section corner on the south boundary of section thirty-four (34) of said township and range; thence easterly on the township line between townships twelve (12) and thirteen (13) south, range seventy-eight (78) west, to the northwest corner of township thirteen (13) south, range seventy-seven (77) west; thence southerly on the range line between ranges seventy-seven (77) and seventy-eight (78) west to the southwest corner of section six (6), township thirteen (13) south, range seventy-seven (77) west; thence easterly on the section line between sections six (6) and seven (7), five (5) and eight (8), and four (4) and nine (9) to the southeast corner of section four (4) of said township and range; thence northerly on the section line between sections three (3) and four (4) of said township and range and sections thirty-three (33) and thirty-four (34), township twelve (12) south, range seventy-seven (77) west, to the northeast corner of section thirty-three (33) of said last-named township and range; thence easterly on the section line between sections twenty-seven (27) and thirty-four (34) to the southeast corner of section twenty-seven (27) of said township and range; thence northerly on the section line between sections twenty-six (26) and twenty-seven (27), twenty-two (22) and twenty-three (23), fourteen (14) and fifteen (15), ten (10) and eleven (11), and two (2) and three (3) of said township and range and sections thirty-four (34) and thirty-five (35), township eleven (11) south, range seventy-seven (77) west, to the northeast corner of section thirty-four (34) of said township and range; thence westerly on the section line between sections twenty-seven (27) and thirty-four (34) to the northwest corner of said section thirty-four (34); thence northerly on the section line between sections twenty-seven (27) and twenty-eight (28) to the northeast corner of section twenty-eight (28) of said township and range; thence westerly on the section line between sections twenty-one (21) and twenty-eight (28), twenty (20) and twenty-nine (29), and nineteen (19) and thirty (30) to the northwest corner of section thirty (30) of said township and range;

thence northerly on the range line between ranges seventy-seven (77) and seventy-eight (78) west to the northeast corner of township eleven (11) south, range seventy-eight (78) west; thence easterly on the second (2d) correction line south to the southeast corner of township ten (10) south, range seventy-eight (78) west; thence northerly on the range line between ranges seventy-seven (77) and seventy-eight (78) west to the southwest corner of section eighteen (18), township nine (9) south, range seventy-seven (77) west; thence easterly on the section line between sections eighteen (18) and nineteen (19), seventeen (17) and twenty (20), sixteen (16) and twenty-one (21), and fifteen (15) and twenty-two (22) to the southeast corner of section fifteen (15) of said township and range; thence northerly on the section line between sections fourteen (14) and fifteen (15) and ten (10) and eleven (11) to the southwest corner of section two (2) of said township and range; thence easterly on the section line between sections two (2) and eleven (11) and one (1) and twelve (12) to the southeast corner of section one (1) of said township and range; thence northerly on the range line between ranges seventy-six (76) and seventy-seven (77) west to the southwest corner of township eight (8) south, range seventy-six (76) west; thence easterly on the township line between townships eight (8) and nine (9) south, range seventy-six (76) west, to the southeast corner of section thirty-one (31), township eight (8) south, range seventy-six (76) west; thence northerly on the section line between sections thirty-one (31) and thirty-two (32) to the southwest corner of section twenty-nine (29) of said township and range; thence easterly on the section line between sections twenty-nine (29) and thirty-two (32) to the southeast corner of said section twenty-nine (29); thence northerly on the section line between sections twenty-eight (28) and twenty-nine (29) and twenty (20) and twenty-one (21) to the southwest corner of section sixteen (16) of said township and range; thence easterly on the section line between sections sixteen (16) and twenty-one (21) to the southeast corner of said section sixteen (16); thence northerly on the section line between sections fifteen (15) and sixteen (16), nine (9) and ten (10), and three (3) and four (4) of said township and range, and sections thirty-three (33) and thirty-four (34), township seven (7) south, range seventy-six (76) west, to the southwest corner of section twenty-seven (27) of said township and range; thence easterly on the section line between sections twenty-seven (27) and thirty-four (34), twenty-six (26) and thirty-five (35), and twenty-five (25) and thirty-six (36) of said township and range, and sections thirty (30) and thirty-one (31), twenty-nine (29) and thirty-two (32), twenty-eight (28) and thirty-three (33), and twenty-seven (27) and thirty-four (34), township seven (7) south, range seventy-five (75) west, to the northwest corner of section thirty-five (35) of said township and range; thence southerly on the section line between sections thirty-four (34) and thirty-five (35) of said township and range and sections two (2) and three (3), ten (10) and eleven (11), fourteen (14) and fifteen (15), twenty-two (22) and twenty-three (23), twenty-six (26) and twenty-seven (27), and thirty-four (34) and thirty-five (35), township eight (8) south, range seventy-five (75) west, to the southwest corner of section thirty-five (35) of said township and range; thence easterly on the township line between townships eight (8) and nine (9) south, range seventy-five (75) west, to the northwest corner of township nine (9) south, range seventy-four (74) west; thence southerly on the range line between ranges seventy-four (74) and seventy-five (75) west to the southwest corner of township ten (10) south, range seventy-four (74) west; thence easterly on the second (2d) correction line south to the northwest corner of township eleven (11) south, range seventy-three (73) west; thence southerly on the range line between ranges seventy-three (73) and seventy-four (74) west to the northeast corner of section thirteen (13), township twelve (12) south, range seventy-four (74) west; thence westerly on the section line between sections twelve (12) and thirteen (13) and eleven (11) and fourteen (14) of said township and range to the quarter-section corner between said sections eleven (11) and fourteen (14); thence southerly through the middle of sections fourteen (14), twenty-three (23), and twenty-six (26) to the center of section twenty-six (26) of said township and range; thence easterly through the middle of sections twenty-six (26) and twenty-five (25) to the quarter-section corner on the range line between section twenty-five (25), township twelve (12) south, range seventy-four (74) west, and section thirty (30), township twelve (12) south, range seventy-three (73) west; thence southerly on said range line to the southwest corner of township twelve (12) south, range seventy-three (73) west; thence easterly on the township line between townships twelve (12) and thirteen (13) south to the southeast corner of township twelve (12) south, range seventy-three (73) west; thence southerly on the range line between ranges seventy-two (72) and seventy-three (73) west to the northeast corner of section twenty-four (24), township thirteen (13) south, range seventy-three (73) west; thence westerly on the section line between sections thirteen (13) and twenty-four (24), fourteen (14) and twenty-three (23), fifteen (15) and twenty-two (22), sixteen (16) and twenty-one (21), seventeen (17) and twenty (20), and eighteen (18) and nineteen (19) to the northwest corner of section nineteen (19) of said township and range; thence southerly on the range line between ranges seventy-three (73) and seventy-four (74) west to the quarter-section corner on the west boundary of section eighteen (18), township fourteen (14) south, range seventy-three (73) west; thence easterly through the middle of sections eighteen (18) and seventeen (17), sixteen (16), fifteen (15), fourteen (14), and thirteen (13), township fourteen (14) south, range seventy-three (73) west, and sections eighteen (18) and seventeen (17), township fourteen (14) south, range seventy-two (72) west, to the quarter-section corner between sections seventeen (17) and sixteen (16) of said last-named township and range; thence northerly on the section line between sections sixteen (16) and seventeen (17) and eight (8) and nine (9) to the northeast corner of section eight (8) of said township and range; thence easterly on the section line between sections four (4) and nine (9), three (3) and ten (10), two (2) and eleven (11), and one (1) and twelve (12) to the southeast corner of section one (1) of said township and range; thence northerly on the range line between ranges seventy-one (71) and seventy-two (72) west to the southwest corner of township thirteen (13) south, range seventy-one (71) west; thence easterly on the township line between townships thirteen (13) and fourteen (14) south to the southeast corner of section thirty-three (33), township thirteen (13) south, range seventy-one (71) west; thence northerly on the section line between sections thirty-three (33) and thirty-four (34), twenty-seven (27) and twenty-eight (28), twenty-one (21) and twenty-two (22), fifteen (15) and sixteen (16), nine (9) and ten (10), and three (3) and four (4) of said township and range, and between sections thirty-three (33) and thirty-four (34), twenty-seven (27) and twenty-eight (28), twenty-one (21) and twenty-two (22), fifteen (15) and sixteen (16), nine (9) and ten (10), and three (3) and four (4), township twelve (12) south, range seventy-one (71) west, and between sections thirty-three (33) and thirty-four (34), twenty-seven (27) and twenty-eight (28), twenty-one (21) and twenty-two (22), fifteen (15) and sixteen (16), nine (9) and ten (10), and three (3) and four (4), township eleven (11) south, range seventy-one (71) west, to the northeast corner of section four (4) of said last-named township and range; thence easterly on the second (2d) correction line south to the southeast corner of section thirty-three (33), township ten (10) south, range seventy-one (71) west; thence northerly on the section line between sections thirty-three (33) and thirty-four (34) of said township and range to the middle of the channel of the South Platte River; thence down the middle of the channel of the said river to its confluence with the North Fork of the South Platte River, the place of beginning, to be known as the South Platte Forest Reserve.

Excepting from the force and effect of this proclamation all lands which may have been prior to the date hereof embraced in any legal entry or covered by any lawful filing duly of record in the proper United States land office, or upon which any valid settlement has been made pursuant to law and the statutory period within which to make entry or filing of record has not expired, and all mining claims duly located and held according to the laws of the United States and rules and regulations not in conflict therewith.

Provided, That this exception shall not continue to apply to any particular tract of land unless the entryman, settler, or claimant continues to comply with the law under which the entry, filing, settlement, or location was made.

Warning is hereby expressly given to all persons not to enter or make settlement upon the tract of land reserved by this proclamation.

In witness whereof I have hereunto set my hand and caused the seal of the United States to be affixed.

[SEAL.]   Done at the city of Washington, this 9th day of December, A. D. 1892, and of the Independence of the United States the one hundred and seventeenth.

BENJ. HARRISON.

By the President:

JOHN W. FOSTER,
Secretary of State.

BY THE PRESIDENT OF THE UNITED STATES OF AMERICA.

A PROCLAMATION.

Whereas it is provided by section 24 of the act of Congress approved March 3, 1891, entitled "An act to repeal timber-culture laws, and for other purposes"—

That the President of the United States may from time to time set apart and reserve in any State or Territory having public land bearing forests, in any part of the public lands wholly or in part covered with timber or undergrowth, whether of commercial value or not, as public reservations; and the President shall by public proclamation declare the establishment of such reservations and the limits thereof.

And whereas the public lands in the State of California within the limits hereinafter described are in part covered with timber, and it appears that the public good would be promoted by setting apart and reserving said lands as a public reservation:

Now, therefore, I, Benjamin Harrison, President of the United States, by virtue of the power in me vested by section 24 of the aforesaid act of Congress, do hereby make known and proclaim that there is hereby reserved from entry or settlement and set apart as a public reservation all those certain tracts, pieces, or parcels of land lying and being situate in the State of California and particularly described as follows, to wit:

Beginning at the northeast corner of township three (3) north, range six (6) west of the San Bernardino meridian; thence westerly on the surveyed and unsurveyed township line between townships three (3) and four (4) north, ranges six (6) and seven (7) west, to the northeast corner of township three (3) north, range eight (8) west; thence northerly on the unsurveyed and surveyed range line between ranges seven (7) and (8) west to the northeast corner of section twenty-four (24), township four (4) north, range eight (8) west; thence westerly on the surveyed and unsurveyed section line between sections thirteen (13) and twenty-four (24), fourteen (14) and twenty-three (23), fifteen (15) and twenty-two (22), sixteen (16) and twenty-one (21), seventeen (17) and twenty (20), and eighteen (18) and nineteen (19) of said township and range to the point for the northwest corner of section nineteen (19) of said township and range; thence northerly on the unsurveyed and surveyed range line between ranges eight (8) and nine (9) west to the northeast corner of township four (4) north, range nine (9) west; thence westerly on the township line between townships four (4) and five (5) north, range nine (9) west, to the southeast corner of township five (5) north, range ten (10) west; thence northerly on the range line between ranges nine (9) and ten (10) west to the northeast corner of section thirty-six (36) of said township and range; thence westerly on the section line between sections twenty-five (25) and thirty-six (36), twenty-six (26) and thirty-five (35), and twenty-seven (27) and thirty-four (34) to the southeast corner of section twenty-eight (28) of said township and range; thence northerly on the section line between sections twenty-seven (27) and twenty-eight (28) to the northeast corner of said section twenty-eight (28); thence westerly on the section line between sections twenty-one (21) and twenty-eight (28), twenty (20) and twenty-nine (29), and nineteen (19) and thirty (30) of said last-named township and range, and on the unsurveyed section line between sections twenty-four (24) and twenty-five (25), twenty-three (23) and twenty-six (26), twenty-two (22) and twenty-seven (27), twenty-one (21) and twenty-eight (28), twenty (20) and twenty-nine (29), and nineteen (19) and thirty (30), township five (5) north, range eleven (11) west, to the point for the northwest corner of section thirty (30) of said last-named township and range; thence southerly on the range line between ranges eleven (11) and twelve (12) west to the southeast corner of township five (5) north, range twelve (12) west; thence westerly on the township line between townships four (4) and five (5) north to the southwest corner of township five (5) north, range twelve (12) west; thence southerly on the range line between ranges twelve (12) and thirteen (13) west to the northeast corner of section twenty-four (24), township four (4) north, range thirteen (13) west; thence westerly on the section line between sections thirteen (13) and twenty-four (24), fourteen (14) and twenty-three (23), fifteen (15) and twenty-two (22), sixteen (16) and twenty-one (21), seventeen (17) and twenty (20), and eighteen (18) and nineteen (19) of said township and range, and sections thirteen (13) and twenty-four (24), fourteen (14) and twenty-three (23), fifteen (15) and twenty-two (22), sixteen (16) and twenty-one (21), seventeen (17) and twenty (20), and eighteen (18) and nineteen (19), township four (4) north, range fourteen (14) west, to the northwest corner of section nineteen (19) of said last-named township and range; thence southerly on the surveyed and unsurveyed range line between ranges fourteen (14) and fifteen (15) west to the point for the southwest corner of township three (3) north, range fourteen (14) west; thence easterly on the unsurveyed township line between townships two (2) and three (3) north, range fourteen (14) west, to a point for the northwest corner of section four (4), township two (2) north, range fourteen (14) west; thence southerly on the unsurveyed section line between sections four (4) and five (5) to the point for the southwest corner of said section four (4); thence easterly on the unsurveyed section line between sections four (4) and nine (9), three (3) and ten (10), two (2) and eleven (11), and one (1) and twelve (12) to a point for the southeast corner of section one (1) of said township and range; thence southerly on the range line between ranges thirteen (13) and fourteen (14) west to the southwest corner of section seven (7), township two (2) north, range thirteen (13) west; thence easterly on the surveyed and unsurveyed section line between sections seven (7) and eighteen (18), eight (8) and seventeen (17), nine (9) and sixteen (16), ten (10) and fifteen (15), eleven (11) and fourteen (14), and twelve (12) and (13) to a point for the northeast corner of section thirteen (13) of said township and range; thence southerly on the range line between ranges twelve (12) and thirteen (13) west to the southwest corner of township two (2) north, range twelve (12) west; thence easterly on the surveyed and unsurveyed township line between townships one (1) and two (2) north, range twelve (12) west, to the point for the northwest corner of section one (1), township one (1) north, range twelve (12) west; thence southerly on the unsurveyed section line between sections one (1) and two (2) to the point for the southwest corner of said section one (1); thence easterly on the unsurveyed section line between sections one (1) and twelve (12) to the point for the southeast corner of said section one (1); thence southerly on the range line between ranges eleven (11) and twelve (12) west to the southwest corner of section seven (7), township one (1) north, range eleven (11) west; thence easterly on the section line between sections seven (7) and eighteen (18), eight (8) and seventeen (17), nine (9) and sixteen (16), ten (10) and fifteen (15), eleven (11) and fourteen (14), and twelve (12) and thirteen (13) of said township and range, and sections seven (7) and eighteen (18), eight (8) and seventeen (17), nine (9) and sixteen (16), ten (10) and fifteen (15), eleven (11) and fourteen (14), and twelve (12) and thirteen (13), township one (1) north, range ten (10) west, to the southeast corner of section twelve (12) of said last-named township and range; thence southerly on the range line between ranges nine (9) and ten (10) west to the southwest corner of section eighteen (18), township one (1) north, range nine (9) west; thence easterly on the section line between sections eighteen (18) and nineteen (19), seventeen (17) and twenty (20), sixteen (16) and twenty-one (21), fifteen (15) and twenty-two (22), fourteen (14) and twenty-three (23), and thirteen (13) and twenty-four (24) of said township and range, and sections eighteen (18) and nineteen (19), seventeen (17) and twenty (20), sixteen (16) and twenty-one (21), fifteen (15) and twenty-two (22), fourteen (14) and twenty-three (23), and thirteen (13) and twenty-four (24), township one (1) north, range eight (8) west, to the southeast corner of section thirteen (13) of said last-named township and range; thence northerly on the range line between ranges seven (7) and eight (8) west to the southwest corner of section seven (7), township one (1) north, range seven (7) west; thence easterly on the section line between sections seven (7) and eighteen

(18), eight (8) and seventeen (17), nine (9) and sixteen (16), ten (10) and fifteen (15), eleven (11) and fourteen (14), and twelve (12) and thirteen (13) of said township and range, and on the surveyed and unsurveyed section line between sections seven (7) and eighteen (18), eight (8) and seventeen (17), nine (9) and sixteen (16), ten (10) and fifteen (15), eleven (11) and fourteen (14), and twelve (12) and thirteen (13), township one (1) north, range six (6) west, to the point for the southeast corner of section twelve (12) of said last-named township and range; thence northerly on the unsurveyed and surveyed range line between ranges five (5) and six (6) west to the northeast corner of township three (3) north, range six (6) west, the place of beginning.

Excepting from the force and effect of this proclamation all lands which may have been prior to the date hereof embraced in any legal entry or covered by any lawful filing duly of record in the proper United States land office, or upon which any valid settlement has been made pursuant to law and the statutory period within which to make entry or filing of record has not expired, and all mining claims duly located and held according to the laws of the United States and rules and regulations not in conflict therewith.

Provided, That this exception shall not continue to apply to any particular tract of land unless the entryman, settler, or claimant continues to comply with the law under which the entry, filing, settlement, or location was made.

Warning is hereby expressly given to all persons not to enter or make settlement upon the tract of land reserved by this proclamation.

In witness whereof I have hereunto set my hand and caused the seal of the United States to be affixed.

[SEAL.]   Done at the city of Washington, this 20th day of December, A. D. 1892, and of the Independence of the United States the one hundred and seventeenth.

                                        BENJ. HARRISON.

By the President:
    JOHN W. FOSTER,
        Secretary of State.

BY THE PRESIDENT OF THE UNITED STATES OF AMERICA.

A PROCLAMATION.

Whereas it is provided by section 24 of the act of Congress approved March 3, 1891, entitled "An act to repeal timber-culture laws, and for other purposes"—

That the President of the United States may from time to time set apart and reserve in any State or Territory having public land bearing forests, in any part of the public lands wholly or in part covered with timber or undergrowth, whether of commercial value or not, as public reservations; and the President shall by public proclamation declare the establishment of such reservations and the limits thereof.

And whereas it is provided by section 14 of said above-mentioned act that the public lands in the Territory of Alaska reserved for public purposes shall not be subject to occupation and sale; and

Whereas the public lands in the Territory of Alaska known as Afognak Island are in part covered with timber and are required for public purposes in order that salmon fisheries in the waters of the island, and salmon and other fish and sea animals, and other animals and birds, and the timber, undergrowth, grass, moss, and other growth in, on, and about said island may be protected and preserved unimpaired, and it appears that the public good would be promoted by setting apart and reserving said lands as a public reservation; and

Whereas the United States Commissioner of Fish and Fisheries has selected Afognak Bay, River, and Lake, with their tributary streams and the sources thereof, and the lands including the same on said Afognak Island and within 1 mile from the shores thereof, as a reserve for the purpose of establishing fish-culture stations and the use of the United States Commission of Fish and Fisheries, the boundary lines of which include the headsprings of the tributaries above mentioned and the lands the drainage of which is into the same:

Now, therefore, I, Benjamin Harrison, President of the United States, by virtue of the power in me vested by sections 24 and 14 of the aforesaid act of Congress and by other laws of the United States, do reserve and do hereby make known and proclaim that there is hereby reserved from occupation and sale and set apart as a public reservation, including use for fish-culture stations, said Afognak Island, Alaska, and its adjacent bays and rocks and territorial waters, including among others the Sea Lion Rocks and Sea Otter Island: *Provided*, That this proclamation shall not be so construed as to deprive any *bona fide* inhabitant of said island of any valid right he may possess under the treaty for the cession of the Russian possessions in North America to the United States, concluded at Washington on the 30th day of March, 1867.

Warning is hereby expressly given to all persons not to enter upon or to occupy the tract or tracts of land or waters reserved by this proclamation, or to fish in or use any of the waters herein described or mentioned, and that all persons or corporations now occupying said island or any of said premises except under said treaty shall depart therefrom.

In witness whereof I have hereunto set my hand and caused the seal of the United States to be affixed.

[SEAL.] Done at the city of Washington, this 24th day of December, A. D. 1892, and of the Independence of the United States the one hundred and seventeenth.

BENJ. HARRISON.

By the President:
JOHN W. FOSTER,
Secretary of State.

BY THE PRESIDENT OF THE UNITED STATES OF AMERICA.

A PROCLAMATION.

Whereas it is provided by section 24 of the act of Congress approved March 3, 1891, entitled "An act to repeal timber-culture laws, and for other purposes"—

That the P esident of the United States may from time to time set apart and reserve in any State or Territory having public land bearing forests, in any part of the public lands wholly or in part covered with timber or undergrowth, whether of commercial value or not, as public reservations; and the President shall by public proclamation declare the establishment of such reservations and the limits thereof.

And whereas the public lands in the State of Colorado within the limits hereinafter described are in part covered with timber, and it appears that the public good would be promoted by setting apart and reserving said lands as a public reservation:

Now, therefore, I, Benjamin Harrison, President of the United States, by virtue of the power in me vested by section 24 of the aforesaid act of Congress, do hereby make known and proclaim that there is hereby reserved from entry or settlement and set apart as a public reservation all those certain tracts, pieces, or parcels of land lying and being situate in the State of Colorado and particularly described as follows, to wit:

Beginning at the northeast corner of township seven (7) south, range ninety-three (93) west of the sixth (6th) principal meridian; thence westerly along the township line between townships six (6) and seven (7) south to the northwest corner of township seven (7) south, range ninety-three (93) west; thence southerly along the range line between ranges ninety-three (93) and ninety-four (94) west to the northwest corner of section nineteen (19), township seven (7) south, range ninety-three (93) west; thence westerly along the unsurveyed section line between sections thirteen (13) and twenty-four (24), fourteen (14) and twenty-three (23), fifteen (15) and twenty-two (22), sixteen (16) and twenty-one (21), seventeen (17) and twenty (20), and eighteen (18) and nineteen (19), township seven (7) south, range ninety-four (94) west, to the northwest corner of section nineteen (19) of said township and range; thence southerly along the range line between ranges ninety-four (94) and ninety-five (95) west to the northwest corner of township eight (8) south, range ninety-four (94) west; thence westerly along the township line between townships seven (7) and eight (8) south to the northwest corner of section three (3), township eight (8) south, range ninety-five (95) west; thence southerly along the section line between sections three (3) and four (4), nine (9) and ten (10), and fifteen (15) and sixteen (16) to the northwest corner of section twenty-two (22) of said township and range; thence westerly along the section line between sections sixteen (16) and twenty-one (21), seventeen (17) and twenty (20), and eighteen (18) and nineteen

(19) of said township and range, and sections thirteen (13) and twenty-four (24), fourteen (14) and twenty-three (23), and fifteen (15) and twenty-two (22), township eight (8) south, range ninety-six (96) west, to the northwest corner of section twenty-two (22) of said township and range; thence southerly along the section line between sections twenty-one (21) and twenty-two (22), twenty-seven (27) and twenty-eight (28), and thirty-three (33) and thirty-four (34) of said township and range to the northwest corner of section three (3), township nine (9) south, range ninety-six (96) west; thence westerly along the township line between townships eight (8) and nine (9) south to the northwest corner of section three (3), township nine (9) south, range ninety-seven (97) west; thence southerly along the section line between sections three (3) and four (4), nine (9) and ten (10), fifteen (15) and sixteen (16), twenty-one (21) and twenty-two (22), twenty-seven (27) and twenty-eight (28), and thirty-three (33) and thirty-four (34) to the southwest corner of section thirty-four (34) of said township and range; thence easterly along the township line between townships nine (9) and ten (10) south to the southeast corner of township nine (9) south, range ninety-six (96) west; thence northerly along the range line between ranges ninety-five (95) and ninety-six (96) west to the southeast corner of section thirteen (13), township nine (9) south, range ninety-six (96) west; thence easterly along the section line between sections eighteen (18) and nineteen (19), seventeen (17) and twenty (20), sixteen (16) and twenty-one (21), fifteen (15) and twenty-two (22), fourteen (14) and twenty-three (23), and thirteen (13) and twenty-four (24), township nine (9) south, range ninety-five (95) west, to the southeast corner of section thirteen (13) of said township and range; thence northerly along the range line between ranges ninety-four (94) and ninety-five (95) west to the southeast corner of township eight (8) south, range ninety-five (95) west; thence easterly along the township line between townships eight (8) and nine (9) south to the southwest corner of township eight (8) south, range ninety-two (92) west; thence southerly along the range line between ranges ninety-two (92) and ninety-three (93) west to the southwest corner of township ten (10) south, range ninety-two (92) west; thence westerly along the second (2d) correction line south between townships ten (10) and eleven (11) south to the northwest corner of township eleven (11) south, range ninety-six (96) west; thence southerly along the range line between ranges ninety-six (96) and ninety-seven (97) west to the northwest corner of township twelve (12) south, range ninety-six (96) west; thence westerly along the township line between townships eleven (11) and twelve (12) south to the northwest corner of fractional section two (2), fractional township twelve (12) south, fractional range ninety-eight (98) west; thence southerly along the range line between fractional range ninety-eight (98) west of the sixth (6th) principal meridian and range two (2) east of the Ute principal meridian to the southwest corner of fractional section thirty-five

(35), fractional township thirteen (13) south, fractional range ninety-eight (98) west of the sixth (6th) principal meridian; thence easterly along the township line between township thirteen (13) and fractional township fourteen (14) south to the southwest corner of township thirteen (13) south, range ninety-six (96) west; thence southerly along the range line between ranges ninety-six (96) and ninety-seven (97) west to the southwest corner of township fourteen (14) south, range ninety-six (96) west; thence easterly along the township line between townships fourteen (14) and fifteen (15) south to the southeast corner of section thirty-three (33), township fourteen (14) south, range ninety-five (95) west; thence northerly along the section line between sections thirty-three (33) and thirty-four (34), twenty-seven (27) and twenty-eight (28), twenty-one (21) and twenty-two (22), fifteen (15) and sixteen (16), nine (9) and ten (10), and three (3) and four (4), townships fourteen (14) and thirteen (13) south, range ninety-five (95) west, and sections thirty-three (33) and thirty-four (34), twenty-seven (27) and twenty-eight (28), and twenty-one (21) and twenty-two (22), township twelve (12) south, range ninety-five (95) west, to the southeast corner of section sixteen (16) of said township and range; thence easterly along the section line between sections fifteen (15) and twenty-two (22), fourteen (14) and twenty-three (23), and thirteen (13) and twenty-four (24), township twelve (12) south, range ninety-five (95) west, and sections eighteen (18) and nineteen (19), seventeen (17) and twenty (20), sixteen (16) and twenty-one (21), fifteen (15) and twenty-two (22), fourteen (14) and twenty-three (23), and thirteen (13) and twenty-four (24), township twelve (12) south, range (94) west, to the southwest corner of section eighteen (18), township twelve (12) south, range ninety-three (93) west; thence southerly along the range line between ranges ninety-three (93) and ninety-four (94) west to the southwest corner of township twelve (12) south, range ninety-three (93) west; thence easterly along the township line between townships twelve (12) and thirteen (13) south to the southeast corner of township twelve (12) south, range ninety-two (92) west; thence northerly along the range line between ranges ninety-one (91) and ninety-two (92) west to the southeast corner of township eleven (11) south, range ninety-two (92) west; thence easterly along the township line between townships eleven (11) and twelve (12) south to the southwest corner of township eleven (11) south, range ninety (90) west; thence southerly along the range line between ranges ninety (90) and ninety-one (91) west to the southwest corner of township twelve (12) south, range ninety (90) west; thence easterly along the township line between townships twelve (12) and thirteen (13) south to the southeast corner of township twelve (12) south, range eighty-nine (89) west; thence northerly along the surveyed and unsurveyed range line between ranges eighty-eight (88) and eighty-nine (89) west to the northeast corner of township eleven (11) south, range eighty-nine (89) west; thence easterly along the second (2d) correction line south to the southeast corner of township ten (10) south, range eighty-nine (89) west; thence northerly along the range line between ranges eighty-eight (88) and eighty-nine (89) west to the northeast corner of township nine (9) south, range eighty-nine (89) west; thence westerly along the township line between townships eight (8) and nine (9) south to the northeast corner of township nine (9) south, range ninety (90) west; thence northerly along the range line between ranges eighty-nine (89) and ninety (90) west to the northeast corner of township eight (8) south, range ninety (90) west; thence westerly along the surveyed and unsurveyed township line between townships seven (7) and eight (8) south to the northeast corner of township eight (8) south, range ninety-three (93) west; thence northerly along the range line between ranges ninety-two (92) and ninety-three (93) west to the northeast corner of township seven (7) south, range ninety-three (93) west, the place of beginning.

Excepting from the force and effect of this proclamation all lands which may have been prior to the date hereof embraced in any legal entry or covered by any lawful filing duly of record in the proper United States land office, or upon which any valid settlement has been made pursuant to law and the statutory period within which to make entry or filing of record has not expired, and all mining claims duly located and held according to the laws of the United States and rules and regulations not in conflict therewith.

Provided, That this exception shall not continue to apply to any particular tract of land unless the entryman, settler, or claimant continues to comply with the law under which the entry, filing, settlement, or location was made.

Warning is hereby expressly given to all persons not to enter or make settlement upon the tract of land reserved by this proclamation.

In witness whereof I have hereunto set my hand and caused the seal of the United States to be affixed.

[SEAL.] Done at the city of Washington, this 24th day of December, A. D. 1892, and of the Independence of the United States the one hundred and seventeenth.

BENJ. HARRISON.

By the President:

JOHN W. FOSTER, *Secretary of State.*

BY THE PRESIDENT OF THE UNITED STATES OF AMERICA.

A PROCLAMATION.

Whereas, pursuant to section 3 of the act of Congress approved October 1, 1890, entitled ''An act to reduce the revenue and equalize duties on imports, and for other purposes,'' the Secretary of State of the United States of America communicated to the Government of Salvador the action of the Congress of the United States of America, with a view to secure reciprocal trade, in declaring the articles enumerated in said section 3 to be exempt from duty upon their importation into the United States of America; and

Whereas the minister for foreign affairs for the Republic of Salvador has communicated to the envoy extraordinary and minister plenipotentiary of the United States to Salvador that the Congress of Salvador has by due legal enactment authorized the executive power to conclude a definitive commercial arrangement with the United States to supersede the existing provisional arrangement; and

Whereas, in reciprocity for the admission into the United States of America free of all duty of the articles enumerated in section 3 of said act, the Government of Salvador will admit free of all duty from and after December 31, 1892, into all the established ports of entry of Salvador the articles or merchandise named in the following schedule, provided that the same is the manufacture or product of the United States:

PRODUCTS AND MANUFACTURES OF THE UNITED STATES TO BE ADMITTED INTO SALVADOR FREE OF CUSTOMS DUTIES AND OF ALL CHARGES, WHETHER NATIONAL OR PROVINCIAL.

1. Cotton-seed oil.
2. Live animals.
3. Tar, vegetable and mineral.
4. Wire, barbed, and staples for fences.
5. Apparatus for distilling liquors.
6. Plows, cultivators, hoes, axes, machetes, shovels, and rakes.
7. Quicksilver.
8. Barrels, casks, and tanks of iron for water.
9. Mineral ores.
10. Boats, lighters, tackle, anchors, chains, girtlines, sails, and all other articles for vessels, to be used in the ports, lakes, and rivers of the Republic.
11. Coal, mineral.
12. Roman cement and hydraulic lime.
13. Kettles for making salt.
14. Wooden staves, barrel heads and hoops.
15. Houses of wood and iron, complete and in parts.
16. Beans, potatoes, and onions.
17. Fruits, fresh.
18. Guano and other fertilizers, natural and artificial.
19. Guys for mining purposes.
20. Hay and straw for forage.
21. Furnaces and instruments for assaying metals.
22. Scientific instruments.
23. Loadstones.
24. Bricks, fire bricks, and crucibles for melting.
25. Hops.
26. Printed books, pamphlets and newspapers, bound or unbound, maps, photographs, printed music, and paper for music.
27. Corn, rice, barley, and rye.
28. Marble, dressed, for furniture, statues, fountains, gravestones, and building purposes.

29. Machinery of all kinds, including sewing machines, and separate or extra parts for the same.

30. Materials of all kinds for the construction and operation of railroads.

31. Materials of all kinds for the construction and operation of telegraphic and telephonic lines.

32. Materials of all kinds for lighting by electricity and gas.

33. Materials of all kinds for the construction of wharves in ports, lakes, or rivers.

34. Wood of all kinds for building, in trunks or pieces, beams, rafters, planks, boards, shingles, and flooring.

35. Molds for making sugar.

36. Models of machinery and buildings.

37. Printing materials, including presses, ink, and all other accessories.

38. Samples of merchandise the duties on which do not exceed $1.

39. Gold and silver in bars, dust, or coin.

40. Preparations of flour in biscuits, crackers, not sweetened, macaroni, vermicelli, and tallarin.

41. Plates of iron for building purposes.

42. Kettles for making sugar.

43. Sulphate of quinine.

44. Tubes of iron and all other accessories for water supply.

45. Wagons, carts, and carriages of all kinds, and separate parts for the same.

It is understood that the packages or coverings in which the articles named in the foregoing schedule are imported shall be free of duty if they are usual and proper for the purpose.

And whereas the Government of Salvador has further stipulated that the laws and regulations adopted to protect its revenue and prevent fraud in the declarations and proof that the articles named in the foregoing schedule are the product or manufacture of the United States of America shall impose no additional charges on the importer nor undue restrictions on the articles imported; and

Whereas the envoy extraordinary and minister plenipotentiary of the United States to Salvador has informed the Government of Salvador that its action in granting freedom of duties to the products and manufactures of the United States of America on their importation into Salvador is accepted as a due reciprocity for the action of Congress as set forth in section 3 of said act:

Now, therefore, be it known that I, Benjamin Harrison, President of the United States of America, have caused the above-stated modifications of the tariff laws of Salvador to be made public for the information of the citizens of the United States of America.

In testimony whereof I have hereunto set my hand and caused the seal of the United States to be affixed.

[SEAL.] Done at the city of Washington, this 27th day of December, A. D. 1892, and of the Independence of the United States the one hundred and seventeenth.

BENJ. HARRISON.

By the President:
JOHN W. FOSTER,
Secretary of State.

BY THE PRESIDENT OF THE UNITED STATES OF AMERICA.

A PROCLAMATION.

Whereas Congress by a statute approved March 22, 1882, and by statutes in furtherance and amendment thereof defined the crimes of bigamy, polygamy, and unlawful cohabitation in the Territories and other places within the exclusive jurisdiction of the United States and prescribed a penalty for such crimes; and

Whereas on or about the 6th day of October, 1890, the Church of the Latter-day Saints, commonly known as the Mormon Church, through its president issued a manifesto proclaiming the purpose of said church no longer to sanction the practice of polygamous marriages and calling upon all members and adherents of said church to obey the laws of the United States in reference to said subject-matter; and

Whereas it is represented that since the date of said declaration the members and adherents of said church have generally obeyed said laws and have abstained from plural marriages and polygamous cohabitation; and

Whereas by a petition dated December 19, 1891, the officials of said church, pledging the membership thereof to a faithful obedience to the laws against plural marriage and unlawful cohabitation, have applied to me to grant amnesty for past offenses against said laws, which request a very large number of influential non-Mormons residing in the Territories have also strongly urged; and

Whereas the Utah Commission in their report bearing date September 15, 1892, recommend that said petition be granted and said amnesty proclaimed, under proper conditions as to the future observance of the law, with a view to the encouragement of those now disposed to become law-abiding citizens; and

Whereas during the past two years such amnesty has been granted to individual applicants in a very large number of cases, conditioned upon the faithful observance of the laws of the United States against unlawful cohabitation, and there are now pending many more such applications:

Now, therefore, I, Benjamin Harrison, President of the United States, by virtue of the powers in me vested, do hereby declare and grant a full amnesty and pardon to all persons liable to the penalties of said act by reason of unlawful cohabitation under the color of polygamous or plural marriage who have since November 1, 1890, abstained from such unlawful cohabitation, but upon the express condition that they shall in the future faithfully obey the laws of the United States hereinbefore named, and not otherwise.   Those who shall fail to avail themselves of the clemency hereby offered will be vigorously prosecuted.

In witness whereof I have hereunto set my hand and caused the seal of the United States to be affixed.

[SEAL.]   Done at the city of Washington, this 4th day of January, A. D. 1893, and of the Independence of the United States the one hundred and seventeenth.

BENJ. HARRISON.

By the President:
JOHN W. FOSTER, *Secretary of State.*

BY THE PRESIDENT OF THE UNITED STATES OF AMERICA.

A PROCLAMATION.

Whereas it is provided by section 24 of the act of Congress approved March 3, 1891, entitled "An act to repeal timber-culture laws, and for other purposes"—

That the President of the United States may from time to time set apart and reserve in any State or Territory having public land bearing forests, in any part of the public lands wholly or in part covered with timber or undergrowth, whether of commercial value or not, as public reservations; and the President shall by public proclamation declare the establishment of such reservations and the limits thereof.

And whereas the public lands in the State of California within the limits hereinafter described are in part covered with timber, and it appears that the public good would be promoted by setting apart and reserving said lands as a public reservation:

Now, therefore, I, Benjamin Harrison, President of the United States, by virtue of the power in me vested by section 24 of the aforesaid act of Congress, do hereby make known and proclaim that there is hereby reserved from entry or settlement and set apart as a public reservation all those certain tracts, pieces, or parcels of land lying and being situate in the State of California and within the boundaries particularly described as follows, to wit:

Beginning at the northeast corner of township five (5) south, range thirty (30) east, on the first (1st) standard parallel south, Mount Diablo meridian, California; thence westerly along said first (1st) standard parallel to the northwest corner of township five (5) south, range twenty-one (21) east; thence southerly on the range line between ranges twenty (20) and twenty-one (21) east to the southwest corner of township six (6) south, range twenty-one (21) east; thence easterly on the township line between townships six (6) and seven (7) south to the southeast corner of township six (6) south, range twenty-one (21) east; thence southerly on the range line between ranges twenty-one (21) and twenty-two (22) east to the southwest corner of township seven (7) south, range twenty-two (22) east; thence easterly along the township line between townships seven (7) and eight (8) south to the southeast corner of township seven (7) south, range twenty-two (22) east; thence southerly along the range line between ranges twenty-two (22) and twenty-three (23) east to the southwest corner of township eight (8) south, range twenty-three (23) east; thence easterly along the second (2d) standard parallel south to the northeast corner of township nine (9) south, range twenty-three (23) east; thence southerly along the unsurveyed and surveyed range line between ranges twenty-three (23) and twenty-four (24) east to the southwest corner of township nine (9) south, range twenty-four (24) east; thence easterly along the township line between townships nine (9) and ten (10) south to the southeast corner of township nine (9) south, range twenty-four (24) east; thence southerly along the range line between ranges twenty-four (24) and twenty-five (25) east to the southwest corner of township ten (10) south, range twenty-five (25) east; thence easterly along the township line between townships ten (10) and eleven (11) south to the southeast corner of township ten (10) south, range twenty-five (25) east; thence southerly along the unsurveyed and surveyed range line between ranges twenty-five (25) and twenty-six (26) east to the southwest corner of township twelve (12) south, range twenty-six (26) east; thence easterly along the third (3d) standard parallel south to the northwest corner of township thirteen (13) south, range twenty-seven (27) east; thence southerly along the range line between ranges twenty-six (26) and twenty-seven (27) east to the southwest corner of township thirteen (13) south, range twenty-seven (27) east; thence easterly along the township line between townships thirteen (13) and fourteen (14) south to the southeast corner of township thirteen (13) south, range twenty-seven (27) east; thence northerly along the boundary line of "General Grant National Park" to the northwest corner, easterly to the northeast corner, southerly to the southeast corner, and westerly to the southwest corner of said park; thence southerly along the range line between ranges twenty-seven (27) and twenty-eight (28) east to the southwest corner of township fourteen (14) south, range twenty-eight (28) east; thence easterly along the township line between townships fourteen (14) and fifteen (15) south to the southwest corner of township fourteen (14) south, range thirty-one (31) east; thence southerly along the range line between ranges thirty (30) and thirty-one (31) east to the fourth (4th) standard parallel south; thence westerly along said fourth (4th) standard parallel to the northwest corner of township seventeen (17) south, range thirty-one (31) east; thence southerly along the range line between ranges thirty (30) and thirty-one (31) east to the southwest corner of township seventeen (17) south, range thirty-one (31) east; thence easterly along the township line between townships seventeen (17) and eighteen (18) south to the southeast corner of township seventeen (17) south, range thirty-one (31) east; thence southerly along the range line between ranges thirty-one (31) and thirty-two (32) east to the southwest corner of township eighteen (18) south, range thirty-two (32) east; thence westerly along the township line between townships

eighteen (18) and nineteen (19) south to the northwest corner of township nineteen (19) south, range thirty (30) east; thence southerly along
the range line between ranges twenty-nine (29) and thirty (30) east to
the fifth (5th) standard parallel south; thence westerly along said fifth
(5th) standard parallel to the northwest corner of township twenty-one
(21) south, range thirty (30) east; thence southerly along the range line
between ranges twenty-nine (29) and thirty (30) east to a point on said
range line where it intersects the northern boundary line of the ''Tule
River Indian Reservation;'' thence easterly and northeasterly along the
northern boundary line of said reservation to the northeast corner thereof,
located in the southwest quarter of section twenty-one (21), township
twenty-one (21) south, range thirty-one (31) east; thence southerly along
the eastern boundary of said reservation to the southeast corner thereof,
located in the northwest quarter of sect on thirty-three (33), township
twenty-two (22) south, range thirty-one (31) east; thence westerly and
southwesterly along the southern boundary of said reservation to a point
where it is intersected by the range line between ranges twenty-nine
(29) and thirty (30) east; thence southerly along said range line to the
southwest corner of township twenty-three (23) south, range thirty (30)
east; thence easterly along the township line between townships twenty-
three (23) and twenty-four (24) south to the southeast corner of township twenty-three (23) south, range thirty (30) east; thence southerly
along the range line between ranges thirty (30) and thirty-one (31) east
to the sixth (6th) standard parallel south; thence westerly along said
sixth (6th) standard parallel to the northwest corner of township twenty-
five (25) south, range thirty-one (31) east; thence southerly along the
range line between ranges thirty (30) and thirty-one (31) east to the
southwest corner of township twenty-six (26) south, range thirty-one
(31) east; thence westerly along the township line between townships
twenty-six (26) and twenty-seven (27) south to the northwest corner of
township twenty-seven (27) south, range thirty (30) east; thence southerly along the range line between ranges twenty-nine (29) and thirty
(30) east to the seventh (7th) standard parallel south; thence easterly
along said seventh (7th) standard parallel to the southeast corner of
township twenty-eight (28) south, range thirty-seven (37) east; thence
northerly along the range line between ranges thirty-seven (37) and
thirty-eight (38) east to the sixth (6th) standard parallel south; thence
easterly along said sixth (6th) standard parallel to the southeast corner
of township twenty-four (24) south, range thirty-seven (37) east; thence
northerly along the range line between ranges thirty-seven (37) and
thirty-eight (38) east to the northeast corner of township twenty-four
(24) south, range thirty-seven (37) east; thence easterly along the township line between townships twenty-three (23) and twenty-four (24)
south to the southeast corner of township twenty-three (23) south, range
thirty-seven (37) east; thence northerly along the range line between

ranges thirty-seven (37) and thirty-eight (38) east to the fifth (5th) standard parallel south; thence westerly along said fifth (5th) standard parallel south to the southeast corner of section thirty-one (31), township twenty (20) south, range thirty-seven (37) east; thence northerly along the western boundary line of sections thirty-two (32), twenty-nine (29), twenty (20), seventeen (17), eight (8), and five (5) to the northwest corner of section five (5) in said township and range; thence westerly along the township line between townships nineteen (19) and twenty (20) south to the southeast corner of township nineteen (19) south, range thirty-six (36) east; thence northerly along the range line between ranges thirty-six (36) and thirty-seven (37) east to the quarter-section corner on the east line of section thirty-six (36), township nineteen (19) south, range thirty-six (36) east, westerly on a line through the centers of sections thirty-six (36) and thirty-five (35) to the center of section thirty-five (35), northerly on a line through the centers of sections thirty-five (35), twenty-six (26), twenty-three (23), and fourteen (14) to the center of section fourteen (14), easterly on a line through the center of section fourteen (14) to the quarter-section corner between said section fourteen (14) and section thirteen (13), and northerly along the section lines on the west boundary of sections thirteen (13), twelve (12), and one (1) to the northwest corner of section one (1), all of said township and range; thence northerly along the section lines on the west boundary of sections thirty-six (36) and twenty-five (25), township eighteen (18) south, range thirty-six (36) east, to the northwest corner of said section twenty-five (25), easterly along the section line between sections twenty-four (24) and twenty-five (25) to the quarter-section corner between said sections, northerly through the centers of sections twenty-four (24) and thirteen (13) to the quarter-section corner between sections thirteen (13) and twelve (12), westerly along the section line to the southwest corner of section twelve (12), and northerly along the section lines on the west boundary of sections twelve (12) and one (1) to the northwest corner of section one (1) of said township and range; thence northerly along the section line on the west boundary of section thirty-six (36), township seventeen (17) south, range thirty-six (36) east, to the quarter-section corner between sections thirty-five (35) and thirty-six (36), westerly to the center of section thirty-five (35), northerly on a line through the centers of sections thirty-five (35), twenty-six (26), twenty-three (23), fourteen (14), and eleven (11) to the quarter-section corner between sections eleven (11) and two (2), westerly along the section line to the southwest corner of section two (2), and northerly along the section line to the northwest corner of section two (2), all of said township and range; thence westerly along the surveyed and unsurveyed line of the fourth (4th) standard parallel south to the southwest corner of township sixteen (16) south, range thirty-four (34) east; thence northerly along the range line between ranges thirty-three (33) and thirty-four

(34) east to the northwest corner of township fifteen (15) south, range thirty-four (34) east; thence easterly along the township line between townships fourteen (14) and fifteen (15) south to the southwest corner of township fourteen (14) south, range thirty-five (35) east; thence northerly on the range line between ranges thirty-four (34) and thirty-five (35) east to the northwest corner of township fourteen (14) south, range thirty-five (35) east; thence westerly along the township line between townships thirteen (13) and fourteen (14) south to the southwest corner of section thirty-five (35), township thirteen (13) south, range thirty-four (34) east, northerly along the section line to the quarter-section corner between sections thirty-four (34) and thirty-five (35), westerly to the center of section thirty-four (34), northerly on a line through the centers of sections thirty-four (34) and twenty-seven (27) to the center of section twenty-seven (27), easterly through section twenty-seven (27) to the quarter-section corner between sections twenty-seven (27) and twenty-six (26), northerly along the section lines on the west boundary of sections twenty-six (26), twenty-three (23), fourteen (14), eleven (11), and two (2) to the northwest corner of west lot one (1) in section two (2), easterly to the southwest corner of the east lot two (2) in section two (2), and northerly to the northwest corner of the west half of east lot six (6), section two (2), all of said township and range; thence westerly along the third (3d) standard parallel south to the southwest corner of section thirty-four (34), township twelve (12) south, range thirty-four (34) east, northerly along the section line to the quarter-section corner between sections thirty-four (34) and thirty-three (33), westerly to the center of section thirty-three (33), northerly to the quarter-section corner between sections thirty-three (33) and twenty-eight (28), westerly on the section line to the southwest corner of section twenty-eight (28), northerly along the section lines on the west boundary of sections twenty-eight (28), twenty-one (21), sixteen (16), nine (9), and four (4) to the quarter-section corner between sections four (4) and five (5), westerly to the center of section five (5), and northerly to the quarter-section corner on the north boundary of said section five (5), all of said township and range; thence westerly along the township line between townships eleven (11) and twelve (12) south to the southwest corner of section thirty-two (32), township eleven (11) south, range thirty-four (34) east, northerly along the section lines on the west boundary of sections thirty-two (32), twenty-nine (29), twenty (20), seventeen (17), and eight (8) to the quarter-section corner between sections seven (7) and eight (8), westerly on a line through the center of section seven (7), township eleven (11) south, range thirty-four (34) east, and sections twelve (12) and eleven (11), township eleven (11) south, range thirty-three (33) east, to the center of said section eleven (11), and northerly on a central line through sections eleven (11) and two (2) to the quarter-section corner on the north line of section two (2), township eleven (11) south, range thirty-three

(33) east; thence westerly on the township line between townships ten (10) and eleven (11) south to the southwest corner of section thirty-five (35), township ten (10) south, range thirty-three (33) east, northerly to the quarter-section corner between sections thirty-five (35) and thirty-four (34), westerly to the center of section thirty-four (34), northerly on a line through the centers of sections thirty-four (34), twenty-seven (27), and twenty-two (22) to the center of section twenty-two (22), easterly to the center of section twenty-three (23), northerly through the centers of sections twenty-three (23), fourteen (14), and eleven (11) to the center of section eleven (11), easterly to the quarter-section corner between sections eleven (11) and twelve (12), northerly along the section line to the northwest corner of section twelve (12), easterly along the section line to the quarter-section corner between sections twelve (12) and one (1), northerly to the center of section one (1), easterly to the quarter-section corner on the east line of section one (1), and northerly to the northeast corner of section one (1), all of said township and range; thence westerly along the unsurveyed township line between townships ten (10) and nine (9) south to the southeast corner of township nine (9) south, range thirty-two (32) east; thence northerly along the range line between ranges thirty-two (32) and thirty-three (33) east to the northeast corner of township nine (9) south, range thirty-two (32) east; thence westerly along the second (2d) standard parallel south to the southeast corner of township eight (8) south, range thirty-one (31) east; thence northerly along the surveyed and unsurveyed range line between ranges thirty-one (31) and thirty-two (32) east to the northeast corner of township eight (8) south, range thirty-one (31) east; thence westerly along the township line between townships seven (7) and eight (8) south to the southeast corner of township seven (7) south, range thirty (30) east; thence northerly along the range line between ranges thirty (30) and thirty-one (31) east to the northeast corner of township five (5) south, range thirty (30) east, the place of beginning.

Excepting from the force and effect of this proclamation all lands which may have been prior to the date hereof embraced in any legal entry or covered by any lawful filing duly of record in the proper United States land office, or upon which any valid settlement has been made pursuant to law and the statutory period within which to make entry or filing of record has not expired, and all mining claims duly located and held according to the laws of the United States and the rules and regulations not in conflict therewith.

Provided, That this exception shall not continue to apply to any particular tract of land unless the entryman, settler, or claimant continues to comply with the law under which the entry, filing, settlement, or location was made.

Warning is hereby expressly given to all persons not to enter or make settlement upon the tract of land reserved by this proclamation.

In witness whereof I have hereunto set my hand and caused the seal of
the United States to be affixed.

[SEAL.]   Done at the city of Washington, this 14th day of February,
A. D. 1893, and of the Independence of the United States the
one hundred and seventeenth.

BENJ. HARRISON.

By the President:

JOHN W. FOSTER, *Secretary of State.*

BY THE PRESIDENT OF THE UNITED STATES OF AMERICA.

A PROCLAMATION.

Whereas it is provided by section 24 of the act of Congress approved
March 3, 1891, entitled "An act to repeal timber-culture laws, and for
other purposes"—

That the President of the United States may from time to time set apart and reserve
in any State or Territory having public land bearing forests, in any part of the public
lands wholly or in part covered with timber or undergrowth, whether of commercial
value or not, as public reservations; and the President shall by public proclamation
declare the establishment of such reservations and the limits thereof.

And whereas the public lands in the State of Washington within the
limits hereinafter described are in part covered with timber, and it appears
that the public good would be promoted by setting apart and reserving
said lands as a public reservation:

Now, therefore, I, Benjamin Harrison, President of the United States,
by virtue of the power in me vested by section 24 of the aforesaid act of
Congress, do hereby make known and proclaim that there is hereby reserved from entry or settlement and set apart as a public reservation all
those certain tracts, pieces, or parcels of land lying and being situate in
the State of Washington and within the boundaries particularly described
as follows, to wit:

Beginning at the southwest corner of township thirteen (13) north,
range fifteen (15) east of the Willamette base and meridian; thence
northerly along the surveyed and unsurveyed range line between ranges
fourteen (14) and fifteen (15) east, subject to the proper easterly or westerly offset on the fourth (4th) standard parallel north, to the point for
the northeast corner of township eighteen (18) north, range fourteen
(14) east; thence westerly along the unsurveyed township line between
townships eighteen (18) and nineteen (19) north to the southeast corner
of township nineteen (19) north, range seven (7) east; thence southerly
along the unsurveyed range line between ranges seven (7) and eight (8)
east, subject to the proper easterly or westerly offsets on the township
line between townships seventeen (17) and eighteen (18) north, and the
fourth (4th) standard parallel north to the point for the southwest corner of township thirteen (13) north, range eight (8) east; thence easterly
along the unsurveyed township line between townships twelve (12) and

thirteen (13) north to the southwest corner of township thirteen (13) north, range fifteen (15) east, the place of beginning.

Excepting from the force and effect of this proclamation all lands which may have been prior to the date hereof embraced in any legal entry or covered by any lawful filing duly of record in the proper United States land office, or upon which any valid settlement has been made pursuant to law and the statutory period within which to make entry or filing of record has not expired, and all mining claims duly located and held according to the laws of the United States and rules and regulations not in conflict therewith.

Provided, That this exception shall not continue to apply to any particular tract of land unless the entryman, settler, or claimant continues to comply with the law under which the entry, filing, settlement, or location was made.

Warning is hereby expressly given to all persons not to enter or make settlement upon the tract of land reserved by this proclamation.

In witness whereof I have hereunto set my hand and caused the seal of the United States to be affixed.

[SEAL.]　　　Done at the city of Washington, this 20th day of February, A. D. 1893, and of the Independence of the United States the one hundred and seventeenth.

BENJ. HARRISON.

By the President:

JOHN W. FOSTER, *Secretary of State.*

BY THE PRESIDENT OF THE UNITED STATES OF AMERICA.

A PROCLAMATION.

Whereas it is provided by section 24 of the act of Congress approved March 3, 1891, entitled "An act to repeal timber-culture laws, and for other purposes"—

That the President of the United States may from time to time set apart and reserve in any State or Territory having public land bearing forests, in any part of the public lands wholly or in part covered with timber or undergrowth, whether of commercial value or not, as public reservations; and the President shall by public proclamation declare the establishment of such reservations and the limits thereof.

And whereas the public lands in the Territory of Arizona within the limits hereinafter described are in part covered with timber, and it appears that the public good would be promoted by setting apart and reserving said lands as a public reservation:

Now, therefore, I, Benjamin Harrison, President of the United States, by virtue of the power in me vested by section 24 of the aforesaid act of Congress, do hereby make known and proclaim that there is hereby reserved from entry or settlement and set apart as a public reservation all those certain tracts, pieces, or parcels of land lying and being situate in the Territory of Arizona and within the boundaries particularly described as follows, to wit :

Beginning at the point of intersection of the parallel of thirty-six (36) degrees thirty (30) minutes north latitude with the meridian of one hundred and eleven (111) degrees forty-five (45) minutes of longitude west from Greenwich ; thence westerly along said parallel of latitude to its intersection with the meridian of one hundred and twelve (112) degrees forty-five (45) minutes west longitude; thence southerly along said meridian of longitude to its intersection with the parallel of thirty-five (35) degrees forty-five (45) minutes north latitude; thence easterly along said parallel of latitude to its intersection with the meridian of one hundred and eleven (111) degrees forty-five (45) minutes west longitude ; thence northerly along said meridian of longitude to its intersection with the parallel of thirty-six (36) degrees thirty (30) minutes north latitude, the place of beginning.

Excepting from the force and effect of this proclamation all lands which may have been prior to the date hereof embraced in any legal entry or covered by any lawful filing duly of record in the proper United States land office, or upon which any valid settlement has been made pursuant to law and the statutory period within which to make entry or filing of record has not expired, and all mining claims duly located and held according to the laws of the United States and rules and regulations not in conflict therewith.

Provided, That this exception shall not continue to apply to any particular tract of land unless the entryman, settler, or claimant continues to comply with the law under which the entry, filing, settlement, or location was made.

Warning is hereby expressly given to all persons not to enter or make settlement upon the tract of land reserved by this proclamation.

In witness whereof I have hereunto set my hand and caused the seal of the United States to be affixed.

[SEAL.] Done at the city of Washington, this 20th day of February, A. D. 1893, and of the Independence of the United States the one hundred and seventeenth.

BENJ. HARRISON.

By the President :

JOHN W. FOSTER, *Secretary of State.*

BY THE PRESIDENT OF THE UNITED STATES OF AMERICA.

A PROCLAMATION.

Whereas by my proclamation of August 18, 1892,* and in pursuance of the authority conferred on me by an act of Congress approved July 26, 1892, entitled "An act to enforce the reciprocal commercial relations

* See pp. 5725-5727.

between the United States and Canada, and for other purposes," I directed "that from and after September 1, 1892, until further notice a toll of 20 cents per ton be levied, collected, and paid on all freight of whatever kind or description passing through the St. Marys Falls Canal in transit to any port of the Dominion of Canada, whether carried in vessels of the United States or of other nations," and to that extent thereby suspended "from and after said date the right of free passage through said St. Marys Falls Canal of any and all cargoes or portions of cargoes in transit to Canadian ports;" and

Whereas the above order was issued in consequence of the imposition by the government of the Dominion of Canada of a discriminating toll whereby unjust and unreasonable burdens were placed, in violation of Article XXVII of the treaty of Washington, upon the carrying of passengers and cargoes through the Welland Canal in transit to ports of the United States, as is fully set forth in the said proclamation; and

Whereas by an order in council dated February 13, 1893, the Governor-General of the Dominion of Canada has directed that—

For the season of 1893 the canal tolls for the passage of the following food products, wheat, Indian corn, pease, barley, rye, oats, flaxseed, and buckwheat, for passage eastward through the Welland Canal be 10 cents per ton, and for passage westward through the St. Lawrence canals only 10 cents per ton; payment of the said toll of 10 cents per ton for passage through the Welland Canal to entitle these products to free passage through the St. Lawrence canals.

And whereas I have received satisfactory assurances that this order revokes during the season of 1893 the discriminating provisions above referred to and secures to citizens of the United States equality with British subjects as regards the use of said canals:

Now, therefore, I, Benjamin Harrison, President of the United States of America, by virtue of the said act of Congress approved July 26, 1892, do hereby declare and proclaim that from and after the date hereof and until further notice the provisions of my said proclamation of August 18, 1892,* are suspended in so far as they direct that a toll of 20 cents per ton be levied, collected, and paid on all freight of whatever kind or description passing through the St. Marys Falls Canal in transit to any port of the Dominion of Canada, whether carried in vessels of the United States or of other nations.

In testimony whereof I have hereunto set my hand and caused the seal of the United States to be affixed.

[SEAL.] Done at the city of Washington, this 21st day of February, 1893, and of the Independence of the United States of America the one hundred and seventeenth.

BENJ. HARRISON

By the President:
JOHN W. FOSTER,
    Secretary of State.

* See pp. 5725–5727.

By the President of the United States of America.

A PROCLAMATION.

Whereas it is provided by section 24 of the act of Congress approved March 3, 1891, entitled "An act to repeal timber-culture laws, and for other purposes"—

That the President of the United States may from time to time set apart and reserve in any State or Territory having public land bearing forests, in any part of the public lands wholly or in part covered with timber or undergrowth, whether of commercial value or not, as public reservations; and the President shall by public proclamation declare the establishment of such reservations and the limits thereof.

And whereas the public lands in the State of California within the limits hereinafter described are in part covered with timber, and it appears that the public good would be promoted by setting apart and reserving said lands as a public reservation:

Now, therefore, I, Benjamin Harrison, President of the United States, by virtue of the power in me vested by section 24 of the aforesaid act of Congress, do hereby make known and proclaim that there is hereby reserved from entry or settlement and set apart as a public reservation all those certain tracts, pieces, or parcels of land lying and being situate in the State of California and within the boundaries particularly described as follows, to wit:

Beginning at the northeast corner of section thirteen (13), township five (5) south, range six (6) west, of the San Bernardino base and meridian; thence westerly along the surveyed and unsurveyed section line to the point for the southwest corner of section ten (10), said township and range; thence northerly along the surveyed and unsurveyed section line to the northwest corner of section three (3), said township and range; thence westerly along the surveyed and unsurveyed township line to the point for the northwest corner of section three (3), township five (5) south, range seven (7) west; thence southerly along the surveyed and unsurveyed section line to the southeast corner of section thirty-three (33), said township and range; thence easterly along the surveyed and unsurveyed township line to the northeast corner of township six (6) south, range seven (7) west; thence southerly to the southwest corner of township five (5) south, range six (6) west; thence easterly to the point for the quarter-section corner on the north line of section six (6), township six (6) south, range six (6) west; thence southerly on a central line to the center of section nineteen (19), said township and range; thence easterly to the quarter-section corner on the east boundary of said section nineteen (19); thence southerly on the section line to the point of intersection with the north boundary of the "Rancho Mission Viejo or La Paz;" thence in a southeasterly direction along said boundary line to the point of intersection with the township line between townships six (6) and seven (7) south; thence easterly along said township line to the southeast corner of township six (6) south, range six (6) west; thence northerly along the range line between ranges five (5) and six (6) west to the northeast corner of section thirteen (13), township five (5) south, range six (6) west, the place of beginning.

Excepting from the force and effect of this proclamation all lands which may have been prior to the date hereof embraced in any legal entry or covered by any lawful filing duly of record in the proper United States land office, or upon which any valid settlement has been made pursuant to law and the statutory period within which to make entry or filing of record has not expired, and all mining claims duly located and held according to the laws of the United States and rules and regulations not in conflict therewith.

Provided, That this exception shall not continue to apply to any particular tract of land unless the entryman, settler, or claimant continues to comply with the law under which the entry, filing, settlement, or location was made.

Warning is hereby expressly given to all persons not to enter or make settlement upon the tract of land reserved by this proclamation.

In witness whereof I have hereunto set my hand and caused the seal of the United States to be affixed.

[SEAL.]   Done at the city of Washington, this 25th day of February, A. D. 1893, and of the Independence of the United States the one hundred and seventeenth.

                              BENJ. HARRISON.

By the President:
    WILLIAM F. WHARTON,
              Acting Secretary of State.

BY THE PRESIDENT OF THE UNITED STATES OF AMERICA.

A PROCLAMATION.

Whereas it is provided by section 24 of the act of Congress approved March 3, 1891, entitled "An act to repeal timber-culture laws, and for other purposes"—

That the President of the United States may from time to time set apart and reserve in any State or Territory having public land bearing forests, in any part of the public lands wholly or in part covered with timber or undergrowth, whether of commercial value or not, as public reservations; and the President shall by public proclamation declare the establishment of such reservations and the limits thereof.

And whereas the public lands in the State of California within the limits hereinafter described are in part covered with timber, and it appears that the public good would be promoted by setting apart and reserving said lands as a public reservation:

Now, therefore, I, Benjamin Harrison, President of the United States,

by virtue of the power in me vested by section 24 of the aforesaid act of Congress, do hereby make known and proclaim that there is hereby reserved from entry or settlement and set apart as a public reservation all those certain tracts, pieces, or parcels of land lying and being situate in the State of California and within the boundaries particularly described as follows, to wit:

Beginning at the northwest corner of township three (3) north, range five (5) west, San Bernardino meridian, California; thence southerly along the surveyed and unsurveyed range line between ranges five (5) and six (6) west to the northwest corner of section eighteen (18), township one (1) north, range five (5) west; thence easterly along the section line between sections seven (7) and eighteen (18) to the western boundary of the "Rancho Muscupiabe;" thence easterly, following the western and northern boundary of said rancho, to the point where said boundary intersects the section line between sections nineteen (19) and thirty (30), township one (1) north, range three (3) west; thence easterly along the section lines to the northeast corner of section twenty-five (25), said township and range; thence southerly along the range line between ranges two (2) and three (3) west to the San Bernardino base line; thence easterly along said base line to the northeast corner of section four (4), township one (1) south, range two (2) west, southerly along the unsurveyed and surveyed section lines to the northeast corner of section (16), easterly along the section lines to the northeast corner of section thirteen (13), and southerly to the southeast corner of section thirteen (13), all of said township and range; thence easterly to a point for the center of township one (1) south, range one (1) west; thence southerly to a point for the southwest corner of section thirty-four (34) in said township and range; thence easterly along the surveyed and unsurveyed township line between townships one (1) and two (2) south to the San Bernardino meridian; thence southerly along said meridian to the northeast corner of township three (3) south, range one (1) west; thence easterly through the Maronge Indian Reservation to the southeast corner of township two (2) south, range three (3) east; thence northerly along the surveyed and unsurveyed range line to the northeast corner of said township; thence easterly to a point for the southeast corner of township one (1) south, range four (4) east; thence northerly along the surveyed and unsurveyed range line between ranges four (4) and five (5) east to the northeast corner of section twenty-four (24), township three (3) north, range four (4) east; thence westerly along the surveyed and unsurveyed section lines to the southwest corner of section eighteen (18), township three (3) north, range (3) east; thence northerly along the range line between ranges two (2) and three (3) east to the northeast corner of township three (3) north, range two (2) east; thence westerly along the township line between townships three (3) and four (4) north to the northwest corner of township three (3) north, range (5) west, the place of beginning.

Excepting from the force and effect of this proclamation all lands which may have been prior to the date hereof embraced in any legal entry or covered by any lawful filing duly of record in the proper United States land office, or upon which any valid settlement has been made pursuant to law and the statutory period within which to make entry or filing of record has not expired, and all mining claims duly located and held according to the laws of the United States and rules and regulations not in conflict therewith.

Provided, That this exception shall not continue to apply to any particular tract of land unless the entryman, settler, or claimant continues to comply with the law under which the entry, filing, settlement, or location was made.

Warning is hereby expressly given to all persons not to enter or make settlement upon the tract of land reserved by this proclamation.

In witness whereof I have hereunto set my hand and caused the seal of the United States to be affixed.

[SEAL.]   Done at the city of Washington, this 25th day of February, A. D. 1893, and of the Independence of the United States the one hundred and seventeenth.

BENJ. HARRISON.

By the President:
WILLIAM F. WHARTON,
Acting Secretary of State.

BY THE PRESIDENT OF THE UNITED STATES OF AMERICA.

A PROCLAMATION.

Whereas public interests require that the Senate should be convened at 12 o'clock on the 4th day of March next to receive such communications as may be made by the Executive:

Now, therefore, I, Benjamin Harrison, President of the United States, do hereby proclaim and declare that an extraordinary occasion requires the Senate of the United States to convene at the Capitol, in the city of Washington, on the 4th day of March next, at 12 o'clock noon, of which all persons who shall at that time be entitled to act as members of that body are hereby required to take notice.

Given under my hand and the seal of the United States, at Washington, this 25th day of February, A. D. 1893, and of the Independence of the United States of America the one hundred and seventeenth.

[SEAL.]

BENJ. HARRISON.

By the President:
WILLIAM F. WHARTON,
Acting Secretary of State.

EXECUTIVE ORDERS.

AMENDMENT OF CIVIL-SERVICE RULES.

JANUARY 5, 1893.

Section 2 of Postal Rule I is hereby amended so as to read as follows:

The classification of the postal service made by the Postmaster-General under section 6 of the act of January 16, 1883, is hereby extended to all free-delivery post-offices; and hereafter whenever any post-office becomes a free-delivery office the said classification or any then existing classification made by the Postmaster-General under said section and act shall apply thereto; and the Civil Service Commission shall provide examinations to test the fitness of persons to fill vacancies in all free-delivery post-offices, and these rules shall be in force therein; but this shall not include any post-office made an experimental free-delivery office under the authority contained in the appropriation act of March 3, 1891. Every revision of the classification of any post-office under section 6 of the act of January 16, 1883, and every inclusion of a post-office within the classified postal service shall be reported to the President.

BENJ. HARRISON.

GENERAL ORDERS, NO. 4.

HEADQUARTERS OF THE ARMY,
ADJUTANT-GENERAL'S OFFICE,
Washington, January 19, 1893.

I. The following proclamation [order] has been received from the President:

EXECUTIVE MANSION,
Washington, D. C., January 18, 1893.

To the People of the United States:

The death of Rutherford B. Hayes, who was President of the United States from March 4, 1877, to March 4, 1881, at his home in Fremont, Ohio, at 11 p. m. yesterday, is an event the announcement of which will be received with very general and very sincere sorrow. His public service extended over many years and over a wide range of official duty. He was a patriotic citizen, a lover of the flag and of our free institutions, an industrious and conscientious civil officer, a soldier of dauntless courage, a loyal comrade and friend, a sympathetic and helpful neighbor, and the honored head of a happy Christian home. He has steadily grown in the public esteem, and the impartial historian will not fail to recognize the conscientiousness, the manliness, and the courage that so strongly characterized his whole public career.

As an expression of the public sorrow it is ordered that the Executive Mansion and the several Executive Departments at Washington be draped in mourning and the flags thereon placed at half-staff for a period of thirty days, and that on the day of the funeral all public business in the Departments be suspended, and that suitable military and naval honors, under the orders of the Secretaries of War and of the Navy, be rendered on that day.

Done at the city of Washington, this 18th day of January, A. D. 1893, [SEAL.] and of the Independence of the United States of America the one hundred and seventeenth.   BENJ. HARRISON.

By the President.
       JOHN W. FOSTER, *Secretary of State.*

II. In compliance with the instructions of the President, on the day of the funeral, at each military post, the troops and cadets will be paraded and this order read to them, after which all labors of the day will cease.

The national flag will be displayed at half-staff.

At dawn of day thirteen guns will be fired, and afterwards at intervals of thirty minutes between the rising and setting of the sun a single gun, and at the close of the day a national salute of forty-four guns.

The officers of the Army will wear crape on the left arm and on their swords and the colors of the Battalion of Engineers, of the several regiments, and of the United States Corps of Cadets will be put in mourning for a period of six months.

The date of the funeral will be communicated to department commanders by telegraph, and by them to their subordinate commanders.

By command of Major-General Schofield:
       R. WILLIAMS, *Adjutant-General.*

GENERAL ORDER No. 406.

NAVY DEPARTMENT,
Washington, D. C., January 19, 1893.

The President of the United States announces the death of ex-President Rutherford B. Hayes in the following proclamation [order]:

[For order see preceding page.]

It is hereby directed, in pursuance of the instructions of the President, that on the day of the funeral, where this order may be received in time, otherwise on the day after its receipt, the ensign at each naval station and of each of the vessels of the United States Navy in commission be hoisted at half-mast from sunrise to sunset, and at each naval station and on board of flagships and vessels acting singly a gun be fired at intervals of every half hour from sunrise to sunset.

The officers of the Navy and Marine Corps will wear the usual badge of mourning attached to the sword hilt and on the left arm for a period of thirty days.

                    JAMES R. SOLEY,
                    Acting Secretary of the Navy.

Executive Mansion,
Washington, January 27, 1893.

To the People of the United States:

It is my painful duty to announce to the people of the United States the death of James Gillespie Blaine, which occurred in this city to-day at 11 o'clock.

For a full generation this eminent citizen has occupied a conspicuous and influential position in the nation. His first public service was in the legislature of his State. Afterwards for fourteen years he was a member of the national House of Representatives, and was three times chosen its Speaker. In 1876 he was elected to the Senate. He resigned his seat in that body in 1881 to accept the position of Secretary of State in the Cabinet of President Garfield. After the tragic death of his chief he resigned from the Cabinet, and, devoting himself to literary work, gave to the public in his Twenty Years of Congress a most valuable and enduring contribution to our political literature. In March, 1889, he again became Secretary of State, and continued to exercise this office until June, 1892. His devotion to the public interests, his marked ability, and his exalted patriotism have won for him the gratitude and affection of his countrymen and the admiration of the world. In the varied pursuits of legislation, diplomacy, and literature his genius has added new luster to American citizenship.

As a suitable expression of the national appreciation of his great public services and of the general sorrow caused by his death, I direct that on the day of his funeral all the Departments of the executive branch of the Government at Washington be closed, and that on all public buildings throughout the United States the national flag shall be displayed at half-staff, and that for a period of thirty days the Department of State be draped in mourning.

Done at the city of Washington, this 27th day of January, A. D. 1893, [SEAL.] and of the Independence of the United States of America the one hundred and seventeenth.

BENJ. HARRISON.

By the President:
John W. Foster,
Secretary of State.

Grover Cleveland

March 4, 1893, to March 4, 1897

SEE VOLUME XI.

Volume eleven is not only an index to the other volumes, not only a key that unlocks the treasures of the entire publication, but it is in itself an alphabetically arranged brief history or story of the great controlling events constituting the History of the United States.

Under its proper alphabetical classification the story is told of every great subject referred to by any of the Presidents in their official Messages, and at the end of each story the official utterances of the Presidents themselves are cited upon the subject, so that you may readily turn to the page in the body of the work itself for this original information.

Next to the possession of knowledge is the ability to turn at will to where knowledge is to be found.

Grover Cleveland

[For portrait and biographical sketch see Vol. VII, pp. 4882-4884.]

INAUGURAL ADDRESS.

My Fellow-Citizens: In obedience to the mandate of my country-men I am about to dedicate myself to their service under the sanction of a solemn oath. Deeply moved by the expression of confidence and personal attachment which has called me to this service, I am sure my gratitude can make no better return than the pledge I now give before God and these witnesses of unreserved and complete devotion to the interests and welfare of those who have honored me.

I deem it fitting on this occasion, while indicating the opinions I hold concerning public questions of present importance, to also briefly refer to the existence of certain conditions and tendencies among our people which seem to menace the integrity and usefulness of their Government.

While every American citizen must contemplate with the utmost pride and enthusiasm the growth and expansion of our country, the sufficiency of our institutions to stand against the rudest shocks of violence, the wonderful thrift and enterprise of our people, and the demonstrated superiority of our free government, it behooves us to constantly watch for every symptom of insidious infirmity that threatens our national vigor.

The strong man who in the confidence of sturdy health courts the sternest activities of life and rejoices in the hardihood of constant labor may still have lurking near his vitals the unheeded disease that dooms him to sudden collapse.

It can not be doubted that our stupendous achievements as a people and our country's robust strength have given rise to heedlessness of those laws governing our national health which we can no more evade than human life can escape the laws of God and nature.

Manifestly nothing is more vital to our supremacy as a nation and to the beneficent purposes of our Government than a sound and stable currency. Its exposure to degradation should at once arouse to activity the most enlightened statesmanship, and the danger of depreciation in the purchasing power of the wages paid to toil should furnish the strongest incentive to prompt and conservative precaution.

In dealing with our present embarrassing situation as related to this subject we will be wise if we temper our confidence and faith in our national strength and resources with the frank concession that even these will not permit us to defy with impunity the inexorable laws of finance and trade.   At the same time, in our efforts to adjust differences of opinion we should be free from intolerance or passion, and our judgments should be unmoved by alluring phrases and unvexed by selfish interests.

I am confident that such an approach to the subject will result in prudent and effective remedial legislation.   In the meantime, so far as the executive branch of the Government can intervene, none of the powers with which it is invested will be withheld when their exercise is deemed necessary to maintain our national credit or avert financial disaster.

Closely related to the exaggerated confidence in our country's greatness which tends to a disregard of the rules of national safety, another danger confronts us not less serious.   I refer to the prevalence of a popular disposition to expect from the operation of the Government especial and direct individual advantages.

The verdict of our voters which condemned the injustice of maintaining protection for protection's sake enjoins upon the people's servants the duty of exposing and destroying the brood of kindred evils which are the unwholesome progeny of paternalism.   This is the bane of republican institutions and the constant peril of our government by the people.   It degrades to the purposes of wily craft the plan of rule our fathers established and bequeathed to us as an object of our love and veneration.   It perverts the patriotic sentiments of our countrymen and tempts them to pitiful calculation of the sordid gain to be derived from their Government's maintenance.   It undermines the self-reliance of our people and substitutes in its place dependence upon governmental favoritism.   It stifles the spirit of true Americanism and stupefies every ennobling trait of American citizenship.

The lessons of paternalism ought to be unlearned and the better lesson taught that while the people should patriotically and cheerfully support their Government its functions do not include the support of the people.

The acceptance of this principle leads to a refusal of bounties and subsidies, which burden the labor and thrift of a portion of our citizens to aid ill-advised or languishing enterprises in which they have no concern.   It leads also to a challenge of wild and reckless pension expenditure, which overleaps the bounds of grateful recognition of patriotic service and prostitutes to vicious uses the people's prompt and generous impulse to aid those disabled in their country's defense.

Every thoughtful American must realize the importance of checking at its beginning any tendency in public or private station to regard frugality and economy as virtues which we may safely outgrow.   The toleration of this idea results in the waste of the people's money by their chosen servants and encourages prodigality and extravagance in the home life of our countrymen.

Under our scheme of government the waste of public money is a crime against the citizen, and the contempt of our people for economy and frugality in their personal affairs deplorably saps the strength and sturdiness of our national character.

It is a plain dictate of honesty and good government that public expenditures should be limited by public necessity, and that this should be measured by the rules of strict economy; and it is equally clear that frugality among the people is the best guaranty of a contented and strong support of free institutions.

One mode of the misappropriation of public funds is avoided when appointments to office, instead of being the rewards of partisan activity, are awarded to those whose efficiency promises a fair return of work for the compensation paid to them. To secure the fitness and competency of appointees to office and remove from political action the demoralizing madness for spoils, civil-service reform has found a place in our public policy and laws. The benefits already gained through this instrumentality and the further usefulness it promises entitle it to the hearty support and encouragement of all who desire to see our public service well performed or who hope for the elevation of political sentiment and the purification of political methods.

The existence of immense aggregations of kindred enterprises and combinations of business interests formed for the purpose of limiting production and fixing prices is inconsistent with the fair field which ought to be open to every independent activity. Legitimate strife in business should not be superseded by an enforced concession to the demands of combinations that have the power to destroy, nor should the people to be served lose the benefit of cheapness which usually results from wholesome competition. These aggregations and combinations frequently constitute conspiracies against the interests of the people, and in all their phases they are unnatural and opposed to our American sense of fairness. To the extent that they can be reached and restrained by Federal power the General Government should relieve our citizens from their interference and exactions.

Loyalty to the principles upon which our Government rests positively demands that the equality before the law which it guarantees to every citizen should be justly and in good faith conceded in all parts of the land. The enjoyment of this right follows the badge of citizenship wherever found, and, unimpaired by race or color, it appeals for recognition to American manliness and fairness.

Our relations with the Indians located within our border impose upon us responsibilities we can not escape. Humanity and consistency require us to treat them with forbearance and in our dealings with them to honestly and considerately regard their rights and interests. Every effort should be made to lead them, through the paths of civilization and education, to self-supporting and independent citizenship. In the meantime, as the nation's wards, they should be promptly defended against the cupidity of designing men and shielded from every influence or temptation that retards their advancement.

The people of the United States have decreed that on this day the control of their Government in its legislative and executive branches shall be given to a political party pledged in the most positive terms to the accomplishment of tariff reform. They have thus determined in favor of a more just and equitable system of Federal taxation. The agents they have chosen to carry out their purposes are bound by their promises not less than by the command of their masters to devote themselves unremittingly to this service.

While there should be no surrender of principle, our task must be undertaken wisely and without heedless vindictiveness. Our mission is not punishment, but the rectification of wrong. If in lifting burdens from the daily life of our people we reduce inordinate and unequal advantages too long enjoyed, this is but a necessary incident of our return to right and justice. If we exact from unwilling minds acquiescence in the theory of an honest distribution of the fund of the governmental beneficence treasured up for all, we but insist upon a principle which underlies our free institutions. When we tear aside the delusions and misconceptions which have blinded our countrymen to their condition under vicious tariff laws, we but show them how far they have been led away from the paths of contentment and prosperity. When we proclaim that the necessity for revenue to support the Government furnishes the only justification for taxing the people, we announce a truth so plain that its denial would seem to indicate the extent to which judgment may be influenced by familiarity with perversions of the taxing power. And when we seek to reinstate the self-confidence and business enterprise of our citizens by discrediting an abject dependence upon governmental favor, we strive to stimulate those elements of American character which support the hope of American achievement.

Anxiety for the redemption of the pledges which my party has made and solicitude for the complete justification of the trust the people have reposed in us constrain me to remind those with whom I am to cooperate that we can succeed in doing the work which has been especially set before us only by the most sincere, harmonious, and disinterested effort. Even if insuperable obstacles and opposition prevent the consummation of our task, we shall hardly be excused; and if failure can be traced to our fault or neglect we may be sure the people will hold us to a swift and exacting accountability.

The oath I now take to preserve, protect, and defend the Constitution of the United States not only impressively defines the great responsibility

I assume, but suggests obedience to constitutional commands as the rule by which my official conduct must be guided. I shall to the best of my ability and within my sphere of duty preserve the Constitution by loyally protecting every grant of Federal power it contains, by defending all its restraints when attacked by impatience and restlessness, and by enforcing its limitations and reservations in favor of the States and the people.

Fully impressed with the gravity of the duties that confront me and mindful of my weakness, I should be appalled if it were my lot to bear unaided the responsibilities which await me. I am, however, saved from discouragement when I remember that I shall have the support and the counsel and cooperation of wise and patriotic men who will stand at my side in Cabinet places or will represent the people in their legislative halls.

I find also much comfort in remembering that my countrymen are just and generous and in the assurance that they will not condemn those who by sincere devotion to their service deserve their forbearance and approval.

Above all, I know there is a Supreme Being who rules the affairs of men and whose goodness and mercy have always followed the American people, and I know He will not turn from us now if we humbly and reverently seek His powerful aid.

MARCH 4, 1893.

SPECIAL MESSAGES.

EXECUTIVE MANSION,
Washington, March 9, 1893.

To the Senate of the United States:

I transmit herewith a report submitted by the Secretary of State in compliance with the resolution of the Senate of the 3d instant, calling for information relating to the capture and imprisonment of Captain Pharos B. Brubaker by Honduras officials.

GROVER CLEVELAND.

EXECUTIVE MANSION,
Washington, March 9, 1893.

To the Senate of the United States:

For the purpose of reexamination I withdraw the treaty of annexation between the United States and the Provisional Government of the Hawaiian Islands, now pending in the Senate, which was signed February 14, 1893, and transmitted to the Senate on the 15th of the same month, and I therefore request that said treaty be returned to me.

GROVER CLEVELAND.

PROCLAMATIONS.

By the President of the United States of America.

A PROCLAMATION.

The following provisions of the laws of the United States are hereby published for the information of all concerned:

Section 1956, Revised Statutes, chapter 3, Title XXIII, enacts that—

No person shall kill any otter, mink, marten, sable, or fur seal, or other fur-bearing animal within the limits of Alaska Territory or in the waters thereof; and every person guilty thereof shall for each offense be fined not less than $200 nor more than $1,000, or imprisoned not more than six months, or both; and all vessels, their tackle, apparel, furniture, and cargo, found engaged in violation of this section shall be forfeited; but the Secretary of the Treasury shall have power to authorize the killing of any such mink, marten, sable, or other fur-bearing animal, except fur seals, under such regulations as he may prescribe; and it shall be the duty of the Secretary to prevent the killing of any fur seal and to provide for the execution of the provisions of this section until it is otherwise provided by law, nor shall he grant any special privileges under this section.

Section 3 of the act entitled "An act to provide for the protection of the salmon fisheries of Alaska," approved March 2, 1889, provides that—

Sec. 3. That section 1956 of the Revised Statutes of the United States is hereby declared to include and apply to all the dominion of the United States in the waters of Bering Sea; and it shall be the duty of the President at a timely season in each year to issue his proclamation, and cause the same to be published for one month in at least one newspaper (if any such there be) published at each United States port of entry on the Pacific coast, warning all persons against entering said waters for the purpose of violating the provisions of said section; and he shall also cause one or more vessels of the United States to diligently cruise said waters and arrest all persons and seize all vessels found to be or to have been engaged in any violation of the laws of the United States therein.

Articles I, II, and III of a convention between the United States of America and Great Britain for the renewal of the existing *modus vivendi* in Bering Sea, concluded April 18, 1892, are published for the same purpose:

Article I. Her Majesty's Government will prohibit during the pendency of the arbitration seal killing in that part of Bering Sea lying eastward of the line of demarcation described in Article No. I of the treaty of 1867 between the United States and Russia, and will promptly use its best efforts to insure the observance of this prohibition by British subjects and vessels.

Art. II. The United States Government will prohibit seal killing for the same period in the same part of Bering Sea and on the shores and islands thereof the property of the United States (in excess of 7,500 to be taken on the islands for the subsistence of the natives), and will promptly use its best efforts to insure the observance of this prohibition by United States citizens and vessels.

Art. III. Every vessel or person offending against this prohibition in the said waters of Bering Sea outside of the ordinary territorial limits of the United States may be seized and detained by the naval or other duly commissioned officers of either of the high contracting parties, but they shall be handed over as soon as practicable to the authorities of the nation to which they respectively belong, who alone shall have jurisdiction to try the offense and impose the penalties for the same. The witnesses and proof necessary to establish the offense shall also be sent with them.

Now, therefore, I, Grover Cleveland, President of the United States, hereby warn all persons against entering the waters of Bering Sea within the dominion of the United States for the purpose of violating the provisions of said section 1956 of the Revised Statutes and of the said articles of said convention, and I hereby proclaim that all persons found to be or to have been engaged in any violation of the laws of the United States or of the provisions of said convention in said waters will be arrested, proceeded against, and punished as above provided.

In testimony whereof I have hereunto set my hand and caused the seal of the United States to be affixed.

[SEAL.]   Done at the city of Washington, this 8th day of April, 1893, and of the Independence of the United States the one hundred and seventeenth.

GROVER CLEVELAND.

By the President:

W. Q. GRESHAM, *Secretary of State.*

BY THE PRESIDENT OF THE UNITED STATES OF AMERICA.

A PROCLAMATION.

Whereas it is provided by section 13 of the act of Congress of March 3, 1891, entitled "An act to amend Title LX, chapter 3, of the Revised Statutes of the United States, relating to copyrights," that said act "shall only apply to a citizen or subject of a foreign state or nation when such foreign state or nation permits to citizens of the United States of America the benefit of copyright on substantially the same basis as its own citizens, or when such foreign state or nation is a party to an international agreement which provides for reciprocity in the granting of copyright, by the terms of which agreement the United States of America may at its pleasure become a party to such agreement;" and

Whereas it is also provided by said section that "the existence of either of the conditions aforesaid shall be determined by the President of the United States by proclamation made from time to time as the purposes of this act may require;" and

Whereas satisfactory official assurances have been given that in Denmark the law permits to citizens of the United States the benefit of copyright on substantially the same basis as to the subjects of Denmark:

Now, therefore, I, Grover Cleveland, President of the United States of America, do declare and proclaim that the first of the conditions specified in section 13 of the act of March 3, 1891, now exists and is fulfilled in respect to the subjects of Denmark.

In testimony whereof I have hereunto set my hand and caused the seal of the United States to be affixed.

[SEAL.]   Done at the city of Washington, this 8th day of May, 1893, and of the Independence of the United States the one hundred and seventeenth.

GROVER CLEVELAND.

By the President:

W. Q. GRESHAM, *Secretary of State.*

EXECUTIVE MANSION,
Washington, D. C., June 30, 1893.

Whereas the distrust and apprehension concerning the financial situation which pervade all business circles have already caused great loss and damage to our people and threaten to cripple our merchants, stop the wheels of manufacture, bring distress and privation to our farmers, and withhold from our workingmen the wage of labor; and

Whereas the present perilous condition is largely the result of a financial policy which the executive branch of the Government finds embodied in unwise laws, which must be executed until repealed by Congress:

Now, therefore, I, Grover Cleveland, President of the United States, in performance of a constitutional duty, do by this proclamation declare that an extraordinary occasion requires the convening of both Houses of the Congress of the United States at the Capitol, in the city of Washington, on the 7th day of August next, at 12 o'clock noon, to the end that the people may be relieved through legislation from present and impending danger and distress.

All those entitled to act as members of the Fifty-third Congress are required to take notice of this proclamation and attend at the time and place above stated.

Given under my hand and the seal of the United States, at the city of Washington, on the 30th day of June, A. D. 1893, and of the

[SEAL.]   Independence of the United States the one hundred and seventeenth.

GROVER CLEVELAND.

By the President:

ALVEY A. ADEE, *Acting Secretary of State.*

BY THE PRESIDENT OF THE UNITED STATES OF AMERICA.

A PROCLAMATION.

Whereas an act of Congress amendatory of an act in relation to aiding vessels wrecked or disabled in the waters conterminous to the United States and the Dominion of Canada was approved May 24, 1890, the said act being in the following words:

Be it enacted by the Senate and House of Representatives of the United States of America in Congress assembled, That an act entitled "An act to aid vessels wrecked or disabled in the waters conterminous to the United States and the Dominion of

LANDING U. S. TROOPS AT SIBONEY, CUBA

LANDING TROOPS ON THE CUBAN SHORE

General Shafter's army of 17,000 men were disembarked on the 22d, 23d and 24th days of June, 1898. The main landing place was Daiquiri, but Kent's division landed at Siboney, as shown in the illustration. Two soldiers perished when a boat capsized. Considering the squally weather and the weight of the accoutrements carried by each man it is a wonder that more did not drown. At Daiquiri some of the boats were run up on the beach, so that the troops might wade ashore, while others ran up to a ramshackle old wharf, to which the men jumped when the boat rose on a wave.

The need of a merchant marine was made apparent by the events of the war. The Government paid steamship owners two and three times their commercial freight rates for the use of vessels as transports and supply ships. (Great Britain pays 10 per cent. more than the commercial rates.) Nevertheless, before turning over their vessels to the Government the owners carefully removed the accessories of a passenger steamer — beds, linen, towels, etc., converting the ships into mere tramp steamers. When the coast of Cuba had been reached and the troops disembarked, the captains of these vessels would take fright at the least sound of firing and run twenty miles out to sea, bearing rations and supplies in their holds, while the troops on the firing line went without their hardtack, bacon and coffee.

The men called the transports prisons, and the landing was like a pleasure-seeking excursion. They sang in chorus to the rhythm of the oars, waded ashore with howls of triumph, stripped and hung their uniforms to dry before the fire, then plunged naked into the surf, still shouting and dancing. At night the searchlights of the fleet made the picturesque scene light as day.

The article, "Spanish-American War," recites the history of the struggle briefly. President McKinley's wartime messages form the official history.

Canada," approved June 19, 1878, be, and the same is hereby, amended so that the same will read as follows:

"That Canadian vessels and wrecking appurtenance may render aid and assistance to Canadian or other vessels and property wrecked, disabled, or in distress in the waters of the United States contiguous to the Dominion of Canada: *Provided*, That this act shall not take effect until proclamation by the President of the United States that the privilege of aiding American or other vessels and property wrecked, disabled, or in distress in Canadian waters contiguous to the United States has been extended by the government of the Dominion of Canada to American vessels and wrecking appliances of all descriptions. This act shall be construed to apply to the Welland Canal, the canal and improvement of the waters between Lake Erie and Lake Huron, and to the waters of the St. Marys River and Canal: *And provided further*, That this act shall cease to be in force from and after the date of the proclamation of the President of the United States to the effect that said reciprocal privilege has been withdrawn, revoked, or rendered inoperative by the said government of the Dominion of Canada."

And whereas an act of Congress making appropriation for the legislative, executive, and judicial expenses of the Government for the fiscal year ending June 30, 1894, and for other purposes, approved March 3, 1893, further amended the act of May 24, 1890, as follows:

That an act approved May 24, 1890, entitled "An act to amend an act entitled 'An act to aid vessels wrecked or disabled in the waters conterminous to the United States and the Dominion of Canada,' approved June 19, 1878," be, and is hereby, amended by striking out the words "the Welland Canal."

And whereas by an order in council dated May 17, 1893, the government of the Dominion of Canada has proclaimed an act entitled "An act respecting aid by United States wreckers in Canadian waters" to take effect June 1, 1893, said act reading as follows:

Her Majesty, by and with the advice and consent of the senate and house of commons of Canada, enacts as follows:

1. United States vessels and wrecking appliances may salve any property wrecked and may render aid and assistance to any vessels wrecked, disabled, or in distress in the waters of Canada contiguous to the United States.

2. Aid and assistance include all necessary towing incident thereto.

3. Nothing in the customs or coasting laws of Canada shall restrict the salving operations of such vessels or wrecking appliances.

4. This act shall come into force from and after a date to be named in a proclamation by the Governor-General, which proclamation may be issued when the Governor in council is advised that the privilege of salving any property wrecked or of aiding any vessels wrecked, disabled, or in distress in United States waters contiguous to Canada will be extended to Canadian vessels and wrecking appliances to the extent to which such privilege is granted by this act to United States vessels and wrecking appliances.

5. This act shall cease to be in force from and after a date to be named in a proclamation to be issued by the Governor-General to the effect that the said reciprocal privilege has been withdrawn, revoked, or rendered inoperative with respect to Canadian vessels or wrecking appliances in United States waters contiguous to Canada.

And whereas said proclamation of the Governor-General of Canada was communicated to this Government by Her Britannic Majesty's ambassador on the 2d day of June last:

Now, therefore, being thus satisfied that the privilege of aiding American or other vessels and property wrecked, disabled, or in distress in

Canadian waters contiguous to the United States has been extended by the government of the Dominion of Canada to American vessels and wrecking appliances of all descriptions, I, Grover Cleveland, President of the United States of America, in virtue of the authority conferred upon me by the aforesaid act of Congress approved May 24, 1890, do proclaim that the condition specified in the legislation of Congress aforesaid now exists and is fulfilled, and that the provisions of said act of May 24, 1890, whereby Canadian vessels and wrecking appliances may render aid and assistance to Canadian and other vessels and property wrecked, disa-bled, or in distress in the waters of the United States contiguous to the Dominion of Canada, including the canal and improvement of the waters between Lake Erie and Lake Huron and the waters of the St. Marys River and Canal, are now in full force and effect.

In testimony whereof I have hereunto set my hand and caused the seal of the United States of America to be hereunto affixed.

[SEAL.]   Done at the city of Washington, this 17th day of July, A. D. 1893, and of the Independence of the United States the one hundred and eighteenth.

GROVER CLEVELAND.

By the President:

W. Q. GRESHAM, *Secretary of State.*

BY THE PRESIDENT OF THE UNITED STATES OF AMERICA.

A PROCLAMATION.

Whereas it is provided by section 13 of the act of Congress of March 3, 1891, entitled "An act to amend Title LX, chapter 3, of the Revised Stat-utes of the United States, relating to copyrights," that said act "shall only apply to a citizen or subject of a foreign state or nation when such foreign state or nation permits to citizens of the United States of America the benefit of copyright on substantially the same basis as its own citi-zens, or when such foreign state or nation is a party to an international agreement which provides for reciprocity in the granting of copyright, by the terms of which agreement the United States of America may at its pleasure become a party to such agreement;" and

Whereas it is also provided by said section that "the existence of either of the conditions aforesaid shall be determined by the President of the United States by proclamation made from time to time as the pur-poses of this act may require;" and

Whereas satisfactory official assurances have been given that in Portu-gal the law permits to citizens of the United States the benefit of copy-right on substantially the same basis as to the subjects of Portugal:

Now, therefore, I, Grover Cleveland, President of the United States of America, do declare and proclaim that the first of the conditions specified in section 13 of the act of March 3, 1891, now exists and is fulfilled in respect to the subjects of Portugal.

In testimony whereof I have hereunto set my hand and caused the seal of the United States to be affixed.

[SEAL.]   Done at the city of Washington, this 20th day of July, A. D. 1893, and of the Independence of the United States the one hundred and eighteenth.

GROVER CLEVELAND.

By the President:

W. Q. GRESHAM, *Secretary of State.*

EXECUTIVE ORDERS.

AMENDMENT OF CIVIL-SERVICE RULES.

Departmental Rule VII is hereby amended by adding thereto the following section:

8. The First Comptroller of the Treasury having advised the Secretary of the Treasury that under the operation of section 5 of the legislative, executive, and judicial appropriation act making appropriations for the fiscal year ending June 30, 1894, the employment of substitutes in the departmental service must cease from and after July 1, 1893, it is hereby ordered, in view of the fact that the substitutes now employed were appointed by regular certification under section 7 of this rule, that such of said substitutes as shall not be appointed to regular places before the employment of substitutes shall cease shall be eligible for appointment to regular places by reinstatement under the provisions of Departmental Rule X, in the order of their employment as substitutes as provided in said section 7, notwithstanding the prohibition contained in the second proviso of said section; and said substitutes shall have preference for appointment in the manner herein provided over all other eligibles.

This section shall become inoperative and cease to be a part of the civil-service rules when all of the substitutes now employed in the several Departments shall have been appointed as herein provided or shall have ceased to be eligible for appointment by reason of the expiration of the time within which a reinstatement can be made under Rule X.

Approved, April 12, 1893.   GROVER CLEVELAND.

EXECUTIVE MANSION, *May 8, 1893.*

It has become apparent after two months' experience that the rules heretofore promulgated regulating interviews with the President have wholly failed in their operation. The time which under these rules was set apart for the reception of Senators and Representatives has been almost entirely spent in listening to applications for office, which have been bewildering in volume, perplexing and exhausting in their iteration, and impossible of remembrance.

A due regard for public duty, which must be neglected if present conditions continue, and an observance of the limitations placed upon human endurance oblige me to decline from and after this date all personal interviews with those seeking appointments to office, except as I on my own

5832 Messages and Papers of the Presidents

motion may especially invite them. The same considerations make it impossible for me to receive those who merely desire to pay their respects except on the days and during the hours especially designated for that purpose.

I earnestly request Senators and Representatives to aid me in securing for them uninterrupted interviews by declining to introduce their constituents and friends when visiting the Executive Mansion during the hours designated for their reception. Applicants for office will only prejudice their prospects by repeated importunity and by remaining in Washington to await results.

GROVER CLEVELAND.

EXECUTIVE MANSION, May 26, 1893.

It is hereby ordered, That the several Executive Departments and the Government Printing Office be closed on Tuesday, the 30th instant, to enable the employees to participate in the decoration of the graves of the soldiers and sailors who fell in the defense of the Union during the War of the Rebellion.

GROVER CLEVELAND.

AMENDMENTS OF CIVIL-SERVICE RULES.

Special Departmental Rule No. 1 is hereby amended as follows: Include among the places excepted from examination therein the following:

6. In the Department of Agriculture:

In the office of the Secretary: The assistant chiefs of the following divisions: Of economic ornithology and mammalogy, of pomology, of microscopy, of vegetable pathology, of records and editing, and one property clerk.

In the Weather Bureau: The assistant chief of the Bureau, the three professors of meteorology of highest grade, executive officer, superintendent of telegraph lines, and one property clerk.

In the United States Commission of Fish and Fisheries the following: Scientific or professional experts to be temporarily employed in investigations authorized by Congress, but not to include any persons regularly employed in that Commission nor any person whose duties are not scientific or professional and who are not experts in the particular line of scientific inquiry in which they are to be employed.

EXECUTIVE MANSION, June 6, 1893.

The foregoing amendments are hereby approved.

GROVER CLEVELAND.

AMENDMENTS OF CIVIL-SERVICE RULES.

Postal Rule No. 2 is hereby amended as follows:

Strike out all of section 1 except the last paragraph, relating to noncompetitive examinations, and insert in lieu thereof the following:

1. To test the fitness for admission to the classified postal service one or more examinations shall be provided, as the Commission may determine, which shall not

include more than the following subjects: Orthography, copying, penmanship, arithmetic (fundamental rules, fractions, and percentage), elements of the geography of the United States, local delivery, reading addresses, physical tests: *Provided,* That when special examinations are needed to test fitness for any place requiring special or technical knowledge or skill the examination shall include, in addition to the special subjects required, such of the subjects of the regular examination as the Commission may determine.

Strike out section 2 and insert in lieu thereof the following:

No person shall be examined for the position of letter carrier if under 21 or over 40 years of age, and no person shall be examined for any other position in the classified postal service if under 18 years of age.

EXECUTIVE MANSION, *June 6, 1893.*

The foregoing amendments are hereby approved.

GROVER CLEVELAND.

EXECUTIVE MANSION,
Washington, June 16, 1893.

In accordance with section 16 of the act of Congress approved April 25, 1890, and entitled "An act to provide for celebrating the four hundredth anniversary of the discovery of America by Christopher Columbus by holding an international exhibition of arts, industries, manufactures, and the product of the soil, mine, and sea in the city of Chicago, in the State of Illinois," the designations of the following-named persons as members of the board of control and management of the Government exhibit at the World's Columbian Exhibition are hereby approved:

W. W. Rockhill, chief clerk of the Department of State, to represent that Department, *vice* William E. Curtis.

Lieutenant-Commander E. D. Taussig, United States Navy, to represent the Navy Department, *vice* Captain R. W. Meade, United States Navy.

Frank W. Clark, chemist, United States Geological Survey, to represent the Department of the Interior, *vice* Horace A. Taylor.

GROVER CLEVELAND.

SPECIAL SESSION MESSAGE.

EXECUTIVE MANSION, *August 8, 1893.*

To the Congress of the United States:

The existence of an alarming and extraordinary business situation, involving the welfare and prosperity of all our people, has constrained me to call together in extra session the people's representatives in Congress, to the end that through a wise and patriotic exercise of the legislative duty, with which they solely are charged, present evils may be mitigated and dangers threatening the future may be averted.

Our unfortunate financial plight is not the result of untoward events nor of conditions related to our natural resources, nor is it traceable to any of the afflictions which frequently check national growth and prosperity.   With plenteous crops, with abundant promise of remunerative production and manufacture, with unusual invitation to safe investment, and with satisfactory assurance to business enterprise, suddenly financial distrust and fear have sprung up on every side.   Numerous moneyed institutions have suspended because abundant assets were not immediately available to meet the demands of frightened depositors.   Surviving corporations and individuals are content to keep in hand the money they are usually anxious to loan, and those engaged in legitimate business are surprised to find that the securities they offer for loans, though heretofore satisfactory, are no longer accepted.   Values supposed to be fixed are fast becoming conjectural, and loss and failure have invaded every branch of business.

I believe these things are principally chargeable to Congressional legislation touching the purchase and coinage of silver by the General Government.

This legislation is embodied in a statute passed on the 14th day of July, 1890, which was the culmination of much agitation on the subject involved, and which may be considered a truce, after a long struggle, between the advocates of free silver coinage and those intending to be more conservative.

Undoubtedly the monthly purchases by the Government of 4,500,000 ounces of silver, enforced under that statute, were regarded by those interested in silver production as a certain guaranty of its increase in price. The result, however, has been entirely different, for immediately following a spasmodic and slight rise the price of silver began to fall after the passage of the act, and has since reached the lowest point ever known. This disappointing result has led to renewed and persistent effort in the direction of free silver coinage.

Meanwhile not only are the evil effects of the operation of the present law constantly accumulating, but the result to which its execution must inevitably lead is becoming palpable to all who give the least heed to financial subjects.

This law provides that in payment for the 4,500,000 ounces of silver bullion which the Secretary of the Treasury is commanded to purchase monthly there shall be issued Treasury notes redeemable on demand in gold or silver coin, at the discretion of the Secretary of the Treasury, and that said notes may be reissued.   It is, however, declared in the act to be "the established policy of the United States to maintain the two metals on a parity with each other upon the present legal ratio or such ratio as may be provided by law."   This declaration so controls the action of the Secretary of the Treasury as to prevent his exercising the discretion nominally vested in him if by such action the parity between gold and silver may be disturbed. Manifestly a refusal by the Secretary to pay these Treasury notes in gold if demanded would necessarily result in their discredit and depreciation as obligations payable only in silver, and would destroy the parity between the two metals by establishing a discrimination in favor of gold.

Up to the 15th day of July, 1893, these notes had been issued in payment of silver-bullion purchases to the amount of more than $147,000,000. While all but a very small quantity of this bullion remains uncoined and without usefulness in the Treasury, many of the notes given in its purchase have been paid in gold. This is illustrated by the statement that between the 1st day of May, 1892, and the 15th day of July, 1893, the notes of this kind issued in payment for silver bullion amounted to a little more than $54,000,000, and that during the same period about $49,-000,000 were paid by the Treasury in gold for the redemption of such notes.

The policy necessarily adopted of paying these notes in gold has not spared the gold reserve of $100,000,000 long ago set aside by the Government for the redemption of other notes, for this fund has already been subjected to the payment of new obligations amounting to about $150,000,000 on account of silver purchases, and has as a consequence for the first time since its creation been encroached upon.

We have thus made the depletion of our gold easy and have tempted other and more appreciative nations to add it to their stock. That the opportunity we have offered has not been neglected is shown by the large amounts of gold which have been recently drawn from our Treasury and exported to increase the financial strength of foreign nations. The excess of exports of gold over its imports for the year ending June 30, 1893, amounted to more than $87,500,000.

Between the 1st day of July, 1890, and the 15th day of July, 1893, the gold coin and bullion in our Treasury decreased more than $132,000,000, while during the same period the silver coin and bullion in the Treasury increased more than $147,000,000. Unless Government bonds are to be constantly issued and sold to replenish our exhausted gold, only to be again exhausted, it is apparent that the operation of the silver-purchase law now in force leads in the direction of the entire substitution of silver for the gold in the Government Treasury, and that this must be followed by the payment of all Government obligations in depreciated silver.

At this stage gold and silver must part company and the Government must fail in its established policy to maintain the two metals on a parity with each other. Given over to the exclusive use of a currency greatly depreciated according to the standard of the commercial world, we could no longer claim a place among nations of the first class, nor could our Government claim a performance of its obligation, so far as such an obligation has been imposed upon it, to provide for the use of the people the best and safest money.

If, as many of its friends claim, silver ought to occupy a larger place in our currency and the currency of the world through general international cooperation and agreement, it is obvious that the United States will not be in a position to gain a hearing in favor of such an arrangement so long as we are willing to continue our attempt to accomplish the result single-handed.

The knowledge in business circles among our own people that our Government can not make its fiat equivalent to intrinsic value nor keep inferior money on a parity with superior money by its own independent efforts has resulted in such a lack of confidence at home in the stability of currency values that capital refuses its aid to new enterprises, while millions are actually withdrawn from the channels of trade and commerce to become idle and unproductive in the hands of timid owners. Foreign investors, equally alert, not only decline to purchase American securities, but make haste to sacrifice those which they already have.

It does not meet the situation to say that apprehension in regard to the future of our finances is groundless and that there is no reason for lack of confidence in the purposes or power of the Government in the premises. The very existence of this apprehension and lack of confidence, however caused, is a menace which ought not for a moment to be disregarded. Possibly, if the undertaking we have in hand were the maintenance of a specific known quantity of silver at a parity with gold, our ability to do so might be estimated and gauged, and perhaps, in view of our unparalleled growth and resources, might be favorably passed upon. But when our avowed endeavor is to maintain such parity in regard to an amount of silver increasing at the rate of $50,000,000 yearly, with no fixed termination to such increase, it can hardly be said that a problem is presented whose solution is free from doubt.

The people of the United States are entitled to a sound and stable currency and to money recognized as such on every exchange and in every market of the world. Their Government has no right to injure them by financial experiments opposed to the policy and practice of other civilized states, nor is it justified in permitting an exaggerated and unreasonable reliance on our national strength and ability to jeopardize the soundness of the people's money.

This matter rises above the plane of party politics. It vitally concerns every business and calling and enters every household in the land. There is one important aspect of the subject which especially should never be overlooked. At times like the present, when the evils of unsound finance threaten us, the speculator may anticipate a harvest gathered from the misfortune of others, the capitalist may protect himself by hoarding or may even find profit in the fluctuations of values; but the wage earner—the first to be injured by a depreciated currency and the last to receive the benefit of its correction—is practically defenseless. He relies for work upon the ventures of confident and contented capital. This failing him, his condition is without alleviation, for he can neither prey on the misfortunes of others nor hoard his labor. One of the greatest statesmen our country has known, speaking more than fifty years ago, when a derangement of the currency had caused commercial distress, said:

The very man of all others who has the deepest interest in a sound currency and who suffers most by mischievous legislation in money matters is the man who earns his daily bread by his daily toil.

These words are as pertinent now as on the day they were uttered, and ought to impressively remind us that a failure in the discharge of our duty at this time must especially injure those of our countrymen who labor, and who because of their number and condition are entitled to the most watchful care of their Government.

It is of the utmost importance that such relief as Congress can afford in the existing situation be afforded at once. The maxim "He gives twice who gives quickly" is directly applicable. It may be true that the embarrassments from which the business of the country is suffering arise as much from evils apprehended as from those actually existing. We may hope, too, that calm counsels will prevail, and that neither the capitalists nor the wage earners will give way to unreasoning panic and sacrifice their property or their interests under the influence of exaggerated fears. Nevertheless, every day's delay in removing one of the plain and principal causes of the present state of things enlarges the mischief already done and increases the responsibility of the Government for its existence. Whatever else the people have a right to expect from Congress, they may certainly demand that legislation condemned by the ordeal of three years' disastrous experience shall be removed from the statute books as soon as their representatives can legitimately deal with it.

It was my purpose to summon Congress in special session early in the coming September, that we might enter promptly upon the work of tariff reform, which the true interests of the country clearly demand, which so large a majority of the people, as shown by their suffrages, desire and expect, and to the accomplishment of which every effort of the present Administration is pledged. But while tariff reform has lost nothing of its immediate and permanent importance and must in the near future engage the attention of Congress, it has seemed to me that the financial condition of the country should at once and before all other subjects be considered by your honorable body.

I earnestly recommend the prompt repeal of the provisions of the act passed July 14, 1890, authorizing the purchase of silver bullion, and that other legislative action may put beyond all doubt or mistake the intention and the ability of the Government to fulfill its pecuniary obligations in money universally recognized by all civilized countries.

GROVER CLEVELAND.

SPECIAL MESSAGE.

EXECUTIVE MANSION,
Washington, October 18, 1893.

To the Senate of the United States:

In response to the resolution of the Senate of the 10th instant, concerning the attitude of the Government of China with regard to an extension of the time for the registration of Chinese laborers in the United States under the act of May 5, 1892, I transmit a report of the Secretary of State on the subject.   GROVER CLEVELAND.

PROCLAMATIONS.

BY THE PRESIDENT OF THE UNITED STATES OF AMERICA.

A PROCLAMATION.

Whereas, pursuant to section 10 of the act of Congress approved March 3, 1893, entitled "An act making appropriations for current and contingent expenses and fulfilling treaty stipulations with Indian tribes for fiscal year ending June 30, 1894," the Cherokee Nation of Indians, by a written agreement made on the 17th day of May, 1893, has ratified the agreement for the cession of certain lands hereinafter described, as amended by said act of March 3, 1893, and thereby ceded, conveyed, transferred, relinquished, and surrendered all its title, claim, and interest of every kind and character in and to that part of the Indian Territory bounded on the west by the one hundredth degree (100°) of west longitude, on the north by the State of Kansas, on the east by the ninety-sixth degree (96°) of west longitude, and on the south by the Creek Nation, the Territory of Oklahoma, and the Cheyenne and Arapahoe Reservation created or defined by Executive order dated August 10, 1869: *Provided,* That any citizen of the Cherokee Nation who prior to the 1st day of November, 1891, was a *bona fide* resident upon and, further, had, as a farmer and for farming purposes, made permanent and valuable improvements upon any part of the land so ceded, and who has not disposed of the same, but desires to occupy the particular lands so improved as a homestead and for farming purposes, shall have the right to select one-eighth of a section of land, to conform, however, to the United States surveys; such selection to embrace, as far as the above limitation will admit, such improvements; the wife and children of any such citizen shall have the same right of selection that is above given to the citizen, and they shall have the preference in making selections to take any lands improved by the husband and father that he can not take until all of his improved land shall be taken; and that any citizen of the Cherokee Nation not a resident within the land so ceded who prior to the 1st day of November, 1891, had for farming purposes made valuable and permanent improvements upon any of the land so ceded shall have the right to select one-eighth of a section of land, to conform to the United States surveys; such selection to embrace, as far as the above limitation will admit, such improvements; but the allotments so provided for shall not exceed seventy (70) in number and the land allotted shall not exceed five thousand and six hundred (5,600) acres; and such allotments shall be made and confirmed under such rules and regulations as shall be prescribed by the Secretary of the Interior, and when so made and confirmed shall be conveyed to the allottees respectively by the United States in fee simple; and from the price to be paid to the Cherokee Nation for the cession so made there shall be deducted the sum of one dollar and forty cents ($1.40) for each acre so taken in allotment: *And provided,* That D. W. Bushyhead having made permanent or valuable improvements prior to the 1st day of November, 1891, on the lands so ceded, he may select a quarter section of the lands ceded, whether reserved or otherwise, prior to the opening of said lands to public settlement, but he shall be required to pay for such selection at the same rate per acre as other settlers, into the Treasury of the United States, in such manner as the Secretary of the Interior shall direct; and

Whereas it is provided in section 10 of the aforesaid act of Congress approved March 3, 1893, that—

Said lands, except the portion to be allotted as provided in said agreement, shall, upon the payment of the sum of $295,736, herein appropriated, to be immediately paid, become and be taken to be and treated as a part of the public domain; but in any opening of the same to settlement sections 16 and 36 in each township, whether surveyed or unsurveyed, shall be, and are hereby, reserved for the use and benefit of the public schools to be established within the limits of such lands, under such conditions and regulations as may be hereafter enacted by Congress. * * *

Sections 13, 14, 15, 16, 21, 22, 23, 24, 25, 26, 27, 28, and the east half of sections 17, 20, and 29, all in township No. 29 north of range No. 2 east of the Indian meridian, the same being lands reserved by Executive order dated July 12, 1884, for use of and in connection with the Chilocco Indian Industrial School, in the Indian Territory, shall not be subject to public settlement, but shall until the further action of Congress continue to be reserved for the purposes for which they were set apart in the said Executive order; and the President of the United States, in any order or proclamation which he shall make for the opening of the lands for settlement, may make such other reservations of lands for public purposes as he may deem wise and desirable.

The President of the United States is hereby authorized, at any time within six months after the approval of this act and the acceptance of the same by the Cherokee Nation as herein provided, by proclamation, to open to settlement any or all of the lands not allotted or reserved in the manner provided in section 13 of the act of Congress approved March 2, 1889, entitled "An act making appropriations for the current and contingent expenses of the Indian Department and for fulfilling treaty stipulations with various Indian tribes for the year ending June 30, 1890, and for other purposes" (25 U. S. Statutes at Large, p. 1005); and also subject to the provisions of the act of Congress approved May 2, 1890, entitled "An act to provide a temporary government for the Territory of Oklahoma, to enlarge the jurisdiction of the United States court in the Indian Territory, and for other purposes;" also subject to the second proviso of section 17, the whole of section 18, of the act of March 3, 1891, entitled "An act making appropriations for the current expenses of the Indian Department and for fulfilling treaty stipulations with various Indian tribes for the year ending June 30, 1892, and for other purposes;" except as to so much of said acts and sections as may conflict with the provisions of this act. Each settler on the lands so to be opened to settlement as aforesaid shall before receiving a patent for his homestead pay to the United States for the lands so taken by him, in addition to the fees provided by law, the sum of $2.50 per acre for any land east of 97½° west longitude, the sum of $1.50 per acre for any land between 97½° west longitude and 98½° west longitude, and the sum of $1 per acre for any land west of 98½° west longitude, and shall also pay interest upon the amount so to be paid for said land from the date of entry to the date of final payment therefor at the rate of 4 per cent per annum.

No person shall be permitted to occupy or enter upon any of the lands herein referred to except in the manner prescribed by the proclamation of the President opening the same to settlement, and any person otherwise occupying or entering upon any of said lands shall forfeit all right to acquire any of said lands. The Secretary of the Interior shall, under the direction of the President, prescribe rules and regulations, not inconsistent with this act, for the occupation and settlement of said lands, to be incorporated in the proclamation of the President, which shall be issued at least twenty days before the time fixed for the opening of said lands.

And whereas by a written agreement made on the 21st day of October, 1891, the Tonkawa tribe of Indians, in the Territory of Oklahoma, ceded, conveyed, and forever relinquished to the United States all their right, title, claim, and interest of every kind and character in and to the lands particularly described in Article I of the agreement: *Provided*, That the allotments of land to said Tonkawa tribe of Indians theretofore made or to be made under said agreement and the provisions of the general allotment act approved February 8, 1887, and an act amendatory thereof, approved February 28, 1891, shall be confirmed: *And provided*, That in all cases where the allottee has died since land has been set off and scheduled to such person the law of descent and partition in force in Oklahoma Territory shall apply thereto, any existing law to the contrary notwithstanding; and

Whereas by a certain other agreement with the Pawnee tribe of Indians, in said Territory, made on the 23d day of November, 1892, said tribe ceded, conveyed, released, relinquished, and surrendered to the United States all its title, claim, and interest of every kind and character in and to the lands particularly described in Article I of the agreement: *Provided*, That the allotments made or to be made to said Indians in the manner and subject to the conditions contained in said agreement shall be confirmed; and

Whereas it is provided in section 13 of the act of Congress accepting, ratifying, and confirming said agreements with the Tonkawa Indians and the Pawnee Indians, specified in sections 11 and 12 of the same act, approved March 3, 1893, entitled "An act making appropriations for current and contingent expenses and fulfilling treaty stipulations with Indian tribes for fiscal year ending June 30, 1894 ''—

That the lands acquired by the agreements specified in the two preceding sections are hereby declared to be a part of the public domain. Sections 16 and 36 in each township, whether surveyed or unsurveyed, are hereby reserved from settlement for the use and benefit of public schools, as provided in section 10 relating to lands acquired from the Cherokee Nation of Indians; and the lands so acquired by the agreements specified in the two preceding sections not so reserved shall be opened to settlement by proclamation of the President at the same time and in the manner and subject to the same conditions and regulations provided in section 10 relating to the opening of the lands acquired from the Cherokee Nation of Indians; and each settler on the lands so to be opened as aforesaid shall before receiving a patent for his homestead pay to the United States for the lands so taken by him, in addition to the fees provided by law, the sum of $2.50 per acre, and shall also pay interest upon the amount so to be paid for said land from the date of entry to the date of final payment at the rate of 4 per cent per annum.

And whereas the thirteenth section of the act approved March 2, 1889, the act approved May 2, 1890, and the second proviso of section 17 and the whole of section 18 of the act approved March 3, 1891, are referred to in the tenth section of the act approved March 3, 1893, and thereby made applicable in the disposal of the lands in the Cherokee Outlet hereinbefore mentioned, the provisions of which acts, so far as they affect the opening to settlement and the disposal of said lands, are more particularly set forth hereinafter in connection with the rules and regulations prescribed by the Secretary of the Interior for the occupation and settlement of the lands hereby opened according to said tenth section; and

Whereas the lands acquired by the three several agreements hereinbefore mentioned have been divided into counties by the Secretary of the Interior, as required by said last-mentioned act of Congress before the same shall be opened to settlement, and lands have been reserved for county-seat purposes, to be entered under sections 2387 and 2388 of the Revised Statutes of the United States, as therein required, as follows, to wit:

For County K, the southeast quarter of section 23 and the northeast quarter of section 26, township 28 north, range 2 east of the Indian meridian, excepting 4 acres reserved for the site of a court-house, to be designated by lot and block upon the official plat of survey of said reservation for county-seat purposes hereafter to be issued by the Commissioner of the General Land Office; said reservation to be additional to the reservations for parks, schools, and other public purposes required to be made by section 22 of the act of May 2, 1890.

For County L, the southwest quarter of section 1 and the southeast quarter of section 2, township 25 north, range 6 west of the Indian meridian, excepting 4 acres reserved for the site of a court-house, to be designated by lot and block upon the official plat of survey of said reservation for county-seat purposes hereafter to be issued by the Commissioner of the General Land Office; said reservation to be additional to the reservations for parks, schools, and other public purposes required to be made by section 22 of the act of May 2, 1890.

For County M, the south half of the northeast quarter and the north half of the southeast quarter of section 23 and the south half of the northwest quarter and the north half of the southwest quarter of section 24, township 27 north, range 14 west of the Indian meridian, excepting 1 acre reserved for Government use for the site of a land office and 4 acres to be reserved for the site of a court-house, which tracts are to be contiguous and to be designated by lot and block upon the official plat of survey of said reservation for county-seat purposes hereafter to be issued by the Commissioner of the General Land Office; said reservations to be additional to the reservations for parks, schools, and other public purposes required to be made by section 22 of the act of May 2, 1890.

For County N, the south half of section 25, township 23 north, range 21 west of the Indian meridian, excepting 1 acre reserved for Government use for the site of a land office and 4 acres to be reserved for the site of a court-house, which tracts are to be contiguous and to be designated by lot and block upon the official plat of survey of said reservation for county-seat purposes hereafter to be issued by the Commissioner of the General Land Office; said reservations to be additional to the reservations for parks, schools, and other public purposes required to be made by section 22 of the act of May 2, 1890.

For County O, the southeast quarter of section 7 and the southwest quarter of section 8, township 22 north, range 6 west of the Indian meridian, excepting 1 acre reserved for Government use for the site of a land office and 4 acres to be reserved for the site of a court-house, which tracts are to be contiguous and to be designated by lot and block upon the official plat of survey of said reservation for county-seat purposes hereafter to be issued by the Commissioner of the General Land Office; said reservations to be additional to the reservations for parks, schools, and other public purposes required to be made by section 22 of the act of May 2, 1890.

For County P, the northeast quarter of section 22 and the northwest quarter of section 23, township 21 north, range 1 west of the Indian meridian, excepting 1 acre reserved for Government use for the site of a land office and 4 acres reserved for the site of a court-house, which tracts are to be contiguous and to be designated by lot and block upon the official plat of survey of said reservation for county-seat purposes hereafter to be issued by the Commissioner of the General Land Office; said reservations to be additional to the reservations for parks, schools, and other public purposes required to be made by section 22 of the act of May 2, 1890; and

For County Q, the southeast quarter of section 31, the west half of the southwest quarter of section 32, township 22 north, range 5 east, lot 4 of section 5, and lot 1 of section 6, township 21 north, range 5 east of the

Indian meridian, excepting 4 acres reserved for the site of a court-house, to be designated by lot and block upon the official plat of survey of said reservation for county-seat purposes hereafter to be issued by the Commissioner of the General Land Office; said reservation to be additional to the reservations for parks, schools, and other public purposes required to be made by section 22 of the act of May 2, 1890.

Whereas it is provided by act of Congress for temporary government of Oklahoma, approved May 2, 1890, section 23 (26 U. S. Statutes at Large, p. 92), that there shall be reserved public highways 4 rods wide between each section of land in said Territory, the section lines being the center of said highways; but no deduction shall be made, where cash payments are provided for, in the amount to be paid for each quarter section of land by reason of such reservation; and

Whereas all the terms, conditions, and considerations required by said agreements made with said nation and tribes of Indians and by the laws relating thereto precedent to opening said lands to settlement have been, as I hereby declare, complied with:

Now, therefore, I, Grover Cleveland, President of the United States, by virtue of the power in me vested by the statutes hereinbefore mentioned and by other the laws of the United States and by said several agreements, do hereby declare and make known that all the lands acquired from the Cherokee Nation of Indians, the Tonkawa tribe of Indians, and the Pawnee tribe of Indians by the three several agreements aforesaid will at the hour of 12 o'clock noon (central standard time) on Saturday, the 16th day of the month of September, A. D. 1893, and not before, be opened to settlement under the terms of and subject to all the conditions, limitations, reservations, and restrictions contained in said agreements, the statutes above specified, the laws of the United States applicable thereto, and the conditions prescribed by this proclamation, saving and excepting lands described and identified as follows, to wit: The lands set apart for the Osage and Kansas Indians, being a tract of country bounded on the north by the State of Kansas, on the east by the ninety-sixth degree of west longitude, on the south and west by the Creek country and the main channel of the Arkansas River; the lands set apart for the Confederated Otoe and Missouria tribes of Indians, described as follows, to wit: Township 22 north, range 1 east; township 23 north, range 1 east; township 22 north, range 2 east; township 23 north, range 2 east; township 22 north, range 3 east; and that portion of township 23 north, range 3 east, lying west of the Arkansas River; and the lands set apart for the Ponca tribe of Indians, described as follows, to wit: Township 24 north, range 1 east; township 25 north, range 1 east; fractional township 24 north, range 2 east; fractional township 25 north, range 2 east; fractional township 24 north, range 3 east; fractional township 25 north, range 3 east; fractional township 24 north, range 4 east; fractional township 25 north, range 4 east, the said fractional townships lying on the right bank of the Arkansas

River; excepting also the lands allotted to the Indians as in said agreements provided; excepting also the lands reserved by Executive orders dated April 18, 1882, and January 17, 1883 (known as Camp Supply Military Reservation), described as follows, to wit: Township 24 north, range 22 west; the south half of township 25 north, range 22 west; and the southwest quarter of township 25 north, range 21 west; excepting also 1 acre of land in each of the reservations for county-seat purposes in Counties M, N, O, and P, which tracts are hereby reserved for Government use as sites for land offices, and 4 acres in each reservation for county-seat purposes hereinbefore named, which tracts are hereby reserved as sites for court-houses; and excepting also the reservations for the use of and in connection with the Chilocco Indian Industrial School and for county-seat purposes hereinbefore described; excepting also the saline lands covered by three leases made by the Cherokee Nation prior to March 3, 1893, known as the Eastern, Middle, and Western Saline reserves, under authority of the act of Congress of August 7, 1882 (22 U. S. Statutes at Large, p. 349), said lands being described and identified as follows: The Eastern Saline Reserve embracing all of section 6; lots 3 and 4 of section 4; the south half of the northeast quarter, the south half of the northwest quarter, the north half of the southwest quarter, and lots 1, 2, 3, and 4 of section 5; and the northeast quarter of the northwest quarter and lots 1 and 2 of section 7, township 25 north, range 9 west. All of sections 6, 7, 8, 17, 18, 19, 20, 21, 27, 28, 29, 30, 31, 32, and 33; the southwest quarter, the southwest quarter of the northwest quarter, and lots 2, 3, 4, 5, 6, and 7 of section 5; the southwest quarter, the southwest quarter of the northwest quarter, the southwest quarter of the southeast quarter, and lot 1 of section 9; the west half of the southwest quarter of section 15; the west half, the southeast quarter, the west half of the northeast quarter, and the southeast quarter of the northeast quarter of section 16; the west half, the west half of the southeast quarter, and the southeast quarter of the southeast quarter of section 22; the west half, the west half of the southeast quarter, the northeast quarter of the southeast quarter, and the southwest quarter of the northeast quarter of section 26; the northwest quarter, the north half of the southwest quarter, the west half of the northeast quarter, and the northeast quarter of the northeast quarter of section 34; and the northwest quarter of the northwest quarter of section 35, township 26 north, range 9 west. All of section 31; the southwest quarter of the southeast quarter, the southeast quarter of the southwest quarter, and lot 4 of section 30; and lots 3 and 4 of section 32, township 27 north, range 9 west. All of sections 1, 2, 3, 4, 9, 10, and 11; the southeast quarter, the south half of the northeast quarter, the east half of the southwest quarter, the southeast quarter of the northwest quarter, and lots 1, 2, and 3 of section 5; the east half, the southwest quarter, and the east half of the northwest quarter of section 8; the north half, the north half of the southwest quarter, the southwest quarter of the southwest quarter, and the northwest quarter of the southeast quarter of section 12; the northwest quarter, the northwest quarter of the northeast quarter, the north half of the southwest quarter, and the southwest quarter of the southwest quarter of section 14; the north half, the southeast quarter and the north half of the southwest quarter of section 15; and the northeast quarter and the north half of the northwest quarter of section 16, township 25 north, range 10 west. All of sections 1, 2, 3, 10, 11, 12, 13, 14, 15, 16, 21, 22, 23, 24, 25, 26, 27, 28, 33, 34, 35, and 36; the south half of the northeast quarter, the southeast quarter of the northwest quarter, the southeast quarter, the east half of the southwest quarter, and lots 1, 2, and 3 of section 4; the east half, the southwest quarter, the east half of the northwest quarter, and the southwest quarter of the northwest quarter of section 9; the southeast quarter of the southeast quarter of section 17; the east half of the northeast quarter and the east half of the southeast quarter of section 20; the southeast quarter and the east half of the northeast quarter of section 29; and the east half and the southeast quarter of the southwest quarter of section 32 of township 26 north, range 10 west. All of sections 22, 26, 27, 34, 35, and 36; the east half of the northeast quarter and the east half of the southeast quarter of section 21; the southwest quarter, the west half of the southeast quarter, the south half of the northwest quarter, and lots 1 and 6 of section 23; the southwest quarter, the west half of the southeast quarter, the southeast quarter of the southeast quarter, the south half of the northwest quarter, and lot 1 of section 25; the east half of section 28; and the east half and the southeast quarter of the southwest quarter of section 33, township 27 north, range 10 west. The Middle Saline Reserve embracing the southwest quarter of the northeast quarter, the southeast quarter of the northwest quarter, the west half of the southeast quarter, the east half of the southwest quarter, and lots 2, 3, 4, 5, 6, and 7 of section 6; and the northwest quarter of the northeast quarter, the northeast quarter of the northwest quarter, and lot 1 of section 7, township 26 north, range 18 west. The southwest quarter of the southeast quarter, the southeast quarter of the southwest quarter, and lot 7 of section 6; the west half of the northeast quarter, the east half of the northwest quarter, the west half of the southeast quarter, the east half of the southwest quarter, and lots 1, 2, 3, and 4 of section 7; the west half of the northeast quarter, the east half of the northwest quarter, the west half of the southeast quarter, the east half of the southwest quarter, and lots 1, 2, 3, and 4 of section 18; the west half of the northeast quarter, the east half of the northwest quarter, the west half of the southeast quarter, the east half of the southwest quarter, and lots 1, 2, 3, and 4 of section 19; the northwest quarter of the northeast quarter, the northeast quarter of the northwest quarter, and lots 1, 2, 3, 4, 6, 7, and 8 of section 30; and the west half of the northeast quarter, the east half of the northwest quarter, the west half of the southeast quarter, the east half of the southwest quarter, and lots 1, 2, 3, and 4 of section 31, township 27 north, range 18 west. All of sections 1 to 6, inclusive; the north half of the north half of sections 8, 9, 10, 11, and 12; and the north half of the northeast quarter, the northeast quarter of the northwest quarter, and lot 1 of section 7, township 26 north, range 19 west. All of sections 7 to 36, inclusive; the south half of the south half of sections 1, 2, 3, 4, and 5, and the south half of the southeast quarter, the southeast of the southwest quarter, and lot 7 of section 6, township 27 north, range 19 west. All of sections 1 and 2; the south half of the northeast quarter, the southeast quarter, and lots 1 and 2 of section 3; the north half of the northeast quarter of section 10; and the north half of the north half of sections 11 and 12, township 26 north, range 20 west. All of sections 11, 12, 13, 14, 23, 24, 25, 26, 35, and 36; the south half of the southeast quarter and lot 7 of section 1; the southwest quarter of the southwest quarter and lot 6 of section 2; the south half of the southeast quarter of section 3; and the east half of sections 10, 15, 22, 27, and 34, township 27 north, range 20 west. And the Western Saline Reserve embracing all of sections 18, 19, 30, and 31, township 29 north, range 20 west; and all of sections 13, 14, 23, 24, 25, 26, 35, and 36, township 29 north, range 21 west. Excepting also that section 13 in each township, which has not been otherwise reserved or disposed of, is hereby reserved for university, agricultural-college, and normal-school purposes, subject to the action of Congress; excepting also that section 33 in each township, which has not been otherwise reserved or disposed of, is hereby reserved for public buildings; excepting also sections 16 and 36 in each township, which are reserved by law for the use and benefit of the public schools; excepting also all selections and allotments made under the law and the agreements herein referred to, the lands covered by said selections and allotments to be particularly described and identified; said descriptions to be furnished by the Commissioner of the General Land Office and posted in the several booths hereinafter referred to as those where certain preliminary declarations are to be made prior to the day named in this proclamation as that when the strip will be open to settlement.

Said lands so to be opened as herein proclaimed shall be entered upon and occupied only in the manner and under the provisions following, to wit:

A strip of land 100 feet in width around and immediately within the outer boundaries of the entire tract of country to be opened to settlement under this proclamation is hereby temporarily set apart for the following purposes and uses, viz:

Said strip, the inner boundary of which shall be 100 feet from the exterior boundary of the country known as the Cherokee Outlet, shall be open to occupancy in advance of the day and hour named for the opening of said country by persons expecting and intending to make settlement pursuant to this proclamation. Such occupancy shall not be regarded as trespass or in violation of this proclamation or of the law under which it is made, nor shall any settlement rights be gained thereby.

The Commissioner of the General Land Office shall, under the direction of the Secretary of the Interior, establish on said 100-foot strip booths, to be located as follows: One in township 29 north, range 2 east; one in township 29 north, range 2 west; one in township 29 north, range 4 west; one in township 29 north, range 8 west; one in township 29 north, range 12 west; one in township 20 north, range 3 east; one in township 20 north, range 2 west; one in township 20 north, range 7 west; and one in township 20 north, range 26 west; and shall place in charge thereof three officers to each booth, who shall be detailed from the General Land Office. Said booths shall be open for the transaction of business on and after Monday, the 11th day of the month of September, A. D. 1893, from 7 a. m. to 12 m. and 1 p. m. to 6 p. m. each business day until the same shall be discontinued by the Secretary of the Interior, who is hereby authorized to discontinue the same at his discretion. Each party desiring to enter upon and occupy as a homestead any of the lands hereby opened to settlement will be required to first appear at one of the before-mentioned booths and make a declaration in writing, to be signed by the party in the presence of one of the officers in charge thereof, which shall be certified by such officer, according to the form hereto attached and made a part hereof marked A, showing his or her qualifications to make homestead entry for said lands, whereupon a certificate will be issued by the officers in charge of the booth to the party making the declaration, which shall be of the form hereto attached and made a part hereof marked D.

Where a party desires to file a soldier's declaratory statement in person, he will be required to make a declaration which shall be of the form hereto attached and made a part hereof marked B, the same to be made and subscribed before one of the officers in charge of the booth and certified by such officer, independently of the affidavit (Form 4–546) to be filed when he presents the certificate of Form D, there given him, to the district officers. Where a party desires to file a declaratory statement through an agent, it will be necessary for him previously to make the affidavit ordinarily required (Form 4–545) before some officer authorized to administer oaths and place the same in the hands of the agent, who, before being permitted to enter upon the lands to be opened in said outlet for the purpose of making the desired filing, will be required to appear before the officers in charge of some one of the booths, to present the said affidavit of the party authorizing him to act as such agent, and to make a declaration in writing, to be subscribed by him in the presence of one of such officers, which shall be certified by such officer, according to the form hereto attached and made a part hereof marked C, whereupon a certificate of Form D will be given him by said officer. The agent should be provided with affidavits of Form 4–545 made in duplicate—one for presentation to the officers in charge of the booth and the other for presentation to the district officers when formal filing is to be made.

Each party desiring to enter upon said lands for the purpose of set‑tling upon a town lot will be required to first appear at one of the before‑mentioned booths and make a declaration in writing, to be signed by the party in the presence of one of the officers in charge thereof, which shall be certified by such officer, according to the form hereto attached and made a part hereof marked E, whereupon a certificate will be issued by the officers in charge of the booth to the party making the declaration, which shall be of the form hereto attached and made a part hereof marked F.

The said declarations made before the officers in charge shall be given consecutive numbers, beginning at No. 1 at each booth, and the certificate issued to the party making the declaration shall be given the same number as is given the declaration. The declaration shall be carefully preserved by the officers in charge of the booths, and when the booths are discontinued said declarations shall be transmitted, together with the duplicate affidavits (Form 4–545) hereinbefore required to be presented in case of agents proposing to act for soldiers in filing declaratory statements, to the General Land Office for filing as a part of the records pertaining to the disposal of said lands.

The certificate will be evidence only that the party named therein is permitted to go in upon the lands opened to settlement by this proclamation at the time specified herein, and the certificate of Form D must be surrendered when application to enter or file is presented to the district officers, and the party's right to make a filing, homestead entry, or settlement shall be passed upon by the district land officers at the proper time and in the usual manner. The holder of such certificate will be required when he makes his homestead affidavit, or, if a soldier or soldier's agent, when he files a declaratory statement at the district office, to allege under oath before the officers taking such homestead affidavit or to whom said declaratory statement is presented for filing that all the statements contained in the declaration made by him, upon which said certificate is based, are true in every particular, such oath to be added to affidavit of Form 4–102, as shown on form hereto attached and made a part hereof marked 102*d*.

After the hour and day hereinbefore named when said lands will be opened to settlement all parties holding such certificates (Form D or F) will be permitted to occupy or enter upon the lands so opened, and parties holding a certificate of Form D may initiate a homestead claim, either by settlement upon the land or by entry or filing at the proper district office; but no person not holding any such certificate shall be permitted to occupy or enter upon any of said lands until after the booths shall have been discontinued by direction of the Secretary of the Interior. Until then the officers of the United States are expressly charged to permit no party without a certificate to occupy or enter upon any of said lands.

The following rules and regulations have been prescribed by the Sec retary of the Interior, under the direction of the President, as provided by section 10 of said act of March 3, 1893, for the occupation and settlement of the lands hereby opened, to wit:

The thirteenth section of the act approved March 2, 1889, the act approved May 2, 1890, the second proviso of section 17 and the whole of section 18 of the act approved March 3, 1891, are by section 10 of the act of March 3, 1893, made applicable in disposing of the lands under said section 10, and said lands are thereby rendered subject to disposal under the homestead and town-site laws only, with certain modifications, which laws as so modified contain provisions substantially as follows:

1. Any party will be entitled to initiate a homestead claim to a tract of said lands who is over 21 years of age or the head of a family; who is a citizen of the United States or has declared his intention to become such; who has not exhausted his homestead right either by perfecting a homestead entry for 160 acres of land under any law, excepting what is known as the commuted provision of the homestead law contained in section 2301 of the United States Revised Statutes, or by making or commuting a homestead entry since March 2, 1889; who has not entered since August 30, 1890, under the land laws of the United States or filed upon a quantity of land agricultural in character and not mineral which with the tracts sought to be entered in any case would make more than 320 acres; who is not the owner in fee simple of 160 acres of land in any State or Territory, and who has not entered upon or occupied the lands hereby opened in violation of this the President's proclamation opening the same to settlement and entry. (See section 2289, U. S. Revised Statutes; act of March 2, 1889, 25 U. S. Statutes at Large, p. 854; section 13 of the act of March 2, 1889, 25 U. S. Statutes at Large, p. 1005; act of August 30, 1890, 26 U. S. Statutes at Large, p. 391; section 20, act of May 2, 1890, 26 U. S. Statutes at Large, p. 91, and section 10, act of March 3, 1893, 27 U. S. Statutes at Large, p. 640.)

2. Each entry shall be in a compact body, according to the rectangular subdivisions of the public surveys, and in a square form, as nearly as reasonably practicable consistently with such surveys; and no person shall be permitted to enter more than one quarter section in quantity of said lands. (See section 13, act of March 2, 1889, 25 U. S. Statutes at Large, p. 1005.)

3. Parties who own and reside upon land (not acquired by them under the homestead law) not amounting in quantity to a quarter section may, if otherwise qualified, enter other land lying contiguous to their own to an amount which shall not with the land already owned by them exceed in the aggregate 160 acres. (See section 2289, U. S. Revised Statutes.)

4. Any party who has made a homestead entry prior to March 2, 1889, for less than one quarter section of land and who still owns and occupies the land so entered may, if otherwise qualified, enter an additional tract of land lying contiguous to the land embraced in the original entry, which

shall not with the land first entered exceed in the aggregate 160 acres; but such additional entry will not be permitted, or if permitted will be canceled, if the original entry should fail for any reason prior to patent or should appear to be illegal or fraudulent. The final proof of residence and cultivation made on the original entry, together with the payment of the prescribed price for the land, will be sufficient to entitle the party to a final certificate for the land so entered without further proof. (See section 5 of the act of March 2, 1889, 25 U. S. Statutes at Large, p. 854.)

5. Parties who have complied with the conditions of the law with regard to a homestead entry for less than 160 acres of land made prior to March 2, 1889, and have had the final papers issued therefor, may, if otherwise qualified, make an additional entry, by legal subdivisions, of so much land as added to the quantity previously so entered shall not exceed 160 acres. Parties making entry under the provisions set forth in this paragraph will be required to reside upon and cultivate the land embraced therein for the prescribed period and to submit proof of residence and cultivation of a like character with that required in ordinary homestead entries before the issuance of a final certificate. (See section 6, act of March 2, 1889, 25 U. S. Statutes at Large, p. 854.)

6. Any officer, soldier, seaman, or marine who served for not less than ninety days in the Army or Navy of the United States during the War of the Rebellion and who was honorably discharged and has remained loyal to the Government, or, in case of his death, his widow, or, in case of her death or remarriage, his minor orphan children, by a guardian duly appointed and officially accredited at the Department of the Interior, may, either in person or by agent, file a declaratory statement for a tract of land and have six months thereafter within which to make actual entry and commence residence and improvements upon the land. (See sections 2304, 2307, and 2309, U. S. Revised Statutes.)

7. Every person entitled under the preceding paragraph to enter a homestead who, or whose deceased husband or father, in case of the widow or minor children, may have prior to June 22, 1874, entered under the homestead laws a quantity of land less than 160 acres may, if otherwise qualified, enter so much land as when added to the quantity previously entered shall not exceed 160 acres; but the party must make affidavit that the entry is made for actual settlement and cultivation, and the proof of such settlement and cultivation prescribed by existing homestead laws and regulations thereunder will be required to be produced before the issue of final certificate. (See section 2306, U. S. Revised Statutes, and section 18 of the act of May 2, 1890, 26 U. S. Statutes at Large, p. 90.)

8. Parties may initiate claims under the homestead law either by settlement on the land or by entry at the district office. In the former case the party will have three months after settlement within which to file his application for the tract at the district office; in the latter case the party

will have six months after entry at that office within which to establish residence and begin improvements upon the land. (See sections 2290 and 2297, U. S. Revised Statutes, and section 3 of the act of May 14, 1880, 21 U. S. Statutes at Large, p. 140.)

9. The homestead affidavits required to be filed with the application must be executed before the register or receiver of the proper district land office (see section 2290, U. S. Revised Statutes) or before any other officer who may be found duly qualified at the time to administer such oaths, according to the provisions of the act of Congress of May 26, 1890 (26 U. S. Statutes at Large, p. 121).

10. Parties applying to make homestead entry will be required to tender with the application the legal fee and commissions, which are as follows: For an entry of over 80 acres a fee of $10, and for an entry of 80 acres or less a fee of $5, and in both cases, in addition, commissions of 2 per cent upon the Government price of the land, computed at the rate of $1.25 per acre, the ordinary minimum price of public lands under the general provisions of section 2357, United States Revised Statutes. (See sections 2238 and 2290, U. S. Revised Statutes.)

11. Homestead applicants appearing in great number at the local office to make entry at the time of opening will be required to form in line, in order that their applications may be presented and acted upon in regular order.

12. Soldiers' declaratory statements can only be made by the parties entitled or by their agents in person, and will not be received if sent by mail. A party acting as agent and appearing in line, as contemplated under the eleventh paragraph, will be allowed to make one entry or filing in his individual character, if he so desires, and to file one declaratory statement in his representative character as agent, if such he shall be, and thereupon he will be required to step out of line, giving place to the next person in order, and, if he desires to make any other filings, to take his place at the end of the line and await his proper turn before doing so, and thus to proceed in order until all the filings desired by him shall be made.

13. Section 2301 of the Revised Statutes of the United States, providing for commutation of homestead entries, is not applicable to said lands. (See section 18 of the act of May 2, 1890, 26 U. S. Statutes at Large, p. 90.)

14. Proof of five years' residence, cultivation, and improvement and the payment prescribed by the statute, as hereinbefore mentioned, must be made before a party will be entitled to a patent under the homestead law, and such proof is required to be made within seven years from the date of the entry. Commissions equal to 2 per cent upon the Government price for the land, computed at $1.25 per acre, under section 2357, United States Revised Statutes, must also be tendered with the final proof. Interest at 4 per cent per annum on the purchase price of the land must

be paid from the date of the entry to date of final payment of purchase money. (See sections 2238 and 2291, U. S. Revised Statutes, and sections 10 and 13 of the act of March 3, 1893, 27 U. S. Statutes at Large, p. 640.)

15. The parties named in paragraph 6 of these regulations are entitled to have the term of service in the Army or Navy under which the claim is made, not exceeding four years, deducted from the period of five years' residence or cultivation required as stated in the preceding paragraph, or, if the party was discharged from service on account of wounds or disabilities incurred in the line of duty, the whole term of enlistment, not exceeding four years, may be deducted. (See section 2305, U. S. Revised Statutes.)

16. Where a homestead settler dies before the consummation of his claim, the widow, or, in case of her death, the heirs or devisee, may continue settlement or cultivation and obtain title upon requisite proof at the proper time. If the widow proves up, title will pass to her; if she dies before proving up and the heirs or devisee make the proof, the title will vest in them, respectively. (See section 2291, U. S. Revised Statutes.)

17. Where both parents die, leaving infant children, the homestead may be sold for cash for the benefit of such children, and the purchaser will receive title from the United States. (See section 2292, U. S. Revised Statutes.)

18. In case of the death of a person after having entered a homestead the failure of the widow, children, or devisee of the deceased to fulfill the demands of the letter of the law as to residence on the lands will not necessarily subject the entry to forfeiture on the ground of abandonment. If the land is cultivated in good faith, the law will be considered as having been substantially complied with.

19. Town-site claims may be initiated upon said lands under the statutes by two methods, which are separate and distinct in character. The regulations under the first method are hereinafter set forth in paragraphs 20, 21, and 22, and under the second method in paragraphs 23 to 28, inclusive. Provision is further made for town-site entries in cases where lands entered under the homestead law are required for town-site purposes, as set forth in paragraph 30.

20. Parties having founded or who desire to found a city or town on the public lands must file with the recorder of the county in which land is situate a plat thereof, describing the exterior boundaries of the land according to the lines of public surveys. Such plat must state the name of the city or town, exhibit the streets, squares, blocks, lots, and alleys, and specify the size of the same, with measurements and area of each municipal subdivision the lots in which shall not exceed 4,200 square feet, with a statement of the extent and general character of the improvements. The plat and statement must be verified by the oath of the party, acting for and in behalf of the occupants and inhabitants of the town or

city. Within one month after filing the plat with the recorder of the county a verified copy of said plat and statement must be sent to the General Land Office, accompanied by the testimony of two witnesses that such town or city has been established in good faith, and a similar map and statement must be filed with the register and receiver of the proper district office. Thereafter the President may cause the lots embraced within the limits of such city or town to be offered at public sale to the highest bidder, subject to a minimum of $10 for each lot; and such lots as may not be disposed of at public sale shall thereafter be liable to private entry at such minimum or at such reasonable increase or diminution thereafter as the Secretary of the Interior may order from time to time, after at least three months' notice, in view of the increase or decrease in the value of the municipal property. Any actual settler upon any lot and upon any additional lot upon which he may have substantial improvements shall be entitled to prove up and purchase the same as a preemption, at such minimum, at any time before the day fixed for the public sale. (See section 2382, U. S. Revised Statutes.)

21. In case the parties interested shall fail or refuse within twelve months after founding a city or town to file in the General Land Office a transcript map, with the statement and testimony, as required in paragraph 20, the Secretary of the Interior may cause a survey and plat to be made of said city or town, and thereafter the lots will be sold at an increase of 50 per cent on the minimum price of $10 per lot. (See section 2384, U. S. Revised Statutes.)

22. When lots vary in size from the limitation of 4,200 square feet and the lots, buildings, and improvements cover an area greater than 640 acres, such variance as to size of lots or excess in area will prove no bar to entry, but the price of the lots may be increased to such reasonable amount as the Secretary of the Interior may by rule establish. (See section 2385, U. S. Revised Statutes.)

23. Under the second method lands actually settled upon and occupied as a town site, and therefore not subject to entry under the homestead laws, may be entered as a town site at the proper district land office. (See section 2387, U. S. Revised Statutes.)

24. If the town is incorporated, the entry may be made by the corporate authorities thereof through the mayor or other principal officer duly authorized so to do. If the town is not incorporated, the entry may be made by the judge of the county court for the county in which said town is situated. In either case the entry must be made in trust for the use and benefit of the occupants thereof according to their respective interests. The execution of such trust as to the disposal of lots and the proceeds of sales is to be conducted under regulations prescribed by the territorial laws. Acts of trustees not in accordance with such regulations are void. (See sections 2387 and 2391, U. S. Revised Statutes.)

25. The officer authorized to enter a town site may make entry at once,

or he may initiate an entry by filing a declaratory statement of the purpose of the inhabitants to make a town-site entry of the land described. The entry or declaratory statement shall include only such land as is actually occupied by the town and the title to which is in the United States, and its exterior limits must conform to the legal subdivisions of the public lands. (See sections 2388 and 2389, U. S. Revised Statutes.)

26. The amount of land that may be entered under this method is proportionate to the number of inhabitants. One hundred and less than 200 inhabitants may enter not to exceed 320 acres; 200 and less than 1,000 inhabitants may enter not to exceed 640 acres; and where the inhabitants number 1,000 and over an amount not to exceed 1,280 acres may be entered, and for each additional 1,000 inhabitants, not to exceed 5,000 in all, a further amount of 320 acres may be allowed. When the number of inhabitants of a town is less than 100, the town site shall be restricted to the land actually occupied for town purposes by legal subdivisions. (See section 2389, U. S. Revised Statutes.)

27. Where an entry is made of less than the maximum quantity of land allowed for town-site purposes, additional entries may be made of contiguous tracts occupied for town purposes which when added to the previous entry or entries will not exceed 2,560 acres; but no additional entry can be allowed which will make the total area exceed the area to which the town may be entitled by virtue of its population at date of additional entry. (See section 4 of the act of March 3, 1877, 19 U. S. Statutes at Large, p. 392.)

28. The land must be paid for at the Government price per acre, and proof must be furnished relating, first, to municipal occupation of the land; second, number of inhabitants; third, extent and value of town improvements; fourth, date when land was first used for town-site purposes; fifth, official character and authority of officer making entry; sixth, if an incorporated town, proof of incorporation, which should be a certified copy of the act of incorporation, and, seventh, that a majority of the occupants or owners of the lots within the town desire that such action be taken. Thirty days' publication of notice of intention to make proof must be made and proof of publication furnished. (See section 2387, U. S. Revised Statutes.)

29. All surveys for town sites on said lands shall contain reservations for parks (of substantially equal area if more than one park) and for schools and other public purposes, embracing in the aggregate not less than 10 nor more than 20 acres, and patents for such reservations, to be maintained for such purposes, will be issued to the towns respectively when organized as municipalities. (See section 22, act of May 2, 1890, 26 U. S. Statutes at Large, p. 92.)

30. In case any of said lands which may be entered under the homestead laws by a person who is entitled to perfect his title thereto under such laws are required for town-site purposes, the entryman may apply

to the Secretary of the Interior to purchase the lands embraced in said homestead, or any part thereof not less than a legal subdivision, for town-site purposes. The party must file in the district office with his application a plat of the proposed town site and evidence of his qualifications to perfect title under the homestead law and of his compliance with all the requirements of the law and the instructions thereunder, and must deposit with the Secretary of the Interior the sum of $10 per acre for all the lands embraced in such town site, except the lands to be donated and maintained for public purposes as mentioned in the preceding paragraph. (See section 22, act of May 2, 1890, 26 U. S. Statutes at Large, p. 92.)

Notice, moreover, is hereby given that it is by law enacted that no person shall be permitted to occupy or enter upon any of the lands herein .eferred to except in the manner prescribed by this proclamation, and any person otherwise occupying or entering upon any of said lands shall forfeit all right to acquire any of said lands, and that the officers of the United States will be required to enforce this provision.

And further notice is hereby given that four land districts have been established in Oklahoma Territory, with boundaries as follows:

The Perry district, bounded and described as follows: Beginning at the middle of the main channel of the Arkansas River where the same is intersected by the northern boundary of Oklahoma Territory; thence west to the northwest corner of township 29 north, range 2 west of the Indian meridian; thence south on the range line between ranges 2 and 3 west to the southwest corner of lot 3 of section 31, township 20 north, range 2 west; thence east to the southeast corner of lot 4 of section 36, township 20 north, range 4 east; thence south on the range line between ranges 4 and 5 east to the middle of the main channel of the Cimarron River; thence down said river, in the middle of the main channel thereof, to the western boundary of the Creek country; thence north to the northwest corner of the Creek country; thence east on the northern boundary of said Creek country to the middle of the main channel of the Arkansas River; thence up said river, in the middle of the main channel thereof, to the place of beginning; the local land office of which will be located at the town of Perry, in County P.

The Enid district, bounded and described as follows: Beginning at the northeast corner of township 29 north, range 3 west of the Indian meridian; thence west to the northwest corner of township 29 north, range 8 west; thence scuth on the range line between ranges 8 and 9 west to the southwest corner of lot 3 of section 31, township 20 north, range 8 west; thence east to the southeast corner of lot 4 of section 36, township 20 north, range 3 west; thence north on the range line between ranges 2 and 3 west to the place of beginning; the local land office of which will be located at the town of Enid, in County O.

The Alva district, bounded and described as follows: Beginning at the northeast corner of township 29 north, range 9 west of the Indian meridian; thence west to the northwest corner of township 29 north, range 16 west; thence south on the range line between ranges 16 and 17 west to the southwest corner of lot 3 of section 31, township 20 north, range 16 west; thence east to the southeast corner of lot 4 of section 36, township 20 north, range 9 west; thence north on the range line between ranges 8 and 9 west to the place of beginning; the local land office of which will be located at the town of Alva, in County M.

The Woodward land district, bounded and described as follows: Beginning at the northeast corner of township 29 north, range 17 west of the Indian meridian; thence west to the northwest corner of township 29 north, range 26 west; thence south to the southwest corner of lot 3 of section 32, township 20 north, range 26 west; thence east to the southeast corner of lot 4 of section 36, township 20 north, range 17 west; thence north on the range line between ranges 16 and 17 west to the place of beginning; the local land office of which will be located at the town of Woodward, in County N.

And further notice is hereby given that the line of 97½° west longitude, named herein for the purpose of disposing of the land hereby opened to settlement, is held to fall on the west line of sections 2, 11, 14, 23, 26, and 35 of the townships in range 3 west of the Indian meridian, and the line of 98½° of west longitude is held to fall on the line running due north and south through the centers of sections 4, 9, 16, 21, 28, and 33 of the townships in range 12 west of the Indian meridian, and said lines have been so laid down upon the township plats on file in the General Land Office.

In witness whereof I have hereunto set my hand and caused the seal of the United States to be affixed.

[SEAL.]   Done at the city of Washington, this 19th day of August, A. D. 1893, and of the Independence of the United States the one hundred and eighteenth.

GROVER CLEVELAND.

By the President:

    W. Q. GRESHAM,
       Secretary of State.

A.

DECLARATION REQUIRED BY PRESIDENT'S PROCLAMATION OF AUGUST 19, 1893, PREPARATORY TO OCCUPYING OR ENTERING UPON THE LANDS OF THE CHEROKEE OUTLET FOR THE PURPOSE OF MAKING A HOMESTEAD ENTRY.

No. ——.

BOOTH IN T. —— N., R. ——, ——, *1893.*

I, ——, of ——, being desirous of occupying or entering upon the lands opened to settlement by the President's proclamation of August 19, 1893, for the purpose of making a homestead entry, do solemnly declare that I am over 21 years of age or the head of a family; that I am a citizen of the United States (or have declared my intention to become such); that I have not perfected a homestead entry for 160 acres of land under any law except what is known as the commuted provision of the homestead law contained in section 2301, Revised Statutes, nor have I made or commuted a homestead entry since March 2, 1889;* —— that I have not entered since August 30, 1890, under the land laws of the United States or filed upon a quantity of land agricultural in character and not mineral which with the tracts now desired would make more than 320 acres; that I am not the owner in fee simple of 160 acres of land in any State or Territory; that I have not entered upon or occupied, nor will I enter upon or occupy, the lands to be opened to settlement by the President's proclamation of August 19, 1893, in violation of the requirements of said proclamation; that I desire to make entry for the purpose of actual settlement and cultivation, and not for the benefit of any other person, persons, or corporation; that I will faithfully and honestly endeavor to comply with all the requirements of law as to settlement, residence, and cultivation necessary to acquire title to the land I may select; that I am not acting as agent of any person, corporation, or syndicate in entering upon said lands, nor in collusion with any person, corporation, or syndicate to give them the benefit of the land I may enter, or any part thereof, or the timber thereon; that I do not apply to enter upon said lands for the purpose of speculation, but in good faith to obtain a home for myself; and that I have not, directly or indirectly, made and will not make any agreement or contract in any way or manner with any person or persons, corporation, or syndicate whatsoever by which the title which I may acquire from the Government of the United States should inure in whole or in part to the benefit of any person except myself. —— ——.

I certify that the foregoing declaration was made and subscribed before me this —— day of ——, 1893.

—— ——, *Officer in Charge.*

*NOTE.—If the party has made a homestead entry since March 2, 1889, but has failed or is unable to perfect title to the land covered thereby because of a valid adverse claim or other invalidity existing at the date of its inception, strike out the words "made or" and insert in the blank space *that I have made a homestead entry since March 2, 1889, but have failed or am unable to perfect title to the land covered thereby because of a valid adverse claim or other invalidity existing at the date of its inception.*

B.

DECLARATION REQUIRED BY PRESIDENT'S PROCLAMATION OF AUGUST 19, 1893, PREPARATORY TO OCCUPYING OR ENTERING UPON THE LANDS OF THE CHEROKEE OUTLET FOR THE PURPOSE OF FILING A SOLDIER'S DECLARATORY STATEMENT IN PERSON.

No. ——.

BOOTH IN T. —— N., R. ——, ——, *1893.*

I, ——, of —— County and State or Territory of ——, do solemnly declare that I served for a period of —— in the Army of the United States during the War of the Rebellion and was honorably discharged therefrom, as shown by a statement of such service herewith, and that I have remained loyal to the Government; that I have not perfected a homestead entry for 160 acres of land under any law except what is known as the commuted provision of the homestead law contained in section 2301, Revised Statutes, nor have I filed a declaratory statement under sections 2304 and 2309 of the Revised Statutes or made or commuted a homestead entry since March 2, 1889;* —— that I have not entered since August 30, 1890, under the land laws of the United States or filed upon a quantity of land agricultural in character and not mineral which with the tracts now desired would make more than 320 acres; that I am not the owner in fee simple of 160 acres of land in any State or Territory; that I have not entered upon or occupied, nor will I enter upon or occupy, the lands to be opened to settlement by the President's proclamation of August 19, 1893, in violation of said proclamation; that I intend to file a soldier's declaratory statement upon said lands, which location will be made for my exclusive use and benefit, for the purpose of my actual settlement and cultivation, and not, either directly or indirectly, for the use and benefit of any other person. —— ——.

I certify that the foregoing declaration was made and subscribed before me this —— day of ——, 1893.

—— ——, *Officer in Charge.*

> *NOTE.—If the party has made an entry or filing since March 2, 1889, to which he is unable to perfect title because of a valid adverse claim or other invalidity existing at the date of its inception, strike out the words "filed a declaratory statement under sections 2304 and 2309 of the Revised Statutes, or made or" and insert in the blank space *that I have made an entry or filing since March 2, 1889, but have failed or am unable to perfect title to the land covered thereby because of a valid adverse claim or other invalidity existing at the date of its inception.*

C.

DECLARATION REQUIRED BY PRESIDENT'S PROCLAMATION OF AUGUST 19, 1893, PREPARATORY TO ENTERING UPON THE LANDS OF THE CHEROKEE OUTLET FOR THE PURPOSE OF FILING A SOLDIER'S DECLARATORY STATEMENT AS AGENT.

No. ——.

BOOTH IN T. —— N., R. ——, ——, *1893.*

I, ——, of ——, desiring to enter upon the Cherokee Outlet for the purpose of filing a soldier's declaratory statement under sections 2304 and 2309, United States Revised Statutes, as agent of ——, do hereby declare that I have no interest or authority in the matter, present or prospective, beyond the filing of such declaratory statement as the true and lawful attorney of the said —— as provided by said sections 2304 and 2309. —— ——.

I certify that the foregoing declaration was made and subscribed before me this —— day of ——, 1893.

—— ——, *Officer in Charge.*

D.

CERTIFICATE THAT MUST BE HELD BY PARTY DESIRING TO OCCUPY OR TO ENTER UPON THE LANDS OPENED TO SETTLEMENT BY THE PRESIDENT'S PROCLAMATION OF AUGUST 19, 1893, FOR THE PURPOSE OF MAKING A HOMESTEAD ENTRY OR FILING A SOLDIER'S DECLARATORY STATEMENT.

No. ——.

BOOTH IN T. —— N., R. ——, ——, *1893.*

This certifies that —— has this day made the declaration before me required by the President's proclamation of August 19, 1893, and he is therefore permitted to go in upon the lands opened to settlement by said proclamation at the time named therein for the purpose of making a homestead entry or filing a soldier's declaratory statement.

It is agreed and understood that this certificate will not prevent the district land officers from passing upon the holder's qualifications to enter or file for any of said lands at the proper time and in the usual manner, and that the holder will be required when he makes his homestead affidavit, or, if a soldier or a soldier's agent, when he files a declaratory statement at the district office, to allege under oath before the officer taking such homestead affidavit or to whom said declaratory statement is presented for filing that all of the statements contained in the declaration made by him, upon which this certificate is based, are true in every particular.

—— ——, *Officer in Charge.*

> This certificate is not transferable. The holder will display the certificate, if demanded, after locating on claim.

E.

DECLARATION REQUIRED BY PRESIDENT'S PROCLAMATION OF AUGUST 19, 1893, PREPARATORY TO OCCUPYING OR ENTERING UPON THE LANDS OF THE CHEROKEE OUTLET FOR THE PURPOSE OF SETTLING UPON A TOWN LOT.

No. ——. BOOTH IN T. —— N., R. ——, ——, *1893*.

I, ——, of ——, being desirous of occupying or entering upon lands opened to settlement by the President's proclamation of August 19, 1893, do solemnly declare that I have not entered upon or occupied, nor will I enter upon or occupy, any of the lands to be opened to settlement by the President's proclamation of August 19, 1893, in violation of the requirements of said proclamation, and that I desire to go in upon said lands for the purpose of settling upon a town lot. —— ——.

I certify that the foregoing declaration was made and subscribed before me this —— day of ——, 1893.

—— ——, *Officer in Charge*.

F.

CERTIFICATE THAT MUST BE HELD BY PARTY DESIRING TO OCCUPY OR ENTER UPON THE LANDS OPENED TO SETTLEMENT BY THE PRESIDENT'S PROCLAMATION OF AUGUST 19, 1893, FOR THE PURPOSE OF SETTLING UPON A TOWN LOT.

No. ——. BOOTH IN T. —— N., R. ——, ——, *1893*.

This certifies that —— has this day made the declaration before me required by the President's proclamation of August 19, 1893, and he is therefore permitted to go in upon the lands opened to settlement by said proclamation at the time named therein for the purpose of settling upon a town lot.

—— ——, *Officer in Charge*.

This certificate is not transferable. The holder will display the certificate, if demanded, after locating on claim.

4–102*d*.

AFFIDAVIT.

LAND OFFICE AT ——, ——, *1893*.

I, ——, of ——, applying to enter (or file for) a homestead, do solemnly swear that I did not enter upon and occupy any portion of the lands described and declared open to entry in the President's proclamation dated August 19, 1893, prior to 12 o'clock noon of September 16, 1893; also that all of the statements contained in a certain declaration made by me as foundation for obtaining permission to enter upon the Cherokee Outlet in pursuance of requirements of the President's proclamation opening said outlet to settlement are true in every particular. —— ——.

Sworn to and subscribed before me this —— day of ——, 189—. —— ——.

NOTE.—This affidavit must be made before the register or receiver of the proper district land office or before some officer authorized to administer oaths and using a seal.

BY THE PRESIDENT OF THE UNITED STATES OF AMERICA.

A PROCLAMATION.

Whereas it is provided by section 24 of the act of Congress approved March 3, 1891, entitled "An act to repeal timber-culture laws, and for other purposes"—

That the President of the United States may from time to time set apart and reserve in any State or Territory having public land bearing forests, in any part of the public lands wholly or in part covered with timber or undergrowth, whether of commercial value or not, as public reservations; and the President shall by public proclamation declare the establishment of such reservations and the limits thereof.

And whereas the public lands in the State of Oregon within the limits hereinafter described are in part covered with timber, and it appears that the public good would be promoted by setting apart and reserving said lands as a public reservation:

Now, therefore, I, Grover Cleveland, President of the United States, by virtue of the power in me vested by section 24 of the aforesaid act of Congress, do hereby make known and proclaim that there is hereby reserved from entry or settlement and set apart as a public reservation all those certain tracts, pieces, or parcels of land lying and being situate in the State of Oregon and particularly described as follows, to wit:

Beginning at the meander corner at the intersection of the range line between ranges six (6) and seven (7) east, township two (2) north, Willamette meridian, Oregon, with the mean high-water mark on the south bank of the Columbia River in said State; thence northeasterly along said mean high-water mark to its intersection with the township line between townships two (2) and three (3) north; thence easterly along said township line to the northeast corner of township two (2) north, range eight (8) east; thence southerly along the range line between ranges eight (8) and nine (9) east to the southwest corner of township two (2) north, range nine (9) east; thence westerly along the township line between townships one (1) and two (2) north to the northwest corner of township one (1) north, range nine (9) east; thence southerly along the range line between ranges eight (8) and nine (9) east to the southwest corner of township one (1) north, range nine (9) east; thence easterly along the base line to the northeast corner of township one (1) south, range ten (10) east; thence southerly along the range line between ranges ten (10) and eleven (11) east to the southeast corner of township four (4) south, range ten (10) east; thence westerly along the township line between townships four (4) and five (5) south to the southwest corner of township four (4) south, range nine (9) east; thence southerly along the west boundary of township five (5) south, range nine (9) east, to its intersection with the west boundary of the Warm Springs Indian Reservation; thence southwesterly along said Indian-reservation boundary to the southwest corner of said reservation; thence southeasterly along the south boundary of said Indian reservation to a point on the north line of section three (3), township twelve (12) south, range nine (9) east, where said boundary crosses the township line between townships eleven (11) and twelve (12) south, range nine (9) east; thence easterly to the northeast corner of township twelve (12) south, range nine (9) east; thence southerly along the range line between ranges nine (9) and ten (10) east to the southeast corner of township thirteen (13) south, range nine (9) east; thence westerly along the third (3d) standard parallel south to the northeast corner of township fourteen (14) south, range nine (9) east; thence southerly along the range line between ranges nine (9) and ten (10) east to the southeast corner of township fifteen (15) south, range nine (9) east; thence easterly along the third (3d) standard parallel south to the northeast corner of township sixteen (16) south, range nine (9) east; thence southerly along the range line between ranges nine (9) and ten (10) east to the southeast corner of township twenty (20) south, range nine (9) east; thence easterly along the fourth (4th) standard parallel south to the northeast corner of township twenty-one (21) south, range nine (9) east; thence southerly along the range line between ranges nine (9) and ten (10) east to the southeast corner of township twenty-three (23) south, range nine (9) east; thence westerly along the township line between townships twenty-three (23) and twenty-four (24) south to the southeast corner of township twenty-three (23) south, range six (6) east; thence southerly along the range line between ranges six (6) and seven (7) east to the southwest corner of township twenty-five (25) south, range seven (7) east; thence westerly along the fifth (5th) standard parallel south to the point for the northwest corner of township twenty-six (26) south, range seven (7) east; thence southerly along the surveyed and unsurveyed west boundaries of townships twenty-six (26), twenty-seven (27), twenty-eight (28), twenty-nine (29), and thirty (30) south to the southwest corner of township thirty (30) south, range seven (7) east; thence westerly along the unsurveyed sixth (6th) standard parallel south to the point for the northwest corner of township thirty-one (31) south, range seven and one-half (7½) east; thence southerly along the surveyed and unsurveyed west boundaries of townships thirty-one (31), thirty-two (32), and thirty-three (33) south, range seven and one-half (7½) east, to the southwest corner of township thirty-three (33) south, range seven and one-half (7½) east; thence easterly along the township line between townships thirty-three (33) and thirty-four (34) south to the northeast corner of township thirty-four (34) south, range six (6) east; thence southerly along the east boundaries of townships thirty-four (34) and thirty-five (35) south, range six (6) east, to the point of intersection of the east boundary of township thirty-five (35) south, range six (6) east, with the west shore of Upper Klamath Lake; thence along said shore of said lake to its intersection with the range line between ranges six (6) and seven (7) east in township thirty-six (36) south; thence southerly along the range line between ranges six (6) and seven (7) east to the southeast corner of township thirty-seven (37) south, range six (6) east; thence westerly along the township line between townships thirty-seven (37) and thirty-eight (38) south to the southwest corner of township thirty-seven (37) south, range four (4) east; thence northerly along the range line between ranges three (3) and four (4) east to the northwest corner of township thirty-six (36) south, range four (4) east; thence easterly along the eighth (8th) standard parallel south to the southwest corner of township thirty-five (35) south, range four (4) east; thence northerly along the range line between ranges three (3) and four (4) east to the southwest corner of township thirty-one (31) south, range four (4) east; thence westerly along the township line between townships thirty-one (31) and thirty-two (32) south to the southwest corner of township thirty-one (31) south, range one (1) east; thence northerly along the surveyed and unsurveyed Willamette meridian to the northwest corner of township twenty (20) south, range one (1) east; thence easterly along the township line between townships nineteen (19) and twenty (20) south to the northeast corner of township twenty (20) south, range one (1) east; thence northerly along the range line between ranges one (1) and two (2) east to the northwest corner of township eighteen (18) south, range two (2) east; thence easterly along the township line between townships seventeen (17) and eighteen (18) south to the southeast corner of township seventeen (17) south, range two (2) east; thence northerly along the range line between ranges two (2) and three (3) east to the southwest corner of township seventeen (17) south, range three (3) east; thence easterly along the surveyed and unsurveyed township line between townships seventeen (17) and eighteen (18) south to the point for the southeast corner of township seventeen (17) south, range four (4) east; thence northerly along the surveyed and unsurveyed range line between ranges four (4) and five (5) east, subject to the proper easterly or westerly offsets on the third (3d), second (2d), and first (1st) standard parallels south, to the northwest corner of township five (5) south, range five (5) east; thence easterly along the township line between townships four (4) and five (5) south to the southeast corner of township four (4) south, range six (6) east; thence northerly along the range line between ranges six (6) and seven (7) east to the northwest corner of township four (4) south, range seven (7) east; thence easterly along the township line between townships three (3) and four (4) south to the southwest corner of section thirty-four (34), township three (3) south, range seven (7) east; thence northerly along the surveyed and unsurveyed section line between sections thirty-three (33) and thirty-four (34), twenty-seven (27) and twenty-eight (28), twenty-one (21) and twenty-two (22), fifteen (15) and sixteen (16), nine (9) and ten (10), and three (3) and four (4) to the northwest corner of section three (3) of said township and range; thence easterly along the surveyed and unsurveyed township line between townships two (2) and three (3) south to the point for the southeast corner of township two (2) south, range eight (8) east; thence northerly along the unsurveyed range line between ranges eight (8) and nine (9) east to the southeast corner of township one (1) south, range eight (8) east; thence westerly along the township line between townships one (1) and two (2) south to the southeast corner of section thirty-four (34), township one (1) south, range eight (8) east; thence northerly along the section line between sections thirty-four (34) and thirty-five (35), twenty-six (26) and twenty-seven (27), and twenty-two (22) and twenty-three (23) to the northeast corner of section twenty-two (22); thence westerly along the section line between sections fifteen (15) and twenty-two (22) to the southeast corner of section sixteen (16); thence northerly on the section line between sections fifteen (15) and sixteen (16) to the point for the northeast corner of section sixteen (16); thence westerly along the section line between sections nine (9) and sixteen (16) to the southeast corner of section eight (8); thence northerly along the section line between sections eight (8) and nine (9) and four (4) and five (5) to the northwest corner of section four (4), township one (1) south, range eight (8) east; thence easterly along the base line to the southeast corner of section thirty-three (33), township one (1) north, range eight (8) east; thence along the unsurveyed section lines northerly to the point for the northeast corner of section thirty-three (33), westerly to the point for the northeast corner of section thirty-two (32), northerly to the point for the northeast corner of section eight (8), westerly to the point for the southwest corner of section six (6); thence northerly along the unsurveyed range line between ranges seven (7) and eight (8) east to the point for the northwest corner of township one (1) north, range eight (8) east; thence westerly along the unsurveyed township line between townships one (1) and two (2) north to the northwest corner of township one (1) north, range seven (7) east; thence northerly along the surveyed and unsurveyed range line between ranges six (6) and seven (7) east to the meander corner at its intersection with the mean high-water mark on the south bank of the Columbia River, the place of beginning.

Excepting from the force and effect of this proclamation all lands which may have been prior to the date hereof embraced in any legal entry or covered by any lawful filing duly of record in the proper United States land office, or upon which any valid settlement has been made pursuant to law and the statutory period within which to make entry or filing of record has not expired, and all mining claims duly located and held according to the laws of the United States and rules and regulations not in conflict therewith.

Provided, That this exception shall not continue to apply to any particular tract of land unless the entryman, settler, or claimant continues to comply with the law under which the entry, filing, settlement, or location was made.

Warning is hereby expressly given to all persons not to enter or make settlement upon the tract of land reserved by this proclamation.

In witness whereof I have hereunto set my hand and caused the seal of the United States to be affixed.

[SEAL.] Done at the city of Washington, this 28th day of September, A. D. 1893, and of the Independence of the United States the one hundred and eighteenth.

GROVER CLEVELAND.

By the President:

ALVEY A. ADEE,
Acting Secretary of State.

By the President of the United States of America.

A PROCLAMATION.

Whereas it is provided by section 24 of the act of Congress approved March 3, 1891, entitled "An act to repeal timber-culture laws, and for other purposes"—

That the President of the United States may from time to time set apart and reserve in any State or Territory having public land bearing forests, in any part of the public lands wholly or in part covered with timber or undergrowth, whether of commercial value or not, as public reservations; and the President shall by public proclamation declare the establishment of such reservations and the limits thereof.

And whereas the public lands in the State of Oregon within the limits hereinafter described are in part covered with timber, and it appears that the public good would be promoted by setting apart and reserving said lands as a public reservation:

Now, therefore, I, Grover Cleveland, President of the United States, by virtue of the power in me vested by section 24 of the aforesaid act of Congress, do hereby make known and proclaim that there is hereby reserved from entry or settlement and set apart as a public reservation all those certain tracts, pieces, or parcels of land lying and being situate in the State of Oregon and within the boundaries particularly described as follows, to wit:

Beginning at the northeast corner of section twenty-seven (27), township thirty-nine (39) south, range one (1) east, Willamette meridian; thence westerly along the surveyed and unsurveyed section line to the northwest corner of section twenty-five (25), township thirty-nine (39) south, range one (1) west; thence southerly along the section line to the southwest corner of section thirty-six (36), said township and range; thence westerly along the ninth (9th) standard parallel south to the northwest corner of section one (1), township forty (40) south, range one (1) west; thence southerly along the section line to the southwest corner of section thirteen (13), said township and range; thence easterly along the surveyed and unsurveyed section line to the point for the southeast corner of section fourteen (14), township forty (40) south, range one (1) east; thence northerly along the surveyed and unsurveyed section line to the northeast corner of section thirty-five (35), township thirty-nine (39) south, range one (1) east; thence westerly to the northwest corner of said section thirty-five (35); thence northerly to the northeast corner of section twenty-seven (27), said township and range, the place of beginning.

Excepting from the force and effect of this proclamation all lands which may have been prior to the date hereof embraced in any legal entry or covered by any lawful filing duly of record in the proper United States land office, or upon which any valid settlement has been made pursuant to law and the statutory period within which to make entry or filing of record has not expired, and all mining claims duly located and held according to the laws of the United States and rules and regulations not in conflict therewith.

Provided, That this exception shall not continue to apply to any particular tract of land unless the entryman, settler, or claimant continues to comply with the law under which the entry, filing, settlement, or location was made.

Warning is hereby expressly given to all persons not to enter or make settlement upon the tract of land reserved by this proclamation.

In witness whereof I have hereunto set my hand and caused the seal of the United States to be affixed.

[SEAL.]   Done at the city of Washington, this 28th day of September, A. D. 1893, and of the Independence of the United States the one hundred and eighteenth.

GROVER CLEVELAND.

By the President:

ALVEY A. ADEE, *Acting Secretary of State.*

BY THE PRESIDENT OF THE UNITED STATES OF AMERICA.

A PROCLAMATION.

While the American people should every day remember with praise and thanksgiving the divine goodness and mercy which have followed them since their beginning as a nation, it is fitting that one day in each year should be especially devoted to the contemplation of the blessings we have received from the hand of God and to the grateful acknowledgment of His loving kindness.

Therefore, I, Grover Cleveland, President of the United States, do hereby designate and set apart Thursday, the 30th day of the present month of November, as a day of thanksgiving and praise to be kept and observed by all the people of our land. On that day let us forego our ordinary work and employments and assemble in our usual places of worship, where we may recall all that God has done for us and where from grateful hearts our united tribute of praise and song may reach the Throne of Grace. Let the reunion of kindred and the social meeting of friends lend cheer and enjoyment to the day, and let generous gifts of charity for the relief of the poor and needy prove the sincerity of our thanksgiving.

Witness my hand and the seal of the United States, which I have caused to be hereto affixed.

[SEAL.]   Done at the city of Washington on the 3d day of November, A. D. 1893, and of the Independence of the United States the one hundred and eighteenth.

GROVER CLEVELAND.

By the President:

W. Q. GRESHAM, *Secretary of State.*

EXECUTIVE ORDER.

AMENDMENTS OF CIVIL-SERVICE RULES.

UNITED STATES CIVIL SERVICE COMMISSION,
Washington, D. C.

Clause 2 of Departmental Rule VIII is hereby amended by insert-ing after the letter "*d*" in parentheses in line 2 the following: "until after absolute appointment and," and by striking out all after the word "transferred" in line 4 to and including the word "made" in line 7; so that as amended the clause will read:

2. No person may be transferred as herein authorized, except as provided in sec-tion 1, clause (*d*), until after absolute appointment and until the Commission shall have certified to the officer making the transfer requisition that the person whom it is proposed to transfer has passed an examination to test fitness for the place to which he is to be transferred: *Provided*, That no person who has been appointed from the copyist register shall be transferred to a place the salary of which is more than $900 per annum until one year after appointment.

EXECUTIVE MANSION,
Washington, August 19, 1893.

The above amendments to clause 2 of Departmental Rule VIII and said rule as so amended are hereby approved.

GROVER CLEVELAND.

FIRST ANNUAL MESSAGE.

EXECUTIVE MANSION,
Washington, December 4, 1893.

To the Congress of the United States:

The constitutional duty which requires the President from time to time to give to the Congress information of the state of the Union and recommend to their consideration such measures as he shall judge neces-sary and expedient is fittingly entered upon by commending to the Con-gress a careful examination of the detailed statements and well-supported recommendations contained in the reports of the heads of Departments, who are chiefly charged with the executive work of the Government. In an effort to abridge this communication as much as is consistent with its purpose I shall supplement a brief reference to the contents of these departmental reports by the mention of such executive business and incidents as are not embraced therein and by such recommendations as appear to be at this particular time appropriate.

While our foreign relations have not at all times during the past year been entirely free from perplexity, no embarrassing situation remains that will not yield to the spirit of fairness and love of justice which, joined with consistent firmness, characterize a truly American foreign policy.

My predecessor having accepted the office of arbitrator of the long-standing Missions boundary dispute, tendered to the President by the Argentine Republic and Brazil, it has been my agreeable duty to receive the special envoys commissioned by those States to lay before me evidence and arguments in behalf of their respective Governments.

The outbreak of domestic hostilities in the Republic of Brazil found the United States alert to watch the interests of our citizens in that country, with which we carry on important commerce. Several vessels of our new Navy are now and for some time have been stationed at Rio de Janeiro. The struggle being between the established Government, which controls the machinery of administration, and with which we maintain friendly relations, and certain officers of the navy employing the vessels of their command in an attack upon the national capital and chief seaport, and lacking as it does the elements of divided administration, I have failed to see that the insurgents can reasonably claim recognition as belligerents.

Thus far the position of our Government has been that of an attentive but impartial observer of the unfortunate conflict. Emphasizing our fixed policy of impartial neutrality in such a condition of affairs as now exists, I deemed it necessary to disavow in a manner not to be misunderstood the unauthorized action of our late naval commander in those waters in saluting the revolted Brazilian admiral, being indisposed to countenance an act calculated to give gratuitous sanction to the local insurrection.

The convention between our Government and Chile having for its object the settlement and adjustment of the demand of the two countries against each other has been made effective by the organization of the claims commission provided for. The two Governments failing to agree upon the third member of the commission, the good offices of the President of the Swiss Republic were invoked, as provided in the treaty, and the selection of the Swiss representative in this country to complete the organization was gratifying alike to the United States and Chile.

The vexatious question of so-called legation asylum for offenders against the state and its laws was presented anew in Chile by the unauthorized action of the late United States minister in receiving into his official residence two persons who had just failed in an attempt at revolution and against whom criminal charges were pending growing out of a former abortive disturbance. The doctrine of asylum as applied to this case is not sanctioned by the best precedents, and when allowed tends to encourage sedition and strife. Under no circumstances can the representatives of this Government be permitted, under the ill-defined fiction of extraterritoriality, to interrupt the administration of criminal justice in the countries to which they are accredited. A temperate demand having been made by the Chilean Government for the correction of this conduct in the instance mentioned, the minister was instructed no longer to harbor the offenders.

The legislation of last year known as the Geary law, requiring the registration of all Chinese laborers entitled to residence in the United States and the deportation of all not complying with the provisions of the act within the time prescribed, met with much opposition from Chinamen in this country. Acting upon the advice of eminent counsel that the law was unconstitutional, the great mass of Chinese laborers, pending judicial inquiry as to its validity, in good faith declined to apply for the certificates required by its provisions. A test case upon proceeding by *habeas corpus* was brought before the Supreme Court, and on May 15, 1893, a decision was made by that tribunal sustaining the law.

It is believed that under the recent amendment of the act extending the time for registration the Chinese laborers thereto entitled who desire to reside in this country will now avail themselves of the renewed privilege thus afforded of establishing by lawful procedure their right to remain, and that thereby the necessity of enforced deportation may to a great degree be avoided.

It has devolved upon the United States minister at Peking, as dean of the diplomatic body, and in the absence of a representative of Sweden and Norway, to press upon the Chinese Government reparation for the recent murder of Swedish missionaries at Sung-pu. This question is of vital interest to all countries whose citizens engage in missionary work in the interior.

By Article XII of the general act of Brussels, signed July 2, 1890, for the suppression of the slave trade and the restriction of certain injurious commerce in the Independent State of the Kongo and in the adjacent zone of central Africa, the United States and the other signatory powers agreed to adopt appropriate means for the punishment of persons selling arms and ammunition to the natives and for the confiscation of the inhibited articles. It being the plain duty of this Government to aid in suppressing the nefarious traffic, impairing as it does the praiseworthy and civilizing efforts now in progress in that region, I recommend that an act be passed prohibiting the sale of arms and intoxicants to natives in the regulated zone by our citizens.

Costa Rica has lately testified its friendliness by surrendering to the United States, in the absence of a convention of extradition, but upon duly submitted evidence of criminality, a noted fugitive from justice. It is trusted that the negotiation of a treaty with that country to meet recurring cases of this kind will soon be accomplished. In my opinion treaties for reciprocal extradition should be concluded with all those countries with which the United States has not already conventional arrangements of that character.

I have deemed it fitting to express to the Governments of Costa Rica and Colombia the kindly desire of the United States to see their pending boundary dispute finally closed by arbitration in conformity with the spirit of the treaty concluded between them some years ago.

Our relations with the French Republic continue to be intimate and cordial. I sincerely hope that the extradition treaty with that country, as amended by the Senate, will soon be operative.

While occasional questions affecting our naturalized citizens returning to the land of their birth have arisen in our intercourse with Germany, our relations with that country continue satisfactory.

The questions affecting our relations with Great Britain have been treated in a spirit of friendliness.

Negotiations are in progress between the two Governments with a view to such concurrent action as will make the award and regulations agreed upon by the Bering Sea Tribunal of Arbitration practically effective, and it is not doubted that Great Britain will cooperate freely with this country for the accomplishment of that purpose.

The dispute growing out of the discriminating tolls imposed in the Welland Canal upon cargoes of cereals bound to and from the lake ports of the United States was adjusted by the substitution of a more equitable schedule of charges, and my predecessor thereupon suspended his proclamation imposing discriminating tolls upon British transit through our canals.*

A request for additions to the list of extraditable offenses covered by the existing treaty between the two countries is under consideration.

During the past year an American citizen employed in a subordinate commercial position in Hayti, after suffering a protracted imprisonment on an unfounded charge of smuggling, was finally liberated on judicial examination. Upon urgent representation to the Haytian Government a suitable indemnity was paid to the sufferer.

By a law of Hayti a sailing vessel, having discharged her cargo, is refused clearance until the duties on such cargo have been paid. The hardship of this measure upon American shipowners, who conduct the bulk of the carrying trade of that country, has been insisted on with a view of securing the removal of this cause of complaint.

Upon receiving authentic information of the firing upon an American mail steamer touching at the port of Amapala because her captain refused to deliver up a passenger in transit from Nicaragua to Guatemala upon demand of the military authorities of Honduras, our minister to that country, under instructions, protested against the wanton act and demanded satisfaction. The Government of Honduras, actuated by a sense of justice and in a spirit of the utmost friendship, promptly disavowed the illegal conduct of its officers and expressed sincere regret for the occurrence.

It is confidently anticipated that a satisfactory adjustment will soon be reached of the questions arising out of the seizure and use of American

*See pp. 5812-5813.

vessels by insurgents in Honduras and the subsequent denial by the successful Government of commercial privileges to those vessels on that account.

A notable part of the southeasterly coast of Liberia between the Cavally and San Pedro rivers, which for nearly half a century has been generally recognized as belonging to that Republic by cession and purchase, has been claimed to be under the protectorate of France in virtue of agreements entered into by the native tribes, over whom Liberia's control has not been well maintained.

More recently negotiations between the Liberian representative and the French Government resulted in the signature at Paris of a treaty whereby as an adjustment certain Liberian territory is ceded to France. This convention at last advices had not been ratified by the Liberian Legislature and Executive.

Feeling a sympathetic interest in the fortunes of the little Commonwealth, the establishment and development of which were largely aided by the benevolence of our countrymen, and which constitutes the only independently sovereign state on the west coast of Africa, this Government has suggested to the French Government its earnest concern lest territorial impairment in Liberia should take place without her unconstrained consent.

Our relations with Mexico continue to be of that close and friendly nature which should always characterize the intercourse of two neighboring republics.

The work of relocating the monuments marking the boundary between the two countries from Paso del Norte to the Pacific is now nearly completed.

The commission recently organized under the conventions of 1884 and 1889 it is expected will speedily settle disputes growing out of the shifting currents of the Rio Grande River east of El Paso.

Nicaragua has recently passed through two revolutions, the party at first successful having in turn been displaced by another. Our newly appointed minister by his timely good offices aided in a peaceful adjustment of the controversy involved in the first conflict. The large American interests established in that country in connection with the Nicaragua Canal were not molested.

The canal company has unfortunately become financially seriously embarrassed, but a generous treatment had been extended to it by the Government of Nicaragua. The United States are especially interested in the successful achievement of the vast undertaking this company has in charge. That it should be accomplished under distinctively American auspices, and its enjoyment assured not only to the vessels of this country as a channel of communication between our Atlantic and Pacific seaboards, but to the ships of the world in the interests of civilization, is a proposition which, in my judgment, does not admit of question.

Guatemala has also been visited by the political vicissitudes which have afflicted her Central American neighbors, but the dissolution of its Legislature and the proclamation of a dictatorship have been unattended with civil war.

An extradition treaty with Norway has recently been exchanged and proclaimed.

The extradition treaty with Russia signed in March, 1887, and amended and confirmed by the Senate in February last, was duly proclaimed last June.

Led by a desire to compose differences and contribute to the restoration of order in Samoa, which for some years previous had been the scene of conflicting foreign pretensions and native strife, the United States, departing from its policy consecrated by a century of observance, entered four years ago into the treaty of Berlin, thereby becoming jointly bound with England and Germany to establish and maintain Malietoa Laupepa as King of Samoa. The treaty provided for a foreign court of justice; a municipal council for the district of Apia, with a foreign president thereof, authorized to advise the King; a tribunal for the settlement of native and foreign land titles, and a revenue system for the Kingdom. It entailed upon the three powers that part of the cost of the new Government not met by the revenue of the islands.

Early in the life of this triple protectorate the native dissensions it was designed to quell revived. Rivals defied the authority of the new King, refusing to pay taxes and demanding the election of a ruler by native suffrage. Mataafa, an aspirant to the throne, and a large number of his native adherents were in open rebellion on one of the islands. Quite lately, at the request of the other powers and in fulfillment of its treaty obligation, this Government agreed to unite in a joint military movement of such dimensions as would probably secure the surrender of the insurgents without bloodshed.

The war ship *Philadelphia* was accordingly put under orders for Samoa, but before she arrived the threatened conflict was precipitated by King Malietoa's attack upon the insurgent camp. Mataafa was defeated and a number of his men killed. The British and German naval vessels present subsequently secured the surrender of Mataafa and his adherents. The defeated chief and ten of his principal supporters were deported to a German island of the Marshall group, where they are held as prisoners under the joint responsibility and cost of the three powers.

This incident and the events leading up to it signally illustrate the impolicy of entangling alliances with foreign powers.

More than fifteen years ago this Government preferred a claim against Spain in behalf of one of our citizens for property seized and confiscated in Cuba. In 1886 the claim was adjusted, Spain agreeing to pay unconditionally, as a fair indemnity, $1,500,000. A respectful but earnest note was recently addressed to the Spanish Government insisting upon prompt fulfillment of its long-neglected obligation.

Other claims preferred by the United States against Spain in behalf of American citizens for property confiscated in Cuba have been pending for many years.

At the time Spain's title to the Caroline Islands was confirmed by arbitration that Government agreed that the rights which had been acquired there by American missionaries should be recognized and respected. It is sincerely hoped that this pledge will be observed by allowing our missionaries, who were removed from Ponape to a place of safety by a United States war ship during the late troubles between the Spanish garrison and the natives, to return to their field of usefulness.

The reproduced caravel *Santa Maria*, built by Spain and sent to the Columbian Exposition, has been presented to the United States in token of amity and in commemoration of the event it was designed to celebrate. I recommend that in accepting this gift Congress make grateful recognition of the sincere friendship which prompted it.

Important matters have demanded attention in our relations with the Ottoman Porte.

The firing and partial destruction by an unrestrained mob of one of the school buildings of Anatolia College, established by citizens of the United States at Marsovan, and the apparent indifference of the Turkish Government to the outrage, notwithstanding the complicity of some of its officials, called for earnest remonstrance, which was followed by promise of reparation and punishment of the offenders.

Indemnity for the injury to the buildings has already been paid, permission to rebuild given, registration of the school property in the name of the American owners secured, and efficient protection guaranteed.

Information received of maltreatment suffered by an inoffensive American woman engaged in missionary work in Turkish Koordistan was followed by such representations to the Porte as resulted in the issuance of orders for the punishment of her assailants, the removal of a delinquent official, and the adoption of measures for the protection of our citizens engaged in mission and other lawful work in that quarter.

Turkey complains that her Armenian subjects obtain citizenship in this country not to identify themselves in good faith with our people, but with the intention of returning to the land of their birth and there engaging in sedition. This complaint is not wholly without foundation. A journal published in this country in the Armenian language openly counsels its readers to arm, organize, and participate in movements for the subversion of Turkish authority in the Asiatic provinces. The Ottoman Government has announced its intention to expel from its dominions Armenians who have obtained naturalization in the United States since 1868.

The right to exclude any or all classes of aliens is an attribute of sovereignty. It is a right asserted and, to a limited extent, enforced by the United States, with the sanction of our highest court. There being no naturalization treaty between the United States and Turkey, our minister at Constantinople has been instructed that, while recognizing the right of that Government to enforce its declared policy against naturalized Armenians, he is expected to protect them from unnecessary harshness of treatment.

In view of the impaired financial resources of Venezuela consequent upon the recent revolution there, a modified arrangement for the satisfaction of the awards of the late revisory claims commission, in progressive installments, has been assented to, and payments are being regularly made thereunder.

The boundary dispute between Venezuela and British Guiana is yet unadjusted. A restoration of diplomatic intercourse between that Republic and Great Britain and reference of the question to impartial arbitration would be a most gratifying consummation.

The ratification by Venezuela of the convention for the arbitration of the long-deferred claim of the Venezuelan Transportation Company is awaited.

It is hardly necessary for me to state that the questions arising from our relations with Hawaii have caused serious embarrassment. Just prior to the installation of the present Administration the existing Government of Hawaii had been suddenly overthrown and a treaty of annexation had been negotiated between the Provisional Government of the islands and the United States and submitted to the Senate for ratification. This treaty I withdrew for examination and dispatched Hon. James H. Blount, of Georgia, to Honolulu as a special commissioner to make an impartial investigation of the circumstances attending the change of government and of all the conditions bearing upon the subject of the treaty. After a thorough and exhaustive examination Mr. Blount submitted to me his report, showing beyond all question that the constitutional Government of Hawaii had been subverted with the active aid of our representative to that Government and through the intimidation caused by the presence of an armed naval force of the United States, which was landed for that purpose at the instance of our minister. Upon the facts developed it seemed to me the only honorable course for our Government to pursue was to undo the wrong that had been done by those representing us and to restore as far as practicable the status existing at the time of our forcible intervention. With a view of accomplishing this result within the constitutional limits of executive power, and recognizing all our obligations and responsibilities growing out of any changed conditions brought about by our unjustifiable interference, our present minister at Honolulu has received appropriate instructions to that end. Thus far no information of the accomplishment of any definite results has been received from him.

Additional advices are soon expected. When received they will be promptly sent to the Congress, together with all other information at hand, accompanied by a special Executive message fully detailing all the facts necessary to a complete understanding of the case and presenting a history of all the material events leading up to the present situation.

By a concurrent resolution passed by the Senate February 14, 1890, and by the House of Representatives on the 3d of April following the President was requested to "invite from time to time, as fit occasions may arise, negotiations with any government with which the United States has or may have diplomatic relations, to the end that any differences or disputes arising between the two governments which can not be adjusted by diplomatic agency may be referred to arbitration and be peaceably adjusted by such means." April 18, 1890, the International American Conference of Washington by resolution expressed the wish that all controversies between the republics of America and the nations of Europe might be settled by arbitration, and recommended that the government of each nation represented in that conference should communicate this wish to all friendly powers. A favorable response has been received from Great Britain in the shape of a resolution adopted by Parliament July 16 last, cordially sympathizing with the purpose in view and expressing the hope that Her Majesty's Government will lend ready cooperation to the Government of the United States upon the basis of the concurrent resolution above quoted.

It affords me signal pleasure to lay this parliamentary resolution before the Congress and to express my sincere gratification that the sentiment of two great and kindred nations is thus authoritatively manifested in favor of the rational and peaceable settlement of international quarrels by honorable resort to arbitration.

Since the passage of the act of March 3, 1893, authorizing the President to raise the grade of our envoys to correspond with the rank in which foreign countries accredit their agents here, Great Britain, France, Italy, and Germany have conferred upon their representatives at this capital the title of ambassador, and I have responded by accrediting the agents of the United States in those countries with the same title. A like elevation of mission is announced by Russia, and when made will be similarly met. This step fittingly comports with the position the United States hold in the family of nations.

During my former Administration I took occasion to recommend a recast of the laws relating to the consular service, in order that it might become a more efficient agency in the promotion of the interests it was intended to subserve. The duties and powers of consuls have been expanded with the growing requirements of our foreign trade. Discharging important duties affecting our commerce and American citizens abroad, and in certain countries exercising judicial functions, these officers should be men of character, intelligence, and ability.

Upon proof that the legislation of Denmark secures copyright to American citizens on equal footing with its own, the privileges of our copyright laws have been extended by proclamation to subjects of that country.*

The Secretary of the Treasury reports that the receipts of the Government from all sources during the fiscal year ended June 30, 1893, amounted to $461,716,561.94 and its expenditures to $459,374,674.29. There was collected from customs $205,355,016.73 and from internal revenue $161,027,623.93. Our dutiable imports amounted to $421,856,711, an increase of $52,453,907 over the preceding year, and importations free of duty amounted to $444,544,211, a decrease from the preceding year of $13,455,447. Internal-revenue receipts exceeded those of the preceding year by $7,147,445.32. The total tax collected on distilled spirits was $94,720,260.55, on manufactured tobacco $31,889,711.74, and on fermented liquors $32,548,983.07. We exported merchandise during the year amounting to $847,665,194, a decrease of $182,612,954 from the preceding year. The amount of gold exported was larger than any previous year in the history of the Government, amounting to $108,-680,844, and exceeding the amount exported during the preceding year by $58,485,517.

The sum paid from the Treasury for sugar bounty was $9,375,130.88, an increase over the preceding year of $2,033,053.09.

It is estimated upon the basis of present revenue laws that the receipts of the Government for the year ending June 30, 1894, will be $430,121,-365.38 and its expenditures $458,121,365.28, resulting in a deficiency of $28,000,000.

On the 1st day of November, 1893, the amount of money of all kinds in circulation, or not included in Treasury holdings, was $1,718,544,682. an increase for the year of $112,404,947. Estimating our population at 67,426,000 at the time mentioned, the per capita circulation was $25.49. On the same date there was in the Treasury gold bullion amounting to $96,657,273 and silver bullion which was purchased at a cost of $126,261,553.

The purchases of silver under the law of July 14, 1890, during the last fiscal year aggregated 54,008,162.59 fine ounces, which cost $45,531,-374.53. The total amount of silver purchased from the time that law became operative until the repeal of its purchasing clause, on the 1st day of November, 1893, was 168,674,590.46 fine ounces, which cost $155,-930,940.84. Between the 1st day of March, 1873, and the 1st day of November, 1893, the Government purchased under all laws 503,003,717 fine ounces of silver, at a cost of $516,622,948. The silver dollars that have been coined under the act of July 14, 1890, number 36,087,285. The seigniorage arising from such coinage was $6,977,098.39, leaving on hand in the mints 140,699,760 fine ounces of silver, which cost $126,-758,218.

Our total coinage of all metals during the last fiscal year consisted of

*See pp. 5827–5828.

97,280,875 pieces, valued at $43,685,178.80, of which there was $30,-038,140 in gold coin, $5,343,715 in silver dollars, $7,217,220.90 in subsidiary silver coin, and $1,086,102.90 in minor coins.

During the calendar year 1892 the production of precious metals in the United States was estimated to be 1,596,375 fine ounces of gold of the commercial and coinage value of $33,000,000 and 58,000,000 fine ounces of silver of the bullion or market value of $50,750,000 and of the coinage value of $74,989,900.

It is estimated that on the 1st day of July, 1893, the metallic stock of money in the United States, consisting of coin and bullion, amounted to $1,213,559,169, of which $597,697,685 was gold and $615,861,484 was silver.

One hundred and nineteen national banks were organized during the year ending October 31, 1893, with a capital of $11,230,000. Forty-six went into voluntary liquidation and 158 suspended. Sixty-five of the suspended banks were insolvent, 86 resumed business, and 7 remain in the hands of the bank examiners, with prospects of speedy resumption. Of the new banks organized, 44 were located in the Eastern States, 41 west of the Mississippi River, and 34 in the Central and Southern States. The total number of national banks in existence on October 31, 1893, was 3,796, having an aggregate capital of $695,558,120. The net increase in the circulation of these banks during the year was $36,886,972.

The recent repeal of the provision of law requiring the purchase of silver bullion by the Government as a feature of our monetary scheme has made an entire change in the complexion of our currency affairs. I do not doubt that the ultimate result of this action will be most salutary and far-reaching. In the nature of things, however, it is impossible to know at this time precisely what conditions will be brought about by the change, or what, if any, supplementary legislation may in the light of such conditions appear to be essential or expedient. Of course, after the recent financial perturbation, time is necessary for the reestablishment of business confidence. When, however, through this restored confidence, the money which has been frightened into hoarding places is returned to trade and enterprise, a survey of the situation will probably disclose a safe path leading to a permanently sound currency, abundantly sufficient to meet every requirement of our increasing population and business.

In the pursuit of this object we should resolutely turn away from alluring and temporary expedients, determined to be content with nothing less than a lasting and comprehensive financial plan. In these circumstances I am convinced that a reasonable delay in dealing with this subject, instead of being injurious, will increase the probability of wise action.

The monetary conference which assembled at Brussels upon our invitation was adjourned to the 30th day of November of the present year. The considerations just stated and the fact that a definite proposition

CUBAN GUERRILLAS JOINING U. S. TROOPS AT SIBONEY

MARCHING THROUGH SIBONEY

From Siboney went two trails to Santiago, which, three miles away from Siboney, merged into one road. This meeting-place, uninhabited by man and surrounded with dense jungle, is called Las Guasimas. Here the Spaniards took position, posting riflemen in pits on the eastern trail and others in the jungle on the western. Shafter's advance on Santiago was led by Wheeler, who sent five hundred Rough Riders by the western, and five hundred negro cavalrymen of the Tenth Regular Regiment by the eastern trail. The Rough Riders performed the more notable part of the work. Having learned that the enemy was near at hand their column halted and deployed into the jungle on either side and into the valley, so as to establish communication with the other column on the eastern trail. Presently a volley rang out and a hail of Mauser bullets whistled through the foliage about three feet above the ground. The troops stumbled through the rank vegetation toward the sound. Sight was almost useless in the bewildering tangle. Our troops at last encountered a curtain of wild grapevines so closely intertwined and festooned with parasitic growths that they could proceed no farther. From behind this curtain came the volleys. After pouring lead into the spot, Roosevelt ordered them to move on knees and stomachs to the left. A skirmish line was thus formed that ran from the eastern trail into the valley and up the slope, to the western trail, outflanking the Spanish ambush. The Rough Riders' part of this line went forward in short dashes, each man seeking his own shelter. An hour and a half of such fighting drove the Spaniards a mile and a half from their first line of battle. The rifle pits on the eastern slope had not been carried, however. The Rough Riders then charged the enemy's principal stronghold, a house on the ridge, and carried it. This made the rifle pits untenable and the enemy retreated toward Santiago.

President McKinley wrote the official history of the war in his messages, just as Madison, Polk and Lincoln wrote the official histories of the War of 1812, and the Mexican and Civil wars. The article, "Spanish-American War," in the encyclopedic index (volume eleven), recites the facts briefly. There are articles on the principal battles, "Santiago," "Santiago Harbor," "Manila Harbor," "Guantanamo," and "San Juan."

from us seemed to be expected upon the reassembling of the conference led me to express a willingness to have the meeting still further
postponed.

It seems to me that it would be wise to give general authority to the
President to invite other nations to such a conference at any time when
there should be a fair prospect of accomplishing an international agree
ment on the subject of coinage.

I desire also to earnestly suggest the wisdom of amending the existing
statutes in regard to the issuance of Government bonds. The authority
now vested in the Secretary of the Treasury to issue bonds is not as clear
as it should be, and the bonds authorized are disadvantageous to the
Government both as to the time of their maturity and rate of interest.

The Superintendent of Immigration, through the Secretary of the
Treasury, reports that during the last fiscal year there arrived at our ports
440,793 immigrants. Of these, 1,063 were not permitted to land under
the limitations of the law and 577 were returned to the countries from
whence they came by reason of their having become public charges.
The total arrivals were 141,034 less than for the previous year.

The Secretary in his report gives an account of the operation of the
Marine-Hospital Service and of the good work done under its supervision
in preventing the entrance and spread of contagious diseases.

The admonitions of the last two years touching our public health and
the demonstrated danger of the introduction of contagious diseases from
foreign ports have invested the subject of national quarantine with increased interest. A more general and harmonious system than now
exists, acting promptly and directly everywhere and constantly operating
by preventive means to shield our country from the invasion of disease,
and at the same time having due regard to the rights and duties of local
agencies, would, I believe, add greatly to the safety of our people.

The Secretary of War reports that the strength of the Army on the
30th day of September last was 25,778 enlisted men and 2,144 officers.

The total expenditures of the Department for the year ending June 30,
1893, amounted to $51,966,074.89. Of this sum $1,992,581.95 was for
salaries and contingent expenses, $23,377,828.35 for the support of the
military establishment, $6,077,033.18 for miscellaneous objects, and $20,-
518,631.41 for public works. This latter sum includes $15,296,876.46
for river and harbor improvements and $3,266,141.20 for fortifications
and other works of defense.

The total enrollment of the militia of the several States was on the 31st
of October of the current year 112,597 officers and enlisted men. The
officers of the Army detailed for the inspection and instruction of this
reserve of our military force report that increased interest and marked
progress are apparent in the discipline and efficiency of the organization.

Neither Indian outbreaks nor domestic violence have called the Army
into service during the year, and the only active military duty required

of it has been in the Department of Texas, where violations of the neutrality laws of the United States and Mexico were promptly and efficiently dealt with by the troops, eliciting the warm approval of the civil and military authorities of both countries.

The operation of wise laws and the influences of civilization constantly tending to relieve the country from the dangers of Indian hostilities, together with the increasing ability of the States, through the efficiency of the National Guard organizations, to protect their citizens from domestic violence, lead to the suggestion that the time is fast approaching when there should be a reorganization of our Army on the lines of the present necessities of the country. This change contemplates neither increase in number nor added expense, but a redistribution of the force and an encouragement of measures tending to greater efficiency among the men and improvement of the service.

The adoption of battalion formations for infantry regiments, the strengthening of the artillery force, the abandonment of smaller and unnecessary posts, and the massing of the troops at important and accessible stations all promise to promote the usefulness of the Army. In the judgment of army officers, with but few exceptions, the operation of the law forbidding the reenlistment of men after ten years' service has not proved its wisdom, and while the arguments that led to its adoption were not without merit the experience of the year constrains me to join in the recommendation for its repeal.

It is gratifying to note that we have begun to attain completed results in the comprehensive scheme of seacoast defense and fortification entered upon eight years ago. A large sum has been already expended, but the cost of maintenance will be inconsiderable as compared with the expense of construction and ordnance. At the end of the current calendar year the War Department will have nine 12-inch guns, twenty 10-inch, and thirty-four 8-inch guns ready to be mounted on gun lifts and carriages, and seventy-five 12-inch mortars. In addition to the product of the Army Gun Factory, now completed at Watervliet, the Government has contracted with private parties for the purchase of one hundred guns of these calibers, the first of which should be delivered to the Department for test before July 1, 1894.

The manufacture of heavy ordnance keeps pace with current needs, but to render these guns available for the purposes they are designed to meet emplacements must be prepared for them. Progress has been made in this direction, and it is desirable that Congress by adequate appropriations should provide for the uninterrupted prosecution of this necessary work.

After much preliminary work and exhaustive examination in accordance with the requirements of the law, the board appointed to select a magazine rifle of modern type with which to replace the obsolete Springfield rifle of the infantry service completed its labors during the last year, and the work of manufacture is now in progress at the national armory at Springfield. It is confidently expected that by the end of the current year our infantry will be supplied with a weapon equal to that of the most progressive armies of the world.

The work on the projected Chickamauga and Chattanooga National Military Park has been prosecuted with zeal and judgment, and its opening will be celebrated during the coming year. Over 9 square miles of the Chickamauga battlefield have been acquired, 25 miles of roadway have been constructed, and permanent tablets have been placed at many historical points, while the invitation to the States to mark the positions of their troops participating in the battle has been very generally accepted.

The work of locating and preserving the lines of battle at the Gettysburg battlefield is making satisfactory progress on the plans directed by the last Congress.

The reports of the Military Academy at West Point and the several schools for special instruction of officers show marked advance in the education of the Army and a commendable ambition among its officers to excel in the military profession and to fit themselves for the highest service to the country.

Under the supervision of Adjutant-General Robert Williams, lately retired, the Bureau of Military Information has become well established and is performing a service that will put in possession of the Government in time of war most valuable information, and at all times serve a purpose of great utility in keeping the Army advised of the world's progress in all matters pertaining to the art of war.

The report of the Attorney-General contains the usual summary of the affairs and proceedings of the Department of Justice for the past year, together with certain recommendations as to needed legislation on various subjects. I can not too heartily indorse the proposition that the fee system as applicable to the compensation of United States attorneys, marshals, clerks of Federal courts, and United States commissioners should be abolished with as little delay as possible. It is clearly in the interest of the community that the business of the courts, both civil and criminal, shall be as small and as inexpensively transacted as the ends of justice will allow.

The system is therefore thoroughly vicious which makes the compensation of court officials depend upon the volume of such business, and thus creates a conflict between a proper execution of the law and private gain, which can not fail to be dangerous to the rights and freedom of the citizen and an irresistible temptation to the unjustifiable expenditure of public funds. If in addition to this reform another was inaugurated which would give to United States commissioners the final disposition of petty offenses within the grade of misdemeanors, especially those coming under the internal-revenue laws, a great advance would be made toward a more decent administration of the criminal law.

In my first message to Congress, dated December 8, 1885,* I strongly recommended these changes and referred somewhat at length to the evils of the present system. Since that time the criminal business of the Federal courts and the expense attending it have enormously increased. The number of criminal prosecutions pending in the circuit and district courts of the United States on the 1st day of July, 1885, was 3,808, of which 1,884 were for violations of the internal-revenue laws, while the number of such prosecutions pending on the 1st day of July, 1893, was 9,500, of which 4,200 were for violations of the internal-revenue laws. The expense of the United States courts, exclusive of judges' salaries, for the year ending July 1, 1885, was $2,874,733.11 and for the year ending July 1, 1893, $4,528,676.87.

It is therefore apparent that the reasons given in 1885 for a change in the manner of enforcing the Federal criminal law have gained cogency and strength by lapse of time.

I also heartily join the Attorney-General in recommending legislation fixing degrees of the crime of murder within Federal jurisdiction, as has been done in many of the States; authorizing writs of error on behalf of the Government in cases where final judgment is rendered against the sufficiency of an indictment or against the Government upon any other question arising before actual trial; limiting the right of review in cases of felony punishable only by fine and imprisonment to the circuit court of appeals, and making speedy provision for the construction of such prisons and reformatories as may be necessary for the confinement of United States convicts.

The report of the Postmaster-General contains a detailed statement of the operations of the Post-Office Department during the last fiscal year and much interesting information touching this important branch of the public service.

The business of the mails indicates with absolute certainty the condition of the business of the country, and depression in financial affairs inevitably and quickly reduces the postal revenues. Therefore a larger discrepancy than usual between the post-office receipts and expenditures is the expected and unavoidable result of the distressing stringency which has prevailed throughout the country during much of the time covered by the Postmaster-General's report. At a date when better times were anticipated it was estimated by his predecessor that the deficiency on the 30th day of June, 1893, would be but a little over a million and a half dollars. It amounted, however, to more than five millions. At the same time and under the influence of like anticipations estimates were made for the current fiscal year, ending June 30, 1894, which exhibited a surplus of revenue over expenditures of $872,245.71; but now, in view of the actual receipts and expenditures during that part of the current fiscal year already expired, the present Postmaster-General estimates

* See pp. 4938-4940.

that at its close instead of a surplus there will be a deficiency of nearly $8,000,000.

The post-office receipts for the last fiscal year amounted to $75,896,-933.16 and its expenditures to $81,074,104.90. This post-office deficiency would disappear or be immensely decreased if less matter were carried free through the mails, an item of which is upward of 300 tons of seeds and grain from the Agricultural Department.

The total number of post-offices in the United States on the 30th day of June, 1893, was 68,403, an increase of 1,284 over the preceding year. Of these, 3,360 were Presidential, an increase in that class of 204 over the preceding year.

Forty-two free-delivery offices were added during the year to those already existing, making a total of 610 cities and towns provided with free delivery on June 30, 1893. Ninety-three other cities and towns are now entitled to this service under the law, but it has not been accorded them on account of insufficient funds to meet the expenses of its establishment.

I am decidedly of the opinion that the provisions of the present law permit as general an introduction of this feature of mail service as is necessary or justifiable, and that it ought not to be extended to smaller communities than are now designated.

The expenses of free delivery for the fiscal year ending June 30, 1894, will be more than $11,000,000, and under legislation now existing there must be a constant increase in this item of expenditure.

There were 6,401 additions to the domestic money-order offices during the last fiscal year, being the largest increase in any year since the inauguration of the system. The total number of these offices at the close of the year was 18,434. There were 13,309,735 money orders issued from these offices, being an increase over the preceding year of 1,240,293, and the value of these orders amounted to $127,576,433.65, an increase of $7,509,632.58. There were also issued during the year postal notes amounting to $12,903,076.73.

During the year 195 international money-order offices were added to those already provided, making a total of 2,407 in operation on June 30, 1893. The number of international money orders issued during the year was 1,055,999, an increase over the preceding year of 72,525, and their value was $16,341,837.86, an increase of $1,221,506.31. The number of orders paid was 300,917, an increase over the preceding year of 13,503, and their value was $5,283,375.70, an increase of $94,094.83.

From the foregoing statements it appears that the total issue of money orders and postal notes for the year amounted to $156,821,348.24.

The number of letters and packages mailed during the year for special delivery was 3,375,693, an increase over the preceding year of nearly 22 per cent. The special-delivery stamps used upon these letters and packages amounted to $337,569.30, and the messengers' fees paid for their delivery amounted to $256,592.71, leaving a profit to the Government of $80,976.59.

The Railway Mail Service not only adds to the promptness of mail delivery at all offices, but it is the especial instrumentality which puts the smaller and way places in the service on an equality in that regard with the larger and terminal offices. This branch of the postal service has therefore received much attention from the Postmaster-General, and though it is gratifying to know that it is in a condition of high efficiency and great usefulness, I am led to agree with the Postmaster-General that there is room for its further improvement.

There are now connected to the Post-Office establishment 28,324 employees who are in the classified service. The head of this great Department gives conclusive evidence of the value of civil-service reform when, after an experience that renders his judgment on the subject absolutely reliable, he expresses the opinion that without the benefit of this system it would be impossible to conduct the vast business intrusted to him.

I desire to commend as especially worthy of prompt attention the suggestions of the Postmaster-General relating to a more sensible and businesslike organization and a better distribution of responsibility in his Department.

The report of the Secretary of the Navy contains a history of the operations of his Department during the past year and exhibits a most gratifying condition of the personnel of our Navy. He presents a satisfactory account of the progress which has been made in the construction of vessels and makes a number of recommendations to which attention is especially invited.

During the past six months the demands for cruising vessels have been many and urgent. There have been revolutions calling for vessels to protect American interests in Nicaragua, Guatemala, Costa Rica, Honduras, Argentina, and Brazil, while the condition of affairs in Honolulu has required the constant presence of one or more ships. With all these calls upon our Navy it became necessary, in order to make up a sufficient fleet to patrol the Bering Sea under the *modus vivendi* agreed upon with Great Britain, to detail to that service one vessel from the Fish Commission and three from the Revenue Marine.

Progress in the construction of new vessels has not been as rapid as was anticipated. There have been delays in the completion of unarmored vessels, but for the most part they have been such as are constantly occurring even in countries having the largest experience in naval shipbuilding. The most serious delays, however, have been in the work upon armored ships. The trouble has been the failure of contractors to deliver armor as agreed. The difficulties seem now, however, to have been all overcome, and armor is being delivered with satisfactory promptness. As a result of the experience acquired by shipbuilders and designers and material men, it is believed that the dates when vessels will be completed can now be estimated with reasonable accuracy. Great guns, rapid-fire guns, torpedoes, and powder are being promptly supplied.

The following vessels of the new Navy have been completed and are now ready for service: The double-turreted coast-defense monitor *Miantonomoh*, the double-turreted coast-defense monitor *Monterey*, the armored cruiser *New York*, the protected cruisers *Baltimore, Chicago, Philadelphia, Newark, San Francisco, Charleston, Atlanta*, and *Boston*, the cruiser *Detroit*, the gunboats *Yorktown, Concord, Bennington, Machias, Castine*, and *Petrel*, the dispatch vessel *Dolphin*, the practice vessel *Bancroft*, and the dynamite gunboat *Vesuvius*. Of these the *Bancroft, Machias, Detroit*, and *Castine* have been placed in commission during the current calendar year.

The following vessels are in process of construction: The second-class battle ships *Maine* and *Texas*, the cruisers *Montgomery* and *Marblehead*, and the coast-defense monitors *Terror, Puritan, Amphitrite*, and *Monadnock*, all of which will be completed within one year; the harbor-defense ram *Katahdin* and the protected cruisers *Columbia, Minneapolis, Olympia, Cincinnati*, and *Raleigh*, all of which will be completed prior to July 1, 1895; the first-class battle ships *Iowa, Indiana, Massachusetts*, and *Oregon*, which will be completed February 1, 1896, and the armored cruiser *Brooklyn*, which will be completed by August 1 of that year. It is also expected that the three gunboats authorized by the last Congress will be completed in less than two years.

Since 1886 Congress has at each session authorized the building of one or more vessels, and the Secretary of the Navy presents an earnest plea for the continuance of this plan. He recommends the authorization of at least one battle ship and six torpedo boats.

While I am distinctly in favor of consistently pursuing the policy we have inaugurated of building up a thorough and efficient Navy, I can not refrain from the suggestion that the Congress should carefully take into account the number of unfinished vessels on our hands and the depleted condition of our Treasury in considering the propriety of an appropriation at this time to begin new work.

The method of employing mechanical labor at navy-yards through boards of labor and making efficiency the sole test by which laborers are employed and continued is producing the best results, and the Secretary is earnestly devoting himself to its development. Attention is invited to the statements of his report in regard to the workings of the system.

The Secretary of the Interior has the supervision of so many important subjects that his report is of especial value and interest.

On the 30th day of June, 1893, there were on the pension rolls 966,012 names, an increase of 89,944 over the number on the rolls June 30, 1892. Of these there were 17 widows and daughters of Revolutionary soldiers, 86 survivors of the War of 1812, 5,425 widows of soldiers of that war, 21,518 survivors and widows of the Mexican War, 3,882 survivors and widows of Indian wars, 284 army nurses, and 475,645 survivors and widows and children of deceased soldiers and sailors of the War of the Rebellion. The latter number represents those pensioned on account of disabilities or death resulting from army and navy service. The number of persons remaining on the rolls June 30, 1893, who were pensioned under the act of June 27, 1890, which allows pensions on account of death and disability not chargeable to army service, was 459,155.

The number added to the rolls during the year was 123,634 and the number dropped was 33,690. The first payments on pensions allowed during the year amounted to $33,756,549.98. This includes arrears, or the accumulation between the time from which the allowance of pension dates and the time of actually granting the certificate.

Although the law of 1890 permits pensions for disabilities not related to military service, yet as a requisite to its benefits a disability must exist incapacitating applicants "from the performance of manual labor to such a degree as to render them unable to earn a support." The execution of this law in its early stages does not seem to have been in accord with its true intention, but toward the close of the last Administration an authoritative construction was given to the statute, and since that time this construction has been followed. This has had the effect of limiting the operation of the law to its intended purpose. The discovery having been made that many names had been put upon the pension roll by means of wholesale and gigantic frauds, the Commissioner suspended payments upon a number of pensions which seemed to be fraudulent or unauthorized pending a complete examination, giving notice to the pensioners, in order that they might have an opportunity to establish, if possible, the justice of their claims notwithstanding apparent invalidity.

This, I understand, is the practice which has for a long time prevailed in the Pension Bureau; but after entering upon these recent investigations the Commissioner modified this rule so as not to allow until after a complete examination interference with the payment of a pension apparently not altogether void, but which merely had been fixed at a rate higher than that authorized by law.

I am unable to understand why frauds in the pension rolls should not be exposed and corrected with thoroughness and vigor. Every name fraudulently put upon these rolls is a wicked imposition upon the kindly sentiment in which pensions have their origin; every fraudulent pensioner has become a bad citizen; every false oath in support of a pension has made perjury more common, and false and undeserving pensioners rob the people not only of their money, but of the patriotic sentiment which the survivors of a war fought for the preservation of the Union ought to inspire. Thousands of neighborhoods have their well-known fraudulent pensioners, and recent developments by the Bureau establish appalling conspiracies to accomplish pension frauds. By no means the least wrong done is to brave and deserving pensioners, who certainly ought not to be condemned to such association.

Those who attempt in the line of duty to rectify these wrongs should not be accused of enmity or indifference to the claims of honest veterans.

The sum expended on account of pensions for the year ending June 30, 1893, was $156,740,467.14.

The Commissioner estimates that $165,000,000 will be required to pay pensions during the year ending June 30, 1894.

The condition of the Indians and their ultimate fate are subjects which are related to a sacred duty of the Government and which strongly appeal to the sense of justice and the sympathy of our people.

Our Indians number about 248,000. Most of them are located on 161 reservations, containing 86,116,531 acres of land. About 110,000 of these Indians have to a large degree adopted civilized customs. Lands in severalty have been allotted to many of them. Such allotments have been made to 10,000 individuals during the last fiscal year, embracing about 1,000,000 acres. The number of Indian Government schools opened during the year was 195, an increase of 12 over the preceding year. Of this total 170 were on reservations, of which 73 were boarding schools and 97 were day schools. Twenty boarding schools and 5 day schools supported by the Government were not located on reservations. The total number of Indian children enrolled during the year as attendants of all schools was 21,138, an increase of 1,231 over the enrollment for the previous year.

I am sure that secular education and moral and religious teaching must be important factors in any effort to save the Indian and lead him to civilization. I believe, too, that the relinquishment of tribal relations and the holding of land in severalty may in favorable conditions aid this consummation. It seems to me, however, that allotments of land in severalty ought to be made with great care and circumspection. If hastily done, before the Indian knows its meaning, while yet he has little or no idea of tilling a farm and no conception of thrift, there is great danger that a reservation life in tribal relations may be exchanged for the pauperism of civilization instead of its independence and elevation.

The solution of the Indian problem depends very largely upon good administration. The personal fitness of agents and their adaptability to the peculiar duty of caring for their wards are of the utmost importance.

The law providing that, except in special cases, army officers shall be detailed as Indian agents it is hoped will prove a successful experiment.

There is danger of great abuses creeping into the prosecution of claims for Indian depredations, and I recommend that every possible safeguard be provided against the enforcement of unjust and fictitious claims of this description.

The appropriations on account of the Indian Bureau for the year ending June 30, 1894, amount to $7,954,962.99, a decrease as compared with the year preceding it of $387,131.95.

The vast area of land which but a short time ago constituted the public domain is rapidly falling into private hands. It is certain that in the transfer the beneficent intention of the Government to supply from its domain homes to the industrious and worthy home seekers is often frustrated. Though the speculator, who stands with extortionate purpose between the land office and those who, with their families, are invited by the Government to settle on the public lands, is a despicable character who ought not to be tolerated, yet it is difficult to thwart his schemes. The recent opening to settlement of the lands in the Cherokee Outlet, embracing an area of 6,500,000 acres, notwithstanding the utmost care in framing the regulations governing the selection of locations and notwithstanding the presence of United States troops, furnished an exhibition, though perhaps in a modified degree, of the mad scramble, the violence, and the fraudulent occupation which have accompanied previous openings of public land.

I concur with the Secretary in the belief that these outrageous incidents can not be entirely prevented without a change in the laws on the subject, and I hope his recommendations in that direction will be favorably considered.

I especially commend to the attention of the Congress the statements contained in the Secretary's report concerning forestry. The time has come when efficient measures should be taken for the preservation of our forests from indiscriminate and remediless destruction.

The report of the Secretary of Agriculture will be found exceedingly interesting, especially to that large part of our citizens intimately concerned in agricultural occupations.

On the 7th day of March, 1893, there were upon its pay rolls 2,430 employees. This number has been reduced to 1,850 persons. In view of a depleted public Treasury and the imperative demand of the people for economy in the administration of their Government, the Secretary has entered upon the task of rationally reducing expenditures by the elimination from the pay rolls of all persons not needed for an efficient conduct of the affairs of the Department.

During the first quarter of the present year the expenses of the Department aggregated $345,876.76, as against $402,012.42 for the corresponding period of the fiscal year ending June 30, 1893. The Secretary makes apparent his intention to continue this rate of reduction by submitting estimates for the next fiscal year less by $994,280 than those for the present year.

Among the heads of divisions in this Department the changes have been exceedingly few. Three vacancies occurring from death and resignations have been filled by the promotion of assistants in the same divisions.

These promotions of experienced and faithful assistants have not only been in the interest of efficient work, but have suggested to those in the

Department who look for retention and promotion that merit and devotion to duty are their best reliance.

The amount appropriated for the Bureau of Animal Industry for the current fiscal year is $850,000. The estimate for the ensuing year is $700,000.

The regulations of 1892 concerning Texas fever have been enforced during the last year and the large stock yards of the country have been kept free from infection. Occasional local outbreaks have been largely such as could have been effectually guarded against by the owners of the affected cattle.

While contagious pleuro-pneumonia in cattle has been eradicated, animal tuberculosis, a disease widespread and more dangerous to human life than pleuro-pneumonia, is still prevalent. Investigations have been made during the past year as to the means of its communication and the method of its correct diagnosis. Much progress has been made in this direction by the studies of the division of animal pathology, but work ought to be extended, in cooperation with local authorities, until the danger to human life arising from this cause is reduced to a minimum.

The number of animals arriving from Canada during the year and inspected by Bureau officers was 462,092, and the number from transatlantic countries was 1,297. No contagious diseases were found among the imported animals.

The total number of inspections of cattle for export during the past fiscal year was 611,542. The exports show a falling off of about 25 per cent from the preceding year, the decrease occurring entirely in the last half of the year. This suggests that the falling off may have been largely due to an increase in the price of American export cattle.

During the year ending June 30, 1893, exports of inspected pork aggregated 20,677,410 pounds, as against 38,152,874 pounds for the preceding year. The falling off in this export was not confined, however, to inspected pork, the total quantity exported for 1892 being 665,490,616 pounds, while in 1893 it was only 527,308,695 pounds.

I join the Secretary in recommending that hereafter each applicant for the position of inspector or assistant inspector in the Bureau of Animal Industry be required, as a condition precedent to his appointment, to exhibit to the United States Civil Service Commission his diploma from an established, regular, and reputable veterinary college, and that this be supplemented by such an examination in veterinary science as the Commission may prescribe.

The exports of agricultural products from the United States for the fiscal year ending June 30, 1892, attained the enormous figure of $800,-000,000, in round numbers, being 78.7 per cent of our total exports. In the last fiscal year this aggregate was greatly reduced, but nevertheless reached 615,000,000, being 75.1 per cent of all American commodities exported.

A review of our agricultural exports with special reference to their destination will show that in almost every line the United Kingdom of Great Britain and Ireland absorbs by far the largest proportion. Of cattle the total exports aggregated in value for the fiscal year ending June 30, 1893, $26,000,000, of which Great Britain took considerably over $25,000,000. Of beef products of all kinds our total exports were $28,000,000, of which Great Britain took $24,000,000. Of pork products the total exports were $84,000,000, of which Great Britain took $53,000,000. In breadstuffs, cotton, and minor products like proportions sent to the same destination are shown.

The work of the statistical division of the Department of Agriculture deals with all that relates to the economics of farming.

The main purpose of its monthly reports is to keep the farmers informed as fully as possible of all matters having any influence upon the world's markets, in which their products find sale. Its publications relate especially to the commercial side of farming.

It is therefore of profound importance and vital concern to the farmers of the United States, who represent nearly one-half of our population, and also of direct interest to the whole country, that the work of this division be efficiently performed and that the information it has gathered be promptly diffused.

It is a matter for congratulation to know that the Secretary will not spare any effort to make this part of his work thoroughly useful.

In the year 1839 the Congress appropriated $1,000, to be taken from the Patent Office funds, for the purpose of collecting and distributing rare and improved varieties of seeds and for prosecuting agricultural investigations and procuring agricultural statistics. From this small beginning the seed division of the Department of Agriculture has grown to its present unwieldy and unjustifiably extravagant proportions.

During the last fiscal year the cost of seeds purchased was $66,548.61. The remainder of an appropriation of $135,000 was expended in putting them up and distributing them. It surely never could have entered the minds of those who first sanctioned appropriations of public money for the purchase of new and improved varieties of seeds for gratuitous distribution that from this would grow large appropriations for the purchase and distribution by members of Congress of ordinary seeds, bulbs, and cuttings which are common in all the States and Territories and everywhere easily obtainable at low prices.

In each State and Territory an agricultural experiment station has been established. These stations, by their very character and name, are the proper agencies to experiment with and test new varieties of seeds; and yet this indiscriminate and wasteful distribution by legislation and legislators continues, answering no purpose unless it be to remind constituents that their representatives are willing to remember them with gratuities at public cost.

Under the sanction of existing legislation there was sent out from the Agricultural Department during the last fiscal year enough of cabbage seed to plant 19,200 acres of land, a sufficient quantity of beans to plant 4,000 acres, beet seed enough to plant 2,500 acres, sweet corn enough to plant 7,800 acres, sufficient cucumber seed to cover 2,025 acres with vines, and enough muskmelon and watermelon seeds to plant 2,675 acres. The total quantity of flower and vegetable seeds thus distributed was contained in more than 9,000,000 packages, and they were sufficient if planted to cover 89,596 acres of land.

In view of these facts this enormous expenditure without legitimate returns of benefit ought to be abolished. Anticipating a consummation so manifestly in the interest of good administration, more than $100,000 has been stricken from the estimate made to cover this object for the year ending June 30, 1895; and the Secretary recommends that the remaining $35,000 of the estimate be confined strictly to the purchase of new and improved varieties of seeds, and that these be distributed through experiment stations.

Thus the seed will be tested, and after the test has been completed by the experiment station the propagation of the useful varieties and the rejection of the valueless may safely be left to the common sense of the people.

The continued intelligent execution of the civil-service law and the increasing approval by the people of its operation are most gratifying. The recent extension of its limitations and regulations to the employees at free-delivery post-offices, which has been honestly and promptly accomplished by the Commission, with the hearty cooperation of the Postmaster-General, is an immensely important advance in the usefulness of the system.

I am, if possible, more than ever convinced of the incalculable benefits conferred by the civil-service law, not only in its effect upon the public service, but also, what is even more important, in its effect in elevating the tone of political life generally.

The course of civil-service reform in this country instructively and interestingly illustrates how strong a hold a movement gains upon our people which has underlying it a sentiment of justice and right and which at the same time promises better administration of their Government.

The law embodying this reform found its way to our statute book more from fear of the popular sentiment existing in its favor than from any love for the reform itself on the part of legislators, and it has lived and grown and flourished in spite of the covert as well as open hostility of spoilsmen and notwithstanding the querulous impracticability of many self-constituted guardians. Beneath all the vagaries and sublimated theories which are attracted to it there underlies this reform a sturdy common-sense principle not only suited to this mundane sphere, but whose application our people are more and more recognizing to be absolutely essential to the most successful operation of their Government, if not to its perpetuity.

It seems to me to be entirely inconsistent with the character of this reform, as well as with its best enforcement, to oblige the Commission to rely for clerical assistance upon clerks detailed from other Departments. There ought not to be such a condition in any Department that clerks hired to do work there can be spared to habitually work at another place, and it does not accord with a sensible view of civil-service reform that persons should be employed on the theory that their labor is necessary in one Department when in point of fact their services are devoted to entirely different work in another Department.

I earnestly urge that the clerks necessary to carry on the work of the Commission be regularly put upon its roster and that the system of obliging the Commissioners to rely upon the services of clerks belonging to other Departments be discontinued. This ought not to increase the expense to the Government, while it would certainly be more consistent and add greatly to the efficiency of the Commission.

Economy in public expenditure is a duty that can not innocently be neglected by those intrusted with the control of money drawn from the people for public uses. It must be confessed that our apparently endless resources, the familiarity of our people with immense accumulations of wealth, the growing sentiment among them that the expenditure of public money should in some manner be to their immediate and personal advantage, the indirect and almost stealthy manner in which a large part of our taxes is exacted, and a degenerated sense of official accountability have led to growing extravagance in governmental appropriations.

At this time, when a depleted public Treasury confronts us, when many of our people are engaged in a hard struggle for the necessaries of life, and when enforced economy is pressing upon the great mass of our countrymen, I desire to urge with all the earnestness at my command that Congressional legislation be so limited by strict economy as to exhibit an appreciation of the condition of the Treasury and a sympathy with the straitened circumstances of our fellow-citizens.

The duty of public economy is also of immense importance in its intimate and necessary relation to the task now in hand of providing revenue to meet Government expenditures and yet reducing the people's burden of Federal taxation.

After a hard struggle tariff reform is directly before us. Nothing so important claims our attention and nothing so clearly presents itself as both an opportunity and a duty—an opportunity to deserve the gratitude of our fellow-citizens and a duty imposed upon us by our oft-repeated professions and by the emphatic mandate of the people. After full discussion our countrymen have spoken in favor of this reform, and they have confided the work of its accomplishment to the hands of those who are solemnly pledged to it.

If there is anything in the theory of a representation in public places of the people and their desires, if public officers are really the servants of the people, and if political promises and professions have any binding force, our failure to give the relief so long awaited will be sheer recreancy. Nothing should intervene to distract our attention or disturb our effort until this reform is accomplished by wise and careful legislation.

While we should stanchly adhere to the principle that only the necessity of revenue justifies the imposition of tariff duties and other Federal taxation and that they should be limited by strict economy, we can not close our eyes to the fact that conditions have grown up among us which in justice and fairness call for discriminating care in the distribution of such duties and taxation as the emergencies of our Government actually demand.

Manifestly if we are to aid the people directly through tariff reform, one of its most obvious features should be a reduction in present tariff charges upon the necessaries of life. The benefits of such a reduction would be palpable and substantial, seen and felt by thousands who would be better fed and better clothed and better sheltered. These gifts should be the willing benefactions of a Government whose highest function is the promotion of the welfare of the people.

Not less closely related to our people's prosperity and well-being is the removal of restrictions upon the importation of the raw materials necessary to our manufactures. The world should be open to our national ingenuity and enterprise. This can not be while Federal legislation through the imposition of high tariff forbids to American manufacturers as cheap materials as those used by their competitors. It is quite obvious that the enhancement of the price of our manufactured products resulting from this policy not only confines the market for these products within our own borders, to the direct disadvantage of our manufacturers, but also increases their cost to our citizens.

The interests of labor are certainly, though indirectly, involved in this feature of our tariff system. The sharp competition and active struggle among our manufacturers to supply the limited demand for their goods soon fill the narrow market to which they are confined. Then follows a suspension of work in mills and factories, a discharge of employees, and distress in the homes of our workingmen.

Even if the often-disproved assertion could be made good that a lower rate of wages would result from free raw materials and low tariff duties, the intelligence of our workmen leads them quickly to discover that their steady employment, permitted by free raw materials, is the most important factor in their relation to tariff legislation.

A measure has been prepared by the appropriate Congressional committee embodying tariff reform on the lines herein suggested, which will be promptly submitted for legislative action. It is the result of much patriotic and unselfish work, and I believe it deals with its subject consistently and as thoroughly as existing conditions permit.

I am satisfied that the reduced tariff duties provided for in the proposed legislation, added to existing internal-revenue taxation, will in the near future, though perhaps not immediately, produce sufficient revenue to meet the needs of the Government.

The committee, after full consideration and to provide against a temporary deficiency which may exist before the business of the country adjusts itself to the new tariff schedules, have wisely embraced in their plan a few additional internal-revenue taxes, including a small tax upon incomes derived from certain corporate investments.

These new adjustments are not only absolutely just and easily borne, but they have the further merit of being such as can be remitted without unfavorable business disturbance whenever the necessity of their imposition no longer exists.

In my great desire for the success of this measure I can not restrain the suggestion that its success can only be attained by means of unselfish counsel on the part of the friends of tariff reform and as a result of their willingness to subordinate personal desires and ambitions to the general good. The local interests affected by the proposed reform are so numerous and so varied that if all are insisted upon the legislation embodying the reform must inevitably fail.

In conclusion my intense feeling of responsibility impels me to invoke for the manifold interests of a generous and confiding people the most scrupulous care and to pledge my willing support to every legislative effort for the advancement of the greatness and prosperity of our beloved country.

GROVER CLEVELAND.

SPECIAL MESSAGES.

EXECUTIVE MANSION,
Washington, December 18, 1893.

To the Senate and House of Representatives:

In my recent annual message to the Congress I briefly referred to our relations with Hawaii and expressed the intention of transmitting further information on the subject when additional advices permitted.

Though I am not able now to report a definite change in the actual situation, I am convinced that the difficulties lately created both here and in Hawaii, and now standing in the way of a solution through Executive action of the problem presented, render it proper and expedient that the matter should be referred to the broader authority and discretion of Congress, with a full explanation of the endeavor thus far made to deal with the emergency and a statement of the considerations which have governed my action.

I suppose that right and justice should determine the path to be followed in treating this subject. If national honesty is to be disregarded and a desire for territorial extension or dissatisfaction with a form of government not our own ought to regulate our conduct, I have entirely misapprehended the mission and character of our Government and the behavior which the conscience of our people demands of their public servants.

When the present Administration entered upon its duties, the Senate had under consideration a treaty providing for the annexation of the Hawaiian Islands to the territory of the United States. Surely under our Constitution and laws the enlargement of our limits is a manifestation of the highest attribute of sovereignty, and if entered upon as an Executive act all things relating to the transaction should be clear and free from suspicion. Additional importance attached to this particular treaty of annexation because it contemplated a departure from unbroken American tradition in providing for the addition to our territory of islands of the sea more than 2,000 miles removed from our nearest coast.

These considerations might not of themselves call for interference with the completion of a treaty entered upon by a previous Administration, but it appeared from the documents accompanying the treaty when submitted to the Senate that the ownership of Hawaii was tendered to us by a Provisional Government set up to succeed the constitutional ruler of the islands, who had been dethroned, and it did not appear that such Provisional Government had the sanction of either popular revolution or suffrage. Two other remarkable features of the transaction naturally attracted attention. One was the extraordinary haste, not to say precipitancy, characterizing all the transactions connected with the treaty. It appeared that a so-called committee of safety, ostensibly the source of the revolt against the constitutional Government of Hawaii, was organized on Saturday, the 14th day of January; that on Monday, the 16th, the United States forces were landed at Honolulu from a naval vessel lying in its harbor; that on the 17th the scheme of a Provisional Government was perfected, and a proclamation naming its officers was on the same day prepared and read at the Government building; that immediately thereupon the United States minister recognized the Provisional Government thus created; that two days afterwards, on the 19th day of January, commissioners representing such Government sailed for this country in a steamer especially chartered for the occasion, arriving in San Francisco on the 28th day of January and in Washington on the 3d day of February; that on the next day they had their first interview with the Secretary of State, and another on the 11th, when the treaty of annexation was practically agreed upon, and that on the 14th it was formally concluded and on the 15th transmitted to the Senate. Thus between the initiation of the scheme for a Provisional Government in Hawaii, on the 14th day of January, and the submission to the Senate of the treaty of annexation concluded with such Government the entire interval was thirty-two days, fifteen of which were spent by the Hawaiian commissioners in their journey to Washington.

In the next place, upon the face of the papers submitted with the treaty it clearly appeared that there was open and undetermined an issue of fact of the most vital importance. The message of the President accompanying the treaty* declared that "the overthrow of the monarchy was not in any way promoted by this Government," and in a letter to the President from the Secretary of State, also submitted to the Senate with the treaty, the following passage occurs:

At the time the Provisional Government took possession of the Government buildings no troops or officers of the United States were present or took any part whatever in the proceedings. No public recognition was accorded to the Provisional Government by the United States minister until after the Queen's abdication and when they were in effective possession of the Government buildings, the archives, the treasury, the barracks, the police station, and all the potential machinery of the Government.

But a protest also accompanied said treaty, signed by the Queen and her ministers at the time she made way for the Provisional Government, which explicitly stated that she yielded to the superior force of the United States, whose minister had caused United States troops to be landed at Honolulu and declared that he would support such Provisional Government.

The truth or falsity of this protest was surely of the first importance. If true, nothing but the concealment of its truth could induce our Government to negotiate with the semblance of a government thus created, nor could a treaty resulting from the acts stated in the protest have been knowingly deemed worthy of consideration by the Senate. Yet the truth or falsity of the protest had not been investigated.

I conceived it to be my duty, therefore, to withdraw the treaty from the Senate for examination, and meanwhile to cause an accurate, full, and impartial investigation to be made of the facts attending the subversion of the constitutional Government of Hawaii and the installment in its place of the Provisional Government. I selected for the work of investigation the Hon. James H. Blount, of Georgia, whose service of eighteen years as a member of the House of Representatives and whose experience as chairman of the Committee of Foreign Affairs in that body, and his consequent familiarity with international topics, joined with his high character and honorable reputation, seemed to render him peculiarly fitted for the duties intrusted to him. His report detailing his action under the instructions given to him and the conclusions derived from his investigation accompany this message.

These conclusions do not rest for their acceptance entirely upon Mr. Blount's honesty and ability as a man, nor upon his acumen and

*See pp. 5783–5784.

impartiality as an investigator. They are accompanied by the evidence upon which they are based, which evidence is also herewith transmitted, and from which it seems to me no other deductions could possibly be reached than those arrived at by the commissioner.

The report, with its accompanying proofs and such other evidence as is now before the Congress or is herewith submitted, justifies, in my opinion, the statement that when the President was led to submit the treaty to the Senate with the declaration that "the overthrow of the monarchy was not in any way promoted by this Government," and when the Senate was induced to receive and discuss it on that basis, both President and Senate were misled.

The attempt will not be made in this communication to touch upon all the facts which throw light upon the progress and consummation of this scheme of annexation. A very brief and imperfect reference to the facts and evidence at hand will exhibit its character and the incidents in which it had its birth.

It is unnecessary to set forth the reasons which in January, 1893, led a considerable proportion of American and other foreign merchants and traders residing at Honolulu to favor the annexation of Hawaii to the United States. It is sufficient to note the fact and to observe that the project was one which was zealously promoted by the minister representing the United States in that country. He evidently had an ardent desire that it should become a fact accomplished by his agency and during his ministry, and was not inconveniently scrupulous as to the means employed to that end. On the 19th day of November, 1892, nearly two months before the first overt act tending toward the subversion of the Hawaiian Government and the attempted transfer of Hawaiian territory to the United States, he addressed a long letter to the Secretary of State, in which the case for annexation was elaborately argued on moral, political, and economical grounds. He refers to the loss to the Hawaiian sugar interests from the operation of the McKinley bill and the tendency to still further depreciation of sugar property unless some positive measure of relief is granted. He strongly inveighs against the existing Hawaiian Government and emphatically declares for annexation. He says:

In truth, the monarchy here is an absurd anachronism. It has nothing on which it logically or legitimately stands. The feudal basis on which it once stood no longer existing, the monarchy now is only an impediment to good government—an obstruction to the prosperity and progress of the islands.

He further says:

As a Crown colony of Great Britain or a Territory of the United States the government modifications could be made readily and good administration of the law secured. Destiny and the vast future interests of the United States in the Pacific clearly indicate who at no distant day must be responsible for the government of these islands. Under a Territorial government they could be as easily governed as any of the existing territories of the United States. * * * Hawaii has reached the parting of the ways. She must now take the road which leads to Asia, or the other, which outlets her in America, gives her an American civilization, and binds her to the care of American destiny.

He also declares:

One of two courses seems to me absolutely necessary to be followed—either bold and vigorous measures for annexation or a "customs union," an ocean cable from the Californian coast to Honolulu, Pearl Harbor perpetually ceded to the United States, with an implied but not expressly stipulated American protectorate over the islands. I believe the former to be the better, that which will prove much the more advantageous to the islands and the cheapest and least embarrassing in the end to the United States. If it was wise for the United States, through Secretary Marcy, thirty-eight years ago, to offer to expend $100,000 to secure a treaty of annexation, it certainly can not be chimerical or unwise to expend $100,000 to secure annexation in the near future. To-day the United States has five times the wealth she possessed in 1854, and the reasons now existing for annexation are much stronger than they were then. I can not refrain from expressing the opinion with emphasis that the golden hour is near at hand.

These declarations certainly show a disposition and condition of mind which may be usefully recalled when interpreting the significance of the minister's conceded acts or when considering the probabilities of such conduct on his part as may not be admitted.

In this view it seems proper to also quote from a letter written by the minister to the Secretary of State on the 8th day of March, 1892, nearly a year prior to the first step taken toward annexation. After stating the possibility that the existing Government of Hawaii might be overturned by an orderly and peaceful revolution, Minister Stevens writes as follows:

Ordinarily, in like circumstances, the rule seems to be to limit the landing and movement of United States forces in foreign waters and dominion exclusively to the protection of the United States legation and of the lives and property of American citizens; but as the relations of the United States to Hawaii are exceptional, and in former years the United States officials here took somewhat exceptional action in circumstances of disorder, I desire to know how far the present minister and naval commander may deviate from established international rules and precedents in the contingencies indicated in the first part of this dispatch.

To a minister of this temper, full of zeal for annexation, there seemed to arise in January, 1893, the precise opportunity for which he was watchfully waiting—an opportunity which by timely "deviation from established international rules and precedents" might be improved to successfully accomplish the great object in view; and we are quite prepared for the exultant enthusiasm with which, in a letter to the State Department dated February 1, 1893, he declares:

The Hawaiian pear is now fully ripe, and this is the golden hour for the United States to pluck it.

As a further illustration of the activity of this diplomatic representative, attention is called to the fact that on the day the above letter was written, apparently unable longer to restrain his ardor, he issued a proclamation whereby, "in the name of the United States," he assumed the protection of the Hawaiian Islands and declared that said action was "taken pending and subject to negotiations at Washington." Of course this assumption of a protectorate was promptly disavowed by our Government, but the American flag remained over the Government building at Honolulu and the forces remained on guard until April, and after Mr. Blount's arrival on the scene, when both were removed.

A brief statement of the occurrences that led to the subversion of the constitutional Government of Hawaii in the interests of annexation to the United States will exhibit the true complexion of that transaction.

On Saturday, January 14, 1893, the Queen of Hawaii, who had been contemplating the proclamation of a new constitution, had, in deference to the wishes and remonstrances of her cabinet, renounced the project for the present at least. Taking this relinquished purpose as a basis of action, citizens of Honolulu numbering from fifty to one hundred, mostly resident aliens, met in a private office and selected a so-called committee of safety, composed of thirteen persons, seven of whom were foreign subjects, and consisted of five Americans, one Englishman, and one German. This committee, though its designs were not revealed, had in view nothing less than annexation to the United States, and between Saturday, the 14th, and the following Monday, the 16th of January—though exactly what action was taken may not be clearly disclosed—they were certainly in communication with the United States minister. On Monday morning the Queen and her cabinet made public proclamation, with a notice which was specially served upon the representatives of all foreign governments, that any changes in the constitution would be sought only in the methods provided by that instrument. Nevertheless, at the call and under the auspices of the committee of safety, a mass meeting of citizens was held on that day to protest against the Queen's alleged illegal and unlawful proceedings and purposes. Even at this meeting the committee of safety continued to disguise their real purpose and contented themselves with procuring the passage of a resolution denouncing the Queen and empowering the committee to devise ways and means "to secure the permanent maintenance of law and order and the protection of life, liberty, and property in Hawaii." This meeting adjourned between 3 and 4 o'clock in the afternoon. On the same day, and immediately after such adjournment, the committee, unwilling to take further steps without the cooperation of the United States minister, addressed him a note representing that the public safety was menaced and that lives and property were in danger, and concluded as follows:

We are unable to protect ourselves without aid, and therefore pray for the protec. tion of the United States forces.

Whatever may be thought of the other contents of this note, the absolute truth of this latter statement is incontestable. When the note was written and delivered the committee, so far as it appears, had neither a man nor a gun at their command, and after its delivery they became so panic-stricken at their position that they sent some of their number to interview the minister and request him not to land the United States forces till the next morning. But he replied that the troops had been ordered and whether the committee were ready or not the landing should take place. And so it happened that on the 16th day of January, 1893, between 4 and 5 o'clock in the afternoon, a detachment of marines from the United States steamer *Boston*, with two pieces of artillery, landed at Honolulu. The men, upward of 160 in all, were supplied with double cartridge belts filled with ammunition and with haversacks and canteens, and were accompanied by a hospital corps with stretchers and medical supplies.

This military demonstration upon the soil of Honolulu was of itself an act of war, unless made either with the consent of the Government of Hawaii or for the *bona fide* purpose of protecting the imperiled lives and property of citizens of the United States. But there is no pretense of any such consent on the part of the Government of the Queen, which at that time was undisputed and was both the *de facto* and the *de jure* Government. In point of fact the existing Government, instead of requesting the presence of an armed force, protested against it. There is as little basis for the pretense that such forces were landed for the security of American life and property. If so, they would have been stationed in the vicinity of such property and so as to protect it, instead of at a distance and so as to command the Hawaiian Government building and palace. Admiral Skerrett, the officer in command of our naval force on the Pacific station, has frankly stated that in his opinion the location of the troops was inadvisable if they were landed for the protection of American citizens, whose residences and places of business, as well as the legation and consulate, were in a distant part of the city; but the location selected was a wise one if the forces were landed for the purpose of supporting the Provisional Government. If any peril to life and property calling for any such martial array had existed, Great Britain and other foreign powers interested would not have been behind the United States in activity to protect their citizens. But they made no sign in that direction. When these armed men were landed the city of Honolulu was in its customary orderly and peaceful condition. There was no symptom of riot or disturbance in any quarter. Men, women, and children were about the streets as usual, and nothing varied the ordinary routine or disturbed the ordinary tranquillity except the landing of the *Boston's* marines and their march through the town to the quarters assigned them. Indeed, the fact that after having called for the landing of the United States forces on the plea of danger to life and property the committee of safety themselves requested the minister to postpone action exposed the untruthfulness of their representations of present peril to life and property. The peril they saw was an anticipation growing out of guilty intentions on their part and something which, though not then existing, they knew would certainly follow their attempt to overthrow the Government of the Queen without the aid of the United States forces.

Thus it appears that Hawaii was taken possession of by the United States forces without the consent or wish of the Government of the islands, or of anybody else so far as shown except the United States minister. Therefore the military occupation of Honolulu by the United States on the day mentioned was wholly without justification, either as an occupation by consent or as an occupation necessitated by dangers threatening American life and property. It must be accounted for in some other way and on some other ground, and its real motive and purpose are neither obscure nor far to seek.

The United States forces being now on the scene and favorably stationed, the committee proceeded to carry out their original scheme. They met the next morning, Tuesday, the 17th, perfected the plan of temporary government, and fixed upon its principal officers, ten of whom were drawn from the thirteen members of the committee of safety. Between 1 and 2 o'clock, by squads and by different routes to avoid notice, and having first taken the precaution of ascertaining whether there was anyone there to oppose them, they proceeded to the Government building to proclaim the new Government. No sign of opposition was manifest, and thereupon an American citizen began to read the proclamation from the steps of the Government building, almost entirely without auditors. It is said that before the reading was finished quite a concourse of persons, variously estimated at from 50 to 100, some armed and some unarmed, gathered about the committee to give them aid and confidence. This statement is not important, since the one controlling factor in the whole affair was unquestionably the United States marines, who, drawn up under arms and with artillery in readiness only 76 yards distant, dominated the situation.

The Provisional Government thus proclaimed was by the terms of the proclamation "to exist until terms of union with the United States had been negotiated and agreed upon." The United States minister, pursuant to prior agreement, recognized this Government within an hour after the reading of the proclamation, and before 5 o'clock, in answer to an inquiry on behalf of the Queen and her cabinet, announced that he had done so.

When our minister recognized the Provisional Government, the only basis upon which it rested was the fact that the committee of safety had in the manner above stated declared it to exist. It was neither a government *de facto* nor *de jure*. That it was not in such possession of the Government property and agencies as entitled it to recognition is conclusively proved by a note found in the files of the legation at Honolulu, addressed by the declared head of the Provisional Government to Minister Stevens, dated January 17, 1893, in which he acknowledges with expressions of appreciation the minister's recognition of the Provisional

Government, and states that it is not yet in the possession of the station house (the place where a large number of the Queen's troops were quartered), though the same had been demanded of the Queen's officers in charge. Nevertheless, this wrongful recognition by our minister placed the Government of the Queen in a position of most perilous perplexity. On the one hand she had possession of the palace, of the barracks, and of the police station, and had at her command at least 500 fully armed men and several pieces of artillery. Indeed, the whole military force of her Kingdom was on her side and at her disposal, while the committee of safety, by actual search, had discovered that there were but very few arms in Honolulu that were not in the service of the Government.

In this state of things, if the Queen could have dealt with the insurgents alone, her course would have been plain and the result unmistakable. But the United States had allied itself with her enemies, had recognized them as the true Government of Hawaii, and had put her and her adherents in the position of opposition against lawful authority. She knew that she could not withstand the power of the United States, but she believed that she might safely trust to its justice. Accordingly, some hours after the recognition of the Provisional Government by the United States minister, the palace, the barracks, and the police station, with all the military resources of the country, were delivered up by the Queen upon the representation made to her that her cause would thereafter be reviewed at Washington, and while protesting that she surrendered to the superior force of the United States, whose minister had caused United States troops to be landed at Honolulu and declared that he would support the Provisional Government, and that she yielded her authority to prevent collision of armed forces and loss of life, and only until such time as the United States, upon the facts being presented to it, should undo the action of its representative and reinstate her in the authority she claimed as the constitutional sovereign of the Hawaiian Islands.

This protest was delivered to the chief of the Provisional Government, who indorsed thereon his acknowledgment of its receipt. The terms of the protest were read without dissent by those assuming to constitute the Provisional Government, who were certainly charged with the knowledge that the Queen, instead of finally abandoning her power, had appealed to the justice of the United States for reinstatement in her authority; and yet the Provisional Government, with this unanswered protest in its hand, hastened to negotiate with the United States for the permanent banishment of the Queen from power and for a sale of her Kingdom.

Our country was in danger of occupying the position of having actually set up a temporary government on foreign soil for the purpose of acquiring through that agency territory which we had wrongfully put in its possession. The control of both sides of a bargain acquired in such a manner is called by a familiar and unpleasant name when found in private transactions. We are not without a precedent showing how scrupulously we avoided such accusations in former days. After the people of Texas had declared their independence of Mexico they resolved that on the acknowledgment of their independence by the United States they would seek admission into the Union. Several months after the battle of San Jacinto, by which Texan independence was practically assured and established, President Jackson declined to recognize it, alleging as one of his reasons that in the circumstances it became us ''to beware of a too early movement, as it might subject us, however unjustly, to the imputation of seeking to establish the claim of our neighbors to a territory with a view to its subsequent acquisition by ourselves.'' This is in marked contrast with the hasty recognition of a government openly and concededly set up for the purpose of tendering to us territorial annexation.

I believe that a candid and thorough examination of the facts will force the conviction that the Provisional Government owes its existence to an armed invasion by the United States. Fair-minded people, with the evidence before them, will hardly claim that the Hawaiian Government was overthrown by the people of the islands or that the Provisional Government had ever existed with their consent. I do not understand that any member of this Government claims that the people would uphold it by their suffrages if they were allowed to vote on the question.

While naturally sympathizing with every effort to establish a republican form of government, it has been the settled policy of the United States to concede to people of foreign countries the same freedom and independence in the management of their domestic affairs that we have always claimed for ourselves, and it has been our practice to recognize revolutionary governments as soon as it became apparent that they were supported by the people. For illustration of this rule I need only to refer to the revolution in Brazil in 1889, when our minister was instructed to recognize the Republic ''so soon as a majority of the people of Brazil should have signified their assent to its establishment and maintenance;'' to the revolution in Chile in 1891, when our minister was directed to recognize the new Government ''if it was accepted by the people,'' and to the revolution in Venezuela in 1892, when our recognition was accorded on condition that the new Government was ''fully established, in possession of the power of the nation, and accepted by the people.''

As I apprehend the situation, we are brought face to face with the following conditions:

The lawful Government of Hawaii was overthrown without the drawing of a sword or the firing of a shot by a process every step of which, it may safely be asserted, is directly traceable to and dependent for its success upon the agency of the United States acting through its diplomatic and naval representatives.

But for the notorious predilections of the United States minister for annexation the committee of safety, which should be called the committee of annexation, would never have existed.

But for the landing of the United States forces upon false pretexts respecting the danger to life and property the committee would never have exposed themselves to the pains and penalties of treason by undertaking the subversion of the Queen's Government.

But for the presence of the United States forces in the immediate vicinity and in position to afford all needed protection and support the committee would not have proclaimed the Provisional Government from the steps of the Government building.

And finally, but for the lawless occupation of Honolulu under false pretexts by the United States forces, and but for Minister Stevens's recognition of the Provisional Government when the United States forces were its sole support and constituted its only military strength, the Queen and her Government would never have yielded to the Provisional Government, even for a time and for the sole purpose of submitting her case to the enlightened justice of the United States.

Believing, therefore, that the United States could not, under the circumstances disclosed, annex the islands without justly incurring the imputation of acquiring them by unjustifiable methods, I shall not again submit the treaty of annexation to the Senate for its consideration, and in the instructions to Minister Willis, a copy of which accompanies this message, I have directed him to so inform the Provisional Government.

But in the present instance our duty does not, in my opinion, end with refusing to consummate this questionable transaction. It has been the boast of our Government that it seeks to do justice in all things without regard to the strength or weakness of those with whom it deals. I mistake the American people if they favor the odious doctrine that there is no such thing as international morality; that there is one law for a strong nation and another for a weak one, and that even by indirection a strong power may with impunity despoil a weak one of its territory.

By an act of war, committed with the participation of a diplomatic representative of the United States and without authority of Congress, the Government of a feeble but friendly and confiding people has been overthrown. A substantial wrong has thus been done which a due regard for our national character as well as the rights of the injured people requires we should endeavor to repair. The Provisional Government has not assumed a republican or other constitutional form, but has remained a mere executive council or oligarchy, set up without the assent of the people. It has not sought to find a permanent basis of popular support and has given no evidence of an intention to do so. Indeed, the representatives of that Government assert that the people of Hawaii are unfit for popular government and frankly avow that they can be best ruled by arbitrary or despotic power.

The law of nations is founded upon reason and justice, and the rules of conduct governing individual relations between citizens or subjects of a civilized state are equally applicable as between enlightened nations.

The considerations that international law is without a court for its en-forcement and that obedience to its commands practically depends upon good faith instead of upon the mandate of a superior tribunal only give additional sanction to the law itself and brand any deliberate infraction of it not merely as a wrong, but as a disgrace. A man of true honor protects the unwritten word which binds his conscience more scrupu-lously, if possible, than he does the bond a breach of which subjects him to legal liabilities, and the United States, in aiming to maintain itself as one of the most enlightened nations, would do its citizens gross injustice if it applied to its international relations any other than a high stand-ard of honor and morality. On that ground the United States can not properly be put in the position of countenancing a wrong after its com-mission any more than in that of consenting to it in advance. On that ground it can not allow itself to refuse to redress an injury inflicted through an abuse of power by officers clothed with its authority and wearing its uniform; and on the same ground, if a feeble but friendly state is in danger of being robbed of its independence and its sovereignty by a misuse of the name and power of the United States, the United States can not fail to vindicate its honor and its sense of justice by an earnest effort to make all possible reparation.

These principles apply to the present case with irresistible force when the special conditions of the Queen's surrender of her sovereignty are recalled. She surrendered, not to the Provisional Government, but to the United States. She surrendered, not absolutely and permanently, but temporarily and conditionally until such time as the facts could be considered by the United States. Furthermore, the Provisional Govern-ment acquiesced in her surrender in that manner and on those terms, not only by tacit consent, but through the positive acts of some members of that Government, who urged her peaceable submission, not merely to avoid bloodshed, but because she could place implicit reliance upon the justice of the United States and that the whole subject would be finally considered at Washington.

I have not, however, overlooked an incident of this unfortunate affair which remains to be mentioned. The members of the Provisional Gov-ernment and their supporters, though not entitled to extreme sympathy, have been led to their present predicament of revolt against the Govern-ment of the Queen by the indefensible encouragement and assistance of our diplomatic representative. This fact may entitle them to claim that in our effort to rectify the wrong committed some regard should be had for their safety. This sentiment is strongly seconded by my anxiety to do nothing which would invite either harsh retaliation on the part of the Queen or violence and bloodshed in any quarter. In the belief that the Queen, as well as her enemies, would be willing to adopt such a course as would meet these conditions, and in view of the fact that both the Queen and the Provisional Government had at one time apparently acquiesced in a reference of the entire case to the United States Government, and considering the further fact that in any event the Provisional Government by its own declared limitation was only "to exist until terms of union with the United States of America have been negotiated and agreed upon," I hoped that after the assurance to the members of that Government that such union could not be consummated I might compass a peaceful adjustment of the difficulty.

Actuated by these desires and purposes, and not unmindful of the inherent perplexities of the situation nor of the limitations upon my power, I instructed Minister Willis to advise the Queen and her supporters of my desire to aid in the restoration of the status existing before the lawless landing of the United States forces at Honolulu on the 16th of January last if such restoration could be effected upon terms providing for clemency as well as justice to all parties concerned. The conditions suggested, as the instructions show, contemplate a general amnesty to those concerned in setting up the Provisional Government and a recognition of all its *bona fide* acts and obligations. In short, they require that the past should be buried and that the restored Government should reassume its authority as if its continuity had not been interrupted These conditions have not proved acceptable to the Queen, and though she has been informed that they will be insisted upon and that unless acceded to the efforts of the President to aid in the restoration of her Government will cease, I have not thus far learned that she is willing to yield them her acquiescence. The check which my plans have thus encountered has prevented their presentation to the members of the Provisional Government, while unfortunate public misrepresentations of the situation and exaggerated statements of the sentiments of our people have obviously injured the prospects of successful Executive mediation.

I therefore submit this communication, with its accompanying exhibits, embracing Mr. Blount's report, the evidence and statements taken by him at Honolulu, the instructions given to both Mr. Blount and Minister Willis, and correspondence connected with the affair in hand.

In commending this subject to the extended powers and wide discretion of the Congress I desire to add the assurance that I shall be much gratified to cooperate in any legislative plan which may be devised for the solution of the problem before us which is consistent with American honor, integrity, and morality.

GROVER CLEVELAND.

EXECUTIVE MANSION,
Washington, December 18, 1893.

To the Senate of the United States:

In compliance with a resolution passed by the Senate on the 6th instant, I hereby transmit reports of the Secretaries of State and of the Navy, with copies of all instructions given to the respective diplomatic and naval representatives of the United States in the Hawaiian Islands since the 4th day of March, 1881, touching the matters specified in the resolution.

It has seemed convenient to include in the present communication to the Senate copies of the diplomatic correspondence concerning the political condition of Hawaii, prepared for transmission to the House of Representatives in response to a later resolution passed by that body on the 13th instant.

GROVER CLEVELAND.

EXECUTIVE MANSION,
Washington, December 18, 1893.

To the House of Representatives:

In compliance with a resolution passed by your honorable body on the 13th instant, I hereby transmit a report of the Secretary of State, with copies of the instructions given to Mr. Albert S. Willis, the representative of the United States now in the Hawaiian Islands, and also the correspondence since the 4th day of March, 1889, concerning the relations of this Government to those islands.

In making this communication I have withheld only a dispatch from the former minister to Hawaii, numbered 70, under date of October 8, 1892, and a dispatch from the present minister, numbered 3, under date of November 16, 1893, because in my opinion the publication of these two papers would be incompatible with the public interest.

GROVER CLEVELAND.

EXECUTIVE MANSION, *January 4, 1894.*

To the Senate of the United States:

I transmit herewith a report of the Secretary of State, submitted in compliance with the resolution of October 17 last, in the matter of the claim of certain persons against the Government of Spain for illegal arrest off the coast of Yucatan in the year 1850, and subsequent imprisonment.

GROVER CLEVELAND.

EXECUTIVE MANSION, *January 13, 1894.*

To the Congress:

I transmit herewith copies of all dispatches from our minister at Hawaii relating in any way to political affairs in that country, except such as have been heretofore laid before the Congress.

I also transmit a copy of the last instructions sent to our minister, dated January 12, 1894, being the only instructions to him not already sent to the Congress.

In transmitting certain correspondence with my message dated December 18, 1893, I withheld a dispatch from our present minister, numbered 3

and dated November 16, 1893, and also a dispatch from our former minister, numbered 70 and dated October 8, 1892. Inasmuch as the contents
of the dispatch of November 16, 1893, are referred to in the dispatches of
a more recent date, now sent to Congress, and inasmuch as there seems
no longer to be sufficient reason for withholding said dispatch, a copy of
the same is herewith submitted. The dispatch numbered 70 and dated
October 8, 1892, above referred to, is still withheld for the reason that
such a course still appears to be justifiable and proper.

                                          GROVER CLEVELAND.

To the Congress: EXECUTIVE MANSION, *January 20, 1894.*

I transmit herewith dispatches received yesterday from our minister
at Hawaii, with certain correspondence which accompanied the same,
including a most extraordinary letter, dated December 27, 1893, signed
by Sanford B. Dole, minister of foreign affairs of the Provisional Government, addressed to our minister, Mr. Willis, and delivered to him a number of hours after the arrival at Honolulu of a copy of my message to
Congress on the Hawaiian question, with copies of instructions given
to our minister.   GROVER CLEVELAND.

To the Congress: EXECUTIVE MANSION, *January 22, 1894.*

I transmit herewith copies of dispatches received from our minister to
Hawaii after the arrival of those copies which accompanied my message
of the 20th instant. I also inclose, for the information of Congress,
copies of reports and a copy of an order just received by the Secretary
of the Navy from Rear-Admiral Irwin, commanding our naval forces at
Honolulu.   GROVER CLEVELAND.

To the Congress: EXECUTIVE MANSION, *February 2, 1894.*

I transmit a communication from the Secretary of State, accompanying
a dispatch received a few days ago from our minister at Hawaii.

                                          GROVER CLEVELAND.

                            EXECUTIVE MANSION,
                        Washington, February 12, 1894.
To the Congress:

I transmit herewith two dispatches received a few days ago from our
minister at Hawaii, and a reply to one of them from the Secretary of
State, in which a correct version is given of an interview which occurred
November 14, 1893, between the Secretary of State and Mr. Thurston,
representing the Provisional Government at Washington.

                                          GROVER CLEVELAND.

EXECUTIVE MANSION, *February 16, 1894.*

To the Senate and House of Representatives:

I transmit herewith, for the information of Congress, a communication from the Secretary of State, covering the report of the Director of the Bureau of the American Republics for the year 1893.

GROVER CLEVELAND.

EXECUTIVE MANSION, *February 19, 1894.*

To the House of Representatives:

I herewith transmit copies of certain dispatches recently received from our minister at Honolulu.

GROVER CLEVELAND.

To the Senate: EXECUTIVE MANSION, *February 19, 1894.*

On the evening of the 16th instant I received a copy of a resolution passed by the Senate, requesting the transmission to that body of all reports and dispatches from our minister at Hawaii, and especially a certain letter written to him by Mr. Dole, President of the Provisional Government.

On the same day I received from the State Department a copy of a dispatch from Minister Willis, accompanied by various exhibits. I was not able to send them to the Senate on that day. The Senate adjourned that afternoon until to-day, and thus prevented the submission until now of these papers.

The next day after the receipt of the Senate resolution, and on the 17th instant, other dispatches were received from Mr. Willis at the State Department. They were copied with all possible haste, and are now submitted at the first meeting of the Senate since their receipt. They include the letter mentioned in the Senate resolution and the answer of Minister Willis to the same.

Since the 18th day of December last, when I submitted to the "broader authority and discretion of the Congress" all matters connected with our relations with Hawaii, I have with the utmost promptness transmitted to the Congress all dispatches and reports relative to the subject, and I am not aware of any dispatches or documents in the remotest way connected with these relations which have come to the possession of the State Department or the Executive and been withheld from the Senate.

GROVER CLEVELAND.

EXECUTIVE MANSION,
Washington, March 7, 1894.

To the Senate of the United States:

I transmit herewith a report submitted by the Secretary of State in response to the resolution of the Senate dated January 23, 1894, requesting communication of correspondence exchanged between the Government of the United States and the Governments of Colombia, Venezuela, and Hayti.

GROVER CLEVELAND.

To the Congress:		Executive Mansion, *March 7, 1894.*

I transmit herewith copies of certain dispatches lately received from our minister at Hawaii, together with copies of the inclosures which accompanied such dispatches.

GROVER CLEVELAND.

Executive Mansion, *March 8, 1894.*

To the Senate of the United States:

I transmit herewith a report furnished by the Secretary of State in response to a resolution of the Senate of the 1st instant, making inquiry respecting the present condition of the *Virginius* indemnity fund.

GROVER CLEVELAND.

Executive Mansion,
Washington, D. C., March 14, 1894.

To the Senate:

I herewith transmit a report* of the Secretary of State of the 14th instant, concerning the several inquiries in the resolution of the Senate addressed to him under date of the 9th instant.

GROVER CLEVELAND.

Executive Mansion,
Washington, March 19, 1894.

To the Senate:

I transmit herewith, with a view to its ratification, a convention concluded at this capital on the 17th instant between the United States and China concerning the subject of emigration between those two countries.

GROVER CLEVELAND.

Executive Mansion,
Washington, March 19, 1894.

To the Senate:

I transmit herewith a report from the Secretary of State, concerning the landing of British troops at Bluefields, Nicaragua, in answer to the resolution of the Senate of the 7th instant on that subject.

GROVER CLEVELAND.

* Relating to the coined silver money and the products of India, Russia, and the Argentine Republic.

EXECUTIVE MANSION, *March 19, 1894.*
To the Congress:

I transmit herewith a copy of a dispatch received from our minister at Hawaii, together with copies of the inclosures which accompanied said dispatch.

GROVER CLEVELAND.

EXECUTIVE MANSION,
Washington, April 3, 1894.
To the Senate:

I transmit herewith report from the Secretary of State, inclosing the final report of the agent of the United States before the Paris Tribunal, also the protocols thus far received and certain other papers relating to that arbitration.

GROVER CLEVELAND.

EXECUTIVE MANSION,
Washington, April 13, 1894.
To the Congress:

I transmit herewith copies of certain dispatches from the United States minister at Honolulu, received by the Secretary of State since my message of March 19, 1894.

GROVER CLEVELAND.

EXECUTIVE MANSION,
Washington, April 21, 1894.
To the Congress:

I transmit herewith a communication from the Secretary of State, covering a dispatch from the United States minister at Honolulu and reply thereto.

GROVER CLEVELAND.

EXECUTIVE MANSION,
Washington, D. C., May 1, 1894.
To the Senate and House of Representatives:

I transmit herewith the ninth annual report of the Commissioner of Labor. This report relates entirely to building and loan associations in the United States.

GROVER CLEVELAND.

EXECUTIVE MANSION,
Washington, May 9, 1894.
To the Senate of the United States:

I transmit herewith, in response to the resolution of the Senate of April 6, 1894, a report of the Secretary of State, containing the requested information as to the present condition of affairs in the Samoan Islands, with copies of the correspondence in relation thereto, including that with the Governments of Great Britain and Germany.

GROVER CLEVELAND.

EXECUTIVE MANSION,
Washington, May 9, 1894.

To the Congress:

I transmit herewith a communication from the Secretary of State, in regard to recent dispatches from the United States minister at Honolulu, received since my message of April 21, 1894, and also a dispatch from the minister dated April 14, 1894.

GROVER CLEVELAND.

EXECUTIVE MANSION,
Washington, May 29, 1894.

To the Congress:

I herewith transmit, having regard to my message of May 9, 1894, a communication from the Secretary of State, covering a dispatch from the United States minister at Honolulu.

GROVER CLEVELAND.

EXECUTIVE MANSION,
Washington, June 20, 1894.

To the Senate:

I transmit herewith, in response to the resolution of the Senate of December 20, 1893, a report from the Acting Secretary of State, covering the desired copies of correspondence in the matter of the claim of Antonio Maximo Mora against Spain.

GROVER CLEVELAND.

EXECUTIVE MANSION,
Washington, June 23, 1894.

To the Congress:

I herewith transmit a communication covering dispatches from the United States minister at Honolulu.

GROVER CLEVELAND.

EXECUTIVE MANSION, *June 25, 1894.*

To the Senate and House of Representatives:

The shocking intelligence has been received that the President of the French Republic met his death yesterday at the hands of an assassin. This terrible event which has overtaken a sister Republic can not fail to deeply arouse the sympathies of the American nation, while the violent termination of a career promising so much in aid of liberty and advancing civilization should be mourned as an affliction to mankind.

GROVER CLEVELAND.

EXECUTIVE MANSION, *June 29, 1894.*

To the Senate of the United States:

Answering a resolution of your honorable body dated the 13th instant, I transmit herewith a report* of the Secretary of State, with an

---

* Relating to the probable retaliatory action of foreign governments for the proposed imposition by the United States of a duty on sugar.

accompanying document, which contain all the information in my possession touching the matters embraced in said resolution.

GROVER CLEVELAND.

EXECUTIVE MANSION,
Washington, July 9, 1894.

To the Senate:

I transmit herewith, in further response to the Senate resolution of April 6, 1894, a report from the Secretary of State, accompanied by copies of certain correspondence relating to Samoan affairs.

GROVER CLEVELAND.

EXECUTIVE MANSION, *July 19, 1894.*

To the Senate of the United States:

In compliance with a resolution of the Senate of the 18th instant, the House of Representatives concurring, I return herewith the bill (S. 1105) entitled ''An act for the relief of Albert Redstone.''

GROVER CLEVELAND.

EXECUTIVE MANSION,
Washington, July 24, 1894.

To the Congress:

I herewith transmit a communication from the Secretary of State, covering a dispatch from the United States minister at Honolulu.

GROVER CLEVELAND.

EXECUTIVE MANSION,
Washington, D. C., July 27, 1894.

To the Senate and House of Representatives:

I transmit herewith the seventh special report of the Commissioner of Labor. This report relates to what is generally known as the slums of cities, and has been prepared in accordance with a joint resolution approved July 20, 1892.

GROVER CLEVELAND.

EXECUTIVE MANSION,
Washington, July 30, 1894.

To the Congress:

I herewith transmit a communication from the Secretary of State, covering two dispatches from the United States minister at Honolulu.

GROVER CLEVELAND.

VETO MESSAGES.

EXECUTIVE MANSION, *January 17, 1894.*

To the House of Representatives:

I return without my approval House bill No. 71, entitled "An act for the relief of purchasers of timber and stone lands under the act of June 3, 1878."

This bill permits the proofs and affidavits which under present statutes parties desiring to acquire certain public lands are required to make before the registers and receivers of the land offices within which such lands are located to be made before any commissioner of the United States circuit court or before the judge or clerk of any court of records of the county or parish in which the lands are situated.

A similar bill was passed by the Fifty-second Congress and was disapproved by the Commissioner of the General Land Office and the Secretary of the Interior. The successors of these officers oppose the present bill on the ground that in its operation it would open the door to fraud and to a perversion of the intentions of the Government in relation to the public lands.

It is difficult, with the most scrupulous care, to guard the alienation of our public lands from fraud and illegal practices. It is perfectly plain, however, that the prospect of accomplishing this result is better under present laws, which require the necessary proofs to be made before land officers who are appointed for that purpose and who are under the control of the General Land Office and amenable to its regulations, than it would be by substituting other officers over whom the Land Office has no control.

Certain rules and orders of the Land Office are now in force which regulate the taking of the necessary proofs and permit oral examinations by registers and receivers. These regulations are of the utmost importance if our land laws are to be justly and honestly administered.

I fully concur in the objections made to this bill by the officers having charge of the public lands in the last Administration and by their successors who are now charged with that responsibility. I am convinced that such a relaxation of our existing land laws as is contemplated by the bill under consideration would not be in the interest of good administration.

GROVER CLEVELAND.

EXECUTIVE MANSION, *January 20, 1894.*

To the House of Representatives:

I hereby return without my approval House bill No. 3289, entitled "An act to authorize the New York and New Jersey Bridge Companies to construct and maintain a bridge across the Hudson River between New York City and the State of New Jersey.''

This bill authorizes the construction of a bridge over the North River between the States of New York and New Jersey, the terminus of which in the city of New York shall not be below Sixty-sixth street. It contemplates the construction of a bridge upon piers placed in the river. No mention is made of a single span crossing the entire river, nor is there anything in the bill indicating that it was within the intention of the Congress that there should be a bridge built without piers. I am by no means certain that the Secretary of War, who is invested by the terms of the bill with considerable discretion so far as the plans for the structure are concerned, would have the right to exact of the promoters of this enterprise the erection of a bridge spanning the entire river.

Much objection has been made to the location of any piers in the river for the reason that they would seriously interfere with the commerce which seeks the port of New York through that channel. It is certainly very questionable whether piers should be permitted at all in the North River at the point designated for the location of this bridge. It seems absolutely certain that within a few years a great volume of shipping will extend to that location, which would be seriously embarrassed by such obstruction.

I appreciate fully the importance of securing some means by which railroad traffic can cross this river, and no one can fail to realize the serious inconvenience to travel caused by lack of facilities of that character. At the same time, it is a plain dictate of wisdom and expediency that the commerce of the river be not unnecessarily interfered with by bridges or in any other manner.

Engineers whose judgment upon the matter can not be questioned, including the engineer of the company proposing to build this bridge, have expressed the opinion that the entire river can be spanned safely and effectively by a suspension bridge, or a construction not needing the use of piers.

The company to which the permission to bridge the river is granted in the bill under consideration was created by virtue of an act of the legislature of the State of New York which became a law, by reason of the failure of the governor to either approve or veto the same, on the 30th day of April, 1890. It may be safely assumed that the members of the legislature which passed this law knew what was necessary for the protection of the commerce of the city of New York and had informed themselves concerning the plan of a bridge that should be built in view of all the interests concerned.

By paragraph 24 of the law creating this company it is provided that ''the said bridge shall be constructed with a single span over the entire river between towers or piers located between the span and the existing pier-head lines in either State,'' and that ''no pier or tower or other obstruction of a permanent character shall be placed or built in the river between said towers or piers under this act.''

In view of such professional judgment, and considering the interests which would be interfered with by the location of piers in the river, and having due regard to the judgment of the legislature of the State of New York, it seems to me that a plan necessitating the use of piers in the bed of the river should be avoided. The question of increased expense of construction or the compromise of conflicting interests should not outweigh the other important considerations involved.

I notice the bill provides that the companies availing themselves of its privileges shall receive no greater pay for transporting the mails across the bridge than is allowed per mile to railroads using the same. If this is intended, as the language seems to import, to authorize this bridge company to charge the United States Government a toll for the carriage of its mails across the bridge equal to the amount which may be paid per mile by the Government for carrying the mails by railroads crossing the bridge, it seems to me it should not be allowed. The expense to the Government for carrying the mails over the structure should beyond any doubt be limited to the compensation paid the railroads for transportation.

An exceedingly important objection to the bill remains to be considered. In 1890 the North River Bridge Company was incorporated by an act of Congress for the purpose of constructing a bridge across the North River, the New York terminus of which was located at or near Twenty-third street in the city of New York. The proposition to construct the bridge at that point was a subject very carefully and thoroughly examined at that time and during the agitation of the project for a number of years prior to the passage of the act. As a result of such examination and much discussion, Congress granted permission to this company to construct a bridge having a single span and suspended from towers on each side of the river, and in the act especially prohibited the placing of any piers in the river, either of a temporary or of a permanent character, in connection with said bridge. This plan to bridge the river without piers was at that time considered feasible by the engineers of the company, and it accepted the terms of the act. Before this permission was finally granted a number of bills were introduced in the Congress covering the same subject, which were referred to Government engineers. Reports were made by these officers in every case insisting upon a construction with a single span and without piers in the bed of the river.

The eighth subdivision of the bill herewith returned provides that any company heretofore created for the purpose of bridging the river may avail itself of the provisions of the act, and makes such company subject to all its provisions. This, of course, has reference to the North River Bridge Company and releases that company from the prohibition of the act under which it was permitted to span the river and permits it to construct piers in the river. It seems to me that the language of the bill under consideration, so far as it relates to this particular feature, is equivalent to a new grant to that company, differing very materially from the grant which was thought expedient at the time it was before the Congress, and removes the guaranty that in the construction of its bridge there shall be no obstructions in the river such as were especially guarded against by the bill originally passed for its benefit. In effect a new charter is granted to a company not named in the bill, and with no apparent reason for the important enlargement of its privileges thus accomplished. It is entirely apparent that the reasons against obstructions in the North River which might interfere with commerce and navigation and the beneficial use of the harbor of New York are immensely strengthened when they are applied to a location in the river far below the location of the bridge which is permitted in the bill now before me.

Whatever question there may be about the injurious character of the obstruction at Sixty-sixth street in New York City, I believe there can be no doubt whatever that piers placed in the river more than 2 miles below, at Twenty-third street, would be very serious impediments. If this thoroughfare, so important to the commerce of the country and the State of New York, is to be crossed by bridges, each scheme for that purpose should be considered by itself and its merits and advisability determined by the circumstances which naturally belong to it. The objection to piers in the river for the purpose of supporting bridges is in any event so serious that the considerations which would determine the question of a bridge located at Sixty-sixth street ought not in such an indirect manner as is done by this bill be applied to a like structure at Twenty-third street.

GROVER CLEVELAND.

EXECUTIVE MANSION, *March 29, 1894.*

To the House of Representatives:

I return without my approval House bill No. 4956, entitled "An act directing the coinage of the silver bullion held in the Treasury, and for other purposes."

My strong desire to avoid disagreement with those in both Houses of Congress who have supported this bill would lead me to approve it if I could believe that the public good would not be thereby endangered and that such action on my part would be a proper discharge of official duty. Inasmuch, however, as I am unable to satisfy myself that the proposed legislation is either wise or opportune, my conception of the obligations and responsibilities attached to the great office I hold forbids the indulgence of my personal desire and inexorably confines me to that course which is dictated by my reason and judgment and pointed out by a sincere purpose to protect and promote the general interests of our people.

The financial disturbance which swept over the country during the last year was unparalleled in its severity and disastrous consequences. There seemed to be almost an entire displacement of faith in our financial ability and a loss of confidence in our fiscal policy. Among those who attempted to assign causes for our distress it was very generally conceded that the operation of a provision of law then in force which required the Government to purchase monthly a large amount of silver bullion and issue its notes in payment therefor was either entirely or to a large extent responsible for our condition. This led to the repeal on the 1st day of November, 1893, of this statutory provision.

We had, however, fallen so low in the depths of depression and timidity and apprehension had so completely gained control in financial circles that our rapid recuperation could not be reasonably expected. Our recovery has, nevertheless, steadily progressed, and though less than five months have elapsed since the repeal of the mischievous silver-purchase requirement a wholesome improvement is unmistakably apparent. Confidence in our absolute solvency is to such an extent reinstated and faith in our disposition to adhere to sound financial methods is so far restored as to produce the most encouraging results both at home and abroad. The wheels of domestic industry have been slowly set in motion and the tide of foreign investment has again started in our direction.

Our recovery being so well under way, nothing should be done to check our convalescence; nor should we forget that a relapse at this time would almost surely reduce us to a lower stage of financial distress than that from which we are just emerging.

I believe that if the bill under consideration should become a law it would be regarded as a retrogression from the financial intentions indicated by our recent repeal of the provision forcing silver-bullion purchases; that it would weaken, if it did not destroy, returning faith and confidence in our sound financial tendencies, and that as a consequence our progress to renewed business health would be unfortunately checked and a return to our recent distressing plight seriously threatened.

This proposed legislation is so related to the currency conditions growing out of the law compelling the purchase of silver by the Government that a glance at such conditions and a partial review of the law referred to may not be unprofitable.

Between the 14th day of August, 1890, when the law became operative, and the 1st day of November, 1893, when the clause it contained directing the purchase of silver was repealed, there were purchased by the Secretary of the Treasury more than 168,000,000 ounces of silver bullion. In payment for this bullion the Government issued its Treasury notes, of various denominations, amounting to nearly $156,000,000, which notes were immediately added to the currency in circulation among our people. Such notes were by the law made legal tender in payment of all debts, public and private, except when otherwise expressly stipulated, and were made receivable for customs, taxes, and all public dues, and when so received might be reissued. They were also permitted to be held by banking associations as a part of their lawful reserves.

On the demand of the holders these Treasury notes were to be redeemed in gold or silver coin, in the discretion of the Secretary of the Treasury; but it was declared as a part of this redemption provision that it was "the established policy of the United States to maintain the two metals on a parity with each other upon the present legal ratio or such ratio as may be provided by law." The money coined from such bullion was to be standard silver dollars, and after directing the immediate coinage of a little less than 28,000,000 ounces the law provided that as much of the remaining bullion should be thereafter coined as might be necessary to provide for the redemption of the Treasury notes issued on its purchase, and that "any gain or seigniorage arising from such coinage shall be accounted for and paid into the Treasury."

This gain or seigniorage evidently indicates so much of the bullion owned by the Government as should remain after using a sufficient amount to coin as many standard silver dollars as should equal in number the dollars represented by the Treasury notes issued in payment of the entire quantity of bullion. These Treasury notes now outstanding and in circulation amount to $152,951,280, and although there has been thus far but a comparatively small amount of this bullion coined, yet the so-called gain or seigniorage, as above defined, which would arise from the coinage of the entire mass has been easily ascertained to be a quantity of bullion sufficient to make when coined 55,156,681 standard silver dollars.

Considering the present intrinsic relation between gold and silver, the maintenance of the parity between the two metals, as mentioned in this law, can mean nothing less than the maintenance of such a parity in the estimation and confidence of the people who use our money in their daily transactions. Manifestly the maintenance of this parity can only be accomplished, so far as it is affected by these Treasury notes and in the estimation of the holders of the same, by giving to such holders on their redemption the coin, whether it is gold or silver, which they prefer. It follows that while in terms the law leaves the choice of coin to be paid on such redemption to the discretion of the Secretary of the Treasury, the exercise of this discretion, if opposed to the demands of the holder, is entirely inconsistent with the effective and beneficial maintenance of the parity between the two metals.

If both gold and silver are to serve us as money and if they together are to supply to our people a safe and stable currency, the necessity of preserving this parity is obvious. Such necessity has been repeatedly conceded in the platforms of both political parties and in our Federal statutes. It is nowhere more emphatically recognized than in the recent law which repealed the provision under which the bullion now on hand was purchased. This law insists upon the "maintenance of the parity in value of the coins of the two metals and the equal power of every dollar at all times in the markets and in the payment of debts."

The Secretary of the Treasury has therefore, for the best of reasons, not only promptly complied with every demand for the redemption of these Treasury notes in gold, but the present situation as well as the letter and spirit of the law appear plainly to justify, if they do not enjoin upon him, a continuation of such redemption.

The conditions I have endeavored to present may be thus summarized:

First. The Government has purchased and now has on hand sufficient silver bullion to permit the coinage of all the silver dollars necessary to redeem in such dollars the Treasury notes issued for the purchase of said silver bullion, and enough besides to coin, as gain or seigniorage, 55,156,681 additional standard silver dollars.

Second. There are outstanding and now in circulation Treasury notes issued in payment of the bullion purchased amounting to $152,951,280. These notes are legal tender in payment of all debts, public and private, except when otherwise expressly stipulated; they are receivable for customs, taxes, and all public dues; when held by banking associations they may be counted as part of their lawful reserves, and they are redeemed by the Government in gold at the option of the holders. These advantageous attributes were deliberately attached to these notes at the time of their issue. They are fully understood by our people to whom such notes have been distributed as currency, and have inspired confidence in their safety and value, and have undoubtedly thus induced their continued and contented use as money, instead of anxiety for their redemption.

Having referred to some incidents which I deem relevant to the subject, it remains for me to submit a specific statement of my objections to the bill now under consideration.

This bill consists of two sections, excluding one which merely appropriates a sum sufficient to carry the act into effect. The first section provides for the immediate coinage of the silver bullion in the Treasury which represents the so-called gain or seigniorage, or which would arise from the coinage of all the bullion on hand, which gain or seigniorage this section declares to be $55,156,681. It directs that the money so coined or the certificates issued thereon shall be used in the payment of public expenditures, and provides that if the needs of the Treasury demand it the Secretary of the Treasury may, in his discretion, issue silver certificates in excess of such coinage, not exceeding the amount of seigniorage in said section authorized to be coined.

The second section directs that as soon as possible after the coinage of this seigniorage the remainder of the bullion held by the Government shall be coined into legal-tender standard silver dollars, and that they shall be held in the Treasury for the redemption of the Treasury notes issued in the purchase of said bullion. It provides that as fast as the bullion shall be coined for the redemption of said notes they shall not be reissued, but shall be canceled and destroyed in amounts equal to the coin held at any time in the Treasury derived from the coinage provided for, and that silver certificates shall be issued on such coin in the manner now provided by law. It is, however, especially declared in said section that the act shall not be construed to change existing laws relating to the legal-tender character or mode of redemption of the Treasury notes issued for the purchase of the silver bullion to be coined.

The entire bill is most unfortunately constructed. Nearly every sentence presents uncertainty and invites controversy as to its meaning and intent. The first section is especially faulty in this respect, and it is extremely doubtful whether its language will permit the consummation of its supposed purposes. I am led to believe that the promoters of the bill intended in this section to provide for the coinage of the bullion constituting the gain or seigniorage, as it is called, into standard silver dollars, and yet there is positively nothing in the section to prevent its coinage into any description of silver coins now authorized under any existing law.

I suppose this section was also intended, in case the needs of the Treasury called for money faster than the seigniorage bullion could actually be coined, to permit the issue of silver certificates in advance of such coinage; but its language would seem to permit the issuance of such certificates to double the amount of seigniorage as stated, one-half of which would not represent an ounce of silver in the Treasury. The debate upon this section in the Congress developed an earnest and positive difference of opinion as to its object and meaning. In any event, I am clear that the present perplexities and embarrassments of the Secretary of the Treasury ought not to be augmented by devolving upon him the execution of a law so uncertain and confused.

I am not willing, however, to rest my objection to this section solely on these grounds. In my judgment sound finance does not commend a further infusion of silver into our currency at this time unaccompanied by further adequate provision for the maintenance in our Treasury of a safe gold reserve.

Doubts also arise as to the meaning and construction of the second section of the bill. If the silver dollars therein directed to be coined are, as the section provides, to be held in the Treasury for the redemption of Treasury notes, it is suggested that, strictly speaking, certificates can not be issued on such coin "in the manner now provided by law," because these dollars are money held in the Treasury for the express purpose of redeeming Treasury notes on demand, which would ordinarily mean that they were set apart for the purpose of substituting them for these Treasury notes. They are not, therefore, held in such a way as to furnish a basis for certificates according to any provision of existing law.

If however, silver certificates can properly be issued upon these dollars, there is nothing in the section to indicate the characteristics and functions of these certificates. If they were to be of the same character as silver certificates in circulation under existing laws, they would at best be receivable only for customs, taxes, and all public dues; and under the language of this section it is, to say the least, extremely doubtful whether the certificates it contemplates would be lawfully received even for such purposes.

Whatever else may be said of the uncertainties of expression in this bill, they certainly ought not to be found in legislation affecting subjects so important and far-reaching as our finances and currency. In stating other and more important reasons for my disapproval of this section I shall, however, assume that under its provisions the Treasury notes issued in payment for silver bullion will continue to be redeemed as heretofore, in silver or gold, at the option of the holders, and that if when they are presented for redemption or reach the Treasury in any other manner there are in the Treasury coined silver dollars equal in nominal value to such Treasury notes, then and in that case the notes will be destroyed and silver certificates to an equal amount be substituted.

I am convinced that this scheme is ill advised and dangerous. As an ultimate result of its operation Treasury notes, which are legal tender for all debts, public and private, and which are redeemable in gold or silver at the option of the holder, will be replaced by silver certificates, which, whatever may be their character and description, will have none of these qualities. In anticipation of this result and as an immediate effect the Treasury notes will naturally appreciate in value and desirability. The fact that gold can be realized upon them and the further fact that their destruction has been decreed when they reach the Treasury must tend to their withdrawal from general circulation to be immediately presented for gold redemption or to be hoarded for presentation at a more convenient season. The sequel of both operations will be a large addition to the silver currency in our circulation and a corresponding reduction of gold in the Treasury. The argument has been made that these things will not occur at once, because a long time must elapse before the coinage of anything but the seigniorage can be entered upon. If the physical effects of the execution of the second section of this bill are not to be realized until far in the future, this may furnish a strong reason why it should not be passed so much in advance; but the postponement of its actual operation can not prevent the fear and loss of confidence and nervous precaution which would immediately follow its passage and bring about its worst consequences. I regard this section of the bill as embodying a plan by which the Government will be obliged to pay out its scanty store of gold for no other purpose than to force an unnatural addition of silver money into the hands of our people. This is an exact reversal of the policy which safe finance dictates if we are to preserve parity between gold and silver and maintain sensible bimetallism.

We have now outstanding more than $338,000,000 in silver certificates issued under existing laws. They are serving the purpose of money usefully and without question. Our gold reserve, amounting to only a little more than $100,000,000, is directly charged with the redemption of $346,000,000 of United States notes. When it is proposed to inflate our silver currency it is a time for strengthening our gold reserve instead of depleting it. I can not conceive of a longer step toward silver monometallism than we take when we spend our gold to buy silver certificates for circulation, especially in view of the practical difficulties surrounding the replenishment of our gold.

This leads me to earnestly present the desirability of granting to the Secretary of the Treasury a better power than now exists to issue bonds to protect our gold reserve when for any reason it should be necessary. Our currency is in such a confused condition and our financial affairs are apt to assume at any time so critical a position that it seems to me such a course is dictated by ordinary prudence.

I am not insensible to the arguments in favor of coining the bullion seigniorage now in the Treasury, and I believe it could be done safely and with advantage if the Secretary of the Treasury had the power to issue bonds at a low rate of interest under authority in substitution of that now existing and better suited to the protection of the Treasury.

I hope a way will present itself in the near future for the adjustment of our monetary affairs in such a comprehensive and conservative manner as will accord to silver its proper place in our currency; but in the meantime I am extremely solicitous that whatever action we take on this subject may be such as to prevent loss and discouragement to our people at home and the destruction of confidence in our financial management abroad.

GROVER CLEVELAND.

EXECUTIVE MANSION, *August 7, 1894.*
To the House of Representatives:

I herewith return without approval House bill No. 2637, entitled "An act for the relief of Eugene Wells, late captain, Twelfth Infantry, and second lieutenant, First Artillery, United States Army."

This bill authorizes the President to nominate and, by and with the advice and consent of the Senate, to appoint the beneficiary therein named a second lieutenant of artillery in the Army of the United States, and it directs that when so appointed he shall be placed upon the retired list on account of disability, thus dispensing with the usual examination and finding by a retiring board and all other ordinary prerequisites of retirement.

Appointments to the Army under the authority of special legislation which names the proposed appointee, and the purpose of which is the immediate retirement of the appointee, are open to serious objections,

though I confess I have been persuaded through sympathy and sentiment on a number of occasions to approve such legislation. When,
however, it is proposed to make the retirement compulsory and without
reference to age or previous examination, a most objectionable feature is
introduced.

The cases covered by the special enactments referred to are usually
such as should, if worthy of any consideration, be provided for under
general or private pension laws, leaving the retired list of the Army to
serve the legitimate purpose for which it was established.

A recent discussion in the House of Representatives upon a bill similar
to the one now before me drew from a member of the House Committee
on Military Affairs the declaration that hundreds of such bills were before
that committee and that there were fifty precedents for the passage of
the particular one then under discussion.

It seems to me that this condition suggests such an encroachment
upon the retired list of the Army as should lead to the virtual abandonment of the legislation referred to.

In addition to the objections to such legislation based upon sound
policy and good administration, there are facts connected with the case
covered by the bill now before me which, in my judgment, forbid its
favorable consideration.

The beneficiary named in this bill entered the military service as first
lieutenant in 1861. In September or October, 1870, then being a captain, a charge of conduct unbecoming an officer and a gentleman was
preferred against him with a view to his trial on said charge before a
court-martial.

The Articles of War provide that any officer convicted of this offense
shall be dismissed the service.

The first specification under this charge alleged that Captain Wells
did violently and without just cause or provocation assault First Lieutenant P. H. Breslin "by furiously striking and hitting him (Lieutenant
Breslin) upon the head with a hickory stick, the butt end of a billiard
cue, and did continue the assault (upon Lieutenant Breslin) until forced
to desist therefrom by First Lieutenant Carl Veitenhimer, Fourth United
States Infantry, thereby endangering the life of Lieutenant Breslin and
disgracing himself (Captain Wells) as an officer of the United States
Army."

The second specification alleged that Captain Wells "did become so
much under the influence of intoxicating liquor as to behave himself in
a scandalous manner by violently attacking the person of First Lieutenant P. H. Breslin, Fourth United States Infantry."

These offenses were charged to have been committed on the 3d day of
September, 1870, at Fort Fetterman, in Wyoming Territory.

On the 15th day of July, 1870, a law was passed, among other things,
to bring about a reduction of the Army, which law provided that the

President should before the 1st day of July, 1871, reduce the number of enlisted men in the Army to 30,000, and authorized him in his discretion to honorably discharge from the service of the United States officers of the Army who might apply therefor on or before January 1, 1871.

Before the trial by court-martial upon the charge then pending against him Captain Wells applied for his discharge under the provision of the law above recited, whereupon the charge against him was withdrawn and canceled, and on the 27th day of October, 1870, his application for a discharge was granted.

On the 6th day of July, 1875, he was again appointed to the Army as second lieutenant in the artillery, against which a remonstrance was made by certain officers in the Army.

In August, 1877, Second Lieutenant Wells was charged with being "drunk on duty, in violation of the thirty-eighth article of war."

He was also charged with "conduct to the prejudice of good order and military discipline."

The first specification under the latter charge alleged that the accused did "engage in an affray with First Lieutenant E. Van A. Andruss, First Artillery." The second specification under said charge alleged that the accused addressed his superior officer in a defiant and disrespectful manner and neglected and hesitated to promptly obey the order of said superior officer.

All these offenses were alleged to have been committed at Reading, Pa., on the d day of August, 1877.

Soon after these charges were preferred a court-martial was convened for the trial of the accused thereon. He pleaded not guilty to the charges and specifications, but was convicted of them all and sentenced "to be dismissed the service of the United States."

On the 6th day of October the proceedings, findings, and sentence of the court-martial were approved by the President, who ordered the sentence to be executed; and on the 13th day of October, 1877, in pursuance thereof, Lieutenant Eugene Wells was dismissed from the service.

Since that time repeated efforts have been made to vacate this judgment and restore the dismissed officer to the service. While a number of committees in Congress have made reports favorable to such action, at least two committees have recommended a denial of legislative relief. Both of these reports were made on behalf of House Committees on Military Affairs by distinguished soldiers, who, after patient examination and with an inclination to be not only just but generous to a fellow-soldier, were constrained to recommend a refusal of the application for restoration. One of these reports was made to the Forty-seventh and the other to the Forty-ninth Congress.

I am impressed with the belief that legislation of the kind proposed is of extremely doubtful expediency in any save very exceptional cases, and I am thoroughly convinced by the facts now before me that the discipline and efficiency of our Army, as well as justice to its meritorious members, do not permit my approval on any ground of the bill herewith returned.

GROVER CLEVELAND.

To the Senate:

EXECUTIVE MANSION, *August 11, 1894.*

I hereby return without my approval Senate bill No. 1438, entitled "An act for the relief of Louis A. Yorke."

In the year 1886 the beneficiary named in this bill was a passed assistant paymaster in the Navy. In December of that year he appeared before a naval examining board convened pursuant to law for the purpose of passing upon his fitness to be promoted to the grade of paymaster.

The investigation of the board was conducted fairly and thoroughly. Much of the evidence relating to the candidate's moral fitness for promotion was documentary, and the examination touching his professional competency was of the usual character in such cases.

Considerable evidence was before the board showing quite a large amount of personal indebtedness owing by the candidate, and it appeared that in a few instances his accounts with the Navy Department had not been promptly settled. It was also shown that he had not at all times deposited the Government money intrusted to his care in the places required by law and the regulations of the Navy. In connection with his personal indebtedness incidents and circumstances were brought to light which certainly indicated that he entertained very lax ideas of honest dealing and fairness and which developed a disregard of the obligations and requirements of his position as an officer in the Navy. He was given abundant opportunity to meet and explain every damaging allegation and every adverse inference arising from the evidence, and his claim, not without foundation it appeared, that the charges against him were instigated by malice was doubtless given full weight.

The examining board on the evidence made the following decisions and findings:

The written examination of the candidate shows that he is deficient in his knowledge of the duties appertaining to the next higher grade; and the record evidence puts in question his moral fitness, and he has failed to establish both his professional and moral qualifications for promotion to the satisfaction of the board.

Therefore we hereby certify that Passed Assistant Paymaster Louis A. Yorke, United States Navy, has the mental fitness to perform efficiently all the duties, both at sea and on shore, of the next higher grade, but he has not the professional and moral qualifications required, and we do not recommend him for promotion.

After the board had thus disposed of the case and had adjourned it was, at the request of the candidate, reconvened by order of the Secretary of the Navy, who issued for its guidance the following directions, among others:

The board will inform Passed Assistant Paymaster Yorke of its findings and of the evidence upon which it finds him to be not morally qualified for promotion, and will

GOING INTO ACTION AT SAN JUAN

GOING INTO ACTION AT SAN JUAN

From June 24th to June 30th, 1898, the army rested on the trail leading from Siboney to Santiago, having its most advanced outpost at El Paso, one and a half miles from San Juan Hill. On June 30th the advance began and on July 1st, at dawn, the artillery commenced shelling El Caney and San Juan Hill. General Sumner's command of seven thousand men was to capture San Juan. General Chaffee, with five thousand, was to capture El Caney.

The troops in the photograph are the Seventy-first New York Volunteers, part of General Sumner's command, fording the river just before they reach the line of battle at the edge of the woods. Later in the day so many wounded crawled hither to drink that this ford received the appellation "Bloody Bend." When the photograph was made the men were under fire, shrapnel and Mauser bullets making the place exceedingly uncomfortable.

The index article, "Santiago (Cuba), Battle of," in the encyclopedic index (volume eleven), gives a detailed description of the operations of the day, both at San Juan Hill and El Caney. The article, "Spanish-American War," narrates the causes, events and consequences of the brief struggle in Cuba.

afford him a further hearing and an opportunity to present such evidence as he may desire as to his moral fitness for promotion.

The board met pursuant to such order on the 4th day of January, 1887, when the findings of the board were read to the candidate for promotion, and also the evidence upon which said findings were based, and he was informed that the board would accord him a further hearing as to his moral fitness for promotion and would afford him a reasonable time in which to submit his case. Thereupon he requested the board to allow him until the 26th day of January to produce the necessary witnesses in his behalf. This request was granted, but on the day appointed, upon his representation that he was then unable to submit his defense, he was upon his request allowed another day for that purpose.

In availing himself of the opportunity thus afforded him to present evidence in defense or explanation of the matters charged against him he examined no witnesses and contented himself with presenting his own statement, containing little more than a reiteration of statements he had already made before the board at previous hearings, supplemented by slight documentary evidence which established no new facts in his favor.

The board thereupon reviewed all the evidence and proofs which had been submitted during the entire examination, and after full consideration decided that there was nothing in the additional evidence produced to warrant a modification of the original finding, and the board therefore again certified and decided that the candidate had not the moral qualifications to perform efficiently the duties of the grade to which he sought promotion.

The Secretary of the Navy transmitted the record, proceedings, and findings of said examining board to the President, with a recommendation that the same be approved and that the candidate be discharged from the Navy with one year's pay, pursuant to a statute passed on the 5th day of August, 1882, directing a discharge from the service in such cases.

Thereupon, and on the 19th day of February, 1887, the record, proceedings, and findings of said board were approved by the President, and Passed Assistant Paymaster Yorke was ordered discharged from the naval service with one year's pay.

The bill now under consideration provides that the action of the examining board above recited "be set aside and declared null and void." It also authorizes the President "to appoint the beneficiary to the office to which he would have been promoted but for said action and to retire him in that grade as of the date he was wholly retired."

The authority attempted by the bill to be given to the President to thus make an appointment to the office of paymaster in the Navy without the interposition of the Senate appears to be inadmissible under that clause of the Constitution which only permits the President to appoint certain officers "by and with the advice and consent of the Senate."

The bill provides for the immediate retirement of the beneficiary. He is now but 47 years old, thus lacking fifteen years of the time when he would be entitled to retirement on account of age. There is no suggestion that he is physically incapacitated. On the contrary, when he was examined for promotion a medical board certified that he was physically qualified to perform all his duties at sea, and the candidate himself not only certified to the same thing, but further declared that he was "free from all bodily ailments." If this condition continues and if he should be restored to the Navy at all, he should be sent to duty on the active list instead of being retired. On the facts as presented he would seem to be out of place among those who, though still compensated by the Government, have been on account of age, long and honorable service, or disabilities incurred in the discharge of duty relieved from further activity.

A careful investigation of the facts submitted to the examining board and a consideration of all the statements made on behalf of the beneficiary named in the bill utterly fail, in my opinion, to justify the impeachment of the findings and determination of the board.

I have no doubt malicious feeling growing out of domestic difficulties entered into the affair and gave impetus to the search after inculpating evidence, but facts were nevertheless established beyond any reasonable doubt which abundantly uphold these findings.

I feel obliged to disapprove the bill herewith returned because I believe the power to appoint a paymaster in the Navy ought not, under the Constitution, be conferred upon the President alone; because if the beneficiary were restored to the Navy there would be no justice or propriety in placing him upon the retired list, and because upon the merits of the case I am of the opinion the judgment of the examining board ought not to be reversed.

GROVER CLEVELAND.

PROCLAMATIONS.

BY THE PRESIDENT OF THE UNITED STATES OF AMERICA.

A PROCLAMATION.

Whereas an act of Congress entitled "An act to give effect to the award rendered by the Tribunal of Arbitration at Paris under the treaty between the United States and Great Britain concluded at Washington February 29, 1892, for the purpose of submitting to arbitration certain questions concerning the preservation of the fur seals," was approved April 6, 1894, and reads as follows:

Whereas the following articles of the award of the Tribunal of Arbitration constituted under the treaty concluded at Washington the 29th of February, 1892, between the United States of America and Her Majesty the Queen of the United Kingdom of

Great Britain and Ireland were delivered to the agents of the respective Governments on the 15th day of August, 1893:

"ARTICLE 1. The Governments of the United States and Great Britain shall forbid their citizens and subjects, respectively, to kill, capture, or pursue at any time and in any manner whatever the animals commonly called fur seals within a zone of 60 miles around the Pribilof Islands, inclusive of the territorial waters.

"The miles mentioned in the preceding paragraph are geographical miles, of 60 to a degree of latitude.

"ART. 2. The two Governments shall forbid their citizens and subjects, respectively, to kill, capture, or pursue in any manner whatever during the season extending each year from the 1st of May to the 31st of July, both inclusive, the fur seals on the high sea in the part of the Pacific Ocean, inclusive of the Bering Sea, which is situated to the north of the thirty-fifth degree of north latitude and eastward of the one hundred and eightieth degree of longitude from Greenwich till it strikes the water boundary described in Article I of the treaty of 1867 between the United States and Russia, and following that line up to Bering Strait.

"ART. 3. During the period of time and in the waters in which the fur-seal fishing is allowed only sailing vessels shall be permitted to carry on or take part in fur-seal fishing operations. They will, however, be at liberty to avail themselves of the use of such canoes or undecked boats, propelled by paddles, oars, or sails, as are in common use as fishing boats.

"ART. 4. Each sailing vessel authorized to fish for fur seals must be provided with a special license issued for that purpose by its Government, and shall be required to carry a distinguishing flag to be prescribed by its Government.

"ART. 5. The masters of the vessels engaged in fur-seal fishing shall enter accurately in their official log book the date and place of each fur-seal fishing operation, and also the number and sex of the seals captured upon each day. These entries shall be communicated by each of the two Governments to the other at the end of each fishing season.

"ART. 6. The use of nets, firearms, and explosives shall be forbidden in the fur-seal fishing. This restriction shall not apply to shotguns when such fishing takes place outside of Bering Sea during the season when it may be lawfully carried on.

"ART. 7. The two Governments shall take measures to control the fitness of the men authorized to engage in fur-seal fishing. These men shall have been proved fit to handle with sufficient skill the weapons by means of which this fishing may be carried on.

"ART. 8. The regulations contained in the preceding articles shall not apply to Indians dwelling on the coast of the territory of the United States or of Great Britain and carrying on fur-seal fishing in canoes or undecked boats not transported by or used in connection with other vessels, and propelled wholly by paddles, oars, or sails and manned by not more than five persons each in the way hitherto practiced by the Indians, provided such Indians are not in the employment of other persons, and provided that when so hunting in canoes or undecked boats they shall not hunt fur seals outside of territorial waters under contract for the delivery of the skins to any person.

"This exemption shall not be construed to affect the municipal law of either country, nor shall it extend to the waters of Bering Sea or the waters of the Aleutian passes.

"Nothing herein contained is intended to interfere with the employment of Indians as hunters or otherwise in connection with fur-sealing vessels as heretofore.

"ART. 9. The concurrent regulations hereby determined with a view to the protection and preservation of the fur seals shall remain in force until they have been in whole or in part abolished or modified by common agreement between the Governments of the United States and of Great Britain.

"The said concurrent regulations shall be submitted every five years to a new examination, so as to enable both interested Governments to consider whether, in the light of past experience, there is occasion for any modification thereof.''

Now, therefore, be it enacted by the Senate and House of Representatives of the United States of America in Congress assembled, That no citizen of the United States or person owing the duty of obedience to the laws or the treaties of the United States, nor any person belonging to or on board of a vessel of the United States, shall kill, capture, or pursue at any time or in any manner whatever outside of territorial waters any fur seal in the waters surrounding the Pribilof Islands within a zone of 60 geographical miles (60 to a degree of latitude) around said islands, exclusive of the territorial waters.

SEC. 2. That no citizen of the United States or person above described in section 1 of this act, nor any person belonging to or on board of a vessel of the United States, shall kill, capture, or pursue in any manner whatever during the season extending from the 1st day of May to the 31st day of July, both inclusive, in each year any fur seal on the high seas outside of the zone mentioned in section 1, and in that part of the Pacific Ocean, including Bering Sea, which is situated to the north of the thirty-fifth degree of north latitude and to the east of the one hundred and eightieth degree of longitude from Greenwich till it strikes the water boundary described in Article I of the treaty of 1867 between the United States and Russia, and following that line up to Bering Strait.

SEC. 3. No citizen of the United States or person above described in the first section of this act shall during the period and in the waters in which by section 2 of this act the killing of fur seals is not prohibited use or employ any vessel, nor shall any vessel of the United States be used or employed, in carrying on or taking part in fur-seal fishing operations, other than a sailing vessel propelled by sails exclusively and such canoes or undecked boats propelled by paddles, oars, or sails as may belong to and be used in connection with such sailing vessels; nor shall any sailing vessel carry on or take part in such operations without a special license obtained from the Government for that purpose and without carrying a distinctive flag prescribed by the Government for the same purpose.

SEC. 4. That every master of a vessel licensed under this act to engage in fur-seal fishing operations shall accurately enter in his official log book the date and place of every such operation, and also the number and sex of the seals captured each day; and on coming into port and before landing cargo the master shall verify on oath such official log book as containing a full and true statement of the number and character of his fur-seal fishing operations, including the number and sex of seals captured; and for any false statement willfully made by a person so licensed by the United States in this behalf he shall be subject to the penalties of perjury, and any seal skins found in excess of the statement in the official log book shall be forfeited to the United States.

SEC. 5. That no person or vessel engaging in fur-seal fishing operations under this act shall use or employ in such operations any net, firearm, air gun, or explosive: *Provided, however,* That this prohibition shall not apply to the use of shotguns in such operations outside of Bering Sea during the season when the killing of fur seals is not there prohibited by this act.

SEC. 6. That the foregoing sections of this act shall not apply to Indians dwelling on the coast of the United States and taking fur seals in canoes or undecked boats propelled wholly by paddles, oars, or sails, and not transported by or used in connection with other vessels or manned by more than five persons, in the manner heretofore practiced by the said Indians: *Provided, however,* That the exception made in this section shall not apply to Indians in the employment of other persons, or who shall kill, capture, or pursue fur seals outside of territorial waters under contract to deliver the skins to other persons, nor to the waters of Bering Sea or of the passes between the Aleutian Islands.

SEC. 7. That the President shall have power to make regulations respecting the special license and the distinctive flag mentioned in this act, and regulations otherwise suitable to secure the due execution of the provisions of this act, and from time to time to add to, modify, amend, or revoke such regulations as in his judgment may seem expedient.

SEC. 8. That, except in the case of a master making a false statement under oath in violation of the provisions of the fourth section of this act, every person guilty of a violation of the provisions of this act or of the regulations made thereunder shall for each offense be fined not less than $200 or imprisoned not more than six months, or both; and all vessels, their tackle, apparel, furniture, and cargo at any time used or employed in violation of this act or of the regulations made thereunder shall be forfeited to the United States.

SEC. 9. That any violation of this act or the regulations made thereunder may be prosecuted either in the district court of Alaska or in any district court of the United States in California, Oregon, or Washington.

SEC. 10. That if any unlicensed vessel of the United States shall be found within the waters to which this act applies, and at a time when the killing of fur seals is by this act there prohibited, having on board seal skins or bodies of seals or apparatus or implements suitable for killing or taking seals, or if any licensed vessel shall be found in the waters to which this act applies having on board apparatus or implements suitable for taking seals, but forbidden then and there to be used, it shall be presumed that the vessel in the one case and the apparatus or implements in the other was or were used in violation of this act until it is otherwise sufficiently proved.

SEC. 11. That it shall be the duty of the President to cause a sufficient naval force to cruise in the waters to which this act is applicable to enforce its provisions; and it shall be the duty of the commanding officer of any vessel belonging to the naval or revenue service of the United States, when so instructed by the President, to seize and arrest all vessels of the United States found by him to be engaged, used, or employed in the waters last aforesaid in violation of any of the prohibitions of this act or of any regulations made thereunder, and to take the same, with all persons on board thereof, to the most convenient port in any district of the United States mentioned in this act, there to be dealt with according to law.

SEC. 12. That any vessel or citizen of the United States or person described in the first section of this act offending against the prohibitions of this act or the regulations thereunder may be seized and detained by the naval or other duly commissioned officers of Her Majesty the Queen of Great Britain, but when so seized and detained they shall be delivered as soon as practicable, with any witnesses and proofs on board, to any naval or revenue officer or other authorities of the United States, whose courts alone shall have jurisdiction to try the offense and impose the penalties for the same: *Provided, however,* That British officers shall arrest and detain vessels and persons as in this section specified only after, by appropriate legislation, Great Britain shall have authorized officers of the United States duly commissioned and instructed by the President to that end to arrest, detain, and deliver to the authorities of Great Britain vessels and subjects of that Government offending against any statutes or regulations of Great Britain enacted or made to enforce the award of the treaty mentioned in the title of this act.

Now, therefore, be it known that I, Grover Cleveland, President of the United States of America, have caused the said act specially to be proclaimed, to the end that its provisions may be known and observed; and I hereby proclaim that every person guilty of a violation of the provisions of said act will be arrested and punished as therein provided, and all vessels so employed, their tackle, apparel, furniture, and cargo, will be seized and forfeited.

In testimony whereof I have hereunto set my hand and caused the seal of the United States to be affixed.

[SEAL.]   Done at the city of Washington, this 9th day of April, A. D. 1894, and of the Independence of the United States the one hundred and eighteenth.

GROVER CLEVELAND.

By the President:

    W. Q. GRESHAM,
        Secretary of State.

BY THE PRESIDENT OF THE UNITED STATES OF AMERICA.

A PROCLAMATION.

Whereas satisfactory proof has been given to me that no light-house and light dues, tonnage dues, beacon and buoy dues, or other equivalent taxes of any kind are imposed upon vessels of the United States in the ports of the island of Grenada, one of the British West India Islands:

Now, therefore, I, Grover Cleveland, President of the United States of America, by virtue of the authority vested in me by section 11 of the act of Congress entitled "An act to abolish certain fees for official services to American vessels and to amend the laws relating to shipping commissioners, seamen, and owners of vessels, and for other purposes," approved June 19, 1886, and in virtue of the further act amendatory thereof, entitled "An act to amend the laws relating to navigation, and for other purposes," approved April 4, 1888, do hereby declare and proclaim that from and after the date of this my proclamation shall be suspended the collection of the whole of the tonnage duty which is imposed by said section 11 of the act approved June 19, 1886, upon vessels entered in the ports of the United States from any of the ports of the island of Grenada.

Provided, That there shall be excluded from the benefits of the suspension hereby declared and proclaimed the vessels of any foreign country in whose ports the fees or dues of any kind or nature imposed on vessels of the United States or the import or export duties on their cargoes are in excess of the fees, dues, or duties imposed on the vessels of such country or on the cargoes of such vessels; but this proviso shall not be held to be inconsistent with the special regulation by foreign countries of duties and other charges on their own vessels and the cargoes thereof engaged in their coasting trade, or with the existence between such countries and other states of reciprocal stipulations founded on special conditions and equivalents, and thus not within the treatment of American vessels under the most-favored-nation clause in treaties between the United States and such countries.

And the suspension hereby declared and proclaimed shall continue so long as the reciprocal exemption of vessels belonging to citizens of the United States and their cargoes shall be continued in the said ports of the island of Grenada, and no longer.

In witness whereof I have hereunto set my hand and caused the seal of the United States to be affixed.

[SEAL.] Done at the city of Washington, this 2d day of May, A. D. 1894, and of the Independence of the United States the one hundred and eighteenth.

GROVER CLEVELAND.

By the President:
W. Q. GRESHAM,
Secretary of State.

BY THE PRESIDENT OF THE UNITED STATES OF AMERICA.

A PROCLAMATION.

Whereas, by reason of unlawful obstructions, combinations, and assemblages of persons, it has become impracticable, in the judgment of the President, to enforce by the ordinary course of judicial proceedings the laws of the United States within the State of Illinois, and especially in the city of Chicago within said State; and

Whereas, for the purpose of enforcing the faithful execution of the laws of the United States and protecting its property and removing obstructions to the United States mails in the State and city aforesaid, the President has employed a part of the military forces of the United States:

Now, therefore, I, Grover Cleveland, President of the United States, do hereby admonish all good citizens and all persons who may be or may come within the city and State aforesaid against aiding, countenancing, encouraging, or taking any part in such unlawful obstructions, combinations, and assemblages; and I hereby warn all persons engaged in or in any way connected with such unlawful obstructions, combinations, and assemblages to disperse and retire peaceably to their respective abodes on or before 12 o'clock noon on the 9th day of July instant.

Those who disregard this warning and persist in taking part with a riotous mob in forcibly resisting and obstructing the execution of the laws of the United States or interfering with the functions of the Government or destroying or attempting to destroy the property belonging to the United States or under its protection can not be regarded otherwise than as public enemies.

Troops employed against such a riotous mob will act with all the moderation and forbearance consistent with the accomplishment of the desired end, but the stern necessities that confront them will not with certainty permit discrimination between guilty participants and those who are mingled with them from curiosity and without criminal intent. The only safe course, therefore, for those not actually unlawfully participating is to abide at their homes, or at least not to be found in the neighborhood of riotous assemblages.

While there will be no hesitation or vacillation in the decisive treatment of the guilty, this warning is especially intended to protect and save the innocent.

In testimony whereof I have hereunto set my hand and caused the seal of the United States to be hereto affixed.

[SEAL.]   Done at the city of Washington, this 8th day of July, A. D. 1894, and of the Independence of the United States the one hundred and nineteenth.

GROVER CLEVELAND.

By the President:

W. Q. GRESHAM,
        Secretary of State.

A PROCLAMATION.

Whereas, by reason of unlawful obstructions, combinations, and assemblages of persons, it has become impracticable, in the judgment of the President, to enforce by the ordinary course of judicial proceedings the laws of the United States at certain points and places within the States of North Dakota, Montana, Idaho, Washington, Wyoming, Colorado, and California and the Territories of Utah and New Mexico, and especially along the lines of such railways traversing said States and Territories as are military roads and post routes and are engaged in interstate commerce and in carrying United States mails; and

Whereas, for the purpose of enforcing the faithful execution of the laws of the United States and protecting property belonging to the United States or under its protection, and of preventing obstructions of the United States mails and of commerce between the States and Territories, and of securing to the United States the right guaranteed by law to the use of such roads for postal, military, naval, and other Government service, the President has employed a part of the military forces of the United States:

Now, therefore, I, Grover Cleveland, President of the United States, do hereby command all persons engaged in or in any way connected with such unlawful obstructions, combinations, and assemblages to disperse and retire peaceably to their respective abodes on or before 3 o'clock in the afternoon on the 10th day of July instant.

In witness whereof I have hereunto set my hand and caused the seal of the United States to be hereto affixed.

[SEAL.] Done at the city of Washington, this 9th day of **July, A. D.** 1894, and of the Independence of the United States the one hundred and nineteenth.

GROVER CLEVELAND.

By the President:

W. Q. GRESHAM,
Secretary of State.

BY THE PRESIDENT OF THE UNITED STATES OF AMERICA.

A PROCLAMATION.

Whereas an act of Congress entitled "An act to adopt regulations for preventing collisions at sea" was approved August 19, 1890, the said act being in the following words:

Be it enacted by the Senate and House of Representatives of the United States of America in Congress assembled, That the following regulations for preventing collisions at sea shall be followed by all public and private vessels of the United States upon the high seas and in all waters connected therewith navigable by seagoing vessels :

PRELIMINARY.

In the following rules every steam vessel which is under sail and not under steam is to be considered a sailing vessel, and every vessel under steam, whether under sail or not, is to be considered a steam vessel.

The words "steam vessel" shall include any vessel propelled by machinery.

A vessel is "under way" within the meaning of these rules when she is not at anchor or made fast to the shore or aground.

RULES CONCERNING LIGHTS, ETC.

The word "visible" in these rules when applied to lights shall mean visible on a dark night with a clear atmosphere.

ARTICLE 1. The rules concerning lights shall be complied with in all weathers from sunset to sunrise, and during such time no other lights which may be mistaken for the prescribed lights shall be exhibited.

ART. 2. A steam vessel when under way shall carry—

(*a*) On or in front of the foremast, or if a vessel without a foremast, then in the fore part of the vessel, at a height above the hull of not less than 20 feet, and if the breadth of the vessel exceeds 20 feet, then at a height above the hull not less than such breadth, so, however, that the light need not be carried at a greater height above the hull than 40 feet a bright white light so constructed as to show an unbroken light over an arc of the horizon of 20 points of the compass, so fixed as to throw the light 10 points on each side of the vessel—namely, from right ahead to 2 points abaft the beam on either side—and of such a character as to be visible at a distance of at least 5 miles.

(*b*) On the starboard side a green light so constructed as to show an unbroken light over an arc of the horizon of 10 points of the compass, so fixed as to throw the light from right ahead to 2 points abaft the beam on the starboard side, and of such a character as to be visible at a distance of at least 2 miles.

(*c*) On the port side a red light so constructed as to show an unbroken light over an arc of the horizon of 10 points of the compass, so fixed as to throw the light from right ahead to 2 points abaft the beam on the port side, and of such a character as to be visible at a distance of at least 2 miles.

(*d*) The said green and red side lights shall be fitted with inboard screens projecting at least 3 feet forward from the light, so as to prevent these lights from being seen across the bow.

(*e*) A steam vessel when under way may carry an additional white light similar in construction to the light mentioned in subdivision (*a*). These two lights shall be so placed in line with the keel that one shall be at least 15 feet higher than the other and in such a position with reference to each other that the lower light shall be forward of the upper one. The vertical distance between these lights shall be less than the horizontal distance.

ART. 3. A steam vessel when towing another vessel shall, in addition to her side lights, carry two bright white lights in a vertical line one over the other, not less than 6 feet apart, and when towing more than one vessel shall carry an additional bright white light 6 feet above or below such light if the length of the tow measuring from the stern of the towing vessel to the stern of the last vessel towed exceeds 600 feet. Each of these lights shall be of the same construction and character and shall be carried in the same position as the white light mentioned in article 2 (*a*), excepting the additional light, which may be carried at a height of not less than 14 feet above the hull.

Such steam vessel may carry a small white light abaft the funnel or aftermast for the vessel towed to steer by, but such light shall not be visible forward of the beam.

ART. 4. (*a*) A vessel which from any accident is not under command shall carry at the same height as a white light mentioned in article 2 (*a*), where they can best be seen, and if a steam vessel in lieu of that light, two red lights in a vertical line one over the other, not less than 6 feet apart, and of such a character as to be visible all around the horizon at a distance of at least 2 miles; and shall by day carry in a vertical line one over the other, not less than 6 feet apart, where they can best be seen, two black balls or shapes each 2 feet in diameter.

(*b*) A vessel employed in laying or in picking up a telegraph cable shall carry in the same position as the white light mentioned in article 2 (*a*), and if a steam vessel in lieu of that light, three lights in a vertical line one over the other, not less than 6 feet apart. The highest and lowest of these lights shall be red and the middle light shall be white, and they shall be of such a character as to be visible all around the horizon at a distance of at least 2 miles. By day she shall carry in a vertical line one over the other, not less than 6 feet apart, where they can best be seen, three shapes not less than 2 feet in diameter, of which the highest and lowest shall be globular in shape and red in color and the middle one diamond in shape and white.

(*c*) The vessels referred to in this article, when not making way through the water, shall not carry the side lights, but when making way shall carry them.

(*d*) The lights and shapes required to be shown by this article are to be taken by other vessels as signals that the vessel showing them is not under command and can not, therefore, get out of the way.

These signals are not signals of vessels in distress and requiring assistance. Such signals are contained in article 31.

ART. 5. A sailing vessel under way and any vessel being towed shall carry the same lights as are prescribed by article 2 for a steam vessel under way, with the exception of the white lights mentioned therein, which they shall never carry.

ART. 6. Whenever, as in the case of small vessels under way during bad weather, the green and red side lights can not be fixed, these lights shall be kept at hand, lighted and ready for use, and shall on the approach of or to other vessels be exhibited on their respective sides, in sufficient time to prevent collision, in such manner as to make them most visible and so that the green light shall not be seen on the port side nor the red light on the starboard side, nor, if practicable, more than 2 points abaft the beam on their respective sides.

To make the use of these portable lights more certain and easy the lanterns containing them shall each be painted outside with the color of the light they respectively contain and shall be provided with proper screens.

ART. 7. Steam vessels of less than 40 and vessels under oars or sails of less than 20 tons gross tonnage, respectively, when under way shall not be obliged to carry the lights mentioned in article 2 (*a*), (*b*), and (*c*), but if they do not carry them they shall be provided with the following lights:

First. Steam vessels of less than 40 tons shall carry—

(*a*) In the fore part of the vessel or on or in front of the funnel, where it can best be seen, and at a height above the gunwale of not less than 9 feet, a bright white light constructed and fixed as prescribed in article 2 (*a*) and of such a character as to be visible at a distance of at least 2 miles.

(*b*) Green and red side lights constructed and fixed as prescribed in article 2 (*b*) and (*c*) and of such a character as to be visible at a distance of at least 1 mile, or a combined lantern showing a green light and a red light from right ahead to 2 points abaft the beam on their respective sides. Such lanterns shall be carried not less than 3 feet below the white light.

Second. Small steamboats, such as are carried by seagoing vessels, may carry the white light at a less height than 9 feet above the gunwale, but it shall be carried above the combined lantern mentioned in subdivision 1 (*b*).

Third. Vessels under oars or sails of less than 20 tons shall have ready at hand a lantern with a green glass on one side and a red glass on the other, which on the approach of or to other vessels shall be exhibited, in sufficient time to prevent collision, so that the green light shall not be seen on the port side nor the red light on the starboard side.

The vessels referred to in this article shall not be obliged to carry the lights prescribed by article 4 (*a*) and article 11, last paragraph.

ART. 8. Pilot vessels when engaged on their station on pilotage duty shall not show the lights required for other vessels, but shall carry a white light at the masthead, visible all around the horizon, and shall also exhibit a flare-up light or flare-up lights at short intervals, which shall never exceed fifteen minutes.

On the near approach of or to other vessels they shall have their side lights lighted, ready for use, and shall flash or show them at short intervals to indicate the direction in which they are heading; but the green light shall not be shown on the port side nor the red light on the starboard side.

A pilot vessel of such a class as to be obliged to go alongside of a vessel to put a pilot on board may show the white light instead of carrying it at the masthead, and may, instead of the colored lights above mentioned, have at hand, ready for use, a lantern with a green glass on the one side and a red glass on the other, to be used as prescribed above.

Pilot vessels when not engaged on their station on pilotage duty shall carry lights similar to those of other vessels of their tonnage.

ART. 9. Fishing vessels and fishing boats when under way and when not required by this article to carry or show the lights therein named shall carry or show the lights prescribed for vessels of their tonnage under way.

(*a*) Vessels and boats when fishing with drift nets shall exhibit two white lights from any part of the vessel where they can best be seen. Such lights shall be placed so that the vertical distance between them shall be not less than 6 feet and not more than 10 feet, and so that the horizontal distance between them measured in a line with the keel shall be not less than 5 feet and not more than 10 feet. The lower of these two lights shall be the more forward, and both of them shall be of such a character as to show all around the horizon and to be visible at a distance of not less than 3 miles.

(*b*) Vessels when engaged in trawling, by which is meant the dragging of an apparatus along the bottom of the sea—

First. If steam vessels, shall carry in the same position as the white light mentioned in article 2 (*a*) a tricolored lantern so constructed and fixed as to show a white light from right ahead to 2 points on each bow and a green light and a red light over an arc of the horizon from 2 points on either bow to 2 points abaft the beam on the starboard and port sides, respectively, and not less than 6 nor more than 12 feet below the tricolored lantern, a white light in a lantern so constructed as to show a clear, uniform, and unbroken light all around the horizon.

Second. If sailing vessels of 7 tons gross tonnage and upward, shall carry a white light in a lantern so constructed as to show a clear, uniform, and unbroken light all around the horizon, and shall also be provided with a sufficient supply of red pyrotechnic lights, which shall each burn for at least 30 seconds, and shall be shown on the approach of or to other vessels in sufficient time to prevent collision.

In the Mediterranean Sea the vessels referred to in subdivision (*b*) 2 may use a flare-up light in lieu of a pyrotechnic light.

All lights mentioned in subdivision (*b*) 1 and 2 shall be visible at a distance of at least 2 miles.

Third. If sailing vessels of less than 7 tons gross tonnage, shall not be obliged to carry the white light mentioned in subdivision (*b*) 2 of this article, but if they do not carry such light they shall have at hand, ready for use, a lantern showing a bright white light, which shall on the approach of or to other vessels be exhibited where it can best be seen, in sufficient time to prevent collision; and they shall also show a red pyrotechnic light, as prescribed in subdivision (*b*) 2, or in lieu thereof a flare-up light.

(*c*) Vessels and boats when line fishing with their lines out and attached to their lines, and when not at anchor or stationary, shall carry the same lights as vessels fishing with drift nets.

(*d*) Fishing vessels and fishing boats may at any time use a flare-up light in addition to the lights which they are by this article required to carry and show. All flare-up lights exhibited by a vessel when trawling or fishing with any kind of dragnet shall be shown at the after part of the vessel, excepting that if the vessel is hanging by the stern to her fishing gear they shall be exhibited from the bow.

(*e*) Every fishing vessel and every boat when at anchor shall exhibit a white light visible all around the horizon at a distance of at least 1 mile.

(*f*) If a vessel or boat when fishing becomes stationary in consequence of her gear getting fast to a rock or other obstruction, she shall show the light and make the fog signal prescribed for a vessel at anchor, respectively. (See article 15 (*d*), (*e*), and last paragraph.)

(*g*) In fog, mist, falling snow, or heavy rain storms drift-net vessels attached to their nets, and vessels when trawling, dredging, or fishing with any kind of dragnet, and vessels line fishing with their lines out shall, if of 20 tons gross tonnage or upward, respectively, at intervals of not more than one minute make a blast—if steam vessels, with the whistle or siren, and if sailing vessels, with the fog horn—each blast to be followed by ringing the bell.

(*h*) Sailing vessels or boats fishing with nets or lines or trawls when under way shall in daytime indicate their occupation to an approaching vessel by displaying a basket or other efficient signal where it can best be seen.

The vessels referred to in this article shall not be obliged to carry the lights prescribed by article 4 (*a*) and article 11, last paragraph.

ART. 10. A vessel which is being overtaken by another shall show from her stern to such last-mentioned vessel a white light or a flare-up light.

The white light required to be shown by this article may be fixed and carried in a lantern, but in such case the lantern shall be so constructed, fitted, and screened that it shall throw an unbroken light over an arc of the horizon of 12 points of the compass—namely, for 6 points from right aft on each side of the vessel—so as to be visible at a distance of at least 1 mile. Such light shall be carried as nearly as practicable on the same level as the side lights.

ART. 11. A vessel under 150 feet in length when at anchor shall carry forward, where it can best be seen, but at a height not exceeding 20 feet above the hull, a white light in a lantern so constructed as to show a clear, uniform, and unbroken light visible all around the horizon at a distance of at least 1 mile.

A vessel of 150 feet or upward in length when at anchor shall carry in the forward part of the vessel, at a height of not less than 20 and not exceeding 40 feet above the hull, one such light, and at or near the stern of the vessel, and at such a height that it shall be not less than 15 feet lower than the forward light, another such light.

The length of a vessel shall be deemed to be the length appearing in her certificate of registry.

A vessel aground in or near a fairway shall carry the above light or lights and the two red lights prescribed by article 4 (*a*).

ART. 12. Every vessel may, if necessary in order to attract attention, in addition to the lights which she is by these rules required to carry, show a flare-up light or use any detonating signal that can not be mistaken for a distress signal.

ART. 13. Nothing in these rules shall interfere with the operation of any special rules made by the government of any nation with respect to additional station and signal lights for two or more ships of war or for vessels sailing under convoy, or with the exhibition of recognition signals adopted by shipowners which have been authorized by their respective governments and duly registered and published.

ART. 14. A steam vessel proceeding under sail only, but having her funnel up, shall carry in daytime forward, where it can best be seen, one black ball or shape 2 feet in diameter.

SOUND SIGNALS FOR FOG, ETC.

ART. 15. All signals prescribed by this article for vessels under way shall be given—
1. By "steam vessels," on the whistle or siren.
2. By "sailing vessels" and "vessels towed," on the fog horn.

The words "prolonged blast" used in this article shall mean a blast of from four to six seconds' duration.

A steam vessel shall be provided with an efficient whistle or siren, sounded by steam or by some substitute for steam, so placed that the sound may not be intercepted by any obstruction, and with an efficient fog horn, to be sounded by mechanical means, and also with an efficient bell. (In all cases where the rules require a bell to be used a drum may be substituted on board Turkish vessels or a gong where such articles are used on board small seagoing vessels.) A sailing vessel of 20 tons gross tonnage or upward shall be provided with a similar fog horn and bell.

In fog, mist, falling snow, or heavy rain storms, whether by day or night, the signals described in this article shall be used as follows, viz:

(*a*) A steam vessel having way upon her shall sound at intervals of not more than two minutes a prolonged blast.

(*b*) A steam vessel under way, but stopped and having no way upon her, shall sound at intervals of not more than two minutes two prolonged blasts with an interval of about one second between them.

(*c*) A sailing vessel under way shall sound at intervals of not more than one minute, when on the starboard tack one blast, when on the port tack two blasts in succession, and when with the wind abaft the beam three blasts in succession.

(*d*) A vessel when at anchor shall at intervals of not more than one minute ring the bell rapidly for about five seconds.

(*e*) A vessel at anchor at sea, when not in ordinary anchorage ground and when in such a position as to be an obstruction to vessels under way, shall sound, if a steam vessel, at intervals of not more than two minutes, two prolonged blasts with her whistle or siren, followed by ringing her bell; or, if a sailing vessel, at intervals of not more than one minute two blasts with her fog horn, followed by ringing her bell.

(*f*) A vessel when towing shall, instead of the signals prescribed in subdivisions (*a*) and (*c*) of this article, at intervals of not more than two minutes sound three blasts in succession, namely, one prolonged blast followed by two short blasts. A vessel towed may give this signal, and she shall not give any other.

(*g*) A steam vessel wishing to indicate to another "The way is off my vessel; you may feel your way past me" may sound three blasts in succession, namely, short, long, short, with intervals of about one second between them.

(*h*) A vessel employed in laying or picking up a telegraph cable shall on hearing the fog signal of an approaching vessel sound in answer three prolonged blasts in succession.

(*i*) A vessel under way which is unable to get out of the way of an approaching vessel through being not under command or unable to maneuver as required by these rules shall on hearing the fog signal of an approaching vessel sound in answer four short blasts in succession.

Sailing vessels and boats of less than 20 tons gross tonnage shall not be obliged to give the above-mentioned signals, but if they do not they shall make some other efficient sound signal at intervals of not more than one minute.

SPEED OF SHIPS TO BE MODERATE IN FOG, ETC.

ART. 16. Every vessel shall in a fog, mist, falling snow, or heavy rain storm go at a moderate speed, having careful regard to the existing circumstances and conditions.

A steam vessel hearing, apparently forward of her beam, the fog signal of a vessel the position of which is not ascertained shall, so far as the circumstances of the case admit, stop her engines, and then navigate with caution until danger of collision is over.

STEERING AND SAILING RULES.

PRELIMINARY.—RISK OF COLLISION.

Risk of collision can, when circumstances permit, be ascertained by carefully watching the compass bearing of an approaching vessel. If the bearing does not appreciably change, such risk should be deemed to exist.

ART. 17. When two sailing vessels are approaching one another so as to involve risk of collision, one of them shall keep out of the way of the other as follows, namely:

(*a*) A vessel which is running free shall keep out of the way of a vessel which is closehauled.

(*b*) A vessel which is closehauled on the port tack shall keep out of the way of a vessel which is closehauled on the starboard tack.

(*c*) When both are running free with the wind on different sides, the vessel which has the wind on the port side shall keep out of the way of the other.

(*d*) When both are running free with the wind on the same side, the vessel which is to the windward shall keep out of the way of the vessel which is to leeward.

(*e*) A vessel which has the wind aft shall keep out of the way of the other vessel.

ART. 18. When two steam vessels are meeting end on or nearly end on, so as to involve risk of collision, each shall alter her course to starboard, so that each may pass on the port side of the other.

This article only applies to cases where vessels are meeting end on or nearly end on in such a manner as to involve risk of collision, and does not apply to two vessels which must if both keep on their respective courses pass clear of each other.

The only cases to which it does apply are when each of the two vessels is end on or nearly end on to the other; in other words, to cases in which by day each vessel sees the masts of the other in a line or nearly in a line with her own, and by night to cases in which each vessel is in such a position as to see both the side lights of the other.

It does not apply by day to cases in which a vessel sees another ahead crossing her own course, or by night to cases where the red light of one vessel is opposed to the red light of the other, or where the green light of one vessel is opposed to the green light of the other, or where a red light without a green light or a green light without a red light is seen ahead, or where both green and red lights are seen anywhere but ahead.

ART. 19. When two steam vessels are crossing, so as to involve risk of collision, the vessel which has the other on her own starboard side shall keep out of the way of the other.

ART. 20. When a steam vessel and a sailing vessel are proceeding in such directions as to involve risk of collision, the steam vessel shall keep out of the way of the sailing vessel.

ART. 21. Where by any of these rules one of two vessels is to keep out of the way, the other shall keep her course and speed.

ART. 22. Every vessel which is directed by these rules to keep out of the way of another vessel shall, if the circumstances of the case admit, avoid crossing ahead of the other.

ART. 23. Every steam vessel which is directed by these rules to keep out of the way of another vessel shall on approaching her, if necessary, slacken her speed or stop or reverse.

ART. 24. Notwithstanding anything contained in these rules every vessel overtaking any other shall keep out of the way of the overtaken vessel.

Every vessel coming up with another vessel from any direction more than 2 points abaft her beam—that is, in such a position with reference to the vessel which she is overtaking that at night she would be unable to see either of that vessel's side lights—shall be deemed to be an overtaking vessel, and no subsequent alteration of the bearing between the two vessels shall make the overtaking vessel a crossing vessel within the meaning of these rules or relieve her of the duty of keeping clear of the overtaken vessel until she is finally past and clear.

As by day the overtaking vessel can not always know with certainty whether she is forward of or abaft this direction from the other vessel, she should if in doubt assume that she is an overtaking vessel and keep out of the way.

ART. 25. In narrow channels every steam vessel shall, when it is safe and practicable, keep to that side of the fairway or mid-channel which lies on the starboard side of such vessel.

ART. 26. Sailing vessels under way shall keep out of the way of sailing vessels or boats fishing with nets or lines or trawls. This rule shall not give to any vessel or boat engaged in fishing the right of obstructing a fairway used by vessels other than fishing vessels or boats.

ART. 27. In obeying and construing these rules due regard shall be had to all dangers of navigation and collision and to any special circumstances which may render a departure from the above rules necessary in order to avoid immediate danger.

SOUND SIGNALS FOR VESSELS IN SIGHT OF ONE ANOTHER.

ART. 28. The words "short blast" used in this article shall mean a blast of about one second's duration.

When vessels are in sight of one another, a steam vessel under way, in taking any course authorized or required by these rules, shall indicate that course by the following signals on her whistle or siren, namely:

One short blast to mean, "I am directing my course to starboard."

Two short blasts to mean, "I am directing my course to port."

Three short blasts to mean, "My engines are going at full speed astern."

NO VESSEL UNDER ANY CIRCUMSTANCES TO NEGLECT PROPER PRECAUTIONS.

ART. 29. Nothing in these rules shall exonerate any vessel or the owner or master or crew thereof from the consequences of any neglect to carry lights or signals, or of any neglect to keep a proper lookout, or of the neglect of any precaution which may be required by the ordinary practice of seamen or by the special circumstances of the case.

RESERVATION OF RULES FOR HARBORS AND INLAND NAVIGATION.

ART. 30. Nothing in these rules shall interfere with the operation of a special rule duly made by local authority relative to the navigation of any harbor, river, or inland waters.

DISTRESS SIGNALS.

ART. 31. When a vessel is in distress and requires assistance from other vessels or from the shore, the following shall be the signals to be used or displayed by her, either together or separately, namely:

In the daytime—
First. A gun fired at intervals of about a minute.
Second. The international code signal of distress, indicated by N C.
Third. The distance signal, consisting of a square flag, having either above or below it a ball or anything resembling a ball.
Fourth. Rockets or shells as prescribed below for use at night.
Fifth. A continuous sounding with any fog-signal apparatus.
At night—
First. A gun fired at intervals of about a minute.
Second. Flames on the vessel (as from a burning tar barrel, oil barrel, etc.).
Third. Rockets or shells bursting in the air with a loud report and throwing stars of any color or description, fired one at a time at short intervals.
Fourth. A continuous sounding with any fog-signal apparatus.

SEC. 2. That all laws or parts of laws inconsistent with the foregoing regulations for preventing collisions at sea for the navigation of all public and private vessels of the United States upon the high seas and in all waters connected therewith navigable by seagoing vessels are hereby repealed.

SEC. 3. That this act shall take effect at a time to be fixed by the President by proclamation issued for that purpose.

And whereas an act of Congress entitled "An act to amend an act approved August 19, 1890, entitled 'An act to adopt regulations for preventing collisions at sea,'" was approved May 28, 1894, the said act being in the following words:

Be it enacted by the Senate and House of Representatives of the United States of America in Congress assembled, That article 7 of the act approved August 19, 1890, entitled "An act to adopt regulations for preventing collisions at sea," be amended to read as follows:

"ART. 7. Steam vessels of less than 40 and vessels under oars or sails of less than 20 tons gross tonnage, respectively, and rowing boats, when under way, shall not be required to carry the lights mentioned in article 2 (*a*), (*b*), and (*c*), but if they do not carry them they shall be provided with the following lights:

"First. Steam vessels of less than 40 tons shall carry—

"(*a*) In the fore part of the vessel or on or in front of the funnel where it can best be seen, and at a height above the gunwale of not less than 9 feet, a bright white light constructed and fixed as prescribed in article 2 (*a*) and of such a character as to be visible at a distance of at least 2 miles.

"(*b*) Green and red side lights constructed and fixed as prescribed in article 2 (*b*) and (*c*) and of such a character as to be visible at a distance of at least 1 mile, or a combined lantern showing a green light and a red light from right ahead to 2 points abaft the beam on their respective sides. Such lanterns shall be carried not less than 3 feet below the white light.

"Second. Small steamboats, such as are carried by seagoing vessels, may carry the white light at a less height than 9 feet above the gunwale, but it shall be carried above the combined lantern mentioned in subdivision 1 (*b*).

"Third. Vessels under oars or sails of less than 20 tons shall have ready at hand a lantern with a green glass on one side and a red glass on the other, which on the approach of or to other vessels shall be exhibited, in sufficient time to prevent collision, so that the green light shall not be seen on the port side nor the red light on the starboard side.

"Fourth. Rowing boats, whether under oars or sail, shall have ready at hand a lantern showing a white light, which shall be temporarily exhibited in sufficient time to prevent collision.

"The vessels referred to in this article shall not be obliged to carry the lights prescribed by article 4 (*a*) and article 11, last paragraph."

That article 9 be hereby repealed.

That article 21 be amended to read as follows:

"ART. 21. Where by any of these rules one of two vessels is to keep out of the way the other shall keep her course and speed.

"NOTE.—When, in consequence of thick weather or other causes, such vessel finds herself so close that collision can not be avoided by the action of the giving-way vessel alone, she also shall take such action as will best aid to avert collision." (See articles 27 and 29.)

That article 31 be amended to read as follows:

"DISTRESS SIGNALS.

"ART. 31. When a vessel is in distress and requires assistance from other vessels or from the shore the following shall be the signals to be used or displayed by her, either together or separately, namely:

"In the daytime—

"First. A gun or other explosive signal fired at intervals of about a minute.

"Second. The international code signal of distress indicated by N C.

"Third. The distance signal, consisting of a square flag, having either above or below it a ball or anything resembling a ball.

"Fourth. A continuous sounding with any fog-signal apparatus.

"At night—

"First. A gun or other explosive signal fired at intervals of about a minute.

"Second. Flames on the vessel (as from a burning tar barrel, oil barrel, etc.).

"Third. Rockets or shells throwing stars of any color or description, fired one at a time at short intervals.

"Fourth. A continuous sounding with any fog-signal apparatus."

And whereas it is provided by section 3 of the act approved August 19, 1890, that it shall take effect at a time to be fixed by the President by proclamation issued for that purpose:

Now, therefore, I, Grover Cleveland, President of the United States of America, do hereby, in virtue of the authority vested in me by section 3 of the act aforesaid, proclaim the 1st day of March, 1895, as the day on which the said act approved August 19, 1890, as amended by the act approved May 28, 1894, shall take effect.

In testimony whereof I have hereunto set my hand and caused the seal of the United States of America to be affixed.

[SEAL.]   Done at the city of Washington, this 13th day of July, 1894, and of the Independence of the United States the one hundred and nineteenth.

GROVER CLEVELAND.

By the President:

W. Q. GRESHAM, *Secretary of State.*

BY THE PRESIDENT OF THE UNITED STATES OF AMERICA.

A PROCLAMATION.

Whereas Congress by a statute approved March 22, 1882, and by statutes in furtherance and amendment thereof defined the crimes of bigamy, polygamy, and unlawful cohabitation in the Territories and other places within the exclusive jurisdiction of the United States and prescribed a penalty for such crimes; and

Whereas on or about the 6th day of October, 1890, the Church of the Latter-day Saints, commonly known as the Mormon Church, through its president issued a manifesto proclaiming the purpose of said church no longer to sanction the practice of polygamous marriages and calling upon all members and adherents of said church to obey the laws of the United States in reference to said subject-matter; and

Whereas on the 4th day of January, A. D. 1893,* Benjamin Harrison, then President of the United States, did declare and grant a full pardon and amnesty to certain offenders under said acts upon condition of future obedience to their requirements, as is fully set forth in said proclamation of amnesty and pardon; and

Whereas upon the evidence now furnished me I am satisfied that the members and adherents of said church generally abstain from plural marriages and polygamous cohabitation and are now living in obedience to the laws, and that the time has now arrived when the interests of public justice and morality will be promoted by the granting of amnesty and pardon to all such offenders as have complied with the conditions of said proclamation, including such of said offenders as have been convicted under the provisions of said act:

Now, therefore, I, Grover Cleveland, President of the United States, by virtue of the powers in me vested, do hereby declare and grant a full amnesty and pardon to all persons who have in violation of said acts committed either of the offenses of polygamy, bigamy, adultery, or unlawful cohabitation under the color of polygamous or plural marriage, or who, having been convicted of violations of said acts, are now suffering deprivations of civil rights in consequence of the same, excepting all persons who have not complied with the conditions contained in said executive proclamation of January 4, 1893.

* See pp. 5803-5804.

In witness whereof I have hereunto set my hand and caused the seal of the United States to be affixed.

[SEAL.]   Done at the city of Washington, this 25th day of September, A. D. 1894, and of the Independence of the United States the one hundred and nineteenth.

                          GROVER CLEVELAND.

By the President:

    W. Q. GRESHAM, *Secretary of State.*

BY THE PRESIDENT OF THE UNITED STATES OF AMERICA.

A PROCLAMATION.

The American people should gratefully render thanksgiving and praise to the Supreme Ruler of the Universe, who has watched over them with kindness and fostering care during the year that has passed; they should also with humility and faith supplicate the Father of All Mercies for continued blessings according to their needs, and they should by deeds of charity seek the favor of the Giver of Every Good and Perfect Gift.

Therefore, I, Grover Cleveland, President of the United States, do hereby appoint and set apart Thursday, the 29th day of November instant, as a day of thanksgiving and prayer to be kept and observed by all the people of the land.

On that day let our ordinary work and business be suspended and let us meet in our accustomed places of worship and give thanks to Almighty God for our preservation as a nation, for our immunity from disease and pestilence, for the harvests that have rewarded our husbandry, for a renewal of national prosperity, and for every advance in virtue and intelligence that has marked our growth as a people.

And with our thanksgiving let us pray that these blessings may be multiplied unto us, that our national conscience may be quickened to a better recognition of the power and goodness of God, and that in our national life we may clearer see and closer follow the path of righteousness.

And in our places of worship and praise, as well as in the happy reunions of kindred and friends on that day, let us invoke divine approval by generously remembering the poor and needy. Surely He who has given us comfort and plenty will look upon our relief of the destitute and our ministrations of charity as the work of hearts truly grateful and as proofs of the sincerity of our thanksgiving.

Witness my hand and the seal of the United States, which I have caused to be hereto affixed.

[SEAL.]   Done at the city of Washington on the 1st day of November, A. D. 1894, and of the Independence of the United States the one hundred and nineteenth.

                          GROVER CLEVELAND.

By the President:

    W. Q. GRESHAM, *Secretary of State.*

A PROCLAMATION.

Whereas by the sixteenth section of the act of Congress approved March 2, 1889 (25 U. S. Statutes at Large, p. 888), the agreements entered into between the Chicago, Milwaukee and St. Paul Railway Company and the Sioux Indians for the right of way and occupation of certain lands for station purposes in that portion of the Sioux Reservation, in the State of South Dakota, relinquished by said Indians were ratified upon the condition that said railway company shall within three years after the said act takes effect construct, complete, and put into operation its line of road as therein provided for, due location of which was to be made within nine months after said act took effect; and in case of failure to so construct said road "the lands granted for right of way, station grounds, or other railway purposes as in this act provided shall without any further act or ceremony be declared by proclamation of the President forfeited, and shall without entry or further action on the part of the United States revert to the United States and be subject to entry under the other provisions of this act;" and

Whereas under previous proclamation* said act took effect on February 10, 1890, and more than three years have elapsed and no construction has been reported of the said road beyond the town of Chamberlain, in the State of South Dakota, as evidenced by the report of the Secretary of the Interior dated December 3, 1894:

Now, therefore, I, Grover Cleveland, President of the United States, do declare that the said lands granted for right of way and station purposes, to wit, that tract of land known as lots 2, 3, and 4 and the southeast quarter of the southwest quarter of section 10, and lots 1 and 9 in section 15, township 104 north, range 71 west, containing 188 acres, as shown by a plat approved January 24, 1891, being the tract selected by the Chicago, Milwaukee and St. Paul Railway Company under the sixteenth section of the act of March 2, 1889 (25 U. S. Statutes at Large, p. 888), also the 640 acres in said township 104 north, ranges 71 and 72 west, fifth principal meridian, in the State of South Dakota, plat of which was approved by the Secretary of the Interior January 24, 1889, and now on file in the General Land Office, are forfeited to the United States and will be subject to entry under the homestead laws as provided by said act of March 2, 1889, whenever the Secretary of the Interior shall give due notice to the local officers of this declaration of forfeiture.

Given under my hand, at the city of Washington, this 5th day of December, A. D. 1894.

GROVER CLEVELAND,
President of the United States.

By the President:
S. W. LAMOREUX,
Commissioner of the General Land Office.

* See pp. 5529-5532.

EXECUTIVE ORDERS.

CIVIL SERVICE.—REVOCATION OF PROMOTION REGULATIONS.

DECEMBER 11, 1893.

The promotion regulations applied to the War Department May 7, 1887, under authority contained in amended Civil-Service Rule VI are hereby revoked, and hereafter promotions in that Department, until otherwise provided, will be made in accordance with the provisions of Departmental Rule IX and the order of the Secretary of War of March 2, 1892, or such other and further orders as the said Secretary may make not inconsistent with the civil-service rules and the order of the President of December 4, 1891, directing the keeping of an efficiency record with a view to the placing of promotions wholly upon the basis of merit.

GROVER CLEVELAND.

AMENDMENTS OF CIVIL-SERVICE RULES.

GENERAL RULE III.

Amend General Rule III by striking out clause (*e*) of section 2.

DEPARTMENTAL RULE II.

Amend Departmental Rule II by striking out the whole of section 1 and substituting therefor the following:

1. To test fitness for the classified departmental service there shall be a clerk-copyist examination and such supplementary and special examinations as the Commission may provide to meet the special requirements of the service. The clerk-copyist examination shall not include more than the following subjects: Orthography, copying, penmanship, arithmetic (fundamental rules, fractions, percentage, interest, and discount), elements of bookkeeping and accounts, elements of the English language, letter writing, elements of the geography, history, and government of the United States.

DEPARTMENTAL RULE VI.

Amend Departmental Rule VI as follows:

In section 1, line 1, strike out the words "copyist and of the clerk" and insert in lieu thereof the words "clerk-copyist," and in the same line strike out the final letter in the word "examinations." In section 4 strike out all after the word "the" where it occurs the second time in line 6 down to and including the word "separated" in line 8 and insert in lieu thereof the words "clerk-copyist," and strike out the final letter of the word "examinations" in line 9. In section 9, line 1, strike out the words "the copyist and the clerk" and insert in lieu thereof the word "all," and strike out all after the word "register" in line 3 to the end of the section.

DEPARTMENTAL RULE VII.

Amend Departmental Rule VII as follows:

In section 1, after the word "clerk" in line 3, insert a hyphen and the word "copyist." In section 3, after the word "the" where it occurs the second time in line 1, strike out the words "copyist or the clerk" and insert in lieu thereof the words "clerk-copyist." Strike out all of section 4 and change the numbering of the sections following as required.

DEPARTMENTAL RULE IX.

Amend Departmental Rule IX as follows:

In section 2, after the word "clerk" in line 1, insert a hyphen and the word "copyist." In section 3, after the word "clerk" in line 1, insert a hyphen and the word "copyist." Strike out the period at the end of section 5 and insert in lieu thereof a comma, and add to the section the following:

But the provisions of clause 1 of this rule shall cease to be operative when, by reason of the consolidation of the clerk and copyist examinations, there shall no longer be any persons in the departmental service to whom they apply.

POSTAL RULE IV.

Postal Rule IV is hereby amended by adding thereto the following section:

4. In case of the sudden occurrence of a vacancy in a position within the classified service of any post-office which the public interest requires shall be immediately filled, and which can not be so filled by certification from the eligible registers, such vacancy may be filled by temporary appointment until a regular appointment can be made under the provisions of sections 1 and 2 of this rule: *Provided,* Such temporary appointment shall in no case continue longer than ninety days: *And provided further,* That no person shall serve more than ninety days in any one year under such temporary appointment. Every such temporary appointment and also the discontinuance of the same shall at once be reported to the Commission.

Approved, January 5, 1894. GROVER CLEVELAND.

AMENDMENT OF CIVIL-SERVICE RULES.

Departmental Rule VII is hereby amended by adding thereto the following section:

9. In case of the sudden occurrence of a vacancy in the position of observer in the Weather Bureau of the Department of Agriculture which the public interest requires shall be immediately filled, and which can not be so filled by certification from the eligible registers of the Commission, the Secretary of Agriculture may fill such vacancy by temporary appointment until a regular appointment can be made under the provisions of sections 1, 2, and 3 of this rule: *Provided,* Such temporary appointment shall in no case continue longer than ninety days. Every such temporary appointment and the discontinuance of the same shall at once be reported to the Commission.

Approved, January 5, 1894. GROVER CLEVELAND.

CIVIL SERVICE.—EXECUTIVE ORDER WITHDRAWING FISH CULTURISTS FROM THE LIST OF PLACES TO BE FILLED BY NONCOMPETITIVE EXAMINATION.

EXECUTIVE MANSION, *January 20, 1894.*

So much of Executive orders heretofore issued under General Rule III, section 2, clause (*d*), as provides for the appointment of fish culturists upon noncompetitive examination is hereby revoked, and hereafter fish culturists will be appointed upon competitive examination.

GROVER CLEVELAND.

AMENDMENT OF CIVIL-SERVICE RULES.

SPECIAL INDIAN RULE NO. I.

EXECUTIVE MANSION, *March 6, 1894.*

Exceptions from examination are hereby made as follows: One superintendent and the necessary teachers, not exceeding four in number, for the organization and equipment of a normal school to be established at Albuquerque, N. Mex., this rule to expire by limitation six months after the date of its approval.

Approved:
GROVER CLEVELAND.

AMENDMENT OF CIVIL-SERVICE RULES.

EXECUTIVE MANSION, *March 20, 1894.*

So much of clause 6 of Special Departmental Rule No. 1, providing for exceptions from examination in the office of the Secretary in the Department of Agriculture, as excepts "clerk to act as appointment clerk" is hereby revoked, and that position will hereafter be treated as subject to competitive examination.

Approved:
GROVER CLEVELAND.

AMENDMENTS OF CIVIL-SERVICE RULES.

Section 6 of Special Departmental Rule No. 1 is hereby amended by striking from the list of excepted places in the Weather Bureau of the Department of Agriculture enumerated therein the following:

The three professors of meteorology of highest grade.

Said section is further amended by adding thereto the following:

Noncompetitive examinations shall be held, on such dates and at such places as the Commission may from time to time determine, to test the competency of inspectors and assistant inspectors in the Bureau of Animal Industry in the Department of Agriculture employed elsewhere than at Washington, who were so employed on the date inspectors and assistant inspectors were included in the classified service and have been continued in the service of the Department until opportunity has been provided for their noncompetitive examination. The results of such examination shall be reported by the Commission to the Secretary of Agriculture.

Approved, May 1, 1894.   GROVER CLEVELAND.

AMENDMENTS OF CIVIL-SERVICE RULES.

EXECUTIVE MANSION, *May 11, 1894.*

SPECIAL DEPARTMENTAL RULE NO. 1.

Special Departmental Rule No. 1 is hereby amended by adding to the exceptions from examination therein made in the Department of the Treasury the following:

In the office of the Second Auditor: One skilled laborer with duties exclusively of a carpenter and cabinetmaker.

In the Bureau of Engraving and Printing: Custodian of proving presses and modeler.

SPECIAL CUSTOMS RULE NO. 1.

Special Customs Rule No. 1, authorizing certain exceptions from examination in the classified customs service, is hereby amended by adding to the statement of places therein excepted the following:

In the customs district of Vermont: One deputy collector and inspector, to be stationed at Halifax during the winter and at Quebec during the time the St. Lawrence River is open to navigation.

RAILWAY MAIL RULE IV.

Railway Mail Rule IV, section 2, clause (*b*), of the civil-service rules is hereby amended by striking out all after the word "averages" in line 3 to and including the word "territory" in line 10, and the word "further" in line 10; so that as amended the clause will read:

The Commission shall certify from the register of the State or Territory in which the vacancy exists the names of the three eligibles thereon having the highest averages: *Provided*, That if upon the register of the State or Territory in which the vacancy exists there are the names of eligibles having a claim of preference under section 1754, Revised Statutes, the names of such eligibles shall be certified before the names of other eligibles of higher grade: *Provided further*, That on a line on which the service does not require the full time of a clerk, and one can be employed jointly with the railroad company, the appointment may be made without examination and certification, with the consent of the Commission, upon a statement of the facts by the general superintendent; but no clerk so appointed shall be eligible for transfer or appointment to any other place in the service.

Section 6 of said rule is hereby amended by adding after the word "substitutes" in line 6 the words "resident in the counties which are supplied wholly or in part by the road on which the vacancy exists;" so that as amended the section will read:

6. There may be certified and appointed in each State and Territory, in the manner provided for in this rule, such number of substitute clerks, not exceeding the ratio of one substitute to ten regular clerks, in such State or Territory as the Postmaster-General may authorize, and any vacancies occurring in class 1 in any State

or Territory in which substitutes have been appointed shall be filled by the appointment thereto of those substitutes resident in the counties which are supplied wholly or in part by the road on which the vacancy exists, in the order of their appointment as substitutes, without further certification. The time during which any substitute is actually employed in the service shall be counted as part of his probation.

GENERAL RULE III.

Section 2 of General Rule III is hereby amended by adding thereto the following clause:

(*h*) For the appointment of an Indian as assistant teacher in the Indian-school service.

INDIAN RULE IV.

Indian Rule IV is hereby amended by adding thereto the following section:

6. Upon the nomination by the Commissioner of Indian Affairs, through the Secretary of the Interior, of an Indian for appointment as assistant teacher, the Commission shall give such Indian noncompetitive examination under General Rule III, section 2, clause (*h*), upon passing which at the required grade he shall be certified and appointed for the probationary period provided for in section 3 of this rule, at the end of which period he shall be absolutely appointed or discharged from the service in accordance with the provisions of said section. Any Indian appointed assistant teacher as herein provided may be, any time after absolute appointment, appointed teacher upon the certification of the Commission that he has passed the teacher's examination.

Approved:
                                    GROVER CLEVELAND.

CIVIL SERVICE.—AMENDMENT OF CLASSIFICATION OF THE INDIAN SERVICE AS MADE BY THE SECRETARY OF THE INTERIOR APRIL 13, 1891.

EXECUTIVE MANSION, *May 11, 1894.*

In the exercise of the power vested in the President by the third paragraph of section 6 of the act entitled "An act to regulate and improve the civil service of the United States," approved January 16, 1883, I hereby direct the Secretary of the Interior to revise the classification of the Indian service made by him, by direction of the President, on the 13th day of April, 1891, and to include in class 3 of said classification assistant teachers.

Approved:
                                    GROVER CLEVELAND.

By THE PRESIDENT OF THE UNITED STATES.

EXECUTIVE ORDER.

EXECUTIVE MANSION, *May 26, 1894.*

It is hereby ordered, That the several Executive Departments and the Government Printing Office be closed on Wednesday, the 30th instant, to enable the employees to participate in the decoration of the graves of the soldiers and sailors who fell in defense of the Union during the War of the Rebellion.
                                    GROVER CLEVELAND.

AMENDMENT OF CIVIL-SERVICE RULES.

Special Indian Rule No. 1 is hereby amended by adding to the places excepted from examination therein the following:

Kindergarten teachers, to be employed as such, not exceeding twenty in number.

Approved, June 21, 1894.

GROVER CLEVELAND.

AMENDMENT OF CIVIL-SERVICE RULES.

Special Customs Rule No. 1 is hereby amended by adding to the places excepted from examination therein the following:

In the customs district of Boston, office of the collector: One superintendent of warehouses.

In the customs district of Philadelphia, office of the collector: Five chiefs of division.

Approved, June 21, 1894.

GROVER CLEVELAND.

AMENDMENTS OF CIVIL-SERVICE RULES.

EXECUTIVE MANSION, *July 9, 1894.*

DEPARTMENTAL RULE II.

Departmental Rule II, clause 3 (*f*), is hereby amended by adding at the end thereof the following words:

Except in the Department of Agriculture the chiefs of the following divisions: Entomology and economic ornithology and mammalogy.

SPECIAL DEPARTMENTAL RULE NO. I.

Special Departmental Rule No. 1 is hereby amended by dropping from among the places therein excepted from examination the following:

In the Department of Agriculture, office of the Secretary, the assistant chiefs of the following divisions: Of entomology and of economic ornithology and mammalogy.

Approved:

GROVER CLEVELAND.

CIVIL SERVICE.—AMENDMENT OF CLASSIFICATION OF THE DEPARTMENT OF THE INTERIOR.

EXECUTIVE MANSION, *July 25, 1894.*

In the exercise of the power vested in the President by the third paragraph of section 6 of the act entitled "An act to regulate and improve the civil service of the United States," approved January 16, 1883, I hereby direct the Secretary of the Interior to revise the classification of the Department of the Interior so as to include therein the chief clerk and the assistant chief clerk at the Indian warehouse at New York.

Approved:

GROVER CLEVELAND.

AMENDMENT OF CIVIL-SERVICE RULES.

Special Departmental Rule No. 1 is hereby amended by adding to the places therein excepted from examination in the Department of the Treasury the following:

In the Bureau of Statistics: One expert in mechanical designs and in diagramming commercial and financial facts.

Approved, November 2, 1894.   GROVER CLEVELAND.

AMENDMENTS OF CIVIL-SERVICE RULES.

DEPARTMENTAL RULE II.

Departmental Rule II, clause 3 (*f*), is hereby amended by adding at the end thereof the following words: "and of pomology;" so that as amended the paragraph will read:

(*f*) Chiefs of divisions, except in the Department of Agriculture the chiefs of the following divisions: Entomology, economic ornithology and mammalogy, and of pomology.

SPECIAL DEPARTMENTAL RULE NO. 1.

Special Departmental Rule No. 1 is hereby amended by dropping from among the places therein excepted from examination the following:

In the Department of Agriculture, office of the Secretary: The assistant chief of the division of pomology.

Approved, November 2, 1894.   GROVER CLEVELAND.

AMENDMENTS OF CIVIL-SERVICE RULES.

EXECUTIVE MANSION, *November 2, 1894.*

INDIAN RULE IV

Section 6 of Indian Rule IV is hereby amended by inserting the following proviso at the end of the first sentence:

Provided, That the certificates of graduation of the Indian graduates of the normal classes at Santa Fe, N. Mex.; Salem, Oreg.; Haskell Institute, Lawrence, Kans.; Carlisle, Pa., and Hampton, Va., may be accepted by the Commission as the basis of certification in lieu of the examination herein provided.

As amended the section will read:

6. Upon the nomination by the Commissioner of Indian Affairs, through the Secretary of the Interior, of an Indian for appointment as assistant teacher, the Commission shall give such Indian noncompetitive examination, under General Rule III, section 2, clause (*h*), upon passing which at the required grade he shall be certified and appointed for the probationary period provided for in section 3 of this rule, at the end of which period he shall be absolutely appointed or discharged from the

service in accordance with the provisions of said section: *Provided*, That the cer‑ tificates of graduation of the Indian graduates of the normal classes at Santa Fe. N. Mex.; Salem, Oreg.; Haskell Institute, Lawrence, Kans.; Carlisle, Pa., and Hamp‑ ton, Va., may be accepted by the Commission as the basis of certification in lieu of the examination herein provided for. Any Indian appointed assistant teacher as herein provided may at any time after absolute appointment be appointed teacher upon the certification of the Commission that he has passed the teacher examination.

SPECIAL INDIAN RULE NO. I.

Special Indian Rule No. 1 is hereby amended by inserting after the words "New Mexico" in line 3 the words "also one normal teacher each at the Salem (Oreg.) school and the Haskell Institute, Lawrence, Kans." As amended the rule will read:

Exceptions from examination are hereby made as follows: One superintendent and the necessary teachers, not exceeding four in number, for the organization and equipment of one normal school to be established at Santa Fe, N. Mex.; also one normal teacher each at the Salem (Oreg.) school and the Haskell Institute, Law‑ rence, Kans.; this rule to expire by limitation six months after the date of its approval.

Approved:

GROVER CLEVELAND.

AMENDMENTS OF CIVIL-SERVICE RULES.

Postal Rule II is hereby amended by striking out all of section 5 and inserting in lieu thereof the following:

5. Exceptions from examination in the classified postal service are hereby made as follows:

(*a*) Assistant postmaster or the chief assistant to the postmaster, by whatever designation known.

(*b*) One secretary to the postmaster, when authorized by law and allowed by the Post-Office Department.

(*c*) Cashier, when authorized by law and employed under that roster title.

(*d*) Assistant cashier, when authorized by law and employed under that roster title.

(*e*) Superintendents of station or branch post-offices at which letter carriers are employed.

(*f*) Printers and pressmen, when authorized by law and allowed by the Post-Office Department and employed as such.

6. No person appointed to a place under any exception made by any postal rule shall be transferred to any other place not also excepted from examination.

Postal Rule IV is hereby amended by inserting after the word "man‑ ner," in section 1, line 3, the following:

Provided, That superintendents of mail shall be selected from among the em‑ ployees of the railway mail service or of the mailing division of the post-office at which they are respectively to serve.

Postal Rule VIII is hereby amended as follows:

In clause (*a*), line 2, after the word "by," insert the word "any," and in the same line strike out "II, clause 5."

Approved, November 2, 1894.

GROVER CLEVELAND.

AMENDMENT OF CIVIL-SERVICE RULES.

EXECUTIVE MANSION, *November 2, 1894.*

Departmental Rule VII, clause 1, is hereby amended by inserting at the end of line 6 the following:

Vacancies in places authorized to be filled by noncompetitive examination may be filled without examination for a period not exceeding thirty days, until a regular appointment can be made upon certification made by the Commission.

Every such appointment and the reasons therefor shall be at once reported to the Commission.

Approved:

GROVER CLEVELAND.

CIVIL SERVICE.—AMENDMENT OF CLASSIFICATION.

In pursuance of the authority contained in the third paragraph of section 6 of the act entitled "An act to regulate and improve the civil service of the United States," approved January 16, 1883, the heads of the several Executive Departments are hereby directed to amend their several classifications so as to include among the employees classified thereunder messengers, assistant messengers, and watchmen.

Approved, November 2, 1894.

GROVER CLEVELAND.

CIVIL SERVICE.—AMENDMENT OF CLASSIFICATION.

In pursuance of the authority contained in the third paragraph of section 6 of the act entitled "An act to regulate and improve the civil service of the United States," approved January 16, 1883, the Postmaster-General is hereby directed to amend the classification of the Post-Office Department so as to include among the classes covered thereby clerks to post-office inspectors.

Approved, November 2, 1894.

GROVER CLEVELAND.

AMENDMENTS OF CIVIL-SERVICE RULES.

GENERAL RULE III.

General Rule III is hereby amended by striking out clause (*b*) of section 2 and relettering the remaining clauses of the section accordingly.

DEPARTMENTAL RULES.

Departmental Rule II is hereby amended as follows:

In section 4, line 1, strike out the word "hereby," and insert after the word "made," at the end of the line, the words "by any departmental rule;" in line 2, after the word "shall," strike out the words "within one year after appointment;" substitute a period for the semicolon in line 3 and strike out the remainder of the section. As amended the section will read:

4. No person appointed to a place under the exceptions to examination made by any departmental rule shall be transferred from such place to a place not also excepted from examination.

Departmental Rule XI is hereby amended as follows:

In clause (*a*), line 2, insert the word "any" before the word "departmental," and strike out in line 3 all after the word "rule."

RAILWAY MAIL RULES.

Railway Mail Rule II is hereby amended as follows:

In section 6, line 2, after the word "shall," strike out the words "within one year after appointment;" substitute a period for the semicolon in line 3 and strike out the remainder of the section. As amended the section will read:

6. No person appointed to a place under any exception to examination hereby made shall be transferred to another place not also excepted from examination.

Approved, November 2, 1894.

GROVER CLEVELAND.

AMENDMENTS OF CIVIL-SERVICE RULES.

Customs Rule I is hereby amended as follows:

In section 2, line 2, strike out the word "fifty" and insert in lieu thereof the word "twenty."

Customs Rule II is hereby amended as follows:

In section 6, line 1, strike out the word "hereby," and after the word "made," at the end of the line, insert the words "by any customs rule;" in line 2, after the word "shall," strike out the words "within one year after appointment;" substitute a period for the semicolon in line 3 and strike out the remainder of the section. As amended the clause will read:

No person appointed to a place under any exception to examination made by any customs rule shall be transferred from such place to another place not also excepted from examination.

Customs Rule VIII is hereby amended as follows:

In clause (*a*), line 2, after the word "by," insert the word "any," and in the same line strike out " II, clause 5."

Approved, November 2, 1894.

GROVER CLEVELAND.

AMENDMENTS OF CIVIL-SERVICE RULES.

DEPARTMENTAL RULE VII.

Departmental Rule VII is hereby amended by adding to the first paragraph of section 1 the following proviso:

Provided further, That sea post clerks in the Post-Office Department shall be appointed by transfer from the classified railway mail service or the classified postal service, and shall be eligible at any time for retransfer to the service from which transferred, but shall not be transferred to any other department or branch of the service, nor to any other place in the Post-Office Department, without examination and certification by the Commission.

RAILWAY MAIL RULE II.

Railway Mail Rule II is hereby amended as follows:
In section 5 strike out clauses (*e*) and (*f*).

RAILWAY MAIL RULE IV.

Railway Mail Rule IV is hereby amended as follows:
In the last proviso of clause (*b*) of section 2, in line 2 of that proviso, after the word "line," insert the words "or at a transfer station or on a steamboat;" in the same line strike out the words "on which" and substitute therefor the word "where," and in line 3, after the word "railroad," insert the words "or steamboat;" so that as amended the proviso will read:

Provided further, That on a line or at a transfer station or on a steamboat where the service does not require the full time of a clerk, and one can be employed jointly with the railroad or steamboat company, the appointment may be made without examination and certification, with the consent of the Commission, upon a statement of the facts by the general superintendent; but no clerk so appointed shall be eligible for transfer or appointment to any other place in the service.

Approved, November 17, 1894.   GROVER CLEVELAND.

SECOND ANNUAL MESSAGE.

EXECUTIVE MANSION, *December 3, 1894.*
To the Congress of the United States:

The assemblage within the nation's legislative halls of those charged with the duty of making laws for the benefit of a generous and free people impressively suggests the exacting obligation and inexorable responsibility involved in their task. At the threshold of such labor now to be undertaken by the Congress of the United States, and in the discharge of an executive duty enjoined by the Constitution, I submit this communication, containing a brief statement of the condition of our national affairs and recommending such legislation as seems to me necessary and expedient.

The history of our recent dealings with other nations and our peaceful relations with them at this time additionally demonstrate the advantage of consistently adhering to a firm but just foreign policy, free from envious or ambitious national schemes and characterized by entire honesty and sincerity.

During the past year, pursuant to a law of Congress commissioners were appointed to the Antwerp Industrial Exposition. Though the participation of American exhibitors fell far short of completely illustrating our national ingenuity and industrial achievements, yet it was quite creditable in view of the brief time allowed for preparation.

I have endeavored to impress upon the Belgian Government the needlessness and positive harmfulness of its restrictions upon the importation of certain of our food products, and have strongly urged that the rigid supervision and inspection under our laws are amply sufficient to prevent the exportation from this country of diseased cattle and unwholesome meat.

The termination of the civil war in Brazil has been followed by the general prevalence of peace and order. It appearing at an early stage of the insurrection that its course would call for unusual watchfulness on the part of this Government, our naval force in the harbor of Rio de Janeiro was strengthened. This precaution, I am satisfied, tended to restrict the issue to a simple trial of strength between the Brazilian Government and the insurgents and to avert complications which at times seemed imminent. Our firm attitude of neutrality was maintained to the end. The insurgents received no encouragement of eventual asylum from our commanders, and such opposition as they encountered was for the protection of our commerce and was clearly justified by public law.

A serious tension of relations having arisen at the close of the war between Brazil and Portugal by reason of the escape of the insurgent admiral Da Gama and his followers, the friendly offices of our representatives to those countries were exerted for the protection of the subjects of either within the territory of the other.

Although the Government of Brazil was duly notified that the commercial arrangement existing between the United States and that country based on the third section of the tariff act of 1890 was abrogated on August 28, 1894, by the taking effect of the tariff law now in force, that Government subsequently notified us of its intention to terminate such arrangement on the 1st day of January, 1895, in the exercise of the right reserved in the agreement between the two countries. I invite attention to the correspondence between the Secretary of State and the Brazilian minister on this subject.

The commission organized under the convention which we had entered into with Chile for the settlement of the outstanding claims of each Government against the other adjourned at the end of the period stipulated for its continuance leaving undetermined a number of American cases which had been duly presented. These claims are not barred, and negotiations are in progress for their submission to a new tribunal.

On the 17th of March last a new treaty with China in further regulation of emigration was signed at Washington, and on August 13 it received the sanction of the Senate. Ratification on the part of China and formal exchange are awaited to give effect to this mutually beneficial convention.

A gratifying recognition of the uniform impartiality of this country toward all foreign states was manifested by the coincident request of the Chinese and Japanese Governments that the agents of the United States should within proper limits afford protection to the subjects of the other during the suspension of diplomatic relations due to a state of war. This delicate office was accepted, and a misapprehension which gave rise to the belief that in affording this kindly unofficial protection our agents would exercise the same authority which the withdrawn agents of the belligerents had exercised was promptly corrected. Although the war between China and Japan endangers no policy of the United States, it deserves our gravest consideration by reason of its disturbance of our growing commercial interests in the two countries and the increased dangers which may result to our citizens domiciled or sojourning in the interior of China.

Acting under a stipulation in our treaty with Korea (the first concluded with a western power), I felt constrained at the beginning of the controversy to tender our good offices to induce an amicable arrangement of the initial difficulty growing out of the Japanese demands for administrative reforms in Korea, but the unhappy precipitation of actual hostilities defeated this kindly purpose.

Deploring the destructive war between the two most powerful of the eastern nations and anxious that our commercial interests in those countries may be preserved and that the safety of our citizens there shall not be jeopardized, I would not hesitate to heed any intimation that our friendly aid for the honorable termination of hostilities would be acceptable to both belligerents.

A convention has been finally concluded for the settlement by arbitration of the prolonged dispute with Ecuador growing out of the proceedings against Emilio Santos, a naturalized citizen of the United States.

Our relations with the Republic of France continue to be such as should exist between nations so long bound together by friendly sympathy and similarity in their form of government.

The recent cruel assassination of the President of this sister Republic called forth such universal expressions of sorrow and condolence from our people and Government as to leave no doubt of the depth and sincerity of our attachment. The resolutions passed by the Senate and House of Representatives on the occasion have been communicated to the widow of President Carnot.

Acting upon the reported discovery of Texas fever in cargoes of American cattle, the German prohibition against importations of live stock and fresh meats from this country has been revived. It is hoped that Germany will soon become convinced that the inhibition is as needless as it is harmful to mutual interests.

The German Government has protested against that provision of the customs tariff act which imposes a discriminating duty of one-tenth of 1 cent a pound on sugars coming from countries paying an export bounty thereon, claiming that the exaction of such duty is in contravention of Articles V and IX of the treaty of 1828 with Prussia.

In the interests of the commerce of both countries and to avoid even the accusation of treaty violation, I recommend the repeal of so much of the statute as imposes that duty, and I invite attention to the accompanying report of the Secretary of State, containing a discussion of the questions raised by the German protests.

Early in the present year an agreement was reached with Great Britain concerning instructions to be given to the naval commanders of the two Governments in Bering Sea and the contiguous North Pacific Ocean for their guidance in the execution of the award of the Paris Tribunal of Arbitration and the enforcement of the regulations therein prescribed for the protection of seal life in the waters mentioned. An understanding has also been reached for the payment by the United States of $425,000 in full satisfaction of all claims which may be made by Great Britain for damages growing out of the controversy as to fur seals in Bering Sea or the seizure of British vessels engaged in taking seal in those waters. The award and findings of the Paris Tribunal to a great extent determined the facts and principles upon which these claims should be adjusted, and they have been subjected by both Governments to a thorough examination upon the principles as well as the facts which they involve. I am convinced that a settlement upon the terms mentioned would be an equitable and advantageous one, and I recommend that provision be made for the prompt payment of the stated sum.

Thus far only France and Portugal have signified their willingness to adhere to the regulations established under the award of the Paris Tribunal of Arbitration.

Preliminary surveys of the Alaskan boundary and a preparatory examination of the question of protection of food fish in the contiguous waters of the United States and the Dominion of Canada are in progress.

The boundary of British Guiana still remains in dispute between Great Britain and Venezuela. Believing that its early settlement on some just basis alike honorable to both parties is in the line of our established policy to remove from this hemisphere all causes of difference with powers beyond the sea, I shall renew the efforts heretofore made to bring about a restoration of diplomatic relations between the disputants and to induce a reference to arbitration—a resort which Great Britain so conspicuously favors in principle and respects in practice and which is earnestly sought by her weaker adversary.

Since communicating the voluminous correspondence in regard to Hawaii and the action taken by the Senate and House of Representatives on certain questions submitted to the judgment and wider discretion of Congress the organization of a government in place of the provisional arrangement which followed the deposition of the Queen has been announced, with evidence of its effective operation. The recognition usual in such cases has been accorded the new Government.

Under our present treaties of extradition with Italy miscarriages of justice have occurred owing to the refusal of that Government to surrender its own subjects. Thus far our efforts to negotiate an amended convention obviating this difficulty have been unavailing.

Apart from the war in which the Island Empire is engaged, Japan attracts increasing attention in this country by her evident desire to cultivate more liberal intercourse with us and to seek our kindly aid in furtherance of her laudable desire for complete autonomy in her domestic affairs and full equality in the family of nations. The Japanese Empire of to-day is no longer the Japan of the past, and our relations with this progressive nation should not be less broad and liberal than those with other powers.

Good will, fostered by many interests in common, has marked our relations with our nearest southern neighbor. Peace being restored along her northern frontier, Mexico has asked the punishment of the late disturbers of her tranquillity. There ought to be a new treaty of commerce and navigation with that country to take the place of the one which terminated thirteen years ago. The friendliness of the intercourse between the two countries is attested by the fact that during this long period the commerce of each has steadily increased under the rule of mutual consideration, being neither stimulated by conventional arrangements nor retarded by jealous rivalries or selfish distrust.

An indemnity tendered by Mexico as a gracious act for the murder in 1887 of Leon Baldwin, an American citizen, by a band of marauders in Durango has been accepted and is being paid in installments.

The problem of the storage and use of the waters of the Rio Grande for irrigation should be solved by appropriate concurrent action of the two interested countries. Rising in the Colorado heights, the stream flows intermittently, yielding little water during the dry months to the irrigation channels already constructed along its course. This scarcity is often severely felt in the regions where the river forms a common boundary. Moreover, the frequent changes in its course through level sands often raise embarrassing questions of territorial jurisdiction.

Prominent among the questions of the year was the Bluefields incident, in what is known as the Mosquito Indian Strip, bordering on the Atlantic Ocean and within the jurisdiction of Nicaragua. By the treaty of 1860 between Great Britain and Nicaragua the former Government expressly recognized the sovereignty of the latter over the strip, and a limited form of self-government was guaranteed to the Mosquito Indians, to be exercised according to their customs, for themselves and other dwellers within its limits. The so-called native government, which grew to be largely made up of aliens, for many years disputed the sovereignty of Nicaragua over the strip and claimed the right to maintain therein a practically independent municipal government. Early in the past year efforts of Nicaragua to maintain sovereignty over the Mosquito territory led to serious disturbances, culminating in the suppression of the native government and the attempted substitution of an impracticable composite administration in which Nicaragua and alien residents were to participate. Failure was followed by an insurrection, which for a time subverted Nicaraguan rule, expelling her officers and restoring the old organization. This in turn gave place to the existing local government established and upheld by Nicaragua.

Although the alien interests arrayed against Nicaragua in these transactions have been largely American and the commerce of that region for some time has been and still is chiefly controlled by our citizens, we can not for that reason challenge the rightful sovereignty of Nicaragua over this important part of her domain.

For some months one, and during part of the time two, of our naval ships have been stationed at Bluefields for the protection of all legitimate interests of our citizens. In September last the Government at Managua expelled from its territory twelve or more foreigners, including two Americans, for alleged participation in the seditious or revolutionary movements against the Republic at Bluefields already mentioned; but through the earnest remonstrance of this Government the two Americans have been permitted to return to the peaceful management of their business. Our naval commanders at the scene of these disturbances by their constant exhibition of firmness and good judgment contributed largely to the prevention of more serious consequences and to the restoration of quiet and order. I regret that in the midst of these occurrences there happened a most grave and irritating failure of Nicaraguan justice. An American citizen named Wilson, residing at Rama, in the Mosquito territory, was murdered by one Argüello, the acting governor of the town. After some delay the murderer was arrested, but so insecurely confined or guarded that he escaped, and notwithstanding our repeated demands it is claimed that his recapture has been impossible by reason of his flight beyond Nicaraguan jurisdiction.

The Nicaraguan authorities, having given notice of forfeiture of their concession to the canal company on grounds purely technical and not embraced in the contract, have receded from that position.

Peru, I regret to say, shows symptoms of domestic disturbance, due probably to the slowness of her recuperation from the distresses of the war of 1881. Weakened in resources, her difficulties in facing international obligations invite our kindly sympathy and justify our forbearance in pressing long-pending claims. I have felt constrained to testify this sympathy in connection with certain demands urgently preferred by other powers.

The recent death of the Czar of Russia called forth appropriate expressions of sorrow and sympathy on the part of our Government with his bereaved family and the Russian people. As a further demonstration of respect and friendship our minister at St. Petersburg was directed to represent our Government at the funeral ceremonies.

The sealing interests of Russia in Bering Sea are second only to our own. A *modus vivendi* has therefore been concluded with the Imperial Government restrictive of poaching on the Russian rookeries and of sealing in waters which were not comprehended in the protected area defined in the Paris award.

Occasion has been found to urge upon the Russian Government equality of treatment for our great life-insurance companies whose operations have been extended throughout Europe. Admitting as we do foreign corporations to transact business in the United States, we naturally expect no less tolerance for our own in the ample fields of competition abroad.

But few cases of interference with naturalized citizens returning to Russia have been reported during the current year. One Krzeminski was arrested last summer in a Polish province on a reported charge of unpermitted renunciation of Russian allegiance, but it transpired that the proceedings originated in alleged malfeasance committed by Krzeminski while an imperial official a number of years ago. Efforts for his release, which promised to be successful, were in progress when his death was reported.

The Government of Salvador having been overthrown by an abrupt popular outbreak, certain of its military and civil officers, while hotly pursued by infuriated insurgents, sought refuge on board the United States war ship *Bennington*, then lying in a Salvadorean port. Although the practice of asylum is not favored by this Government, yet in view of the imminent peril which threatened the fugitives and solely from considerations of humanity they were afforded shelter by our naval commander, and when afterwards demanded under our treaty of extradition with Salvador for trial on charges of murder, arson, and robbery I directed that such of them as had not voluntarily left the ship be conveyed to one of our nearest ports where a hearing could be had before a judicial officer, in compliance with the terms of the treaty. On their arrival at San Francisco such a proceeding was promptly instituted before the United States district judge, who held that the acts constituting the alleged offenses were political and discharged all the accused except one Cienfuegos, who was held for an attempt to murder. Thereupon I was constrained to direct his release for the reason that an attempt to murder was not one of the crimes charged against him and upon which his surrender to the Salvadorean authorities had been demanded.

Unreasonable and unjust fines imposed by Spain on the vessels and commerce of the United States have demanded from time to time during the last twenty years earnest remonstrance on the part of our Government. In the immediate past exorbitant penalties have been imposed upon our vessels and goods by customs authorities of Cuba and Puerto Rico for clerical errors of the most trivial character in the manifests or bills of lading. In some cases fines amounting to thousands of dollars have been levied upon cargoes or the carrying vessels when the goods in question were entitled to free entry. Fines have been exacted even when the error had been detected and the Spanish authorities notified before the arrival of the goods in port.

This conduct is in strange contrast with the considerate and liberal treatment extended to Spanish vessels and cargoes in our ports in like cases. No satisfactory settlement of these vexatious questions has yet been reached.

The Mora case, referred to in my last annual message, remains unsettled. From the diplomatic correspondence on this subject which has been laid before the Senate it will be seen that this Government has offered to conclude a convention with Spain for disposal by arbitration of outstanding claims between the two countries, except the Mora claim, which, having been long ago adjusted, now only awaits payment as stipulated, and of course it could not be included in the proposed convention. It was hoped that this offer would remove parliamentary obstacles encountered by the Spanish Government in providing payment of the Mora indemnity. I regret to say that no definite reply to this offer has yet been made and all efforts to secure payment of this settled claim have been unavailing.

In my last annual message I adverted to the claim on the part of Turkey of the right to expel as persons undesirable and dangerous Armenians naturalized in the United States and returning to Turkish jurisdiction.* Numerous questions in this relation have arisen. While this Government acquiesces in the asserted right of expulsion, it will not consent that Armenians may be imprisoned or otherwise punished for no other reason than having acquired without imperial consent American citizenship.

Three of the assailants of Miss Melton, an American teacher in Mosul, have been convicted by the Ottoman courts, and I am advised that an appeal against the acquittal of the remaining five has been taken by the Turkish prosecuting officer.

A convention has been concluded with Venezuela for the arbitration of a long-disputed claim growing out of the seizure of certain vessels the property of citizens of the United States. Although signed, the treaty of extradition with Venezuela is not yet in force, owing to the insistence of that Government that when surrendered its citizens shall in no case be liable to capital punishment.

The rules for the prevention of collisions at sea which were framed by the maritime conference held in this city in 1889, having been concurrently incorporated in the statutes of the United States and Great Britain,

* See pp. 5872–5873.

have been announced to take effect March 1, 1895, and invitations have been extended to all maritime nations to adhere to them. Favorable responses have thus far been received from Austria, France, Portugal, Spain, and Sweden.

In my last annual message I referred briefly to the unsatisfactory state of affairs in Samoa under the operation of the Berlin treaty as signally illustrating the impolicy of entangling alliances with foreign powers,* and on May 9, 1894, in response to a resolution of the Senate, I sent a special message† and documents to that body on the same subject, which emphasized my previously expressed opinions. Later occurrences, the correspondence in regard to which will be laid before the Congress, further demonstrate that the Government which was devised by the three powers and forced upon the Samoans against their inveterate hostility can be maintained only by the continued presence of foreign military force and at no small sacrifice of life and treasure.

The suppression of the Mataafa insurrection by the powers and the subsequent banishment of the leader and eleven other chiefs, as recited in my last message, did not bring lasting peace to the islands. Formidable uprisings continued, and finally a rebellion broke out in the capital island, Upolu, headed in Aana, the western district, by the younger Tamasese, and in Atua, the eastern district, by other leaders. The insurgents ravaged the country and fought the Government's troops up to the very doors of Apia. The King again appealed to the powers for help, and the combined British and German naval forces reduced the Atuans to apparent subjection, not, however, without considerable loss to the natives. A few days later Tamasese and his adherents, fearing the ships and the marines, professed submission.

Reports received from our agents at Apia do not justify the belief that the peace thus brought about will be of long duration. It is their conviction that the natives are at heart hostile to the present Government, that such of them as profess loyalty to it do so from fear of the powers, and that it would speedily go to pieces if the war ships were withdrawn. In reporting to his Government on the unsatisfactory situation since the suppression of the late revolt by foreign armed forces, the German consul at Apia stated:

That peace will be lasting is hardly to be presumed. The lesson given by firing on Atua was not sufficiently sharp and incisive to leave a lasting impression on the forgetful Samoan temperament. In fact, conditions are existing which show that peace will not last and is not seriously intended. Malietoa, the King, and his chiefs are convinced that the departure of the war ships will be a signal for a renewal of war. The circumstance that the representatives of the villages of all the districts which were opposed to the Government have already withdrawn to Atua to hold meetings, and that both Atua and Aana have forbidden inhabitants of those districts which fought on the side of the Government to return to their villages, and have already partly burned down the latter, indicates that a real conciliation of the parties is still far off.

* See p. 5871.   † See p. 5909.

And in a note of the 10th ultimo, inclosing a copy of that report for the information of this Government, the German ambassador said:

The contents of the report awakened the Imperial Government's apprehension that under existing circumstances the peace concluded with the rebels will afford no assurance of the lasting restoration of tranquillity in the islands.

The present Government has utterly failed to correct, if indeed it has not aggravated, the very evils it was intended to prevent. It has not stimulated our commerce with the islands. Our participation in its establishment against the wishes of the natives was in plain defiance of the conservative teachings and warnings of the wise and patriotic men who laid the foundations of our free institutions, and I invite an expression of the judgment of Congress on the propriety of steps being taken by this Government looking to the withdrawal from its engagements with the other powers on some reasonable terms not prejudicial to any of our existing rights.

The Secretary of the Treasury reports that the receipts of the Government from all sources of revenue during the fiscal year ending June 30, 1894, amounted to $372,802,498.29 and its expenditures to $442,605,758.87, leaving a deficit of $69,803,260.58. There was a decrease of $15,952,674.66 in the ordinary expense of the Government as compared with the fiscal year 1893.

There was collected from customs $131,818,530.62 and from internal revenue $147,168,449.70. The balance of the income for the year, amounting to $93,815,517.97, was derived from the sales of lands and other sources.

The value of our total dutiable imports amounted to $275,199,086, being $146,657,625 less than during the preceding year, and the importations free of duty amounted to $379,795,536, being $64,748,675 less than during the preceding year. The receipts from customs were $73,536,486.11 less and from internal revenue $13,836,539.97 less than in 1893.

The total tax collected from distilled spirits was $85,259,250.25, on manufactured tobacco $28,617,898.62, and on fermented liquors $31,414,788.04.

Our exports of merchandise, domestic and foreign, amounted during the year to $892,140,572, being an increase over the preceding year of $44,495,378.

The total amount of gold exported during the fiscal year was $76,898,061, as against $108,680,444 during the fiscal year 1893. The amount imported was $72,449,119, as against $21,174,381 during the previous year.

The imports of silver were $13,286,552 and the exports were $50,451,265.

The total bounty paid upon the production of sugar in the United States for the fiscal year was $12,100,208.89, being an increase of $2,725,078.01

over the payments made during the preceding year. The amount of bounty paid from July 1, 1894, to August 28, 1894, the time when further payments ceased by operation of law, was $966,185.84. The total expenses incurred in the payment of the bounty upon sugar during the fiscal year was $130,140.85.

It is estimated that upon the basis of the present revenue laws the receipts of the Government during the current fiscal year, ending June 30, 1895, will be $424,427,748.44 and its expenditures $444,427,748.44, resulting in a deficit of $20,000,000.

On the 1st day of November, 1894, the total stock of money of all kinds in the country was $2,240,773,888, as against $2,204,651,000 on the 1st day of November, 1893, and the money of all kinds in circulation, or not included in the Treasury holdings, was $1,672,093,422, or $24.27 per capita upon an estimated population of 68,887,000. At the same date there was held in the Treasury gold bullion amounting to $44,615,-177.55 and silver bullion which was purchased at a cost of $127,772,988. The purchase of silver bullion under the act of July 14, 1890, ceased on the 1st day of November, 1893, and up to that time there had been purchased during the fiscal year 11,917,658.78 fine ounces, at a cost of $8,715,-521.32, an average cost of $0.7313 per fine ounce. The total amount of silver purchased from the time that law took effect until the repeal of its purchasing clause, on the date last mentioned, was 168,674,682.53 fine ounces, which cost $155,931,002.25, the average price per fine ounce being $0.9244.

The total amount of standard silver dollars coined at the mints of the United States since the passage of the act of February 28, 1878, is $421,-776,408, of which $378,166,793 were coined under the provisions of that act, $38,531,143 under the provisions of the act of July 14, 1890, and $5,078,472 under the act providing for the coinage of trade-dollar bullion.

The total coinage of all metals at our mints during the last fiscal year consisted of 63,485,220 pieces, valued at $106,216,730.06, of which there were $99,474,912.50 in gold coined, $758 in standard silver dollars, $6,024,140.30 in subsidiary silver coin, and $716,919.26 in minor coin.

During the calendar year 1893 the production of precious metals in the United States was estimated at 1,739,323 fine ounces of gold of the commercial and coinage value of $35,955,000 and 60,000,000 fine ounces of silver of the bullion or market value of $46,800,000 and of the coinage value of $77,576,000. It is estimated that on the 1st day of July, 1894, the stock of metallic money in the United States, consisting of coin and bullion, amounted to $1,251,640,958, of which $627,923,201 was gold and $624,347,757 was silver.

Fifty national banks were organized during the year ending October 31, 1894, with a capital of $5,285,000, and 79, with a capital of $10,475,-000, went into voluntary liquidation. Twenty-one banks, with a capital of $2,770,000, were placed in the hands of receivers. The total number of national banks in existence on the 31st day of October last was 3,756, being 40 less than on the 31st day of October, 1893. The capital stock paid in was $672,671,365, being $9,678,491 less than at the same time in the previous year, and the surplus fund and individual profits, less expenses and taxes paid, amounted to $334,121,082.10, which was $16,-089,780 less than on October 31, 1893. The circulation was decreased $1,741,563. The obligations of the banks to each other were increased $117,268,334 and the individual deposits were $277,294,489 less than at the corresponding date in the previous year. Loans and discounts were $161,206,923 more than at the same time the previous year, and checks and other cash items were $90,349,963 more. The total resources of the banks at the date mentioned amounted to $3,473,922,055, as against $3,109,563,284.36 in 1893.

From the report of the Secretary of War it appears that the strength of the Army on September 30, 1894, was 2,135 officers and 25,765 enlisted men. Although this is apparently a very slight decrease compared with the previous year, the actual effective force has been increased to the equivalent of nearly two regiments through the reorganization of the system of recruiting and the consequent release to regimental duty of the large force of men hitherto serving at the recruiting depots. The abolition of these depots, it is predicted, will furthermore effect an annual reduction approximating $250,000 in the direct expenditures, besides promoting generally the health, morale, and discipline of the troops.

The execution of the policy of concentrating the Army at important centers of population and transportation, foreshadowed in the last annual report of the Secretary, has resulted in the abandonment of fifteen of the smaller posts, which was effected under a plan which assembles organizations of the same regiments hitherto widely separated. This renders our small forces more readily effective for any service which they may be called upon to perform, increases the extent of the territory under protection without diminishing the security heretofore afforded to any locality, improves the discipline, training, and *esprit de corps* of the Army, besides considerably decreasing the cost of its maintenance.

Though the forces of the Department of the East have been somewhat increased, more than three-fourths of the Army is still stationed west of the Mississippi. This carefully matured policy, which secures the best and greatest service in the interests of the general welfare from the small force comprising our Regular Army, should not be thoughtlessly embarrassed by the creation of new and unnecessary posts through acts of Congress to gratify the ambitions or interests of localities.

While the maximum legal strength of the Army is 25,000 men, the effective strength, through various causes, is but little over 20,000 men. The purpose of Congress does not, therefore, seem to be fully attained by the existing condition. While no considerable increase in the Army is, in my judgment, demanded by recent events, the policy of seacoast fortification, in the prosecution of which we have been steadily engaged for some years, has so far developed as to suggest that the effective strength of the Army be now made at least equal to the legal strength. Measures taken by the Department during the year, as indicated, have already considerably augmented the effective force, and the Secretary of War presents a plan, which I recommend to the consideration of Congress, to attain the desired end. Economies effected in the Department in other lines of its work will offset to a great extent the expenditure involved in the proposition submitted. Among other things this contemplates the adoption of the three-battalion formation of regiments, which for several years has been indorsed by the Secretaries of War and the Generals Commanding the Army. Compact in itself, it provides a skeleton organization, ready to be filled out in the event of war, which is peculiarly adapted to our strength and requirements; and the fact that every other nation, with a single exception, has adopted this formation to meet the conditions of modern warfare should alone secure for the recommendation an early consideration.

It is hardly necessary to recall the fact that in obedience to the commands of the Constitution and the laws, and for the purpose of protecting the property of the United States, aiding the process of Federal courts, and removing lawless obstructions to the performance by the Government of its legitimate functions, it became necessary in various localities during the year to employ a considerable portion of the regular troops. The duty was discharged promptly, courageously, and with marked discretion by the officers and men, and the most gratifying proof was thus afforded that the Army deserves that complete confidence in its efficiency and discipline which the country has at all times manifested.

The year has been free from disturbances by Indians, and the chances of further depredations on their part are constantly becoming more remote and improbable.

The total expenditures for the War Department for the year ended June 30, 1894, amounted to $56,039,009.34. Of this sum $2,000,614.99 was for salaries and contingent expenses, $23,665,156.16 for the support of the military establishment, $5,001,682.23 for miscellaneous objects, and $25,371,555.96 for public works. This latter sum includes $19,-494,037.49 for river and harbor improvements and $3,947,863.56 for fortifications and other works of defense. The appropriations for the current year aggregate $52,429,112.78, and the estimates submitted by the Secretary of War for the next fiscal year call for appropriations amounting to $52,318,629.55.

The skill and industry of our ordnance officers and inventors have, it is believed, overcome the mechanical obstacles which have heretofore delayed the armament of our coasts, and this great national undertaking upon which we have entered may now proceed as rapidly as Congress shall determine. With a supply of finished guns of large caliber already on hand, to which additions should now rapidly follow, the wisdom of providing carriages and emplacements for their mount can not be too strongly urged.

The total enrollment of the militia of the several States is 117,533 officers and enlisted men, an increase of 5,343 over the number reported at the close of the previous year. The reports of militia inspections by Regular Army officers show a marked increase in interest and efficiency among the State organizations, and I strongly recommend a continuance of the policy of affording every practical encouragement possible to this important auxiliary of our military establishment.

The condition of the Apache Indians held as prisoners by the Government for eight years at a cost of half a million dollars has been changed during the year from captivity to one which gives them an opportunity to demonstrate their capacity for self-support and at least partial civilization. Legislation enacted at the late session of Congress gave the War Department authority to transfer the survivors, numbering 346, from Mount Vernon Barracks, in Alabama, to any suitable reservation. The Department selected as their future home the military lands near Fort Sill, Ind. T., where, under military surveillance, the former prisoners have been established in agriculture under conditions favorable to their advancement.

In recognition of the long and distinguished military services and faithful discharge of delicate and responsible civil duties by Major-General John M. Schofield, now the General Commanding the Army, it is suggested to Congress that the temporary revival of the grade of lieutenant-general in his behalf would be a just and gracious act and would permit his retirement, now near at hand, with rank befitting his merits.

The report of the Attorney-General notes the gratifying progress made by the Supreme Court in overcoming the arrears of its business and in reaching a condition in which it will be able to dispose of cases as they arise without any unreasonable delay. This result is of course very largely due to the successful working of the plan inaugurating circuit courts of appeals. In respect to these tribunals the suggestion is made in quarters entitled to the highest consideration that an additional circuit judge for each circuit would greatly strengthen these courts and the confidence reposed in their adjudications, and that such an addition would not create a greater force of judges than the increasing business of such courts requires. I commend the suggestion to the careful consideration of the Congress. Other important topics are adverted to in the report, accompanied by recommendations, many of which have been treated at large in previous messages, and at this time, therefore, need only be named. I refer to the abolition of the fee system as a measure of compensation to Federal officers; the enlargement of the powers of United States commissioners, at least in the Territories; the allowance of writs of error in criminal cases on behalf of the United States, and the establishment of degrees in the crime of murder. A topic dealt with by the Attorney-General of much importance is the condition of the administration of justice in the Indian Territory. The permanent solution of what is called the Indian problem is probably not to be expected at once, but meanwhile such ameliorations of present conditions as the existing system will admit of ought not to be neglected. I am satisfied there should be a Federal court established for the Territory, with sufficient judges, and that this court should sit within the Territory and have the same jurisdiction as to Territorial affairs as is now vested in the Federal courts sitting in Arkansas and Texas.

Another subject of pressing moment referred to by the Attorney-General is the reorganization of the Union Pacific Railway Company on a basis equitable as regards all private interests and as favorable to the Government as existing conditions will permit. The operation of a railroad by a court through a receiver is an anomalous state of things which should be terminated on all grounds, public and private, at the earliest possible moment. Besides, not to enact the needed enabling legislation at the present session postpones the whole matter until the assembling of a new Congress and inevitably increases all the complications of the situation, and could not but be regarded as a signal failure to solve a problem which has practically been before the present Congress ever since its organization.

Eight years ago in my annual message I urged upon the Congress as strongly as I could the location and construction of two prisons for the confinement of United States prisoners.* A similar recommendation has been made from time to time since, and a few years ago a law was passed providing for the selection of sites for three such institutions. No appropriation has, however, been made to carry the act into effect, and the old and discreditable condition still exists.

It is not my purpose at this time to repeat the considerations which make an impregnable case in favor of the ownership and management by the Government of the penal institutions in which Federal prisoners are confined. I simply desire to again urge former recommendations on the subject and to particularly call the attention of the Congress to that part of the report of the Secretary of War in which he states that the military prison at Fort Leavenworth, Kans., can be turned over to the Government as a prison for Federal convicts without the least difficulty and with an actual saving of money from every point of view.

Pending a more complete reform, I hope that by the adoption of the suggestion of the Secretary of War this easy step may be taken in the direction of the proper care of its convicts by the Government of the United States.

The report of the Postmaster-General presents a comprehensive statement of the operations of the Post-Office Department for the last fiscal year.

* See pp. 5102–5103.

The receipts of the Department during the year amounted to $75,-080,479.04 and the expenditures to $84,324,414.15.

The transactions of the postal service indicate with barometric certainty the fluctuations in the business of the country. Inasmuch, therefore, as business complications continued to exist throughout the last year to an unforeseen extent, it is not surprising that the deficiency of revenue to meet the expenditures of the Post-Office Department, which was estimated in advance at about $8,000,000, should be exceeded by nearly $1,225,000. The ascertained revenues of the last year, which were the basis of calculation for the current year, being less than estimated, the deficiency for the current year will be correspondingly greater, though the Postmaster-General states that the latest indications are so favorable that he confidently predicts an increase of at least 8 per cent in the revenues of the current year over those of the last year.

The expenditures increase steadily and necessarily with the growth and needs of the country, so that the deficiency is greater or less in any year, depending upon the volume of receipts.

The Postmaster-General states that this deficiency is unnecessary and might be obviated at once if the law regulating rates upon mail matter of the second class was modified. The rate received for the transmission of this second-class matter is 1 cent per pound, while the cost of such transmission to the Government is eight times that amount. In the general terms of the law this rate covers newspapers and periodicals. The extensions of the meaning of these terms from time to time have admitted to the privileges intended for legitimate newspapers and periodicals a surprising range of publications and created abuses the cost of which amounts in the aggregate to the total deficiency of the Post-Office Department. Pretended newspapers are started by business houses for the mere purpose of advertising goods, complying with the law in form only and discontinuing the publications as soon as the period of advertising is over. "Sample copies" of pretended newspapers are issued in great numbers for a like purpose only. The result is a great loss of revenue to the Government, besides its humiliating use as an agency to aid in carrying out the scheme of a business house to advertise its goods by means of a trick upon both its rival houses and the regular and legitimate newspapers. Paper-covered literature, consisting mainly of trashy novels, to the extent of many thousands of tons is sent through the mails at 1 cent per pound, while the publishers of standard works are required to pay eight times that amount in sending their publications. Another abuse consists in the free carriage through the mails of hundreds of tons of seed and grain uselessly distributed through the Department of Agriculture. The Postmaster-General predicts that if the law be so amended as to eradicate these abuses not only will the Post-Office Department show no deficiency, but he believes that in the near future all legitimate newspapers and periodical magazines might be properly transmitted through the mails to their subscribers free of cost. I invite your prompt consideration of this subject and fully indorse the views of the Postmaster-General.

The total number of post-offices in the United States on the 30th day of June, 1894, was 69,805, an increase of 1,403 over the preceding year. Of these, 3,428 were Presidential, an increase in that class of 68 over the preceding year.

Six hundred and ten cities and towns are provided with free delivery. Ninety-three other cities and towns entitled to this service under the law have not been accorded it on account of insufficient funds. The expense of free delivery for the current fiscal year will be more than $12,300,000, and under existing legislation this item of expenditure is subject to constant increase. The estimated cost of rural free delivery generally is so very large that it ought not to be considered in the present condition of affairs.

During the year 830 additional domestic money-order offices were established. The total number of these offices at the close of the year was 19,264. There were 14,304,041 money orders issued during the year, being an increase over the preceding year of 994,306. The value of these orders amounted to $138,793,579.49, an increase of $11,217,145.84. There were also issued during the year postal notes amounting to $12,-649,094.55.

During the year 218 international money-order offices were added to those already established, making a total of 2,625 such offices in operation June 30, 1894. The number of international money orders issued during the year was 917,823, a decrease in number of 138,176, and their value was $13,792,455.31, a decrease in amount of $2,549,382.55. The number of orders paid was 361,180, an increase over the preceding year of 60,263, and their value was $6,568,493.78, an increase of $1,285,118.08.

From the foregoing statements it appears that the total issue of money orders and postal notes for the year amounted to $165,235,129.35.

The number of letters and packages mailed during the year for special delivery was 3,436,970. The special-delivery stamps used upon these letters and packages amounted to $343,697. The messengers' fees paid for their delivery amounted to $261,209.70, leaving a balance in favor of the Government of $82,487.30.

The report shows most gratifying results in the way of economies worked out without affecting the efficiency of the postal service. These consist in the abrogation of steamship subsidy contracts, reletting of mail transportation contracts, and in the cost and amount of supplies used in the service, amounting in all to $16,619,047.42.

This report also contains a valuable contribution to the history of the Universal Postal Union, an arrangement which amounts practically to the establishment of one postal system for the entire civilized world. Special attention is directed to this subject at this time in view of the fact that the next congress of the union will meet in Washington in 1897, and it is hoped that timely action will be taken in the direction of perfecting preparations for that event.

The Postmaster-General renews the suggestion made in a previous report that the Department organization be increased to the extent of creating a direct district supervision of all postal affairs, and in this suggestion I fully concur.

There are now connected with the Post-Office establishment 32,661 employees who are in the classified service. This includes many who have been classified upon the suggestion of the Postmaster-General. He states that another year's experience at the head of the Department serves only to strengthen the conviction as to the excellent working of the civil-service law in this branch of the public service.

Attention is called to the report of the Secretary of the Navy, which shows very gratifying progress in the construction of ships for our new Navy. All the vessels now building, including the three torpedo boats authorized at the last session of Congress and excepting the first-class battle ship *Iowa*, will probably be completed during the coming fiscal year.

The estimates for the increase of the Navy for the year ending June 30, 1896, are large, but they include practically the entire sum necessary to complete and equip all the new ships not now in commission, so that unless new ships are authorized the appropriations for the naval service for the fiscal year ending June 30, 1897, should fall below the estimates for the coming year by at least $12,000,000.

The Secretary presents with much earnestness a plea for the authorization of three additional battle ships and ten or twelve torpedo boats. While the unarmored vessels heretofore authorized, including those now nearing completion, will constitute a fleet which it is believed is sufficient for ordinary cruising purposes in time of peace, we have now completed and in process of construction but four first-class battle ships and but few torpedo boats. If we are to have a navy for warlike operations, offensive and defensive, we certainly ought to increase both the number of battle ships and torpedo boats.

The manufacture of armor requires expensive plants and the aggregation of many skilled workmen. All the armor necessary to complete the vessels now building will be delivered before the 1st of June next. If no new contracts are given out, contractors must disband their workmen and their plants must lie idle. Battle ships authorized at this time would not be well under way until late in the coming fiscal year, and at least three years and a half from the date of the contract would be required for their completion. The Secretary states that not more than 15 per cent of the cost of such ships need be included in the appropriations for the coming year.

I recommend that provision be made for the construction of additional battle ships and torpedo boats.

The Secretary recommends the manufacture not only of a reserve supply of ordnance and ordnance material for ships of the Navy, but also a supply for the auxiliary fleet. Guns and their appurtenances should be provided and kept on hand for both these purposes. We have not to-day a single gun that could be put upon the ships *Paris* or *New York* of the International Navigation Company or any other ship of our reserve Navy.

The manufacture of guns at the Washington Navy-Yard is proceeding satisfactorily, and none of our new ships will be required to wait for their guns or ordnance equipment.

An important order has been issued by the Secretary of the Navy coordinating the duties of the several bureaus concerned in the construction of ships. This order, it is believed, will secure to a greater extent than has heretofore been possible the harmonious action of these several bureaus and make the attainment of the best results more certain.

During the past fiscal year there has been an unusual and pressing demand in many quarters of the world for the presence of vessels to guard American interests.

In January last, during the Brazilian insurrection, a large fleet was concentrated in the harbor of Rio de Janeiro. The vigorous action of Rear-Admiral Benham in protecting the personal and commercial rights of our citizens during the disturbed conditions afforded results which will, it is believed, have a far-reaching and wholesome influence whenever in like circumstances it may become necessary for our naval commanders to interfere on behalf of our people in foreign ports.

The war now in progress between China and Japan has rendered it necessary or expedient to dispatch eight vessels to those waters.

Both the Secretary of the Navy and the Secretary of the Treasury recommend the transfer of the work of the Coast Survey proper to the Navy Department. I heartily concur in this recommendation. Excluding Alaska and a very small area besides, all the work of mapping and charting our coasts has been completed. The hydrographic work, which must be done over and over again by reason of the shifting and varying depths of water consequent upon the action of streams and tides, has heretofore been done under the direction of naval officers in subordination to the Superintendent of the Coast Survey. There seems to be no good reason why the Navy should not have entire charge hereafter of such work, especially as the Hydrographic Office of the Navy Department is now and has been for many years engaged in making efficient maps entirely similar to those prepared by the Coast Survey.

I feel it my imperative duty to call attention to the recommendation of the Secretary in regard to the personnel of the line of the Navy. The stagnation of promotion in this the vital branch of the service is so great as to seriously impair its efficiency.

I consider it of the utmost importance that the young and middle-aged officers should before the eve of retirement be permitted to reach a grade entitling them to active and important duty.

The system adopted a few years ago regulating the employment of labor at the navy-yards is rigidly upheld and has fully demonstrated its usefulness and expediency. It is within the domain of civil-service reform inasmuch as workmen are employed through a board of labor selected at each navy-yard and are given work without reference to politics and in the order of their application, preference, however, being given to Army and Navy veterans and those having former navy-yard experience.

Amendments suggested by experience have been made to the rules regulating the system. Through its operation the work at our navy-yards has been vastly improved in efficiency and the opportunity to work has been honestly and fairly awarded to willing and competent applicants.

It is hoped that if this system continues to be strictly adhered to there will soon be as a natural consequence such an equalization of party benefit as will remove all temptation to relax or abandon it.

The report of the Secretary of the Interior exhibits the situation of the numerous and interesting branches of the public service connected with his Department. I commend this report and the valuable recommendations of the Secretary to the careful attention of the Congress.

The public land disposed of during the year amounted to 10,406,100.77 acres, including 28,876.05 of Indian lands.

It is estimated that the public domain still remaining amounts to a little more than 600,000,000 acres, including, however, about 360,000,000 acres in Alaska, as well as military reservations and railroad and other selections of lands yet unadjudicated.

The total cash receipts from sale of lands amounted to $2,674,285.79, including $91,981.03 received for Indian lands.

Thirty-five thousand patents were issued for agricultural lands, and 3,100 patents were issued to Indians on allotments of their holdings in severalty, the land so allotted being inalienable by the Indian allottees for a period of twenty-five years after patent.

There were certified and patented on account of railroad and wagon-road grants during the year 865,556.45 acres of land, and at the close of the year 29,000,000 acres were embraced in the lists of selections made by railroad and wagon-road companies and awaited settlement.

The selections of swamp lands and that taken as indemnity therefor since the passage of the act providing for the same in 1849 amount to nearly or quite 80,500,000 acres, of which 58,000,000 have been patented to States. About 138,000 acres were patented during the last year. Nearly 820,000 acres of school and education grants were approved during the year, and at its close 1,250,363.81 acres remained unadjusted.

It appears that the appropriation for the current year on account of special service for the protection of the public lands and the timber thereon is much less than those for previous years, and inadequate for an efficient performance of the work. A larger sum of money than has been appropriated during a number of years past on this account has been returned to the Government as a result of the labors of those employed in the particular service mentioned, and I hope it will not be crippled by insufficient appropriation.

I fully indorse the recommendation of the Secretary that adequate protection be provided for our forest reserves and that a comprehensive forestry system be inaugurated. Such keepers and superintendents as are necessary to protect the forests already reserved should be provided. I am of the opinion that there should be an abandonment of the policy sanctioned by present laws under which the Government, for a very small consideration, is rapidly losing title to immense tracts of land covered with timber, which should be properly reserved as permanent sources of timber supply.

The suggestion that a change be made in the manner of securing surveys of the public lands is especially worthy of consideration. I am satisfied that these surveys should be made by a corps of competent surveyors under the immediate control and direction of the Commissioner of the General Land Office.

An exceedingly important recommendation of the Secretary relates to the manner in which contests and litigated cases growing out of efforts to obtain Government land are determined. The entire testimony upon which these controversies depend in all their stages is taken before the local registers and receivers, and yet these officers have no power to subpœna witnesses or to enforce their attendance to testify. These cases, numbering three or four thousand annually, are sent by the local officers to the Commissioner of the General Land Office for his action. The exigencies of his other duties oblige him to act upon the decisions of the registers and receivers without an opportunity of thorough personal examination. Nearly 2,000 of these cases are appealed annually from the Commissioner to the Secretary of the Interior. Burdened with other important administrative duties, his determination of these appeals must be almost perfunctory and based upon the examination of others, though this determination of the Secretary operates as a final adjudication upon rights of very great importance.

I concur in the opinion that the Commissioner of the General Land Office should be relieved from the duty of deciding litigated land cases, that a nonpartisan court should be created to pass on such cases, and that the decisions of this court should be final, at least so far as the decisions of the Department are now final. The proposed court might be given authority to certify questions of law in matters of especial importance to the Supreme Court of the United States or the court of appeals for the District of Columbia for decision. The creation of such a tribunal would expedite the disposal of cases and insure decisions of a more satisfactory character. The registers and receivers who originally hear and decide these disputes should be invested with authority to compel witnesses to attend and testify before them.

Though the condition of the Indians shows a steady and healthy progress, their situation is not satisfactory at all points. Some of them to whom allotments of land have been made are found to be unable or disinclined to follow agricultural pursuits or to otherwise beneficially manage their land. This is especially true of the Cheyennes and Arapahoes, who, as it appears by reports of their agent, have in many instances never been located upon their allotments, and in some cases do not even know where their allotments are. Their condition has deteriorated. They are not self-supporting and they live in camps and spend their time in idleness.

I have always believed that allotments of reservation lands to Indians in severalty should be made sparingly, or at least slowly, and with the utmost caution. In these days, when white agriculturists and stock raisers of experience and intelligence find their lot a hard one, we ought not to expect Indians, unless far advanced in civilization and habits of industry, to support themselves on the small tracts of land usually allotted to them.

If the self-supporting scheme by allotment fails, the wretched pauperism of the allottees which results is worse than their original condition of regulated dependence. It is evident that the evil consequences of ill-advised allotment are intensified in cases where the false step can not be retraced on account of the purchase by the Government of reservation lands remaining after allotments are made and the disposition of such remaining lands to settlers or purchasers from the Government.

I am convinced that the proper solution of the Indian problem and the success of every step taken in that direction depend to a very large extent upon the intelligence and honesty of the reservation agents and the interest they have in their work. An agent fitted for his place can do much toward preparing the Indians under his charge for citizenship and allotment of their lands, and his advice as to any matter concerning their welfare will not mislead. An unfit agent will make no effort to advance the Indians on his reservation toward civilization or preparation for allotment of lands in severalty, and his opinion as to their condition in this and other regards is heedless and valueless.

The indications are that the detail of army officers as Indian agents will result in improved management on the reservations.

Whenever allotments are made and any Indian on the reservation has previously settled upon a lot and cultivated it or shown a disposition to improve it in any way, such lot should certainly be allotted to him, and this should be made plainly obligatory by statute.

In the light of experience and considering the uncertainty of the Indian situation and its exigencies in the future, I am not only disposed to be very cautious in making allotments, but I incline to agree with the Secretary of the Interior in the opinion that when allotments are made the balance of reservation land remaining after allotment, instead of being bought by the Government from the Indians and opened for settlement

BLOCKHOUSE AND CHARGE OF SAN JUAN HILL

CAPTURE OF SAN JUAN HILL

While our army rested from June 24th to 30th, the Spaniards diligently entrenched themselves on San Juan Hill. By the time we attacked (July 1st), their position was nearly all that military skill could make it. Sumner's division of seven thousand lay at the edge of the woods in the valley, within a half-mile range, while the Spaniards from their trenches fired in volleys so systematically that each rod of ground received its due proportion of lead.

Grimes's battery threw its shrapnel over the heads of our troops into the blockhouse and trenches.

Finally, the Spanish fire made their position absolutely untenable; they were forced to get out of it. Retreat was impossible, because the trail was choked with men. Their only means of escape was to advance. According to an eyewitness, Roosevelt rode out of the woods at the head of his men, but found the negroes of the Ninth Cavalry in his way. "If you don't wish to go forward, please let my men pass," he said. The negroes, for answer, sprang in line beside the Rough Riders. Then commenced the famous charge. Picturesque details were sadly lacking. The grass offered about as much resistance as water waist high, and the climb was made slowly and stubbornly by a single line of men, slipping and scrambling over the ground. The crest of the hill sputtered little jets of flame at them; some tumbled out of sight in the grass, but like a rising tide, the troops plodded on. Near the top the lessening area drew the men closer together. They broke into a run. That was all the Spaniards could endure, so they fled.

See the articles "Spanish-American War," "Santiago," "Santiago Harbor," and "Guantanamo" in the encyclopedic index (volume eleven). President McKinley's wartime messages from the official record of the war.

with such scandals and unfair practices as seem unavoidable, should remain for a time at least as common land or be sold by the Government on behalf of the Indians in an orderly way and at fixed prices, to be determined by its location and desirability, and that the proceeds, less expenses, should be held in trust for the benefit of the Indian proprietors.

The intelligent Indian-school management of the past year has been followed by gratifying results. Efforts have been made to advance the work in a sound and practical manner. Five institutes of Indian teachers have been held during the year, and have proved very beneficial through the views exchanged and methods discussed particularly applicable to Indian education.

Efforts are being made in the direction of a gradual reduction of the number of Indian contract schools, so that in a comparatively short time they may give way altogether to Government schools, and it is hoped that the change may be so gradual as to be perfected without too great expense to the Government or undue disregard of investments made by those who have established and are maintaining such contract schools.

The appropriation for the current year, ending June 30, 1895, applicable to the ordinary expenses of the Indian service amounts to $6,733,-003.18, being less by $663,240.64 than the sum appropriated on the same account for the previous year.

At the close of the last fiscal year, on the 30th day of June, 1894, there were 969,544 persons on our pension rolls, being a net increase of 3,532 over the number reported at the end of the previous year.

These pensioners may be classified as follows: Soldiers and sailors survivors of all wars, 753,968; widows and relatives of deceased soldiers, 215,162; army nurses in the War of the Rebellion, 414. Of these pensioners 32,039 are surviving soldiers of Indian and other wars prior to the late Civil War and the widows or relatives of such soldiers.

The remainder, numbering 937,505, are receiving pensions on account of the rebellion, and of these 469,344 are on the rolls under the authority of the act of June 27, 1890, sometimes called the dependent-pension law.

The total amount expended for pensions during the year was $139,-804,461.05, leaving an unexpended balance from the sum appropriated of $25,205,712.65.

The sum necessary to meet pension expenditures for the year ending June 30, 1896, is estimated at $140,000,000.

The Commissioner of Pensions is of the opinion that the year 1895, being the thirtieth after the close of the War of the Rebellion, must, according to all sensible human calculation, see the highest limit of the pension roll, and that after that year it must begin to decline.

The claims pending in the Bureau have decreased more than 90,000 during the year. A large proportion of the new claims filed are for increase of pension by those now on the rolls.

The number of certificates issued was 80,213.

The names dropped from the rolls for all causes during the year num bered 37,951.

Among our pensioners are 9 widows and 3 daughters of soldiers of the Revolution and 45 survivors of the War of 1812.

The barefaced and extensive pension frauds exposed under the direction of the courageous and generous veteran soldier now at the head of the Bureau leave no room for the claim that no purgation of our pension rolls was needed or that continued vigilance and prompt action are not necessary to the same end.

The accusation that an effort to detect pension frauds is evidence of unfriendliness toward our worthy veterans and a denial of their claims to the generosity of the Government suggests an unfortunate indifference to the commission of any offense which has for its motive the securing of a pension and indicates a willingness to be blind to the existence of mean and treacherous crimes which play upon demagogic fears and make sport of the patriotic impulse of a grateful people.

The completion of the Eleventh Census is now in charge of the Commissioner of Labor. The total disbursements on account of the work for the fiscal year ending June 30, 1894, amounted to $10,365,676.81. At the close of the year the number of persons employed in the Census Office was 679; at present there are about 400. The whole number of volumes necessary to comprehend the Eleventh Census will be 25, and they will contain 22,270 printed pages. The assurance is confidently made that before the close of the present calendar year the material still incomplete will be practically in hand, and the census can certainly be closed by the 4th of March, 1895. After that the revision and proof reading necessary to bring out the volumes will still be required.

The text of the census volumes has been limited as far as possible to the analysis of the statistics presented. This method, which is in accordance with law, has caused more or less friction and in some instances individual disappointment, for when the Commissioner of Labor took charge of the work he found much matter on hand which according to this rule he was compelled to discard. The census is being prepared according to the theory that it is designed to collect facts and certify them to the public not to elaborate arguments or to present personal views.

The Secretary of Agriculture in his report reviews the operations of his Department for the last fiscal year and makes recommendations for the further extension of its usefulness. He reports a saving in expenditures during the year of $600,000, which is covered back into the Treasury. This sum is 23 per cent of the entire appropriation.

A special study has been made of the demand for American farm products in all foreign markets, especially Great Britain. That country received from the United States during the nine months ending September 30, 1894, 305,910 live beef cattle, valued at $26,500,000, as against 182,611 cattle, valued at $16,634,000, during the same period for 1893.

During the first six months of 1894 the United Kingdom took also 112,000,000 pounds of dressed beef from the United States, valued at nearly $10,000,000.

The report shows that during the nine months immediately preceding September 30, 1894, the United States exported to Great Britain 222,-676,000 pounds of pork; of apples, 1,900,000 bushels, valued at $2,500,-000, and of horses 2,811, at an average value of $139 per head. There was a falling off in American wheat exports of 13,500,000 bushels, and the Secretary is inclined to believe that wheat may not in the future be the staple export cereal product of our country, but that corn will continue to advance in importance as an export on account of the new uses to which it is constantly being appropriated.

The exports of agricultural products from the United States for the fiscal year ending June 30, 1894, amounted to $628,363,038, being 72.28 per cent of American exports of every description, and the United Kingdom of Great Britain took more than 54 per cent of all farm products finding foreign markets.

The Department of Agriculture has undertaken during the year two new and important lines of research. The first relates to grasses and forage plants, with the purpose of instructing and familiarizing the people as to the distinctive grasses of the United States and teaching them how to introduce valuable foreign forage plants which may be adapted to this country. The second relates to agricultural soils and crop production, involving the analyses of samples of soils from all sections of the American Union, to demonstrate their adaptability to particular plants and crops. Mechanical analyses of soils may be of such inestimable utility that it is foremost in the new lines of agricultural research, and the Secretary therefore recommends that a division having it in charge be permanently established in the Department.

The amount appropriated for the Weather Bureau was $951,100. Of that sum $138,500, or 14 per cent, has been saved and is returned to the Treasury.

As illustrating the usefulness of this service it may be here stated that the warnings which were very generally given of two tropical storms occurring in September and October of the present year resulted in detaining safely in port 2,305 vessels, valued at $36,283,913, laden with cargoes of probably still greater value. What is much more important and gratifying, many human lives on these ships were also undoubtedly saved.

The appropriation to the Bureau of Animal Industry was $850,000, and the expenditures for the year were only $495,429.24, thus leaving unexpended $354,570.76. The inspection of beef animals for export and interstate trade has been continued, and 12,944,056 head were inspected during the year, at a cost of 1¾ cents per head, against 4¾ cents for 1893. The amount of pork microscopically examined was 35,437,937 pounds, against 20,677,410 pounds in the preceding year. The cost of this inspection has been diminished from 8¾ cents per head in 1893 to 6½ cents in 1894.

The expense of inspecting the pork sold in 1894 to Germany and France by the United States was $88,922.10. The quantity inspected was greater by 15,000,000 pounds than during the preceding year, when the cost of such inspection was $172,367.08. The Secretary of Agriculture recommends that the law providing for the microscopic inspection of export and interstate meat be so amended as to compel owners of the meat inspected to pay the cost of such inspection, and I call attention to the arguments presented in his report in support of this recommendation.

The live beef cattle exported and tagged during the year numbered 353,535. This is an increase of 69,533 head over the previous year.

The sanitary inspection of cattle shipped to Europe has cost an average of 10¾ cents for each animal, and the cost of inspecting Southern cattle and the disinfection of cars and stock yards averages 2.7 cents per animal.

The scientific inquiries of the Bureau of Animal Industry have progressed steadily during the year. Much tuberculin and mallein have been furnished to State authorities for use in the agricultural colleges and experiment stations for the treatment of tuberculosis and glanders.

Quite recently this Department has published the results of its investigations of bovine tuberculosis, and its researches will be vigorously continued. Certain herds in the District of Columbia will be thoroughly inspected and will probably supply adequate scope for the Department to intelligently prosecute its scientific work and furnish sufficient material for purposes of illustration, description, and definition.

The sterilization of milk suspected of containing the bacilli of tuberculosis has been during the year very thoroughly explained in a leaflet by Dr. D. E. Salmon, the Chief of the Bureau, and given general circulation throughout the country.

The Office of Experiment Stations, which is a part of the United States Department of Agriculture, has during the past year engaged itself almost wholly in preparing for publication works based upon the reports of agricultural experiment stations and other institutions for agricultural inquiry in the United States and foreign countries.

The Secretary in his report for 1893 called attention to the fact that the appropriations made for the support of the experiment stations throughout the Union were the only moneys taken out of the National Treasury by act of Congress for which no accounting to Federal authorities was required. Responding to this suggestion, the Fifty-third Congress, in making the appropriation for the Department for the present fiscal year, provided that—

The Secretary of Agriculture shall prescribe the form of annual financial statement required by section 3 of said act of March 2, 1887; shall ascertain whether the expenditures under the appropriation hereby made are in accordance with the provisions of said act, and shall make report thereon to Congress.

In obedience to this law the Department of Agriculture immediately sent out blank forms of expense accounts to each station, and proposes in addition to make, through trusted experts, systematic examination of the several stations during each year for the purpose of acquiring by personal investigation the detailed information necessary to enable the Secretary of Agriculture to make, as the statute provides, a satisfactory report to Congress. The boards of management of the several stations with great alacrity and cordiality have approved the amendment to the law providing this supervision of their expenditures, anticipating that it will increase the efficiency of the stations and protect their directors and managers from loose charges concerning their use of public funds, besides bringing the Department of Agriculture into closer and more confidential relations with the experimental stations, and through their joint service largely increasing their usefulness to the agriculture of the country.

Acting upon a recommendation contained in the report of 1893, Congress appropriated $10,000 "to enable the Secretary of Agriculture to investigate and report upon the nutritive value of the various articles and commodities used for human food, with special suggestions of full, wholesome, and edible rations less wasteful and more economical than those in common use."

Under this appropriation the Department has prepared and now has nearly ready for distribution an elementary discussion of the nutritive value and pecuniary economy of food. When we consider that fully one-half of all the money earned by the wage earners of the civilized world is expended by them for food, the importance and utility of such an investigation is apparent.

The Department expended in the fiscal year 1893 $2,354,809.56, and out of that sum the total amount expended in scientific research was 45.6 per cent. But in the year ending June 30, 1894, out of a total expenditure of $1,948,988.38, the Department applied 51.8 per cent of that sum to scientific work and investigation. It is therefore very plainly observable that the economies which have been practiced in the administration of the Department have not been at the expense of scientific research.

The recommendation contained in the report of the Secretary for 1893 that the vicious system of promiscuous free distribution of its departmental documents be abandoned is again urged. These publications may well be furnished without cost to public libraries, educational institutions, and the officers and libraries of States and of the Federal Government; but from all individuals applying for them a price covering the cost of the document asked for should be required. Thus the publications and documents would be secured by those who really desire them for proper purposes. Half a million of copies of the report of the

Secretary of Agriculture are printed for distribution, at an annual cost of about $300,000. Large numbers of them are cumbering storerooms at the Capitol and the shelves of secondhand-book stores throughout the country. All this labor and waste might be avoided if the recommendations of the Secretary were adopted.

The Secretary also again recommends that the gratuitous distribution of seeds cease and that no money be appropriated for that purpose except to experiment stations. He reiterates the reasons given in his report for 1893 for discontinuing this unjustifiable gratuity, and I fully concur in the conclusions which he has reached.

The best service of the statistician of the Department of Agriculture is the ascertainment, by diligence and care, of the actual and real conditions, favorable or unfavorable, of the farmers and farms of the country, and to seek the causes which produce these conditions, to the end that the facts ascertained may guide their intelligent treatment.

A further important utility in agricultural statistics is found in their elucidation of the relation of the supply of farm products to the demand for them in the markets of the United States and of the world.

It is deemed possible that an agricultural census may be taken each year through the agents of the statistical division of the Department. Such a course is commended for trial by the chief of that division. Its scope would be:

(1) The area under each of the more important crops.

(2) The aggregate products of each of such crops.

(3) The quantity of wheat and corn in the hands of farmers at a date after the spring sowings and plantings and before the beginning of harvest, and also the quantity of cotton and tobacco remaining in the hands of planters, either at the same date or at some other designated time.

The cost of the work is estimated at $500,000.

Owing to the peculiar quality of the statistician's work and the natural and acquired fitness necessary to its successful prosecution, the Secretary of Agriculture expresses the opinion that every person employed in gathering statistics under the chief of that division should be admitted to that service only after a thorough, exhaustive, and successful examination at the hands of the United States Civil Service Commission. This has led him to call for such examination of candidates for the position of assistant statisticians, and also of candidates for chiefs of sections in that division.

The work done by the Department of Agriculture is very superficially dealt with in this communication, and I commend the report of the Secretary and the very important interests with which it deals to the careful attention of the Congress.

The advantages to the public service of an adherence to the principles of civil-service reform are constantly more apparent, and nothing is so encouraging to those in official life who honestly desire good government as the increasing appreciation by our people of these advantages. A vast majority of the voters of the land are ready to insist that the time and attention of those they select to perform for them important public duties should not be distracted by doling out minor offices, and they are growing to be unanimous in regarding party organization as something that should be used in establishing party principles instead of dictating the distribution of public places as rewards of partisan activity.

Numerous additional offices and places have lately been brought within civil-service rules and regulations, and some others will probably soon be included.

The report of the Commissioners will be submitted to the Congress, and I invite careful attention to the recommendations it contains.

I am entirely convinced that we ought not to be longer without a national board of health or national health officer charged with no other duties than such as pertain to the protection of our country from the invasion of pestilence and disease. This would involve the establishment by such board or officer of proper quarantine precautions, or the necessary aid and counsel to local authorities on the subject; prompt advice and assistance to local boards of health or health officers in the suppression of contagious disease, and in cases where there are no such local boards or officers the immediate direction by the national board or officer of measures of suppression; constant and authentic information concerning the health of foreign countries and all parts of our own country as related to contagious diseases, and consideration of regulations to be enforced in foreign ports to prevent the introduction of contagion into our cities and the measures which should be adopted to secure their enforcement.

There seems to be at this time a decided inclination to discuss measures of protection against contagious diseases in international conference, with a view of adopting means of mutual assistance. The creation of such a national health establishment would greatly aid our standing in such conferences and improve our opportunities to avail ourselves of their benefits.

I earnestly recommend the inauguration of a national board of health or similar national instrumentality, believing the same to be a needed precaution against contagious disease and in the interest of the safety and health of our people.

By virtue of a statute of the United States passed in 1888 I appointed in July last Hon. John D. Kernan, of the State of New York, and Hon. Nicholas E. Worthington, of the State of Illinois, to form, with Hon. Carroll D. Wright, Commissioner of Labor, who was designated by said statute, a commission for the purpose of making careful inquiry into the causes of the controversies between certain railroads and their employees which had resulted in an extensive and destructive strike, accompanied by much violence and dangerous disturbance, with considerable loss of life and great destruction of property.

The report of the commissioners has been submitted to me and will be transmitted to the Congress with the evidence taken upon their investigation.

Their work has been well done, and their standing and intelligence give assurance that the report and suggestions they make are worthy of careful consideration.

The tariff act passed at the last session of the Congress needs important amendments if it is to be executed effectively and with certainty. In addition to such necessary amendments as will not change rates of duty, I am still very decidedly in favor of putting coal and iron upon the free list.

So far as the sugar schedule is concerned, I would be glad, under existing aggravations, to see every particle of differential duty in favor of refined sugar stricken out of our tariff law. If with all the favor now accorded the sugar-refining interest in our tariff laws it still languishes to the extent of closed refineries and thousands of discharged workmen, it would seem to present a hopeless case for reasonable legislative aid. Whatever else is done or omitted, I earnestly repeat here the recommendation I have made in another portion of this communication, that the additional duty of one-tenth of a cent per pound laid upon sugar imported from countries paying a bounty on its export be abrogated. It seems to me that exceedingly important considerations point to the propriety of this amendment.

With the advent of a new tariff policy not only calculated to relieve the consumers of our land in the cost of their daily life, but to invite a better development of American thrift and create for us closer and more profitable commercial relations with the rest of the world, it follows as a logical and imperative necessity that we should at once remove the chief if not the only obstacle which has so long prevented our participation in the foreign carrying trade of the sea. A tariff built upon the theory that it is well to check imports and that a home market should bound the industry and effort of American producers was fitly supplemented by a refusal to allow American registry to vessels built abroad, though owned and navigated by our people, thus exhibiting a willingness to abandon all contest for the advantages of American transoceanic carriage. Our new tariff policy, built upon the theory that it is well to encourage such importations as our people need, and that our products and manufactures should find markets in every part of the habitable globe, is consistently supplemented by the greatest possible liberty to our citizens in the ownership and navigation of ships in which our products and manufactures may be transported. The millions now paid to foreigners for carrying American passengers and products across the sea should be turned into American hands. Shipbuilding, which has been protected to strangulation, should be revived by the prospect of profitable employment for ships when built, and the American sailor should be resurrected and again take his place—a sturdy and industrious citizen in time of peace and a patriotic and safe defender of American interests in the day of conflict.

The ancient provision of our law denying American registry to ships built abroad and owned by Americans appears in the light of present conditions not only to be a failure for good at every point, but to be nearer a relic of barbarism than anything that exists under the permission of a statute of the United States. I earnestly recommend its prompt repeal.

During the last month the gold reserved in the Treasury for the purpose of redeeming the notes of the Government circulating as money in the hands of the people became so reduced and its further depletion in the near future seemed so certain that in the exercise of proper care for the public welfare it became necessary to replenish this reserve and thus maintain popular faith in the ability and determination of the Government to meet as agreed its pecuniary obligations.

It would have been well if in this emergency authority had existed to issue the bonds of the Government bearing a low rate of interest and maturing within a short period; but the Congress having failed to confer such authority, resort was necessarily had to the resumption act of 1875, and pursuant to its provisions bonds were issued drawing interest at the rate of 5 per cent per annum and maturing ten years after their issue, that being the shortest time authorized by the act. I am glad to say, however, that on the sale of these bonds the premium received operated to reduce the rate of interest to be paid by the Government to less than 3 per cent.

Nothing could be worse or further removed from sensible finance than the relations existing between the currency the Government has issued, the gold held for its redemption, and the means which must be resorted to for the purpose of replenishing such redemption fund when impaired. Even if the claims upon this fund were confined to the obligations originally intended and if the redemption of these obligations meant their cancellation, the fund would be very small. But these obligations when received and redeemed in gold are not canceled, but are reissued and may do duty many times by way of drawing gold from the Treasury. Thus we have an endless chain in operation constantly depleting the Treasury's gold and never near a final rest. As if this was not bad enough, we have, by a statutory declaration that it is the policy of the Government to maintain the parity between gold and silver, aided the force and momentum of this exhausting process and added largely to the currency obligations claiming this peculiar gold redemption. Our small gold reserve is thus subject to drain from every side. The demands that increase our danger also increase the necessity of protecting this reserve against depletion, and it is most unsatisfactory to know that the protection afforded is only a temporary palliation.

It is perfectly and palpably plain that the only way under present conditions by which this reserve when dangerously depleted can be replenished is through the issue and sale of the bonds of the Government for gold, and yet Congress has not only thus far declined to authorize the issue of bonds best suited to such a purpose, but there seems a disposition in some quarters to deny both the necessity and power for the issue of bonds at all.

I can not for a moment believe that any of our citizens are deliberately willing that their Government should default in its pecuniary obligations or that its financial operations should be reduced to a silver basis.   At any rate, I should not feel that my duty was done if I omitted any effort I could make to avert such a calamity.   As long, therefore, as no provision is made for the final redemption or the putting aside of the currency obligation now used to repeatedly and constantly draw from the Government its gold, and as long as no better authority for bond issues is allowed than at present exists, such authority will be utilized whenever and as often as it becomes necessary to maintain a sufficient gold reserve, and in abundant time to save the credit of our country and make good the financial declarations of our Government.

Questions relating to our banks and currency are closely connected with the subject just referred to, and they also present some unsatisfactory features.   Prominent among them are the lack of elasticity in our currency circulation and its frequent concentration in financial centers when it is most needed in other parts of the country.

The absolute divorcement of the Government from the business of banking is the ideal relationship of the Government to the circulation of the currency of the country.

This condition can not be immediately reached, but as a step in that direction and as a means of securing a more elastic currency and obviating other objections to the present arrangement of bank circulation the Secretary of the Treasury presents in his report a scheme modifying present banking laws and providing for the issue of circulating notes by State banks free from taxation under certain limitations.

The Secretary explains his plan so plainly and its advantages are developed by him with such remarkable clearness that any effort on my part to present argument in its support would be superfluous.   I shall therefore content myself with an unqualified indorsement of the Secretary's proposed changes in the law and a brief and imperfect statement of their prominent features.

It is proposed to repeal all laws providing for the deposit of United States bonds as security for circulation; to permit national banks to issue circulating notes not exceeding in amount 75 per cent of their paid-up and unimpaired capital, provided they deposit with the Government as a guaranty fund, in United States legal-tender notes, including Treasury notes of 1890, a sum equal in amount to 30 per cent of the notes they desire to issue, this deposit to be maintained at all times, but whenever any bank retires any part of its circulation a proportional part of its guaranty fund shall be returned to it; to permit the Secretary of the Treasury to prepare and keep on hand ready for issue in case an increase in circulation is desired blank national-bank notes for each bank having circulation and to repeal the provisions of the present law imposing limitations and restrictions upon banks desiring to reduce or increase their circulation, thus permitting such increase or reduction within the limit of 75 per cent of capital to be quickly made as emergencies arise.

In addition to the guaranty fund required, it is proposed to provide a safety fund for the immediate redemption of the circulating notes of failed banks by imposing a small annual tax, say one-half of 1 per cent, upon the average circulation of each bank until the fund amounts to 5 per cent of the total circulation outstanding. When a bank fails its guaranty fund is to be paid into this safety fund and its notes are to be redeemed in the first instance from such safety fund thus augmented, any impairment of such fund caused thereby to be made good from the immediately available cash assets of said bank, and if these should be insufficient such impairment to be made good by *pro rata* assessment among the other banks, their contributions constituting a first lien upon the assets of the failed bank in favor of the contributing banks. As a further security it is contemplated that the existing provision fixing the individual liability of stockholders is to be retained and the bank's indebtedness on account of its circulating notes is to be made a first lien on all its assets.

For the purpose of meeting the expense of printing notes, official supervision, cancellation, and other like charges there shall be imposed a tax of say one-half of 1 per cent per annum upon the average amount of notes in circulation.

It is further provided that there shall be no national-bank notes issued of a less denomination than $10; that each national bank, except in case of a failed bank, shall redeem or retire its notes in the first instance at its own office or at agencies to be designated by it, and that no fixed reserve need be maintained on account of deposits.

Another very important feature of this plan is the exemption of State banks from taxation by the United States in cases where it is shown to the satisfaction of the Secretary of the Treasury and Comptroller of the Currency by banks claiming such exemption that they have not had outstanding their circulating notes exceeding 75 per cent of their paid-up and unimpaired capital; that their stockholders are individually liable for the redemption of their circulating notes to the full extent of their ownership of stock; that the liability of said banks upon their circulating notes constitutes under their State law a first lien upon their assets; that such banks have kept and maintained a guaranty fund in United States legal-tender notes, including Treasury notes of 1890, equal to 30 per cent of their outstanding circulating notes, and that such banks have promptly redeemed their circulating notes when presented at their principal or branch offices.

It is quite likely that this scheme may be usefully amended in some of its details, but I am satisfied it furnishes a basis for a very great improvement in our present banking and currency system.

I conclude this communication fully appreciating that the responsibility for all legislation affecting the people of the United States rests upon their representatives in the Congress, and assuring them that, whether in accordance with recommendations I have made or not, I shall be glad to cooperate in perfecting any legislation that tends to the prosperity and welfare of our country.

GROVER CLEVELAND.

SPECIAL MESSAGES.

EXECUTIVE MANSION, *December 6, 1894.*

To the Senate of the United States:

In compliance with the resolution of the Senate of the 24th of July, 1894, directing the Secretary of State to furnish copies of all papers, correspondence, diplomatic or otherwise, on file in the State Department in connection with the arrest and imprisonment at Arequipa, Peru, of Victor H. McCord, I transmit herewith the correspondence indicated.

GROVER CLEVELAND.

EXECUTIVE MANSION,
Washington, December 10, 1894.

To the Congress of the United States:

I transmit herewith a communication from the Secretary of State, inclosing the report, with accompanying papers, of the commission of the United States for the Columbian Historical Exposition in Madrid in 1892 and 1893, constituted in virtue of the act of Congress approved May 13, 1892.

GROVER CLEVELAND.

EXECUTIVE MANSION, *December 10, 1894.*

To the Senate and House of Representatives:

I transmit herewith the report on the Chicago strike of June and July, 1894, forwarded to me by the Strike Commission appointed July 26, 1894, under the provisions of section 6 of chapter 1063 of the laws of the United States, passed October 1, 1888.

The testimony taken by the commission and the suggestions and recommendations made to it accompany the report in the form of appendixes.

GROVER CLEVELAND.

EXECUTIVE MANSION,
Washington, December 11, 1894.

To the Senate of the United States:

In response to the resolution of the Senate dated December 6, 1894, requesting that copies of correspondence in regard to the claim of Antonio Maximo Mora against the Government of Spain exchanged since my last message to the Senate on the same subject, dated June 20, 1894,* be communicated to it, if not incompatible with the public interests, I transmit herewith the report of the Secretary of State on the matter, with accompanying copies of correspondence.

GROVER CLEVELAND.

EXECUTIVE MANSION, *December 11, 1894.*

To the Senate of the United States:

I have received a copy of the following resolution of the Senate, passed on 3d instant:

Resolved, That the President be requested, if in his judgment it be not incompatible with the public interest, to communicate to the Senate any information he may have received in regard to alleged cruelties committed upon Armenians in Turkey, and especially whether any such cruelties have been committed upon citizens who have declared their intention to become naturalized in this country or upon persons because of their being Christians.

And further, to inform the Senate whether any expostulations have been addressed by this Government to the Government of Turkey in regard to such matters or any proposals made by or to this Government to act in concert with other Christian powers regarding the same.

In response to said resolution I beg leave to inform the Senate that I have no information concerning cruelties committed upon Armenians in Turkey or upon persons because of their being Christians, except such information as has been derived from newspapers and statements emanating from the Turkish Government denying such cruelties and two telegraphic reports from our minister at Constantinople.

One of these reports, dated November 28, 1894, is in answer to an inquiry by the State Department touching reports in the press alleging the killing of Armenians, and is as follows:

Reports in American papers of Turkish atrocities at Sassoun are sensational and exaggerated. The killing was in a conflict between armed Armenians and Turkish soldiers. The grand vizier says it was necessary to suppress insurrection, and that about fifty Turks were killed; between three and four hundred Armenian guns were picked up after the fight, and reports that about that number of Armenians were killed. I give credit to his statement.

The other dispatch referred to is dated December 2, 1894, and is as follows:

Information from British ambassador indicates far more loss of lives in Armenia, attended with atrocities, than stated in my telegram of 28th.

*See p. 5910.

I have received absolutely no information concerning any cruelties committed "upon citizens who have declared their intention to become naturalized in this country," or upon any persons who had a right to claim or have claimed for any reason the protection of the United States Government.

In the absence of such authentic detailed knowledge on the subject as would justify our interference no "expostulations have been addressed by this Government to the Government of Turkey in regard to such matters."

The last inquiry contained in the resolution of the Senate touching these alleged cruelties seeks information concerning "any proposals made by or to this Government to act in concert with other Christian powers regarding the same."

The first proposal of the kind referred to was made by the Turkish Government through our minister on the 30th day of November, when the Sultan then expressed a desire that a consul of the United States be sent with a Turkish commission to investigate these alleged atrocities on Armenians. This was construed as an invitation on the part of the Turkish Government to actually take part with a Turkish commission in an investigation of these affairs and any report to be made thereon, and the proposition came before our minister's second dispatch was received and at a time when the best information in the possession of our Government was derived from his first report, indicating that the statements made in the press were sensational and exaggerated and that the atrocities alleged really did not exist. This condition very much weakened any motive for an interference based on considerations of humanity, and permitted us without embarrassment to pursue a course plainly marked out by other controlling incidents.

By a treaty entered into at Berlin in the year 1878 between Turkey and various other governments Turkey undertook to guarantee protection to the Armenians, and agreed that it would "periodically make known the steps taken to this effect to the powers, who will superintend their application."

Our Government was not a party to this treaty, and it is entirely obvious that in the face of the provisions of such treaty above recited our interference in the proposed investigation, especially without the invitation of any of the powers which had assumed by treaty obligations to secure the protection of these Armenians, might have been exceedingly embarrassing, if not entirely beyond the limits of justification or propriety.

The Turkish invitation to join the investigation set on foot by that Government was therefore, on the 2d day of December, declined. On the same day, and after this declination had been sent, our minister at Constantinople forwarded his second dispatch, tending to modify his former report as to the extent and character of Armenian slaughter. At the same time the request of the Sultan for our participation in the investigation was repeated, and Great Britain, one of the powers which joined in the treaty of Berlin, made a like request.

In view of changed conditions and upon reconsideration of the subject it was determined to send Mr. Jewett, our consul at Sivas, to the scene of the alleged outrages, not for the purpose of joining with any other government in an investigation and report, but to the end that he might be able to inform this Government as to the exact truth.

Instructions to this effect were sent to Mr. Jewett, and it is supposed he has already entered upon the duty assigned him.

I submit with this communication copies of all correspondence and dispatches in the State Department on this subject and the report to me of the Secretary of State thereon. GROVER CLEVELAND.

EXECUTIVE MANSION,
Washington, January 3, 1895.

To the Senate of the United States:

In response to the resolution of the Senate of the 4th ultimo, requesting "any reports or correspondence relating to affairs at Bluefields, in the Mosquito territory," and also information as to "whether any American citizens have been arrested or the rights of any American citizens at Bluefields have been interfered with during the past two years by the Government of Nicaragua," I transmit herewith a report from the Secretary of State, with accompanying papers.

GROVER CLEVELAND.

EXECUTIVE MANSION, *January 9, 1895.*

To the Senate and House of Representatives:

I submit herewith certain dispatches from our minister at Hawaii and the documents which accompanied the same.

They disclose the fact that the Hawaiian Government desires to lease to Great Britain one of the uninhabited islands belonging to Hawaii as a station for a submarine telegraph cable to be laid from Canada to Australia, with a connection between the island leased and Honolulu.

Both the Hawaiian Government and the representatives of Great Britain in this negotiation concede that the proposed lease can not be effected without the consent of the United States, for the reason that in our reciprocity treaty with the King of Hawaii he agreed that as long as said treaty remained in force he would not "lease or otherwise dispose of or create any lien upon any port, harbor, or other territory in his dominion, or grant any special privilege or right of use therein, to any other power, state, or government."

At the request of the Hawaiian Government this subject is laid before the Congress for its determination upon the question of so modifying the treaty agreement above recited as to permit the proposed lease.

It will be seen that the correspondence which is submitted between the Hawaiian and British negotiators negatives the existence on the part of Hawaii of any suspicion of British unfriendliness or the fear of British aggression.

The attention of the Congress is directed to the following statement contained in a communication addressed to the Hawaiian Government by the representatives of Great Britain:

We propose to inform the British Government of your inquiry whether they would accept the sovereignty of Nicker Island or some other uninhabited island on condition that no subsidy is required from you. As we explained, we have not felt at liberty to entertain that question ourselves, as we were definitely instructed not to ask for the sovereignty of any island, but only for a lease simply for the purpose of the cable.

Some of the dispatches from our minister, which are submitted, not only refer to the project for leasing an uninhabited island belonging to Hawaii, but contain interesting information concerning recent occurrences in that country and its political and social condition. This information is valuable because it is based upon the observation and knowledge necessarily within the scope of the diplomatic duties which are intrusted solely to the charge of this intelligent diplomatic officer representing the United States Government at Hawaii.

I hope the Congress will see fit to grant the request of the Hawaiian Government, and that our consent to the proposed lease will be promptly accorded. It seems to me we ought not by a refusal of this request to stand in the way of the advantages to be gained by isolated Hawaii through telegraphic communication with the rest of the world, especially in view of the fact that our own communication with that country would thereby be greatly improved without apparent detriment to any legitimate American interest.

GROVER CLEVELAND.

EXECUTIVE MANSION, *January 11, 1895.*

To the Senate of the United States:

In response to the resolution of the Senate of the 19th ultimo, requesting the record of the extradition proceedings in the case of General Ezeta, etc., I transmit herewith a letter from the Secretary of State, with accompanying papers.

GROVER CLEVELAND.

EXECUTIVE MANSION,
Washington, January 15, 1895.

To the Senate of the United States:

I transmit a report from the Secretary of State, with accompanying papers, in response to the resolution of the Senate of the 3d instant, requesting "all correspondence or other papers relating to the delivery by the United States consul at Shanghai of two Japanese citizens to the Chinese authorities," and information "whether the said Japanese were put to death after being tortured, and whether there was any understanding with the Chinese Government that officers of the United States should aid, assist, and give comfort to any Japanese citizen desiring to leave China, and whether the United States consul at Hankow was reprimanded by Chinese officials for aiding Japanese citizens to leave the country, and whether all information was refused to the United States consul at Ningpo when he made inquiries as to the charges against certain Japanese citizens arrested there."

GROVER CLEVELAND.

EXECUTIVE MANSION, *January 28, 1895.*

To the Senate and House of Representatives:

In my last annual message I commended to the serious consideration of the Congress the condition of our national finances, and in connection with the subject indorsed a plan of currency legislation which at that time seemed to furnish protection against impending danger.* This plan has not been approved by the Congress. In the meantime the situation has so changed and the emergency now appears so threatening that I deem it my duty to ask at the hands of the legislative branch of the Government such prompt and effective action as will restore confidence in our financial soundness and avert business disaster and universal distress among our people.

Whatever may be the merits of the plan outlined in my annual message as a remedy for ills then existing and as a safeguard against the depletion of the gold reserve then in the Treasury, I am now convinced that its reception by the Congress and our present advanced stage of financial perplexity necessitate additional or different legislation.

With natural resources unlimited in variety and productive strength and with a people whose activity and enterprise seek only a fair opportunity to achieve national success and greatness, our progress should not be checked by a false financial policy and a heedless disregard of sound monetary laws, nor should the timidity and fear which they engender stand in the way of our prosperity.

It is hardly disputed that this predicament confronts us to-day. Therefore no one in any degree responsible for the making and execution of our laws should fail to see a patriotic duty in honestly and sincerely attempting to relieve the situation. Manifestly this effort will not succeed unless it is made untrammeled by the prejudice of partisanship and with a steadfast determination to resist the temptation to accomplish party advantage. We may well remember that if we are threatened with

* See pp. 5985-5988.

financial difficulties all our people in every station of life are concerned; and surely those who suffer will not receive the promotion of party interests as an excuse for permitting our present troubles to advance to a disastrous conclusion. It is also of the utmost importance that we approach the study of the problems presented as free as possible from the tyranny of preconceived opinions, to the end that in a common danger we may be able to seek with unclouded vision a safe and reasonable protection.

The real trouble which confronts us consists in a lack of confidence, widespread and constantly increasing, in the continuing ability or disposition of the Government to pay its obligations in gold. This lack of confidence grows to some extent out of the palpable and apparent embarrassment attending the efforts of the Government under existing laws to procure gold and to a greater extent out of the impossibility of either keeping it in the Treasury or canceling obligations by its expenditure after it is obtained.

The only way left open to the Government for procuring gold is by the issue and sale of its bonds. The only bonds that can be so issued were authorized nearly twenty-five years ago and are not well calculated to meet our present needs. Among other disadvantages, they are made payable in coin instead of specifically in gold, which in existing conditions detracts largely and in an increasing ratio from their desirability as investments. It is by no means certain that bonds of this description can much longer be disposed of at a price creditable to the financial character of our Government.

The most dangerous and irritating feature of the situation, however, remains to be mentioned. It is found in the means by which the Treasury is despoiled of the gold thus obtained without canceling a single Government obligation and solely for the benefit of those who find profit in shipping it abroad or whose fears induce them to hoard it at home. We have outstanding about five hundred millions of currency notes of the Government for which gold may be demanded, and, curiously enough, the law requires that when presented and, in fact, redeemed and paid in gold they shall be reissued. Thus the same notes may do duty many times in drawing gold from the Treasury; nor can the process be arrested as long as private parties, for profit or otherwise, see an advantage in repeating the operation. More than $300,000,000 in these notes have already been redeemed in gold, and notwithstanding such redemption they are all still outstanding.

Since the 17th day of January, 1894, our bonded interest-bearing debt has been increased $100,000,000 for the purpose of obtaining gold to replenish our coin reserve. Two issues were made amounting to fifty millions each, one in January and the other in November. As a result of the first issue there was realized something more than $58,000,000 in gold. Between that issue and the succeeding one in November, comprising a period of about ten months, nearly $103,000,000 in gold were drawn from the Treasury. This made the second issue necessary, and upon that more than fifty-eight millions in gold was again realized. Between the date of this second issue and the present time, covering a period of only about two months, more than $69,000,000 in gold have been drawn from the Treasury. These large sums of gold were expended without any cancellation of Government obligations or in any permanent way benefiting our people or improving our pecuniary situation.

The financial events of the past year suggest facts and conditions which should certainly arrest attention.

More than $172,000,000 in gold have been drawn out of the Treasury during the year for the purpose of shipment abroad or hoarding at home.

While nearly $103,000,000 of this amount was drawn out during the first ten months of the year, a sum aggregating more than two-thirds of that amount, being about $69,000,000, was drawn out during the following two months, thus indicating a marked acceleration of the depleting process with the lapse of time.

The obligations upon which this gold has been drawn from the Treasury are still outstanding and are available for use in repeating the exhausting operation with shorter intervals as our perplexities accumulate.

Conditions are certainly supervening tending to make the bonds which may be issued to replenish our gold less useful for that purpose.

An adequate gold reserve is in all circumstances absolutely essential to the upholding of our public credit and to the maintenance of our high national character.

Our gold reserve has again reached such a stage of diminution as to require its speedy reenforcement.

The aggravations that must inevitably follow present conditions and methods will certainly lead to misfortune and loss, not only to our national credit and prosperity and to financial enterprise, but to those of our people who seek employment as a means of livelihood and to those whose only capital is their daily labor.

It will hardly do to say that a simple increase of revenue will cure our troubles. The apprehension now existing and constantly increasing as to our financial ability does not rest upon a calculation of our revenue. The time has passed when the eyes of investors abroad and our people at home were fixed upon the revenues of the Government. Changed conditions have attracted their attention to the gold of the Government. There need be no fear that we can not pay our current expenses with such money as we have. There is now in the Treasury a comfortable surplus of more than $63,000,000, but it is not in gold, and therefore does not meet our difficulty.

I can not see that differences of opinion concerning the extent to which silver ought to be coined or used in our currency should interfere with the counsels of those whose duty it is to rectify evils now apparent in our financial situation. They have to consider the question of national credit and the consequences that will follow from its collapse. Whatever ideas may be insisted upon as to silver or bimetallism, a proper solution of the question now pressing upon us only requires a recognition of gold as well as silver and a concession of its importance, rightfully or wrongfully acquired, as a basis of national credit, a necessity in the honorable discharge of our obligations payable in gold, and a badge of solvency. I do not understand that the real friends of silver desire a condition that might follow inaction or neglect to appreciate the meaning of the present exigency if it should result in the entire banishment of gold from our financial and currency arrangements.

Besides the Treasury notes, which certainly should be paid in gold, amounting to nearly $500,000,000, there will fall due in 1904 one hundred millions of bonds issued during the last year, for which we have received gold, and in 1907 nearly six hundred millions of 4 per cent bonds issued in 1877. Shall the payment of these obligations in gold be repudiated? If they are to be paid in such a manner as the preservation of our national honor and national solvency demands, we should not destroy or even imperil our ability to supply ourselves with gold for that purpose.

While I am not unfriendly to silver and while I desire to see it recognized to such an extent as is consistent with financial safety and the preservation of national honor and credit, I am not willing to see gold entirely banished from our currency and finances. To avert such a consequence I believe thorough and radical remedial legislation should be promptly passed. I therefore beg the Congress to give the subject immediate attention.

In my opinion the Secretary of the Treasury should be authorized to issue bonds of the Government for the purpose of procuring and maintaining a sufficient gold reserve and the redemption and cancellation of the United States legal-tender notes and the Treasury notes issued for the purchase of silver under the law of July 14, 1890. We should be relieved from the humiliating process of issuing bonds to procure gold to be immediately and repeatedly drawn out on these obligations for purposes not related to the benefit of our Government or our people. The principal and interest of these bonds should be payable on their face in gold, because they should be sold only for gold or its representative, and because there would now probably be difficulty in favorably disposing of bonds not containing this stipulation. I suggest that the bonds be issued in denominations of twenty and fifty dollars and their multiples and that they bear interest at a rate not exceeding 3 per cent per annum. I do not see why they should not be payable fifty years from their date. We of the present generation have large amounts to pay if we meet our obligations, and long bonds are most salable. The Secretary of the Treasury might well be permitted at his discretion to receive on the sale of bonds the legal-tender and Treasury notes to be retired, and of course when they are thus retired or redeemed in gold they should be canceled.

These bonds under existing laws could be deposited by national banks as security for circulation, and such banks should be allowed to issue circulation up to the face value of these or any other bonds so deposited, except bonds outstanding bearing only 2 per cent interest and which sell in the market at less than par. National banks should not be allowed to take out circulating notes of a less denomination than $10, and when such as are now outstanding reach the Treasury, except for redemption and retirement, they should be canceled and notes of the denomination of $10 and upward issued in their stead. Silver certificates of the denomination of $10 and upward should be replaced by certificates of the denominations under $10.

As a constant means for the maintenance of a reasonable supply of gold in the Treasury, our duties on imports should be paid in gold, allowing all other dues to the Government to be paid in any other form of money.

I believe all the provisions I have suggested should be embodied in our laws if we are to enjoy a complete reinstatement of a sound financial condition. They need not interfere with any currency scheme providing for the increase of the circulating medium through the agency of national or State banks that may commend itself to the Congress, since they can easily be adjusted to such a scheme. Objection has been made to the issuance of interest-bearing obligations for the purpose of retiring the noninterest-bearing legal-tender notes. In point of fact, however, these notes have burdened us with a large load of interest, and it is still accumulating. The aggregate interest on the original issue of bonds, the proceeds of which in gold constituted the reserve for the payment of these notes, amounted to $70,326,250 on January 1, 1895, and the annual charge for interest on these bonds and those issued for the same purpose during the last year will be $9,145,000, dating from January 1, 1895.

While the cancellation of these notes would not relieve us from the obligations already incurred on their account, these figures are given by way of suggesting that their existence has not been f⁻ ˍ from interest charges and that the longer they are outstanding, judging from the experience of the last year, the more expensive they will become.

In conclusion I desire to frankly confess my reluctance to issuing more bonds in present circumstances and with no better results than have lately followed that course. I can not, however, refrain from adding to an assurance of my anxiety to cooperate with the present Congress in any reasonable measure of relief an expression of my determination to leave nothing undone which furnishes a hope for improving the situation or checking a suspicion of our disinclination or disability to meet with the strictest honor every national obligation.

GROVER CLEVELAND.

EXECUTIVE MANSION, *January 30, 1895.*

To the House of Representatives:

In compliance with a resolution of the House of Representatives of the 28th instant, the Senate concurring, I herewith return the bill (H. R. 6186) entitled "An act to pension Maria Davis."

GROVER CLEVELAND.

EXECUTIVE MANSION,
Washington, February 4, 1895.

To the Senate of the United States:

In response to the resolution of the Senate dated December 6, 1894, requesting that copies of correspondence in regard to the claim of Antonio Maximo Mora against the Government of Spain exchanged since my last message to the Senate on the same subject, dated June 20, 1894,* be communicated to it if not incompatible with the public interests, I transmit herewith a report of the Secretary of State, inclosing copies of further correspondence exchanged between the Governments of the United States and Spain since the date of my last message to the Senate, December 11, 1894.†

GROVER CLEVELAND.

EXECUTIVE MANSION,
Washington, February 4, 1895.

To the House of Representatives:

In response to the resolution of the House of Representatives of the 1st instant, calling for certain information touching the recent insurrection in the Hawaiian Islands, I transmit herewith a report of the Secretary of State, with accompanying papers.

GROVER CLEVELAND.

EXECUTIVE MANSION, *February 5, 1895.*

To the House of Representatives:

In compliance with a resolution of the House of Representatives of the 2d instant, the Senate concurring, I return herewith the bill (H.R.5377) entitled "An act granting a pension to Richard R. Knight."

GROVER CLEVELAND.

EXECUTIVE MANSION,
Washington, February 7, 1895.

To the Senate:

I transmit herewith, in response to a resolution of the Senate of the 16th ultimo, a report from the Secretary of State, accompanied by copies of certain correspondence touching the enforcement of the provisions of the tariff act of 1894.

GROVER CLEVELAND.

*See p. 5910.　　　　　†See p. 5989.

EXECUTIVE MANSION, *February 8, 1895*

To the Congress of the United States:

Since my recent communication to the Congress calling attention to our financial condition and suggesting legislation which I deemed essential to our national welfare and credit* the anxiety and apprehension then existing in business circles have continued.

As a precaution, therefore, against the failure of timely legislative aid through Congressional action, cautious preparations have been pending to employ to the best possible advantage, in default of better means, such Executive authority as may without additional legislation be exercised for the purpose of reenforcing and maintaining in our Treasury an adequate and safe gold reserve.

In the judgment of those especially charged with this responsibility the business situation is so critical and the legislative situation is so unpromising, with the omission thus far on the part of Congress to beneficially enlarge the powers of the Secretary of the Treasury in the premises, as to enjoin immediate Executive action with the facilities now at hand.

Therefore, in pursuance of section 3700 of the Revised Statutes, the details of an arrangement have this day been concluded with parties abundantly able to fulfill their undertaking whereby bonds of the United States authorized under the act of July 14, 1875, payable in coin thirty years after their date, with interest at the rate of 4 per cent per annum, to the amount of a little less than $62,400,000, are to be issued for the purchase of gold coin, amounting to a sum slightly in excess of $65,000,000, to be delivered to the Treasury of the United States, which sum added to the gold now held in our reserve will so restore such reserve as to make it amount to something more than $100,000,000. Such a premium is to be allowed to the Government upon the bonds as to fix the rate of interest upon the amount of gold realized at 3¾ per cent per annum. At least one-half of the gold to be obtained is to be supplied from abroad, which is a very important and favorable feature of the transaction.

The privilege is especially reserved to the Government to substitute at par within ten days from this date, in lieu of the 4 per cent coin bonds, other bonds in terms payable in gold and bearing only 3 per cent interest if the issue of the same should in the meantime be authorized by the Congress.

The arrangement thus completed, which after careful inquiry appears in present circumstances and considering all the objects desired to be the best attainable, develops such a difference in the estimation of investors between bonds made payable in coin and those specifically made payable in gold in favor of the latter as is represented by three-fourths of a cent in annual interest. In the agreement just concluded the annual saving

*See pp. 5993-5997.

in interest to the Government if 3 per cent gold bonds should be substituted for 4 per cent coin bonds under the privilege reserved would be $539,159, amounting in thirty years, or at the maturity of the coin bonds, to $16,174,770.

Of course there never should be a doubt in any quarter as to the redemption in gold of the bonds of the Government which are made payable in coin. Therefore the discrimination, in the judgment of investors, between our bond obligations payable in coin and those specifically made payable in gold is very significant. It is hardly necessary to suggest that, whatever may be our views on the subject, the sentiments or preferences of those with whom we must negotiate in disposing of our bonds for gold are not subject to our dictation.

I have only to add that in my opinion the transaction herein detailed for the information of the Congress promises better results than the efforts previously made in the direction of effectively adding to our gold reserve through the sale of bonds, and I believe it will tend, as far as such action can in present circumstances, to meet the determination expressed in the law repealing the silver-purchasing clause of the act of July 14, 1890, and that, in the language of such repealing act, the arrangement made will aid our efforts to "insure the maintenance of the parity in value of the coins of the two metals and the equal power of every dollar at all times in the markets and in the payment of debts."

GROVER CLEVELAND.

EXECUTIVE MANSION, *February 8, 1895.*

To the Senate and House of Representatives:

I transmit herewith, for the information of the Congress, a copy of a telegraphic dispatch just received from Mr. Willis, our minister to Hawaii, with a copy of the reply thereto which was immediately sent by the Secretary of State.

GROVER CLEVELAND.

EXECUTIVE MANSION, *February 11, 1895.*

To the Senate:

On the 8th day of January I received a copy of the following Senate resolution:

Resolved, That the President be requested, if not incompatible with the public interests, to communicate to the Senate all reports, documents, and other papers, including logs of vessels, relating to the enforcement of the regulations respecting fur seals adopted by the Governments of the United States and Great Britain in accordance with the decision of the Tribunal of Arbitration convened at Paris and the resolutions under which said reports are required to be made, as well as relating to the number of seals taken during the season of 1894 by pelagic hunters and by the lessees of the Pribilof and Commander islands; also relating to the steps which may have been taken to extend the said regulations to the Asiatic waters of the

North Pacific Ocean and Bering Sea and to secure the concurrence of other nations in said regulations, and, further, all papers not heretofore published, including communications of the agent of the United States before said tribunal at Paris, relating to the claims of the British Government on account of the seizure of the sealing vessels in Bering Sea.

In compliance with said request I herewith transmit sundry papers, documents, and reports which have been returned to me by the Secretary of State, the Secretary of the Treasury, and the Secretary of the Navy, to whom said resolution was referred. I am not in possession of any further information touching the various subjects embodied in such resolution.

It will be seen from a letter of the Secretary of the Navy accompanying the papers and documents sent from his Department that it is impossible to furnish at this time the complete log books of some of the naval vessels referred to in the resolution, but I venture to express the hope that the reports of the commanders of such vessels herewith submitted will be found to contain in substance so much of the matters recorded in said log books as are important in answering the inquiries addressed to me by the Senate.   GROVER CLEVELAND.

EXECUTIVE MANSION,
Washington, February 12, 1895.

To the Senate and House of Representatives:

I transmit herewith, for the information of the Congress, a communication from the Secretary of State, covering the report of the Director of the Bureau of the American Republics for the year 1894.

GROVER CLEVELAND.

EXECUTIVE MANSION, *February 14, 1895.*

To the Senate and House of Representatives:

I transmit herewith the eighth special report of the Commissioner of Labor, which relates to "the housing of the working people" in different countries.   GROVER CLEVELAND.

EXECUTIVE MANSION,
Washington, February 26, 1895.

To the Senate:

I transmit herewith, in response to a resolution of the Senate of the 29th ultimo, a report from the Secretary of State, accompanied by copies of correspondence touching Samoan affairs.

GROVER CLEVELAND.

VETO MESSAGES.

EXECUTIVE MANSION, *January 14, 1895.*

To the House of Representatives:

I herewith return without my approval House bill No. 7451, entitled "An act to authorize the entry of land for gravel pits and reservoir purposes and authorizing the grant of right of way for pipe lines."

The first section of this bill permits the sale to railroad companies, in the discretion of the Secretary of the Interior, under certain restrictions and at an appraised value, certain public lands to be used by said companies for gravel pits or the construction of reservoirs. It also permits grants of the right of way for pipe lines connecting such reservoirs with the railways of said companies.

The second, third, and fourth sections of the bill relate to the purchase by any citizen of the United States, or any association of citizens, or any ditch or water company, of public lands suitable for reservoir purposes at such a price as the Secretary of the Interior shall prescribe, not less than $2 per acre.

The right to purchase these lands is given by the sections last referred to "under rules and regulations prescribed by the Secretary of the Interior."

I think the expediency and propriety of disposing of these lands for the purposes specified should in each case be determined by the Secretary of the Interior, as well as the rules and regulations governing such disposition.

The objections to the bill, however, which appear to be the most serious are found in its fifth and last section, which provides:

That any State or any county or district organization duly organized under the laws of any State or Territory may apply for any of the storage-reservoir sites not reserved by the United States, situated on unentered public lands, for the storage of water for irrigating, mining, or other useful purposes, whereupon the Secretary of the Interior shall set aside and withdraw from public sale or other disposition such site or sites and permit the use thereof for either or all of such purposes.

These provisions do not seem to be in harmony with prior laws by which, under certain conditions, arid lands may be conveyed to States for the purpose of irrigation, and it is not clear what is intended by the words "any of the storage-reservoir sites not reserved by the United States."

The apparent purpose and effect of the section is to give to the organizations mentioned the right to select such land as may present eligible reservoir sites not reserved and upon unentered lands, and demand of the Secretary of the Interior a grant of the same, leaving no discretion on the subject to him or to any other officer of the Government; and these grants are to be made without any compensation to the Government and without any specific requirement of the amount or kind of work to be done or improvements to be made upon such sites.

The grants may be demanded not only for the storage of water for irrigating purposes, but for "mining and other useful purposes." Inasmuch as no officer of the Government is vested with any discretion in the premises, the pretext that the "purpose" to be accomplished is "useful" might result in the use of these sites in a manner prejudicial to the surrounding public domain and destructive of the utilization of such sites for irrigating purposes.

The wise and prudent safeguards which have been incorporated in other legislation relating to the disposition of arid public lands and their irrigation seem to have been to such an extent overlooked in the construction of the bill under consideration that, in my judgment, if it should become the law a beneficent policy which the Government has entered upon in the interest of agriculture would be seriously endangered.

GROVER CLEVELAND.

To the Senate: EXECUTIVE MANSION, *February 1, 1895.*

I herewith return without my approval Senate bill No. 2338, entitled "An act granting to the Gila Valley, Globe and Northern Railway Company a right of way through the San Carlos Indian Reservation, in the Territory of Arizona."

The reservation through which it is proposed to construct a railroad under the provisions of this bill is inhabited by tribes of Indians which in the past have been most troublesome and whose depredations on more than one occasion have caused loss of life, destruction of property, and serious alarm to the people of the surrounding country; and their condition as to civilization is not now so far improved as to give assurance that in the future they may not upon occasion make trouble.

The discontent among the Indians which has given rise to disturbances in the past has been largely caused by trespass upon their lands and interference with their rights by the neighboring whites. I am in very great doubt whether in any circumstances a road through their reservation should at this time be permitted, and especially since the route, which is rather indefinitely described in the bill, appears to pass through the richest and most desirable part of their lands. In any event, I am thoroughly convinced that the construction of the road should not be permitted without first obtaining the consent of these Indians. This is a provision which has been insisted upon, so far as I am aware, in all the like bills which have been approved for a long time, and I think it should especially be inserted in this bill if, even upon any conditions, it is thought expedient to permit a railroad to traverse this reservation.

The importance of this consent does not rest solely upon the extent to which the Indians have the right of ownership over this land. The fact that the procurement of this consent is the most effective means of allaying the discontent which might arise and perhaps develop into a train of lamentable and destructive outbreaks of violence particularly emphasizes its importance.

GROVER CLEVELAND.

EXECUTIVE MANSION, *February 5, 1895.*

To the House of Representatives:

I return herewith without approval House bill No. 5368, entitled "An act for the relief of H. W. McConnell."

The reports of both the Senate and House committees, which favorably reported this bill, disclose an intention to partially relieve the former postmaster at Jacksboro, in the State of Texas, from liability on account of two remittances of postal funds which he dispatched at different times during the year 1883 to be deposited at Dallas, in the same State, and which were lost by robberies of the stage conveying the same. In dealing with the first remittance the committees report that the postmaster should be relieved of liability to the amount of only $94, the loss of the remainder of the money being chargeable to his neglect and violation of postal regulations. As to the second remittance, the committees report that by reason of like neglect and violation of regulations the postmaster should be held responsible for the loss of all the money transmitted except the sum of $42.

For these two sums, amounting to $136, an appropriation is made for the benefit of H. W. McConnell.

The name of the postmaster intended to be relieved is H. H. McConnell, as appears by the records of the Post-Office Department. The person to whom the money appropriated should be paid is therefore not correctly named in the bill.

An examination of this postmaster's accounts discloses the further fact that the amount proposed to be appropriated for his relief is too large by $42, that being the sum allowed him by reason of the second stage robbery. This item has already been credited to him in the adjustment of his accounts at the Post-Office Department, and the claim for its reimbursement has been thereby extinguished.

GROVER CLEVELAND.

EXECUTIVE MANSION, *February 12, 1895.*

To the Senate:

I return herewith without approval Senate bill No. 143, entitled "An act for the relief of the heirs of D. Fulford."

This bill directs the Secretary of the Treasury "to redeem, in favor of the heirs at law of D. Fulford, four bonds of the United States, consols of 1867, of the denomination of $500, $100, $50, and $50, and known as five-twenties, said bonds having been destroyed by fire the 9th day of

FORT AND BLOCKHOUSE AT EL CANEY

THE FIGHT AT EL CANEY

General Shafter had planned to envelop Santiago by driving in the out-posts at San Juan and El Caney. The pictures regarding the San Juan charge appear elsewhere. The illustration on the reverse shows the block-house and fort at El Caney where occurred the gallant defense of Brigadier-General Vera de Rey, who died fighting. After Capron's battery had shelled the town from its position 2,400 yards distant, Major-General Adna R. Chaffee sent his men forward with one hundred rounds of ammunition apiece. Approaching from three directions, their fire nearly encircled the town. The enemy were strongly posted in a church, a stone fort, a block-house, trenches and various redoubts, like that shown in another picture. Our troops, who were forced to economize their ammunition, drove the Spaniards from their trenches into the blockhouses and fort, from whence they poured an exceedingly damaging fire. Capron's battery concentrated on the fort and it was soon rent and shattered. Then our infantry charged forward and captured the fort, but not until every man of the defenders was killed or wounded. The Spanish blockhouses were forced to surrender at the same time. Out of General de Rey's five hundred and twenty men only one hundred remained alive at the end of the action.

The reader will observe the shattered condition of the stone fort, the barbed-wire fencing on the hillside, and the snarled appearance of the fence about the blockhouse where our troops in their charges attempted to cut the wires.

President McKinley's messages form the official history of the war. The encyclopedic index covers it by the articles entitled " Spanish-American War," " Spain," " Spain, Treaties with," " Cuba," " Santiago, Battle of," " Santiago Harbor, Battle of," " Guantanamo, Battle of," and " Manila Bay, Battle of."

July, 1872, and to pay to the heirs at law of said D. Fulford the amount of said bonds, together with accrued interest from July 1, 1872, to the date of the maturity of said bonds."

The bill further provides that the heirs to whom the payment is to be made shall execute and file with the Secretary of the Treasury a bond "conditioned to save harmless the United States from loss or liability on account of said bonds or the interest accrued thereon, and to contain such words as to cover any liability resulting from any mistake in the designation or description of the bonds, so that in no event shall the United States be called upon by a rightful claimant for a second payment thereof."

The proposition is that the Government shall pay bonds alleged to have been destroyed by fire nearly twenty-three years ago.

The Secretary of the Treasury states that an application for the payment of these bonds, made by Mr. Fulford himself, was rejected by the Department because he was unable to describe the bonds in such a way as to permit their identification and because the evidence of their destruction by fire was inconclusive.

The Senate Committee on Claims, however, in their report on the bill under consideration, state that they are entirely satisfied that Mr. Fulford was the owner of four Government bonds, one for $500, one for $100, and two for $50, and that they were burned with his residence, which was destroyed by fire on the 9th day of July, 1872, and that while he could not furnish the numbers or descriptions of said bonds he understood all these bonds were of the class known as consols of 1867, and that he had collected the coupons thereon for the interest due July 1, 1872.

The particular class of bonds mentioned were dated July 1, 1867, and were payable or redeemable not less than five nor more than twenty years from their date. The short period expired, therefore, on the 1st day of July, 1872. That was the date when the last coupons on Mr. Fulford's bonds, which it is alleged were detached and collected, became due, and only nine days before the supposed destruction of the bonds by fire.

A letter from the Secretary of the Treasury dated July 20, 1892, attached to the report of the Senate committee made upon a bill similar to this which was pending at that time, discloses the fact that among the consols of 1867 then outstanding there were 107 of the denomination of $500, 167 of the denomination of $100, and 85 of the denomination of $50. This statement merely shows that there were numerous bonds precisely similar to those described as belonging to Mr. Fulford which had not in July, 1892, been redeemed, though the extreme limit of their maturity expired on the 1st day of July, 1887. The letter of the Secretary further discloses, however, that there were two of these outstanding bonds of the denomination of $500 and two of the denomination of $100 upon which coupons of interest had not been paid since July 1, 1872. Of course this lends plausibility to the suggestion that two of these four bonds, one of each denomination, were those destroyed when Mr. Fulford's house was burned in July, 1872; but this suggestion loses its force under the additional statement in the letter of the Secretary of the Treasury that in July, 1892, there were no consols of 1867 of the denomination of $50 whose last coupon was paid July 1, 1872. This shows conclusively that no fifty-dollar bonds of this class were destroyed by fire in Mr. Fulford's house and casts great uncertainty upon the description of the other bonds, inasmuch as the theory of the claimants seems to be that all the bonds destroyed belonged to the same class.

In 1893, upon an examination of the records of the Treasury Department, it was found that the two unpaid bonds for $500 reported in 1892 as outstanding, from which no coupons had been paid since July 1, 1872, still remained unredeemed, but that one of the two one-hundred-dollar bonds which were in that condition in 1892 had been since that time paid and canceled. I think it must be conceded that this late redemption of this bond greatly weakens any presumption that the other three will not be presented for payment.

It is perfectly clear that so far as this bill directs the payment to the persons therein named of two consols of 1867 of the denomination of $50 each on the ground that such bonds were destroyed by fire in July, 1872, it requires the payment of money to those not entitled to it, since it is shown that these consols could not have been destroyed at the time stated, because coupons due on all consols of that denomination unredeemed have been paid since that date.

While the objections to the payment of the amount of the other two bonds mentioned in the bill are less conclusive, there seem to be so much doubt and uncertainty concerning their description and character, and their identification as unredeemed consols of 1867 is so unsatisfactory, that, in my opinion, it is not safe to assume, as is done in this bill, that they are represented among those bonds of that class recorded as still outstanding whose coupons for some reason have not been presented for payment since July 1, 1872.

I do not believe that an indemnity bond could be drawn which, as against the strict rights of sureties, would protect the Government against double liability in case all the payments directed by this bill were made. Even if the payments were confined to the two larger consols described, there would be great difficulty in framing a bond which would surely indemnify the Government.

There should always be a willingness to save the holders of Government securities from damage through their loss or destruction, but, in my judgment, a bad precedent would be established by paying obligations whose destruction and identification are not more satisfactorily established than in this case.

GROVER CLEVELAND.

EXECUTIVE MANSION, *February 19, 1895.*

To the House of Representatives:

I return herewith without approval House bill No. 6244, entitled "An act to remove the charge of desertion from the military record of Jacob Eckert."

This bill directs the Secretary of War "to cause the records of the War Department to be so amended as to remove the charge of desertion from the service record of Jacob Eckert, of New Philadelphia, Ohio, late a private in Company B, Sixty-first Ohio Volunteer Infantry, and to grant an honorable discharge to said Jacob Eckert from the service of the United States Army as of date when said company was mustered out of service."

The regiment and company to which this soldier belonged, except such members as reenlisted as veterans, were mustered out of the service October 17, 1864.

Jacob Eckert did not reenlist and was not mustered out with his comrades for the reason that he was then under arrest on a charge of desertion. In November, 1864, he was tried by a general court-martial and convicted of having deserted on the 1st of September, 1864, and again on the 2d day of September, 1864, and upon such conviction he was sentenced to forfeit all pay due him from September 1, the date of his first desertion, until the expiration of his term of service, to be dishonorably discharged and confined at hard labor for twelve months.

This sentence was approved by the reviewing authority, and I assume the convicted soldier served his term of imprisonment, since the statement contained in the report of the House committee to whom this bill was referred that he was dishonorably discharged in 1865 can be accounted for in no other way.

It seems to me that the provisions of this bill amount to a legislative reversal of the judgment of a regularly constituted court and a legislative pardon of the offense of which this soldier was convicted. If this doubtful authority is to be exercised by Congress, it should be done in such a manner as not to restore a man properly convicted and sentenced as a deserter, without even the allegation of injustice, to the rights of pay, allowance, and pension belonging to those who faithfully and honorably served in the military service of their country according to the terms of their enlistment.

GROVER CLEVELAND.

EXECUTIVE MANSION, *February 20, 1895.*

To the Senate:

I return herewith without approval Senate bill No. 1526, entitled "An act for the relief of Henry Halteman."

This bill directs the Secretary of War "to grant an honorable discharge from the United States service to Henry Halteman, late of Company F, Second United States Artillery."

It is conceded that this soldier enlisted in the Regular Army on the 18th day of December, 1860, for the term of five years and that he deserted on the 18th day of August, 1865. The only excuse or palliation offered for his offense is found in the statement that his desertion was provoked by his company's being ordered to California so near the termination of his enlistment that his term would have expired before or soon after his company could have reached California, and "that his return would have been both tedious and somewhat perilous, if not expensive."

The fact must not be overlooked that this soldier enlisted in the Regular Army and that his term had no relation to the duration of the war or the immediate need of the Government for troops at the time of his desertion. The morale and discipline of the Regular Army are therefore directly involved in the proposed legislation.

The soldier's name remained on the records of the War Department as a deserter at large for twenty-three years, and until the year 1888. In August of that year application was made to the Department for the removal of the charge of desertion against him, which was refused on the ground that it was not shown that such charge was founded in error. Thereupon he applied for a discharge without character, as it is called, as of the date of his desertion. This was granted on the 21st day of September, 1888. Such discharges, which were not uncommon at that time, omitted the certificate of character which entitled the soldier to reenlistment.

In 1892 a bill similar to that now under consideration was referred to the Adjutant-General of the Army and was returned with an adverse report.

The record of the War Department on the subject of this soldier's separation from the Army is absolutely correct as it stands, and no sufficient reason is apparent why another record should be substituted. If this deserter is to be allowed an honorable discharge, I do not see why every deserter should not be absolved from the consequences of his unfaithfulness.

The effect of this bill if it should become a law would be to allow the beneficiary not only a pensionable status, but arrears of pay and clothing allowances up to the date of his desertion and travel allowance from the place of his desertion to the place of his enlistment.

It is not denied that all these things have been justly forfeited by deliberate and inexcusable desertion. In the case presented it seems to me that the laws and regulations adopted for the purpose of maintaining the discipline and efficiency of the Army ought not to be set aside.

GROVER CLEVELAND.

EXECUTIVE MANSION, *February 23, 1895.*

To the House of Representatives:

I return herewith without approval House bill No. 8165, entitled "An act authorizing the Kansas City, Oklahoma and Pacific Railway Company to construct and operate a railway through Indian reservations in the

Indian Territory and the Territories of Oklahoma and New Mexico, and for other purposes."

This bill contains concessions more comprehensive and sweeping than any ever presented for my approval, and it seems to me the rights and interests of the Indians and the Government are the least protected.

The route apparently desired, though passing through or into one State and three Territories, is described as indefinitely as possible, and does not seem to be subject to the approval in its entirety of the Secretary of the Interior or any other governmental agency having relation to the interest involved.

There is no provision for obtaining the consent of the Indians through whose territory and reservations the railroad may be located.

Though it is proposed to build the railroad through territories having local courts convenient to their inhabitants, all controversies that may arise out of the location and building of the road are by the provisions of the bill to be passed upon by the United States circuit and district courts for the district of Kansas "and such other courts as may be authorized by Congress."

The bill provides that "the civil jurisdiction of said courts is hereby extended within the limits of said Indian reservations, without distinction as to citizenship of the parties, so far as may be necessary to carry out the provisions of this act." This provision permits the subordination of the jurisdiction of Indian courts, which we are bound by treaty to protect, to the "provisions of this act" and to the interests and preferences of the railroad company for whose benefit the bill under consideration is intended.

A plan of appraisal is provided for in the bill in case an agreement can not be reached as to the amount of compensation to be paid for the taking of lands held by individual occupants according to the laws, customs, and usages of any of the Indian nations or tribes or by allotment or agreement with the Indians. It is, however, further provided that in case either party is dissatisfied with the award of the referees to be appointed an appeal may be taken to the district court held at Wichita, Kans., no matter where on the proposed route of the road the controversy may originate. If upon the hearing of said appeal the judgment of the court shall be for the same sum as the award of the referees, the costs shall be adjudged against the appellant, and if said judgment shall be for a smaller sum the costs shall be adjudged against the party claiming damages. It does not seem to me that the interests of an Indian occupant or allottee are properly regarded when he is obliged, if dissatisfied with an award for the taking of his land, to go to the district court of Kansas for redress, at the risk of incurring costs and expenses that may not only exceed the award originally made to him, but leave him in debt.

It is probable that there are other valid objections to this bill. I have only attempted to suggest enough to justify my action in disapproving it.

In constructing legislation of this description it should not be forgotten that the rights and interests of the Indians are important in every view and should be scrupulously protected.

GROVER CLEVELAND.

EXECUTIVE MANSION, *February 23, 1895.*

To the House of Representatives:

I return herewith without approval House bill No. 5740, entitled "An act incorporating the Society of American Florists."

No sufficient reason is apparent for the incorporation of this organization under Federal laws. There is not the least difficulty in the way of the accomplishment under State laws by the incorporators named in the bill of every purpose which can legitimately belong to their corporate existence. The creation of such a corporation by a special act of Congress establishes a vexatious and troublesome precedent.

There appears to be no limit in the bill to the value of the real and personal property which the proposed corporation may hold if acquired by donation or bequest. The limit of $50,000 applies only to property acquired by purchase.

A conclusive objection to the bill is found in the fact that it fails to carry out the purposes and objects of those interested in its passage. The promoters of the bill are florists, who undoubtedly seek to advance floriculture. The declared object of the proposed incorporation is, however, stated in the bill to be "the elevation and advancement of horticulture in all its branches, to increase and diffuse the knowledge thereof, and for kindred purposes in the interest of horticulture."

It is entirely clear that the interests of florists would be badly served by a corporation confined to the furtherance of garden culture.

GROVER CLEVELAND.

EXECUTIVE MANSION, *February 23, 1895.*

To the House of Representatives:

I return herewith without approval House bill No. 4658, entitled "An act granting a pension to Hiram R. Rhea and repealing an act approved March 3, 1871."

The person named in the title of this bill was pensioned under the provisions of a private act passed March 3, 1871. In 1892 a letter from the Commissioner of Pensions was presented to Congress exhibiting facts which established in a most satisfactory manner that the claim for pension allowed by said special act was a barefaced and impudent fraud, supported by deliberate perjury. This letter appears to be the moving cause of the passage of the bill now before me. Payment of pension under the fraudulent act has been suspended since January 28, 1893, and since that time no information has been received from the fraudulent pensioner.

The circumstances developed called for the repeal of the law of 1871 placing him upon the pension roll. This is accomplished in the second section of the bill under consideration, which section I would be glad to approve. This repeal, however, is accompanied by a provision in the first section of the bill directing the Secretary of the Interior to place upon the pension roll this identical fraudulent pensioner, under a certificate numbered precisely the same as that heretofore issued to him, "at a rate proportionate to the degree of disability from such gunshot wounds as may be shown to the satisfaction of said Secretary to have been received at the hands of Confederate soldiers or sympathizers while said Rhea was attempting to cooperate with the Union forces," etc.

Inasmuch as the letter of the Commissioner of Pensions to which reference has been made, and which forms part of the committee's report on this bill, is the basis of this repealing provision, and inasmuch as this letter furnishes evidence that the pensioner was when injured a very disreputable member of a band of armed rebels and was wounded by Union soldiers, I can not understand why the same bill which for this reason purges the pension rolls of his name should in the same breath undo this work and direct his name to be rewritten on the rolls.

If the facts before Congress justify the repeal of the law under which this man fraudulently received a pension for nearly twenty-two years, they certainly do not justify the provision directing his name to be put on the rolls again with a view to further examination of his case or for any other purpose.

GROVER CLEVELAND.

EXECUTIVE MANSION, *February 27, 1895.*

To the House of Representatives:

I return herewith without approval House bill No. 2051, entitled "An act to grant a pension to Eunice Putman."

This bill provides for a pension to the beneficiary therein named as the helpless daughter of John Putman, who served as a private in the War of the Rebellion from August 27, 1864, to June 2, 1865. In 1870, when the beneficiary was not 2 years old, her mother died, and her father married again in 1872. He applied for a pension in 1884, but died the same year. His claim was allowed, however, in 1891, and his pension which had accrued between the date of his application and his death was paid to his widow, Jeanette S. Putman. Immediately thereafter a pension was allowed the widow in her own right, dating from the soldier's death, in 1884, with $2 additional per month for each of the two minor children. The beneficiary was not included because she had reached the age of 16 years prior to her father's death.

The report of the committee to whom this bill was referred states that no claim for pension on account of the soldier's death has ever been filed in the Pension Bureau, and it seems that upon this theory it was proposed to pension the daughter. I do not suppose it was intended that a double pension should be allowed. In point of fact, the widow has already been pensioned, and no such pension allowance has been made for the minor children. There is no suggestion that the widow has died or remarried.

If this bill should become a law, two full pensions would be in force at the same time, one to the widow and another to the daughter, each predicated upon the services and death of the same soldier.

GROVER CLEVELAND.

EXECUTIVE MANSION, *February 27, 1895.*

To the House of Representatives:

I herewith return without approval House bill No. 6868, entitled "An act for the relief of Catherine Ott, widow of Joseph Ott."

An application by the beneficiary named in this bill, under the law of 1890, was rejected on the ground that her husband died in the service, and therefore had not been honorably discharged, as required by that law.

It appears that after he had served a number of years in a cavalry regiment, and having been once discharged for reenlistment, he was transferred to the Veteran Reserve Corps and was in that service at the time of his death.

In these circumstances the rejection of the beneficiary's claim on the ground stated is held, under present rulings of the Pension Bureau, to have been erroneous, and such claim can now be favorably adjudicated upon proof of continued widowhood of the applicant and the lack of other means of support than her daily labor.

If such proof is supplied, she would be entitled to a pension dating from July 14, 1890, which would be much more advantageous than the relief afforded by the bill herewith returned.

If the beneficiary can justly claim a pension dating from her application to the Pension Bureau in 1890, the benefits accruing to her therefrom should not be superseded by this special legislation, which allows relief only from the date of its enactment.

GROVER CLEVELAND.

EXECUTIVE MANSION, *February 28, 1895.*

To the House of Representatives:

I herewith return without approval House bill No. 8681, entitled "An act authorizing the Arkansas Northwestern Railway Company to construct and operate a railway through the Indian Territory, and for other purposes.''

The contemplated route of this railway, so far as it is disclosed in the bill, would run from a point in the southwestern corner of the State of Missouri, across the northeastern corner of the Indian Territory, to a point in the southeastern part of the State of Kansas. This route necessarily runs through the lands of the Cherokee Indians or through the small reservations of the Quapaws, the Peorias, the Ottawas, the Wyandottes, and the Senecas.

There is no provision in the bill requiring the consent of the Indians whose lands are to be thus traversed.

There is no provision requiring the entire line to be located and approved by the Secretary of the Interior before the work of building is commenced.

The bill provides for compensation to individual occupants or allottees by a process of appraisal by referees, with the right of appeal to the district court held at Fort Smith, in the State of Arkansas.

In the case of allotted land or land held in individual occupancy by the Indians great care should be exercised in interfering with their holdings. Their land is given them for cultivation and with a view of making them self-supporting and industrious citizens. If their land is invaded and cut up by railroads, the purpose of allotment is in danger of being defeated. Money compensation is of but little use to them, and no amount can compensate for the disturbance in the cultivation of their lands and their consequent discontent and discouragement.

These considerations, it seems to me, emphasize the necessity of the exact location of the entire line of the contemplated railroad and such control over it by the Secretary of the Interior as will enable him to avoid as much as possible interference with individual Indian occupants and other difficulties.

This supervision and regulation of the line can be done with much more safety and effectiveness in considering the entire line than it can be done in sections of 25 miles each, as is provided in the bill.

The United States circuit and district courts for the districts of Kansas and the district of Arkansas and such other courts as may be authorized by Congress are given concurrent jurisdiction of all controversies arising between the railway company and the nations and tribes of Indians through whose territory the railway shall be constructed, or between said company and the members of said nations or tribes, without reference to the amount in controversy, and the civil jurisdiction of said courts is extended within the limits of said Indian Territory, without distinction as to the citizenship of parties, so far as may be necessary to carry out the provisions of the act.

The requirement that an Indian shall be obliged to seek a distant court for the adjudication of his rights in his controversies, great and small, with this railway company would result in many cases to a denial of justice.

I am convinced of the growing necessity, in this period of change in our relations with the Indians, of caution and certainty in the grants given to railroads to pass through Indian lands and of the exercise of care in allowing interference with their occupation.

GROVER CLEVELAND.

EXECUTIVE MANSION, *February 28, 1895.*

To the House of Representatives:

I herewith return without approval House bill No. 5624, entitled "An act to authorize the Oklahoma Central Railroad to construct and operate a railway through the Indian and Oklahoma Territories, and for other purposes."

The railroad proposed to be built under authority of this bill commences at a point in the Creek Nation called Sapulpa and runs through the Indian Territory to Oklahoma City, in Oklahoma, and thence through the Kiowa and Comanche Reservation to a point at or near the Red River, on the west line of said reservation.

There is no provision in this bill requiring the consent of the Indians through whose lands it is proposed to build the road.

The character and situation of these Indians are such as to make this consent important.

The first section gives the railroad company the right to build not only its line of road, but " such tracks, turn-outs, branches, sidings, and extensions as said company may deem it to their interest to construct."

If under an apparent grant to build a railroad the route of which is in a general way defined this company is to be allowed to build such branches and extensions as it may deem it to its interest to construct, the grant, I am sure, is more comprehensive than was intended by the Congress.

It seems to me that the entire line of the proposed railroad should be precisely located and subjected to the approval of the Secretary of the Interior before the work of construction is entered upon. This bill provides that it shall be approved in sections of 25 miles before construction on such sections shall be commenced.

Our relations to the Indians on reservations and their welfare and quiet are better preserved and protected when the entire line of road can be settled upon at one time and all uncertainty and doubt on the subject removed. The object sought by submitting the line to the supervision and determination of the Secretary of the Interior can be better and more intelligently accomplished if it is dealt with in its entirety instead of in sections.

GROVER CLEVELAND.

PROCLAMATIONS.

BY THE PRESIDENT OF THE UNITED STATES OF AMERICA.

A PROCLAMATION.

The following provisions of the laws of the United States are hereby published for the information of all concerned:

Section 1956, Revised Statutes, chapter 3, Title XXIII, enacts that—

No person shall kill any otter, mink, marten, sable, or fur seal, or other fur-bearing animal within the limits of Alaska Territory or in the waters thereof; and every person guilty thereof shall for each offense be fined not less than $200 nor more than $1,000, or imprisoned not more than six months, or both; and all vessels, their tackle, apparel, furniture, and cargo, found engaged in violation of this section shall be forfeited; but the Secretary of the Treasury shall have power to authorize the killing of any such mink, marten, sable, or other fur-bearing animal, except fur seals, under such regulations as he may prescribe; and it shall be the duty of the Secretary to prevent the killing of any fur seal and to provide for the execution of the provisions of this section until it is otherwise provided by law, nor shall he grant any special privileges under this section.

Section 3 of the act entitled "An act to provide for the protection of the salmon fisheries of Alaska," approved March 2, 1889, provides—

SEC. 3. That section 1956 of the Revised Statutes of the United States is hereby declared to include and apply to all the dominion of the United States in the waters of Bering Sea; and it shall be the duty of the President at a timely season in each year to issue his proclamation, and cause the same to be published for one month in at least one newspaper (if any such there be) published at each United States port of entry on the Pacific coast, warning all persons against entering said waters for the purpose of violating the provisions of said section; and he shall also cause one or more vessels of the United States to diligently cruise said waters and arrest all persons and seize all vessels found to be or to have been engaged in any violation of the laws of the United States therein.

Now, therefore, I, Grover Cleveland, President of the United States, hereby warn all persons against entering the waters of Bering Sea within the dominion of the United States for the purpose of violating the provisions of said section 1956 of the Revised Statutes; and I hereby proclaim that all persons found to be or to have been engaged in any violation of the laws of the United States in said waters will be arrested, proceeded against, and punished as above provided.

In testimony whereof I have hereunto set my hand and caused the seal of the United States to be affixed.

[SEAL.]   Done at the city of Washington, this 18th day of February, A. D. 1895, and of the Independence of the United States the one hundred and nineteenth.

GROVER CLEVELAND.

By the President:
W. Q. GRESHAM,
Secretary of State.

By the President of the United States of America.

A PROCLAMATION.

Whereas an act of Congress entitled "An act to postpone the enforcement of the act of August 19, 1890, entitled 'An act to adopt regulations for preventing collisions at sea,'" was approved February 23, 1895:

Now, therefore, I, Grover Cleveland, President of the United States of America, do hereby give notice that said act of August 19, 1890, as amended by the act of May 28, 1894, will not go into force on March 1, 1895, the date fixed in my proclamation of July 13, 1894,* but on such future date as may be designated in a proclamation of the President to be issued for that purpose.

In testimony whereof I have hereunto set my hand and caused the seal of the United States of America to be affixed.

[SEAL.]   Done at the city of Washington, this 25th day of February, 1895, and of the Independence of the United States the one hundred and nineteenth.   GROVER CLEVELAND.

By the President:

W. Q. GRESHAM, *Secretary of State.*

By the President of the United States of America.

A PROCLAMATION.

Whereas, pursuant to section 1 of the act of Congress approved July 13, 1892, entitled "An act making appropriations for the current and contingent expenses of the Indian Department and for fulfilling treaty stipulations with various Indian tribes for the fiscal year ending June 30, 1893, and for other purposes," certain articles of agreement were made and concluded at the Yankton Indian Agency, S. Dak., on the 31st day of December, 1892, by and between the United States of America and the Yankton tribe of Sioux or Dakota Indians upon the Yankton Reservation, whereby the said Yankton tribe of Sioux or Dakota Indians, for the consideration therein mentioned, ceded, sold, relinquished, and conveyed to the United States all their claim, right, title, and interest in and to all the unallotted lands within the limits of the reservation set apart to said tribe by the first article of the treaty of April 19, 1858, between said tribe and the United States; and

Whereas it is further stipulated and agreed by article 8 that such part of the surplus lands by said agreement ceded and sold to the United States as may be occupied by the United States for agency, schools, and other purposes shall be reserved from sale to settlers until they are no longer required for such purposes, but all of the other lands so ceded and sold shall immediately after the ratification of the agreement by Congress be offered for

*See pp. 5933-5942.

sale through the proper land office, to be disposed of under the existing land laws of the United States to actual and *bona fide* settlers only; and

Whereas it is also stipulated and agreed by article 10 that any religious society or other organization shall have the right for two years from the date of the ratification of the said agreement within which to purchase the lands occupied by it under proper authority for religious or educational work among the Indians, at a valuation fixed by the Secretary of the Interior, which shall not be less than the average price paid to the Indians for the surplus lands; and

Whereas it is provided in the act of Congress accepting, ratifying, and confirming the said agreement, approved August 15, 1894, section 12 (Pamphlet Statutes, Fifty-third Congress, second session, pp. 314–319)—

That the lands by said agreement ceded to the United States shall upon proclamation by the President be opened to settlement, and shall be subject to disposal only under the homestead and town-site laws of the United States, excepting the sixteenth and thirty-sixth sections in each Congressional township, which shall be reserved for common-school purposes and be subject to the laws of the State of South Dakota: *Provided*, That each settler on said lands shall, in addition to the fees provided by law, pay to the United States for the land so taken by him the sum of $3.75 per acre, of which sum he shall pay 50 cents at the time of making his original entry and the balance before making final proof and receiving a certificate of final entry; but the rights of honorably discharged Union soldiers and sailors as defined and described in sections 2304 and 2305 of the Revised Statutes of the United States shall not be abridged except as to the sum to be paid as aforesaid.

That the Secretary of the Interior, upon proper plats and description being furnished, is hereby authorized to issue patents to Charles Picotte and Felix Brunot and W. T. Selwyn, United States interpreters, for not to exceed 1 acre of land each, so as to embrace their houses near the agency buildings upon said reservation, but not to embrace any buildings owned by the Government, upon the payment by each of said persons of the sum of $3.75.

That every person who shall sell or give away any intoxicating liquors or other intoxicants upon any of the lands by said agreement ceded, or upon any of the lands included in the Yankton Sioux Indian Reservation as created by the treaty of April 19, 1858, shall be punishable by imprisonment for not more than two years and by a fine of not more than $300.

And whereas all the terms, conditions, and considerations required by said agreement made with said tribes of Indians and by the laws relating thereto precedent to opening said lands to settlement have been, as I hereby declare, complied with:

Now, therefore, I, Grover Cleveland, President of the United States, by virtue of the power in me vested by the statutes hereinbefore mentioned, do hereby declare and make known that all of the lands acquired from the Yankton tribe of Sioux or Dakota Indians by the said agreement, saving and excepting the lands reserved in pursuance of the provisions of said agreement and the act of Congress ratifying the same, will, at and after the hour of 12 o'clock noon (central standard time) on the 21st day of May, 1895, and not before, be open to settlement under the terms of and subject to all the conditions, limitations, reservations, and restrictions contained in said agreement, the statutes hereinbefore specified, and the laws of the United States applicable thereto.

The lands to be so opened to settlement are for greater convenience particularly described in the accompanying schedule, entitled "Schedule of lands within the Yankton Reservation, S. Dak., to be opened to settlement by proclamation of the President," and which schedule is made a part hereof.

In witness whereof I have hereunto set my hand and caused the seal of the United States to be affixed.

[SEAL.]   Done at the city of Washington, this 16th day of May, A. D. 1895, and of the Independence of the United States the one hundred and nineteenth.

GROVER CLEVELAND.

By the President:

EDWIN F. UHL, *Acting Secretary of State.*

BY THE PRESIDENT OF THE UNITED STATES OF AMERICA.

A PROCLAMATION.

Whereas, pursuant to section 1 of the act of Congress approved July 13, 1892, entitled "An act making appropriations for the current and contingent expenses of the Indian Department and for fulfilling treaty stipulations with various Indian tribes for the fiscal year ending June 30, 1893, and for other purposes," certain articles of cession and agreement were made and concluded at the Siletz Agency, Oreg., on the 31st day of October, 1892, by and between the United States of America and the Alsea and other Indians on Siletz Reservation in Oregon, whereby said Alsea and other Indians, for the consideration therein mentioned, ceded and conveyed to the United States all their claim, right, title, and interest in and to all the unallotted lands within the limits of said reservation, except the five sections described in article 4 of the agreement, viz: Section 9, township 9 south, range 11 west of the Willamette meridian; and the west half of the west half of section 5, and the east half of section 6, and the east half of the west half of section 6, township 10 south, range 10 west; and the south half of section 8, and the north half of section 17, and section 16, township 9 south, range 9 west; and the east half of the northeast quarter and lot 3, section 20, and south half and south half of north half of section 21, township 8, range 10 west; and

Whereas it is further stipulated and agreed by article 6 that any religious society or other organization shall have the right for two years from the date of the ratification of this agreement within which to purchase the lands occupied by it with proper authority for religious or educational work among the Indians, at the rate of $2.50 per acre, the same to be conveyed to such society or organization by patent; and

Whereas it is provided in the act of Congress accepting, ratifying, and

confirming said agreement, approved August 15, 1894 (Pamphlet Statutes, pp. 286–338), section 15, that—

The mineral lands shall be disposed of under the laws applicable thereto, and the
balance of the land so ceded shall be disposed of until further provided by law under
the town-site law and under the provisions of the homestead law: *Provided, however,*
That each settler under and in accordance with the provisions of said homestead laws
shall at the time of making his original entry pay the sum of 50 cents per acre in addition to the fees now required by law, and at the time of making final proof shall pay
the further sum of $1 per acre, final proof to be made within five years from the date
of entry; and three years' actual residence on the land shall be established by such
evidence as is now required in homestead proofs as a prerequisite to title or patent.

And whereas it is provided—

That immediately after the passage of this act the Secretary of the Interior shall,
under such regulations as he may prescribe, open said lands to settlement, after proclamation by the President and sixty days' notice.

And whereas all the terms, conditions, and considerations required by
said agreement made with said tribe of Indians hereinbefore mentioned
and the laws relating thereto precedent to opening said lands to settlement have been, as I hereby declare, provided for, paid, and complied with:

Now, therefore, I, Grover Cleveland, President of the United States, by
virtue of the power in me vested by the statutes hereinbefore mentioned
and by said agreement, do hereby declare and make known that all of the
lands acquired from the Alsea and other Indians by said agreement will,
at and after the hour of 12 o'clock noon (Pacific standard time) on the
25th day of July, 1895, and not before, be opened to settlement under
the terms of and subject to all the conditions, limitations, reservations,
and restrictions contained in said agreement, the statutes above specified, and the laws of the United States applicable thereto.

The lands to be so opened to settlement are for greater convenience
particularly described in the accompanying schedule, entitled "Schedule
of lands within the Siletz Indian Reservation, in Oregon, opened to settlement by proclamation of the President dated May 16, 1895," and which
schedule is made a part hereof.

Warning is hereby given that no person entering upon and occupying
said lands before said hour of 12 o'clock noon of the 25th day of July,
1895, hereinbefore fixed, will ever be permitted to enter any of said lands
or acquire any rights thereto, and that the officers of the United States
will be required to strictly enforce this provision, which is authorized by
the act of August 15, 1894, hereinbefore mentioned.

In witness whereof I have hereunto set my hand and caused the seal of
the United States to be affixed.

[SEAL.] Done at the city of Washington, this 16th day of May, A. D.
1895, and of the Independence of the United States the one
hundred and nineteenth.

GROVER CLEVELAND.

By the President:

EDWIN F. UHL, *Acting Secretary of State.*

BY THE PRESIDENT OF THE UNITED STATES OF AMERICA.

A PROCLAMATION.

Whereas by a written agreement made on the 9th day of September, 1891, the Kickapoo Nation of Indians, in the Territory of Oklahoma, ceded, conveyed, transferred, and relinquished, forever and absolutely, without any reservation whatever, all their claim, title, and interest of every kind and character in and to the lands particularly described in article 1 of the agreement: *Provided*, That in said tract of country there shall be allotted to each and every member, native and adopted, of said Kickapoo tribe of Indians 80 acres of land, in the manner and under the conditions stated in said agreement, and that when the allotments of land shall have been made and approved by the Secretary of the Interior the title thereto shall be held in trust for the allottees respectively for the period of twenty-five years in the manner and to the extent provided for in the act of Congress approved February 8, 1887 (24 U. S. Statutes at Large, p. 388); and

Whereas it is further stipulated and agreed by article 6 of the agreement that wherever in this reservation any religious society or other organization is now occupying any portion of said reservation for religious or educational work among the Indians the land so occupied may be allotted and confirmed to such society or organization, not, however, to exceed 160 acres of land to any one society or organization, so long as the same shall be so occupied and used: and such land shall not be subject to homestead entry; and

Whereas it is provided in the act of Congress accepting, ratifying, and confirming the said agreement with the Kickapoo Indians, approved March 3, 1893 (27 U. S. Statutes at Large, pp. 557–563), section 3—

That whenever any of the lands acquired by this agreement shall by operation of law or proclamation of the President of the United States be open to settlement or entry they shall be disposed of (except sections 16 and 36 in each township thereof) to actual settlers only under the provisions of the homestead and town-site laws, except section 2301 of the Revised Statutes of the United States, which shall not apply: *Provided, however*, That each settler on said lands shall before making a final proof and receiving a certificate of entry pay to the United States for the land so taken by him, in addition to the fees provided by law and within five years from the date of the first original entry, the sum of $1.50 an acre, one-half of which shall be paid within two years; but the rights of honorably discharged Union soldiers and sailors as defined and described in sections 2304 and 2305 of the Revised Statutes of the United States shall not be abridged except as to the sum to be paid as aforesaid. Until said lands are opened to settlement by proclamation of the President of the United States no person shall be permitted to enter upon or occupy any of said lands, and any person violating this provision shall never be permitted to make entry of any of said lands or acquire any title thereto: *Provided*, That any person having attempted to but for any cause failed to acquire a title in fee under existing law, or who made entry under what is known as the commuted provision of the homestead law, shall be qualified to make homestead entry upon said lands.

And whereas allotments of land in severalty to said Kickapoo Indians

U. S. FIELD HOSPITAL AND SPANISH FORT AT EL CANEY

UNITES STATES FIELD HOSPITAL AND SPANISH FORT AT EL CANEY

Many observers have commented on the behavior of the wounded. They were usually silent under suffering, uncomplaining and patient. Some even tried to laugh at their injuries. Frequently the surgeon's or hospital steward's inquiries would elicit the response: "Oh, I've got a punctured tire, that's all!" One phase of the battle is disgraceful to the Spaniards. Their sharpshooters fired at wounded men in the stretchers and at the surgeons and stewards working over them, whom they repeatedly killed and wounded. The right-hand tent seems to be a sort of waiting-room, while an operation is in progress in the center tent. The interior of the left-hand tent cannot be discerned, but the bandage on the soldier's hand would indicate that it, too, was an operating-room.

The character of the small fort in the lower panel is worth noting. It could be constructed very quickly and yet would prove as good a shelter against rifle-balls as walls three feet thick. Barb wire was an important part of Spanish engineering in Cuba. This typical redoubt guarded the entrance to El Caney.

See the article "Santiago" for the story of the fight at San Juan and El Caney. See the article "Spanish-American War" for a brief history. See McKinley's wartime messages for the official history of the struggle.

have been made and approved in accordance with law and the provisions of the before-mentioned agreement with them; and

Whereas it is provided by the act of Congress for the temporary government of Oklahoma, approved May 2, 1890, section 23 (26 U. S. Statutes at Large, p. 92), that there shall be reserved public highways 4 rods wide between each section of land in said Territory, the section lines being the center of said highways; but no deduction shall be made, where cash payments are provided for, in the amount to be paid for each quarter section of land by reason of such reservation; and

Whereas it is provided in the act of Congress approved February 10, 1894 (28 U. S. Statutes at Large, p. 37)—

That every homestead settler on the public lands on the left bank of the Deep Fork River in the former Iowa Reservation, in the Territory of Oklahoma, who entered less than 160 acres of land may enter under the homestead laws other lands adjoining the land embraced in his original entry when such additional lands become subject to entry, which additional entry shall nôt with the lands originally entered exceed in the aggregate 160 acres: *Provided*, That where such adjoining entry is made residence shall not be required upon the lands so entered, but the residence and cultivation by the settler upon and of the land embraced in his original entry shall be considered residence and cultivation for the same length of time upon the land embraced in his additional entry; but such lands so entered shall be paid for conformably to the terms of the act acquiring the same and opening it to homestead entry.

And whereas it is further provided in the act of Congress approved March 2, 1895 (28 U. S. Statutes at Large, p. 899)—

That any State or Territory entitled to indemnity school lands or entitled to select lands for educational purposes under existing law may select such lands within the boundaries of any Indian reservation in such State or Territory from the surplus lands thereof purchased by the United States, after allotments have been made to the Indians of such reservation and prior to the opening of such reservation to settlement.

And whereas all the terms, conditions, and considerations required by said agreement made with said tribes of Indians and by the laws relating thereto precedent to opening said lands to settlement have been, as I hereby declare, complied with:

Now, therefore, I, Grover Cleveland, President of the United States, by virtue of the power in me vested by the statutes hereinbefore mentioned and by other the laws of the United States and by the said agreement, do hereby declare and make known that all of said lands hereinbefore described, acquired from the Kickapoo Indians by the agreement aforesaid, will, at and after the hour of 12 o'clock noon (central standard time), Thursday, the 23d day of the month of May, A. D. 1895, and not before, be open to settlement under the terms of and subject to all the conditions, limitations, reservations, and restrictions contained in the said agreement, the statutes above specified, and the laws of the United States applicable thereto, saving and excepting such tracts as have been allotted, reserved, or selected under the laws herein referred to and such tracts as may be properly selected by the Territory of Oklahoma under and in accordance with the provisions of the act of March 2, 1895, hereinbefore quoted, prior to the time herein fixed for the opening of said lands to settlement.

The lands to be so opened to settlement are for greater convenience particularly described in the accompanying schedule, entitled "Schedule of lands within the Kickapoo Reservation, Oklahoma Territory, to be opened to settlement by proclamation of the President;" but notice is hereby given that should any of the lands described in the accompanying schedule be properly selected by the Territory of Oklahoma under and in accordance with the provisions of said act of Congress approved March 2, 1895, prior to the time herein fixed for the opening of said lands to settlement such tracts will not be subject to settlement or entry.

Notice, moreover, is hereby given that it is by law enacted that until said lands are opened to settlement by proclamation no person shall be permitted to enter upon or occupy the same, and any person violating this provision shall never be permitted to make entry of any of said lands or acquire any title thereto. The officers of the United States will be required to enforce this provision.

And further notice is hereby given that all of said lands lying north of the township line between townships 13 and 14 north are now attached to the Eastern land district, the office of which is at Guthrie, Oklahoma Territory, and all of said lands lying south of the township line between townships 13 and 14 north are now attached to the Oklahoma land district, the office of which is at Oklahoma, Oklahoma Territory.

In witness whereof I have hereunto set my hand and caused the seal or the United States to be affixed.

[SEAL.]   Done at the city of Washington, this 18th day of May, A. D. 1895, and of the Independence of the United States the one hundred and nineteenth.

GROVER CLEVELAND.

By the President:

Edwin F. Uhl,
Acting Secretary of State.

A PROCLAMATION

By the President of the United States.

Walter Q. Gresham, Secretary of State of the United States, is dead.

The President in making this distressing announcement to his fellow-countrymen speaks from the depths of a personal affliction to remind them that they too have lost a pure and able public servant, a wise and patriotic guardian of all their rights and interests, a manly and loyal American, and a generous and lovable man.

As a suitable expression of national bereavement, I direct that the diplomatic representatives of the United States in all foreign countries display the flags over their embassies and legations at half-mast for ten days; that for a like period the flag of the United States be displayed at half-mast at all forts and military posts and at all naval stations and on all vessels of the United States.

I further order that on the day of the funeral the Executive Departments in the city of Washington be closed and that on all public buildings throughout the United States the national flag be displayed at half-mast.

Done at the city of Washington, this 28th day of May, A. D. 1895, and of the Independence of the United States of America the one hundred and nineteenth.

[SEAL.]

GROVER CLEVELAND.

By the President:

EDWIN F. UHL,
Acting Secretary of State.

BY THE PRESIDENT OF THE UNITED STATES.

A PROCLAMATION.

Whereas the island of Cuba is now the seat of serious civil disturbances, accompanied by armed resistance to the authority of the established Government of Spain, a power with which the United States are and desire to remain on terms of peace and amity; and

Whereas the laws of the United States prohibit their citizens, as well as all others being within and subject to their jurisdiction, from taking part in such disturbances adversely to such established Government, by accepting or exercising commissions for warlike service against it, by enlistment or procuring others to enlist for such service, by fitting out or arming or procuring to be fitted out and armed ships of war for such service, by augmenting the force of any ship of war engaged in such service and arriving in a port of the United States, and by setting on foot or providing or preparing the means for military enterprises to be carried on from the United States against the territory of such Government:

Now, therefore, in recognition of the laws aforesaid and in discharge of the obligations of the United States toward a friendly power, and as a measure of precaution, and to the end that citizens of the United States and all others within their jurisdiction may be deterred from subjecting themselves to legal forfeitures and penalties, I, Grover Cleveland, President of the United States of America, do hereby admonish all such citizens and other persons to abstain from every violation of the laws hereinbefore referred to, and do hereby warn them that all violations of such laws will be rigorously prosecuted; and I do hereby enjoin upon all officers of the United States charged with the execution of said laws the utmost diligence in preventing violations thereof and in bringing to trial and punishment any offenders against the same.

In testimony whereof I have hereunto set my hand and caused the seal of the United States to be affixed.

[SEAL.]   Done at the city of Washington, this 12th day of June, A. D. 1895, and of the Independence of the United States of America the one hundred and nineteenth.

GROVER CLEVELAND.

By the President:
RICHARD OLNEY,
Secretary of State.

BY THE PRESIDENT OF THE UNITED STATES OF AMERICA.

A PROCLAMATION.

Whereas it is provided by section 13 of the act of Congress of March 3, 1891, entitled "An act to amend Title LX, chapter 3, of the Revised Statutes of the United States, relating to copyrights," that said act "shall only apply to a citizen or subject of a foreign state or nation when such foreign state or nation permits to citizens of the United States of America the benefit of copyright on substantially the same basis as its own citizens, or when such foreign state or nation is a party to an international agreement which provides for reciprocity in the granting of copyright, by the terms of which agreement the United States of America may at its pleasure become a party to such agreement;" and

Whereas it is also provided by said section that "the existence of either of the conditions aforesaid shall be determined by the President of the United States by proclamation made from time to time as the purposes of this act may require;" and

Whereas satisfactory official assurances have been given that in Spain and her provinces and colonial possessions the law permits to citizens of the United States the benefit of copyright on substantially the same basis as to the subjects of Spain:

Now, therefore, I, Grover Cleveland, President of the United States of America, do declare and proclaim that the first of the conditions specified in section 13 of the act of March 3, 1891, now exists and is fulfilled in respect to the subjects of Spain.

In testimony whereof I have hereunto set my hand and caused the seal of the United States to be affixed.

[SEAL.]   Done at the city of Washington, this 10th day of July, 1895, and of the Independence of the United States the one hundred and twentieth.

GROVER CLEVELAND.

By the President:
ALVEY A. ADEE,
Acting Secretary of State.

By the President of the United States.

A PROCLAMATION.

The constant goodness and forbearance of Almighty God which have been vouchsafed to the American people during the year which is just past call for their sincere acknowledgment and devout gratitude.

To the end, therefore, that we may with thankful hearts unite in extolling the loving care of our Heavenly Father, I, Grover Cleveland, President of the United States, do hereby appoint and set ap rt Thursday, the 28th day of the present month of November, as a day o' thanksgiving and prayer to be kept and observed by all our people.

On that day let us forego our usual occupations and in our accustomed places of worship join in rendering thanks to the Giver of Every Good and Perfect Gift for the bounteous returns that have rewarded our labors in the fields and in the busy marts of trade, for the peace and order that have prevailed throughout the land, for our protection from pestilence and dire calamity, and for the other blessings that have been showered upon us from an open hand.

And with our thanksgiving let us humbly beseech the Lord to so incline the hearts of our people unto Him that He will not leave us nor forsake us as a nation, but will continue to us His mercy and protecting care, guiding us in the path of national prosperity and happiness, enduing us with rectitude and virtue, and keeping alive within us a patriotic love for the free institutions which have been given to us as our national heritage.

And let us also on the day of our thanksgiving especially remember the poor and needy, and by deeds of charity let us show the sincerity of our gratitude.

In witness whereof I have hereunto set my hand and caused the seal of the United States to be affixed.

[SEAL.]   Done at the city of Washington, this 4th day of November, A. D. 1895, and in the one hundred and twentieth year of the Independence of the United States.

GROVER CLEVELAND.

By the President:

RICHARD OLNEY,
Secretary of State.

By the President of the United States of America.

A PROCLAMATION.

Whereas section 17 of the act of August 28, 1894, entitled "An act to reduce taxation, to provide revenue for the Government, and for other purposes," prohibits "the importation of neat cattle and the hides of neat cattle from any foreign country into the United States;" and

Whereas it is provided by the act of Congress approved March 2, 1895, entitled "An act making appropriations for the Department of Agriculture for the fiscal year ending June 30, 1896"—

That whenever the Secretary of Agriculture shall certify to the President of the United States what countries or parts of countries are free from contagious or infectious diseases of domestic animals, and that neat cattle and hides can be imported from such countries without danger to the domestic animals of the United States, the President of the United States may suspend the prohibition of the importation of neat cattle and hides in the manner provided by law.

And whereas the Secretary of Agriculture has now certified to me that the countries of Norway, Sweden, Holland, Great Britain, Ireland, the Channel Islands, and the countries of North, Central, and South America, including Mexico, are so far free from contagious or infectious diseases of domestic animals that neat cattle may be imported from those countries into the United States, under the sanitary regulations prescribed by the Secretary of Agriculture, without danger to the domestic animals of the United States, and that so far as the countries above named, as well as all other countries from which hides are imported into the United States, are concerned, they are so far free from contagious or infectious diseases of domestic animals that hides of neat cattle can be imported from all parts of the world, under proper regulations prescribed by the Secretary of the Treasury, without danger to the domestic animals of the United States:

Now, therefore, I, Grover Cleveland, President of the United States, do hereby suspend the prohibition of the importation of neat cattle from the countries of Norway, Sweden, Holland, Great Britain, Ireland, the Channel Islands, and the countries of North, Central, and South America, including Mexico, and of the hides of neat cattle from all parts of the world; but all importations of neat cattle shall be made under the sanitary regulations prescribed by the Secretary of Agriculture and all importations of hides shall be made under proper regulations prescribed by the Secretary of the Treasury.

In testimony whereof I have hereunto set my hand and caused the seal of the United States to be affixed.

[SEAL.]　　Done at the city of Washington, this 8th day of November, 1895, and of the Independence of the United States of America the one hundred and twentieth.

GROVER CLEVELAND.

By the President:

RICHARD OLNEY, *Secretary of State.*

BY THE PRESIDENT OF THE UNITED STATES OF AMERICA.

A PROCLAMATION.

Whereas, pursuant to section 5 of the act of Congress approved February 8, 1887 (24 U. S. Statutes at Large, p. 388), entitled "An act to provide for the allotment of lands in severalty to the Indians on the various reservations and to extend the protection of the laws of the United

States and the Territories over the Indians, and for other purposes,'' certain articles of cession and agreement were made and concluded at the Nez Percé Agency, Idaho, on the 1st day of May, 1893, by and between the United States of America and the Nez Percé Indians, whereby said Indians, for the consideration therein mentioned, ceded and conveyed to the United States all their claim, right, title, and interest to all the unallotted lands set apart as a home for their use and occupation by the second article of the treaty between said Indians and the United States concluded June 9, 1863 (14 U. S. Statutes at Large, p. 647), and included in the following boundaries, to wit:

Commencing at the northeast corner of Lake Wa-ha and running thence northerly to a point on the north bank of the Clearwater River 3 miles below the mouth of the Lapwai; thence down the north bank of the Clearwater to the mouth of the Hatwai Creek; thence due north to a point 7 miles distant; thence eastwardly to a point on the North Fork of the Clearwater 7 miles distant from its mouth; thence to a point on Oro Fino Creek 5 miles above its mouth; thence to a point on the North Fork of the South Fork of the Clearwater 1 mile above the bridge on the road leading to Elk City (so as to include all the Indian farms now within the forks); thence in a straight line westwardly to the place of beginning.

Saving and excepting the sixteenth and thirty-sixth sections of each Congressional township, which shall be reserved for common-school purposes and be subject to the laws of Idaho, and excepting the tracts described in articles 1 and 2 of the agreement, viz:

The said Nez Percé Indians hereby cede, sell, relinquish, and convey to the United States all their claim, right, title, and interest in and to all the unallotted lands within the limits of said reservation, saving and excepting the following-described tracts of lands, which are hereby retained by the said Indians, viz:

In township 34, range 4 west: Northeast quarter, north half and southeast of northwest quarter, northeast quarter of southwest quarter, north half and east half of southwest quarter, and the southeast quarter of southeast quarter, section 13; 440 acres.

In township 34, range 3 west: Sections 10, 15, 36; 1,920 acres.

In township 33, range 3 west: Section 1; northwest quarter of northeast quarter, north half of northwest quarter, section 12; 760 acres.

In township 35, range 2 west: South half of northeast quarter, northwest quarter, north half and southeast quarter of southwest quarter, southeast quarter, section 3; east half, east half of northwest quarter, southwest quarter, section 10; section 11; north half, north half of south half, section 21; east half of northeast quarter, section 20; sections 22, 27, 35; 4,200 acres.

In township 34, range 2 west: North half, southwest quarter, north half and southwest quarter and west half of southeast quarter of southeast quarter, section 13; section 14; north half, section 23; west half of east half and west half of northeast quarter, northwest quarter, north half of southwest quarter, west half of east half and northwest quarter and east half of southwest quarter of southeast quarter, section 24; section 29; 2,700 acres.

In township 33, range 2 west: West half and southeast quarter, section 6; sections 16, 22, 27; north half and north half of south half, section 34; 2,880 acres.

In township 34, range 1 west: West half, section 2; sections 3, 4: north half and southwest quarter, section 8; north half, section 9; north half and north half of southwest quarter, section 18; northwest quarter, section 17; 2,960 acres.

In township 37, range 1 east: Section 20; section 21, less south half of south half of southwest quarter of southeast quarter (10 acres); 1,270 acres.

In township 36, range 1 east: South half of sections 3, 4; sections 11, 12; 1,920 acres.

In township 36, range 2 east: Sections 16, 17, 18, 20; all of section 25 west of boundary line of reservation; sections 26, 27; 4,240 acres.

In township 35, range 2 east: North half of sections 16, 17; section 27; north half of section 34; 1,600 acres.

In township 34, range 2 east: East half and east half of west half of southeast quarter, section 24; 100 acres.

In township 34, range 3 east: South half of sections 19, 20; north half, north half of south half, southwest quarter and north half of southeast quarter of southwest quarter, north half of south half of southeast quarter, section 23; north half, north half and north half of southwest quarter and southeast quarter of southwest quarter, southeast quarter, section 24; north half and southeast quarter of northeast quarter, north half of northwest quarter, section 25; south half of northeast quarter of northeast quarter, section 26; section 29; northeast quarter of northeast quarter and south half, section 30; northwest quarter and north half of southwest quarter, section 31, northeast quarter, north half and southeast quarter of northwest quarter, section 32; northwest quarter, north half of southwest quarter, section 33; 3,700 acres.

In township 33, range 4 east: South half of southeast quarter, section 18; northeast quarter and fraction northeast of river in east half of northwest quarter, section 19; fraction west of boundary line of reservation in section 22; west half and southeast quarter of section 35; 1,440 acres.

In township 32, range 4 east: Fraction in west half of northeast quarter of southwest quarter, fraction in northwest quarter of southeast quarter, section 1; section 2; south half of section 6; west half and southeast quarter of northeast quarter of section 9; 1,410 acres.

In township 31, range 4 east: South half of northeast quarter, southeast quarter of northwest quarter, northeast quarter of southwest quarter, southeast quarter, section 17; northwest quarter, section 21; 480 acres.

Total, 32,020 acres.

ART. II. It is also stipulated and agreed that the place known as "the boom" on the Clearwater River, near the mouth of Lapwai Creek, shall be excepted from this cession and reserved for the common use of the tribe, with full right of access thereto, and that the tract of land adjoining said boom now occupied by James Moses shall be allotted to him in such manner as not to interfere with such right; also that there shall be reserved from said cession the land described as follows: " Commencing at a point at the margin of Clearwater River, on the south side thereof, which is 300 yards below where the middle thread of Lapwai Creek empties into said river; run thence up the margin of said Clearwater River at low-water mark 900 yards to a point; run thence south 250 yards to a point; thence southwesterly in a line to the southeast corner of a stone building partly finished as a church; thence west 300 yards to a point; thence from said point northerly in a straight line to the point of beginning; and also the adjoining tract of land lying southerly of said tract, on the south end thereof, commencing at the said corner of said church, and at the point 300 yards west thereof and run a line from each of said points, one of said lines running on the east side and the other on the west of said Lapwai Creek, along the foothills of each side of said creek, up the same sufficiently far so that a line being drawn east and west to intersect the aforesaid lines shall embrace within its boundaries, together with the first above-described tract of land, a sufficient quantity of land as to include and comprise 640 acres."

And excepting the land embraced in the William Craig donation claim, in township 35 north, range 3 west. (See case of Caldwell *vs.* Robinson, Federal Reporter, vol. 59, p. 653); and

Whereas it is further stipulated and agreed by article 6 of the agreement that any religious society or other organization now occupy-ing under proper authority, for religious or educational work among the Indians, any of the lands ceded shall have the right for two years from the date of the ratification of this agreement within which to purchase the land so occupied, at the rate of $3 per acre, the same to be conveyed to such society or organization by patent in the usual form; and

Whereas it is further agreed by article 9 of the agreement that the lands by this agreement ceded, those retained, and those allotted to the said Nez Percé Indians shall be subject for a period of twenty-five years to all the laws of the United States prohibiting the introduction of intox-icants into the Indian country, and that the Nez Percé Indian allottees, whether under the care of an Indian agent or not, shall for a like period be subject to all the laws of the United States prohibiting the sale or other disposition of intoxicants to Indians; and

Whereas it is provided in the act of Congress accepting, ratifying, and confirming said agreement, approved August 15, 1894 (28 U. S. Statutes at Large, pp. 286–338), section 16—

That immediately after the issuance and receipt by the Indians of trust patents for the allotted lands, as provided for in said agreement, the lands so ceded, sold, relin-quished, and conveyed to the United States shall be opened to settlement by procla-mation of the President and shall be subject to disposal only under the homestead, town-site, stone and timber, and mining laws of the United States, excepting the sixteenth and thirty-sixth sections in each Congressional township, which shall be reserved for common-school purposes and be subject to the laws of Idaho: *Provided*, That each settler on said lands shall before making final proof and receiving a cer-tificate of entry pay to the United States for the lands so taken by him, in addition to the fees provided by law, the sum of $3.75 per acre for agricultural lands, one-half of which shall be paid within three years from the date of original entry, and the sum of $5 per acre for stone, timber, and mineral lands, subject to the regulations pre-scribed by existing laws; but the rights of honorably discharged Union soldiers and sailors as defined and described in sections 2304 and 2305 of the Revised Statutes of the United States shall not be abridged except as to the sum to be paid as aforesaid.

And whereas all the terms, conditions, and considerations required by said agreement made with said tribe of Indians hereinbefore men-tioned and the laws relating thereto precedent to opening said lands to settlement have been, as I hereby declare, provided for, paid, and complied with:

Now, therefore, I, Grover Cleveland, President of the United States, by virtue of the power in me vested by the statutes hereinbefore men-tioned and by said agreement, do hereby declare and make known that all of the unallotted and unreserved lands acquired from the Nez Percé Indians by said agreement will, at and after the hour of 12 o'clock noon (Pacific standard time) on the 18th day of November, 1895, and not before, be opened to settlement under the terms of and subject to all the conditions, limitations, reservations, and restrictions contained in said agreement, the statutes above specified, and the laws of the United States applicable thereto,

The lands to be so opened to settlement are for greater convenience particularly described in the accompanying schedule, entitled "Schedule of lands within the Nez Percé Indian Reservation, Idaho, to be opened to settlement by proclamation of the President," and which schedule is made a part hereof.

In witness whereof I have hereunto set my hand and caused the seal of the United States to be affixed.

[SEAL.]   Done at the city of Washington, this 8th day of November, A. D. 1895, and of the Independence of the United States the one hundred and twentieth.

GROVER CLEVELAND.

By the President:
    RICHARD OLNEY,
       Secretary of State.

EXECUTIVE ORDERS.

AMENDMENT OF CIVIL-SERVICE RULES.

Special Departmental Rule No. 1 is hereby amended by striking out the whole of the paragraph in section 3, Department of the Interior, relating to the Geological Survey and substituting in lieu thereof the following:

In the Geological Survey: Geologist, assistant geologist, paleontologist, assistant paleontologist, chief photographer, photographer, chief chemist, chemist, assistant chemist, chief engraver, engraver, assistant engraver, lithographic engraver, map printer, lithographic printer, assistant lithographic printer, map reviser, statistical experts temporarily employed.

Approved, December 4, 1894.

GROVER CLEVELAND.

AMENDMENT OF CIVIL-SERVICE RULES.

Departmental Rule VII is hereby amended by adding thereto the following section, to be numbered 9:

The Commission shall certify for transfer and reappointment to any classified non-excepted place in the departmental service, upon the requisition of the head of a Department, any person who at the time of making such requisition is holding an office outside the classified service in any Executive Department at Washington to which he was appointed from a classified place in the departmental service; and upon the requisition of any head of Department the Commission shall certify for reinstatement in the classified service of said Department any such officer who within one year next preceding the date of the requisition, by the abolition of his office or otherwise, has without delinquency or misconduct been separated from said office: *Provided*, That this section shall not authorize the reappointment to the classified service of any such officer or ex-officer who was appointed to his office from an excepted place, unless his appointment to such excepted place was by promotion from a nonexcepted place.

Approved, December 15, 1894.   GROVER CLEVELAND.

AMENDMENTS OF CIVIL-SERVICE RULES.

EXECUTIVE MANSION, *January 3, 1895.*

Postal Rule II, clause 5, is amended by striking out paragraph (*e*) and relettering paragraph (*f*) as (*e*), so that as amended the clause will read:

5. Exceptions from examination in the classified postal service are hereby made as follows:

(*a*) Assistant postmaster, or the chief assistant to the postmaster, by whatever designation known.

(*b*) One secretary to the postmaster, when authorized by law and allowed by the Post-Office Department.

(*c*) Cashier, when authorized by law and employed under that roster title.

(*d*) Assistant cashier, when authorized by law and employed under that roster title.

(*e*) Printers and pressmen, when authorized by law and allowed by the Post-Office Department and employed as such.

Approved: GROVER CLEVELAND.

AMENDMENTS OF CIVIL-SERVICE RULES.

EXECUTIVE MANSION, *February 12, 1895.*

Departmental Rule VII, clause 8, is hereby amended to read as follows:

In case of the occurrence of a vacancy in any Department which the public interest requires shall be immediately filled, and which can not be so filled by certification from the eligible registers of the Commission, such vacancy may be filled by temporary appointment outside the civil service until a regular appointment can be made under the provisions of sections 1, 2, and 3 of this rule: *Provided,* That such temporary appointment shall in no case continue longer than ninety days, and shall expire by limitation at the end of that time: *And provided further,* That no person shall serve longer than the period herein prescribed in any one year under such temporary appointment.

The year limitation in regard to reappointment shall begin to run on the date of the original appointment.

Every such temporary appointment and the discontinuance of the same shall at once be reported to the Commission.

Postal Rule IV, clause 4, is hereby amended to read as follows:

4. In case of the occurrence of a vacancy in a position within the classified service of any post-office which the public interest requires shall be immediately filled, where there is no eligible remaining on the proper register, such vacancy may be filled by temporary appointment outside the civil service until a regular appointment can be made under the provisions of sections 1 and 2 of this rule: *Provided,* That such temporary appointment shall in no case continue longer than ninety days, and shall expire by limitation at the end of that time: *And provided further,* That no person shall serve more than ninety days in any one year under such temporary appointment.

The year limitation in regard to reappointment shall begin to run on the date of the original appointment.

Every such temporary appointment and also the discontinuance of the same shall at once be reported to the Commission.

Approved:

GROVER CLEVELAND.

AMENDMENTS OF CIVIL-SERVICE RULES.

GENERAL RULES.

General Rule II: Strike out the word "five" in line 1 and insert in lieu thereof the word "six," and add at the end of the rule a new clause, as follows:

6. The classified internal-revenue service.

General Rule III, section 5: Insert after the word "may" in line 1 the words "in its discretion," and after the word "appointment" in line 2 the following: "or an applicant who has been guilty of a crime or of infamous or notoriously disgraceful conduct." As amended the section will read:

5. The Commission may, in its discretion, refuse to examine an applicant who would be physically unable to perform the duties of the place to which he desires appointment or an applicant who has been guilty of a crime or of infamous or notoriously disgraceful conduct. The reason for any such action shall be entered on the minutes of the Commission.

Section 9: In line 1 strike out the word "departmental," and after the word "service" in the same line and in line 2 the words "and the classified railway mail service."

General Rule V: In line 2 change the order of words and insert other words so as to make the phrase amended read as follows: "and postmasters and customs and internal-revenue officers and custodians of public buildings."

General Rule IV, section 2: Insert after the word "may" in line 1 the words "in its discretion."

DEPARTMENTAL RULES.

Departmental Rule II: In section 1, line 2, after the word "such," insert the word "other" and strike out the words "supplementary and special." In section 2, line 2, strike out the words "supplementary and special" and insert in lieu thereof the word "other."

Departmental Rule IV: In section 1, after the semicolon following the word "age" in line 4, insert the following: "or for the position of messenger or assistant messenger who is not under 18 years of age, or for the position of page or messenger boy who is not under 14 nor over 18 years of age."

Departmental Rule V: In section 2, paragraph 6, line 1, after the word "postal," insert the words "internal-revenue."

Departmental Rule VI: In section 1, line 2, after the word "of," strike out the words "special and supplementary" and insert in lieu thereof the word "other." In section 4, line 7, after the words "clerk-copyist," insert the words "or the messenger and watchman." In section 5, line 3, after the word "printing," insert the words "or for page or messenger boy."

Departmental Rule VII: In section 3, at the beginning of line 2, before the word "register," insert the words "the messenger or the watchman." In the second paragraph of the same section, in line 2, after the word "assistant," insert the words "or page or messenger boy."

Departmental Rule VIII: In section 1 insert a clause, to be lettered (*c*), as follows:

(*c*) From a bureau of the Treasury Department in which business relating to the internal revenue is transacted to a classified internal-revenue district, and from such a district to such a bureau in the Treasury Department, upon requisition by the Secretary of the Treasury.

The remaining clauses of the section to be relettered (*d*) and (*e*), respectively. In section 2, line 2, strike out the letter "*d*" in parentheses and insert in lieu thereof the letter "*e*," and at the end of the section add the following proviso:

Provided, That a person may be transferred from a place in one Department to a place requiring no higher examination in another Department without examination.

Departmental Rule IX: Strike out the whole of section 1 and insert in lieu thereof the following:

1. Until promotion regulations have been applied to a Department under the provisions of section 6 of General Rule III promotions therein may be made as follows:

(*a*) Any person appointed from the appropriate register to the position of messenger, assistant messenger, watchman, or other subordinate position below the positions of clerk and copyist may at any time after absolute appointment, if not barred by age limitations, be transferred to any other of said subordinate positions, but shall not be promoted to the position of clerk or copyist or to any place the duties of which are clerical: *Provided*, That printers' assistants in the Bureau of Engraving and Printing, Treasury Department, shall only be eligible for transfer to the grade of operative in that Bureau.

Strike out sections 2, 3, and 5 and renumber section 4 as 2.

Approved, March 2, 1895.   GROVER CLEVELAND.

AMENDMENT OF CIVIL-SERVICE RULES.

EXECUTIVE MANSION, *March 18, 1895.*

Indian Rule IV is amended by adding at the end thereof a new section, to read as follows:

7. Graduates of Indian normal schools and of normal classes in Indian schools may be employed in the Indian-school service as assistant teachers or day-school

teachers without further examination: *Provided*, That certificates of satisfactory pro-
ficiency, of good moral character, and of physical soundness, signed by the proper
officials, be transmitted at the time of appointment to the Civil Service Commission:
And provided further, That until the 1st of July, 1896, graduates of the senior classes
of Carlisle, Hampton, Lincoln Institute, Chilocco, Haskell Institute, and other Indian
schools of equal grade may be included in the provisions of this rule. Such teachers shall become eligible for promotion to advanced positions on presentation to the
Civil Service Commission of satisfactory certificates of efficiency and fidelity in their
work and of a progressive spirit in their professional interests, signed by their immediate official superiors and by the superintendent of Indian schools, and forwarded
with his approval by the Secretary of the Interior, the Commission reserving to itself
the right to decide as to the satisfactoriness of such certificates.

Approved:

GROVER CLEVELAND.

EXECUTIVE MANSION, *March 20, 1895.*

The Executive order dated February 26, 1891,* establishing limits of
punishment for enlisted men of the Army, under an act of Congress approved September 27, 1890, and which was published in General Orders,
No. 21, 1891, Headquarters of the Army, is amended so as to prescribe as
follows:

ARTICLE I.

In all cases of desertion the sentence may include dishonorable discharge and forfeiture of pay and allowances.

Subject to the modifications authorized in section 3 of this article, the
limit of the term of confinement (at hard labor) for desertion shall be as
follows:

SECTION 1. In case of surrender—

(*a*) When the deserter surrenders himself after an absence of not
more than thirty days, one year.

(*b*) When the surrender is made after an absence of more than thirty
days, eighteen months.

SEC. 2. In case of apprehension—

(*a*) When at the time of desertion the deserter shall not have been
more than six months in the service, eighteen months.

(*b*) When he shall have been more than six months in the service,
two and one-half years.

SEC. 3. The foregoing limitations are subject to modification under
the following conditions:

(*a*) The punishment of a deserter may be increased by one year of
confinement at hard labor in consideration of each previous conviction
of desertion.

(*b*) The punishment for desertion when joined in by two or more
soldiers in the execution of a conspiracy or for desertion in the presence of an outbreak of Indians or of any unlawful assemblage which the

*See pp. 5602–5607.

troops may be opposing shall not exceed dishonorable discharge, forfeiture of all pay and allowances, and confinement at hard labor for five years.

ARTICLE II.

Except as herein otherwise indicated punishments shall not exceed the limits prescribed in the following table:

Offenses.	Limits of punishment.
Under seventeenth article of war.	
Selling horse or arms, or both......	Dishonorable discharge, forfeiture of all pay and allowances, and confinement at hard labor for 3 years.
Selling accouterments.............	Four months' confinement at hard labor and forfeiture of $10 per month for the same period; for noncommissioned officer, reduction in addition thereto.
Selling clothing	Two months' confinement at hard labor and forfeiture of $10 per month for the same period; for noncommissioned officer, reduction in addition thereto.
Losing or spoiling horse or arms through neglect.	Four months' confinement at hard labor and forfeiture of $10 per month for the same period; for noncommissioned officer, reduction in addition thereto.
Losing or spoiling accouterments or clothing through neglect.	One month's confinement at hard labor and forfeiture of $10; for noncommissioned officer, reduction in addition thereto.
Under twentieth article of war.	
Behaving himself with disrespect to his commanding officer.	Six months' confinement at hard labor and forfeiture of $10 per month for the same period; for noncommissioned officer, reduction in addition thereto.
Under twenty-fourth article of war.	
Refusal to obey or using violence to officer or noncommissioned officer while quelling quarrels or disorders.	Dishonorable discharge, with forfeiture of all pay and allowances, and confinement at hard labor for 2 years.
Under thirty-first article of war.	
Lying out of quarters..............	Forfeiture of $2; corporal, $3; sergeant, $4.
Under thirty-second article of war.	
Absence without leave—*	
Less than 1 hour...............	Forfeiture of $1; corporal, $2; sergeant, $3; first sergeant or noncommissioned officer of higher grade, $4.
From 1 to 6 hours†.............	Forfeiture of $2; corporal, $3; sergeant, $4; first sergeant or noncommissioned officer of higher grade, $5.
From 6 to 12 hours..............	Forfeiture of $3; corporal, $4; sergeant, $6; first sergeant or noncommissioned officer of higher grade, $7.
From 12 to 24 hours.............	Forfeiture of $5; corporal, $6; sergeant, $7; first sergeant or noncommissioned officer of higher grade, $10.
From 24 to 48 hours.............	Forfeiture of $6 and 5 days' confinement at hard labor; for corporal, forfeiture of $8; sergeant, $10; first sergeant or noncommissioned officer of higher grade, $12, or, for all noncommissioned officers, reduction.
From 2 to 10 days...............	Forfeiture of $10 and 10 days' confinement at hard labor; for noncommissioned officer, reduction in addition thereto.
From 10 to 30 days.............	Forfeiture of $20 and 1 month's confinement at hard labor; for noncommissioned officer, reduction in addition thereto.

*Upon trial for desertion and conviction of absence without leave only, the court may, in addition to the limit prescribed for such absence, award a stoppage of the amount paid for apprehension.

†Including first and excluding last.

Offenses.	Limits of punishment.
Under thirty-second article of war —continued.	
Absence without leave—continued.	
From 30 to 90 days	Three months' confinement at hard labor and forfeiture of $10 per month for same period; for noncommissioned officer, reduction in addition thereto.
For 90 or more than 90 days	Dishonorable discharge and forfeiture of all pay and allowances and 6 months' confinement at hard labor.
Under thirty-third article of war.	
Failure to repair at the time fixed, etc., to the place of parade for—	
Reveille or retreat roll call and 11 p. m. inspection.	Forfeiture of $1; corporal, $2; sergeant, $3; first sergeant, $4.
Guard detail	Forfeiture of $5; corporal, $8; sergeant, $10.
Fatigue detail...................	
Dress parade...................	
The weekly inspection	
Target practice	Forfeiture of $2; corporal, $3; sergeant, $5.
Drill	
Guard mounting (by musician).	
Stable duty..................	
Under thirty-eighth article of war.	
Drunkenness on—	
Guard	Six months' confinement at hard labor and forfeiture of $10 per month for the same period; for noncommissioned officer, reduction in addition thereto.
Duty as company cook.........	Forfeiture of $20.
Extra or special duty	
At drill........................	
At target practice.............	
At parade	Forfeiture of $12; for noncommissioned officer, reduction and forfeiture of $20.
At inspection	
At inspection of company guard detail	
At stable duty.................	
Under fortieth article of war.	
Quitting guard....................	Six months' confinement at hard labor and forfeiture of $10 per month for the same period; for noncommissioned officer, reduction in addition thereto.
Under fifty-first article of war.	
Persuading soldiers to desert.......	Dishonorable discharge, forfeiture of all pay and allowances, and 1 year's confinement at hard labor.
Under sixtieth article of war	Dishonorable discharge, forfeiture of all pay and allowances, and 4 years' confinement at hard labor.
Under sixty-second article of war.	
Manslaughter.....................	Dishonorable discharge, forfeiture of all pay and allowances, and 10 years' confinement at hard labor.
Assault with intent to kill.........	Dishonorable discharge, forfeiture of all pay and allowances, and 10 years' confinement at hard labor.
Burglary	Dishonorable discharge, forfeiture of all pay and allowances, and 5 years' confinement at hard labor.
Forgery........................	Dishonorable discharge, forfeiture of all pay and allowances, and 4 years' confinement at hard labor.
Perjury	Dishonorable discharge, forfeiture of all pay and allowances, and 4 years' confinement at hard labor.

Offenses.	Limits of punishment.
Under sixty-second article of war—continued.	
False swearing	Dishonorable discharge, forfeiture of all pay and allowances, and 2 years' confinement at hard labor.
Robbery...........................	Dishonorable discharge, forfeiture of all pay and allowances, and 6 years' confinement at hard labor.
Larceny or embezzlement of property of the value of—*	
More than $100................	Dishonorable discharge, forfeiture of all pay and allowances, and 4 years' confinement at hard labor.
$100 or less and more than $50..	Dishonorable discharge, forfeiture of all pay and allowances, and 3 years' confinement at hard labor.
$50 or less and more than $20 ...	Dishonorable discharge, forfeiture of all pay and allowances, and 2 years' confinement at hard labor.
$20 or less	Dishonorable discharge, forfeiture of all pay and allowances, and 1 year's confinement at hard labor.
Fraudulent enlistment procured by false representation or concealment of a fact in regard to a prior enlistment or discharge or in regard to conviction of a civil or military crime.	Dishonorable discharge, forfeiture of all pay and allowances, and confinement at hard labor for 1 year.
Fraudulent enlistment, other cases of.	Dishonorable discharge, forfeiture of all pay and allowances, and confinement at hard labor for 6 months.
Disobedience of orders, involving willful defiance of the authority of a noncommissioned officer in the execution of his office.	Six months' confinement at hard labor and forfeiture of $10 per month for the same period; for noncommissioned officer, reduction in addition thereto.
Using threatening or insulting language or behaving in an insubordinate manner to a noncommissioned officer while in the execution of his office.	One month's confinement at hard labor and forfeiture of $10; for noncommissioned officer, reduction in addition thereto.
Absence from fatigue duty	Forfeiture of $4; corporal, $5; sergeant, $6.
Absence from extra or special duty.	Forfeiture of $4; corporal, $5; sergeant, $6.
Absence from duty as company or hospital cook.	Forfeiture of $10.
Introducing liquor into post or camp in violation of standing orders.	Forfeiture of $3; for noncommissioned officer, reduction and forfeiture of $5.
Drunkenness at post or in quarters.	Forfeiture of $3; for noncommissioned officer, reduction and forfeiture of $5.
Drunkenness and disorderly conduct, causing the offender's arrest and conviction by civil authorities at a place within 10 miles of his station.	Forfeiture of $10 and 7 days' confinement at hard labor; for noncommissioned officer, reduction and forfeiture of $12.
Noisy or disorderly conduct in quarters.	Forfeiture of $4; corporal, $7; sergeant, $10.
Abuse by noncommissioned officer of his authority over an inferior.	Reduction, 3 months' confinement at hard labor, and forfeiture of $10 per month for the same period.
Noncommissioned officer encouraging gambling.	Reduction and forfeiture of $5.
Noncommissioned officer making false report.	Reduction, forfeiture of $8, and 10 days' confinement at hard labor.
Sentinel allowing a prisoner under his charge to escape through neglect.	Six months' confinement at hard labor and forfeiture of $10 per month for the same period.
Sentinel willfully suffering prisoner under his charge to escape.	Dishonorable discharge, forfeiture of all pay and allowances, and 1 year's confinement at hard labor.

*In specifications to charges of larceny or embezzlement the value of the property shall be stated.

Offenses.	Limits of punishment.
Under sixty-second article of war—continued.	
Sentinel allowing a prisoner under his charge to obtain liquor.	Two months' confinement at hard labor and forfeiture of $10 per month for the same period.
Sentinel or member of guard drinking liquor with prisoners.	Two months' confinement at hard labor and forfeiture of $10 per month for the same period.
Disrespect or affront to a sentinel..	Two months' confinement at hard labor and forfeiture of $10 per month for the same period; for noncommissioned officer, reduction in addition thereto.
Resisting or disobeying sentinel in lawful execution of his duty.	Six months' confinement at hard labor and forfeiture of $10 per month for the same period; for noncommissioned officer, reduction in addition thereto.
Lewd or indecent exposure of person	Three months' confinement at hard labor and forfeiture of $10 per month for the same period; for noncommissioned officer, reduction in addition thereto.

ARTICLE III.

SECTION 1. When a soldier shall be convicted of an offense the punishment for which, as authorized by Article II of this order or the custom of the service, does not exceed that which an inferior court-martial may award, the punishment so authorized may be increased by one-half for every previous conviction of one or more offenses within eighteen months preceding the trial and during the current enlistment: *Provided,* That the increase of punishment for five or more previous convictions shall not exceed that thus authorized when there are four previous convictions, and that when one or more of such five or more previous convictions shall have been by general court-martial or when such convictions shall have occurred within one year preceding the trial the limit of punishment shall be dishonorable discharge, forfeiture of all pay and allowances, and confinement at hard labor for three months.

When the conviction is of an offense punishable under Article II of this order or the custom of the service with a greater punishment than an inferior court-martial can award, but not punishable with dishonorable discharge, the sentence may on proof of five or more previous convictions within eighteen months and during the current enlistment impose dishonorable discharge and forfeiture of all pay and allowances in addition to the authorized confinement, and when this confinement is less than three months it may be increased to three months.

When a noncommissioned officer is convicted of an offense not punishable with reduction, he may, if he shall have been convicted of a military offense within a year and during the current enlistment, be sentenced to reduction in addition to the punishment already authorized.

SEC. 2. In every case when an offense on trial before a court-martial is of a character admitting of the introduction of evidence of previous convictions and the accused is convicted the court, after determining its findings, will be opened for the purpose of ascertaining whether there is such evidence, and, if so, of hearing it. These convictions must be proved by the records of previous trials or by duly authenticated orders promulgating the same, except in the cases of conviction by summary court, when a duly authenticated copy of the record of said court shall be deemed sufficient proof. Charges forwarded to the authority ordering a general court-martial or submitted to a summary, garrison, or regimental court must be accompanied by the proper evidence of such previous convictions as may have to be considered in determining upon a sentence.

ARTICLE IV.

When a soldier shall on one arraignment be convicted of two or more offenses none of which is punishable under Article II of this order or the custom of the service with dishonorable discharge, but the aggregate term of confinement for which may exceed six months, dishonorable discharge with forfeiture of pay and allowances may be awarded in addition to the authorized confinement.

ARTICLE V.

This order prescribes the *maximum* limit of punishment for the offenses named, and this limit is intended for those cases in which the severest punishment should be awarded. In other cases the punishment should be graded down according to the extenuating circumstances. Offenses not herein provided for remain punishable as authorized by the Articles of War and the custom of the service.

ARTICLE VI.

Summary courts are subject to the restrictions named in the eighty-third article of war. Soldiers against whom charges may be preferred for trial by summary court shall not be confined in the guardhouse, but shall be placed in arrest in quarters before and during trial and while awaiting sentence, except when in particular cases restraint may be necessary.

ARTICLE VII.

The following substitutions for punishments named in Article II of this order are authorized at the discretion of the court:

Two days' confinement at hard labor for $1 forfeiture; one day's solitary confinement on bread and water diet for two days' confinement at hard labor or for $1 forfeiture: *Provided*, That a noncommissioned officer not sentenced to reduction shall not be subject to confinement: *And provided*, That solitary confinement shall not exceed fourteen days at one time nor be repeated until fourteen days have elapsed, and shall not exceed eighty-four days in one year. Whenever the limit herein prescribed for an offense or offenses may be brought within the punishing power of inferior courts-martial, as defined by the eighty-third article of war, by substitution of punishment under the provisions of this article, the said courts have jurisdiction of such offense or offenses.

ARTICLE VIII.

Noncommissioned officers above the rank of corporal shall not, if they object thereto, be brought to trial before regimental, garrison, or summary courts-martial without the authority of the officer competent to order their trial by general court-martial, nor shall sergeants of the post noncommissioned staff or hospital stewards be reduced, but they may be dishonorably discharged whenever reduction is included in the limit of punishment. GROVER CLEVELAND.

AMENDMENT OF CIVIL-SERVICE RULES.

EXECUTIVE MANSION, *April 15, 1895.*

Whereas on November 2, 1894, Departmental Rule II, section 4, Customs Rule II, section 6, Postal Rule II, section 6, Railway Mail Rule II, section 6, were amended to declare that no person appointed to a place under any exception to examination should be transferred from such place to another place not also excepted from examination; and

Whereas it was not my intention that these several amendments should be retroactive in their effect:

I therefore direct that the word "hereafter" be inserted after the word "person" in the first line of each of said sections as of the date of said amendments, viz, November 2, 1894.

Approved: GROVER CLEVELAND.

CIVIL SERVICE.—INTERNAL-REVENUE RULES.

ADOPTING AND PROMULGATING ORDER.

MAY 7, 1895.

In the exercise of the power vested in him by the Constitution, by the seventeen hundred and fifty-third section of the Revised Statutes, and the act entitled "An act to regulate and improve the civil service of the United States," approved January 16, 1883, the President hereby makes and promulgates the following rules concerning the classified internal-revenue service, to be known as the Internal-Revenue Rules:

INTERNAL-REVENUE RULE I.

The classified internal-revenue service shall include all the clerks, storekeepers, storekeepers and gaugers, and gaugers classified under the provisions of section 6 of the act to regulate and improve the civil service of the United States, approved January 16, 1883.

INTERNAL-REVENUE RULE II.

1. To test fitness for admission to the classified internal-revenue service, examinations of a practical character shall be provided on such subjects as the Commission may direct.

2. The following age limitations shall apply to applicants for the classified internal-revenue service: For clerk, not under 18 years of age; for storekeepers, storekeepers and gaugers, and for gaugers, not under 21 years of age.

3. Blank forms of application shall be furnished by the secretaries of the several internal-revenue boards of examiners to any person desiring to be examined who applies therefor in person or by letter in his own handwriting.

4. The date of reception of each application and also of its approval by the board shall be noted on the application paper.

5. Exceptions from examination in the classified internal-revenue service are hereby made as follows:

6. No person appointed to a place excepted from examination by any internal-revenue rule shall be transferred from such place to another place not also excepted from examination.

INTERNAL-REVENUE RULE III.

1. The Commission shall appoint in each classified internal-revenue district a board of examiners, which shall—

(*a*) Conduct all examinations for admission to or promotion in the classified service of the internal-revenue district in which the board is located.

(*b*) Conduct such other examinations as the Commission may direct.

(*c*) Mark the papers of such examinations as the Commission may direct.

2. The papers of every examination shall be marked under the direction of the Commission, and each competitor shall be graded on a scale of 100, according to general average determined by the marks of the examiners.

3. Immediately after the general average shall have been ascertained each competitor shall be notified that he has passed or has failed to pass.

4. No competitor who has failed to pass an examination and no eligible during the period of his eligibility shall be allowed reexamination unless he shall furnish satisfactory evidence to the Commission that at the time of his examination he was, because of illness or other good cause, incapable of doing himself justice; and his rating on such reexamination, if an eligible, shall cancel and be a substitute for his rating on his previous examination.

5. All competitors whose claim to preference under section 1754, Revised Statutes, has been allowed by the Commission who attain a general average of 65 per cent or over, and all other competitors who attain a general average of 70 per cent or over, shall be eligible for appointment to the place for which they were examined, and the names of all the eligibles shall be entered in the order of grade on the proper register of eligibles.

6. When two or more eligibles are of the same grade, preference in certification shall be determined by the order in which their application papers were filed.

7. The period of eligibility shall be one year from the date on which the name of the eligible is entered on the register.

INTERNAL-REVENUE RULE IV.

1. All vacancies, unless filled by promotion, reduction, transfer, or reappointment, shall be filled in the following manner:

(*a*) When a vacancy occurs in any district, the collector thereof shall report the fact to the Commissioner of Internal Revenue, stating the class in which the vacancy occurs and whether in his judgment the place should be filled. If the Commissioner decides that the good of the public service requires that it be filled, he shall request the secretary of the board of examiners of that district to certify to him the names of persons eligible to the vacant place.

(*b*) If fitness for the vacant place is tested by competitive examination, the names of the three eligibles highest in grade on the proper register who have not been three times certified shall be certified; but if the request indicates the sex of the eligibles desired the three highest in grade of that sex shall be certified: *Provided*, That the eligibles upon any register who have been allowed preference under section 1754 of the Revised Statutes shall be certified, according to their grade, before all other eligibles thereon: *Provided further*, That no certification for an appointment shall be made under this clause while there are persons in the district in which any vacancy may exist, who have been removed from the service in that district on account of a reduction of the force or otherwise, who are eligible for reinstatement under Internal-Revenue Rule VII, and who are willing to reenter the service by reinstatement. Every collector of internal revenue shall keep a list of all such persons in his office, and said persons shall have preference for reinstatement to the service in the order of their separation therefrom.

(*c*) No eligible shall be certified more than three times.

2. Of the three names certified to him the Commissioner of Internal Revenue shall select one, and may select more than one if more than one vacancy exists at the time the certification is made. If the vacancy is in the class of clerk, the Commissioner shall certify the name of the person selected by him to the collector of the district in which the vacancy occurs and the collector shall make the appointment. If the vacancy is in the storekeepers', gaugers', or storekeepers and gaugers' class, the Commissioner of Internal Revenue shall certify the name to the Secretary of the Treasury with his recommendation that the person whose name is thus certified be appointed: *Provided*, That if any objection is made under section 3 of General Rule IV to any eligible certified, and is sustained by the Commission, another eligible shall be certified in the place of the one objected to.

3. Each person thus selected for appointment shall be notified, and upon indicating his acceptance shall be appointed for a probationary period of six months, at the end of which period, if his conduct and capacity be satisfactory to the appointing officer, he shall receive absolute appointment; but if his conduct and capacity be not satisfactory to said officer he shall be so notified, and this notification shall be his discharge from the service: *Provided*, That any probationer may be discharged during probation for misconduct or evident unfitness or incapacity.

4. The Commissioner of Internal Revenue shall require the collector under whom a probationer is serving to carefully observe and report in writing upon the services rendered by and the character and qualifications of such probationer as to punctuality, industry, habits, ability, and adaptability. These reports shall be preserved on file in the office of the collector, and copies thereof shall be filed with the Commissioner of Internal Revenue for such disposition as the Secretary of the Treasury may direct. The Civil Service Commission may prescribe the form and manner in which these reports shall be made.

5. In case of the occurrence of a vacancy in the classified service of any internal-revenue collection district which the public interest requires shall be immediately filled, and there is no eligible entitled to reinstatement under section 1, clause (*b*), of this rule or remaining on the proper register, such vacancy, if in the class of storekeeper, storekeeper and gauger, or clerk, may be filled without examination and certification by a temporary designation by the collector of the district of some suitable person to perform the duties of the position until a regular appointment can be made under the provisions of sections 1, 2, and 3 of this rule: *Provided*, That service under such temporary designation shall in no case continue longer than six months, and shall expire by limitation at the end of that time: *And provided further*, That no person shall serve more than six months in any one year under such temporary designation, the year limitation in regard to such designation to begin to run on the date thereof.

Every such temporary designation and also the discontinuance of the same shall at once be reported to the Commission.

INTERNAL-REVENUE RULE V.

Until promotion regulations shall have been applied to a classified internal-revenue collection district promotions therein may be made upon any test of fitness determined upon by the Commissioner of Internal Revenue, with the approval of the

Commission: *Provided*, That no employee shall be promoted to any grade he could not enter by appointment under the minimum age limitation applied thereto by section 2 of Internal-Revenue Rule II.

INTERNAL-REVENUE RULE VI.

Transfers may be made as follows:

From one classified internal-revenue collection district to another, from any classified internal-revenue collection district to a bureau in the Treasury Department in which business relating to the internal revenue is transacted, and from such a bureau in the Treasury Department to such a district, upon the requisition of the Secretary of the Treasury and the certification of the Commission, the appointment upon such transfer to be made by the Secretary of the Treasury, upon the recommendation of the Commissioner of Internal Revenue, if the place to be filled by such transfer is that of storekeeper, storekeeper and gauger, or gauger: *Provided*, That no person shall be transferred as herein authorized who is not within the age limitations prescribed by the civil-service rules for the place to which he is to be transferred and who has not been absolutely appointed, or, if appointed without civil-service examination, who has not served six months continuously in the district or bureau from which he is to be transferred.

INTERNAL-REVENUE RULE VII.

Upon the requisition of the Commissioner of Internal Revenue the secretary of the board of examiners for his district shall certify for reinstatement in a grade requiring no higher examination than the one in which he was formerly employed any person who within one year next preceding the date of the requisition has through no delinquency or misconduct been separated from the classified service of said district: *Provided*, That certification may be made, subject to the other conditions of this rule, for the reinstatement of any person who served in the military or naval service of the United States in the late War of the Rebellion and was honorably discharged therefrom, or the widow of any such person, without regard to the length of time he or she has been separated from the service.

INTERNAL-REVENUE RULE VIII.

Each collector in the classified internal-revenue service shall report to the board of examiners—

(*a*) Every probational and every absolute appointment and every appointment to an excepted or to an unclassified place in the internal-revenue service under him.

(*b*) Every refusal to make an absolute appointment and the reason therefor, and every refusal to accept an appointment.

(*c*) Every separation from the internal-revenue service under him and the cause of such separation, whether death, resignation, or dismissal.

(*d*) Every restoration to the internal-revenue service under him.

GROVER CLEVELAND.

AMENDMENT OF CUSTOMS RULE IV.

Customs Rule IV is hereby amended by adding thereto the following section, to be numbered 5:

5. In case of the occurrence of a vacancy in the classified service of any customs district which the public interest requires shall be immediately filled, and there is no eligible remaining on the proper register, such vacancy may be filled by temporary appointment without examination and certification until a regular appointment can be made under the provisions of sections 1 and 2 of this rule: *Provided*, That

such temporary appointment shall in no case continue longer than ninety days and shall expire by limitation at the end of that time: *And provided further*, That no person shall serve more than ninety days in any one year under such temporary appointment, the year limitation in regard to such appointment to begin to run on the date thereof.

Every such temporary appointment and also the discontinuance of the same shall at once be reported to the Commission.

Approved, May 18, 1895.   GROVER CLEVELAND.

AMENDMENT OF CIVIL-SERVICE RULES.

EXECUTIVE MANSION,
Washington, D. C., May 16, 1895.

Special Departmental Rule No. 1 is hereby amended as follows:

Include among the places excepted from examination therein the following:

6. In the Department of Agriculture: The chief of the dairy division.

Approved, May 24, 1895.

GROVER CLEVELAND, *President.*

CIVIL SERVICE.—EXECUTIVE ORDER REVOKED.

EXECUTIVE MANSION, *May 24, 1895.*

The Executive order heretofore issued under General Rule III, section 2, clause (*c*), that provides for the appointment of four clerks in the division of accounts and disbursements in the Department of Agriculture by noncompetitive examination is hereby revoked, and hereafter these positions will be filled through competitive examination.

Approved: GROVER CLEVELAND.

CIVIL SERVICE.—AMENDMENT OF CLASSIFICATION.

EXECUTIVE MANSION, *May 24, 1895.*

In pursuance of the authority contained in the third paragraph of section 6 of the act entitled "An act to regulate and improve the civil service of the United States," approved January 16, 1883, the Secretary of Agriculture is hereby directed to amend the classification of the Department of Agriculture so as to include among the classes covered thereby clerks, microscopists, assistant microscopists, stock examiners, taggers, agents, and all other employees, except temporary laborers in the Bureau of Animal Industry of the Department of Agriculture outside of Washington, D. C., all State statistical agents of the Department of Agriculture outside of Washington, D. C., and all messengers in the Weather Bureau of the Department of Agriculture outside of Washington, D. C. The classification when so amended shall take effect on July 1, 1895.

Approved: GROVER CLEVELAND.

THE WRECK OF THE *CHRISTOBAL COLON*

THE WRECK OF THE *CRISTOBAL COLON*

Photographs like this reinforce the arguments of our Presidents for a navy sufficient to protect our extensive coasts from the depredations of any naval power. Here is a vessel, which it required not less than two years to build, totally destroyed after a two-hour engagement. Cervera's fleet bore with them to the bottom every hope that Spain had of winning the war. They were vanquished because their marksmanship was inferior to that of the American gun-crews. A war with any first-class power would not give us such an advantage, as their gunners are trained to an efficiency equal to ours. The chances of war would play a part, and it might be our fate to see an American fleet destroyed as quickly and as totally as Cervera's. We need a navy strong enough to make other nations want to keep peace with us. We believe we have such a navy now, but it behooves us to take care that the present superb fleet does not suffer the neglect and parsimony that lowered our navy from first place in 1865 to the lowest in 1874.

The Presidents' discussions of naval policy may be referred to by consulting the encyclopedic index under the heading "Navy." The article bearing that title is worth reading.

AMENDMENT OF CIVIL-SERVICE RULES.

EXECUTIVE MANSION, *May 24, 1895.*

Special Departmental Rule No. 1, section 6, is hereby amended by striking out the whole of said section and substituting therefor the following:

6. In the Department of Agriculture, in the office of the Secretary: Private secretary to the chief clerk, and wood engravers; scientific or professional experts employed for a period of not exceeding six months outside of Washington, D. C., in investigations specially authorized by Congress, but no such expert shall be reappointed as an expert unless the United States Civil Service Commission shall certify that such person has passed a suitable examination and is eligible for such appointment. This exception does not include any person to be employed in that Department in Washington, D. C., nor any person whose duties are not scientific or professional or who is not expert in the particular line of scientific or professional inquiry in which such person is to be employed.

Approved:

GROVER CLEVELAND.

AMENDMENT OF CIVIL-SERVICE RULES.

EXECUTIVE MANSION, *May 24, 1895.*

Special Departmental Rule No. 1, clause 3, is hereby amended by adding to the places excepted from examination in the Department of the Interior the following:

In the Bureau of Education: Specialist in foreign educational systems and specialist in education as a preventive of pauperism and crime.

Approved:

GROVER CLEVELAND.

AMENDMENTS OF CIVIL-SERVICE RULES.

DEPARTMENTAL RULE II.

EXECUTIVE MANSION, *May 24, 1895.*

Section 3 is hereby amended as follows: At the end of clause (*b*) add the following: "nor the cashier, nor the two clerks employed as assistant disbursing clerks in the division of accounts and disbursements in the Department of Agriculture."

At the end of clause (*c*) add the following: "but not including the disbursing clerk in the division of accounts and disbursements in the Department of Agriculture."

At the end of clause (*e*) add the following: "except those of the Weather Bureau and the Bureau of Animal Industry, in the Department of Agriculture."

At the end of clause (*f*) add the following: "except all chiefs of division in the Department of Agriculture."

The section as amended will read:

3. Exceptions from examination in the classified departmental service are hereby made as follows:

(*a*) One private secretary or one confidential clerk of the head of each classified Department and of each Assistant Secretary thereof, and also of each head of bureau appointed by the President by and with the advice and consent of the Senate.

(*b*) Direct custodians of money for whose fidelity another officer is under official bond; but this exception shall not include any officer below the grade of assistant cashier or assistant teller, nor the cashier, nor the two clerks employed as assistant disbursing clerks in the division of accounts and disbursements in the Department of Agriculture.

(*c*) Disbursing officers who give bonds, but not including the disbursing clerk in the division of accounts and disbursements in the Department of Agriculture.

(*d*) Persons employed exclusively in the secret service of the Government.

(*e*) Chief clerks, except those of the Weather Bureau and of the Bureau of Animal Industry, in the Department of Agriculture.

(*f*) Chiefs of division, except all chiefs of division in the Department of Agriculture.

GROVER CLEVELAND.

EXECUTIVE MANSION, *May 28, 1895.*

To the Heads of the Executive Departments:

As a mark of respect to the memory of the Hon. Walter Q. Gresham, late Secretary of State, the President directs that the several Executive Departments and the Government Printing Office, in the city of Washington, be closed on Wednesday, the 29th day of May, 1895, the day of the funeral.

HENRY T. THURBER,
Private Secretary.

EXECUTIVE MANSION, *May 28, 1895.*

It is hereby ordered, That the several Executive Departments and the Government Printing Office be closed on Thursday, the 30th instant, to enable the employees to participate in the decoration of the graves of the soldiers and sailors who fell in defense of the Union during the War of the Rebellion.

GROVER CLEVELAND.

CIVIL SERVICE.—GOVERNMENT PRINTING OFFICE RULES.

ADOPTING AND PROMULGATING ORDER.

EXECUTIVE MANSION, *June 13, 1895.*

In the exercise of the power vested in him by the Constitution, by the seventeen hundred and fifty-third section of the Revised Statutes, and the act entitled "An act to regulate and improve the civil service of the United States," approved January 16, 1883, the President hereby makes and promulgates the following rules concerning the classified service of the Government Printing Office, to be known as the Government Printing Office Rules:

RULE I.

1. The classified service of the Government Printing Office shall include all persons employed in that office except those appointed by and with the advice and consent of the Senate and unskilled laborers or workmen.

2. The officers, clerks, and other employees of the Government Printing Office are hereby arranged in the following classes:

Class 1.—All persons receiving an annual salary of less than $720, or a compensation at the rate of less than $720 per annum.

Class 2.—All persons receiving an annual salary of $720 or more, or a compensation at the rate of $720 or more, but less than $840 per annum.

Class 3.—All persons receiving an annual salary of $840 or more, or a compensation at the rate of $840 or more, but less than $900 per annum.

Class 4.—All persons receiving an annual salary of $900 or more, or a compensation at the rate of $900 or more, but less than $1,000 per annum.

Class 5.—All persons receiving an annual salary of $1,000 or more, or a compensation at the rate of $1,000 or more, but less than $1,200 per annum.

Class 6.—All persons receiving an annual salary of $1,200 or more, or a compensation at the rate of $1,200 or more, but less than $1,400 per annum.

Class 7.—All persons receiving an annual salary of $1,400 or more, or a compensation at the rate of $1,400 or more, but less than $1,600 per annum.

Class 8.—All persons receiving an annual salary of $1,600 or more, or a compensation at the rate of $1,600 or more, but less than $1,800 per annum.

Class 9.—All persons receiving an annual salary of $1,800 or more, or a compensation at the rate of $1,800 or more, but less than $2,000 per annum.

Class 10.—All persons receiving an annual salary of $2,000 or more, or a compensation at the rate of $2,000 or more per annum.

RULE II.

1. To test fitness for admission to the classified service of the Government Printing Office, examinations of a practical character shall be provided by the Commission. If the trade or occupation is such that a competitive test can not be made, the Commission shall provide regulations for the registration of applicants without competitive tests.

2. Any male citizen of the United States not under 21 or over 45 years of age and any female citizen not under 18 or over 35 years of age may be examined for positions in the Government Printing Office.

3. No application for a position in the Government Printing Office which belongs to one of the recognized mechanical trades shall be received from any applicant who has not served at least five years at the particular trade to which the position for which he applies belongs, one year of which service must have been rendered as a journeyman.

4. Blank forms of application shall be furnished by the Commission, and the date of reception and also of approval by the Commission of each application shall be entered on the application paper.

RULE III.

1. The grade or standing of every competitor shall be determined under regulations made by the Commission, and each competitor shall be duly notified whether or not he is eligible for appointment.

2. No competitor who has failed to obtain an eligible standing shall be admitted

to another test within six months from the date of failure unless he shall furnish satisfactory evidence to the Commission that at the time of his examination he was unable to do himself justice because of illness or other good cause.

3. No eligible shall be admitted to a test during the period of his eligibility unless he shall furnish satisfactory evidence to the Commission that at the time of his examination he was unable to do himself justice because of illness or other good cause.

4. All competitors whose claims of preference under section 1754 of the Revised Statutes have been allowed by the Commission who attain a general average of 65 per cent or over, and all other competitors who attain a general average of 70 per cent or over, shall be eligible for appointment to the place for which they were examined. The names of all competitors thus rendered eligible shall be entered in the order of grade on the proper register of eligibles.

5. The Commission shall establish regulations for the order of certification of applicants who are registered without competitive examinations under the provisions of Rule II, paragraph 1.

6. When two or more eligibles are of the same grade, preference in certification shall be determined by the order in which the application papers are filed.

7. The period of eligibility to appointment shall be one year from the date on which the name of the eligible is entered on the register, unless otherwise determined by regulations by the Commission.

RULE IV.

1. All vacancies, unless filled by promotion, transfer, or reappointment, shall be filled in the following manner:

(*a*) The Public Printer shall, in form and manner to be prescribed by the Commission, request the certification to him of either males or females, or both, eligible to the vacant place.

(*b*) If fitness for the vacant place is tested by competitive examination, the Commission shall certify from the proper register the names of the three eligibles thereon, of the sex or sexes called for, having the highest averages, who have not been three times certified: *Provided*, That the eligibles upon any register who have been allowed preference under section 1754 of the Revised Statutes shall be certified according to their grade before all other eligibles thereon: *And provided further*, That if the vacancy is in a position for which a competitive examination can not be provided certification shall be made of the names of the first three eligibles on the register, of the sex or sexes called for, who have not been three times certified.

2. Of the three names certified to him the Public Printer shall select one, and if at the time of making this selection there are more vacancies than one he may select more than one: *Provided*, That if the Public Printer shall object in writing to any eligible named in the certification, stating that because of physical incapacity or for other good cause particularly specified such eligible is not capable of properly performing the duties of the vacant place, the Commission may, upon investigation and ascertainment of the fact that the objection made is good and well founded, direct the certification of another eligible in place of the eligible to whom objection is made.

3. When a person designated for appointment shall have reported in person to the Public Printer, he shall be appointed for a probational period of six months, at the end of which period, if his conduct and capacity be satisfactory to the Public Printer, he shall receive absolute appointment; but if his conduct and capacity be not satisfactory he shall be notified that he will not receive absolute appointment, and this notification shall discharge him from the service. The Public Printer shall require the officer under whom the probationer may be serving to carefully observe and report in writing upon the services rendered by and the character and qualifications of

such probationer as to punctuality, industry, habits, ability, and adaptability. These reports shall be preserved on file, and the Commission may prescribe the form and manner in which they shall be made.

4. Any person appointed to a position which belongs to one of the recognized mechanical trades may upon reporting for appointment be subjected to a practical test under the supervision of a board designated by the Commission, and if he or she fails to attain a general average of 70 per cent on a maximum of 100 per cent he or she shall be rejected for appointment.

5. In case of public and pressing exigency, demanding the immediate employment of skilled and experienced workmen who can not be at once supplied in the manner provided for in section 2 of this rule, or by transfer under Rule VI, or reinstatement under Rule VII, there may be employed without examination or certification for a period not to exceed thirty days, which with the consent of the Commission may be extended in periods of thirty days each, any persons who have the requisite knowledge or experience who may be available: *Provided*, That no person shall serve more than ninety days in any one year under such temporary appointment. The year limitation in regard to appointment shall begin to run at the date of the original appointment. Every such temporary appointment and also the discontinuance of the same shall be at once reported to the Commission.

RULE V.

1. Until promotion regulations shall have been applied to the classified service of the Government Printing Office promotions therein may be made upon any test of fitness determined upon by the Public Printer if not disapproved by the Commission.

RULE VI.

1. Transfers may be made as follows:

(*a*) From a position in the classified service of the Government Printing Office requiring a knowledge of some mechanical trade to a position in any one of the Executive Departments requiring a knowledge of the same mechanical trade, upon requisition from the head of the Department to which the transfer is to be made and the consent of the Public Printer: *Provided*, That a person so transferred shall not be transferred to another position in one of the Executive Departments unless such other position requires a knowledge of the same mechanical trade upon which the original transfer was based, nor until he has served one year in the position to which he was originally transferred.

(*b*) From any Executive Department to the classified service of the Government Printing Office upon requisition from the Public Printer and the consent of the head of the Department from which the transfer is to be made.

2. No person shall be transferred as herein authorized until after absolute appointment and until the Commission shall have certified to the officer making the transfer requisition that the person whom it is proposed to transfer has passed an examination to test fitness for the place to which he or she is to be transferred. No person shall be transferred to any place from which he or she may be barred by age limitations for original entrance or by the rules regulating the apportionment of appointments among the several States and Territories and the District of Columbia.

RULE VII.

Upon requisition of the Public Printer the Commission shall certify for reinstatement in the Government Printing Office, in a grade requiring no higher examination than the one in which he was formerly employed, any person who within one year next preceding the date of the requisition has through no delinquency or misconduct been separated from the classified service of the Government Printing

Office: *Provided*, That certification may be made, subject to the other conditions of this rule, for the reinstatement of any person who served in the military or naval service of the United States in the late War of the Rebellion and was honorably discharged therefrom, or the widow of any such person, without regard to the length of time he or she has been separated from the service.

RULE VIII.

The Public Printer shall report to the Commission—

(*a*) Every probational and every absolute appointment to the service of the Government Printing Office.

(*b*) Every refusal to make an absolute appointment and the reason therefor, and every declination of an appointment.

(*c*) Every separation from the service of the Government Printing Office and the cause of such separation, whether death, resignation, or dismissal.

Approved:

GROVER CLEVELAND.

CIVIL SERVICE.—EXECUTIVE ORDER WITHDRAWING ENGINEERS AND ASSISTANT ENGINEERS FROM THE LIST OF PLACES TO BE FILLED BY NONCOMPETITIVE EXAMINATION.

So much of Executive orders heretofore issued under General Rule III, section 2, clause (*c*), as provides for the appointment of engineers and assistant engineers by noncompetitive examination is hereby revoked, and hereafter engineers and assistant engineers will be appointed by competitive examination.

Approved, June 25, 1895.

GROVER CLEVELAND.

In the exercise of the power vested in him by the Constitution, by the seventeen hundred and fifty-third section of the Revised Statutes, and the act entitled "An act to regulate and improve the civil service of the United States," approved January 16, 1883, the President hereby makes and promulgates the following rule to cancel and be in lieu of Customs Rule V of the Revised Civil-Service Rules:

CUSTOMS RULE V.

1. Until promotion regulations have been applied to a classified customs district the following promotions may be made therein at any time after absolute appointment:

(*a*) Any employee in any grade, upon any test of fitness determined upon by the nominating officer, to any vacant place in the class next above the one in which he may be serving, except to the positions of weigher and gauger.

(*b*) Any employee in any grade may be promoted or transferred to a vacancy in the lowest class of the grade of examiner after passing the examiner examination, to a vacancy in the lowest class of the grade of weigher after passing the weigher examination, to a vacancy in the lowest class of the grade of gauger after passing the gauger examination, or to a vacancy in the lowest class of any other grade than the one in which he may be serving upon passing the examination provided for that grade.

Approved, July 11, 1895.

GROVER CLEVELAND.

CIVIL SERVICE.—CLASSIFICATION OF THE PENSION AGENCIES OF THE INTERIOR DEPARTMENT.

EXECUTIVE MANSION, *July 15, 1895.*

In the exercise of the power vested in the President by the third paragraph of section 6 of the act entitled "An act to regulate and improve the civil service of the United States," approved January 16, 1883, I hereby direct the Secretary of the Interior to amend the classification of the Department of the Interior so as to include among the employees classified thereunder the officers, clerks, and other employees of the pension agencies of said Department.

GROVER CLEVELAND.

AMENDMENT OF CIVIL-SERVICE RULES.

DEPARTMENTAL RULE VIII.

Section 1, clause (*a*), is hereby amended as follows: Strike out the period after the word "made" in the second line, insert a semicolon, and add the following:

But transfers from a pension agency of the Interior Department may be made only as follows: From a pension agency of the Interior Department to the office of the Secretary of the Interior, or of the Assistant Attorney-General for the Interior Department, or to the Pension Office, or from any of the above-named offices to a pension agency, or from one pension agency to another pension agency, upon requisition of the Secretary of the Interior: *Provided,* That a transfer from a pension agency to a position in the Interior Department shall not be made when the person to be transferred would not be eligible to original appointment in the departmental service under the law requiring an apportionment of appointments among the States, Territories, and the District of Columbia according to population.

The section and clause as amended will read:

1. Transfers may be made as follows:

(*a*) From one Department to another, upon requisition by the head of the Department to which the transfer is to be made; but transfers from a pension agency of the Interior Department may be made only as follows: From a pension agency of the Interior Department to the office of the Secretary of the Interior, or of the Assistant Attorney-General for the Interior Department, or to the Pension Office, or from any of the above-named offices to a pension agency, or from one pension agency to another pension agency, upon requisition of the Secretary of the Interior: *Provided,* That a transfer from a pension agency to a position in the Interior Department shall not be made when the person to be transferred would not be eligible to original appointment in the departmental service under the law requiring an apportionment of appointments among the States, Territories, and the District of Columbia according to population.

Approved, July 15, 1895.

GROVER CLEVELAND.

AMENDMENTS OF CIVIL-SERVICE RULES.

DEPARTMENTAL RULE II.

Section 3, providing for exceptions from examination in the classified departmental service, is hereby amended as follows by the insertion of clause (*g*):

One designated clerk at each pension agency (designated to sign official checks for the pension agent).

Section 4 is hereby amended as follows: In the third line, after the word "examination," add the following proviso:

Provided, That any person employed in an excepted place in any office or bureau at the time when said office or bureau is brought into the classified service, or any person transferred directly from a nonexcepted to an excepted place in the office or bureau in which he is serving, may at any time be directly transferred from such excepted place to any nonexcepted place in the office or bureau in which he is serving.

The section as amended will read:

4. No person hereafter appointed to a place under the exceptions to examination made by any departmental rule shall be transferred from such place to a place not also excepted from examination: *Provided*, That any person employed in an excepted place in any office or bureau at the time when said office or bureau is brought into the classified service, or any person transferred directly from a nonexcepted to an excepted place in the office or bureau in which he is serving, may at any time be directly transferred from such excepted place to any nonexcepted place in the office or bureau in which he is serving.

Approved, July 15, 1895.   GROVER CLEVELAND.

AMENDMENT OF CIVIL-SERVICE RULES.

EXECUTIVE MANSION, *July 15, 1895.*

Special Departmental Rule I is hereby amended by striking out the whole of the paragraph in section 3, Department of the Interior, relating to the Geological Survey and substituting in lieu thereof the following:

In the Geological Survey: Professional experts and special agents employed for short periods at per diem salaries and paid only when actually employed.

Approved: GROVER CLEVELAND.

AMENDMENTS OF CIVIL-SERVICE RULES.

DEPARTMENTAL RULE VII.

Section 2 is hereby amended as follows: At the end of the section, after the word "law," add the following proviso:

Provided, That appointments to positions at pension agencies shall not be charged to the apportionment.

The section as amended will read as follows:

2. Certifications hereunder shall be made in such a manner as to maintain as nearly as possible the apportionment of appointments among the several States and Territories and the District of Columbia as required by law: *Provided*, That appointments to positions at pension agencies shall not be charged to the apportionment.

Section 3, paragraph 2, is hereby amended as follows: In the second line, after the word "register," insert the following: "or when certification is made from any register to fill a vacancy at any pension agency."

The paragraph as amended will read:

When certification is made from a supplementary or special register or the printer's assistant or page and messenger-boy register, or when certification is made from any register to fill a vacancy at any pension agency, and there are more vacancies than one to be filled, the appointing officer may select from the three names certified more than one.

Section 6 is hereby amended as follows: Strike out the word "and" at the beginning of line 9, and in line 12, after the word "appointment," insert the following proviso:

And provided further, That at each pension agency at the time of the quarterly payment of pensions such temporary appointments may be made as the needs of the service may demand for a period not to exceed thirty days, which appointments shall not be extended or renewed until the date of the next quarterly payment of pensions.

The section as amended will read:

6. In case of the occurrence of a vacancy ᵣn any Department which the public interest requires shall be immediately filled, and which can not be so filled by certification from the eligible registers of the Commission, such vacancy may be filled by temporary appointment outside the civil service until a regular appointment can be made under the provisions of sections 1, 2, and 3 of this rule: *Provided*, That such temporary appointment shall in no case continue longer than ninety days, and shall expire by limitation at the end of that time: *Provided further*, That no person shall serve longer than the period herein prescribed in any one year under such temporary appointment. The year limitation in regard to reappointment shall begin to run on the date of the original appointment: *And provided further*, That at each pension agency at the time of the quarterly payment of pensions such temporary appointments may be made as the needs of the service may demand for a period not to exceed thirty days, which appointments shall not be extended or renewed until the date of the next quarterly payment of pensions. Every such temporary appointment and the discontinuance of the same shall at once be reported to the Commission.

Approved, July 15, 1895.

GROVER CLEVELAND.

CIVIL SERVICE.—AMENDMENT OF CLASSIFICATION.

EXECUTIVE MANSION, *July 15, 1895.*

In pursuance of the authority contained in the third paragraph of section 6 of the act entitled "An act to regulate and improve the civil service of the United States," approved January 16, 1883, the heads of the several

Executive Departments are hereby directed to amend their several classifications so as to include firemen among the employees classified thereunder.

GROVER CLEVELAND.

AMENDMENT OF CIVIL-SERVICE RULES.

EXECUTIVE MANSION, *July 15, 1895.*

Executive orders heretofore issued designating the places to be filled by noncompetitive examination under clause (*c*) of General Rule III are hereby amended so as to include among those places in the Department of the Interior, in the Geological Survey, the editor and the photographer.

Approved:

GROVER CLEVELAND.

AMENDMENT OF CIVIL-SERVICE RULES.

Special Departmental Rule I is hereby amended by adding to the list of places excepted from examination in the Treasury Department—

In the Bureau of Immigration: One statistician and stenographer, with power to act as immigrant inspector.

Approved, July 30, 1895.

GROVER CLEVELAND.

AMENDMENT OF CIVIL-SERVICE RULES.

Departmental Rule IX, clause 1, paragraph 2, is hereby amended by striking out in line 1 the words "appointed from the appropriate register to" and substituting therefor the word "occupying;" by adding before the word "messenger" in line 2 the following: "engineers, assistant engineers, firemen;" by striking out in line 3 the words "below the positions of clerk and copyist" and substituting therefor the words "the educational test for appointment to which is below the grade of the educational test required for the position of clerk or copyist;" and by adding in line 7, after the words "printers' assistants," the words "and skilled helpers." As amended the paragraph will read as follows:

Any person occupying the position of engineer, assistant engineer, fireman, messenger, assistant messenger, watchman, or other subordinate position the educational test for appointment to which is below the grade of the educational test required for the position of clerk or copyist may at any time after absolute appointment, if not barred by age limitations, be transferred to any other of said subordinate positions, but shall not be promoted to the position of clerk or copyist or to any place the duties of which are clerical: *Provided,* That printers' assistants and skilled helpers in the Bureau of Engraving and Printing, Treasury Department, shall only be eligible for transfer to the grade of operator in that Bureau.

Approved, August 5, 1895.

GROVER CLEVELAND.

CIVIL SERVICE.—EXECUTIVE ORDER WITHDRAWING COMPOSITORS AND PRESSMEN FROM THE LIST OF PLACES TO BE FILLED BY NONCOMPETITIVE EXAMINATION.

EXECUTIVE MANSION, *August 16, 1895.*

So much of Executive orders heretofore issued under General Rule III, section 2, clause (*c*), as provides for the appointment of compositors and pressmen by noncompetitive examination is hereby revoked, and hereafter compositors and pressmen will be appointed by competitive examination.

Approved: GROVER CLEVELAND.

AMENDMENT OF CIVIL-SERVICE RULES.

EXECUTIVE MANSION, *August 22, 1895.*

Government Printing Office Rule II, section 2, is hereby amended by omitting in line 1, after the words "under 21," the words "or over 45," and in line 2, after the words "under 18," the words "or over 35." The section as amended will read as follows:

2. Any male citizen of the United States not under 21 years of age and any female citizen not under 18 years of age may be examined for positions in the Government Printing Office.

Approved: GROVER CLEVELAND.

AMENDMENT OF CIVIL-SERVICE RULES.

EXECUTIVE MANSION, *September 5, 1895.*

Special Departmental Rule I is hereby amended by striking out from the list of places excepted from examination in all the Departments "bookbinders."

Approved: GROVER CLEVELAND.

AMENDMENT OF CIVIL-SERVICE RULES.

Special Departmental Rule I is hereby amended to except from examination in the Department of the Treasury, in the Bureau of Printing and Engraving, forty-three compositors and eight pressmen now temporarily employed under authority of the sundry civil act of March 2, 1895, such employment to cease prior to March 14, 1896. Vacancies occurring in this force shall be filled only by competitive examination under the civil-service rules.

Approved, September 16, 1895. GROVER CLEVELAND.

EXECUTIVE MANSION, *September 20, 1895.*

It being of great importance that the consuls and commercial agents of the United States shall possess the proper qualifications for their respective positions, to be ascertained either through a satisfactory record of previous actual service under the Department of State or through an appropriate examination:

It is hereby ordered, That any vacancy in a consulate or commercial agency now or hereafter existing the salary of which is not more than $2,500 nor less than $1,000, or the compensation of which, if derived from official fees, exclusive of notarial and other unofficial receipts, does not exceed $2,500 nor fall below $1,000, shall be filled (*a*) by a transfer or promotion from some other position under the Department of State of a character tending to qualify the incumbent for the position to be filled, or (*b*) by appointment of a person not under the Department of State, but having previously served thereunder to its satisfaction in a capacity tending to qualify him for the position to be filled, or (*c*) by the appointment of a person who, having furnished the customary evidence of character, responsibility, and capacity, and being thereupon selected by the President for examination, is found upon such examination to be qualified for the position.

For the purposes of this order notarial and unofficial fees shall not be regarded, but the compensation of a consulate or commercial agency shall be ascertained, if the office is salaried, by reference to the last preceding appropriation act, and if the office is not salaried by reference to the returns of official fees for the last preceding fiscal year.

The examination hereinbefore provided for shall be by a board of three persons designated by the Secretary of State, who shall also prescribe the subjects to which such examinations shall relate and the general mode of conducting the same by the board.

A vacancy in a consulate will be filled at discretion only when a suitable appointment can not be made in any of the modes indicated in the second paragraph of this order.

GROVER CLEVELAND.

EXECUTIVE MANSION,
Washington, September 30, 1895.

Lieutenant-General John M. Schofield having reached the age entitling him to relief from active military service, he is, in accordance with the provisions of law, hereby placed upon the retired list of the Army, to date September 29, 1895, with all the pay and allowances belonging to his rank upon such retirement.

It is with much regret that the President makes the announcement that the country is thus to lose from the command of its Army this distinguished general, who has done so much for its honor and efficiency. His gallantry in war challenges the admiration of all his countrymen, while they will not fail to gratefully remember and appreciate how faithfully he has served his country in times of peace by his splendid and successful performance of civil as well as military duty.

Lieutenant-General Schofield's career, exhibiting an unvarying love for his profession, a jealous care for its honor and good name, a just apprehension of the subordination it exacts, and a constant manifestation of the best traits of true Americanism, furnishes to the Army an example of inestimable value, and should teach all our people that the highest soldierly qualities are built upon the keenest sense of the obligations belonging to good citizenship.

GROVER CLEVELAND.

AMENDMENT OF CIVIL-SERVICE RULES.

EXECUTIVE MANSION, *November 6, 1895.*

Section 2 of Postal Rule I is hereby amended by inserting after the word "thereto" in line 6 the following:

And whenever, by order of the Postmaster-General, any post-office shall be consolidated with and made part of another post-office where free delivery is established, all the employees of the office thus consolidated whose names appear on the roster of said office approved by the Post-Office Department, and including the postmaster thereof, shall from the date of said order be employees of said free-delivery office, and the person holding on the date of said order the position of postmaster at the office thus consolidated with said free-delivery office may be assigned to any position therein and given any appropriate designation under the classification act which the Postmaster-General may direct.

The section as amended shall read as follows:

2. The classification of the postal service made by the Postmaster-General under section 6 of the act of January 16, 1883, is hereby extended to all free-delivery post-offices, and hereafter whenever any post-office becomes a free-delivery office the said classification or any then existing classification made by the Postmaster-General under said section and act shall apply thereto; and whenever, by order of the Postmaster-General, any post-office shall be consolidated with and made part of another post-office where free delivery is established, all the employees of the office thus consolidated whose names appear on the roster of said office approved by the Post-Office Department, and including the postmaster thereof, shall from the date of said order be employees of said free-delivery office, and the person holding on the date of said order the position of postmaster at the office thus consolidated with said free-delivery office may be assigned to any position therein and given any appropriate designation under the classification act which the Postmaster-General may direct; and the Civil Service Commission shall provide examinations to test the fitness of persons to fill vacancies in all free-delivery post-offices, and these rules shall be in force therein; but this shall not include any post-office made an experimental free-delivery office under the authority contained in the appropriation act of March 3, 1891. Every revision of the classification of any post-office under section 6 of the act of January 16, 1883, and every inclusion of a post-office within the classified postal service shall be reported to the President.

Approved:

GROVER CLEVELAND.

THIRD ANNUAL MESSAGE.

EXECUTIVE MANSION, *December 2, 1895.*

To the Congress of the United States:

The present assemblage of the legislative branch of our Government occurs at a time when the interests of our pecple and the needs of the country give especial prominence to the condition of our foreign relations and the exigencies of our national finances. The reports of the heads of the several administrative Departments of the Government fully and plainly exhibit what has been accomplished within the scope of their respective duties and present such recommendations for the betterment of our country's condition as patriotic and intelligent labor and observation suggest.

I therefore deem my executive duty adequately performed at this time by presenting to the Congress the important phases of our situation as related to our intercourse with foreign nations and a statement of the financial problems which confront us, omitting, except as they are related to these topics, any reference to departmental operations.

I earnestly invite, however, not only the careful consideration but the severely critical scrutiny of the Congress and my fellow-countrymen to the reports concerning these departmental operations. If justly and fairly examined, they will furnish proof of assiduous and painstaking care for the public welfare. I press the recommendations they contain upon the respectful attention of those charged with the duty of legislation, because I believe their adoption would promote the people's good.

By amendatory tariff legislation in January last the Argentine Republic, recognizing the value of the large market opened to the free importation of its wools under our last tariff act, has admitted certain products of the United States to entry at reduced duties. It is pleasing to note that the efforts we have made to enlarge the exchanges of trade on a sound basis of mutual benefit are in this instance appreciated by the country from which our woolen factories draw their needful supply of raw material.

The Missions boundary dispute between the Argentine Republic and Brazil, referred to the President of the United States as arbitrator during the term of my predecessor, and which was submitted to me for determination, resulted in an award in favor of Brazil upon the historical and documentary evidence presented, thus ending a long-protracted controversy and again demonstrating the wisdom and desirability of settling international boundary disputes by recourse to friendly arbitration.

Negotiations are progressing for a revival of the United States and Chilean Claims Commission, whose work was abruptly terminated last year by the expiration of the stipulated time within which awards could be made.

The resumption of specie payments by Chile is a step of great interest and importance both in its direct consequences upon her own welfare and as evincing the ascendency of sound financial principles in one of the most influential of the South American Republics.

The close of the momentous struggle between China and Japan, while relieving the diplomatic agents of this Government from the delicate duty they undertook at the request of both countries of rendering such service to the subjects of either belligerent within the territorial limits of the other as our neutral position permitted, developed a domestic condition in the Chinese Empire which has caused much anxiety and called for prompt and careful attention. Either as a result of a weak control by the central Government over the provincial administrations, following a diminution of traditional governmental authority under the stress of an overwhelming national disaster, or as a manifestation upon good opportunity of the aversion of the Chinese population to all foreign ways and undertakings, there have occurred in widely separated provinces of China serious outbreaks of the old fanatical spirit against foreigners, which, unchecked by the local authorities, if not actually connived at by them, have culminated in mob attacks on foreign missionary stations, causing much destruction of property and attended with personal injuries as well as loss of life.

Although but one American citizen was reported to have been actually wounded, and although the destruction of property may have fallen more heavily upon the missionaries of other nationalities than our own, it plainly behooved this Government to take the most prompt and decided action to guard against similar or perhaps more dreadful calamities befalling the hundreds of American mission stations which have grown up throughout the interior of China under the temperate rule of toleration, custom, and imperial edict. The demands of the United States and other powers for the degradation and punishment of the responsible officials of the respective cities and provinces who by neglect or otherwise had permitted uprisings, and for the adoption of stern measures by the Emperor's Government for the protection of the life and property of foreigners, were followed by the disgrace and dismissal of certain provincial officials found derelict in duty and the punishment by death of a number of those adjudged guilty of actual participation in the outrages.

This Government also insisted that a special American commission should visit the province where the first disturbances occurred for the purpose of investigation. The latter commission, formed after much opposition, has gone overland from Tientsin, accompanied by a suitable Chinese escort, and by its demonstration of the readiness and ability of our Government to protect its citizens will act, it is believed, as a most influential deterrent of any similar outbreaks.

The energetic steps we have thus taken are all the more likely to result in future safety to our citizens in China because the Imperial Government is, I am persuaded, entirely convinced that we desire only the liberty and protection of our own citizens and redress for any wrongs they may have suffered, and that we have no ulterior designs or objects, political or otherwise. China will not forget either our kindly service to her citizens during her late war nor the further fact that, while furnishing all the facilities at our command to further the negotiation of a peace between her and Japan, we sought no advantages and interposed no counsel.

The Governments of both China and Japan have, in special dispatches transmitted through their respective diplomatic representatives, expressed in a most pleasing manner their grateful appreciation of our assistance to their citizens during the unhappy struggle and of the value of our aid in paving the way to their resumption of peaceful relations.

The customary cordial relations between this country and France have been undisturbed, with the exception that a full explanation of the treatment of John L. Waller by the expeditionary military authorities of France still remains to be given. Mr. Waller, formerly United States consul at Tamatav, remained in Madagascar after his term of office expired, and was apparently successful in procuring business concessions from the Hovas of greater or less value. After the occupation of Tamatav and the declaration of martial law by the French he was arrested upon various charges, among them that of communicating military information to the enemies of France, was tried and convicted by a military tribunal, and sentenced to twenty years' imprisonment.

Following the course justified by abundant precedents, this Government requested from that of France the record of the proceedings of the French tribunal which resulted in Mr. Waller's condemnation. This request has been complied with to the extent of supplying a copy of the official record, from which appear the constitution and organization of the court, the charges as formulated, and the general course and result of the trial, and by which it is shown that the accused was tried in open court and was defended by counsel; but the evidence adduced in support of the charges, which was not received by the French minister for foreign affairs till the first week in October, has thus far been withheld, the French Government taking the ground that its production in response to our demand would establish a bad precedent. The efforts of our ambassador to procure it, however, though impeded by recent changes in the French ministry, have not been relaxed, and it is confidently expected that some satisfactory solution of the matter will shortly be reached. Meanwhile it appears that Mr. Waller's confinement has every alleviation which the state of his health and all the other circumstances of the case demand or permit.

In agreeable contrast to the difference above noted respecting a matter of common concern, where nothing is sought except such a mutually satisfactory outcome as the true merits of the case require, is the recent resolution of the French Chambers favoring the conclusion of a permanent treaty of arbitration between the two countries.

An invitation has been extended by France to the Government and people of the United States to participate in a great international exposition at Paris in 1900 as a suitable commemoration of the close of this the world's marvelous century of progress. I heartily recommend its acceptance, together with such legislation as will adequately provide for a due representation of this Government and its people on the occasion.

Our relations with the States of the German Empire are in some aspects typical of a condition of things elsewhere found in countries whose productions and trade are similar to our own. The close rivalries of competing industries; the influence of the delusive doctrine that the internal development of a nation is promoted and its wealth increased by a policy which, in undertaking to reserve its home markets for the exclusive use of its own producers, necessarily obstructs their sales in foreign markets and prevents free access to the products of the world; the desire to retain trade in time-worn ruts, regardless of the inexorable laws of new needs and changed conditions of demand and supply, and our own halting tardiness in inviting a freer exchange of commodities, and by this means imperiling our footing in the external markets naturally open to us, have created a situation somewhat injurious to American export interests, not only in Germany, where they are perhaps most noticeable, but in adjacent countries. The exports affected are largely American cattle and other food products, the reason assigned for unfavorable discrimination being that their consumption is deleterious to the public health. This is all the more irritating in view of the fact that no European state is as jealous of the excellence and wholesomeness of its exported food supplies as the United States, nor so easily able, on account of inherent soundness, to guarantee those qualities.

Nor are these difficulties confined to our food products designed for exportation. Our great insurance companies, for example, having built up a vast business abroad and invested a large share of their gains in foreign countries in compliance with the local laws and regulations then existing, now find themselves within a narrowing circle of onerous and unforeseen conditions, and are confronted by the necessity of retirement from a field thus made unprofitable, if, indeed, they are not summarily expelled, as some of them have lately been from Prussia.

It is not to be forgotten that international trade can not be one-sided. Its currents are alternating, and its movements should be honestly reciprocal. Without this it almost necessarily degenerates into a device to gain advantage or a contrivance to secure benefits with only the semblance of a return. In our dealings with other nations we ought to be open-handed and scrupulously fair. This should be our policy as a producing nation, and it plainly becomes us as a people who love generosity and the moral aspects of national good faith and reciprocal forbearance.

These considerations should not, however, constrain us to submit to unfair discrimination nor to silently acquiesce in vexatious hindrances to the enjoyment of our share of the legitimate advantages of proper trade relations. If an examination of the situation suggests such measures on our part as would involve restrictions similar to those from which we suffer, the way to such a course is easy. It should, however, by no means be lightly entered upon, since the necessity for the inauguration of such a policy would be regretted by the best sentiment of our people and because it naturally and logically might lead to consequences of the gravest character.

I take pleasure in calling to your attention the encomiums bestowed on those vessels of our new Navy which took part in the notable ceremony of the opening of the Kiel Canal. It was fitting that this extraordinary achievement of the newer German nationality should be celebrated in the presence of America's exposition of the latest developments of the world's naval energy.

Our relations with Great Britain, always intimate and important, have demanded during the past year even a greater share of consideration than is usual.

Several vexatious questions were left undetermined by the decision of the Bering Sea Arbitration Tribunal. The application of the principles laid down by that august body has not been followed by the results they were intended to accomplish, either because the principles themselves lacked in breadth and definiteness or because their execution has been more or less imperfect. Much correspondence has been exchanged between the two Governments on the subject of preventing the exterminating slaughter of seals. The insufficiency of the British patrol of Bering Sea under the regulations agreed on by the two Governments has been pointed out, and yet only two British ships have been on police duty during this season in those waters.

The need of a more effective enforcement of existing regulations as well as the adoption of such additional regulations as experience has shown to be absolutely necessary to carry out the intent of the award have been earnestly urged upon the British Government, but thus far without effective results. In the meantime the depletion of the seal herds by means of pelagic hunting has so alarmingly progressed that unless their slaughter is at once effectively checked their extinction within a few years seems to be a matter of absolute certainty.

The understanding by which the United States was to pay and Great Britain to receive a lump sum of $425,000 in full settlement of all British claims for damages arising from our seizure of British sealing vessels unauthorized under the award of the Paris Tribunal of Arbitration was not confirmed by the last Congress, which declined to make the necessary appropriation. I am still of the opinion that this arrangement was a judicious and advantageous one for the Government, and I earnestly recommend that it be again considered and sanctioned. If, however, this does not meet with the favor of Congress, it certainly will hardly dissent from the proposition that the Government is bound by every consideration of honor and good faith to provide for the speedy adjustment of these claims by arbitration as the only other alternative. A treaty of arbitration has therefore been agreed upon, and will be immediately laid before the Senate, so that in one of the modes suggested a final settlement may be reached.

Notwithstanding that Great Britain originated the proposal to enforce international rules for the prevention of collisions at sea, based on the recommendations of the Maritime Conference of Washington, and concurred in, suggesting March 11, 1895, as the date to be set by proclamation for carrying these rules into general effect, Her Majesty's Government, having encountered opposition on the part of British shipping interests, announced its inability to accept that date, which was consequently canceled. The entire matter is still in abeyance, without prospect of a better condition in the near future.

The commissioners appointed to mark the international boundary in Passamaquoddy Bay according to the description of the treaty of Ghent have not yet fully agreed.

The completion of the preliminary survey of that Alaskan boundary which follows the contour of the coast from the southernmost point of Prince of Wales Island until it strikes the one hundred and forty-first meridian at or near the summit of Mount St. Elias awaits further necessary appropriation, which is urgently recommended. This survey was undertaken under the provisions of the convention entered into by this country and Great Britain July 22, 1892, and the supplementary convention of February 3, 1894.

As to the remaining section of the Alaskan boundary, which follows the one hundred and forty-first meridian northwardly from Mount St. Elias to the Frozen Ocean, the settlement of which involves the physical location of the meridian mentioned, no conventional agreement has yet been made. The ascertainment of a given meridian at a particular point is a work requiring much time and careful observations and surveys. Such observations and surveys were undertaken by the United States Coast and Geodetic Survey in 1890 and 1891, while similar work in the same quarters, under British auspices, is believed to give nearly coincident results; but these surveys have been independently conducted, and no international agreement to mark those or any other parts of the one hundred and forty-first meridian by permanent monuments has yet been made. In the meantime the valley of the Yukon is becoming a highway through the hitherto unexplored wilds of Alaska, and abundant mineral wealth has been discovered in that region, especially at or near the junction of the boundary meridian with the Yukon and its tributaries. In these circumstances it is expedient, and, indeed, imperative, that the jurisdictional limits of the respective Governments in this new region be speedily determined. Her Britannic Majesty's Government has proposed a joint delimitation of the one hundred and forty-first meridian by an international commission of experts, which, if Congress will authorize it and make due provision therefor, can be accomplished with no unreasonable delay. It is impossible to overlook the vital importance of continuing the work already entered upon and supplementing it by further effective measures looking to the exact location of this entire boundary line.

I call attention to the unsatisfactory delimitation of the respective jurisdictions of the United States and the Dominion of Canada in the Great Lakes at the approaches to the narrow waters that connect them. The waters in question are frequented by fishermen of both nationalities and their nets are there used. Owing to the uncertainty and ignorance as to the true boundary, vexatious disputes and injurious seizures of boats and nets by Canadian cruisers often occur, while any positive settlement thereof by an accepted standard is not easily to be reached. A joint commission to determine the line in those quarters on a practical basis, by measured courses following range marks on shore, is a necessity for which immediate provision should be made.

It being apparent that the boundary dispute between Great Britain and the Republic of Venezuela concerning the limits of British Guiana was approaching an acute stage, a definite statement of the interest and policy of the United States as regards the controversy seemed to be required both on its own account and in view of its relations with the friendly powers directly concerned. In July last, therefore, a dispatch was addressed to our ambassador at London for communication to the British Government in which the attitude of the United States was fully and distinctly set forth. The general conclusions therein reached and formulated are in substance that the traditional and established policy of this Government is firmly opposed to a forcible increase by any European power of its territorial possessions on this continent; that this policy is as well founded in principle as it is strongly supported by numerous precedents; that as a consequence the United States is bound to protest against the enlargement of the area of British Guiana in derogation of the rights and against the will of Venezuela; that considering the disparity in strength of Great Britain and Venezuela the territorial dispute between them can be reasonably settled only by friendly and impartial arbitration, and that the resort to such arbitration should include the whole controversy, and is not satisfied if one of the powers concerned is permitted to draw an arbitrary line through the territory in debate and to declare that it will submit to arbitration only the portion lying on one side of it. In view of these conclusions, the dispatch in question called upon the British Government for a definite answer to the question whether it would or would not submit the territorial controversy between itself and Venezuela in its entirety to impartial arbitration. The answer of the British Government has not yet been received, but is expected shortly, when further communication on the subject will probably be made to the Congress.

Early in January last an uprising against the Government of Hawaii was promptly suppressed. Martial law was forthwith proclaimed and numerous arrests were made of persons suspected of being in sympathy with the Royalist party. Among these were several citizens of the United States, who were either convicted by a military court and sentenced to death, imprisonment, or fine or were deported without trial. The United States, while denying protection to such as had taken the Hawaiian oath of allegiance, insisted that martial law, though altering the forms of justice, could not supersede justice itself, and demanded stay of execution until the proceedings had been submitted to this Government and knowledge obtained therefrom that our citizens had received fair trial. The death sentences were subsequently commuted or were remitted on condition of leaving the islands. The cases of certain Americans arrested and expelled by arbitrary order without formal charge or trial have had attention, and in some instances have been found to justify remonstrance and a claim for indemnity, which Hawaii has not thus far conceded.

Mr. Thurston, the Hawaiian minister, having furnished this Government abundant reason for asking that he be recalled, that course was pursued, and his successor has lately been received.

The deplorable lynching of several Italian laborers in Colorado was naturally followed by international representations, and I am happy to say that the best efforts of the State in which the outrages occurred have been put forth to discover and punish the authors of this atrocious crime. The dependent families of some of the unfortunate victims invite by their deplorable condition gracious provision for their needs.

These manifestations against helpless aliens may be traced through successive stages to the vicious *padroni* system, which, unchecked by our immigration and contract-labor statutes, controls these workers from the moment of landing on our shores and farms them out in distant and often rude regions, where their cheapening competition in the fields of bread-winning toil brings them into collision with other labor interests. While welcoming, as we should, those who seek our shores to merge themselves in our body politic and win personal competence by honest effort, we can not regard such assemblages of distinctively alien laborers, hired out in the mass to the profit of alien speculators and shipped hither and thither as the prospect of gain may dictate, as otherwise than repugnant to the spirit of our civilization, deterrent to individual advancement, and hindrances to the building up of stable communities resting upon the wholesome ambitions of the citizen and constituting the prime factor in the prosperity and progress of our nation. If legislation can reach this growing evil, it certainly should be attempted.

Japan has furnished abundant evidence of her vast gain in every trait and characteristic that constitutes a nation's greatness. We have reason for congratulation in the fact that the Government of the United States, by the exchange of liberal treaty stipulations with the new Japan, was the first to recognize her wonderful advance and to extend to her the consideration and confidence due to her national enlightenment and progressive character.

The boundary dispute which lately threatened to embroil Guatemala and Mexico has happily yielded to pacific counsels, and its determination has, by the joint agreement of the parties, been submitted to the sole arbitration of the United States minister to Mexico.

The commission appointed under the convention of February 18, 1889, to set new monuments along the boundary between the United States and Mexico has completed its task.

As a sequel to the failure of a scheme for the colonization in Mexico of negroes, mostly immigrants from Alabama under contract, a great number of these helpless and suffering people, starving and smitten with contagious disease, made their way or were assisted to the frontier, where, in wretched plight, they were quarantined by the Texas authorities. Learning of their destitute condition, I directed rations to be temporarily furnished them through the War Department. At the expiration of their quarantine they were conveyed by the railway companies at comparatively nominal rates to their homes in Alabama, upon my assurance, in the absence of any fund available for the cost of their transportation, that I would recommend to Congress an appropriation for its payment. I now strongly urge upon Congress the propriety of making such an appropriation. It should be remembered that the measures taken were dictated not only by sympathy and humanity, but by a conviction that it was not compatible with the dignity of this Government that so large a body of our dependent citizens should be thrown for relief upon the charity of a neighboring state.

In last year's message I narrated at some length the jurisdictional questions then freshly arisen in the Mosquito Indian Strip of Nicaragua. Since that time, by the voluntary act of the Mosquito Nation, the territory reserved to them has been incorporated with Nicaragua, the Indians formally subjecting themselves to be governed by the general laws and regulations of the Republic instead of by their own customs and regulations, and thus availing themselves of a privilege secured to them by the treaty between Nicaragua and Great Britain of January 28, 1860.

After this extension of uniform Nicaraguan administration to the Mosquito Strip, the case of the British vice-consul, Hatch, and of several of his countrymen who had been summarily expelled from Nicaragua and treated with considerable indignity provoked a claim by Great Britain upon Nicaragua for pecuniary indemnity, which, upon Nicaragua's refusal to admit liability, was enforced by Great Britain. While the sovereignty and jurisdiction of Nicaragua was in no way questioned by Great Britain, the former's arbitrary conduct in regard to British subjects furnished the ground for this proceeding.

A British naval force occupied without resistance the Pacific seaport of Corinto, but was soon after withdrawn upon the promise that the sum demanded would be paid. Throughout this incident the kindly offices of the United States were invoked and were employed in favor of as peaceful a settlement and as much consideration and indulgence toward Nicaragua as were consistent with the nature of the case. Our efforts have since been made the subject of appreciative and grateful recognition by Nicaragua.

The coronation of the Czar of Russia at Moscow in May next invites the ceremonial participation of the United States, and in accordance with usage and diplomatic propriety our minister to the imperial court has been directed to represent our Government on the occasion.

Correspondence is on foot touching the practice of Russian consuls within the jurisdiction of the United States to interrogate citizens as to their race and religious faith, and upon ascertainment thereof to deny to Jews authentication of passports or legal documents for use in Russia. Inasmuch as such a proceeding imposes a disability which in the case of succession to property in Russia may be found to infringe the treaty rights of our citizens, and which is an obnoxious invasion of our territorial jurisdiction, it has elicited fitting remonstrance, the result of which, it is hoped, will remove the cause of complaint. The pending claims of sealing vessels of the United States seized in Russian waters remain unadjusted. Our recent convention with Russia establishing a *modus vivendi* as to imperial jurisdiction in such cases has prevented further difficulty of this nature.

The Russian Government has welcomed in principle our suggestion for a *modus vivendi*, to embrace Great Britain and Japan, looking to the better preservation of seal life in the North Pacific and Bering Sea and the extension of the protected area defined by the Paris Tribunal to all Pacific waters north of the thirty-fifth parallel. It is especially noticeable that Russia favors prohibition of the use of firearms in seal hunting throughout the proposed area and a longer closed season for pelagic sealing.

In my last two annual messages I called the attention of the Congress to the position we occupied as one of the parties to a treaty or agreement by which we became jointly bound with England and Germany to so interfere with the government and control of Samoa as in effect to assume the management of its affairs.* On the 9th day of May, 1894, I transmitted to the Senate a special message,† with accompanying documents, giving information on the subject and emphasizing the opinion I have at all times entertained, that our situation in this matter was inconsistent with the mission and traditions of our Government, in violation of the principles we profess, and in all its phases mischievous and vexatious.

I again press this subject upon the attention of the Congress and ask for such legislative action or expression as will lead the way to our relief from obligations both irksome and unnatural.

*See pp. 5871, 5963-5964.   † See p. 5909.

Cuba is again gravely disturbed. An insurrection in some respects more active than the last preceding revolt, which continued from 1868 to 1878, now exists in a large part of the eastern interior of the island, menacing even some populations on the coast. Besides deranging the commercial exchanges of the island, of which our country takes the predominant share, this flagrant condition of hostilities, by arousing sentimental sympathy and inciting adventurous support among our people, has entailed earnest effort on the part of this Government to enforce obedience to our neutrality laws and to prevent the territory of the United States from being abused as a vantage ground from which to aid those in arms against Spanish sovereignty.

Whatever may be the traditional sympathy of our countrymen as individuals with a people who seem to be struggling for larger autonomy and greater freedom, deepened, as such sympathy naturally must be, in behalf of our neighbors, yet the plain duty of their Government is to observe in good faith the recognized obligations of international relationship. The performance of this duty should not be made more difficult by a disregard on the part of our citizens of the obligations growing out of their allegiance to their country, which should restrain them from violating as individuals the neutrality which the nation of which they are members is bound to observe in its relations to friendly sovereign states. Though neither the warmth of our people's sympathy with the Cuban insurgents, nor our loss and material damage consequent upon the futile endeavors thus far made to restore peace and order, nor any shock our humane sensibilities may have received from the cruelties which appear to especially characterize this sanguinary and fiercely conducted war, have in the least shaken the determination of the Government to honestly fulfill every international obligation, yet it is to be earnestly hoped on every ground that the devastation of armed conflict may speedily be stayed and order and quiet restored to the distracted island, bringing in their train the activity and thrift of peaceful pursuits.

One notable instance of interference by Spain with passing American ships has occurred. On March 8 last the *Allianca*, while bound from Colon to New York, and following the customary track for vessels near the Cuban shore, but outside the 3-mile limit, was fired upon by a Spanish gunboat. Protest was promptly made by the United States against this act as not being justified by a state of war, nor permissible in respect of vessels on the usual paths of commerce, nor tolerable in view of the wanton peril occasioned to innocent life and property. The act was disavowed, with full expression of regret and assurance of nonrecurrence of such just cause of complaint, while the offending officer was relieved of his command. Military arrests of citizens of the United States in Cuba have occasioned frequent reclamations. Where held on criminal charges their delivery to the ordinary civil jurisdiction for trial has been demanded and obtained in conformity with treaty provisions, and where

THE SURRENDER OF THE *OQUENDO*

THE SURRENDER OF THE *OQUENDO*

In the photograph, the cutter carrying the white flag bears Lieutenant Blue, who was charged with the mission of demanding the surrender. The crew of the *Oquendo* is seen on the deck. Some Spanish sailors, who have swum ashore, are visible on the beach.

As she lies on the beach, with her punctured sides, dismounted guns and snarled iron work, with fire blazing in the hold, she is a striking example of the destructive power of modern projectiles.

The article, "Santiago Harbor, Battle of," gives a complete history of the decisive naval engagement of the war.

merely detained by way of military precaution under a proclaimed state of siege, without formulated accusation, their release or trial has been insisted upon. The right of American consular officers in the island to prefer protests and demands in such cases having been questioned by the insular authority, their enjoyment of the privilege stipulated by treaty for the consuls of Germany was claimed under the most-favored-nation provision of our own convention and was promptly recognized.

The long-standing demand of Antonio Maximo Mora against Spain has at last been settled by the payment, on the 14th of September last, of the sum originally agreed upon in liquidation of the claim. Its distribution among the parties entitled to receive it has proceeded as rapidly as the rights of those claiming the fund could be safely determined.

The enforcement of differential duties against products of this country exported to Cuba and Puerto Rico prompted the immediate claim on our part to the benefit of the minimum tariff of Spain in return for the most favorable treatment permitted by our laws as regards the production of Spanish territories. A commercial arrangement was concluded in January last securing the treatment so claimed.

Vigorous protests against excessive fines imposed on our ships and merchandise by the customs officers of these islands for trivial errors have resulted in the remission of such fines in instances where the equity of the complaint was apparent, though the vexatious practice has not been wholly discontinued.

Occurrences in Turkey have continued to excite concern. The reported massacres of Christians in Armenia and the development there and in other districts of a spirit of fanatic hostility to Christian influences naturally excited apprehension for the safety of the devoted men and women who, as dependents of the foreign missionary societies in the United States, reside in Turkey under the guaranty of law and usage and in the legitimate performance of their educational and religious mission. No efforts have been spared in their behalf, and their protection in person and property has been earnestly and vigorously enforced by every means within our power.

I regret, however, that an attempt on our part to obtain better information concerning the true condition of affairs in the disturbed quarter of the Ottoman Empire by sending thither the United States consul at Sivas to make investigation and report was thwarted by the objections of the Turkish Government. This movement on our part was in no sense meant as a gratuitous entanglement of the United States in the so-called Eastern question nor as an officious interference with the right and duty which belong by treaty to certain great European powers calling for their intervention in political matters affecting the good government and religious freedom of the non-Mussulman subjects of the Sultan, but it arose solely from our desire to have an accurate knowledge of the conditions in our efforts to care for those entitled to our protection.

The presence of our naval vessels which are now in the vicinity of the disturbed localities affords opportunities to acquire a measure of familiarity with the condition of affairs and will enable us to take suitable steps for the protection of any interests of our countrymen within reach of our ships that might be found imperiled.

The Ottoman Government has lately issued an imperial *irade* exempting forever from taxation an American college for girls at Scutari. Repeated assurances have also been obtained by our envoy at Constantinople that similar institutions maintained and administered by our countrymen shall be secured in the enjoyment of all rights and that our citizens throughout the Empire shall be protected.

The Government, however, in view of existing facts, is far from relying upon such assurances as the limit of its duty. Our minister has been vigilant and alert in affording all possible protection in individual cases where danger threatened or safety was imperiled. We have sent ships as far toward the points of actual disturbance as it is possible for them to go, where they offer refuge to those obliged to flee, and we have the promise of other powers which have ships in the neighborhood that our citizens as well as theirs will be received and protected on board those ships. On the demand of our minister orders have been issued by the Sultan that Turkish soldiers shall guard and escort to the coast American refugees.

These orders have been carried out, and our latest intelligence gives assurance of the present personal safety of our citizens and missionaries. Though thus far no lives of American citizens have been sacrificed, there can be no doubt that serious loss and destruction of mission property have resulted from riotous conflicts and outrageous attacks.

By treaty several of the most powerful European powers have secured a right and have assumed a duty not only in behalf of their own citizens and in furtherance of their own interests, but as agents of the Christian world. Their right is to enforce such conduct of Turkish government as will restrain fanatical brutality, and if this fails their duty is to so interfere as to insure against such dreadful occurrences in Turkey as have lately shocked civilization. The powers declare this right and this duty to be theirs alone, and it is earnestly hoped that prompt and effective action on their part will not be delayed.

The new consulates at Erzerum and Harpoot, for which appropriation was made last session, have been provisionally filled by trusted employees of the Department of State. These appointees, though now in Turkey, have not yet received their exequaturs.

The arbitration of the claim of the Venezuela Steam Transportation Company under the treaty of January 19, 1892, between the United States and Venezuela, resulted in an award in favor of the claimant.

The Government has used its good offices toward composing the differences between Venezuela on the one hand and France and Belgium on the other growing out of the dismissal of the representatives of those powers on the ground of a publication deemed offensive to Venezuela. Although that dismissal was coupled with a cordial request that other more personally agreeable envoys be sent in their stead, a rupture of intercourse ensued and still continues.

In view of the growth of our interests in foreign countries and the encouraging prospects for a general expansion of our commerce, the question of an improvement in the consular service has increased in importance and urgency. Though there is no doubt that the great body of consular officers are rendering valuable services to the trade and industries of the country, the need of some plan of appointment and control which would tend to secure a higher average of efficiency can not be denied.

The importance of the subject has led the Executive to consider what steps might properly be taken without additional legislation to answer the need of a better system of consular appointments. The matter having been committed to the consideration of the Secretary of State, in pursuance of his recommendations an Executive order was issued on the 20th of September, 1895,* by the terms of which it is provided that after that date any vacancy in a consulate or commercial agency with an annual salary or compensation from official fees of not more than $2,500 or less than $1,000 should be filled either by transfer or promotion from some other position under the Department of State of a character tending to qualify the incumbent for the position to be filled, or by the appointment of a person not under the Department of State, but having previously served thereunder and shown his capacity and fitness for consular duty, or by the appointment of a person who, having been selected by the President and sent to a board for examination, is found upon such examination to be qualified for the position. Posts which pay less than $1,000 being usually, on account of their small compensation, filled by selection from residents of the locality, it was not deemed practicable to put them under the new system.

The compensation of $2,500 was adopted as the maximum limit in the classification for the reason that consular officers receiving more than that sum are often charged with functions and duties scarcely inferior in dignity and importance to those of diplomatic agents, and it was therefore thought best to continue their selection in the discretion of the Executive without subjecting them to examination before a board. Excluding 71 places with compensation at present less than $1,000 and 53 places above the maximum in compensation, the number of positions remaining within the scope of the order is 196. This number will undoubtedly be increased by the inclusion of consular officers whose remuneration in fees, now less than $1,000, will be augmented with the growth of our foreign commerce and a return to more favorable business conditions.

In execution of the Executive order referred to the Secretary of State has designated as a board to conduct the prescribed examinations the

*See p. 6056.

Third Assistant Secretary of State, the Solicitor of the Department of State, and the Chief of the Consular Bureau, and has specified the subjects to which such examinations shall relate.

It is not assumed that this system will prove a full measure of consular reform. It is quite probable that actual experience will show particulars in which the order already issued may be amended and demonstrate that for the best results appropriate legislation by Congress is imperatively required.

In any event, these efforts to improve the consular service ought to be immediately supplemented by legislation providing for consular inspection. This has frequently been a subject of Executive recommendation, and I again urge such action by Congress as will permit the frequent and thorough inspection of consulates by officers appointed for that purpose or by persons already in the diplomatic or consular service. The expense attending such a plan would be insignificant compared with its usefulness, and I hope the legislation necessary to set it on foot will be speedily forthcoming.

I am thoroughly convinced that in addition to their salaries our ambassadors and ministers at foreign courts should be provided by the Government with official residences. The salaries of these officers are comparatively small and in most cases insufficient to pay, with other necessary expenses, the cost of maintaining household establishments in keeping with their important and delicate functions. The usefulness of a nation's diplomatic representative undeniably depends much upon the appropriateness of his surroundings, and a country like ours, while avoiding unnecessary glitter and show, should be certain that it does not suffer in its relations with foreign nations through parsimony and shabbiness in its diplomatic outfit. These considerations and the other advantages of having fixed and somewhat permanent locations for our embassies would abundantly justify the moderate expenditure necessary to carry out this suggestion.

As we turn from a review of our foreign relations to the contemplation of our national financial situation we are immediately aware that we approach a subject of domestic concern more important than any other that can engage our attention, and one at present in such a perplexing and delicate predicament as to require prompt and wise treatment.

We may well be encouraged to earnest effort in this direction when we recall the steps already taken toward improving our economic and financial situation and when we appreciate how well the way has been prepared for further progress by an aroused and intelligent popular interest in these subjects.

By command of the people a customs-revenue system designed for the protection and benefit of favored classes at the expense of the great mass of our countrymen, and which, while inefficient for the purpose of revenue, curtailed our trade relations and impeded our entrance to the markets of the world, has been superseded by a tariff policy which in principle is based upon a denial of the right of the Government to obstruct the avenues to our people's cheap living or lessen their comfort and contentment for the sake of according especial advantages to favorites, and which, while encouraging our intercourse and trade with other nations, recognizes the fact that American self-reliance, thrift, and ingenuity can build up our country's industries and develop its resources more surely than enervating paternalism.

The compulsory purchase and coinage of silver by the Government, unchecked and unregulated by business conditions and heedless of our currency needs, which for more than fifteen years diluted our circulating medium, undermined confidence abroad in our financial ability, and at last culminated in distress and panic at home, has been recently stopped by the repeal of the laws which forced this reckless scheme upon the country.

The things thus accomplished, notwithstanding their extreme importance and beneficent effects, fall far short of curing the monetary evils from which we suffer as a result of long indulgence in ill-advised financial expedients.

The currency denominated United States notes and commonly known as greenbacks was issued in large volume during the late Civil War and was intended originally to meet the exigencies of that period. It will be seen by a reference to the debates in Congress at the time the laws were passed authorizing the issue of these notes that their advocates declared they were intended for only temporary use and to meet the emergency of war. In almost if not all the laws relating to them some provision was made contemplating their voluntary or compulsory retirement. A large quantity of them, however, were kept on foot and mingled with the currency of the country, so that at the close of the year 1874 they amounted to $381,999,073.

Immediately after that date, and in January, 1875, a law was passed providing for the resumption of specie payments, by which the Secretary of the Treasury was required whenever additional circulation was issued to national banks to retire United States notes equal in amount to 80 per cent of such additional national-bank circulation until such notes were reduced to $300,000,000. This law further provided that on and after the 1st day of January, 1879, the United States notes then outstanding should be redeemed in coin, and in order to provide and prepare for such redemption the Secretary of the Treasury was authorized not only to use any surplus revenues of the Government, but to issue bonds of the United States and dispose of them for coin and to use the proceeds for the purposes contemplated by the statute.

In May, 1878, and before the date thus appointed for the redemption and retirement of these notes, another statute was passed forbidding their further cancellation and retirement. Some of them had, however, been previously redeemed and canceled upon the issue of additional national-bank circulation, as permitted by the law of 1875, so that the amount outstanding at the time of the passage of the act forbidding their further retirement was $346,681,016.

The law of 1878 did not stop at distinct prohibition, but contained in addition the following express provision:

And when any of said notes may be redeemed or be received into the Treasury under any law from any source whatever, and shall belong to the United States, they shall not be retired, canceled, or destroyed, but they shall be reissued and paid out again and kept in circulation.

This was the condition of affairs on the 1st day of January, 1879, which had been fixed upon four years before as the date for entering upon the redemption and retirement of all these notes, and for which such abundant means had been provided.

The Government was put in the anomalous situation of owing to the holders of its notes debts payable in gold on demand which could neither be retired by receiving such notes in discharge of obligations due the Government nor canceled by actual payment in gold. It was forced to redeem without redemption and to pay without acquittance.

There had been issued and sold $95,500,000 of the bonds authorized by the resumption act of 1875, the proceeds of which, together with other gold in the Treasury, created a gold fund deemed sufficient to meet the demands which might be made upon it for the redemption of the outstanding United States notes. This fund, together with such other gold as might be from time to time in the Treasury available for the same purpose, has been since called our gold reserve, and $100,000,000 has been regarded as an adequate amount to accomplish its object. This fund amounted on the 1st day of January, 1879, to $114,193,360, and though thereafter constantly fluctuating it did not fall below that sum until July, 1892. In April, 1893, for the first time since its establishment, this reserve amounted to less than $100,000,000, containing at that date only $97,011,330.

In the meantime, and in July, 1890, an act had been passed directing larger governmental monthly purchases of silver than had been required under previous laws, and providing that in payment for such silver Treasury notes of the United States should be issued payable on demand in gold or silver coin, at the discretion of the Secretary of the Treasury. It was, however, declared in the act to be "the established policy of the United States to maintain the two metals on a parity with each other upon the present legal ratio or such ratio as may be provided by law." In view of this declaration it was not deemed permissible for the Secretary of the Treasury to exercise the discretion in terms conferred on him by refusing to pay gold on these notes when demanded, because by such discrimination in favor of the gold dollar the so-called parity of the two metals would be destroyed and grave and dangerous consequences would be precipitated by affirming or accentuating the constantly widening disparity between their actual values under the existing ratio.

It thus resulted that the Treasury notes issued in payment of silver purchases under the law of 1890 were necessarily treated as gold obligations at the option of the holder. These notes on the 1st day of November, 1893, when the law compelling the monthly purchase of silver was repealed, amounted to more than $155,000,000. The notes of this description now outstanding added to the United States notes still undiminished by redemption or cancellation constitute a volume of gold obligations amounting to nearly $500,000,000.

These obligations are the instruments which ever since we had a gold reserve have been used to deplete it.

This reserve, as has been stated, had fallen in April, 1893, to $97,-011,330. It has from that time to the present, with very few and unimportant upward movements, steadily decreased, except as it has been temporarily replenished by the sale of bonds.

Among the causes for this constant and uniform shrinkage in this fund may be mentioned the great falling off of exports under the operation of the tariff law until recently in force, which crippled our exchange of commodities with foreign nations and necessitated to some extent the payment of our balances in gold; the unnatural infusion of silver into our currency and the increasing agitation for its free and unlimited coinage, which have created apprehension as to our disposition or ability to continue gold payments; the consequent hoarding of gold at home and the stoppage of investments of foreign capital, as well as the return of our securities already sold abroad; and the high rate of foreign exchange, which induced the shipment of our gold to be drawn against as a matter of speculation.

In consequence of these conditions the gold reserve on the 1st day of February, 1894, was reduced to $65,438,377, having lost more than $31,-000,000 during the preceding nine months, or since April, 1893. Its replenishment being necessary and no other manner of accomplishing it being possible, resort was had to the issue and sale of bonds provided for by the resumption act of 1875. Fifty millions of these bonds were sold, yielding $58,633,295.71, which was added to the reserve fund of gold then on hand. As a result of this operation this reserve, which had suffered constant and large withdrawals in the meantime, stood on the 6th day of March, 1894, at the sum of $107,446,802. Its depletion was, however, immediately thereafter so accelerated that on the 30th day of June, 1894, it had fallen to $64,873,025, thus losing by withdrawals more than $42,000,000 in five months and dropping slightly below its situation when the sale of $50,000,000 in bonds was effected for its replenishment.

This depressed condition grew worse, and on the 24th day of November, 1894, our gold reserve being reduced to $57,669,701, it became necessary to again strengthen it.

This was done by another sale of bonds amounting to $50,000,000, from which there was realized $58,538,500, with which the fund was increased to $111,142,021 on the 4th day of December, 1894.

Again disappointment awaited the anxious hope for relief. There was not even a lull in the exasperating withdrawals of gold. On the contrary, they grew larger and more persistent than ever. Between the 4th day of December, 1894, and early in February, 1895, a period of scarcely more than two months after the second reenforcement of our gold reserve by the sale of bonds, it had lost by such withdrawals more than $69,000,000 and had fallen to $41,340,181. Nearly $43,000,000 had been withdrawn within the month immediately preceding this situation.

In anticipation of impending trouble I had on the 28th day of January, 1895, addressed a communication* to the Congress fully setting forth our difficulties and dangerous position and earnestly recommending that authority be given the Secretary of the Treasury to issue bonds bearing a low rate of interest, payable by their terms in gold, for the purpose of maintaining a sufficient gold reserve and also for the redemption and cancellation of outstanding United States notes and the Treasury notes issued for the purchase of silver under the law of 1890. This recommendation did not, however, meet with legislative approval.

In February, 1895, therefore, the situation was exceedingly critical. With a reserve perilously low and a refusal of Congressional aid, everything indicated that the end of gold payments by the Government was imminent. The results of prior bond issues had been exceedingly unsatisfactory, and the large withdrawals of gold immediately succeeding their public sale in open market gave rise to a reasonable suspicion that a large part of the gold paid into the Treasury upon such sales was promptly drawn out again by the presentation of United States notes or Treasury notes, and found its way to the hands of those who had only temporarily parted with it in the purchase of bonds.

In this emergency, and in view of its surrounding perplexities, it became entirely apparent to those upon whom the struggle for safety was devolved not only that our gold reserve must, for the third time in less than thirteen months, be restored by another issue and sale of bonds bearing a high rate of interest and badly suited to the purpose, but that a plan must be adopted for their disposition promising better results than those realized on previous sales. An agreement was therefore made with a number of financiers and bankers whereby it was stipulated that bonds described in the resumption act of 1875, payable in coin thirty years after their date, bearing interest at the rate of 4 per cent per annum, and amounting to about $62,000,000, should be exchanged for gold, receivable by weight, amounting to a little more than $65,000,000.

This gold was to be delivered in such installments as would complete its delivery within about six months from the date of the contract, and

*See pp. 5993-5997.

at least one-half of the amount was to be furnished from abroad. It was also agreed by those supplying this gold that during the continuance of the contract they would by every means in their power protect the Government against gold withdrawals. The contract also provided that if Congress would authorize their issue bonds payable by their terms in gold and bearing interest at the rate of 3 per cent per annum might within ten days be substituted at par for the 4 per cent bonds described in the agreement.

On the day this contract was made its terms were communicated to Congress by a special Executive message,* in which it was stated that more than $16,000,000 would be saved to the Government if gold bonds bearing 3 per cent interest were authorized to be substituted for those mentioned in the contract.

The Congress having declined to grant the necessary authority to secure this saving, the contract, unmodified, was carried out, resulting in a gold reserve amounting to $107,571,230 on the 8th day of July, 1895. The performance of this contract not only restored the reserve, but checked for a time the withdrawals of gold and brought on a period of restored confidence and such peace and quiet in business circles as were of the greatest possible value to every interest that affects our people. I have never had the slightest misgiving concerning the wisdom or propriety of this arrangement, and am quite willing to answer for my full share of responsibility for its promotion. I believe it averted a disaster the imminence of which was, fortunately, not at the time generally understood by our people.

Though the contract mentioned stayed for a time the tide of gold withdrawal, its good results could not be permanent. Recent withdrawals have reduced the reserve from $107,571,230 on the 8th day of July, 1895, to $79,333,966. How long it will remain large enough to render its increase unnecessary is only matter of conjecture, though quite large withdrawals for shipment in the immediate future are predicted in well-informed quarters. About $16,000,000 has been withdrawn during the month of November.

The foregoing statement of events and conditions develops the fact that after increasing our interest-bearing bonded indebtedness more than $162,000,000 to save our gold reserve we are nearly where we started, having now in such reserve $79,333,966, as against $65,438,377 in February, 1894, when the first bonds were issued.

Though the amount of gold drawn from the Treasury appears to be very large as gathered from the facts and figures herein presented, it actually was much larger, considerable sums having been acquired by the Treasury within the several periods stated without the issue of bonds. On the 28th of January, 1895, it was reported by the Secretary of the Treasury that more than $172,000,000 of gold had been withdrawn for

*See pp. 5999-6000.

hoarding or shipment during the year preceding.   He now reports that from January 1, 1879, to July 14, 1890, a period of more than eleven years, only a little over $28,000,000 was withdrawn, and that between July 14, 1890, the date of the passage of the law for an increased purchase of silver, and the 1st day of December, 1895, or within less than five and a half years, there was withdrawn nearly $375,000,000, making a total of more than $403,000,000 drawn from the Treasury in gold since January 1, 1879, the date fixed in 1875 for the retirement of the United States notes.

Nearly $327,000,000 of the gold thus withdrawn has been paid out on these United States notes, and yet every one of the $346,000,000 is still uncanceled and ready to do service in future gold depletions.

More than $76,000,000 in gold has since their creation in 1890 been paid out from the Treasury upon the notes given on the purchase of silver by the Government, and yet the whole, amounting to $155,000,000, except a little more than $16,000,000 which has been retired by exchanges for silver at the request of the holders, remains outstanding and prepared to join their older and more experienced allies in future raids upon the Treasury's gold reserve.

In other words, the Government has paid in gold more than nine-tenths of its United States notes and still owes them all.   It has paid in gold about one-half of its notes given for silver purchases without extinguishing by such payment one dollar of these notes.

When, added to all this, we are reminded that to carry on this astounding financial scheme the Government has incurred a bonded indebtedness of $95,500,000 in establishing a gold reserve and of $162,315,400 in efforts to maintain it; that the annual interest charge on such bonded indebtedness is more than $11,000,000; that a continuance of our present course may result in further bond issues, and that we have suffered or are threatened with all this for the sake of supplying gold for foreign shipment or facilitating its hoarding at home, a situation is exhibited which certainly ought to arrest attention and provoke immediate legislative relief.

I am convinced the only thorough and practicable remedy for our troubles is found in the retirement and cancellation of our United States notes, commonly called greenbacks, and the outstanding Treasury notes issued by the Government in payment of silver purchases under the act of 1890.

I believe this could be quite readily accomplished by the exchange of these notes for United States bonds, of small as well as large denominations, bearing a low rate of interest.   They should be long-term bonds, thus increasing their desirability as investments, and because their payment could be well postponed to a period far removed from present financial burdens and perplexities, when with increased prosperity and resources they would be more easily met.

To further insure the cancellation of these notes and also provide a way by which gold may be added to our currency in lieu of them, a feature in the plan should be an authority given to the Secretary of the Treasury to dispose of the bonds abroad for gold if necessary to complete the contemplated redemption and cancellation, permitting him to use the proceeds of such bonds to take up and cancel any of the notes that may be in the Treasury or that may be received by the Government on any account.

The increase of our bonded debt involved in this plan would be amply compensated by renewed activity and enterprise in all business circles, the restored confidence at home, the reinstated faith in our monetary strength abroad, and the stimulation of every interest and industry that would follow the cancellation of the gold-demand obligations now afflicting us. In any event, the bonds proposed would stand for the extinguishment of a troublesome indebtedness, while in the path we now follow there lurks the menace of unending bonds, with our indebtedness still undischarged and aggravated in every feature. The obligations necessary to fund this indebtedness would not equal in amount those from which we have been relieved since 1884 by anticipation and payment beyond the requirements of the sinking fund out of our surplus revenues.

The currency withdrawn by the retirement of the United States notes and Treasury notes, amounting to probably less than $486,000,000, might be supplied by such gold as would be used on their retirement or by an increase in the circulation of our national banks. Though the aggregate capital of those now in existence amounts to more than $664,000,000, their outstanding circulation based on bond security amounts to only about $190,000,000. They are authorized to issue notes amounting to 90 per cent of the bonds deposited to secure their circulation, but in no event beyond the amount of their capital stock, and they are obliged to pay 1 per cent tax on the circulation they issue.

I think they should be allowed to issue circulation equal to the par value of the bonds they deposit to secure it, and that the tax on their circulation should be reduced to one-fourth of 1 per cent, which would undoubtedly meet all the expense the Government incurs on their account. In addition they should be allowed to substitute or deposit in lieu of the bonds now required as security for their circulation those which would be issued for the purpose of retiring the United States notes and Treasury notes.

The banks already existing, if they desired to avail themselves of the provisions of law thus modified, could issue circulation, in addition to that already outstanding, amounting to $478,000,000, which would nearly or quite equal the currency proposed to be canceled. At any rate, I should confidently expect to see the existing national banks or others to be organized avail themselves of the proposed encouragements to issue circulation and promptly fill any vacuum and supply every currency need

It has always seemed to me that the provisions of law regarding the capital of national banks, which operate as a limitation to their location, fail to make proper compensation for the suppression of State banks, which came near to the people in all sections of the country and readily furnished them with banking accommodations and facilities. Any inconvenience or embarrassment arising from these restrictions on the location of national banks might well be remedied by better adapting the present system to the creation of banks in smaller communities or by permitting banks of large capital to establish branches in such localities as would serve the people, so regulated and restrained as to secure their safe and conservative control and management.

But there might not be the necessity for such an addition to the currency by new issues of bank circulation as at first glance is indicated. If we should be relieved from maintaining a gold reserve under conditions that constitute it the barometer of our solvency, and if our Treasury should no longer be the foolish purveyor of gold for nations abroad or for speculation and hoarding by our citizens at home, I should expect to see gold resume its natural and normal functions in the business affairs of the country and cease to be an object attracting the timid watch of our people and exciting their sensitive imaginations.

I do not overlook the fact that the cancellation of the Treasury notes issued under the silver-purchasing act of 1890 would leave the Treasury in the actual ownership of sufficient silver, including seigniorage, to coin nearly $178,000,000 in standard dollars. It is worthy of consideration whether this might not from time to time be converted into dollars or fractional coin and slowly put into circulation, as in the judgment of the Secretary of the Treasury the necessities of the country should require.

Whatever is attempted should be entered upon fully appreciating the fact that by careless, easy descent we have reached a dangerous depth, and that our ascent will not be accomplished without laborious toil and struggle. We shall be wise if we realize that we are financially ill and that our restoration to health may require heroic treatment and unpleasant remedies.

In the present stage of our difficulty it is not easy to understand how the amount of our revenue receipts directly affects it. The important question is not the quantity of money received in revenue payments, but the kind of money we maintain and our ability to continue in sound financial condition. We are considering the Government's holdings of gold as related to the soundness of our money and as affecting our national credit and monetary strength.

If our gold reserve had never been impaired; if no bonds had ever been issued to replenish it; if there had been no fear and timidity concerning our ability to continue gold payments; if any part of our revenues were now paid in gold, and if we could look to our gold receipts as a means of maintaining a safe reserve, the amount of our revenues would be an influential factor in the problem. But, unfortunately, all the circumstances that might lend weight to this consideration are entirely lacking.

In our present predicament no gold is received by the Government in payment of revenue charges, nor would there be if the revenues were increased. The receipts of the Treasury, when not in silver certificates, consist of United States notes and Treasury notes issued for silver purchases. These forms of money are only useful to the Government in paying its current ordinary expenses, and its quantity in Government possession does not in the least contribute toward giving us that kind of safe financial standing or condition which is built on gold alone.

If it is said that these notes if held by the Government can be used to obtain gold for our reserve, the answer is easy. The people draw gold from the Treasury on demand upon United States notes and Treasury notes, but the proposition that the Treasury can on demand draw gold from the people upon them would be regarded in these days with wonder and amusement; and even if this could be done there is nothing to prevent those thus parting with their gold from regaining it the next day or the next hour by the presentation of the notes they received in exchange for it.

The Secretary of the Treasury might use such notes taken from a surplus revenue to buy gold in the market. Of course he could not do this without paying a premium. Private holders of gold, unlike the Government, having no parity to maintain, would not be restrained from making the best bargain possible when they furnished gold to the Treasury; but the moment the Secretary of the Treasury bought gold on any terms above par he would establish a general and universal premium upon it, thus breaking down the parity between gold and silver, which the Government is pledged to maintain, and opening the way to new and serious complications. In the meantime the premium would not remain stationary, and the absurd spectacle might be presented of a dealer selling gold to the Government and with United States notes or Treasury notes in his hand immediately clamoring for its return and a resale at a higher premium.

It may be claimed that a large revenue and redundant receipts might favorably affect the situation under discussion by affording an opportunity of retaining these notes in the Treasury when received, and thus preventing their presentation for gold. Such retention to be useful ought to be at least measurably permanent; and this is precisely what is prohibited, so far as United States notes are concerned, by the law of 1878, forbidding their further retirement. That statute in so many words provides that these notes when received into the Treasury and belonging to the United States shall be "paid out again and kept in circulation."

It will, moreover, be readily seen that the Government could not refuse to pay out United States notes and Treasury notes in current transactions when demanded, and insist on paying out silver alone, and still maintain the parity between that metal and the currency representing gold. Besides, the accumulation in the Treasury of currency of any kind exacted from the people through taxation is justly regarded as an evil, and it can not proceed far without vigorous protest against an unjustifiable retention of money from the business of the country and a denunciation of a scheme of taxation which proves itself to be unjust when it takes from the earnings and income of the citizen money so much in excess of the needs of Government support that large sums can be gathered and kept in the Treasury. Such a condition has heretofore in times of surplus revenue led the Government to restore currency to the people by the purchase of its unmatured bonds at a large premium and by a large increase of its deposits in national banks, and we easily remember that the abuse of Treasury accumulation has furnished a most persuasive argument in favor of legislation radically reducing our tariff taxation.

Perhaps it is supposed that sufficient revenue receipts would in a sentimental way improve the situation by inspiring confidence in our solvency and allaying the fear of pecuniary exhaustion. And yet through all our struggles to maintain our gold reserve there never has been any apprehension as to our ready ability to pay our way with such money as we had, and the question whether or not our current receipts met our current expenses has not entered into the estimate of our solvency. Of course the general state of our funds, exclusive of gold, was entirely immaterial to the foreign creditor and investor. His debt could only be paid in gold, and his only concern was our ability to keep on hand that kind of money.

On July 1, 1892, more than a year and a half before the first bonds were issued to replenish the gold reserve, there was a net balance in the Treasury, exclusive of such reserve, of less than $13,000,000, but the gold reserve amounted to more than $114,000,000, which was the quieting feature of the situation. It was when the stock of gold began rapidly to fall that fright supervened and our securities held abroad were returned for sale and debts owed abroad were pressed for payment. In the meantime extensive shipments of gold and other unfavorable indications caused restlessness and fright among our people at home. Thereupon the general state of our funds, exclusive of gold, became also immaterial to them, and they too drew gold from the Treasury for hoarding against all contingencies. This is plainly shown by the large increase in the proportion of gold withdrawn which was retained by our own people as time and threatening incidents progressed. During the fiscal year ending June 30, 1894, nearly $85,000,000 in gold was withdrawn from the Treasury and about $77,000,000 was sent abroad, while during the fiscal year ending June 30, 1895, over $117,000,000 was drawn out, of which only about $66,000,000 was shipped, leaving the large balance of such withdrawals to be accounted for by domestic hoarding.

Inasmuch as the withdrawal of our gold has resulted largely from fright, there is nothing apparent that will prevent its continuance or recurreuce, with its natural consequences, except such a change in our financial methods as will reassure the frightened and make the desire for gold less intense. It is not clear how an increase in revenue, unless it be in gold, can satisfy those whose only anxiety is to gain gold from the Government's store.

It can not, therefore, be safe to rely upon increased revenues as a cure for our present troubles.

It is possible that the suggestion of increased revenue as a remedy foɪ the difficulties we are considering may have originated in an intimation or distinct allegation that the bonds which have been issued ostensibly to replenish our gold reserve were really issued to supply insufficient revenue. Nothing can be further from the truth. Bonds were issued to obtain gold for the maintenance of our national credit. As has been shown, the gold thus obtained has been drawn again from the Treasury upon United States notes and Treasury notes. This operation would have been promptly prevented if possible; but these notes having thus been passed to the Treasury, they became the money of the Government, like any other ordinary Government funds, and there was nothing to do but to use them in paying Government expenses when needed.

At no time when bonds have been issued has there been any consideration of the question of paying the expenses of Government with their proceeds. There was no necessity to consider that question. At the time of each bond issue we had a safe surplus in the Treasury for ordinary operations, exclusive of the gold in our reserve. In February, 1894, when the first issue of bonds was made, such surplus amounted to over $18,000,000; in November, when the second issue was made, it amounted to more than $42,000,000, and in February, 1895, when bonds for the third time were issued, such surplus amounted to more than $100,000,000. It now amounts to $98,072,420.30.

Besides all this, the Secretary of the Treasury had no authority whatever to issue bonds to increase the ordinary revenues or pay current expenses.

I can not but think there has been some confusion of ideas regarding the effects of the issue of bonds and the results of the withdrawal of gold. It was the latter process, and not the former, that, by substituting in the Treasury United States notes and Treasury notes for gold, increased by their amount the money which was in the first instance subject to ordinary Government expenditure.

Although the law compelling an increased purchase of silver by the Government was passed on the 14th day of July, 1890, withdrawals of gold from the Treasury upon the notes given in payment on such purchases did not begin until October, 1891. Immediately following that date the withdrawals upon both these notes and United States notes increased very largely, and have continued to such an extent that since the passage of that law there has been more than thirteen times as much gold taken out of the Treasury upon United States notes and Treasury notes issued for silver purchases as was thus withdrawn during the eleven and a half years immediately prior thereto and after the 1st day of January, 1879, when specie payments were resumed.

It is neither unfair nor unjust to charge a large share of our present financial perplexities and dangers to the operation of the laws of 1878 and 1890 compelling the purchase of silver by the Government, which not only furnished a new Treasury obligation upon which its gold could be withdrawn, but so increased the fear of an overwhelming flood of silver and a forced descent to silver payments that even the repeal of these laws did not entirely cure the evils of their existence.

While I have endeavored to make a plain statement of the disordered condition of our currency and the present dangers menacing our prosperity and to suggest a way which leads to a safer financial system, I have constantly had in mind the fact that many of my countrymen, whose sincerity I do not doubt, insist that the cure for the ills now threatening us may be found in the single and simple remedy of the free coinage of silver. They contend that our mints shall be at once thrown open to the free, unlimited, and independent coinage of both gold and silver dollars of full legal-tender quality, regardless of the action of any other government and in full view of the fact that the ratio between the metals which they suggest calls for 100 cents' worth of gold in the gold dollar at the present standard and only 50 cents in intrinsic worth of silver in the silver dollar.

Were there infinitely stronger reasons than can be adduced for hoping that such action would secure for us a bimetallic currency moving on lines of parity, an experiment so novel and hazardous as that proposed might well stagger those who believe that stability is an imperative condition of sound money.

No government, no human contrivance or act of legislation, has ever been able to hold the two metals together in free coinage at a ratio appreciably different from that which is established in the markets of the world.

Those who believe that our independent free coinage of silver at an artificial ratio with gold of 16 to 1 would restore the parity between the metals, and consequently between the coins, oppose an unsupported and improbable theory to the general belief and practice of other nations and to the teaching of the wisest statesmen and economists of the world, both in the past and present, and, what is far more conclusive, they run counter to our own actual experiences.

Twice in our earlier history our lawmakers, in attempting to establish a bimetallic currency, undertook free coinage upon a ratio which accidentally varied from the actual relative values of the two metals not more than 3 per cent. In both cases, notwithstanding greater difficulties and cost of transportation than now exist, the coins whose intrinsic worth was undervalued in the ratio gradually and surely disappeared from our circulation and went to other countries where their real value was better recognized.

Acts of Congress were impotent to create equality where natural causes decreed even a slight inequality.

Twice in our recent history we have signally failed to raise by legislation the value of silver. Under an act of Congress passed in 1878 the Government was required for more than twelve years to expend annually at least $24,000,000 in the purchase of silver bullion for coinage. The act of July 14, 1890, in a still bolder effort, increased the amount of silver the Government was compelled to purchase and forced it to become the buyer annually of 54,000,000 ounces, or practically the entire product of our mines. Under both laws silver rapidly and steadily declined in value. The prophecy and the expressed hope and expectation of those in the Congress who led in the passage of the last-mentioned act that it would reestablish and maintain the former parity between the two metals are still fresh in our memory.

In the light of these experiences, which accord with the experiences of other nations, there is certainly no secure ground for the belief that an act of Congress could now bridge an inequality of 50 per cent between gold and silver at our present ratio, nor is there the least possibility that our country, which has less than one-seventh of the silver money in the world, could by its action alone raise not only our own but all silver to its lost ratio with gold. Our attempt to accomplish this by the free coinage of silver at a ratio differing widely from actual relative values would be the signal for the complete departure of gold from our circulation, the immediate and large contraction of our circulating medium, and a shrinkage in the real value and monetary efficiency of all other forms of currency as they settled to the level of silver monometallism. Everyone who receives a fixed salary and every worker for wages would find the dollar in his hand ruthlessly scaled down to the point of bitter disappointment, if not to pinching privation.

A change in our standard to silver monometallism would also bring on a collapse of the entire system of credit, which, when based on a standard which is recognized and adopted by the world of business, is many times more potent and useful than the entire volume of currency and is safely capable of almost indefinite expansion to meet the growth of trade and enterprise. In a self-invited struggle through darkness and uncertainty our humiliation would be increased by the consciousness that we had parted company with all the enlightened and progressive nations of the world and were desperately and hopelessly striving to meet the stress of modern commerce and competition with a debased and unsuitable currency and in association with the few weak and laggard nations which have silver alone as their standard of value.

All history warns us against rash experiments which threaten violent changes in our monetary standard and the degradation of our currency. The past is full of lessons teaching not only the economic dangers but the national immorality that follow in the train of such experiments. I will not believe that the American people can be persuaded after sober deliberation to jeopardize their nation's prestige and proud standing by encouraging financial nostrums, nor that they will yield to the false allurements of cheap money when they realize that it must result in the weakening of that financial integrity and rectitude which thus far in our history has been so devotedly cherished as one of the traits of true Americanism.

Our country's indebtedness, whether owing by the Government or existing between individuals, has been contracted with reference to our present standard. To decree by act of Congress that these debts shall be payable in less valuable dollars than those within the contemplation and intention of the parties when contracted would operate to transfer by the fiat of law and without compensation an amount of property and a volume of rights and interests almost incalculable.

Those who advocate a blind and headlong plunge to free coinage in the name of bimetallism, and professing the belief, contrary to all experience, that we could thus establish a double standard and a concurrent circulation of both metals in our coinage, are certainly reckoning from a cloudy standpoint. Our present standard of value is the standard of the civilized world and permits the only bimetallism now possible, or at least that is within the independent reach of any single nation, however powerful that nation may be. While the value of gold as a standard is steadied by almost universal commercial and business use, it does not despise silver nor seek its banishment. Wherever this standard is maintained there is at its side in free and unquestioned circulation a volume of silver currency sometimes equaling and sometimes even exceeding it in amount both maintained at a parity notwithstanding a depreciation or fluctuation in the intrinsic value of silver.

There is a vast difference between a standard of value and a currency for monetary use. The standard must necessarily be fixed and certain. The currency may be in divers forms and of various kinds. No silver-standard country has a gold currency in circulation, but an enlightened and wise system of finance secures the benefits of both gold and silver as currency and circulating medium by keeping the standard stable and all other currency at par with it. Such a system and such a standard also give free scope for the use and expansion of safe and conservative credit, so indispensable to broad and growing commercial transactions and so well substituted for the actual use of money. If a fixed and stable standard is maintained, such as the magnitude and safety of our commercial transactions and business require, the use of money itself is conveniently minimized.

Every dollar of fixed and stable value has through the agency of confident credit an astonishing capacity of multiplying itself in financial work. Every unstable and fluctuating dollar fails as a basis of credit, and in its use begets gambling speculation and undermines the foundations of honest enterprise.

I have ventured to express myself on this subject with earnestness and plainness of speech because I can not rid myself of the belief that there lurk in the proposition for the free coinage of silver, so strongly approved and so enthusiastically advocated by a multitude of my countrymen, a serious menace to our prosperity and an insidious temptation of our people to wander from the allegiance they owe to public and private integrity. It is because I do not distrust the good faith and sincerity of those who press this scheme that I have imperfectly but with zeal submitted my thoughts upon this momentous subject. I can not refrain from begging them to reexamine their views and beliefs in the light of patriotic reason and familiar experience and to weigh again and again the consequences of such legislation as their efforts have invited. Even the continued agitation of the subject adds greatly to the difficulties of a dangerous financial situation already forced upon us.

In conclusion I especially entreat the people's representatives in the Congress, who are charged with the responsibility of inaugurating measures for the safety and prosperity of our common country, to promptly and effectively consider the ills of our critical financial plight. I have suggested a remedy which my judgment approves. I desire, however, to assure the Congress that I am prepared to cooperate with them in perfecting any other measure promising thorough and practical relief, and that I will gladly labor with them in every patriotic endeavor to further the interests and guard the welfare of our countrymen, whom in our respective places of duty we have undertaken to serve.

GROVER CLEVELAND.

SPECIAL MESSAGES.

EXECUTIVE MANSION, *December 17, 1895*

To the Congress:

In my annual message addressed to the Congress on the 3d instant I called attention to the pending boundary controversy between Great Britain and the Republic of Venezuela and recited the substance of a representation made by this Government to Her Britannic Majesty's Government suggesting reasons why such dispute should be submitted to arbitration for settlement and inquiring whether it would be so submitted.*

The answer of the British Government, which was then awaited, has since been received, and, together with the dispatch to which it is a reply, is hereto appended.

*See p. 6064.

Such reply is embodied in two communications addressed by the British prime minister to Sir Julian Pauncefote, the British ambassador at this capital. It will be seen that one of these communications is devoted exclusively to observations upon the Monroe doctrine, and claims that in the present instance a new and strange extension and development of this doctrine is insisted on by the United States; that the reasons justifying an appeal to the doctrine enunciated by President Monroe are generally inapplicable "to the state of things in which we live at the present day," and especially inapplicable to a controversy involving the boundary line between Great Britain and Venezuela.

Without attempting extended argument in reply to these positions, it may not be amiss to suggest that the doctrine upon which we stand is strong and sound, because its enforcement is important to our peace and safety as a nation and is essential to the integrity of our free institutions and the tranquil maintenance of our distinctive form of government. It was intended to apply to every stage of our national life and can not become obsolete while our Republic endures. If the balance of power is justly a cause for jealous anxiety among the Governments of the Old World and a subject for our absolute noninterference, none the less is an observance of the Monroe doctrine of vital concern to our people and their Government.

Assuming, therefore, that we may properly insist upon this doctrine without regard to "the state of things in which we live" or any changed conditions here or elsewhere, it is not apparent why its application may not be invoked in the present controversy.

If a European power by an extension of its boundaries takes possession of the territory of one of our neighboring Republics against its will and in derogation of its rights, it is difficult to see why to that extent such European power does not thereby attempt to extend its system of government to that portion of this continent which is thus taken. This is the precise action which President Monroe declared to be "dangerous to our peace and safety," and it can make no difference whether the European system is extended by an advance of frontier or otherwise.

It is also suggested in the British reply that we should not seek to apply the Monroe doctrine to the pending dispute because it does not embody any principle of international law which "is founded on the general consent of nations," and that "no statesman, however eminent, and no nation, however powerful, are competent to insert into the code of international law a novel principle which was never recognized before and which has not since been accepted by the government of any other country."

Practically the principle for which we contend has peculiar, if not exclusive, relation to the United States. It may not have been admitted in so many words to the code of international law, but since in international councils every nation is entitled to the rights belonging to it, if the enforcement of the Monroe doctrine is something we may justly claim it has its place in the code of international law as certainly and as securely as if it were specifically mentioned; and when the United States is a suitor before the high tribunal that administers international law the question to be determined is whether or not we present claims which the justice of that code of law can find to be right and valid.

The Monroe doctrine finds its recognition in those principles of international law which are based upon the theory that every nation shall have its rights protected and its just claims enforced.

Of course this Government is entirely confident that under the sanction of this doctrine we have clear rights and undoubted claims. Nor is this ignored in the British reply. The prime minister, while not admitting that the Monroe doctrine is applicable to present conditions, states:

In declaring that the United States would resist any such enterprise if it was contemplated, President Monroe adopted a policy which received the entire sympathy of the English Government of that date.

He further declares:

Though the language of President Monroe is directed to the attainment of objects which most Englishmen would agree to be salutary, it is impossible to admit that they have been inscribed by any adequate authority in the code of international law.

Again he says:

They [Her Majesty's Government] fully concur with the view which President Monroe apparently entertained, that any disturbance of the existing territorial distribution in that hemisphere by any fresh acquisitions on the part of any European State would be a highly inexpedient change.

In the belief that the doctrine for which we contend was clear and definite, that it was founded upon substantial considerations and involved our safety and welfare, that it was fully applicable to our present conditions and to the state of the world's progress, and that it was directly related to the pending controversy, and without any conviction as to the final merits of the dispute, but anxious to learn in a satisfactory and conclusive manner whether Great Britain sought under a claim of boundary to extend her possessions on this continent without right, or whether she merely sought possession of territory fairly included within her lines of ownership, this Government proposed to the Government of Great Britain a resort to arbitration as the proper means of settling the question, to the end that a vexatious boundary dispute between the two contestants might be determined and our exact standing and relation in respect to the controversy might be made clear.

It will be seen from the correspondence herewith submitted that this proposition has been declined by the British Government upon grounds which in the circumstances seem to me to be far from satisfactory. It is deeply disappointing that such an appeal, actuated by the most friendly feelings toward both nations directly concerned, addressed to the sense of justice and to the magnanimity of one of the great powers of the world, and touching its relations to one comparatively weak and small, should have produced no better results.

The course to be pursued by this Government in view of the present condition does not appear to admit of serious doubt. Having labored faithfully for many years to induce Great Britain to submit this dispute to impartial arbitration, and having been now finally apprised of her refusal to do so, nothing remains but to accept the situation, to recognize its plain requirements, and deal with it accordingly. Great Britain's present proposition has never thus far been regarded as admissible by Venezuela, though any adjustment of the boundary which that country may deem for her advantage and may enter into of her own free will can not of course be objected to by the United States.

Assuming, however, that the attitude of Venezuela will remain unchanged, the dispute has reached such a stage as to make it now incumbent upon the United States to take measures to determine with sufficient certainty for its justification what is the true divisional line between the Republic of Venezuela and British Guiana. The inquiry to that end should of course be conducted carefully and judicially, and due weight should be given to all available evidence, records, and facts in support of the claims of both parties.

In order that such an examination should be prosecuted in a thorough and satisfactory manner, I suggest that the Congress make an adequate appropriation for the expenses of a commission, to be appointed by the Executive, who shall make the necessary investigation and report upon the matter with the least possible delay. When such report is made and accepted it will, in my opinion, be the duty of the United States to resist by every means in its power, as a willful aggression upon its rights and interests, the appropriation by Great Britain of any lands or the exercise of governmental jurisdiction over any territory which after investigation we have determined of right belongs to Venezuela.

In making these recommendations I am fully alive to the responsibility incurred and keenly realize all the consequences that may follow.

I am, nevertheless, firm in my conviction that while it is a grievous thing to contemplate the two great English-speaking peoples of the world as being otherwise than friendly competitors in the onward march of civilization and strenuous and worthy rivals in all the arts of peace, there is no calamity which a great nation can invite which equals that which follows a supine submission to wrong and injustice and the consequent loss of national self-respect and honor, beneath which are shielded and defended a people's safety and greatness.

GROVER CLEVELAND.

EXECUTIVE MANSION,
Washington, December 19, 1895.

To the Senate of the United States:

In response to the resolution of the Senate of the 4th instant, requesting the President, "if in his judgment not incompatible with the public

CLOSE VIEW OF THE RUINED OQUENDO

CLOSE VIEW OF THE RUINED *OQUENDO*

The reader will, no doubt, be interested to compare the damage wrought by American gunners on the *Oquendo,* of Cervera's fleet, with the effect of Japanese fire on the Russian warships in the illustration in Volume IX.

The stories of both wars are told in the encyclopedic index in the articles "Spanish-American War" and "Russo-Japanese War."

interest, to communicate to the Senate all information which has been received by him or by the State Department in regard to injuries inflicted upon the persons or property of American citizens in Turkey and in regard to the condition of affairs there in reference to the oppression or cruelties practiced upon the Armenian subjects of the Turkish Government; also to inform the Senate whether all the American consuls in the Turkish Empire are at their posts of duty, and, if not, to state any circumstances which have interfered with the performance of the duties of such consuls," I transmit herewith a report from the Secretary of State.

GROVER CLEVELAND.

To the Congress: EXECUTIVE MANSION, *December 20, 1895.*

In my last annual message the evils of our present financial system were plainly pointed out and the causes and means of the depletion of Government gold were explained. It was therein stated that after all the efforts that had been made by the executive branch of the Government to protect our gold reserve by the issuance of bonds amounting to more than $162,000,000, such reserve then amounted to but little more than $79,000,000; that about $16,000,000 had been withdrawn from such reserve during the month next previous to the date of that message, and that quite large withdrawals for shipment in the immediate future were predicted.

The contingency then feared has reached us, and the withdrawals of gold since the communication referred to and others that appear inevitable threaten such a depletion in our Government gold reserve as brings us face to face to the necessity of further action for its protection. This condition is intensified by the prevalence in certain quarters of sudden and unusual apprehension and timidity in business circles.

We are in the midst of another season of perplexity caused by our dangerous and fatuous financial operations. These may be expected to recur with certainty as long as there is no amendment in our financial system. If in this particular instance our predicament is at all influenced by a recent insistence upon the position we should occupy in our relation to certain questions concerning our foreign policy, this furnishes a signal and impressive warning that even the patriotic sentiment of our people is not an adequate substitute for a sound financial policy.

Of course there can be no doubt in any thoughtful mind as to the complete solvency of our nation, nor can there be any just apprehension that the American people will be satisfied with less than an honest payment of our public obligations in the recognized money of the world. We should not overlook the fact, however, that aroused fear is unreasoning and must be taken into account in all efforts to avert possible loss and the sacrifice of our people's interests.

The real and sensible cure for our recurring troubles can only be effected by a complete change in our financial scheme. Pending that the executive branch of the Government will not relax its efforts nor abandon its determination to use every means within its reach to maintain before the world American credit, nor will there be any hesitation in exhibiting its confidence in the resources of our country and the constant patriotism of our people.

In view, however, of the peculiar situation now confronting us, I have ventured to herein express the earnest hope that the Congress, in default of the inauguration of a better system of finance, will not take a recess from its labors before it has by legislative enactment or declaration done something not only to remind those apprehensive among our own people that the resources of their Government and a scrupulous regard for honest dealing afford a sure guaranty of unquestioned safety and soundness, but to reassure the world that with these factors and the patriotism of our citizens the ability and determination of our nation to meet in any circumstances every obligation it incurs do not admit of question.

I ask at the hands of the Congress such prompt aid as it alone has the power to give to prevent in a time of fear and apprehension any sacrifice of the people's interests and the public funds or the impairment of our public credit in an effort by Executive action to relieve the dangers of the present emergency.   GROVER CLEVELAND.

EXECUTIVE MANSION,
Washington, December 30, 1895.

To the Senate of the United States:

In response to the resolution of the Senate of the 21st instant, relative to the refusal of the Turkish Government to grant exequaturs to the vice-consuls of the United States at Erzerum and Harpoot, I transmit herewith a report from the Secretary of State.

GROVER CLEVELAND.

EXECUTIVE MANSION,
Washington, January 10, 1896.

To the Senate of the United States:

I transmit herewith, in response to the Senate resolution of December 18, 1895, addressed to the Secretary of State, a report of that officer, with the accompanying correspondence, in relation to the arrest and imprisonment of Victor Hugo McCord at Arequipa, Peru, requested by said resolution.   GROVER CLEVELAND.

EXECUTIVE MANSION, *January 17, 1896.*

To the Congress:

I desire to invite attention to the necessity for prompt legislation in order to remove the limitation of the time within which suits may be brought by the Government to annul unlawful or unauthorized grants of public lands.

By the act of March 3, 1887 (24 U. S. Statutes at Large, p. 556), the Secretary of the Interior is directed to adjust each of the railroad land grants which may be unadjusted, and it is provided, if it shall appear upon the completion of such adjustment or sooner that the lands have been from any cause erroneously certified or patented by the United States to or for the use of a company claiming under any of said grants, it shall be the duty of the Secretary of the Interior to demand a reconveyance of the title to all lands so erroneously certified or patented, and on failure of the company to make such reconveyance within ninety days the Attorney-General is required to institute and prosecute in the proper courts necessary proceedings to restore title to said lands to the United States. The demands made under this act have been numerous, and in some cases have resulted in the reinvestment of title to the lands in the United States upon demand, but in most cases the demand has been refused and suits have been necessary.

The work of adjustment has been unavoidably slow. The said act makes provision for the reinstatement of entries erroneously canceled on account of railroad withdrawals, and, upon certain conditions, provides for the confirmation of titles derived by purchase from the companies of lands shown to be excepted from the grants. It contemplates a disposition of every tract, described by the granting act, situated within the primary or granted limits; an inspection of each tract certified or patented to the company within such limit, to determine whether such certification or patenting was proper; the listing of those tracts shown to be erroneously certified, and the determination for what tracts lost to the grant indemnity is to be allowed.

It is necessary in making such an adjustment that all questions of conflicting claims, either between settlers and the road or between two roads the grants for which conflict or overlap, be finally disposed of, so that a proper disposition of the land can be shown in the adjustment. While adjustments have proceeded with the utmost rapidity consistent with a due regard for the rights of the settlers, of the United States, and the railroad companies, and while to this end the force of adjusters has been largely augmented in the General Land Office, many of the grants yet remain unadjusted.

In some of the grants, notably the corporation grants, the lack of surveys up to the present time made the completion of the work impossible.

Decisions rendered by the Interior Department in numerous conflicts have been carried into the courts. The construction of the Interior Department has generally been sustained when final determination has been reached, but many of the cases are still pending in the courts, not yet having been decided. Some of these cases, while involving immediately the title to only one particular tract, will when decided furnish a rule of construction to control the disposition of the title to thousands of acres of other lands in the same situation. Until the courts pass upon these questions final adjustments can not be made.

By section 8 of the act of March 3, 1891 (26 U. S. Statutes at Large, p. 1099), it is expressly enacted that suits by the United States to vacate and annul any patent theretofore issued "shall only be brought within five years from the passage of this act." This period of five years will expire on the 3d of March, 1896. Of course no suit by the United States to secure the cancellation of a patent in this class of cases after that date would be effective. Indeed, it is now too late to initiate proceedings looking to any such suit, inasmuch as demand has to be first made on the company, and thereafter ninety days must be allowed for compliance or refusal, in accordance with the provisions of the act of March 3, 1887. Before the expiration of this period the statute would bar the right of recovery by the Government, and the benefits of anticipated favorable decisions of the courts would be lost so far as they might determine the character and disposition of grants similar to those directly involved in pending cases.

It will be readily seen that if this act of limitations is to remain on the statute books the portion of the adjustment act referred to would be rendered nugatory. Indeed, there would be but little use in continuing the adjustment of many of the land grants, inasmuch as ascertained rights of the United States or of settlers could not be enforced by law.

Legislation establishing limitations against the right of the Government to sue is an innovation not entirely consistent with the general history of the rights of the Government, for it has uniformly been held that time did not bar the sovereign power from the assertion of a right.

The early adjudications of the Land Department construed the grants with a degree of liberality toward the grantees which later decisions of the courts and of the Department have not sustained. It seems clear that the further progress of adjustments will develop facts and transactions in connection with these land grants which ought to be the subjects of legal examination and scrutiny before they are allowed to become final and conclusive. The Government should not be prevented from going into the courts to right wrongs perpetrated by its agents or any other parties, and by which much of the public domain may be diverted from the people at large to corporate uses.

In these circumstances it seems to me that the act of 1891 should be so amended as not to apply to suits brought to recover title to lands certified or patented on account of railroad or other grants; and I respectfully urge upon Congress speedy action to the end suggested, so that the adjustment of these grants may proceed without the interposition of a bar, through lapse of time, against the right of recovery by the Government in proper cases.

GROVER CLEVELAND.

EXECUTIVE MANSION,
Washington, January 20, 1896.

To the House of Representatives:

In response to the resolution of the House of Representatives of December 28, 1895, I transmit herewith a report from the Secretary of State and accompanying papers, relating to certain speeches made by Thomas F. Bayard, ambassador of the United States to Great Britain.

In response to that part of said resolution which requests information as to the action taken by the President concerning the speeches therein referred to, I reply that no action has been taken thereon by the President except such as is indicated in the report and correspondence herewith submitted.

GROVER CLEVELAND.

EXECUTIVE MANSION,
Washington, January 22, 1896.

To the House of Representatives:

I transmit herewith, in compliance with the resolution of the House of Representatives of December 28, 1895, a report from the Secretary of State, with copies of all the correspondence of record in the Department of State in relation to the schooner *Henry Crosby*, fired upon while at anchor at Azua, Santo Domingo, December 10, 1893.

GROVER CLEVELAND.

EXECUTIVE MANSION, *January 22, 1896.*

To the Senate of the United States:

In response to the resolution adopted by the Senate on December 16, 1895, respecting what action had been taken in regard to the payment of the appropriation for the bounty on sugar contained in the sundry civil bill approved March 2, 1895, I herewith transmit a communication received from the Secretary of the Treasury, which contains all the information I have upon the subject.

GROVER CLEVELAND.

EXECUTIVE MANSION,
Washington, January 23, 1896.

To the Senate:

I transmit herewith a report from the Secretary of State, in answer to a resolution of the Senate of the 16th instant, requesting information in regard to the treatment of naturalized citizens of the United States of Armenian origin, and their families, by the Turkish Government.

GROVER CLEVELAND.

EXECUTIVE MANSION,
Washington, January 27, 1896.

To the House of Representatives:

I transmit herewith a report from the Secretary of State, with copies of all correspondence of record relating to the failure of the scheme for the colonization of negroes in Mexico, necessitating their return to their home in Alabama.

I referred to this matter in my message to Congress at the beginning of the present session, and for the reasons then given* I again urge the propriety of making an appropriation to cover the cost of transportation furnished by the railroad companies.

GROVER CLEVELAND.

EXECUTIVE MANSION,
Washington, January 30, 1896.

To the House of Representatives:

I transmit herewith a communication from the Secretary of State, accompanying the reports of the consuls of the United States on trade and commerce. In view of the evident value of this compilation to our business interests, I indorse the recommendation of the Secretary that Congress authorize the printing of a special edition of 10,000 copies of the General Summary of the Commerce of the World for distribution by the Department of State, and of 2,500 copies of Commercial Relations (including this summary) to enable the Department to meet the increasing demand for commercial information.

GROVER CLEVELAND.

EXECUTIVE MANSION,
Washington, February 3, 1896.

To the Congress:

In my last annual message allusion was made to the lawless killing of certain Italian laborers in the State of Colorado,† and it was added that "the dependent families of some of the unfortunate victims invite by their deplorable condition gracious provision for their needs."

It now appears that in addition to three of these laborers who were riotously killed two others, who escaped death by flight, incurred pitiable disabilities through exposure and privation.

Without discussing the question of the liability of the United States for these results, either by reason of treaty obligations or under the general rules of international law, I venture to urge upon the Congress the propriety of making from the public Treasury prompt and reasonable pecuniary provision for those injured and for the families of those who were killed.

*See p. 6066.   †See p. 6065.

To aid in the consideration of the subject I append hereto a report of the Secretary of State, accompanied by certain correspondence which quite fully presents all the features of the several cases.

GROVER CLEVELAND.

To the House of Representatives:

Pursuant to the request made in a House resolution passed on the 30th day of January, 1896, I herewith transmit the report, with accompanying maps and exhibits, of the board of engineers under the provisions of chapter 189 of laws of 1895, for the purpose of ascertaining the feasibility, permanence, and cost of the construction and completion of the Nicaragua Canal by the route contemplated and provided for by the act which passed the Senate January 28, 1895, entitled "An act to amend an act entitled 'An act to incorporate the Maritime Canal Company of Nicaragua,' approved February 20, 1889."

FEBRUARY 7, 1896.

GROVER CLEVELAND.

EXECUTIVE MANSION,
Washington, February 10, 1896.

To the Senate of the United States:

I transmit herewith, in answer to the resolution of the Senate of December 18, 1895, a report by the Secretary of State, accompanied by copies of correspondence touching the establishment or attempted establishment of post routes by Great Britain or the Dominion of Canada over or upon United States territory in Alaska; also as to the occupation or attempted occupation by any means of any portion of that territory by the military or civil authorities of Great Britain or of Canada.

GROVER CLEVELAND.

EXECUTIVE MANSION,
Washington, February 10, 1896.

To the Senate:

I transmit herewith, for the consideration of the Senate with a view to its ratification, a convention signed at Washington the 8th instant between the Governments of the United States of America and of Her Britannic Majesty, providing for the settlement of the claims presented by Great Britain against the United States in virtue of the convention of February 29, 1892, and of the findings of the Paris Tribunal of Arbitration pursuant to article 8 of said convention, as well as of the additional claims specified in paragraph 5 of the preamble of the present convention.

GROVER CLEVELAND.

EXECUTIVE MANSION,
Washington, February 11, 1896.

To the Senate of the United States:

I transmit herewith, in answer to the resolution of the Senate of December 9, 1895, a report from the Secretary of State, accompanied by copies of correspondence and other papers in regard to the case of John L. Waller, a citizen of the United States, at present in the custody of the French Government.

It will be seen upon examination, as would of course be expected, that there is a slight conflict of evidence upon some of the features of Mr. Waller's case. Nevertheless, upon a fair and just consideration of all the facts and circumstances as presented, and especially in view of Mr. Waller's own letters, the conclusions set forth in the report of the Secretary of State do not appear to admit of any reasonable doubt nor to leave open to the Executive any other course of action than that adopted and acted upon as therein stated.

It is expected that Mr. Waller's release from imprisonment will be immediately forthcoming. GROVER CLEVELAND.

[A similar message was sent to the House of Representatives in answer to a resolution of that body of December 28, 1895.]

EXECUTIVE MANSION,
Washington, February 11, 1896.

To the House of Representatives:

In response to the resolution of the House of Representatives of December 28 last, as follows—

Resolved, That the Secretary of State be directed to communicate to the House of Representatives, if not inconsistent with the public interests, copies of all correspondence relating to affairs in Cuba since February last—

I transmit herewith a communication from the Secretary of State and such portions of the correspondence requested as I deem it not inconsistent with the public interests to communicate.

GROVER CLEVELAND.

EXECUTIVE MANSION,
Washington, February 14, 1896.

To the Senate:

In response to the resolution of the Senate of January 7, 1896, I transmit herewith a report from the Secretary of State, with an accompanying report of the special agent of the United States sent to the Fiji Islands to investigate the claims of B. H. Henry and other American citizens for compensation for certain lands alleged to have been owned by them and claimed to have been appropriated by the British Government.

GROVER CLEVELAND.

EXECUTIVE MANSION,
Washington, February 14, 1896.

To the Senate of the United States:

I transmit, with the accompanying papers, a report from the Secretary of State, answering the resolution of the Senate of January 16, 1896, addressed to him, calling for information concerning the claims against Peru of Thomas W. Sparrow, N. B. Noland, and others, members of the commission known as the Hydrographic Commission of the Amazon, employed by the Government of Peru, for compensation for their services on said commission.

GROVER CLEVELAND.

EXECUTIVE MANSION,
Washington, February 14, 1896.

To the Senate and House of Representatives:

I transmit herewith, for the information of Congress, a communication from the Secretary of State, covering the report of the Director of the Bureau of the American Republics for the year 1895.

GROVER CLEVELAND.

EXECUTIVE MANSION,
Washington, February 17, 1896.

To the House of Representatives:

I transmit herewith, in compliance with the resolution of the House of Representatives of February 1, 1896, a report from the Secretary of State, with copies of the correspondence of record in the Department of State in relation to the exclusion of life-insurance companies of the United States from transacting business in Germany.

GROVER CLEVELAND.

EXECUTIVE MANSION, *February 18, 1896.*

To the House of Representatives:

In compliance with a resolution of the House of Representatives, the Senate concurring, I return herewith Senate bill 879, entitled "An act to amend an act entitled 'An act to grant to the Gainesville, McAlester and St. Louis Railroad Company a right of way through the Indian Territory.'"

GROVER CLEVELAND.

EXECUTIVE MANSION,
Washington, February 28, 1896.

To the Senate:

I transmit herewith, in response to the resolutions of the Senate of the 18th and 19th instant, a report of the Secretary of State, in regard to the claim of A. H. Lazare against the Government of Hayti.

GROVER CLEVELAND.

EXECUTIVE MANSION,
Washington, March 9, 1896.

To the Senate:

I transmit herewith, in answer to the resolution of the Senate of the 24th ultimo, a report from the Secretary of State, in relation to the claim of the legal representatives of Lieutenant George C. Foulke against the Government of the United States.   GROVER CLEVELAND.

EXECUTIVE MANSION, *March 9, 1896.*

To the Senate:

I transmit herewith, in response to the Senate's resolution of February 6, 1896, addressed to the Secretary of State, copies, in translation, of the decrees or orders of the Governments of Germany, France, Belgium, and Denmark placing restrictions upon the importation of certain American products.   GROVER CLEVELAND.

EXECUTIVE MANSION,
Washington, March 13, 1896.

To the Senate:

I transmit herewith, in response to a resolution of the Senate of March 2, a report from the Secretary of State, accompanied by copies of correspondence touching the arrest in Havana of Marcus E. Rodriguez, Luis Someillau y Azpeitia, and Luis Someillau y Vidal, citizens of the United States.   GROVER CLEVELAND.

EXECUTIVE MANSION,
Washington, March 13, 1896.

To the House of Representatives:

In response to the resolution of the House of Representatives of February 13, 1896, I transmit a report from the Secretary of State and accompanying papers, relating to the claim of Bernard Campbell against the Government of Hayti.   GROVER CLEVELAND.

EXECUTIVE MANSION, *April 14, 1896*

To the Senate of the United States:

In compliance with a resolution of the Senate, the House of Representatives concurring, I return herewith the enrolled joint resolution (S. R. 116) authorizing the Public Printer to print the Annual Report of the United States Coast and Geodetic Survey in quarto form and to bind it in one volume.   GROVER CLEVELAND.

EXECUTIVE MANSION,
Washington, April 15, 1896.

To the Senate of the United States:

In response to the resolution of March 24, 1896, requesting that the Senate be furnished with the correspondence of the Department of State between November 5, 1875, and the date of the pacification of Cuba in 1878 relating to the subject of mediation or intervention by the United States in the affairs of that island, I transmit a report from the Secretary of State, forwarding such papers as seem to be called for by the resolution in question.

GROVER CLEVELAND.

EXECUTIVE MANSION,
Washington, April 30, 1896.

To the House of Representatives:

I transmit herewith, in response to the resolution of the House of Representatives of the 9th instant, addressed to the Secretary of State, a report of that officer, accompanied by copies of the correspondence in regard to the imprisonment of Mrs. Florence E. Maybrick.

GROVER CLEVELAND.

EXECUTIVE MANSION,
Washington, May 16, 1896.

To the Senate:

I transmit herewith, in response to the resolution of the Senate dated the 9th instant and addressed to the Secretary of State, a report of that officer, accompanied by copies of printed documents containing the information desired respecting the historical archives deposited in the Department of State.

GROVER CLEVELAND.

EXECUTIVE MANSION,
Washington, May 23, 1896.

To the Senate of the United States:

I transmit herewith, in response to a resolution of the Senate of the 16th instant, a report of the Secretary of State, to which are attached copies in English and Spanish of the original text of a protocol executed January 12, 1877, between the minister plenipotentiary of the United States of America to the Court of Spain and the minister of state of His Majesty the King of Spain.

It being, in my judgment, incompatible with the public service, I am constrained to refrain from communicating to the Senate at this time copies of the correspondence described in the third paragraph of said resolution.

GROVER CLEVELAND.

EXECUTIVE MANSION, *May 28, 1896.*

To the House of Representatives:

In compliance with a resolution of the House of Representatives of the 27th instant, the Senate concurring, I return herewith the bill (H. R. 5731) entitled "An act to regulate the practice of medicine and surgery, to license physicians and surgeons, and to punish persons violating the provisions thereof in the District of Columbia."

GROVER CLEVELAND.

EXECUTIVE MANSION, *June 3, 1896.*

To the House of Representatives:

In compliance with a resolution of the House of Representatives of the 2d instant, the Senate concurring, I return herewith the bill (H. R. 3279) entitled "An act to authorize the reassessment of water-main taxes or assessments in the District of Columbia, and for other purposes."

GROVER CLEVELAND.

To the Senate: EXECUTIVE MANSION, *June 8, 1896.*

I transmit herewith a report of the Secretary of State, in answer to the resolution of the Senate of May 9, 1896, directing that "the Secretary of State, the Secretary of the Treasury, the Secretary of War, the Secretary of the Navy, the Secretary of the Interior, the Secretary of Agriculture, the Postmaster-General, and the Attorney-General cause a careful and thorough inquiry to be made regarding the number of aliens employed in their respective Departments, and to communicate the result of said inquiry to the Senate at the earliest practicable day."

GROVER CLEVELAND.

VETO MESSAGES.

EXECUTIVE MANSION, *February 28, 1896.*

To the House of Representatives:

I herewith return without my approval House bill No. 2769, entitled "An act to authorize the leasing of lands for educational purposes in Arizona."

This bill provides for the leasing of all the public lands reserved to the Territory of Arizona for the benefit of its universities and schools, "under such laws and regulations as may be hereafter prescribed by the legislature of said Territory."

If the proposed legislation granted no further authority than this, it would, in terms at least, recognize the safety and propriety of leaving the desirability of leasing these lands and the limitations and safeguards egulating such leasing to be determined by the local legislature chosen by the people to make their laws and protect their interests.

Instead of stopping here, however, the bill further provides that until such legislative action the governor, the secretary of the Territory, and the superintendent of public instruction shall constitute a board for the leasing of said lands under the rules and regulations heretofore prescribed by the Secretary of the Interior. It is specifically declared that it shall not be necessary to submit said leases to the Secretary of the Interior for approval, and that no leases shall be made for a longer term than five years nor for a term extending beyond the date of the admission of the Territory to statehood.

Under these provisions the lands reserved for university and school purposes, whose value largely depends upon their standing timber, and in which every citizen of the Territory has a deep interest, may be leased and denuded of their timber by officers none of whom have been chosen by the people, and without the sanction of any law or regulation made by their representatives in the local legislature. Even the measure of protection which would be afforded the citizens of the Territory by a submission to the Secretary of the Interior of the leases proposed, and thus giving him an opportunity to ascertain whether or not they comply with his regulations, is especially withheld.

It was hardly necessary to provide in this bill that these lands might be leased "under such laws and regulations as may be hereafter prescribed by the legislature of said Territory" if the action of the legislature was to be forestalled and rendered nugatory by the immediate and unrestrained action of the officers constituted "a board for the leasing of said lands" pending such legislative consideration. These are inconsistencies which are not satisfactorily accounted for by the suggestion that the time that would elapse before the legislature could consider the subject would be important.

The protests I have received from numerous and influential citizens of the Territory indicate considerable opposition to this bill among those interested in the preservation and proper management' of these school lands.

GROVER CLEVELAND.

To the Senate: EXECUTIVE MANSION, *April 21, 1896.*

I herewith return without my approval Senate bill No. 894, entitled "An act granting a pension to Nancy G. Allabach."

This bill provides for the payment of a pension of $30 a month to the beneficiary named as the widow of Peter H. Allabach.

This soldier served for nine months in the Army during the War of the Rebellion, having also served in the war with Mexico.

He was mustered out of his last service on the 23d day of May, 1863, and died on the 11th of February, 1892.

During his life he made no application for pension on account of disabilities. It is not now claimed that he was in the least disabled as an incident of his military service, nor is it alleged that his death, which occurred nearly twenty-nine years after his discharge from the Army, was in any degree related to such service.

His widow was pensioned after his death under the statute allowing pensions to widows of soldiers of the Mexican War without reference to the cause of the death of their husbands. Her case is also, indirectly, one of those provided for by the general act passed in 1890, commonly called the dependent-pension law.

It is proposed, however, by the special act under consideration to give this widow a pension of $30 a month without the least suggestion of the death or disability of her husband having been caused by his military service, and solely, as far as is discoverable, upon the ground that she is poor and needs the money.

This condition is precisely covered by existing general laws; and if a precedent is to be established by the special legislation proposed, I do not see how the same relief as is contained in this bill can be denied to the many thousand widows who in a similar situation are now on the pension rolls under general laws.

GROVER CLEVELAND.

EXECUTIVE MANSION, *April 21, 1896.*

To the Senate:

I return herewith without my approval Senate bill No. 249, entitled "An act granting a pension to Charles E. Jones."

The beneficiary named in this bill was a photographer who accompanied one of the regiments of the Union Army in the War of the Rebellion. He was injured, apparently not very seriously, while taking photographs and when no battle was in actual progress. He was not enlisted, and was in no manner in the military service of the United States.

Aside from the question as to whether his present sad condition is attributable to the injury mentioned, it seems to me the extension of pension relief to such cases would open the door to legislation hard to justify and impossible to restrain from abuse.

GROVER CLEVELAND.

EXECUTIVE MANSION, *April 25, 1896.*

To the House of Representatives:

I herewith return without my approval House bill No. 1094, entitled "An act granting a pension to Francis E. Hoover."

It is proposed by this bill to grant a pension of $50 a month to the beneficiary named, who served as a private for about one year and nine months in the Union Army during the War of the Rebellion.

I do not understand it is claimed in any quarter that the present helpless condition of this soldier is at all attributable to his army service.

He himself never applied for a pension until after the passage of the law of 1890, providing for a pension for those who had served in the Army and are unable to maintain themselves by manual labor on account of disability not chargeable to army service. The committee of the House of Representatives in reporting this bill declare: ''The testimony does not show the disease of the soldier to be of service origin.''

The beneficiary is now receiving the largest pension permitted under the law of 1890.

His condition may well excite our sympathy, but to grant him a pension of $50 a month without the least suggestion that his pitiable disability is related to his army service, and in view of the fact that he is now receiving the highest pension allowed by a general law enacted to expressly meet such cases, it seems to me would result in an unfair discrimination as against many thousand worthy soldiers similarly situated, and would invite applications which, while difficult to refuse in the face of such a precedent, must certainly lead to the breaking down of all the limitations and restrictions provided by our laws regulating pensions.

The value of pension legislation depends as much upon fairness and justice in its administration as it does upon its liberality and generosity.

GROVER CLEVELAND.

EXECUTIVE MANSION, *May 19, 1896.*

To the House of Representatives:

I return herewith without approval House bill No. 1139, entitled ''An act granting a pension to Caroline D. Mowatt.''

The beneficiary mentioned in this bill was married in 1858 to Alfred B. Soule, who served as major of a Maine regiment of volunteers in the War of the Rebellion from September 10, 1862, to July 15, 1863, when he was mustered out of the service. He died in February, 1864, and in 1866 a pension was granted to the beneficiary as his widow at the rate of $25 a month, dating from the time of her husband's death, two years before.

The widow continued to receive the pension allowed her until June 17, 1869, when she was married to Henry T. Mowatt, which under the law terminated her pensionable right. It appears, however, that a small pension was allowed two minor children of the soldier at the time of their mother's remarriage, which continued until 1876, more than seven years after such remarriage, when the youngest of said children became 16 years of age.

In 1878, nine years after he became the second husband of the beneficiary, Henry T. Mowatt died.

Though twenty-seven years have passed since the beneficiary ceased to be the widow of the deceased soldier, and though she has been the widow of Henry T. Mowatt for eighteen years, it is proposed by the bill under consideration to again place her name upon the pension roll "as widow of Alfred B. Soule, late major of the Twenty-third Regiment Maine Volunteers."

Of course the propriety of the law which terminates the pension of a soldier's widow upon her remarriage will not be questioned. I suppose no one would suggest the renewal of such pension during the lifetime of her second husband. Her pensionable relation to the Government as the widow of her deceased soldier husband, under any reasonable pension theory, absolutely terminated with her remarriage.

If she is to be again pensioned because her second husband does not survive her, the transaction has more the complexion of an adjustment of a governmental insurance on the life of the second husband than the allowance of a pension on just and reasonable grounds.

Legislation of this description is sure to establish a precedent which it will be difficult to disclaim, and which if followed can not fail to lead to abuse.

GROVER CLEVELAND.

EXECUTIVE MANSION, *May 20, 1896.*

To the House of Representatives:

I return herewith without approval House bill No. 577, entitled "An act granting a pension to Lydia A. Taft."

In 1858 the beneficiary named in this bill became the wife of Lowell Taft, who afterwards enlisted in the Union Army as a private in a Connecticut regiment and served from August, 1862, until June, 1865. The records of the War Department show that he was captured by the enemy June 15, 1863, and paroled July 14, 1863.

No application for a pension was ever made by him, though he lived until 1891, when he died at a soldiers' home in Connecticut.

No suggestion is made that he incurred any disability in the service or that his death was in any manner related to such service.

In 1882, nearly twenty-four years after her marriage to the soldier and seventeen years after his discharge from the Army, the beneficiary obtained a divorce from him upon the grounds of habitual drunkenness and failure to afford her a support.

It is now proposed, five years after the soldier's death, to pension as his widow the wife who was divorced from him at her own instance fourteen years ago.

A government's generous care for widows deprived of a husband's support and companionship by the casualties or disabilities of war rests upon grounds which all must cheerfully approve; but it is difficult to place upon these grounds the case of this proposed beneficiary, who has renounced a wife's relation, with all its duties and all its rights, and who by her own act placed herself beyond the possibility of becoming the widow of her soldier husband.

If, as stated in the report of the House committee on this bill, the beneficiary for some reason contributed something toward the soldier's support after her divorce and paid the expense of his burial, the fact still remains that this soldier died in a soldiers' home wifeless and leaving no one surviving who, claiming to be his widow, should be allowed to profit by his death.

GROVER CLEVELAND.

EXECUTIVE MANSION, *May 21, 1896.*

To the House of Representatives:

I herewith return without approval House bill No. 1185, entitled "An act granting a pension to Rachel Patton."

John H. Patton, the husband of the beneficiary, was a captain in an Illinois regiment, and was killed in action June 25, 1863.

In December, 1863, the beneficiary was pensioned as his widow at the rate of $20 a month.

She received this pension for thirteen years and until 1876, when she married one William G. Culbertson. Thereupon, because of such marriage, her name was dropped from the pension rolls, pursuant to law.

In 1889, thirteen years after her remarriage and the termination of her pension, she procured a decree of divorce against her second husband on the ground of desertion.

She has a small income, but it does not appear that alimony was allowed her in the divorce proceedings.

It is proposed by this bill to pension her at the same rate which was allowed her while she remained the widow of the deceased soldier.

It can not be denied that the remarriage of this beneficiary terminated her pensionable relation to the Government as completely as if it never existed. The statute which so provides simply declares what is approved by a fair and sensible consideration of pension principles. As a legal proposition, the pensionable status of a soldier's widow, lost by her remarriage, can not be recovered by the dissolution of the second marriage. Waiving, however, the application of strictly legal principles to the subject, there does not appear to be any sentiment which should restore to the pension rolls as the widow of a deceased soldier a divorced wife who has relinquished the title of soldier's widow to again become a wife, and who to secure the expected advantages and comforts of a second marriage has been quite willing to forego the provision which was made for her by the Government solely on the grounds of her soldier widowhood.

GROVER CLEVELAND.

EXECUTIVE MANSION, *May 23, 1896.*

To the House of Representatives:

I herewith return without approval House bill No. 4804, entitled "An act to amend subdivision 10 of section 2238 of the Revised Statutes of the United States."

The subdivision of the section of the law proposed to be amended by this bill has reference to the fees allowed receivers and registers at public-land offices. This subdivision now reads as follows:

Tenth. Registers and receivers are allowed jointly at the rate of 15 cents per hundred words for testimony reduced by them to writing for claimants in establishing preemption and homestead rights.

The bill under consideration so amends this subdivision that in the first clause a compensation of 10 cents per hundred words is allowed to the registers and receivers for reducing to writing the testimony of claimants "in all cases," instead of 15 cents per hundred words for reducing to writing testimony "in establishing preemption and homestead rights," as provided in the old law.

Whether this reduction of fees preserves an adequate and just compensation to the officers affected I suppose has been duly considered by the Congress.

The bill, however, after providing for this change in compensation, contains the following words:

And in all cases where they [the registers and receivers] can secure a competent person to reduce the testimony to writing for a sum less per folio than the sum herein prescribed it shall be their duty to do so.

By the addition of these words the bill seems to give certain fees by way of official compensation to the officers named for certain services to be performed by them and at the same time to provide that if they can secure other persons willing to perform these services for a less sum than the amount allowed to them they shall forego their fees in favor of such persons.

It is very important that the fees and perquisites of public officers should be definitely and clearly fixed, so that the official may know precisely the items of his lawful compensation and the people be protected from extortion and imposition.

A public officer ought not to be expected to search very industriously for a person to underbid him for official work, and if such a person appeared the temptation to combination and conspiracy would in many cases lead to abuse.

It will be observed that the officers are not given by this amendment the option to do this work themselves at 10 cents per folio or secure a competent person to do it at a less rate, nor, if they desire, are they allowed to compete with those willing to accept a less compensation. They may charge a fixed rate for the service if performed by them, but in any event if they can procure another party to perform the services for a less sum they must do so.

I am convinced that this bill in its present form, perhaps through unfortunate phraseology, if it became a law would lead to confusion and uncertainty and would invite practices against which the public service ought to be carefully guarded.   GROVER CLEVELAND.

EXECUTIVE MANSION, *May 26, 1896.*

To the House of Representatives:

I return herewith without approval House bill No. 7161, entitled "An act for the relief of Benjamin F. Jones."

This bill directs the payment to the beneficiary, late postmaster at Beauregard, Miss., or to his order, of the sum of $50, in full compensation for services and expenses in carrying and distributing the mails between Wesson and Beauregard, in the State of Mississippi, in 1883.

It appears from the report of the House committee recommending the passage of this bill that on April 22, 1883, while Mr. Jones was postmaster at Beauregard, a cyclone destroyed every building in the place, including that in which the post-office was kept; that in consequence of this disaster the mails for Beauregard were for a period of thirty-five days, and until May 27, 1883, deposited at Wesson, 1 mile distant; that during that time it became necessary to transport such mails from Wesson to Beauregard, and that the postmaster caused this to be done, at an expense of $97.

A report from the Postmaster-General discloses the fact that this claim was presented to the Department in 1884 and was rejected on the ground that if the service was performed as alleged it was not authorized or directed by the Department.

In 1885 a suit was instituted against this postmaster and his sureties for a balance due the Government from him on his official accounts for the quarter ending June 30, 1883.

It will be observed that this quarter covered the period within which the alleged services were performed.

In the suit referred to a judgment was recovered by the Government against the postmaster for $190.45, being the balance found due from him. This judgment still remains unpaid.

In this condition of affairs it is quite plain that in fairness and justice no appropriation should be made in favor of the claimant.

It is the opinion of the Auditor of the Post-Office Department that even if this bill becomes a law payment of the money appropriated should be withheld under a section of the Revised Statutes which provides:

No money shall be paid to any person for his compensation who is in arrears to the United States until he has accounted for and paid into the Treasury all sums for which he may be liable.

GROVER CLEVELAND.

EXECUTIVE MANSION, *May 29, 1896.*

To the House of Representatives:

I return herewith without approval House bill No. 7977, entitled "An act making appropriations for the construction, repair, and preservation of certain public works on rivers and harbors, and for other purposes."

There are 417 items of appropriation contained in this bill, and every part of the country is represented in the distribution of its favors.

It directly appropriates or provides for the immediate expenditure of nearly $14,000,000 for river and harbor work. This sum is in addition to appropriations contained in another bill for similar purposes amounting to a little more than $3,000,000, which have already been favorably considered at the present session of Congress.

The result is that the contemplated immediate expenditures for the objects mentioned amount to about $17,000,000.

A more startling feature of this bill is its authorization of contracts for river and harbor work amounting to more than $62,000,000. Though the payments on these contracts are in most cases so distributed that they are to be met by future appropriations, more than $3,000,000 on their account are included in the direct appropriations above mentioned. Of the remainder, nearly $20,000,000 will fall due during the fiscal year ending June 30, 1898, and amounts somewhat less in the years immediately succeeding. A few contracts of a like character authorized under previous statutes are still outstanding, and to meet payments on these more than $4,000,000 must be appropriated in the immediate future.

If, therefore, this bill becomes a law, the obligations which will be imposed on the Government, together with the appropriations made for immediate expenditure on account of rivers and harbors, will amount to about $80,000,000. Nor is this all. The bill directs numerous surveys and examinations which contemplate new work and further contracts and which portend largely increased expenditures and obligations.

There is no ground to hope that in the face of persistent and growing demands the aggregate of appropriations for the smaller schemes, not covered by contracts, will be reduced or even remain stationary. For the fiscal year ending June 30, 1898, such appropriations, together with the installments on contracts which will fall due in that year, can hardly be less than $30,000,000; and it may reasonably be apprehended that the prevalent tendency toward increased expenditures of this sort and the concealment which postponed payments afford for extravagance will increase the burdens chargeable to this account in succeeding years.

In view of the obligation imposed upon me by the Constitution, it seems to me quite clear that I only discharge a duty to our people when I interpose my disapproval of the legislation proposed.

Many of the objects for which it appropriates public money are not related to the public welfare, and many of them are palpably for the benefit of limited localities or in aid of individual interests.

On the face of the bill it appears that not a few of these alleged improvements have been so improvidently planned and prosecuted that after an unwise expenditure of millions of dollars new experiments for their accomplishment have been entered upon.

While those intrusted with the management of public funds in the interest of all the people can hardly justify questionable expenditures for public work by pleading the opinions of engineers or others as to the practicability of such work, it appears that some of the projects for which appropriations are proposed in this bill have been entered upon without the approval or against the objections of the examining engineers.

I learn from official sources that there are appropriations contained in the bill to pay for work which private parties have actually agreed with the Government to do in consideration of their occupancy of public property.

Whatever items of doubtful propriety may have escaped observation or may have been tolerated in previous Executive approvals of similar bills, I am convinced that the bill now under consideration opens the way to insidious and increasing abuses and is in itself so extravagant as to be especially unsuited to these times of depressed business and resulting disappointment in Government revenue. This consideration is emphasized by the prospect that the public Treasury will be confronted with other appropriations made at the present session of Congress amounting to more than $500,000,000.

Individual economy and careful expenditure are sterling virtues which lead to thrift and comfort. Economy and the exaction of clear justification for the appropriation of public moneys by the servants of the people are not only virtues, but solemn obligations.

To the extent that the appropriations contained in this bill are instigated by private interests and promote local or individual projects their allowance can not fail to stimulate a vicious paternalism and encourage a sentiment among our people, already too prevalent, that their attachment to our Government may properly rest upon the hope and expectation of direct and especial favors and that the extent to which they are realized may furnish an estimate of the value of governmental care.

I believe no greater danger confronts us as a nation than the unhappy decadence among our people of genuine and trustworthy love and affection for our Government as the embodiment of the highest and best aspirations of humanity, and not as the giver of gifts, and because its mission is the enforcement of exact justice and equality, and not the allowance of unfair favoritism.

I hope I may be permitted to suggest, at a time when the issue of Government bonds to maintain the credit and financial standing of the country is a subject of criticism, that the contracts provided for in this bill would create obligations of the United States amounting to $62,000,000 no less binding than its bonds for that sum.

GROVER CLEVELAND.

EXECUTIVE MANSION, *May 29, 1896.*

To the Senate:

I herewith return without approval Senate bill No. 147, entitled "An act granting a pension to Elvira Bachelder."

This bill provides for a pension to the beneficiary as dependent mother of "J. K. P. Bachelder, late a private in Company D, Seventh New Hampshire Volunteer Infantry."

On the merits of the case I am satisfied this mother deserves a pension. I withhold my approval of the bill intended to grant her this relief solely because I am advised that the law would be inoperative for the reason that the deceased soldier never served in the Seventh New Hampshire Infantry, and should have been described in the bill as a member of Company D, First New Hampshire Heavy Artillery.

GROVER CLEVELAND.

EXECUTIVE MANSION, *May 29, 1896.*

To the House of Representatives:

I herewith return without approval House bill No. 900, entitled "An act to provide for the payment of the claim of William H. Mahoney."

This bill directs the Secretary of the Treasury to receive and pay to W. H. Mahoney, without the indorsement of N. A. Rogers, a certain bond issued by the United States in 1861 for the sum of $500, such payment to be made upon the giving by said Mahoney of a bond to hold harmless the United States against repayment of said bond.

The bond mentioned is one of a large issue which was authorized under an act passed March 2, 1861, and known as Oregon war-debt bonds. They were made payable in 1881.

In 1864 an act was passed directing the Secretary of the Treasury to issue or cause to be issued to E. F. and Samuel A. Ward duplicates of nineteen of these bonds, particularly described by their numbers and otherwise. Among others are mentioned "Nos. 1352 to 1359, inclusive." This of course includes the bond numbered 1358, which is directed to be paid in the bill under consideration. Nothing can now be discovered to indicate the occasion for the issuance of these duplicates, but from the fact that a bond of indemnity was required it is inferred that they were issued because of the loss or destruction of the original bonds.

Pursuant to this act a duplicate of the bond in question, among others, was issued and made payable to the order of Thomas Pritchard, attorney, who was the payee in the original bond.

In 1881 this duplicate was paid by the Treasury Department and is now in possession of the Government. The indorsement of the payee, "Thomas Pritchard, attorney," appears thereon and all other proper indorsements to show title in the party to whom the payment was made.

The Government has therefore once paid the amount of this bond to the party apparently entitled to it. If the beneficiary named in this bill has a better right to the money, the Government, not being in default, should be protected against double payment. I suppose to sustain a claim upon the indemnity bond given when the duplicate was issued in 1864 we should be prepared to show that the second payment on the original bond was made upon such a state of facts as compelled or at least justified it. The passage of an act simply directing such payment would alone not be sufficient. The bond directed to be given by this bill would afford the Government no protection, since it only provides against repayment of the bond in the future, whereas the payment we should suffer from has already been made.

I suggest that an act be passed directing the Secretary of the Treasury to investigate the entire subject with a view of determining to whom this money should be paid, in a manner to bind, if possible, by the results of the examination the party to whom it has already been paid, and who should refund if another has a better right.

GROVER CLEVELAND.

EXECUTIVE MANSION, *May 30, 1896.*

To the House of Representatives:

I return without approval House bill No. 6037, entitled "An act grant-ing a pension to Mrs. Amanda Woodcock."

The bill provides for the granting of a pension to the beneficiary therein named, describing her as the "widow of Robert Woodcock, deceased, late a private in the Fourth United States Volunteer Infantry in the Mexican War."

My action in this case is based upon the following statement concern-ing the bill from the Pension Bureau:

The bill, if approved, would be inoperative, inasmuch as there was no such organ-ization in the Mexican War as named in the bill (Fourth United States Volunteer Infantry), and the service alleged by the soldier having been in the Fourth Kentucky Volunteer Infantry.

GROVER CLEVELAND.

EXECUTIVE MANSION, *May 30, 1896.*

To the House of Representatives:

I herewith return without approval House bill No. 4526, entitled "An act granting a pension to Jonathan Scott."

This bill directs that the Secretary of the Interior place upon the pen-sion roll, at the rate of $72 per month, subject to the provisions and lim-itations of the pension laws, the name of Jonathan Scott, late of Company M, Sixth Regiment Iowa Volunteer Cavalry.

The beneficiary was dropped from the pension roll in October, 1895, after a very thorough examination, for fraud, it appearing to the satisfac-tion of the Pension Bureau that the disability for which he was pensioned was not due to his army service. There certainly ought to be a strong presumption that the case was fairly and justly determined by the Bureau, and the evidence strongly tends to support the conclusion reached. If restored to the rolls, such restoration would still be "subject to the provisions and limitations of the pension laws," and he would not be exempt from further investigation if circumstances or newly developed facts justified such a course.

Whatever may be the merits of the case, however, I am advised by the Pension Bureau that the bill, if it becomes a law in its present form, would be inoperative for the reason that the beneficiary is therein described as having been a member of the Sixth Regiment of Iowa Volunteer Cavalry, whereas he actually served in the Fifth Regiment of the Volunteer Cavalry of that State.

GROVER CLEVELAND.

To the Senate: EXECUTIVE MANSION, *June 1, 1896.*

I herewith return without approval Senate bill No. 149, entitled "An act granting a pension to Helen M. Jacob."

The purpose of this bill is to grant a pension of $12 per month to "Helen M. Jacob, of Rochester, Ind., widow of Benjamin Oden West."

It appears from the records of the War Department that Benjamin O. West served in the Mexican War from January to November in the year 1847. The beneficiary named in this bill was married to him in 1850, and he died in 1856. She was pensioned as his widow, and received such pension from the date of her husband's death until April 17, 1861. On that date she was married to William W. Jacob, whereupon her pension ceased, but two minor children were awarded pensions and continued in receipt of the same until January, 1873, when the youngest child became 16 years of age.

The entire absence of any fixed or reasonable principle or rule regulating private pension legislation at this time suggests the danger of its near approach in many cases to caprice and favoritism.

Though I have in a number of instances deferred to the judgment of Congress and refrained from interposing objections to bills of this character which seemed to me to be of doubtful merit, I am unwilling to follow such a wide departure from a palpably just pension theory and assent to the establishment of such an unfortunate precedent as this bill involves.

There is no duty or obligation due from the Government to a soldier's widow except it be worked out through the deceased soldier. She is pensioned only because he served his country and because through his death she as his wife has lost his support. In other words, she becomes a beneficiary of the Government because she is a soldier's widow. When she marries again, and thus displaces the memory of her soldier husband and surrenders all that belongs to soldier widowhood, she certainly ought not on the death of her second husband to be allowed to claim that she is again the soldier's widow.

GROVER CLEVELAND.

EXECUTIVE MANSION, *June 6, 1896.*

To the House of Representatives:

I hereby return without my approval House bill No. 8293, entitled "An act making appropriations to supply deficiencies in the appropriations for the fiscal year ending June 30, 1896, and for prior years, and for other purposes."

To the extent that the Constitution has devolved upon the President a participation in legislation I suppose his action on bills presented to him for approval involves a duty to be performed, like others pertaining to his office, with care and circumspection and in full view of his responsibility to the people and his obligation to subserve the public welfare. It is difficult to understand why under the Constitution it should be necessary to submit proposed legislation to Executive scrutiny and approval except to invoke the exercise of Executive judgment and invite independent Executive action.

The unpleasant incidents which accompany the use of the veto power would tempt its avoidance if such a course did not involve an abandonment of constitutional duty and an assent to legislation for which the Executive is not willing to share the responsibility.

I regret that I am constrained to disapprove an important appropriation bill so near the close of the present session of Congress. I have, however, by immediate action after the receipt of the bill, endeavored to delay as little as possible a reconsideration of this proposed legislation, though I am thus obliged to content myself with a less complete explanation of my objections than would otherwise be submitted.

This bill is in many of its features far removed from a legitimate deficiency bill, and it contains a number of appropriations which seem to me to be exceedingly questionable. Without noticing in detail many of these items, I shall refer to two of them which, in my judgment, justify my action in the premises.

The bill appropriates $1,027,314.09 for a partial payment upon claims which originated in depredations upon our commerce by French cruisers and vessels during the closing years of the last century. They have become quite familiar to those having Congressional experience, as they have been pressed for recognition and payment, with occasional intervals of repose, for nearly one hundred years.

These claims are based upon the allegations that France, being at war with England, seized and condemned many American vessels and cargoes in violation of the rules of international law and treaty provisions and contrary to the duty she owed to our country as a neutral power and to our citizens; that by reason of these acts claims arose in favor of such of our citizens as were damnified against the French nation, which claims our Government attempted to enforce, and that in concluding a treaty with France in the year 1800 these claims were abandoned or relinquished in consideration of the relinquishment of certain claims which France charged against us.

Upon these statements it is insisted by those interested that we as a nation having reaped a benefit in our escape from these French demands against us through the abandonment of the claims of our citizens against France, the Government became equitably bound as between itself and its citizens to pay the claims thus relinquished.

I do not understand it to be asserted that there exists any legal liability against the Government on account of its relation to these claims. At the term of the Supreme Court just finished the Chief Justice, in an opinion concerning them and the action of Congress in appropriating for their payment, said:

We think that payments thus prescribed to be made were purposely brought within the category of payments by way of gratuity—payments of grace and not of right.

From the time the plan was conceived to charge the Government with the payment of these claims they have abided in the atmosphere of controversy. Every proposition presented in their support has been stoutly disputed and every inference suggested in their favor has been promptly challenged.

Thus, inasmuch as it must, I think, be conceded that if a state of war existed between our country and France at the time these depredations were committed our Government was not justified in claiming indemnity for our citizens, it is asserted that we were at the time actually engaged in war with the French nation. This position seems to be sustained by an opinion of the Attorney-General of the United States written in 1798 and by a number of decisions of the Supreme Court delivered soon after that time.

We had certainly abrogated treaties with France, and our cruisers and armed ships were roaming the seas capturing her vessels and property.

So, also, when it is asserted that the validity of these claims was acknowledged in the treaty negotiations by the representatives of France, their declarations to a contrary purport are exhibited.

And when it is alleged that the abandonment of these claims against France was in consideration of great benefits to the Government, it is as confidently alleged that they were in point of fact abandoned because their enforcement was hopeless and that even if any benefit really accrued to us by insistence upon their settlement in the course of diplomatic negotiation such result gave no pretext for taxing the Government with liability to the claimants.

Without noticing other considerations and contentions arising from the alleged origin of these claims, a brief reference to their treatment in the past and the development of their presentation may be useful and pertinent.

It is, I believe, somewhat the fashion in interested quarters to speak of the failure by the Government to pay these claims as such neglect as amounts to repudiation and a denial of justice to citizens who have

RETURN OF OUR BATTLE-SCARRED BUT TRIUMPHANT FLEET

THE RETURN OF THE FLEET, 1898

The hearts of the American people swelled with pride and joy when their victorious navy returned to their shores, and the ovation received by all who wore the navy uniform, from tars to Rear-Admirals, will be long remembered. The navy is the best tangible evidence of the resources and power of the Government. It is an asset of the State Department and monies expended on it may be considered as insurance premiums against the incalculable damage which a foreign navy could do to our coasts. The recent cruise of the battle-ship fleet around the world was a demonstration of the navy's readiness for action and ability to remain at sea for long periods.

The articles "Navy," "Navy Department," and "Cruise of the Battleship Fleet," in the encyclopedic index (volume eleven), will give interesting information, and the discussions of our naval policy by the Presidents will reveal the matter in all its bearings, military and diplomatic.

suffered. Of course the original claimants have for years been beyond the reach of relief; but as their descendants in each generation become more numerous the volume of advocacy, importunity, and accusation correspondingly increases. If injustice has been done in the refusal of these claims, it began early in the present century and may be charged against men then in public life more conversant than we can be with the facts involved and whose honesty and sense of right ought to be secure from suspicion.

As early as 1802 a committee of the House of Representatives reported the facts connected with these claims, but apparently without recommendation. No action was taken on the report. In 1803 a resolution declaring that indemnity ought to be paid was negatived by a vote of the same body. A favorable committee report was made in 1807, but it seems that no legislative action resulted. In 1818 an adverse report was made to the Senate, followed by the passage of a resolution declaring "that the relief asked by the memorialists and petitioners ought not to be granted." In 1822 and again in 1824 adverse committee reports on the subject were made to the House, concluding with similar resolutions.

The presumption against these claims arising from such unfavorable reports and resolutions and from the failure of Congress to provide for their payment at a time so near the events upon which they are based can not be destroyed by the interested cry of injustice and neglect of the rights of our citizens.

Until 1846 these claims were from time to time pressed upon the attention of Congress with varying fortunes, but never with favorable legislative action. In that year, however, a bill was passed for their ascertainment and satisfaction, and $5,000,000 were appropriated for their payment. This bill was vetoed by President Polk,* who declared that he could "perceive no legal or equitable ground upon which this large appropriation can rest." This veto was sustained by the House of Representatives.

Nine years afterwards, and in 1855, another bill was passed similar to the one last mentioned, and appropriating for the settlement of these claims a like sum of money. This bill was also vetoed,† President Pierce concluding a thorough discussion of its demerits with these words:

In view of what has been said there would seem to be no ground on which to raise a liability of the United States, unless it be the assumption that the United States are to be considered the insurer and the guarantor of all claims, of whatever nature, which any individual citizen may have against a foreign nation.

This veto was also sustained by the House of Representatives.

I think it will be found that in all bills proposed in former times for the payment of these claims the sum to be appropriated for that purpose did not exceed $5,000,000. It is now estimated that those already passed upon, with those still pending for examination in the Court of

*See pp. 2316–2319. †See pp. 2840–2855.

Claims, may amount to $25,000,000. This indicates either that the actual sufferers or those nearer to them in time and blood than the present claimants underestimated their losses or that there has been a great development in the manner of their presentation.

Nothwithstanding persistent efforts to secure payment from the Government and the importunity of those interested, no appropriation has ever been made for that purpose except a little more than $1,300,000, which was placed in the general deficiency bill in the very last hours of the session of Congress on March 3, 1891.

In the long list of beneficiaries who are provided for in the bill now before me on account of these claims 152 represent the owners of ships and their cargoes and 186 those who lost as insurers of such vessels or cargoes.

These insurers by the terms of their policies undertook and agreed "to bear and take upon themselves all risks and perils of the sea, men-of-war, fire, enemies, rovers, thieves, jettison, letters of mart and counter mart, surprisals, takings at sea, arrests, restraints, and detainments of all kings, princes, or people of what nation, condition, or quality whatsoever."

The premiums received on these policies were large, and the losses were precisely those within the contemplation of the insurers. It is well known that the business of insurance is entered upon with the expectation that the premiums received will pay all losses and yield a profit to the insurance in addition; and yet, without any showing that the business did not result in a profit to these insurance claimants, it is proposed that the Government shall indemnify them against the precise risks they undertook, notwithstanding the fact that the money appropriated is not to be paid except "by way of gratuity—payments as of grace and not of right."

The appropriations to indemnify against insurance losses rest upon weaker grounds, it seems to me, than those of owners; but in the light of all the facts and circumstances surrounding these spoliation claims, as they are called, none of them, in my opinion, should be paid by the Government.

Another item in this bill which seems to me especially objectionable is an appropriation in favor of Charles P. Chouteau, survivor, etc., of $174,445.75, in full satisfaction of all claims arising out of the construction of the ironclad steam battery *Etlah*.

The contract for the construction of this battery was made by the Government with Charles W. McCord during the war, and he was to be paid therefor the sum of $386,000. He was paid this sum and $210,991 for extras, and in May, 1866, gave his receipt in full. The assignee of McCord in bankruptcy assigned to Chouteau and his associates in 1868 all claims of McCord against the United States for the precise extras for which he had receipted in full two years before. Chouteau brought suit in the Court of Claims for such extras and was defeated. I can not gather from the facts I have been able to collect concerning this appropriation that it is justified on any ground.

In 1890 my immediate predecessor vetoed a bill allowing the matter to be examined again by the Court of Claims.*

If the additional payment proposed in this bill was made, the cost of the battery in question would be almost double that of the contract price.

I have determined to submit this incomplete presentation of my objections to this bill at once in order that the Congress may act thereon without embarrassment or the interruption of plans for an early adjournment.

GROVER CLEVELAND.

EXECUTIVE MANSION, *June 10, 1896.*
To the House of Representatives:

I herewith return without my approval House bill No. 225, entitled "An act to provide for the lease of Fort Omaha Military Reservation to the State of Nebraska."

This bill authorizes and directs the Secretary of War, when Fort Crook, near the city of Omaha, is ready for occupancy, to lease for a nominal rent to the State of Nebraska the possession of Fort Omaha Military Reservation, containing about 80 acres, with all the buildings, appurtenances, and improvements thereof. It is declared that the lease shall be conditional upon the use of said reservation by the State of Nebraska as a place of rendezvous and school of instruction for the National Guard of said State; that the State of Nebraska shall while it is in possession of said reservation keep the buildings and improvements thereon in as good condition and repair as at the date it shall enter into possession thereof, and that at any time when, in the judgment of the Secretary of War, the interests of the United States shall require such action he shall take possession of said military reservation for the use of the Government, together with all the buildings, appurtenances, and improvements thereon.

On the 23d day of July, 1888, an act was passed authorizing the Secretary of War to purchase suitable grounds, of not less than 640 acres in extent, to be situate within 10 miles of the city of Omaha, and to construct the necessary buildings thereon for a ten-company military post, to be known as Fort Omaha, and a necessary sum, not exceeding $200,000, was appropriated to enable the Secretary of War to carry out the provisions of said act.

The said act also authorized the Secretary of War, when the purchase of the new site should be effected, to sell the military reservation known as Fort Omaha and such of the buildings and improvements thereon as could not be economically removed to the new site, and to cause the said reservation, for the purposes of said sale, to be platted in blocks, streets,

*See p. 5528.

and alleys, if in his judgment it would inure to the benefit of the Government in making a sale of such site.

The new site provided for by this act has been purchased, a large sum of money has been spent by the Government in preparing it for use, and I understand it will soon be ready for occupancy. The authority to sell the old site has not been exercised. This may be accounted for by the fact that the Government has not thus far been able to dispense with its use or because the depression in land values at Omaha has rendered it unadvisable.

The authority to sell and to remove any of the buildings from the old reservation to the new site still remains, however, unimpaired. In this condition of affairs it is now proposed to lease this land and these buildings to the State of Nebraska at a nominal rent, allowing the Government to repossess it only "when the interests of the United States shall require such action."

Of course it would be claimed that this language, in view of the statute of 1888, should not be construed as permitting the Government to retake the property for the purpose of selling it, because that is not stipulated in the bill. For that reason it would be plausibly urged that the lease was paramount to the power of sale contained in the law of 1888 and that the omission of any provision that possession might be resumed for the purpose of sale plainly indicated that "the interests of the United States" which allow such resumption contemplate some other and different emergency.

As a practical question, we all know that transactions of this character relating to Government property amount to a permanent alienation, or certainly pave the way for an absolute grant.

I do not think there should be anything done with this valuable property which will in the least embarrass the Government in its sale, and to that extent reimbursing itself for the cost of the new military post, which was plainly contemplated in the law of 1888.

GROVER CLEVELAND.

PROCLAMATIONS.

By the President of the United States of America.

A PROCLAMATION.

Whereas the Congress of the United States passed an act, which was approved on the 16th day of July, 1894, entitled "An act to enable the people of Utah to form a constitution and State government and to be admitted into the Union on an equal footing with the original States," which act provided for the election of delegates to a constitutional convention to meet at the seat of government of the Territory of Utah on the first Monday in March, 1895, for the purpose of declaring the adoption of the Constitution of the United States by the people of the proposed State and forming a constitution and State government for such State; and

Whereas delegates were accordingly elected, who met, organized, and declared on behalf of the people of said proposed State their adoption of the Constitution of the United States, all as provided in said act; and

Whereas said convention, so organized, did, by ordinance irrevocable without the consent of the United States and the people of said State, as required by said act, provide that perfect toleration of religious sentiment shall be secured and that no inhabitant of said State shall ever be molested in person or property on account of his or her mode of religious worship, but that polygamous or plural marriages are forever prohibited, and did also by said ordinance make the other various stipulations recited in section 3 of said act; and

Whereas said convention thereupon formed a constitution and State government for said proposed State, which constitution, including said ordinance, was duly submitted to the people thereof at an election held on the Tuesday next after the first Monday of November, 1895, as directed by said act; and

Whereas the return of said election has been made and canvassed and the result thereof certified to me, together with a statement of the votes cast and a copy of said constitution and ordinance, all as provided in said act, showing that a majority of the votes lawfully cast at such election was for the ratification and adoption of said constitution and ordinance; and

Whereas the constitution and government of said proposed State are republican in form, said constitution is not repugnant to the Constitution of the United States and the Declaration of Independence, and all the provisions of said act have been complied with in the formation of said constitution and government:

Now, therefore, I, Grover Cleveland, President of the United States of America, in accordance with the act of Congress aforesaid and by authority thereof, announce the result of said election to be as so certified and do hereby declare and proclaim that the terms and conditions prescribed by the Congress of the United States to entitle the State of Utah to admission into the Union have been duly complied with and that the creation of said State and its admission into the Union on an equal footing with the original States is now accomplished.

In testimony whereof I have hereunto set my hand and caused the seal of the United States to be affixed.

[SEAL.] Done at the city of Washington, this 4th day of January, A. D. 1896, and of the Independence of the United States of America the one hundred and twentieth.

GROVER CLEVELAND.

By the President:
RICHARD OLNEY, *Secretary of State.*

BY THE PRESIDENT OF THE UNITED STATES OF AMERICA.

A PROCLAMATION.

Whereas it is provided by section 13 of the act of Congress of March 3, 1891, entitled "An act to amend Title LX, chapter 3, of the Revised Statutes of the United States, relating to copyrights," that said act "shall only apply to a citizen or subject of a foreign state or nation when such foreign state or nation permits to citizens of the United States of America the benefit of copyright on substantially the same basis as its own citizens, or when such foreign state or nation is a party to an international agreement which provides for reciprocity in the granting of copyright, by the terms of which agreement the United States of America may at its pleasure become a party to such agreement;" and

Whereas it is also provided by said section that "the existence of either of the conditions aforesaid shall be determined by the President of the United States by proclamation made from time to time as the purposes of this act may require;" and

Whereas satisfactory official assurances have been given that in the United States of Mexico the law permits to citizens of the United States of America the benefit of copyright on substantially the same basis as to the citizens of that Republic:

Now, therefore, I, Grover Cleveland, President of the United States of America, do declare and proclaim that the first of the conditions specified in section 13 of the act of March 3, 1891, now exists and is fulfilled in respect to the citizens of the United States of Mexico.

In testimony whereof I have hereunto set my hand and caused the seal of the United States to be affixed.

[SEAL.]   Done at the city of Washington, this 27th day of February, 1896, and of the Independence of the United States the one hundred and twentieth.

GROVER CLEVELAND.

By the President:

RICHARD OLNEY, *Secretary of State.*

BY THE PRESIDENT OF THE UNITED STATES OF AMERICA.

A PROCLAMATION.

Whereas in a suit between the United States and the State of Texas involving the title to and jurisdiction over all that territory lying between the North and South forks of the Red River and the one hundredth degree of longitude, known and styled as "Greer County, Tex.," the Supreme Court of the United States has decided that the title to and jurisdiction over said territory is vested in the United States; and

Whereas the Choctaw Nation claims that the title to these lands passed to said nation by virtue of treaties with the United States and that the title of said nation to said lands has not been extinguished, but that said Choctaw Nation has a right and interest therein; and

Whereas it is claimed that divers persons settled upon said lands prior to the 30th day of December, 1887, acting in good faith upon the belief that the same belonged to and were subject to the jurisdiction of the State of Texas and that Congress will be asked to extend to all such settlers suitable relief:

Now, therefore, I, Grover Cleveland, President of the United States, by virtue of the authority in me vested, not admitting in any wise the validity of such claim on behalf of the Choctaw Nation, but for the purpose of preserving the status of said lands intact until such time as said claim of the Choctaw Nation thereto may be duly determined, and that the settlers hereinbefore referred to shall not be disturbed until Congress shall have fully considered their claims for relief, do hereby withdraw said lands from disposition under the public-land laws of the United States and declare the same to be in a state of reservation until such time as this order of withdrawal may be revoked; and I do further warn and admonish all persons against entering upon said lands with a view to occupying the same or settling thereon under the public-land laws during the existence of this order.

In witness whereof I have hereunto set my hand and caused the seal of the United States to be affixed.

[SEAL.]   Done at the city of Washington, this 16th day of March, A. D. 1896, and of the Independence of the United States the one hundred and twentieth.

GROVER CLEVELAND.

By the President:
RICHARD OLNEY, *Secretary of State.*

BY THE PRESIDENT OF THE UNITED STATES OF AMERICA.

A PROCLAMATION.

The following provisions of the laws of the United States are published hereby for the information of all concerned:

Section 1956, Revised Statutes, chapter 3, Title XXIII, enacts that—

No person shall kill any otter, mink, marten, sable, or fur seal, or other fur-bearing animal within the limits of Alaska Territory or in the waters thereof; and every person guilty thereof shall for each offense be fined not less than $200 nor more than $1,000, or imprisoned not more than six months, or both; and all vessels, their tackle, apparel, furniture, and cargo, found engaged in violation of this section shall be forfeited; but the Secretary of the Treasury shall have power to authorize the killing of any such mink, marten, sable, or other fur-bearing animal, except fur seals, under such regulations as he may prescribe; and it shall be the duty of the Secretary to prevent the killing of any fur seal and to provide for the execution of the provisions of this section until it is otherwise provided by law, nor shall he grant any special privileges under this section.

Section 3 of the act entitled "An act to provide for the protection of the salmon fisheries of Alaska," approved March 2, 1889, provides—

SEC. 3. That section 1956 of the Revised Statutes of the United States is hereby declared to include and apply to all the dominion of the United States in the waters of Bering Sea; and it shall be the duty of the President at a timely season in each year to issue his proclamation, and cause the same to be published for one month in at least one newspaper (if any such there be) published at each United States port of entry on the Pacific coast, warning all persons against entering said waters for the purpose of violating the provisions of said section; and he shall also cause one or more vessels of the United States to diligently cruise said waters and arrest all persons and seize all vessels found to be or to have been engaged in any violation of the laws of the United States therein.

The act entitled "An act to extend to the North Pacific Ocean the provisions of the statutes for the protection of the fur seals and other fur-bearing animals," approved February 21, 1893, provides—

That whenever the Government of the United States shall conclude an effective international arrangement for the protection of fur seals in the North Pacific Ocean by agreement with any power or as a result of the decision of the Tribunal of Arbitration under the convention concluded between the United States and Great Britain February 29, 1892, and so long as such arrangement shall continue, the provisions of section 1956 of the Revised Statutes and all other provisions of the statutes of the United States, so far as the same may be applicable, relative to the protection of fur seals and other fur-bearing animals within the limits of Alaska or in the waters thereof shall be extended to and over all that portion of the Pacific Ocean included in such international arrangement. Whenever an effective international arrangement is concluded as aforesaid it shall be the duty of the President to declare that fact by proclamation and to designate the portion of the Pacific Ocean to which it is applicable and that this act has become operative, and likewise when such arrangement ceases to declare that fact and that this act has become inoperative; and his proclamation in respect thereto shall be conclusive. During the extension as aforesaid of said laws for the protection of fur seals or other fur-bearing animals all violations thereof in said designated portion of the Pacific Ocean shall be held to be the same as if committed within the limits of Alaska or in the waters thereof, but they may be prosecuted either in the district court of Alaska or in any district court of the United States in California, Oregon, or Washington.

An arrangement having been made for the protection of fur seals as a result of the decision of the Tribunal of Arbitration under the convention concluded as aforesaid February 29, 1892, which prohibits the killing of seals at any time within a radius of 60 miles around the Pribilof Islands or during May, June, and July of each year in that portion of the Pacific Ocean, inclusive of Bering Sea, situated to the north of the thirty-fifth degree of north latitude and eastward of the one hundred and eightieth degree of longitude from Greenwich until it strikes the water boundary described in Article I of the treaty of 1867 between the United States and Russia, and following that line up to Bering Strait:

Now, therefore, be it known that I, Grover Cleveland, President of the United States of America, hereby declare that the said act of Congress of February 21, 1893, has become operative; that in accordance therewith section 1956 of the Revised Statutes is applicable to the waters above mentioned, included in the award of the tribunal at Paris given under the said convention of February 29, 1892, and that I have caused the foregoing laws specially to be proclaimed to the end that their provisions may be known and observed.

I hereby proclaim that every person guilty of a violation of the provisions of said laws and of any other provisions of the statutes of the United States, so far as the same may be applicable, relative to the protection of fur-bearing animals within the limits of Alaska or in the waters thereof will be arrested and punished as therein provided, and all vessels so engaged, their tackle, apparel, furniture, and cargo, will be seized and forfeited.

In testimony whereof I have hereunto set my hand and caused the seal of the United States to be affixed.

[SEAL.]   Done at the city of Washington, this 14th day of April, A. D. 1896, and of the Independence of the United States the one hundred and twentieth.   GROVER CLEVELAND.

By the President:
RICHARD OLNEY,
Secretary of State.

BY THE PRESIDENT OF THE UNITED STATES OF AMERICA.

A PROCLAMATION.

Whereas it is provided by section 13 of the act of Congress of March 3, 1891, entitled "An act to amend Title LX, chapter 3, of the Revised Statutes of the United States, relating to copyrights," that said act "shall only apply to a citizen or subject of a foreign state or nation when such foreign state or nation permits to citizens of the United States of America the benefit of copyright on substantially the same basis as its own citizens, or when such foreign state or nation is a party to an international agreement which provides for reciprocity in the granting of copyright, by the terms of which agreement the United States of America may at its pleasure become a party to such agreement;" and

Whereas it is also provided by said section that "the existence of either of the conditions aforesaid shall be determined by the President of the United States by proclamation made from time to time as the purposes of this act may require;" and

Whereas satisfactory official assurances have been given that in the Republic of Chile the law permits to citizens of the United States of America the benefit of copyright on substantially the same basis as to the citizens of that Republic:

Now, therefore, I, Grover Cleveland, President of the United States of America, do declare and proclaim that the first of the conditions specified in section 13 of the act of March 3, 1891, now exists and is fulfilled in respect to the citizens of the Republic of Chile.

In testimony whereof I have hereunto set my hand and caused the seal of the United States to be affixed.

[SEAL.]　　　Done at the city of Washington, this 25th day of May, 1896, and of the Independence of the United States the one hundred and twentieth.

GROVER CLEVELAND.

By the President:

RICHARD OLNEY,
　　Secretary of State.

BY THE PRESIDENT OF THE UNITED STATES OF AMERICA.

A PROCLAMATION.

Whereas by a proclamation dated the 12th day of June, A. D. 1895,* attention was called to the serious civil disturbances, accompanied by armed resistance to the established Government of Spain, then prevailing in the island of Cuba, and citizens of the United States and all other persons were admonished to abstain from taking part in such disturbances in contravention of the neutrality laws of the United States; and

Whereas said civil disturbances and armed resistance to the authority of Spain, a power with which the United States are on terms of peace and amity, continue to prevail in said island of Cuba; and

Whereas since the date of said proclamation said neutrality laws of the United States have been the subject of authoritative exposition by the judicial tribunal of last resort, and it has thus been declared that any combination of persons organized in the United States for the purpose of proceeding to and making war upon a foreign country with which the United States are at peace, and provided with arms to be used for such purpose, constitutes a "military expedition or enterprise" within the meaning of said neutrality laws, and that the providing or preparing of the means for such "military expedition or enterprise," which is expressly prohibited by said laws, includes furnishing or aiding in transportation for such "military expedition or enterprise;" and

Whereas, by express enactment, if two or more persons conspire to commit an offense against the United States any act of one conspirator to effect the object of such conspiracy renders all the conspirators liable to fine and imprisonment; and

Whereas there is reason to believe that citizens of the United States and others within their jurisdiction fail to apprehend the meaning and operation of the neutrality laws of the United States as authoritatively interpreted as aforesaid, and may be misled into participation in transactions which are violations of said laws and will render them liable to the severe penalties provided for such violations:

Now, therefore, that the laws above referred to, as judicially con-

*See pp. 6023-6024.

strued, may be duly executed, that the international obligations of the United States may be fully satisfied, and that their citizens and all others within their jurisdiction, being seasonably apprised of their legal duty in the premises, may abstain from disobedience to the laws of the United States and thereby escape the forfeitures and penalties legally consequent thereon, I, Grover Cleveland, President of the United States, do hereby solemnly warn all citizens of the United States and all others within their jurisdiction against violations of the said laws, interpreted as hereinbefore explained, and give notice that all such violations will be vigorously prosecuted; and I do hereby invoke the cooperation of all good citizens in the enforcement of said laws and in the detection and apprehension of any offenders against the same, and do hereby enjoin upon all the executive officers of the United States the utmost diligence in preventing, prosecuting, and punishing any infractions thereof.

In testimony whereof I have hereunto set my hand and caused the seal of the United States to be affixed.

[SEAL.] Done at the city of Washington, this 27th day of July, A. D. 1896, and of the Independence of the United States the one hundred and twenty-first.

GROVER CLEVELAND.

By the President:
RICHARD OLNEY,
Secretary of State.

BY THE PRESIDENT OF THE UNITED STATES.

THANKSGIVING PROCLAMATION.

The people of the United States should never be unmindful of the gratitude they owe the God of Nations for His watchful care, which has shielded them from dire disaster and pointed out to them the way of peace and happiness. Nor should they ever refuse to acknowledge with contrite hearts their proneness to turn away from God's teachings and to follow with sinful pride after their own devices.

To the end that these thoughts may be quickened it is fitting that on a day especially appointed we should join together in approaching the Throne of Grace with praise and supplication.

Therefore, I, Grover Cleveland, President of the United States, do hereby designate and set apart Thursday, the 26th day of the present month of November, to be kept and observed as a day of thanksgiving and prayer throughout our land.

On that day let all our people forego their usual work and occupation, and, assembled in their accustomed places of worship, let them with one accord render thanks to the Ruler of the Universe for our preservation as a nation and our deliverance from every threatened danger, for the peace that has dwelt within our boundaries, for our defense against disease and pestilence during the year that has passed, for the plenteous rewards that have followed the labors of our husbandmen, and for all the other blessings that have been vouchsafed to us.

And let us, through the mediation of Him who has taught us how to pray, implore the forgiveness of our sins and a continuation of heavenly favor.

Let us not forget on this day of thanksgiving the poor and needy, and by deeds of charity let our offerings of praise be made more acceptable in the sight of the Lord.

Witness my hand and the seal of the United States, which I have caused to be hereto affixed.

[SEAL.]　　Done at the city of Washington, this 4th day of November, A. D. 1896, and of the Independence of the United States of America the one hundred and twenty-first.

GROVER CLEVELAND

By the President:

RICHARD OLNEY,
Secretary of State.

BY THE PRESIDENT OF THE UNITED STATES.

A PROCLAMATION.

Whereas on June 21, 1890, the President of the United States by proclamation reserved certain lands in Juneau and Douglas City, Fort Wrangell and Sitka, in the Territory of Alaska, for public buildings, barracks, parade grounds, parks, wharves, coaling stations, etc., which are fully set forth and particularly described in said proclamation; and

Whereas a treaty of cession was exchanged and proclaimed on June 20, 1867, whereby the Russian Empire ceded to the United States the Territory of Alaska; and

Whereas said treaty, by Article II, provided, *inter alia*, that—

It is, however, understood and agreed that the churches which have been built in the ceded territory by the Russian Government shall remain the property of such members of the Greek Oriental Church resident in the territory as may choose to worship therein.

And whereas there were included among the lands hereinbefore referred to as reserved on June 21, 1890, certain lands in and about the town of Sitka, in said Territory of Alaska, which are claimed by the Holy Orthodox Catholic Apostolic Oriental Church, commonly styled the Greco-Russian Church, and described in the said treaty as the Greek Oriental Church:

Now, therefore, I, Grover Cleveland, President of the United States, by virtue of the authority in me vested, do hereby declare, proclaim, and make known that the Executive order of June 21, 1890, making said reservations of lands in the Territory of Alaska, therein particularly described, is hereby modified, and said reservations are diminished so that the following property, described in Inventory B attached to and referred to in the protocol of transfer signed by the representatives of Russia and the United States on October 26, 1867, and being in and about the town of Sitka aforesaid, be excluded therefrom, to wit:

The Cathedral Church of St. Michael, built of timber, situated in the center of the city.

The Church of Resurrection, of timber, commonly called the Kalochian Church, situated near the battery number at the palisade separating the city from the Indian village.

102. A double-storied timber building for bishop house, with outbuildings, appurtenances, and grounds.

35. A timber house for church warden.

98. A timber house for the deacon.

104
105
114 } Three timber houses, with their appurtenances and outbuildings, for lodging of priests.

F
G
H
I } Four lots of ground belonging to the parsonages.

a The place commemorative of the old church.

b A tomb.

Three cemeteries, two outside palisades and one by the Church of the Resurrection.

In witness whereof I have hereunto set my hand and caused the seal of the United States to be affixed.

[SEAL.]   Done at the city of Washington, this 14th day of November, in the year 1896, and of the Independence of the United States the one hundred and twenty-first.

GROVER CLEVELAND.

By the President:

RICHARD OLNEY,
Secretary of State.

BY THE PRESIDENT OF THE UNITED STATES.

A PROCLAMATION.

Whereas by a proclamation of the President of the United States dated January 26, 1888,* upon proof then appearing satisfactory that no tonnage or light-house dues or any equivalent tax or taxes whatever were

* See pp. 5326–5327.

imposed upon American vessels entering the ports of the Empire of Germany, either by the Imperial Government or by the governments of the German maritime States, and that vessels belonging to the United States of America and their cargoes were not required in German ports to pay any fee or due of any kind or nature or any import due higher or other than was payable by German vessels or their cargoes in the United States, the President did thereby declare and proclaim, from and after the date of his said proclamation of January 26, 1888, the suspension of the collection of the whole of the duty of 6 cents per ton, not to exceed 30 cents per ton per annum, imposed upon vessels entered in the ports of the United States from any of the ports of the Empire of Germany by section 11 of the act of Congress approved June 19, 1886, entitled "An act to abolish certain fees for official services to American vessels and to amend the laws relating to shipping commissioners, seamen, and owners of vessels, and for other purposes;" and

Whereas the President did further declare and proclaim in his proclamation of January 26, 1888, that the said suspension should continue so long as the reciprocal exemption of vessels belonging to citizens of the United States and their cargoes should be continued in the said ports of the Empire of Germany, and no longer; and

Whereas it now appears upon satisfactory proof that tonnage or lighthouse dues or a tax or taxes equivalent thereto are in fact imposed upon American vessels and their cargoes entered in German ports higher and other than those imposed upon German vessels or their cargoes entered in ports of the United States, so that said proclamation of January 26, 1888, in its operation and effect contravenes the meaning and intent of said section 11 of the act of Congress approved June 19, 1886:

Now, therefore, I, Grover Cleveland, President of the United States of America, by virtue of the aforesaid section 11 of the act aforesaid, as well as in pursuance of the terms of said proclamation itself, do hereby revoke my said proclamation of January 26, 1888, suspending the collection of the whole of the duty of 6 cents per ton, not to exceed 30 cents per ton per annum, which is imposed by the aforesaid section of said act upon vessels entered in the ports of the United States from any of the ports of the German Empire, this revocation of said proclamation to take effect on and after the 2d day of January, 1897.

In witness whereof I have hereunto set my hand and caused the seal of the United States to be affixed.

[SEAL.]   Done at the city of Washington, this 3d day of December, A. D. 1896, and of the Independence of the United States the one hundred and twenty-first.

GROVER CLEVELAND.

By the President:
    RICHARD OLNEY,
        Secretary of State.

EXECUTIVE ORDERS.

AMENDMENT OF CIVIL-SERVICE RULES.

EXECUTIVE MANSION, *December 2, 1895.*

Special Departmental Rule No. 1, clause 8, is hereby amended by striking from the list of places excepted from examination in the Department of Labor statistical experts and temporary experts.

Approved:
GROVER CLEVELAND.

AMENDMENT OF CIVIL-SERVICE RULES.

EXECUTIVE MANSION, *December 2, 1895.*

So much of Executive orders heretofore issued under General Rule III, section 2, clause (*c*), as provides for the appointment of special agents in the Department of Labor by noncompetitive examination is hereby revoked.

Approved:
GROVER CLEVELAND.

AMENDMENT OF CIVIL-SERVICE RULES.

EXECUTIVE MANSION, *January 18, 1896.*

Section 5 of Internal-Revenue Rule IV is hereby amended by adding at the end of the first paragraph thereof the following:

And provided further, That whenever an emergency shall arise requiring that a vacant position in any internal-revenue district shall be filled before a certificate can be issued by the Commission and an appointment made thereto in the manner provided in these rules, such position may be filled without regard to the provisions of these rules by temporary appointment for a period not to exceed fifteen days, and only for such period as may be required for the execution of the necessary details of an appointment thereto in accordance with said provisions; but no person shall receive such emergency appointment who within the sixty days next previous thereto has been separated from a position in said district to which he was temporarily appointed under the provisions of this section.

The section as amended shall read as follows:

5. In the case of the occurrence of a vacancy in the classified service of any internal-revenue collection district which the public interest requires shall be immediately filled and there is no eligible entitled to reinstatement under section 1, clause (*b*), of this rule or remaining on the proper register, such vacancy in the class of storekeeper, storekeeper and gauger, or clerk may be filled without examination and certification by a temporary designation by the collector of the district of some suitable person to perform the duties of the position until a regular appointment can be made under the provisions of sections 1, 2, and 3 of this rule: *Provided,* That service under such temporary designation shall in no case continue longer than six months, and shall expire by limitation at the end of that time: *And provided further,* That no person shall serve more than six months in any one year under such temporary

designation, the year limitation in regard to such designation to begin to run on the date thereof: *And provided further*, That whenever an emergency shall arise requiring that a vacant position in any internal-revenue district shall be filled before a certificate can be issued by the Commission and an appointment made thereto in the manner provided in these rules, such position may be filled without regard to the provisions of these rules by temporary appointment for a period not to exceed fifteen days, and only for such period as may be required for the execution of the necessary details of an appointment thereto in accordance with said provisions; but no person shall receive such emergency appointment who within the sixty days next previous thereto has been separated from a position in said district to which he was temporarily appointed under the provisions of this section.

Every such temporary designation, and also the discontinuance of the same, shall be at once reported to the Commission.

Approved:

GROVER CLEVELAND.

AMENDMENT OF CIVIL-SERVICE RULES.

EXECUTIVE MANSION, *January 18, 1896.*

Section 5 of Customs Rule II is hereby amended by adding thereto the following:

(*i*) Any person appointed to a position which requires only a portion of his time and attention for the performance of its duties, pays him a compensation not exceeding $300 per annum, and permits of his pursuing other regular business or occupation, such person being conveniently located for the performance of said duties.

The section as amended shall read as follows:

5. Exceptions from examination in the classified customs service are hereby made as follows:

(*a*) Deputy collectors who do not also act as inspectors, examiners, or clerks.
(*b*) Cashier of the collector.
(*c*) Assistant cashier of the collector.
(*d*) Auditor of the collector.
(*e*) Chief acting disbursing officer.
(*f*) Deputy naval officers.
(*g*) Deputy surveyors.
(*h*) One private secretary or one confidential clerk of each nominating officer.
(*i*) Any person appointed to a position which requires only a portion of his time and attention for the performance of its duties, pays him a compensation not exceeding $300 per annum, and permits of his pursuing other regular business or occupation, such person being conveniently located for the performance of said duties.

Approved:

GROVER CLEVELAND.

CIVIL SERVICE.—EXTENSION OF THE CLASSIFIED DEPARTMENTAL AND INDIAN SERVICES.

In the exercise of the power vested in the President by the third paragraph of section 6 of the act entitled "An act to regulate and improve the civil service of the United States," approved January 16, 1883, I hereby direct the Secretary of the Interior to amend the classification of the Interior Department so as to include among the positions classified thereunder and subject to competitive examination clerk, assistant clerk, issue clerk, property clerk, storekeeper, and all other clerical positions at Indian agencies and Indian schools; likewise to amend the classification of the Indian service so as to include among the positions classified thereunder supervisor of Indian schools, day-school inspector, disciplinarian, industrial teacher, teacher of industries, kindergarten teacher, farmer, nurse, assistant matron, and seamstress.

But Indians shall be eligible to appointment to any of said positions on such test of fitness as may be required by the Secretary of the Interior and without examination or certification by the Civil Service Commission; but they shall not be transferred from said positions to the departmental service.

Approved, March 20, 1896.

GROVER CLEVELAND.

AMENDMENT OF CIVIL-SERVICE RULES.

EXECUTIVE MANSION, *March 28, 1896.*

So much of the Executive orders heretofore issued under General Rule III, section 2, clause (*c*), as provides for the appointment of members of the board of pension appeals in the Department of the Interior by noncompetitive examination is hereby revoked, and these places will hereafter be treated as subject to competitive examination.

Approved:

GROVER CLEVELAND.

AMENDMENT OF CIVIL-SERVICE RULES.

EXECUTIVE MANSION, *March 28, 1896.*

Special Departmental Rule No. 1, clause 3, is hereby amended by striking from the list of places excepted from examination in the Department of the Interior assistant attorneys and law clerks, and these places will hereafter be treated as subject to competitive examination.

Approved:

GROVER CLEVELAND.

CIVIL-SERVICE RULES.

In the exercise of power vested in him by the Constitution and of authority given to him by the seventeen hundred and fifty-third section of the Revised Statutes and by an act to regulate and improve the civil service of the United States, approved January 16, 1883, the President hereby makes and promulgates the following rules and revokes all others:

RULE I.

1. The United States Civil Service Commission shall have authority to prescribe regulations in pursuance of and for the execution of the provisions of these rules and of the civil-service act.

2. The several terms hereinafter mentioned, wherever used in these rules or the regulations of the Commission, shall be construed as follows:

(*a*) The term "civil-service act" refers to "An act to regulate and improve the civil service of the United States," approved January 16, 1883.

(*b*) The term "classified service" refers to all that part of the executive civil service of the United States included within the provisions of the civil-service act.

(*c*) The term "grade" in connection with employees or positions refers to a group of employees or positions in the classified service arranged upon the basis of duties performed, without regard to salaries received.

(*d*) The term "class" in connection with employees or positions refers to a group of employees or positions in any grade arranged upon the basis of salaries received, in pursuance of the provisions of section 163 of the Revised Statutes and of section 6 of the civil-service act.

(*e*) The term "excepted position" refers to any position within the provisions of the civil-service act, but excepted from the requirement of competitive examination or registration for appointment thereto.

RULE II.

1. Any person in the executive civil service of the United States who shall willfully violate any of the provisions of the civil-service act or of these rules shall be dismissed from office.

2. No person in the executive civil service shall use his official authority or official influence for the purpose of interfering with an election or controlling the result thereof.

3. No person in the executive civil service shall dismiss, or cause to be dismissed, or make any attempt to procure the dismissal of, or in any manner change the official rank or compensation of, any other person therein because of his political or religious opinions or affiliations.

4. No question in any examination or form of application shall be so framed as to elicit information concerning, nor shall any inquiry be made concerning, nor any other attempt be made to ascertain, the political or religious opinions or affiliations of any applicant, competitor, or eligible; and all disclosures thereof shall be discountenanced, and no discrimination shall be exercised, threatened, or promised against or in favor of any applicant, competitor, or eligible because of his political or religious opinions or affiliations.

5. No recommendation of an applicant, competitor, or eligible involving any disclosure of his political or religious opinions or affiliations shall be received, filed, or considered by the Commission, by any board of examiners, or by any nominating or appointing officer.

6. In making removals or reductions or in imposing punishment for delinquency or misconduct penalties like in character shall be imposed for like offenses, and action thereupon shall be taken irrespective of the political or religious opinions or affiliations of the offenders.

7. A person holding a position on the date said position is classified under the civil-service act shall be entitled to all the rights and benefits possessed by persons of the same class or grade appointed upon examination under the provisions of said act.

RULE III.

1. All that part of the executive civil service of the United States which has been or may hereafter be classified under the civil-service act shall be arranged in branches as follows: The departmental service, the custom-house service, the post-office service, the Government printing service, and the internal-revenue service.

2. The departmental service shall include officers and employees as follows, except those in the service of the Government Printing Office and in the service of the several custom-houses, post-offices, and internal-revenue districts:

(*a*) All officers and employees, of whatever designation, except persons merely employed as laborers or workmen and persons who have been nominated for confirmation by the Senate, however or for whatever purpose employed, whether compensated by a fixed salary or otherwise, who are serving in or on detail from—

The several Executive Departments, the commissions, and offices in the District of Columbia.

The railway mail service.

The Indian service.

The several pension agencies.

The steamboat-inspection service.

The marine-hospital service.

The light-house service.

The life-saving service.

The several mints and assay offices.

The revenue-cutter service.

The force employed under custodians of public buildings.

The several subtreasuries.

The engineer department at large.

(*b*) All executive officers and employees outside of the District of Columbia not covered in (*a*), of whatever designation, whether compensated by a fixed salary or otherwise—

Who are serving in a clerical capacity or whose duties are in whole or in part of a clerical nature.

Who are serving in the capacity of watchman or messenger.

Who are serving in the capacity of physician, hospital steward, nurse, or whose duties are of a medical nature.

Who are serving in the capacity of draftsman, civil engineer, steam engineer, electrical engineer, computer, or fireman.

Who are in the service of the Supervising Architect's Office in the capacity of superintendent of construction, superintendent of repair, or foreman.

Who are in the service of the Treasury Department in any capacity except those in the life-saving service.

3. The custom-house service shall include the officers and employees serving in any customs district whose employees number as many as five who have been or may hereafter be classified under the civil-service act; and whenever in any customs district whose officers and employees number less than five the number of officers and employees shall be increased to as many as five the Secretary of the Treasury shall at once notify the Commission of such increase and the officers and employees in said district shall be included within the classified service from the date of said increase.

4. The post-office service shall include the officers and employees in any free-delivery post-office who have been or may hereafter be classified under the civil-service act; and whenever the free-delivery system shall be established in any post-office the Postmaster-General shall at once notify the Commission of such establishment and the officers or employees of said office shall be included within the classified service from the date of such establishment; and whenever by order of the Postmaster-General any post-office shall be consolidated with and made a part of a free-delivery post-office the Postmaster-General shall at once notify the Commission of such consolidation and from the date of said order the employees of the office thus made a part of the free-delivery office whose names appear on the roster of the Post-Office Department shall be employees of said free-delivery office, and the person holding on the date of said order the position of postmaster at the office thus made a part of said free-delivery office may be made an employee in said free-delivery office and may at the time of classification be assigned to any position therein and given any appropriate designation which the Postmaster-General may direct.

5. The Government printing service shall include the officers and employees in the Government Printing Office who have been or may hereafter be classified under the civil-service act.

6. The internal-revenue service shall include the officers and employees who have been or may hereafter be classified under the civil-service act in any internal-revenue district.

7. All officers and employees who have heretofore been classified under the civil-service act shall be considered as still classified and subject to the provisions of these rules.

8. The following-mentioned positions or employees shall not be subject to the provisions of these rules:

(*a*) Any position filled by a person whose place of private business is conveniently located for the performance of the duties of said position, or any position filled by a person remunerated in one sum both for services rendered therein and for necessary rent, fuel, and lights furnished for the performance of the duties thereof: *Provided*, That in either case the performance of the duties of said position requires only a portion of the time and attention of the occupant, paying him a compensation not exceeding, for his personal salary only, $300 per annum, and permitting of his pursuing other regular business or occupation.

(*b*) Any person in the military or naval service of the United States who is detailed for the performance of civil duties.

(*c*) Any person employed in a foreign country under the State Department or temporarily employed in a confidential capacity in a foreign country.

(*d*) Any position whose duties are of a quasi military or quasi naval character and for the performance of whose duties a person is enlisted for a term of years.

RULE IV.

1. In pursuance of the provisions of section 2 of the civil-service act, there shall be provided, to test fitness for admission to positions which have been or may hereafter be classified under the civil-service act, examinations of a practical and suitable character involving such subjects and tests as the Commission may direct.

2. No person shall be appointed to or be employed in any position which has been or may hereafter be classified under the civil-service act until he shall have passed the examination provided therefor or unless he is especially exempt from examination by the provisions of said act or the rules made in pursuance thereof.

3. In pursuance of the provisions of section 2 of the civil-service act, wherever competent persons can be found who are willing to compete, no noncompetitive examination shall be given except as follows:

(*a*) To test fitness for transfer or for promotion in a part of the service to which promotion regulations have not been applied.

(*b*) To test fitness for appointment of Indians as superintendents, teachers, teachers of industries, kindergartners, and physicians in the Indian service at large.

The noncompetitive examinations of Indians for the positions mentioned shall consist of such tests of fitness, not disapproved by the Commission, as may be determined upon by the Secretary of the Interior. A statement of the result of every noncompetitive test and all appointments, transfers, or promotions based thereon shall be immediately forwarded to the Commission.

4. In pursuance of the provisions of section 3 of the civil-service act, examinations shall be provided at such places and upon such dates as the Commission shall deem most practicable to subserve the convenience of applicants and the needs of the service.

5. In pursuance of the provisions of section 3 of the civil-service act, the Commission shall appoint from persons in the Government service such boards of examiners as it may deem necessary. The members of said boards shall perform such duties as the Commission may direct in connection with examinations, appointments, and promotions in any part of the service which has been or may hereafter be classified. The members of any board of examiners in the performance of their duties as such shall be under the direct and sole control and authority of the Commission. The duties performed by the members of any board of examiners in their capacity as such shall be considered part of the duties of the office in which they are serving, and time shall be allowed for the performance of said duties during the office hours of said office. The members of any board of examiners shall not all be adherents of one political party when persons of other political parties are available and competent to serve upon said board.

6. In pursuance of the provisions of section 3 of the civil-service act, all **executive**

officers of the United States shall facilitate civil-service examinations, and postmasters, customs officers, internal-revenue officers, and custodians of public buildings at places where such examinations are to be held shall for the purpose of such examinations permit and arrange for the use of suitable rooms under their charge and for heating, lighting, and furnishing the same.

RULE V.

1. Every applicant for examination must be a citizen of the United States, must be of proper age, and must make an application under oath upon a form prescribed by the Commission and accompanied by such certificates as may be prescribed.

2. No application for examination shall be accepted from any person serving in the Army, the Navy, or Marine Corps of the United States unless the written consent of the head of the department under which said person is enlisted is filed with his application.

3. The Commission may, in its discretion, refuse to examine an applicant or to certify an eligible who is physically so disabled as to be rendered unfit for the performance of the duties of the position to which he seeks appointment, or who has been guilty of a crime or of infamous or notoriously disgraceful conduct, or who has been dismissed from the service for delinquency or misconduct within one year next preceding the date of his application, or who has intentionally made a false statement in any material fact or practiced or attempted to practice any deception or fraud in securing his registration or appointment. Any of the foregoing disqualifications shall be good cause for the removal of an eligible from the service after his appointment.

4. No application for examination shall be accepted unless the applicant is within the age limitations fixed herein for entrance to the position to which he seeks to be appointed: *Provided*, That, subject to the other conditions of these rules, the application of any person whose claim of preference under the provisions of section 1754 of the Revised Statutes has been allowed by the Commission may be accepted without regard to his age. The age limitations for entrance to positions in the different branches of the service shall be as follows:

	Minimum.	Maximum.
Departmental service:		
Page or messenger boy	14	18
Apprentice (or student)	16	20
Printer's assistant and messenger	18	No limit.
Positions in railway mail service	18	35
Superintendent, physician, supervisor, day-school inspector, Indian service	25	55
All other positions in the Indian service	21	45
All other positions	20	No limit.
(These limitations shall not apply in the cases of wives of superintendents of Indian schools who apply for examination for the position of teacher or matron.)		
Custom-house service:		
Clerk and messenger	20	No limit.
Other positions	21	No limit.
Post-office service:		
Letter carrier	21	40
Other positions	18	No limit.
Government printing service:		
All positions (male)	21	No limit.
All positions (female)	18	No limit.
Internal-revenue service:		
Clerk	18	No limit.
Other positions	21	No limit.

5. No application shall be accepted for examination for a position which belongs to one of the recognized mechanical trades unless it shall be shown that the applicant has served as apprentice or as journeyman or as apprentice and journeyman at said trade for such periods as the Commission may prescribe.

RULE VI.

The following-named employees or positions which have been or may hereafter be classified under the civil-service act shall be excepted from the requirement of examination or registration:

Departmental service.—(*a*) Private secretaries or confidential clerks (not exceeding two) to the President or to the head of each of the eight Executive Departments; (*b*) Indians employed in the Indian service at large, except those employed as superintendents, teachers, teachers of industries, kindergartners, and physicians.

Custom-house service.—(*a*) One cashier in each customs district; (*b*) one chief or principal deputy or assistant collector in each customs district whose employees number as many as 150.

Post-office service.—(*a*) One assistant postmaster, or chief assistant to the postmaster, of whatever designation, at each post-office; (*b*) one cashier of each first-class post-office when employed under the roster title of cashier only.

Internal-revenue service.—One cashier in each internal-revenue district.

RULE VII.

1. Examination papers shall be rated on a scale of 100, and the subjects therein shall be given such relative weights as the Commission may prescribe. After a competitor's papers have been rated he shall be duly notified of the result thereof.

2. Every competitor who attains an average percentage of 70 or over shall be eligible for appointment to the position for which he was examined, and the names of eligibles shall be entered in the order of their average percentages on the proper register of eligibles: *Provided,* That the names of all competitors whose claims to preference under the provisions of section 1754 of the Revised Statutes have been allowed by the Commission, and who attain an average percentage of 65 or over, shall be placed in the order of their average percentages at the head of the proper register of eligibles.

3. For filling vacancies in positions for which competitive tests are not practicable the registration of applicants shall be in the order in which they fulfill the requirements prescribed therefor by regulation of the Commission: *Provided,* That persons who served in the military or naval service of the United States in the late War of the Rebellion and were honorably discharged therefrom, and persons who have been separated from such positions above mentioned through no delinquency or misconduct, shall be placed at the head of the proper register in the order of their fulfillment of said requirements.

4. The term of eligibility shall be one year from the date on which the name of the eligible is entered upon the register.

RULE VIII.

In pursuance of the provisions of section 2 of the civil-service act, whenever a vacancy occurs in any position which has been or may hereafter be classified under the civil-service act, and which is not an excepted position, the filling of said vacancy, unless filled through noncompetitive examination or by reinstatement, transfer, promotion, or reduction, shall be governed as follows:

1. The appointing or nominating officer shall request certification to him of the names of eligibles for the position vacant, and the Commission shall certify to said officer from the proper register the three names at the head thereof which have not been three times certified to the Department or office in which the vacancy

exists: *Provided*, That certification for temporary appointment shall not be counted as one of the three certifications to which an eligible is entitled: *And provided further*, That whenever the sex of those whose names are to be certified is fixed by any law, rule, or regulation or is specified in the request for certification the names of those of the sex so fixed or specified shall be certified, but in other cases certification shall be made without regard to sex.

2. Of the three names certified the nominating or appointing officer shall select one, and if at the time of selection there are more vacancies than one he may select more than one name, unless otherwise directed by the Commission.

3. If an eligible who is not entitled to certification is certified and appointed, his appointment shall be immediately revoked by the appointing officer upon notification from the Commission.

4. A person selected for appointment shall be notified of his selection by the appointing or nominating officer, and upon his acceptance shall receive from the appointing officer a certificate of appointment for a probationary period of six months, at the end of which period, if the conduct and capacity of the probationer are satisfactory to the appointing officer, his retention in the service shall be equivalent to his absolute appointment; but if his conduct or capacity be not satisfactory he shall be notified by the appointing officer that he will not receive absolute appointment because of such unsatisfactory conduct or want of capacity, and such notification shall discharge him from the service: *Provided*, That the probation of an employee in the Indian-school service shall terminate at the end of the school year in which he is appointed: *And provided further*, That the time which an employee has actually served as substitute in parts of the service where substitutes are authorized shall be counted as part of the probationary period of his regular appointment, but that time served under a temporary appointment shall not be so counted.

5. If the appointing or nominating officer shall object to an eligible named in the certificate, stating that because of some physical defect, mental unsoundness, or moral disqualification, particularly specified, said eligible would be incompetent or unfit for the performance of the duties of the vacant position, and if said officer shall sustain such objection with evidence satisfactory to the Commission, the Commission may certify the eligible on the register who is in average percentage next below those already certified in place of the one to whom objection is made and sustained.

6. Certifications for appointment of persons for service in or on direct detail from any Department or office in Washington, D. C., shall be so made as to maintain as nearly as possible the apportionment of such appointments among the several States and Territories and District of Columbia upon the basis of population, except to appointments in the Government Printing Office, to the position of printer's assistant, skilled helper, and operative in the Bureau of Engraving and Printing, to positions in the post quartermaster's office, in the pension agency, and other local offices in the District of Columbia, and to the positions of page and messenger boy and apprentice or student.

7. Within any part of the service to which promotion regulations have been or may hereafter be applied certification of those eligible to original appointment shall not be made for filling a vacancy in a position above the lowest class in any grade whenever there is any person eligible and willing to be promoted to said vacancy: *Provided*, That a vacancy in any position requiring the exercise of technical or professional knowledge may be filled by original appointment.

8. When two or more eligibles on a register have the same average percentage, preference in certification shall be determined by the order in which their applications were filed.

9. For filling vacancies in positions outside of the District of Columbia and in positions in the pension agency, the depot quartermaster's office, and other local offices in the District of Columbia the territory of the United States shall be arranged in

such sections or districts as the Commission may determine, and an eligible shall be certified in his order to vacancies in the section or district in which he resides, and, upon his written request, to vacancies in any one or more of the other sections or districts: *Provided*, That in the custom-house service, post-office service, or internal-revenue service an eligible shall be certified only to vacancies in the customs district, post-office, or internal-revenue district where he was examined.

10. In any part of the service in which the employment of substitutes is not prohibited by law there may be certified and appointed in the manner provided for in this rule only such number of substitutes as are actually needed for the performance of substitute duty.

11. In any part of the service in which substitutes are employed certifications of those eligible to original appointment shall be made for filling vacancies in substitute positions only, and vacancies in regular positions shall be filled by the appointment or promotion thereto of substitutes in the order of their original appointment as substitutes whenever there are substitutes of the required sex who are eligible and willing to be so appointed or promoted. Substitutes so appointed or promoted shall, however, be subject to the provisions of these rules relating to probation and permanent appointment.

12. Upon request of the appointing or nominating officer preference in certification may be given to the wife of the superintendent of an Indian school for filling a vacancy in the position of teacher or matron in said school.

13. Whenever there shall occur a vacancy which the public interest requires shall be immediately filled and which can not be so filled in time to meet the emergency by certification from the eligible registers, such vacancy may, subject to the approval of the Commission, be filled by temporary appointment without examination until a regular appointment can be made. Such temporary appointment shall in no case continue longer than ninety days, and shall expire by limitation at the end of that time. No person shall serve longer than ninety days in any one year under such temporary appointment or appointments, and in any event only until a regular appointment can be made through examination and certification. Said year limitation shall begin to run in the case of any person on the date of his first such appointment: *Provided*, That whenever an emergency shall arise requiring that a vacant position in any internal-revenue district shall be filled before a certificate can be issued by the Commission and an appointment made thereto in the manner provided in these rules such position may be filled without regard to the provisions of these rules by temporary appointment for a period not to exceed thirty days, and only for such period as may be required for the execution of the necessary details of an appointment thereto in accordance with said provisions; but no person shall receive such temporary appointment who within the ninety days next previous thereto has been separated from a position in said district to which he was temporarily appointed under the provisions of this section.

14. Whenever a temporary appointment shall be made through certification from the eligible registers of the Commission in the manner provided in these rules, such temporary appointment shall in no case continue longer than six months, and shall expire by limitation at the end of that period.

RULE IX.

A vacancy in any position which has been or may hereafter be classified under the civil-service act may, upon requisition of the proper officer and the certificate of the Commission, be filled by the reinstatement without examination of any person who within one year next preceding the date of said requisition has through no delinquency or misconduct been separated from a classified position at the date of said requisition and in that Department or office and that branch of the service in which said vacancy exists: *Provided*, That for original entrance to the position proposed

By the President of the United States of America.

A Proclamation.

Whereas: The Congress of the United States passed an Act which was approved on the sixteenth day of July, eighteen hundred and ninety four, entitled "An Act to enable the people of Utah to form a Constitution and State Government and to be admitted into the Union on an equal footing with the original States," which Act provided for the election of delegates to a Constitutional Convention to meet at the seat of government of the Territory of Utah, on the first Monday in March eighteen hundred and ninety-five, for the purpose of declaring the adoption of the Constitution of the United States by the people of the proposed State and forming a Constitution and State Government for such State;

And whereas, delegates were accordingly elected who met, organized and declared on behalf of the people of said proposed State their adoption of the Constitution of the United States, all as provided in said Act;

And whereas, said Convention, so organized, did by ordinance irrevocable without the consent of the United States and the people of said State, as required

PRESIDENT CLEVELAND'S PROCLAMATION ON UTAH'S
ADMISSION TO THE UNION.

the United States to be affixed.

Done at the city of Washington this fourth day of January in the year of our Lord one thousand eight hundred and ninety six, and of the Independence of the United States of America the one hundred and twentieth.

Grover Cleveland

By the President.

Richard Olney
Secretary of State.

PRESIDENT CLEVELAND'S SIGNATURE TO PROCLAMATION
ADMITTING UTAH INTO THE UNION.

to be filled by reinstatement there is not required by these rules, in the opinion of the Commission, an examination involving essential tests different from or higher than those involved in the examination for original entrance to the position formerly held by the person proposed to be reinstated: *And provided further*, That, subject to the other conditions of these rules, any person who served in the military or naval service of the United States in the late War of the Rebellion and was honorably discharged therefrom, or the widow of any such person, may be reinstated without regard to the length of time he or she has been separated from the service.

RULE X.

Within that part of the civil service of the United States which has been or may hereafter be classified under the civil-service act transfers shall be governed as follows:

1. A person in any Department or office may be transferred within the same Department or office and the same branch of the service upon any test of fitness, not disapproved by the Commission, which may be determined upon by the appointing officer, subject to the limitations of the provisos of section 2 of this rule.

2. A person who has received absolute appointment may be transferred without examination from any Department, office, or branch of the service upon requisition and consent of the proper officers and the certificate of the Commission: *Provided*, That no transfer shall be made of a person to a position within the same Department or office and the same branch of the service, or to a position in another Department, office, or branch of the service, if from original entrance to such position said person is barred by the age limitations prescribed therefor or by the provisions regulating apportionment, or if in said position there is not required, in the judgment of the Commission, the performance of the same class of work or the practice of the same mechanical trade performed or practiced in the position from which transfer is proposed: *And provided further*, That transfer shall not be made without examination, provided by the Commission, to a position for original entrance to which, in the judgment of the Commission, there is required by these rules an examination involving essential tests different from or higher than those involved in the examination required for original entrance to the position from which transfer is proposed; but a person employed in any grade shall not because of such employment be barred from the open competitive examination provided for original entrance to any other grade.

3. Upon requisition of the proper officer and the certificate of the Commission transfer may be made without examination from the office of the President of the United States, after continuous service therein for the two years next preceding the date of said requisition, to any position classified under the civil-service act, if in said position there is required, in the judgment of the Commission, the performance of the same class of work that is required to be performed in the position from which transfer is proposed.

4. Transfer shall not be made from an excepted position to a position not excepted: *Provided*, That a person holding an excepted position at the time said position is classified under the civil-service act, or a person holding an excepted position which he entered prior to the President's order of November 2, 1894, may, subject to the other conditions and provisions of this rule, be transferred to a position not excepted.

5. Transfer shall not be made from a position not classified under the civil-service act to a classified position: *Provided*, That a person who by promotion or transfer from a classified position has entered a position appointment to which is made by the President by and with the advice and consent of the Senate, and has served continuously therein from the date of said promotion or transfer, may be transferred from said Presidential appointment to the position from which he was so transferred or to any position to which transfer could be made therefrom.

6. Transfer shall not be made from a position outside the District of Columbia to a position within the District of Columbia except upon the certificate of the Commission, subject to the other conditions and provisions of this rule.

7. Any person who has been transferred from a classified position to another classified position may be retransferred to the position in which he was formerly employed or to any position to which transfer could be made therefrom without regard to the limitations of this rule.

8. All transfers herein authorized shall be made only after the issuance by the Commission of the certificates therefor, except those which may be specifically exempted from such condition by regulation of the Commission.

9. Whenever a person is proposed for transfer from one branch of the service to another branch of the service and from a part of the service not within the provisions regulating apportionment to a part of the service within said provisions, and the transfer is one which under the provisions of this rule may be allowed without examination, such person shall be required precedent to his transfer to file a statement under oath setting forth the same facts, accompanied by the same certificates or vouchers relating to residence, as may be required in an application for examination.

RULE XI.

1. In pursuance of the requirements of section 7 of the civil-service act, competitive tests or examinations shall, as far as practicable and useful, be established to test fitness for promotion in any part of the civil service of the United States which has been or may hereafter be classified under the civil-service act.

2. The details regulating promotions shall be formulated by the Commission after consultation with the heads of the several Departments, bureaus, or offices. It shall be the duty of the head of each Department, bureau, or office when such regulations have been formulated to promulgate the same, and any amendments or revocations thereof shall be approved by the Commission before going into effect.

3. The Commission shall, upon the nomination of the head of each Department, bureau, or office, designate and select a suitable number of persons, not less than three, in said Department, bureau, or office to be members of a board of promotion. In the Departments, bureaus, or offices in Washington and in all other offices the members of any board of examiners shall not all be adherents of one political party when persons of other political parties are available and competent to serve upon said board.

4. Until the regulations herein authorized have been approved for any Department, bureau, or office in which promotion regulations approved by the Commission are not in force promotions therein may be made from one class to another class which is in the same grade and from one grade to another grade upon any test of fitness, not disapproved by the Commission, which may be determined upon by the promoting officer: *Provided*, That no promotion of a person shall be made, except upon examination provided by the Commission, from one class to another class or from one grade to another grade if for original entrance to said class or grade to which promotion is proposed there is required by these rules an examination involving essential tests different from or higher than those involved in the examination required for original entrance to the class or grade from which promotion is proposed: *And provided further*, That no promotion of a person shall be made, except upon examination provided by the Commission, to a position in which, in the judgment of the Commission, there is not required the performance of the same class of work or the practice of the same mechanical trade which is required to be performed or practiced in the position from which promotion is proposed, but a person employed in any grade shall not because of such employment be barred from the open competitive examination provided for original entrance to any other grade: *And provided further*, That

no promotion of a person shall be made to a class or grade from original entrance to which such person is barred by the age limitations prescribed therefor or by the provisions regulating apportionment.

RULE XII.

1. In pursuance of the provisions of section 2 of the civil-service act every nominating or appointing officer in the executive civil service of the United States shall furnish to the Commission a list of all the positions and employments under his control and authority, together with the names, designations, compensations, and dates of appointment or employment of all persons serving in said positions or employments, said list to be arranged as follows: (*a*) Classified positions not excepted from examination; (*b*) classified positions excepted from examination; (*c*) unclassified positions.

2. Every nominating or appointing officer in the executive civil service shall report in detail to the Commission, in form and manner to be prescribed by the Commission, all changes as soon as made, and the dates thereof, in the service under his control and authority, setting forth among other things the following: The position to which an appointment or reinstatement is made; the position from which a separation is made, whether the same was caused by dismissal, resignation, or death, and the posiion from which and the position to which a transfer or promotion is made; the compensation of every position from which or to which a change is made; the name of every person appointed, reinstated, promoted, transferred, or separated from the service, and every failure to accept an appointment and the reasons therefor.

Approved, May 6, 1896.

GROVER CLEVELAND.

EXECUTIVE MANSION,
Washington, D. C., May 7, 1896.

In the exercise of the authority vested in the President by the seventeen hundred and fifty-third (1753d) section of the Revised Statutes—

It is ordered, That the office of the Interstate Commerce Commission be, and the same is hereby, classified as a part of the classified departmental service, and for the purpose of applying the civil-service rules thereto the officers, clerks, and other employees of said Commission are hereby arranged in the following classes, viz:

Class A.—All persons receiving an annual salary of less than $720, or a compensation at the rate of less than $720 per annum.

Class B.—All persons receiving an annual salary of $720 or more, or a compensation at the rate of $720 or more, but less than $840 per annum.

Class C.—All persons receiving an annual salary of $840 or more, or a compensation at the rate of $840 or more, but less than $900 per annum.

Class D.—All persons receiving a salary of $900 or more, or a compensation at the rate of $900 or more, but less than $1,000 per annum.

Class E.—All persons receiving an annual salary of $1,000 or more, or a compensation at the rate of $1,000 or more, but less than $1,200 per annum.

Class 1.—All persons receiving an annual salary of $1,200 or more, or a compensation at the rate of $1,200 or more, but less than $1,400 per annum.

Class 2.—All persons receiving an annual salary of $1,400 or more per annum, or a compensation at the rate of $1,400 or more, but less than $1,600 per annum.

Class 3.—All persoLs receiving an annual salary of $1,600 or more per annum, or an annual compensation at the rate of $1,600 or more, but less than $1,800 per annum.

Class 4.—All persons receiving an annual salary of $1,800 or more per annum, or a compensation at the rate of $1,800 or more, but less than $2,000 per annum.

Class 5.—All persons receiving an annual salary of $2,000 or more or a compensation at the rate of $2,000 or more per annum.

Provided, That no person who may be appointed to an office by and with the advice and consent of the Senate and that no person who may be employed merely as a workman or laborer shall be considered as within this classification, and no person so employed shall be assigned to the duties of a classified place.

Provided further, That no person shall be admitted to any place not excepted from examination by the civil-service rules in any of the classes above designated until he or she shall have passed an appropriate examination under the United States Civil Service Commission and his or her eligibility has been certified to by said Commission.

GROVER CLEVELAND.

AMENDMENTS OF CIVIL-SERVICE RULES.

EXECUTIVE MANSION, *May 13, 1896.*

The civil-service rules are hereby amended as follows:

Rule III, clause 2 (*a*), is amended by adding after the words "the light-house service" the words "the life-saving service."

Paragraph (*b*) of the same rule and clause is amended by striking out after the words "who are in the service of the Treasury Department in any capacity" the words "except those in the life-saving service."

Approved:

GROVER CLEVELAND.

AMENDMENTS OF CIVIL-SERVICE RULES.

The civil-service rules as revised May 6, 1896, are hereby amended as follows:

Rule I, section 2, clause (*b*): In the third line, after the word "act," insert "and these rules;" so that as amended the clause will read:

(*b*) The term "classified service" refers to all that part of the executive civil service of the United States included within the provisions of the civil-service act and these rules.

Rule III, section 2, clause (*a*), is amended by adding thereto the following clause:

The Ordnance Department at large.

Rule III, section 2, clause (*a*), is amended by striking out after "persons" in the third line the words "who have been nominated for" and inserting in lieu thereof the words "whose appointments are subject to."

Rule III, section 2 clause (*b*), is amended by inserting in the second line, after the word "designation," the words "except persons merely employed as laborers or workmen and persons whose appointments are subject to confirmation by the Senate."

Rule III, section 2, clause (*b*), is amended by adding thereto the following words:

Who are employed in the Department of Justice under the annual appropriation for the investigation of official acts, records, and accounts of officers of the courts.

Rule III, section 3, is amended to read as follows:

3. The custom-house service shall include such officers and employees as have been or may hereafter be classified under the civil-service act who are serving in any customs district whose officers and employees number as many as five; and whenever in any customs district whose officers and employees number less than five the number of officers and employees shall be increased to as many as five the Secretary of the Treasury shall at once notify the Commission of such increase, and the officers and employees of said district shall be included within the classified service from the date of said increase.

Rule III, section 6, is amended by inserting in the second line, after the word "employees," the following: "in any internal-revenue district;" and in the third line, after the word "act," by striking out the following: "in any internal-revenue district;" so that as amended the section will read:

6. The internal-revenue service shall include the officers and employees in any internal-revenue district who have been or may hereafter be classified under the civil-service act.

Rule VI is amended by adding in the departmental service an additional clause, making exceptions from examination, to read as follows:

(*c*) Attorneys or assistant attorneys in any Department whose main duties are connected with the management of cases in court.

Amend Rule VI by striking out after "internal-revenue service" the words "one cashier in each internal-revenue district" and inserting in lieu thereof—

One employee in each internal-revenue district who shall act as cashier or chief deputy or assistant collector, as may be determined by the Treasury Department.

Amend Rule VIII by striking out section 3.

Rule IX is amended by striking out in the seventh line the word "classified" and inserting in lieu thereof after the word "position" in the same line the following: "included within the classified service;" so that as amended the line will read: "misconduct, been separated from a position included within the classified service at the."

Rule XI, section 2, is amended by striking out in line 1 the words "The details regulating" and inserting in their stead the words "Regulations to govern;" so that as amended the section will read:

2. Regulations to govern promotions shall be formulated by the Commission after consultation with the heads of the several Departments, bureaus, and offices. It shall be the duty of the head of each Department, bureau, or office when such regulations have been formulated to promulgate the same, and any amendments or revocations thereof shall be approved by the Commission before going into effect.

Rule XI, section 3: The word "examiners" in line 7 is changed to "promotion," making the section read:

3. The Commission shall, upon the nomination of the head of each Department, bureau, or office, designate and select a suitable number of persons, not less than three, in said Department, bureau, or office to be members of a board of promotion. In the Departments, bureaus, or offices in Washington and in all other offices the members of any board of promotion shall not all be adherents of one political party when persons of other political parties are available and competent to serve upon said board.

Approved, November 2, 1896. GROVER CLEVELAND.

CIVIL SERVICE.—EXECUTIVE ORDER.

EXECUTIVE MANSION, *November 2, 1896.*

The regulations of the Navy Department governing the employment of labor at navy-yards having been adopted by the Civil Service Commission as a regulation of the Commission July 29, 1896, under the authority conferred by clause 1, Rule I, of the revised civil-service rules of May 6, 1896, it is hereby ordered that no modification of the existing regulations shall be made without the approval of the Civil Service Commission. GROVER CLEVELAND.

FOURTH ANNUAL MESSAGE.

EXECUTIVE MANSION, *December 7, 1896.*

To the Congress of the United States:

As representatives of the people in the legislative branch of their Government, you have assembled at a time when the strength and excellence of our free institutions and the fitness of our citizens to enjoy popular rule have been again made manifest. A political contest involving momentous consequences, fraught with feverish apprehension, and creating aggressiveness so intense as to approach bitterness and passion has been waged throughout our land and determined by the decree of free and independent suffrage without disturbance of our tranquillity or the least sign of weakness in our national structure.

When we consider these incidents and contemplate the peaceful obedience and manly submission which have succeeded a heated clash of political opinions, we discover abundant evidence of a determination on the part of our countrymen to abide by every verdict of the popular will and to be controlled at all times by an abiding faith in the agencies established for the direction of the affairs of their Government.

Thus our people exhibit a patriotic disposition which entitles them to demand of those who undertake to make and execute their laws such faithful and unselfish service in their behalf as can only be prompted by a serious appreciation of the trust and confidence which the acceptance of public duty invites.

In obedience to a constitutional requirement I herein submit to the Congress certain information concerning national affairs, with the suggestion of such legislation as in my judgment is necessary and expedient. To secure brevity and avoid tiresome narration I shall omit many details concerning matters within Federal control which, though by no means unimportant, are more profitably discussed in departmental reports. I shall also further curtail this communication by omitting a minute recital of many minor incidents connected with our foreign relations which have heretofore found a place in Executive messages, but are now contained in a report of the Secretary of State, which is herewith submitted.

At the outset of a reference to the more important matters affecting our relations with foreign powers it would afford me satisfaction if I could assure the Congress that the disturbed condition in Asiatic Turkey had during the past year assumed a less hideous and bloody aspect and that, either as a consequence of the awakening of the Turkish Government to the demands of humane civilization or as the result of decisive action on the part of the great nations having the right by treaty to interfere for the protection of those exposed to the rage of mad bigotry and cruel fanaticism, the shocking features of the situation had been mitigated. Instead, however, of welcoming a softened disposition or protective intervention, we have been afflicted by continued and not unfrequent reports of the wanton destruction of homes and the bloody butchery of men, women, and children, made martyrs to their profession of Christian faith.

While none of our citizens in Turkey have thus far been killed or wounded, though often in the midst of dreadful scenes of danger, their safety in the future is by no means assured. Our Government at home and our minister at Constantinople have left nothing undone to protect our missionaries in Ottoman territory, who constitute nearly all the individuals residing there who have a right to claim our protection on the score of American citizenship. Our efforts in this direction will not be relaxed; but the deep feeling and sympathy that have been aroused among our people ought not to so far blind their reason and judgment as to lead them to demand impossible things. The outbreaks of blind fury which lead to murder and pillage in Turkey occur suddenly and without notice, and an attempt on our part to force such a hostile presence there as might be effective for prevention or protection would not only be resisted by the Ottoman Government, but would be regarded as an interruption of their plans by the great nations who assert their exclusive right to intervene in their own time and method for the security of life and property in Turkey.

Several naval vessels are stationed in the Mediterranean as a measure of caution and to furnish all possible relief and refuge in case of emergency.

We have made claims against the Turkish Government for the pillage and destruction of missionary property at Harpoot and Marash during uprisings at those places. Thus far the validity of these demands has not been admitted, though our minister, prior to such outrages and in anticipation of danger, demanded protection for the persons and property of our missionary citizens in the localities mentioned and notwithstanding that strong evidence exists of actual complicity of Turkish soldiers in the work of destruction and robbery.

The facts as they now appear do not permit us to doubt the justice of these claims, and nothing will be omitted to bring about their prompt settlement.

A number of Armenian refugees having arrived at our ports, an order has lately been obtained from the Turkish Government permitting the wives and children of such refugees to join them here. It is hoped that hereafter no obstacle will be interposed to prevent the escape of all those who seek to avoid the perils which threaten them in Turkish dominions.

Our recently appointed consul to Erzerum is at his post and discharging the duties of his office, though for some unaccountable reason his formal exequatur from the Sultan has not been issued.

I do not believe that the present somber prospect in Turkey will be long permitted to offend the sight of Christendom. It so mars the humane and enlightened civilization that belongs to the close of the nineteenth century that it seems hardly possible that the earnest demand of good people throughout the Christian world for its corrective treatment will remain unanswered.

The insurrection in Cuba still continues with all its perplexities. It is difficult to perceive that any progress has thus far been made toward the pacification of the island or that the situation of affairs as depicted in my last annual message has in the least improved. If Spain still holds Havana and the seaports and all the considerable towns, the insurgents still roam at will over at least two-thirds of the inland country. If the determination of Spain to put down the insurrection seems but to strengthen with the lapse of time and is evinced by her unhesitating devotion of largely increased military and naval forces to the task, there is much reason to believe that the insurgents have gained in point of numbers and character and resources and are none the less inflexible in their resolve not to succumb without practically securing the great objects for which they took up arms. If Spain has not yet reestablished her authority, neither have the insurgents yet made good their title to be regarded as an independent state. Indeed, as the contest has gone on the pretense that civil government exists on the island, except so far as Spain is able to maintain it, has been practically abandoned. Spain does keep on foot such a government, more or less imperfectly, in the large towns and their immediate suburbs; but that exception being made, the entire country is either given over to anarchy or is subject to the military occupation of one or the other party. It is reported, indeed, on reliable authority that at the demand of the commander in chief of the insurgent army the putative Cuban government has now given up all attempt to exercise its functions, leaving that government confessedly (what there is the best reason for supposing it always to have been in fact) a government merely on paper.

Were the Spanish armies able to meet their antagonists in the open or in pitched battle, prompt and decisive results might be looked for, and the immense superiority of the Spanish forces in numbers, discipline, and equipment could hardly fail to tell greatly to their advantage. But they are called upon to face a foe that shuns general engagements, that can choose and does choose its own ground, that from the nature of the country is visible or invisible at pleasure, and that fights only from ambuscade and when all the advantages of position and numbers are on its side. In a country where all that is indispensable to life in the way of food, clothing, and shelter is so easily obtainable, especially by those born and bred on the soil, it is obvious that there is hardly a limit to the time during which hostilities of this sort may be prolonged. Meanwhile, as in all cases of protracted civil strife, the passions of the combatants grow more and more inflamed and excesses on both sides become more frequent and more deplorable. They are also participated in by bands of marauders, who, now in the name of one party and now in the name of the other, as may best suit the occasion, harry the country at will and plunder its wretched inhabitants for their own advantage. Such a condition of things would inevitably entail immense destruction of property, even if it were the policy of both parties to prevent it as far as practicable; but while such seemed to be the original policy of the Spanish Government, it has now apparently abandoned it and is acting upon the same theory as the insurgents, namely, that the exigencies of the contest require the wholesale annihilation of property that it may not prove of use and advantage to the enemy.

It is to the same end that, in pursuance of general orders, Spanish garrisons are now being withdrawn from plantations and the rural population required to concentrate itself in the towns. The sure result would seem to be that the industrial value of the island is fast diminishing and that unless there is a speedy and radical change in existing conditions it will soon disappear altogether. That value consists very largely, of course, in its capacity to produce sugar—a capacity already much reduced by the interruptions to tillage which have taken place during the last two years. It is reliably asserted that should these interruptions continue during the current year, and practically extend, as is now threatened, to the entire sugar-producing territory of the island, so much time and so much money will be required to restore the land to its normal productiveness that it is extremely doubtful if capital can be induced to even make the attempt.

The spectacle of the utter ruin of an adjoining country, by nature one of the most fertile and charming on the globe, would engage the serious attention of the Government and people of the United States in any cir= cumstances. In point of fact, they have a concern with it which is by no means of a wholly sentimental or philanthropic character. It lies so near to us as to be hardly separated from our territory. Our actual pecun-iary interest in it is second only to that of the people and Government of Spain. It is reasonably estimated that at least from $30,000,000 to $50,000,000 of American capital are invested in plantations and in rail-road, mining, and other business enterprises on the island. The volume of trade between the United States and Cuba, which in 1889 amounted to about $64,000,000, rose in 1893 to about $103,000,000, and in 1894, the year before the present insurrection broke out, amounted to nearly $96,000,000. Besides this large pecuniary stake in the fortunes of Cuba, the United States finds itself inextricably involved in the present contest in other ways, both vexatious and costly.

Many Cubans reside in this country, and indirectly promote the in-surrection through the press, by public meetings, by the purchase and shipment of arms, by the raising of funds, and by other means which the spirit of our institutions and the tenor of our laws do not permit to be made the subject of criminal prosecutions. Some of them, though Cubans at heart and in all their feelings and interests, have taken out papers as naturalized citizens of the United States—a proceeding resorted to with a view to possible protection by this Government, and not un-naturally regarded with much indignation by the country of their origin. The insurgents are undoubtedly encouraged and supported by the wide-spread sympathy the people of this country always and instinctively feel for every struggle for better and freer government, and which, in the case of the more adventurous and restless elements of our population, leads in only too many instances to active and personal participation in the contest. The result is that this Government is constantly called upon to protect American citizens, to claim damages for injuries to per-sons and property, now estimated at many millions of dollars, and to ask explanations and apologies for the acts of Spanish officials whose zeal for the repression of rebellion sometimes blinds them to the immunities belonging to the unoffending citizens of a friendly power. It follows from the same causes that the United States is compelled to actively police a long line of seacoast against unlawful expeditions, the escape of which the utmost vigilance will not always suffice to prevent.

These inevitable entanglements of the United States with the rebellion in Cuba, the large American property interests affected, and considerations of philanthropy and humanity in general have led to a vehement demand in various quarters for some sort of positive intervention on the part of the United States. It was at first proposed that belligerent rights should be accorded to the insurgents—a proposition no longer urged because untimely and in practical operation clearly perilous and injurious to our own interests. It has since been and is now sometimes contended that the independence of the insurgents should be recognized; but imperfect and restricted as the Spanish government of the island may be, no other exists there, unless the will of the military officer in temporary command of a particular district can be dignified as a species of government. It is now also suggested that the United States should buy the island—a suggestion possibly worthy of consideration if there were any evidence of a desire or willingness on the part of Spain to entertain such a proposal. It is urged finally that, all other methods failing, the existing internecine strife in Cuba should be terminated by our intervention, even at the cost of a war between the United States and Spain—a war which its advocates confidently prophesy could neither be large in its proportions nor doubtful in its issue.

The correctness of this forecast need be neither affirmed nor denied. The United States has, nevertheless, a character to maintain as a nation, which plainly dictates that right and not might should be the rule of its conduct. Further, though the United States is not a nation to which peace is a necessity, it is in truth the most pacific of powers and desires nothing so much as to live in amity with all the world. Its own ample and diversified domains satisfy all possible longings for territory, preclude all dreams of conquest, and prevent any casting of covetous eyes upon neighboring regions, however attractive. That our conduct toward Spain and her dominions has constituted no exception to this national disposition is made manifest by the course of our Government, not only thus far during the present insurrection, but during the ten years that followed the rising at Yara in 1868. No other great power, it may safely be said, under circumstances of similar perplexity, would have manifested the same restraint and the same patient endurance. It may also be said that this persistent attitude of the United States toward Spain in connection with Cuba unquestionably evinces no slight respect and regard for Spain on the part of the American people. They in truth do not forget her connection with the discovery of the Western Hemisphere, nor do they underestimate the great qualities of the Spanish people nor fail to fully recognize their splendid patriotism and their chivalrous devotion to the national honor.

They view with wonder and admiration the cheerful resolution with which vast bodies of men are sent across thousands of miles of ocean and an enormous debt accumulated that the costly possession of the gem of the Antilles may still hold its place in the Spanish crown.   And yet neither the Government nor the people of the United States have shut their eyes to the course of events in Cuba or have failed to realize the existence of conceded grievances which have led to the present revolt from the authority of Spain—grievances recognized by the Queen Regent and by the Cortes, voiced by the most patriotic and enlightened of Spanish statesmen, without regard to party, and demonstrated by reforms proposed by the executive and approved by the legislative branch of the Spanish Government.   It is in the assumed temper and disposition of the Spanish Government to remedy these grievances, fortified by indications of influential public opinion in Spain, that this Government has hoped to discover the most promising and effective means of composing the present strife with honor and advantage to Spain and with the achievement of all the reasonable objects of the insurrection.

It would seem that if Spain should offer to Cuba genuine autonomy—a measure of home rule which, while preserving the sovereignty of Spain, would satisfy all rational requirements of her Spanish subjects—there should be no just reason why the pacification of the island might not be effected on that basis.   Such a result would appear to be in the true interest of all concerned.   It would at once stop the conflict which is now consuming the resources of the island and making it worthless for whichever party may ultimately prevail.   It would keep intact the possessions of Spain without touching her honor, which will be consulted rather than impugned by the adequate redress of admitted grievances.   It would put the prosperity of the island and the fortunes of its inhabitants within their own control without severing the natural and ancient ties which bind them to the mother country, and would yet enable them to test their capacity for self-government under the most favorable conditions.   It has been objected on the one side that Spain should not promise autonomy until her insurgent subjects lay down their arms; on the other side, that promised autonomy, however liberal, is insufficient, because without assurance of the promise being fulfilled.

But the reasonableness of a requirement by Spain of unconditional surrender on the part of the insurgent Cubans before their autonomy is conceded is not altogether apparent.   It ignores important features of the situation—the stability two years' duration has given to the insurrection; the feasibility of its indefinite prolongation in the nature of things, and, as shown by past experience, the utter and imminent ruin of the island unless the present strife is speedily composed; above all, the rank abuses which all parties in Spain, all branches of her Government, and all her leading public men concede to exist and profess a desire to remove. Facing such circumstances, to withhold the proffer of needed reforms until the parties demanding them put themselves at mercy by throwing down their arms has the appearance of neglecting the gravest of perils and inviting suspicion as to the sincerity of any professed willingness to grant reforms. The objection on behalf of the insurgents that promised reforms can not be relied upon must of course be considered, though we have no right to assume and no reason for assuming that anything Spain undertakes to do for the relief of Cuba will not be done according to both the spirit and the letter of the undertaking.

Nevertheless, realizing that suspicions and precautions on the part of the weaker of two combatants are always natural and not always unjustifiable, being sincerely desirous in the interest of both as well as on its own account that the Cuban problem should be solved with the least possible delay, it was intimated by this Government to the Government of Spain some months ago that if a satisfactory measure of home rule were tendered the Cuban insurgents and would be accepted by them upon a guaranty of its execution the United States would endeavor to find a way not objectionable to Spain of furnishing such guaranty. While no definite response to this intimation has yet been received from the Spanish Government, it is believed to be not altogether unwelcome, while, as already suggested, no reason is perceived why it should not be approved by the insurgents. Neither party can fail to see the importance of early action, and both must realize that to prolong the present state of things for even a short period will add enormously to the time and labor and expenditure necessary to bring about the industrial recuperation of the island. It is therefore fervently hoped on all grounds that earnest efforts for healing the breach between Spain and the insurgent Cubans upon the lines above indicated may be at once inaugurated and pushed to an immediate and successful issue. The friendly offices of the United States, either in the manner above outlined or in any other way consistent with our Constitution and laws, will always be at the disposal of either party.

Whatever circumstances may arise, our policy and our interests would constrain us to object to the acquisition of the island or an interference with its control by any other power.

It should be added that it can not be reasonably assumed that the hitherto expectant attitude of the United States will be indefinitely maintained. While we are anxious to accord all due respect to the sovereignty of Spain, we can not view the pending conflict in all its features and properly apprehend our inevitably close relations to it and its possible results without considering that by the course of events we may be drawn into such an unusual and unprecedented condition as will fix a limit to our patient waiting for Spain to end the contest, either alone and in her own way or with our friendly cooperation.

When the inability of Spain to deal successfully with the insurrection has become manifest and it is demonstrated that her sovereignty is extinct in Cuba for all purposes of its rightful existence, and when a hopeless struggle for its reestablishment has degenerated into a strife which means nothing more than the useless sacrifice of human life and the utter destruction of the very subject-matter of the conflict, a situation will be presented in which our obligations to the sovereignty of Spain will be superseded by higher obligations, which we can hardly hesitate to recognize and discharge. Deferring the choice of ways and methods until the time for action arrives, we should make them depend upon the precise conditions then existing; and they should not be determined upon without giving careful heed to every consideration involving our honor and interest or the international duty we owe to Spain. Until we face the contingencies suggested or the situation is by other incidents imperatively changed we should continue in the line of conduct heretofore pursued, thus in all circumstances exhibiting our obedience to the requirements of public law and our regard for the duty enjoined upon us by the position we occupy in the family of nations.

A contemplation of emergencies that may arise should plainly lead us to avoid their creation, either through a careless disregard of present duty or even an undue stimulation and ill-timed expression of feeling. But I have deemed it not amiss to remind the Congress that a time may arrive when a correct policy and care for our interests, as well as a regard for the interests of other nations and their citizens, joined by considerations of humanity and a desire to see a rich and fertile country intimately related to us saved from complete devastation, will constrain our Government to such action as will subserve the interests thus involved and at the same time promise to Cuba and its inhabitants an opportunity to enjoy the blessings of peace.

The Venezuelan boundary question has ceased to be a matter of difference between Great Britain and the United States, their respective Governments having agreed upon the substantial provisions of a treaty between Great Britain and Venezuela submitting the whole controversy to arbitration. The provisions of the treaty are so eminently just and fair that the assent of Venezuela thereto may confidently be anticipated.

Negotiations for a treaty of general arbitration for all differences between Great Britain and the United States are far advanced and promise to reach a successful consummation at an early date.

The scheme of examining applicants for certain consular positions to test their competency and fitness, adopted under an Executive order issued on the 20th of September, 1895,* has fully demonstrated the usefulness of this innovation. In connection with this plan of examination promotions and transfers of deserving incumbents have been quite extensively made, with excellent results.

*See p. 6056.

During the past year 35 appointments have been made in the consular service, 27 of which were made to fill vacancies caused by death or resignation or to supply newly created posts, 2 to succeed incumbents removed for cause, 2 for the purpose of displacing alien consular officials by American citizens, and 4 merely changing the official title of incumbent from commercial agent to consul. Twelve of these appointments were transfers or promotions from other positions under the Department of State, 4 of those appointed had rendered previous service under the Department, 8 were made of persons who passed a satisfactory examination, 7 were appointed to places not included in the order of September 20, 1895, and 4 appointments, as above stated, involved no change of incumbency.

The inspection of consular offices provided for by an appropriation for that purpose at the last session of the Congress has been productive of such wholesome effects that I hope this important work will in the future be continued. I know of nothing that can be done with the same slight expense so improving to the service.

I desire to repeat the recommendation contained in my last annual message in favor of providing at public expense official residences for our ambassadors and ministers at foreign capitals. The reasons supporting this recommendation are strongly stated in the report of the Secretary of State, and the subject seems of such importance that I hope it may receive the early attention of the Congress.

We have during the last year labored faithfully and against unfavorable conditions to secure better preservation of seal life in the Bering Sea. Both the United States and Great Britain have lately dispatched commissioners to these waters to study the habits and condition of the seal herd and the causes of their rapid decrease. Upon the reports of these commissioners, soon to be submitted, and with the exercise of patience and good sense on the part of all interested parties, it is earnestly hoped that hearty cooperation may be secured for the protection against threatened extinction of seal life in the Northern Pacific and Bering Sea.

The Secretary of the Treasury reports that during the fiscal year ended June 30, 1896, the receipts of the Government from all sources amounted to $409,475,408.78. During the same period its expenditures were $434,678,654.48, the excess of expenditures over receipts thus amounting to $25,203,245.70. The ordinary expenditures during the year were $4,015,852.21 less than during the preceding fiscal year. Of the receipts mentioned there was derived from customs the sum of $160,021,751.67 and from internal revenue $146,830,615.66. The receipts from customs show an increase of $7,863,134.22 over those from the same source for the fiscal year ended June 30, 1895, and the receipts from internal revenue an increase of $3,584,537.91.

The value of our imported dutiable merchandise during the last fiscal year was $369,757,470 and the value of free goods imported $409,967,-470, being an increase of $6,523,675 in the value of dutiable goods and

$41,231,034 in the value of free goods over the preceding year. Our exports of merchandise, foreign and domestic, amounted in value to $882,606,938, being an increase over the preceding year of $75,068,773. The average *ad valorem* duty paid on dutiable goods imported during the year was 39.94 per cent and on free and dutiable goods taken together 20.55 per cent.

The cost of collecting our internal revenue was 2.78 per cent, as against 2.81 per cent for the fiscal year ending June 30, 1895. The total production of distilled spirits, exclusive of fruit brandies, was 86,588,703 taxable gallons, being an increase of 6,639,108 gallons over the preceding year. There was also an increase of 1,443,676 gallons of spirits produced from fruit as compared with the preceding year. The number of barrels of beer produced was 35,859,250, as against 33,589,784 produced in the preceding fiscal year, being an increase of 2,269,466 barrels.

The total amount of gold exported during the last fiscal year was $112,-409,947 and of silver $60,541,670, being an increase of $45,941,466 of gold and $13,246,384 of silver over the exportations of the preceding fiscal year. The imports of gold were $33,525,065 and of silver $28,-777,186, being $2,859,695 less of gold and $8,566,007 more of silver than during the preceding year.

The total stock of metallic money in the United States at the close of the last fiscal year, ended on the 30th day of June, 1896, was $1,228,-326,035, of which $599,597,964 was in gold and $628,728,071 in silver.

On the 1st day of November, 1896, the total stock of money of all kinds in the country was $2,285,410,590, and the amount in circulation, not including that in the Treasury holdings, was $1,627,055,641, being $22.63 per capita upon an estimated population of 71,902,000.

The production of the precious metals in the United States during the calendar year 1895 is estimated to have been 2,254,760 fine ounces of gold, of the value of $46,610,000, and 55,727,000 fine ounces of silver, of the commercial value of $36,445,000 and the coinage value of $72,051,-000. The estimated production of these metals throughout the world during the same period was 9,688,821 fine ounces of gold, amounting to $200,285,700 in value, and 169,189,249 fine ounces of silver, of the commercial value of $110,654,000 and of the coinage value of $218,738,100 according to our ratio.

The coinage of these metals in the various countries of the world during the same calendar year amounted to $232,701,438 in gold and $121,996,219 in silver.

The total coinage at the mints of the United States during the fiscal year ended June 30, 1896, amounted to $71,188,468.52, of which $58,-878,490 was in gold coins and $12,309,978.52 in standard silver dollars, subsidiary coins, and minor coins.

The number of national banks organized from the time the law authorizing their creation was passed up to October 31, 1896, was 5,051, and of this number 3,679 were at the date last mentioned in active operation, having authorized capital stock of $650,014,895, held by 288,902 shareholders, and circulating notes amounting to $211,412,620.

The total outstanding circulating notes of all national banks on the 31st day of October, 1896, amounted to $234,553,807, including unredeemed but fully secured notes of banks insolvent and in process of liquidation. The increase in national-bank circulation during the year ending on that day was $21,099,429. On October 6, 1896, when the condition of national banks was last reported, the total resources of the 3,679 active institutions were $3,263,685,313.83, which included $1,893,268,839.31 in loans and discounts and $362,165,733.85 in money of all kinds on hand. Of their liabilities $1,597,891,058.03 was due to individual depositors and $209,944,019 consisted of outstanding circulating notes.

There were organized during the year preceding the date last mentioned 28 national banks, located in 15 States, of which 12 were organized in the Eastern States, with a capital of $1,180,000, 6 in the Western States, with a capital of $875,000, and 10 in the Southern States, with a capital of $1,190,000. During the year, however, 37 banks voluntarily abandoned their franchises under the national law, and in the case of 27 others it was found necessary to appoint receivers. Therefore, as compared with the year preceding, there was a decrease of 36 in the number of active banks.

The number of existing banks organized under State laws is 5,708.

The number of immigrants arriving in the United States during the fiscal year was 343,267, of whom 340,468 were permitted to land and 2,799 were debarred on various grounds prescribed by law and returned to the countries whence they came at the expense of the steamship companies by which they were brought in. The increase in immigration over the preceding year amounted to 84,731. It is reported that with some exceptions the immigrants of the past year were of a hardy laboring class, accustomed and able to earn a support for themselves, and it is estimated that the money brought with them amounted to at least $5,000,-000, though it was probably much in excess of that sum, since only those having less than $30 are required to disclose the exact amount, and it is known that many brought considerable sums of money to buy land and build homes. Including all the immigrants arriving who were over 14 years of age, 28.63 per cent were illiterate, as against 20.37 per cent of those of that age arriving during the preceding fiscal year. The number of immigrants over 14 years old, the countries from which they came, and the percentage of illiterates among them were as follows: Italy, 57,515, with 54.59 per cent; Ireland, 37,496, with 7 per cent; Russia, 35,188, with 41.14 per cent; Austria-Hungary and provinces, 57,053, with 38.92 per cent; Germany, 25,334, with 2.96 per cent; Sweden, 18,821, with 1.16 per cent; while from Portugal there came 2,067, of whom 77.69 per cent were illiterate. There arrived from Japan during the year only 1,110 immigrants, and it is the opinion of the immigration authorities that the apprehension heretofore existing to some extent of a large immigration from Japan to the United States is without any substantial foundation.

From the Life-Saving Service it is reported that the number of disasters to documented vessels within the limits of its operations during the year was 437. These vessels had on board 4,608 persons, of whom 4,595 were saved and 13 lost. The value of such vessels is estimated at $8,880,140 and of their cargoes $3,846,380, making the total value of property imperiled $12,726,520. Of this amount $11,292,707 was saved and $1,432,750 was lost. Sixty-seven of the vessels were totally wrecked. There were besides 243 casualties to small undocumented craft, on board of which there were 594 persons, of whom 587 were saved and 7 were lost. The value of the property involved in these latter casualties is estimated at $119,265, of which $114,915 was saved and $4,350 was lost. The life-saving crews during the year also rescued or assisted numerous other vessels and warned many from danger by signals, both by day and night. The number of disasters during the year exceeded that of any previous year in the history of the service, but the saving of both life and property was greater than ever before in proportion to the value of the property involved and to the number of persons imperiled.

The operations of the Marine-Hospital Service, the Revenue-Cutter Service, the Steamboat-Inspection Service, the Light-House Service, the Bureau of Navigation, and other branches of public work attached to the Treasury Department, together with various recommendations concerning their support and improvement, are fully stated in the report of the Secretary of the Treasury, to which the attention of the Congress is especially invited.

The report of the Secretary of War exhibits satisfactory conditions in the several branches of the public service intrusted to his charge.

The limit of our military force as fixed by law is constantly and readily maintained. The present discipline and morale of our Army are excellent, and marked progress and efficiency are apparent throughout its entire organization.

With the exception of delicate duties in the suppression of slight Indian disturbances along our southwestern boundary, in which the Mexican troops cooperated, and the compulsory but peaceful return, with the consent of Great Britain, of a band of Cree Indians from Montana to the British possessions, no active operations have been required of the Army during the year past.

Changes in methods of administration, the abandonment of unnecessary posts and consequent concentration of troops, and the exercise of care and vigilance by the various officers charged with the responsibility in the expenditure of the appropriations have resulted in reducing to a minimum the cost of maintenance of our military establishment.

During the past year the work of constructing permanent infantry and cavalry posts has been continued at the places heretofore designated. The Secretary of War repeats his recommendation that appropriations for barracks and quarters should more strictly conform to the needs of the service as judged by the Department rather than respond to the wishes and importunities of localities. It is imperative that much of the money provided for such construction should now be allotted to the erection of necessary quarters for the garrisons assigned to the coast defenses, where many men will be needed to properly care for and operate modern guns. It is essential, too, that early provision be made to supply the necessary force of artillery to meet the demands of this service.

The entire Army has now been equipped with the new magazine arms, and wise policy demands that all available public and private resources should be so employed as to provide within a reasonable time a sufficient number to supply the State militia with these modern weapons and provide an ample reserve for any emergency.

The organized militia numbers 112,879 men. The appropriations for its support by the several States approximate $2,800,000 annually, and $400,000 is contributed by the General Government. Investigation shows these troops to be usually well drilled and inspired with much military interest, but in many instances they are so deficient in proper arms and equipment that a sudden call to active duty would find them inadequately prepared for field service. I therefore recommend that prompt measures be taken to remedy this condition and that every encouragement be given to this deserving body of unpaid and voluntary citizen soldiers, upon whose assistance we must largely rely in time of trouble.

During the past year rapid progress has been made toward the completion of the scheme adopted for the erection and armament of fortifications along our seacoast, while equal progress has been made in providing the material for submarine defense in connection with these works.

It is peculiarly gratifying at this time to note the great advance that has been made in this important undertaking since the date of my annual message to the Fifty-third Congress at the opening of its second session, in December, 1893. At that time I informed the Congress of the approaching completion of nine 12-inch, twenty 10-inch, and thirty-four 8-inch high-power steel guns and seventy-five 12-inch rifled mortars.

This total then seemed insignificant when compared with the great work remaining to be done. Yet it was none the less a source of satisfaction to every citizen when he reflected that it represented the first installment of the new ordnance of American design and American manufacture and demonstrated our ability to supply from our own resources guns of unexcelled power and accuracy.

At that date, however, there were practically no carriages upon which to mount these guns and only thirty-one emplacements for guns and sixty-four for mortars. Nor were all these emplacements in condition to receive their armament. Only one high-power gun was at that time in position for the defense of the entire coast.

Since that time the number of guns actually completed has been increased to a total of twenty-one 12-inch, fifty-six 10-inch, sixty-one 8-inch high-power breech-loading steel guns, ten rapid-fire guns, and eighty 12-inch rifled mortars. In addition there are in process of construction one 16-inch-type gun, fifty 12-inch, fifty-six 10-inch, twenty-seven 8-inch high-power guns, and sixty-six 12-inch rifled mortars; in all, four hundred and twenty-eight guns and mortars.

During the same year, immediately preceding the message referred to, the first modern gun carriage had been completed and eleven more were in process of construction. All but one were of the nondisappearing type. These, however, were not such as to secure necessary cover for the artillery gunners against the intense fire of modern machine rapid-fire and high-power guns.

The inventive genius of ordnance and civilian experts has been taxed in designing carriages that would obviate this fault, resulting, it is believed, in the solution of this difficult problem. Since 1893 the number of gun carriages constructed or building has been raised to a total of 129, of which 90 are on the disappearing principle, and the number of mortar carriages to 152, while the 95 emplacements which were provided for prior to that time have been increased to 280 built and building.

This improved situation is largely due to the recent generous response of Congress to the recommendations of the War Department.

Thus we shall soon have complete about one-fifth of the comprehensive system the first step in which was noted in my message to the Congress of December 4, 1893.*

When it is understood that a masonry emplacement not only furnishes a platform for the heavy modern high-power gun, but also in every particular serves the purpose and takes the place of the fort of former days, the importance of the work accomplished is better comprehended.

In the hope that the work will be prosecuted with no less vigor in the future, the Secretary of War has submitted an estimate by which, if allowed, there will be provided and either built or building by the end of the next fiscal year such additional guns, mortars, gun carriages, and emplacements as will represent not far from one-third of the total work to be done under the plan adopted for our coast defenses, thus affording a prospect that the entire work will be substantially completed within six years. In less time than that, however, we shall have attained a marked degree of security.

The experience and results of the past year demonstrate that with a continuation of present careful methods the cost of the remaining work will be much less than the original estimate.

We should always keep in mind that of all forms of military preparation coast defense alone is essentially pacific in its nature. While it gives the sense of security due to a consciousness of strength, it is neither the

*See pp. 5882–5883.

purpose nor the effect of such permanent fortifications to involve us in foreign complications, but rather to guarantee us against them. They are not temptation to war, but security against it. Thus they are thoroughly in accord with all the traditions of our national diplomacy.

The Attorney-General presents a detailed and interesting statement of the important work done under his supervision during the last fiscal year.

The ownership and management by the Government of penitentiaries for the confinement of those convicted in United States courts of violations of Federal laws, which for many years has been a subject of Executive recommendation, have at last to a slight extent been realized by the utilization of the abandoned military prison at Fort Leavenworth as a United States penitentiary.

This is certainly a movement in the right direction, but it ought to be at once supplemented by the rebuilding or extensive enlargement of this improvised prison and the construction of at least one more, to be located in the Southern States. The capacity of the Leavenworth Penitentiary is so limited that the expense of its maintenance, calculated at a per capita rate upon the number of prisoners it can accommodate, does not make as economical an exhibit as it would if it were larger and better adapted to prison purposes; but I am thoroughly convinced that economy, humanity, and a proper sense of responsibility and duty toward those whom we punish for violations of Federal law dictate that the Federal Government should have the entire control and management of the penitentiaries where convicted violators are confined.

It appears that since the transfer of the Fort Leavenworth Military Prison to its new uses the work previously done by prisoners confined there, and for which expensive machinery has been provided, has been discontinued. This work consisted of the manufacture of articles for army use, now done elsewhere. On all grounds it is exceedingly desirable that the convicts confined in this penitentiary be allowed to resume work of this description.

It is most gratifying to note the satisfactory results that have followed the inauguration of the new system provided for by the act of May 28, 1896, under which certain Federal officials are compensated by salaries instead of fees. The new plan was put in operation on the 1st day of July, 1896, and already the great economy it enforces, its prevention of abuses, and its tendency to a better enforcement of the laws are strikingly apparent. Detailed evidence of the usefulness of this long-delayed but now happily accomplished reform will be found clearly set forth in the Attorney-General's report.

Our Post-Office Department is in good condition, and the exhibit made of its operations during the fiscal year ended June 30, 1896, if allowance is made for imperfections in the laws applicable to it, is very satisfactory. The total receipts during the year were $82,499,208.40. The total expenditures were $90,626,296.84, exclusive of the $1,559,898.27 which was earned by the Pacific Railroad for transportation and credited on their debt to the Government. There was an increase of receipts over the previous year of $5,516,080.21, or 7.1 per cent, and an increase of expenditures of $3,836,124.02, or 4.42 per cent. The deficit was $1,679,-956.19 less than that of the preceding year. The chief expenditures of the postal service are regulated by law and are not in the control of the Postmaster-General. All that he can accomplish by the most watchful administration and economy is to enforce prompt and thorough collection and accounting for public moneys and such minor savings in small expenditures and in letting those contracts, for post-office supplies and star service, which are not regulated by statute.

An effective cooperation between the Auditor's Office and the Post-Office Department and the making and enforcement of orders by the Department requiring immediate notification to their sureties of all delinquencies on the part of postmasters, and compelling such postmasters to make more frequent deposits of postal funds, have resulted in a prompter auditing of their accounts and much less default to the Government than heretofore.

The year's report shows large extensions of both star-route service and railway mail service, with increased postal facilities. Much higher accuracy in handling mails has also been reached, as appears by the decrease of errors in the railway mail service and the reduction of mail matter returned to the Dead-Letter Office.

The deficit for the last year, although much less than that of the last and preceding years, emphasizes the necessity for legislation to correct the growing abuse of second-class rates, to which the deficiency is mainly attributable. The transmission at the rate of 1 cent a pound of serial libraries, advertising sheets, "house organs" (periodicals advertising some particular "house" or institution), sample copies, and the like ought certainly to be discontinued. A glance at the revenues received for the work done last year will show more plainly than any other statement the gross abuse of the postal service and the growing waste of its earnings.

The free matter carried in the mails for the Departments, offices, etc., of the Government and for Congress, in pounds, amounted to 94,480,189.

If this is offset against buildings for post-offices and stations, the rental of which would more than compensate for such free postal service, we have this exhibit:

Weight of mail matter (other than above) transmitted through the mails for the year ending June 30, 1896.

Class.	Weight.	Revenue.
	Pounds.	
1. Domestic and foreign letters and postal cards, etc......	65,337,343	$60,624,464
2. Newspapers and periodicals, 1 cent per pound..........	348,988,648	2,996,403
3. Books, seeds, etc., 8 cents a pound.......................	78,701,148	10,324,069
4. Parcels, etc., 16 cents a pound...........................	19,950,187	3,129,321
Total	512,977,326	77,044,257

The remainder of our postal revenue, amounting to something more than $5,000,000, was derived from box rents, registry fees, money-order business, and other similar items.

The entire expenditures of the Department, including pay for transportation credited to the Pacific railroads, were $92,186,195.11, which may be considered as the cost of receiving, carrying, and delivering the above mail matter. It thus appears that though the second-class matter constituted more than two-thirds of the total that was carried, the revenue derived from it was less than one-thirtieth of the total expense.

The average revenue was—
From each pound of first-class matter ....cents.. 93.0
From each pound of second class* ....mills.. 8.5
From each pound of third class ....cents.. 13.1
From each pound of fourth class...do... 15.6

The growth in weight of second-class matter has been from 299,000,000 pounds in 1894 to 312,000,000 in 1895 and to almost 349,000,000 in 1896, and it is quite evident this increasing drawback is far outstripping any possible growth of postal revenues.

Our mail service should of course be such as to meet the wants and even the conveniences of our people at a direct charge upon them so light as perhaps to exclude the idea of our Post-Office Department being a money-making concern; but in the face of a constantly recurring deficiency in its revenues and in view of the fact that we supply the best mail service in the world it seems to me it is quite time to correct the abuses that swell enormously our annual deficit. If we concede the public policy of carrying weekly newspapers free in the county of publication, and even the policy of carrying at less than one-tenth of their cost other *bona fide* newspapers and periodicals, there can be no excuse for subjecting the service to the further immense and increasing loss involved in carrying at the nominal rate of 1 cent a pound the serial libraries, sometimes including trashy and even harmful literature, and other matter which under the loose interpretation of a loose statute have been gradually given second-class rates, thus absorbing all profitable returns derived from first-class matter, which pays three or four times more than its cost, and producing a large annual loss to be paid by general taxation. If such second-class matter paid merely the cost of its handling, our deficit would disappear and a surplus result which might be used to give the people still better mail facilities or cheaper rates of letter postage. I recommend that legislation be at once enacted to correct these abuses and introduce better business ideas in the regulation of our postal rates.

Experience and observation have demonstrated that certain improvements in the organization of the Post-Office Department must be secured before we can gain the full benefit of the immense sums expended in its administration. This involves the following reforms, which I earnestly recommend:

There should be a small addition to the existing inspector service, to be employed in the supervision of the carrier force, which now numbers

* Of the second class 52,348,297 was county-free matter.

13,000 men and performs its service practically without the surveillance exercised over all other branches of the postal or public service. Of course such a lack of supervision and freedom from wholesome disciplinary restraints must inevitably lead to imperfect service. There should also be appointed a few inspectors who could assist the central office in necessary investigation concerning matters of post-office leases, post-office sites, allowances for rent, fuel, and lights, and in organizing and securing the best results from the work of the 14,000 clerks now employed in first and second class offices.

I am convinced that the small expense attending the inauguration of these reforms would actually be a profitable investment.

I especially recommend such a recasting of the appropriations by Congress for the Post-Office Department as will permit the Postmaster-General to proceed with the work of consolidating post-offices. This work has already been entered upon sufficiently to fully demonstrate by experiment and experience that such consolidation is productive of better service, larger revenues, and less expenditures, to say nothing of the further advantage of gradually withdrawing post-offices from the spoils system.

The Universal Postal Union, which now embraces all the civilized world and whose delegates will represent 1,000,000,000 people, will hold its fifth congress in the city of Washington in May, 1897. The United States may be said to have taken the initiative which led to the first meeting of this congress, at Berne in 1874, and the formation of the Universal Postal Union, which brings the postal service of all countries to every man's neighborhood and has wrought marvels in cheapening postal rates and securing absolutely safe mail communication throughout the world. Previous congresses have met in Berne, Paris, Lisbon, and Vienna, and the respective countries in which they have assembled have made generous provision for their accommodation and for the reception and entertainment of the delegates.

In view of the importance of this assemblage and of its deliberations and of the honors and hospitalities accorded to our representatives by other countries on similar occasions, I earnestly hope that such an appropriation will be made for the expenses necessarily attendant upon the coming meeting in our capital city as will be worthy of our national hospitality and indicative of our appreciation of the event.

The work of the Navy Department and its present condition are fully exhibited in the report of the Secretary.

The construction of vessels for our new Navy has been energetically prosecuted by the present Administration upon the general lines previously adopted, the Department having seen no necessity for radical changes in prior methods, under which the work was found to be progressing in a manner highly satisfactory. It has been decided, however, to provide in every shipbuilding contract that the builder should pay all trial expenses, and it has also been determined to pay no speed premiums in future contracts. The premiums recently earned and some yet to be decided are features of the contracts made before this conclusion was reached.

On March 4, 1893, there were in commission but two armored vessels—the double-turreted monitors *Miantonomoh* and *Monterey*. Since that date, of vessels theretofore authorized, there have been placed in their first commission 3 first-class and 2 second-class battle ships, 2 armored cruisers, 1 harbor-defense ram, and 5 double-turreted monitors, including the *Maine* and the *Puritan*, just completed. Eight new unarmored cruisers and 2 new gunboats have also been commissioned. The *Iowa*, another battle ship, will be completed about March 1, and at least 4 more gunboats will be ready for sea in the early spring.

It is gratifying to state that our ships and their outfits are believed to be equal to the best that can be manufactured elsewhere, and that such notable reductions have been made in their cost as to justify the statement that quite a number of vessels are now being constructed at rates as low as those that prevail in European shipyards.

Our manufacturing facilities are at this time ample for all possible naval contingencies. Three of our Government navy-yards—those at Mare Island, Cal., Norfolk, Va., and Brooklyn, N. Y.—are equipped for shipbuilding, our ordnance plant in Washington is equal to any in the world, and at the torpedo station we are successfully making the highest grades of smokeless powder. The first-class private shipyards at Newport News, Philadelphia, and San Francisco are building battle ships; eleven contractors, situated in the States of Maine, Rhode Island, Pennsylvania, New Jersey, Maryland, Virginia, and the State of Washington, are constructing gunboats or torpedo boats; two plants are manufacturing large quantities of first-class armor, and American factories are producing automobile torpedoes, powder, projectiles, rapid-fire guns, and everything else necessary for the complete outfit of naval vessels.

There have been authorized by Congress since March, 1893, 5 battle ships, 6 light-draft gunboats, 16 torpedo boats, and 1 submarine torpedo boat. Contracts for the building of all of them have been let. The Secretary expresses the opinion that we have for the present a sufficient supply of cruisers and gunboats, and that hereafter the construction of battle ships and torpedo boats will supply our needs.

Much attention has been given to the methods of carrying on departmental business. Important modifications in the regulations have been made, tending to unify the control of shipbuilding as far as may be under the Bureau of Construction and Repair, and also to improve the mode of purchasing supplies for the Navy by the Bureau of Supplies and Accounts. The establishment under recent acts of Congress of a supply fund with which to purchase these supplies in large quantities and other modifications of methods have tended materially to their cheapening and better quality.

The War College has developed into an institution which it is believed will be of great value to the Navy in teaching the science of war, as well as in stimulating professional zeal in the Navy, and it will be especially useful in the devising of plans for the utilization in case of necessity of all the naval resources of the United States.

The Secretary has persistently adhered to the plan he found in operation for securing labor at navy-yards through boards of labor employment, and has done much to make it more complete and efficient. The naval officers who are familiar with this system and its operation express the decided opinion that its results have been to vastly improve the character of the work done at our yards and greatly reduce its cost.

Discipline among the officers and men of the Navy has been maintained to a high standard and the percentage of American citizens enlisted has been very much increased.

The Secretary is considering and will formulate during the coming winter a plan for laying up ships in reserve, thereby largely reducing the cost of maintaining our vessels afloat. This plan contemplates that battle ships, torpedo boats, and such of the cruisers as are not needed for active service at sea shall be kept in reserve with skeleton crews on board to keep them in condition, cruising only enough to insure the efficiency of the ships and their crews in time of activity.

The economy to result from this system is too obvious to need comment.

The Naval Militia, which was authorized a few years ago as an experiment, has now developed into a body of enterprising young men, active and energetic in the discharge of their duties and promising great usefulness. This establishment has nearly the same relation to our Navy as the National Guard in the different States bears to our Army, and it constitutes a source of supply for our naval forces the importance of which is immediately apparent.

The report of the Secretary of the Interior presents a comprehensive and interesting exhibit of the numerous and important affairs committed to his supervision. It is impossible in this communication to do more than briefly refer to a few of the subjects concerning which the Secretary gives full and instructive information.

The money appropriated on account of this Department and for its disbursement for the fiscal year ended June 30, 1896, amounted to more than $157,000,000, or a greater sum than was appropriated for the entire maintenance of the Government for the two fiscal years ended June 30, 1861.

Our public lands, originally amounting to 1,840,000,000 acres, have been so reduced that only about 600,000,000 acres still remain in Government control, excluding Alaska. The balance, being by far the most valuable portion, has been given away to settlers, to new States, and to railroads or sold at a comparatively nominal sum. The patenting of land in execution of railroad grants has progressed rapidly during the year, and since the 4th day of March, 1893, about 25,000,000 acres have thus been conveyed to these corporations.

I agree with the Secretary that the remainder of our public lands should be more carefully dealt with and their alienation guarded by better economy and greater prudence.

The commission appointed from the membership of the National Academy of Sciences, provided for by an act of Congress, to formulate plans for a national forestry system will, it is hoped, soon be prepared to present the result of thorough and intelligent examination of this important subject.

The total Indian population of the United States is 177,235, according to a census made in 1895, exclusive of those within the State of New York and those comprising the Five Civilized Tribes. Of this number there are approximately 38,000 children of school age. During the year 23,393 of these were enrolled in schools. The progress which has attended recent efforts to extend Indian-school facilities and the anticipation of continued liberal appropriations to that end can not fail to afford the utmost satisfaction to those who believe that the education of Indian children is a prime factor in the accomplishment of Indian civilization.

It may be said in general terms that in every particular the improvement of the Indians under Government care has been most marked and encouraging.

The Secretary, the Commissioner of Indian Affairs, and the agents having charge of Indians to whom allotments have been made strongly urge the passage of a law prohibiting the sale of liquor to allottees who have taken their lands in severalty. I earnestly join in this recommendation and venture to express the hope that the Indian may be speedily protected against this greatest of all obstacles to his well-being and advancement.

The condition of affairs among the Five Civilized Tribes, who occupy large tracts of land in the Indian Territory and who have governments of their own, has assumed such an aspect as to render it almost indispensable that there should be an entire change in the relations of these Indians to the General Government. This seems to be necessary in furtherance of their own interests, as well as for the protection of non-Indian residents in their territory. A commission organized and empowered under several recent laws is now negotiating with these Indians for the relinquishment of their courts and the division of their common lands in severalty and are aiding in the settlement of the troublesome question of tribal membership. The reception of their first proffers of negotiation was not encouraging, but through patience and such conduct on their part as demonstrated that their intentions were friendly and in the interest of the tribes the prospect of success has become more promising. The effort should be to save these Indians from the consequences of their own mistakes and improvidence and to secure to the real Indian his rights as against intruders and professed friends who profit by his retrogression. A change is also needed to protect life and property through the operation of courts conducted according to strict justice and strong enough to enforce their mandates.

As a sincere friend of the Indian, I am exceedingly anxious that these reforms should be accomplished with the consent and aid of the tribes and that no necessity may be presented for radical or drastic legislation. I hope, therefore, that the commission now conducting negotiations will soon be able to report that progress has been made toward a friendly adjustment of existing difficulties.

It appears that a very valuable deposit of gilsonite or asphaltum has been found on the reservation in Utah occupied by the Uncompahgre Ute Indians. Every consideration of care for the public interest and every sensible business reason dictate such management or disposal of this important source of public revenue as will except it from the general rules and incidents attending the ordinary disposition of public lands and secure to the Government a fair share at least of its advantages in place of its transfer for a nominal sum to interested individuals.

I indorse the recommendation made by the present Secretary of the Interior, as well as his predecessor, that a permanent commission, consisting of three members, one of whom shall be an army officer, be created to perform the duties now devolving upon the Commissioner and Assistant Commissioner of Indian Affairs. The management of the Bureau involves such numerous and diverse details and the advantages of an uninterrupted policy are so apparent that I hope the change suggested will meet the approval of the Congress.

The diminution of our enormous pension roll and the decrease of pension expenditure, which have been so often confidently foretold, still fail in material realization. The number of pensioners on the rolls at the close of the fiscal year ended June 30, 1896, was 970,678. This is the largest number ever reported. The amount paid exclusively for pensions during the year was $138,214,761.94, a slight decrease from that of the preceding year, while the total expenditures on account of pensions, including the cost of maintaining the Department and expenses attending pension distribution, amounted to $142,206,550.59, or within a very small fraction of one-third of the entire expense of supporting the Government during the same year. The number of new pension certificates issued was 90,640. Of these, 40,374 represent original allowances of claims and 15,878 increases of existing pensions.

The number of persons receiving pensions from the United States, but residing in foreign countries, at the close of the last fiscal year was 3,781, and the amount paid to them during the year was $582,735.38.

The sum appropriated for the payment of pensions for the current fiscal year, ending June 30, 1897, is $140,000,000, and for the succeeding year it is estimated that the same amount will be necessary.

The Commissioner of Pensions reports that during the last fiscal year 339 indictments were found against violators of the pension laws. Upon these indictments 167 convictions resulted.

In my opinion, based upon such statements as these and much other information and observation, the abuses which have been allowed to creep into our pension system have done incalculable harm in demoralizing our people and undermining good citizenship. I have endeavored within my sphere of official duty to protect our pension roll and make it what it should be, a roll of honor, containing the names of those disabled in their country's service and worthy of their country's affectionate remembrance. When I have seen those who pose as the soldiers' friends active and alert in urging greater laxity and more reckless pension expenditure, while nursing selfish schemes, I have deprecated the approach of a situation when necessary retrenchment and enforced economy may lead to an attack upon pension abuses so determined as to overlook the discrimination due to those who, worthy of a nation's care, ought to live and die under the protection of a nation's gratitude.

The Secretary calls attention to the public interests involved in an adjustment of the obligations of the Pacific railroads to the Government. I deem it to be an important duty to especially present this subject to the consideration of the Congress.

On January 1, 1897, with the amount already matured, more than $13,000,000 of the principal of the subsidy bonds issued by the United States in aid of the construction of the Union Pacific Railway, including its Kansas line, and more than $6,000,000 of like bonds issued in aid of the Central Pacific Railroad, including those issued to the Western Pacific Railroad Company, will have fallen due and been paid or must on that day be paid by the Government. Without any reference to the application of the sinking fund now in the Treasury, this will create such a default on the part of these companies to the Government as will give it the right to at once institute proceedings to foreclose its mortgage lien. In addition to this indebtedness, which will be due January 1, 1897, there will mature between that date and January 1, 1899, the remaining principal of such subsidy bonds, which must also be met by the Government. These amount to more than $20,000,000 on account of the Union Pacific lines and exceed $21,000,000 on account of the Central Pacific lines.

The situation of these roads and the condition of their indebtedness to the Government have been fully set forth in the reports of various committees to the present and prior Congresses, and as early as 1887 they were thoroughly examined by a special commission appointed pursuant to an act of Congress. The considerations requiring an adjustment of the Government's relations to the companies have been clearly presented and the conclusion reached with practical uniformity that if these relations are not terminated they should be revised upon a basis securing their safe continuance,

Under section 4 of the act of Congress passed March 3, 1887, the President is charged with the duty, in the event that any mortgage or other incumbrance paramount to the interest of the United States in the property of the Pacific railroads should exist and be lawfully liable to be enforced, to direct the action of the Departments of Treasury and of Justice in the protection of the interest of the United States by redemption or through judicial proceedings, including foreclosures of the Government liens.

In view of the fact that the Congress has for a number of years almost constantly had under consideration various plans for dealing with the conditions existing between these roads and the Government, I have thus far felt justified in withholding action under the statute above mentioned.

In the case of the Union Pacific Company, however, the situation has become especially and immediately urgent. Proceedings have been instituted to foreclose a first mortgage upon those aided parts of the main lines upon which the Government holds a second and subordinate mortgage lien. In consequence of those proceedings and increasing complications, added to the default occurring on the 1st day of January, 1897, a condition will be presented at that date, so far as this company is concerned, that must emphasize the mandate of the act of 1887 and give to Executive duty under its provisions a more imperative aspect. Therefore, unless Congress shall otherwise direct or shall have previously determined upon a different solution of the problem, there will hardly appear to exist any reason for delaying beyond the date of the default above mentioned such Executive action as will promise to subserve the public interests and save the Government from the loss threatened by further inaction.

The Department of Agriculture is so intimately related to the welfare of our people and the prosperity of our nation that it should constantly receive the care and encouragement of the Government. From small beginnings it has grown to be the center of agricultural intelligence and the source of aid and encouragement to agricultural efforts. Large sums of money are annually appropriated for the maintenance of this Department, and it must be confessed that the legislation relating to it has not always been directly in the interest of practical farming or properly guarded against waste and extravagance. So far, however, as public money has been appropriated fairly and sensibly to help those who actually till the soil, no expenditure has been more profitably made or more generally approved by the people.

Under the present management of the Department its usefulness has been enhanced in every direction, and at the same time strict economy has been enforced to the utmost extent permitted by Congressional action. From the report of the Secretary it appears that through careful and prudent financial management he has annually saved a large sum from his appropriations, aggregating during his incumbency and up to the close of the present fiscal year nearly one-fifth of the entire amount appropriated. These results have been accomplished by a conscientious study of the real needs of the farmer and such a regard for economy as the genuine farmer ought to appreciate, supplemented by a rigid adherence to civil-service methods in a Department which should be conducted in the interest of agriculture instead of partisan politics.

The Secretary reports 'hat the value of our exports of farm products during the last fiscal year amounted to $570,000,000, an increase of $17,-000,000 over those of the year immediately preceding. This statement is not the less welcome because of the fact that, notwithstanding such increase, the proportion of exported agricultural products to our total exports of all descriptions fell off during the year. The benefits of an increase in agricultural exports being assured, the decrease in its proportion to our total exports is the more gratifying when we consider that it is owing to the fact that such total exports for the year increased more than $75,000,000.

The large and increasing exportation of our agricultural products suggests the great usefulness of the organization lately established in the Department for the purpose of giving to those engaged in farming pursuits reliable information concerning the condition, needs, and advantages of different foreign markets. Inasmuch as the success of the farmer depends upon the advantageous sale of his products, and inasmuch as foreign markets must largely be the destination of such products, it is quite apparent that a knowledge of the conditions and wants that affect those markets ought to result in sowing more intelligently and reaping with a better promise of profit. Such information points out the way to a prudent foresight in the selection and cultivation of crops and to a release from the bondage of unreasoning monotony of production, a glutted and depressed market, and constantly recurring unprofitable toil.

In my opinion the gratuitous distribution of seeds by the Department as at present conducted ought to be discontinued. No one can read the statement of the Secretary on this subject and doubt the extravagance and questionable results of this practice. The professed friends of the farmer, and certainly the farmers themselves, are naturally expected to be willing to rid a Department devoted to the promotion of farming interests of a feature which tends so much to its discredit.

The Weather Bureau, now attached to the Department of Agriculture, has continued to extend its sphere of usefulness, and by an uninterrupted improvement in the accuracy of its forecasts has greatly increased its efficiency as an aid and protection to all whose occupations are related to weather conditions.

Omitting further reference to the operations of the Department, I commend the Secretary's report and the suggestions it contains to the careful consideration of the Congress.

The progress made in civil-service reform furnishes a cause for the utmost congratulation. It has survived the doubts of its friends as well as the rancor of its enemies and has gained a permanent place among the agencies destined to cleanse our politics and to improve, economize, and elevate the public service.

There are now in the competitive classified service upward of 84,000 places, more than half of these having been included from time to time since March 4, 1893. A most radical and sweeping extension was made by Executive order dated the 6th day of May, 1896,* and if fourth-class postmasterships are not included in the statement it may be said that practically all positions contemplated by the civil-service law are now classified. Abundant reasons exist for including these postmasterships, based upon economy, improved service, and the peace and quiet of neighborhoods. If, however, obstacles prevent such action at present, I earnestly hope that Congress will, without increasing post-office appropriations, so adjust them as to permit in proper cases a consolidation of these post-offices, to the end that through this process the result desired may to a limited extent be accomplished.

The civil-service rules as amended during the last year provide for a sensible and uniform method of promotion, basing eligibility to better positions upon demonstrated efficiency and faithfulness. The absence of fixed rules on this subject has been an infirmity in the system more and more apparent as its other benefits have been better appreciated.

The advantages of civil-service methods in their business aspects are too well understood to require argument. Their application has become a necessity to the executive work of the Government. But those who gain positions through the operation of these methods should be made to understand that the nonpartisan scheme through which they receive their appointments demands from them by way of reciprocity nonpartisan and faithful performance of duty under every Administration and cheerful fidelity to every chief. While they should be encouraged to decently exercise their rights of citizenship and to support through their suffrages the political beliefs they honestly profess, the noisy, pestilent, and partisan employee, who loves political turmoil and contention or who renders lax and grudging service to an Administration not representing his political views, should be promptly and fearlessly dealt with in such a way as to furnish a warning to others who may be likewise disposed.

The annual report of the Commissioners will be duly transmitted, and I commend the important matter they have in charge to the careful consideration of the Congress.

The Interstate Commerce Commission has during the last year supplied abundant evidence of its usefulness and the importance of the work committed to its charge.

Public transportation is a universal necessity, and the question of just and reasonable charges therefor has become of vital importance not only

*See pp. 6133-6143.

to shippers and carriers, but also to the vast multitude of producers and consumers. The justice and equity of the principles embodied in the existing law passed for the purpose of regulating these charges are everywhere conceded, and there appears to be no question that the policy thus entered upon has a permanent place in our legislation.

As the present statute when enacted was in the nature of the case more or less tentative and experimental, it was hardly expected to supply a complete and adequate system. While its wholesome effects are manifest and have amply justified its enactment, it is evident that all desired reforms in transportation methods have not been fully accomplished. In view of the judicial interpretation which some provisions of this statute have received and the defects disclosed by the efforts made for its enforcement, its revision and amendment appear to be essential, to the end that it may more effectually reach the evils designed to be corrected. I hope the recommendations of the Commission upon this subject will be promptly and favorably considered by the Congress.

I desire to recur to the statements elsewhere made concerning the Government's receipts and expenditures for the purpose of venturing upon some suggestions touching our present tariff law and its operation.

This statute took effect on the 28th day of August, 1894. Whatever may be its shortcomings as a complete measure of tariff reform, it must be conceded that it has opened the way to a freer and greater exchange of commodities between us and other countries, and thus furnished a wider market for our products and manufactures.

The only entire fiscal year during which this law has been in force ended on the 30th day of June, 1896. In that year our imports increased over those of the previous year more than $6,500,000, while the value of the domestic products we exported and which found markets abroad was nearly $70,000,000 more than during the preceding year.

Those who insist that the cost to our people of articles coming to them from abroad for their needful use should only be increased through tariff charges to an extent necessary to meet the expenses of the Government, as well as those who claim that tariff charges may be laid upon such articles beyond the necessities of Government revenue and with the additional purpose of so increasing their price in our markets as to give American manufacturers and producers better and more profitable opportunities, must agree that our tariff laws are only primarily justified as sources of revenue to enable the Government to meet the necessary expenses of its maintenance. Considered as to its efficiency in this aspect, the present law can by no means fall under just condemnation. During the only complete fiscal year of its operation it has yielded nearly $8,000,000 more revenue than was received from tariff duties in the preceding year. There was, nevertheless, a deficit between our receipts and expenditures of a little more than $25,000,000. This, however, was not unexpected.

The situation was such in December last, seven months before the close of the fiscal year, that the Secretary of the Treasury foretold a deficiency of $17,000,000. The great and increasing apprehension and timidity in business circles and the depression in all activities intervening since that time, resulting from causes perfectly well understood and entirely disconnected with our tariff law or its operation, seriously checked the imports we would have otherwise received and readily account for the difference between this estimate of the Secretary and the actual deficiency, as well as for a continued deficit. Indeed, it must be confessed that we could hardly have had a more unfavorable period than the last two years for the collection of tariff revenue. We can not reasonably hope that our recuperation from this business depression will be sudden, but it has already set in with a promise of acceleration and continuance.

I believe our present tariff law, if allowed a fair opportunity, will in the near future yield a revenue which, with reasonably economical expenditures, will overcome all deficiencies. In the meantime no deficit that has occurred or may occur need excite or disturb us. To meet any such deficit we have in the Treasury in addition to a gold reserve of one hundred millions a surplus of more than $128,000,000 applicable to the payment of the expenses of the Government, and which must, unless expended for that purpose, remain a useless hoard, or, if not extravagantly wasted, must in any event be perverted from the purpose of its exaction from our people. The payment, therefore, of any deficiency in the revenue from this fund is nothing more than its proper and legitimate use. The Government thus applying a surplus fortunately in its Treasury to the payment of expenses not met by its current revenues is not at all to be likened to a man living beyond his income and thus incurring debt or encroaching on his principal.

It is not one of the functions of our Government to accumulate and make additions to a fund not needed for immediate expenditure. With individuals it is the chief object of struggle and effort. The application of an accumulated fund by the Government to the payment of its running expenses is a duty. An individual living beyond his income and embarrassing himself with debt or drawing upon his accumulated fund of principal is either unfortunate or improvident. The distinction is between a government charged with the duty of expending for the benefit of the people and for proper purposes all the money it receives from any source, and the individual, who is expected to manifest a natural desire to avoid debt or to accumulate as much as possible and to live within the income derived from such accumulations, to the end that they may be increased or at least remain unimpaired for the future use and enjoyment of himself or the objects of his love and affection who may survive him.

It is immeasurably better to appropriate our surplus to the payment of justifiable expenses than to allow it to become an invitation to reckless appropriations and extravagant expenditures.

I suppose it will not be denied that under the present law our people obtain the necessaries of a comfortable existence at a cheaper rate than formerly. This is a matter of supreme importance, since it is the palpable duty of every just government to make the burdens of taxation as light as possible. The people should not be required to relinquish this privilege of cheaper living except under the stress of their Government's necessity made plainly manifest.

This reference to the condition and prospects of our revenues naturally suggests an allusion to the weakness and vices of our financial methods. They have been frequently pressed upon the attention of Congress in previous Executive communications and the inevitable danger of their continued toleration pointed out. Without now repeating these details, I can not refrain from again earnestly presenting the necessity of the prompt reform of a system opposed to every rule of sound finance and shown by experience to be fraught with the gravest peril and perplexity. The terrible Civil War, which shook the foundations of our Government more than thirty years ago, brought in its train the destruction of property, the wasting of our country's substance, and the estrangement of brethren. These are now past and forgotten. Even the distressing loss of life the conflict entailed is but a sacred memory which fosters patriotic sentiment and keeps alive a tender regard for those who nobly died. And yet there remains with us to-day in full strength and activity, as an incident of that tremendous struggle, a feature of its financial necessities not only unsuited to our present circumstances, but manifestly a disturbing menace to business security and an ever-present agent of monetary distress.

Because we may be enjoying a temporary relief from its depressing influence, this should not lull us into a false security nor lead us to forget the suddenness of past visitations.

I am more convinced than ever that we can have no assured financial peace and safety until the Government currency obligations upon which gold may be demanded from the Treasury are withdrawn from circulation and canceled. This might be done, as has been heretofore recommended, by their exchange for long-term bonds bearing a low rate of interest or by their redemption with the proceeds of such bonds. Even if only the United States notes known as greenbacks were thus retired it is probable that the Treasury notes issued in payment of silver purchases under the act of July 14, 1890, now paid in gold when demanded, would not create much disturbance, as they might from time to time, when received in the Treasury by redemption in gold or otherwise, be gradually and prudently replaced by silver coin.

This plan of issuing bonds for the purpose of redemption certainly appears to be the most effective and direct path to the needed reform. In default of this, however, it would be a step in the right direction if currency obligations redeemable in gold whenever so redeemed should be canceled instead of being reissued. This operation would be a slow remedy, but it would improve present conditions.

National banks should redeem their own notes. They should be allowed to issue circulation to the par value of bonds deposited as security for its redemption and the tax on their circulation should be reduced to one-fourth of 1 per cent.

In considering projects for the retirement of United States notes and Treasury notes issued under the law of 1890, I am of the opinion that we have placed too much stress upon the danger of contracting the currency and have calculated too little upon the gold that would be added to our circulation if invited to us by better and safer financial methods. It is not so much a contraction of our currency that should be avoided as its unequal distribution.

This might be obviated and any fear of harmful contraction at the same time removed by allowing the organization of smaller banks and in less populous communities than are now permitted, and also authorizing existing banks to establish branches in small communities under proper restrictions.

The entire case may be presented by the statement that the day of sensible and sound financial methods will not dawn upon us until our Government abandons the banking business and the accumulation of funds and confines its monetary operations to the receipt of the money contributed by the people for its support and to the expenditure of such money for the people's benefit.

Our business interests and all good citizens long for rest from feverish agitation and the inauguration by the Government of a reformed financial policy which will encourage enterprise and make certain the rewards of labor and industry.

Another topic in which our people rightfully take a deep interest may be here briefly considered. I refer to the existence of trusts and other huge aggregations of capital the object of which is to secure the monopoly of some particular branch of trade, industry, or commerce and to stifle wholesome competition. When these are defended, it is usually on the ground that though they increase profits they also reduce prices, and thus may benefit the public. It must be remembered, however, that a reduction of prices to the people is not one of the real objects of these organizations, nor is their tendency necessarily in that direction. If it occurs in a particular case it is only because it accords with the purposes or interests of those managing the scheme.

Such occasional results fall far short of compensating the palpable evils charged to the account of trusts and monopolies. Their tendency is to crush out individual independence and to hinder or prevent the free use of human faculties and the full development of human character. Through them the farmer, the artisan, and the small trader is in danger of dislodgment from the proud position of being his own master, watchful of all that touches his country's prosperity, in which he has an individual lot, and interested in all that affects the advantages of business of which he is a factor, to be relegated to the level of a mere appurtenance to a great machine, with little free will, with no duty but that of passive obedience, and with little hope or opportunity of rising in the scale of responsible and helpful citizenship.

To the instinctive belief that such is the inevitable trend of trusts and monopolies is due the widespread and deep-seated popular aversion in which they are held and the not unreasonable insistence that, whatever may be their incidental economic advantages, their general effect upon personal character, prospects, and usefulness can not be otherwise than injurious.

Though Congress has attempted to deal with this matter by legislation, the laws passed for that purpose thus far have proved ineffective, not because of any lack of disposition or attempt to enforce them, but simply because the laws themselves as interpreted by the courts do not reach the difficulty. If the insufficiencies of existing laws can be remedied by further legislation, it should be done. The fact must be recognized, however, that all Federal legislation on this subject may fall short of its purpose because of inherent obstacles and also because of the complex character of our governmental system, which, while making the Federal authority supreme within its sphere, has carefully limited that sphere by metes and bounds that can not be transgressed. The decision of our highest court on this precise question renders it quite doubtful whether the evils of trusts and monopolies can be adequately treated through Federal action unless they seek directly and purposely to include in their objects transportation or intercourse between States or between the United States and foreign countries.

It does not follow, however, that this is the limit of the remedy that may be applied. Even though it may be found that Federal authority is not broad enough to fully reach the case, there can be no doubt of the power of the several States to act effectively in the premises, and there should be no reason to doubt their willingness to judiciously exercise such power.

In concluding this communication its last words shall be an appeal to the Congress for the most rigid economy in the expenditure of the money it holds in trust for the people. The way to perplexing extravagance is easy, but a return to frugality is difficult. When, however, it is considered that those who bear the burdens of taxation have no guaranty of honest care save in the fidelity of their public servants, the duty of all possible retrenchment is plainly manifest.

When our differences are forgotten and our contests of political opinion are no longer remembered, nothing in the retrospect of our public service will be as fortunate and comforting as the recollection of official duty well performed and the memory of a constant devotion to the interests of our confiding fellow-countrymen.   GROVER CLEVELAND.

SPECIAL MESSAGES.

EXECUTIVE MANSION,
Washington, January 5, 1897.

To the Senate:

I transmit herewith, in response to a resolution of the Senate of the 22d ultimo, a report from the Secretary of State, accompanied by copies of correspondence concerning the death of Charles Govin, a citizen of the United States, in the island of Cuba.

GROVER CLEVELAND.

EXECUTIVE MANSION,
Washington, January 8, 1897.

To the House of Representatives:

I transmit herewith, in response to the resolution of the House of Representatives of May 8, 1896, requesting information as to what had been done by the Department of State to carry out the provision in the act of March 2, 1895, making appropriations for the Department of Agriculture for the year 1896, as to negotiations with Great Britain to secure the abrogation or modification of the regulations requiring the slaughter of cattle from the United States at the port of entry, a report from the Secretary of State, with accompanying papers.

GROVER CLEVELAND.

EXECUTIVE MANSION,
Washington, January 8, 1897.

To the House of Representatives:

I transmit herewith the report of the Secretary of State in response to the resolution of the House of Representatives of June 5, 1896, calling for information concerning the changes made in the force of his Department since the 4th day of March, 1893.

This report has been in my hands since the 9th day of December, 1896, and its transmission to the House of Representatives has been delayed by my inadvertence.

GROVER CLEVELAND.

EXECUTIVE MANSION, *January 11, 1897.*

To the Senate:

I transmit herewith a treaty for the arbitration of all matters in difference between the United States and Great Britain.

The provisions of the treaty are the result of long and patient deliberation and represent concessions made by each party for the sake of agreement upon the general scheme.

Though the result reached may not meet the views of the advocates of immediate, unlimited, and irrevocable arbitration of all international controversies, it is nevertheless confidently believed that the treaty can not fail to be everywhere recognized as making a long step in the right direction and as embodying a practical working plan by which disputes between the two countries will reach a peaceful adjustment as matter of course and in ordinary routine.

In the initiation of such an important movement it must be expected that some of its features will assume a tentative character looking to a further advance, and yet it is apparent that the treaty which has been formulated not only makes war between the parties to it a remote possibility, but precludes those fears and rumors of war which of themselves too often assume the proportions of national disaster.

It is eminently fitting as well as fortunate that the attempts to accomplish results so beneficent should be initiated by kindred peoples, speaking the same tongue and joined together by all the ties of common traditions, common institutions, and common aspirations. The experiment of substituting civilized methods for brute force as the means of settling international questions of right will thus be tried under the happiest auspices. Its success ought not to be doubtful, and the fact that its ultimate ensuing benefits are not likely to be limited to the two countries immediately concerned should cause it to be promoted all the more eagerly. The examples set and the lesson furnished by the successful operation of this treaty are sure to be felt and taken to heart sooner or later by other nations, and will thus mark the beginning of a new epoch in civilization.

Profoundly impressed as I am, therefore, by the promise of transcendent good which this treaty affords, I do not hesitate to accompany its transmission with an expression of my earnest hope that it may commend itself to the favorable consideration of the Senate.

GROVER CLEVELAND.

EXECUTIVE MANSION, *January 18, 1897.*

To the Senate and House of Representatives:

I transmit herewith the report of Messrs. James B. Angell, of Michigan, John E. Russell, of Massachusetts, and Lyman E. Cooley, of Illinois, who were appointed commissioners under the authority of a law passed March 2, 1895, to make inquiry and report, after conference with such similar commissioners as might be appointed on behalf of Great Britain or the Dominion of Canada, concerning the feasibility of the construction of such canals as will enable vessels engaged in ocean commerce to pass between the Great Lakes and the Atlantic Ocean, and the most convenient location and probable cost of such canals, together with other facts and information in said act specified relating to their construction and use.

The commissioners have prosecuted the work assigned them with great zeal and intelligence, resulting in the collection of a mass of information embodied in their report and its accompanying exhibits which is of great importance and interest as related to the project subjected to their examination.

The advantages of direct and unbroken water transportation of the products of our Western States and Territories from convenient points of shipment to our seaboard ports are plainly palpable. The report of the commissioners contains, in my opinion, demonstration of the feasibility of securing such transportation, and gives ground for the anticipation that better and more uninterrupted commerce, through the plan suggested, between the great West and foreign ports, with the increase of national prosperity which must follow in its train, will not long escape American enterprise and activity.

It will be observed that the report of the commissioners, though as comprehensive as the time and facilities at their disposal permitted, does not definitely deal with the cost of the work they were called upon to consider and omits some of the other details related to it. Thus far they have labored without compensation, and a part of the small sum appropriated for the payment of their expenses still remains unexpended.

I suggest to the Congress the propriety of making economical provision for such further prosecution of their work as will more fully develop the information necessary to an exact and complete understanding of this interesting and important subject.   GROVER CLEVELAND.

EXECUTIVE MANSION,
Washington, January 22, 1897.

To the Senate of the United States:

In response to the resolution of the Senate of December 15, 1896, relating to Cuban affairs, I transmit a report from the Secretary of State, submitting a list of the claims filed in the Department of State by citizens of the United States against Spain arising out of the insurrection existing in the island of Cuba, and the accompanying correspondence relating to the vessel called the *Competitor* and the persons claiming American citizenship captured thereon, which I deem it not incompatible with the public interests to communicate.   GROVER CLEVELAND.

EXECUTIVE MANSION,
Washington, January 25, 1897.

To the Senate of the United States:

I transmit herewith, in response to the Senate resolution of December 21, 1896, addressed to the Secretary of State, a report of that officer covering a list of persons claiming to be citizens of the United States who have been arrested on the island of Cuba since February 24, 1895, to the present time.   GROVER CLEVELAND.

EXECUTIVE MANSION,
Washington, February 1, 1897.

To the Senate:

I transmit herewith, in response to a resolution of the Senate of the 6th ultimo, a report from the Secretary of State, accompanied by copies of correspondence concerning the arrest, imprisonment, trial, and condemnation to perpetual imprisonment in chains of Jules Sanguily, a citizen of the United States, by the authorities of Spain in Cuba.

GROVER CLEVELAND.

EXECUTIVE MANSION, *February 5, 1897.*

To the Senate and House of Representatives:

The World's Columbian Commission has delivered to me certain documents and exhibits which they desire should constitute the final report required by section 12 of the act of Congress passed April 25, 1890, providing for the celebration of the four hundredth anniversary of the discovery of America and the holding of an international exhibition in the city of Chicago.

The documents referred to embrace the reports of the president and secretary of the commission and a report of the executive committee on awards, with exhibits relating to the same. They are contained in five boxes of considerable size, which, instead of actually transmitting with this communication, I have deposited in the State Department subject to the action and direction of the Congress.

I am informed that the director-general of the exposition has made a report directly to the Congress, and that no report of the lady managers has yet been made.

The selection of such part of the material mentioned as may be considered necessary to constitute a final exhibit of the action of the commission and the results of the exposition is submitted to the discretion of Congress.

GROVER CLEVELAND.

EXECUTIVE MANSION,
Washington, February 8, 1897.

To the Senate and House of Representatives:

I transmit herewith a communication from the Secretary of State and accompanying reports from diplomatic and consular officers of the United States on the passport regulations of foreign countries. In view of the evident value of the information contained in these reports, especially to American citizens going abroad and sojourning or traveling in foreign lands, I approve the recommendation of the Secretary that Congress authorize the printing of a special edition of 3,000 copies of the work, to be distributed by the Department of State as indicated in the Secretary's report.

GROVER CLEVELAND.

EXECUTIVE MANSION, *February 8, 1897.*

To the Senate and House of Representatives:

I herewith submit the thirteenth annual report of the Civil Service Commission, containing a detailed statement of its important work and exhibiting the present condition of the classified service of the Government.

GROVER CLEVELAND.

EXECUTIVE MANSION, *February 10, 1897.*

To the Senate of the United States:

In compliance with a resolution of the Senate of the 9th instant, the House of Representatives concurring, I return herewith Senate bill No. 3328, entitled ''An act to amend an act entitled 'An act to repeal the timber-culture laws, and for other purposes.'''

GROVER CLEVELAND.

EXECUTIVE MANSION,
Washington, February 11, 1897.

To the Senate of the United States:

In response to the resolution of the Senate of February 4, 1897, I transmit a report from the Secretary of State, submitting copies of correspondence relative to the arrest and detention of Gaspar A. Betancourt, a citizen of the United States, by the Spanish authorities in Cuba.

GROVER CLEVELAND.

EXECUTIVE MANSION,
Washington, February 11, 1897.

To the Senate of the United States:

In response to the resolution of the Senate of February 2, 1897, I transmit a report from the Secretary of State, relative to the killing of Segundo N. Lopez, son of M. F. Lopez, at Sagua la Grande, in Cuba.

GROVER CLEVELAND.

EXECUTIVE MANSION,
Washington, February 20, 1897.

To the Senate:

I transmit herewith, in answer to the resolution of the Senate of the 17th instant, a report from the Secretary of State, touching the reply of the British Government in regard to the failure of the negotiations of the Paris Tribunal to protect the fur-seal herd of Alaska.

GROVER CLEVELAND.

EXECUTIVE MANSION,
Washington, February 20, 1897.

To the Senate:

I transmit herewith, in answer to the resolution of the Senate of the 15th instant, a report from the Secretary of State, accompanied by copies of correspondence with the German Government in reference to American insurance companies.

GROVER CLEVELAND.

EXECUTIVE MANSION,
Washington, February 23, 1897.

To the Senate:

I transmit herewith, in response to the resolution of the Senate of February 6, 1897, a report from the Secretary of State, in regard to the persons claiming American citizenship captured on board of the *Competitor*.

GROVER CLEVELAND.

EXECUTIVE MANSION,
Washington, February 24, 1897

To the Congress:

I transmit herewith a communication from the Secretary of State, covering the report of the joint commission on behalf of the United States and Great Britain, dated December 31, 1896, relative to the preservation of the fisheries in waters contiguous to the United States and Canada, as provided by the joint agreement between the United States and Great Britain dated December 6, 1892.

GROVER CLEVELAND.

EXECUTIVE MANSION,
Washington, February 25, 1897.

To the Senate and House of Representatives:

I transmit herewith, for the information of the Congress, a communication from the Secretary of State, covering the report of the Director of the Bureau of the American Republics for the year 1896.

GROVER CLEVELAND.

EXECUTIVE MANSION,
Washington, February 26, 1897.

To the House of Representatives:

I transmit herewith a communication from the Secretary of State, accompanying the annual reports of the consuls of the United States upon foreign industries and commerce. In view of the value of these reports to the business interests throughout the country, I indorse the recommendation of the Secretary of State that Congress authorize the printing of a special edition of 10,000 copies of the general summary entitled Review of the World's Commerce, and of 5,000 copies of Commercial Relations (including this summary), to enable the Department of State to meet the demand for such information.   GROVER CLEVELAND.

EXECUTIVE MANSION, *March 1, 1897.*

To the Congress:

I transmit herewith the report of the board of lady managers of the World's Columbian Commission.   GROVER CLEVELAND.

EXECUTIVE MANSION,
Washington, March 1, 1897.

To the Senate:

In response to the resolution of the Senate of the 24th ultimo, I transmit herewith a report from the Secretary of State, covering copies of the correspondence and reports of the consul-general of the United States at Havana relating to all American citizens now in prison in the island of Cuba not previously reported on.   GROVER CLEVELAND.

EXECUTIVE MANSION,
Washington, March 2, 1897.

To the Senate:

I transmit herewith, in response to the resolution of the Senate of February 24, 1897, a report from the Secretary of State, in relation to the claim of M. A. Cheek against the Siamese Government, with accompanying papers.   GROVER CLEVELAND.

EXECUTIVE MANSION,
Washington, March 2, 1897.

To the Senate:

I herewith transmit a report of the Secretary of State upon a resolution of the Senate relating to the arrest, imprisonment, and death of Dr. Ricardo Ruiz in the jail of Guanabacoa, on the island of Cuba. Agreeing with the suggestion of the Secretary, I have not thought it compatible with the public interest that the correspondence referred to in the resolution should be communicated pending the public and exhaustive investigation about to be instituted.

Though it seems to be clear that the consul-general should have professional aid in such investigation, that matter, together with the selection of the particular persons to act with him, properly devolves upon my successor in office.   GROVER CLEVELAND.

SHELTER TRENCHES BEFORE MALABON AND CALOOCAN, PHILIPPINES

THE FILIPINO INSURRECTION

Our occupation of Manila was from the outset distinctly distasteful to the natives. The Filipinos had acted as allies in the attack on the city and they resented being excluded from it, as required by our Government. The protocol of peace with Spain gave us control of the "city, bay and harbor of Manila," pending the ratification of a conclusive treaty. Our military authorities thought "city" meant Manila and its suburbs. The Filipinos claimed it meant the walled portion. Finally, under compulsion, the Filipino troops withdrew beyond the line laid down. The whole native population hated our troops, who soon fraternized with the Spanish soldiers but drew a sharp color line against the natives. Under the leadership of Aguinaldo they set up a new government. When McKinley ordered the extension of military rule to all parts of the island, only lack of munitions prevented an immediate outbreak. A month later, on February 4, 1899, however, hostilities began; a Filipino, who refused to halt when challenged, was fired at by a picket; his comrades avenged him; our troops replied; and the day following a battle was fought which drove the insurgents six miles northward. On February 10th was fought the battle of Caloocan. The character of the warfare may be judged by the fact that the Filipinos had 14,623 killed and 3,297 wounded, a striking reversal of the usual proportion of casualties. See the article, "Philippine Islands," in the encyclopedic index (volume eleven).

EXECUTIVE MANSION,
Washington, March 3, 1897.

To the Senate:

I transmit herewith, in reply to the resolution of the Senate of January 23, 1897, a report from the Secretary of State, accompanied by copies of the correspondence therein requested, relating to the Nicaraguan Canal or the Maritime Canal Company of Nicaragua, since 1887.

GROVER CLEVELAND.

VETO MESSAGES.

EXECUTIVE MANSION, *January 14, 1897.*

To the House of Representatives:

I return herewith without my approval House bill No. 9469, entitled "An act to constitute a new division of the eastern judicial district of Texas, and to provide for the holding of terms of court at Beaumont, Tex., and for the appointment of a clerk for said court."

It appears that terms of court are now held at four different places within the eastern judicial district of Texas and that parties having business in the courts are not seriously inconvenienced under present arrangements.

Both the Federal judge and district attorney in this district express themselves in opposition to the bill as unnecessary and an interruption to the transaction of the large volume of business now pending and constantly coming before the court.

I have before me certificates of the clerks of the present divisions of the courts showing that during the last five years the counties which it is proposed shall constitute the new division have contributed but forty-two cases to the calendars of the court.

Conclusive proof is also before me that the additional terms of court provided for in this bill would so interfere with the terms already appointed in the existing divisions that the proper administration of the civil as well as the criminal law would be impracticable.

The criminal docket of the terms held at Paris is so large that under present arrangements and with the utmost industry trials can not now be as promptly disposed of as the ends of justice require. This condition would be further aggravated if terms of the court should be held at Beaumont on the dates proposed in this bill, since they are fixed at such times as to necessarily curtail the period now devoted to the Paris terms.

On the grounds stated and because I am unable to discover how the public interests can possibly be promoted by the proposed legislation I am constrained to withhold my approval of the bill under consideration.

GROVER CLEVELAND.

EXECUTIVE MANSION, *February 22, 1897.*

To the House of Representatives:

I return herewith without my approval House bill No. 2189, entitled "An act granting a pension to Mrs. Mary A. Freeman."

A former husband of the beneficiary, named Andrew V. Pritchard, did service in the Mexican War, and on July 22, 1847, died of disease contracted in such service. Thereupon the beneficiary named in this bill was pensioned as his widow. She continued to receive this pension until 1852, when she married John Freeman, through which she of course lost her pensionable status. Two minor children of the soldier were, however, placed on the pension roll in her stead, and their pension was paid to them until the youngest became 16 years of age, in 1863.

John Freeman died in December, 1871, the beneficiary having been his wife for almost twenty years. It is now proposed to restore her to the pension roll as the widow of her former husband, the Mexican soldier, who died nearly fifty years ago, and notwithstanding the fact that less than five years after his death she relinquished her right to a pension and surrendered her widowhood to become the wife of another husband, with whom she lived for many years.

I am not willing, even by inaction, to be charged with acquiescence in what appears to be such an entire departure from the principle, as well as sentiment, connected with reasonable pension legislation.

GROVER CLEVELAND.

To the Senate: EXECUTIVE MANSION, *February 22, 1897.*

I return herewith without approval Senate bill No. 1323, entitled "An act granting a pension to Maria Somerlat, widow of Valentine Somerlat."

This beneficiary, under the name of Maria Somerlat, was pensioned in 1867 as the widow of Valentine Somerlat, a volunteer soldier, dating from his death, in 1864. She continued to draw the pension allowed her as such widow until 1881, when she married one Hiram Smith. Subsequently, but at what time does not appear, she was divorced from Smith in a suit that seems to have been begun by him, but in which she interposed a cross bill and obtained judgment in her favor. Notwithstanding her remarriage, through which she ceased to be the widow of the dead soldier, it is proposed to pension her again on account of his death.

The rule governing the operation of general pension laws which forfeits a widow's pension on her remarriage seems so reasonable and just and its relaxation must necessarily lead to such a departure from just principles and to such vexatious pension administration that I am convinced it ought to be strictly maintained.

I hope I may be permitted to call the attention of the Senate to the increasing latitude clearly discernible in special pension legislation. It has seemed to me so useless to attempt to stem the tide of this legislation by Executive interference that I have contented myself with nonacquiescence in numerous cases where I could not approve.

There have been already presented to me for Executive action during the present session of the Congress 206 special pension bills, of which I have actually examined 115. The entire number of such bills that have become laws during the four sessions of the Congress since March 4, 1893, is 391. Some of those presented at the present session are not based upon the least pretext that the death or disability involved is related to army service, while in numerous other cases it is extremely difficult to satisfactorily discover such relationship.

There is one feature of this legislation which I am sure deserves attention. I refer to the great number of special bills passed for the purpose of increasing the pensions of those already on the rolls. Of the 115 special pension bills which I have examined since the beginning of the present session of the Congress, 58 granted or restored pensions and 57 increased those already existing, and the appropriation of money necessary to meet these increases exceeds considerably the amount required to pay the original pensions granted or restored by the remaining 58 bills.

I can not discover that these increases are regulated by any rule or principle, and when we remember that there are nearly a million pensioners on our rolls and consider the importunity for such increase that must follow the precedents already made, the relation of the subject to a justifiable increase of our national revenues can not escape attention.

GROVER CLEVELAND.

EXECUTIVE MANSION, *February 22, 1897.*

To the House of Representatives:

I return herewith without my approval House bill No. 6902, entitled "An act granting a pension to Mrs. Mary A. Viel."

This beneficiary was married in 1862 to Major W. D. Sanger, then in the volunteer military service. He died in 1872, never having made any application for pension. His widow made no application for pension, but within three years after her husband's death, and in 1875, became the wife of Paul Viel. Eight years thereafter he died, leaving her his widow, and it is now proposed to pension her as the widow of the soldier, Major Sanger, though she long ago by her own deliberate act surrendered that title and all its incidents.

There is a further objection to granting this pension. I do not find that any claim is made that the death of the soldier, who was the beneficiary's first husband, was at all attributable to his army service. Neither he nor his widow, while she remained such, presented any such claim, nor is it found in reports of the committees in the Senate or House to whom the bill under consideration was referred. On the contrary, the

Senate Committee on Pensions in their report distinctly state that "there is no proof that soldier contracted disease while in the service or that he died of pensionable disabilities."

GROVER CLEVELAND.

EXECUTIVE MANSION, *March 1, 1897.*

To the Senate:

I return herewith without approval Senate bill No. 719, entitled "An act to restore a pension to Harriet M. Knowlton."

Major William Knowlton, a most worthy volunteer soldier, died of wounds received in battle on the 20th day of September, 1864.

In 1865 his widow, the beneficiary named in this bill, was pensioned at the rate of $25 a month, commencing on the day of her husband's death, with an additional allowance for four minor children dating from July, 1866.

She continued to receive this pension and allowance until November, 1867, when she married Albin P. Stinchfield.

Thereupon her name was dropped from the pension roll, she having by her remarriage lost her pensionable condition, and her children were pensioned at a small monthly rate from the date of their mother's remarriage until June 1, 1880, when the youngest became 16 years of age.

The beneficiary, after living with her second husband about twenty-two years, secured a divorce from him in the year 1889, and it is now proposed to pension the divorced wife as the widow of her deceased soldier husband at the rate she received while she was actually his widow, thirty years ago.

Her pensionable relation to the Government terminated with her remarriage, and her divorce from her second husband could not upon any ground of principle restore it. A departure from this rule, even in aid of cases of hardship, can not fail to establish precedents inviting the abandonment of reasonable and justifiable pension theories.

GROVER CLEVELAND.

EXECUTIVE MANSION, *March 1, 1897.*

To the House of Representatives:

I herewith return without approval House bill No. 1299, entitled "An act to pension Harriet Woodbury, of Windsor, Vt."

The beneficiary named in this bill was the wife of Aaron G. Firman at the time of his enlistment in 1863. He died October 2, 1864, and the beneficiary, as his widow, was pensioned in 1865, from the day of her soldier husband's death.

She continued to receive the pension allowed to her as such widow until July 14, 1866, when she married Samuel H. Woodbury. She was thereupon dropped from the pension roll pursuant to law, and in 1868 the minor son of the soldier was allowed a pension of $8 a month, commencing at the date of the remarriage of his mother. This pension was increased to $10 a month in 1873, from July 25, 1866, and was continued until 1880, when the minor child reached the age of 16 years.

On July 26, 1886, twenty years after the beneficiary ceased to be the widow of the soldier Aaron G. Firman and became the wife of the civilian Samuel H. Woodbury, he died and she became his widow.

It is now proposed by this bill to pension her again as the widow of the deceased soldier, notwithstanding her voluntary abandonment of that relation to become the wife of another more than thirty years ago.

No feature of our pension laws is so satisfactory and just as a fair allowance to the widows of our soldiers who have died from causes attributable to their army service. When, however, such a beneficiary by remarriage surrenders her soldier widowhood and turns away from its tender and patriotic associations to assume again the relation and allegiance of wife to another husband, when she discards the soldier's name and in every way terminates her pensionable relationship to the Government, I am unable to discover any principle which justifies her restoration to that relationship upon the death of her second husband.

No one can be insensible to the sad plight of a widow in needy condition, but our pension laws should deal with soldiers' widows. I understand that only the existence of this relationship to a deceased soldier creates through him the Government's duty and justifies the application of public money to the relief of such widows.

GROVER CLEVELAND.

EXECUTIVE MANSION, *March 2, 1897.*

To the House of Representatives:

I herewith return without approval House bill No. 7864, entitled "An act to amend the immigration laws of the United States."

By the first section of this bill it is proposed to amend section 1 of the act of March 3, 1891, relating to immigration by adding to the classes of aliens thereby excluded from admission to the United States the following:

All persons physically capable and over 16 years of age who can not read and write the English language or some other language; but a person not so able to read and write who is over 50 years of age and is the parent or grandparent of a qualified immigrant over 21 years of age and capable of supporting such parent or grandparent may accompany such immigrant, or such a parent or grandparent may be sent for and come to join the family of a child or grandchild over 21 years of age similarly qualified and capable, and a wife or minor child not so able to read and write may accompany or be sent for and come and join the husband or parent similarly qualified and capable.

A radical departure from our national policy relating to immigration is here presented. Heretofore we have welcomed all who came to us from other lands except those whose moral or physical condition or history threatened danger to our national welfare and safety. Relying upon the zealous watchfulness of our people to prevent injury to our political and social fabric, we have encouraged those coming from foreign countries to cast their lot with us and join in the development of our vast domain, securing in return a share in the blessings of American citizenship.

A century s stupendous growth, largely due to the assimilation and thrift of millions of sturdy and patriotic adopted citizens, attests the success of this generous and free-handed policy which, while guarding the people's interests, exacts from our immigrants only physical and moral soundness and a willingness and ability to work.

A contemplation of the grand results of this policy can not fail to arouse a sentiment in its defense, for however it might have been regarded as an original proposition and viewed as an experiment its accomplishments are such that if it is to be uprooted at this late day its disadvantages should be plainly apparent and the substitute adopted should be just and adequate, free from uncertainties, and guarded against difficult or oppressive administration.

It is not claimed, I believe, that the time has come for the further restriction of immigration on the ground that an excess of population overcrowds our land.

It is said, however, that the quality of recent immigration is undesirable. The time is quite within recent memory when the same thing was said of immigrants who, with their descendants, are now numbered among our best citizens.

It is said that too many immigrants settle in our cities, thus dangerously increasing their idle and vicious population. This is certainly a disadvantage. It can not be shown, however, that it affects all our cities, nor that it is permanent; nor does it appear that this condition where it exists demands as its remedy the reversal of our present immigration policy.

The claim is also made that the influx of foreign laborers deprives of the opportunity to work those who are better entitled than they to the privilege of earning their livelihood by daily toil. An unfortunate condition is certainly presented when any who are willing to labor are unemployed, but so far as this condition now exists among our people it must be conceded to be a result of phenomenal business depression and the stagnation of all enterprises in which labor is a factor. With the advent of settled and wholesome financial and economic governmental policies and consequent encouragement to the activity of capital the misfortunes of unemployed labor should, to a great extent at least, be remedied. If it continues, its natural consequences must be to check the further immigration to our cities of foreign laborers and to deplete the ranks of those already there. In the meantime those most willing and best entitled ought to be able to secure the advantages of such work as there is to do.

It is proposed by the bill under consideration to meet the alleged difficulties of the situation by establishing an educational test by which the right of a foreigner to make his home with us shall be determined. Its general scheme is to prohibit from admission to our country all immigrants "physically capable and over 16 years of age who can not read and write the English language or some other language," and it is provided that this test shall be applied by requiring immigrants seeking admission to read and afterwards to write not less than twenty nor more than twenty-five words of the Constitution of the United States in some language, and that any immigrant failing in this shall not be admitted, but shall be returned to the country from whence he came at the expense of the steamship or railroad company which brought him.

The best reason that could be given for this radical restriction of immigration is the necessity of protecting our population against degeneration and saving our national peace and quiet from imported turbulence and disorder.

I can not believe that we would be protected against these evils by limiting immigration to those who can read and write in any language twenty-five words of our Constitution. In my opinion, it is infinitely more safe to admit a hundred thousand immigrants who, though unable to read and write, seek among us only a home and opportunity to work than to admit one of those unruly agitators and enemies of governmental control who can not only read and write, but delights in arousing by inflammatory speech the illiterate and peacefully inclined to discontent and tumult. Violence and disorder do not originate with illiterate laborers. They are, rather, the victims of the educated agitator. The ability to read and write, as required in this bill, in and of itself affords, in my opinion, a misleading test of contented industry and supplies unsatisfactory evidence of desirable citizenship or a proper apprehension of the benefits of our institutions. If any particular element of our illiterate immigration is to be feared for other causes than illiteracy, these causes should be dealt with directly, instead of making illiteracy the pretext for exclusion, to the detriment of other illiterate immigrants against whom the real cause of complaint can not be alleged.

The provisions intended to rid that part of the proposed legislation already referred to from obvious hardship appears to me to be indefinite and inadequate.

A parent, grandparent, wife, or minor child of a qualified immigrant, though unable to read and write, may accompany the immigrant or be sent for to join his family, provided the immigrant is capable of supporting such relative. These exceptions to the general rule of exclusion contained in the bill were made to prevent the separation of families, and yet neither brothers nor sisters are provided for. In order that relatives who are provided for may be reunited, those still in foreign lands must be sent for to join the immigrant here. What formality is necessary to constitute this prerequisite, and how are the facts of relationship and that the relative is sent for to be established? Are the illiterate relatives of immigrants who have come here under prior laws entitled to the advantage of these exceptions? A husband who can read and write and who determines to abandon his illiterate wife abroad will find here under this law an absolutely safe retreat. The illiterate relatives mentioned must not only be sent for, but such immigrant must be capable of supporting them when they arrive. This requirement proceeds upon the assumption that the foreign relatives coming here are in every case, by reason of poverty, liable to become a public charge unless the immigrant is capable of their support. The contrary is very often true. And yet if unable to read and write, though quite able and willing to support themselves and their relatives here besides, they could not be admitted under the provisions of this bill if the immigrant was impoverished, though the aid of his fortunate but illiterate relative might be the means of saving him from pauperism.

The fourth section of this bill provides—

That it shall be unlawful for any male alien who has not in good faith made his declaration before the proper court of his intention to become a citizen of the United States to be employed on any public works of the United States or to come regularly or habitually into the United States by land or water for the purpose of engaging in any mechanical trade or manual labor for wages or salary, returning from time to time to a foreign country.

The fifth section provides—

That it shall be unlawful for any person, partnership, company, or corporation knowingly to employ any alien coming into the United States in violation of the next preceding section of this act.

The prohibition against the employment of aliens upon any public works of the United States is in line with other legislation of a like character. It is quite a different thing, however, to declare it a crime for an alien to come regularly and habitually into the United States for the purpose of obtaining work from private parties, if such alien returns from time to time to a foreign country, and to constitute any employment of such alien a criminal offense.

When we consider these provisions of the bill in connection with our long northern frontier and the boundaries of our States and Territories, often but an imaginary line separating them from the British dominions, and recall the friendly intercourse between the people who are neighbors on either side, the provisions of this bill affecting them must be regarded as illiberal, narrow, and un-American.

The residents of these States and Territories have separate and especial interests which in many cases make an interchange of labor between their people and their alien neighbors most important, frequently with the advantage largely in favor of our citizens. This suggests the inexpediency of Federal interference with these conditions when not necessary to the correction of a substantial evil, affecting the general welfare. Such unfriendly legislation as is proposed could hardly fail to provoke retaliatory measures, to the injury of many of our citizens who now find employment on adjoining foreign soil.

The uncertainty of construction to which the language of these provisions is subject is a serious objection to a statute which describes a crime. An important element in the offense sought to be created by these sections is the coming "regularly or habitually into the United States." These words are impossible of definite and certain construction. The same may be said of the equally important words "returning from time to time to a foreign country."

A careful examination of this bill has convinced me that for the reasons given and others not specifically stated its provisions are unnecessarily harsh and oppressive, and that its defects in construction would cause vexation and its operation would result in harm to our citizens.

GROVER CLEVELAND.

POCKET VETOES.

["An act granting a pension to Mrs. Mary Gould Carr, widow of the late Brigadier and Brevet Major General Joseph B. Carr, United States Volunteers, deceased."]

DECEMBER 30, 1896.

This bill was presented to me on the 16th day of December, 1896. Congress, pursuant to a concurrent resolution adopted by both Houses of Congress, adjourned from the 22d day of December, 1896, to January 5, 1897. I have not approved the bill. GROVER CLEVELAND.

["An act to increase the pension of Caroline A. Hough, widow of Brigadier-General John Hough."]

DECEMBER 31, 1896.

This bill was presented to me on the 16th day of December, 1896. Congress, pursuant to a concurrent resolution adopted by both Houses of Congress, adjourned from the 22d day of December, 1896, to January 5, 1897. I have not approved the bill. GROVER CLEVELAND.

PROCLAMATIONS.

BY THE PRESIDENT OF THE UNITED STATES OF AMERICA.

A PROCLAMATION.

Whereas an act of Congress entitled "An act to adopt regulations for preventing collisions at sea" was approved August 19, 1890, the said act being in the following words:

Be it enacted by the Senate and House of Representatives of the United States of America in Congress assembled, That the following regulations for preventing collisions at sea shall be followed by all public and private vessels of the United States upon the high seas and in all waters connected therewith navigable by seagoing vessels:

PRELIMINARY.

In the following rules every steam vessel which is under sail and not under steam is to be considered a sailing vessel, and every vessel under steam, whether under sail or not, is to be considered a steam vessel.

The words "steam vessel" shall include any vessel propelled by machinery.

A vessel is "under way" within the meaning of these rules when she is not at anchor or made fast to the shore or aground.

RULES CONCERNING LIGHTS, ETC.

The word "visible" in these rules when applied to lights shall mean visible on a dark night with a clear atmosphere.

ARTICLE 1. The rules concerning lights shall be complied with in all weathers from sunset to sunrise, and during such time no other lights which may be mistaken for the prescribed lights shall be exhibited.

ART. 2. A steam vessel when under way shall carry —

(*a*) On or in front of the foremast, or if a vessel without a foremast, then in the fore part of the vessel, at a height above the hull of not less than 20 feet, and if the breadth of the vessel exceeds 20 feet, then at a height above the hull not less than such breadth, so, however, that the light need not be carried at a greater height above the hull than 40 feet a bright white light so constructed as to show an unbroken light over an arc of the horizon of 20 points of the compass, so fixed as to throw the light 10 points on each side of the vessel—namely, from right ahead to 2 points abaft the beam on either side—and of such a character as to be visible at a distance of at least 5 miles.

(*b*) On the starboard side a green light so constructed as to show an unbroken light over an arc of the horizon of 10 points of the compass, so fixed as to throw the light from right ahead to 2 points abaft the beam on the starboard side, and of such a character as to be visible at a distance of at least 2 miles.

(*c*) On the port side a red light so constructed as to show an unbroken light over an arc of the horizon of 10 points of the compass, so fixed as to throw the light from right ahead to 2 points abaft the beam on the port side, and of such a character as to be visible at a distance of at least 2 miles.

(*d*) The said green and red side lights shall be fitted with inboard screens projecting at least 3 feet forward from the light, so as to prevent these lights from being seen across the bow.

(*e*) A steam vessel when under way may carry an additional white light similar in construction to the light mentioned in subdivision (*a*). These two lights shall be so placed in line with the keel that one shall be at least 15 feet higher than the other and in such a position with reference to each other that the lower light shall be forward of the upper one. The vertical distance between these lights shall be less than the horizontal distance.

ART. 3. A steam vessel when towing another vessel shall, in addition to her side lights, carry two bright white lights in a vertical line one over the other, not less than 6 feet apart, and when towing more than one vessel shall carry an additional bright white light 6 feet above or below such light, if the length of the tow measuring from the stern of the towing vessel to the stern of the last vessel towed exceeds 600 feet. Each of these lights shall be of the same construction and character and shall be carried in the same position as the white light mentioned in article 2 (*a*), excepting the additional light, which may be carried at a height of not less than 14 feet above the hull.

Such steam vessel may carry a small white light abaft the funnel or aftermast for the vessel towed to steer by, but such light shall not be visible forward of the beam.

ART. 4. (*a*) A vessel which from any accident is not under command shall carry at the same height as ⌐ white light mentioned in article 2 (*a*), where they can best be seen, and if a steam vessel in lieu of that light, two red lights in a vertical line one over the other, not less than 6 feet apart, and of such a character as to be visible all around the horizon at a distance of at least 2 miles, and shall by day carry in a vertical line one over the other, not less than 6 feet apart, where they can best be seen, two black balls or shapes each 2 feet in diameter.

(*b*) A vessel employed in laying or in picking up a telegraph cable shall carry in the same position as the white light mentioned in article 2 (*a*), and if a steam vessel in lieu of that light, three lights in a vertical line one over the other, not less than 6 feet apart. The highest and lowest of these lights shall be red and the middle light shall be white, and they shall be of such a character as to be visible all around the horizon at a distance of at least 2 miles. By day she shall carry in a vertical line one over the other, not less than 6 feet apart, where they can best be seen, three shapes not less than 2 feet in diameter, of which the highest and lowest shall be globular in shape and red in color and the middle one diamond in shape and white.

(*c*) The vessels referred to in this article when not making way through the water shall not carry the side lights, but when making way shall carry them.

(*d*) The lights and shapes required to be shown by this article are to be taken by other vessels as signals that the vessel showing them is not under command and can not, therefore, get out of the way.

These signals are not signals of vessels in distress and requiring assistance. Such signals are contained in article 31.

ART. 5. A sailing vessel under way and any vessel being towed shall carry the same lights as are prescribed by article 2 for a steam vessel under way, with the exception of the white lights mentioned therein, which they shall never carry.

ART. 6. Whenever, as in the case of small vessels under way during bad weather, the green and red side lights can not be fixed, these lights shall be kept at hand, lighted and ready for use, and shall on the approach of or to other vessels be exhibited on their respective sides, in sufficient time to prevent collision, in such manner as to make them most visible and so that the green light shall not be seen on the port side nor the red light on the starboard side, nor, if practicable, more than 2 points abaft the beam on their respective sides.

To make the use of these portable lights more certain and easy the lanterns containing them shall each be painted outside with the color of the light they respectively contain and shall be provided with proper screens.

ART. 7. Steam vessels of less than 40 and vessels under oars or sails of less than 20 tons gross tonnage, respectively, when under way shall not be obliged to carry the lights mentioned in article 2 (*a*), (*b*), and (*c*), but if they do not carry them they shall be provided with the following lights:

First. Steam vessels of less than 40 tons shall carry—

(*a*) In the fore part of the vessel or on or in front of the funnel, where it can best be seen, and at a height above the gunwale of not less than 9 feet, a bright white light constructed and fixed as prescribed in article 2 (*a*) and of such a character as to be visible at a distance of at least 2 miles.

(*b*) Green and red side lights constructed and fixed as prescribed in article 2 (*b*) and (*c*) and of such a character as to be visible at a distance of at least 1 mile, or a combined lantern showing a green light and a red light from right ahead to 2 points abaft the beam on their respective sides. Such lanterns shall be carried not less than 3 feet below the white light.

Second. Small steamboats, such as are carried by seagoing vessels, may carry the white light at a less height than 9 feet above the gunwale, but it shall be carried above the combined lantern mentioned in subdivision 1 (*b*).

Third. Vessels under oars or sails of less than 20 tons shall have ready at hand a lantern with a green glass on one side and a red glass on the other, which on the approach of or to other vessels shall be exhibited, in sufficient time to prevent collision, so that the green light shall not be seen on the port side nor the red light on the starboard side.

The vessels referred to in this article shall not be obliged to carry the lights prescribed by article 4 (*a*) and article 11, last paragraph.

ART. 8. Pilot vessels when engaged on their station on pilotage duty shall not show the lights required for other vessels, but shall carry a white light at the masthead, visible all around the horizon, and shall also exhibit a flare-up light or flare-up lights at short intervals, which shall never exceed fifteen minutes.

On the near approach of or to other vessels they shall have their side lights lighted ready for use and shall flash or show them at short intervals to indicate the direction in which they are heading; but the green light shall not be shown on the port side nor the red light on the starboard side.

A pilot vessel of such a class as to be obliged to go alongside of a vessel to put a pilot on board may show the white light instead of carrying it at the masthead, and may instead of the colored lights above mentioned have at hand ready for use a lantern with a green glass on the one side and a red glass on the other, to be used as prescribed above.

Pilot vessels when not engaged on their station on pilotage duty shall carry lights similar to those of other vessels of their tonnage.

ART. 9. Fishing vessels and fishing boats when under way and when not required by this article to carry or show the lights therein named shall carry or show the lights prescribed for vessels of their tonnage under way.

(*a*) Vessels and boats when fishing with drift nets shall exhibit two white lights from any part of the vessel where they can best be seen. Such lights shall be placed so that the vertical distance between them shall be not less than 6 feet and not more than 10 feet, and so that the horizontal distance between them measured in a line with the keel shall be not less than 5 feet and not more than 10 feet. The lower of these two lights shall be the more forward, and both of them shall be of such a character as to show all around the horizon and to be visible at a distance of not less than 3 miles.

(*b*) Vessels when engaged in trawling, by which is meant the dragging of an apparatus along the bottom of the sea—

First. If steam vessels, shall carry in the same position as the white light mentioned in article 2 (*a*) a tricolored lantern so constructed and fixed as to show a white light from right ahead to 2 points on each bow and a green light and a red light over an arc of the horizon from 2 points on either bow to 2 points abaft the beam on the starboard and port sides, respectively, and not less than 6 nor more than 12 feet below the tricolored lantern a white light in a lantern so constructed as to show a clear, uniform, and unbroken light all around the horizon.

Second. If sailing vessels of 7 tons gross tonnage and upward, shall carry a white light in a lantern so constructed as to show a clear, uniform, and unbroken light all around the horizon, and shall also be provided with a sufficient supply of red pyrotechnic lights, which shall each burn for at least thirty seconds and shall be shown on the approach of or to other vessels in sufficient time to prevent collision.

In the Mediterranean Sea the vessels referred to in subdivision (*b*) 2 may use a flare-up light in lieu of a pyrotechnic light.

All lights mentioned in subdivision (*b*) 1 and 2 shall be visible at a distance of at least 2 miles.

Third. If sailing vessels of less than 7 tons gross tonnage, shall not be obliged to carry the white light mentioned in subdivision (*b*) 2 of this article, but if they do not carry such light they shall have at hand, ready for use, a lantern showing a bright white light, which shall on the approach of or to other vessels be exhibited where it can best be seen in sufficient time to prevent collision; and they shall also show a red pyrotechnic light, as prescribed in subdivision (*b*) 2, or in lieu thereof a flare-up light.

(*c*) Vessels and boats when line fishing with their lines out and attached to their lines, and when not at anchor or stationary, shall carry the same lights as vessels fishing with drift nets.

(*d*) Fishing vessels and fishing boats may at any time use a flare-up light in addition to the lights which they are by this article required to carry and show. All flare-up lights exhibited by a vessel when trawling or fishing with any kind of drag-net shall be shown at the after part of the vessel, excepting that if the vessel is hanging by the stern to her fishing gear they shall be exhibited from the bow.

(*e*) Every fishing vessel and every boat when at anchor shall exhibit a white light visible all around the horizon at a distance of at least 1 mile.

(*f*) If a vessel or boat when fishing becomes stationary in consequence of her gear getting fast to a rock or other obstruction, she shall show the light and make the fog signal prescribed for a vessel at anchor, respectively. (See article 15 (*d*), (*e*), and last paragraph.)

(*g*) In fog, mist, falling snow, or heavy rain storms drift-net vessels attached to their nets, and vessels when trawling, dredging, or fishing with any kind of drag-net, and vessels line fishing with their lines out shall, if of 20 tons gross tonnage or upward, respectively, at intervals of not more than one minute make a blast—if steam vessels, with the whistle or siren, and if sailing vessels, with the fog horn—each blast to be followed by ringing the bell.

(*h*) Sailing vessels or boats fishing with nets or lines or trawls when under way shall in daytime indicate their occupation to an approaching vessel by displaying a basket or other efficient signal where it can best be seen.

The vessels referred to in this article shall not be obliged to carry the light prescribed by article 4 (*a*) and article 11, last paragraph.

ART. 10. A vessel which is being overtaken by another shall show from her stern to such last-mentioned vessel a white light or a flare-up light.

The white light required to be shown by this article may be fixed and carried in a lantern, but in such case the lantern shall be so constructed, fitted, and screened that it shall throw an unbroken light over an arc of the horizon of 12 points of the compass—namely, for 6 points from right aft on each side of the vessel—so as to be visible at a distance of at least 1 mile. Such light shall be carried as nearly as practicable on the same level as the side lights.

ART. 11. A vessel under 150 feet in length when at anchor shall carry forward, where it can best be seen, but at a height not exceeding 20 feet above the hull, a white light in a lantern so constructed as to show a clear, uniform, and unbroken light visible all around the horizon at a distance of at least 1 mile.

A vessel of 150 feet or upward in length when at anchor shall carry in the forward part of the vessel, at a height of not less than 20 and not exceeding 40 feet above the hull, one such light, and at or near the stern of the vessel, and at such a height that it shall be not less than 15 feet lower than the forward light, another such light.

The length of a vessel shall be deemed to be the length appearing in her certificate of registry.

A vessel aground in or near a fairway shall carry the above light or lights and the two red lights prescribed by article 4 (*a*).

ART. 12. Every vessel may, if necessary in order to attract attention, in addition to the lights which she is by these rules required to carry, show a flare-up light or use any detonating signal that can not be mistaken for a distress signal.

ART. 13. Nothing in these rules shall interfere with the operation of any special rules made by the government of any nation with respect to additional station and signal lights for two or more ships of war or for vessels sailing under convoy, or with the exhibition of recognition signals adopted by ship owners, which have been authorized by their respective governments and duly registered and published.

ART. 14. A steam vessel proceeding under sail only, but having her funnel up, shall carry in daytime forward, where it can best be seen, one black ball or shape 2 feet in diameter.

SOUND SIGNALS FOR FOG, ETC.

ART. 15. All signals prescribed by this article for vessels under way shall be given—

1. By "steam vessels," on the whistle or siren.

2. By "sailing vessels" and "vessels towed," on the fog horn.

The words "prolonged blast" used in this article shall mean a blast of from four to six seconds' duration.

A steam vessel shall be provided with an efficient whistle or siren, sounded by steam or by some substitute for steam, so placed that the sound may not be intercepted by any obstruction, and with an efficient fog horn, to be sounded by mechanical means, and also with an efficient bell. (In all cases where the rules require a bell to be used a drum may be substituted on board Turkish vessels or a gong where such articles are used on board small seagoing vessels.) A sailing vessel of 20 tons gross tonnage or upward shall be provided with a similar fog horn and bell.

In fog, mist, falling snow, or heavy rain storms, whether by day or night, the signals described in this article shall be used as follows, viz:

(*a*) A steam vessel having way upon her shall sound at intervals of not more than two minutes a prolonged blast.

(*b*) A steam vessel under way, but stopped and having no way upon her, shall sound at intervals of not more than two minutes two prolonged blasts, with an interval of about one second between them.

(*c*) A sailing vessel under way shall sound at intervals of not more than one minute, when on the starboard tack one blast, when on the port tack two blasts in succession, and when with the wind abaft the beam three blasts in succession.

(*d*) A vessel when at anchor shall at intervals of not more than one minute ring the bell rapidly for about five seconds.

(*e*) A vessel at anchor at sea, when not in ordinary anchorage ground and when in such a position as to be an obstruction to vessels under way, shall sound, if a steam vessel, at intervals of not more than two minutes, two prolonged blasts with her whistle or siren, followed by ringing her bell, or if a sailing vessel, at intervals of not more than one minute, two blasts with her fog horn, followed by ringing her bell.

(*f*) A vessel when towing shall, instead of the signals prescribed in subdivisions (*a*) and (*c*) of this article, at intervals of not more than two minutes sound three blasts in succession, namely, one prolonged blast followed by two short blasts. A vessel towed may give this signal, and she shall not give any other.

(*g*) A steam vessel wishing to indicate to another "The way is off my vessel; you may feel your way past me" may sound three blasts in succession—namely, short, long, short—with intervals of about one second between them.

(*h*) A vessel employed in laying or picking up a telegraph cable shall on hearing the fog signal of an approaching vessel sound in answer three prolonged blasts in succession.

(*i*) A vessel under way which is unable to get out of the way of an approaching vessel through being not under command or unable to maneuver as required by these rules shall on hearing the fog signal of an approaching vessel sound in answer four short blasts in succession.

Sailing vessels and boats of less than 20 tons gross tonnage shall not be obliged to give the above-mentioned signals, but if they do not they shall make some other efficient sound signal at intervals of not more than one minute.

SPEED OF SHIPS TO BE MODERATE IN FOG, ETC.

ART. 16. Every vessel shall in a fog, mist, falling snow, or heavy rain storms go at a moderate speed, having careful regard to the existing circumstances and conditions.

A steam vessel hearing, apparently forward of her beam, the fog signal of a vessel the position of which is not ascertained shall, so far as the circumstances of the case admit, stop her engines and then navigate with caution until danger of collision is over.

STEERING AND SAILING RULES.

PRELIMINARY.—RISK OF COLLISION.

Risk of collision can, when circumstances permit, be ascertained by carefully watching the compass bearing of an approaching vessel. If the bearing does not appreciably change, such risk should be deemed to exist.

ART. 17. When two sailing vessels are approaching one another so as to involve risk of collision, one of them shall keep out of the way of the other as follows, namely:

(*a*) A vessel which is running free shall keep out of the way of a vessel which is closehauled.

(*b*) A vessel which is closehauled on the port tack shall keep out of the way of a vessel which is closehauled on the starboard tack.

(*c*) When both are running free with the wind on different sides, the vessel which has the wind on the port side shall keep out of the way of the other.

(*d*) When both are running free with the wind on the same side, the vessel which is to the windward shall keep out of the way of the vessel which is to leeward.

(*e*) A vessel which has the wind aft shall keep out of the way of the other vessel.

ART. 18. When two steam vessels are meeting end on or nearly end on, so as to involve risk of collision, each shall alter her course to starboard, so that each may pass on the port side of the other.

This article only applies to cases where vessels are meeting end on or nearly end on in such a manner as to involve risk of collision, and does not apply to two vessels which must, if both keep on their respective courses, pass clear of each other.

The only cases to which it does apply are when each of the two vessels is end on or nearly end on to the other; in other words, to cases in which by day each vessel sees the masts of the other in a line or nearly in a line with her own, and by night to cases in which each vessel is in such a position as to see both the side lights of the other.

It does not apply by day to cases in which a vessel sees another ahead crossing her own course, or by night to cases where the red light of one vessel is opposed to the red light of the other, or where the green light of one vessel is opposed to the green light of the other, or where a red light without a green light or a green light without a red light is seen ahead, or where both green and red lights are seen anywhere but ahead.

ART. 19. When two steam vessels are crossing, so as to involve risk of collision, the vessel which has the other on her own starboard side shall keep out of the way of the other.

ART. 20. When a steam vessel and a sailing vessel are proceeding in such directions as to involve risk of collision, the steam vessel shall keep out of the way of the sailing vessel.

ART. 21. Where by any of these rules one of two vessels is to keep out of the way, the other shall keep her course and speed.

ART. 22. Every vessel which is directed by these rules to keep out of the way of another vessel shall, if the circumstances of the case admit, avoid crossing ahead of the other.

ART. 23. Every steam vessel which is directed by these rules to keep out of the way of another vessel shall on approaching her, if necessary, slacken her speed or stop or reverse.

ART. 24. Notwithstanding anything contained in these rules every vessel overtaking any other shall keep out of the way of the overtaken vessel.

Every vessel coming up with another vessel from any direction more than 2 points abaft her beam — that is, in such a position with reference to the vessel which she is overtaking that at night she would be unable to see either of that vessel's side lights — shall be deemed to be an overtaking vessel, and no subsequent alteration of the bearing between the two vessels shall make the overtaking vessel a crossing vessel within the meaning of these rules or relieve her of the duty of keeping clear of the overtaken vessel until she is finally past and clear.

As by day the overtaking vessel can not always know with certainty whether she is forward of or abaft this direction from the other vessel, she should if in doubt assume that she is an overtaking vessel and keep out of the way.

ART. 25. In narrow channels every steam vessel shall, when it is safe and practicable, keep to that side of the fairway or mid-channel which lies on the starboard side of such vessel.

ART. 26. Sailing vessels under way shall keep out of the way of sailing vessels or boats fishing with nets or lines or trawls. This rule shall not give to any vessel or boat engaged in fishing the right of obstructing a fairway used by vessels other than fishing vessels or boats.

ART. 27. In obeying and construing these rules due regard shall be had to all dangers of navigation and collision and to any special circumstances which may render a departure from the above rules necessary in order to avoid immediate danger.

SOUND SIGNALS FOR VESSELS IN SIGHT OF ONE ANOTHER.

ART. 28. The words "short blast" used in this article shall mean a blast of about one second's duration.

When vessels are in sight of one another, a steam vessel under way in taking any course authorized or required by these rules shall indicate that course by the following signals on her whistle or siren, namely:

One short blast to mean, "I am directing my course to starboard."

Two short blasts to mean, "I am directing my course to port."

Three short blasts to mean, "My engines are going at full speed astern."

NO VESSEL UNDER ANY CIRCUMSTANCES TO NEGLECT PROPER PRECAUTIONS.

ART. 29. Nothing in these rules shall exonerate any vessel or the owner or master or crew thereof from the consequences of any neglect to carry lights or signals, or of any neglect to keep a proper lookout, or of the neglect of any precaution which may be required by the ordinary practice of seamen or by the special circumstances of the case.

RESERVATION OF RULES FOR HARBORS AND INLAND NAVIGATION.

ART. 30. Nothing in these rules shall interfere with the operation of a special rule duly made by local authority relative to the navigation of any harbor, river, or inland waters.

DISTRESS SIGNALS.

ART. 31. When a vessel is in distress and requires assistance from other vessels or from the shore, the following shall be the signals to be used or displayed by her either together or separately, namely:

In the daytime—

First. A gun fired at intervals of about a minute.

Second. The international code signal of distress indicated by N C.

Third. The distance signal, consisting of a square flag, having either above or below it a ball or anything resembling a ball.

Fourth. Rockets or shells as prescribed below for use at night.

Fifth. A continuous sounding with any fog-signal apparatus.

At night—

First. A gun fired at intervals of about a minute.

Second. Flames on the vessel (as from a burning tar barrel, oil barrel, etc.).

Third. Rockets or shells bursting in the air with a loud report and throwing stars of any color or description, fired one at a time at short intervals.

Fourth. A continuous sounding with any fog-signal apparatus.

SEC. 2. That all laws or parts of laws inconsistent with the foregoing regulations for preventing collisions at sea, for the navigation of all public and private vessels of the United States upon the high seas and in all waters connected therewith navigable by seagoing vessels, are hereby repealed.

SEC. 3. That this act shall take effect at a time to be fixed by the President by proclamation issued for that purpose.

And whereas an act of Congress entitled "An act to amend an act approved August 19, 1890, entitled 'An act to adopt regulations for preventing collisions at sea,'" was approved May 28, 1894, the said act being in the following words:

Be it enacted by the Senate and House of Representatives of the United States of America in Congress assembled, That article 7 of the act approved August 19, 1890, entitled "An act to adopt regulations for preventing collisions at sea," be amended to read as follows:

"ART. 7. Steam vessels of less than 40 and vessels under oars or sails of less than 20 tons gross tonnage, respectively, and rowing boats, when under way, shall not be required to carry the lights mentioned in article 2 (*a*), (*b*), and (*c*), but if they do not carry them they shall be provided with the following lights:

"First. Steam vessels of less than 40 tons shall carry—

"(*a*) In the fore part of the vessel or on or in front of the funnel, where it can best be seen, and at a height above the gunwale of not less than 9 feet, a bright white light constructed and fixed as prescribed in article 2 (*a*) and of such a character as to be visible at a distance of at least 2 miles.

"(*b*) Green and red side lights constructed and fixed as prescribed in article 2 (*b*) and (*c*) and of such a character as to be visible at a distance of at least 1 mile, or a combined lantern showing a green light and a red light from right ahead to 2 points abaft the beam on their respective sides. Such lanterns shall be carried not less than 3 feet below the white light.

"Second. Small steamboats, such as are carried by seagoing vessels, may carry the white light at a less height than 9 feet above the gunwale, but it shall be carried above the combined lantern mentioned in subdivision 1 (*b*).

"Third. Vessels under oars or sails of less than 20 tons shall have ready at hand a lantern with a green glass on one side and a red glass on the other, which on the approach of or to other vessels shall be exhibited, in sufficient time to prevent collision, so that the green light shall not be seen on the port side nor the red light on the starboard side.

"Fourth. Rowing boats, whether under oars or sail, shall have ready at hand a lantern showing a white light, which shall be temporarily exhibited in sufficient time to prevent collision.

"The vessels referred to in this article shall not be obliged to carry the lights prescribed by article 4 (*a*) and article 11, last paragraph."

That article 9 be hereby repealed.

That article 21 be amended to read as follows:

"ART. 21. Where by any of these rules one of two vessels is to keep out of the way the other shall keep her course and speed.

" NOTE.—When in consequence of thick weather or other causes such vessel finds herself so close that collision can not be avoided by the action of the giving-way vessel alone, she also shall take such action as will best aid to avert collision." (See articles 27 and 29.)

That article 31 be amended to read as follows:

"DISTRESS SIGNALS.

"ART. 31. When a vessel is in distress and requires assistance from other vessels or from the shore, the following shall be the signals to be used or displayed by her, either together or separately, namely:

" In the daytime—

"First. A gun or other explosive signal fired at intervals of about a minute.

"Second. The international code signal of distress indicated by N C.

"Third. The distance signal, consisting of a square flag, having either above or below it a ball or anything resembling a ball.

"Fourth. A continuous sounding with any fog-signal apparatus.

"At night—

"First. A gun or other explosive signal fired at intervals of about a minute.

"Second. Flames on the vessel (as from a burning tar barrel, oil barrel, etc.).

"Third. Rockets or shells throwing stars of any color or description, fired one at a time at short intervals.

"Fourth. A continuous sounding with any fog-signal apparatus."

And whereas it was provided by section 3 of the said act of August 19, 1890, that it should take effect at a time to be fixed by the President by proclamation issued for that purpose; and

Whereas the President did, in virtue of the authority vested in him by the said section 3 of the act of August 19, 1890, issue a proclamation on the 13th day of July, 1894,* declaring the 1st day of March, 1895, as the day on which the said act approved August 19, 1890, as amended by the act approved May 28, 1894, should take effect; and

Whereas an act of Congress entitled "An act relating to lights on fishing vessels" was approved August 13, 1894, the said act being in the following words:

Be it enacted by the Senate and House of Representatives of the United States of America in Congress assembled, That article 10 of the act approved March 3, 1885, entitled "An act to adopt the 'Revised international regulations for preventing collisions at sea,'" so far as said article relates to lights for fishing vessels, is hereby reenacted and continued in force, anything in the act approved May 28, 1894, entitled "An act to amend an act approved August 19, 1890, entitled 'An act to adopt regulations for preventing collisions at sea,'" to the contrary notwithstanding.

And whereas the said article of the act approved March 3, 1885, entitled "An act to adopt the 'Revised international regulations for preventing collisions at sea,'" reenacted by the said act of August 13, 1894, is as follows:

ART. 10. Open boats and fishing vessels of less than 20 tons net registered tonnage when under way and when not having their nets, trawls, dredges, or lines in the

* See pp. 5933–5942.

water shall not be obliged to carry the colored side lights; but every such boat and vessel shall in lieu thereof have ready at hand a lantern with a green glass on the one side and a red glass on the other side, and on approaching to or being approached by another vessel such lantern shall be exhibited, in sufficient time to prevent collision, so that the green light shall not be seen on the port side nor the red light on the starboard side.

The following portion of this article applies only to fishing vessels and boats when in the sea off the coast of Europe lying north of Cape Finisterre:

(*a*) All fishing vessels and fishing boats of 20 tons net registered tonnage or upward when under way and when not having their nets, trawls, dredges, or lines in the water shall carry and show the same lights as other vessels under way.

(*b*) All vessels when engaged in fishing with drift nets shall exhibit two white lights from any part of the vessel where they can be best seen. Such lights shall be placed so that the vertical distance between them shall be not less than 6 feet and not more than 10 feet and so that the horizontal distance between them measured in a line with the keel of the vessel shall be not less than 5 feet and not more than 10 feet. The lower of these two lights shall be the more forward, and both of them shall be of such a character and contained in lanterns of such construction as to show all round the horizon on a dark night with a clear atmosphere for a distance of not less than 3 miles.

(*c*) All vessels when trawling, dredging, or fishing with any kind of dragnets shall exhibit from some part of the vessel where they can be best seen two lights. One of these lights shall be red and the other shall be white. The red light shall be above the white light and shall be at a vertical distance from it of not less than 6 feet and not more than 12 feet, and the horizontal distance between them, if any, shall not be more than 10 feet. These two lights shall be of such a character and contained in lanterns of such construction as to be visible all round the horizon on a dark night with a clear atmosphere, the white light to a distance of not less than 3 miles and the red light of not less than 2 miles.

(*d*) A vessel employed in line fishing with her lines out shall carry the same lights as a vessel when engaged in fishing with drift nets.

(*e*) If a vessel when fishing with a trawl, dredge, or any kind of dragnet becomes stationary in consequence of her gear getting fast to a rock or other obstruction, she shall show the light and make the fog signal for a vessel at anchor.

(*f*) Fishing vessels and open boats may at any time use a flare-up in addition to the lights which they are by this article required to carry and show. All flare-up lights exhibited by a vessel when trawling, dredging, or fishing with any kind of dragnet shall be shown at the after part of the vessel, excepting that if the vessel is hanging by the stern to her trawl, dredge, or dragnet they shall be exhibited from the bow.

(*g*) Every fishing vessel and every open boat when at anchor between sunset and sunrise shall exhibit a white light visible all round the horizon at a distance of at least 1 mile.

(*h*) In a fog a drift-net vessel attached to her nets, and a vessel when trawling, dredging, or fishing with any kind of dragnet, and a vessel employed in line fishing with her lines out shall at intervals of not more than two minutes make a blast with her fog horn and ring her bell alternately.

And whereas an act of Congress entitled "An act to postpone the enforcement of the act of August 19, 1890, entitled 'An act to adopt regulations for preventing collisions at sea,'" was approved February 23, 1895, the said act being in the following words:

Whereas the President, in accordance with the proposition of Great Britain to enforce on March 1, 1895, the "Revised international regulations for preventing collisions at sea," and on the representations of that Government that those regulations had received the general approval of the several foreign maritime powers, pursuant to section 3 of the act of August 19, 1890, entitled "An act to adopt regulations for preventing collisions at sea," issued on July 13, 1894, his proclamation* fixing March 1, 1895, as the time when the provisions of said act, as amended, embodying said revised international regulations, shall take effect; and

Whereas the Government of Great Britain has withdrawn from the position communicated to this Government on April 25, 1894, that no time should be lost in carrying those regulations into effect, and on January 16, 1895, announced to this Government that the Government of Great Britain now finds it impossible until Parliament has been consulted to fix a date for bringing the regulations into force, and earnestly requests this Government to consent to a temporary postponement of the enforcement of said regulations; and

Whereas it is desirable that the "Revised international regulations for preventing collisions at sea" shall be put into force simultaneously by the maritime powers: Therefore,

Be it enacted by the Senate and House of Representatives of the United States of America in Congress assembled, That said act of August 19, 1890, take effect not on March 1, 1895, but at a subsequent time, to be fixed by the President by proclamation issued for that purpose.

And whereas the President did, in virtue of the authority vested in him by the said act of February 23, 1895, issue a proclamation on the 25th day of February, 1895,† giving notice that the said act of August 19, 1890, as amended by the act of May 28, 1894, would not go into force on March 1, 1895, the date fixed in his said proclamation of July 13, 1894,* but on such future date as might be designated in a proclamation of the President to be issued for that purpose; and

Whereas an act of Congress entitled "An act to amend an act approved August 19, 1890, entitled 'An act to adopt regulations for preventing collisions at sea,' " was approved June 10, 1896, the said act being in the following words:

Be it enacted by the Senate and House of Representatives of the United States of America in Congress assembled, That article 15 of the act approved August 19, 1890, entitled "An act to adopt regulations for preventing collisions at sea," be amended to read as follows:

"ART. 15. All signals prescribed by this article for vessels under way shall be given—

"First. By 'steam vessels,' on the whistle or siren.

"Second. By 'sailing vessels' and 'vessels towed,' on the fog horn.

"The words 'prolonged blast' used in this article shall mean a blast of from four to six seconds' duration.

"A steam vessel shall be provided with an efficient whistle or siren, sounded by steam or some substitute for steam, so placed that the sound may not be intercepted by any obstruction, and with an efficient fog horn to be sounded by mechanical means, and also with an efficient bell. (In all cases where the rules require a bell to be used a drum may be substituted on board Turkish vessels or a gong where such articles are used on board small seagoing vessels.) A sailing vessel of 20 tons gross tonnage or upward shall be provided with a similar fog horn and bell.

"In fog, mist, falling snow, or heavy rain storms, whether by day or night, the signals described in this article shall be used as follows, namely:

"(a) A steam vessel having way upon her shall sound at intervals of not more than two minutes a prolonged blast.

*See pp. 5933–5942.   †See p. 6016.

"(b) A steam vessel under way, but stopped and having no way upon her, shall sound at intervals of not more than two minutes two prolonged blasts with an interval of about one second between.

"(c) A sailing vessel under way shall sound at intervals of not more than one minute, when on the starboard tack one blast, when on the port tack two blasts in succession, and when with the wind abaft the beam three blasts in succession.

"(d) A vessel when at anchor shall at intervals of not more than one minute ring the bell rapidly for about five seconds.

"(e) A vessel when towing, a vessel employed in laying or in picking up a telegraph cable, and a vessel under way which is unable to get out of the way of an approaching vessel through being not under command or unable to maneuver as required by the rules shall, instead of the signals prescribed in subdivisions (a) and (c) of this article, at intervals of not more than two minutes sound three blasts in succession, namely, one prolonged blast followed by two short blasts. A vessel towed may give this signal, and she shall not give any other.

"Sailing vessels and boats of less than 20 tons gross tonnage shall not be obliged to give the above-mentioned signals, but if they do not they shall make some other efficient sound signal at intervals of not more than one minute."

SEC. 2. That said act of August 19, 1890, as amended, shall take effect at a subsequent time to be fixed by the President by proclamation issued for that purpose.

And whereas it was provided by section 2 of the act approved June 10, 1896, that the said act of August 19, 1890, as amended should take effect at a subsequent time to be fixed by the President by proclamation issued for that purpose:

Now, therefore, I, Grover Cleveland, President of the United States of America, do hereby, in virtue of the authority vested in me by section 3 of the act of August 19, 1890, and by section 2 of the act of June 10, 1896, proclaim the 1st day of July, 1897, as the day on which the said act approved August 19, 1890, as amended by the act approved May 28, 1894, by the act approved August 13, 1894, and by the act approved June 10, 1896, shall take effect.

In testimony whereof I have hereunto set my hand and caused the seal of the United States of America to be affixed.

[SEAL.] Done at the city of Washington, this 31st day of December, 1896, and of the Independence of the United States the one hundred and twenty-first. GROVER CLEVELAND.

By the President:
RICHARD OLNEY, *Secretary of State.*

BY THE PRESIDENT OF THE UNITED STATES OF AMERICA.

A PROCLAMATION.

Whereas it is provided by section 24 of the act of Congress approved March 3, 1891, entitled "An act to repeal timber-culture laws, and for other purposes" —

That the President of the United States may from time to time set apart and reserve in any State or Territory having public land bearing forests, in any part of the public lands wholly or in part covered with timber or undergrowth, whether of commercial value or not, as public reservations; and the President shall by public proclamation declare the establishment of such reservations and the limits thereof.

And whereas the public lands in the State of Utah within the limits hereinafter described are in part covered with timber, and it appears that the public good would be promoted by setting apart and reserving said lands as a public reservation:

Now, therefore, I, Grover Cleveland, President of the United States, by virtue of the power in me vested by section 24 of the aforesaid act of Congress, do hereby make known and proclaim that there is hereby reserved from entry or settlement and set apart as a public reservation all those certain tracts, pieces, or parcels of land lying and being situate in the State of Utah and within the boundaries particularly described as follows, to wit:

Beginning at the northwest corner of township one (1) south, range seven (7) east, Salt Lake meridian, Utah; thence easterly along the base line to the southeast corner of township one (1) north, range eight (8) east; thence northerly along the range line to the northeast corner of said township; thence easterly along the township line between townships one (1) and two (2) north to the southeast corner of township two (2) north, range thirteen (13) east; thence northerly along the range line to the northeast corner of said township; thence easterly along the surveyed and unsurveyed township line between townships two (2) and three (3) north to its point of intersection with the Green River; thence in a southeasterly direction along the middle of the channel of said river to the point for the unsurveyed range line between ranges twenty-two (22) and twenty-three (23) east; thence southerly along the unsurveyed and surveyed range line between said ranges to the point for the southeast corner of township two (2) south, range twenty-two (22) east; thence westerly along the unsurveyed and surveyed township line between townships two (2) and three (3) south to the northwest corner of township three (3) south, range nineteen (19) east; thence southerly along the west boundary of said township to its intersection with the east boundary of the Uintah Indian Reservation; thence northwesterly along said Indian-reservation boundary to the northeast corner of said reservation; thence southwesterly along the north boundary of said Indian reservation to the intersection therewith by the range line between ranges six (6) and seven (7) east; thence northerly along said range line, surveyed and unsurveyed, to the northwest corner of township one (1) south, range seven (7) east, the place of beginning.

Excepting from the force and effect of this proclamation all lands which may have been prior to the date hereof embraced in any legal entry or covered by any lawful filing duly of record in the proper United States land office, or upon which any valid settlement has been made pursuant to law and the statutory period within which to make entry or filing of record has not expired, and all mining claims duly located and held according to the laws of the United States and rules and regulations not in conflict therewith.

Provided, That this exception shall not continue to apply to any particular tract of land unless the entryman, settler, or claimant continues to comply with the law under which the entry, filing, settlement, or location was made.

Warning is hereby expressly given to all persons not to enter or make settlement upon the tract of land reserved by this proclamation.

In witness whereof I have hereunto set my hand and caused the seal of the United States to be affixed.

[SEAL.] Done at the city of Washington, this 22d day of February, A. D. 1897, and of the Independence of the United States the one hundred and twenty-first.

GROVER CLEVELAND.

By the President:

RICHARD OLNEY, *Secretary of State.*

BY THE PRESIDENT OF THE UNITED STATES OF AMERICA.

A PROCLAMATION.

Whereas it is provided by section 24 of the act of Congress approved March 3, 1891, entitled "An act to repeal timber-culture laws, and for other purposes"—

That the President of the United States may from time to time set apart and reserve in any State or Territory having public land bearing forests, in any part of the public lands wholly or in part covered with timber or undergrowth, whether of commercial value or not, as public reservations; and the President shall by public proclamation declare the establishment of such reservations and the limits thereof.

And whereas the public lands in the State of California within the limits hereinafter described are in part covered with timber, and it appears that the public good would be promoted by setting apart and reserving said lands as a public reservation:

Now, therefore, I, Grover Cleveland, President of the United States, by virtue of the power in me vested by section 24 of the aforesaid act of Congress, do hereby make known and proclaim that there is hereby reserved from entry or settlement and set apart as a public reservation all those certain tracts, pieces, or parcels of land lying and being situate in the State of California and within the boundaries particularly described as follows, to wit:

Beginning at the southeast corner of township eight (8) south, range eight (8) east, San Bernardino base and meridian, California; thence northerly along the range line to the northeast corner of said township; thence westerly along the township line to the southwest corner of township seven (7) south, range eight (8) east; thence northerly along the range line to the northwest corner of said township; thence westerly along the township line to the southwest corner of township six (6) south, range seven (7) east; thence northerly along the range line to the northwest corner of said township; thence westerly along the unsurveyed and surveyed township line to the southwest corner of township five (5) south, range six (6) east; thence northerly along the range line to the northwest corner of said township; thence westerly along the first (1st) standard parallel south to the southwest corner of township four (4) south, range four (4) east; thence northerly along the range line to the northwest corner of said township; thence westerly along the unsurveyed and surveyed township line between townships three (3) and four (4) south to its intersection with the east boundary line of the "Rancho San Jacinto Neuvo y Potrero;" thence southeasterly along the boundary line of said rancho and the boundary line of "Rancho San Jacinto Viejo" to the most southeasterly point of said last-named rancho; thence westerly along the south boundary of said "Rancho San Jacinto Viejo" to the point of intersection by the section line between sections fifteen (15) and sixteen (16), township five (5) south, range one (1) east; thence southerly along the section line to the southwest corner of section thirty-four (34), township six (6) south, range one (1) east; thence easterly along the township line to the northwest corner of township seven (7) south, range two (2) east; thence southerly along the range line between ranges one (1) and two (2) east to the southwest corner of township eight (8) south, range two (2) east; thence along the second (2d) standard parallel south to the northwest corner of township nine (9) south, range two (2) east; thence southerly along the range line to he southwest corner of said township; thence easterly along the township line between townships nine (9) and ten (10) south to the southeast corner of township nine (9) south, range four (4) east; thence northerly along the range line to the northeast corner of said township; thence easterly along the second (2d) standard parallel south to the northwest corner of township nine (9) south, range seven (7) east; thence southerly along the range line to the southwest corner of section eighteen (18), said township; thence easterly along the section line to the southeast corner of section thirteen (13), said township; thence southerly along the range line between ranges seven (7) and eight (8) east to the southwest corner of township ten (10) south, range eight (8) east; thence easterly along the township line to the southeast corner of said township; thence northerly along the range line between ranges eight (8) and nine (9) east to the northeast corner of township nine (9) south, range eight (8) east; thence westerly along the second (2d) standard parallel south to the southeast corner of township eight (8) south, range eight (8) east, the place of beginning.

Excepting from the force and effect of this proclamation all irrigation rights and lands lawfully acquired therefor and all lands which may have been prior to the date hereof embraced in any legal entry or covered by any lawful filing duly of record in the proper United States land office, or upon which any valid settlement has been made pursuant to law and the statutory period within which to make entry or filing of record has not expired, and all mining claims duly located and held according to the laws of the United States and rules and regulations not in conflict therewith.

Provided, That this exception shall not continue to apply to any particular tract of land unless the entryman, settler, or claimant continues to comply with the law under which the entry, filing, settlement, or location was made.

Warning is hereby expressly given to all persons not to enter or make settlement upon the tract of land reserved by this proclamation.

In witness whereof I have hereunto set my hand and caused the seal of the United States to be affixed.

[SEAL.]   Done at the city of Washington, this 22d day of February, A. D. 1897, and of the Independence of the United States the one hundred and twenty-first.

GROVER CLEVELAND.

By the President:

RICHARD OLNEY,
    Secretary of State.

BY THE PRESIDENT OF THE UNITED STATES OF AMERICA.

A PROCLAMATION.

Whereas it is provided by section 24 of the act of Congress approved March 3, 1891, entitled "An act to repeal timber-culture laws, and for other purposes"—

That the President of the United States may from time to time set apart and reserve in any State or Territory having public land bearing forests, in any part of the public lands wholly or in part covered with timber or undergrowth, whether of commercial value or not, as public reservations; and the President shall by public proclamation declare the establishment of such reservations and the limits thereof.

And whereas the public lands in the State of Washington within the limits hereinafter described are in part covered with timber, and it appears that the public good would be promoted by setting apart and reserving said lands as a public reservation:

Now, therefore, I, Grover Cleveland, President of the United States, by virtue of the power in me vested by section 24 of the aforesaid act of Congress, do hereby make known and proclaim that there is hereby reserved from entry or settlement and set apart as a public reservation all those certain tracts, pieces, or parcels of land lying and being situate in the State of Washington and within the boundaries particularly described as follows, to wit:

Beginning at the southeast corner of township four (4) north, range nine (9) east, Willamette base and meridian, Washington; thence north-erly along the range line between ranges nine (9) and (10) east, subject to the proper offset on the first (1st) standard parallel north to the north-west corner of township six (6) north, range ten (10) east; thence east-erly along the township line to the northeast corner of said township; thence northerly along the range line to the northwest corner of town-ship seven (7) north, range eleven (11) east; thence easterly along the township line between townships seven (7) and eight (8) north to the northeast corner of township seven (7) north, range twelve (12) east; thence northerly along the surveyed and unsurveyed range line between ranges twelve (12) and thirteen (13) east, subject to the proper offset on the second (2d) standard parallel north, to the northwest corner of town-ship (11) north, range thirteen (13) east; thence easterly along the sur-veyed and unsurveyed township line between townships eleven (11) and twelve (12) north to the southwest corner of township twelve (12) north, range (15) east; thence northerly along the surveyed and unsurveyed range line between ranges fourteen (14) and fifteen (15) east, subject to the proper offsets on the third (3d) and fourth (4th) standard parallels north to the point for the northeast corner of township eighteen (18) north, range fourteen (14) east; thence westerly along the unsurveyed and surveyed township line between townships eighteen (18) and nine-teen (19) north to the southwest corner of township nineteen (19) north, range seven (7) east; thence southerly along the surveyed and unsur-veyed range line between ranges six (6) and seven (7) east, subject to the proper offsets on the township line between townships seventeen (17) and eighteen (18) north and on the fourth (4th), third (3d), and second (2d) standard parallels north, to the point for the northeast corner of township five (5) north, range six (6) east; thence westerly along the unsurveyed township line between townships five (5) and (6) north to the southeast corner of township six (6) north, range four (4) east; thence southerly along the unsurveyed range line between ranges four (4) and five (5) east, subject to the proper offset on the first (1st) standard par-allel north, to the point for the southwest corner of township four (4) north, range five (5) east; thence easterly along the unsurveyed and surveyed township line between townships three (3) and four (4) north to the southeast corner of township four (4) north, range nine (9) east, the place of beginning.

Excepting from the force and effect of this proclamation all lands which may have been prior to the date hereof embraced in any legal entry or covered by any lawful filing duly of record in the proper United States land office, or upon which any valid settlement has been made pursuant to law and the statutory period within which to make entry or filing of record has not expired, and all mining claims duly located and held ac-cording to the laws of the United States and rules and regulations not in conflict therewith.

Provided, That this exception shall not continue to apply to any particular tract of land unless the entryman, settler, or claimant continues to comply with the law under which the entry, filing, settlement, or location was made.

Warning is hereby expressly given to all persons not to enter or make settlement upon the tract of land reserved by this proclamation.

Whereas a portion of the land embraced within the limits above described was reserved by proclamation of February 20, 1893, and designated as "The Pacific Forest Reserve," and whereas it appearing proper that the entire area herein described should be distinguished by the name of the most notable landmark within its boundaries, the title "The Pacific Forest Reserve" is hereby abolished, and the reservation established by this proclamation shall be known as "The Mount Rainier Forest Reserve."

In witness whereof I have hereunto set my hand and caused the seal of the United States to be affixed.

[SEAL.] Done at the city of Washington, this 22d day of February, A. D. 1897, and of the Independence of the United States the one hundred and twenty-first.

GROVER CLEVELAND.

By the President:

RICHARD OLNEY,
    Secretary of State.

BY THE PRESIDENT OF THE UNITED STATES OF AMERICA.

A PROCLAMATION.

Whereas it is provided by section 24 of the act of Congress approved March 3, 1891, entitled "An act to repeal timber-culture laws, and for other purposes"—

That the President of the United States may from time to time set apart and reserve in any State or Territory having public land bearing forests, in any part of the public lands wholly or in part covered with timber or undergrowth, whether of commercial value or not, as public reservations; and the President shall by public proclamation declare the establishment of such reservations and the limits thereof.

And whereas the public lands in the State of California within the limits hereinafter described are in part covered with timber, and it appears that the public good would be promoted by setting apart and reserving said lands as a public reservation:

Now, therefore, I, Grover Cleveland, President of the United States, by virtue of the power in me vested by section 24 of the aforesaid act of Congress, do hereby make known and proclaim that there is hereby reserved from entry or settlement and set apart as a public reservation all those certain tracts, pieces, or parcels of land lying and being situate in the State of California and within the boundaries particularly described as follows, to wit:

Beginning at the southeast corner of township three (3) north, range twenty-four (24) east, Mount Diablo base and meridian, California; thence northerly along the range line to the northeast corner of said township; thence westerly along the township line to the northwest corner of said township; thence northerly along the range line to the township line between townships four (4) and five (5) north, range twenty-three (23) east; thence easterly along the township line to the southeast corner of township five (5) north, range twenty-three (23) east; thence northerly along the range line to the northeast corner of said township; thence westerly along the first (1st) standard parallel north to the southwest corner of township six (6) north, range twenty-two (22) east; thence northerly along the range line between ranges twenty-one (21) and twenty-two (22) east to the northeast corner of township seven (7) north, range twenty-one (21) east; thence westerly along the township line to the northwest corner of said township; thence northerly along the range line to the northeast corner of township eight (8) north, range twenty (20) east; thence westerly along the surveyed and unsurveyed township line between townships eight (8) and nine (9) north to the northwest corner of township eight (8) north, range seventeen (17) east; thence southerly along the range line to the southeast corner of township eight (8) north, range sixteen (16) east; thence easterly along the unsurveyed township line to the point for the southeast corner of township eight (8) north, range seventeen (17) east; thence southerly along the unsurveyed and surveyed range line between ranges seventeen (17) and eighteen (18) east, subject to the easterly offset on the first (1st) standard parallel north, to the southeast corner of township four (4) north, range seventeen (17) east; thence easterly along the township line to the northeast corner of township three (3) north, range eighteen (18) east; thence southerly along the range line to the southeast corner of said township; thence easterly along the township line between townships two (2) and three (3) north to the southeast corner of township three (3) north, range twenty-four (24) east, the place of beginning.

Excepting from the force and effect of this proclamation all lands which may have been prior to the date hereof embraced in any legal entry or covered by any lawful filing duly of record in the proper United States land office, or upon which any valid settlement has been made pursuant to law and the statutory period within which to make entry or filing of record has not expired, and all mining claims duly located and held according to the laws of the United States and rules and regulations not in conflict therewith.

Provided, That this exception shall not continue to apply to any particular tract of land unless the entryman, settler, or claimant continues to comply with the law under which the entry, filing, settlement, or location was made.

Warning is hereby expressly given to all persons not to enter or make settlement upon the tract of land reserved by this proclamation.

In witness whereof I have hereunto set my hand and caused the seal of the United States to be affixed.

[SEAL.] Done at the city of Washington, this 22d day of February, A. D. 1897, and of the Independence of the United States the one hundred and twenty-first.

GROVER CLEVELAND.

By the President:

RICHARD OLNEY,
Secretary of State.

BY THE PRESIDENT OF THE UNITED STATES OF AMERICA.

A PROCLAMATION.

Whereas it is provided by section 24 of the act of Congress approved March 3, 1891, entitled "An act to repeal timber-culture laws, and for other purposes"—

That the President of the United States may from time to time set apart and reserve in any State or Territory having public land bearing forests, in any part of the public lands wholly or in part covered with timber or undergrowth, whether of commercial value or not, as public reservations; and the President shall by public proclamation declare the establishment of such reservations and the limits thereof.

And whereas the public lands in the States of Idaho and Montana within the limits hereinafter described are in part covered with timber, and it appears that the public good would be promoted by setting apart and reserving said lands as a public reservation:

Now, therefore, I, Grover Cleveland, President of the United States, by virtue of the power in me vested by section 24 of the aforesaid act of Congress, do hereby make known and proclaim that there is hereby reserved from entry or settlement and set apart as a public reservation all those certain tracts, pieces, or parcels of land lying and being situate in the States of Idaho and Montana and within the boundaries particularly described as follows, to wit:

Beginning at the northeast corner of township thirty-six (36) north, range five (5) east, Boise meridian, Idaho; thence southerly along the surveyed and unsurveyed range line between ranges five (5) and six (6) east to the point of intersection with the Salmon River; thence in an easterly direction along the middle of the channel of said river to the point of intersection for the unsurveyed range line between ranges eighteen (18) and nineteen (19) east; thence northerly along said unsurveyed range line to the point of intersection with the boundary line between the States of Idaho and Montana; thence in an easterly direction along said State boundary line to the point for the unsurveyed range line between ranges nineteen (19) and twenty (20) west, principal meridian, Montana; thence northerly along said range line to the base line; thence westerly along said base line to the southeast corner of township one (1) north, range twenty (20) west; thence northerly along the range line to the northeast corner of said township; thence westerly along the surveyed and unsurveyed township line between townships one (1) and two (2) north to the point for the southeast corner of township two (2) north, range twenty-two (22) west; thence northerly along the unsurveyed range line between ranges twenty-one (21) and twenty-two (22) west, allowing for the proper offsets on the first (1st) and second (2d) standard parallels north, to the point for the northeast corner of township ten (10) north, range twenty-two (22) west; thence westerly along the unsurveyed township line between townships ten (10) and eleven (11) north to the point of intersection with the boundary line between the States of Montana and Idaho; thence along said State boundary line to the point for the unsurveyed township line between townships thirty-eight (38) and thirty-nine (39) north, Idaho; thence westerly along said township line to the point for the northwest corner of township thirty-eight (38) north, range ten (10) east; thence southerly along the unsurveyed range line between ranges nine (9) and ten (10) east to the point for the southwest corner of township thirty-seven (37) north, range ten (10) east; thence westerly along the unsurveyed seventh (7th) standard parallel north to the northeast corner of township thirty-six (36) north, range five (5) east, the place of beginning.

Excepting from the force and effect of this proclamation all lands which may have been prior to the date hereof embraced in any legal entry or covered by any lawful filing duly of record in the proper United States land office, or upon which any valid settlement has been made pursuant to law and the statutory period within which to make entry or filing of record has not expired, and all mining claims duly located and held according to the laws of the United States and rules and regulations not in conflict therewith.

Provided, That this exception shall not continue to apply to any particular tract of land unless the entryman, settler, or claimant continues to comply with the law under which the entry, filing, settlement, or location was made.

Warning is hereby expressly given to all persons not to enter or make settlement upon the tract of land reserved by this proclamation.

In witness whereof I have hereunto set my hand and caused the seal of the United States to be affixed.

[SEAL.]   Done at the city of Washington, this 22d day of February, A. D. 1897, and of the Independence of the United States the one hundred and twenty-first.

GROVER CLEVELAND.

By the President:
RICHARD OLNEY,
    Secretary of State.

By the President of the United States of America.

A PROCLAMATION.

Whereas it is provided by section 24 of the act of Congress approved March 3, 1891, entitled "An act to repeal timber-culture laws, and for other purposes"—

That the President of the United States may from time to time set apart and reserve in any State or Territory having public land bearing forests, in any part of the public lands wholly or in part covered with timber or undergrowth, whether of commercial value or not, as public reservations; and the President shall by public proclamation declare the establishment of such reservations and the limits thereof.

And whereas the public lands in the State of Washington within the limits hereinafter described are in part covered with timber, and it appears that the public good would be promoted by setting apart and reserving said lands as a public reservation:

Now, therefore, I, Grover Cleveland, President of the United States, by virtue of the power in me vested by section 24 of the aforesaid act of Congress, do hereby make known and proclaim that there is hereby reserved from entry or settlement and set apart as a public reservation all those certain tracts, pieces, or parcels of land lying and being situate in the State of Washington and within the boundaries particularly described as follows, to wit:

Beginning at the southeast corner of township twenty-one (21) north, range five (5) west, Willamette base and meridian, Washington; thence northerly along the surveyed and unsurveyed range line between ranges four (4) and five (5) west to the point for the northeast corner of township twenty-three (23) north, range five (5) west; thence easterly along the unsurveyed and surveyed township line to the point for the southeast corner of township twenty-four (24) north, range four (4) west; thence northerly along the unsurveyed range line to the point for the northeast corner of said township; thence easterly along the unsurveyed and surveyed sixth (6th) standard parallel north to the southeast corner of township twenty-five (25) north, range three (3) west; thence northerly along the surveyed and unsurveyed range line between ranges two (2) and three (3) west to the northeast corner of township twenty-nine (29) north, range three (3) west; thence westerly along the surveyed and unsurveyed seventh (7th) standard parallel north to the point for the southeast corner of township thirty (30) north, range nine (9) west; thence northerly along the unsurveyed and surveyed range line to the northeast corner of said township; thence westerly along the township line between townships thirty (30) and thirty-one (31) north to the northeast corner of township thirty (30) north, range fourteen (14) west; thence northerly along the range line to its intersection with the shore of the Strait of Juan de Fuca; thence northwesterly along said shore line to the east boundary of the Makah Indian Reservation; thence southerly along the east boundary to the southeast corner of said reservation and westerly along the south boundary thereof to the high-water mark on the Pacific coast; thence southerly along said coast line to the north boundary of the Quinaielt Indian Reservation; thence southeasterly along the north boundary to the eastern point of said reservation and southwesterly along the south boundary thereof to the point of intersection with the fifth (5th) standard parallel north; thence easterly along said parallel to the southeast corner of township twenty-one (21) north, range five (5) west, the place of beginning.

Excepting from the force and effect of this proclamation all lands which may have been prior to the date hereof embraced in any legal entry or covered by any lawful filing duly of record in the proper United States land office, or upon which any valid settlement has been made pursuant to law and the statutory period within which to make entry or filing of record has not expired, and all mining claims duly located and held according to the laws of the United States and rules and regulations not in conflict therewith.

Provided, That this exception shall not continue to apply to any particular tract of land unless the entryman, settler, or claimant continues to comply with the law under which the entry, filing, settlement, or location was made.

Warning is hereby expressly given to all persons not to enter or make settlement upon the tract of land reserved by this proclamation.

In witness whereof I have hereunto set my hand and caused the seal of the United States to be affixed.

[SEAL.]   Done at the city of Washington, this 22d day of February, A. D. 1897, and of the Independence of the United States the one hundred and twenty-first.

GROVER CLEVELAND.

By the President:
     RICHARD OLNEY,
         Secretary of State.

BY THE PRESIDENT OF THE UNITED STATES OF AMERICA.

A PROCLAMATION.

Whereas it is provided by section 24 of the act of Congress approved March 3, 1891, entitled "An act to repeal timber-culture laws, and for other purposes"—

That the President of the United States may from time to time set apart and reserve in any State or Territory having public land bearing forests, in any part of the public lands wholly or in part covered with timber or undergrowth, whether of commercial value or not, as public reservations; and the President shall by public proclamation declare the establishment of such reservations and the limits thereof.

And whereas the public lands in the State of South Dakota within the limits hereinafter described are in part covered with timber, and it appears that the public good would be promoted by setting apart and reserving said lands as a public reservation:

Now, therefore, I, Grover Cleveland, President of the United States, by virtue of the power in me vested by section 24 of the aforesaid act of Congress, do hereby make known and proclaim that there is hereby reserved from entry or settlement and set apart as a public reservation all those certain tracts, pieces, or parcels of land lying and being situate in the State of South Dakota and within the boundaries particularly described as follows, to wit:

Beginning at the northwest corner of township one (1) south, range seven (7) east, Black Hills meridian, South Dakota; thence westerly along the Black Hills base line to the southwest corner of township one (1) north, range six (6) east; thence northerly along the range line between ranges five (5) and six (6) east to the northwest corner of township two (2) north, range six (6) east; thence westerly along the unsurveyed township line between townships two (2) and three (3) north to the point of intersection with the boundary line between the States of South Dakota and Wyoming; thence southerly along said State boundary line to the point of intersection by the township line between townships six (6) and seven (7) south, Black Hills base line; thence easterly along said township line to the southwest corner of township six (6) south, range four (4) east; thence northerly along the range line to the northwest corner of said township; thence easterly along the township line between townships five (5) and six (6) south to the southwest corner of township five (5) south, range (6) east; thence northerly along the range line to the northwest corner of said township; thence easterly along the first (1st) standard parallel south to the southwest corner of township four (4) south, range seven (7) east; thence northerly along the range line between ranges six (6) and seven (7) east to the northwest corner of township one (1) south, range seven (7) east, the place of beginning.

Excepting from the force and effect of this proclamation all lands which may have been prior to the date hereof embraced in any legal entry or covered by any lawful filing duly of record in the proper United States land office, or upon which any valid settlement has been made pursuant to law and the statutory period within which to make entry or filing of record has not expired, and all mining claims duly located and held according to the laws of the United States and rules and regulations not in conflict therewith.

Provided, That this exception shall not continue to apply to any particular tract of land unless the entryman, settler, or claimant continues to comply with the law under which the entry, filing, settlement, or location was made.

Warning is hereby expressly given to all persons not to enter or make settlement upon the tract of land reserved by this proclamation.

In witness whereof I have hereunto set my hand and caused the seal of the United States to be affixed.

[SEAL.]   Done at the city of Washington, this 22d day of February, A. D. 1897, and of the Independence of the United States the one hundred and twenty-first.

GROVER CLEVELAND.

By the President:

RICHARD OLNEY,
  Secretary of State.

BY THE PRESIDENT OF THE UNITED STATES OF AMERICA.

A PROCLAMATION.

Whereas it is provided by section 24 of the act of Congress approved March 3, 1891, entitled "An act to repeal timber-culture laws, and for other purposes"—

That the President of the United States may from time to time set apart and reserve in any State or Territory having public land bearing forests, in any part of the public lands wholly or in part covered with timber or undergrowth, whether of commercial value or not, as public reservations; and the President shall by public proclamation declare the establishment of such reservations and the limits thereof.

And whereas the public lands in the States of Idaho and Washington within the limits hereinafter described are in part covered with timber, and it appears that the public good would be promoted by setting apart and reserving said lands as a public reservation:

Now, therefore, I, Grover Cleveland, President of the United States, by virtue of the power in me vested by section 24 of the aforesaid act of Congress, do hereby make known and proclaim that there is hereby reserved from entry or settlement and set apart as a public reservation all that tract of land situate in the States of Idaho and Washington embraced within the following boundaries, to wit:

Bounded on the east by the summit of the ridges dividing the waters tributary to the Kootenai River and Priest Lake and River; on the west by the summit of the ridges dividing the waters tributary to the Pend Oreille River or Clark Fork of the Columbia River and Priest Lake and River; on the north by the international boundary line between the States of Idaho and Washington and the British possessions, connecting the east and west boundaries above described; on the south by the township line between townships fifty-six (56) and fifty-seven (57) north of the base line, Idaho, projected to connect the east and west boundaries above described.

Excepting from the force and effect of this proclamation all lands which may have been prior to the date hereof embraced in any legal entry or covered by any lawful filing duly of record in the proper United States land office, or upon which any valid settlement has been made pursuant to law and the statutory period within which to make entry or filing of record has not expired, and all mining claims duly located and held according to the laws of the United States and rules and regulations not in conflict therewith.

Provided, That this exception shall not continue to apply to any particular tract of land unless the entryman, settler, or claimant continues to comply with the law under which the entry, filing, settlement, or location was made.

Warning is hereby expressly given to all persons not to enter or make settlement upon the tract of land reserved by this proclamation.

In witness whereof I have hereunto set my hand and caused the seal of the United States to be affixed.

[SEAL.]   Done at the city of Washington, this 22d day of February, A. D. 1897, and of the Independence of the United States the one hundred and twenty-first.

GROVER CLEVELAND.

By the President:

RICHARD OLNEY,
Secretary of State.

BY THE PRESIDENT OF THE UNITED STATES OF AMERICA.

A PROCLAMATION.

Whereas it is provided by section 24 of the act of Congress approved March 3, 1891, entitled "An act to repeal timber-culture laws, and for other purposes"—

That the President of the United States may from time to time set apart and reserve in any State or Territory having public land bearing forests, in any part of the public lands wholly or in part covered with timber or undergrowth, whether of commercial value or not, as public reservations; and the President shall by public proclamation declare the establishment of such reservations and the limits thereof.

And whereas the public lands in the State of Washington within the limits hereinafter described are in part covered with timber, and it appears that the public good would be promoted by setting apart and reserving said lands as a public reservation:

Now, therefore, I, Grover Cleveland, President of the United States, by virtue of the power in me vested by section 24 of the aforesaid act of Congress, do hereby make known and proclaim that there is hereby reserved from entry or settlement and set apart as a public reservation all those certain tracts, pieces, or parcels of land lying and being situate in the State of Washington and within the boundaries particularly described as follows, to wit:

Beginning at the point for the southwest corner of township twenty-nine (29) north, range eight (8) east, Willamette meridian, Washington;

6220 Messages and Papers of the Presidents

thence northerly along the unsurveyed range line between ranges seven (7) and eight (8) east to the point for the northwest corner of township thirty-two (32) north, range eight (8) east; thence easterly along the unsurveyed eighth (8th) standard parallel north to the point for the southwest corner of township thirty-three (33) north, range twelve (12) east; thence northerly along the unsurveyed range line between ranges eleven (11) and twelve (12) east to the point for the northwest corner of township thirty-six (36) north, range twelve (12) east; thence westerly along the unsurveyed ninth (9th) standard parallel north to the point for the southwest corner of township thirty-seven (37) north, range seven (7) east; thence northerly along the unsurveyed range line between ranges six (6) and seven (7) east to its point of intersection with the international boundary line between the State of Washington and the British possessions; thence easterly along said international boundary line to the point for the unsurveyed range line between ranges twenty-two (22) and twenty-three (23) east; thence southerly along said unsurveyed range line, subject to the proper easterly or westerly offsets on the ninth (9th) and eighth (8th) standard parallels north, to the point for the southeast corner of township twenty-nine (29) north, range twenty-two (22) east; thence westerly along the unsurveyed and surveyed seventh (7th) standard parallel north to the point for the southwest corner of township twenty-nine (29) north, range (8) east, the place of beginning.

Excepting from the force and effect of this proclamation all lands which may have been prior to the date hereof embraced in any legal entry or covered by any lawful filing duly of record in the proper United States land office, or upon which any valid settlement has been made pursuant to law and the statutory period within which to make entry or filing of record has not expired, and all mining claims duly located and held according to the laws of the United States and rules and regulations not in conflict therewith.

Provided, That this exception shall not continue to apply to any particular tract of land unless the entryman, settler, or claimant continues to comply with the law under which the entry, filing, settlement, or location was made.

Warning is hereby expressly given to all persons not to enter or make settlement upon the tract of land reserved by this proclamation.

In witness whereof I have hereunto set my hand and caused the seal of the United States to be affixed.

[SEAL.] Done at the city of Washington, this 22d day of February, A. D. 1897, and of the Independence of the United States the one hundred and twenty-first.

GROVER CLEVELAND

By the President:

RICHARD OLNEY,
Secretary of State.

By the President of the United States of America.

A PROCLAMATION.

Whereas it is provided by section 24 of the act of Congress approved March 3, 1891, entitled "An act to repeal timber-culture laws, and for other purposes"—

That the President of the United States may from time to time set apart and reserve in any State or Territory having public land bearing forests, in any part of the public lands wholly or in part covered with timber or undergrowth, whether of commercial value or not, as public reservations; and the President shall by public proclamation declare the establishment of such reservations and the limits thereof.

And whereas the public lands in the State of Wyoming within the limits hereinafter described are in part covered with timber, and it appears that the public good would be promoted by setting apart and reserving said lands as a public reservation:

Now, therefore, I, Grover Cleveland, President of the United States, by virtue of the power in me vested by section 24 of the aforesaid act of Congress, do hereby make known and proclaim that there is hereby reserved from entry or settlement and set apart as a public reservation all those certain tracts, pieces, or parcels of land lying and being situate in the State of Wyoming and within the boundaries particularly described as follows, to wit:

Beginning at the southeast corner of township forty-three (43) north, range one hundred and ten (110) west, sixth (6th) principal meridian, Wyoming; thence northerly along the surveyed and unsurveyed range line between ranges one hundred and nine (109) and one hundred and ten (110) west to the point of intersection with the south boundary of the Yellowstone National Park Timber Land Reserve as established by proclamation of September 10, 1891;* thence westerly along said boundary to its intersection with the boundary line between the States of Wyoming and Idaho; thence southerly along said State boundary line to the point for the unsurveyed township line between townships forty-two (42) and forty-three (43) north; thence easterly along the unsurveyed and surveyed township line between townships forty-two (42) and forty-three (43) north to the southeast corner of township forty-three (43) north, range one hundred and ten (110) west, the place of beginning.

Excepting from the force and effect of this proclamation all lands which may have been prior to the date hereof embraced in any legal entry or covered by any lawful filing duly of record in the proper United States land office, or upon which any valid settlement has been made pursuant to law and the statutory period within which to make entry or filing of record has not expired, and all mining claims duly located and held according to the laws of the United States and rules and regulations not in conflict therewith.

*See pp. 5590–5591.

Provided, That this exception shall not continue to apply to any particular tract of land unless the entryman, settler, or claimant continues to comply with the law under which the entry, filing, settlement, or location was made.

Warning is hereby expressly given to all persons not to enter or make settlement upon the tract of land reserved by this proclamation.

In witness whereof I have hereunto set my hand and caused the seal of the United States to be affixed.

[SEAL.]   Done at the city of Washington, this 22d day of February, A. D. 1897, and of the Independence of the United States the one hundred and twenty-first.

GROVER CLEVELAND.

By the President:
RICHARD OLNEY,
Secretary of State.

BY THE PRESIDENT OF THE UNITED STATES OF AMERICA.

A PROCLAMATION.

Whereas it is provided by section 24 of the act of Congress approved March 3, 1891, entitled "An act to repeal timber-culture laws, and for other purposes"—

That the President of the United States may from time to time set apart and reserve in any State or Territory having public land bearing forests, in any part of the public lands wholly or in part covered with timber or undergrowth, whether of commercial value or not, as public reservations; and the President shall by public proclamation declare the establishment of such reservations and the limits thereof.

And whereas the public lands in the State of Montana within the limits hereinafter described are in part covered with timber, and it appears that the public good would be promoted by setting apart and reserving said lands as a public reservation:

Now, therefore, I, Grover Cleveland, President of the United States, by virtue of the power in me vested by section 24 of the aforesaid act of Congress, do hereby make known and proclaim that there is hereby reserved from entry or settlement and set apart as a public reservation all those certain tracts, pieces, or parcels of land lying and being situate in the State of Montana and within the boundaries particularly described as follows, to wit:

Beginning at the point on the south boundary of the Blackfeet Indian Reservation where said boundary line is intersected by the range line between ranges eight (8) and nine (9) west, principal meridian, Montana; thence southwesterly along the south boundary to the southwest corner of said reservation and northwesterly along the west boundary thereof as defined and described in the act of Congress approved June 10, 1896, entitled "An act making appropriations for current and contingent expenses of the Indian Department and fulfilling treaty stipulations with various Indian tribes for the fiscal year ending June 30, 1897, and for other purposes," to the point where the unsurveyed range line between ranges twelve (12) and thirteen (13) west will intersect said boundary line; thence southerly along said unsurveyed range line to the point for the northeast corner of township twenty-nine (29) north, range thirteen (13) west; thence westerly along the unsurveyed township line to the point for the northwest corner of said township; thence southerly along the unsurveyed range line to the point for the southwest corner of section eighteen (18), said township; thence westerly along the unsurveyed section line to the point for the northwest corner of section nineteen (19), township twenty-nine (29) north, range fourteen (14) west; thence southerly along the unsurveyed range line to the point for the southwest corner of said township twenty-nine (29) north, range fourteen (14) west; thence westerly along the unsurveyed seventh (7th) standard parallel north to the point for the southeast corner of township twenty-nine (29) north, range seventeen (17) west; thence northerly along the unsurveyed range line to the point for the northeast corner of said township; thence westerly along the unsurveyed township line to the point for the northwest corner of section three (3), said township; thence northerly along the unsurveyed section line to the point for the northeast corner of section four (4), township thirty (30) north, range seventeen (17) west; thence westerly along the unsurveyed township line to the point for the northwest corner of section three (3), township thirty (30) north, range nineteen (19) west; thence southerly along the unsurveyed and surveyed section line, subject to the proper offset on the seventh (7th) standard parallel north, to the southeast corner of section twenty-one (21), township twenty-eight (28) north, range nineteen (19) west; thence easterly along the unsurveyed section line to the point for the southeast corner of section twenty-four (24), said township; thence southerly along the unsurveyed and surveyed range line to the southeast corner of township twenty-seven (27) north, range nineteen (19) west; thence easterly along the surveyed and unsurveyed township line to the point for the northwest corner of section three (3), township twenty-six (26) north, range eighteen (18) west; thence southerly along the unsurveyed section line to the point for the southwest corner of section thirty-four (34), said township; thence westerly along the unsurveyed and surveyed township line to its intersection with the east shore of Flathead Lake; thence southerly along the shore of said lake to the north boundary of the Flathead Indian Reservation; thence easterly along the north boundary to the northeast corner of said reservation and southerly along the east boundary thereof to the point where said boundary line will be intersected by the unsurveyed fourth (4th) standard parallel north; thence easterly along said unsurveyed parallel to the point for the southeast corner of township seventeen (17) north, range seven (7) west; thence northerly along the unsurveyed range line to the point for the northeast corner of said township; thence westerly along the unsurveyed township line to the point for the northwest corner of said township; thence northerly along the unsurveyed range line to the point for the northeast corner of township eighteen (18) north, range eight (8) west; thence westerly along the unsurveyed township line to the point for the southeast corner of township nineteen (19) north, range nine (9) west; thence northerly along the unsurveyed and surveyed range line between ranges eight (8) and nine (9) west, subject to the proper offsets on the fifth (5th), sixth (6th), and seventh (7th) standard parallels north, to the point of intersection with the south boundary of the Blackfeet Indian Reservation, the place of beginning.

Excepting from the force and effect of this proclamation all lands which may have been prior to the date hereof embraced in any legal entry or covered by any lawful filing duly of record in the proper United States land office, or upon which any valid settlement has been made pursuant to law and the statutory period within which to make entry or filing of record has not expired, and all mining claims duly located and held according to the laws of the United States and rules and regulations not in conflict therewith.

Provided, That this exception shall not continue to apply to any particular tract of land unless the entryman, settler, or claimant continues to comply with the law under which the entry, filing, settlement, or location was made.

Warning is hereby expressly given to all persons not to enter or make settlement upon the tract of land reserved by this proclamation.

The rights and privileges reserved to the Indians of the Blackfeet Indian Reservation by Article I of the agreement set forth in and accepted, ratified, and confirmed by the act of Congress approved June 10, 1896, hereinbefore referred to, respecting that portion of their reservation relinquished to the United States by said Article I shall be in no way infringed or modified by reason of the fact that a part of the area so relinquished is embraced within the limits of the boundaries herein described and set apart as a forest reservation, nor shall the right of occupation, location, and purchase of said relinquished lands under the provisions of the mineral-land laws accorded by said act of Congress be abridged.

In witness whereof I have hereunto set my hand and caused the seal of the United States to be affixed.

[SEAL.]   Done at the city of Washington, this 22d day of February, A. D. 1897, and of the Independence of the United States the one hundred and twenty-first.

GROVER CLEVELAND.

By the President:

RICHARD OLNEY,
Secretary of State.

By the President of the United States of America.

A PROCLAMATION.

Whereas it is provided by section 24 of the act of Congress approved March 3, 1891, entitled "An act to repeal timber-culture laws, and for other purposes"—

That the President of the United States may from time to time set apart and reserve in any State or Territory having public land bearing forests, in any part of the public lands wholly or in part covered with timber or undergrowth, whether of commercial value or not, as public reservations; and the President shall by public proclamation declare the establishment of such reservations and the limits thereof.

And whereas the public lands in the State of Wyoming within the limits hereinafter described are in part covered with timber, and it appears that the public good would be promoted by setting apart and reserving said lands as a public reservation:

Now, therefore, I, Grover Cleveland, President of the United States, by virtue of the power in me vested by section 24 of the aforesaid act of Congress, do hereby make known and proclaim that there is hereby reserved from entry or settlement and set apart as a public reservation all those certain tracts, pieces, or parcels of land lying and being situate in the State of Wyoming and within the boundaries particularly described as follows, to wit:

Beginning at the southeast corner of township forty-eight (48) north, range eighty-four (84) west, sixth (6th) principal meridian, Wyoming; thence northerly along the range line to the northeast corner of said township; thence westerly along the twelfth (12th) standard parallel north to the southeast corner of township forty-nine (49) north, range eighty-four (84) west; thence northerly along the range line to the northeast corner of section thirteen (13), township fifty (50) north, range eighty-four (84) west; thence westerly along the section line to the northeast corner of section seventeen (17), said township; thence northerly along the section line to the southeast corner of section twenty-nine (29), township fifty-one (51) north, range eighty-four (84) west; thence easterly along the section line to the southeast corner of section twenty-six (26), said township; thence northerly along the section line to the northeast corner of section two (2), township fifty-two (52) north, range eighty-four (84) west; thence westerly along the thirteenth (13th) standard parallel north to the southeast corner of section thirty-five (35), township fifty-three (53) north, range eighty-four (84) west; thence northerly along the section line to the northeast corner of section fourteen (14), said township; thence westerly along the section line to the northeast corner of section fourteen (14), township fifty-three (53) north, range eighty-five (85) west; thence northerly along the section line to the northeast corner of section two (2), said township; thence westerly along the township line to the northeast corner of section two (2), township fifty-three (53) north, range eighty-six (86) west; thence northerly along the section line to the northeast corner of section two (2), township fifty-four (54) north, range eighty-six (86) west; thence westerly along the township line to the southeast corner of township fifty-five (55) north, range eighty-seven (87) west; thence northerly along the range line to the northeast corner of said township; thence westerly along the township line to the northwest corner of said township; thence southerly along the range line to the southwest corner of said township; thence westerly along the township line to the northwest corner of township fifty-four (54) north, range eighty-eight (88) west; thence northerly along the range line between ranges eighty-eight (88) and eighty-nine (89) west to the northwest corner of township fifty-six (56) north, range eighty-eight (88) west; thence westerly along the fourteenth (14th) standard parallel north to the southwest corner of township fifty-seven (57) north, range eighty-eight (88) west; thence northerly along the range line between ranges eighty-eight (88) and eighty-nine (89) west to the point of intersection with the boundary line between the States of Wyoming and Montana; thence westerly along said State boundary line to the point for the unsurveyed range line between ranges ninety-two (92) and ninety-three (93) west; thence southerly along said unsurveyed range line to the fourteenth (14th) standard parallel north; thence easterly along said standard parallel to the northeast corner of township fifty-six (56) north, range ninety-three (93) west; thence southerly along the range line between ranges ninety-two (92) and ninety-three (93) west to the northwest corner of township fifty-four (54) north, range ninety-two (92) west; thence easterly along the township line to the northeast corner of said township; thence southerly along the range line to the southeast corner of said township; thence easterly along the township line to the northeast corner of township fifty-three (53) north, range ninety-one (91) west; thence southerly along the range line to the southeast corner of said township; thence easterly along the thirteenth (13th) standard parallel north to the northwest corner of township fifty-two (52) north, range eighty-eight (88) west; thence southerly along the range line between ranges eighty-eight (88) and eighty-nine (89) west to the southwest corner of township fifty-one (51) north, range eighty-eight (88) west; thence easterly along the township line to the southeast corner of said township; thence southerly along the range line between ranges eighty-seven (87) and eighty-eight (88) west to the southwest corner of township forty-nine (49) north, range eighty-seven (87) west; thence easterly along the twelfth (12th) standard parallel north to the northwest corner of township forty-eight (48) north, range eighty-seven (87) west; thence southerly along the range line to the southwest corner of said township; thence easterly along the township line between townships forty-seven (47) and forty-eight (48) north to the southeast corner of township forty-eight (48) north, range eighty-four (84) west, the place of beginning.

Excepting from the force and effect of this proclamation all lands which may have been prior to the date hereof embraced in any legal entry or covered by any lawful filing duly of record in the proper United States land office, or upon which any valid settlement has been made pursuant to law and the statutory period within which to make entry or filing of record has not expired, and all mining claims duly located and held according to the laws of the United States and rules and regulations not in conflict therewith.

Provided, That this exception shall not continue to apply to any particular tract of land unless the entryman, settler, or claimant continues to comply with the law under which the entry, filing, settlement, or location was made.

Warning is hereby expressly given to all persons not to enter or make settlement upon the tract of land reserved by this proclamation.

In witness whereof I have hereunto set my hand and caused the seal of the United States to be affixed.

[SEAL.]   Done at the city of Washington, this 22d day of February, A. D. 1897, and of the Independence of the United States the one hundred and twenty-first.

GROVER CLEVELAND.

By the President:

RICHARD OLNEY,
        Secretary of State.

BY THE PRESIDENT OF THE UNITED STATES OF AMERICA.

A PROCLAMATION.

Whereas it is provided by section 24 of the act of Congress approved March 3, 1891, entitled "An act to repeal timber-culture laws, and for other purposes"—

That the President of the United States may from time to time set apart and reserve in any State or Territory having public land bearing forests, in any part of the public lands wholly or in part covered with timber or undergrowth, whether of commercial value or not, as public reservations; and the President shall by public proclamation declare the establishment of such reservations and the limits thereof.

And whereas the public lands in the State of Montana within the limits hereinafter described are in part covered with timber, and it appears that the public good would be promoted by setting apart and reserving said lands as a public reservation:

Now, therefore, I, Grover Cleveland, President of the United States, by virtue of the power in me vested by section 24 of the aforesaid act of Congress, do hereby make known and proclaim that there is hereby reserved from entry or settlement and set apart as a public reservation all those certain tracts, pieces, or parcels of land lying and being situate in the State of Montana and within the boundaries particularly described as follows, to wit:

Beginning at the southwest corner of township thirty-three (33) north, range twenty-five (25) west, principal meridian, Montana; thence easterly along the surveyed and unsurveyed eighth (8th) standard parallel north to the northeast corner of township thirty-two (32) north, range twenty-two (22) west; thence southerly along the range line between ranges twenty-one (21) and twenty-two (22) west to the southeast corner of section thirteen (13) of said township thirty-two (32) north, range twenty-two (22) west; thence easterly along the unsurveyed section line to the point for the southeast corner of section thirteen (13), township thirty-two (32) north, range eighteen (18) west; thence southerly along the unsurveyed range line between ranges seventeen (17) and eighteen (18) west to the northwest corner of township thirty-one (31) north, range seventeen (17) west; thence easterly along the township line between townships thirty-one (31) and thirty-two (32) north to the northwest corner of section two (2), township thirty-one (31) north, range seventeen (17) west; thence along the section lines southerly to the southwest corner of section twenty-three (23) and easterly to the northeast corner of section twenty-five (25), said township; thence southerly along the range line between ranges sixteen (16) and seventeen (17) west to the southeast corner of said township thirty-one (31) north, range seventeen (17) west; thence easterly along the unsurveyed township line between townships thirty (30) and thirty-one (31) north to the point for the southeast corner of township thirty-one (31) north, range sixteen (16) west; thence southerly along the unsurveyed range line between ranges fifteen (15) and sixteen (16) west to the point for the southwest corner of township thirty (30) north, range fifteen (15) west; thence easterly along the unsurveyed township line between townships twenty-nine (29) and thirty (30) north to the point for the southeast corner of said township thirty (30) north; thence northerly along the unsurveyed range line between ranges fourteen (14) and fifteen (15) west to the point for the southeast corner of section thirteen (13), said township thirty (30) north, range fifteen (15) west; thence along the unsurveyed section lines easterly to the point for the southeast corner of section sixteen (16) and northerly to the point for the northeast corner of section four (4), township thirty (30) north, range fourteen (14) west; thence easterly along the unsurveyed township line between townships thirty (30) and thirty-one (31) north to the point for the southeast corner of township thirty-one (31) north, range fourteen (14) west; thence northerly along the unsurveyed range line between ranges thirteen (13) and fourteen (14) west to the point where it will intersect the west boundary of the Blackfeet Indian Reservation as said boundary is defined and described in the act of Congress approved June 10 1896, entitled "An act making appropriations for current and contingent expenses of the Indian Department and fulfilling treaty stipulations with various Indian tribes for the fiscal year ending June 30, 1897, and for other purposes;" thence northwesterly along the boundary of said Indian reservation to its point of intersection with the international boundary line between the State of Montana and the British possessions; thence westerly along said international boundary line to the point for the unsurveyed range line between ranges twenty-five (25) and twenty-six (26) west; thence southerly along the unsurveyed range line between ranges twenty-five (25) and twenty-six (26) west to the ninth (9th) standard parallel north; thence easterly along said parallel to the northeast corner of township thirty-six (36) north, range twenty-six (26) west; thence southerly along the range line between ranges twenty-five (25) and twenty-six (26) west to the southwest corner of township thirty-three (33) north, range twenty-five (25) west, the place of beginning.

Excepting from the force and effect of this proclamation all lands which may have been prior to the date hereof embraced in any legal entry or covered by any lawful filing duly of record in the proper United States land office, or upon which any valid settlement has been made pursuant to law and the statutory period within which to make entry or filing of record has not expired, and all mining claims duly located and held according to the laws of the United States and rules and regulations not in conflict therewith.

Provided, That this exception shall not continue to apply to any particular tract of land unless the entryman, settler, or claimant continues to comply with the law under which the entry, filing, settlement, or location was made.

Warning is hereby expressly given to all persons not to enter or make settlement upon the tract of land reserved by this proclamation.

The rights and privileges reserved to the Indians of the Blackfeet Indian Reservation by Article I of the agreement set forth in and accepted, ratified, and confirmed by the act of Congress approved June 10, 1896, hereinbefore referred to, respecting that portion of their reservation relinquished to the United States by said Article I shall be in no way infringed or modified by reason of the fact that a part of the area so relinquished is embraced within the limits of the boundaries herein described and set apart as a forest reservation, nor shall the right of occupation, location, and purchase of said relinquished lands under the provisions of the mineral-land laws accorded by said act of Congress be abridged.

In witness whereof I have hereunto set my hand and caused the seal of the United States to be affixed.

[SEAL.] Done at the city of Washington, this 22d day of February, A. D. 1897, and of the Independence of the United States the one hundred and twenty-first.

GROVER CLEVELAND.

By the President:

RICHARD OLNEY, *Secretary of State.*

By the President of the United States of America.

A PROCLAMATION.

Whereas public interests require that the Senate should be convened at 12 o'clock on the 4th day of March next to receive such communications as may be made by the Executive:

Now, therefore, I, Grover Cleveland, President of the United States of America, do hereby proclaim and declare that an extraordinary occasion requires the Senate of the United States to convene at the Capitol, in the city of Washington, on the 4th day of March next, at 12 o'clock noon, of which all persons who shall at that time be entitled to act as members of that body are hereby required to take notice.

Given under my hand and the seal of the United States, at Washington, [SEAL.] the 24th day of February, A. D. 1897, and of the Independence of the United States the one hundred and twenty-first.

GROVER CLEVELAND.

By the President:

RICHARD OLNEY,
Secretary of State.

EXECUTIVE ORDERS.

AMENDMENT OF CIVIL-SERVICE RULES.

EXECUTIVE MANSION, *December 23, 1896.*

Amend clause 2 (*b*) of Rule III by adding at the end thereof the following:

And all officers and employees in the penitentiary service who are by law subject to classification.

Approved:

GROVER CLEVELAND.

AMENDMENT OF CIVIL-SERVICE RULES.

EXECUTIVE MANSION, *January 2, 1897.*

Amend Rule VIII by striking out section 12 and substituting therefor the following:

Whenever there are no names of eligibles upon a register for any grade in which a vacancy exists, and the public interest requires that it must be filled before eligibles can be provided by the Commission, such vacancy may, subject to the approval of the Commission, be filled by appointment without examination and certification for such part of three months as will enable the Commission to provide eligibles. Such temporary appointment shall expire by limitation as soon as an eligible shall be provided, and no person shall serve longer than three months in any one year under such temporary appointment or appointments unless by special authority of the Commission previously obtained. Said year limitation shall commence from the date of such first appointment: *Provided*, That whenever an emergency shall arise requiring that a vacancy shall be filled before a certification can be issued and an appointment made thereto in the manner provided in these rules, such vacancy may be filled without regard to the provisions of these rules for such part of thirty days as may be required for the issuance of a certificate and the execution of the necessary details of an appointment thereto in accordance with said provisions. Such appointment shall in no case continue longer than thirty days.

Approved:

GROVER CLEVELAND.

AMENDMENT OF CIVIL-SERVICE RULES.

EXECUTIVE MANSION, *January 2, 1897.*

Amend Rule V, section 4, prescribing age limitations for the classified service, by striking out the table after the tenth line and substituting therefor the following:

	Minimum.	Maximum.
Departmental service:		
Page, messenger boy, apprentice, or student............	14	20
Printer's assistant and messenger......................	18	No limit.
Positions in the railway mail service....................	18	35
Internes and hospital stewards in the marine-hospital service and acting second assistant **engineer** in the revenue-cutter service................................	21	30
Cadet in the revenue-cutter service and aid in the Coast and Geodetic Survey....................................	18	25
Surfmen in the life-saving service.......	18	45
Superintendent, physician, supervisor, day-school inspector, and disciplinarian in the Indian service; inspector and assistant inspector of hulls, an inspector and an assistant inspector of boilers, in the steamboat-inspection service...........	25	55
All other positions	20	No limit.
(The age limitation shall not apply in the case of the wife of the superintendent of an Indian school who applies for examination for the position of teacher or matron.)		
Custom-house service:		
All positions	20	No limit.
Post-office service:		
Letter carrier	21	40
All other positions....................................	18	No limit.
Government printing service:		
All positions (male)...................................	21	No limit.
All positions (female).................................	18	No limit.
Internal-revenue service:		
All positions...	21	No limit.

Approved:

GROVER CLEVELAND.

CIVIL SERVICE.—CLASSIFICATION OF THE OFFICE OF THE PRESIDENT.

EXECUTIVE OFFICE,
Washington, D. C., January 12, 1897.

In accordance with the third clause of section 6 of the act entitled "An act to regulate and improve the civil service of the United States," approved January 16, 1883—

It is ordered, That the officers and employees in or under this office included within the provisions of the civil-service law and rules be, and they are hereby, arranged in the following classes:

Class A.—All persons receiving an annual salary of less than $720, or a compensation at the rate of less than $720 per annum.

Class B.—All persons receiving an annual salary of $720 or more, or a compensation at the rate of $720 or more, but less than $840 per annum.

Class C.—All persons receiving an annual salary of $840 or more, or a compensation at the rate of $840 or more, but less than $900 per annum.

Class D.—All persons receiving an annual salary of $900 or more, or a compensation at the rate of $900 or more, but less than $1,000 per annum.

Class E.—All persons receiving an annual salary of $1,000 or more, or a compensation at the rate of $1,000 or more, but less than $1,200 per annum.

Class 1.—All persons receiving an annual salary of $1,200 or more, or a compensation at the rate of $1,200 or more, but less than $1,400 per annum.

Class 2.—All persons receiving an annual salary of $1,400 or more, or a compensation at the rate of $1,400 or more, but less than $1,600 per annum.

Class 3.—All persons receiving an annual salary of $1,600 or more, or a compensation at the rate of $1,600 or more, but less than $1,800 per annum.

Class 4.—All persons receiving an annual salary of $1,800 or more, or a compensation at the rate of $1,800 or more, but less than $2,000 per annum.

Class 5.—All persons receiving an annual salary of $2,000 or more, or a compensation at the rate of $2,000 or more, but less than $2,500 per annum.

Class 6.—All persons receiving an annual salary of $2,500 or more, or a compensation at the rate of $2,500 or more per annum.

It is provided, That this classification shall not include persons appointed to an office by and with the advice and consent of the Senate nor persons employed as mere laborers or workmen; but all positions whose occupants are designated as laborers or workmen, and who were prior to May 6, 1896, and are now regularly assigned to work of the same grade as that performed by classified employees, shall be included within this classification. Hereafter no person who is appointed as a laborer or workman, without examination under the civil-service rules, shall be assigned to work of the same grade as that performed by classified employees.

It is also ordered, That no person shall be admitted into any place not excepted from examination by the civil-service rules in any of the classes above designated until he shall have passed an appropriate examination prepared by the United States Civil Service Commission and his eligibility has been certified to this office by said Commission.

By direction of the President:

HENRY T. THURBER, *Private Secretary.*

EXECUTIVE MANSION,
Washington, January 12, 1897.

Hon. JUDSON HARMON,
  Attorney-General of the United States.

DEAR SIR: The bill which has been for some time pending before the Congress providing for the adjustment and extension of the indebtedness of the Pacific railroads to the Government of the United States has been defeated in the House of Representatives.

In the case of the Union Pacific Railroad and the Kansas Pacific Railroad, a default in the payment of their indebtedness having occurred and suits having been commenced for the foreclosure of the lien upon said roads which is paramount to the lien and security of the United States, you are hereby directed, pursuant to the provisions of an act of Congress passed March 3, 1887, after taking such precautions and perfecting such arrangements as are possible to assure as far as practicable the payment of their indebtedness to the Government as a result of the suits now pending or others to be instituted, to take such proceedings in the courts as shall be needful to protect and defend the rights and interests of the United States in respect of such indebtedness, and to take steps to foreclose the mortgages or liens of the United States upon the property of these railroad companies.

In the case of the other aided Pacific railroads, as to which no foreclosure suits are pending, a different situation is presented, which requires further consideration before deciding the course to be taken by the Government.

Yours, truly,   GROVER CLEVELAND.

AMENDMENT OF CIVIL-SERVICE RULES.

Rule VI of the civil-service rules is hereby amended by adding to the exceptions from examination in the departmental service a new clause, to read as follows:

(*d*) Assistant Secretary Smithsonian Institution, in charge of United States National Museum.

Approved, January 27, 1897.   GROVER CLEVELAND.

William McKinley

March 4, 1897, to September 14 1901

Messages, Proclamations, Executive Orders, and Last Public Utterance to the People at Buffalo

SEE VOLUME XI.

Volume eleven is not only an index to the other volumes, not only a key that unlocks the treasures of the entire publication, but it is in itself an alphabetically arranged brief history or story of the great controlling events constituting the History of the United States.

Under its proper alphabetical classification the story is told of every great subject referred to by any of the Presidents in their official Messages, and at the end of each story the official utterances of the Presidents themselves are cited upon the subject, so that you may readily turn to the page in the body of the work itself for this original information.

Next to the possession of knowledge is the ability to turn at will to where knowledge is to be found.

HOME AT CANTON, OHIO, OF

WILLIAM McKINLEY

With official portrait engraved from copy of original in steel

William McKinley

WILLIAM McKINLEY, the twenty-fifth President of the United States, was born in Niles, Trumbull County, Ohio, January 29, 1843. His ancestors on the paternal side, who were Scotch-Irish, came from Scotland and located in Pennsylvania. His great-grandfather, David McKinley, after serving in the Revolution, resided in Pennsylvania until 1814, when he went to Ohio, where he died in 1840, at the age of 85. The grandmother of the President, Mary Rose, came from a Puritan family that fled from England to Holland and emigrated to Pennsylvania with William Penn. The father of the President, William McKinley, sr., was born in Pine Township, Mercer County, Pa., in 1807, and married Nancy Campbell Allison, of Columbiana County, Ohio, in 1829. Both the grandfather and father of the President were iron manufacturers. His father was a devout Methodist, a stanch Whig and Republican, and an ardent advocate of a protective tariff. He died during his son's first term as governor of Ohio, in November, 1892, at the age of 85. The mother of the President passed away at Canton, Ohio, in December, 1897, at the advanced age of 89. William McKinley was educated in the public schools of Niles, Union Seminary, at Poland, Ohio, and Allegheny College, at Meadville, Pa. Before attaining his majority taught in the public schools. At the age of 16 became a member of the Methodist Episcopal Church. At the beginning of hostilities in the War between the States Mr. McKinley, who was a clerk in the Poland post-office, volunteered his services, and on June 11, 1861, was enlisted as a private in the Twenty-third Ohio Volunteer Infantry. Participated in all the early engagements in West Virginia, and in the winter's camp at Fayetteville received his first promotion, commissary-sergeant, on April 15, 1862. In recognition of his services at Antietam, Sergeant McKinley was made second lieutenant, his commission dating from September 24, 1862, and on February 7, 1863, while at Camp Piatt, he was again promoted, receiving the rank of first lieutenant. In the retreat near Lynchburg, Va., his regiment marched 180 miles, fighting nearly all the time, with scarcely any rest or food. Lieutenant McKinley conducted himself with gallantry, and at Winchester won additional honors. The Thirteenth West Virginia Regiment failed to retire when the rest of Hayes's brigade fell back, and, being in great danger of capture, the young lieutenant was directed to go and bring it away, which he did in safety, after riding through a heavy fire.   On July 25, 1864, at the age of 21, McKinley was promoted to the rank of captain.   The brigade continued its fighting up and down the Shenandoah Valley.   At Berryville, Va., September 3, 1864, Captain McKinley's horse was shot from under him.   Served successively on the staffs of Generals R. B. Hayes, George Crook, and Winfield S. Hancock, and on March 14, 1865, was brevetted major of United States Volunteers by President Lincoln for gallantry in the battles of Opequan, Cedar Creek, and Fishers Hill. Was detailed as acting assistant adjutant-general of the First Division, First Army Corps, on the staff of General Samuel S. Carroll.   At the close of the war was urged to remain in the Army, but, deferring to the judgment of his father, was mustered out of the service July 26, 1865, and returned to Poland.   At once began the study of law under Glidden & Wilson, of Youngstown, Ohio, and later attended the law school in Albany, N. Y.   Was admitted to the bar in March, 1867, at Warren, Ohio, and the same year removed to Canton, Ohio, which has since been his home.   In 1867 his first political speeches were made in favor of negro suffrage.   In 1869 was elected prosecuting attorney of Stark County, and served one term, being defeated two years later for the same office.   Mr. McKinley took an active interest in State politics, and made speeches in many of the campaigns.   On January 25, 1871, married Miss Ida Saxton.   Two daughters were born to them, both of whom died in early childhood.   In 1876 was elected a member of the National House of Representatives, and for fourteen years represented the Congressional district of which his county was a part, except for a portion of his fourth term, when he was unseated late in the first session.   While in Congress served on the Committees on the Judiciary, Revision of the Laws, Expenditures in the Post-Office Department, Rules, and Ways and Means.   As chairman of the last-named committee in the Fifty-first Congress, reported the tariff law of 1890.   At the beginning of this Congress was defeated in the caucus of his party for the Speakership of the House.   In the meantime, his district having been materially changed, he was defeated for reelection to Congress in November, 1890, though he largely reduced the usual majority against his party in the counties of which the new district was constituted.   In 1891 was elected governor of Ohio by a plurality of 21,500, and in 1893 was reelected by a plurality of 80,995.   In 1884 was a delegate at large to the Republican national convention, and supported James G. Blaine for President; was a member of the committee on resolutions, and presented the platform to the convention.   Also attended the convention of his party in 1888 as a delegate at large from Ohio, supporting John Sherman for President, and as chairman of the committee on resolutions again reported the platform.   In 1892 was again a delegate at large from Ohio, and supported the renomination of Benjamin Harrison, and served as chairman of the convention. At that convention 182 votes were cast for him for President, although he had persistently refused to have his name considered. On June 18, 1896, was nominated for President by the national convention of his party at St. Louis, receiving on the first ballot 661½ out of a total of 922 votes. Was chosen President at the ensuing November election by a plurality in the popular vote of over 600,000, and received 271 electoral votes, against 176 for William J. Bryan of Nebraska. Was again nominated for the Presidency at the National Republican Convention which met at Philadelphia in June, 1900. At the November election he was re-elected, receiving 292 electoral votes, against 155 votes for William J. Bryan.

In September, 1901, he accepted an invitation to attend the Pan-American Exposition at Buffalo. Was shot Sept. 6, 1901, by an assassin in the Music Hall at Buffalo, and died from the effects of the wound, Sept. 14. He was buried at Canton, Ohio.

INAUGURAL ADDRESS.

Fellow-Citizens:

In obedience to the will of the people, and in their presence, by the authority vested in me by this oath, I assume the arduous and responsible duties of President of the United States, relying upon the support of my countrymen and invoking the guidance of Almighty God. Our faith teaches that there is no safer reliance than upon the God of our fathers, who has so singularly favored the American people in every national trial, and who will not forsake us so long as we obey His commandments and walk humbly in His footsteps.

The responsibilities of the high trust to which I have been called—always of grave importance—are augmented by the prevailing business conditions, entailing idleness upon willing labor and loss to useful enterprises. The country is suffering from industrial disturbances from which speedy relief must be had. Our financial system needs some revision; our money is all good now, but its value must not further be threatened. It should all be put upon an enduring basis, not subject to easy attack, nor its stability to doubt or dispute. Our currency should continue under the supervision of the Government. The several forms of our paper money offer, in my judgment, a constant embarrassment to the Government and a safe balance in the Treasury. Therefore I believe it necessary to devise a system which, without diminishing the circulating medium or offering a premium for its contraction, will present a remedy for those arrangements which, temporary in their nature, might well in the years of our prosperity have been displaced by wiser provisions. With adequate revenue secured, but not until then, we can enter upon such changes in our fiscal laws as will, while insuring safety and volume to our money, no longer impose upon the Government the necessity of maintaining so large a gold reserve, with its attendant and inevitable temptations to speculation. Most of our financial laws are the outgrowth of experience and trial, and should not be amended without investigation and demonstration of the wisdom of the proposed changes. We must be both " sure we are right " and " make haste slowly." If, therefore, Congress, in its wisdom, shall deem it expedient to create a commission to take under early consideration the revision of our coinage, banking and currency laws, and give them that exhaustive, careful and dispassionate examination that their importance demands, I shall cordially concur in such action. If such power is vested in the President, it is my purpose to appoint a commission of prominent, well-informed citizens of different parties, who will command public confidence, both on account of their ability and special fitness for the work. Business experience and public training may thus be combined, and the patriotic zeal of the friends of the country be so directed that such a report will be made as to receive the support of all parties, and our finances cease to be the subject of mere partisan contention. The experiment is, at all events, worth a trial, and, in my opinion, it can but prove beneficial to the entire country.

The question of international bimetallism will have early and earnest attention. It will be my constant endeavor to secure it by co-operation with the other great commercial powers of the world. Until that condition is realized when the parity between our gold and silver money springs from and is supported by the relative value of the two metals, the value of the silver already coined and of that which may hereafter be coined, must be kept constantly at par with gold by every resource at our command. The credit of the Government, the integrity of its currency, and the inviolability of its obligations must be preserved. This was the commanding verdict of the people, and it will not be unheeded.

Economy is demanded in every branch of the Government at all times, but especially in periods, like the present, of depression in business and distress among the people. The severest economy must be observed in all public expenditures, and extravagance stopped wherever it is found, and prevented wherever in the future it may be developed. If the revenues are to remain as now, the only relief that can come must be from decreased expenditures. But the present must not become the permanent condition of the Government. It has been our uniform practice to retire, not increase our outstanding obligations, and this policy must again be resumed and vigorously enforced. Our revenues should always be large enough to meet with ease and promptness not only our current needs and the principal and interest of the public debt, but to make proper and liberal provision for that most deserving body of public creditors, the soldiers and sailors and the widows and orphans who are the pensioners of the United States.

The Government should not be permitted to run behind or increase its debt in times like the present. Suitably to provide against this is the mandate of duty — the certain and easy remedy for most of our financial difficulties. A deficiency is inevitable so long as the expenditures of the Government exceed its receipts. It can only be met by loans or an increased revenue. While a large annual surplus of revenue may invite waste and extravagance, inadequate revenue creates distrust and undermines public and private credit. Neither should be encouraged. Between more loans and more revenue there ought to be but one opinion. We should have more revenue, and that without delay, hindrance, or postponement. A surplus in the Treasury created by loans is not a permanent or safe reliance. It will suffice while it lasts, but it can not last long while the outlays of the Government are greater than its receipts, as has been the case during the past two years. Nor must it be forgotten that however much such loans may temporarily relieve the situation, the Government is still indebted for the amount of the surplus thus accrued, which it must ultimately pay, while its ability to pay is not strengthened, but weakened by a continued deficit. Loans are imperative in great emergencies to preserve the Government or its credit, but a failure to supply needed revenue in time of peace for the maintenance of either has no justification.

The best way for the Government to maintain its credit is to pay as it goes — not by resorting to loans, but by keeping out of debt — through an adequate income secured by a system of taxation, external or internal, or both. It is the settled policy of the Government, pursued from the beginning and practised by all parties and Administrations, to raise the bulk of our revenue from taxes upon foreign productions entering the United States for sale and consumption, and avoiding, for the most part, every form of direct taxation, except in time of war. The country is clearly opposed to any needless additions to the subject of internal taxation, and is committed by its latest popular utterance to the system of tariff taxation. There can be no misunderstanding, either, about the principle upon which this tariff taxation shall be levied. Nothing has ever been made plainer at a general election than that the controlling principle in the raising of revenue from duties on imports is zealous care for American interests and American labor. The people have declared that such legislation should be had as will give ample protection and encouragement to the industries and the development of our country. It is, therefore, earnestly hoped and expected that Congress will, at the earliest practicable moment, enact revenue legislation that shall be fair, reasonable, conservative, and just, and which, while supplying sufficient revenue for public purposes, will still be signally beneficial and helpful to every section and every enterprise of the people. To this policy we are all, of whatever party, firmly bound by the voice of the people — a power vastly more potential than the expression of any political platform. The paramount duty of Congress is to stop deficiencies by the restoration of that protective legislation which has always been the firmest prop of the Treasury. The passage of such a law or laws would strengthen the credit of the Government both at home and abroad, and go far toward stopping the drain upon the gold reserve held for the redemption of our currency, which has been heavy and well-nigh constant for several years.

In the revision of the tariff especial attention should be given to the re-enactment and extension of the reciprocity principle of the law of 1890, under which so great a stimulus was given to our foreign trade in new and advantageous markets for our surplus agricultural and manufactured products. The brief trial given this legislation amply justifies a further experiment and additional discretionary power in the making of commercial treaties, the end in view always to be the opening up of new markets for the products of our country, by granting concessions to the products of other lands that we need and cannot produce ourselves, and which do not involve any loss of labor to our own people, but tend to increase their employment.

The depression of the past four years has fallen with especial severity upon the great body of toilers of the country, and upon none more than the holders of small farms. Agriculture has languished and labor suffered. The revival of manufacturing will be a relief to both. No portion of our population is more devoted to the institution of free government nor more loyal in their support, while none bears more cheerfully or fully its proper share in the maintenance of the Government or is better entitled to its wise and liberal care and protection. Legislation helpful to producers is beneficial to all. The depressed condition of industry on the farm and in the mine and factory has lessened the ability of the people to meet the demands upon them, and they rightfully expect that not only a system of revenue shall be established that will secure the largest income with the least burden, but that every means will be taken to decrease, rather than increase, our public expenditures. Business conditions are not the most promising. It will take time to restore the prosperity of former years. If we cannot promptly attain it, we can resolutely turn our faces in that direction and aid its return by friendly legislation. However troublesome the situation may appear, Congress will not, I am sure, be found lacking in disposition or ability to relieve it as far as legislation can do so. The restoration of confidence and the revival of business, which men of all parties so much desire, depend more largely upon the prompt, energetic, and intelligent action of Congress than upon any other single agency affecting the situation.

It is inspiring, too, to remember that no great emergency in the one hundred and eight years of our eventful national life has ever arisen that has not been met with wisdom and courage by the American people, with fidelity to their best interests and highest destiny, and to the honor of the American name. These years of glorious history have exalted mankind and advanced the cause of freedom throughout the world, and immeasurably strengthened the precious free institutions which we enjoy. The people love and will sustain these institutions. The great essential to our happiness and prosperity is that we adhere to the principles upon which the Government was established and insist upon their faithful observance. Equality of rights must prevail, and our laws be always and everywhere respected and obeyed. We may have failed in the discharge of our full duty as citizens of the great Republic, but it is consoling and encouraging to realize that free speech, a free press, free thought, free schools, the free and unmolested right of religious liberty and worship, and free and fair elections are dearer and more universally enjoyed to-day than ever before. These guaranties must be sacredly preserved and wisely strengthened. The constituted authorities must be cheerfully and vigorously upheld. Lynchings must not be tolerated in a great and civilized country like the United States; courts, not mobs, must execute the penalties of the law. The preservation of public order, the right of discussion, the integrity of courts, and the orderly administration of justice must continue forever the rock of safety upon which our Government securely rests.

One of the lessons taught by the late election, which all can rejoice in, is that the citizens of the United States are both law-respecting and law-abiding people, not easily swerved from the path of patriotism and honor. This is in entire accord with the genius of our institutions, and but emphasizes the advantages of inculcating even a greater love for law and order in the future. Immunity should be granted to none who violate the laws, whether individuals, corporations, or communities; and as the Constitution imposes upon the President the duty of both its own execution, and of the statutes enacted in pursuance of its provisions, I shall endeavor carefully to carry them into effect. The declaration of the party now restored to power has been in the past that of "opposition to all combinations of capital organized in trusts, or otherwise, to control arbitrarily the condition of trade among our citizens," and it has supported "such legislation as will prevent the execution of all schemes to oppress the people by undue charges on their supplies, or by unjust rates for the transportation of their products to the market." This purpose will be steadily pursued, both by the enforcement of the laws now in existence and the recommendation and support of such new statutes as may be necessary to carry it into effect.

Our naturalization and immigration laws should be further improved to the constant promotion of a safer, a better, and a higher citizenship. A grave peril to the Republic would be a citizenship too ignorant to understand or too vicious to appreciate the great value and beneficence of our institutions and laws, and against all who come here to make war upon them our gates must be promptly and tightly closed. Nor must we be unmindful of the need of improvement among our own citizens, but with the zeal of our forefathers encourage the spread of knowledge and free education. Illiteracy must be banished from the land if we shall attain that high destiny as the foremost of the enlightened nations of the world which, under Providence, we ought to achieve.

Reforms in the civil service must go on; but the changes should be real and genuine, not perfunctory, or prompted by a zeal in behalf of any party simply because it happens to be in power. As a member of Congress I voted and spoke in favor of the present law, and I shall attempt its enforcement in the spirit in which it was enacted. The purpose in view was to secure the most efficient service of the best men who would accept appointment under the Government, retaining faithful and devoted public servants in office, but shielding none, under the authority of any rule or custom, who are inefficient, incompetent, or unworthy. The best interests of the country demand this, and the people heartily approve the law wherever and whenever it has been thus administrated.

Congress should give prompt attention to the restoration of our American merchant marine, once the pride of the seas in all the great ocean highways of commerce. To my mind, few more important subjects so imperatively demand its intelligent consideration. The United States has progressed with marvelous rapidity in every field of enterprise and endeavor until we have become foremost in nearly all the great lines of inland trade, commerce, and industry. Yet, while this is true, our American merchant marine has been steadily declining until it is now lower, both in the percentage of tonnage and the number of vessels employed, than it was prior to the Civil War. Commendable progress has been made of late years in the upbuilding of the American Navy, but we must supplement these efforts by providing as a proper consort for it a merchant marine amply sufficient for our own carrying trade to foreign countries. The question is one that appeals both to our business necessities and the patriotic aspirations of a great people.

It has been the policy of the United States since the foundation of the Government to cultivate relations of peace and amity with all the nations of the world, and this accords with my conception of our duty now. We have cherished the policy of non-interference with the affairs of foreign governments wisely inaugurated by Washington, keeping ourselves free from entanglement, either as allies or foes, content to leave undisturbed with them the settlement of their own domestic concerns. It will be our aim to pursue a firm and dignified foreign policy, which shall be just, impartial, ever watchful of our national honor, and always insisting upon the enforcement of the lawful rights of American citizens everywhere. Our diplomacy should seek nothing more and accept nothing less than is due us. We want no wars of conquest; we must avoid the temptation of territorial aggression. War should never be entered upon until every agency of peace has failed; peace is preferable to war in almost every contingency. Arbitration is the true method of settlement of international as well as local or individual differences. It was recognized as the best means of adjustment of differences between employers and employees by the Forty-ninth Congress, in 1886, and its application was extended to our diplomatic relations by the unanimous concurrence of the Senate and House of the Fifty-first Congress in 1890. The latter resolution was accepted as the basis of negotiations with us by the British House of Commons in 1893, and upon our invitation a treaty of arbitration between the United States and Great Britain was signed at Washington and transmitted to the Senate for its ratification in January last. Since this treaty is clearly the result of our own initiative; since it has been recognized as the leading feature of our foreign policy throughout our entire national history — the adjustment of difficulties by judicial methods rather than force of arms — and since it presents to the world the glorious example of reason and peace, not passion and war, controlling the relations between two of the greatest nations in the world, an example certain to be followed by others, I respectfully urge the early action of the Senate thereon, not merely as a matter of policy, but as a duty to mankind. The importance and moral influence of the ratification of such a treaty can hardly be overestimated in the cause of advancing civilization. It may well engage the best thought of the statesmen and people of every country, and I cannot but consider it fortunate that it was reserved to the United States to have the leadership in so grand a work.

It has been the uniform practice of each President to avoid, as far as possible, the convening of Congress in extraordinary session. It is an example which, under ordinary circumstances and in the absence of a public necessity, is to be commended. But a failure to convene the representatives of the people in Congress in extra session when it involves neglect of a public duty places the responsibility of such neglect upon the Executive himself. The condition of the public Treasury, as has been indicated, demands the immediate consideration of Congress. It alone has the power to provide revenues for the Government. Not to convene it under such circumstances I can view in no other sense than the neglect of a plain duty. I do not sympathize with the sentiment that Congress in session is dangerous to our general business interests. Its members are the agents of the people, and their presence at the seat of Government in the execution of the sovereign will should not operate as an injury, but a benefit. There could be no better time to put the Government upon a sound financial and economic basis than now. The people have only recently voted that this should be done, and nothing is more binding upon the agents of their will than the obligation of immediate action. It has always seemed to me that the postponement of the meeting of Congress until more than a year after it has been chosen deprived Congress too often of the inspiration of the popular will and the country of the corresponding benefits. It is evident, therefore, that to postpone action in the presence of so great a necessity would be unwise on the part of the Executive because unjust to the interests of the people. Our action now will be freer from mere partisan consideration than if the question of tariff revision was postponed until the regular session of Congress. We are nearly two years from a Congressional election, and politics cannot so greatly distract us as if such contest was immediately pending. We can approach the problem calmly and patriotically, without fearing its effect upon an early election.

Our fellow-citizens who may disagree with us upon the character of this legislation prefer to have the question settled now, even against their preconceived views, and perhaps settled so reasonably, as I trust and believe it will be, as to insure great permanence, than to have further uncertainty menacing the vast and varied business interests of the United States. Again, whatever action Congress may take will be given a fair opportunity for trial before the people are called to pass judgment upon it, and this I consider a great essential to the rightful and lasting settlement of the question. In view of these considerations, I shall deem it my duty as President to convene Congress in extraordinary session on Monday, the 15th day of March, 1897.

In conclusion, I congratulate the country upon the fraternal spirit of the people and the manifestations of good will everywhere so apparent. The recent election not only most fortunately demonstrated the obliteration of sectional or geographical lines, but to some extent also the prejudices which for years have distracted our councils and marred our true greatness as a nation. The triumph of the people, whose verdict is carried into effect to-day, is not the triumph of one section, nor wholly of one party, but of all sections and all the people. The North and the South no longer divide on the old lines, but upon principles and policies; and in this fact surely every lover of the country can find cause for true felicitation. Let us rejoice in and cultivate this spirit; it is ennobling and will be both a gain and a blessing to our beloved country. It will be my constant aim to do nothing, and permit nothing to be done, that will arrest or disturb this growing sentiment of unity and co-operation, this revival of esteem and affiliation which now animates so many thousands in both the old antagonistic sections, but I shall cheerfully do everything possible to promote and increase it.

Let me again repeat the words of the oath administered by the Chief Justice which, in their respective spheres, so far as applicable, I would have all my countrymen observe: "I will faithfully execute the office of President of the United States, and will, to the best of my ability, preserve, protect, and defend the Constitution of the United States."

This is the obligation I have reverently taken before the Lord Most High. To keep it will be my single purpose, my constant prayer; and I shall confidently rely upon the forbearance and assistance of all the people in the discharge of my solemn responsibilities.

MESSAGES.

EXECUTIVE MANSION, *March 15, 1897.*

To the Congress of the United States:

Regretting the necessity which has required me to call you together, I feel that your assembling in extraordinary session is indispensable because of the condition in which we find the revenues of the Government. It is conceded that its current expenditures are greater than its receipts, and that such a condition has existed for now more than three years. With unlimited means at our command, we are presenting the remarkable spectacle of increasing our public debt by borrowing money to meet the ordinary outlays incident upon even an economical and prudent administration of the Government. An examination of the subject discloses this fact in every detail and leads inevitably to the conclusion that the condition of the revenue which allows it is unjustifiable and should be corrected.

We find by the reports of the Secretary of the Treasury that the revenues for the fiscal year ending June 30, 1892, from all sources were $425,868,260.22, and the expenditures for all purposes were $415,953,-806.56, leaving an excess of receipts over expenditures of $9,914,453.66. During that fiscal year $40,570,467.98 were paid upon the public debt, which had been reduced since March 1, 1889, $259,076,890, and the annual interest charge decreased $11,684,576.60. The receipts of the Government from all sources during the fiscal year ending June 30, 1893, amounted to $461,716,561.94, and its expenditures to $459,374,-887.65, showing an excess of receipts over expenditures of $2,341,674.29.

Since that time the receipts of no fiscal year, and with but few exceptions of no month of any fiscal year, have exceeded the expenditures. The receipts of the Government, from all sources, during the fiscal year ending June 30, 1894, were $372,802,498.29, and its expenditures $442,605,758.87, leaving a deficit, the first since the resumption of specie payments, of $69,803,260.58. Notwithstanding there was a decrease of $16,769,128.78 in the ordinary expenses of the Government, as compared with the previous fiscal year, its income was still not sufficient to provide for its daily necessities, and the gold reserve in the Treasury for the redemption of greenbacks was drawn upon to meet them. But this did not suffice, and the Government then resorted to loans to replenish the reserve.

In February, 1894, $50,000,000 in bonds were issued, and in November following a second issue of $50,000,000 was deemed necessary.

The sum of $117,171,795 was realized by the sale of these bonds, but the reserve was steadily decreased until, on February 8, 1895, a third sale of $62,315,400 in bonds, for $65,116,244, was announced to Congress.

The receipts of the Government for the fiscal year ending June 30, 1895, were $390,373,203.30, and the expenditures $433,178,426.48, showing a deficit of $42,805,223.18. A further loan of $100,000,000 was negotiated by the Government in February, 1896, the sale netting $111,166,246, and swelling the aggregate of bonds issued within three years to $262,315,400. For the fiscal year ending June 30, 1896, the revenues of the Government from all sources amounted to $409,475,-408.78, while its expenditures were $434,678,654.48, or an excess of expenditures over receipts of $25,203,245.70. In other words, the total receipts for the three fiscal years ending June 30, 1896, were insufficient by $137,811,729.46 to meet the total expenditures.

Nor has this condition since improved. For the first half of the present fiscal year, the receipts of the Government, exclusive of postal revenues, were $157,507,603.76, and its expenditures, exclusive of postal service, $195,410,000.22, or an excess of expenditures over receipts of $37,902,396.46. In January of this year, the receipts, exclusive of postal revenues, were $24,316,994.05, and the expenditures, exclusive of postal service, $30,269,389.29, a deficit of $5,952,395.24 for the month. In February of this year, the receipts, exclusive of postal revenues, were $24,400,997.38, and expenditures, exclusive of postal service, $28,796,056.66, a deficit of $4,395,059.28; or a total deficiency of $186,061,580.44 for the three years and eight months ending March 1, 1897. Not only are we without a surplus in the Treasury, but with an increase in the public debt there has been a corresponding increase in the annual interest charge, from $22,893,883.20 in 1892, the lowest of any year since 1862, to $34,387,297.60 in 1896, or an increase of $11,493,414.40.

It may be urged that even if the revenues of the Government had been sufficient to meet all its ordinary expenses during the past three years, the gold reserve would still have been insufficient to meet the demands upon it, and that bonds would necessarily have been issued for its repletion. Be this as it may, it is clearly manifest, without denying or affirming the correctness of such a conclusion, that the debt would have been decreased in at least the amount of the deficiency, and business confidence immeasurably strengthened throughout the country.

Congress should promptly correct the existing condition. Ample revenues must be supplied not only for the ordinary expenses of the Government, but for the prompt payment of liberal pensions and the liquidation of the principal and interest of the public debt. In raising revenue, duties should be so levied upon foreign products as to preserve the home market, so far as possible, to our own producers; to revive and increase manufactures; to relieve and encourage agriculture; to increase our domestic and foreign commerce; to aid and develop mining and building; and to render to labor in every field of useful occupation the liberal wages and adequate rewards to which skill and industry are justly entitled. The necessity of the passage of a tariff law which shall provide ample revenue, need not be further urged. The imperative demand of the hour is the prompt enactment of such a measure, and to this object I earnestly recommend that Congress shall make every endeavor. Before other business is transacted, let us first provide sufficient revenue to faithfully administer the Government without the contracting of further debt, or the continued disturbance of our finances. WILLIAM McKINLEY.

EXECUTIVE MANSION, *April 7, 1897.*

To the Senate and House of Representatives:

Information which has recently come to me from the governors of Arkansas, Mississippi, and Louisiana, and from prominent citizens of these States and Tennessee, warrants the conclusion that widespread distress, involving the destruction of a large amount of property and loss of human life, has resulted from the floods which have submerged that section of the country. These are stated, on reliable authority, to be the most destructive floods that have ever devastated the Mississippi Valley, the water being much higher than the highest stage it has reached before. From Marion, Ark., north of Memphis, to Greenville, Miss., a distance of more than 250 miles by river, it is reported there are now at least fifty towns and villages under water, and a territory extending from 100 miles north of Memphis to 200 miles south, and from 5 to 40 miles wide, is submerged. Hundreds of thousands of acres of cultivated soil, with growing crops, are included in the submerged territory. In this section alone there are from 50,000 to 60,000 people whose property has been destroyed and whose business has been suspended. Growing crops have been ruined, thousands of cattle have been drowned, and the inhabitants of certain areas threatened with starvation. As a great majority of the sufferers are small farmers, they have thus been left entirely destitute, and will be unprepared for work even after the floods have subsided.

The entire Mississippi Valley in Arkansas is flooded and communication with many points cut off. In Mississippi a like condition exists. The levees in Louisiana, with a single exception, have held; but the water is rising and the situation there is reported as being extremely critical.

Under such circumstances the citizens of these States look for the co-operation and support of the National Government in relieving the pressing cases of destitution for food, clothing, and shelter, which are beyond the reach of local efforts. The authorities who have communicated with the Executive recognize that their first and most energetic duty is to provide as far as possible the means of caring for their own citizens; but nearly all of them agree in the opinion that after their resources have been exhausted a sum aggregating at least $150,000 and possibly $200,000 will be required for immediate use.

Precedents are not wanting that in such emergencies as this Congress has taken prompt, generous, and intelligent action, involving the expenditure of cor iderable sums of money, with satisfactory results. In 1874 $590,000 was appropriated, and in 1882 $350,000 was also appropriated for relief in same direction, besides large sums in other years.

The citizens' relief committee of Memphis has taken prompt action, has already cared for from 6,000 to 7,000 refugees from the flooded districts, and they are still arriving in that city in large numbers daily. Supplies and provisions have been sent to the various points in Arkansas and Mississippi by this committee, but the utmost that can be done by these efforts is to partly relieve the most acute cases of suffering. No action has yet been taken for the great majority of the inhabitants living in the interior, whose condition has already been described.

Under these conditions and having exerted themselves to the fullest extent, the local authorities have reluctantly confessed their inability to further cope with this distressing situation unaided by relief from the Government. It has therefore seemed to me that the representatives of the people should be promptly informed of the nature and extent of the suffering and needs of these stricken people, and I have communicated these facts in the hope and belief that the legislative branch of the Government will promptly re-enforce the work of the local authorities in the States named.   WILLIAM McKINLEY.

EXECUTIVE MANSION,
Washington, April 14, 1897.
To the Senate and House of Representatives:

I transmit herewith for the consideration of the respective Houses of the Congress, a report of the Secretary of State representing the appropriateness of early action in order that the Government of the United States may be enabled to accept the invitation of that of the French Republic to participate in the Universal Exposition to be held at Paris in 1900.

The recommendations of this report have my most cordial approval, and I urge upon the Congress such timely provision for this great international enterprise as will fittingly respond to the widely testified wish and expectation of our inventors and producers that they may have adequate opportunity again, as in the past, to fortify the important positions that have won in the world's competitive fields of discovery and industry. Nor are the traditional friendships of the United States and France and the mutual advantages to accrue from their enlarged commercial intercourse less important factors than the individual interests to be fostered by renewed participation in a great French exposition, especially when it is remembered that the present display is projected with a degree of completeness and on a scale of magnificence beyond any of the European exhibitions that have marked the close of the century.

It is proper that I should emphasize the need of early action, for if the present session pass without suitable provision being made, the postponement of the matter for nearly a year longer could not but operate greatly to the disadvantage of the United States, in view of the elaborate preparations already making by other governments, and of the danger that further delay may result in an inadequate allotment of space to this country as well as an incomplete organization of the American exhibit. WILLIAM McKINLEY.

EXECUTIVE MANSION.
Washington, May 3, 1897.

To the Congress of the United States:

I transmit a report from the Secretary of State reciting the circumstances attending the lynching at Hahnville, La., on the night of August 8, 1896, of three Italian subjects, named Salvatore Arena, Giuseppe Venturelia, and Lorenzo Salardino, and I recommend the appropriation by Congress, without admitting the liability of the Government of the United States in the premises, of the sum of $6,000, to be paid by the Secretary of State to the Government of Italy, and to be distributed by that government in such manner as it may deem proper among the heirs of the three Italian subjects above named.

WILLIAM McKINLEY.

EXECUTIVE MANSION,
Washington, May 13, 1897.

To the Senate of the United States:

I transmit herewith, in response to the Senate resolution of April 22, 1897, addressed to the Secretary of State, a report from that officer relative to diplomatic and consular reports on postal savings banks systems in foreign countries. WILLIAM McKINLEY.

EXECUTIVE MANSION, *May 17, 1897.*
To the Senate and House of Representatives of the United States:

Official information from our consuls in Cuba establishes the fact that a large number of American citizens in the island are in a state of destitution, suffering for want of food and medicines. This applies particularly to the rural districts of the central and eastern parts.

The agricultural classes have been forced from their farms into the nearest towns, where they are without work or money. The local authorities of the several towns, however kindly disposed, are unable to relieve the needs of their own people, and are altogether powerless to help our citizens.

The latest report of Consul-General Lee estimates six to eight hundred Americans are without means of support. I have assured him that provision would be made at once to relieve them. To that end I recommend that Congress make an appropriation of not less than $50,000, to be immediately available for use, under the direction of the Secretary of State.

It is desirable that a part of the sum which may be appropriated by Congress should, in the discretion of the Secretary of State, also be used for the transportation of American citizens who, desiring to return to the United States, are without means to do so.

WILLIAM McKINLEY.

EXECUTIVE MANSION, *July 1, 1897.*
To the Congress of the United States:

On the 15th ultimo all the buildings of the immigration station at Ellis Island, New York, excepting the heating plant and lighting apparatus, were destroyed by fire.

I transmit herewith a letter from the Secretary of the Treasury, which states the fact and explains the need of rebuilding.

In order that there may be no delay in this important work, I recommend that an appropriation be made at once of $600,000, the sum estimated by the Secretary of the Treasury as required for this purpose.

WILLIAM McKINLEY.

EXECUTIVE MANSION,
Washington, July 23, 1897.
To the Senate of the United States:

I transmit herewith a report from the Acting Secretary of State, with an accompanying paper, in response to the resolution of the Senate of July 12, 1897, requesting the Secretary of State to send to the diplomatic representatives of the United States abroad a circular letter, similar to the one sent by Secretary Blaine on May 20, 1881, instructing them to obtain from the several foreign governments to which they are accredited as full information as possible (including copy of laws relating thereto) as to the nature and practical workings (including expenses, receipts, and rates) of the postal telegraphs, telephones, and postal savings banks of such countries as have adopted the same.

WILLIAM McKINLEY.

EXECUTIVE MANSION, *July 24, 1897.*

To the Congress of the United States:

In my message convening the Congress in extraordinary session I called attention to a single subject — that of providing revenue adequate to meet the reasonable and proper expenses of the Government. I believed that to be the most pressing subject for settlement then. A bill to provide the necessary revenues for the Government has already passed the House of Representatives and the Senate and awaits executive action.

Another question of very great importance is that of the establishment of our currency and banking system on a better basis, which I commented upon in my inaugural address in the following words:

Our financial system needs some revision ; our money is all good now, but its value must not further be threatened. It should all be put upon an enduring basis, not subject to easy attack, nor its stability to doubt or dispute. The several forms of our paper money offer, in my judgment, a constant embarrassment to the Government and imperil a safe balance in the Treasury.

Nothing was settled more clearly at the late national election than the determination upon the part of the people to keep their currency stable in value and equal to that of the most advanced nations of the world.

The soundness of our currency is nowhere questioned. No loss can occur to its holders. It is the system which should be simplified and strengthened, keeping our money just as good as it is now with less expense to the Government and the people.

The sentiment of the country is strongly in favor of early action by Congress in this direction, to revise our currency laws and remove them from partisan contention. A notable assembly of business men with delegates from twenty-nine States and Territories was held at Indianapolis in January of this year. The financial situation commanded their earnest attention, and after a two days' session the convention recommended to Congress the appointment of a monetary commission.

I recommend this report to the consideration of Congress. The authors of the report recommend a commission "to make a thorough investigation of the monetary affairs and needs of this country in all relations and aspects, and to make proper suggestions as to any evils found to exist and the remedies therefor."

This subject should receive the attention of Congress at its special session. It ought not to be postponed until the regular session.

I therefore urgently recommend that a special commission be created, non-partisan in its character, to be composed of well-informed citizens of different parties who will command the confidence of Congress and the country because of their special fitness for the work, whose duty it shall be to make recommendations of whatever changes in our present banking and currency laws may be found necessary and expedient, and to report their conclusions on or before the 1st day of November next, in order that the same may be transmitted by me to Congress for its consideration at its first regular session.

It is to be hoped that the report thus made will be so comprehensive and sound as to receive the support of all parties and the favorable action of Congress. At all events, such a report cannot fail to be of value to the executive branch of the Government, as well as to those charged with public legislation, and to greatly assist in the establishment of an improved system of finance.

WILLIAM McKINLEY.

FIRST ANNUAL MESSAGE.

EXECUTIVE MANSION, *December 6, 1897.*
To the Senate and House of Representatives:

It gives me pleasure to extend greeting to the Fifty-fifth Congress, assembled in regular session at the seat of Government, with many of whose Senators and Representatives I have been associated in the legislative service. Their meeting occurs under felicitous conditions, justifying sincere congratulation and calling for our grateful acknowledgment to a beneficent Providence which has so signally blessed and prospered us as a nation. Peace and good will with all the nations of the earth continue unbroken.

A matter of genuine satisfaction is the growing feeling of fraternal regard and unification of all sections of our country, the incompleteness of which has too long delayed realization of the highest blessings of the Union. The spirit of patriotism is universal and is ever increasing in fervor. The public questions which now most engross us are lifted far above either partisanship, prejudice, or former sectional differences. They affect every part of our common country alike and permit of no division on ancient lines. Questions of foreign policy, of revenue, the soundness of the currency, the inviolability of national obligations, the improvement of the public service, appeal to the individual conscience of every earnest citizen to whatever party he belongs or in whatever section of the country he may reside.

The extra session of this Congress which closed during July last enacted important legislation, and while its full effect has not yet been realized, what it has already accomplished assures us of its timeliness and wisdom. To test its permanent value further time will be required, and the people, satisfied with its operation and results thus far, are in no mind to withhold from it a fair trial.

Tariff legislation having been settled by the extra session of Congress, the question next pressing for consideration is that of the currency.

The work of putting our finances upon a sound basis, difficult as it may seem, will appear easier when we recall the financial operations of the Government since 1866. On the 30th day of June of that year we had outstanding demand liabilities in the sum of $728,868,447.41. On the 1st of January, 1879, these liabilities had been reduced to $443,889,495.88. Of our interest-bearing obligations, the figures are even more striking. On July 1, 1866, the principal of the interest-bearing debt of the Government was $2,332,331,208. On the 1st day of July, 1893, this sum had been reduced to $585,037,100, or an aggregate reduction of $1,747,294,108. The interest-bearing debt of the United States on the 1st day of December, 1897, was $847,365,620. The Government money now outstanding (December 1) consists of $346,681,016 of United States notes, $107,793,280 of Treasury notes issued by authority of the law of 1890, $384,963,504 of silver certificates, and $61,280,761 of standard silver dollars.

With the great resources of the Government, and with the honorable example of the past before us, we ought not to hesitate to enter upon a currency revision which will make our demand obligations less onerous to the Government and relieve our financial laws from ambiguity and doubt.

The brief review of what was accomplished from the close of the war to 1893, makes unreasonable and groundless any distrust either of our financial ability or soundness; while the situation from 1893 to 1897 must admonish Congress of the immediate necessity of so legislating as to make the return of the conditions then prevailing impossible.

There are many plans proposed as a remedy for the evil. Before we can find the true remedy we must appreciate the real evil. It is not that our currency of every kind is not good, for every dollar of it is good; good because the Government's pledge is out to keep it so, and that pledge will not be broken. However, the guaranty of our purpose to keep the pledge will be best shown by advancing toward its fulfillment.

The evil of the present system is found in the great cost to the Government of maintaining the parity of our different forms of money, that is, keeping all of them at par with gold. We surely cannot be longer heedless of the burden this imposes upon the people, even under fairly prosperous conditions, while the past four years have demonstrated that it is not only an expensive charge upon the Government, but a dangerous menace to the National credit.

It is manifest that we must devise some plan to protect the Government against bond issues for repeated redemptions. We must either curtail the opportunity for speculation, made easy by the multiplied redemptions of our demand obligations, or increase the gold reserve for their redemption. We have $900,000,000 of currency which the Government by solemn enactment has undertaken to keep at par with gold. Nobody is obliged to redeem in gold but the Government. The banks are not required to redeem in gold. The Government is obliged to keep equal with gold all its outstanding currency and coin obligations, while its receipts are not required to be paid in gold. They are paid in every kind of money but gold, and the only means by which the Government can with certainty get gold is by borrowing. It can get it in no other way when it most needs it. The Government without any fixed gold revenue is pledged to maintain gold redemption, which it has steadily and faithfully done, and which, under the authority now given, it will continue to do.

The law which requires the Government, after having redeemed its United States notes, to pay them out again as current funds, demands a constant replenishment of the gold reserve. This is especially so in times of business panic and when the revenues are insufficient to meet the expenses of the Government. At such times the Government has no other way to supply its deficit and maintain redemption but through the increase of its bonded debt, as during the Administration of my predecessor, when $262,315,400 of four-and-a-half per cent bonds were issued and sold and the proceeds used to pay the expenses of the Government in excess of the revenues and sustain the gold reserve. While it is true that the greater part of the proceeds of these bonds were used to supply deficient revenues, a considerable portion was required to maintain the gold reserve.

With our revenues equal to our expenses, there would be no deficit requiring the issuance of bonds. But if the gold reserve falls below $100,000,000, how will it be replenished except by selling more bonds? Is there any other way practicable under existing law? The serious question then is, Shall we continue the policy that has been pursued in the past; that is, when the gold reserve reaches the point of danger, issue more bonds and supply the needed gold, or shall we provide other means to prevent these recurring drains upon the gold reserve? If no further legislation is had and the policy of selling bonds is to be continued, then Congress should give the Secretary of the Treasury authority to sell bonds at long or short periods, bearing a less rate of interest than is now authorized by law.

I earnestly recommend, as soon as the receipts of the Government are quite sufficient to pay all the expenses of the Government, that when any of the United States notes are presented for redemption in gold and are redeemed in gold, such notes shall be kept and set apart, and only paid out in exchange for gold. This is an obvious duty. If the holder of the United States note prefers the gold and gets it from the Government, he should not receive back from the Government a United States note without paying gold in exchange for it. The reason for this is made all the more apparent when the Government issues an interest-bearing debt to provide gold for the redemption of United States notes — a non-interest-bearing debt. Surely it should not pay them out again except on demand and for gold. If they are put out in any other way, they may return again to be followed by another bond issue to redeem them — another interest-bearing debt to redeem a non-interest-bearing debt.

In my view, it is of the utmost importance that the Government should be relieved from the burden of providing all the gold required for exchanges and export. This responsibility is alone borne by the Government, without any of the usual and necessary banking powers to help itself. The banks do not feel the strain of gold redemption. The whole strain rests upon the Government, and the size of the gold reserve in the Treasury has come to be, with or without reason, the signal of danger or of security. This ought to be stopped.

If we are to have an era of prosperity in the country, with sufficient receipts for the expenses of the Government, we may feel no immediate embarrassment from our present currency; but the danger still exists, and will be ever present, menacing us so long as the existing system continues. And, besides, it is in times of adequate revenues and business tranquillity that the Government should prepare for the worst. We cannot avoid, without serious consequences, the wise consideration and prompt solution of this question.

The Secretary of the Treasury has outlined a plan, in great detail, for the purpose of removing the threatened recurrence of a depleted gold reserve and save us from future embarrassment on that account. To this plan I invite your careful consideration.

I concur with the Secretary of the Treasury in his recommendation that National banks be allowed to issue notes to the face value of the bonds which they have deposited for circulation, and that the tax on circulating notes secured by deposit of such bonds be reduced to one-half of one per cent per annum. I also join him in recommending that authority be given for the establishment of National banks with a minimum capital of $25,000. This will enable the smaller villages and agricultural regions of the country to be supplied with currency to meet their needs.

I recommend that the issue of National bank notes be restricted to the denomination of ten dollars and upwards. If the suggestions I have herein made shall have the approval of Congress, then I would recommend that National banks be required to redeem their notes in gold.

The most important problem with which this Government is now called upon to deal pertaining to its foreign relations concerns its duty toward Spain and the Cuban insurrection. Problems and conditions more or less in common with those now existing have confronted this Government at various times in the past. The story of Cuba for many years has been one of unrest, growing discontent, an effort toward a larger enjoyment of liberty and self-control, of organized resistance to the mother country, of depression after distress and warfare, and of ineffectual settlement to be followed by renewed revolt. For no enduring period since the enfranchisement of the continental possessions of Spain in the Western Continent has the condition of Cuba or the policy of Spain toward Cuba not caused concern to the United States.

The prospect from time to time that the weakness of Spain's hold upon the island and the political vicissitudes and embarrassments of the home Government might lead to the transfer of Cuba to a continental power called forth between 1823 and 1860 various emphatic declarations of the policy of the United States to permit no disturbance of Cuba's connection with Spain unless in the direction of independence or acquisition by us through purchase, nor has there been any change of this declared policy since upon the part of the Government.

The revolution which began in 1868 lasted for ten years despite the strenuous efforts of the successive peninsular governments to suppress it. Then as now the Government of the United States testified its grave concern and offered its aid to put an end to bloodshed in Cuba. The overtures made by General Grant were refused and the war dragged on, entailing great loss of life and treasure and increased injury to American interests, besides throwing enhanced burdens of neutrality upon this Government. In 1878 peace was brought about by the truce of Zanjon, obtained by negotiations between the Spanish commander, Martinez de Campos, and the insurgent leaders.

The present insurrection broke out in February, 1895. It is not my purpose at this time to recall its remarkable increase or to characterize its tenacious resistance against the enormous forces massed against it by Spain. The revolt and the efforts to subdue it carried destruction to every quarter of the island, developing wide proportions and defying the efforts of Spain for its suppression. The civilized code of war has been disregarded, no less so by the Spaniards than by the Cubans.

The existing conditions can not but fill this Government and the American people with the gravest apprehension. There is no desire on the part of our people to profit by the misfortunes of Spain. We have only the desire to see the Cubans prosperous and contented, enjoying that measure of self-control which is the inalienable right of man, protected in their right to reap the benefit of the exhaustless treasures of their country.

The offer made by my predecessor in April, 1896, tendering the friendly offices of this Government, failed. Any mediation on our part was not accepted. In brief, the answer read: "There is no effectual way to pacify Cuba unless it begins with the actual submission of the rebels to the mother country." Then only could Spain act in the promised direction, of her own motion and after her own plans.

The cruel policy of concentration was initiated February 16, 1896. The productive districts controlled by the Spanish armies were depopulated. The agricultural inhabitants were herded in and about the garrison towns, their lands laid waste and their dwellings destroyed. This policy the late cabinet of Spain justified as a necessary measure of war and as a means of cutting off supplies from the insurgents. It has utterly failed as a war measure. It was not civilized warfare. It was extermination.

Against this abuse of the rights of war I have felt constrained on repeated occasions to enter the firm and earnest protest of this Government. There was much of public condemnation of the treatment of American citizens by alleged illegal arrests and long imprisonment awaiting trial or pending protracted judicial proceedings. I felt it my first duty to make instant demand for the release or speedy trial of all American citizens under arrest. Before the change of the Spanish cabinet in October last twenty-two prisoners, citizens of the United States, had been given their freedom.

For the relief of our own citizens suffering because of the conflict the aid of Congress was sought in a special message,* and under the appropriation of May 24, 1897, effective aid has been given to American citizens in Cuba, many of them at their own request having been returned to the United States.

The instructions given to our new minister to Spain before his departure for his post directed him to impress upon that Government the sincere wish of the United States to lend its aid toward the ending of the war in Cuba by reaching a peaceful and lasting result, just and honorable alike to Spain and to the Cuban people. These instructions recited the character and duration of the contest, the widespread losses it entails, the burdens and restraints it imposes upon us, with constant disturbance of national interests, and the injury resulting from an indefinite continuance of this state of things. It was stated that at this juncture our Government was constrained to seriously inquire if the time was not ripe when Spain of her own volition, moved by her own interests and every sentiment of humanity, should put a stop to this destructive war and make proposals of settlement honorable to herself and just to her Cuban colony. It was urged that as a neighboring nation, with large interests in Cuba, we could be required to wait only a reasonable time for the mother country to establish its authority and restore peace and order within the borders of the island; that we could not contemplate an indefinite period for the accomplishment of this result.

No solution was proposed to which the slightest idea of humiliation to Spain could attach, and, indeed, precise proposals were withheld to avoid embarrassment to that Government. All that was asked or expected was that some safe way might be speedily provided and permanent peace

* See pp. 6248-6249.

restored. It so chanced that the consideration of this offer, addressed to the same Spanish administration which had declined the tenders of my predecessor, and which for more than two years had poured men and treasure into Cuba in the fruitless effort to suppress the revolt, fell to others. Between the departure of General Woodford, the new envoy, and his arrival in Spain the statesman who had shaped the policy of his country fell by the hand of an assassin, and although the cabinet of the late premier still held office and received from our envoy the proposals he bore, that cabinet gave place within a few days thereafter to a new administration, under the leadership of Sagasta.

The reply to our note was received on the 23d day of October. It is in the direction of a better understanding. It appreciates the friendly purposes of this Government. It admits that our country is deeply affected by the war in Cuba and that its desires for peace are just. It declares that the present Spanish government is bound by every consideration to a change of policy that should satisfy the United States and pacify Cuba within a reasonable time. To this end Spain has decided to put into effect the political reforms heretofore advocated by the present premier, without halting for any consideration in the path which in its judgment leads to peace. The military operations, it is said, will continue, but will be humane and conducted with all regard for private rights, being accompanied by political action leading to the autonomy of Cuba while guarding Spanish sovereignty. This, it is claimed, will result in investing Cuba with a distinct personality, the island to be governed by an executive and by a local council or chamber, reserving to Spain the control of the foreign relations, the army and navy, and the judicial administration. To accomplish this the present government proposes to modify existing legislation by decree, leaving the Spanish Cortes, with the aid of Cuban senators and deputies, to solve the economic problem and properly distribute the existing debt.

In the absence of a declaration of the measures that this Government proposes to take in carrying out its proffer of good offices, it suggests that Spain be left free to conduct military operations and grant political reforms, while the United States for its part shall enforce its neutral obligations and cut off the assistance which it is asserted the insurgents receive from this country. The supposition of an indefinite prolongation of the war is denied. It is asserted that the western provinces are already well-nigh reclaimed, that the planting of cane and tobacco therein has been resumed, and that by force of arms and new and ample reforms very early and complete pacification is hoped for.

The immediate amelioration of existing conditions under the new administration of Cuban affairs is predicted, and therewithal the disturbance and all occasion for any change of attitude on the part of the United States. Discussion of the question of the international duties and responsibilities of the United States as Spain understands them is presented, with an apparent disposition to charge us with failure in this regard. This charge is without any basis in fact. It could not have been made if Spain had been cognizant of the constant efforts this Government has made, at the cost of millions and by the employment of .he administrative machinery of the nation at command, to perform its full duty according to the law of nations. That it has successfully prevented the departure of a single military expedition or armed vessel from our shores in violation of our laws would seem to be a sufficient answer. But of this aspect of the Spanish note it is not necessary to speak further now. Firm in the conviction of a wholly performed obligation, due response to this charge has been made in diplomatic course.

Throughout all these horrors and dangers to our own peace this Government has never in any way abrogated its sovereign prerogative of reserving to itself the determination of its policy and course according to its own high sense of right and in consonance with the dearest interests and convictions of our own people should the prolongation of the strife so demand.

Of the untried measures there remain only: Recognition of the insurgents as belligerents; recognition of the independence of Cuba; neutral intervention to end the war by imposing a rational compromise between the contestants, and intervention in favor of one or the other party. I speak not of forcible annexation, for that can not be thought of. That, by our code of morality, would be criminal aggression.

Recognition of the belligerency of the Cuban insurgents has often been canvassed as a possible, if not inevitable, step both in regard to the previous ten years' struggle and during the present war. I am not unmindful that the two Houses of Congress in the spring of 1896 expressed the opinion by concurrent resolution that a condition of public war existed requiring or justifying the recognition of a state of belligerency in Cuba, and during the extra session the Senate voted a joint resolution of like import, which, however, was not brought to a vote in the House of Representatives. In the presence of these significant expressions of the sentiment of the legislative branch it behooves the Executive to soberly consider the conditions under which so important a measure must needs rest for justification. It is to be seriously considered whether the Cuban insurrection possesses beyond dispute the attributes of statehood, which alone can demand the recognition of belligerency in its favor. Possession, in short, of the essential qualifications of sovereignty by the insurgents and the conduct of the war by them according to the received code of war are no less important factors toward the determination of the problem of belligerency than are the influences and consequences of the struggle upon the internal polity of the recognizing state.

The wise utterances of President Grant in his memorable message of December 7, 1875, are signally relevant to the present situation in Cuba, and it may be wholesome now to recall them. At that time a ruinous conflict had for seven years wasted the neighboring island. During all those years an utter disregard of the laws of civilized warfare and of the just demands of humanity, which called forth expressions of condemnation from the nations of Christendom, continued unabated. Desolation and ruin pervaded that productive region, enormously affecting the commerce of all commercial nations, but that of the United States more than any other by reason of proximity and larger trade and intercourse. At that juncture General Grant uttered these words, which now, as then, sum up the elements of the problem:

A recognition of the independence of Cuba being, in my opinion, impracticable and indefensible, the question which next presents itself is that of the recognition of belligerent rights in the parties to the contest.

In a former message to Congress* I had occasion to consider this question, and reached the conclusion that the conflict in Cuba, dreadful and devastating as were its incidents, did not rise to the fearful dignity of war. * * * It is possible that the acts of foreign powers, and even acts of Spain herself, of this very nature, might be pointed to in defense of such recognition. But now, as in its past history, the United States should carefully avoid the false lights which might lead it into the mazes of doubtful law and of questionable propriety, and adhere rigidly and sternly to the rule, which has been its guide, of doing only that which is right and honest and of good report. The question of according or of withholding rights of belligerency must be judged in every case in view of the particular attending facts. Unless justified by necessity, it is always, and justly, regarded as an unfriendly act and a gratuitous demonstration of moral support to the rebellion. It is necessary, and it is required, when the interests and rights of another government or of its people are so far affected by a pending civil conflict as to require a definition of its relations to the parties thereto. But this conflict must be one which will be recognized in the sense of international law as war. Belligerence, too, is a fact. The mere existence of contending armed bodies and their occasional conflicts do not constitute war in the sense referred to. Applying to the existing condition of affairs in Cuba the tests recognized by publicists and writers on international law, and which have been observed by nations of dignity, honesty, and power when free from sensitive or selfish and unworthy motives, I fail to find in the insurrection the existence of such a substantial political organization, real, palpable, and manifest to the world, having the forms and capable of the ordinary functions of government toward its own people and to other states, with courts for the administration of justice, with a local habitation, possessing such organization of force, such material, such occupation of territory, as to take the contest out of the category of a mere rebellious insurrection or occasional skirmishes and place it on the terrible footing of war, to which a recognition of belligerency would aim to elevate it. The contest, moreover, is solely on land; the insurrection has not possessed itself of a single seaport whence it may send forth its flag, nor has it any means of communication with foreign powers except through the military lines of its adversaries. No apprehension of any of those sudden and difficult complications which a war upon the ocean is apt to precipitate upon the vessels, both commercial and national, and upon the consular officers of other powers calls for the definition of their relations to the parties to the contest. Considered as a question of expediency, I regard the accordance of belligerent rights still to be as unwise and premature as I regard it to be, at present, indefensible as a measure of right. Such recognition entails upon the country according the rights which flow from it difficult and complicated duties, and requires

* See pp. 4018-4023.

the exaction from the contending parties of the strict observance of their rights and obligations. It confers the right of search upon the high seas by vessels of both parties; it would subject the carrying of arms and munitions of war, which now may be transported freely and without interruption in the vessels of the United States, to detention and to possible seizure; it would give rise to countless vexatious questions, would release the parent Government from responsibility for acts done by the insurgents, and would invest Spain with the right to exercise the supervision recognized by our treaty of 1795 over our commerce on the high seas, a very large part of which, in its traffic between the Atlantic and the Gulf States and between all of them and the States on the Pacific, passes through the waters which wash the shores of Cuba. The exercise of this supervision could scarce fail to lead, if not to abuses, certainly to collisions perilous to the peaceful relations of the two States. There can be little doubt to what result such supervision would before long draw this nation. It would be unworthy of the United States to inaugurate the possibilities of such result by measures of questionable right or expediency or by any indirection.

Turning to the practical aspects of a recognition of belligerency and reviewing its inconveniences and positive dangers, still further pertinent considerations appear. In the code of nations there is no such thing as a naked recognition of belligerency, unaccompanied by the assumption of international neutrality. Such recognition, without more, will not confer upon either party to a domestic conflict a status not theretofore actually possessed or affect the relation of either party to other states. The act of recognition usually takes the form of a solemn proclamation of neutrality, which recites the *de facto* condition of belligerency as its motive. It announces a domestic law of neutrality in the declaring state. It assumes the international obligations of a neutral in the presence of a public state of war. It warns all citizens and others within the jurisdiction of the proclaimant that they violate those rigorous obligations at their own peril and can not expect to be shielded from the consequences. The right of visit and search on the seas and seizure of vessels and cargoes and contraband of war and good prize under admiralty law must under international law be admitted as a legitimate consequence of a proclamation of belligerency. While according the equal belligerent rights defined by public law to each party in our ports disfavors would be imposed on both, which, while nominally equal, would weigh heavily in behalf of Spain herself. Possessing a navy and controlling the ports of Cuba, her maritime rights could be asserted not only for the military investment of the island, but up to the margin of our own territorial waters, and a condition of things would exist for which the Cubans within their own domain could not hope to create a parallel, while its creation through aid or sympathy from within our domain would be even more impossible than now, with the additional obligations of international neutrality we would perforce assume.

The enforcement of this enlarged and onerous code of neutrality would only be influential within our own jurisdiction by land and sea and applicable by our own instrumentalities. It could impart to the United States no jurisdiction between Spain and the insurgents. It would give the

United States no right of intervention to enforce the conduct of the strife within the paramount authority of Spain according to the international code of war.

For these reasons I regard the recognition of the belligerency of the Cuban insurgents as now unwise, and therefore inadmissible. Should that step hereafter be deemed wise as a measure of right and duty, the Executive will take it.

Intervention upon humanitarian grounds has been frequently suggested and has not failed to receive my most anxious and earnest consideration. But should such a step be now taken, when it is apparent that a hopeful change has supervened in the policy of Spain toward Cuba? A new government has taken office in the mother country. It is pledged in advance to the declaration that all the effort in the world can not suffice to maintain peace in Cuba by the bayonet; that vague promises of reform after subjugation afford no solution of the insular problem; that with a substitution of commanders must come a change of the past system of warfare for one in harmony with a new policy, which shall no longer aim to drive the Cubans to the "horrible alternative of taking to the thicket or succumbing in misery;" that reforms must be instituted in accordance with the needs and circumstances of the time, and that these reforms, while designed to give full autonomy to the colony and to create a virtual entity and self-controlled administration, shall yet conserve and affirm the sovereignty of Spain by a just distribution of powers and burdens upon a basis of mutual interest untainted by methods of selfish expediency.

The first acts of the new government lie in these honorable paths. The policy of cruel rapine and extermination that so long shocked the universal sentiment of humanity has been reversed. Under the new military commander a broad clemency is proffered. Measures have already been set on foot to relieve the horrors of starvation. The power of the Spanish armies, it is asserted, is to be used not to spread ruin and desolation, but to protect the resumption of peaceful agricultural pursuits and productive industries. That past methods are futile to force a peace by subjugation is freely admitted, and that ruin without conciliation must inevitably fail to win for Spain the fidelity of a contented dependency.

Decrees in application of the foreshadowed reforms have already been promulgated. The full text of these decrees has not been received, but as furnished in a telegraphic summary from our minister are: All civil and electoral rights of peninsular Spaniards are, in virtue of existing constitutional authority, forthwith extended to colonial Spaniards. A scheme of autonomy has been proclaimed by decree, to become effective upon ratification by the Cortes. It creates a Cuban parliament, which, with the insular executive, can consider and vote upon all subjects affecting local order and interests, possessing unlimited powers save as to matters of state, war, and the navy, as to which the Governor-General acts by his own authority as the delegate of the central Government. This parliament receives the oath of the Governor-General to preserve faithfully the liberties and privileges of the colony, and to it the colonial secretaries are responsible. It has the right to propose to the central Government, through the Governor-General, modifications of the national charter and to invite new projects of law or executive measures in the interest of the colony.

Besides its local powers, it is competent, first, to regulate electoral registration and procedure and prescribe the qualifications of electors and the manner of exercising suffrage; second, to organize courts of justice with native judges from members of the local bar; third, to frame the insular budget, both as to expenditures and revenues, without limitation of any kind, and to set apart the revenues to meet the Cuban share of the national budget, which latter will be voted by the national Cortes with the assistance of Cuban senators and deputies; fourth, to initiate or take part in the negotiations of the national Government for commercial treaties which may affect Cuban interests; fifth, to accept or reject commercial treaties which the national Government may have concluded without the participation of the Cuban government; sixth, to frame the colonial tariff, acting in accord with the peninsular Government in scheduling articles of mutual commerce between the mother country and the colonies. Before introducing or voting upon a bill the Cuban government or the chambers will lay the project before the central Government and hear its opinion thereon, all the correspondence in such regard being made public. Finally, all conflicts of jurisdiction arising between the different municipal, provincial, and insular assemblies, or between the latter and the insular executive power, and which from their nature may not be referable to the central Government for decision, shall be submitted to the courts.

That the government of Sagasta has entered upon a course from which recession with honor is impossible can hardly be questioned; that in the few weeks it has existed it has made earnest of the sincerity of its professions is undeniable. I shall not impugn its sincerity, nor should impatience be suffered to embarrass it in the task it has undertaken. It is honestly due to Spain and to our friendly relations with Spain that she should be given a reasonable chance to realize her expectations and to prove the asserted efficacy of the new order of things to which she stands irrevocably committed. She has recalled the commander whose brutal orders inflamed the American mind and shocked the civilized world. She has modified the horrible order of concentration and has undertaken to care for the helpless and permit those who desire to resume the cultivation of their fields to do so, and assures them of the protection of the Spanish Government in their lawful occupations. She has just released the *Competitor* prisoners, heretofore sentenced to death, and who have been the subject of repeated diplomatic correspondence during both this and the preceding Administration.

Not a single American citizen is now in arrest or confinement in Cuba of whom this Government has any knowledge. The near future will demonstrate whether the indispensable condition of a righteous peace, just alike to the Cubans and to Spain as well as equitable to all our interests so intimately involved in the welfare of Cuba, is likely to be attained. If not, the exigency of further and other action by the United States will remain to be taken. When that time comes that action will be determined in the line of indisputable right and duty. It will be faced, without misgiving or hesitancy in the light of the obligation this Government owes to itself, to the people who have confided to it the protection of their interests and honor, and to humanity.

Sure of the right, keeping free from all offense ourselves, actuated only by upright and patriotic considerations, moved neither by passion nor selfishness, the Government will continue its watchful care over the rights and property of American citizens and will abate none of its efforts to bring about by peaceful agencies a peace which shall be honorable and enduring. If it shall hereafter appear to be a duty imposed by our obligations to ourselves, to civilization and humanity to intervene with force, it shall be without fault on our part and only because the necessity for such action will be so clear as to command the support and approval of the civilized world.

By a special message dated the 16th day of June last, I laid before the Senate a treaty signed that day by the plenipotentiaries of the United States and of the Republic of Hawaii, having for its purpose the incorporation of the Hawaiian Islands as an integral part of the United States and under its sovereignty. The Senate having removed the injunction of secrecy, although the treaty is still pending before that body, the subject may be properly referred to in this Message because the necessary action of the Congress is required to determine by legislation many details of the eventual union should the fact of annexation be accomplished, as I believe it should be.

While consistently disavowing from a very early period any aggressive policy of absorption in regard to the Hawaiian group, a long series of declarations through three-quarters of a century has proclaimed the vital interest of the United States in the independent life of the Islands and their intimate commercial dependence upon this country. At the same time it has been repeatedly asserted that in no event could the entity of Hawaiian statehood cease by the passage of the Islands under the domination or influence of another power than the United States. Under these circumstances, the logic of events required that annexation, heretofore offered but declined, should in the ripeness of time come about as the natural result of the strengthening ties that bind us to those Islands, and be realized by the free will of the Hawaiian State.

That treaty was unanimously ratified without amendment by the Senate and President of the Republic of Hawaii on the 10th of September last, and only awaits the favorable action of the American Senate to effect the complete absorption of the Islands into the domain of the United States. What the conditions of such a union shall be, the political relation thereof to the United States, the character of the local administration, the quality and degree of the elective franchise of the inhabitants, the extension of the federal laws to the territory or the enactment of special laws to fit the peculiar condition thereof, the regulation if need be of the labor system therein, are all matters which the treaty has wisely relegated to the Congress.

If the treaty is confirmed as every consideration of dignity and honor requires, the wisdom of Congress will see to it that, avoiding abrupt assimilation of elements perhaps hardly yet fitted to share in the highest franchises of citizenship, and having due regard to the geographical conditions, the most just provisions for self-rule in local matters with the largest political liberties as an integral part of our Nation will be accorded to the Hawaiians. No less is due to a people who, after nearly five years of demonstrated capacity to fulfill the obligations of self-governing statehood, come of their free will to merge their destinies in our body-politic.

The questions which have arisen between Japan and Hawaii by reason of the treatment of Japanese laborers emigrating to the Islands under the Hawaiian-Japanese convention of 1888, are in a satisfactory stage of settlement by negotiation. This Government has not been invited to mediate, and on the other hand has sought no intervention in that matter, further than to evince its kindliest disposition toward such a speedy and direct adjustment by the two sovereign States in interest as shall comport with equity and honor. It is gratifying to learn that the apprehensions at first displayed on the part of Japan lest the cessation of Hawaii's national life through annexation might impair privileges to which Japan honorably laid claim, have given place to confidence in the uprightness of this Government, and in the sincerity of its purpose to deal with all possible ulterior questions in the broadest spirit of friendliness.

As to the representation of this Government to Nicaragua, Salvador, and Costa Rica, I have concluded that Mr. William L. Merry, confirmed as minister of the United States to the States of Nicaragua, Salvador and Costa Rica, shall proceed to San José, Costa Rica, and there temporarily establish the headquarters of the United States to those three States. I took this action for what I regarded as the paramount interests of this country. It was developed upon an investigation by the Secretary of State that the Government of Nicaragua, while not unwilling to receive Mr. Merry in his diplomatic quality, was unable to do so because of the compact concluded June 20, 1895, whereby that Republic and those of Salvador and Honduras, forming what is known as the Greater Republic of Central America, had surrendered to the representative Diet thereof their right to receive and send diplomatic agents. The Diet was not willing to accept him because he was not accredited to that body. I could not accredit him to that body because the appropriation law of Congress did not permit it. Mr. Baker, the present minister at Managua, has been directed to present his letters of recall.

Mr. W. Godfrey Hunter has likewise been accredited to the Governments of Guatemala and Honduras, the same as his predecessor. Guatemala is not a member of the Greater Republic of Central America, but Honduras is. Should this latter Government decline to receive him, he has been instructed to report this fact to his Government and await its further instructions.

A subject of large importance to our country, and increasing appreciation on the part of the people, is the completion of the great highway of trade between the Atlantic and Pacific, known as the Nicaragua Canal. Its utility and value to American commerce is universally admitted. The Commission appointed under date of July 24 last "to continue the surveys and examinations authorized by the act approved March 2, 1895," in regard to "the proper route, feasibility, and cost of construction of the Nicaragua Canal, with a view of making complete plans for the entire work of construction of such canal," is now employed in the undertaking. In the future I shall take occasion to transmit to Congress the report of this Commission, making at the same time such further suggestions as may then seem advisable.

Under the provisions of the act of Congress approved March 3, 1897, for the promotion of an international agreement respecting bimetallism, I appointed on the 14th day of April, 1897, Hon. Edward O. Wolcott of Colorado, Hon. Adlai E. Stevenson of Illinois, and Hon. Charles J. Paine of Massachusetts, as special envoys to represent the United States. They have been diligent in their efforts to secure the concurrence and cooperation of European countries in the international settlement of the question, but up to this time have not been able to secure an agreement contemplated by their mission.

The gratifying action of our great sister Republic of France in joining this country in the attempt to bring about an agreement among the principal commercial nations of Europe, whereby a fixed and relative value between gold and silver shall be secured, furnishes assurance that we are not alone among the larger nations of the world in realizing the international character of the problem and in the desire of reaching some wise and practical solution of it. The British Government has published a *résumé* of the steps taken jointly by the French ambassador in London and the special envoys of the United States, with whom our ambassador at London actively co-operated in the presentation of this subject to Her Majesty's Government. This will be laid before Congress.

Our special envoys have not made their final report, as further negotiations between the representatives of this Government and the Governments of other countries are pending and in contemplation. They believe that doubts which have been raised in certain quarters respecting the position of maintaining the stability of the parity between the metals and kindred questions may yet be solved by further negotiations.

Meanwhile it gives me satisfaction to state that the special envoys have already demonstrated their ability and fitness to deal with the subject, and it is to be earnestly hoped that their labors may result in an international agreement which will bring about recognition of both gold and silver as money upon such terms, and with such safeguards as will secure the use of both metals upon a basis which shall work no injustice to any class of our citizens.

In order to execute as early as possible the provisions of the third and fourth sections of the Revenue Act, approved July 24, 1897, I appointed the Hon. John A. Kasson of Iowa, a special commissioner plenipotentiary to undertake the requisite negotiations with foreign countries desiring to avail themselves of these provisions. The negotiations are now proceeding with several Governments, both European and American. It is believed that by a careful exercise of the powers conferred by that Act some grievances of our own and of other countries in our mutual trade relations may be either removed, or largely alleviated, and that the volume of our commercial exchanges may be enlarged, with advantage to both contracting parties.

Most desirable from every standpoint of national interest and patriotism is the effort to extend our foreign commerce. To this end our merchant marine should be improved and enlarged. We should do our full share of the carrying trade of the world. We do not do it now. We should be the laggard no longer. The inferiority of our merchant marine is justly humiliating to the national pride. The Government by every proper constitutional means, should aid in making our ships familiar visitors at every commercial port of the world, thus opening up new and valuable markets to the surplus products of the farm and the factory.

The efforts which had been made during the two previous years by my predecessor to secure better protection to the fur seals in the North Pacific Ocean and Bering Sea, were renewed at an early date by this

Administration, and have been pursued with earnestness. Upon my invitation, the Governments of Japan and Russia sent delegates to Washington, and an international conference was held during the months of October and November last, wherein it was unanimously agreed that under the existing regulations this species of useful animals was threatened with extinction, and that an international agreement of all the interested powers was necessary for their adequate protection.

The Government of Great Britain did not see proper to be represented at this conference, but subsequently sent to Washington, as delegates, the expert commissioners of Great Britain and Canada who had, during the past two years, visited the Pribilof Islands, and who met in conference similar commissioners on the part of the United States. The result of this conference was an agreement on important facts connected with the condition of the seal herd, heretofore in dispute, which should place beyond controversy the duty of the Governments concerned to adopt measures without delay for the preservation and restoration of the herd. Negotiations to this end are now in progress, the result of which I hope to be able to report to Congress at an early day.

International arbitration cannot be omitted from the list of subjects claiming our consideration. Events have only served to strengthen the general views on this question expressed in my inaugural address. The best sentiment of the civilized world is moving toward the settlement of differences between nations without resorting to the horrors of war. Treaties embodying these humane principles on broad lines, without in any way imperiling our interests or our honor, shall have my constant encouragement.

The acceptance by this Government of the invitation of the Republic of France to participate in the Universal Exposition of 1900, at Paris, was immediately followed by the appointment of a special commissioner to represent the United States in the proposed exposition, with special reference to the securing of space for an adequate exhibit on behalf of the United States.

The special commissioner delayed his departure for Paris long enough to ascertain the probable demand for space by American exhibitors. His inquiries developed an almost unprecedented interest in the proposed exposition, and the information thus acquired enabled him to justify an application for a much larger allotment of space for the American section than had been reserved by the exposition authorities. The result was particularly gratifying, in view of the fact that the United States was one of the last countries to accept the invitation of France.

The reception accorded our special commissioner was most cordial, and he was given every reasonable assurance that the United States would receive a consideration commensurate with the proportions of our exhibit. The report of the special commissioner as to the magnitude and importance of the coming exposition, and the great demand for space by American exhibitors, supplies new arguments for a liberal and judicious appropriation by Congress, to the end that an exhibit fairly representative of the industries and resources of our country may be made in an exposition which will illustrate the world's progress during the nineteenth century. That exposition is intended to be the most important and comprehensive of the long series of international exhibitions, of which our own at Chicago was a brilliant example, and it is desirable that the United States should make a worthy exhibit of American genius and skill and their unrivaled achievements in every branch of industry.

The present immediately effective force of the Navy consists of four battle ships of the first class, two of the second, and forty-eight other vessels, ranging from armored cruisers to torpedo boats. There are under construction five battle ships of the first class, sixteen torpedo boats, and one submarine boat. No provision has yet been made for the armor of three of the five battle ships, as it has been impossible to obtain it at the price fixed by Congress. It is of great importance that Congress provide this armor, as until then the ships are of no fighting value.

The present naval force, especially in view of its increase by the ships now under construction, while not as large as that of a few other powers, is a formidable force; its vessels are the very best of each type; and with the increase that should be made to it from time to time in the future, and careful attention to keeping it in a high state of efficiency and repair, it is well adapted to the necessities of the country.

The great increase of the Navy which has taken place in recent years was justified by the requirements for national defense, and has received public approbation. The time has now arrived, however, when this increase, to which the country is committed, should, for a time, take the form of increased facilities commensurate with the increase of our naval vessels. It is an unfortunate fact that there is only one dock on the Pacific Coast capable of docking our largest ships, and only one on the Atlantic Coast, and that the latter has for the last six or seven months been under repair and therefore incapable of use. Immediate steps should be taken to provide three or four docks of this capacity on the Atlantic Coast, at least one on the Pacific Coast, and a floating dock in the Gulf. This is the recommendation of a very competent Board, appointed to investigate the subject. There should also be ample provision made for powder and projectiles, and other munitions of war, and for an increased number of officers and enlisted men. Some additions are also necessary to our navy-yards, for the repair and care of our large number of vessels. As there are now on the stocks five battle ships of the largest class, which cannot be completed for a year or two, I concur with the recommendation of the Secretary of the Navy for an appropriation authorizing the construction of one battle ship for the Pacific Coast, where, at present, there is only one in commission and one under construction, while on the Atlantic Coast there are three in commission and four under construction; and also that several torpedo boats be authorized in connection with our general system of coast defense.

The Territory of Alaska requires the prompt and early attention of Congress. The conditions now existing demand material changes in the laws relating to the Territory. The great influx of population during the past summer and fall and the prospect of a still larger immigration in the spring will not permit us to longer neglect the extension of civil authority within the Territory or postpone the establishment of a more thorough government.

A general system of public surveys has not yet been extended to Alaska and all entries thus far made in that district are upon special surveys. The act of Congress extending to Alaska the mining laws of the United States contained the reservation that it should not be construed to put in force the general land laws of the country. By act approved March 3, 1891, authority was given for entry of lands for town-site purposes and also for the purchase of not exceeding one hundred and sixty acres then or thereafter occupied for purposes of trade and manufacture. The purpose of Congress as thus far expressed has been that only such rights should apply to that Territory as should be specifically named.

It will be seen how much remains to be done for that vast and remote and yet promising portion of our country. Special authority was given to the President by the Act of Congress approved July 24, 1897, to divide that Territory into two land districts and to designate the boundaries thereof and to appoint registers and receivers of said land offices, and the President was also authorized to appoint a surveyor-general for the entire district. Pursuant to this authority, a surveyor-general and receiver have been appointed, with offices at Sitka. If in the ensuing year the conditions justify it, the additional land district authorized by law will be established, with an office at some point in the Yukon Valley. No appropriation, however, was made for this purpose, and that is now necessary to be done for the two land districts into which the Territory is to be divided.

I concur with the Secretary of War in his suggestions as to the necessity for a military force in the Territory of Alaska for the protection of persons and property. Already a small force, consisting of twenty-five men, with two officers, under command of Lieutenant-Colonel Randall, of the Eighth Infantry, has been sent to St. Michael to establish a military post.

As it is to the interest of the Government to encourage the development and settlement of the country and its duty to follow up its citizens there with the benefits of legal machinery, I earnestly urge upon Congress the establishment of a system of government with such flexibility as will enable it to adjust itself to the future areas of greatest population.

The startling though possibly exaggerated reports from the Yukon River country, of the probable shortage of food for the large number of people who are wintering there without the means of leaving the country are confirmed in such measure as to justify bringing the matter to the attention of Congress. Access to that country in winter can be had only by the passes from Dyea and vicinity, which is a most difficult and perhaps an impossible task. However, should these reports of the suffering of our fellow-citizens be further verified, every effort at any cost should be made to carry them relief.

For a number of years past it has been apparent that the conditions under which the Five Civilized Tribes were established in the Indian Territory under treaty provisions with the United States, with the right of self-government and the exclusion of all white persons from within their borders, have undergone so complete a change as to render the continuance of the system thus inaugurated practically impossible. The total number of the Five Civilized Tribes, as shown by the last census, is 45,494, and this number has not materially increased; while the white population is estimated at from 200,000 to 250,000 which, by permission of the Indian Government has settled in the Territory. The present area of the Indian Territory contains 25,694,564 acres, much of which is very fertile land. The United States citizens residing in the Territory, most of whom have gone there by invitation or with the consent of the tribal authorities, have made permanent homes for themselves. Numerous towns have been built in which from 500 to 5,000 white people now reside. Valuable residences and business houses have been erected in many of them. Large business enterprises are carried on in which vast sums of money are employed, and yet these people, who have invested their capital in the development of the productive resources of the country, are without title to the land they occupy, and have no voice whatever in the government either of the Nations or Tribes. Thousands of their children who were born in the Territory are of school age, but the doors of the schools of the Nations are shut against them, and what education they get is by private contribution. No provision for the protection of the life or property of these white citizens is made by the Tribal Governments and Courts.

The Secretary of the Interior reports that leading Indians have absorbed great tracts of land to the exclusion of the common people, and government by an Indian aristocracy has been practically established, to the detriment of the people. It has been found impossible for the United States to keep its citizens out of the Territory, and the executory conditions contained in the treaties with these Nations have for the most part become impossible of execution. Nor has it been possible for the Tribal Governments to secure to each individual Indian his full enjoyment in common with other Indians of the common property of the Nations. Friends of the Indians have long believed that the best interests of the Indians of the Five Civilized Tribes would be found in American citizenship, with all the rights and privileges which belong to that condition.

By section 16, of the act of March 3, 1893, the President was authorized to appoint three commissioners to enter into negotiations with the Cherokee, Choctaw, Chickasaw, Muscogee (or Creek), and Seminole Nations, commonly known as the Five Civilized Tribes in the Indian Territory. Briefly, the purposes of the negotiations were to be: The extinguishment of Tribal titles to any lands within that Territory now held by any and all such Nations or Tribes, either by cession of the same or some part thereof to the United States, or by allotment and division of the same in severalty among the Indians of such Nations or Tribes respectively as may be entitled to the same, or by such other method as may be agreed upon between the several Nations and Tribes aforesaid, or each of them, with the United States, with a view to such an adjustment upon the basis of justice and equity as may, with the consent of the said Nations of Indians so far as may be necessary, be requisite and suitable to enable the ultimate creation of a State or States of the Union which shall embrace the lands within said Indian Territory.

The Commission met much opposition from the beginning. The Indians were very slow to act, and those in control manifested a decided disinclination to meet with favor the propositions submitted to them. A little more than three years after this organization the Commission effected an agreement with the Choctaw Nation alone. The Chickasaws, however, refused to agree to its terms, and as they have a common interest with the Choctaws in the lands of said Nations, the agreement with the latter Nation could have no effect without the consent of the former. On April 23, 1897, the Commission effected an agreement with both tribes — the Choctaws and Chickasaws. This agreement, it is understood, has been ratified by the constituted authorities of the respective Tribes or Nations parties thereto, and only requires ratification by Congress to make it binding.

On the 27th of September, 1897, an agreement was effected with the Creek Nation, but it is understood that the National Council of said Nation has refused to ratify the same. Negotiations are yet to be had with the Cherokees, the most populous of the Five Civilized Tribes, and with the Seminoles, the smallest in point of numbers and territory.

The provision in the Indian Appropriation Act, approved June 10, 1896, makes it the duty of the Commission to investigate and determine the rights of applicants for citizenship in the Five Civilized Tribes, and to make complete census rolls of the citizens of said Tribes. The Commission is at present engaged in this work among the Creeks, and has made appointments for taking the census of these people up to and including the 30th of the present month.

Should the agreement between the Choctaws and Chickasaws be ratified by Congress and should the other Tribes fail to make an agreement with the Commission, then it will be necessary that some legislation shall be had by Congress, which, while just and honorable to the Indians, shall be equitable to the white people who have settled upon these lands by invitation of the Tribal Nations.

Hon. Henry L. Dawes, Chairman of the Commission, in a letter to the Secretary of the Interior, under date of October 11, 1897, says: "Individual ownership is, in their (the Commission's) opinion, absolutely essential to any permanent improvement in present conditions, and the lack of it is the root of nearly all the evils which so grievously afflict these people. Allotment by agreement is the only possible method, unless the United States Courts are clothed with the authority to apportion the lands among the citizen Indians for whose use it was originally granted."

I concur with the Secretary of the Interior that there can be no cure for the evils engendered by the perversion of these great trusts, excepting by their resumption by the Government which created them.

The recent prevalence of yellow fever in a number of cities and towns throughout the South has resulted in much disturbance of commerce, and demonstrated the necessity of such amendments to our quarantine laws as will make the regulations of the national quarantine authorities paramount. The Secretary of the Treasury, in the portion of his report relating to the operation of the Marine Hospital Service, calls attention to the defects in the present quarantine laws, and recommends amendments thereto which will give the Treasury Department the requisite authority to prevent the invasion of epidemic diseases from foreign countries, and in times of emergency, like that of the past summer, will add to the efficiency of the sanitary measures for the protection of the people, and at the same time prevent unnecessary restriction of commerce. I concur in his recommendation.

In further effort to prevent the invasion of the United States by yellow fever, the importance of the discovery of the exact cause of the disease, which up to the present time has been undetermined, is obvious, and to this end a systematic bacteriological investigation should be made. I therefore recommend that Congress authorize the appointment of a commission by the President, to consist of four expert bacteriologists, one to be selected from the medical officers of the Marine Hospital Service, one to be appointed from civil life, one to be detailed from the medical officers of the Army, and one from the medical officers of the Navy.

The Union Pacific Railway, Main Line, was sold under the decree of the United States Court for the District of Nebraska, on the 1st and 2d of November of this year. The amount due the Government consisted of the principal of the subsidy bonds, $27,236,512, and the accrued interest thereon, $31,211,711.75, making the total indebtedness, $58,-448,223.75. The bid at the sale covered the first mortgage lien and the entire mortgage claim of the Government, principal and interest.

The sale of the subsidized portion of the Kansas Pacific Line, upon which the Government holds a second mortgage lien, has been postponed at the instance of the Government to December 16, 1897. The debt of this division of the Union Pacific Railway to the Government on November 1, 1897, was the principal of the subsidy bonds, $6,303,000, and the unpaid and accrued interest thereon, $6,626,-690.33, making a total of $12,929,690.33.

The sale of this road was originally advertised for November 4, but for the purpose of securing the utmost public notice of the event it was postponed until December 16, and a second advertisement of the sale was made. By the decree of the Court, the upset price on the sale of the Kansas Pacific will yield to the Government the sum of $2,500,000 over all prior liens, costs, and charges. If no other or better bid is made, this sum is all that the Government will receive on its claim of nearly $13,000,000. The Government has no information as to whether there will be other bidders or a better bid than the minimum amount herein stated. The question presented therefore is: Whether the Government shall, under the authority given it by the act of March 3, 1887, purchase or redeem the road in the event that a bid is not made by private parties covering the entire Government claim. To qualify the Government to bid at the sales will require a deposit of $900,000, as follows: In the Government cause $500,000 and in each of the first mortgage causes $200,000, and in the latter the deposit must be in cash. Payments at the sale are as follows : Upon the acceptance of the bid a sum which with the amount already deposited shall equal fifteen per cent of the bid ; the balance in installments of twenty-five per cent thirty, forty, and fifty days after the confirmation of the sale. The lien on the Kansas Pacific prior to that of the Government on the 30th July, 1897, principal and interest, amounted to $7,281,048.11. The Government, therefore, should it become the highest bidder, will have to pay the amount of the first mortgage lien.

I believe that under the act of 1887 it has the authority to do this and in absence of any action by Congress I shall direct the Secretary of the Treasury to make the necessary deposit as required by the Court's decree to qualify as a bidder and to bid at the sale a sum which will at least equal the principal of the debt due to the Government; but suggest in order to remove all controversy that an amendment of the law be immediately passed explicitly giving such powers and appropriating in general terms whatever sum is sufficient therefor.

In so important a matter as the Government becoming the possible owner of railroad property which it perforce must conduct and operate, I feel constrained to lay before Congress these facts for its consideration and action before the consummation of the sale. It is clear to my mind that the Government should not permit the property to be sold at a price which will yield less than one-half of the principal of its debt and less than one-fifth of its entire debt, principal and interest. But whether the Government, rather than accept less than its claim, should become a bidder and thereby the owner of the property, I submit to the Congress for action.

The Library building provided for by the act of Congress approved April 15, 1886, has been completed and opened to the public. It should be a matter of congratulation that through the foresight and munificence of Congress the nation possesses this noble treasure-house of knowledge. It is earnestly to be hoped that having done so much toward the cause of education, Congress will continue to develop the Library in every phase of research to the end that it may be not only one of the most magnificent but among the richest and most useful libraries in the world.

The important branch of our Government known as the Civil Service, the practical improvement of which has long been a subject of earnest discussion, has of late years received increased legislative and Executive approval. During the past few months the service has been placed upon a still firmer basis of business methods and personal merit. While the right of our veteran soldiers to reinstatement in deserving cases has been asserted, dismissals for merely political reasons have been carefully guarded against, the examinations for admittance to the service enlarged and at the same time rendered less technical and more practical; and a distinct advance has been made by giving a hearing before dismissal upon all cases where incompetency is charged or demand made for the removal of officials in any of the Departments. This order has been made to give to the accused his right to be heard but without in any way impairing the power of removal, which should always be exercised in cases of inefficiency and incompetency, and which is one of the vital safeguards of the civil service reform system, preventing stagnation and deadwood and keeping every employee keenly alive to the fact that the security of his tenure depends not on favor but on his own tested and carefully watched record of service.

Much of course still remains to be accomplished before the system can be made reasonably perfect for our needs. There are places now in the classified service which ought to be exempted and others not classified may properly be included. I shall not hesitate to exempt cases which I think have been improperly included in the classified service or include those which in my judgment will best promote the public service. The system has the approval of the people and it will be my endeavor to uphold and extend it.

I am forced by the length of this Message to omit many important references to affairs of the Government with which Congress will have to deal at the present session. They are fully discussed in the departmental reports, to all of which I invite your earnest attention.

The estimates of the expenses of the Government by the several Departments will, I am sure, have your careful scrutiny. While the Congress may not find it an easy task to reduce the expenses of the Government, it should not encourage their increase. These expenses will in my judgment admit of a decrease in many branches of the Government without injury to the public service. It is a commanding duty to keep the appropriations within the receipts of the Government, and thus avoid a deficit.   WILLIAM McKINLEY.

EXECUTIVE MANSION,
Washington, December 6, 1897.

To the Congress of the United States:

The act of Congress, approved July 19, 1897, entitled "An act making appropriations to supply deficiencies in the appropriations for the fiscal year ending June 30, 1897, and for prior years, for other purposes," provided for the acceptance by the Government of the United States of the invitation extended by the Republic of France to participate in an international exposition to be held at Paris, from April 15 to November 15, 1900, and authorized the President to appoint a special commissioner with a view to securing all attainable information necessary to a full and complete understanding by Congress in regard to the participation of this Government in that exposition.

Maj. Moses P. Handy of Chicago, was appointed such special commissioner, and I now enclose his report, giving the details of his mission. It is a comprehensive and clear presentation of the situation. He recommends that an appropriation of $919,600 be granted, so that a creditable exhibit on behalf of the United States may be made. The details of this report will show how this appropriation may be profitably expended.

Besides securing a much larger amount of space than had been re-served, Major Handy obtained the gratifying assurance that the United States will be placed on a footing with the most favored nations, and " that in the installation of every important department the United States will have a location commensurate with the dignity and impor-tance of the country and adjoining in every case countries of the first rank."

In view of the magnitude and importance of the approaching expo-sition, and of our standing among the nations which will be there represented, and in view also of our increased population and acknowl-edged progress in arts, science, and manufactures, I earnestly commend the report of Major Handy to your consideration, and trust that a liberal appropriation may be made.

Moreover, the magnificent exhibit of the French Republic at Chicago in 1893, on which a million dollars were expended, should be a strong incentive to reciprocal liberality on the part of the Government of the United States, and suggests to our citizens the necessity as well as the propriety of installing at the Paris Exposition an exhibit on a par with that of the Government and people of France at Chicago, and in keep-ing with the scope and extent of the preparations which are being made by nearly all the important nations of the earth for their proposed ex-hibits in that exposition.

I suggest that the subject be given timely and favorable considera-tion.   WILLIAM McKINLEY.

EXECUTIVE MANSION,
Washington, January 14, 1898.

To the Congress of the United States:

I transmit herewith a report from the Secretary of State in regard to the award of the commissioners appointed pursuant to the stipulations of the convention of February 8, 1896, between the United States and Great Britain, providing for the settlement of the claims presented by the latter against the former in virtue of the convention of February 29, 1892.

The report of the Secretary of State presents a clear epitome of the award and renders unnecessary any extended observations on my part further than to say that I cordially coincide with his recommendation and that our treaty obligations demand prompt and favorable action by Congress, which I urgently hope may be taken, to the end that these long-pending questions may be finally and satisfactorily termi-nated.

The total amount necessary to satisfy the award of the commissioners is $473,151.26, which I recommend be appropriated.

WILLIAM McKINLEY.

EXECUTIVE MANSION,
Washington, January 18, 1898.

To the Congress of the United States:

I transmit herewith a report from the Secretary of State, with accompanying papers, touching the lynching in 1895 at Yreka, Cal., of Luis Moreno, a Mexican citizen, and the demand of the Mexican Government for an indemnity for his relatives on account thereof.

Following the course adopted in the case of the lynching of three Italian subjects at Hahnville, La., on August 8, 1896, I recommend the appropriation by Congress, out of humane consideration and without reference to the question of liability of the Government of the United States in the premises, of the sum of $2,000 to be paid by the Secretary of State to the Government of Mexico, to be by that Government distributed among the heirs of the above-named Luis Moreno.

WILLIAM McKINLEY.

EXECUTIVE MANSION.
Washington, January 26, 1898.

To the Congress:

I transmit herewith a report from the Secretary of State and accompanying papers presenting the claim of Capt. B. Tellefsen, of the Norwegian steamer *Albert*, against the Government of the United States, for $998.96, being the expenses incurred by him in consequence of a violation of Article XIII of the treaty of commerce and navigation of 1827 between the United States and Sweden and Norway.

WILLIAM McKINLEY.

EXECUTIVE MANSION,
Washington, March 22, 1898.

To the Senate:

In connection with Senate Document No. 39, Fifty-fifth Congress, second session, and in further response to the resolution of the Senate of July 12, 1897, I transmit herewith a report from the Secretary of State, with additional papers, relating to postal telegraphs, telephones, and postal savings banks in Austria.   WILLIAM McKINLEY.

EXECUTIVE MANSION, *March 28, 1898.*
To the Congress of the United States:

For some time prior to the visit of the *Maine* to Havana Harbor our consular representatives pointed out the advantages to flow from the visit of national ships to the Cuban waters, in accustoming the people to the presence of our flag as the symbol of good will and of our ships in the fulfillment of the mission of protection to American interests, even though no immediate need therefor might exist.

Accordingly, on the 24th of January last, after conference with the Spanish minister, in which the renewal of visits of our war vessels to Spanish waters was discussed and accepted, the peninsular authorities at Madrid and Havana were advised of the purpose of this Government to resume friendly naval visits at Cuban ports, and that in that view the *Maine* would forthwith call at the port of Havana.

This announcement was received by the Spanish Government with appreciation of the friendly character of the visit of the *Maine* and with notification of intention to return the courtesy by sending Spanish ships to the principal ports of the United States. Meanwhile the *Maine* entered the port of Havana on the 25th of January, her arrival being marked with no special incident besides the exchange of customary salutes and ceremonial visits.

The *Maine* continued in the harbor of Havana during the three weeks following her arrival. No appreciable excitement attended her stay. On the contrary, a feeling of relief and confidence followed the resumption of the long-interrupted friendly intercourse. So noticeable was this immediate effect of her visit that the consul-general strongly urged that the presence of our ships in Cuban waters should be kept up by retaining the *Maine* at Havana, or, in the event of her recall, by sending another vessel there to take her place.

At forty minutes past 9 in the evening of the 15th of February the *Maine* was destroyed by an explosion, by which the entire forward part of the ship was utterly wrecked. In this catastrophe 2 officers and 264 of her crew perished, those who were not killed outright by her explosion being penned between decks by the tangle of wreckage and drowned by the immediate sinking of the hull.

Prompt assistance was rendered by the neighboring vessels anchored in the harbor, aid being especially given by the boats of the Spanish cruiser *Alfonso XII* and the Ward Line steamer *City of Washington*, which lay not far distant. The wounded were generously cared for by the authorities of Havana, the hospitals being freely opened to them, while the earliest recovered bodies of the dead were interred by the municipality in a public cemetery in the city. Tributes of grief and sympathy were offered from all official quarters of the island.

The appalling calamity fell upon the people of our country with crushing force, and for a brief time an intense excitement prevailed, which in a community less just and self-controlled than ours might have led to hasty acts of blind resentment. This spirit, however, soon gave way to the calmer processes of reason and to the resolve to investigate the facts and await material proof before forming a judgment as to the cause, the responsibility, and, if the facts warranted, the remedy due. This course necessarily recommended itself from the outset to the Executive, for only in the light of a dispassionately ascertained certainty could it determine the nature and measure of its full duty in the matter.

The usual procedure was followed, as in all cases of casualty or disaster to national vessels of any maritime state. A naval court of inquiry was at once organized, composed of officers well qualified by rank and practical experience to discharge the onerous duty imposed upon them. Aided by a strong force of wreckers and divers, the court proceeded to make a thorough investigation on the spot, employing every available means for the impartial and exact determination of the causes of the explosion. Its operations have been conducted with the utmost deliberation and judgment, and, while independently pursued, no attainable source of information was neglected, and the fullest opportunity was allowed for a simultaneous investigation by the Spanish authorities.

The finding of the court of inquiry was reached, after twenty-three days of continuous labor, on the 21st of March instant, and, having been approved on the 22d by the commander in chief of the United States naval force on the North Atlantic station, was transmitted to the Executive.

It is herewith laid before the Congress, together with the voluminous testimony taken before the court.

Its purport is, in brief, as follows:

When the *Maine* arrived at Havana, she was conducted by the regular Government pilot to buoy No. 4, to which she was moored in from 5½ to 6 fathoms of water.

The state of discipline on board and the condition of her magazines, boilers, coal bunkers, and storage compartments are passed in review, with the conclusion that excellent order prevailed and that no indication of any cause for an internal explosion existed in any quarter.

At 8 o'clock in the evening of February 15 everything had been reported secure, and all was quiet.

At forty minutes past 9 o'clock the vessel was suddenly destroyed.

There were two distinct explosions, with a brief interval between them. The first lifted the forward part of the ship very perceptibly; the second, which was more open, prolonged, and of greater volume, is attributed by the court to the partial explosion of two or more of the forward magazines.

The evidence of the divers establishes that the after part of the ship was practically intact and sank in that condition a very few moments after the explosion. The forward part was completely demolished.

Upon the evidence of a concurrent external cause the finding of the court is as follows:

At frame 17 the outer shell of the ship, from a point 11½ feet from the middle line of the ship and 6 feet above the keel when in its normal position, has been forced up so as to be now about 4 feet above the surface of the water, therefore about 34 feet above where it would be had the ship sunk uninjured.

The outside bottom plating is bent into a reversed V shape (∧), the after wing of which, about 15 feet broad and 32 feet in length (from frame 17 to frame 25), is doubled back upon itself against the continuation of the same plating, extending forward.

At frame 18 the vertical keel is broken in two and the flat keel bent into an angle similar to the angle formed by the outside bottom plates. This break is now about 6 feet below the surface of the water and about 30 feet above its normal position.

In the opinion of the court this effect could have been produced only by the explosion of a mine situated under the bottom of the ship at about frame 18 and somewhat on the port side of the ship.

The conclusions of the court are:

That the loss of the *Maine* was not in any respect due to fault or negligence on the part of any of the officers or members of her crew;

That the ship was destroyed by the explosion of a submarine mine, which caused the partial explosion of two or more of her forward magazines; and

That no evidence has been obtainable fixing the responsibility for the destruction of the *Maine* upon any person or persons.

I have directed that the finding of the court of inquiry and the views of this Government thereon be communicated to the Government of Her Majesty the Queen Regent, and I do not permit myself to doubt that the sense of justice of the Spanish nation will dictate a course of action suggested by honor and the friendly relations of the two Governments.

It will be the duty of the Executive to advise the Congress of the result, and in the meantime deliberate consideration is invoked.

WILLIAM McKINLEY.

EXECUTIVE MANSION, *March 31, 1898.*

To the Congress:

I transmit herewith, for the information of Congress, a communication from the Secretary of Agriculture covering a detailed report showing the present condition of the beet-sugar industry in this country and the results of experiments made by the Department of Agriculture in the production of sugar from beets in the United States during the past year.   WILLIAM McKINLEY.

EXECUTIVE MANSION,
Washington, April 4, 1898.

To the Senate of the United States:

In response to the resolution of the Senate of January 17, 1898, I transmit a report from the Secretary of State, accompanied by copies of correspondence exchanged between Henry Woodruff, trustee and of counsel for the holders of a majority of the first-mortgage bonds of " The Railway of the East," of Venezuela, *et al.*, and the Department of

State, and by a list of claims of citizens of the United States presented after August 1, 1898, and, so far as appears, not settled by Venezuela, nor disposed of by the commission of 1889–90.

WILLIAM McKINLEY.

EXECUTIVE MANSION, *April 7, 1898.*

To the Senate:

In response to the resolution of the Senate of February 26, 1898, requesting the President " if not incompatible with the public interest, to transmit to the Senate the proceedings of the international commission authorized in the concurrent resolution of Congress of April 29, 1890, and a subsequent international convention between the United States and Mexico of May 6, 1896, and also the correspondence relating thereto with Mexico by the Department of the Interior, Department of War, and Department of Justice, as well as the Department of State, relating to the equitable distribution of the waters of the Rio Grande River, including the draft of an incomplete treaty between said Governments, negotiated between the late Secretary of State, Mr. Olney, on the part of the United States, and Mr. Romero, on the part of Mexico, and all the correspondence between said officials relating thereto," I transmit herewith reports from the Secretary of State, the Secretary of War, the Secretary of the Interior, and the Attorney-General, with accompanying papers.

WILLIAM McKINLEY.

EXECUTIVE MANSION, *April 11, 1898.*

To the Congress of the United States:

Obedient to that precept of the Constitution which commands the President to give from time to time to the Congress information of the state of the Union and to recommend to their consideration such measures as he shall judge necessary and expedient, it becomes my duty to now address your body with regard to the grave crisis that has arisen in the relations of the United States to Spain by reason of the warfare that for more than three years has raged in the neighboring island of Cuba.

I do so because of the intimate connection of the Cuban question with the state of our own Union and the grave relation the course which it is now incumbent upon the nation to adopt must needs bear to the traditional policy of our Government if it is to accord with the precepts laid down by the founders of the Republic and religiously observed by succeeding Administrations to the present day.

The present revolution is but the successor of other similar insurrections which have occurred in Cuba against the dominion of Spain, extending over a period of nearly half a century, each of which during its

SURRENDER OF SANTIAGO—PEACE MAKERS AT PARIS—
McKINLEY SIGNING PEACE PROTOCOL

PEACE NEGOTIATIONS

By July 3, 1898, the Spanish commander in Santiago saw that he would have to surrender. On July 5th he proposed to withdraw but was refused the privilege. From that date until the 10th, skirmishing and parleying were intermittent. On the 16th the final terms of surrender were arranged. It provided that the Spanish Army should have the honors of war. They marched out, stacked arms, and were transported by the United States to Spain.

On August 12, 1898, through the efforts of the French Ambassador, a peace protocol was drawn up and signed by McKinley, thus ending hostilities but little more than a month after their commencement.

On December 10, 1898, the treaty of peace was signed at Paris.

For full details, see President McKinley's wartime messages, which form the official record; and the articles "Spanish-American War," "Santiago (Cuba), Battle of," "Santiago Harbor, Battle of," and "Spain, Treaties With," in the encyclopedic index (volume eleven).

progress has subjected the United States to great effort and expense in enforcing its neutrality laws, caused enormous losses to American trade and commerce, caused irritation, annoyance, and disturbance among our citizens, and, by the exercise of cruel, barbarous, and uncivilized practices of warfare, shocked the sensibilities and offended the humane sympathies of our people.

Since the present revolution began, in February, 1895, this country has seen the fertile domain at our threshold ravaged by fire and sword in the course of a struggle unequaled in the history of the island and rarely paralleled as to the numbers of the combatants and the bitterness of the contest by any revolution of modern times where a dependent people striving to be free have been opposed by the power of the sovereign state.

Our people have beheld a once prosperous community reduced to comparative want, its lucrative commerce virtually paralyzed, its exceptional productiveness diminished, its fields laid waste, its mills in ruins, and its people perishing by tens of thousands from hunger and destitution. We have found ourselves constrained, in the observance of that strict neutrality which our laws enjoin and which the law of nations commands, to police our own waters and watch our own seaports in prevention of any unlawful act in aid of the Cubans.

Our trade has suffered, the capital invested by our citizens in Cuba has been largely lost, and the temper and forbearance of our people have been so sorely tried as to beget a perilous unrest among our own citizens, which has inevitably found its expression from time to time in the National Legislature, so that issues wholly external to our own body politic engross attention and stand in the way of that close devotion to domestic advancement that becomes a self-contained commonwealth whose primal maxim has been the avoidance of all foreign entanglements. All this must needs awaken, and has, indeed, aroused, the utmost concern on the part of this Government, as well during my predecessor's term as in my own.

In April, 1896, the evils from which our country suffered through the Cuban war became so onerous that my predecessor made an effort to bring about a peace through the mediation of this Government in any way that might tend to an honorable adjustment of the contest between Spain and her revolted colony, on the basis of some effective scheme of self-government for Cuba under the flag and sovereignty of Spain. It failed through the refusal of the Spanish government then in power to consider any form of mediation or, indeed, any plan of settlement which did not begin with the actual submission of the insurgents to the mother country, and then only on such terms as Spain herself might see fit to grant. The war continued unabated. The resistance of the insurgents was in no wise diminished.

The efforts of Spain were increased, both by the dispatch of fresh levies to Cuba and by the addition to the horrors of the strife of a new and inhuman phase happily unprecedented in the modern history of civilized Christian peoples. The policy of devastation and concentration, inaugurated by the Captain-General's *bando* of October 21, 1896, in the Province of Pinar del Rio was thence extended to embrace all of the island to which the power of the Spanish arms was able to reach by occupation or by military operations. The peasantry, including all dwelling in the open agricultural interior, were driven into the garrison towns or isolated places held by the troops.

The raising and movement of provisions of all kinds were interdicted. The fields were laid waste, dwellings unroofed and fired, mills destroyed, and, in short, everything that could desolate the land and render it unfit for human habitation or support was commanded by one or the other of the contending parties and executed by all the powers at their disposal.

By the time the present Administration took office, a year ago, reconcentration (so called) had been made effective over the better part of the four central and western provinces—Santa Clara, Matanzas, Havana, and Pinar del Rio.

The agricultural population to the estimated number of 300,000 or more was herded within the towns and their immediate vicinage, deprived of the means of support, rendered destitute of shelter, left poorly clad, and exposed to the most unsanitary conditions. As the scarcity of food increased with the devastation of the depopulated areas of production, destitution and want became misery and starvation. Month by month the death rate increased in an alarming ratio. By March, 1897, according to conservative estimates from official Spanish sources, the mortality among the reconcentrados from starvation and the diseases thereto incident exceeded 50 per cent of their total number.

No practical relief was accorded to the destitute. The overburdened towns, already suffering from the general dearth, could give no aid. So-called "zones of cultivation" established within the immediate areas of effective military control about the cities and fortified camps proved illusory as a remedy for the suffering. The unfortunates, being for the most part women and children, with aged and helpless men, enfeebled by disease and hunger, could not have tilled the soil without tools, seed, or shelter for their own support or for the supply of the cities. Reconcentration, adopted avowedly as a war measure in order to cut off the resources of the insurgents, worked its predestined result. As I said in my message of last December, it was not civilized warfare; it was extermination. The only peace it could beget was that of the wilderness and the grave.

Meanwhile the military situation in the island had undergone a noticeable change. The extraordinary activity that characterized the second year of the war, when the insurgents invaded even the thitherto unharmed fields of Pinar del Rio and carried havoc and destruction up to the walls of the city of Havana itself, had relapsed into a dogged struggle in the central and eastern provinces. The Spanish arms regained a measure of control in Pinar del Rio and parts of Havana, but, under the existing conditions of the rural country, without immediate improvement of their productive situation. Even thus partially restricted, the revolutionists held their own, and their conquest and submission, put forward by Spain as the essential and sole basis of peace, seemed as far distant as at the outset.

In this state of affairs my Administration found itself confronted with the grave problem of its duty. My message of last December * reviewed the situation and narrated the steps taken with a view to relieving its acuteness and opening the way to some form of honorable settlement. The assassination of the prime minister, Canovas, led to a change of government in Spain. The former administration, pledged to subjugation without concession, gave place to that of a more liberal party, committed long in advance to a policy of reform involving the wider principle of home rule for Cuba and Puerto Rico.

The overtures of this Government made through its new envoy, General Woodford, and looking to an immediate and effective amelioration of the condition of the island, although not accepted to the extent of admitted mediation in any shape, were met by assurances that home rule in an advanced phase would be forthwith offered to Cuba, without waiting for the war to end, and that more humane methods should thenceforth prevail in the conduct of hostilities. Coincidentally with these declarations the new government of Spain continued and completed the policy, already begun by its predecessor, of testifying friendly regard for this nation by releasing American citizens held under one charge or another connected with the insurrection, so that by the end of November not a single person entitled in any way to our national protection remained in a Spanish prison.

While these negotiations were in progress the increasing destitution of the unfortunate reconcentrados and the alarming mortality among them claimed earnest attention. The success which had attended the limited measure of relief extended to the suffering American citizens among them by the judicious expenditure through the consular agencies of the money appropriated expressly for their succor by the joint resolution approved May 24, 1897, prompted the humane extension of a similar scheme of aid to the great body of sufferers. A suggestion to this end was acquiesced in by the Spanish authorities.

On the 24th of December last I caused to be issued an appeal to the American people inviting contributions in money or in kind for the succor of the starving sufferers in Cuba, following this on the 8th of January by a similar public announcement of the formation of a central Cuban relief committee, with headquarters in New York City, composed of three members representing the American National Red Cross and the religious and business elements of the community.

The efforts of that committee have been untiring and have accomplished much. Arrangements for free transportation to Cuba have greatly aided the charitable work. The president of the American Red Cross and representatives of other contributory organizations have generously visited Cuba and cooperated with the consul-general and the local authorities to make effective distribution of the relief collected through the efforts of the central committee. Nearly $200,000 in money and supplies has already reached the sufferers, and more is forthcoming. The supplies are admitted duty free, and transportation to the interior has been arranged, so that the relief, at first necessarily confined to Havana and the larger cities, is now extended through most, if not all, of the towns where suffering exists.

Thousands of lives have already been saved. The necessity for a change in the condition of the reconcentrados is recognized by the Spanish Government. Within a few days past the orders of General Weyler have been revoked. The reconcentrados, it is said, are to be permitted to return to their homes and aided to resume the self-supporting pursuits of peace. Public works have been ordered to give them employment and a sum of $600,000 has been appropriated for their relief.

The war in Cuba is of such a nature that, short of subjugation or extermination, a final military victory for either side seems impracticable. The alternative lies in the physical exhaustion of the one or the other party, or perhaps of both—a condition which in effect ended the ten years' war by the truce of Zanjon. The prospect of such a protraction and conclusion of the present strife is a contingency hardly to be contemplated with equanimity by the civilized world, and least of all by the United States, affected and injured as we are, deeply and intimately, by its very existence.

Realizing this, it appeared to be my duty, in a spirit of true friendliness, no less to Spain than to the Cubans, who have so much to lose by the prolongation of the struggle, to seek to bring about an immediate termination of the war. To this end I submitted on the 27th ultimo, as a result of much representation and correspondence, through the United States minister at Madrid, propositions to the Spanish Government looking to an armistice until October 1 for the negotiation of peace with the good offices of the President.

In addition I asked the immediate revocation of the order of reconcentration, so as to permit the people to return to their farms and the needy to be relieved with provisions and supplies from the United States, cooperating with the Spanish authorities, so as to afford full relief.

The reply of the Spanish cabinet was received on the night of the 31st ultimo. It offered, as the means to bring about peace in Cuba, to confide the preparation thereof to the insular parliament, inasmuch as the concurrence of that body would be necessary to reach a final result, it being, however, understood that the powers reserved by the constitution to the central Government are not lessened or diminished. As the Cuban parliament does not meet until the 4th of May next, the Spanish Government would not object for its part to accept at once a suspension of hostilities if asked for by the insurgents from the general in chief, to whom it would pertain in such case to determine the duration and conditions of the armistice.

The propositions submitted by General Woodford and the reply of the Spanish Government were both in the form of brief memoranda, the texts of which are before me and are substantially in the language above given. The function of the Cuban parliament in the matter of "preparing" peace and the manner of its doing so are not expressed in the Spanish memorandum, but from General Woodford's explanatory reports of preliminary discussions preceding the final conference it is understood that the Spanish Government stands ready to give the insular congress full powers to settle the terms of peace with the insurgents, whether by direct negotiation or indirectly by means of legislation does not appear.

With this last overture in the direction of immediate peace, and its disappointing reception by Spain, the Executive is brought to the end of his effort.

In my annual message of December last I said:

Of the untried measures there remain only: Recognition of the insurgents as belligerents; recognition of the independence of Cuba; neutral intervention to end the war by imposing a rational compromise between the contestants, and intervention in favor of one or the other party. I speak not of forcible annexation, for that can not be thought of. That, by our code of morality, would be criminal aggression.

Thereupon I reviewed these alternatives in the light of President Grant's measured words, uttered in 1875, when, after seven years of sanguinary, destructive, and cruel hostilities in Cuba, he reached the conclusion that the recognition of the independence of Cuba was impracticable and indefensible and that the recognition of belligerence was not warranted by the facts according to the tests of public law. I commented especially upon the latter aspect of the question, pointing out the inconveniences and positive dangers of a recognition of belligerence, which, while adding to the already onerous burdens of neutrality within our own jurisdiction, could not in any way extend our influence or effective offices in the territory of hostilities.

Nothing has since occurred to change my view in this regard, and I recognize as fully now as then that the issuance of a proclamation of neutrality, by which process the so-called recognition of belligerents is published, could of itself and unattended by other action accomplish nothing toward the one end for which we labor—the instant pacification of Cuba and the cessation of the misery that afflicts the island.

Turning to the question of recognizing at this time the independence of the present insurgent government in Cuba, we find safe precedents in our history from an early day. They are well summed up in President Jackson's message to Congress, December 21, 1836, on the subject of the recognition of the independence of Texas. He said:

In all the contests that have arisen out of the revolutions of France, out of the disputes relating to the crowns of Portugal and Spain, out of the revolutionary movements of those Kingdoms, out of the separation of the American possessions of both from the European Governments, and out of the numerous and constantly occurring struggles for dominion in Spanish America, so wisely consistent with our just principles has been the action of our Government that we have under the most critical circumstances avoided all censure and encountered no other evil than that produced by a transient estrangement of good will in those against whom we have been by force of evidence compelled to decide.

It has thus been made known to the world that the uniform policy and practice of the United States is to avoid all interference in disputes which merely relate to the internal government of other nations, and eventually to recognize the authority of the prevailing party, without reference to our particular interests and views or to the merits of the original controversy.

* * * * * * *

* * * But on this as on every trying occasion safety is to be found in a rigid adherence to principle.

In the contest between Spain and her revolted colonies we stood aloof and waited, not only until the ability of the new States to protect themselves was fully established, but until the danger of their being again subjugated had entirely passed away. Then, and not till then, were they recognized. Such was our course in regard to Mexico herself. * * * It is true that, with regard to Texas, the civil authority of Mexico has been expelled, its invading army defeated, the chief of the Republic himself captured, and all present power to control the newly organized Government of Texas annihilated within its confines. But, on the other hand, there is, in appearance at least, an immense disparity of physical force on the side of Mexico. The Mexican Republic under another Executive is rallying its forces under a new leader and menacing a fresh invasion to recover its lost dominion.

Upon the issue of this threatened invasion the independence of Texas may be considered as suspended, and were there nothing peculiar in the relative situation of the United States and Texas our acknowledgment of its independence at such a crisis could scarcely be regarded as consistent with that prudent reserve with which we have heretofore held ourselves bound to treat all similar questions.

Thereupon Andrew Jackson proceeded to consider the risk that there might be imputed to the United States motives of selfish interest in view of the former claim on our part to the territory of Texas and of the avowed purpose of the Texans in seeking recognition of independence as an incident to the incorporation of Texas in the Union, concluding thus:

Prudence, therefore, seems to dictate that we should still stand aloof and maintain our present attitude, if not until Mexico itself or one of the great foreign powers shall recognize the independence of the new Government, at least until the lapse of time or the course of events shall have proved beyond cavil or dispute the ability of the people of that country to maintain their separate sovereignty and to uphold the Government constituted by them. Neither of the contending parties can justly complain of this course. By pursuing it we are but carrying out the long-established policy of our Government—a policy which has secured to us respect and influence abroad and inspired confidence at home.

These are the words of the resolute and patriotic Jackson. They are evidence that the United States, in addition to the test imposed by public law as the condition of the recognition of independence by a neutral state (to wit, that the revolted state shall "constitute in fact a body politic, having a government in substance as well as in name, possessed of the elements of stability," and forming *de facto*, "if left to itself, a state among the nations, reasonably capable of discharging the duties of a state"), has imposed for its own governance in dealing with cases like these the further condition that recognition of independent statehood is not due to a revolted dependency until the danger of its being again subjugated by the parent state has entirely passed away.

This extreme test was, in fact, applied in the case of Texas. The Congress to whom President Jackson referred the question as one "probably leading to war," and therefore a proper subject for "a previous understanding with that body by whom war can alone be declared and by whom all the provisions for sustaining its perils must be furnished," left the matter of the recognition of Texas to the discretion of the Executive, providing merely for the sending of a diplomatic agent when the President should be satisfied that the Republic of Texas had become "an independent state." It was so recognized by President Van Buren, who commissioned a chargé d'affaires March 7, 1837, after Mexico had abandoned an attempt to reconquer the Texan territory, and when there was at the time no *bona fide* contest going on between the insurgent province and its former sovereign.

I said in my message of December last:

It is to be seriously considered whether the Cuban insurrection possesses beyond dispute the attributes of statehood, which alone can demand the recognition of belligerency in its favor.

The same requirement must certainly be no less seriously considered when the graver issue of recognizing independence is in question, for no less positive test can be applied to the greater act than to the lesser, while, on the other hand, the influences and consequences of the struggle upon the internal policy of the recognizing state, which form important factors when the recognition of belligerency is concerned, are secondary, if not rightly eliminable, factors when the real question is whether the community claiming recognition is or is not independent beyond peradventure.

Nor from the standpoint of expediency do I think it would be wise or prudent for this Government to recognize at the present time the independence of the so-called Cuban Republic. Such recognition is not necessary in order to enable the United States to intervene and pacify the island. To commit this country now to the recognition of any particular government in Cuba might subject us to embarrassing conditions of international obligation toward the organization so recognized. In case of intervention our conduct would be subject to the approval or disapproval of such government. We would be required to submit to its direction and to assume to it the mere relation of a friendly ally.

When it shall appear hereafter that there is within the island a government capable of performing the duties and discharging the functions of a separate nation, and having as a matter of fact the proper forms and attributes of nationality, such government can be promptly and readily recognized and the relations and interests of the United States with such nation adjusted.

There remain the alternative forms of intervention to end the war, either as an impartial neutral, by imposing a rational compromise between the contestants, or as the active ally of the one party or the other.

As to the first, it is not to be forgotten that during the last few months the relation of the United States has virtually been one of friendly intervention in many ways, each not of itself conclusive, but all tending to the exertion of a potential influence toward an ultimate pacific result, just and honorable to all interests concerned. The spirit of all our acts hitherto has been an earnest, unselfish desire for peace and prosperity in Cuba, untarnished by differences between us and Spain and unstained by the blood of American citizens.

The forcible intervention of the United States as a neutral to stop the war, according to the large dictates of humanity and following many historical precedents where neighboring states have interfered to check the hopeless sacrifices of life by internecine conflicts beyond their borders, is justifiable on rational grounds. It involves, however, hostile constraint upon both the parties to the contest, as well to enforce a truce as to guide the eventual settlement.

The grounds for such intervention may be briefly summarized as follows:

First. In the cause of humanity and to put an end to the barbarities, bloodshed, starvation, and horrible miseries now existing there, and which the parties to the conflict are either unable or unwilling to stop or mitigate. It is no answer to say this is all in another country, belonging to another nation, and is therefore none of our business. It is specially our duty, for it is right at our door.

Second. We owe it to our citizens in Cuba to afford them that protection and indemnity for life and property which no government there can or will afford, and to that end to terminate the conditions that deprive them of legal protection.

Third. The right to intervene may be justified by the very serious injury to the commerce, trade, and business of our people and by the wanton destruction of property and devastation of the island.

Fourth, and which is of the utmost importance. The present condition of affairs in Cuba is a constant menace to our peace and entails upon this Government an enormous expense. With such a conflict waged for years in an island so near us and with which our people have such trade and business relations; when the lives and liberty of our citizens are in constant danger and their property destroyed and themselves ruined; where our trading vessels are liable to seizure and are seized at our very door by war ships of a foreign nation; the expeditions of filibustering that we are powerless to prevent altogether, and the irritating questions and entanglements thus arising—all these and others that I need not mention, with the resulting strained relations, are a constant menace to our peace and compel us to keep on a semi war footing with a nation with which we are at peace.

These elements of danger and disorder already pointed out have been strikingly illustrated by a tragic event which has deeply and justly moved the American people. I have already transmitted to Congress the report of the naval court of inquiry on the destruction of the battle ship *Maine* in the harbor of Havana during the night of the 15th of February.* The destruction of that noble vessel has filled the national heart with inexpressible horror. Two hundred and fifty-eight brave sailors and marines and two officers of our Navy, reposing in the fancied security of a friendly harbor, have been hurled to death, grief and want brought to their homes and sorrow to the nation.

The naval court of inquiry, which, it is needless to say, commands the unqualified confidence of the Government, was unanimous in its conclusion that the destruction of the *Maine* was caused by an exterior explosion—that of a submarine mine. It did not assume to place the responsibility. That remains to be fixed.

In any event, the destruction of the *Maine*, by whatever exterior cause, is a patent and impressive proof of a state of things in Cuba that is intolerable. That condition is thus shown to be such that the Spanish Government can not assure safety and security to a vessel of the American Navy in the harbor of Havana on a mission of peace, and rightfully there.

Further referring in this connection to recent diplomatic correspondence, a dispatch from our minister to Spain of the 26th ultimo contained the statement that the Spanish minister for foreign affairs assured him positively that Spain will do all that the highest honor and justice require in the matter of the *Maine*. The reply above referred to, of the 31st ultimo, also contained an expression of the readiness of Spain to submit to an arbitration all the differences which can arise in this matter, which is subsequently explained by the note of the Spanish minister at Washington of the 10th instant, as follows:

As to the question of fact which springs from the diversity of views between the reports of the American and Spanish boards, Spain proposes that the facts be ascertained by an impartial investigation by experts, whose decision Spain accepts in advance.

To this I have made no reply.

* See pp. 6277-6280.

President Grant, in 1875, after discussing the phases of the contest as it then appeared and its hopeless and apparent indefinite prolongation, said:

In such event I am of opinion that other nations will be compelled to assume the responsibility which devolves upon them, and to seriously consider the only remaining measures possible—mediation and intervention. Owing, perhaps, to the large expanse of water separating the island from the peninsula, * * * the contending parties appear to have within themselves no depository of common confidence to suggest wisdom when passion and excitement have their sway and to assume the part of peacemaker. In this view in the earlier days of the contest the good offices of the United States as a mediator were tendered in good faith, without any selfish purpose, in the interest of humanity and in sincere friendship for both parties, but were at the time declined by Spain, with the declaration, nevertheless, that at a future time they would be indispensable. No intimation has been received that in the opinion of Spain that time has been reached. And yet the strife continues, with all its dread horrors and all its injuries to the interests of the United States and of other nations. Each party seems quite capable of working great injury and damage to the other, as well as to all the relations and interests dependent on the existence of peace in the island; but they seem incapable of reaching any adjustment, and both have thus far failed of achieving any success whereby one party shall possess and control the island to the exclusion of the other. Under these circumstances the agency of others, either by mediation or by intervention, seems to be the only alternative which must, sooner or later, be invoked for the termination of the strife.

In the last annual message of my immediate predecessor, during the pending struggle, it was said:

When the inability of Spain to deal successfully with the insurrection has become manifest and it is demonstrated that her sovereignty is extinct in Cuba for all purposes of its rightful existence, and when a hopeless struggle for its reestablishment has degenerated into a strife which means nothing more than the useless sacrifice of human life and the utter destruction of the very subject-matter of the conflict, a situation will be presented in which our obligations to the sovereignty of Spain will be superseded by higher obligations, which we can hardly hesitate to recognize and discharge.

In my annual message to Congress December last, speaking to this question, I said:

The near future will demonstrate whether the indispensable condition of a righteous peace, just alike to the Cubans and to Spain, as well as equitable to all our interests so intimately involved in the welfare of Cuba, is likely to be attained. If not, the exigency of further and other action by the United States will remain to be taken. When that time comes, that action will be determined in the line of indisputable right and duty. It will be faced, without misgiving or hesitancy, in the light of the obligation this Government owes to itself, to the people who have confided to it the protection of their interests and honor, and to humanity.

Sure of the right, keeping free from all offense ourselves, actuated only by upright and patriotic considerations, moved neither by passion nor selfishness, the Government will continue its watchful care over the rights and property of American citizens and will abate none of its efforts to bring about by peaceful agencies a peace which shall be honorable and enduring. If it shall hereafter appear to be a duty imposed by our obligations to ourselves, to civilization, and humanity to intervene with force, it shall be without fault on our part and only because the necessity for such action will be so clear as to command the support and approval of the civilized world.

The long trial has proved that the object for which Spain has waged the war can not be attained. The fire of insurrection may flame or may smolder with varying seasons, but it has not been and it is plain that it can not be extinguished by present methods. The only hope of relief and repose from a condition which can no longer be endured is the enforced pacification of Cuba. In the name of humanity, in the name of civiliza-tion, in behalf of endangered American interests which give us the right and the duty to speak and to act, the war in Cuba must stop.

In view of these facts and of these considerations I ask the Congress to authorize and empower the President to take measures to secure a full and final termination of hostilities between the Government of Spain and the people of Cuba, and to secure in the island the establishment of a stable government, capable of maintaining order and observing its international obligations, insuring peace and tranquillity and the security of its citizens as well as our own, and to use the military and naval forces of the United States as may be necessary for these purposes.

And in the interest of humanity and to aid in preserving the lives of the starving people of the island I recommend that the distribution of food and supplies be continued and that an appropriation be made out of the public Treasury to supplement the charity of our citizens.

The issue is now with the Congress. It is a solemn responsibility. I have exhausted every effort to relieve the intolerable condition of affairs which is at our doors. Prepared to execute every obligation imposed upon me by the Constitution and the law, I await your action.

Yesterday, and since the preparation of the foregoing message, official information was received by me that the latest decree of the Queen Regent of Spain directs General Blanco, in order to prepare and facilitate peace, to proclaim a suspension of hostilities, the duration and details of which have not yet been communicated to me.

This fact, with every other pertinent consideration, will, I am sure, have your just and careful attention in the solemn deliberations upon which you are about to enter. If this measure attains a successful result, then our aspirations as a Christian, peace-loving people will be realized. If it fails, it will be only another justification for our contemplated action.

WILLIAM McKINLEY.

EXECUTIVE MANSION,
Washington, April 11, 1898.

To the Senate of the United States:

I transmit herewith, in response to a resolution of the Senate of the 14th of February last, calling for information and correspondence in re-gard to the condition of the island of Cuba and to negotiations for com-mercial relations between the United States and that island, a report of the Secretary of State, with its accompanying correspondence, covering the first inquiry of the resolution, together with a report of the special commissioner plenipotentiary charged with commercial negotiations under the provisions of the tariff act approved July 24, 1897, in response to the second inquiry.

WILLIAM McKINLEY.

DEPARTMENT OF STATE,
Washington, April 11, 1898.

The PRESIDENT:

The Secretary of State has had the honor to receive, by reference from the President, a resolution adopted in the Senate of the United States on the 14th of February last, reading as follows:

"*Resolved*, That the President is requested, if in his opinion it is not incompatible with the public service, to send to the Senate copies of the reports of the consul-general and of the consuls of the United States in Cuba written or received since March 4, 1897, which relate to the state of war in that island and the condition of the people there, or that he will send such parts of said reports as will inform the Senate as to these facts.

"Second. That the President inform the Senate whether any agent of a government in Cuba has been accredited to this Government or the President of the United States with authority to negotiate a treaty of reciprocity with the United States, or any other diplomatic or commercial agreement with the United States, and whether such person has been recognized and received as the representative of such government in Cuba."

This resolution contemplates answer being made to two separable inquiries: First, in relation to the present condition of affairs in Cuba, and, secondly, with regard to the action had in view of the overtures of the Government of Spain for a reciprocal commercial agreement covering particularly the trade between the United States and the island of Cuba.

The conduct of commercial negotiations under the authority and in accordance with the conditions found in sections 3, 4, and 5 of the existing tariff act, approved July 24, 1897, having been intrusted to a special commissioner plenipotentiary duly empowered by the President to that end, it has been deemed convenient to leave to the commissioner the preparation of a report in answer to the second part of the Senate resolution, the undersigned reserving to himself the response to the first part thereof, which concerns the political and consular functions of the Department of State. The separate report of the Hon. John A. Kasson, special commissioner plenipotentiary, is therefore herewith independently submitted to the President with a view to its transmission to the Senate, should such a course be, in the President's judgment, not incompatible with the public service.

The Senate resolution, while in terms calling for the submission to that honorable body of all or of a practical selection of the reports of the consul-general and consuls of the United States in Cuba written or received since March 4, 1897, which relate to the state of war in that island and the condition of the people there, appears to leave it to the discretion of the President to direct the scope of the information to be so reported and the manner of its communication. The undersigned, having taken the President's direction on both these points, has the honor to lay before him a selection of the correspondence received by the Department of State from the various consular representatives in Cuba, aiming thereby to show the present situation in the island rather than to give a historical account of all the reported incidents since the date assigned by the resolution.

Respectfully submitted.

JOHN SHERMAN.

DEPARTMENT OF STATE, WASHINGTON,
Office of Special Commissioner Plenipotentiary.

The PRESIDENT:

In response to the following resolution of the Senate, passed under date of Feb. ruary 14, 1898, and which was referred to the undersigned for report, viz—

"Second. That the President inform the Senate whether any agent of a government in Cuba has been accredited to this Government or the President of the United States with authority to negotiate a treaty of reciprocity with the United States, or any other diplomatic or commercial agreement with the United States, and whether such person has been recognized and received as the representative of such government in Cuba"—

I have the honor to submit the following report:

In October, 1897, the minister of Spain at this capital verbally advised the undersigned that so soon as the new government in Spain had leisure to take up the question he would probably be authorized to enter into negotiations with the undersigned for reciprocal trade arrangements with Spain, and that a representative of Cuba would probably be associated for the interests of that island.

Under date of December 9, 1897, the minister of the United States at Madrid was instructed to ascertain the disposition of the Spanish Government in respect to these negotiations.

Under date of January 24, 1898, a dispatch from Mr. Woodford (referred to this office) advised the Secretary of State that arrangements were made for the negotiation of a commercial treaty between Spain and the United States; that separate provisions would be made for Cuba, and that the Cuban insular government would appoint a delegate to represent that island in the negotiations. This was accompanied by a memorandum from the Spanish minister of colonies, stating that the same rules as for Cuba might be applied to Puerto Rico, and suggesting a basis for the negotiations. This communication was referred to this office on the 4th of February.

On the 6th of February the Spanish minister, Mr. Dupuy de Lôme, called on the undersigned and announced that he was authorized to represent Spain in the pending negotiations and that a special representative would arrive from Cuba, under appointment of the insular government, to act as far as the interests of that island were involved. He mentioned the name of Señor Angulo as the gentleman who had been suggested in Cuba for that appointment; but the delegate was not officially notified to this office.

On March 17 a note from the Spanish minister, Señor Polo y Bernabé, addressed, under date of the 16th instant, to the Secretary of State, was referred to this office. In that note his excellency advised this Government of his appointment by Her Majesty the Queen Regent of Spain to conduct these negotiations, assisted by Señor Manuel Rafael Angulo as special delegate of the insular government of Cuba, who would be aided by two technical assistants, also appointed by the Cuban government; and, further, that an officer from the treasury department would be added in the same character.

His excellency announced his readiness to commence the labors of the commission so soon as the Government of the United States should formulate the general plan for carrying on the work.

Respectfully submitted, March 17, 1898.

JOHN A. KASSON,
Special Commissioner Plenipotentiary.

EXECUTIVE MANSION, *April 12, 1898.*

To the Senate of the United States:

In response to a resolution of the Senate of the 4th instant, I inclose herewith a letter from the Secretary of the Navy, inclosing a copy of a report from the Chief of the Bureau of Navigation.

WILLIAM McKINLEY.

NAVY DEPARTMENT,
Washington, April 9, 1898.

The PRESIDENT OF THE UNITED STATES SENATE.

SIR: I have the honor to acknowledge the receipt of Senate resolution of April 4, directing that the Senate be informed "of the total number of human lives that were lost by the sinking of the United States battle ship *Maine* in Havana Harbor, Cuba, on the 15th day of February, 1898, the total number of dead bodies rescued from said ship, the total number remaining unrescued, and what effort, if any, is being made to rescue them," and in reply thereto inclose a copy of a report from the Chief of the Bureau of Navigation covering the above inquiry.

I have the honor to be, sir, very respectfully,

JOHN D. LONG, *Secretary.*

MEMORANDUM FOR THE SECRETARY.

BUREAU OF NAVIGATION,
Washington, D. C., April 8, 1898.

Number on board the U. S. S. *Maine* at the time of the disaster:
Officers	26	
Sailors	290	
Marines	39	
		355

Number saved:
Officers	24	
Sailors	60	
Marines	11	
		95

Number lost:
Officers	2	
Sailors	230	
Marines	28	
		260
		355

Bodies recovered:
Officers	1	
Sailors and marines	177	

Died from injuries:
Sailors and marines	8	
		186

Of the number recovered there were buried—
In the cemetery at Havana	166	
At Key West	19	
At Pittsburg, Pa. (officer)	1	
		186

Number of bodies not recovered:
Officers	1	
Enlisted men and marines	73	
		74

The work of recovery was continued until April 6, when the wrecking tugs were withdrawn, and nothing is now being done in that direction so far as is known; and the last bodies reported as recovered were sent to Key West on the 30th ultimo. No estimate has been made of the portions of bodies which were recovered and buried. The large percentage of bodies not recovered is due, no doubt, to the fact that the men were swinging in their hammocks immediately over that portion of the vessel which was totally destroyed.

A. S. CROWNINSHIELD,
Chief of Bureau.

EXECUTIVE MANSION.
Washington, April 15, 1898.

To the Senate:

In connection with Senate Document No. 39, Fifty-fifth Congress, second session, and in further response to the resolution of the Senate of

July 12, 1897, I transmit herewith a report from the Secretary of State, with accompanying papers relating to postal telegraphs, telephones, and postal savings banks in the colony of Victoria.

WILLIAM McKINLEY.

EXECUTIVE MANSION,
Washington, April 25, 1898.

To the Senate and House of Representatives of the United States of America:

I transmit to the Congress, for its consideration and appropriate action, copies of correspondence recently had with the representative of Spain in the United States, with the United States minister at Madrid, and through the latter with the Government of Spain, showing the action taken under the joint resolution approved April 20, 1898, "for the recognition of the independence of the people of Cuba, demanding that the Government of Spain relinquish its authority and government in the island of Cuba, and to withdraw its land and naval forces from Cuba and Cuban waters, and directing the President of the United States to use the land and naval forces of the United States to carry these resolutions into effect."*

Upon communicating to the Spanish minister in Washington the demand which it became the duty of the Executive to address to the Government of Spain in obedience to said resolution, the minister asked for his passports and withdrew. The United States minister at Madrid was in turn notified by the Spanish minister for foreign affairs that the withdrawal of the Spanish representative from the United States had terminated diplomatic relations between the two countries, and that all official communications between their respective representatives ceased therewith.

I commend to your especial attention the note addressed to the United States minister at Madrid by the Spanish minister for foreign affairs on the 21st instant, whereby the foregoing notification was conveyed. It will be perceived therefrom that the Government of Spain, having cognizance of the joint resolution of the United States Congress, and in view of the things which the President is thereby required and authorized to do, responds by treating the reasonable demands of this Government as measures of hostility, following with that instant and complete severance of relations by its action which by the usage of nations accompanies an existent state of war between sovereign powers.

The position of Spain being thus made known, and the demands of the United States being denied, with a complete rupture of intercourse,

* See pp. 6297-6298.

by the act of Spain, I have been constrained, in exercise of the power
and authority conferred upon me by the joint resolution aforesaid, to
proclaim, under date of April 22, 1898,* a blockade of certain ports of
the north coast of Cuba, lying between Cardenas and Bahia Honda,
and of the port of Cienfuegos, on the south coast of Cuba, and further
in exercise of my constitutional powers and using the authority conferred upon me by the act of Congress approved April 22, 1898, to
issue my proclamation dated April 23, 1898,† calling forth volunteers
in order to carry into effect the said resolution of April 20, 1898.
Copies of these proclamations are hereto appended.

   In view of the measures so taken, and with a view to the adoption
of such other measures as may be necessary to enable me to carry out
the expressed will of the Congress of the United States in the premises, I now recommend to your honorable body the adoption of a joint
resolution declaring that a state of war exists between the United
States of America and the Kingdom of Spain, and I urge speedy action ther on, to the end that the definition of the international status
of the United States as a belligerent power may be made known and
the assertion of all its rights and the maintenance of all its duties in
the conduct of a public war may be assured. ‡

                                        WILLIAM McKINLEY.

JOINT RESOLUTION for the recognition of the independence of the people of Cuba, demanding
   that the Government of Spain relinquish its authority and government in the island of Cuba, and
   to withdraw its land and naval forces from Cuba and Cuban waters, and directing the President
   of the United States to use the land and naval forces of the United States to carry these resolutions into effect.

   Whereas the abhorrent conditions which have existed for more than three years
in the island of Cuba, so near our own borders, have shocked the moral sense of the
people of the United States, have been a disgrace to Christian civilization, culminating, as they have, in the destruction of a United States battle ship, with 266 of its
officers and crew, while on a friendly visit in the harbor of Havana, and cannot
longer be endured, as has been set forth by the President of the United States in his
message to Congress of April 11, 1898,§ upon which the action of Congress was
invited: Therefore,
   *Resolved by the Senate and House of Representatives of the United States of
America in Congress assembled*, First. That the people of the island of Cuba are
and of right ought to be free and independent.
   Second. That it is the duty of the United States to demand, and the Government
of the United States does hereby demand, that the Government of Spain at once
relinquish its authority and government in the island of Cuba and withdraw its land
and naval forces from Cuba and Cuban waters.
   Third. That the President of the United States be, and he hereby is, directed and
empowered to use the entire land and naval forces of the United States and to call
into the actual service of the United States the militia of the several States to such
extent as may be necessary to carry these resolutions into effect.

   * See pp. 6472-6473.   † See pp. 6473-6474.   ‡ See p. 6348.   § See pp. 6291-6292.

Fifty-fifth Congress of the United States of America;

At the Second Session,

Begun and held at the City of Washington on Monday, the sixth day of December, one thousand eight hundred and ninety-seven.

AN ACT

Declaring that war exists between the United States of America and the Kingdom of Spain.

Be it enacted by the Senate and House of Representatives of the United States of America in Congress assembled, First. That war be, and the same is hereby, declared to exist, and that war has existed since the twenty-first day of April, anno Domini eighteen hundred and ninety-eight, including said day, between the United States of America and the Kingdom of Spain.

Second. That the President of the United States be, and he hereby is, directed and empowered to use the entire land and naval forces of the United States, and to call into the actual service of the United States the militia of the several States, to such extent as may be necessary to carry this Act into effect.

Thomas B. Reed
Speaker of the House of Representatives.

Approved
April 25, 1898
Garret A. Hobart
Vice-President of the United States and
President of the Senate.

William McKinley

DECLARATION OF WAR AGAINST SPAIN.

Fourth. That the United States hereby disclaims any disposition or intention to exercise sovereignty, jurisdiction, or control over said island except for the pacification thereof, and asserts its determination, when that is accomplished, to leave the government and control of the island to its people.

Approved, April 20, 1898.

EXECUTIVE MANSION,
Washington, April 27, 1898.

To the Congress:

I transmit herewith a report from the Secretary of State and accompanying papers relating to the claim against the United States of the Russian subject, Gustav Isak Dahlberg, master and principal owner of the Russian bark *Hans*, based on his wrongful and illegal arrest and imprisonment by officers of the United States district court for the southern district of Mississippi, and in view of the opinion expressed by the Department of Justice that the said arrest and detention of the complainant were wrongful and without authority of law, I recommend the appropriation by Congress of the sum of $5,000 to reimburse the master and owners of the vessel for all losses and damages incurred by reason of his said wrongful and illegal arrest and detention.

WILLIAM McKINLEY.

EXECUTIVE MANSION, *May 9, 1898.*

To the Congress of the United States:

On the 24th of April I directed the Secretary of the Navy to telegraph orders to Commodore George Dewey, of the United States Navy, commanding the Asiatic Squadron, then lying in the port of Hongkong, to proceed forthwith to the Philippine Islands, there to commence operations and engage the assembled Spanish fleet.

Promptly obeying that order, the United States squadron, consisting of the flagship *Olympia, Baltimore, Raleigh, Boston, Concord,* and *Petrel,* with the revenue cutter *McCulloch* as an auxiliary dispatch boat, entered the harbor of Manila at daybreak on the 1st of May and immediately engaged the entire Spanish fleet of eleven ships, which were under the protection of the fire of the land forts. After a stubborn fight, in which the enemy suffered great loss, these vessels were destroyed or completely disabled and the water battery at Cavite silenced. Of our brave officers and men not one was lost and only eight injured, and those slightly. All of our ships escaped any serious damage.

By the 4th of May, Commodore Dewey had taken possession of the naval station at Cavite, destroying the fortifications there and at the entrance of the bay and paroling their garrisons. The waters of the bay are under his complete control. He has established hospitals within the

American lines, where 250 of the Spanish sick and wounded are assisted and protected.

The magnitude of this victory can hardly be measured by the ordinary standard of naval warfare. Outweighing any material advantage is the moral effect of this initial success. At this unsurpassed achievement the great heart of our nation throbs, not with boasting or with greed of conquest, but with deep gratitude that this triumph has come in a just cause and that by the grace of God an effective step has thus been taken toward the attainment of the wished-for peace. To those whose skill, courage, and devotion have won the fight, to the gallant commander and the brave officers and men who aided him, our country owes an incalculable debt.

Feeling as our people feel, and speaking in their name, I at once sent a message to Commodore Dewey thanking him and his officers and men for their splendid achievement and overwhelming victory and informing him that I had appointed him an acting rear-admiral.

I now recommend that, following our national precedents and expressing the fervent gratitude of every patriotic heart, the thanks of Congress be given Acting Rear-Admiral George Dewey, of the United States Navy, for highly distinguished conduct in conflict with the enemy, and to the officers and men under his command for their gallantry in the destruction of the enemy's fleet and the capture of the enemy's fortifications in the bay of Manila.

WILLIAM McKINLEY.

EXECUTIVE MANSION, May 16, 1898.

To the House of Representatives:

I transmit herewith a communication from the Secretary of State, accompanying the annual reports of the consuls of the United States upon foreign industries and commerce. In view of the value of these reports to the business interests of the country, I indorse the recommendation of the Secretary of State that Congress authorize the printing of a special edition of 10,000 copies of the general summary entitled "Review of the World's Commerce," and 5,000 copies of Commercial Relations (including this summary), to enable the Department of State to meet the demands for such information.

WILLIAM McKINLEY.

EXECUTIVE MANSION, May 16, 1898.

To the House of Representatives:

I return herewith to the House of Representatives, in which it originated, House bill No. 2219, entitled "An act for the relief of the administrators of Isaac P. Tice, deceased, and others," without my approval.

The object of this bill is to confer upon the Court of Claims jurisdiction to retry and determine a case brought by the representatives of Isaac P. Tice against the United States in the Court of Claims in the year 1873 to recover from the Government the sum of $25,-000, the alleged value of certain meters invented by Isaac P. Tice for the purpose of measuring the quality and strength of distilled spirits.

It was claimed that this amount, together with the sum of $733.33 for storage of said meters, was due to the claimant under a contract made between Tice and the Commissioner of Internal Revenue in pursuance of section 15 of the act of March 2, 1867 (14 Stats., 481). From the report of the case in 13 Court of Claims Reports, 112, it appears that the matter was fully and deliberately tried and argued both on behalf of the claimant and of the United States, and that at December term, 1877, the Court of Claims rendered a decision adverse to the claimant, expressly stating that the claimants had failed to establish their claim both in law and on the facts. Not satisfied with this conclusion of the Court of Claims, the claimants took an appeal to the Supreme Court of the United States, where the case was again argued and was decided, October term, 1878, the judgment of the Court of Claims being declared to be in accordance with the law and therefore affirmed. In these two decisions the law and the facts pertaining to the claim were fully set forth and discussed.

The bill further confers upon the Court of Claims jurisdiction to try and determine certain alleged claims of said Tice and others for money collected on account of the Tice meters, but not paid over to him or them under the regulations of the Treasury.

The amount of the latter claim, according to the report of the committee of the House of Representatives to which this bill was referred, is $140,000. It does not appear from the report of the committee, nor from any documents to which I have access, who are the other persons by whom this latter sum is claimed. The claim for $140,000 must have accrued prior to July, 1871, and therefore at this time is of at least twenty-seven years' standing.

It will thus be perceived that the object of the bill is to remove from the pathway of the claimants two legal bars to the prosecution of their claim in the courts—one, the bar of the statute of limitations, which requires all claimants against the Government to present their claims and bring actions thereon within six years from the time the cause of action accrues; and the other, that bar of estoppel which arises by reason of a former adverse judgment, rendered in a court of competent jurisdiction. This is not a general modification of the law in these respects, but a special application of it to these particular claimants.

If the principle on which the statute of limitations is founded is wise and beneficent, then the effect of it ought not to be impaired by special legislative exemptions in favor of particular persons or cases except upon very clear and just grounds, where no lack of diligence in the prosecution of the claim is apparent. I cannot find in the papers submitted to me any sufficient grounds to justify a special exception from the ordinary rule in favor of these claimants. As to the claim for $140,000, no reason is stated why it was not included in the original suit nor why action upon it was not brought against the Government within the six years allowed by the statute for that purpose. To permit such an action to be brought now is simply, without any reason of a special nature, to grant a privilege to these claimants which is denied to all other citizens of the United States, in accordance with the provisions of the general statute of limitations. The principle underlying statutes of limitations and the reasons for the maintenance of such a rule of litigation are much more cogent when applied to claims against the Government than when applied to claims against individuals.

These claims do not differ in their character from ordinary business transactions such as transpire every day between private persons or business corporations. The Government can only defend itself against claims of this nature through its public officers and with the use of such public records as the Departments may furnish. Great difficulties are experienced by it in contesting fraudulent and unjust claims, and it is only fair in the interest of the public that a rigorous adherence to some rule of limitation should be maintained.

The provision of the bill which practically directs a new trial of the claim for $25,000, decided adversely to the claimants more than twenty years ago, is still more objectionable. These parties had their day in court. They produced their witnesses and were heard both originally and upon appeal, and upon the case they were then able to make the court decided they had no claim against the Government. It is now suggested that other witnesses have been discovered who can supply the lack of proof which was produced on the former trial. Such a ground for a new trial would never be considered in any court of law in the land in a case between private parties where such a length of time had intervened since the former trial. No explanation of a satisfactory nature is furnished for the failure of the claimants to produce these witnesses upon the original trial.

The bill further provides that upon a retrial of the original claim, or upon the trial of the new claim, the claimants shall be at liberty to offer in evidence the depositions of witnesses now on the files of any of the committees of Congress in relation to the aforesaid matters, which may be introduced as evidence in case of the death or disability of the deponents.

This provision will enable the claimants to present *ex-parte* affidavits, prepared by the claimants or their attorneys, without opportunity being afforded to the Government to cross-examine, provided the claimants can show that the deposing witnesses are either dead or under disability, by which, no doubt, is intended any such disability by reason of absence, illness, and the like, as may render them legally incapable of being produced in person to testify upon the retrial. Such a provision as this is most dangerous to the interests of the Government.

I fail to see any reason in the facts connected with these claims for granting to these parties relief of this extraordinary nature.

The Treasury of the United States ought to be very carefully guarded against attacks of those who come forward with stale claims, and especially from the attacks of those who have already been fully heard according to the methods prescribed by the statutes.

To approve this bill would be to furnish a very dangerous precedent which would open the door to demands upon Congress in other cases which have been fully heard and determined.

For these reasons I am constrained to withhold my approval from this bill. WILLIAM McKINLEY.

EXECUTIVE MANSION, *June 1, 1898.*

To the Congress of the United States:

The resolution of Congress passed May 9, 1898, tendering to Commodore George Dewey, United States, Navy commander-in-chief of the United States naval force on the Asiatic station, the thanks of Congress and of the American people for highly distinguished conduct in conflict with the enemy, as displayed by him in the destruction of the Spanish fleet and batteries in the harbor of Manila, Philippine Islands, May 1, 1898, and through him extending the thanks of Congress and the American people to the officers and men under his command for gallantry and skill exhibited by them on that occasion, required the President to communicate the same to Commodore Dewey, and through him to the officers and men under his command. This having been done, through the Secretary of the Navy, on the 15th of May, 1898, the following response has been received, and is hereby transmitted to the Congress:

I desire to express to the Department, and to request that it will be transmitted to the President and to Congress, my most sincere thanks for the great compliment paid to me

WILLIAM McKINLEY

JOINT RESOLUTION tendering the thanks of Congress to Commodore George Dewey, United States Navy, and to the officers and men of the squadron under his command.

Resolved by the Senate and House of Representatives of the United States of America in Congress assembled, That, in pursuance of the recommendation of the President, made in accordance with the provisions of section 1508 of the Revised Statutes, the thanks of Congress and of the American people are hereby tendered to Commodore George Dewey, United States Navy, commander in chief of the United States naval force on the Asiatic station, for highly distinguished conduct in conflict with the enemy, as displayed by him in the destruction of the Spanish fleet and batteries in the harbor of Manila, Philippine Islands, May 1, 1898.

SEC. 2. That the thanks of Congress and the American people are hereby extended through Commodore Dewey to the officers and men under his command for the gallantry and skill exhibited by them on that occasion.

SEC. 3. *Be it further resolved,* That the President of the United States be requested to cause this resolution to be communicated to Commodore Dewey, and through him to the officers and men under his command.

Approved, May 10, 1898.

JOINT RESOLUTION authorizing the Secretary of the Navy to present a sword of honor to Commodore George Dewey, and to cause to be struck bronze medals commemorating the battle of Manila Bay, and to distribute such medals to the officers and men of the ships of the Asiatic Squadron of the United States.

Resolved by the Senate and House of Representatives of the United States of America in Congress assembled, That the Secretary of the Navy be and he hereby is, authorized to present a sword of honor to Commodore George Dewey and to cause to be struck bronze medals commemorating the battle of Manila Bay, and to distribute such medals to the officers and men of the ships of the Asiatic Squadron of the United States under command of Commodore George Dewey on May 1, 1898 ; and that to enable the Secretary to carry out this resolution the sum of $10,000, or so much thereof as may be necessary, is hereby appropriated out of any money in the Treasury not otherwise appropriated.

Approved, June 3, 1898.

EXECUTIVE MANSION,
Washington, June 14, 1898.

To the Congress of the United States:

I transmit herewith (having reference to Senate Document No. 4, Fifty-fifth Congress, second session) a report made by Thomas W. Cridler, Third Assistant Secretary of State, who, upon the death of Maj. Moses P. Handy, I designated to continue the work as special commissioner, under the act of Congress approved July 19, 1897, in relation to the acceptance by the Government of the United States of the invitation of France to participate in the International Exposition to be held at Paris from April 15 to November 5, 1900.

I cordially renew my recommendation that a liberal appropriation be immediately granted. WILLIAM McKINLEY.

EXECUTIVE MANSION, *June 23, 1898.*

To the Senate of the United States:

I transmit herewith a report from the Secretary of the Interior relative to Senate resolution of June 10, 1898, requesting the President "to make such arrangements as may be necessary to secure at the Trans-Mississippi and International Exposition to be held in the city of Omaha, Neb., the attendance of representatives of the Iroquois tribes and Delawares of Canada and of the Abenakis of St. Francis and Becaucourt, and such other Indian nations as have emigrated from the territory now of the United States to Canada.

To carry out this resolution, if it shall be found agreeable to the Government of Canada, it will be necessary for this Government to send an agent to visit the tribes and secure their assent, organize the representative delegations, escort them to the exposition, take charge of and care for them while there and until they are returned to their respective tribes.

The resolution seems to presuppose that there are funds which may be lawfully used to defray the expenses which must necessarily be incurred in the premises By reference to the Secretary's report, it will be seen that there are no moneys lawfully available for that purpose.

It is not to be presumed that the Senate, under such circumstances, would desire the Executive to take the action indicated in the resolution, and I am therefore constrained to await the requisite appropriation by Congress for the payment of the expenses that must be necessarily incurred in the accomplishment of the proposed objects.

WILLIAM McKINLEY.

EXECUTIVE MANSION, *June 27, 1898.*

To the Congress of the United States:

On the 11th of May, 1898, there occurred a conflict in the bay of Cardenas, Cuba, in which the naval torpedo boat *Winslow* was disabled, her commander wounded, and one of her officers and a part of her crew killed by the enemy's fire

In the face of a most galling fire from the enemy's guns the revenue cutter *Hudson*, commanded by First Lieutenant Frank H. Newcomb, United States Revenue-Cutter Service, rescued the disabled *Winslow*, her wounded commander and remaining crew. The commander of the *Hud-son* kept his vessel in the very hottest fire of the action, although in constant danger of going ashore on account of the shallow water, until he finally got a line made fast to the *Winslow* and towed that vessel out of range of the enemy's guns—a deed of special gallantry.

I recommend that in recognition of the signal act of heroism of First Lieutenant Frank H. Newcomb, United States Revenue-Cutter Service, above set forth, the thanks of Congress be extended to him and to his officers and men of the *Hudson*, and that a gold medal of honor be presented to Lieutenant Newcomb, a silver medal of honor to each of his officers, and a bronze medal of honor to each member of his crew who served with him at Cardenas.

It will be remembered that Congress by appropriate action recognized the several commanders of ships of war for their services in the battle of Manila, May 1, 1898.

The commander of the revenue cutter *Hugh McCulloch*, present and in active cooperation with the fleet under Commodore Dewey on that occasion (by Executive order under the provisions of section 2757, Revised Statutes), is the only commander of a national ship to whom promotion or advancement was not and could not be given, because he already held the highest rank known to the Revenue-Cutter Service.

I now recommend that in recognition of the efficient and meritorious services of Captain Daniel B. Hodgsdon, United States Revenue-Cutter Service, who commanded the *Hugh McCulloch* at the battle of Manila (that officer being now in the sixty-third year of his age and having served continuously on active duty for thirty-seven years), he be placed upon the permanent waiting-orders or retired list of the Revenue-Cutter Service on the full-duty pay of his grade.

WILLIAM McKINLEY.

EXECUTIVE MANSION, *June 27, 1898.*

To the Congress of the United States:

On the morning of the 3d of June, 1898, Assistant Naval Constructor Richmond P. Hobson, United States Navy, with a volunteer crew of seven men, in charge of the partially dismantled collier *Merrimac*, entered the fortified harbor of Santiago, Cuba, for the purpose of sinking the collier in the narrowest portion of the channel, and thus interposing a serious obstacle to the egress of the Spanish fleet which had recently entered that harbor. This enterprise, demanding coolness, judgment, and bravery amounting to heroism, was carried into successful execution in the face of a persistent fire from the hostile fleet as well as from the fortifications on shore.

Rear-Admiral Sampson, commander in chief of our naval force in Cuban waters, in an official report dated "Off Santiago de Cuba, June 3, 1898," and addressed to the Secretary of the Navy, referring to Mr. Hobson's gallant exploit, says:

As stated in a recent telegram, before coming here I decided to make the harbor entrance secure against the possibility of egress of the Spanish ships by obstructing the narrow part of the entrance by sinking a collier at that point. Upon calling upon Mr. Hobson for his professional opinion as to a sure method of sinking the ship, he manifested a most lively interest in the problem. After several days' consideration he presented a solution which he considered would insure the immediate sinking of the ship when she had reached the desired point in the channel. * * * The plan contemplated a crew of only seven men and Mr. Hobson, who begged that it might be intrusted to him.

As soon as I reached Santiago and had the collier to work upon, the details were commenced and diligently prosecuted, hoping to complete them in one day, as the moon and tide served best the first night after our arrival. Notwithstanding every effort, the hour of 4 o'clock in the morning arrived and the preparations were scarcely completed. After a careful inspection of the final preparations I was forced to relinquish the plan for that morning, as dawn was breaking. Mr. Hobson begged to try it at all hazards.

This morning proved more propitious, as a prompt start could be made. Nothing could have been more gallantly executed. * * * A careful inspection of the harbor from this ship showed that the *Merrimac* had been sunk in the channel.

I can not myself too earnestly express my appreciation of the conduct of Mr. Hobson and his gallant crew. I venture to say that a more brave and daring thing has not been done since Cushing blew up the *Albemarle*.

The members of the crew who were with Mr. Hobson on this memorable occasion have already been rewarded for their services by advancement, which, under the provisions of law and regulations, the Secretary of the Navy was authorized to make; and the nomination to the Senate of Naval Cadet Powell, who in a steam launch followed the *Merrimac* on her perilous trip for the purpose of rescuing her force after the sinking of that vessel, to be advanced in rank to the grade of ensign has been prepared and will be submitted.

Cushing, with whose gallant act in blowing up the ram *Albemarle* during the Civil War Admiral Sampson compares Mr. Hobson's sinking of the *Merrimac*, received the thanks of Congress, upon recommendation of the President, by name, and was in consequence, under the provisions of section 1508 of the Revised Statutes, advanced one grade, such advancement embracing 56 numbers. The section cited applies, however, to line officers only, and Mr. Hobson, being a member of the staff of the Navy, could not under its provisions be so advanced.

In considering the question of suitably rewarding Assistant Naval Constructor Hobson for his valiant conduct on the occasion referred to, I have deemed it proper to address this message to you with the recommendation that he receive the thanks of Congress and, further, that he be transferred to the line of the Navy and promoted to such position therein as the President, by and with the advice and consent of the Senate, may determine. Mr. Hobson's transfer from the construction corps to the line is fully warranted, he having received the necessary technical training as a graduate of the Naval Academy, where he stood No. 1 in his class; and such action is recommended partly in deference to what is understood to be his own desire, although, he being now a prisoner in the hands of the enemy, no direct communication on the subject has been received from him, and partly for the reason that the abilities displayed by him at Santiago are of such a character as to indicate especial fitness for the duties of the line.

WILLIAM McKINLEY.

SECOND ANNUAL MESSAGE.

EXECUTIVE MANSION, *December 5, 1898.*

To the Senate and House of Representatives:

Notwithstanding the added burdens rendered necessary by the war, our people rejoice in a very satisfactory and steadily increasing degree of prosperity, evidenced by the largest volume of business ever recorded. Manufacture has been productive, agricultural pursuits have yielded abundant returns, labor in all fields of industry is better rewarded, revenue legislation passed by the present Congress has increased the Treasury's receipts to the amount estimated by its authors, the finances of the Government have been successfully administered and its credit advanced to the first rank, while its currency has been maintained at the world's highest standard. Military service under a common flag and for a righteous cause has strengthened the national spirit and served to cement more closely than ever the fraternal bonds between every section of the country.

A review of the relation of the United States to other powers, always appropriate, is this year of primary importance in view of the momentous issues which have arisen, demanding in one instance the ultimate determination by arms and involving far-reaching consequences which will require the earnest attention of the Congress.

In my last annual message* very full consideration was given to the question of the duty of the Government of the United States toward Spain and the Cuban insurrection as being by far the most important problem with which we were then called upon to deal. The considerations then advanced and the exposition of the views therein expressed disclosed my sense of the extreme gravity of the situation. Setting aside as logically unfounded or practically inadmissible the recognition of the Cuban insurgents as belligerents, the recognition of the independence of Cuba, neutral intervention to end the war by imposing a rational compromise between the contestants, intervention in favor of one or the other

* See pp. 6254-6263.

party, and forcible annexation of the island, I concluded it was honestly due to our friendly relations with Spain that she should be given a reasonable chance to realize her expectations of reform to which she had become irrevocably committed. Within a few weeks previously she had announced comprehensive plans which it was confidently asserted would be efficacious to remedy the evils so deeply affecting our own country, so injurious to the true interests of the mother country as well as to those of Cuba, and so repugnant to the universal sentiment of humanity.

The ensuing month brought little sign of real progress toward the pacification of Cuba. The autonomous administrations set up in the capital and some of the principal cities appeared not to gain the favor of the inhabitants nor to be able to extend their influence to the large extent of territory held by the insurgents, while the military arm, obviously unable to cope with the still active rebellion, continued many of the most objectionable and offensive policies of the government that had preceded it. No tangible relief was afforded the vast numbers of unhappy reconcentrados, despite the reiterated professions made in that regard and the amount appropriated by Spain to that end. The proffered expedient of zones of cultivation proved illusory. Indeed no less practical nor more delusive promises of succor could well have been tendered to the exhausted and destitute people, stripped of all that made life and home dear and herded in a strange region among unsympathetic strangers hardly less necessitous than themselves.

By the end of December the mortality among them had frightfully increased. Conservative estimates from Spanish sources placed the deaths among these distressed people at over 40 per cent from the time General Weyler's decree of reconcentration was enforced. With the acquiescence of the Spanish authorities, a scheme was adopted for relief by charitable contributions raised in this country and distributed, under the direction of the consul-general and the several consuls, by noble and earnest individual effort through the organized agencies of the American Red Cross. Thousands of lives were thus saved, but many thousands more were inaccessible to such forms of aid.

The war continued on the old footing, without comprehensive plan, developing only the same spasmodic encounters, barren of strategic result, that had marked the course of the earlier ten years' rebellion as well as the present insurrection from its start. No alternative save physical exhaustion of either combatant, and therewithal the practical ruin of the island, lay in sight, but how far distant no one could venture to conjecture.

At this juncture, on the 15th of February last, occurred the destruction of the battle ship *Maine* while rightfully lying in the harbor of Havana on a mission of international courtesy and good will—a catastrophe the suspicious nature and horror of which stirred the nation's heart profoundly. It is a striking evidence of the poise and sturdy good sense distinguishing our national character that this shocking blow, falling upon a generous people already deeply touched by preceding events in Cuba, did not move them to an instant desperate resolve to tolerate no longer the existence of a condition of danger and disorder at our doors that made possible such a deed, by whomsoever wrought. Yet the instinct of justice prevailed, and the nation anxiously awaited the result of the searching investigation at once set on foot. The finding of the naval board of inquiry established that the origin of the explosion was external, by a submarine mine, and only halted through lack of positive testimony to fix the responsibility of its authorship.

All these things carried conviction to the most thoughtful, even before the finding of the naval court, that a crisis in our relations with Spain and toward Cuba was at hand. So strong was this belief that it needed but a brief Executive suggestion to the Congress to receive immediate answer to the duty of making instant provision for the possible and perhaps speedily probable emergency of war, and the remarkable, almost unique, spectacle was presented of a unanimous vote of both Houses, on the 9th of March, appropriating $50,000,000 ''for the national defense and for each and every purpose connected therewith, to be expended at the discretion of the President.'' That this act of prevision came none too soon was disclosed when the application of the fund was undertaken. Our coasts were practically undefended. Our Navy needed large provision for increased ammunition and supplies, and even numbers to cope with any sudden attack from the navy of Spain, which comprised modern vessels of the highest type of continental perfection. Our Army also required enlargement of men and munitions. The details of the hurried preparation for the dreaded contingency are told in the reports of the Secretaries of War and of the Navy, and need not be repeated here. It is sufficient to say that the outbreak of war when it did come found our nation not unprepared to meet the conflict.

Nor was the apprehension of coming strife confined to our own country. It was felt by the continental powers, which on April 6, through their ambassadors and envoys, addressed to the Executive an expression of hope that humanity and moderation might mark the course of this Government and people, and that further negotiations would lead to an agreement which, while securing the maintenance of peace, would afford all necessary guaranties for the reestablishment of order in Cuba. In responding to that representation I said I shared the hope the envoys had expressed that peace might be preserved in a manner to terminate the chronic condition of disturbance in Cuba, so injurious and menacing to our interests and tranquillity, as well as shocking to our sentiments of humanity; and while appreciating the humanitarian and disinterested character of the communication they had made on behalf of the powers, I stated the confidence of this Government, for its part, that equal appreciation would be shown for its own earnest and unselfish endeavors to fulfill a duty to humanity by ending a situation the indefinite prolongation of which had become insufferable.

Still animated by the hope of a peaceful solution and obeying the dictates of duty, no effort was relaxed to bring about a speedy ending of the Cuban struggle. Negotiations to this object continued actively with the Government of Spain, looking to the immediate conclusion of a six months' armistice in Cuba, with a view to effect the recognition of her people's right to independence. Besides this, the instant revocation of the order of reconcentration was asked, so that the sufferers, returning to their homes and aided by united American and Spanish effort, might be put in a way to support themselves and, by orderly resumption of the well-nigh destroyed productive energies of the island, contribute to the restoration of its tranquillity and well-being. Negotiations continued for some little time at Madrid, resulting in offers by the Spanish Government which could not but be regarded as inadequate. It was proposed to confide the preparation of peace to the insular parliament, yet to be convened under the autonomous decrees of November, 1897, but without impairment in any wise of the constitutional powers of the Madrid Government, which to that end would grant an armistice, if solicited by the insurgents, for such time as the general in chief might see fit to fix. How and with what scope of discretionary powers the insular parliament was expected to set about the "preparation" of peace did not appear. If it were to be by negotiation with the insurgents, the issue seemed to rest on the one side with a body chosen by a fraction of the electors in the districts under Spanish control, and on the other with the insurgent population holding the interior country, unrepresented in the so-called parliament and defiant at the suggestion of suing for peace.

Grieved and disappointed at this barren outcome of my sincere endeavors to reach a practicable solution, I felt it my duty to remit the whole question to the Congress. In the message of April 11, 1898,* I announced that with this last overture in the direction of immediate peace in Cuba and its disappointing reception by Spain the effort of the Executive was brought to an end. I again reviewed the alternative courses of action which had been proposed, concluding that the only one consonant with international policy and compatible with our firm-set historical traditions was intervention as a neutral to stop the war and check the hopeless sacrifice of life, even though that resort involved "hostile constraint upon both the parties to the contest, as well to enforce a truce as to guide the eventual settlement." The grounds justifying that step were the interests of humanity, the duty to protect the life and property of our citizens in Cuba, the right to check injury to our commerce and people through the devastation of the island, and, most important, the need of removing at once and forever the constant menace and the

* See pp. 6281-6292.

burdens entailed upon our Government by the uncertainties and perils of the situation caused by the unendurable disturbance in Cuba. I said:

The long trial has proved that the object for which Spain has waged the war can not be attained. The fire of insurrection may flame or may smolder with varying seasons, but it has not been and it is plain that it can not be extinguished by present methods. The only hope of relief and repose from a condition which can no longer be endured is the enforced pacification of Cuba. In the name of humanity, in the name of civilization, in behalf of endangered American interests which give us the right and the duty to speak and to act, the war in Cuba must stop.

In view of all this the Congress was asked to authorize and empower the President to take measures to secure a full and final termination of hostilities between Spain and the people of Cuba and to secure in the island the establishment of a stable government, capable of maintaining order and observing its international obligations, insuring peace and tranquillity and the security of its citizens as well as our own, and for the accomplishment of those ends to use the military and naval forces of the United States as might be necessary, with added authority to continue generous relief to the starving people of Cuba.

The response of the Congress, after nine days of earnest deliberation, during which the almost unanimous sentiment of your body was developed on every point save as to the expediency of coupling the proposed action with a formal recognition of the Republic of Cuba as the true and lawful government of that island—a proposition which failed of adoption—the Congress, after conference, on the 19th of April, by a vote of 42 to 35 in the Senate and 311 to 6 in the House of Representatives, passed the memorable joint resolution declaring—

First. That the people of the island of Cuba are, and of right ought to be, free and independent.

Second. That it is the duty of the United States to demand, and the Government of the United States does hereby demand, that the Government of Spain at once relinquish its authority and government in the island of Cuba and withdraw its land and naval forces from Cuba and Cuban waters.

Third. That the President of the United States be, and he hereby is, directed and empowered to use the entire land and naval forces of the United States and to call into the actual service of the United States the militia of the several States to such extent as may be necessary to carry these resolutions into effect.

Fourth. That the United States hereby disclaims any disposition or intention to exercise sovereignty, jurisdiction, or control over said island except for the pacification thereof, and asserts its determination when that is accomplished to leave the government and control of the island to its people.

This resolution was approved by the Executive on the next day, April 20. A copy was at once communicated to the Spanish minister at this capital, who forthwith announced that his continuance in Washington had thereby become impossible, and asked for his passports, which were given him. He thereupon withdrew from Washington, leaving the protection of Spanish interests in the United States to the French ambassador and the Austro-Hungarian minister. Simultaneously with its communication to the Spanish minister here, General Woodford, the American minister at Madrid, was telegraphed confirmation of the text of the joint resolution and directed to communicate it to the Government of Spain with the formal demand that it at once relinquish its authority and government in the island of Cuba and withdraw its forces therefrom, coupling this demand with announcement of the intentions of this Government as to the future of the island, in conformity with the fourth clause of the resolution, and giving Spain until noon of April 23 to reply.

That demand, although, as above shown, officially made known to the Spanish envoy here, was not delivered at Madrid. After the instruction reached General Woodford on the morning of April 21, but before he could present it, the Spanish minister of state notified him that upon the President's approval of the joint resolution the Madrid Government, regarding the act as "equivalent to an evident declaration of war," had ordered its minister in Washington to withdraw, thereby breaking off diplomatic relations between the two countries and ceasing all official communication between their respective representatives. General Woodford thereupon demanded his passports and quitted Madrid the same day.

Spain having thus denied the demand of the United States and initiated that complete form of rupture of relations which attends a state of war, the executive powers authorized by the resolution were at once used by me to meet the enlarged contingency of actual war between sovereign states. On April 22 I proclaimed a blockade of the north coast of Cuba, including ports on said coast between Cardenas and Bahia Honda, and the port of Cienfuegos, on the south coast of Cuba,* and on the 23d I called for volunteers to execute the purpose of the resolution.† By my message of April 25 the Congress was informed of the situation, and I recommended formal declaration of the existence of a state of war between the United States and Spain.‡ The Congress accordingly voted on the same day the act approved April 25, 1898, declaring the existence of such war from and including the 21st day of April,§ and reenacted the provision of the resolution of April 20 directing the President to use all the armed forces of the nation to carry that act into effect.‖ Due notification of the existence of war as aforesaid was given April 25 by telegraph to all the governments with which the United States maintain relations, in order that their neutrality might be assured during the war. The various governments responded with proclamations of neutrality, each after its own methods. It is not among the least gratifying incidents of the struggle that the obligations of neutrality were impartially discharged by all, often under delicate and difficult circumstances.

In further fulfillment of international duty I issued, April 26, 1898, a proclamation announcing the treatment proposed to be accorded to vessels and their cargoes as to blockade, contraband, the exercise of the right of search, and the immunity of neutral flags and neutral goods

* See pp. 6472–6473.　　† See pp. 6473–6474.　　‡ See pp. 6296–6297.　　§ See p. 6348.
‖ See pp. 6297–6298.

under enemy's flag.* A similar proclamation was made by the Spanish Government. In the conduct of hostilities the rules of the Declaration of Paris, including abstention from resort to privateering, have accordingly been observed by both belligerents, although neither was a party to that declaration.

Our country thus, after an interval of half a century of peace with all nations, found itself engaged in deadly conflict with a foreign enemy. Every nerve was strained to meet the emergency. The response to the initial call for 125,000 volunteers† was instant and complete, as was also the result of the second call, of May 25, for 75,000 additional volunteers.‡ The ranks of the Regular Army were increased to the limits provided by the act of April 26, 1898.

The enlisted force of the Navy on the 15th day of August, when it reached its maximum, numbered 24,123 men and apprentices. One hundred and three vessels were added to the Navy by purchase, 1 was presented to the Government, 1 leased, and the 4 vessels of the International Navigation Company—the *St. Paul, St. Louis, New York*, and *Paris*—were chartered. In addition to these the revenue cutters and lighthouse tenders were turned over to the Navy Department and became temporarily a part of the auxiliary Navy.

The maximum effective fighting force of the Navy during the war, separated into classes, was as follows:

Four battle ships of the first class, 1 battle ship of the second class, 2 armored cruisers, 6 coast-defense monitors, 1 armored ram, 12 protected cruisers, 3 unprotected cruisers, 18 gunboats, 1 dynamite cruiser, 11 torpedo boats; vessels of the old Navy, including monitors, 14. Auxiliary Navy: 11 auxiliary cruisers, 28 converted yachts, 27 converted tugs, 19 converted colliers, 15 revenue cutters, 4 light-house tenders, and 19 miscellaneous vessels.

Much alarm was felt along our entire Atlantic seaboard lest some attack might be made by the enemy. Every precaution was taken to prevent possible injury to our great cities lying along the coast. Temporary garrisons were provided, drawn from the State militia; infantry and light batteries were drawn from the volunteer force. About 12,000 troops were thus employed. The coast signal service was established for observing the approach of an enemy's ships to the coast of the United States, and the Life-Saving and Light-House services cooperated, which enabled the Navy Department to have all portions of the Atlantic coast, from Maine to Texas, under observation.

The auxiliary Navy was created under the authority of Congress and was officered and manned by the Naval Militia of the several States. This organization patrolled the coast and performed the duty of a second line of defense.

Under the direction of the Chief of Engineers submarine mines were

---

*See pp. 6474-6475.　　　　†See pp. 6473-6474.　　　　‡See p. 6477.

placed at the most exposed points. Before the outbreak of the war permanent mining casemates and cable galleries had been constructed at nearly all important harbors. Most of the torpedo material was not to be found in the market, and had to be specially manufactured. Under date of April 19 district officers were directed to take all preliminary measures short of the actual attaching of the loaded mines to the cables, and on April 22 telegraphic orders were issued to place the loaded mines in position.

The aggregate number of mines placed was 1,535, at the principal harbors from Maine to California. Preparations were also made for the planting of mines at certain other harbors, but owing to the early destruction of the Spanish fleet these mines were not placed.

The Signal Corps was promptly organized, and performed service of the most difficult and important character. Its operations during the war covered the electrical connection of all coast fortifications, the establishment of telephonic and telegraphic facilities for the camps at Manila, Santiago, and in Puerto Rico. There were constructed 300 miles of line at ten great camps, thus facilitating military movements from those points in a manner heretofore unknown in military administration. Field telegraph lines were established and maintained under the enemy's fire at Manila, and later the Manila-Hongkong cable was reopened.

In Puerto Rico cable communications were opened over a discontinued route, and on land the headquarters of the commanding officer was kept in telegraphic or telephonic communication with the division commanders on four different lines of operations.

There was placed in Cuban waters a completely outfitted cable ship, with war cables and cable gear, suitable both for the destruction of communications belonging to the enemy and the establishment of our own. Two ocean cables were destroyed under the enemy's batteries at Santiago. The day previous to the landing of General Shafter's corps, at Caimanera, within 20 miles of the landing place, cable communications were established and a cable station opened giving direct communication with the Government at Washington. This service was invaluable to the Executive in directing the operations of the Army and Navy. With a total force of over 1,300, the loss was by disease in camp and field, officers and men included, only 5.

The national-defense fund of $50,000,000 was expended in large part by the Army and Navy, and the objects for which it was used are fully shown in the reports of the several Secretaries. It was a most timely appropriation, enabling the Government to strengthen its defenses and make preparations greatly needed in case of war.

This fund being inadequate to the requirements of equipment and for the conduct of the war, the patriotism of the Congress provided the means in the war-revenue act of June 13 by authorizing a 3 per cent popular loan not to exceed $400,000,000 and by levying additional imposts and taxes. Of the authorized loan $200,000,000 were offered and promptly taken, the subscriptions so far exceeding the call as to cover it many times over, while, preference being given to the smaller bids, no single allotment exceeded $5,000. This was a most encouraging and significant result, showing the vast resources of the nation and the determination of the people to uphold their country's honor.

It is not within the province of this message to narrate the history of the extraordinary war that followed the Spanish declaration of April 21, but a brief recital of its more salient features is appropriate.

The first encounter of the war in point of date took place April 27, when a detachment of the blockading squadron made a reconnoissance in force at Matanzas, shelled the harbor forts, and demolished several new works in construction.

The next engagement was destined to mark a memorable epoch in maritime warfare. The Pacific fleet, under Commodore George Dewey, had lain for some weeks at Hongkong. Upon the colonial proclamation of neutrality being issued and the customary twenty-four hours' notice being given, it repaired to Mirs Bay, near Hongkong, whence it proceeded to the Philippine Islands under telegraphed orders to capture or destroy the formidable Spanish fleet then assembled at Manila. At daybreak on the 1st of May the American force entered Manila Bay, and after a few hours' engagement effected the total destruction of the Spanish fleet, consisting of ten war ships and a transport, besides capturing the naval station and forts at Cavite, thus annihilating the Spanish naval power in the Pacific Ocean and completely controlling the bay of Manila, with the ability to take the city at will. Not a life was lost on our ships, the wounded only numbering seven, while not a vessel was materially injured. For this gallant achievement the Congress, upon my recommendation, fitly bestowed upon the actors preferment and substantial reward.

The effect of this remarkable victory upon the spirit of our people and upon the fortunes of the war was instant. A prestige of invincibility thereby attached to our arms which continued throughout the struggle. Reenforcements were hurried to Manila under the command of Major-General Merritt and firmly established within sight of the capital, which lay helpless before our guns.

On the 7th day of May the Government was advised officially of the victory at Manila, and at once inquired of the commander of our fleet what troops would be required. The information was received on the 15th day of May, and the first army expedition sailed May 25 and arrived off Manila June 30. Other expeditions soon followed, the total force consisting of 641 officers and 15,058 enlisted men.

Only reluctance to cause needless loss of life and property prevented the early storming and capture of the city, and therewith the absolute military occupancy of the whole group. The insurgents meanwhile had resumed the active hostilities suspended by the uncompleted truce of December, 1897. Their forces invested Manila from the northern and eastern sides, but were constrained by Admiral Dewey and General Merritt from attempting an assault. It was fitting that whatever was to be done in the way of decisive operations in that quarter should be accomplished by the strong arm of the United States alone. Obeying the stern precept of war which enjoins the overcoming of the adversary and the extinction of his power wherever assailable as the speedy and sure means to win a peace, divided victory was not permissible, for no partition of the rights and responsibilities attending the enforcement of a just and advantageous peace could be thought of.

Following the comprehensive scheme of general attack, powerful forces were assembled at various points on our coast to invade Cuba and Puerto Rico. Meanwhile naval demonstrations were made at several exposed points. On May 11 the cruiser *Wilmington* and torpedo boat *Winslow* were unsuccessful in an attempt to silence the batteries at Cardenas, a gallant ensign, Worth Bagley, and four seamen falling. These grievous fatalities were, strangely enough, among the very few which occurred during our naval operations in this extraordinary conflict.

Meanwhile the Spanish naval preparations had been pushed with great vigor. A powerful squadron under Admiral Cervera, which had assembled at the Cape Verde Islands before the outbreak of hostilities, had crossed the ocean, and by its erratic movements in the Caribbean Sea delayed our military plans while baffling the pursuit of our fleets. For a time fears were felt lest the *Oregon* and *Marietta*, then nearing home after their long voyage from San Francisco of over 15,000 miles, might be surprised by Admiral Cervera's fleet, but their fortunate arrival dispelled these apprehensions and lent much-needed reenforcement. Not until Admiral Cervera took refuge in the harbor of Santiago de Cuba, about May 19. was it practicable to plan a systematic naval and military attack upon the Antillean possessions of Spain.

Several demonstrations occurred on the coasts of Cuba and Puerto Rico in preparation for the larger event. On May 13 the North Atlantic Squadron shelled San Juan de Puerto Rico. On May 30 Commodore Schley's squadron bombarded the forts guarding the mouth of Santiago Harbor. Neither attack had any material result. It was evident that well-ordered land operations were indispensable to achieve a decisive advantage.

The next act in the war thrilled not alone the hearts of our countrymen but the world by its exceptional heroism. On the night of June 3 Lieutenant Hobson, aided by seven devoted volunteers, blocked the narrow outlet from Santiago Harbor by sinking the collier *Merrimac* in the channel, under a fierce fire from the shore batteries, escaping with their lives as by a miracle, but falling into the hands of the Spaniards. It is a most gratifying incident of the war that the bravery of this little band of heroes was cordially appreciated by the Spanish admiral, who sent a flag of truce to notify Admiral Sampson of their safety and to compliment them on their daring act. They were subsequently exchanged July 7.

By June 7 the cutting of the last Cuban cable isolated the island. Thereafter the invasion was vigorously prosecuted. On June 10, under a heavy protecting fire, a landing of 600 marines from the *Oregon*, *Marblehead*, and *Yankee* was effected in Guantanamo Bay, where it had been determined to establish a naval station.

This important and essential port was taken from the enemy, after severe fighting, by the marines, who were the first organized force of the United States to land in Cuba.

The position so won was held despite desperate attempts to dislodge our forces. By June 16 additional forces were landed and strongly intrenched. On June 22 the advance of the invading army under Major-General Shafter landed at Daiquiri, about 15 miles east of Santiago. This was accomplished under great difficulties, but with marvelous dispatch. On June 23 the movement against Santiago was begun. On the 24th the first serious engagement took place, in which the First and Tenth Cavalry and the First United States Volunteer Cavalry, General Young's brigade of General Wheeler's division, participated, losing heavily. By nightfall, however, ground within 5 miles of Santiago was won. The advantage was steadily increased. On July 1 a severe battle took place, our forces gaining the outworks of Santiago; on the 2d El Caney and San Juan were taken after a desperate charge, and the investment of the city was completed. The Navy cooperated by shelling the town and the coast forts.

On the day following this brilliant achievement of our land forces, the 3d of July, occurred the decisive naval combat of the war. The Spanish fleet, attempting to leave the harbor, was met by the American squadron under command of Commodore Sampson. In less than three hours all the Spanish ships were destroyed, the two torpedo boats being sunk and the *María Teresa*, *Almirante Oquendo*, *Vizcaya*, and *Cristóbal Colón* driven ashore. The Spanish admiral and over 1,300 men were taken prisoners. While the enemy's loss of life was deplorably large, some 600 perishing, on our side but one man was killed, on the *Brooklyn*, and one man seriously wounded. Although our ships were repeatedly struck, not one was seriously injured. Where all so conspicuously distinguished themselves, from the commanders to the gunners and the unnamed heroes in the boiler rooms, each and all contributing toward the achievement of this astounding victory, for which neither ancient nor modern history affords a parallel in the completeness of the event and the marvelous disproportion of casualties, it would be invidious to single out any for especial honor. Deserved promotion has rewarded the more conspicuous actors. The nation's profoundest gratitude is due to all of these brave men who by their skill and devotion in a few short hours crushed the sea power of Spain and wrought a triumph whose decisiveness and far-reaching consequences can scarcely be measured. Nor can we be unmindful of the achievements of our builders, mechanics, and artisans for their skill in the construction of our war ships.

With the catastrophe of Santiago Spain's effort upon the ocean virtually ceased. A spasmodic effort toward the end of June to send her Mediterranean fleet, under Admiral Camara, to relieve Manila was abandoned, the expedition being recalled after it had passed through the Suez Canal.

The capitulation of Santiago followed. The city was closely besieged by land, while the entrance of our ships into the harbor cut off all relief on that side. After a truce to allow of the removal of noncombatants protracted negotiations continued from July 3 until July 15, when, under menace of immediate assault, the preliminaries of surrender were agreed upon. On the 17th General Shafter occupied the city. The capitulation embraced the entire eastern end of Cuba. The number of Spanish soldiers surrendering was 22,000, all of whom were subsequently conveyed to Spain at the charge of the United States. The story of this successful campaign is told in the report of the Secretary of War, which will be laid before you. The individual valor of officers and soldiers was never more strikingly shown than in the several engagements leading to the surrender of Santiago, while the prompt movements and successive victories won instant and universal applause. To those who gained this complete triumph, which established the ascendency of the United States upon land as the fight off Santiago had fixed our supremacy on the seas, the earnest and lasting gratitude of the nation is unsparingly due. Nor should we alone remember the gallantry of the living; the dead claim our tears, and our losses by battle and disease must cloud any exultation at the result and teach us to weigh the awful cost of war, however rightful the cause or signal the victory.

With the fall of Santiago the occupation of Puerto Rico became the next strategic necessity. General Miles had previously been assigned to organize an expedition for that purpose. Fortunately he was already at Santiago, where he had arrived on the 11th of July with reenforcements for General Shafter's army.

With these troops, consisting of 3,415 infantry and artillery, two companies of engineers, and one company of the Signal Corps, General Miles left Guantanamo on July 21, having nine transports convoyed by the fleet under Captain Higginson with the *Massachusetts* (flagship), *Dixie*, *Gloucester*, *Columbia*, and *Yale*, the two latter carrying troops. The expedition landed at Guanica July 25, which port was entered with little opposition. Here the fleet was joined by the *Annapolis* and the *Wasp*, while the *Puritan* and *Amphitrite* went to San Juan and joined the *New Orleans*, which was engaged in blockading that port. The Major-General Commanding was subsequently reenforced by General Schwan's brigade of the Third Army Corps, by General Wilson with a part of his division, and also by General Brooke with a part of his corps, numbering in all 16,973 officers and men.

On July 27 he entered Ponce, one of the most important ports in the island, from which he thereafter directed operations for the capture of the island.

With the exception of encounters with the enemy at Guayama, Hormigueros, Coamo, and Yauco and an attack on a force landed at Cape San Juan, there was no serious resistance. The campaign was prosecuted with great vigor, and by the 12th of August much of the island was in our possession and the acquisition of the remainder was only a matter of a short time. At most of the points in the island our troops were enthusiastically welcomed. Protestations of loyalty to the flag and gratitude for delivery from Spanish rule met our commanders at every stage. As a potent influence toward peace the outcome of the Puerto Rican expedition was of great consequence, and generous commendation is due to those who participated in it.

The last scene of the war was enacted at Manila, its starting place. On August 15, after a brief assault upon the works by the land forces, in which the squadron assisted, the capital surrendered unconditionally. The casualties were comparatively few. By this the conquest of the Philippine Islands, virtually accomplished when the Spanish capacity for resistance was destroyed by Admiral Dewey's victory of the 1st of May, was formally sealed. To General Merritt, his officers and men, for their uncomplaining and devoted service and for their gallantry in action, the nation is sincerely grateful. Their long voyage was made with singular success, and the soldierly conduct of the men, most of whom were without previous experience in the military service, deserves unmeasured praise.

The total casualties in killed and wounded in the Army during the war with Spain were: Officers killed, 23; enlisted men killed, 257; total, 280; officers wounded, 113; enlisted men wounded, 1,464; total, 1,577. Of the Navy: Killed, 17; wounded, 67; died as result of wounds, 1; invalided from service, 6; total, 91.

It will be observed that while our Navy was engaged in two great battles and in numerous perilous undertakings in blockade and bombardment, and more than 50,000 of our troops were transported to distant lands and were engaged in assault and siege and battle and many skirmishes in unfamiliar territory, we lost in both arms of the service a total of 1,668 killed and wounded; and in the entire campaign by land and sea we did not lose a gun or a flag or a transport or a ship, and, with the exception of the crew of the *Merrimac*, not a soldier or sailor was taken prisoner.

On August 7, forty-six days from the date of the landing of General Shafter's army in Cuba and twenty-one days from the surrender of

Santiago, the United States troops commenced embarkation for home, and our entire force was returned to the United States as early as August 24. They were absent from the United States only two months.

It is fitting that I should bear testimony to the patriotism and devotion of that large portion of our Army which, although eager to be ordered to the post of greatest exposure, fortunately was not required outside of the United States. They did their whole duty, and, like their comrades at the front, have earned the gratitude of the nation. In like manner, the officers and men of the Army and of the Navy who remained in their departments and stations faithfully performing most important duties connected with the war, and whose requests for assignment in the field and at sea I was compelled to refuse because their services were indispensable here, are entitled to the highest commendation. It is my regret that there seems to be no provision for their suitable recognition.

In this connection it is a pleasure for me to mention in terms of cordial appreciation the timely and useful work of the American National Red Cross, both in relief measures preparatory to the campaigns, in sanitary assistance at several of the camps of assemblage, and later, under the able and experienced leadership of the president of the society, Miss Clara Barton, on the fields of battle and in the hospitals at the front in Cuba. Working in conjunction with the governmental authorities and under their sanction and approval, and with the enthusiastic cooperation of many patriotic women and societies in the various States, the Red Cross has fully maintained its already high reputation for intense earnestness and ability to exercise the noble purposes of its international organization, thus justifying the confidence and support which it has received at the hands of the American people. To the members and officers of this society and all who aided them in their philanthropic work the sincere and lasting gratitude of the soldiers and the public is due and is freely accorded.

In tracing these events we are constantly reminded of our obligations to the Divine Master for His watchful care over us and His safe guidance, for which the nation makes reverent acknowledgment and offers humble prayer for the continuance of His favor.

The annihilation of Admiral Cervera's fleet, followed by the capitulation of Santiago, having brought to the Spanish Government a realizing sense of the hopelessness of continuing a struggle now become wholly unequal, it made overtures of peace through the French ambassador, who, with the assent of his Government, had acted as the friendly representative of Spanish interests during the war. On the 26th of July M. Cambon presented a communication signed by the Duke of Almodóvar, the Spanish minister of state, inviting the United States to state the terms upon which it would be willing to make peace. On the 30th of July, by a communication addressed to the Duke of Almodóvar and handed to M. Cambon, the terms of this Government were announced substantially as in the protocol afterwards signed. On the 10th of August the Spanish reply, dated August 7, was handed by M. Cambon to the Secretary of State. It accepted unconditionally the terms imposed as to Cuba, Puerto Rico, and an island of the Ladrones group, but appeared to seek to introduce inadmissible reservations in regard to our demand as to the Philippine Islands. Conceiving that discussion on this point could neither be practical nor profitable, I directed that in order to avoid misunderstanding the matter should be forthwith closed by proposing the embodiment in a formal protocol of the terms upon which the negotiations for peace were to be undertaken. The vague and inexplicit suggestions of the Spanish note could not be accepted, the only reply being to present as a virtual ultimatum a draft of protocol embodying the precise terms tendered to Spain in our note of July 30, with added stipulations of detail as to the appointment of commissioners to arrange for the evacuation of the Spanish Antilles. On August 12 M. Cambon announced his receipt of full powers to sign the protocol so submitted. Accordingly, on the afternoon of August 12, M. Cambon, as the plenipotentiary of Spain, and the Secretary of State, as the plenipotentiary of the United States, signed a protocol providing—

ARTICLE I. Spain will relinquish all claim of sovereignty over and title to Cuba.

ART. II. Spain will cede to the United States the island of Puerto Rico and other islands now under Spanish sovereignty in the West Indies, and also an island in the Ladrones to be selected by the United States.

ART. III. The United States will occupy and hold the city, bay, and harbor of Manila pending the conclusion of a treaty of peace which shall determine the control, disposition, and government of the Philippines.

The fourth article provided for the appointment of joint commissions on the part of the United States and Spain, to meet in Havana and San Juan, respectively, for the purpose of arranging and carrying out the details of the stipulated evacuation of Cuba, Puerto Rico, and other Spanish islands in the West Indies.

The fifth article provided for the appointment of not more than five commissioners on each side, to meet at Paris not later than October 1 and to proceed to the negotiation and conclusion of a treaty of peace, subject to ratification according to the respective constitutional forms of the two countries.

The sixth and last article provided that upon the signature of the protocol hostilities between the two countries should be suspended and that notice to that effect should be given as soon as possible by each Government to the commanders of its military and naval forces.

Immediately upon the conclusion of the protocol I issued a proclamation, of August 12,* suspending hostilities on the part of the United States. The necessary orders to that end were at once given by telegraph The blockade of the ports of Cuba and San Juan de Puerto Rico was in like

* See p. 6487.

manner raised. On the 18th of August the muster out of 100,000 volunteers, or as near that number as was found to be practicable, was ordered.

On the 1st of December 101,165 officers and men had been mustered out and discharged from the service, and 9,002 more will be mustered out by the 10th of this month; also a corresponding number of general and general staff officers have been honorably discharged the service.

The military commissions to superintend the evacuation of Cuba, Puerto Rico, and the adjacent islands were forthwith appointed—for Cuba, Major-General James F. Wade, Rear-Admiral William T. Sampson, Major-General Matthew C. Butler; for Puerto Rico, Major-General John R. Brooke, Rear-Admiral Winfield S. Schley, Brigadier-General William W. Gordon—who soon afterwards met the Spanish commissioners at Havana and San Juan, respectively. The Puerto Rican Joint Commission speedily accomplished its task, and by the 18th of October the evacuation of the island was completed. The United States flag was raised over the island at noon on that day. The administration of its affairs has been provisionally intrusted to a military governor until the Congress shall otherwise provide. The Cuban Joint Commission has not yet terminated its labors. Owing to the difficulties in the way of removing the large numbers of Spanish troops still in Cuba, the evacuation can not be completed before the 1st of January next.

Pursuant to the fifth article of the protocol, I appointed William R. Day, lately Secretary of State; Cushman K. Davis, William P. Frye, and George Gray, Senators of the United States, and Whitelaw Reid to be the peace commissioners on the part of the United States. Proceeding in due season to Paris, they there met on the 1st of October five commissioners similarly appointed on the part of Spain. Their negotiations have made hopeful progress, so that I trust soon to be able to lay a definitive treaty of peace before the Senate, with a review of the steps leading to its signature.

I do not discuss at this time the government or the future of the new possessions which will come to us as the result of the war with Spain. Such discussion will be appropriate after the treaty of peace shall be ratified. In the meantime and until the Congress has legislated otherwise it will be my duty to continue the military governments which have existed since our occupation and give to the people security in life and property and encouragement under a just and beneficent rule.

As soon as we are in possession of Cuba and have pacified the island it will be necessary to give aid and direction to its people to form a government for themselves. This should be undertaken at the earliest moment consistent with safety and assured success. It is important that our relations with this people shall be of the most friendly character and our commercial relations close and reciprocal. It should be our duty to assist in every proper way to build up the waste places of the island, encourage the industry of the people, and assist them to form a government which shall be free and independent, thus realizing the best aspirations of the Cuban people.

Spanish rule must be replaced by a just, benevolent, and humane government, created by the people of Cuba, capable of performing all international obligations, and which shall encourage thrift, industry, and prosperity and promote peace and good will among all of the inhabitants, whatever may have been their relations in the past. Neither revenge nor passion should have a place in the new government. Until there is complete tranquillity in the island and a stable government inaugurated military occupation will be continued.

With the one exception of the rupture with Spain, the intercourse of the United States with the great family of nations has been marked with cordiality, and the close of the eventful year finds most of the issues that necessarily arise in the complex relations of sovereign states adjusted or presenting no serious obstacle to a just and honorable solution by amicable agreement.

A long unsettled dispute as to the extended boundary between the Argentine Republic and Chile, stretching along the Andean crests from the southern border of the Atacama Desert to Magellan Straits, nearly a third of the length of the South American continent, assumed an acute stage in the early part of the year, and afforded to this Government occasion to express the hope that the resort to arbitration, already contemplated by existing conventions between the parties, might prevail despite the grave difficulties arising in its application. I am happy to say that arrangements to this end have been perfected, the questions of fact upon which the respective commissioners were unable to agree being in course of reference to Her Britannic Majesty for determination. A residual difference touching the northern boundary line across the Atacama Desert, for which existing treaties provided no adequate adjustment, bids fair to be settled in like manner by a joint commission, upon which the United States minister at Buenos Ayres has been invited to serve as umpire in the last resort.

I have found occasion to approach the Argentine Government with a view to removing differences of rate charges imposed upon the cables of an American corporation in the transmission between Buenos Ayres and the cities of Uruguay and Brazil of through messages passing from and to the United States. Although the matter is complicated by exclusive concessions by Uruguay and Brazil to foreign companies, there is strong hope that a good understanding will be reached and that the important channels of commercial communication between the United States and the Atlantic cities of South America may be freed from an almost prohibitory discrimination.

In this relation I may be permitted to express my sense of the fitness of an international agreement whereby the interchange of messages over connecting cables may be regulated on a fair basis of uniformity. The world has seen the postal system developed from a congeries of independent and exclusive services into a well-ordered union, of which all countries enjoy the manifold benefits. It would be strange were the nations not in time brought to realize that modern civilization, which owes so much of its progress to the annihilation of space by the electric force, demands that this all-important means of communication be a heritage of all peoples, to be administered and regulated in their common behoof. A step in this direction was taken when the international convention of 1884 for the protection of submarine cables was signed, and the day is, I trust, not far distant when this medium for the transmission of thought from land to land may be brought within the domain of international concert as completely as is the material carriage of commerce and correspondence upon the face of the waters that divide them.

The claim of Thomas Jefferson Page against Argentina, which has been pending many years, has been adjusted. The sum awarded by the Congress of Argentina was $4,242.35.

The sympathy of the American people has justly been offered to the ruler and the people of Austria-Hungary by reason of the affliction that has lately befallen them in the assassination of the Empress-Queen of that historic realm.

On the 10th of September, 1897, a conflict took place at Lattimer, Pa., between a body of striking miners and the sheriff of Luzerne County and his deputies, in which 22 miners were killed and 44 wounded, of whom 10 of the killed and 12 of the wounded were Austrian and Hungarian subjects. This deplorable event naturally aroused the solicitude of the Austro-Hungarian Government, which, on the assumption that the killing and wounding involved the unjustifiable misuse of authority, claimed reparation for the sufferers. Apart from the searching investigation and peremptory action of the authorities of Pennsylvania, the Federal Executive took appropriate steps to learn the merits of the case, in order to be in a position to meet the urgent complaint of a friendly power. The sheriff and his deputies, having been indicted for murder, were tried, and acquitted, after protracted proceedings and the hearing of hundreds of witnesses, on the ground that the killing was in the line of their official duty to uphold law and preserve public order in the State. A representative of the Department of Justice attended the trial and reported its course fully. With all the facts in its possession, this Government expects to reach a harmonious understanding on the subject with that of Austria-Hungary, notwithstanding the renewed claim of the latter, after learning the result of the trial, for indemnity for its injured subjects.

Despite the brief time allotted for preparation, the exhibits of this country at the Universal Exposition at Brussels in 1897 enjoyed the singular distinction of a larger proportion of awards, having regard to the number and classes of articles entered than those of other countries.

The worth of such a result in making known our national capacity to supply the world's markets is obvious.

Exhibitions of this international character are becoming more frequent as the exchanges of commercial countries grow more intimate and varied. Hardly a year passes that this Government is not invited to national participation at some important foreign center, but often on too short notice to permit of recourse to Congress for the power and means to do so. My predecessors have suggested the advisability of providing by a general enactment and a standing appropriation for accepting such invitations and for representation of this country by a commission. This plan has my cordial approval.

I trust that the Belgian restrictions on the importation of cattle from the United States, originally adopted as a sanitary precaution, will at an early day be relaxed as to their present features of hardship and discrimination, so as to admit live cattle under due regulation of their slaughter after landing. I am hopeful, too, of favorable change in the Belgian treatment of our preserved and salted meats. The growth of direct trade between the two countries, not alone for Belgian consumption and Belgian products, but by way of transit from and to other continental states, has been both encouraging and beneficial. No effort will be spared to enlarge its advantages by seeking the removal of needless impediments and by arrangements for increased commercial exchanges.

The year's events in Central America deserve more than passing mention.

A menacing rupture between Costa Rica and Nicaragua was happily composed by the signature of a convention between the parties, with the concurrence of the Guatemalan representative as a mediator, the act being negotiated and signed on board the United States steamer *Alert*, then lying in Central American waters. It is believed that the good offices of our envoy and of the commander of that vessel contributed toward this gratifying outcome.

In my last annual message the situation was presented with respect to the diplomatic representation of this Government in Central America created by the association of Nicaragua, Honduras, and Salvador under the title of the Greater Republic of Central America, and the delegation of their international functions to the Diet thereof. While the representative character of the Diet was recognized by my predecessor and has been confirmed during my Administration by receiving its accredited envoy and granting exequaturs to consuls commissioned under its authority, that recognition was qualified by the distinct understanding that the responsibility of each of the component sovereign Republics toward the United States remained wholly unaffected.

This proviso was needful inasmuch as the compact of the three Republics was at the outset an association whereby certain representative functions were delegated to a tripartite commission rather than a federation possessing centralized powers of government and administration. In this view of their relation and of the relation of the United States to the several Republics, a change in the representation of this country in Central America was neither recommended by the Executive nor initiated by Congress, thus leaving one of our envoys accredited, as heretofore, separately to two States of the Greater Republic, Nicaragua and Salvador, and to a third State, Costa Rica, which was not a party to the compact, while our other envoy was similarly accredited to a union State, Honduras, and a nonunion State, Guatemala. The result has been that the one has presented credentials only to the President of Costa Rica, the other having been received only by the Government of Guatemala.

Subsequently the three associated Republics entered into negotiations for taking the steps forecast in the original compact. A convention of their delegates framed for them a federal constitution under the name of the United States of Central America, and provided for a central federal government and legislature. Upon ratification by the constituent States, the 1st of November last was fixed for the new system to go into operation. Within a few weeks thereafter the plan was severely tested by revolutionary movements arising, with a consequent demand for unity of action on the part of the military power of the federal States to suppress them. Under this strain the new union seems to have been weakened through the withdrawal of its more important members. This Government was not officially advised of the installation of the federation and has maintained an attitude of friendly expectancy, while in no wise relinquishing the position held from the outset that the responsibilities of the several States toward us remained unaltered by their tentative relations among themselves.

The Nicaragua Canal Commission, under the chairmanship of Rear-Admiral John G. Walker, appointed July 24, 1897, under the authority of a provision in the sundry civil act of June 4 of that year, has nearly completed its labors, and the results of its exhaustive inquiry into the proper route, the feasibility, and the cost of construction of an interoceanic canal by a Nicaraguan route will be laid before you. In the performance of its task the commission received all possible courtesy and assistance from the Governments of Nicaragua and Costa Rica, which thus testified their appreciation of the importance of giving a speedy and practical outcome to the great project that has for so many years engrossed the attention of the respective countries.

As the scope of the recent inquiry embraced the whole subject, with the aim of making plans and surveys for a canal by the most convenient route, it necessarily included a review of the results of previous surveys and plans, and in particular those adopted by the Maritime Canal Company under its existing concessions from Nicaragua and Costa Rica, so that to this extent those grants necessarily hold as essential a part in the deliberations and conclusions of the Canal Commission as they have held and must needs hold in the discussion of the matter by the Congress. Under these circumstances and in view of overtures made to the Governments of Nicaragua and Costa Rica by other parties for a new canal concession predicated on the assumed approaching lapse of the contracts of the Maritime Canal Company with those States, I have not hesitated to express my conviction that considerations of expediency and international policy as between the several governments interested in the construction and control of an interoceanic canal by this route require the maintenance of the *status quo* until the Canal Commission shall have reported and the United States Congress shall have had the opportunity to pass finally upon the whole matter during the present session, without prejudice by reason of any change in the existing conditions.

Nevertheless, it appears that the Government of Nicaragua, as one of its last sovereign acts before merging its powers in those of the newly formed United States of Central America, has granted an optional concession to another association, to become effective on the expiration of the present grant. It does not appear what surveys have been made or what route is proposed under this contingent grant, so that an examination of the feasibility of its plans is necessarily not embraced in the report of the Canal Commission. All these circumstances suggest the urgency of some definite action by the Congress at this session if the labors of the past are to be utilized and the linking of the Atlantic and Pacific oceans by a practical waterway is to be realized. That the construction of such a maritime highway is now more than ever indispensable to that intimate and ready intercommunication between our eastern and western seaboards demanded by the annexation of the Hawaiian Islands and the prospective expansion of our influence and commerce in the Pacific, and that our national policy now more imperatively than ever calls for its control by this Government, are propositions which I doubt not the Congress will duly appreciate and wisely act upon.

A convention providing for the revival of the late United States and Chilean Claims Commission and the consideration of claims which were duly presented to the late commission, but not considered because of the expiration of the time limited for the duration of the commission, was signed May 24, 1897, and has remained unacted upon by the Senate. The term therein fixed for effecting the exchange of ratifications having elapsed, the convention falls unless the time be extended by amendment, which I am endeavoring to bring about, with the friendly concurrence of the Chilean Government.

The United States has not been an indifferent spectator of the extraordinary events transpiring in the Chinese Empire, whereby portions of its maritime provinces are passing under the control of various European powers; but the prospect that the vast commerce which the energy of our citizens and the necessity of our staple productions for Chinese uses has built up in those regions may not be prejudiced through any exclusive treatment by the new occupants has obviated the need of our country becoming an actor in the scene. Our position among nations, having a large Pacific coast and a constantly expanding direct trade with the farther Orient, gives us the equitable claim to consideration and friendly treatment in this regard, and it will be my aim to subserve our large interests in that quarter by all means appropriate to the constant policy of our Government. The territories of Kiao-chow, of Wei-hai-wei, and of Port Arthur and Talienwan, leased to Germany, Great Britain, and Russia, respectively, for terms of years, will, it is announced, be open to international commerce during such alien occupation; and if no discriminating treatment of American citizens and their trade be found to exist or be hereafter developed, the desire of this Government would appear to be realized.

In this relation, as showing the volume and value of our exchanges with China and the peculiarly favorable conditions which exist for their expansion in the normal course of trade, I refer to the communication addressed to the Speaker of the House of Representatives by the Secretary of the Treasury on the 14th of last June, with its accompanying letter of the Secretary of State, recommending an appropriation for a commission to study the commercial and industrial conditions in the Chinese Empire and report as to the opportunities for and obstacles to the enlargement of markets in China for the raw products and manufactures of the United States. Action was not taken thereon during the late session. I cordially urge that the recommendation receive at your hands the consideration which its importance and timeliness merit.

Meanwhile there may be just ground for disquietude in view of the unrest and revival of the old sentiment of opposition and prejudice to alien people which pervades certain of the Chinese provinces. As in the case of the attacks upon our citizens in Szechuen and at Kutien in 1895, the United States minister has been instructed to secure the fullest measure of protection, both local and imperial, for any menaced American interests, and to demand, in case of lawless injury to person or property, instant reparation appropriate to the case. War ships have been stationed at Tientsin for more ready observation of the disorders which have invaded even the Chinese capital, so as to be in a position to act should need arise, while a guard of marines has been sent to Peking to afford the minister the same measure of authoritative protection as the representatives of other nations have been constrained to employ.

Following close upon the rendition of the award of my predecessor as arbitrator of the claim of the Italian subject Cerruti against the Republic of Colombia, differences arose between the parties to the arbitration in regard to the scope and extension of the award, of which certain articles were contested by Colombia, while Italy claimed their literal fulfillment. The award having been made by the President of the United States, as an act of friendly consideration and with the sole view to an impartial composition of the matter in dispute, I could not but feel deep concern at such a miscarriage, and while unable to accept the Colombian theory that I, in my official capacity, possessed continuing functions as arbitrator, with power to interpret or revise the terms of the award, my best efforts were lent to bring the parties to a harmonious agreement as to the execution of its provisions.

A naval demonstration by Italy resulted in an engagement to pay the liabilities claimed upon their ascertainment; but this apparent disposition of the controversy was followed by a rupture of diplomatic intercourse between Colombia and Italy, which still continues, although, fortunately, without acute symptoms having supervened. Notwithstanding this, efforts are reported to be continuing for the ascertainment of Colombia's contingent liability on account of Cerruti's debts under the fifth article of the award.

A claim of an American citizen against the Dominican Republic for a public bridge over the Ozama River, which has been in diplomatic controversy for several years, has been settled by expert arbitration and an award in favor of the claimant amounting to about $90,000. It, however, remains unpaid, despite urgent demands for its settlement according to the terms of the compact.

There is now every prospect that the participation of the United States in the Universal Exposition to be held in Paris in 1900 will be on a scale commensurate with the advanced position held by our products and industries in the world's chief marts.

The preliminary report of Mr. Moses P. Handy, who, under the act approved July 19, 1897, was appointed special commissioner with a view to securing all attainable information necessary to a full and complete understanding by Congress in regard to the participation of this Government in the Paris Exposition, was laid before you by my message of December 6, 1897, and showed the large opportunities opened to make known our national progress in arts, science, and manufactures, as well as the urgent need of immediate and adequate provision to enable due advantage thereof to be taken. Mr. Handy's death soon afterwards rendered it necessary for another to take up and complete his unfinished work, and on January 11 last Mr. Thomas W. Cridler, Third Assistant Secretary of State, was designated to fulfill that task. His report was laid before you by my message of June 14, 1898, with the gratifying result of awakening renewed interest in the projected display. By a provision in the sundry civil appropriation act of July 1, 1898, a sum not to exceed $650,000 was allotted for the organization of a commission to care for the proper preparation and installation of American exhibits and for the display of suitable exhibits by the several Executive Departments, particularly by the Department of Agriculture, the Fish Commission, and the Smithsonian Institution, in representation of the Government of the United States.

Pursuant to that enactment I appointed Mr. Ferdinand W. Peck, of Chicago, commissioner-general, with an assistant commissioner-general and a secretary. Mr. Peck at once proceeded to Paris, where his success in enlarging the scope and variety of the United States exhibit has been most gratifying. Notwithstanding the comparatively limited area of the exposition site—less than one-half that of the World's Fair at Chicago—the space assigned to the United States has been increased from the absolute allotment of 157,403 square feet reported by Mr. Handy to some 202,000 square feet, with corresponding augmentation of the field for a truly characteristic representation of the various important branches of our country's development. Mr. Peck's report will be laid before you. In my judgment its recommendations will call for your early consideration, especially as regards an increase of the appropriation to at least one million dollars in all, so that not only may the assigned space be fully taken up by the best possible exhibits in every class, but the preparation and installation be on so perfect a scale as to rank among the first in that unparalleled competition of artistic and inventive production, and thus counterbalance the disadvantage with which we start as compared with other countries whose appropriations are on a more generous scale and whose preparations are in a state of much greater forwardness than our own.

Where our artisans have the admitted capacity to excel, where our inventive genius has initiated many of the grandest discoveries of these later days of the century, and where the native resources of our land are as limitless as they are valuable to supply the world's needs, it is our province, as it should be our earnest care, to lead in the march of human progress, and not rest content with any secondary place. Moreover, if this be due to ourselves, it is no less due to the great French nation whose guests we become, and which has in so many ways testified its wish and hope that our participation shall befit the place the two peoples have won in the field of universal development.

The commercial arrangement made with France on the 28th of May, 1898, under the provisions of section 3 of the tariff act of 1897, went into effect on the 1st day of June following. It has relieved a portion of our export trade from serious embarrassment. Further negotiations are now pending under section 4 of the same act with a view to the increase of trade between the two countries to their mutual advantage. Negotiations with other governments, in part interrupted by the war with Spain, are in progress under both sections of the tariff act. I hope to be able to announce some of the results of these negotiations during the present session of Congress.

Negotiations to the same end with Germany have been set on foot. Meanwhile no effort has been relaxed to convince the Imperial Government of the thoroughness of our inspection of pork products for exportation, and it is trusted that the efficient administration of this measure by the Department of Agriculture will be recognized as a guaranty of the healthfulness of the food staples we send abroad to countries where their use is large and necessary.

I transmitted to the Senate on the 10th of February last information touching the prohibition against the importation of fresh fruits from this country, which had then recently been decreed by Germany on the ground of danger of disseminating the San José scale insect. This precautionary measure was justified by Germany on the score of the drastic steps taken in several States of the Union against the spread of the pest, the elaborate reports of the Department of Agriculture being put in evidence to show the danger to German fruit-growing interests should the scale obtain a lodgment in that country. Temporary relief was afforded in the case of large consignments of fruit then on the way by inspection and admission when found noninfected. Later the prohibition was extended to dried fruits of every kind, but was relaxed so as to apply only to unpeeled fruit and fruit waste. As was to be expected, the alarm reached to other countries, and Switzerland has adopted a similar inhibition. Efforts are in progress to induce the German and Swiss Governments to relax the prohibition in favor of dried fruits shown to have been cured under circumstances rendering the existence of animal life impossible.

Our relations with Great Britain have continued on the most friendly footing. Assenting to our request, the protection of Americans and their interests in Spanish jurisdiction was assumed by the diplomatic and consular representatives of Great Britain, who fulfilled their delicate and arduous trust with tact and zeal, eliciting high commendation. I may be allowed to make fitting allusion to the instance of Mr. Ramsden, Her Majesty's consul at Santiago de Cuba, whose untimely death after distinguished service and untiring effort during the siege of that city was sincerely lamented.

In the early part of April last, pursuant to a request made at the instance of the Secretary of State by the British ambassador at this capital, the Canadian government granted facilities for the passage of four United States revenue cutters from the Great Lakes to the Atlantic coast by way of the Canadian canals and the St. Lawrence River. The vessels had reached Lake Ontario and were there awaiting the opening of navigation when war was declared between the United States and Spain. Her Majesty's Government thereupon, by a communication of the latter part of April, stated that the permission granted before the outbreak of hostilities would not be withdrawn provided the United States Government gave assurance that the vessels in question would proceed direct to a United States port without engaging in any hostile operation. This Government promptly agreed to the stipulated condition, it being understood that the vessels would not be prohibited from resisting any hostile attack.

It will give me especial satisfaction if I shall be authorized to communicate to you a favorable conclusion of the pending negotiations with Great Britain in respect to the Dominion of Canada. It is the earnest wish of this Government to remove all sources of discord and irritation in our relations with the neighboring Dominion. The trade between the two countries is constantly increasing, and it is important to both countries that all reasonable facilities should be granted for its development.

The Government of Greece strongly urges the onerousness of the duty here imposed upon the currants of that country, amounting to 100 per cent or more of their market value. This fruit is stated to be exclusively a Greek product, not coming into competition with any domestic product. The question of reciprocal commercial relations with Greece, including the restoration of currants to the free list, is under consideration.

The long-standing claim of Bernard Campbell for damages for injuries sustained from a violent assault committed against him by military authorities in the island of Haiti has been settled by the agreement of that Republic to pay him $10,000 in American gold. Of this sum $5,000 has already been paid. It is hoped that other pending claims of American citizens against that Republic may be amicably adjusted.

Pending the consideration by the Senate of the treaty signed June 16, 1897, by the plenipotentiaries of the United States and of the Republic of Hawaii, providing for the annexation of the islands, a joint resolution to accomplish the same purpose by accepting the offered cession and incorporating the ceded territory into the Union was adopted by the Congress and approved July 7, 1898. I thereupon directed the United States steamship *Philadelphia* to convey Rear-Admiral Miller to Honolulu, and intrusted to his hands this important legislative act, to be delivered to the President of the Republic of Hawaii, with whom the Admiral and the United States minister were authorized to make appropriate arrangements for transferring the sovereignty of the islands to the United States. This was simply but impressively accomplished on the 12th of August last by the delivery of a certified copy of the resolution to President Dole, who thereupon yielded up to the representative of the Government of the United States the sovereignty and public property of the Hawaiian Islands.

Pursuant to the terms of the joint resolution and in exercise of the authority thereby conferred upon me, I directed that the civil, judicial, and military powers theretofore exercised by the officers of the Government of the Republic of Hawaii should continue to be exercised by those officers until Congress shall provide a government for the incorporated territory, subject to my power to remove such officers and to fill vacancies. The President, officers, and troops of the Republic thereupon took the oath of allegiance to the United States, thus providing for the uninterrupted continuance of all the administrative and municipal functions of the annexed territory until Congress shall otherwise enact.

Following the further provision of the joint resolution, I appointed the Hons. Shelby M. Cullom, of Illinois, John T. Morgan, of Alabama, Robert R. Hitt, of Illinois, Sanford B. Dole, of Hawaii, and Walter F. Frear, of Hawaii, as commissioners to confer and recommend to Congress such legislation concerning the Hawaiian Islands as they should deem necessary or proper. The commissioners having fulfilled the mission confided to them, their report will be laid before you at an early day. It is believed that their recommendations will have the earnest consideration due to the magnitude of the responsibility resting upon you to give such shape to the relationship of those mid-Pacific lands to our home Union as will benefit both in the highest degree, realizing the aspirations of the community that has cast its lot with us and elected to share our political heritage, while at the same time justifying the foresight of those who for three-quarters of a century have looked to the assimilation of Hawaii as a natural and inevitable consummation, in harmony with our needs and in fulfillment of our cherished traditions.

The questions heretofore pending between Hawaii and Japan growing out of the alleged mistreatment of Japanese treaty immigrants were, I am pleased to say, adjusted before the act of transfer by the payment of a reasonable indemnity to the Government of Japan.

Under the provisions of the joint resolution, the existing customs relations of the Hawaiian Islands with the United States and with other countries remain unchanged until legislation shall otherwise provide. The consuls of Hawaii here and in foreign countries continue to fulfill their commercial agencies, while the United States consulate at Honolulu is maintained for all appropriate services pertaining to trade and the revenue. It would be desirable that all foreign consuls in the Hawaiian Islands should receive new exequaturs from this Government.

The attention of Congress is called to the fact that, our consular offices having ceased to exist in Hawaii and being about to cease in other countries coming under the sovereignty of the United States, the provisions for the relief and transportation of destitute American seamen in these countries under our consular regulations will in consequence terminate. It is proper, therefore, that new legislation should be enacted upon this subject in order to meet the changed conditions.

The interpretation of certain provisions of the extradition convention of December 11, 1861, has been at various times the occasion of controversy with the Government of Mexico. An acute difference arose in the case of the Mexican demand for the delivery of Jesús Guerra, who, having led a marauding expedition near the border with the proclaimed purpose of initiating an insurrection against President Diaz, escaped into Texas. Extradition was refused on the ground that the alleged offense was political in its character, and therefore came within the treaty proviso of nonsurrender. The Mexican contention was that the exception only related to purely political offenses, and that as Guerra's acts were admixed with the common crime of murder, arson, kidnaping, and robbery, the option of nondelivery became void, a position which this Government was unable to admit in view of the received international doctrine and practice in the matter. The Mexican Government, in view of this, gave notice January 24, 1898, of the termination of the convention, to take effect twelve months from that date, at the same time inviting the conclusion of a new convention, toward which negotiations are on foot.

In this relation I may refer to the necessity of some amendment of our existing extradition statute. It is a common stipulation of such treaties that neither party shall be bound to give up its own citizens, with the added proviso in one of our treaties, that with Japan, that it may surrender if it see fit. It is held in this country by an almost uniform course of decisions that where a treaty negatives the obligation to surrender the President is not invested with legal authority to act. The conferment of such authority would be in the line of that sound morality which shrinks from affording secure asylum to the author of a heinous crime. Again, statutory provision might well be made for what is styled extradition by way of transit, whereby a fugitive surrendered by one foreign government to another may be conveyed across the territory of the United States to the jurisdiction of the demanding state. A recommendation in this behalf made in the President's message of 1886* was not acted upon. The matter is presented for your consideration.

The problem of the Mexican free zone has been often discussed with regard to its inconvenience as a provocative of smuggling into the United States along an extensive and thinly guarded land border. The effort made by the joint resolution of March 1, 1895, to remedy the abuse charged by suspending the privilege of free transportation in bond across the territory of the United States to Mexico failed of good result, as is stated in Report No. 702 of the House of Representatives, submitted in the last session, March 11, 1898. As the question is one to be conveniently met by wise concurrent legislation of the two countries looking to the protection of the revenues by harmonious measures operating equally on either side of the boundary, rather than by conventional arrangements, I suggest that Congress consider the advisability of authorizing and inviting a conference of representatives of the Treasury Departments of the United States and Mexico to consider the subject in all its complex bearings, and make report with pertinent recommendations to the respective Governments for the information and consideration of their Congresses.

The Mexican Water Boundary Commission has adjusted all matters submitted to it to the satisfaction of both Governments save in three important cases—that of the "Chamizal" at El Paso, Tex., where the two commissioners failed to agree, and wherein, for this case only, this Government has proposed to Mexico the addition of a third member;

* See pp. 5086-5088.

the proposed elimination of what are known as "Bancos," small isolated islands formed by the cutting off of bends in the Rio Grande, from the operation of the treaties of 1884 and 1889, recommended by the commissioners and approved by this Government, but still under consideration by Mexico; and the subject of the "Equitable distribution of the waters of the Rio Grande," for which the commissioners recommended an international dam and reservoir, approved by Mexico, but still under consideration by this Government. Pending these questions it is necessary to extend the life of the commission, which expires December 23 next.

The coronation of the young Queen of the Netherlands was made the occasion of fitting congratulations.

The claim of Victor H. McCord against Peru, which for a number of years has been pressed by this Government and has on several occasions attracted the attention of the Congress, has been satisfactorily adjusted. A protocol was signed May 17, 1898, whereby, the fact of liability being admitted, the question of the amount to be awarded was submitted to the chief justice of Canada as sole arbitrator. His award sets the indemnity due the claimant at $40,000.

The Government of Peru has given the prescribed notification of its intention to abrogate the treaty of friendship, commerce, and navigation concluded with this country August 31, 1887. As that treaty contains many important provisions necessary to the maintenance of commerce and good relations, which could with difficulty be replaced by the negotiation of renewed provisions within the brief twelve months intervening before the treaty terminates, I have invited suggestions by Peru as to the particular provisions it is desired to annul, in the hope of reaching an arrangement whereby the remaining articles may be provisionally saved.

His Majesty the Czar having announced his purpose to raise the Imperial Russian mission at this capital to the rank of an embassy, I responded, under the authority conferred by the act of March 3, 1893, by commissioning and accrediting the actual representative at St. Petersburg in the capacity of ambassador extraordinary and plenipotentiary. The Russian ambassador to this country has since presented his credentials.

The proposal of the Czar for a general reduction of the vast military establishments that weigh so heavily upon many peoples in time of peace was communicated to this Government with an earnest invitation to be represented in the conference which it is contemplated to assemble with a view to discussing the means of accomplishing so desirable a result. His Majesty was at once informed of the cordial sympathy of this Government with the principle involved in his exalted proposal and of the readiness of the United States to take part in the conference. The active military force of the United States, as measured by our population, territorial area, and taxable wealth, is, and under any conceivable prospective conditions must continue to be, in time of peace so conspicuously less than that of the armed powers to whom the Czar's appeal is especially addressed that the question can have for us no practical importance save as marking an auspicious step toward the betterment of the condition of the modern peoples and the cultivation of peace and good will among them; but in this view it behooves us as a nation to lend countenance and aid to the beneficent project.

The claims of owners of American sealing vessels for seizure by Russian cruisers in Bering Sea are being pressed to a settlement. The equities of the cases justify the expectation that a measure of reparation will eventually be accorded in harmony with precedent and in the light of the proven facts.

The recommendation made in my special message of April 27 last is renewed, that appropriation be made to reimburse the master and owners of the Russian bark *Hans* for wrongful arrest of the master and detention of the vessel in February, 1896, by officers of the United States district court for the southern district of Mississippi. The papers accompanying my said message make out a most meritorious claim and justify the urgency with which it has been presented by the Government of Russia.

Malietoa Laupepa, King of Samoa, died on August 22 last. According to Article I of the general act of Berlin, ''his successor shall be duly elected according to the laws and customs of Samoa.''

Arrangements having been agreed upon between the signatories of the general act for the return of Mataafa and the other exiled Samoan chiefs, they were brought from Jaluit by a German war vessel and landed at Apia on September 18 last.

Whether the death of Malietoa and the return of his old-time rival Mataafa will add to the undesirable complications which the execution of the tripartite general act has heretofore developed remains to be seen. The efforts of this Government will, as heretofore, be addressed toward a harmonious and exact fulfillment of the terms of the international engagement to which the United States became a party in 1889.

The Cheek claim against Siam, after some five years of controversy, has been adjusted by arbitration under an agreement signed July 6, 1897, an award of 706,721 ticals (about $187,987.78), with release of the Cheek estate from mortgage claims, having been rendered March 21, 1898, in favor of the claimant by the arbitrator, Sir Nicholas John Hannen, British chief justice for China and Japan.

An envoy from Siam has been accredited to this Government and has presented his credentials.

Immediately upon the outbreak of the war with Spain the Swiss Government, fulfilling the high mission it has deservedly assumed as the patron of the International Red Cross, proposed to the United States and Spain that they should severally recognize and carry into execution, as a *modus vivendi*, during the continuance of hostilities, the additional articles proposed by the international conference of Geneva, October 20, 1868, extending the effects of the existing Red Cross convention of 1864 to the conduct of naval war. Following the example set by France and Germany in 1870 in adopting such a *modus vivendi*, and in view of the accession of the United States to those additional articles in 1882, although the exchange of ratifications thereof still remained uneffected, the Swiss proposal was promptly and cordially accepted by us, and simultaneously by Spain.

This Government feels a keen satisfaction in having thus been enabled to testify its adherence to the broadest principles of humanity even amidst the clash of war, and it is to be hoped that the extension of the Red Cross compact to hostilities by sea as well as on land may soon become an accomplished fact through the general promulgation of the additional naval Red Cross articles by the maritime powers now parties to the convention of 1864.

The important question of the claim of Switzerland to the perpetual cantonal allegiance of American citizens of Swiss origin has not made hopeful progress toward a solution, and controversies in this regard still continue.

The newly accredited envoy of the United States to the Ottoman Porte carries instructions looking to the disposal of matters in controversy with Turkey for a number of years. He is especially charged to press for a just settlement of our claims for indemnity by reason of the destruction of the property of American missionaries resident in that country during the Armenian troubles of 1895, as well as for the recognition of older claims of equal justness.

He is also instructed to seek an adjustment of the dispute growing out of the refusal of Turkey to recognize the acquired citizenship of Ottoman-born persons naturalized in the United States since 1869 without prior imperial consent, and in the same general relation he is directed to endeavor to bring about a solution of the question which has more or less acutely existed since 1869 concerning the jurisdictional rights of the United States in matters of criminal procedure and punishment under Article IV of the treaty of 1830. This latter difficulty grows out of a verbal difference, claimed by Turkey to be essential, between the original Turkish text and the promulgated translation.

After more than two years from the appointment of a consul of this country to Erzerum, he has received his exequatur.

The arbitral tribunal appointed under the treaty of February 2, 1897, between Great Britain and Venezuela, to determine the boundary line between the latter and the colony of British Guiana, is to convene at Paris during the present month. It is a source of much gratification to this Government to see the friendly resort of arbitration applied to the settlement of this controversy, not alone because of the earnest part we have had in bringing about the result, but also because the two members named on behalf of Venezuela, Mr. Chief Justice Fuller and Mr. Justice Brewer, chosen from our highest court, appropriately testify the continuing interest we feel in the definitive adjustment of the question according to the strictest rules of justice. The British members, Lord Herschell and Sir Richard Collins, are jurists of no less exalted repute, while the fifth member and president of the tribunal, M. F. De Martens, has earned a world-wide reputation as an authority upon international law.

The claim of Felipe Scandella against Venezuela for arbitrary expulsion and injury to his business has been adjusted by the revocation of the order of expulsion and by the payment of the sum of $16,000.

I have the satisfaction of being able to state that the Bureau of the American Republics, created in 1890 as the organ for promoting commercial intercourse and fraternal relations among the countries of the Western Hemisphere, has become a more efficient instrument of the wise purposes of its founders, and is receiving the cordial support of the contributing members of the international union which are actually represented in its board of management. A commercial directory, in two volumes, containing a mass of statistical matter descriptive of the industrial and commercial interests of the various countries, has been printed in English, Spanish, Portuguese, and French, and a monthly bulletin published in these four. languages and distributed in the Latin-American countries as well as in the United States has proved to be a valuable medium for disseminating information and furthering the varied interests of the international union.

During the past year the important work of collecting information of practical benefit to American industries and trade through the agency of the diplomatic and consular officers has been steadily advanced, and in order to lay such data before the public with the least delay the practice was begun in January, 1898, of issuing the commercial reports from day to day as they are received by the Department of State. It is believed that for promptitude as well as fullness of information the service thus supplied to our merchants and manufacturers will be found to show sensible improvement and to merit the liberal support of Congress.

The experiences of the last year bring forcibly home to us a sense of the burdens and the waste of war. We desire, in common with most civilized nations, to reduce to the lowest possible point the damage sustained in time of war by peaceable trade and commerce. It is true we may suffer in such cases less than other communities, but all nations are damaged more or less by the state of uneasiness and apprehension into which an outbreak of hostilities throws the entire commercial world. It should be our object, therefore, to minimize, so far as practicable, this inevitable loss and disturbance. This purpose can probably best be accomplished by an international agreement to regard all private property at sea as exempt from capture or destruction by the forces of belligerent powers. The United States Government has for many years advocated this humane and beneficent principle, and is now in position to recommend it to other powers without the imputation of selfish motives. I therefore suggest for your consideration that the Executive be authorized to correspond with the governments of the principal maritime powers with a view of incorporating into the permanent law of civilized nations the principle of the exemption of all private property at sea, not contraband of war, from capture or destruction by belligerent powers.

The Secretary of the Treasury reports that the receipts of the Government from all sources during the fiscal year ended June 30, 1898, including $64,751,223 received from sale of Pacific railroads, amounted to $405,321,335, and its expenditures to $443,368,582. There was collected from customs $149,575,062 and from internal revenue $170,900,641. Our dutiable imports amounted to $324,635,479, a decrease of $58,156,690 over the preceding year, and importations free of duty amounted to $291,-414,175, a decrease from the preceding year of $90,524,068. Internal-revenue receipts exceeded those of the preceding year by $24,212,067.

The total tax collected on distilled spirits was $92,546,999; on manufactured tobacco, $36,230,522, and on fermented liquors, $39,515,421. We exported merchandise during the year amounting to $1,231,482,330, an increase of $180,488,774 from the preceding year.

It is estimated upon the basis of present revenue laws that the receipts of the Government for the year ending June 30, 1899, will be $577,-874,647, and its expenditures $689,874,647, resulting in a deficiency of $112,000,000.

On the 1st of December, 1898, there was held in the Treasury gold coin amounting to $138,441,547, gold bullion amounting to $138,502,545, silver bullion amounting to $93,359,250, and other forms of money amounting to $451,963,981.

On the same date the amount of money of all kinds in circulation, or not included in Treasury holdings, was $1,886,879,504, an increase for the year of $165,794,966. Estimating our population at 75,194,000 at the time mentioned, the per capita circulation was $25.09. On the same date there was in the Treasury gold bullion amounting to $138,502,545.

The provisions made for strengthening the resources of the Treasury in connection with the war have given increased confidence in the purpose and power of the Government to maintain the present standard, and have established more firmly than ever the national credit at home and abroad. A marked evidence of this is found in the inflow of gold to the Treasury. Its net gold holdings on November 1, 1898, were $239,-885,162 as compared with $153,573,147 on November 1, 1897, and an increase of net cash of $207,756,100, November 1, 1897, to $300,238,275, November 1, 1898. The present ratio of net Treasury gold to outstanding Government liabilities, including United States notes, Treasury notes of 1890, silver certificates, currency certificates, standard silver dollars, and fractional silver coin, November 1, 1898, was 25.35 per cent, as compared with 16.96 per cent, November 1, 1897.

I renew so much of my recommendation of December, 1897, as follows:

That when any of the United States notes are presented for redemption in gold and are redeemed in gold, such notes shall be kept and set apart and only paid out in exchange for gold. This is an obvious duty. If the holder of the United States note prefers the gold and gets it from the Government, he should not receive back from the Government a United States note without paying gold in exchange for it. The reason for this is made all the more apparent when the Government issues an interest-bearing debt to provide gold for the redemption of United States notes— a non-interest-bearing debt. Surely it should not pay them out again except on demand and for gold. If they are put out in any other way, they may return again, to be followed by another bond issue to redeem them—another interest-bearing debt to redeem a non-interest-bearing debt.

This recommendation was made in the belief that such provisions of law would insure to a greater degree the safety of the present standard, and better protect our currency from the dangers to which it is subjected from a disturbance in the general business conditions of the country.

In my judgment the present condition of the Treasury amply justifies the immediate enactment of the legislation recommended one year ago, under which a portion of the gold holdings should be placed in a trust fund from which greenbacks should be redeemed upon presentation, but when once redeemed should not thereafter be paid out except for gold.

It is not to be inferred that other legislation relating to our currency is not required; on the contrary, there is an obvious demand for it.

The importance of adequate provision which will insure to our future a money standard related as our money standard now is to that of our commercial rivals is generally recognized.

The companion proposition that our domestic paper currency shall be kept safe and yet be so related to the needs of our industries and internal commerce as to be adequate and responsive to such needs is a proposition scarcely less important. The subject, in all its parts, is commended to the wise consideration of the Congress.

The annexation of Hawaii and the changed relations of the United States to Cuba, Puerto Rico, and the Philippines resulting from the war, compel the prompt adoption of a maritime policy by the United States. There should be established regular and frequent steamship communication, encouraged by the United States, under the American flag, with the newly acquired islands. Spain furnished to its colonies, at an annual cost of about $2,000,000, steamship lines communicating with a portion of the world's markets, as well as with trade centers of the home Government. The United States will not undertake to do less. It is our duty to furnish the people of Hawaii with facilities, under national control, for their export and import trade. It will be conceded that the present situation calls for legislation which shall be prompt, durable, and liberal.

The part which American merchant vessels and their seamen performed in the war with Spain demonstrates that this service, furnishing both pickets and the second line of defense, is a national necessity, and should be encouraged in every constitutional way. Details and methods for the accomplishment of this purpose are discussed in the report of the Secretary of the Treasury, to which the attention of Congress is respectfully invited.

In my last annual message I recommended that Congress authorize the appointment of a commission for the purpose of making systematic investigations with reference to the cause and prevention of yellow fever. This matter has acquired an increased importance as a result of the military occupation of the island of Cuba and the commercial intercourse between this island and the United States which we have every reason to expect. The sanitary problems connected with our new relations with the island of Cuba and the acquisition of Puerto Rico are no less important than those relating to finance, commerce, and administration. It is my earnest desire that these problems may be considered by competent experts and that everything may be done which the most recent advances in sanitary science can offer for the protection of the health of our soldiers in those islands and of our citizens who are exposed to the dangers of infection from the importation of yellow fever. I therefore renew my recommendation that the authority of Congress may be given and a suitable appropriation made to provide for a commission of experts to be appointed for the purpose indicated.

Under the act of Congress approved April 26, 1898, authorizing the President in his discretion, ''upon a declaration of war by Congress, or a declaration by Congress that war exists,'' I directed the increase of the Regular Army to the maximum of 62,000, authorized in said act.

There are now in the Regular Army 57,862 officers and men. In said act it was provided—

That at the end of any war in which the United States may become involved the Army shall be reduced to a peace basis by the transfer in the same arm of the service or absorption by promotion or honorable discharge, under such regulations as the Secretary of War may establish, of supernumerary commissioned officers and the honorable discharge or transfer of supernumerary enlisted men; and nothing contained in this act shall be construed as authorizing the permanent increase of the commissioned or enlisted force of the Regular Army beyond that now provided by the law in force prior to the passage of this act, except as to the increase of twenty-five majors provided for in section 1 hereof.

The importance of legislation for the permanent increase of the Army is therefore manifest, and the recommendation of the Secretary of War for that purpose has my unqualified approval. There can be no question that at this time, and probably for some time in the future, 100,000 men will be none too many to meet the necessities of the situation. At all events, whether that number shall be required permanently or not, the power should be given to the President to enlist that force if in his discretion it should be necessary; and the further discretion should be given him to recruit for the Army within the above limit from the inhabitants of the islands with the government of which we are charged. It is my purpose to muster out the entire Volunteer Army as soon as the Congress shall provide for the increase of the regular establishment. This will be only an act of justice and will be much appreciated by the brave men who left their homes and employments to help the country in its emergency.

In my last annual message I stated:

The Union Pacific Railway, main line, was sold under the decree of the United States court for the district of Nebraska on the 1st and 2d of November of this year. The amount due the Government consisted of the principal of the subsidy bonds, $27,236,-512, and the accrued interest thereon, $31,211,711.75, making the total indebtedness $58,448,223.75. The bid at the sale covered the first-mortgage lien and the entire mortgage claim of the Government, principal and interest.

This left the Kansas Pacific case unconcluded. By a decree of the court in that case an upset price for the property was fixed at a sum which would yield to the Government only $2,500,000 upon its lien. The sale, at the instance of the Government, was postponed first to December 15, 1897, and later, upon the application of the United States, was postponed to the 16th day of February, 1898.

Having satisfied myself that the interests of the Government required that an effort should be made to obtain a larger sum, I directed the Secretary of the Treasury, under the act passed March 3, 1887, to pay out of the Treasury to the persons entitled to receive the same the amounts due upon all prior mortgages upon the Eastern and Middle divisions of said railroad out of any money in the Treasury not otherwise appropriated, whereupon the Attorney-General prepared a petition to be presented to the court, offering to redeem said prior liens in such manner as the court might direct, and praying that thereupon the United States might be held to be subrogated to all the rights of said prior lien holders and that a receiver might be appointed to take possession of the mortgaged premises and maintain and operate the same until the court or Congress otherwise directed. Thereupon the reorganization committee agreed that if said petition was withdrawn and the sale allowed to proceed on the 16th of February, 1898, they would bid a sum at the sale which would realize to the Government the entire principal of its debt, $6,303,000.

Believing that no better price could be obtained and appreciating the difficulties under which the Government would labor if it should become the purchaser of the road at the sale, in the absence of any authority by Congress to take charge of and operate the road I directed that upon the guaranty of a minimum bid which should give the Government the principal of its debt the sale should proceed. By this transaction the

Government secured an advance of $3,803,000 over and above the sum which the court had fixed as the upset price, and which the reorganization committee had declared was the maximum which they would pay for the property.

It is a gratifying fact that the result of these proceedings against the Union Pacific system and the Kansas Pacific line is that the Government has received on account of its subsidy claim the sum of $64,751,223.75, an increase of $18,997,163.76 over the sum which the reorganization committee originally agreed to bid for the joint property, the Government receiving its whole claim, principal and interest, on the Union Pacific, and the principal of its debt on the Kansas Pacific Railroad.

Steps had been taken to foreclose the Government's lien upon the Central Pacific Railroad Company, but before action was commenced Congress passed an act, approved July 7, 1898, creating a commission consisting of the Secretary of the Treasury, the Attorney-General, and the Secretary of the Interior, and their successors in office, with full power to settle the indebtedness to the Government growing out of the issue of bonds in aid of the construction of the Central Pacific and Western Pacific bond-aided railroads, subject to the approval of the President.

No report has yet been made to me by the commission thus created. Whatever action is had looking to a settlement of the indebtedness in accordance with the act referred to will be duly submitted to the Congress.

I deem it my duty to call to the attention of Congress the condition of the present building occupied by the Department of Justice. The business of that Department has increased very greatly since it was established in its present quarters. The building now occupied by it is neither large enough nor of suitable arrangement for the proper accommodation of the business of the Department. The Supervising Architect has pronounced it unsafe and unsuited for the use to which it is put. The Attorney-General in his report states that the library of the Department is upon the fourth floor, and that all the space allotted to it is so crowded with books as to dangerously overload the structure. The first floor is occupied by the Court of Claims. The building is of an old and dilapidated appearance, unsuited to the dignity which should attach to this important Department.

A proper regard for the safety, comfort, and convenience of the officers and employees would justify the expenditure of a liberal sum of money in the erection of a new building of commodious proportions and handsome appearance upon the very advantageous site already secured for that purpose, including the ground occupied by the present structure and adjoining vacant lot, comprising in all a frontage of 201 feet on Pennsylvania avenue and a depth of 136 feet.

In this connection I may likewise refer to the inadequate accommodations provided for the Supreme Court in the Capitol, and suggest the wisdom of making provision for the erection of a separate building for the court and its officers and library upon available ground near the Capitol.

The postal service of the country advances with extraordinary growth. Within twenty years both the revenues and the expenditures of the Post-Office Department have multiplied threefold. In the last ten years they have nearly doubled. Our postal business grows much more rapidly than our population. It now involves an expenditure of $100,000,000 a year, numbers 73,000 post-offices, and enrolls 200,000 employees. This remarkable extension of a service which is an accurate index of the public conditions presents gratifying evidence of the advancement of education, of the increase of communication and business activity, and of the improvement of mail facilities leading to their constantly augmenting use.

The war with Spain laid new and exceptional labors on the Post-Office Department. The mustering of the military and naval forces of the United States required special mail arrangements for every camp and every campaign. The communication between home and camp was naturally eager and expectant. In some of the larger places of rendezvous as many as 50,000 letters a day required handling. This necessity was met by the prompt detail and dispatch of experienced men from the established force and by directing all the instrumentalities of the railway mail and post-office service, so far as necessary, to this new need. Congress passed an act empowering the Postmaster-General to establish offices or branches at every military camp or station, and under this authority the postal machinery was speedily put into effective operation.

Under the same authority, when our forces moved upon Cuba, Puerto Rico, and the Philippines they were attended and followed by the postal service. Though the act of Congress authorized the appointment of postmasters where necessary, it was early determined that the public interests would best be subserved, not by new designations, but by the detail of experienced men familiar with every branch of the service, and this policy was steadily followed. When the territory which was the theater of conflict came into our possession, it became necessary to reestablish mail facilities for the resident population as well as to provide them for our forces of occupation, and the former requirement was met through the extension and application of the latter obligation. I gave the requisite authority, and the same general principle was applied to this as to other branches of civil administration under military occupation. The details are more particularly given in the report of the Postmaster-General, and, while the work is only just begun, it is pleasing to be able to say that the service in the territory which has come under our control is already materially improved.

The following recommendations of the Secretary of the Navy relative to the increase of the Navy have my earnest approval:

1. Three seagoing sheathed and coppered battle ships of about 13,500 tons trial displacement, carrying the heaviest armor and most powerful

ordnance for vessels of their class, and to have the highest practicable speed and great radius of action. Estimated cost, exclusive of armor and armament, $3,600,000 each.

2. Three sheathed and coppered armored cruisers of about 12,000 tons trial displacement, carrying the heaviest armor and most powerful ordnance for vessels of their class; and to have the highest practicable speed and great radius of action. Estimated cost, exclusive of armor and armament, $4,000,000 each.

3. Three sheathed and coppered protected cruisers of about 6,000 tons trial displacement, to have the highest practicable speed and great radius of action, and to carry the most powerful ordnance suitable for vessels of their class. Estimated cost, exclusive of armor and armament, $2,150,000 each.

4. Six sheathed and coppered cruisers of about 2,500 tons trial displacement, to have the highest speed compatible with good cruising qualities, great radius of action, and to carry the most powerful ordnance suited to vessels of their class. Estimated cost, exclusive of armament, $1,141,800 each.

I join with the Secretary of the Navy in recommending that the grades of admiral and vice-admiral be temporarily revived, to be filled by officers who have specially distinguished themselves in the war with Spain.

I earnestly urge upon Congress the importance of early legislation providing for the taking of the Twelfth Census. This is necessary in view of the large amount of work which must be performed in the preparation of the schedules preparatory to the enumeration of the population.

There were on the pension rolls on June 30, 1898, 993,714 names, an increase of nearly 18,000 over the number on the rolls on the same day of the preceding year. The amount appropriated by the act of December 22, 1896, for the payment of pensions for the fiscal year of 1898 was $140,000,000. Eight million seventy thousand eight hundred and seventy-two dollars and forty-six cents was appropriated by the act of March 31, 1898, to cover deficiencies in army pensions, and repayments in the sum of $12,020.33, making a total of $148,082,892.79 available for the payment of pensions during the fiscal year 1898. The amount disbursed from that sum was $144,651,879.80, leaving a balance of $3,431,012.99 unexpended on the 30th of June, 1898, which was covered into the Treasury. There were 389 names added to the rolls during the year by special acts passed at the second session of the Fifty-fifth Congress, making a total of 6,486 pensioners by Congressional enactments since 1861.

The total receipts of the Patent Office during the past year were $1,253,948.44. The expenditures were $1,081,633.79, leaving a surplus of $172,314.65.

The public lands disposed of by the Government during the year reached 8,453,896.92 acres, an increase of 614,780.26 acres over the previous year. The total receipts from public lands during the fiscal year amounted to $2,277,995.18, an increase of $190,063.90 over the preceding year. The lands embraced in the eleven forest reservations which were suspended by the act of June 4, 1897, again became subject to the operations of the proclamations of February 22, 1897, creating them, which added an estimated amount of 19,951,360 acres to the area embraced in the reserves previously created. In addition thereto two new reserves were created during the year—the Pine Mountain and Zaca Lake Reserve, in California, embracing 1,644,594 acres, and the Prescott Reserve, in Arizona, embracing 10,240 acres—while the Pecos River Reserve, in New Mexico, has been changed and enlarged to include 120,000 additional acres.

At the close of the year thirty forest reservations, not including those of the Afognak Forest and the Fish-Culture Reserve, in Alaska, had been created by Executive proclamations under section 24 of the act of March 3, 1891, embracing an estimated area of 40,719,474 acres.

The Department of the Interior has inaugurated a forest system, made possible by the act of July, 1898, for a graded force of officers in control of the reserves. This system has only been in full operation since August, but good results have already been secured in many sections. The reports received indicate that the system of patrol has not only prevented destructive fires from gaining headway, but has diminished the number of fires.

The special attention of the Congress is called to that part of the report of the Secretary of the Interior in relation to the Five Civilized Tribes. It is noteworthy that the general condition of the Indians shows marked progress. But one outbreak of a serious character occurred during the year, and that among the Chippewa Indians of Minnesota, which happily has been suppressed.

While it has not yet been practicable to enforce all the provisions of the act of June 28, 1898, "for the protection of the people of the Indian Territory, and for other purposes," it is having a salutary effect upon the nations composing the five tribes. The Dawes Commission reports that the most gratifying results and greater advance toward the attainment of the objects of the Government have been secured in the past year than in any previous year. I can not too strongly indorse the recommendation of the commission and of the Secretary of the Interior for the necessity of providing for the education of the 30,000 white children resident in the Indian Territory.

The Department of Agriculture has been active in the past year. Explorers have been sent to many of the countries of the Eastern and Western hemispheres for seeds and plants that may be useful to the United States, and with the further view of opening up markets for our surplus products. The Forestry Division of the Department is giving special attention to the treeless regions of our country and is introducing species specially adapted to semiarid regions. Forest fires, which seriously interfere with production, especially in irrigated regions, are being studied, that losses from this cause may be avoided. The Department is inquiring into the use and abuse of water in many States of the West, and collating information regarding the laws of the States, the decisions of the courts, and the customs of the people in this regard, so that uniformity may be secured. Experiment stations are becoming more effective every year. The annual appropriation of $720,000 by Congress is supplemented by $400,000 from the States. Nation-wide experiments have been conducted to ascertain the suitableness as to soil and climate and States for growing sugar beets. The number of sugar factories has been doubled in the past two years, and the ability of the United States to produce its own sugar from this source has been clearly demonstrated.

The Weather Bureau forecast and observation stations have been extended around the Caribbean Sea, to give early warning of the approach of hurricanes from the south seas to our fleets and merchant marine.

In the year 1900 will occur the centennial anniversary of the founding of the city of Washington for the permanent capital of the Government of the United States by authority of an act of Congress approved July 16, 1790. In May, 1800, the archives and general offices of the Federal Government were removed to this place. On the 17th of November, 1800, the National Congress met here for the first time and assumed exclusive control of the Federal district and city. This interesting event assumes all the more significance when we recall the circumstances attending the choosing of the site, the naming of the capital in honor of the Father of his Country, and the interest taken by him in the adoption of plans for its future development on a magnificent scale.

These original plans have been wrought out with a constant progress and a signal success even beyond anything their framers could have foreseen. The people of the country are justly proud of the distinctive beauty and government of the capital and of the rare instruments of science and education which here find their natural home.

A movement lately inaugurated by the citizens to have the anniversary celebrated with fitting ceremonies, including, perhaps, the establishment of a handsome permanent memorial to mark so historical an occasion and to give it more than local recognition, has met with general favor on the part of the public.

I recommend to the Congress the granting of an appropriation for this purpose and the appointment of a committee from its respective bodies. It might also be advisable to authorize the President to appoint a committee from the country at large, which, acting with the Congressional and District of Columbia committees, can complete the plans for an appropriate national celebration.

The alien contract law is shown by experience to need some amendment; a measure providing better protection for seamen is proposed; the rightful application of the eight-hour law for the benefit of labor and of the principle of arbitration are suggested for consideration; and I commend these subjects to the careful attention of the Congress.

The several departmental reports will be laid before you. They give in great detail the conduct of the affairs of the Government during the past year and discuss many questions upon which the Congress may feel called upon to act. WILLIAM McKINLEY.

AN ACT declaring that war exists between the United States of America and the Kingdom of Spain.

Be it enacted by the Senate and House of Representatives of the United States of America in Congress assembled, First. That war be, and the same is hereby, declared to exist, and that war has existed since the 21st day of April, A. D. 1898, including said day, between the United States of America and the Kingdom of Spain.

Second. That the President of the United States be, and he hereby is, directed and empowered to use the entire land and naval forces of the United States and to call into the actual service of the United States the militia of the several States to such extent as may be necessary to carry this act into effect.

Approved, April 25, 1898.

EXECUTIVE MANSION, *December 6, 1898.*
To the Congress of the United States:

I transmit herewith, for the information of the Congress, the report of the Hawaiian Commission appointed in pursuance of the "Joint resolution to provide for annexing the Hawaiian Islands to the United States," approved July 7, 1898, together with a copy of the civil and penal laws of Hawaii. WILLIAM McKINLEY.

EXECUTIVE MANSION, *December 14, 1898.*
To the Congress of the United States:

I transmit herewith, for the information and use of the Congress, a communication from the Secretary of Agriculture, which is accompanied by a report on the market for American horses in foreign countries.
WILLIAM McKINLEY.

EXECUTIVE MANSION, *January 5, 1899.*
To the Senate and House of Representatives:

I transmit herewith a report of the Secretary of Agriculture on the work and expenditures of the agricultural experiment stations established under the act of Congress of March 2, 1887, for the fiscal year ending June 30, 1898, in accordance with the act making appropriations for the Department of Agriculture for the said fiscal year.
WILLIAM McKINLEY.

EXECUTIVE MANSION, *January 5, 1899.*
To the Senate:

In response to the resolution of the Senate of December 21, 1898, requesting the President, "If it be not inconsistent with the public service, to inform the Senate whether authentic information is in possession of the Government as to the alleged dissolution of the Government of the United States of Central America." I transmit herewith a report from the Secretary of State with accompanying papers.

WILLIAM McKINLEY.

EXECUTIVE MANSION,
Washington, January 6, 1899.
To the Senate of the United States:

I transmit herewith in answer to the resolution of the Senate of December 15, 1898, a communication from the Secretary of State covering a preliminary report from the Nicaraguan Canal Commission, dated December 26, 1898, relative to its progress in investigating the question of the proper route, the feasibility, and cost of construction of the Nicaragua Canal.

WILLIAM McKINLEY.

EXECUTIVE MANSION,
Washington, January 6, 1899.
To the Senate and House of Representatives:

I transmit herewith a communication from the Secretary of State, inclosing the annual report of the Director of the Bureau of the American Republics, with accompanying documents. In view of the improved condition and increasing usefulness of the Bureau, to which I have already called attention in my annual message, and the welcome assurances of greater activity on the part of the other American republics in support of its purposes, I cordially indorse the recommendations of the Secretary of State. It will doubtless be as gratifying to Congress as it is to me to be informed that the Argentine Republic has decided to renew its relations with the Bureau, and that there are grounds for hoping that the International American Union, created by the impressive conference of the representatives of our sister republics and those of the United States in Washington in 1889-90, will soon be perfected by the adhesion of the Republic of Chile to the compact for the support of the Bureau as the organ of the union. The interest of the United States in giving the fullest possible effect to the laudable desire of the international conference to promote not only trade intercourse but a closer fellowship among the various republics of this hemisphere is so evident that I am satisfied the progress made by the bureau, as a practical agency for attaining these objects, will receive the commendation and support of Congress.

WILLIAM McKINLEY.

EXECUTIVE MANSION,
Washington, January 11, 1899.

To the Senate of the United States:

In response to the resolution of the Senate of June 6, 1898, I transmit a report from the Secretary of State, inclosing copies of all papers on file in the Department of State relating to the case of Hugo O. Loewi, including those printed in Document No. 186, Senate, Fifty-fifth Congress, second session.   WILLIAM McKINLEY.

EXECUTIVE MANSION, *January 17, 1899.*
To the Senate and House of Representatives:

It will be remembered that in the month of October, 1897, reports were received here of the probable loss of the whaling fleet in the Arctic regions, and of the likelihood that nearly 300 men, composing the officers and crews of the fleet, would perish from hunger unless succor could reach them early in the spring.

The revenue cutter *Bear* was known to be *en route* from the Arctic Ocean to Puget Sound, Washington. Her arrival was anxiously awaited, as no other suitable Government vessel could be made available for Arctic work. That ship arrived at Seattle, Wash., on the 6th of November, after a six-months' cruise in the Arctic, and I at once ordered an expedition prepared for the relief of the imperiled whalemen,

The preparation of the *Bear* was commenced on the 11th of November, under the direction of the Secretary of the Treasury. Her officers and men of the Revenue-Cutter Service all volunteered for the perilous work, and the ship was completely fitted out, and, under the command of Capt. Francis Tuttle, of the Revenue-Cutter Service, sailed on her errand of mercy November 29, 1897, within nineteen days from the inception of the movement.

The plan of the expedition was briefly as follows:

The ship was to be fully provided with rations for the ice-imperiled whalemen, which were to be conveyed to them as soon as the ice conditions in Bering Strait would permit the passage through. An overland expedition was to be landed from the *Bear* as soon as practicable, at some point on the coast of Alaska, in Bering Sea, to be determined upon by Captain Tuttle. The problem of getting food to the imperiled people at the earliest time possible was the all-important consideration, for it was fully understood that the *Bear* could not, under the most favorable conditions of ice navigation in that region, reach their neighborhood before the following July or August. The utter lack of transportation of any kind in this far-off land suggested the idea, which was adopted as the only possible plan, of driving reindeer overland, to be slaughtered on arrival, for food to last until the arrival of the *Bear* with supplies the following summer. The reindeer were to be collected by the overland expedition from several points in Alaska, notably Cape Prince of Wales and Point Rodney, and, with such aid as could be procured from natives and others, driven to Point Barrow.

The overland expedition was formed, and consisted of First Lieut. David H. Jarvis, Revenue-Cutter Service, commanding; Second Lieut. Ellsworth P. Bertholf, Revenue-Cutter Service, and Dr. Samuel J. Call, surgeon of the *Bear*, all volunteers. This overland expedition was landed from the *Bear* at Cape Vancouver, in Bering Sea, Alaska, on the 16th of December, 1897, and commenced its toilsome and dreary journey through an arctic night to Point Barrow, Captain Tuttle returning with his command to winter at Dutch Harbor, Alaska, and from there to take advantage of the first opportunity in the early summer of 1898 to get north.

The overland expedition worked its way to the reindeer stations named, and succeeded in getting together about 450 deer. They were materially aided by Mr. W. T. Lopp, agent of the American Missionary Society at Cape Prince of Wales, and Artisarlook, a native of that region, both of whom, at great personal sacrifice, left their families and accompanied the reindeer herd to Point Barrow.

The overland expedition, after a difficult and hazardous journey of nearly 2,000 miles through the storms and bitter cold of an arctic winter, reached Point Barrow with the herd on the 29th of March, 1898, three months and twelve days from their landing from the *Bear* at Cape Vancouver, Alaskan coast of Bering Sea. They arrived none too soon. From the lack of an authoritative head, supplemented by bad sanitary conditions and want of proper food, the men from the whale ships quartered there were found upon the verge of great suffering, while sickness had broken out among them. Lieutenant Jarvis, under the instructions given him by the Secretary of the Treasury, at once assumed charge, in the name of the Government, of the camp and locality of Point Barrow, and he and Dr. Call devoted themselves with intelligent energy to correcting the wretched conditions found to exist. Order was at once inaugurated. Fresh meat from the reindeer herd was supplied, the sanitary conditions were improved, and the general health and comfort of the whalemen received immediate attention. Lieutenant Jarvis and Dr. Call remained at Point Barrow in charge until the arrival of the *Bear*, July 28, 1898, a period of four months. As soon as the *Bear* arrived Captain Tuttle began the distribution of ample supplies to the whalemen on shipboard and on shore. Having supplied all demands generously, succored the needy to the number of 275 between Point Barrow and Kotzebue Sound, taking on board the *Bear* 146 whalemen, 91 of whom were brought to the Pacific coast (the remainder having of their own volition left the ship *en route*), the vessel arrived back at Seattle on the 13th of September, after an absence in the bleak and dreary regions of Bering Sea and the Arctic Ocean of about seventeen months.

The hardships and perils encountered by the members of the overland expedition in their great journey through an almost uninhabited region, a barren waste of ice and snow, facing death itself every day for nearly four months, over a route never before traveled by white men, with no refuge but at the end of the journey, carrying relief and cheer to 275 distressed citizens of our country, all make another glorious page in the history of American seamen. They reflect by their heroic and gallant struggles the highest credit upon themselves and the Government which they faithfully served. I commend this heroic crew to the grateful consideration of Congress and the American people.

The year just closed has been fruitful of noble achievements in the field of war; and while I have commended to your consideration the names of heroes who have shed luster upon the American name in valorous contests and battles by land and sea, it is no less my pleasure to invite your attention to a victory of peace the results of which cannot well be magnified, and the dauntless courage of the men engaged stamps them as true heroes, whose services cannot pass unrecognized.

I have therefore the honor to submit the following recommendations and to ask your favorable action thereon :

1. That the thanks of Congress be voted to Capt. Francis Tuttle, Revenue-Cutter Service, and the officers and enlisted men composing his command for their able and gallant services.

2. That the thanks of Congress be extended to the members of the overland expedition; First Lieut. David H. Jarvis, Revenue-Cutter Service, commanding the overland expedition; to Second Lieut. Ellsworth P. Bertholf, Revenue-Cutter Service, and to Dr. Samuel J. Call, Surgeon.

3. That gold medals of honor of appropriate design, to be approved by the Secretary of the Treasury, be awarded to Lieutenants Jarvis and Bertholf and Dr. Call, commemorative of their heroic struggles in aid of suffering fellow-men.

4. That the sum of $2,500 be appropriated to be disbursed by the Secretary of the Treasury in bestowing rewards upon W. T. Lopp, Artisarlook, and native herders, who rendered material aid to the relief expedition.   WILLIAM McKINLEY.

EXECUTIVE MANSION, *January 19, 1899.*
To the Senate and House of Representatives:

I transmit herewith a second report on the investigations of the agricultural capabilities of Alaska for the year 1898, in accordance with the acts of Congress making appropriations for the Department of Agriculture for the fiscal years ending June 30, 1898, and June 30, 1899.
                    WILLIAM McKINLEY.

EXECUTIVE MANSION, *January 19, 1899.*

To the Senate of the United States:

I herewith return without approval Senate bill No. 708, entitled "An act for the relief of Albert E. Redstone."

My objections to the bill are:

First. It assumes that the beneficiary, Albert E. Redstone, sustained a loss by the incorporation of his preemption claim within the limits of the Sierra Forest Reserve. This reserve was established by executive proclamation of February 14, 1893 (27 Stats., 1059), issued under section 24 of the act of March 8, 1891 (26 Stats., 1103), and contains the following saving clause for the protection of existing claims under the public land laws:

* * * Excepting from the force and effect of this proclamation all lands which may have been, prior to the date hereof, embraced in any legal entry or covered by any lawful filing duly of record in the proper United States Land Office, or upon which any valid settlement has been made pursuant to law, and the statutory period within which to make entry or filing of record has not expired; * * *

Mr. Redstone did not sustain any loss by the creation of this reserve, because his rights, if he had any at that time, were fully recognized and protected by this provision in the proclamation.

Second. Mr. Redstone's preemption declaratory statement was filed April 6, 1889, and alleged settlement upon the same day. The land covered thereby had not been proclaimed for sale, and under sections 2265 and 2267 of the Revised Statutes, Mr. Redstone had thirty-three months from the date of his settlement within which to make proof and payment for the land, but in fact he never attempted to make such proof or payment. His preemption claim had therefore expired by operation of law long before the creation of this reserve. After his filing had thus expired Mr. Redstone was cited by the Land Department to show cause why his claim should not be declared at an end, and his filing formally canceled upon the public records, but he made no response or defense, and the filing was accordingly canceled.

Third. The Commissioner of the General Land Office reports that an investigation, made under the supervision of his office, shows that Mr. Redstone had actually abandoned the land covered by his preemption claim before the reserve was established.

Fourth. The Commissioner of the General Land Office reports that an examination, made under the supervision of his office, shows that the improvements placed upon this land during the life of this preemption claim and thereafter abandoned were less than $200 in value, while the amount appropriated in this bill is $1,800.

WILLIAM McKINLEY.

EXECUTIVE MANSION, *January 27, 1899.*

To the Senate and House of Representatives:

In accordance with a provision in the act making appropriations for the Department of Agriculture for the fiscal year ending June 30, 1899, I transmit herewith a report of the Secretary of Agriculture "upon the forestry investigations and work of the Department of Agriculture."

WILLIAM McKINLEY.

EXECUTIVE MANSION, *February 9, 1899.*

To the Senate of the United States:

I transmit herewith, in response to a resolution of the Senate of the 2nd instant, requesting information "whether any franchises or concessions of any character are being or have been granted by any municipality in Cuba or Puerto Rico since the military occupation thereof by the United States," etc., a report from the Secretary of War and accompanying papers.

WILLIAM McKINLEY,

EXECUTIVE MANSION,
Washington, February 10, 1899.

To the Senate and House of Representatives:

As a consequence of the ratification of the treaty of peace between the United States and Spain and its expected ratification by the Spanish Government, the United States will come into possession of the Philippine Islands, on the farther shores of the Pacific. The Hawaiian Islands and Guam becoming United States territory and forming convenient stopping places on the way across the sea, the necessity for speedy cable communication between the United States and all these Pacific islands has become imperative. Such communication should be established in such a way as to be wholly under the control of the United States, whether in time of peace or of war. At present the Philippines can be reached only by cables which pass through many foreign countries, and the Hawaiian Islands and Guam can only be communicated with by steamers, involving delays in each instance of at least a week. The present condition should not be allowed to continue for a moment longer than is absolutely necessary.

So long ago as 1885 reference was made in an executive message to Congress to the necessity for cable communication between the United States and Hawaii. This necessity has greatly increased since then. The question has been discussed in the Fifty-second, Fifty-fourth, and Fifty-fifth Congresses, in each of which some effort has been made looking toward laying a cable, at least as far as the Hawaiian Islands. The time has now arrived when a cable in the Pacific must extend at least as far as Manila, touching at the Hawaiian Islands and Guam on the way. Two methods of establishing this cable communication at once suggest themselves. First, construction and maintenance of such a cable by and at the expense of the United States Government; and, second, construction and maintenance of such a cable by a private United States corporation under such safeguards as Congress shall impose.

I do not make any recommendations to Congress as to which of these methods would be the more desirable. A cable of the length of that proposed requires so much time for construction and laying that it is estimated that at least two years must elapse after giving the order for the cable before the entire system could be successfully laid and put in operation. Further deep-sea soundings must be taken west of the Hawaiian Islands before the final route for the cable can be selected. Under these circumstances, it becomes a paramount necessity that measures should be taken before the close of the present Congress to provide such means as may seem most suitable for the establishment of a cable system.

I commend the whole subject to the careful consideration of the Congress and to such prompt action as may seem advisable.

WILLIAM McKINLEY.

EXECUTIVE MANSION,
Washington, February 11, 1899.

To the House of Representatives:

I transmit herewith the response of the Secretary of State to the resolution of the House of Representatives of February 4, 1899, calling for information in his possession concerning certain alleged outrages committed upon the person of Bishop Earl Cranston and other American citizens in the city of Peking, China. WILLIAM McKINLEY.

EXECUTIVE MANSION,
Washington, February 18, 1899.

To the Senate:

I transmit herewith the response of the Secretary of Agriculture to the resolution of the Senate of February 8, 1899, calling for information in his possession regarding the practical usefulness of reservoirs to agriculture in the irrigated region of the United States, especially as affecting the distribution of water to crops, the area and value of reclaimed land, and the stability and unprofitableness of farming where irrigation is practised. WILLIAM McKINLEY.

EXECUTIVE MANSION,
Washington, February 21, 1899.

To the Senate and House of Representatives:

I transmit herewith a communication from the Secretary of State, accompanying the commercial relations of the United States for the year 1898, being the annual reports of the consular officers upon the industries and commerce of foreign countries. In view of the value of these reports to the manufacturing and exporting interests of the country, I indorse the recommendation of the Secretary of State that Congress authorize the printing of the usual editions of 10,000 copies of the general summary, entitled "Review of the World's Commerce" and of 5,000 copies of "Commercial Relations" (including this summary), to enable the Department of State to meet the demand for such information.

WILLIAM McKINLEY.

EXECUTIVE MANSION, *April 11, 1899.*

Whereas a treaty of peace between the United States of America and Her Majesty the Queen Regent of Spain, in the name of her august son, Don Alfonso XIII, was concluded and signed by their respective plenipotentiaries at Paris on the 10th day of December, 1898, the original of which, being in the English and Spanish languages, is word for word as follows : (Here the full text of the treaty is inserted.) And whereas the said convention has been duly ratified on both parts and the ratifications of the two Governments were exchanged in the City of Washington on the 11th day of April, 1899 : Now, therefore, be it known that I, William McKinley, President of the United States of America, have caused the said convention to be made public, to the end that the same and every article and clause thereof may be observed and fulfilled with good faith by the United States and the citizens thereof.

WILLIAM McKINLEY.

EXECUTIVE MANSION, *December 5, 1899.*

To the Senate and House of Representatives:

At the threshold of your deliberations you are called to mourn with your countrymen the death of Vice-President Hobart, who passed from this life on the morning of November 21 last. His great soul now rests in eternal peace. His private life was pure and elevated, while his public career was ever distinguished by large capacity, stainless integrity, and exalted motives. He has been removed from the high office which he honored and dignified, but his lofty character, his devotion to duty, his honesty of purpose, and noble virtues remain with us as a priceless legacy and example.

The Fifty-sixth Congress convenes in its first regular session with the country in a condition of unusual prosperity, of universal good will among the people at home, and in relations of peace and friendship with every government of the world. Our foreign commerce has shown great increase in volume and value. The combined imports and exports for the year are the largest ever shown by a single year in all our history. Our exports for 1899 alone exceeded by more than a billion dollars our imports and exports combined in 1870. The imports per capita are 20 per cent less than in 1870, while the exports per capita are 58 per cent more than in 1870, showing the enlarged capacity of the United States to satisfy the wants of its own increasing population, as well as to contribute to those of the peoples of other nations.

Exports of agricultural products were $784,776,142. Of manufactured products we exported in value $339,592,146, being larger than any previous year. It is a noteworthy fact that the only years in all our history when the products of our manufactories sold abroad exceeded those bought abroad were 1898 and 1899.

Government receipts from all sources for the fiscal year ended June 30, 1899, including $11,798,314.14, part payment of the Central Pacific Railroad indebtedness, aggregated $610,982,004.35. Customs receipts were $206,128,481.75, and those from internal revenue $273,-437,161.51.

For the fiscal year the expenditures were $700,093,564.02, leaving a deficit of $89,111,559.67.

The Secretary of the Treasury estimates that the receipts for the current fiscal year will aggregate $640,958,112, and upon the basis of present appropriations the expenditures will aggregate $600,958,112, leaving a surplus of $40,000,000.

For the fiscal year ended June 30, 1899, the internal-revenue receipts were increased about $100,000,000.

The present gratifying strength of the Treasury is shown by the fact that on December 1, 1899, the available cash balance was $278,-004,837.72, of which $239,744,905.36 was in gold coin and bullion. The conditions of confidence which prevail throughout the country have brought gold into more general use and customs receipts are now almost entirely paid in that coin.

The strong position of the Treasury with respect to cash on hand and the favorable showing made by the revenues have made it possible for the Secretary of the Treasury to take action under the provisions of section 3694, Revised Statutes, relating to the sinking fund. Receipts exceeded expenditures for the first five months of the current fiscal year by $13,413,389.91, and, as mentioned above, the Secretary of the Treasury estimates that there will be a surplus of approximately $40,000,000 at the end of the year. Under such conditions it was deemed advisable and proper to resume compliance with the provisions of the sinking-fund law, which for eight years has not been done because of deficiencies in the revenues. The Treasury Department therefore offered to purchase during November $25,000,000 of the 5 per cent loan of 1904, or the 4 per cent funded loan of 1907, at the current market price. The amount offered and purchased during November was $18,408,600. The premium paid by the Government on such purchases was $2,263,521 and the net saving in interest was about $2,885,000. The success of this operation was sufficient to induce the Government to continue the offer to purchase bonds to and including the 23d day of December, instant, unless the remainder of the $25,000,000 called for should be presented in the meantime for redemption.

Increased activity in industry, with its welcome attendant — a larger employment for labor at higher wages — gives to the body of the people a larger power to absorb the circulating medium. It is further true that year by year, with larger areas of land under cultivation, the increasing volume of agricultural products, cotton, corn, and wheat, calls for a larger volume of money supply. This is especially noticeable at the crop-harvesting and crop-moving period.

In its earlier history the National Banking Act seemed to prove a reasonable avenue through which needful additions to the circulation could from time to time be made. Changing conditions have apparently rendered it now inoperative to that end. The high margin in bond securities required, resulting from large premiums which Government bonds command in the market, or the tax on note issues, or both operating together, appear to be the influences which impair its public utility.

The attention of Congress is respectfully invited to this important matter, with the view of ascertaining whether or not such reasonable modifications can be made in the National Banking Act as will render its service in the particulars here referred to more responsive to the people's needs. I again urge that national banks be authorized to organize with a capital of $25,000.

I urgently recommend that to support the existing gold standard, and to maintain "the parity in value of the coins of the two metals (gold and silver) and the equal power of every dollar at all times in the market and in the payment of debts," the Secretary of the Treasury be given additional power and, charged with the duty to sell United States bonds and to employ such other effective means as may be necessary to these ends. The authority should include the power to sell bonds on long and short time, as conditions may require, and should provide for a rate of interest lower than that fixed by the act of January 14, 1875. While there is now no commercial fright which withdraws gold from the Government, but, on the contrary, such widespread confidence that gold seeks the Treasury demanding paper money in exchange, yet the very situation points to the present as the most fitting time to make adequate provision to insure the continuance of the gold standard and of public confidence in the ability and purpose of the Government to meet all its obligations in the money which the civilized world recognizes as the best. The financial transactions of the Government are conducted upon a gold basis. We receive gold when we sell United States bonds and use gold for their payment. We are maintaining the parity of all the money issued or coined by authority of the Government. We are doing these things with the means at hand. Happily at the present time we are not compelled to resort to loans to supply gold. It has been done in the past, however, and may have to be done in the future. It behooves us, therefore, to provide at once the best means to meet the emergency when it arises, and the best means are those which are the most certain and economical. Those now authorized have the virtue neither of directness nor economy. We have already eliminated one of the causes of our financial plight and embarrassment during the years 1893, 1894, 1895, and 1896. Our receipts now equal our expenditures; deficient revenues no longer create alarm. Let us remove the only remaining cause by conferring the full and necessary power on the Secretary of the Treasury and impose upon him the duty to uphold the present gold standard and preserve the coins of the two metals on a parity with each other, which is the repeatedly declared policy of the United States.

In this connection I repeat my former recommendations that a portion of the gold holdings shall be placed in a trust fund from which greenbacks shall be redeemed upon presentation, but when once redeemed shall not thereafter be paid out except for gold.

The value of an American merchant marine to the extension of our commercial trade and the strengthening of our power upon the sea invites the immediate action of the Congress. Our national development will be one-sided and unsatisfactory so long as the remarkable growth of our inland industries remains unaccompanied by progress on the seas. There is no lack of constitutional authority for legislation which shall give to the country maritime strength commensurate with its industrial achievements and with its rank among the nations of the earth.

The past year has recorded exceptional activity in our shipyards, and the promises of continual prosperity in shipbuilding are abundant. Advanced legislation for the protection of our seamen has been enacted. Our coast trade, under regulations wisely framed at the beginning of the Government and since, shows results for the past fiscal year unequaled in our records or those of any other power. We shall fail to realize our opportunities, however, if we complacently regard only matters at home and blind ourselves to the necessity of securing our share in the valuable carrying trade of the world.

Last year American vessels transported a smaller share of our exports and imports than during any former year in all our history, and the measure of our dependence upon foreign shipping was painfully manifested to our people. Without any choice of our own, but from necessity, the Departments of the Government charged with military and naval operations in the East and West Indies had to obtain from foreign flags merchant vessels essential for those operations.

The other great nations have not hesitated to adopt the required means to develop their shipping as a factor in national defense and as one of the surest and speediest means of obtaining for their producers a share in foreign markets. Like vigilance and effort on our part cannot fail to improve our situation, which is regarded with humiliation at home and with surprise abroad. Even the seeming sacrifices, which at the beginning may be involved, will be offset later by more than equivalent gains.

The expense is as nothing compared to the advantage to be achieved. The reestablishment of our merchant marine involves in a large measure our continued industrial progress and the extension of our commercial triumphs. I am satisfied the judgment of the country favors the policy of aid to our merchant marine, which will broaden our commerce and markets and upbuild our sea-carrying capacity for the products of agriculture and manufacture; which, with the increase of our Navy, mean more work and wages to our countrymen, as well as a safeguard to American interests in every part of the world.

Combinations of capital organized into trusts to control the conditions of trade among our citizens, to stifle competition, limit production, and determine the prices of products used and consumed by the people, are justly provoking public discussion, and should early claim the attention of the Congress.

The Industrial Commission, created by the act of the Congress of June 18, 1898, has been engaged in extended hearings upon the disputed questions involved in the subject of combinations in restraint

of trade and competition.   They have not yet completed their investigation of this subject, and the conclusions and recommendations at
which they may arrive are undetermined.

The subject is one giving rise to many divergent views as to the
nature and variety or cause and extent of the injuries to the public
which may result from large combinations concentrating more or less
numerous enterprises and establishments, which previously to the
formation of the combination were carried on separately.

It is universally conceded that combinations which engross or control the market of any particular kind of merchandise or commodity
necessary to the general community, by suppressing natural and ordinary competition, whereby prices are unduly enhanced to the general consumer, are obnoxious not only to the common law but also to
the public welfare.   There must be a remedy for the evils involved
in such organizations.   If the present law can be extended more certainly to control or check these monopolies or trusts, it should be
done without delay.   Whatever power the Congress possesses over
this most important subject should be promptly ascertained and asserted.

President Harrison in his annual message of December 3, 1889,
says:

Earnest attention should be given by Congress to a consideration of the question how far the restraint of those combinations of capital commonly called "trusts"
is matter of Federal jurisdiction.   When organized, as they often are, to crush out
all healthy competition and to monopolize the production or sale of an article of
commerce and general necessity they are dangerous conspiracies against the public
good, and should be made the subject of prohibitory and even penal legislation.

An act to protect trade and commerce against unlawful restraints
and monopolies was passed by Congress on the 2d of July, 1890.
The provisions of this statute are comprehensive and stringent.   It
declares every contract or combination, in the form of a trust or
otherwise, or conspiracy in the restraint of trade or commerce among
the several States or with foreign nations, to be unlawful.   It denom-
inates as a criminal every person who makes any such contract or
engages in any such combination or conspiracy, and provides a punishment by fine or imprisonment.   It invests the several circuit
courts of the United States with jurisdiction to prevent and restrain
violations of the act, and makes it the duty of the several United
States district attorneys, under the direction of the Attorney-General,
to institute proceedings in equity to prevent and restrain such violations.   It further confers upon any person who shall be injured in
his business or property by any other person or corporation by reason
of anything forbidden or declared to be unlawful by the act, the
power to sue therefor in any circuit court of the United States without respect to the amount in controversy, and to recover threefold

the damages by him sustained and the costs of the suit, including reasonable attorney fees. It will be perceived that the act is aimed at every kind of combination in the nature of a trust or monopoly in restraint of interstate or international commerce.

The prosecution by the United States of offenses under the act of 1890 has been frequently resorted to in the Federal courts, and notable efforts in the restraint of interstate commerce, such as the Trans-Missouri Freight Association and the Joint Traffic Association, have been successfully opposed and suppressed.

President Cleveland in his annual message of December 7, 1896 — more than six years subsequent to the enactment of this law — after stating the evils of these trust combinations, says:

> Though Congress has attempted to deal with this matter by legislation, the laws passed for that purpose thus far have proved ineffective, not because of any lack of disposition or attempt to enforce them, but simply because the laws themselves as interpreted by the courts do not reach the difficulty. If the insufficiencies of existing laws can be remedied by further legislation, it should be done. The fact must be recognized, however, that all Federal legislation on this subject may fall short of its purpose because of inherent obstacles, and also because of the complex character of our governmental system, which, while making the Federal authority supreme within its sphere, has carefully limited that sphere by metes and bounds which cannot be transgressed. The decision of our highest court on this precise question renders it quite doubtful whether the evils of trusts and monopolies can be adequately treated through Federal action, unless they seek directly and purposely to include in their objects transportation or intercourse between States or between the United States and foreign countries.
>
> It does not follow, however, that this is the limit of the remedy that may be applied. Even though it may be found that Federal authority is not broad enough to fully reach the case, there can be no doubt of the power of the several States to act effectively in the premises, and there should be no reason to doubt their willingness to judiciously exercise such power.

The State legislation to which President Cleveland looked for relief from the evils of trusts has failed to accomplish fully that object. This is probably due to a great extent to the fact that different States take different views as to the proper way to discriminate between evil and injurious combinations and those associations which are beneficial and necessary to the business prosperity of the country. The great diversity of treatment in different States arising from this cause and the intimate relations of all parts of the country to each other without regarding State lines in the conduct of business have made the enforcement of State laws difficult.

It is apparent that uniformity of legislation upon this subject in the several States is much to be desired. It is to be hoped that such uniformity founded in a wise and just discrimination between what is injurious and what is useful and necessary in business operations may be obtained and that means may be found for the Congress within the limitations of its constitutional power so to supplement an effective code of State legislation as to make a complete system of laws throughout the United States adequate to compel a general observance of the salutary rules to which I have referred.

The whole question is so important and far-reaching that I am sure no part of it will be lightly considered, but every phase of it will have the studied deliberation of the Congress, resulting in wise and judicious action.

A review of our relations with foreign States is presented with such recommendations as are deemed appropriate.

The long-pending boundary dispute between the Argentine Republic and Chile was settled in March last by the award of an arbitral commission, on which the United States minister at Buenos Ayres served as umpire.

Progress has been made toward the conclusion of a convention of extradition with the Argentine Republic. Having been advised and consented to by the United States Senate and ratified by Argentina, it only awaits the adjustment of some slight changes in the text before exchange.

In my last annual message I adverted to the claim of the Austro-Hungarian Government for indemnity for the killing of certain Austrian and Hungarian subjects by the authorities of the State of Pennsylvania, at Lattimer, while suppressing an unlawful tumult of miners, September 10, 1897. In view of the verdict of acquittal rendered by the court before which the sheriff and his deputies were tried for murder, and following the established doctrine that the Government may not be held accountable for injuries suffered by individuals at the hands of the public authorities while acting in the line of duty in suppressing disturbance of the public peace, this Government, after due consideration of the claim advanced by the Austro-Hungarian Government, was constrained to decline liability to indemnify the sufferers.

It is gratifying to be able to announce that the Belgian Government has mitigated the restrictions on the importation of cattle from the United States, to which I referred in my last annual message.

Having been invited by Belgium to participate in a congress, held at Brussels, to revise the provisions of the general act of July 2, 1890, for the repression of the African slave trade, to which the United States was a signatory party, this Government preferred not to be represented by a plenipotentiary, but reserved the right of accession to the result. Notable changes were made, those especially concerning this country being in the line of the increased restriction of the deleterious trade in spirituous liquors with the native tribes, which this Government has from the outset urgently advocated. The amended general act will be laid before the Senate, with a view to its advice and consent.

Early in the year the peace of Bolivia was disturbed by a successful insurrection. The United States minister remained at his post, attending to the American interests in that quarter, and using besides his good offices for the protection of the interests of British subjects in the absence of their national representative. On the establishment of the new Government, our minister was directed to enter into relations therewith.

General Pando was elected President of Bolivia on October 23.

Our representative has been instructed to use all permissible friendly endeavors to induce the Government of Bolivia to amend its marriage laws so as to give legal status to the non-Catholic and civil marriages of aliens within its jurisdiction, and strong hopes are entertained that the Bolivian law in this regard will be brought, as was that of Peru some years ago, into harmony with the general practice of modern States.

A convention of extradition with Brazil, signed May 14, 1897, has been ratified by the Brazilian Legislature.

During the past summer two national ships of the United States have visited Brazilian ports on a friendly mission and been cordially received. The voyage of the *Wilmington* up the Amazon River gave rise to a passing misunderstanding, owing to confusion in obtaining permission to visit the interior and make surveys in the general interest of navigation, but the incident found a ready adjustment in harmony with the close relations of amity which this Government has always sedulously sought to cultivate with the commonwealths of the Western Continent.

The claim growing out of the seizure of the American-owned newspaper "The Panama Star and Herald" by the authorities of Colombia has been settled, after a controversy of several years, by an agreement assessing at $30,000 the indemnity to be paid by the Colombian Government, in three installments of $10,000 each.

The good will of Colombia toward our country has been testified anew by the cordial extension of facilities to the Nicaraguan Canal Commission in their approaching investigation of the Panama Canal and other projected routes across the Isthmus of Darien.

Toward the end of October an insurrectionary disturbance developed in the Colombian Republic. This movement has thus far not attained any decisive result and is still in progress.

Discussion of the questions raised by the action of Denmark in imposing restrictions on the importation of American meats has continued without substantial result in our favor.

The neighboring island Republic of Santo Domingo has lately been the scene of revolution, following a long period of tranquillity. It began with the killing of President Heureaux in July last, and culminated in the relinquishment by the succeeding Vice-President of the reins of government to the insurgents. The first act of the provisional government was the calling of a presidential and constituent election. Juan Isidro Jimenez, having been elected President, was inaugurated on the 14th of November. Relations have been entered into with the newly established Government.

The experimental association of Nicaragua, Honduras, and Salvador, under the title of the Greater Republic of Central America, when apparently on the threshold of a complete federal organization by the adoption of a constitution and the formation of a national legislature, was disrupted in the last days of November, 1898, by the withdrawal of Salvador. Thereupon Nicaragua and Honduras abandoned the joint compact, each resuming its former independent sovereignty. This was followed by the reception of Minister Merry by the Republics of Nicaragua and Salvador, while Minister Hunter in turn presented his credentials to the Government of Honduras, thus reverting to the old distribution of the diplomatic agencies of the United States in Central America for which our existing statutes provide. A Nicaraguan envoy has been accredited to the United States.

An insurrectionary movement, under General Reyes, broke out at Bluefields in February last, and for a time exercised actual control in the Mosquito Territory. The *Detroit* was promptly sent thither for the protection of American interests. After a few weeks the Reyes government renounced the conflict, giving place to the restored supremacy of Nicaragua. During the interregnum certain public dues accruing under Nicaraguan law were collected from American merchants by the authorities for the time being in effective administrative control. Upon the titular government regaining power, a second payment of these dues was demanded. Controversy arose touching the validity of the original payment of the debt to the *de facto* regent of the territory. An arrangement was effected in April last by the United States minister and the foreign secretary of Nicaragua whereby the amounts of the duplicate payments were deposited with the British consul pending an adjustment of the matter by direct agreement between the Governments of the United States and Nicaragua. The controversy is still unsettled.

The contract of the Maritime Canal Company of Nicaragua was declared forfeited by the Nicaraguan Government on the 10th of October, on the ground of nonfulfillment within the ten years' term stipulated in the contract. The Maritime Canal Company has lodged a protest against this action, alleging rights in the premises which appear worthy of consideration. This Government expects that Nicaragua will afford the protestants a full and fair hearing upon the merits of the case.

The Nicaragua Canal Commission, which had been engaged upon the work of examination and survey for a ship-canal route across Nicaragua, having completed its labors and made its report, was dissolved on May 31, and on June 10 a new commission, known as the Isthmian Canal Commission, was organized under the terms of the act approved March 3, 1899, for the purpose of examining the American Isthmus with a view to determining the most practicable and feasible route for a ship canal across that Isthmus, with its probable cost, and other essential details.

This Commission, under the presidency of Rear-Admiral John G. Walker, U. S. N. (retired), entered promptly upon the work intrusted to it, and is now carrying on examinations in Nicaragua along the route of the Panama Canal, and in Darien from the Atlantic, in the neighborhood of the Atrato River, to the Bay of Panama, on the Pacific side. Good progress has been made, but under the law a comprehensive and complete investigation is ca'led for, which will require much labor and considerable time for its accomplishment. The work will be prosecuted as expeditiously as possible and a report made at the earliest practicable date.

The great importance of this work cannot be too often or too strongly pressed upon the attention of the Congress. In my message of a year ago I expressed my views of the necessity of a canal which would link the two great oceans, to which I again invite your consideration. The reasons then presented for early action are even stronger now.

A pleasing incident in the relations of this Government with that of Chile occurred in the generous assistance given to the war ship *Newark* when in distress in Chilean waters. Not alone in this way has the friendly disposition of Chile found expression. That country has acceded to the convention for the establishment of the Bureau of the American Republics, in which organization every independent State of the continent now shares.

The exchange of ratifications of a convention for the revival of the United States and Chilean Claims Commission and for the adjudication of claims heretofore presented but not determined during the life of the previous Commission has been delayed by reason of the necessity for fresh action by the Chilean Senate upon the amendments attached to the ratification of the treaty by the United States Senate. This formality is soon to be accomplished.

In view of disturbances in the populous provinces of northern China, where are many of our citizens, and of the imminence of disorder near the capital and toward the seaboard, a guard of marines was landed from the *Boston* and stationed during last winter in the legation compound at Peking. With the restoration of order this protection was withdrawn.

The interests of our citizens in that vast Empire have not been neglected during the past year. Adequate protection has been secured for our missionaries and some injuries to their property have been redressed.

American capital has sought and found various opportunities of competing to carry out the internal improvements which the Imperial Government is wisely encouraging, and to develop the natural resources of the Empire. Our trade with China has continued to grow, and our commercial rights under existing treaties have been everywhere maintained during the past year, as they will be in the future.

The extension of the area open to international foreign settlement at Shanghai and the opening of the ports of Nanking, Tsing-tao (Kiao chao), and Ta-lien-wan to foreign trade and settlement will doubtless afford American enterprise additional facilities and new fields, of which it will not be slow to take advantage.

In my message to Congress of December 5, 1898, I urged that the recommendation which had been made to the Speaker of the House of Representatives by the Secretary of the Treasury on the 14th of June, 1898, for an appropriation for a commission to study the commercial and industrial conditions in the Chinese Empire and report as to the opportunities for, and obstacles to, the enlargement of markets in China for the raw products and manufactures of the United States, should receive at your hands the consideration which its importance and timeliness merited, but the Congress failed to take action.

I now renew this recommendation, as the importance of the subject has steadily grown since it was first submitted to you, and no time should be lost in studying for ourselves the resources of this great field for American trade and enterprise.

The death of President Faure in February last called forth those sincere expressions of sympathy which befit the relations of two Republics as closely allied by unbroken historic ties as are the United States and France.

Preparations for the representation of the industries, arts, and products of the United States at the World's Exposition to be held in Paris next year continue on an elaborate and comprehensive scale, thanks to the generous appropriation provided by Congress and to the friendly interest the French Government has shown in furthering a typical exhibit of American progress.

There has been allotted to the United States a considerable addition of space, which, while placing our country in the first rank among exhibitors, does not suffice to meet the increasingly urgent demands of our manufacturers. The efforts of the Commissioner-General are ably directed toward a strictly representative display of all that most characteristically marks American achievement in the inventive arts, and most adequately shows the excellence of our natural productions.

In this age of keen rivalry among nations for mastery in commerce, the doctrine of evolution and the rule of the survival of the fittest must be as inexorable in their operation as they are positive in the results they bring about. The place won in the struggle by an industrial people can only be held by unrelaxed endeavor and constant advance in achievement. The present extraordinary impetus in every line of American exportation and the astounding increase in the volume and value of our share in the world's markets may not be attributed to accidental conditions.

The reasons are not far to seek. They lie deep in our national character and find expression year by year in every branch of handicraft, in every new device whereby the materials we so abundantly produce are subdued to the artisan's will and made to yield the largest, most practical, and most beneficial return. The American exhibit at Paris should, and I am confident will, be an open volume, whose lessons of skillfully directed endeavor, unfaltering energy, and consummate performance may be read by all on every page, thus spreading abroad a clearer knowledge of the worth of our productions and the justice of our claim to an important place in the marts of the world. To accomplish this by judicious selection, by recognition of paramount merit in whatever walk of trade or manufacture it may appear, and by orderly classification and attractive installation is the task of our Commission.

The United States Government building is approaching completion, and no effort will be spared to make it worthy, in beauty of architectural plan and in completeness of display, to represent our nation. It has been suggested that a permanent building of similar or appropriate design be erected on a convenient site, already given by the municipality, near the exposition grounds, to serve in commemoration of the part taken by this country in this great enterprise, as an American National Institute, for our countrymen resorting to Paris for study.

I am informed by our Commissioner-General that we shall have in the American sections at Paris over 7,000 exhibitors, from every State in our country, a number ten times as great as those which were represented at Vienna in 1873, six times as many as those in Paris in 1878, and four times as many as those who exhibited in Paris in 1889. This statement does not include the exhibits from either Cuba, Puerto Rico, or Hawaii, for which arrangements have been made.

A number of important international congresses on special topics affecting public interests are proposed to be held in Paris next summer in connection with the exposition. Effort will be made to have the several technical branches of our administration efficiently represented at those conferences, each in its special line, and to procure the largest possible concourse of State representatives, particularly at the Congresses of Public Charity and Medicine.

Our relations with Germany continue to be most cordial. The increasing intimacy of direct association has been marked during the year by the granting permission in April for the landing on our shores of a cable from Borkum Emden, on the North Sea, by way of the Azores, and also by the conclusion on September 2 of a Parcels Post Convention with the German Empire. In all that promises closer relations of intercourse and commerce and a better understanding between two races having so many traits in common, Germany can be assured of the most cordial cooperation of this Government and people. We may be rivals in many material paths, but our rivalry should be generous and open, ever aiming toward the attainment of larger results and the mutually beneficial advancement of each in the line of its especial adaptabilities.

The several governments of the Empire seem reluctant to admit the natural excellence of our food productions and to accept the evidence we constantly tender of the care with which their purity is guarded by rigid inspection from the farm, through the slaughterhouse and the packing establishments, to the port of shipment. Our system of control over exported food staples invites examination from any quarter and challenges respect by its efficient thoroughness.

It is to be hoped that in time the two Governments will act in common accord toward the realization of their common purpose to safeguard the public health and to insure the purity and wholesomeness of all food products imported by either country from the other. Were the Congress to authorize an invitation to Germany, in connection with the pending reciprocity negotiations, for the constitution of a joint commission of scientific experts and practical men of affairs to conduct a searching investigation of food production and exportation in both countries and report to their respective legislatures for the adoption of such remedial measures as they might recommend for either, the way might be opened for the desirable result indicated.

Efforts to obtain for American life insurance companies a full hearing as to their business operations in Prussia have, after several years of patient representation, happily succeeded, and one of the most important American companies has been granted a concession to continue business in that Kingdom.

I am also glad to announce that the German insurance companies have been readmitted by the superintendent of insurance to do business in the State of New York.

Subsequent to the exchange of our peace treaty with Spain, Germany acquired the Caroline Islands by purchase, paying therefor $5,000,000. Assurances have been received from the German Government that the rights of American missionaries and traders there will be considerately observed.

In my last annual message I referred to the pending negotiations with Great Britain in respect to the Dominion of Canada. By means of an executive agreement, a Joint High Commission had been created for the purpose of adjusting all unsettled questions between the United States and Canada, embracing twelve subjects, among which were the questions of the fur seals, the fisheries of the coast and contiguous inland waters, the Alaskan boundary, the transit of merchandise in bond, the alien labor laws, mining rights, reciprocity in trade, revision of the agreement respecting naval vessels in the Great Lakes, a more complete marking of parts of the boundary, provision for the conveyance of criminals, and for wrecking and salvage.

Much progress had been made by the Commission toward the adjustment of many of these questions, when it became apparent that an irreconcilable difference of views was entertained respecting the delimitation of the Alaskan boundary. In the failure of an agreement as to the meaning of Articles III and IV of the treaty of 1825 between Russia and Great Britain, which defined the boundary between Alaska and Canada, the American Commissioners proposed that the subject of the boundary be laid aside, and that the remaining questions of difference be proceeded with, some of which were so far advanced as to assure the probability of a settlement. This being declined by the British Commissioners, an adjournment was taken until the boundary should be adjusted by the two Governments. The subject has been receiving the careful attention which its importance demands, with the result that a *modus vivendi* for provisional demarcations in the region about the head of Lynn Canal has been agreed upon; and it is hoped that the negotiations now in progress between the two Governments will end in an agreement for the establishment and delimitation of a permanent boundary.

Apart from these questions growing out of our relationship with our northern neighbor, the most friendly disposition and ready agreement have marked the discussion of numerous matters arising in the vast and intimate intercourse of the United States with Great Britain.

This Government has maintained an attitude of neutrality in the unfortunate contest between Great Britain and the Boer States of Africa. We have remained faithful to the precept of avoiding entangling alliances as to affairs not of our direct concern. Had circumstances suggested that the parties to the quarrel would have welcomed any kindly expression of the hope of the American people that war might be averted, good offices would have been gladly tendered. The United States representative at Pretoria was early instructed to see that all neutral American interests be respected by the combatants. This has been an easy task in view of the positive declarations of both British and Boer authorities that the personal and property rights of our citizens should be observed.

Upon the withdrawal of the British agent from Pretoria the United States consul was authorized, upon the request of the British Government and with the assent of the South African and Orange Free State Governments, to exercise the customary good offices of a neutral for the care of British interests. In the discharge of this function, I am happy to say that abundant opportunity has been afforded to show the impartiality of this Government toward both the combatants.

For the fourth time in the present decade, question has arisen with the Government of Italy in regard to the lynching of Italian subjects. The latest of these deplorable events occurred at Tallulah, Louisiana, whereby five unfortunates of Italian origin were taken from jail and hanged.

The authorities of the State and a representative of the Italian Embassy having separately investigated the occurrence, with discrepant results, particularly as to the alleged citizenship of the victims, and it not appearing that the State had been able to discover and punish the violators of the law, an independent investigation has been set on foot, through the agency of the Department of State, and is still in progress. The result will enable the Executive to treat the question with the Government of Italy in a spirit of fairness and justice. A satisfactory solution will doubtless be reached

The recurrence of these distressing manifestations of blind mob fury directed at dependents or natives of a foreign country suggests that the contingency has arisen for action by Congress in the direction of conferring upon the Federal courts jurisdiction in this class of international cases where the ultimate responsibility of the Federal Government may be involved. The suggestion is not new. In his annual message of December 9, 1891, my predecessor, President Harrison, said:

It would, I believe, be entirely competent for Congress to make offenses against the treaty rights of foreigners domiciled in the United States cognizable in the Federal courts. This has not, however, been done, and the Federal officers and courts have no power in such cases to intervene either for the protection of a foreign citizen or for the punishment of his slayers. It seems to me to follow, in this state of the law, that the officers of the State charged with police and judicial powers in such cases must, in the consideration of international questions growing out of such incidents, be regarded in such sense as Federal agents as to make this Government answerable for their acts in cases where it would be answerable if the United States had used its constitutional power to define and punish crimes against treaty rights.

A bill to provide for the punishment of violations of treaty rights of aliens was introduced in the Senate March 1, 1892, and reported favorably March 30. Having doubtless in view the language of that part of Article III of the treaty of February 26, 1871, between the United States and Italy, which stipulates that " The citizens of each of the high contracting parties shall receive, in the States and Territories of the other, most constant protection and security for their persons and property, and shall enjoy in this respect the same rights and privileges as are or shall be granted to the natives, on their submitting themselves to the conditions imposed upon the natives," the bill so introduced and reported provided that any act committed in any State or Territory of the United States in violation of the rights of a citizen or subject of a foreign country secured to such citizen or subject by treaty between the United States and such foreign country and constituting a crime under the laws of the State or Territory shall constitute a like crime against the United States and be cognizable in the Federal courts. No action was taken by Congress in the matter.

I earnestly recommend that the subject be taken up anew and acted upon during the present session. The necessity for some such provision abundantly appears. Precedent for constituting a Federal jurisdiction in criminal cases where aliens are sufferers is rationally deducible from the existing statute, which gives to the district and circuit courts of the United States jurisdiction of civil suits brought by aliens where the amount involved exceeds a certain sum. If such jealous solicitude be shown for alien rights in cases of merely civil and pecuniary import, how much greater should be the public duty to take cognizance of matters affecting the lives and the rights of aliens under the settled principles of international law no less than under treaty stipulation, in cases of such transcendent wrong-doing as mob murder, especially when experience has shown that local justice is too often helpless to punish the offenders.

After many years of endeavor on the part of this Government to that end the Italian Government has consented to enter into negotiations for a naturalization convention, having for one of its objects the regulation of the status of Italians (except those of an age for active military service) who, having been naturalized in the United States, may revisit Italy. It is hoped that with the mutually conciliatory spirit displayed a successful conclusion will be reached.

The treaty of commerce and navigation between the United States and Japan on November 22, 1894, took effect in accordance with the terms of its XIXth Article on the 17th of July last; simultaneously with the enforcement of like treaties with the other powers, except France, whose convention did not go into operation until August 4, the United States being, however, granted up to that date all the privileges and rights accorded to French citizens under the old French treaty. By this notable conventional reform Japan's position as a fully independent sovereign power is assured, control being gained of taxation, customs revenues, judicial administration, coasting trade, and all other domestic functions of government, and foreign extra-territorial rights being renounced.

Comprehensive codes of civil and criminal procedure according to western methods, public instruction, patents and copyrights, municipal administration, including jurisdiction over the former foreign settlements, customs tariffs and procedure, public health, and other administrative measures have been proclaimed. The working of the new system has given rise to no material complaints on the part of the American citizens or interests, a circumstance which attests the ripe consideration with which the change has been prepared.

Valuable assistance was rendered by the Japanese authorities to the United States transport ship *Morgan City* while stranded at Kobe. Permission has been granted to land and pasture army horses at Japanese ports of call on the way to the Philippine Islands. These kindly evidences of good will are highly appreciated.

The Japanese Government has shown a lively interest in the proposition of the Pacific Cable Company to add to its projected cable lines to Hawaii, Guam, and the Philippines a branch connection with the coast of Japan. It would be a gratifying consummation were the utility of the contemplated scheme enhanced by bringing Japan and the United States into direct telegraphic relation.

Without repeating the observations of my special message of February 10, 1899, concerning the necessity of a cable to Manila, I respectfully invite attention to it.

I recommend that, in case the Congress should not take measures to bring about this result by direct action of the Government, the Postmaster-General be authorized to invite competitive bids for the establishment of a cable; the company making the best responsible bid to be awarded the contract; the successful company to give ample bonds to insure the completion of the work within a reasonable time.

The year has been marked by constant increase in the intimacy of our relations with Mexico and in the magnitude of mutually advantageous interchanges. This Government has omitted no opportunity to show its strong desire to develop and perpetuate the ties of cordiality now so long happily unbroken.

Following the termination on January 20, 1899, by Mexico of the convention of extradition of December 11, 1861, a new treaty more in accordance with the ascertained needs of both countries was signed February 22, 1899, and exchanged in the City of Mexico on the 22d of April last. Its operation thus far has been effective and satisfactory. A recent case has served to test the application of its IVth Article, which provides that neither party shall be bound to deliver up its own citizens, but that the executive authority of each shall have the power to deliver them up if in its discretion it be deemed proper to do so.

The extradition of Mrs. Mattie Rich, a citizen of the United States, charged with homicide committed in Mexico, was after mature consideration directed by me in the conviction that the ends of justice would be thereby subserved. Similar action, on appropriate occasion, by the Mexican Executive will not only tend to accomplish the desire of both Governments that grave crimes go not unpunished, but also to repress lawlessness along the border of the two countries. The new treaty stipulates that neither Government shall assume jurisdiction in the punishment of crimes committed exclusively within the territory of the other. This will obviate in future the embarrassing controversies which have heretofore arisen through Mexico's assertion of a claim to try and punish an American citizen for an offense committed within the jurisdiction of the United States.

The International Water Boundary Commission, organized by the convention of March 1, 1889, for the adjustment of questions affecting the Rio Grande frontier, has not yet completed its labors. A further extension of its term for one year, until December 24, 1899, was effected by a convention signed December 2, 1898, and exchanged and proclaimed in February last.

An invitation extended to the President of Mexico to visit Chicago in October, on the occasion of laying the corner stone of the United States Government building in that city, was cordially accepted by him, with the necessary consent of the Mexican Congress, but the illness of a member of his family prevented his attendance. The Minister of Foreign Relations, however, came as the personal representative of President Diaz, and in that high character was duly honored.

Claims growing out of the seizure of American sealing vessels in Bering Sea have been under discussion with the Government of Russia for several years, with the recent happy result of an agreement to submit them to the decision of a single arbitrator. By this act Russia affords proof of her adherence to the beneficent principle of arbitration which her plenipotentiaries conspicuously favored at The Hague Disarmament Conference when it was advocated by the representatives of the United States.

A suggestion for a permanent exposition of our products and manufactures in Russia, although not yet fully shaped, has been so cordially welcomed by the Imperial Government that it may not inaptly take a fitting place in whatever legislation the Congress may adopt looking to enlargement of our commercial opportunities abroad.

Important events have occurred in the Samoan Islands. The election, according to the laws and customs of Samoa, of a successor to the late King, Malietoa Laupepa, developed a contest as to the validity of the result, which issue, by the terms of the General Act, was to be decided by the Chief Justice. Upon his rendering a judgment in favor of Malietoa Tanu, the rival chief, Mataafa, took up arms. The active intervention of American and British war ships became imperative to restore order, at the cost of sanguinary encounters. In this emergency a joint commission of representatives of the United States, Germany, and Great Britain was sent to Samoa to investigate the situation and provide a temporary remedy. By its active efforts a peaceful solution was reached for the time being, the kingship being abolished and a provisional government established. Recommendations unanimously made by the commission for a permanent adjustment of the Samoan question were taken under consideration by the three powers parties to the General Act. But the more they were examined the more evident it became that a radical change was necessary in the relations of the powers to Samoa.

The inconveniences and possible perils of the tripartite scheme of supervision and control in the Samoan group by powers having little interest in common in that quarter beyond commercial rivalry had been once more emphasized by the recent events. The suggested remedy of the Joint Commission, like the scheme it aimed to replace, amounted to what has been styled a *tridominium*, being the exercise of the functions of sovereignty by an unanimous agreement of three powers. The situation had become far more intricate and embarrassing from every point of view than it was when my predecessor, in 1894, summed up its perplexities and condemned the participation in it of the United States.

The arrangement under which Samoa was administered had proved impracticable and unacceptable to all the powers concerned. To withdraw from the agreement and abandon the islands to Germany and Great Britain would not be compatible with our interests in the archipelago. To relinquish our rights in the harbor of Pago Pago, the best anchorage in the Pacific, the occupancy of which had been leased to the United States in 1878 by the first foreign treaty ever concluded by Samoa, was not to be thought of either as regards the needs of our Navy or the interests of our growing commerce with the East. We could not have considered any proposition for the abrogation of the tripartite control which did not confirm us in all our rights and safeguard all our national interests in the islands.

Our views commended themselves to the other powers. A satisfactory arrangement was concluded between the Governments of Germany and of England, by virtue of which England retired from Samoa in view of compensations in other directions, and both powers renounced in favor of the United States all their rights and claims over and in respect to that portion of the group lying to the east of the one hundred and seventy-first degree of west longitude, embracing the islands of Tutuila, Ofoo, Olosenga, and Manua. I transmit to the Senate, for its constitutional action thereon, a convention, which besides the provisions above mentioned also guarantees us the same privileges and conditions in respect to commerce and commercial vessels in all of the islands of Samoa as those possessed by Germany.

Claims have been preferred by white residents of Samoa on account of injuries alleged to have been suffered through the acts of the treaty Governments in putting down the late disturbances. A convention has been made between the three powers for the investigation and settlement of these claims by a neutral arbitrator, to which the attention of the Senate will be invited.

My annual message of last year was necessarily devoted in great part to a consideration of the Spanish War and of the results it wrought and the conditions it imposed for the future. I am gratified to announce that the treaty of peace has restored friendly relations between the two powers. Effect has been given to its most important provisions. The evacuation of Puerto Rico having already been accomplished on the 18th of October, 1898, nothing remained necessary there but to continue the provisional military control of the island until the Congress should enact a suitable government for the ceded territory. Of the character and scope of the measures to that end I shall treat in another part of this message.

The withdrawal of the authority of Spain from the island of Cuba was effected by the 1st of January, so that the full re-establishment of peace found the relinquished territory held by us in trust for the inhabitants, maintaining, under the direction of the Executive, such government and control therein as should conserve public order, restore the productive conditions of peace so long disturbed by the instability and disorder which prevailed for the greater part of the preceding three decades, and build up that tranquil development of the domestic state whereby alone can be realized the high purpose, as proclaimed in the joint resolution adopted by the Congress on the 19th of April, 1898, by which the United States disclaimed any disposition or intention to exercise sovereignty, jurisdiction, or control over Cuba, except for the pacification thereof, and asserted its determination when that was accomplished to leave the government and control of the island to its people. The pledge contained in this resolution is of the highest honorable obligation and must be sacredly kept.

I believe that substantial progress has been made in this direction. All the administrative measures adopted in Cuba have aimed to fit it for a regenerated existence by enforcing the supremacy of law and justice; by placing wherever practicable the machinery of administration in the hands of the inhabitants; by instituting needed sanitary reforms; by spreading education; by fostering industry and trade; by inculcating public morality, and, in short, by taking every rational step to aid the Cuban people to attain to that plane of self-conscious respect and self-reliant unity which fits an enlightened community for self-government within its own sphere, while enabling it to fulfill all outward obligations.

This nation has assumed before the world a grave responsibility for the future good government of Cuba. We have accepted a trust the fulfillment of which calls for the sternest integrity of purpose and the exercise of the highest wisdom. The new Cuba yet to arise from the ashes of the past must needs be bound to us by ties of singular intimacy and strength if its enduring welfare is to be assured. Whether those ties shall be organic or conventional, the destinies of Cuba are in some rightful form and manner irrevocably linked with our own, but how and how far is for the future to determine in the ripeness of events. Whatever be the outcome, we must see to it that free Cuba be a reality, not a name, a perfect entity, not a hasty experiment bearing within itself the elements of failure. Our mission, to accomplish which we took up the wager of battle, is not to be fulfilled by turning adrift any loosely framed commonwealth to face the vicissitudes which too often attend weaker States whose natural wealth and abundant resources are offset by the incongruities of their political organization and the recurring occasions for internal rivalries to sap their strength and dissipate their energies. The greatest blessing which can come to Cuba is the restoration of her agricultural and industrial prosperity, which will give employment to idle men and re-establish the pursuits of peace. This is her chief and immediate need.

On the 19th of August last an order was made for the taking of the census in the island, to be completed on the 30th of November. By the treaty of peace the Spanish people on the island have until April 11, 1900, to elect whether they will remain citizens of Spain or become citizens of Cuba. Until then it cannot be definitely ascertained who shall be entitled to participate in the formation of the government of Cuba. By that time the results of the census will have been tabulated and we shall proceed to provide for elections which will commit the municipal governments of the island to the officers elected by the people. The experience thus acquired will prove of great value in the formation of a representative convention of the people to draft a constitution and establish a general system of independent government for the island. In the meantime and so long as we exercise control over the island the products of Cuba should have a market in the United States on as good terms and with as favorable rates of duty as are given to the West India Islands under treaties of reciprocity which shall be made.

For the relief of the distressed in the island of Cuba the War Department has issued supplies to destitute persons through the officers of the Army, which have amounted to 5,493,000 rations, at a cost of $1,417,554.07.

To promote the disarmament of the Cuban volunteer army, and in the interest of public peace and the welfare of the people, the sum of $75 was paid to each Cuban soldier borne upon the authenticated rolls, on condition that he should deposit his arms with the authorities designated by the United States. The sum thus disbursed aggregated $2,547,750, which was paid from the emergency fund provided by the act of January 5, 1899, for that purpose.

Out of the Cuban island revenues during the six months ending June 30, 1899, $1,712,014.20 was expended for sanitation, $293,881.70 for charities and hospitals, and $88,944.03 for aid to the destitute.

Following the exchange of ratifications of the treaty of peace the two Governments accredited ministers to each other, Spain sending to Washington the Duke of Arcos, an eminent diplomatist, previously stationed in Mexico, while the United States transferred to Madrid Hon. Bellamy Storer, its minister at Brussels. This was followed by the respective appointment of consuls, thereby fully resuming the relations interrupted by the war. In addition to its consular representation in the United States, the Spanish Government has appointed consuls for Cuba, who have been provisionally recognized during the military administration of the affairs of that island.

Judicial intercourse between the courts of Cuba and Puerto Rico and of Spain has been established, as provided by the treaty of peace. The Cuban political prisoners in Spanish penal stations have been and are being released and returned to their homes, in accordance with Article VI of the treaty. Negotiations are about to be had for defining the conventional relations between the two countries, which fell into abeyance by reason of the war. I trust that these will include a favorable arrangement for commercial reciprocity under the terms of sections 3 and 4 of the current tariff act. In these, as in all matters of international concern, no effort will be spared to respond to the good disposition of Spain, and to cultivate in all practicable ways the intimacy which should prevail between two nations whose past history has so often and in so many ways been marked by sincere friendship and by community of interests.

I would recommend appropriate legislation in order to carry into execution Article VII of the Treaty of Peace with Spain, by which the United States assured the payment of certain claims for indemnity of its citizens against Spain.

The United States minister to Turkey continues, under instructions, to press for a money payment in satisfaction of the just claims for injuries suffered by American citizens in the disorders of several years past and for wrongs done to them by the Ottoman authorities. Some of these claims are of many years' standing. This Government is hopeful of a general agreement in this regard.

In the Turkish Empire the situation of our citizens remains unsatisfactory. Our efforts during nearly forty years to bring about a convention of naturalization seem to be on the brink of final failure through the announced policy of the Ottoman Porte to refuse recognition of the alien status of native Turkish subjects naturalized abroad since 1867. Our statutes do not allow this Government to admit any distinction between the treatment of native and naturalized Americans abroad, so that ceaseless controversy arises in cases where persons owing in the eye of international law a dual allegiance are prevented from entering Turkey or are expelled after entrance. Our law in this regard contrasts with that of the European States. The British act, for instance, does not claim effect for the naturalization of an alien in the event of his return to his native country, unless the change be recognized by the law of that country or stipulated by treaty between it and the naturalizing State.

The arbitrary treatment, in some instances, of American productions in Turkey has attracted attention of late, notably in regard to our flour. Large shipments by the recently opened direct steamship line to Turkish ports have been denied entrance on the score that, although of standard composition and unquestioned purity, the flour was pernicious to health because of deficient "elasticity" as indicated by antiquated and untrustworthy tests. Upon due protest by the American minister, and it appearing that the act was a virtual discrimination against our product, the shipments in question were admitted. In these, as in all instances, wherever occurring, when American products may be subjected in a foreign country, upon specious pretexts, to discrimination compared with the like products of another country, this Government will use its earnest efforts to secure fair and equal treatment for its citizens and their goods. Failing this, it will not hesitate to apply whatever corrective may be provided by the statutes.

The International Commission of Arbitration, appointed under the Anglo-Venezuelan treaty of 1897, rendered an award on October 3 last, whereby the boundary line between Venezuela and British Guiana is determined, thus ending a controversy which has existed for the greater part of the century. The award, as to which the arbitrators were unanimous, while not meeting the extreme contention of either party, gives to Great Britain a large share of the interior territory in dispute and to Venezuela the entire mouth of the Orinoco, including Barima Point and the Caribbean littoral for some distance to the eastward. The decision appears to be equally satisfactory to both parties.

Venezuela has once more undergone a revolution. The insurgents, under General Castro, after a sanguinary engagement in which they suffered much loss, rallied in the mountainous interior and advanced toward the capital. The bulk of the army having sided with the movement, President Andrade quitted Caracas, where General Castro set up a provisional government with which our minister and the representatives of other powers entered into diplomatic relations on the 20th of November, 1899.

The fourth section of the Tariff Act approved July 24, 1897, appears to provide only for commercial treaties which should be entered into by the President and also ratified by the Senate within two years from its passage. Owing to delays inevitable in negotiations of this nature, none of the treaties initiated under that section could be concluded in time for ratification by the Senate prior to its adjournment on the 4th of March last. Some of the pending negotiations, however, were near conclusion at that time, and the resulting conventions have since been signed by the plenipotentiaries. Others, within both the third and fourth sections of the act, are still under consideration. Acting under the constitutional power of the Executive in respect to treaties, I have deemed it my duty, while observing the limitations of concession provided by the fourth section, to bring to a conclusion all pending negotiations, and submit them to the Senate for its advice and consent.

Conventions of reciprocity have been signed during the Congressional recess with Great Britain for the respective colonies of British Guiana, Barbados, Bermuda, Jamaica, and Turks and Caicos Islands, and with the Republic of Nicaragua.

Important reciprocal conventions have also been concluded with France and with the Argentine Republic.

In my last annual message the progress noted in the work of the diplomatic and consular officers in collecting information as to the industries and commerce of other countries, and in the care and promptitude with which their reports are printed and distributed, has continued during the past year, with increasingly valuable results in suggesting new sources of demand for American products and in pointing out the obstacles still to be overcome in facilitating the remarkable expansion of our foreign trade. It will doubtless be gratifying to Congress to learn that the various agencies of the Department of State are co-operating in these endeavors with a zeal and effectiveness which are not only receiving the cordial recognition of our business interests, but are exciting the emulation of other Governments. In any rearrangement of the great and complicated work of obtaining official data of an economic character which Congress may undertake it is most important, in my judgment, that the results already secured by the efforts of the Department of State should be carefully considered with a view to a judicious development and increased utility to our export trade.

The interest taken by the various States forming the International Union of American Republics in the work of its organic bureau is evidenced by the fact that for the first time since its creation in 1890 all the Republics of South and Central America are now represented in it.

The unanimous recommendation of the International American Conference, providing for the International Union of American Republics, stated that it should continue in force during a term of ten years from the date of its organization, and no country becoming a member of the union should cease to be a member until the end of said period of ten years, and unless twelve months before the expiration of said period a majority of the members of the union had given to the Secretary of State of the United States official notice of their wish to terminate the union at the end of its first period, that the union should continue to be maintained for another period of ten years, and thereafter, under the same conditions, for successive periods of ten years each.

The period for notification expired on July 14, 1899, without any of the members having given the necessary notice of withdrawal. Its maintenance is therefore assured for the next ten years. In view of this fact and of the numerous questions of general interest and common benefit to all of the Republics of America, some of which were considered by the first International American Conference, but not finally settled, and others which have since then grown to importance, it would seem expedient that the various Republics constituting the Union should be invited to hold at an early date another conference in the capital of one of the countries other than the United States, which has already enjoyed this honor.

The purely international character of the work being done by the bureau and the appreciation of its value are further emphasized by the active co-operation which the various Governments of the Latin-American Republics and their diplomatic representatives in this capital are now exhibiting and the zealous endeavors they are making to extend its field of usefulness, to promote through it commercial intercourse, and strengthen the bonds of amity and confidence between its various members and the nations of this continent.

The act to encourage the holding of the Pan-American Exposition on the Niagara frontier, within the county of Erie or Niagara, in the State of New York, in the year 1901, was approved on March 3, 1899.

This exposition, which will be held in the city of Buffalo, in the near vicinity of the great Niagara cataract, and within a day's journey of which reside 40,000,000 of our people, will be confined entirely to the Western Hemisphere. Satisfactory assurances have already been given by the diplomatic representatives of Great Britain, Mexico, the Central and South American Republics, and most of the States of the United States that these countries and States will make an unique, interesting, and instructive exhibit, peculiarly illustrative of their material progress during the century which is about to close.

The law provides an appropriation of $500,000 for the purpose of making an exhibit at the exposition by the Government of the United States from its Executive Departments and from the Smithsonian Institution and National Museum, the United States Commission of Fish and Fisheries, the Department of Labor, and the Bureau of the American Republics. To secure a complete and harmonious arrangement of this Government exhibit a board of management has already been created, and charged with the selection, purchase, preparation, transportation, arrangement, and safe-keeping of the articles and materials to be exhibited. This board has been organized and has already entered upon the performance of its duties, as provided for by the law.

I have every reason to hope and believe that this exposition will tend more firmly to cement the cordial relations between the nations on this continent.

In accordance with an act of Congress approved December 21, 1898, and under the auspices of the Philadelphia Commercial Museum, a most interesting and valuable exposition of products and manufactures especially adapted to export trade was held in Philadelphia from the 14th of September to the 1st of December, 1899. The representative character of the exhibits and the widespread interest manifested in the special objects of the undertaking afford renewed encouragement to those who look confidently to the steady growth of our enlarged exportation of manufactured goods, which has been the most remarkable fact in the economic development of the United States in recent years. A feature of this exposition which is likely to become of permanent and increasing utility to our industries is the collection of samples of merchandise produced in various countries with special reference to particular markets, providing practical object lessons to United States manufacturers as to qualities, styles, and prices of goods such as meet the special demands of consumers and may be exported with advantage.

In connection with the exposition an International Commercial Congress was held, upon the invitation of the Philadelphia Commercial Museum, transmitted by the Department of State to the various foreign Governments, for an exchange of information and opinions with the view to the promotion of international trade. This invitation met with general and cordial acceptance, and the Congress, which began its sessions at the exposition on the 13th of October, proved to be of great practical importance, from the fact that it developed a general recognition of the interdependence of nations in trade and a most gratifying spirit of accommodation with reference to the gradual removal of existing impediments to reciprocal relations, without injury to the industrial interests of either party.

In response to the invitation of His Majesty, the Emperor of Russia, delegates from twenty-six countries were assembled at The Hague on the 18th of May, as members of a conference in the interest of peace. The commission from the United States consisted of the Hon. Andrew D. White, the Hon. Seth Low, the Hon. Stanford Newel, Captain Alfred T. Mahan, of the United States Navy, Captain William Crozier, of the United States Army, and the Hon. Frederick W. Holls, secretary. The occasion seemed to be opportune for the serious consideration of a plan for the pacific adjustment of international differences, a subject in which the American people have been deeply interested for many years, and a definite project for a permanent international tribunal was included in the instructions to the delegates of the United States.

The final act of the conference includes conventions upon the amelioration of the laws and customs of war on land, the adaptation to maritime warfare of the principles of the Geneva Convention of 1864, and the extension of judicial methods to international cases. The Convention for the Pacific Settlement of International Conflicts embodies the leading features of the American plan, with such modifications as were rendered necessary by the great diversity of views and interests represented by the delegates. The four titles of the convention provide for the maintenance of general peace, the exercise of good offices and mediation, the formation of commissions of inquiry, and international arbitration.

The mediation provided for by the convention is purely voluntary and advisory, and is intended to avoid any invasion or limitation of the sovereign rights of the adhering States. The commissions of inquiry proposed consists of delegations to be specifically constituted for particular purposes by means of conventions between the contesting parties, having for their object the clear understanding of international differences before resorting to the use of force. The provision for arbitration contemplates the formation of a permanent tribunal before which disputed cases may be brought for settlement by the mutual consent of the litigants in each separate case. The advantages of such a permanent tribunal over impromptu commissions of arbitration are conceived to be the actual existence of a competent court, prepared to administer justice, the greater economy resulting from a well-devised system, and the accumulated judicial skill and experience which such a tribunal would soon possess.

While earnestly promoting the idea of establishing a permanent international tribunal, the delegation of the United States was not unmindful of the inconveniences which might arise from an obtrusive exercise of mediation, and in signing the convention carefully guarded the historic position of the United States by the following declaration:

Nothing contained in this convention shall be so construed as to require the United States of America to depart from its traditional policy of not intruding upon, interfering with or entangling itself in the political questions or policy or internal administration of any foreign state ; nor shall anything contained in the said convention be construed to imply a relinquishment by the United States of America of its traditional attitude toward purely American questions.

Thus interpreted, the Convention for the Pacific Settlement of International Conflicts may be regarded as realizing the earnest desire of great numbers of American citizens, whose deep sense of justice, expressed in numerous resolutions and memorials, has urged them to labor for this noble achievement. The general character of this convention, already signed by the delegates of more than twenty sovereign States, further commends it to the favorable action of the Senate of the United States, whose ratification it still awaits.

Since my last annual message, and in obedience to the acts of the Congress of April 22 and 26, 1898, the remaining volunteer force enlisted for the Spanish War, consisting of 34,834 regulars and 110,· 202 volunteers, with over 5,000 volunteer officers, has been discharged from the military service. Of the volunteers, 667 officers and 14,831 men were serving in the Philippines, and 1,650 of the regulars, who were entitled to be mustered out after the ratification of the treaty of peace. They voluntarily remained at the front until their places could be filled by new troops. They were returned home in the order in which they went to Manila, and are now all of them out of the service and in the ranks of citizenship. I recommend that the Congress provide a special medal of honor for the volunteers, regulars, sailors, and marines on duty in the Philippines who voluntarily remained in the service after their terms of enlistment had expired.

By the act of March 2, 1899, Congress gave authority to increase the Regular Army to a maximum not exceeding 65,000 enlisted men, and to enlist a force of 35,000 volunteers, to be recruited from the country at large. By virtue of this authority the Regular Army has been increased to the number of 61,999 enlisted men and 2,248 officers, and new volunteer regiments have been organized aggregating 33,050 enlisted men and 1,524 officers. Two of these volunteer regiments are made up of colored men, with colored line officers. The new troops to take the places of those returning from the Philippines have been transported to Manila to the number of 581 officers and 26,322 enlisted men of the Regular Army and 594 officers and 15,388 enlisted men of the new volunteer force, while 504 officers and 14,119 men of the volunteer force are on the ocean *en route* to Manila.

The force now in Manila consists of 905 officers and 30,578 regulars, and 594 officers and 15,388 of the volunteers, making an aggregate of 1,499 officers and 45,966 men. When the troops now under orders shall reach Manila the force in the archipelago will comprise 2,051 officers and 63,483 men. The muster out of the great volunteer army organized for the Spanish War and the creation of a new army, the transportation from Manila to San Francisco of those entitled to discharge and the transportation of the new troops to take their places have been a work of great magnitude well and ably done, for which too much credit cannot be given the War Department.

During the past year we have reduced our force in Cuba and Puerto Rico. In Cuba we now have 334 officers and 10,796 enlisted men;

in Puerto Rico, 87 officers and 2,855 enlisted men and a battalion of 400 men composed of native Puerto Ricans; while stationed throughout the United States are 910 officers and 17,317 men, and in Hawaii 12 officers and 453 enlisted men.

The operations of the Army are fully presented in the report of the Secretary of War. I cannot withhold from officers and men the highest commendation for their soldierly conduct in trying situations, their willing sacrifices for their country, and the integrity and ability with which they have performed unusual and difficult duties in our island possessions.

In the organization of the volunteer regiments authorized by the act of March 2, 1899, it was found that no provision had been made for chaplains. This omission was doubtless from inadvertence. I recommend the early authorization for the appointment of one chaplain for each of said regiments. These regiments are now in the Philippines, and it is important that immediate action be had.

In restoring peaceful conditions, orderly rule, and civic progress in Cuba, Puerto Rico, and, so far as practicable, in the Philippines, the rehabilitation of the postal service has been an essential and important part of the work. It became necessary to provide mail facilities both for our forces of occupation and for the native population. To meet this requirement has involved a substantial reconstruction. The existing systems were so fragmentary, defective, and inadequate that a new and comprehensive organization had to be created. American trained officials have been assigned to the directing and executive positions, while natives have been chiefly employed in making up the body of the force. In working out this plan the merit rule has been rigorously and faithfully applied.

The appointment of Director-General of Posts of Cuba was given to an expert who had been Chief Post-Office Inspector and Assistant Postmaster-General, and who united large experience with administrative capacity. For the postmastership at Havana the range of skilled and available men was scanned, and the choice fell upon one who had been twenty years in the service as deputy postmaster and postmaster of a large city. This principle governed and determined the selection of the American officials sent not only to Cuba, but to Puerto Rico and the Philippines, and they were instructed to apply it so far as practicable in the employment of the natives as minor postmasters and clerks. The postal system in Cuba, though remaining under the general guidance of the Postmaster-General, was made essentially independent. It was felt that it should not be a burden upon the postal service of the United States, and provision was made that any deficit in the postal revenue should be a charge upon the general revenues of the island.

Though Puerto Rico and the Philippines hold a different relation to the United States, yet, for convenience of administration, the same principle of an autonomous system has been extended to them. The development of the service in all of the islands has been rapid and successful. It has moved forward on American lines, with free delivery, money order, and registry systems, and has given the people mail facilities far greater and more reliable than any they have ever before enjoyed. It is thus not only a vital agency of industrial, social, and business progress, but an important influence in diffusing a just understanding of the true spirit and character of American administration.

The domestic postal service continues to grow with extraordinary rapidity. The expenditures and the revenues will each exceed $100,000,000 during the current year. Fortunately, since the revival of prosperous times the revenues have grown much faster than the expenditures, and there is every indication that a short period will witness the obliteration of the annual deficit. In this connection the report of the Postmaster-General embodies a statement of some evils which have grown up outside of the contemplation of law in the treatment of some classes of mail matter which wrongly exercise the privilege of the pound rate, and shows that if this matter had been properly classified and had paid the rate which it should have paid, instead of a postal deficit for the last fiscal year of $6,610,000, there would have been on one basis a surplus of $17,637,570, and on another of $5,733,836. The reform thus suggested, in the opinion of the Postmaster-General, would not only put the postal service at once on a self-sustaining basis, but would permit great and valuable improvements, and I commend the subject to the consideration of the Congress.

The Navy has maintained the spirit and high efficiency which have always characterized that service, and has lost none of the gallantry in heroic action which has signalized its brilliant and glorious past. The Nation has equal pride in its early and later achievements. Its habitual readiness for every emergency has won the confidence and admiration of the country. The people are interested in the continued preparation and prestige of the Navy and will justify liberal appropriations for its maintenance and improvement. The officers have shown peculiar adaptation for the performance of new and delicate duties which our recent war has imposed.

It cannot be doubted that Congress will at once make necessary provision for the armor plate for the vessels now under contract and building. Its attention is respectfully called to the report of the Secretary of the Navy, in which the subject is fully presented. I unite in his recommendation that the Congress enact such special legislation as may be necessary to enable the Department to make contracts early in the coming year for armor of the best quality that can be obtained in this country for the *Maine, Ohio*, and *Missouri*, and that the provision of the act of March 3, 1899, limiting the price of armor to $300 per ton be removed.

In the matter of naval construction Italy and Japan, of the great powers, laid down less tonnage in the year 1899 than this country, and Italy alone has less tonnage under construction. I heartily concur in the recommendations for the increase of the Navy, as suggested by the Secretary.

Our future progress and prosperity depend upon our ability to equal, if not surpass, other nations in the enlargement and advance of science, industry, and commerce. To invention we must turn as one of the most powerful aids to the accomplishment of such a result. The attention of the Congress is directed to the report of the Commissioner of Patents, in which will be found valuable suggestions and recommendations.

On the 30th of June, 1899, the pension roll of the United States numbered 991,519. These include the pensioners of the Army and Navy in all our wars. The number added to the rolls during the year was 40,991. The number dropped by reason of death, remarriage, minors by legal limitation, failure to claim within three years, and other causes, was 43,186, and the number of claims disallowed was 107,919. During the year 89,054 pension certificates were issued, of which 37,077 were for new or original pensions. The amount disbursed for army and navy pensions during the year was $138,355,052.95, which was $1,651,461.61 less than the sum of the appropriations.

The Grand Army of the Republic at its recent national encampment held in Philadelphia has brought to my attention and to that of the Congress the wisdom and justice of a modification of the third section of the act of June 27, 1890, which provides pensions for the widows of officers and enlisted men who served ninety days or more during the War of the Rebellion and were honorably discharged, provided that such widows are without other means of support than their daily labor and were married to the soldier, sailor, or marine on account of whose service they claim pension prior to the date of the act.

The present holding of the Department is that if the widow's income aside from her daily labor does not exceed in amount what her pension would be, to wit, $96 per annum, she would be deemed to be without other means of support than her daily labor, and would be entitled to a pension under this act; while if the widow's income independent of the amount received by her as the result of her daily labor exceeds $96, she would not be pensionable under the act. I am advised by the Commissioner of Pensions that the amount of the income allowed before title to pension would be barred has varied widely under different administrations of the Pension Office, as well as during different periods of the same administration, and has been the cause of just complaint and criticism.

With the approval of the Secretary of the Interior the Commissioner of Pensions recommends that, in order to make the practice at all times uniform and to do justice to the dependent widow, the amount of income allowed independent of the proceeds of her daily labor should be not less than $250 per annum, and he urges that the Congress shall so amend the act as to permit the Pension Office to grant pensionable status to widows under the terms of the third section of the act of June 27, 1890, whose income aside from the proceeds of daily labor is not in excess of $250 per annum. I believe this to be a simple act of justice and heartily recommend it.

The Dawes Commission reports that gratifying progress has been made in its work during the preceding year. The field-work of enrollment of four of the nations has been completed. I recommend that Congress at an early day make liberal appropriation for educational purposes in the Indian Territory.

In accordance with the act of Congress approved March 3, 1899, the preliminary work in connection with the Twelfth Census is now fully under way. The officers required for the proper administration of the duties imposed have been selected. The provision for securing a proper enumeration of the population, as well as to secure evidence of the industrial growth of the Nation, is broader and more comprehensive than any similar legislation in the past. The Director advises that every needful effort is being made to push this great work to completion in the time limited by the statute. It is believed that the Twelfth Census will emphasize our remarkable advance in all that pertains to national progress.

Under the authority of the act of Congress approved July 7, 1898, the commission consisting of the Secretary of the Treasury, the Attorney-General, and the Secretary of the Interior has made an agreement of settlement, which has had my approval, of the indebtedness to the Government growing out of the issue of bonds to aid in the construction of the Central Pacific and Western Pacific railroads. The agreement secures to the Government the principal and interest of said bonds, amounting to $58,812,715.48. There has been paid thereon $11,762,543.12, which has been covered into the Treasury, and the remainder, payable within ten years, with interest at the rate of 3 per cent per annum, payable semiannually, is secured by the deposit of an equal amount of first-mortgage bonds of the Pacific Railway companies. The amounts paid and secured to be paid to the Government on account of the Pacific Railroad subsidy claims are:

Union Pacific, cash	$58,448,223.75
Kansas Pacific, cash	6,303,000.00
Central and Western Pacific, cash	11,798,314.14
Notes, secured	47,050,172.36
Kansas Pacific—dividends for deficiency due United States, cash	821,897.70
Making a total of	124,421,607.95

The whole indebtedness was about $130,000,000, more than half of which consisted of accrued interest, for which sum the Government has realized the entire amount less about $6,000,000 within a period of two years.

On June 30, 1898, there were thirty forest reservations (exclusive of the Afognak Forest and Fish Culture Reserve in Alaska), embracing an estimated area of 40,719,474 acres. During the past year two of the existing forest reserves, the Trabuco Canyon (California) and Black Hills (South Dakota and Wyoming), have been considerably enlarged, the area of the Mount Rainier Reserve, in the State of Washington, has been somewhat reduced, and six additional reserves have been established, namely, the San Francisco Mountains (Arizona), the Black Mesa (Arizona), Lake Tahoe (California), Gallatin (Montana), Gila River (New Mexico), and Fish Lake (Utah), the total estimated area of which is 5,205,775 acres. This makes at the present time a total of thirty-six forest reservations, embracing an estimated area of 46,021,899 acres. This estimated area is the aggregated areas within the boundaries of the reserves. The lands actually reserved are, however, only the vacant public lands therein, and these have been set aside and reserved for sale or settlement in order that they may be of the greatest use to the people.

Protection of the national forests, inaugurated by the Department of the Interior in 1897, has been continued during the past year and much has been accomplished in the way of preventing forest fires and the protection of the timber. There are now large tracts covered by forests which will eventually be reserved and set apart for forest uses. Until that can be done Congress should increase the appropriations for the work of protecting the forests.

The Department of Agriculture is constantly consulting the needs of producers in all the States and Territories. It is introducing seeds and plants of great value and promoting fuller diversification of crops. Grains, grasses, fruits, legumes, and vegetables are imported for all parts of the United States. Under this encouragement the sugar-beet factory multiplies in the North and far West, semitropical plants are sent to the South, and congenial climates are sought for the choice productions of the far East. The hybridizing of fruit trees and grains is conducted in the search for varieties adapted to exacting conditions. The introduction of tea gardens into the Southern States promises to provide employment for idle hands, as well as to supply the home market with tea. The subject of irrigation where it is of vital importance to the people is being carefully studied, steps are being taken to reclaim injured or abandoned lands, and information for the people along these lines is being printed and distributed.

Markets are being sought and opened up for surplus farm and factory products in Europe and in Asia. The outlook for the education of the young farmer through agricultural college and experiment station, with opportunity given to specialize in the Department of Agriculture, is very promising. The people of Hawaii, Puerto Rico, and the Philippine Islands should be helped, by the establishment of experiment stations, to a more scientific knowledge of the production of coffee, india rubber, and other tropical products, for which there is demand in the United States.

There is widespread interest in the improvement of our public highways at the present time, and the Department of Agriculture is co-operating with the people in each locality in making the best possible roads from local material and in experimenting with steel tracks. A more intelligent system of managing the forests of the country is being put in operation and a careful study of the whole forestry problem is being conducted throughout the United States. A very extensive and complete exhibit of the agricultural and horticultural products of the United States is being prepared for the Paris Exposition.

On the 10th of December, 1898, the treaty of peace between the United States and Spain was signed. It provided, among other things, that Spain should cede to the United States the archipelago known as the Philippine Islands, that the United States should pay to Spain the sum of twenty millions of dollars, and that the civil rights and political status of the native inhabitants of the territories thus ceded to the United States should be determined by the Congress. The treaty was ratified by the Senate on the 6th of February, 1899, and by the Government of Spain on the 19th of March following. The ratifications were exchanged on the 11th of April and the treaty publicly proclaimed. On the 2d of March the Congress voted the sum contemplated by the treaty, and the amount was paid over to the Spanish Government on the 1st of May.

In this manner the Philippines came to the United States. The islands were ceded by the Government of Spain, which had been in undisputed possession of them for centuries. They were accepted not merely by our authorized commissioners in Paris, under the direction of the Executive, but by the constitutional and well-considered action of the representatives of the people of the United States in both Houses of Congress. I had every reason to believe, and I still believe that this transfer of sovereignty was in accordance with the wishes and the aspirations of the great mass of the Filipino people.

From the earliest moment no opportunity was lost of assuring the people of the islands of our ardent desire for their welfare and of the intention of this Government to do everything possible to advance their interests. In my order of the 19th of May, 1898, the commander of the military expedition dispatched to the Philippines was instructed to declare that we came not to make war upon the people of that country, "nor upon any party or faction among them, but to protect them in their homes, in their employments, and in their personal and religious rights." That there should be no doubt as to the paramount authority there, on the 17th of August it was directed that "there must be no joint occupation with the insurgents"; that the United States must preserve the peace and protect persons and property within the territory occupied by their military and naval forces; that the insurgents and all others must recognize the military occupation and authority of the United States. As early as December 4, before the cession, and in anticipation of that event, the commander in Manila was urged to restore peace and tranquillity and to undertake the establishment of a beneficent government, which should afford the fullest security for life and property.

On the 21st of December, after the treaty was signed, the commander of the forces of occupation was instructed "to announce and proclaim in the most public manner that we come, not as invaders and conquerors, but as friends to protect the natives in their homes, in their employments, and in their personal and religious rights." On the same day, while ordering General Otis to see that the peace should be preserved in Iloilo, he was admonished that: "It is most important that there should be no conflict with the insurgents." On the 1st day of January, 1899, urgent orders were reiterated that the kindly intentions of this Government should be in every possible way communicated to the insurgents.

On the 21st of January I announced my intention of dispatching to Manila a commission composed of three gentlemen of the highest character and distinction, thoroughly acquainted with the Orient, who, in association with Admiral Dewey and Major-General Otis, were instructed "to facilitate the most humane and effective extension of authority throughout the islands, and to secure with the least possible delay the benefits of a wise and generous protection of life and property to the inhabitants." These gentlemen were Dr. Jacob

Gould Schurman, president of Cornell University; the Hon. Charles Denby, for many years minister to China, and Prof. Dean C. Worcester, of the University of Michigan, who had made a most careful study of life in the Philippines. While the treaty of peace was under consideration in the Senate, these Commissioners set out on their mission of good will and liberation. Their character was a sufficient guaranty of the beneficent purpose with which they went, even if they had not borne the positive instructions of this Government, which made their errand pre-eminently one of peace and friendship.

But before their arrival at Manila the sinister ambition of a few leaders of the Filipinos had created a situation full of embarrassment for us and most grievous in its consequences to themselves. The clear and impartial preliminary report of the Commissioners, which I transmit herewith, gives so lucid and comprehensive a history of the present insurrectionary movement that the story need not be here repeated. It is enough to say that the claim of the rebel leader that he was promised independence by an officer of the United States in return for his assistance has no foundation in fact and is categorically denied by the very witnesses who were called to prove it. The most the insurgent leader hoped for when he came back to Manila was the liberation of the islands from the Spanish control, which they had been laboring for years without success to throw off.

The prompt accomplishment of this work by the American Army and Navy gave him other ideas and ambitions, and insidious suggestions from various quarters perverted the purposes and intentions with which he had taken up arms. No sooner had our army captured Manila than the Filipino forces began to assume an attitude of suspicion and hostility which the utmost efforts of our officers and troops were unable to disarm or modify. Their kindness and forbearance were taken as a proof of cowardice. The aggressions of the Filipinos continually increased until finally, just before the time set by the Senate of the United States for a vote upon the treaty, an attack, evidently prepared in advance, was made all along the American lines, which resulted in a terribly destructive and sanguinary repulse of the insurgents.

Ten days later an order of the insurgent government was issued to its adherents who had remained in Manila, of which General Otis justly observes that "for barbarous intent it is unequaled in modern times." It directs that at 8 o'clock on the night of the 15th of February the "territorial militia" shall come together in the streets of San Pedro armed with their *bolos*, with guns and ammunition where convenient; that Filipino families only shall be respected; but that all other individuals, of whatever race they may be, shall be exterminated without any compassion, after the extermination of the army of occupation, and adds: "Brothers, we must avenge ourselves on the Americans and exterminate them, that we may take our revenge for the infamies and treacheries which they have committed upon us Have no compassion upon them; attack with vigor." A copy of this fell by good fortune into the hands of our officers and they were able to take measures to control the rising, which was actually attempted on the night of February 22, a week later than was originally contemplated. Considerable numbers of armed insurgents entered the city by waterways and swamps and in concert with confederates inside attempted to destroy Manila by fire. They were kept in check during the night and the next day driven out of the city with heavy loss.

This was the unhappy condition of affairs which confronted our Commissioners on their arrival in Manila. They had come with the hope and intention of co-operating with Admiral Dewey and Major-General Otis in establishing peace and order in the archipelago and the largest measure of self-government compatible with the true welfare of the people. What they actually found can best be set forth in their own words:

Deplorable as war is, the one in which we are now engaged was unavoidable by us. We were attacked by a bold, adventurous, and enthusiastic army. No alternative was left to us except ignominious retreat.

It is not to be conceived of that any American would have sanctioned the surrender of Manila to the insurgents. Our obligations to other nations and to the friendly Filipinos and to ourselves and our flag demanded that force should be met by force. Whatever the future of the Philippines may be, there is no course open to us now except the prosecution of the war until the insurgents are reduced to submission. The Commission is of the opinion that there has been no time since the destruction of the Spanish squadron by Admiral Dewey when it was possible to withdraw our forces from the island either with honor to ourselves or with safety to the inhabitants.

The course thus clearly indicated has been unflinchingly pursued. The rebellion must be put down. Civil government cannot be thoroughly established until order is restored. With a devotion and gallantry worthy of its most brilliant history, the Army, ably and loyally assisted by the Navy, has carried on this unwelcome but most righteous campaign with richly deserved success. The noble self-sacrifice with which our soldiers and sailors whose terms of service had expired refused to avail themselves of their right to return home as long as they were needed at the front forms one of the brightest pages in our annals. Although their operations have been somewhat interrupted and checked by a rainy season of unusual violence and duration, they have gained ground steadily in every direction, and now look forward confidently to a speedy completion of their task.

The unfavorable circumstances connected with an active campaign have not been permitted to interfere with the equally important work of reconstruction. Again I invite your attention to the report of the Commissioners for the interesting and encouraging details of the work already accomplished in the establishment of peace and order and the inauguration of self-governing municipal life in many portions of the archipelago. A notable beginning has been made in the establishment of a government in the island of Negros which is deserving of special consideration. This was the first island to accept American sovereignty. Its people unreservedly proclaimed allegiance to the United States and adopted a constitution looking to the establishment of a popular government. It was impossible to guarantee to the people of Negros that the constitution so adopted should be the ultimate form of government. Such a question, under the treaty with Spain and in accordance with our own Constitution and laws, came exclusively within the jurisdiction of the Congress. The government actually set up by the inhabitants of Negros eventually proved unsatisfactory to the natives themselves. A new system was put into force by order of the Major-General Commanding the Department, of which the following are the most important elements:

It was ordered that the government of the island of Negros should consist of a military governor appointed by the United States military governor of the Philippines, and a civil governor and an advisory council elected by the people. The military governor was authorized to appoint secretaries of the treasury, interior, agriculture, public instruction, an attorney-general, and an auditor. The seat of government was fixed at Bacolod. The military governor exercises the supreme executive power. He is to see that the laws are executed, appoint to office, and fill all vacancies in office not otherwise provided for, and may, with the approval of the military governor of the Philippines, remove any officer from office. The civil governor advises the military governor on all public civil questions and presides over the advisory council. He, in general, performs the duties which are performed by secretaries of state in our own system of government.

The advisory council consists of eight members elected by the people within territorial limits which are defined in the order of the commanding general.

The times and places of holding elections are to be fixed by the military governor of the island of Negros. The qualifications of voters are as follows:

(1) A voter must be a male citizen of the island of Negros. (2) Of the age of 21 years. (3) He shall be able to speak, read, and write the English, Spanish, or Visayan language, or he must own

real property worth $500, or pay a rental on real property of the value of $1,000. (4) He must have resided in the island not less than one year preceding, and in the district in which he offers to register as a voter not less than three months immediately preceding the time he offers to register. (5) He must register at a time fixed by law before voting. (6) Prior to such registration he shall have paid all taxes due by him to the Government. Provided, that no insane person shall be allowed to register or vote.

The military governor has the right to veto all bills or resolutions adopted by the advisory council, and his veto is final if not disapproved by the military governor of the Philippines.

The advisory council discharges all the ordinary duties of a legislature. The usual duties pertaining to said offices are to be performed by the secretaries of the treasury, interior, agriculture, public instruction, the attorney-general, and the auditor.

The judicial power is vested in three judges, who are to be appointed by the military governor of the island. Inferior courts are to be established.

Free public schools are to be established throughout the populous districts of the island, in which the English language shall be taught, and this subject will receive the careful consideration of the advisory council.

The burden of government must be distributed equally and equitably among the people. The military authorities will collect and receive the customs revenue, and will control postal matters and Philippine inter-island trade and commerce.

The military governor, subject to the approval of the military governor of the Philippines, determines all questions not specifically provided for and which do not come under the jurisdiction of the advisory council.

The authorities of the Sulu Islands have accepted the succession of the United States to the rights of Spain, and our flag floats over that territory. On the 10th of August, 1899, Brig.-Gen. J. C. Bates, United States Volunteers, negotiated an agreement with the Sultan and his principal chiefs, which I transmit herewith. By Article I the sovereignty of the United States over the whole archipelago of Jolo and its dependencies is declared and acknowledged.

The United States flag will be used in the archipelago and its dependencies, on land and sea. Piracy is to be suppressed, and the Sultan agrees to co-operate heartily with the United States authorities to that end and to make every possible effort to arrest and bring to justice all persons engaged in piracy. All trade in domestic products of the archipelago of Jolo when carried on with any part of the Philippine Islands and under the American flag shall be free, unlimited, and undutiable. The United States will give full protection to the Sultan in case any foreign nation should attempt to impose upon him. The United States will not sell the island of Jolo or any other island of the Jolo archipelago to any foreign nation without the consent of the Sultan. Salaries for the Sultan and his associates in the administration of the islands have been agreed upon to the amount of $760 monthly.

Article X provides that any slave in the archipelago of Jolo shall have the right to purchase freedom by paying to the master the usual market value. The agreement by General Bates was made subject to confirmation by the President and to future modifications by the consent of the parties in interest. I have confirmed said agreement, subject to the action of the Congress, and with the reservation, which I have directed shall be communicated to the Sultan of Jolo, that this agreement is not to be deemed in any way to authorize or give the consent of the United States to the existence of slavery in the Sulu archipelago. I communicate these facts to the Congress for its information and action.

Everything indicates that with the speedy suppression of the Tagalo rebellion life in the archipelago will soon resume its ordinary course under the protection of our sovereignty, and the people of those favored islands will enjoy a prosperity and a freedom which they have never before known. Already hundreds of schools are open and filled with children. Religious freedom is sacredly assured and enjoyed. The courts are dispensing justice. Business is beginning to circulate in its accustomed channels. Manila, whose inhabitants were fleeing to the country a few months ago, is now a populous and thriving mart of commerce. The earnest and unremitting endeavors of the Commission and the Admiral and Major-General Commanding the Department of the Pacific to assure the people of the beneficent intentions of this Government have had their legitimate effect in convincing the great mass of them that peace and safety and prosperity and stable government can only be found in a loyal acceptance of the authority of the United States.

The future government of the Philippines rests with the Congress of the United States. Few graver responsibilities have ever been confided to us. If we accept them in a spirit worthy of our race and our traditions, a great opportunity comes with them. The islands lie under the shelter of our flag. They are ours by every title of law and equity. They cannot be abandoned. If we desert them we leave them at once to anarchy and finally to barbarism. We fling them, a golden apple of discord, among the rival powers, no one of which could permit another to seize them unquestioned. Their rich plains and valleys would be the scene of endless strife and bloodshed. The advent of Dewey's fleet in Manila Bay instead of being, as we hope, the dawn of a new day of freedom and progress, will have been the beginning of an era of misery and violence worse than any which has darkened their unhappy past. The suggestion has been made that we could renounce our authority over the islands and, giving them independence, could retain a protectorate over them. This proposition will not be found, I am sure, worthy of your serious attention. Such an arrangement would involve at the outset a cruel breach of faith. It would place the peaceable and loyal majority, who ask nothing better than to accept our authority, at the mercy of the minority of armed insurgents. It would make us responsible for the acts of the insurgent leaders and give us no power to control them. It would charge us with the task of protecting them against each other and defending them against any foreign power with which they chose to quarrel. In short, it would take from the Congress of the United States the power of declaring war and vest that tremendous prerogative in the Tagal leader of the hour.

It does not seem desirable that I should recommend at this time a specific and final form of government for these islands. When peace shall be restored it will be the duty of Congress to construct a plan of government which shall establish and maintain freedom and order and peace in the Philippines. The insurrection is still existing, and when it terminates further information will be required as to the actual condition of affairs before inaugurating a permanent scheme of civil government. The full report of the Commission, now in preparation, will contain information and suggestions which will be of value to Congress, and which I will transmit as soon as it is completed. As long as the insurrection continues the military arm must necessarily be supreme. But there is no reason why steps should not be taken from time to time to inaugurate governments essentially popular in their form as fast as territory is held and controlled by our troops. To this end I am considering the advisability of the return of the Commission, or such of the members thereof as can be secured, to aid the existing authorities and facilitate this work throughout the islands. I have believed that reconstruction should not begin by the establishment of one central civil government for all the islands, with its seat at Manila, but rather that the work should be commenced by building up from the bottom, first establishing municipal governments and then provincial governments, a central government at last to follow.

Until Congress shall have made known the formal expression of its will I shall use the authority vested in me by the Constitution and the statutes to uphold the sovereignty of the United States in those distant islands as in all other places where our flag rightfully floats. I shall put at the disposal of the Army and Navy all the means which the liberality of Congress and the people have provided to cause this unprovoked and wasteful insurrection to cease.

If any orders of mine were required to insure the merciful conduct of military and naval operations, they would not be lacking; but every step of the progress of our troops has been marked by a humanity which has surprised even the misguided insurgents. The truest kindness to them will be a swift and effective defeat of their present leader. The hour of victory will be the hour of clemency and reconstruction.

No effort will be spared to build up the waste places desolated by war and by long years of misgovernment. We shall not wait for the end of strife to begin the beneficent work. We shall continue, as we have begun, to open the schools and the churches, to set the courts in operation, to foster industry and trade and agriculture, and in every way in our power to make these people whom Providence has brought within our jurisdiction feel that it is their liberty and not our power, their welfare and not our gain, we are seeking to enhance. Our flag has never waved over any community but in blessing. I believe the Filipinos will soon recognize the fact that it has not lost its gift of benediction in its world-wide journey to their shores.

Some embarrassment in administration has occurred by reason of the peculiar status which the Hawaiian Islands at present occupy under the joint resolution of annexation approved July 7, 1898. While by that resolution the Republic of Hawaii as an independent nation was extinguished, its separate sovereignty destroyed, and its property and possessions vested in the United States, yet a complete establishment for its government under our system was not effected. While the municipal laws of the islands not enacted for the fulfillment of treaties and not inconsistent with the joint resolution or contrary to the Constitution of the United States or any of its treaties remain in force, yet these laws relate only to the social and internal affairs of the islands, and do not touch many subjects of importance which are of a broader national character. For example, the Hawaiian Republic was divested of all title to the public lands in the islands, and is not only unable to dispose of lands to settlers desiring to take up homestead sites, but is without power to give complete title in cases where lands have been entered upon under lease or other conditions which carry with them the right to the purchaser, lessee, or settler to have a full title granted to him upon compliance with the conditions prescribed by law or by his particular agreement of entry.

Questions of doubt and difficulty have also arisen with reference to the collection of tonnage tax on vessels coming from Hawaiian ports; with reference to the status of Chinese in the islands, their entrance and exit therefrom; as to patents and copyrights; as to the register

THE BOXER UPRISING

THE BOXER UPRISING

These pictures suggest some very interesting reading. The Boxer uprising, the story of which is told in the article entitled "Boxers," in the encyclopedic index (volume eleven), caused increased diplomatic intercourse between the young Republic and the immemorial Empire. Other nations regarded China as the vandals regarded a fallen city; there was loot to be had and each with steel in hand determined to get his share. The indemnity first demanded was $735,000,000; through the chivalrous good offices of the United States the amount was lowered to $387,500,000. Then our share in this amount was remitted entirely. The incidents of our intercourse with China are narrated in the articles "Chinese Indemnity," "Chinese Loan," "Chinese Immigration," "China," "China, Treaties with," in the encyclopedic index (volume eleven).

The Chinese Army, which revolted and joined forces with the Boxers, was made up of men like those shown in the upper panel. All sorts of horrible fates were predicted for those who dared to enter the hallowed precincts where the American troops are encamping. Relief was sent to the beleaguered legations through the breach in the wall. The lowest panel shows the ruins of the Chinese section of Peking after the bombardment.

of vessels under the navigation laws; as to the necessity of holding elections in accordance with the provisions of the Hawaiian statutes for the choice of various officers, and as to several other matters of detail touching the interests both of the island and of the Federal Government.

By the resolution of annexation the President was directed to appoint five commissioners to recommend to Congress such legislation concerning the islands as they should deem necessary or proper. These commissioners were duly appointed and after a careful investigation and study of the system of laws and government prevailing in the islands, and of the conditions existing there, they prepared a bill to provide a government under the title of "The Territory of Hawaii." The report of the Commission, with the bill which they prepared, was transmitted by me to Congress on December 6, 1898, but the bill still awaits final action.

The people of these islands are entitled to the benefits and privileges of our Constitution, but in the absence of any act of Congress providing for Federal courts in the islands, and for a procedure by which appeals, writs of error, and other judicial proceedings necessary for the enforcement of civil rights may be prosecuted, they are powerless to secure their enforcement by the judgment of the courts of the United States. It is manifestly important, therefore, that an act shall be passed as speedily as possible erecting these islands into a judicial district, providing for the appointment of a judge and other proper officers and methods of procedure in appellate proceedings, and that the government of this newly acquired territory under the Federal Constitution shall be fully defined and provided for.

A necessity for immediate legislative relief exists in the Territory of Alaska. Substantially the only law providing a civil government for this Territory is the act of May 17, 1884. This is meager in its provisions, and is fitted only for the administration of affairs in a country sparsely inhabited by civilized people and unimportant in trade and production, as was Alaska at the time this act was passed. The increase in population by immigration during the past few years, consequent upon the discovery of gold, has produced such a condition as calls for more ample facilities for local self-government and more numerous conveniences of civil and judicial administration. Settlements have grown up in various places, constituting in point of population and business cities of thousands of inhabitants, yet there is no provision of law under which a municipality can be organized or maintained.

In some localities the inhabitants have met together and voluntarily formed a municipal organization for the purposes of local government, adopting the form of a municipal constitution and charter, under which said officials have been appointed; and ordinances creating and regulating a police force, a fire department, a department of health, and making provision for the care of the insane and indigent poor and sick and for public schools, have been passed. These proceedings and the ordinances passed by such municipalities are without statutory authority and have no sanction, except as they are maintained by the popular sentiment of the community. There is an entire absence of authority to provide the ordinary instruments of local police control and administration, the population consisting of the usual percentage of lawless adventurers of the class that always flock to new fields of enterprise or discovery, and under circumstances which require more than ordinary provision for the maintenance of peace, good order, and lawful conduct.

The whole vast area of Alaska comprises but one judicial district, with one judge, one marshal, and one district attorney, yet the civil and criminal business has more than doubled within the past year, and is many times greater both in volume and importance than it was in 1884. The duties of the judge require him to travel thousands of miles to discharge his judicial duties at the various places designated for that purpose. The Territory should be divided into at least two districts, and an additional judge, district attorney, marshal, and other appropriate officers be provided.

There is practically no organized form of government in the Territory. There is no authority, except in Congress, to pass any law, no matter how local or trivial, and the difficulty of conveying to the Congress an adequate conception and understanding of the various needs of the people in the different communities is easily understood. I see no reason why a more complete form of Territorial organization should not be provided. Following the precedent established in the year 1805, when a temporary government was provided for the recently acquired territory, then known under the name of Louisiana, it seems to me that it would be advantageous to confer greater executive power upon the governor and to establish, as was done in the case of the Territory of Louisiana, a legislative council having power to adopt ordinances which shall extend to all the rightful subjects of local legislation, such ordinances not to take effect until reported to and approved by the Congress if in session, and if that body is not in session then by the President. In this manner a system of laws providing for the incorporation and government of towns and cities having a certain population, giving them the power to establish and maintain a system of education to be locally supported, and ordinances providing for police, sanitary, and other such purposes, could be speedily provided. I believe a provision of this kind would be satisfactory to the people of the Territory. It is probable that the area is too vast and the population too scattered and transitory to make it wise at the present time to provide for an elective legislative body, but the conditions calling for local self-government will undoubtedly very soon exist, and will be facilitated by the measures which I have recommended.

I recommend that legislation to the same end be had with reference to the government of Puerto Rico. The time is ripe for the adoption of a temporary form of government for this island; and many suggestions made with reference to Alaska are applicable also to Puerto Rico.

The system of civil jurisprudence now adopted by the people of this island is described by competent lawyers who are familiar with it, as thoroughly modern and scientific, so far as it relates to matters of internal business, trade, production, and social and private right in general. The cities of the island are governed under charters which probably require very little or no change. So that with relation to matters of local concern and private right, it is not probable that much, if any, legislation is desirable; but with reference to public administration and the relations of the island to the Federal Government, there are many matters which are of pressing urgency. The same necessity exists for legislation on the part of Congress to establish Federal courts and Federal jurisdiction in the island as has been previously pointed out by me with reference to Hawaii. Besides the administration of justice, there are the subjects of the public lands; the control and improvement of rivers and harbors; the control of the waters or streams' not navigable, which, under the Spanish law, belonged to the Crown of Spain, and have by the treaty of cession passed to the United States; the immigration of people from foreign countries; the importation of contract labor; the imposition and collection of internal revenue; the application of the navigation laws; the regulation of the current money; the establishment of post-offices and post-roads; the regulation of tariff rates on merchandise imported from the island into the United States; the establishment of ports of entry and delivery; the regulation of patents and copyrights; these, with various other subjects which rest entirely within the power of the Congress, call for careful consideration and immediate action.

It must be borne in mind that since the cession Puerto Rico has been denied the principal markets she had long enjoyed and our tariffs have been continued against her products as when she was under Spanish sovereignty. The markets of Spain are closed to her products except upon terms to which the commerce of all nations is subjected. The island of Cuba, which used to buy her cattle and tobacco without customs duties, now imposes the same duties upon these products as from any other country entering her ports. She has therefore lost her free intercourse with Spain and Cuba without any compensating benefits in this market. Her coffee was little known and not in use by our people, and therefore there was no demand here for this, one of her chief products. The markets of the United States should be opened up to her products. Our plain duty is to abolish all customs tariffs between the United States and Puerto Rico and give her products free access to our markets.

As a result of the hurricane which swept over Puerto Rico on the 8th of August, 1899, over 100,000 people were reduced to absolute destitution, without homes, and deprived of the necessaries of life. To the appeal of the War Department the people of the United States made prompt and generous response. In addition to the private charity of our people, the War Department has expended for the relief of the distressed $392,342.63, which does not include the cost of transportation.

It is desirable that the government of the island under the law of belligerent right, now maintained through the Executive Department, should be superseded by an administration entirely civil in its nature. For present purposes I recommend that Congress pass a law for the organization of a temporary government, which shall provide for the appointment by the President, subject to confirmation by the Senate, of a governor and such other officers as the general administration of the island may require, and that for legislative purposes upon subjects of a local nature not partaking of a Federal character a legislative council, composed partly of Puerto Ricans and partly of citizens of the United States, shall be nominated and appointed by the President, subject to confirmation by the Senate, their acts to be subject to the approval of the Congress or the President prior to going into effect. In the municipalities and other local subdivisions I recommend that the principle of local self-government be applied at once, so as to enable the intelligent citizens of the island to participate in their own government and to learn by practical experience the duties and requirements of a self-contained and self-governing people. I have not thought it wise to commit the entire government of the island to officers selected by the people, because I doubt whether in habits, training, and experience they are such as to fit them to exercise at once so large a degree of self-government; but it is my judgment and expectation that they will soon arrive at an attainment of experience and wisdom and self-control that will justify conferring upon them a much larger participation in the choice of their insular officers.

The fundamental requirement for these people, as for all people, is education. The free schoolhouse is the best preceptor for citizenship. In the introduction of modern educational methods care, however, must be exercised that changes be not made too abruptly and that the history and racial peculiarities of the inhabitants shall be given due weight. Systems of education in these new possessions founded upon common-sense methods, adapted to existing conditions and looking to the future moral and industrial advancement of the people, will commend to them in a peculiarly effective manner the blessings of free government.

The love of law and the sense of obedience and submission to the lawfully constituted judicial tribunals are embedded in the hearts of our people, and any violation of these sentiments and disregard of their obligations justly arouses public condemnation. The guaranties of life, liberty, and of civil rights should be faithfully upheld; the right of trial by jury respected and defended. The rule of the courts should assure the public of the prompt trial of those charged with criminal offenses, and upon conviction the punishment should be commensurate with the enormity of the crime.

Those who, in disregard of law and the public peace, unwilling to await the judgment of court and jury, constitute themselves judges and executioners should not escape the severest penalties for their crimes.

What I said in my inaugural address of March 4, 1897, I now repeat:

The constituted authorities must be cheerfully and vigorously upheld. Lynchings must not be tolerated in a great and civilized country like the United States. Courts, not mobs, must execute the penalties of the laws. The preservation of public order, the right of discussion, the integrity of courts, and the orderly administration of justice must continue forever the rock of safety upon which our Government securely rests.

In accordance with the act of Congress providing for an appropriate national celebration in the year 1900 of the establishment of the seat of Government in the District of Columbia, I have appointed a committee, consisting of the governors of all the States and Territories of the United States, who have been invited to assemble in the city of Washington on the 21st of December, 1899, which, with the committees of the Congress and the District of Columbia, are charged with the proper conduct of this celebration.

Congress at its last session appropriated five thousand dollars "to enable the Chief of Engineers of the Army to continue the examination of the subject and to make or secure designs, calculations, and estimates for a memorial bridge from the most convenient point of the Naval Observatory grounds, or adjacent thereto, across the Potomac River to the most convenient point of the Arlington estate property." In accordance with the provisions of this act, the Chief of Engineers has selected four eminent bridge engineers to submit competitive designs for a bridge combining the elements of strength and durability and such architectural embellishment and ornamentation as will fitly apply to the dedication, "A memorial to American patriotism." The designs are now being prepared, and as soon as completed will be submitted to the Congress by the Secretary of War. The proposed bridge would be a convenience to all the people from every part of the country who visit the national cemetery, an ornament to the Capital of the Nation, and forever stand as a monument to American patriotism. I do not doubt that Congress will give to the enterprise still further proof of its favor and approval.

The executive order of May 6, 1896, extending the limits of the classified service, brought within the operation of the civil-service law and rules nearly all of the executive civil service not previously classified.

Some of the inclusions were found wholly illogical and unsuited to the work of the several Departments. The application of the rules to many of the places so included was found to result in friction and embarrassment. After long and very careful consideration, it became evident to the heads of the Departments, responsible for their efficiency, that in order to remove these difficulties and promote an efficient and harmonious administration certain amendments were necessary. These amendments were promulgated by me in executive order dated May 29, 1899.

The principal purpose of the order was to except from competitive examination certain places involving fiduciary responsibilities or duties of a strictly confidential, scientific, or executive character which it was thought might better be filled either by noncompetitive examination, or in the discretion of the appointing officer, than by open competition. These places were comparatively few in number. The order provides for the filling of a much larger number of places, mainly in the outside service of the War Department, by what is known as the registration system, under regulations to be approved by the President, similar to those which have produced such admirable results in the navy-yard service.

All of the amendments had for their main object a more efficient and satisfactory administration of the system of appointments established by the civil-service law. The results attained show that under their operation the public service has improved and that the civil-service system is relieved of many objectionable features which heretofore subjected it to just criticism and the administrative officers to the charge of unbusinesslike methods in the conduct of public affairs. It is believed that the merit system has been greatly strengthened and its permanence assured. It will be my constant aim in the administration of government in our new possessions to make fitness, character, and merit essential to appointment to office, and to give to the capable and deserving inhabitants preference in appointments.

The 14th of December will be the One Hundredth Anniversary of the death of Washington. For a hundred years the Republic has had the priceless advantage of the lofty standard of character and conduct which he bequeathed to the American people. It is an inheritance which time, instead of wasting, continually increases and enriches. We may justly hope that in the years to come the benignant influence of the Father of his Country may be even more potent for good than in the century which is drawing to a close. I have been glad to learn that in many parts of the country the people will fittingly observe this historic anniversary.

Presented to this Congress are great opportunities. With them come great responsibilities. The power confided to us increases the weight of our obligations to the people, and we must be profoundly sensible of them as we contemplate the new and grave problems which confront us. Aiming only at the public good, we cannot err. A right interpretation of the people's will and of duty cannot fail to insure wise measures for the welfare of the islands which have come under the authority of the United States, and inure to the common interest and lasting honor of our country. Never has this Nation had more abundant cause than during the past year for thankfulness to God for manifold blessings and mercies, for which we make reverent acknowledgment. WILLIAM McKINLEY.

EXECUTIVE MANSION,
Washington, December 11, 1899.
To the Senate and House of Representatives:

I transmit herewith, for the consideration of the Congress, a communication from the secretary of the Chamber of Commerce of the State of New York, inclosing resolutions unanimously adopted by that chamber on June 1, 1899, requesting legislation authorizing the appointment of commercial *attachés* to the principal embassies and legations of the United States. WILLIAM McKINLEY.

EXECUTIVE MANSION, *January 4, 1900.*
To the Senate of the United States:

In compliance with a resolution of the Senate of December 20, 1899, I transmit herewith a copy of the report of the commission appointed by the President to investigate the conduct of the War Department in the war with Spain, together with a copy of all the testimony taken by said commission. WILLIAM McKINLEY.

EXECUTIVE MANSION,
Washington, February 1, 1900.

To the Senate of the United States:

In compliance with the resolution of the Senate of January 24, 1900, I transmit herewith a copy of the report and all accompanying papers of Brig-Gen. John C. Bates, in relation to the negotiations of a treaty or agreement made by him with the Sultan of Sulu on the 20th day of August, 1899.

I reply to the request and said resolution for further information that the payments of money provided for by the agreement will be made from the revenues of the Philippine Islands, unless Congress shall otherwise direct.

Such payments are not for specific services but are a part consideration due to the Sulu tribe or nation under the agreement, and they have been stipulated for subject to the action of Congress in conformity with the practice of this Government from the earliest times in its agreements with the various Indian nations occupying and governing portions of the territory subject to the sovereignty of the United States.   WILLIAM McKINLEY.

EXECUTIVE MANSION, *February 2, 1900.*

To the Senate and House of Representatives:

I transmit herewith, for the information of the Congress, a report of a commission appointed by me on January 20, 1899, to investigate affairs in the Philippine Islands.   WILLIAM McKINLEY.

EXECUTIVE MANSION, *February 21, 1900.*

To the House of Representatives:

I transmit herewith a report from the Secretary of State, in response to the resolution of the House of Representatives of February 19, 1900, calling upon him to inform the House of Representatives —

1. If "Charles E. Macrum, as consul of the American Government, informed the State Department that his official mail had been opened and read by the British censor at Durban, and if so, what steps, if any, have been taken in relation thereto; and

2. "What truth there is in the charge that a secret alliance exists between the Republic of the United States and the Empire of Great Britain."   WILLIAM McKINLEY.

EXECUTIVE MANSION, *March 5, 1900.*

To the Senate :

In response to the following resolution of the Senate of January 17, 1900, requesting the President —

If in his judgment not incompatible with the public interest, to communicate to the Senate all communications which have been received by him or by any Department or officer, civil or military, from Aguinaldo or any other person undertaking to represent the people in arms against the United States in the Philippine Islands, or any alleged government or public authority of said people, and all replies to such communications;

Also, the proclamation sent by him to be issued to the people of the Philippine Islands, as actually directed by him to be issued, and the same as actually proclaimed by General Otis, if in any respect it was altered or any part of it was omitted;

Also, to inform the Senate whether any approval or disapproval was expressed by his authority, or that of the War Department, of such change, if any;

Also, all constitutions, forms of government, or proclamations issued by Aguinaldo, or any congress or legislative assembly or body claiming to be such, or convention of the people of the Philippine Islands, or any part thereof, or claiming to represent them or any part thereof, of which information may have come to him or to any Department of the Government;

Also, all instructions given by him to the commissioners of the Philippine Islands, or either of them;

Also, any information which may have come to him, or any Department of the Government, since January 1, 1898, in regard to any plans of the people in arms against the United States for the pillage of Manila, for risings in the city, or for the destruction of foreign property and the massacre of foreign residents;

Also, any information that may have come to him, or any Department of the Government, of the treatment of the other inhabitants of the Philippines by those in arms against the authority of the United States, and of the attitude and feeling of such other inhabitants or tribes toward the so-called government of Aguinaldo and his armed followers;

Also, any information that may have come to him, or any Department of the Government, of the treatment of prisoners, either Spanish or American, by the people in arms against the authority of the United States;

Also, any information that may have come to him, or any Department of the Government, as to any aid or encouragement received by Aguinaldo and his followers from persons in the United States; as to what pamphlets, speeches, or other documents emanating from the United States and adverse to its authority and to its policy were circulated in whole or in part among the Filipinos in arms against the United States, among the other inhabitants of the islands, or among the soldiers of the United States, and any information as to the effect, if any, of such pamphlets, speeches, and other documents, or of similar utterances in the United States upon the course of the rebellion against the United States;

Also, any further or other information which would tend to throw light upon the conduct and events of the insurrection against the authority of the United States in the Philippine Islands, and of the military movements for its suppression since January 1, 1898.

And that the President be further requested to communicate, without delay, so much of such information as is now in his possession or in that of any Department at Washington, without waiting to obtain so much of said information as may require considerable delay or communication with the Philippine Islands, and to communicate the remainder of the information as soon thereafter as it can be obtained,

I transmit herewith the following papers:

First. Copies of all communications which have been received by me, or by any Department or officer, civil or military, from Aguinaldo, or any other person undertaking to represent the people in arms against the United States in the Philippine Islands, or any alleged government or public authority of said people, and copies of all replies to such communications, so far as such communications and replies have been reported to me or to any Executive Department. Said copies of documents are appended hereto marked " I."

Second. Copy of instructions relating to a proclamation sent to General Otis and of the proclamation issued by General Otis pursuant thereto. Said copies of documents are appended hereto, marked " II." No disapproval of the said proclamation was expressed by my authority or that of the War Department. It was, in fact, approved by me, although no formal communication to that effect was sent to General Otis.

Also, among the papers marked " II," a letter of instructions to Maj.-Gen. Wesley Merritt, commanding the army in the Philippines, under date of May 28, 1898, and a proclamation issued by him to the people of the Philippines dated August 14, 1898.

Third. Copies of English translations of all constitutions, forms of government, or proclamations issued by Aguinaldo, or any congress or legislative assembly or body claiming to be such, or convention of the people of the Philippine Islands, or any part thereof, or claiming to represent them, or any part thereof, of which information has come to me or to any Department of the Government. Said copies of documents are appended hereto marked " III."

Fourth. Copies of all written instructions given by me to the commissioners to the Philippine Islands, or either of them. Said copies of documents are appended hereto marked " IV."

Fifth. Such information as has come to me, or any Department of the Government, since January 1, 1898, in regard to any plans of the people in arms against the United States for the pillage of Manila, for risings in the city, or for the destruction of foreign property and the massacre of foreign residents. Said copies of documents are appended hereto marked " V."

Sixth. The information which has come to me, or any Department of the Government, of the treatment of the other inhabitants of the Philippines by those in arms against the authority of the United States, and of the attitude and feeling of such other inhabitants or tribes toward the so-called government of Aguinaldo and his armed followers, is contained in the preliminary statement of the Philippine Commission, dated November 2, 1899, in the report of the Philippine Commission, dated January 31, 1900, and transmitted by me to Congress February 2, 1900, together with the preliminary statement, and the report of Maj.-Gen. E. S. Otis, United States Volunteers, commanding the Department of the Pacific and Eighth Army Corps, dated August 31, 1899, and transmitted to Congress with the report of the Secretary of War, dated November 29, 1899, with the accompanying documents.

Seventh. The information which has come to me, or any Department of the Government, of the treatment of prisoners, either Spanish or American, by the people in arms against the authority of the United States, is contained in the same documents.

Eighth. The information that has come to me, or any Department of the Government, as to any aid or encouragement received by Aguinaldo and his followers from persons in the United States, as to what pamphlets, speeches, or other documents emanating from the United States, and adverse to its authority and to its policy, were circulated, in whole or in part, among the Filipinos in arms against the United States, among the other inhabitants of the islands, or among the soldiers of the United States, and any information as to the effect, if any, of such pamphlets, speeches, and other documents, or of similar utterances in the United States upon the course of the rebellion against the United States is contained in the same documents, and the copies of documents appended hereto marked "VI." WILLIAM McKINLEY.

EXECUTIVE MANSION, *March 15, 1900.*
To the Senate of the United States:

In response to the resolution of the Senate of March 12, 1900, calling for the correspondence touching the request of the Government of the South African Republics for my intervention with a view to the cessation of hostilities, I transmit herewith a report of the Secretary of State furnishing the requested papers. WILLIAM McKINLEY.

EXECUTIVE MANSION, *March 21, 1900.*
To the Senate:

In response to the resolution of the Senate of January 23, 1900, requesting the President, "if in his opinion it is not incompatible with the public interest, to furnish the Senate with copies of the correspondence with the Republic of Colombia in relation to the Panama Canal and to the treaty between this Government and New Granada concluded December 12, 1846, not heretofore communicated," I transmit herewith a report from the Secretary of State, with accompanying papers.

WILLIAM McKINLEY.

EXECUTIVE MANSION,
Washington, March 27, 1900.
To the House of Representatives:

In response to the resolution of the House of Representatives of March 24, 1900, reading as follows:

WHEREAS the commercial community of the United States is deeply interested n ascertaining the conditions which are to govern trade in such parts of the Chinese

Empire as are claimed by various foreign powers to be within their "areas of interest"; and

WHEREAS bills are now pending before both Houses of Congress for the dispatch of a mission to China to study its economic condition: Therefore, be it

Resolved, That the President of the United States be requested to transmit to the House of Representatives, if not incompatible with the public service, such correspondence as may have passed between the Department of State and various foreign Governments concerning the maintenance of the "open door" policy in China,

I transmit herewith a report from the Secretary of State, with accompanying papers.   WILLIAM McKINLEY.

EXECUTIVE MANSION,
Washington, April 2, 1900.
To the Senate and House of Representatives:

I transmit herewith a copy of a letter from Mr. Ferdinand W. Peck, Commissioner-General of the United States to the Paris Exposition of 1900, dated November 17, 1899, submitting a detailed statement of the expenditures incurred under authority of law.

WILLIAM McKINLEY.

EXECUTIVE MANSION, *April 17, 1900.*
To the House of Representatives:

I transmit herewith a report from the Secretary of State in response to the resolution of the House of Representatives of March 23, 1900, calling for copies of any and all letters on file in the Department of State from citizens of the United States resident in the South African Republic from January 1, 1899, to the present time, making complaints of treatment by the South African Republic.

WILLIAM McKINLEY.

EXECUTIVE MANSION,
Washington, May 3, 1900.
To the House of Representatives:

I herewith return, without approval, House bill No. 4001, entitled "An act authorizing the rights of settlers on the Navajo Indian Reservation, Territory of Arizona." My objections to the bill are embodied in the following statement:

This tribe has a population of about 20,500 souls, of whom 1,000 dress in the manner of white men, 250 can read, and 500 use enough English for ordinary conversation. Last year they cultivated 8,000 acres, and possessed approximately 1,000,000 sheep, 250,000 goats, 100,500 cattle, 1,200 swine, and very considerable herds of horses and ponies.

Prior to January last the reservation, which is in the extreme northeastern portion of the Territory of Arizona, consisted of lands set apart for the use of these Indians under the treaty of June 1, 1863 (15 Stat., 667), and subsequent executive orders. On account of the conditions naturally prevailing in that section, the reservation, as then constituted, was altogether inadequate for the purpose for which it was set apart. There was not a sufficient supply of grass or water within its borders for the flocks and herds of the tribe, and in consequence more than one-third of the Indians were habitually off the reservation with their flocks and herds, and were in frequent contention and strife with whites over pasturage and water.

After most careful inquiry and inspection of the reservation as it then existed, and of adjacent land by efficient officers in the Indian service, the Commission of Indian Affairs, with the concurrence of the Secretary of the Interior, recommended that the limits of the reservation be extended westward so as to embrace the lands lying between the Navajo and Moqui Indian reservations on the east and the Colorado and Little Colorado Rivers and the Grand Canyon Forest Reserve on the west. This recommendation was supported by a very numerously signed petition from the white residents of that section, and also by a letter from the Governor of the Territory of Arizona, in which it was said:

I understand that a petition has been forwarded asking that the western limit be fixed at the Little Colorado River, as being better for all concerned and less liable to cause friction between the Indians and the whites. I earnestly hope that the prayer of the petitioners be granted, for the reason that the Little Colorado could be made a natural dividing line, distinct and well defined, and would extend the grazing territory of the Navajoes to a very considerable extent without seriously encroaching upon the interests of white settlers who have their property in that neighborhood.

I think great care should be exercised in questions of this nature because of possible serious friction which may occur if the interests of all concerned are not carefully protected.

The investigation which preceded this recommendation, and upon which it was in part based, showed that with the boundaries of the reservation thus extended the Indians would be able to obtain within the limits of the reservation sufficient grass and water for their flocks and herds, and the Government would therefore be justified in confining them to the reservation, thus avoiding the prior contention and friction between them and the whites.

It appearing that but little aid had been extended to these Indians by the Government for many years, that they had taken on habits of industry and husbandry, which entitled them to encouragement, and that it was neither just nor possible to confine them to the limits of a reservation which would not sustain their flocks and herds, an order was issued by me January 8 last, extending the reservation boundaries as recommended. The Indians have accepted this as an evidence of the good faith of the Government toward them, and it is now the belief of those charged with the administration of Indian affairs that further contention and friction between the Indians and whites will be avoided, if this arrangement is not disturbed.

The present bill proposes to open to miners and prospectors, and to the operation of the mining laws, a substantial portion of this reservation, including a part of the lands covered by the recent order. There has been no effort to obtain from the Indians a concession of this character, nor has any reason been presented why, if these lands are to be taken from them — for that will practically result from this bill, if it becomes a law, even though not so intended — it should not be done in pursuance of negotiations had with the Indians as in other instances.

The Indians could not understand how lands given to them in January as necessary for their use should be taken away without previous notice in May of the same year. While the Indians are the wards of the Government, and must submit to that which is deemed for their best interests by the sovereign guardian, they should, nevertheless, be dealt with in a manner calculated to give them confidence in the Government and to assist them in passing through the inevitable transition to a state of civilization and full citizenship. Believing that due consideration has not been given to the status and interests of the Indians, I withhold my approval from the bill.   WILLIAM McKINLEY.

EXECUTIVE MANSION,
Washington, May 12, 1900.

To the Senate of the United States:

In reply to the resolution of the Senate, dated March 2, 1900, I send herewith copy of an order to the provost marshal general of Manila, dated March 8, 1900, and the various endorsements and reports thereon, whereby it appears that the traffic in wine, beer, and liquor in the city of Manila is now controlled under a rigidly enforced high-license system; that the number of places where the liquor is sold has greatly decreased; that all such places are required to be closed at 8:30 in the evening on week days and to be kept closed on Sundays, and that the orderly condition of the city compares favorably with cities of similar size in the United States.   WILLIAM McKINLEY.

EXECUTIVE MANSION, *May 12, 1900.*

To the Senate of the United States:

In response to a resolution of the Senate of April 11, 1900, reading as follows:

Resolved, That the President be, and is hereby, requested, if not incompatible with public interest, to inform the Senate whether persons have been executed in Puerto

Rico by the Spanish method of garrote since he has been governing that country as Commander-in-Chief of the Army and Navy of the United States; and if so, the President is requested to inform the Senate why this mode of execution was adopted,

I transmit herewith copies of reports from Brig.-Gen. George W. Davis, United States Volunteers, military governor of Puerto Rico, which contain the information called for.   WILLIAM McKINLEY.

EXECUTIVE MANSION,
Washington, May 19, 1900.

To the Senate:

In response to the following resolution of the Senate of April 28, 1900:

Resolved, That the President be, and he is hereby requested, if not incompatible with the public interest, to inform the Senate whether General Torres, one of the officers of the Philippine army, came to General Otis with a flag of truce on February 5, 1899, the day after the fighting commenced between our forces and those of the Filipinos, and stated to General Otis that General Aguinaldo declared that fighting had been begun accidentally, and was not authorized by him, and that Aguinaldo wished to have it stopped, and that to bring about a conclusion of hostilities he proposed the establishment of a neutral zone between the two armies of a width that would be agreeable to General Otis, so that during the peace negotiations there might be no further danger of conflict between the two armies, and whether General Otis replied that fighting having once begun, must go on to the grim end. Was General Otis directed by the Secretary of War to make such an answer? Did General Otis telegraph the Secretary of War on February 9, 1899, as follows: "Aguinaldo now applies for a cessation of hostilities and conference. Have declined to answer?" And did General Otis afterwards reply? Was he directed by the Secretary of War to reply, and what answer, if any, did he or the Secretary of War make to the application to cease fighting?

The President is also requested to inform the Senate whether the flag of the Philippine Republic was ever saluted by Admiral Dewey or any of the vessels of his fleet at any time since May 1, 1898. Did Admiral Dewey, at the request of Aguinaldo, or any officer under him, send the vessels *Concord* and *Raleigh* to Subig Bay to assist Aguinaldo's forces in the capture of the Spanish garrison at that place? Did said vessels assist in the capture of the Spanish garrison, and after the capture did they turn the prisoners thus taken over to the Philippine forces?"

I herewith transmit a copy of a cable dispatch to General Otis, dated April 30, 1900, and of his reply, dated May 1, 1900.

General Otis was not directed by the Secretary of War to make such an answer as is set forth in the resolution, nor were any answers to communications upon the subject of the cessation of hostilities prescribed by the Secretary of War to General Otis, but he was left to exercise in respect thereof his own judgment, based upon his superior knowledge of the conditions surrounding the troops under his command.

I also transmit a copy of a cable dispatch from General Otis, sent from Manila February 8, 1899, received in Washington February 9,

1899, being the same dispatch to which he refers in his reply of May 1, 1900 as misleading. So far as I am informed, General Otis did not afterwards reply, except as set forth in his dispatch of May 1, 1900. He was not directed by the Secretary of War to reply, and no answer was made by him or the Secretary of War to an application to cease fighting. There appears to have been no such application.

I further transmit a copy of a letter from the Secretary of the Navy to Admiral George Dewey, dated May 14, 1900, and a copy of the Admiral's reply, dated May 17, 1900.　　　WILLIAM McKINLEY.

EXECUTIVE MANSION, *May 22, 1900.*
To the Senate and House of Representatives:

I transmit herewith a report from the Secretary of State, with accompanying papers, relative to the status of Chinese persons in the Philippine Islands.　　　WILLIAM McKINLEY.

EXECUTIVE MANSION, *May 22, 1900.*
To the Senate and House of Representatives:

I transmit herewith, for the information of Congress, a communication from the Secretary of Agriculture, forwarding a report on the progress of the beet-sugar industry in the United States during the year 1899. It embraces the observations made by a special agent on the various phases of the beet-sugar industry of the Hawaiian Islands; also the results of analyses of sugar-beets received by the Department of Agriculture from the different States and Territories, together with much other information relating to the sugar industry.

Your attention is invited to the recommendation of the Secretary of Agriculture that 20,000 copies of the report be printed for the use of the Department, in addition to such number as may be desired for the use of the Senate and House of Representatives.
　　　WILLIAM McKINLEY.

EXECUTIVE MANSION,
　　　　　　Washington, May 26, 1900.
To the Senate:

I transmit herewith, in answer to the resolution of the Senate of May 22, 1900, a report from the Secretary of State showing that the consul of the United States at Pretoria was directed on May 8, 1900, to forward copies of the constitutions of the South African Republic and the Orange Free State by return mail. Translations thereof will be communicated to the Senate at the earliest practicable date.
　　　WILLIAM McKINLEY.

EXECUTIVE MANSION,
Washington, June 2, 1900.

To the Senate of the United States:

I transmit herewith, in further reply to the resolution of the Senate of April 10, 1900, having reference to Senate Document No. 336, Fifty-sixth Congress, first session, a further report from the Secretary of State, showing the places of residence of experts, clerks, officers, and employees of the Commission of the United States to the Paris Exposition of 1900, as well as the items of expenditures of the Commission for the months of January, February, and March, 1900, amounting to $211,583.25. WILLIAM McKINLEY.

EXECUTIVE MANSION,
Washington, June 6, 1900.

To the Senate of the United States:

In further response to the resolution of the Senate of January 17, 1900, requesting, among other things, information tending to throw light upon the conduct and events of the insurrection against the authority of the United States in the Philippine Islands, I transmit herewith a correspondence between the Secretary of War and the officers of the Second Division of the Eighth Army Corps.

WILLIAM McKINLEY.

EXECUTIVE MANSION, *December 3, 1900.*
To the Senate and House of Representatives:

At the outgoing of the old and the incoming of the new century you begin the last session of the Fifty-sixth Congress with evidences on every hand of individual and national prosperity and with proof of the growing strength and increasing power for good of Republican institutions. Your countrymen will join with you in felicitation that American liberty is more firmly established than ever before, and that love for it and the determination to preserve it are more universal than at any former period of our history.

The Republic was never so strong, because never so strongly intrenched in the hearts of the people as now. The Constitution, with few amendments, exists as it left the hands of its authors. The additions which have been made to it proclaim larger freedom and more extended citizenship. Popular government has demonstrated in its one hundred and twenty-four years of trial here its stability and security, and its efficiency as the best instrument of national development and the best safeguard to human rights.

When the Sixth Congress assembled in November, 1800, the population of the United States was 5,308,483. It is now 76,304,799.

Then we had sixteen States. Now we have forty-five. Then our territory consisted of 909,050 square miles. It is now 3,846,595 square miles. Education, religion, and morality have kept pace with our advancement in other directions, and while extending its power the Government has adhered to its foundation principles and abated none of them in dealing with our new peoples and possessions. A nation so preserved and blessed gives reverent thanks to God and invokes His guidance and the continuance of His care and favor.

In our foreign intercourse the dominant question has been the treatment of the Chinese problem. Apart from this our relations with the powers have been happy.

The recent troubles in China spring from the antiforeign agitation which for the past three years has gained strength in the northern provinces. Their origin lies deep in the character of the Chinese races and in the traditions of their Government. The Taiping rebellion and the opening of Chinese ports to foreign trade and settlement disturbed alike the homogeneity and the seclusion of China.

Meanwhile foreign activity made itself felt in all quarters, not alone on the coast, but along the great river arteries and in the remoter districts, carrying new ideas and introducing new associations among a primitive people which had pursued for centuries a national policy of isolation.

The telegraph and the railway spreading over their land, the steamers plying on their waterways, the merchant and the missionary penetrating year by year farther to the interior, became to the Chinese mind types of an alien invasion, changing the course of their national life and fraught with vague forebodings of disaster to their beliefs and their self-control.

For several years before the present troubles all the resources of foreign diplomacy, backed by moral demonstrations of the physical force of fleets and arms, have been needed to secure due respect for the treaty rights of foreigners and to obtain satisfaction from the responsible authorities for the sporadic outrages upon the persons and property of unoffending sojourners, which from time to time occurred at widely separated points in the northern provinces, as in the case of the outbreaks in Sze-chuen and Shan-tung.

Posting of antiforeign placards became a daily occurrence, which the repeated reprobation of the Imperial power failed to check or punish. These inflammatory appeals to the ignorance and superstition of the masses, mendacious and absurd in their accusations and deeply hostile in their spirit, could not but work cumulative harm. They aimed at no particular class of foreigners; they were impartial in attacking everything foreign.

An outbreak in Shan-tung, in which German missionaries were slain, was the too natural result of these malevolent teachings. The posting of seditious placards, exhorting to the utter destruction of foreigners and of every foreign thing, continued unrebuked. Hostile demonstrations toward the stranger gained strength by organization.

The sect, commonly styled the Boxers, developed greatly in the provinces north of the Yang-Tse, and with the collusion of many notable officials, including some in the immediate councils of the Throne itself, became alarmingly aggressive. No foreigner's life, outside of the protected treaty ports, was safe. No foreign interest was secure from spoliation.

The diplomatic representatives of the powers in Peking strove in vain to check this movement. Protest was followed by demand and demand by renewed protest, to be met with perfunctory edicts from the Palace and evasive and futile assurances from the Tsung-li Yamen. The circle of the Boxer influence narrowed about Peking, and while nominally stigmatized as seditious, it was felt that its spirit pervaded the capital itself, that the Imperial forces were imbued with its doctrines, and that the immediate counselors of the Empress Dowager were in full sympathy with the antiforeign movement.

The increasing gravity of the conditions in China and the imminence of peril to our own diversified interests in the Empire, as well as to those of all the other treaty governments, were soon appreciated by this Government, causing it profound solicitude. The United States from the earliest days of foreign intercourse with China had followed a policy of peace, omitting no occasions to testify good will, to further the extension of lawful trade, to respect the sovereignty of its Government, and to insure by all legitimate and kindly but earnest means the fullest measure of protection for the lives and property of our law-abiding citizens and for the exercise of their beneficent callings among the Chinese people.

Mindful of this, it was felt to be appropriate that our purposes should be pronounced in favor of such course as would hasten united action of the powers at Peking to promote the administrative reforms so greatly needed for strengthening the Imperial Government and maintaining the integrity of China, in which we believed the whole western world to be alike concerned. To these ends I caused to be addressed to the several powers occupying territory and maintaining spheres of influence in China the circular proposals of 1899, inviting from them declarations of their intentions and views as to the desirability of the adoption of measures insuring the benefits of equality of treatment of all foreign trade throughout China.

With gratifying unanimity the responses coincided in this common policy, enabling me to see in the successful termination of these negotiations proof of the friendly spirit which animates the various powers interested in the untrammeled development of commerce and industry in the Chinese Empire as a source of vast benefit to the whole commercial world.

In this conclusion, which I had the gratification to announce as a completed engagement to the interested powers on March 20, 1900, I hopefully discerned a potential factor for the abatement of the distrust of foreign purposes which for a year past had appeared to inspire the policy of the Imperial Government, and for the effective exertion by it of power and authority to quell the critical antiforeign movement in the northern provinces most immediately influenced by the Manchu sentiment.

Seeking to testify confidence in the willingness and ability of the Imperial administration to redress the wrongs and prevent the evils we suffered and feared, the marine guard, which had been sent to Peking in the autumn of 1899 for the protection of the legation, was withdrawn at the earliest practicable moment, and all pending questions were remitted, as far as we were concerned, to the ordinary resorts of diplomatic intercourse.

The Chinese Government proved, however, unable to check the rising strength of the Boxers and appeared to be a prey to internal dissensions. In the unequal contest the antiforeign influences soon gained the ascendancy under the leadership of Prince Tuan. Organized armies of Boxers, with which the Imperial forces affiliated, held the country between Peking and the coast, penetrated into Manchuria up to the Russian borders, and through their emissaries threatened a like rising throughout northern China.

Attacks upon foreigners, destruction of their property, and slaughter of native converts were reported from all sides. The Tsung-li Yamen, already permeated with hostile sympathies, could make no effective response to the appeals of the legations. At this critical juncture, in the early spring of this year, a proposal was made by the other powers that a combined fleet should be assembled in Chinese waters as a moral demonstration, under cover of which to exact of the Chinese Government respect for foreign treaty rights and the suppression of the Boxers.

The United States, while not participating in the joint demonstration, promptly sent from the Philippines all ships that could be spared for service on the Chinese coast. A small force of marines was landed at Taku and sent to Peking for the protection of the American legation. Other powers took similar action, until some four hundred men were assembled in the capital as legation guards.

Still the peril increased. The legations reported the development of the seditious movement in Peking and the need of increased provision for defense against it. While preparations were in progress for a larger expedition, to strengthen the legation guards and keep the railway open, an attempt of the foreign ships to make a landing at Taku was met by a fire from the Chinese forts. The forts were thereupon shelled by the foreign vessels, the American admiral taking no part in the attack, on the ground that we were not at war with China and that a hostile demonstration might consolidate the antiforeign elements and strengthen the Boxers to oppose the relieving column.

Two days later the Taku forts were captured after a sanguinary conflict. Severance of communication with Peking followed, and a combined force of additional guards, which was advancing to Peking by the Pei-Ho, was checked at Langfang. The isolation of the legations was complete.

The siege and the relief of the legations has passed into undying history. In all the stirring chapter which records the heroism of the devoted band, clinging to hope in the face of despair, and the undaunted spirit that led their relievers through battle and suffering to the goal, it is a memory of which my countrymen may be justly proud that the honor of our flag was maintained alike in the siege and the rescue, and that stout American hearts have again set high, in fervent emulation with true men of other race and language, the indomitable courage that ever strives for the cause of right and justice.

By June 19 the legations were cut off. An identical note from the Yamen ordered each minister to leave Peking, under a promised escort, within twenty-four hours. To gain time they replied, asking prolongation of the time, which was afterwards granted, and requesting an interview with the Tsung-li Yamen on the following day. No reply being received, on the morning of the 20th the German minister, Baron von Ketteler, set out for the Yamen to obtain a response, and on the way was murdered.

An attempt by the legation guard to recover his body was foiled by the Chinese. Armed forces turned out against the legations. Their quarters were surrounded and attacked. The mission compounds were abandoned, their inmates taking refuge in the British legation, where all the other legations and guards gathered for more effective defense. Four hundred persons were crowded in its narrow compass. Two thousand native converts were assembled in a nearby palace under protection of the foreigners. Lines of defense were strengthened, trenches dug, barricades raised, and preparations made to stand a siege, which at once began.

From June 20 until July 17, writes Minister Conger, "there was scarcely an hour during which there was not firing upon some part of our lines and into some of the legations, varying from a single shot to a general and continuous attack along the whole line."

Artillery was placed around the legations and on the over-looking palace walls, and thousands of 3-inch shot and shell were fired, destroying some buildings and damaging all. So thickly did the balls rain, that, when the ammunition of the besieged ran low, five quarts of Chinese bullets were gathered in an hour in one compound and recast.

Attempts were made to burn the legations by setting neighboring houses on fire, but the flames were successfully fought off, although the Austrian, Belgian, Italian, and Dutch legations were then and subsequently burned. With the aid of the native converts, directed by the missionaries, to whose helpful co-operation Mr. Conger awards unstinted praise, the British legation was made a veritable fortress. The British minister, Sir Claude MacDonald, was chosen general commander of the defense, with the secretary of the American legation, Mr. E. G. Squiers, as chief of staff.

To save life and ammunition the besieged sparingly returned the incessant fire of the Chinese soldiery, fighting only to repel attack or make an occasional successful sortie for strategic advantage, such as that of fifty-five American, British, and Russian marines led by Captain Myers, of the United States Marine Corps, which resulted in the capture of a formidable barricade on the wall that gravely menaced the American position. It was held to the last, and proved an invaluable acquisition, because commanding the water gate through which the relief column entered.

During the siege the defenders lost 65 killed, 135 wounded, and 7 by disease—the last all children.

On July 14 the besieged had their first communication with the Tsung-li Yamen, from whom a message came inviting to a conference, which was declined. Correspondence, however, ensued and a sort of armistice was agreed upon, which stopped the bombardment and lessened the rifle fire for a time. Even then no protection whatever was afforded, nor any aid given, save to send to the legations a small supply of fruit and three sacks of flour.

Indeed, the only communication had with the Chinese Government related to the occasional delivery or dispatch of a telegram or to the demands of the Tsung-li Yamen for the withdrawal of the legations to the coast under escort. Not only are the protestations of the Chinese Government that it protected and succored the legations positively contradicted, but irresistible proof accumulates that the attacks upon them were made by Imperial troops, regularly uniformed, armed, and officered, belonging to the command of Jung Lu, the Imperial commander in chief. Decrees encouraging the Boxers, organizing them under prominent Imperial officers, provisioning them, and even granting them large sums in the name of the Empress Dowager, are known to exist. Members of the Tsung-li

Yamen who counseled protection of the foreigners were beheaded. Even in the distant provinces men suspected of foreign sympathy were put to death, prominent among these being Chang Yen-hoon, formerly Chinese minister in Washington.

With the negotiation of the partial armistice of July 14, a proceeding which was doubtless promoted by the representations of the Chinese envoy in Washington, the way was opened for the conveyance to Mr. Conger of a test message sent by the Secretary of State through the kind offices of Minister Wu Ting-fang. Mr. Conger's reply, dispatched from Peking on July 18 through the same channel, afforded to the outside world the first tidings that the inmates of the legations were still alive and hoping for succor.

This news stimulated the preparations for a joint relief expedition in numbers sufficient to overcome the resistance which for a month had been organizing between Taku and the capital. Reinforcements sent by all the co-operating Governments were constantly arriving. The United States contingent, hastily assembled from the Philippines or dispatched from this country, amounted to some 5,000 men, under the able command first of the lamented Colonel Liscum and afterwards of General Chaffee.

Toward the end of July the movement began. A severe conflict followed at Tientsin, in which Colonel Liscum was killed. The city was stormed and partly destroyed. Its capture afforded the base of operations from which to make the final advance, which began in the first days of August, the expedition being made up of Japanese, Russian, British, and American troops at the outset.

Another battle was fought and won at Yangtsun. Thereafter the disheartened Chinese troops offered little show of resistance. A few days later the important position of Ho-si-woo was taken. A rapid march brought the united forces to the populous city of Tung Chow, which capitulated without a contest.

On August 14 the capital was reached. After a brief conflict beneath the walls the relief column entered and the legations were saved. The United States soldiers, sailors, and marines, officers and men alike, in those distant climes and unusual surroundings, showed the same valor, discipline, and good conduct and gave proof of the same high degree of intelligence and efficiency which have distinguished them in every emergency.

The Imperial family and the Government had fled a few days before. The city was without visible control. The remaining Imperial soldiery had made on the night of the 13th a last attempt to exterminate the besieged, which was gallantly repelled. It fell to the occupying forces to restore order and organize a provisional administration.

Happily the acute disturbances were confined to the northern provinces. It is a relief to recall and a pleasure to record the loyal conduct of the viceroys and local authorities of the southern and eastern provinces. Their efforts were continuously directed to the pacific control of the vast populations under their rule and to the scrupulous observance of foreign treaty rights. At critical moments they did not hesitate to memorialize the Throne, urging the protection of the legations, the restoration of communication, and the assertion of the Imperial authority against the subversive elements. They maintained excellent relations with the official representatives of foreign powers. To their kindly disposition is largely due the success of the consuls in removing many of the missionaries from the interior to places of safety. In this relation the action of the consuls should be highly commended. In Shan-tung and eastern Chi-li the task was difficult, but, thanks to their energy and the co-operation of American and foreign naval commanders, hundreds of foreigners, including those of other nationalities than ours, were rescued from imminent peril.

The policy of the United States through all this trying period was clearly announced and scrupulously carried out. A circular note to the powers dated July 3 proclaimed our attitude. Treating the condition in the north as one of virtual anarchy, in which the great provinces of the south and southeast had no share, we regarded the local authorities in the latter quarters as representing the Chinese people with whom we sought to remain in peace and friendship. Our declared aims involved no war against the Chinese nation. We adhered to the legitimate office of rescuing the imperiled legation, obtaining redress for wrongs already suffered, securing wherever possible the safety of American life and property in China, and preventing a spread of the disorders or their recurrence.

As was then said, "The policy of the Government of the United States is to seek a solution which may bring about permanent safety and peace to China, preserve Chinese territorial and administrative entity, protect all rights guaranteed to friendly powers by treaty and international law, and safeguard for the world the principle of equal and impartial trade with all parts of the Chinese Empire."

Faithful to those professions which, as it proved, reflected the views and purposes of the other co-operating Governments, all our efforts have been directed toward ending the anomalous situation in China by negotiations for a settlement at the earliest possible moment. As soon as the sacred duty of relieving our legation and its dependents was accomplished we withdrew from active hostilities, leaving our legation under an adequate guard in Peking as a channel of negotiation and settlement — a course adopted by others of the interested powers. Overtures of the empowered representatives of the Chinese Emperor have been considerately entertained.

The Russian proposition looking to the restoration of the Imperial power in Peking has been accepted as in full consonance with our own desires, for we have held and hold that effective reparation for wrongs suffered and an enduring settlement that will make their recurrence impossible can best be brought about under an authority which the Chinese nation reverences and obeys. While so doing we forego no jot of our undoubted right to exact exemplary and deterrent punishment of the responsible authors and abettors of the criminal acts whereby we and other nations have suffered grievous injury.

For the real culprits, the evil counselors who have misled the Imperial judgment and diverted the sovereign authority to their own guilty ends, full expiation becomes imperative within the rational limits of retributive justice. Regarding this as the initial condition of an acceptable settlement between China and the powers, I said in my message of October 18 to the Chinese Emperor:

> I trust that negotiations may begin so soon as we and the other offended Governments shall be effectively satisfied of Your Majesty's ability and power to treat with just sternness the principal offenders, who are doubly culpable, not alone toward the foreigners, but toward Your Majesty, under whose rule the purpose of China to dwell in concord with the world had hitherto found expression in the welcome and protection assured to strangers.

Taking, as a point of departure, the Imperial edict appointing Earl Li Hung Chang and Prince Ching plenipotentiaries to arrange a settlement, and the edict of September 25, whereby certain high officials were designated for punishment, this Government has moved, in concert with the other powers, toward the opening of negotiations, which Mr. Conger, assisted by Mr. Rockhill, has been authorized to conduct on behalf of the United States.

General bases of negotiation formulated by the Government of the French Republic have been accepted with certain reservations as to details, made necessary by our own circumstances, but, like similar reservations by other powers, open to discussion in the progress of the negotiations. The disposition of the Emperor's Government to admit liability for wrongs done to foreign Governments and their nationals, and to act upon such additional designation of the guilty persons as the foreign ministers at Peking may be in a position to make, gives hope of a complete settlement of all questions involved, assuring foreign rights of residence and intercourse on terms of equality for all the world.

I regard as one of the essential factors of a durable adjustment the securement of adequate guarantees for liberty of faith, since insecurity of those natives who may embrace alien creeds is a scarcely less effectual assault upon the rights of foreign worship and teaching than would be the direct invasion thereof.

The matter of indemnity for our wronged citizens is a question of grave concern. Measured in money alone, a sufficient reparation may prove to be beyond the ability of China to meet. All the powers concur in emphatic disclaimers of any purpose of aggrandizement through the dismemberment of the Empire. I am disposed to think that due compensation may be made in part by increased guarantees of security for foreign rights and immunities, and, most important of all, by the opening of China to the equal commerce of all the world. These views have been and will be earnestly advocated by our representatives.

The Government of Russia has put forward a suggestion, that in the event of protracted divergence of views in regard to indemnities the matter may be relegated to the Court of Arbitration at The Hague. I favorably incline to this, believing that high tribunal could not fail to reach a solution no less conducive to the stability and enlarged prosperity of China itself than immediately beneficial to the powers.

Ratifications of a treaty of extradition with the Argentine Republic were exchanged on June 2 last.

While the Austro-Hungarian Government has in the many cases that have been reported of the arrest of our naturalized citizens for alleged evasion of military service faithfully observed the provisions of the treaty and released such persons from military obligations, it has in some instances expelled those whose presence in the community of their origin was asserted to have a pernicious influence. Representations have been made against this course whenever its adoption has appeared unduly onerous.

We have been urgently solicited by Belgium to ratify the International Convention of June, 1899, amendatory of the previous Convention of 1890 in respect to the regulation of the liquor trade in Africa. Compliance was necessarily withheld, in the absence of the advice and consent of the Senate thereto. The principle involved has the cordial sympathy of this Government, which in the revisionary negotiations advocated more drastic measures, and I would gladly see its extension, by international agreement, to the restriction of the liquor traffic with all uncivilized peoples, especially in the Western Pacific.

A conference will be held at Brussels December 11, 1900, under the Convention for the protection of industrial property, concluded at Paris March 20, 1883, to which delegates from this country have been appointed. Any lessening of the difficulties that our inventors encounter in obtaining patents abroad for their inventions and that our farmers, manufacturers, and merchants may have in the protection of their trade-marks is worthy of careful consideration, and your attention will be called to the results of the conference at the proper time.

In the interest of expanding trade between this country and South America, efforts have been made during the past year to conclude conventions with the southern republics for the enlargement of postal facilities. Two such agreements, signed with Bolivia on April 24, of which that establishing the money-order system is undergoing certain changes suggested by the Post-Office Department, have not yet been ratified by this Government. A treaty of extradition with that country, signed on the same day, is before the Senate.

A boundary dispute between Brazil and Bolivia over the territory of Acre is in a fair way of friendly adjustment, a protocol signed in December, 1899, having agreed on a definite frontier and provided for its demarcation by a joint commission.

Conditions in Brazil have weighed heavily on our export trade to that country in marked contrast to the favorable conditions upon which Brazilian products are admitted into our markets. Urgent representations have been made to that Government on the subject and some amelioration has been effected. We rely upon the reciprocal justice and good will of that Government to assure to us a further improvement in our commercial relations.

The Convention signed May 24, 1897, for the final settlement of claims left in abeyance upon the dissolution of the Commission of 1893, was at length ratified by the Chilean Congress and the supplemental Commission has been organized.

It remains for the Congress to appropriate for the necessary expenses of the Commission.

The insurrectionary movement which disturbed Colombia in the latter part of 1899 has been practically suppressed, although guerrillas still operate in some departments. The executive power of that Republic changed hands in August last by the act of Vice-President Marroquin in assuming the reins of government during the absence of President San Clemente from the capital. The change met with no serious opposition, and, following the precedents in such cases, the United States minister entered into relations with the new *de facto* Government on September 17.

It is gratifying to announce that the residual questions between Costa Rica and Nicaragua growing out of the Award of President

Cleveland in 1888 have been adjusted through the choice of an American engineer, General E. P. Alexander, as umpire to run the disputed line. His task has been accomplished to the satifaction of both contestants.

A revolution in the Dominican Republic toward the close of last year resulted in the installation of President Jimenez, whose Government was formally recognized in January. Since then final payment has been made of the American claim in regard to the Ozama bridge.

The year of the exposition has been fruitful in occasions for displaying the good will that exists between this country and France. This great competition brought together from every nation the best in natural productions, industry, science, and the arts, submitted in generous rivalry to a judgment made all the more searching because of that rivalry. The extraordinary increase of exportations from this country during the past three years and the activity with which our inventions and wares had invaded new markets caused much interest to center upon the American exhibit, and every encouragement was offered in the way of space and facilities to permit of its being comprehensive as a whole and complete in every part.

It was, however, not an easy task to assemble exhibits that could fitly illustrate our diversified resources and manufactures. Singularly enough, our national prosperity lessened the incentive to exhibit. The dealer in raw materials knew that the user must come to him; the great factories were contented with the phenomenal demand for their output, not alone at home, but also abroad, where merit had already won a profitable trade.

Appeals had to be made to the patriotism of exhibitors to induce them to incur outlays promising no immediate return. This was especially the case where it became needful to complete an industrial sequence or illustrate a class of processes. One manufacturer after another had to be visited and importuned, and at times, after a promise to exhibit in a particular section had been obtained, it would be withdrawn, owing to pressure of trade orders, and a new quest would have to be made.

The installation of exhibits, too, encountered many obstacles and involved unexpected cost. The exposition was far from ready at the date fixed for its opening. The French transportation lines were congested with offered freight. Belated goods had to be hastily installed in unfinished quarters with whatever labor could be obtained in the prevailing confusion. Nor was the task of the Commission lightened by the fact that, owing to the scheme of classification adopted, it was impossible to have the entire exhibit of any one country in the same building or more than one group of exhibits in the same part of any building. Our installations were scattered on both sides of the Seine and in widely remote suburbs of Paris, so that additional assistants were needed for the work of supervision and arrangement.

Despite all these drawbacks the contribution of the United States was not only the largest foreign display, but was among the earliest in place and the most orderly in arrangement. Our exhibits were shown in one hundred and one out of one hundred and twenty-one classes, and more completely covered the entire classification than those of any other nation. In total number they ranked next after those of France, and the attractive form in which they were presented secured general attention.

A criterion of the extent and success of our participation and of the thoroughness with which our exhibits were organized is seen in the awards granted to American exhibitors by the international jury, namely, grand prizes, 240; gold medals, 597; silver medals, 776; bronze medals, 541, and honorable mentions, 322 — 2,476 in all, being the greatest total number given to the exhibit of any exhibiting nation, as well as the largest number in each grade. This significant recognition of merit in competition with the chosen exhibits of all other nations and at the hands of juries almost wholly made up of representatives of France and other competing countries is not only most gratifying, but is especially valuable, since it sets us to the front in international questions of supply and demand, while the large proportion of awards in the classes of art and artistic manufactures afforded unexpected proof of the stimulation of national culture by the prosperity that flows from natural productiveness joined to industrial excellence.

Apart from the exposition several occasions for showing international good will occurred. The inauguration in Paris of the Lafayette Monument, presented by the school children of the United States, and the designing of a commemorative coin by our Mint and the presentation of the first piece struck to the President of the Republic, were marked by appropriate ceremonies, and the Fourth of July was especially observed in the French capital.

Good will prevails in our relations with the German Empire. An amicable adjustment of the long-pending question of the admission of our life-insurance companies to do business in Prussia has been reached. One of the principal companies has already been readmitted and the way is opened for the others to share the privilege.

The settlement of the Samoan problem, to which I adverted in my last message, has accomplished good results. Peace and contentment prevail in the islands, especially in Tutuila, where a convenient administration that has won the confidence and esteem of the kindly disposed natives has been organized under the direction of the commander of the United States naval station at Pago-Pago.

An Imperial meat-inspection law has been enacted for Germany. While it may simplify the inspections, it prohibits certain products heretofore admitted. There is still great uncertainty as to whether our well-nigh extinguished German trade in meat products can revive under its new burdens. Much will depend upon regulations not yet promulgated, which we confidently hope will be free from the discriminations which attended the enforcement of the old statutes.

The remaining link in the new lines of direct telegraphic communication between the United States and the German Empire has recently been completed, affording a gratifying occasion for exchange of friendly congratulations with the German Emperor.

Our friendly relations with Great Britain continue. The war in Southern Africa introduced important questions. A condition unusual in international wars was presented in that while one belligerent had control of the seas, the other had no ports, shipping, or direct trade, but was only accessible through the territory of a neutral. Vexatious questions arose through Great Britain's action in respect to neutral cargoes, not contraband in their own nature, shipped to Portuguese South Africa, on the score of probable or suspected ultimate destination to the Boer States.

Such consignments in British ships, by which alone direct trade is kept up between our ports and Southern Africa, were seized in application of a municipal law prohibiting British vessels from trading with the enemy without regard to any contraband character of the goods, while cargoes shipped to Delagoa Bay in neutral bottoms were arrested on the ground of alleged destination to enemy's country. Appropriate representations on our part resulted in the British Government agreeing to purchase outright all such goods shown to be the actual property of American citizens, thus closing the incident to the satisfaction of the immediately interested parties, although, unfortunately, without a broad settlement of the question of a neutral's right to send goods not contraband *per se* to a neutral port adjacent to a belligerent area.

The work of marking certain provisional boundary points, for convenience of administration, around the head of Lynn Canal, in accordance with the temporary arrangement of October, 1899, was completed by a joint survey in July last. The *modus vivendi* has so far worked without friction, and the Dominion Government has provided rules and regulations for securing to our citizens the benefit of the reciprocal stipulation that the citizens or subjects of either power found by that arrangement within the temporary jurisdiction of the other shall suffer no diminution of the rights and privileges they have hitherto enjoyed. But however necessary such an expedient may have been to tide over the grave emergencies of the situation, it is at best but an unsatisfactory makeshift, which should not be suffered to delay the speedy and complete establishment of the frontier line to which we are entitled under the Russo-American treaty for the cession of Alaska.

In this relation I may refer again to the need of definitely marking the Alaskan boundary where it follows the one hundred and forty-first meridian. A convention to that end has been before the Senate for some two years, but as no action has been taken I contemplate negotiating a new convention for a joint determination of the meridian by telegraphic observations. These, it is believed, will give more accurate and unquestionable results than the sidereal methods heretofore independently followed, which, as is known, proved discrepant at several points on the line, although not varying at any place more than 700 feet.

The pending claim of R. H. May against the Guatemalan Government has been settled by arbitration, Mr. George F. B. Jenner, British minister at Guatemala, who was chosen as sole arbitrator, having awarded $143,750.73 in gold to the claimant.

Various American claims against Haiti have been or are being advanced to the resort of arbitration.

As the result of negotiations with the Government of Honduras in regard to the indemnity demanded for the murder of Frank H. Pears in Honduras, that Government has paid $10,000 in settlement of the claim of the heirs

The assassination of King Humbert called forth sincere expressions of sorrow from this Government and people, and occasion was fitly taken to testify to the Italian nation the high regard here felt for the memory of the lamented ruler.

In my last message I referred at considerable length to the lynching of five Italians at Tallulah. Notwithstanding the efforts of the Federal Government, the production of evidence tending to inculpate the authors of this grievous offense against our civilization, and the repeated inquests set on foot by the authorities of the State of Louisiana, no punishments have followed. Successive grand juries have failed to indict. The representations of the Italian Government in the face of this miscarriage have been most temperate and just.

Setting the principle at issue high above all consideration of merely pecuniary indemnification, such as this Government made in the three previous cases, Italy has solemnly invoked the pledges of existing treaty and asked that the justice to which she is entitled shall be meted in regard to her unfortunate countrymen in our territory with the same full measure she herself would give to any American were his reciprocal treaty rights contemned.

I renew the urgent recommendations I made last year that the Congress appropriately confer upon the Federal courts jurisdiction in this class of international cases where the ultimate responsibility of the Federal Government may be involved, and I invite action upon the bills to accomplish this which were introduced in the Senate and House. It is incumbent upon us to remedy the statutory omission which has led, and may again lead, to such untoward results. I have pointed out the necessity and the precedent for legislation of this character. Its enactment is a simple measure of previsory justice toward the nations with which we as a sovereign equal make treaties requiring reciprocal observance.

While the Italian Government naturally regards such action as the primary and, indeed, the most essential element in the disposal of the Tallulah incident, I advise that, in accordance with precedent, and in view of the improbability of that particular case being reached by the bill now pending, Congress make gracious provision for indemnity to the Italian sufferers in the same form and proportion as heretofore.

In my inaugural address I referred to the general subject of lynching in these words:

Lynching must not be tolerated in a great and civilized country like the United States; courts, not mobs, must execute the penalties of the law. The preservation of public order, the right of discussion, the integrity of courts, and the orderly administration of justice must continue forever the rock of safety upon which our Government securely rests.

This I most urgently reiterate and again invite the attention of my countrymen to this reproach upon our civilization.

The closing year has witnessed a decided strengthening of Japan's relations to other States. The development of her independent judicial and administrative functions under the treaties which took effect July 17, 1899, has proceeded without international friction, showing the competence of the Japanese to hold a foremost place among modern peoples.

In the treatment of the difficult Chinese problems Japan has acted in harmonious concert with the other powers, and her generous cooperation materially aided in the joint relief of the beleaguered legations in Peking and in bringing about an understanding preliminary to a settlement of the issues between the powers and China. Japan's declarations in favor of the integrity of the Chinese Empire and the conservation of open world trade therewith have been frank and positive. As a factor for promoting the general interests of peace, order, and fair commerce in the Far East the influence of Japan can hardly be overestimated.

The valuable aid and kindly courtesies extended by the Japanese Government and naval officers to the battle ship *Oregon* are gratefully appreciated.

Complaint was made last summer of the discriminatory enforcement of a bubonic quarantine against Japanese on the Pacific coast and of interference with their travel in California and Colorado under the health laws of those States. The latter restrictions have been adjudged by a Federal court to be unconstitutional. No recurrence of either cause of complaint is apprehended.

No noteworthy incident has occurred in our relations with our important southern neighbor. Commercial intercourse with Mexico continues to thrive, and the two Governments neglect no opportunity to foster their mutual interests in all practicable ways.

Pursuant to the declaration of the Supreme Court that the awards of the late Joint Commission in the La Abra and Weil claims were obtained through fraud, the sum awarded in the first case, $403,030.08, has been returned to Mexico, and the amount of the Weil award will be returned in like manner.

A Convention indefinitely extending the time for the labors of the United States and Mexican International (Water) Boundary Commission has been signed.

It is with satisfaction that I am able to announce the formal notification at The Hague, on September 4, of the deposit of ratifications of the Convention for the Pacific Settlement of International Disputes by sixteen powers, namely, the United States, Austria, Belgium, Denmark, England, France, Germany, Italy, Persia, Portugal, Roumania, Russia, Siam, Spain, Sweden and Norway, and the Netherlands. Japan also has since ratified the Convention.

The Administrative Council of the Permanent Court of Arbitration has been organized and has adopted rules of order and a constitution for the International Arbitration Bureau. In accordance with Article XXIII of the Convention providing for the appointment by each signatory power of persons of known competency in questions of international law as arbitrators, I have appointed as members of this Court, Hon. Benjamin Harrison, of Indiana, ex-President of the United States; Hon. Melville W. Fuller, of Illinois, Chief Justice of the United States; Hon. John W. Griggs, of New Jersey, Attorney-General of the United States; and Hon. George Gray, of Delaware, a judge of the circuit court of the United States.

As an incident of the brief revolution in the Mosquito district of Nicaragua early in 1899 the insurgents forcibly collected from American merchants duties upon imports. On the restoration of order the Nicaraguan authorities demanded a second payment of such duties on the ground that they were due to the titular Government and that their diversion had aided the revolt.

This position was not accepted by us. After prolonged discussion a compromise was effected under which the amount of the second payments was deposited with the British consul at San Juan del Norte in trust until the two Governments should determine whether the first payments had been made under compulsion to a *de facto* authority. Agreement as to this was not reached, and the point was waived by the act of the Nicaraguan Government in requesting the British consul to return the deposits to the merchants.

Menacing differences between several of the Central American States have been accommodated, our ministers rendering good offices toward an understanding.

The all-important matter of an interoceanic canal has assumed a new phase. Adhering to its refusal to reopen the question of the forfeiture of the contract of the Maritime Canal Company, which was terminated for alleged nonexecution in October, 1899, the Government of Nicaragua has since supplemented that action by declaring the so-styled Eyre-Cragin option void for nonpayment of the stipulated advance. Protests in relation to these acts have been filed in the State Department and are under consideration. Deeming itself relieved from existing engagements, the Nicaraguan Government shows a disposition to deal freely with the canal question either in the way of negotiations with the United States or by taking measures to promote the waterway.

Overtures for a convention to effect the building of a canal under the auspices of the United States are under consideration. In the meantime, the views of the Congress upon the general subject, in the light of the report of the Commission appointed to examine the comparative merits of the various trans-Isthmian ship-canal projects, may be awaited.

I commend to the early attention of the Senate the Convention with Great Britain to facilitate the construction of such a canal and to remove any objection which might arise out of the Convention commonly called the Clayton-Bulwer Treaty.

The long-standing contention with Portugal, growing out of the seizure of the Delagoa Bay Railway, has been at last determined by a favorable award of the tribunal of arbitration at Berne, to which it was submitted. The amount of the award, which was deposited in London awaiting arrangements by the Governments of the United

States and Great Britain for its disposal, has recently been paid over to the two Governments.

A lately signed Convention of Extradition with Peru as amended by the Senate has been ratified by the Peruvian Congress.

Another illustration of the policy of this Government to refer international disputes to impartial arbitration is seen in the agreement reached with Russia to submit the claims on behalf of American sealing vessels seized in Bering Sea to determination by Mr. T. M. C. Asser, a distinguished statesman and jurist of the Netherlands.

Thanks are due to the Imperial Russian Government for the kindly aid rendered by its authorities in eastern Siberia to American missionaries fleeing from Manchuria.

Satisfactory progress has been made toward the conclusion of a general treaty of friendship and intercourse with Spain, in replacement of the old treaty, which passed into abeyance by reason of the late war. A new convention of extradition is approaching completion, and I should be much pleased were a commercial arrangement to follow. I feel that we should not suffer to pass any opportunity to reaffirm the cordial ties that existed between us and Spain from the time of our earliest independence, and to enhance the mutual benefits of that commercial intercourse which is natural between the two countries.

By the terms of the Treaty of Peace the line bounding the ceded Philippine group in the southwest failed to include several small islands lying westward of the Sulus, which have always been recognized as under Spanish control. The occupation of Sibutú and Cagayan Sulu by our naval forces elicited a claim on the part of Spain, the essential equity of which could not be gainsaid. In order to cure the defect of the treaty by removing all possible ground of future misunderstanding respecting the interpretation of its third article, I directed the negotiation of a supplementary treaty, which will be forthwith laid before the Senate, whereby Spain quits all title and claim of title to the islands named as well as to any and all islands belonging to the Philippine Archipelago lying outside the lines described in said third article, and agrees that all such islands shall be comprehended in the cession of the archipelago as fully as if they had been expressly included within those lines. In consideration of this cession the United States is to pay to Spain the sum of $100,000.

A bill is now pending to effect the recommendation made in my last annual message that appropriate legislation be had to carry into execution Article VII of the Treaty of Peace with Spain, by which the United States assumed the payment of certain claims for indemnity of its citizens against Spain. I ask that action be taken to fulfill this obligation.

The King of Sweden and Norway has accepted the joint invitation of the United States, Germany, and Great Britain to arbitrate claims growing out of losses sustained in the Samoan Islands in the course of military operations made necessary by the disturbances in 1899.

Our claims upon the Government of the Sultan for reparation for injuries suffered by American citizens in Armenia and elsewhere give promise of early and satisfactory settlement. His Majesty's good disposition in this regard has been evinced by the issuance of an irade for rebuilding the American college at Harpoot.

The failure of action by the Senate at its last session upon the commercial conventions then submitted for its consideration and approval, although caused by the great pressure of other legislative business, has caused much disappointment to the agricultural and industrial interests of the country, which hoped to profit by their provisions. The conventional periods for their ratification having expired, it became necessary to sign additional articles extending the time for that purpose. This was requested on our part, and the other Governments interested have concurred with the exception of one convention, in respect to which no formal reply has been received.

Since my last communication to the Congress on this subject special commercial agreements under the third section of the tariff act have been proclaimed with Portugal, with Italy, and with Germany. Commercial conventions under the general limitations of the fourth section of the same act have been concluded with Nicaragua, with Ecuador, with the Dominican Republic, with Great Britain on behalf of the island of Trinidad, and with Denmark on behalf of the island of St. Croix. These will be early communicated to the Senate. Negotiations with other Governments are in progress for the improvement and security of our commercial relations.

The policy of reciprocity so manifestly rests upon the principles of international equity and has been so repeatedly approved by the people of the United States that there ought to be no hesitation in either branch of the Congress in giving to it full effect.

This Government desires to preserve the most just and amicable commercial relations with all foreign countries, unmoved by the industrial rivalries necessarily developed in the expansion of international trade. It is believed that the foreign Governments generally entertain the same purpose, although in some instances there are clamorous demands upon them for legislation specifically hostile to American interests. Should these demands prevail I shall communicate with the Congress with the view of advising such legislation as may be necessary to meet the emergency.

The exposition of the resources and products of the Western Hemisphere to be held at Buffalo next year promises important results not only for the United States but for the other participating countries. It is gratifying that the Latin-American States have evinced the liveliest interest, and the fact that an International American Congress will be held in the City of Mexico while the exposition is in progress encourages the hope of a larger display at Buffalo than might otherwise be practicable. The work of preparing an exhibit of our national resources is making satisfactory progress under the direction of different officials of the Federal Government, and the various States of the Union have shown a disposition toward the most liberal participation in the enterprise.

The Bureau of the American Republics continues to discharge, with the happiest results, the important work of promoting cordial relations between the United States and the Latin-American countries, all of which are now active members of the International Union. The Bureau has been instrumental in bringing about the agreement for another International American Congress, which is to meet in the City of Mexico in October, 1901. The Bureau's future for another term of ten years is assured by the international compact, but the congress will doubtless have much to do with shaping new lines of work and a general policy. Its usefulness to the interests of Latin-American trade is widely appreciated and shows a gratifying development.

The practical utility of the consular service in obtaining a wide range of information as to the industries and commerce of other countries and the opportunities thereby afforded for introducing the sale of our goods have kept steadily in advance of the notable expansion of our foreign trade, and abundant evidence has been furnished, both at home and abroad, of the fact that the Consular Reports including many from our diplomatic representatives, have to a considerable extent pointed out ways and means of disposing of a great variety of manufactured goods which otherwise might not have found sale abroad.

Testimony of foreign observers to the commercial efficiency of the consular corps seems to be conclusive, and our own manufacturers and exporters highly appreciate the value of the services rendered not only in the printed reports but also in the individual efforts of consular officers to promote American trade. An increasing part of the work of the Bureau of Foreign Commerce, whose primary duty it is to compile and print the reports, is to answer inquiries from trade organizations, business houses, etc., as to conditions in various parts of the world, and, notwithstanding the smallness of the force employed, the work has been so systematized that responses are made with such promptitude and accuracy as to elicit flattering encomiums. The experiment of printing the Consular Reports daily for immediate use by trade bodies, exporters, and the press, which was begun in January, 1898, continues to give general satisfaction.

It is gratifying to be able to state that the surplus revenues for the fiscal year ended June 30, 1900, were $79,527,060.18. For the six preceding years we had only deficits, the aggregate of which from 1894 to 1899, inclusive, amounted to $283,022,991.14. The receipts for the year from all sources, exclusive of postal revenues, aggregated $567,240,851.89, and expenditures for all purposes, except for the administration of the postal department, aggregated $487,713,791.71. The receipts from customs were $233,164,871.16, an increase over the preceding year of $27,036,389.41. The receipts from internal revenue were $295,327,926.76, an increase of $21,890,765.25 over 1899. The receipts from miscellaneous sources were $38,748,053.97, as against $36,394,976.92 for the previous year.

It is gratifying also to note that during the year a considerable reduction is shown in the expenditures of the Government. The War Department expenditures for the fiscal year 1900 were $134,774,767.78, a reduction of $95,066,486.69 over those of 1899. In the Navy Department the expenditures were $55,953,077.72 for the year 1900, as against $63,942,104.25 for the preceding year, a decrease of $7,989,026.53. In the expenditures on account of Indians there was a decrease in 1900 over 1899 of $2,630,604.38; and in the civil and miscellaneous expenses for 1900 there was a reduction of $13,418,065.74.

Because of the excess of revenues over expenditures the Secretary of the Treasury was enabled to apply bonds and other securities to the sinking fund to the amount of $56,544,556.06. The details of the sinking fund are set forth in the report of the Secretary of the Treasury, to which I invite attention. The Secretary of the Treasury estimates that the receipts for the current fiscal year will aggregate $580,000,000 and the expenditures $500,000,000, leaving an excess of revenues over expenditures of $80,000,000. The present condition of the Treasury is one of undoubted strength. The available cash balance November 30 was $139,303,794.50. Under the form of statement prior to the financial law of March 14 last there would have been included in the statement of available cash gold coin and bullion held for the redemption of United States notes.

If this form were pursued, the cash balance including the present gold reserve of $150,000,000, would be $289,303,794.50. Such balance November 30, 1899, was $296,495,301.55. In the general fund, which is wholly separate from the reserve and trust funds, there was on November 30, $70,090,073.15 in gold coin and bullion, to which should be added $22,957,300 in gold certificates subject to issue, against which there is held in the Division of Redemption gold coin and bullion, making a total holding of free gold amounting to $93,-047,373.15.

It will be the duty as I am sure it will be the disposition of the Congress to provide whatever further legislation is needed to insure the continued parity under all conditions between our two forms of metallic money, silver and gold.

Our surplus revenues have permitted the Secretary of the Treasury since the close of the fiscal year to call in the funded loan of 1891 continued at 2 per cent, in the sum of $25,364,500. To and including November 30, $23,458,100 of these bonds have been paid. This sum, together with the amount which may accrue from further redemptions under the call, will be applied to the sinking fund.

The law of March 14, 1900, provided for refunding into 2 per cent thirty-year bonds, payable, principal and interest, in gold coin of the present standard value, that portion of the public debt represented by the 3 per cent bonds of 1908, the 4 percents of 1907, and the 5 percents of 1904, of which there was outstanding at the date of said law $839,149,930. The holders of the old bonds presented them for exchange between March 14 and November 30 to the amount of $364,943,750. The net saving to the Government on these transactions aggregates $9,106,166.

Another effect of the operation, as stated by the Secretary, is to reduce the charge upon the Treasury for the payment of interest from the dates of refunding to February 1, 1904, by the sum of more than seven million dollars annually. From February 1, 1904, to July 1, 1907, the annual interest charge will be reduced by the sum of more than five millions, and for the thirteen months ending August 1, 1908, by about one million. The full details of the refunding are given in the annual report of the Secretary of the Treasury.

The beneficial effect of the financial act of 1900, so far as it relates to a modification of the national banking act, is already apparent. The provision for the incorporation of national banks with a capital of not less than $25,000 in places not exceeding three thousand inhabitants has resulted in the extension of banking facilities to many small communities hitherto unable to provide themselves with banking institutions under the national system. There were organized from the enactment of the law up to and including November 30, 369 national banks, of which 266 were with capital less than $50,000, and 103 with capital of $50,000 or more.

It is worthy of mention that the greater number of banks being organized under the new law are in sections where the need of banking facilities has been most pronounced. Iowa stands first, with 30 banks of the smaller class, while Texas, Oklahoma, Indian Territory, and the middle and western sections of the country have also availed themselves largely of the privileges under the new law.

A large increase in national-bank-note circulation has resulted from the provision of the act which permits national banks to issue circulating notes to the par value of the United States bonds deposited as security instead of only 90 per cent thereof, as heretofore. The increase in circulating notes from March 14 to November 30 is $77,889,570.

The party in power is committed to such legislation as will better make the currency responsive to the varying needs of business at all seasons and in all sections.

Our foreign trade shows a remarkable record of commercial and industrial progress. The total of imports and exports for the first time in the history of the country exceeded two billions of dollars. The exports are greater than they have ever been before, the total for the fiscal year 1900 being $1,394,483,082, an increase over 1899 of $167,459,780, an increase over 1898 of $163,000,752, over 1897 of $343,489,526, and greater than 1896 by $511,876,144.

The growth of manufactures in the United States is evidenced by the fact that exports of manufactured products largely exceed those of any previous year, their value for 1900 being $433,851,756, against $339,592,146 in 1899, an increase of 28 per cent.

Agricultural products were also exported during 1900 in greater volume than in 1899, the total for the year being $835,858,123, against $784,776,142 in 1899.

The imports for the year amounted to $849,941,184, an increase over 1899 of $152,792,695. This increase is largely in materials for manufacture, and is in response to the rapid development of manufacturing in the United States. While there was imported for use in manufactures in 1900 material to the value of $79,768,972 in excess of 1899, it is reassuring to observe that there is a tendency toward decrease in the importation of articles manufactured ready for consumption, which in 1900 formed 15.17 per cent of the total imports, against 15.54 per cent in 1899 and 21.09 per cent in 1896.

I recommend that the Congress at its present session reduce the internal-revenue taxes imposed to meet the expenses of the war with

Spain in the sum of thirty millions of dollars. This reduction should be secured by the remission of those taxes which experience has shown to be the most burdensome to the industries of the people.

I specially urge that there be included in whatever reduction is made the legacy tax on bequests for public uses of a literary, educational, or charitable character.

American vessels during the past three years have carried about 9 per cent of our exports and imports. Foreign ships should carry the least, not the greatest, part of American trade. The remarkable growth of our steel industries, the progress of shipbuilding for the domestic trade, and our steadily maintained expenditures for the Navy have created an opportunity to place the United States in the first rank of commercial maritime powers.

Besides realizing a proper national aspiration this will mean the establishment and healthy growth along all our coasts of a distinctive national industry, expanding the field for the profitable employment of labor and capital. It will increase the transportation facilities and reduce freight charges on the vast volume of products brought from the interior to the seaboard for export, and will strengthen an arm of the national defense upon which the founders of the Government and their successors have relied. In again urging immediate action by the Congress on measures to promote American shipping and foreign trade, I direct attention to the recommendations on the subject in previous messages, and particularly to the opinion expressed in the message of 1899:

I am satisfied the judgment of the country favors the policy of aid to our merchant marine, which will broaden our commerce and markets and upbuild our sea-carrying capacity for the products of agriculture and manufacture, which, with the increase of our Navy, mean more work and wages to our countrymen, as well as a safeguard to American interests in every part of the world.

The attention of the Congress is invited to the recommendation of the Secretary of the Treasury in his annual report for legislation in behalf of the Revenue-Cutter Service, and favorable action is urged.

In my last annual message to the Congress I called attention to the necessity for early action to remedy such evils as might be found to exist in connection with combinations of capital organized into trusts, and again invite attention to my discussion of the subject at that time, which concluded with these words:

It is apparent that uniformity of legislation upon this subject in the several States is much to be desired. It is to be hoped that such uniformity, founded in a

wise and just discrimination between what is injurious and what is useful and necessary in business operations, may be obtained, and that means may be found for
the Congress, within the limitations of its constitutional power, so to supplement
an effective code of State legislation as to make a complete system of laws throughout the United States adequate to compel a general observance of the salutary rules
to which I have referred.

The whole question is so important and far-reaching that I am sure no part of it
will be lightly considered, but every phase of it will have the studied deliberation
of the Congress, resulting in wise and judicious action.

Restraint upon such combinations as are injurious, and which
are within Federal jurisdiction, should be promptly applied by the
Congress.

In my last annual message I dwelt at some length upon the condition of affairs in the Philippines. While seeking to impress upon
you that the grave responsibility of the future government of those
islands rests with the Congress of the United States, I abstained
from recommending at that time a specific and final form of government for the territory actually held by the United States forces and
in which as long as insurrection continues the military arm must
necessarily be supreme. I stated my purpose, until the Congress
shall have made the formal expression of its will, to use the authority vested in me by the Constitution and the statutes to uphold the
sovereignty of the United States in those distant islands as in all
other places where our flag rightfully floats, placing, to that end, at
the disposal of the army and navy all the means which the liberality
of the Congress and the people have provided. No contrary expression of the will of the Congress having been made, I have steadfastly
pursued the purpose so declared, employing the civil arm as well toward the accomplishment of pacification and the institution of local
governments within the lines of authority and law.

Progress in the hoped-for direction has been favorable. Our forces
have successfully controlled the greater part of the islands, overcoming the organized forces of the insurgents and carrying order and
administrative regularity to all quarters. What opposition remains
is for the most part scattered, obeying no concerted plan of strategic
action, operating only by the methods common to the traditions of
guerrilla warfare, which, while ineffective to alter the general control
now established, are still sufficient to beget insecurity among the
populations that have felt the good results of our control and thus
delay the conferment upon them of the fuller measures of local self-
government, of education, and of industrial and agricultural development which we stand ready to give to them.

By the spring of this year the effective opposition of the dissatisfied Tagals to the authority of the United States was virtually ended,
thus opening the door for the extension of a stable administration

over much of the territory of the Archipelago. Desiring to bring this about, I appointed in March last a civil Commission composed of the Hon William H. Taft, of Ohio; Prof. Dean C. Worcester, of Michigan; the Hon. Luke I. Wright, of Tennessee; the Hon. Henry C. Ide, of Vermont, and Prof. Bernard Moses, of California. The aims of their mission and the scope of their authority are clearly set forth in my instructions of April 7, 1900, addressed to the Secretary of War to be transmitted to them:

In the message transmitted to the Congress on the 5th of December, 1899, I said, speaking of the Philippine Islands: " As long as the insurrection continues the military arm must necessarily be supreme. But there is no reason why steps should not be taken from time to time to inaugurate governments essentially popular in their form as fast as territory is held and controlled by our troops. To this end I am considering the advisability of the return of the Commission, or such of the members thereof as can be secured, to aid the existing authorities and facilitate this work throughout the islands."

To give effect to the intention thus expressed, I have appointed Hon. William H. Taft, of Ohio; Prof. Dean C. Worcester, of Michigan; Hon. Luke I. Wright, of Tennessee; Hon. Henry C. Ide, of Vermont, and Prof. Bernard Moses, of California, Commissioners to the Philippine Islands to continue and perfect the work of organizing and establishing civil government already commenced by the military authorities, subject in all respects to any laws which Congress may hereafter enact.

The Commissioners named will meet and act as a board, and the Hon. William H. Taft is designated as president of the board. It is probable that the transfer of authority from military commanders to civil officers will be gradual and will occupy a considerable period. Its successful accomplishment and the maintenance of peace and order in the meantime will require the most perfect co-operation between the civil and military authorities in the islands, and both should be directed during the transition period by the same Executive Department. The Commission will therefore report to the Secretary of War, and all their action will be subject to your approval and control.

You will instruct the Commission to proceed to the city of Manila, where they will make their principal office, and to communicate with the Military Governor of the Philippine Islands, whom you will at the same time direct to render to them every assistance within his power in the performance of their duties. Without hampering them by too specific instructions, they should in general be enjoined, after making themselves familiar with the conditions and needs of the country, to devote their attention in the first instance to the establishment of municipal governments, in which the natives of the islands, both in the cities and in the rural communities, shall be afforded the opportunity to manage their own local affairs to the fullest extent of which they are capable and subject to the least degree of supervision and control which a careful study of their capacities and observation of the workings of native control show to be consistent with the maintenance of law, order, and loyalty.

The next subject in order of importance should be the organization of government in the larger administrative divisions corresponding to counties, departments, or provinces, in which the common interests of many or several municipalities falling within the same tribal lines, or the same natural geographical limits, may best be subserved by a common administration. Whenever the Commission is of the opinion that the condition of affairs in the islands is such that the central administration may safely be transferred from military to civil control they will report that conclusion to you, with their recommendations as to the form of central government to be established for the purpose of taking over the control.

Beginning with the 1st day of September, 1900, the authority to exercise, subject to my approval, through the Secretary of War, that part of the power of government in the Philippine Islands which is of a legislative nature is to be transferred from the Military Governor of the islands to this Commission, to be thereafter exercised by them in the place and stead of the Military Governor, under such rules and regulations as you shall prescribe, until the establishment of the civil central government for the islands contemplated in the last foregoing paragraph, or until Congress shall otherwise provide. Exercise of this legislative authority will include the making of rules and orders, having the effect of law, for the raising of revenue by taxes, customs duties, and imposts; the appropriation and expenditure of public funds of the islands; the establishment of an educational system throughout the islands; the establishment of a system to secure an efficient civil service; the organization and establishment of courts; the organization and establishment of municipal and departmental governments, and all other matters of a civil nature for which the Military Governor is now competent to provide by rules or orders of a legislative character.

The Commission will also have power during the same period to appoint to office such officers under the judicial, educational, and civil-service systems and in the municipal and departmental governments as shall be provided for. Until the complete transfer of control the Military Governor will remain the chief executive head of the government of the islands, and will exercise the executive authority now possessed by him and not herein expressly assigned to the Commission, subject, however, to the rules and orders enacted by the Commission in the exercise of the legislative powers conferred upon them. In the meantime the municipal and departmental governments will continue to report to the Military Governor and be subject to his administrative supervision and control, under your direction, but that supervision and control will be confined within the narrowest limits consistent with the requirement that the powers of government in the municipalities and departments shall be honestly and effectively exercised and that law and order and individual freedom shall be maintained.

All legislative rules and orders, establishments of government, and appointments to office by the Commission will take effect immediately, or at such times as they shall designate, subject to your approval and action upon the coming in of the Commission's reports, which are to be made from time to time as their action is taken. Wherever civil governments are constituted under the direction of the Commission such military posts, garrisons, and forces will be continued for the suppression of insurrection and brigandage and the maintenance of law and order as the Military Commander shall deem requisite, and the military forces shall be at all times subject, under his orders, to the call of the civil authorities for the maintenance of law and order and the enforcement of their authority.

In the establishment of municipal governments the Commission will take as the basis of their work the governments established by the Military Governor under his order of August 8, 1899, and under the report of the board constituted by the Military Governor by his order of January 29, 1900, to formulate and report a plan of municipal government, of which His Honor Cayetano Arellano, President of the Audiencia, was chairman, and they will give to the conclusions of that board the weight and consideration which the high character and distinguished abilities of its members justify.

In the constitution of departmental or provincial governments they will give especial attention to the existing government of the island of Negros, constituted, with the approval of the people of that island, under the order of the Military Governor of July 22, 1899, and after verifying, so far as may be practicable. the reports of the successful working of that government they will be guided by the experience thus acquired so far as it may be applicable to the condition existing in other portions of the Philippines. They will avail themselves, to the fullest degree practicable, of the conclusions reached by the previous Commission to the Philippines.

In the distribution of powers among the governments organized by the Commission, the presumption is always to be in favor of the smaller subdivision, so that all the powers which can properly be exercised by the municipal government shall be vested in that government, and all the powers of a more general character which can be exercised by the departmental government shall be vested in that government, and so that in the governmental system, which is the result of the process, the central government of the islands, following the example of the distribution of the powers between the States and the National Government of the United States, shall have no direct administration except of matters of purely general concern, and shall have only such supervision and control over local governments as may be necessary to secure and enforce faithful and efficient administration by local officers.

The many different degrees of civilization and varieties of custom and capacity among the people of the different islands preclude very definite instruction as to the part which the people shall take in the selection of their own officers; but these general rules are to be observed: That in all cases the municipal officers, who administer the local affairs of the people, are to be selected by the people, and that wherever officers of more extended jurisdiction are to be selected in any way, natives of the islands are to be preferred, and if they can be found competent and willing to perform the duties, they are to receive the offices in preference to any others.

It will be necessary to fill some offices for the present with Americans which after a time may well be filled by natives of the islands. As soon as practicable a system for ascertaining the merit and fitness of candidates for civil office should be put in force. An indispensable qualification for all offices and positions of trust and authority in the islands must be absolute and unconditional loyalty to the United States, and absolute and unhampered authority and power to remove and punish any officer deviating from that standard must at all times be retained in the hands of the central authority of the islands.

In all the forms of government and administrative provisions which they are authorized to prescribe the Commission should bear in mind that the government which they are establishing is designed not for our satisfaction, or for the expression of our theoretical views, but for the happiness, peace, and prosperity of the people of the Philippine Islands, and the measures adopted should be made to conform to their customs, their habits, and even heir prejudices, to the fullest extent consistent with the accomplishment of the indispensable requisites of just and effective government.

At the same time the Commission should bear in mind, and the people of the islands should be made plainly to understand, that there are certain great principles of government which have been made the basis of our governmental system which we deem essential to the rule of law and the maintenance of individual freedom, and of which they have, unfortunately, been denied the experience possessed by us; that there are also certain practical rules of government which we have found to be essential to the preservation of these great principles of liberty and law, and that these principles and these rules of government must be established and maintained in their islands for the sake of their liberty and happiness, however much they may conflict with the customs or laws of procedure with which they are familiar.

It is evident that the most enlightened thought of the Philippine Islands fully appreciates the importance of these principles and rules, and they will inevitably within a short time command universal assent. Upon every division and branch of the government of the Philippines, therefore, must be imposed these inviolable rules:

That no person shall be deprived of life, liberty, or property without due process of law; that private property shall not be taken for public use without just compensation; that in all criminal prosecutions the accused shall enjoy the right to a speedy and public trial, to be informed of the nature and cause of the accusation, to be confronted with the witnesses against him, to have compulsory process for obtaining witnesses in his favor, and to have the assistance of counsel for his defense; that excessive bail shall not be required, nor excessive fines imposed, nor cruel and unusual punishment inflicted; that no person shall be put twice in jeopardy for the same offense, or be compelled in any criminal case to be a witness against himself; that the right to be secure against unreasonable searches and seizures shall not be violated; that neither slavery nor involuntary servitude shall exist except as a punishment for crime; that no bill of attainder or *ex-post-facto* law shall be passed; that no law shall be passed abridging the freedom of speech or of the press, or the rights of the people to peaceably assemble and petition the Government for a redress of grievances; that no law shall be made respecting an establishment of religion, or prohibiting the free exercise thereof, and that the free exercise and enjoyment of religious profession and worship without discrimination or preference shall forever be allowed.

It will be the duty of the Commission to make a thorough investigation into the titles to the large tracts of land held or claimed by individuals or by religious orders; into the justice of the claims and complaints made against such landholders by the people of the island or any part of the people, and to seek by wise and peaceable measures a just settlement of the controversies and redress of wrongs which have caused strife and bloodshed in the past. In the performance of this duty the Commission is enjoined to see that no injustice is done; to have regard for substantial rights and equity, disregarding technicalities so far as substantial right permits, and to observe the following rules:

That the provision of the Treaty of Paris pledging the United States to the protection of all rights of property in the islands, and as well the principle of our own Government which prohibits the taking of private property without due process of law, shall not be violated; that the welfare of the people of the islands, which should be a paramount consideration, shall be attained consistently with this rule of property right; that if it becomes necessary for the public interest of the people of the islands to dispose of claims to property which the Commission finds to be not lawfully acquired and held disposition shall be made thereof by due legal procedure, in which there shall be full opportunity for fair and impartial hearing and judgment; that if the same public interests require the extinguishment of property rights lawfully acquired and held due compensation shall be made out of the public treasury therefor; that no form of religion and no minister of religion shall be forced upon any community or upon any citizen of the islands; that, upon the other hand, no minister of religion shall be interfered with or molested in following his calling, and that the separation between State and Church shall be real, entire, and absolute.

It will be the duty of the Commission to promote and extend, and, as they find occasion, to improve the system of education already inaugurated by the military authorities. In doing this they should regard as of first importance the extension of a system of primary education which shall be free to all, and which shall tend to fit the people for the duties of citizenship and for the ordinary avocations of a civilized community. This instruction should be given in the first instance in every part of the islands in the language of the people. In view of the great number of languages spoken by the different tribes, it is especially important to the prosperity of the islands that a common medium of communication may be established, and it is obviously desirable that this medium should be the English language. Especial attention should be at once given to affording full opportunity to all the people of the islands to acquire the use of the English language.

It may be well that the main changes which should be made in the system of taxation and in the body of the laws under which the people are governed, except such changes as have already been made by the military government, should be relegated to the civil government which is to be established under the auspices of the Commission. It will, however, be the duty of the Commission to inquire diligently as to whether there are any further changes which ought not to be delayed, and if so, they are authorized to make such changes subject to your approval. In doing so they are to bear in mind that taxes which tend to penalize or repress industry and enterprise are to be avoided; that provisions for taxation should be simple, so that they may be understood by the people; that they should affect the fewest practicable subjects of taxation which will serve for the general distribution of the burden.

The main body of the laws which regulate the rights and obligations of the people should be maintained with as little interference as possible. Changes made should be mainly in procedure, and in the criminal laws to secure speedy and impartial trials, and at the same time effective administration and respect for individual rights.

In dealing with the uncivilized tribes of the islands the Commission should adopt the same course followed by Congress in permitting the tribes of our North American Indians to maintain their tribal organization and government, and under which many of those tribes are now living in peace and contentment, surrounded by a civilization to which they are unable or unwilling to conform. Such tribal governments should, however, be subjected to wise and firm regulation, and, without undue or petty interference, constant and active effort should be exercised to prevent barbarous practices and introduce civilized customs.

Upon all officers and employees of the United States, both civil and military, should be impressed a sense of the duty to observe not merely the material but the personal and social rights of the people of the islands, and to treat them with the same courtesy and respect for their personal dignity which the people of the United States are accustomed to require from each other.

The articles of capitulation of the city of Manila on the 13th of August, 1898, concluded with these words:

"This city, its inhabitants, its churches and religious worship, its educational establishments, and its private property of all descriptions, are placed under the special safeguard of the faith and honor of the American Army."

I believe that this pledge has been faithfully kept. As high and sacred an obligation rests upon the Government of the United States to give protection for property and life, civil and religious freedom, and wise, firm, and unselfish guidance in the paths of peace and prosperity to all the people of the Philippine Islands. I charge this Commission to labor for the full performance of this obligation, which concerns the honor and conscience of their country, in the firm hope that through their labors all the inhabitants of the Philippine Islands may come to look back with gratitude to the day when God gave victory to American arms at Manila and set their land under the sovereignty and the protection of the people of the United States.

Coincidently with the entrance of the Commission upon its labors I caused to be issued by General MacArthur, the Military Governor of the Philippines, on June 21, 1900, a proclamation of amnesty in generous terms, of which many of the insurgents took advantage, among them a number of important leaders.

This Commission, composed of eminent citizens representing the diverse geographical and political interests of the country, and bringing to their task the ripe fruits of long and intelligent service in educational, administrative, and judicial careers, made great progress from the outset. As early as August 21, 1900, it submitted a preliminary report, which will be laid before the Congress, and from which it appears that already the good effects of returning order are felt; that business, interrupted by hostilities, is improving as peace extends; that a larger area is under sugar cultivation than ever before; that the customs revenues are greater than at any time during the Spanish rule; that economy and efficiency in the military administration have created a surplus fund of $6,000,000, available for needed public improvements; that a stringent civil-service law is in preparation; that railroad communications are expanding, opening up rich districts, and that a comprehensive scheme of education is being organized.

Later reports from the Commission show yet more encouraging advance toward insuring the benefits of liberty and good government to the Filipinos, in the interest of humanity and with the aim of building up an enduring, self-supporting, and self-administering community in those far eastern seas. I would impress upon the Congress that whatever legislation may be enacted in respect to the Philippine Islands should be along these generous lines. The fortune of war has thrown upon this nation an unsought trust which should be unselfishly discharged, and devolved upon this Government a moral as well as material responsibility toward these millions whom we have freed from an oppressive yoke.

I have on another occasion called the Filipinos "the wards of the nation." Our obligation as guardian was not lightly assumed; it must not be otherwise than honestly fulfilled, aiming first of all to benefit those who have come under our fostering care. It is our duty so to treat them that our flag may be no less beloved in the mountains of Luzon and the fertile zones of Mindanao and Negros than it is at home, that there as here it shall be the revered symbol of liberty, enlightenment, and progress in every avenue of development

The Filipinos are a race quick to learn and to profit by knowledge He would be rash who, with the teachings of contemporaneous history in view, would fix a limit to the degree of culture and advancement yet within the reach of these people if our duty toward them be faithfully performed.

The civil government of Puerto Rico provided for by the act of the Congress approved April 12, 1900, is in successful operation The courts have been established. The Governor and his associates, working intelligently and harmoniously, are meeting with commendable success.

On the 6th of November a general election was held in the island for members of the Legislature, and the body elected has been called to convene on the first Monday of December.

I recommend that legislation be enacted by the Congress conferring upon the Secretary of the Interior supervision over the public lands in Puerto Rico, and that he be directed to ascertain the location and quantity of lands the title to which remained in the Crown of Spain at the date of cession of Puerto Rico to the United States, and that appropriations necessary for surveys be made, and that the methods of the disposition of such lands be prescribed by law.

On the 25th of July, 1900, I directed that a call be issued for an election in Cuba for members of a constitutional convention to frame a constitution as a basis for a stable and independent government in the island. In pursuance thereof the Military Governor issued the following instructions:

Whereas the Congress of the United States, by its joint resolution of April 20, 1898, declared —

"That the people of the island of Cuba are, and of right ought to be, free and independent.

"That the United States hereby disclaims any disposition or intention to exercise sovereignty, jurisdiction, or control over said island except for the pacification thereof, and asserts its determination, when that is accomplished, to leave the government and control of the island to its people;"

And whereas, the people of Cuba have established municipal governments, deriving their authority from the suffrages of the people given under just and equal laws, and are now ready, in like manner, to proceed to the establishment of a general government which shall assume and exercise sovereignty, jurisdiction, and control over the island:

Therefore, it is ordered that a general election be held in the island of Cuba on the third Saturday of September, in the year nineteen hundred, to elect delegates to a convention to meet in the city of Havana at twelve o'clock noon on the first Monday of November, in the year nineteen hundred, to frame and adopt a constitution for the people of Cuba, and as a part thereof to provide for and agree with the Government of the United States upon the relations to exist between that Government and the Government of Cuba, and to provide for the election by the people of officers under such constitution and the transfer of government to the officers so elected.

The election will be held in the several voting precincts of the island under, and pursuant to, the provisions of the electoral law of April 18, 1900, and the amendments thereof.

The election was held on the 15th of September, and the convention assembled on the 5th of November, 1900, and is now in session.

In calling the convention to order, the Military Governor of Cuba made the following statement:

As Military Governor of the island, representing the President of the United States, I call this convention to order.

It will be your duty, first, to frame and adopt a constitution for Cuba, and when that has been done to formulate what in your opinion ought to be the relations between Cuba and the United States.

The constitution must be adequate to secure a stable, orderly, and free government.

When you have formulated the relations which in your opinion ought to exist between Cuba and the United States the Government of the United States will doubtless take such action on its part as shall lead to a final and authoritative agreement between the people of the two countries to the promotion of their common interests.

All friends of Cuba will follow your deliberations with the deepest interest, earnestly desiring that you shall reach just conclusions, and that by the dignity, individual self-restraint, and wise conservatism which shall characterize your proceedings the capacity of the Cuban people for representative government may be signally illustrated.

The fundamental distinction between true representative government and dictatorship is that in the former every representative of the people, in whatever office, confines himself strictly within the limits of his defined powers. Without such restraint there can be no free constitutional government.

Under the order pursuant to which you have been elected and convened you have no duty and no authority to take part in the present government of the island. Your powers are strictly limited by the terms of that order.

When the convention concludes its labors I will transmit to the Congress the constitution as framed by the convention for its consideration and for such action as it may deem advisable.

I renew the recommendation made in my special message of February 10, 1899, as to the necessity for cable communication between the United States and Hawaii, with extension to Manila. Since then circumstances have strikingly emphasized this need. Surveys have shown the entire feasibility of a chain of cables which at each stopping place shall touch on American territory, so that the system shall be under our own complete control. Manila once within telegraphic reach, connection with the systems of the Asiatic coast would open increased and profitable opportunities for a more direct cable route from our shores to the Orient than is now afforded by the trans-Atlantic, continental, and trans-Asian lines. I urge attention to this important matter.

The present strength of the Army is 100,000 men — 65,000 regulars and 35,000 volunteers. Under the act of March 2, 1899, on the 30th of June next the present volunteer force will be discharged and the Regular Army will be reduced to 2,447 officers and 29,025 enlisted men.

In 1888 a Board of Officers convened by President Cleveland adopted a comprehensive scheme of coast-defense fortifications which involved the outlay of something over one hundred million dollars

This plan received the approval of the Congress, and since then regular appropriations have been made and the work of fortification has steadily progressed.

More than sixty millions of dollars have been invested in a great number of forts and guns, with all the complicated and scientific machinery and electrical appliances necessary for their use. The proper care of this defensive machinery requires men trained in its use. The number of men necessary to perform this duty alone is ascertained by the War Department, at a minimum allowance, to be 18,420.

There are fifty-eight or more military posts in the United States other than the coast-defense fortifications.

The number of these posts is being constantly increased by the Congress. More than $22,000,000 have been expended in building and equipment, and they can only be cared for by the Regular Army. The posts now in existence and others to be built provide for accommodations for, and if fully garrisoned require, 26,000 troops. Many of these posts are along our frontier or at important strategic points, the occupation of which is necessary.

We have in Cuba between 5,000 and 6,000 troops. For the present our troops in that island cannot be withdrawn or materially diminished, and certainly not until the conclusion of the labors of the constitutional convention now in session and a government provided by the new constitution shall have been established and its stability assured.

In Puerto Rico we have reduced the garrisons to 1,636, which includes 879 native troops. There is no room for further reduction here.

We will be required to keep a considerable force in the Philippine Islands for some time to come. From the best information obtainable we will need there for the immediate future from 45,000 to 60,000 men. I am sure the number may be reduced as the insurgents shall come to acknowledge the authority of the United States, of which there are assuring indications.

It must be apparent that we will require an army of about 60,000, and that during present conditions in Cuba and the Philippines the President should have authority to increase the force to the present number of 100,000. Included in this number authority should be given to raise native troops in the Philippines up to 15,000, which the Taft Commission believe will be more effective in detecting and suppressing guerrillas, assassins, and ladrones than our own soldiers.

The full discussion of this subject by the Secretary of War in his annual report is called to your earnest attention.

I renew the recommendation made in my last annual message that the Congress provide a special medal of honor for the volunteers, regulars, sailors, and marines on duty in the Philippines who vol-untarily remained in the service after their terms of enlistment had expired.

I favor the recommendation of the Secretary of War for the detail of officers from the line of the Army when vacancies occur in the Adjutant-General's Department, Inspector-General's Department, Quartermaster's Department, Subsistence Department, Pay Depart-ment, Ordnance Department, and Signal Corps.

The Army cannot be too highly commended for its faithful and effective service in active military operations in the field and the difficult work of civil administration.

The continued and rapid growth of the postal service is a sure index of the great and increasing business activity of the country. Its most striking new development is the extension of rural free delivery. This has come almost wholly within the last year. At the beginning of the fiscal year 1899–1900 the number of routes in operation was only 391, and most of these had been running less than twelve months. On the 15th of November, 1900, the number had increased to 2,614, reaching into forty-four States and Terri-tories, and serving a population of 1,801,524. The number of appli-cations now pending and awaiting action nearly equals all those granted up to the present time, and by the close of the current fiscal year about 4,000 routes will have been established, providing for the daily delivery of mails at the scattered homes of about three and a half millions of rural population.

This service ameliorates the isolation of farm life, conduces to good roads, and quickens and extends the dissemination of general information. Experience thus far has tended to allay the appre-hension that it would be so expensive as to forbid its general adop-tion or make it a serious burden. Its actual application has shown that it increases postal receipts, and can be accompanied by reduc-tions in other branches of the service, so that the augmented reve-nues and the accomplished savings together materially reduce the net cost. The evidences which point to these conclusions are pre-sented in detail in the annual report of the Postmaster-General, which with its recommendations is commended to the consideration of the Congress. The full development of this special service, how-ever, requires such a large outlay of money that it should be under-taken only after a careful study and thorough understanding of all that it involves.

Very efficient service has been rendered by the Navy in connection with the insurrection in the Philippines and the recent disturbance in China.

A very satisfactory settlement has been made of the long-pending question of the manufacture of armor plate. A reasonable price has been secured and the necessity for a Government armor plant avoided.

I approve of the recommendations of the Secretary for new vessels and for additional officers and men which the required increase of the Navy makes necessary. I commend to the favorable action of the Congress the measure now pending for the erection of a statue to the memory of the late Admiral David D. Porter. I commend also the establishment of a national naval reserve and of the grade of vice-admiral. Provision should be made, as recommended by the Secretary, for suitable rewards for special merit. Many officers who rendered the most distinguished service during the recent war with Spain have received in return no recognition from the Congress.

The total area of public lands as given by the Secretary of the Interior is approximately 1,071,881,662 acres, of which 917,135,880 acres are undisposed of and 154,745,782 acres have been reserved for various purposes. The public lands disposed of during the year amount to 13,453,887.96 acres, including 62,423.09 acres of Indian lands, an increase of 4,271,474.80 over the preceding year. The total receipts from the sale of public lands during the fiscal year were $4,379,758.10, an increase of $1,309,620.76 over the preceding year.

The results obtained from our forest policy have demonstrated its wisdom and the necessity in the interest of the public for its continuance and increased appropriations by the Congress for the carrying on of the work. On June 30, 1900, there were thirty-seven forest reserves, created by Presidential proclamations under section 24 of the act of March 3, 1891, embracing an area of 46,425,529 acres.

During the past year the Olympic Reserve, in the State of Washington, was reduced 265,040 acres, leaving its present area at 1,923,840 acres. The Prescott Reserve, in Arizona, was increased from 10,240 acres to 423,680 acres, and the Big Horn Reserve, in Wyoming, was increased from 1,127,680 acres to 1,180,800 acres. A new reserve, the Santa Ynez, in California, embracing an area of 145,000 acres, was created during this year. On October 10, 1900, the Crow Creek Forest Reserve, in Wyoming, was created, with an area of 56,320 acres.

At the end of the fiscal year there were on the pension roll 993,529 names, a net increase of 2,010 over the fiscal year 1899. The number added to the rolls during the year was 45,344. The amount disbursed for Army pensions during the year was $134,700,597.24 and for Navy pensions $3,761,533.41, a total of $138,462,130.65, leaving an unexpended balance of $5,542,768.25 to be covered into the Treasury, which shows an increase over the previous year's expenditure of $107,077.70. There were 684 names added to the rolls during the year by special acts passed at the first session of the Fifty-sixth Congress.

The act of May 9, 1900, among other things provides for an extension of income to widows pensioned under said act to $250 per annum. The Secretary of the Interior believes that by the operations of this act the number of persons pensioned under it will increase and the increased annual payment for pensions will be between $3,000,000 and $4,000,000.

The Government justly appreciates the services of its soldiers and sailors by making pension payments liberal beyond precedent to them, their widows and orphans.

There were 26,540 letters patent granted, including reissues and designs, during the fiscal year ended June 30, 1900; 1,660 trademarks, 682 labels, and 93 prints registered. The number of patents which expired was 19,988. The total receipts for patents were $1,358,228.35. The expenditures were $1,247,827.58, showing a surplus of $110,400.77.

The attention of the Congress is called to the report of the Secretary of the Interior touching the necessity for the further establishment of schools in the Territory of Alaska, and favorable action is invited thereon.

Much interesting information is given in the report of the Governor of Hawaii as to the progress and development of the islands during the period from July 7, 1898, the date of the approval of the joint resolution of the Congress providing for their annexation, up to April 30, 1900, the date of the approval of the act providing a government for the Territory, and thereafter.

The last Hawaiian census, taken in the year 1896, gives a total population of 109,020, of which 31,019 were native Hawaiians. The number of Americans reported was 8,485. The results of the Federal census, taken this year, show the islands to have a total population of 154,001, showing an increase over that reported in 1896 of 44,981, or 41.2 per cent.

There has been marked progress in the educational, agricultural, and railroad development of the islands.

In the Territorial act of April 30, 1900, section 7 of said act repeals Chapter 34 of the Civil Laws of Hawaii whereby the Government was to assist in encouraging and developing the agricultural resources of the Republic, especially irrigation. The Governor of Hawaii recommends legislation looking to the development of such water supply as may exist on the public lands, with a view of promoting land settlement. The earnest consideration of the Congress is invited to this important recommendation and others, as embodied in the report of the Secretary of the Interior.

The Director of the Census states that the work in connection with the Twelfth Census is progressing favorably. This national undertaking, ordered by the Congress each decade, has finally resulted in the collection of an aggregation of statistical facts to determine the industrial growth of the country, its manufacturing and mechanical resources, its richness in mines and forests, the number of its agriculturists, their farms and products, its educational and religious opportunities, as well as questions pertaining to sociological conditions.

The labors of the officials in charge of the Bureau indicate that the four important and most-desired subjects, namely, population, agricultural, manufacturing, and vital statistics, will be completed within the limit prescribed by the law of March 3, 1899.

The field work incident to the above inquiries is now practically finished, and as a result the population of the States and Territories, including the Hawaiian Islands and Alaska, has been announced. The growth of population during the last decade amounts to over 13,000,000, a greater numerical increase than in any previous census in the history of the country.

Bulletins will be issued as rapidly as possible giving the population by States and Territories, by minor civil divisions. Several announcements of this kind have already been made, and it is hoped that the list will be completed by January 1. Other bulletins giving the results of the manufacturing and agricultural inquiries will be given to the public as rapidly as circumstances will admit.

The Director, while confident of his ability to complete the different branches of the undertaking in the allotted time, finds himself embarrassed by the lack of a trained force properly equipped for statistical work, thus raising the question whether in the interest of economy and a thorough execution of the census work there should not be retained in the Government employ a certain number of experts not only to aid in the preliminary organization prior to the taking of the decennial census, but in addition to have the advantage in the field and office work of the Bureau of trained assistants to facilitate the early completion of this enormous undertaking.

I recommend that the Congress at its present session apportion representation among the several States as provided by the Constitution.

The Department of Agriculture has been extending its work during the past year, reaching farther for new varieties of seeds and plants; co-operating more fully with the States and Territories in research along useful lines; making progress in meteorological work relating to lines of wireless telegraphy and forecasts for ocean-going vessels; continuing inquiry as to animal disease; looking into the extent and character of food adulteration; outlining plans for the care, preservation, and intelligent harvesting of our woodlands; studying soils that producers may cultivate with better knowledge of conditions, and helping to clothe desert places with grasses suitable to our arid regions. Our island possessions are being considered that their peoples may be helped to produce the tropical products now so extensively brought into the United States. Inquiry into methods of improving our roads has been active during the year; help has been given to many localities, and scientific investigation of material in the States and Territories has been inaugurated. Irrigation problems in our semiarid regions are receiving careful and increased consideration.

An extensive exhibit at Paris of the products of agriculture has made the peoples of many countries more familiar with the varied products of our fields and their comparative excellence.

The collection of statistics regarding our crops is being improved and sources of information are being enlarged, to the end that producers may have the earliest advices regarding crop conditions. There has never been a time when those for whom it was established have shown more appreciation of the services of the Department.

In my annual message of December 5, 1898, I called attention to the necessity for some amendment of the alien contract law. There still remain important features of the rightful application of the eight-hour law for the benefit of labor and of the principle of arbitration, and I again commend these subjects to the careful attention of the Congress.

That there may be secured the best service possible in the Philippine Islands, I have issued, under date of November 30, 1900, the following order:

The United States Civil Service Commission is directed to render such assistance as may be practicable to the Civil Service Board, created under the act of the United States Philippine Commission, for the establishment and maintenance of an honest and efficient civil service in the Philippine Islands, and for that purpose to conduct examinations for the civil service of the Philippine Islands, upon the request of the Civil Service Board of said islands, under such regulations as may be agreed upon by the said Board and the said United States Civil Service Commission.

The Civil Service Commission is greatly embarrassed in its work for want of an adequate permanent force for clerical and other assistance. Its needs are fully set forth in its report. I invite attention to the report, and especially urge upon the Congress that this important bureau of the public service, which passes upon the qualifications and character of so large a number of the officers and employees of the Government, should be supported by all needed appropriations to secure promptness and efficiency.

I am very much impressed with the statement made by the heads of all the Departments of the urgent necessity of a hall of public records. In every departmental building in Washington, so far as I am informed, the space for official records is not only exhausted, but the walls of rooms are lined with shelves, the middle floor space of many rooms is filled with file cases, and garrets and basements, which were never intended and are unfitted for their accommodation, are crowded with them. Aside from the inconvenience there is great danger, not only from fire, but from the weight of these records upon timbers not intended for their support. There should be a separate building especially designed for the purpose of receiving and preserving the annually accumulating archives of the several Executive Departments. Such a hall need not be a costly structure, but should be so arranged as to admit of enlargement from time to time. I urgently recommend that the Congress take early action in this matter.

I transmit to the Congress a resolution adopted at a recent meeting of the American Bar Association concerning the proposed celebration of John Marshall Day, February 4, 1901. Fitting exercises have been arranged, and it is earnestly desired by the committee that the Congress may participate in this movement to honor the memory of the great jurist.

The transfer of the Government to this city is a fact of great historical interest. Among the people there is a feeling of genuine pride in the Capital of the Republic.

It is a matter of interest in this connection that in 1800 the population of the District of Columbia was 14,093; to-day it is 278,718. The population of the city of Washington was then 3,210; to-day it is 218,196.

The Congress having provided for "an appropriate national celebration of the Centennial Anniversary of the Establishment of the Seat of the Government in the District of Columbia," the committees authorized by it have prepared a programme for the 12th of December, 1900, which date has been selected as the anniversary day.

Deep interest has been shown in the arrangements for the celebration by the members of the committees of the Senate and House of Representatives, the committee of Governors appointed by the President, and the committees appointed by the citizens and inhabitants of the District of Columbia generally. The programme, in addition to a reception and other exercises at the Executive Mansion, provides commemorative exercises to be held jointly by the Senate and House of Representatives in the Hall of the House of Representatives, and a reception in the evening at the Corcoran Gallery of Art in honor of the Governors of the States and Territories.

In our great prosperity we must guard against the danger it invites of extravagance in Government expenditures and appropriations; and the chosen representatives of the people will, I doubt not, furnish an example in their legislation of that wise economy which in a season of plenty husbands for the future. In this era of great business activity and opportunity caution is not untimely. It will not abate, but strengthen, confidence. It will not retard, but promote, legitimate industrial and commercial expansion. Our growing power brings with it temptations and perils requiring constant vigilance to avoid. It must not be used to invite conflicts, nor for oppression, but for the more effective maintenance of those principles of equality and justice upon which our institutions and happiness depend. Let us keep always in mind that the foundation of our Government is liberty; its superstructure peace. WILLIAM McKINLEY.

EXECUTIVE MANSION,
Washington, December 4, 1900.
To the Senate and House of Representatives:

I transmit herewith, for the information of Congress, copy of a letter from the Commissioner-General of the United States to the Paris Exposition of 1900, of November 17, 1900, giving a detailed statement of the expenditures of the commission for the year ended November 15, 1900. WILLIAM McKINLEY.

EXECUTIVE MANSION,
Washington, December 6, 1900.
To the Senate and House of Representatives:

I transmit herewith the report from the Secretary of State and accompanying papers relating to the claim against the United States of the Russian subject, Gustav Isak Dahlberg, master and principal owner of the Russian bark *Hans*, based on his wrongful and illegal arrest and imprisonment by officers of the United States District Court for the southern district of Mississippi, and, in view of the opinion expressed by the Department of Justice that the said arrest and detention of the complainant were wrongful and without the authority of law, I recommend the appropriation by Congress of the sum of $5,000 to reimburse the master and owners of the vessel for all losses and damages incurred by reason of his said wrongful and illegal arrest and detention.   WILLIAM McKINLEY.

EXECUTIVE MANSION,
Washington, December 6, 1900.

To the Congress of the United States:

I transmit herewith a report from the Secretary of State, with accompanying papers, in relation to the lynching, in La Salle County, Tex., on October 5, 1895, of Florentino Suaste, a Mexican citizen.

Following the course pursued in the case of the lynching of three Italian subjects at Hahnville, La., on August 8, 1896, and in that of the lynching of the Mexican citizen, Luis Moreno, at Yreka, Cal., in August, 1895, I recommend the appropriation by Congress, out of humane consideration, and without reference to the question of liability of the Government of the United States, of the sum of $2,000, to be paid by the Secretary of State to the Government of Mexico, and by that Government distributed to the heirs of the above-mentioned Florentino Suaste.   WILLIAM McKINLEY.

EXECUTIVE MANSION, *January 3, 1901.*

To the Senate of the United States:

In reply to a resolution of the Senate of December 19, 1900, directing the Secretary of War "to transmit to the Senate the report of Abraham L. Lawshe, giving in detail the result of his investigations, made under the direction of the War Department, into the receipts and expenditures of Cuban funds," the Senate is informed that for the reasons stated in the accompanying communication from the Secretary of War, dated December 28, 1900, it is not deemed compatible with the public interest to transmit the report to the Senate at this time.

WILLIAM McKINLEY.

EXECUTIVE MANSION,
Washington, January 16, 1901.

To the Senate and House of Representatives:

I transmit herewith for the information of the Congress a letter from the Secretary of Agriculture, in which he presents a preliminary report of investigations upon the forests of the southern Appalachian Mountain region. Upon the basis of the facts established by this investigation the Secretary of Agriculture recommends the purchase of land for a national forest reserve in western North Carolina, eastern Tennessee, and adjacent States. I commend to the favorable consideration of Congress the reasons upon which this recommendation rests.

WILLIAM McKINLEY.

EXECUTIVE MANSION, January 25, 1901.

To the Senate and House of Representatives:

For the information of the Congress and with a view to such action on its part as it may deem wise and appropriate I transmit a report of the Secretary of War, made to me under date of January 24, 1901, containing the reports of the Taft commission, its several acts of legislation, and other important information relating to the conditions and immediate wants of the Philippine Islands.

I earnestly recommend legislation under which the government of the islands may have authority to assist in their peaceful industrial development in the directions indicated by the Secretary of War.

WILLIAM McKINLEY.

EXECUTIVE MANSION,
Washington, January 29, 1901.

To the Congress:

I transmit herewith a report from the Secretary of State relating to the treaty between the United States and Spain, signed at Washington, November 7, 1900, providing for the cession of any and all islands of the Philippine Archipelago lying outside of the lines described in Article III of the treaty of peace of December 10, 1898.

I recommend the appropriation by Congress during the present session of the sum of one hundred thousand dollars for the purpose of carrying out the obligations of the United States under the treaty.

WILLIAM McKINLEY.

EXECUTIVE MANSION,
Washington, January 29, 1901.

To the Congress:

I transmit herewith a report from the Secretary of State relating to the lynching of two Italian subjects at Tallulah, La., on July 20, 1899.

I renew the recommendation made in my annual message to the Congress on December 3, 1900, that in accordance with precedent Congress make gracious provision for indemnity to the families of the victims in the same form as heretofore.

WILLIAM McKINLEY.

EXECUTIVE MANSION,
Washington, January 29, 1901.

To the Senate and House of Representatives:

I transmit herewith a communication from the Secretary of State accompanying the Commercial Relations of the United States for the year 1900, being the annual and other reports of consular and diplomatic officers upon the industries and commerce of foreign countries, with particular reference to the growing share of the United States in international trade. The advance in the general efficiency of our consular service in promoting trade, which was noted in my message of March 1, 1900, transmitting the reports for 1899, was even more marked than last year. The promptitude with which the reports of the consuls are printed and distributed, the generous recognition which is being increasingly accorded by our business interests to the practical value of their efforts for enlarging trade, and the continued testimony of competent foreign authorities to the general superiority of their commercial work, have naturally had a stimulating effect upon its consular corps as a whole, and experience in the discharge of their duties adds greatly to their efficiency. It is gratifying to be able to state that the improvement in the service, following closely upon the steady progress in expediting the publication of reports, has enabled the Department of State this year to submit the annual reports a month in advance of the usual time, and to make them as nearly as possible a contemporaneous picture of the trade of the world. In view of the great importance of these reports to our producers, manufacturers, exporters, and business interest generally, I cordially approve the recommendation of the Secretary of State that Congress shall authorize the printing as heretofore of an edition of 10,000 copies of the summary, entitled "Review of the World's Commerce," and of 5,000 copies of Commercial Relations (including this summary), to be distributed by the Department of State.

WILLIAM McKINLEY.

EXECUTIVE MANSION, *February 14, 1901.*

To the Senate and House of Representatives:

During our recent war with Spain the United States naval force on the North Atlantic Station was charged with varied and important duties, chief among which were the maintenance of the blockade of Cuba, aiding the army, and landing troops and in subsequent operations, and particularly in the pursuit, blockade, and destruction of the Spanish Squadron under Admiral Cervera.

This naval campaign, embracing objects of wide scope and grave responsibilities, was conducted with great ability on the part of the commander-in-chief, and of the officers and enlisted men under his command. It culminated in the annihilation of the Spanish fleet in the battle of July 3, 1898, one of the most memorable naval engagements in history.

The result of this battle was the freeing of our Atlantic coast from the possibilities to which it had been exposed from Admiral Cervera's fleet, and the termination of the war upon the seas.

I recommend that, following our national precedents, especially that in the case of Admiral Dewey and the Asiatic Squadron, the thanks of Congress be given to Rear-Admiral William T. Sampson, United States Navy, and to the officers and men under his command for highly distinguished conduct in conflict with the enemy, and in carrying on the blockade and naval campaign on the Cuban coast, resulting in the destruction of the Spanish fleet at Santiago de Cuba July 3, 1898.

WILLIAM McKINLEY.

EXECUTIVE MANSION, *February 21, 1901.*

To the Senate and House of Representatives:

I transmit herewith, for the information of the Congress and with a view to its publication in suitable form, if such action is deemed desirable, a special report of the United States Board on Geographic Names, relating to geographic names in the Philippine Islands, and invite attention to the recommendation of the Board:

"That in addition to the usual number, there be printed 15,000 copies: 2,000 copies for the use of the Senate, 3,000 copies for the use of the House of Representatives, and 10,000 copies for distribution by the Board to the Executive Departments and the public."

WILLIAM McKINLEY.

EXECUTIVE MANSION,
Washington, February 26, 1901.

To the Congress:

I transmit herewith, for the consideration of Congress, in connection with my message of January 29, 1901, relative to the lynching of certain Italian subjects at Tallulah, La., a report by the Secretary of State touching a claim for $5,000 presented by the Italian ambassador at Washington on behalf of Gaiseppe Defina, on account of his being obliged to abandon his home and business.

WILLIAM McKINLEY.

EXECUTIVE MANSION,
Washington, February 28, 1901.

To the Senate and House of Representatives:

I transmit herewith, in pursuance of the act of Congress approved July 1, 1898 (U. S. Stat. L., vol. 30, pp. 645, 646), the report of Mr

Ferdinand W. Peck, commissioner-general of the United States to the International Exposition held at Paris, France, during the year 1900.

WILLIAM McKINLEY.

EXECUTIVE MANSION,
Washington, March 1, 1901.

To the House of Representatives:

I return herewith, without approval, House bill No. 3204, entitled "An act to refer certain claims for Indian depredations to the Court of Claims."

General relief has been extended to citizens who have lost property by reason of Indian depredations by the act of March 3, 1891, conferring jurisdiction upon the Court of Claims to hear and determine such cases. That act provides for payment for damages growing out of depredations committed by any Indian or Indians belonging to a band, tribe, or nation in amity with the United States, excluding from consideration all claims which originated during the existence of actual hostilities between the United States and the Indian tribe.

In making this discrimination the act of 1891 follows the general principle which has been asserted in all general legislation which has ever been enacted for the payment of claims for property destroyed by Indians. The first act which promised such indemnity, that of May 19, 1796, contained the same restriction, and it was reported in every subsequent general act of Congress dealing with the subject. This policy, which has been clearly manifested from the beginning, is in accord with the recognized principle that the nation is not liable for damage to the private property of its citizens caused by the act of the public enemy. This statute has been thoroughly considered by the Court of Claims and by the Supreme Court and its interpretation fixed, and it has been declared to be in accord not only with the policy of Congress as expressed through the legislation of the century, but with the general principles of international law.

I am informed that the records of the Court of Claims show that the claims of four of the five beneficiaries named in the present bill have been presented to that court under the general law and decided adversely, the court having held that a state of war existed between the United States and the Sioux Indians in the year 1862 when the claims arose. The remaining claim, which originated under the same circumstances and at the same time, would, of course, be subject to the same defense if presented.

The bill provides that these claims shall be sent back to the Court of Claims for trial according to the principles and rules which governed the commission appointed under the act of February 16, 1863. That act which was a special act relating to losses occurring during the

hostilities of the previous year, did not, of course, impose the requirement of amity, the claims allowed by the commission being paid out of
the funds belonging to the hostile Indians sequestered by the statute.
The effect of this bill, if it became a law, would be to provide for the
payment out of the Treasury of the United States of these claims which
were not presented for payment out of the Indian funds and which have
been rejected by the courts under the general law. There are many
hundreds of cases, aggregating a large amount claimed, which have
been filed in the Court of Claims, but which are excluded from its
jurisdiction for the same reason which necessitated the dismissal of the
petitions filed by these claimants. There is no legal obligation on the
part of the United States, and no promise, express or implied, for the
payment of such claims.

The measure of governmental liability is fulfilled by the passage of
the act of March 3, 1891, and the prompt payment of the judgments
rendered thereunder. To single out for payment a few claims of this
large class to the exclusion of all others would, in my judgment, be
unjust; and such action would also with reason be cited as a precedent
for extending governmental aid in all similar cases.

For the reasons given I am constrained to withhold my approval
from the bill.   WILLIAM McKINLEY.

EXECUTIVE MANSION, *March 1, 1901.*
To the House of Representatives:

I transmit herewith a report from the Secretary of State in response
to the resolution of the House of Representatives of February 19, 1901,
requesting him to furnish that body "all the information in the possession of the State Department relating to the shipment of horses and
mules from New Orleans in large numbers for the use of the British
army in the war in South Africa."

                                                  WILLIAM McKINLEY.

EXECUTIVE MANSION,
                                    Washington, March 2, 1901.
To the House of Representatives:

I return herewith, without approval, House bill No. 321, entitled
"An act for the relief of the legal representative of Samuel Tewksbury,
deceased."

This bill provides for the payment to the legal representative of Samuel Tewksbury, late of Scranton, Allegheny County, Pa., the sum of
$5,697 in full compensation for the use and occupation by the United
States Government of the brick building and premises owned by him
in the city of Scranton, Pa., as a depot or barracks for United States

troops by the Provost Marshal of the United States from June, 1862, to June, 1865, inclusive.

The records of the War Department show that about April 26, 1865, Col. J. G. Johnson, Chief Quartermaster, forwarded to the office of the Quartermaster-General a claim of Samuel Tewksbury for use of a building at Scranton, Pa., from February 24, 1864, to February 3, 1865, stated at $1,133.33, and damage to said building at $1,400, total $2,533.33.

In forwarding these papers Colonel Johnson states as follows:

In the spring of 1864 Mr. Samuel Tewksbury presented to me through his agents a claim against the United States Government for use of the premises mentioned in the enclosed account accompanying the papers.

I learn from Mr. S. N. Bradford, Provost Marshal of the Twelfth District of Pennsylvania at Scranton, that lodgings were furnished to persons in military service at that place by Gardiner and Atkinson under a contract with the Provost Marshal, also that the contractors rented the building used for the above purpose from Mr. Tewksbury.

Considering it a matter entirely between that gentleman and his tenants, Messrs. Gardiner and Atkinson, I at that time refused to take any action in the matter whatever.

The claim was again submitted to the office of the Quartermaster-General on September 30, 1865, by Major W. B. Lane, and was returned on May 1, 1866, with the information that the United States had already paid for lodging of the troops under the control of the Provost Marshal at Scranton, Pa., during the time for which charge for rent is made.

The claimant was referred to the officer or person by whom the building was taken for compensation for its use. No other record of this case is found in the War Department, although it will be observed that the bill covers a period from June, 1862, to June, 1865, inclusive, while the claim as originally presented to the War Department was for occupancy of the building at Scranton, Pa., from February 24, 1864, to February 3, 1865.

It thus appears that when this claim was originally presented it was examined by the proper representative of the Government, and was rejected; that no such use and occupation as the United States Government had of claimant's building was under a contract between the Government and the tenants of claimant, and that payment therefor was duly made by the Government. Now after a lapse of some thirty-seven years the period of use and occupation covered by the claim has increased threefold, and the compensation asked therefor has more than doubled. Under the circumstances of this case I do not feel at liberty to approve the bill. WILLIAM McKINLEY.

PRESIDENT McKINLEY'S SECOND INAUG-
URAL ADDRESS.

My Fellow-Citizens:

When we assembled here on the 4th of March, 1897, there was great anxiety with regard to our currency and credit. None exists now. Then our Treasury receipts were inadequate to meet the current obligations of the Government. Now they are sufficient for all public needs, and we have a surplus instead of a deficit. Then I felt constrained to convene the Congress in extraordinary session to devise revenues to pay the ordinary expenses of the Government. Now I have the satisfaction to announce that the Congress just closed has reduced taxation in the sum of $41,000,000. Then there was deep solicitude because of the long depression in our manufacturing, mining, agricultural, and mercantile industries and the consequent distress of our laboring population. Now every avenue of production is crowded with activity, labor is well employed, and American products find good markets at home and abroad.

Our diversified productions, however, are increasing in such unprecedented volume as to admonish us of the necessity of still further enlarging our foreign markets by broader commercial relations. For this purpose reciprocal trade arrangements with other nations should in liberal spirit be carefully cultivated and promoted.

The national verdict of 1896 has for the most part been executed. Whatever remains unfulfilled is a continuing obligation resting with undiminished force upon the Executive and the Congress. But fortunate as our condition is, its permanence can only be assured by sound business methods and strict economy in national administration and legislation. We should not permit our great prosperity to lead us to reckless ventures in business or profligacy in public expenditures. While the Congress determines the objects and the sum of appropriations, the officials of the executive departments are responsible for honest and faithful disbursement, and it should be their constant care to avoid waste and extravagance.

Honesty, capacity, and industry are nowhere more indispensable than in public employment. These should be fundamental requisites to original appointment and the surest guaranties against removal.

Four years ago we stood on the brink of war without the people knowing it and without any preparation or effort at preparation for the impending peril. I did all that in honor could be done to avert the war, but without avail. It became inevitable; and the Congress at its first regular session, without party division, provided money in anticipation of the crisis and in preparation to meet it. It came.

WILLIAM McKINLEY PROCEEDING TO HIS SECOND INAUGURATION

SECOND INAUGURATION OF McKINLEY

The pathos of McKinley's death is emphasized by this photograph. In March he left the White House and journeyed through streets lined with acclaiming people, to a ceremony of investiture representing the highest honor achievable by an American citizen. In September, he who was trusted and beloved to a degree never witnessed since the death of Lincoln, died by the hand of an assassin.

As a President, McKinley's record includes the restoration of the protective tariff system; the just and humane, but vigorous, prosecution of a war; a generous participation in the settlement of China's difficulties, by which the Nation won not only the gratitude of China, but the respect of the world; and a cautious and conscientious reorganization of the shattered governments of Cuba, Porto Rico and the Philippines. The article "McKinley, William," in the encyclopedic index is a brief narrative of his administration.

His private life was so pure, his personality so lovable, his conduct during suffering so noble, and the whole tenor of his thought so humbly Christian, that when the grave closed over his corpse the whole nation grieved.

The result was signally favorable to American arms and in the highest degree honorable to the Government. It imposed upon us obligations from which we cannot escape and from which it would be dishonorable to seek escape. We are now at peace with the world, and it is my fervent prayer that if differences arise between us and other powers they may be settled by peaceful arbitration and that hereafter we may be spared the horrors of war.

Intrusted by the people for a second time with the office of President, I enter upon its administration appreciating the great responsibilities which attach to this renewed honor and commission, promising unreserved devotion on my part to their faithful discharge and reverently invoking for my guidance the direction and favor of Almighty God. I should shrink from the duties this day assumed if I did not feel that in their performance I should have the co-operation of the wise and patriotic men of all parties. It encourages me for the great task which I now undertake to believe that those who voluntarily committed to me the trust imposed upon the Chief Executive of the Republic will give to me generous support in my duties to "preserve, protect, and defend, the Constitution of the United States" and to "care that the laws be faithfully executed." The national purpose is indicated through a national election. It is the constitutional method of ascertaining the public will. When once it is registered it is a law to us all, and faithful observance should follow its decrees.

Strong hearts and helpful hands are needed, and, fortunately, we have them in every part of our beloved country. We are reunited. Sectionalism has disappeared. Division on public questions can no longer be traced by the war maps of 1861. These old differences less and less disturb the judgment. Existing problems demand the thought and quicken the conscience of the country, and the responsibility for their presence, as well as for their righteous settlement, rests upon us all — no more upon me than upon you. There are some national questions in the solution of which patriotism should exclude partisanship. Magnifying their difficulties will not take them off our hands nor facilitate their adjustment. Distrust of the capacity, integrity, and high purposes of the American people will not be an inspiring theme for future political contests. Dark pictures and gloomy forebodings are worse than useless. These only becloud, they do not help to point the way of safety and honor. "Hope maketh not ashamed." The prophets of evil were not the builders of the Republic, nor in its crises since have they saved or served it. The faith of the fathers was a mighty force in its creation, and the faith of their descendants has wrought its progress and furnished its defenders. They are obstructionists who despair, and who would destroy confidence in the ability of our people to solve wisely and for civilization the mighty problems resting upon them. The American people, intrenched in freedom at home, take their love for it with them wherever they go, and they reject as mistaken and unworthy the doctrine that we lose our own liberties by securing the enduring foundations of liberty to others. Our institutions will not deteriorate by extension, and our sense of justice will not abate under tropic suns in distant seas. As heretofore, so hereafter will the nation demonstrate its fitness to administer any new estate which events devolve upon it, and in the fear of God will "take occasion by the hand and make the bounds of freedom wider yet." If there are those among us who would make our way more difficult, we must not be disheartened, but the more earnestly dedicate ourselves to the task upon which we have rightly entered. The path of progress is seldom smooth. New things are often found hard to do. Our fathers found them so. We find them so. They are inconvenient. They cost us something. But are we not made better for the effort and sacrifice, and are not those we serve lifted up and blessed?

We will be consoled, too, with the fact that opposition has confronted every onward movement of the Republic from its opening hour until now, but without success. The Republic has marched on and on, and its step has exalted freedom and humanity. We are undergoing the same ordeal as did our predecessors nearly a century ago. We are following the course they blazed. They triumphed. Will their successors falter and plead organic impotency in the nation? Surely after 125 years of achievement for mankind we will not now surrender our equality with other powers on matters fundamental and essential to nationality. With no such purpose was the nation created. In no such spirit has it developed its full and independent sovereignty. We adhere to the principle of equality among ourselves, and by no act of ours will we assign to ourselves a subordinate rank in the family of nations.

My fellow-citizens, the public events of the past four years have gone into history. They are too near to justify recital. Some of them were unforeseen; many of them momentous and far-reaching in their consequences to ourselves and our relations with the rest of the world. The part which the United States bore so honorably in the thrilling scenes in China, while new to American life, has been in harmony with its true spirit and best traditions, and in dealing with the results its policy will be that of moderation and fairness.

We face at this moment a most important question — that of the future relations of the United States and Cuba. With our near neighbors we must remain close friends. The declaration of the purposes of this Government in the resolution of April 20, 1898, must be made good. Ever since the evacuation of the island by the army of Spain the Executive, with all practicable speed, has been assisting its people in the successive steps necessary to the establishment of a free and independent government prepared to assume and perform the obligations of international law which now rest upon the United States under the treaty of Paris. The convention elected by the people to frame a constitution is approaching the completion of its labors. The transfer of American control to the new government is of such great importance, involving an obligation resulting from our intervention and the treaty of peace, that I am glad to be advised by the recent act of Congress of the policy which the legislative branch of the Government deems essential to the best interests of Cuba and the United States. The principles which led to our intervention require that the fundamental law upon which the new government rests should be adapted to secure a government capable of performing the duties and discharging the functions of a separate nation, of observing its international obligations of protecting life and property, insuring order, safety, and liberty, and conforming to the established and historical policy of the United States in its relation to Cuba.

The peace which we are pledged to leave to the Cuban people must carry with it the guaranties of permanence. We became sponsors for the pacification of the island, and we remain accountable to the Cubans, no less than to our own country and people, for the reconstruction of Cuba as a free commonwealth on abiding foundations of right, justice, liberty, and assured order. Our enfranchisement of the people will not be completed until free Cuba shall "be a reality, not a name; a perfect entity, not a hasty experiment bearing within itself the elements of failure."

While the treaty of peace with Spain was ratified on the 6th of February, 1899, and ratifications were exchanged nearly two years ago, the Congress has indicated no form of government for the Philippine Islands. It has, however, provided an army to enable the Executive to suppress insurrection, restore peace, give security to the inhabitants, and establish the authority of the United States throughout the archipelago. It has authorized the organization of native troops as auxiliary to the regular force. It has been advised from time to time of the acts of the military and naval officers in the islands, of my action in appointing civil commissions, of the instructions with which they were charged, of their duties and powers, of their recommendations, and of their several acts under executive commission, together with the very complete general information they have submitted. These reports fully set forth the conditions, past and present, in the islands, and the instructions clearly show the principles which will guide the Executive until the Congress shall, as it is required to do by the treaty, determine "the civil rights and political status of the native inhabitants." The Congress having added the sanction of its authority to the powers already possessed and exercised by the Executive under the Constitution, thereby leaving with the Executive the responsibility for the government of the Philippines, I shall continue the efforts already begun until order shall be restored throughout the islands, and as fast as conditions permit will establish local governments, in the formation of which the full co-operation of the people has been already invited, and when established will encourage the people to administer them. The settled purpose, long ago proclaimed, to afford the inhabitants of the islands self-government as fast as they were ready for it will be pursued with earnestness and fidelity. Already something has been accomplished in this direction. The Government's representatives, civil and military, are doing faithful and noble work in their mission of emancipation and merit the approval and support of their countrymen. The most liberal terms of amnesty have already been communicated to the insurgents, and the way is still open for those who have raised their arms against the Government for honorable submission to its authority. Our countrymen should not be deceived. We are not waging war against the inhabitants of the Philippine Islands. A portion of them are making war against the United States. By far the greater part of the inhabitants recognize American sovereignty and welcome it as a guaranty of order and of security for life, property, liberty, freedom of conscience, and the pursuit of happiness. To them full protection will be given. They shall not be abandoned. We will not leave the destiny of the loyal millions in the islands to the disloyal thousands who are in rebellion against the United States. Order under civil institutions will come as soon as those who now break the peace shall keep it. Force will not be needed or used when those who make war against us shall make it no more. May it end without further bloodshed, and there be ushered in the reign of peace to be made permanent by a government of liberty under law!

MARCH 4, 1901.

PROCLAMATIONS.

BY THE PRESIDENT OF THE UNITED STATES OF AMERICA.

A PROCLAMATION.

Whereas public interests require that the Congress of the United States should be convened in extra session at twelve o'clock on the 15th day of March, 1897, to receive such communication as may be made by the Executive:

Now, therefore, I, William McKinley, President of the United States of America, do hereby proclaim and declare that an extraordinary occasion requires the Congress of the United States to convene in extra session at the Capitol in the city of Washington on the 15th day of March, 1897, at twelve o'clock, noon, of which all persons who shall at that time be entitled to act as members thereof, are hereby required to take notice.

Given under my hand and the seal of the United States at Washington the 6th day of March in the year of our Lord one thousand eight hundred and ninety-seven, and of the Independence of the United States the one hundred and twenty-first.

[SEAL.]

WILLIAM McKINLEY.

By the President:
JOHN SHERMAN,
Secretary of State.

BY THE PRESIDENT OF THE UNITED STATES.

THANKSGIVING PROCLAMATION.

In remembrance of God's goodness to us during the past year, which has been so abundant, "let us offer unto Him our thanksgiving and pay our vows unto the Most High." Under His watchful providence industry has prospered, the conditions of labor have been improved, the rewards of the husbandman have been increased, and the comforts of our homes multiplied. His mighty hand has preserved peace and protected the nation. Respect for law and order has been strengthened, love of free institutions cherished, and all sections of our beloved country brought into closer bonds of fraternal regard and generous co-operation.

For these great benefits it is our duty to praise the Lord in a spirit of humility and gratitude and to offer up to Him our most earnest supplications. That we may acknowledge our obligation as a people to Him who has so graciously granted us the blessings of free government and material prosperity, I, William McKinley, President of the United States, do hereby designate and set apart Thursday, the twenty-fifth day of November, for national thanksgiving and prayer, which all of the people are invited to observe with appropriate religious services in their respective places of worship. On this day of rejoicing and domestic reunion let our prayers ascend to the Giver of every good and perfect gift for the continuance of His love and favor to us, that our hearts may be filled with charity and good will, and we may be ever worthy of His beneficent concern.

In witness whereof I have hereunto set my hand and caused the seal of the United States to be affixed.

Done at the city of Washington this 29th day of October, in the year of our Lord one thousand eight hundred and ninety-

[SEAL.]   seven, and of the Independence of the United States the one hundred and twenty-second.

WILLIAM McKINLEY.

By the President:

JOHN SHERMAN,
Secretary of State.

BY THE PRESIDENT OF THE UNITED STATES OF AMERICA.

A PROCLAMATION.

Whereas satisfactory proof has been given me that vessels of the United States in ballast which proceed to Mexico with the object of devoting themselves to pearl fishery and fishing on the Mexican coasts or for the purpose of receiving and carrying passengers and mail or of loading cattle, wood, or any other Mexican product and which shall go directly to ports open to general commerce so that thence they may be dispatched to their destination, and steam vessels of the United States are exempted from tonnage duties in Mexican ports;

Now, therefore, I, William McKinley, President of the United States of America, by virtue of the authority vested in me by the act of Congress approved July 24, 1897, entitled "An act to authorize the President to suspend discriminating duties imposed on foreign vessels and commerce," do hereby declare and proclaim that from and after the date of this, my proclamation, Mexican vessels in ballast which proceed to the United States with the object of fishing on the coast thereof or for the purpose of receiving and carrying passengers and mail or of loading cattle, wood, or any other product of the United States and which shall go directly to ports open to general commerce so that thence they may be despatched to their destination, and Mexican steam vessels shall be exempted from the payment of the tonnage duties imposed by section 4219 of the Revised Statutes of the United States.

And this proclamation shall remain in force and effect until otherwise ordered by the President of the United States.

In witness whereof I have set my hand and caused the seal of the United States to be hereunto affixed.

Done at the city of Washington this 12th day of November, in the year of our Lord one thousand eight hundred and ninety-

[SEAL.]   seven, and of the Independence of the United States the one hundred and twenty-second.

WILLIAM McKINLEY.

By the President:
     JOHN SHERMAN,
          Secretary of State.

BY THE PRESIDENT OF THE UNITED STATES OF AMERICA.

A PROCLAMATION.

Whereas by a joint resolution passed by the Congress and approved April 20, 1898,* and communicated to the Government of Spain, it was demanded that said Government at once relinquish its authority and government in the island of Cuba and withdraw its land and naval forces from Cuba and Cuban waters, and the President of the United States was directed and empowered to use the entire land and naval forces of the United States and to call into the actual service of the United States the militia of the several States to such extent as might be necessary to carry said resolution into effect; and

Whereas in carrying into effect said resolution the President of the United States deems it necessary to set on foot and maintain a blockade of the north coast of Cuba, including all ports on said coast between Cardenas and Bahia Honda, and the port of Cienfuegos, on the south coast of Cuba:

Now, therefore, I, William McKinley, President of the United States, in order to enforce the said resolution, do hereby declare and proclaim that the United States of America have instituted and will maintain a blockade of the north coast of Cuba, including ports on said coast between Cardenas and Bahia Honda, and the port of Cienfuegos, on the south coast of Cuba, aforesaid, in pursuance of the laws of the United States and the law of nations applicable to such cases. An efficient force will be posted so as to prevent the entrance and exit of vessels from the ports aforesaid. Any neutral vessel approaching any of said

* See pp. 6297-6298.

ports or attempting to leave the same without notice or knowledge of the establishment of such blockade will be duly warned by the commander of the blockading forces, who will indorse on her register the fact and the date of such warning, where such indorsement was made; and if the same vessel shall again attempt to enter any blockaded port she will be captured and sent to the nearest and convenient port for such proceedings against her and her cargo as prize as may be deemed advisable.

Neutral vessels lying in any of said ports at the time of the establishment of such blockade will be allowed thirty days to issue therefrom.

In witness whereof I have hereunto set my hand and caused the seal of the United States to be affixed.

Done at the city of Washington, this 22d day of April, [SEAL.] A. D., 1898, and of the Independence of the United States the one hundred and twenty-second.

WILLIAM McKINLEY.

By the President:

JOHN SHERMAN,
    Secretary of State.

BY THE PRESIDENT OF THE UNITED STATES.

A PROCLAMATION.

Whereas a joint resolution of Congress was approved on the 20th day of April, 1898,* entitled "Joint resolution for the recognition of the independence of the people of Cuba, demanding that the Government of Spain relinquish its authority and government in the island of Cuba and to withdraw its land and naval forces from Cuba and Cuban waters, and directing the President of the United States to use the land and naval forces of the United States to carry these resolutions into effect;" and

Whereas by an act of Congress entitled "An act to provide for temporarily increasing the military establishment of the United States in time of war, and for other purposes," approved April 22, 1898, the President is authorized, in order to raise a volunteer army, to issue his proclamation calling for volunteers to serve in the Army of the United States:

Now, therefore, I, William McKinley, President of the United States, by virtue of the power vested in me by the Constitution and the laws, and deeming sufficient occasion to exist, have thought fit to call forth, and hereby do call forth, volunteers to the aggregate number of 125,000 in order to carry into effect the purpose of the said resolution, the same

* See pp. 6297-6298.

to be apportioned, as far as practicable, among the several States and Territories and the District of Columbia according to population and to serve for two years unless sooner discharged. The details for this object will be immediately communicated to the proper authorities through the War Department.

In witness whereof I have hereunto set my hand and caused the seal of the United States to be affixed.

Done at the city of Washington, this 23d day of April, [SEAL.] A. D. 1898, and of the Independence of the United States the one hundred and twenty-second.

WILLIAM McKINLEY.

By the President:
    JOHN SHERMAN,
        Secretary of State.

BY THE PRESIDENT OF THE UNITED STATES OF AMERICA.

A PROCLAMATION.

Whereas by an act of Congress approved April 25, 1898,* it is declared that war exists and that war has existed since the 21st day of April, A. D. 1898, including said day, between the United States of America and the Kingdom of Spain; and

Whereas, it being desirable that such war should be conducted upon principles in harmony with the present views of nations and sanctioned by their recent practice, it has already been announced that the policy of this Government will be not to resort to privateering, but to adhere to the rules of the Declaration of Paris:

Now, therefore, I, William McKinley, President of the United States of America, by virtue of the power vested in me by the Constitution and the laws, do hereby declare and proclaim:

1. The neutral flag covers enemy's goods with the exception of contraband of war.

2. Neutral goods not contraband of war are not liable to confiscation under the enemy's flag.

3. Blockades in order to be binding must be effective.

4. Spanish merchant vessels in any ports or places within the United States shall be allowed till May 21, 1898, inclusive, for loading their cargoes and departing from such ports or places; and such Spanish merchant vessels, if met at sea by any United States ship, shall be permitted to continue their voyage if on examination of their papers it shall appear that their cargoes were taken on board before the expiration of the above term: *Provided,* That nothing herein contained shall

*See p. 6348.

apply to Spanish vessels having on board any officer in the military or naval service of the enemy, or any coal (except such as may be necessary for their voyage), or any other article prohibited or contraband of war, or any dispatch of or to the Spanish Government.

5. Any Spanish merchant vessel which prior to April 21, 1898, shall have sailed from any foreign port bound for any port or place in the United States shall be permitted to enter such port or place and to discharge her cargo, and afterwards forthwith to depart without molestation; and any such vessel, if met at sea by any United States ship, shall be permitted to continue her voyage to any port not blockaded.

6. The right of search is to be exercised with strict regard for the rights of neutrals, and the voyages of mail steamers are not to be interfered with except on the clearest grounds of suspicion of a violation of law in respect of contraband or blockade.

In witness whereof I have hereunto set my hand and caused the seal of the United States to be affixed.

Done at the city of Washington on the 26th day of April, [SEAL.]   A. D. 1898, and of the Independence of the United States the one hundred and twenty-second.

WILLIAM McKINLEY.

By the President:

ALVEY A. ADEE,
Acting Secretary of State.

BY THE PRESIDENT OF THE UNITED STATES OF AMERICA.

A PROCLAMATION.

Whereas it is provided by section twenty-four of the act of Congress, approved March third, eighteen hundred and ninety-one, entitled, "An act to repeal timber-culture laws, and for other purposes." "That the President of the United States may, from time to time, set apart and reserve, in any State or Territory having public land bearing forests, in any part of the public lands wholly or in part covered with timber or undergrowth, whether of commercial value or not, as public reservations, and the President shall, by public proclamation, declare the establishment of such reservations and the limits thereof;"

And whereas, the public lands in the Territory of Arizona, within the limits hereinafter described, are in part covered with timber, and it appears that the public good would be promoted by setting apart and reserving said lands as a public reservation;

Now, therefore, I, William McKinley, President of the United States, by virtue of the power in me vested by section twenty-four of the aforesaid act of Congress, do hereby make known and proclaim that there is hereby reserved from entry or settlement and set apart as a Public Reservation all those certain tracts, pieces, or parcels of land lying and being situate in the Territory of Arizona, and within the boundaries particularly described as follows, to wit:

Beginning at the northeast corner of Section twelve (12), Township thirteen (13) North, Range three (3) West, Gila and Salt River Meridian, Arizona; thence southerly along the range line to the point for the southeast corner of Section twenty-five (25), said Township; thence westerly along the unsurveyed section line to the point for the southwest corner of Section twenty-eight (28), said Township; thence northerly alone the unsurveyed section line to the point for the northwest corner of Section nine (9), said Township; thence easterly along the unsurveyed and surveyed section line to the northeast corner of Section twelve (12), said Township, the place of beginning.

Excepting from the force and effect of this proclamation all lands which may have been, prior to the date hereof, embraced in any legal entry or covered by any lawful filing duly of record in the proper United States Land Office, or upon which any valid settlement has been made pursuant to law, and the statutory period within which to make entry or filing of record has not expired; and all mining claims duly located and held according to the laws of the United States and rules and regulations not in conflict therewith;

Provided, that this exception shall not continue to apply to any particular tract of land unless the entryman, settler, or claimant continues to comply with the law under which the entry, filing, settlement, or location was made.

Warning is hereby expressly given to all persons not to enter or make settlement upon the tract of land reserved by this proclamation.

In witness whereof I have hereunto set my hand and caused the seal of the United States to be affixed.

Done at the city of Washington, this 10th day of May, in the year of our Lord one thousand eight hundred and ninety-eight, [SEAL.] and of the Independence of the United States the one hundred and twenty-second.

WILLIAM McKINLEY.

By the President:
   WILLIAM R. DAY,
         Secretary of State.

By the President of the United States.

A PROCLAMATION.

Whereas an act of Congress was approved on the 25th day of April, 1898,* entitled "An act declaring that war exists between the United States of America and the Kingdom of Spain;" and

Whereas by an act of Congress entitled "An act to provide for temporarily increasing the military establishment of the United States in time of war and for other purposes," approved April 22, 1898, the President is authorized, in order to raise a volunteer army, to issue his proclamation calling for volunteers to serve in the Army of the United States:

Now, therefore, I, William McKinley, President of the United States, by virtue of the power vested in me by the Constitution and the laws, and deeming sufficient occasion to exist, have thought fit to call forth, and hereby do call forth, volunteers to the aggregate number of 75,000 in addition to the volunteers called forth by my proclamation of the 23d of April, in the present year,† the same to be apportioned, as far as practicable, among the several States and Territories and the District of Columbia according to population and to serve for two years unless sooner discharged. The proportion of each arm and the details of enlistment or organization will be made known through the War Department.

In witness whereof I have hereunto set my hand and caused the seal of the United States to be affixed.

Done at the city of Washington, this 25th day of May, [SEAL.] A. D. 1898, and of the Independence of the United States the one hundred and twenty-second.

WILLIAM McKINLEY.

By the President:

William R. Day,
Secretary of State.

By the President of the United States of America.

A PROCLAMATION.

Whereas it is provided by section twenty-four of the act of Congress approved March third, eighteen hundred and ninety-one, entitled, "An act to repeal timber-culture laws, and for other purposes," "That the President of the United States may, from time to time, set apart and reserve, in any State or Territory having public land bearing forests, in

*See p. 6348.   †See pp. 6473–6474.

any part of the public lands wholly or in part covered with timber or undergrowth, whether of commercial value or not, as public reservations, and the President shall, by public proclamation, declare the establishment of such reservations and the limits thereof;"

And whereas it is further provided by the act of Congress, approved June fourth, eighteen hundred and ninety-seven, entitled, "An act making appropriations for sundry civil expenses of the Government for the fiscal year ending June thirtieth, eighteen hundred and ninety-eight, and for other purposes," that "The President is hereby authorized at any time to modify any executive order that has been or may hereafter be made establishing any forest reserve, and by such modification may reduce the area or change the boundary lines of such reserve, or may vacate altogether any order creating such reserve;"

And whereas the public lands in the Territory of New Mexico, within the limits hereinafter described, are in part covered with timber, and it appears that the public good would be promoted by setting apart and reserving said lands as a public reservation;

Now, therefore, I, William McKinley, President of the United States, by virtue of the power in me vested by the aforesaid acts of Congress, do hereby make known and proclaim that the boundary lines of the Forest Reservation in the Territory of New Mexico, known as "The Pecos River Forest Reserve," created by proclamation of January eleventh, eighteen hundred and ninety-two, are hereby so changed and enlarged as to include all those certain tracts, pieces, or parcels of land lying and being situate in the Territory of New Mexico, and within the boundaries particularly described as follows, to wit:

Beginning at the southwest corner of Township seventeen (17) North, Range thirteen (13) East, New Mexico Principal Meridian, New Mexico; thence easterly along the Fourth (4th) Standard Parallel North, to its intersection with the west boundary line of the Las Vegas Grant; thence northerly along the west boundary lines of the Las Vegas and Mora Grants to the point of intersection with the southeast boundary line of the Rancho del Rio Grande Grant; thence along the boundary line of said grant in a southwesterly direction to the most southerly point thereof; thence southerly to the line of the Santa Barbary Grant; thence southeasterly and southerly to the southeast corner thereof; thence westerly along the south boundary line of said grant to the southwest corner thereof, and continuing westerly to the east boundary line of the Las Trampas Grant; thence in a general southwesterly direction following the boundary lines of the Las Trampas, Las Truchas, and San Fernando Santiago Grants to the point of intersection with the unsurveyed range line between Ranges ten (10) and eleven (11) East; thence southerly along the range line to the point for the southwest corner of Section eighteen (18), Fractional Township sixteen (16) North, Range eleven (11) East; thence easterly along the unsurveyed section line to the point for the southeast corner of Section thirteen (13), said town-ship; thence northerly along the range line to the northeast corner of Township seventeen (17) North, Range eleven (11) East; thence easterly along the township line to the southeast corner of Township eighteen (18) North, Range twelve (12) East; thence southerly along the range line to the southwest corner of Township seventeen (17) North, Range thirteen (13) East, the place of beginning.

Excepting from the force and effect of this proclamation all lands which may have been, prior to the date hereof, embraced in any legal entry or covered by any lawful filing duly of record in the proper United States Land Office, or upon which any valid settlement has been made pursuant to law, and the statutory period within which to make entry or filing of record has not expired; and all mining claims duly located and held according to the laws of the United States and rules and regulations not in conflict therewith;

Provided, that this exception shall not continue to apply to any particular tract of land unless the entryman, settler, or claimant continues to comply with the law under which the entry, filing, settlement, or location was made.

Warning is hereby expressly given to all persons not to enter or make settlement upon the tract of land reserved by this proclamation.

In witness whereof I have hereunto set my hand and caused the seal of the United States to be affixed.

Done at the city of Washington, this 27th day of May, in the year of our Lord one thousand eight hundred and ninety-eight, [SEAL.] and of the Independence of the United States the one hundred and twenty-second.

WILLIAM McKINLEY.

By the President:

J. B. MOORE,
Acting Secretary of State.

BY THE PRESIDENT OF THE UNITED STATES OF AMERICA.

A PROCLAMATION.

Whereas pursuant to section 3 of the act of Congress approved July 24, 1897, entitled "An Act to provide revenue for the Government and to encourage the industries of the United States," the Governments of the United States and of the French Republic have in the spirit of amity, and with a desire to improve their commercial relations, entered into a Commercial Agreement in which reciprocal and equivalent concessions have been in the judgment of the President secured according to the provisions of said section, whereby the following articles of commerce, being the products and manufactures of the United States, are to be admitted into France on and after the 1st day of June, 1898, at the minimum rate of duty, not exceeding the rates respectively appearing in the following table, namely:

Canned meats	15	francs per 100 kilogs.
Table fruits, fresh:		
Lemons, oranges, cedrats and their varieties not mentioned	5	" " " "
Mandarin oranges	10	" " " "
Common table grapes	8	" " " "
Apples and pears:		
For the table	2	" " " "
For cider and perry	1. 50	" " " "
Other fruits except hothouse grapes and fruits	3	" " " "
Fruits dried or pressed (excluding raisins):		
Apples and pears:		
For the table	10	" " " "
For cider and perry	4	" " " "
Prunes	10	" " " "
Other fruits	5	" " " "
Common woods, logs	0. 65	" " " "
Sawed or squared timber 80 mm. or more in thickness	1	" " " "
Squared or sawed lumber exceeding 35 mm. and less than 80 mm. in thickness	1. 25	" " " "
Wood sawed 35 mm. or less in thickness	1. 75	" " " "
Paving blocks	1. 75	" " " "
Staves	0. 75	" " " "
Hops	30	" " " "
Apples and pears crushed, or cut and dried	1. 50	" " " "
Manufactured and prepared Pork meats	50	" " " "
Lard and its compounds	25	" " " "

Therefore, in further execution of the provisions of said section it is hereby declared that on and after the 1st day of June, 1898, and during the continuance in force of the Agreement aforesaid, and until otherwise declared, the imposition and collection of the duties heretofore imposed and collected upon the following named articles, the products of France, by virtue of said act are hereby suspended, and in place thereof the duties shall be imposed and collected thereon according to the provisions of said section 3 as follows:

On argols, or crude tartar, or wine lees, crude, five *per centum ad valorem.*

On brandies, or other spirits manufactured or distilled from grain or other materials, one dollar and seventy-five cents per proof gallon.

On paintings in oil or water colors, pastels, pen and ink drawings, and statuary, fifteen *per centum ad valorem.*

It is further declared that the rates of duty heretofore imposed and collected on still wines and vermuth, the product of France, under the provisions of the United States Tariff Act of 1897 are conditionally suspended, and in place thereof shall be imposed and collected on and after the 1st day of June next as follows, namely:

On still wines and vermuth, in casks, thirty-five cents per gallon; in bottles or jugs, per case of one dozen bottles or jugs containing each not more than one quart and more than one pint, or twenty-four bottles or jugs containing each not more than one pint, one dollar and twenty-five cents per case, and any excess beyond these quantities found in such bottles or jugs shall be subject to a duty of four cents per pint or fractional part thereof, but no separate or additional duty shall be assessed upon the bottles or jugs.

Now, therefore, be it known that I, William McKinley, President of the United States of America, have caused the above stated modifications of the customs duties of the respective countries to be made public for the information of the citizens of the United States of America.

In testimony whereof I have hereunto set my hand and caused the seal of the United States to be affixed.

Done at the city of Washington, this 30th day of May, one thousand eight hundred and ninety-eight, and of the Independence [SEAL.] of the United States of America the one hundred and twenty-second.

WILLIAM McKINLEY.

By the President:
> WILLIAM R. DAY,
> *Secretary of State.*

BY THE PRESIDENT OF THE UNITED STATES OF AMERICA.

A PROCLAMATION.

Whereas, for the reasons set forth in my proclamation of April 22, 1898,* a blockade of the ports on the northern coast of Cuba from Cardenas to Bahia Honda, inclusive, and of the port of Cienfuegos, on the south coast of Cuba, was declared to have been instituted; and

Whereas it has become desirable to extend the blockade to other Spanish ports:

Now, therefore, I, William McKinley, President of the United States, do hereby declare and proclaim that in addition to the blockade of the ports specified in my proclamation of April 22, 1898, the United States of America has instituted and will maintain an effective blockade of all the ports on the south coast of Cuba from Cape Frances to Cape Cruz, inclusive, and also of the port of San Juan, in the island of Puerto Rico.

*See pp. 6472-6473.

Neutral vessels lying in any of the ports to which the blockade is by the present proclamation extended will be allowed thirty days to issue therefrom with cargo.

In witness whereof I have hereunto set my hand and caused the seal of the United States to be affixed.

        Done at the city of Washington, this 27th day of June, A. D.,
[SEAL.]   1898, and of the Independence of the United States the one hundred and twenty-second.

                      WILLIAM McKINLEY.

By the President:
    J. B. MOORE,
        Acting Secretary of State.

BY THE PRESIDENT OF THE UNITED STATES OF AMERICA.

A PROCLAMATION.

Whereas it is provided by section twenty-four of the act of Congress, approved March third, eighteen hundred and ninety-one, entitled "An act to repeal timber-culture laws, and for other purposes," "That the President of the United States may, from time to time, set apart and reserve, in any State or Territory having public land bearing forests, in any part of the public lands wholly or in part covered with timber or undergrowth, whether of commercial value or not, as public reservations, and the President shall, by public proclamation, declare the establishment of such reservations and the limits thereof;"

And whereas it is further provided by the act of Congress, approved June fourth, eighteen hundred and ninety-seven, entitled "An act making appropriations for sundry civil expenses of the Government for the fiscal year ending June thirtieth, eighteen hundred and ninety-eight, and for other purposes," that "The President is hereby authorized at any time to modify any executive order that ha. been or may hereafter be made establishing any forest reserve, and by such modification may reduce the area or change the boundary lines of such reserve, or may vacate altogether any order creating such reserve;"

And whereas the public lands in the State of California, within the limits hereinafter described, are in part covered with timber, and it appears that the public good would be promoted by setting apart and reserving said lands as a public reservation;

Now, therefore, I, William McKinley, President of the United States, by virtue of the power in me vested by the aforesaid acts of Congress, do hereby make known and proclaim that the boundary lines of the Forest Reservation in the State of California, known as "the Pine Mountain and Zaca Lake Forest Reserve," created by proclamation of

March second, eighteen hundred and ninety-eight, are hereby so changed and enlarged as to include all those certain tracts, pieces, or parcels of land lying and being situate in the State of California, and within the boundaries particularly described as follows, to wit:

Beginning at the northwest corner of fractional Township twelve (12) North, Range thirty (30) West, San Bernardino Base and Meridian, California; thence southerly along the range line to the southwest corner of said fractional township; thence westerly along the township line to the northwest corner of Section three (3), Township eleven (11) North, Range thirty-one (31) West; thence southerly along the section line to the southwest corner of Section twenty-two (22), said township; thence westerly along the section line to the northwest corner of Section thirty (30), said township; thence southerly along the range line between Ranges thirty-one (31) and thirty-two (32) West, to the northern boundary of the rancho Sisquoc; thence in a general southeasterly direction along the boundaries of the ranchos Sisquoc, La Laguna, Cañada de los Pinos or College Rancho, Tequepis, San Marcos, and Los Prietos y Najalayegua, to the range line between Ranges twenty-four (24) and twenty-five (25) West; thence southerly along said range line to the southeast corner of Township five (5) North, Range twenty-five (25) West; thence easterly along the township line between Townships four (4) and five (5) North, to the western boundary of the rancho Temascal; thence along the western, northern, and eastern boundary of said rancho to its intersection with the northern boundary of the rancho San Francisco; thence along the northern and eastern boundary of said rancho to its southeast corner and continuing southerly to the northern boundary of the Ex Mission de San Fernando Grant; thence along the northern boundary of said grant to its intersection with the range line between Ranges fourteen (14) and fifteen (15) West; thence northerly along said range line to the northeast corner of Section twenty-four (24), Township four (4) North, Range fifteen (15) West; thence easterly along the section line to the southeast corner of Section thirteen (13), Township four (4) North, Range thirteen (13) West; thence northerly along the range line to the southwest corner of Township five (5) North, Range twelve (12) West; thence easterly along the township line to the southeast corner of said township; thence northerly along the range line to the northeast corner of Section twelve (12) of said township; thence westerly along the section line to the northwest corner of Section seven (7), said township; thence northerly along the range line to the First (1st) Standard Parallel North; thence westerly along the First (1st) Standard Parallel North to the southeast corner of Township six (6) North, Range thirteen (13) West; thence northerly along the range line to the northeast corner of Section thirteen (13), said township; thence westerly along the section line to the northwest corner of Section thirteen (13), Township six (6) North,

Range fourteen (14) West; thence northerly along the section line to the northeast corner of Section two (2), said township; thence westerly along the township line to the northwest corner of Section four (4), said township; thence northerly along the section line to the northeast corner of Section five (5), Township seven (7) North, Range fourteen (14) West; thence westerly along the township line to the northwest corner of fractional Section one (1), Township seven (7) North, Range seventeen (17) West; thence northerly along the section line to the intersection with the southern boundary of the rancho La Liebre; thence northwesterly along the boundaries of the ranchos La Liebre and Los Alamos y Agua Caliente to the township line between Townships eight (8) and nine (9) North; thence westerly along said township line to the southeast corner of Township nine (9) North, Range twenty-two (22) West; thence northerly along the township line to the northeast corner of said township; thence westerly along the township line to the intersection with the southern boundary of the rancho Cuyama; thence westerly and northwesterly along the southern boundaries of the ranchos Cuyama to the Eighth (8th) Standard Parallel South; thence westerly along said parallel to the northwest corner of fractional Township twelve (12) North, Range thirty (30) West, the place of beginning.

Excepting from the force and effect of this proclamation all irrigation rights and lands lawfully acquired therefor and all lands which may have been, prior to the date hereof, embraced in any legal entry or covered by any lawful filing duly of record in the proper United States Land Office, or upon which any valid settlement has been made pursuant to law, and the statutory period within which to make entry or filing of record has not expired; and all mining claims duly located and held according to the laws of the United States and rules and regulations not in conflict therewith;

Provided, that this exception shall not continue to apply to any particular tract of land unless the entryman, settler, or claimant continues to comply with the law under which the entry, filing, settlement, or location was made.

Warning is hereby expressly given to all persons not to enter or make settlement upon the tract of land reserved by this proclamation.

In witness whereof I have hereunto set my hand and caused the seal of the United States to be affixed.

Done at the city of Washington, this 29th day of June, in the year of our Lord one thousand eight hundred and ninety-eight, and [SEAL.] of the Independence of the United States the one hundred and twenty-second.

WILLIAM McKINLEY

By the President:
J. B. MOORE,
Acting Secretary of State.

BY THE PRESIDENT OF THE UNITED STATES OF AMERICA.

A PROCLAMATION.

Whereas satisfactory proof has been given to me that no tonnage or light-house dues or any equivalent tax or taxes whatever are imposed upon vessels of the United States in the port of Copenhagen, in the Kingdom of Denmark;

Now, therefore, I, William McKinley, President of the United States of America, by virtue of the authority vested in me by section eleven of the act of Congress, entitled "An Act to abolish certain fees for official services to American vessels, and to amend the laws relating to shipping commissioners, seamen, and owners of vessels, and for other purposes," approved June nineteenth, one thousand eight hundred and eighty-six, and in virtue of the further act amendatory thereof, entitled "An act to amend the laws relating to navigation and for other purposes," approved April four, one thousand eight hundred and eighty-eight, do hereby declare and proclaim that from and after the date of this, my Proclamation, shall be suspended the collection of the whole of the tonnage duty which is imposed by said section eleven of the act approved June nineteenth, one thousand eight hundred and eighty-six, upon vessels entered in the ports of the United States directly from the port of Copenhagen, in the Kingdom of Denmark.

Provided, that there shall be excluded from the benefits of the suspension hereby declared and proclaimed, the vessels of any foreign country in whose ports the fees or dues of any kind or nature imposed on vessels of the United States, or the import or export duties on their cargoes, are in excess of the fees, dues, or duties imposed on the vessels of such country or on the cargoes of such vessels; but this proviso shall not be held to be inconsistent with the special regulation by foreign countries of duties and other charges on their own vessels, and the cargoes thereof, engaged in their coasting trade, or with the existence between such countries and other States of reciprocal stipulations founded on special conditions and equivalents, and thus not within the treatment of American vessels under the most favored nation clause in treaties between the United States and such countries.

And the suspension hereby declared and proclaimed shall continue so long as the reciprocal exemption of vessels belonging to citizens of the United States and their cargoes, shall be continued in the said port of Copenhagen and no longer.

In witness whereof I have hereunto set my hand and caused the seal of the United States to be affixed.

Done at the city of Washington, this 19th day of July, in the year of our Lord one thousand eight hundred and ninety-eight, and [SEAL.] of the Independence of the United States the one hundred and twenty-third.

WILLIAM McKINLEY.

By the President:

WILLIAM R. DAY,
Secretary of State.

BY THE PRESIDENT OF THE UNITED STATES OF AMERICA.

A PROCLAMATION.

Whereas in the opening of the Cherokee Outlet, pursuant to section ten, of the act of Congress, approved March third, eighteen hundred and ninety-three, the lands known as the Eastern, Middle, and Western Saline Reserves, were excepted from settlement in view of three leases made by the Cherokee Nation prior to March third, eighteen hundred and ninety-three, under authority of the act of Congress, approved August seventh, eighteen hundred and eighty-two;

And whereas it appears that said leases were never approved as provided by law;

Now, therefore, I, William McKinley, President of the United States, by virtue of the power in me vested by section ten of said act of March third, eighteen hundred and ninety-three, do hereby declare and make known that all the lands in said saline reserves, as described in a proclamation dated August nineteenth, eighteen hundred and ninety-three, are hereby restored to the public domain and will be disposed of under the laws of the United States relating to public lands in said Cherokee Outlet, subject to the policy of the Government in disposing of saline lands.

In witness whereof, I have hereunto set my hand and caused the seal of the United States to be affixed.

Done at the city of Washington, this 27th day of July, in the year of our Lord, one thousand eight hundred and ninety- [SEAL.] eight, and of the Independence of the United States the one hundred and twenty-third.

WILLIAM McKINLEY.

By the President:

WILLIAM R. DAY,
Secretary of State.

BY THE PRESIDENT OF THE UNITED STATES OF AMERICA.

A PROCLAMATION.

Whereas by a protocol concluded and signed August 12, 1898,* by William R. Day, Secretary of State of the United States, and His Excellency Jules Cambon, ambassador extraordinary and plenipotentiary of the Republic of France at Washington, respectively representing for this purpose the Government of the United States and the Government of Spain, the United States and Spain have formally agreed upon the terms on which negotiations for the establishment of peace between the two countries shall be undertaken; and

Whereas it is in said protocol agreed that upon its conclusion and signature hostilities between the two countries shall be suspended and that notice to that effect shall be given as soon as possible by each Government to the commanders of its military and naval forces:

Now, therefore, I, William McKinley, President of the United States, do, in accordance with the stipulations of the protocol, declare and proclaim on the part of the United States a suspension of hostilities and do hereby command that orders be immediately given through the proper channels to the commanders of the military and naval forces of the United States to abstain from all acts inconsistent with this proclamation.

In witness whereof I have hereunto set my hand and caused the seal of the United States to be affixed.

Done at the city of Washington, this 12th day of August,
[SEAL.]   A. D. 1898, and of the Independence of the United States the one hundred and twenty-third.

WILLIAM McKINLEY.

By the President:
WILLIAM R. DAY,
Secretary of State.

BY THE PRESIDENT OF THE UNITED STATES OF AMERICA.

A PROCLAMATION.

Whereas it is provided by section twenty-four of the act of Congress, approved March third, eighteen hundred and ninety-one, entitled, "An act to repeal timber-culture laws, and for other purposes," "That the President of the United States may, from time to time, set apart and reserve, in any State or Territory having public land bearing

* See p. 6321.

forests, in any part of the public lands wholly or in part covered with timber or undergrowth, whether of commercial value or not, as public reservations, and the President shall, by public proclamation, declare the establishment of such reservations and the limits thereof;''

And whereas it is further provided by the act of Congress, approved June fourth, eighteen hundred and ninety-seven, entitled, ''An act making appropriations for sundry civil expenses of the Government for the fiscal year ending June thirtieth, eighteen hundred and ninety-eight, and for other purposes,'' that ''The President is hereby authorized at any time to modify any Executive order that has been or may hereafter be made establishing any forest reserve, and by such modification may reduce the area or change the boundary lines of such reserve, or may vacate altogether any order creating such reserve;''

And whereas, the public lands in the States of South Dakota and Wyoming, within the limits hereinafter described, are in part covered with timber, and it appears that the public good would be promoted by setting apart and reserving said lands as a public reservation;

Now, therefore, I, William McKinley, President of the United States, by virtue of the power in me vested by the aforesaid acts of Congress, do hereby make known and proclaim that the boundary lines of the Forest Reservation in the State of South Dakota, known as ''The Black Hills Forest Reserve,'' created by proclamation of February twenty-second, eighteen hundred and ninety-seven, are hereby so changed and enlarged as to include all those certain tracts, pieces or parcels of land lying and being situate in the States of South Dakota and Wyoming, and within the boundaries particularly described as follows, to wit:

Beginning at the southeast corner of Township five (5) South, Range five (5) East, Black Hills Meridian, South Dakota; thence northerly to the northeast corner of said township; thence easterly to the southeast corner of Section thirty-three (33), Township four (4) South, Range six (6) East; thence northerly to the southeast corner of Section nine (9), said township; thence easterly to the southeast corner of Section twelve (12), said township; thence northerly along the range line to the northeast corner of Section thirteen (13), Township one (1) North, Range six (6) East; thence westerly to the northwest corner of said section; thence northerly to the northeast corner of Section two (2), said township; thence westerly to the northwest corner of said section; thence northerly to the northeast corner of Section twenty-two (22), Township two (2) North, Range six (6) East; thence westerly to the southeast corner of Section seventeen (17), said township; thence northerly to the northeast corner of said section; thence westerly to the northwest corner of said section; thence northerly to the southeast corner of Section thirty (30), Township three (3) North, Range

six (6) East; thence easterly to the southeast corner of Section twenty-
seven (27), said township; thence northerly to the northeast corner of
Section twenty-two (22), said township; thence westerly to the northwest corner of said section; thence northerly to the northeast corner of
Section sixteen (16), said township; thence westerly to the northwest
corner of said section; thence northerly to the northeast corner of Section eight (8), said township; thence westerly to the northwest corner
of said section; thence northerly to the northeast corner of Section
nineteen (19), Township four (4) North, Range six (6) East; thence
westerly to the northwest corner of said section; thence northerly to
the northeast corner of Section twelve (12), Township four (4) North,
Range five (5) East; thence westerly to the northwest corner of said
section; thence northerly to the northeast corner of Section thirty-five
(35), Township five (5) North, Range five (5) East; thence westerly
to the northwest corner of said section; thence northerly to the
northeast corner of Section twenty-seven (27), said township; thence
westerly to the northwest corner of said section; thence northerly to
the northeast corner of Section twenty-one (21), said township; thence
westerly to the southeast corner of Section thirteen (13), Township
five (5) North, Range four (4) East; thence northerly to the northeast
corner of said section; thence westerly to the northwest corner of said
section; thence northerly to the northeast corner of Section two (2),
said township; thence westerly to the northwest corner of Section four
(4), said township; thence southerly to the southwest corner of said
section; thence westerly to the southeast corner of Section two (2),
Township five (5) North, Range three (3) East; thence northerly to
the northeast corner of said section; thence westerly to the southeast
corner of Section thirty-five (35), Township six (6) North, Range two
(2) East; thence northerly to the northeast corner of Section twenty-
six (26) said township; thence westerly to the southeast corner of
Section twenty-four (24), Township six (6) North, Range one (1)
East; thence northerly to the northeast corner of said section; thence
westerly along the section line to its intersection with the boundary line
between the States of South Dakota and Wyoming; thence southerly
along said State boundary line to its intersection with the section line
between Sections twenty-eight (28) and thirty-three (33), Township
fifty-two (52) North, Range sixty (60) West, Sixth (6th) Principal
Meridian, Wyoming; thence westerly to the northwest corner of Section thirty-six (36), Township fifty-two (52) North, Range sixty-one
(61) West; thence southerly along the section line to its intersection
with the Twelfth (12th) Standard Parallel North; thence easterly along
said parallel to its intersection with the boundary line between the
States of Wyoming and South Dakota; thence southerly along said
State boundary line to its intersection with the section line between Sections eighteen (18) and nineteen (19), Township three (3) South,

Range one (1) East, Black Hills Meridian, South Dakota; thence easterly to the northwest corner of Section twenty-two (22), said township, thence southerly to the southwest corner of Section thirty-four (34), said township; thence easterly to the southeast corner of said township; thence southerly to the southwest corner of Section thirty (30), Township four (4) South, Range two (2) East; thence easterly to the southeast corner of Section twenty-seven (27), said township; thence southerly to the southwest corner of Section eleven (11), Township five (5) South, Range two (2) East; thence easterly to the northwest corner of Section eighteen (18), Township five (5) South, Range four (4) East; thence southerly to the southwest corner of said township; thence easterly to the southeast corner of Township five (5) South, Range five (5) East, the place of beginning; excepting and excluding from reservation all those certain tracts, pieces or parcels of land lying and being situate within the boundaries particularly described as follows, to wit:

Beginning at the northeast corner of Section twenty-four (24), Township five (5) North, Range three (3) East, Black Hills Meridian; thence westerly to the northwest corner of Section nineteen (19), said township; thence southerly to the northwest corner of Section thirty-one (31), said township; thence westerly to the northwest corner of Section thirty-six (36), Township five (5) North, Range two (2) East; thence southerly to the southwest corner of Section thirteen (13), Township four (4) North, Range two (2) East; thence easterly to the southeast corner of Section fifteen (15), Township four (4) North, Range three (3) East; thence northerly to the southwest corner of Section two (2), said township; thence easterly to the southeast corner of said section; thence northerly to the northeast corner of said section; thence easterly to the southeast corner of Township five (5) North, Range three (3) East; thence northerly to the northeast corner of Section twenty-four (24), said township, the place of beginning.

Excepting from the force and effect of this proclamation all lands which may have been, prior to the date hereof, embraced in any legal entry or covered by any lawful filing duly of record in the proper United States Land Office, or upon which any valid settlement has been made pursuant to law, and the statutory period within which to make entry or filing of record has not expired; and all mining claims duly located and held according to the laws of the United States and rules and regulations not in conflict therewith; *Provided,* That this exception shall not continue to apply to any particular tract of land unless the entryman, settler, or claimant continues to comply with the law under which the entry, filing, settlement, or location was made.

Warning is hereby expressly given to all persons not to enter or make settlement upon the tract of land reserved by this proclamation.

In witness whereof I have hereunto set my hand and caused the seal of the United States to be affixed.

Done at the city of Washington, this 19th day of September, in the year of our Lord, one thousand eight hundred and ninety-eight, and of the Independence of the United States the one hundred and twenty-third.

[SEAL.]

WILLIAM McKINLEY.

By the President:

ALVEY A. ADEE,

Acting Secretary of State.

BY THE PRESIDENT OF THE UNITED STATES.

THANKSGIVING PROCLAMATION.

The approaching November brings to mind the custom of our ancestors, hallowed by time and rooted in our most sacred traditions, of giving thanks to Almighty God for all the blessings He has vouchsafed to us during the year.

Few years in our history have afforded such cause for thanksgiving as this. We have been blessed by abundant harvests; our trade and commerce have wonderfully increased; our public credit has been improved and strengthened; all sections of our common country have been brought together and knitted into closer bonds of national purpose and unity.

The skies have been for a time darkened by the cloud of war, but as we were compelled to take up the sword in the cause of humanity we are permitted to rejoice that the conflict has been of brief duration and the losses we have had to mourn, though grievous and important, have been so few, considering the great results accomplished, as to inspire us with gratitude and praise to the Lord of Hosts. We may laud and magnify His holy name that the cessation of hostilities came so soon as to spare both sides the countless sorrows and disasters that attend protracted war.

I do therefore invite all my fellow-citizens, as well those who may be at sea or sojourning in foreign lands as those at home, to set apart and observe Thursday, the 24th day of November, as a day of national thanksgiving, to come together in their several places of worship for a service of praise and thanks to Almighty God for all the blessings of the year, for the mildness of the seasons and the fruitfulness of the soil, for the continued prosperity of the people, for the devotion and valor of our countrymen, for the glory of our victory and the hope of a righteous peace, and to pray that the divine guidance which has brought us heretofore to safety and honor may be graciously continued in the years to come.

In witness whereof I have hereunto set my hand and caused the seal of the United States to be affixed.

Done at the city of Washington, this 28th day of October, [SEAL.]   A. D. 1898, and of the Independence of the United States the one hundred and twenty-third.

WILLIAM McKINLEY.

By the President:
    JOHN HAY,
        Secretary of State.

BY THE PRESIDENT OF THE UNITED STATES.

A PROCLAMATION.

Whereas by joint resolution "to provide for annexing the Hawaiian Islands to the United States," approved July 7, 1898, the cession by the Government of the Republic of Hawaii to the United States of America, of all rights of sovereignty of whatsoever kind in and over the Hawaiian Islands and their dependencies, and the transfer to the United States of the absolute fee and ownership of all public, Government, or crown lands, public buildings, or edifices, ports, harbors, military equipment, and all other public property of every kind and description belonging to the Government of the Hawaiian Islands, was duly accepted, ratified, and confirmed, and the said Hawaiian Islands and their dependencies annexed as a part of the territory of the United States and made subject to the sovereign dominion thereof, and all and singular the property and rights hereinbefore mentioned vested in the United States of America; and

Whereas it was further provided in said resolution that the existing laws of the United States relative to public lands shall not apply to such lands in the Hawaiian Islands, but the Congress of the United States shall enact special laws for their management and disposition; and

Whereas it is deemed necessary in the public interests that certain lots and plats of land in the city of Honolulu be immediately reserved for naval purposes;

Now, therefore, I, William McKinley, President of the United States, by virtue of the authority in me vested, do hereby declare, proclaim, and make known that the following described lots or plats of land be and the same are hereby reserved for naval purposes until such time as the Congress of the United States shall otherwise direct, to wit:

1st. The water front lying between the Bishop Estate and the line of Richards Street including the site of prospective wharves, slips, and their approaches.

2d. The blocks of land embracing lots No. 86 to 91, 100 to 131, including Mililani Street to the intersection of Halekauwali Street; and the Government water lots lying between the Bishop Estate and Punchbowl and Allen Streets.

In witness whereof I have hereunto set my hand, and caused the seal of the United States to be affixed.

Done at the city of Washington, this 2d day of November, in the year one thousand eight hundred and ninety-eight, and of the [SEAL.] Independence of the United States the one hundred and twenty-third.

WILLIAM McKINLEY.

By the President:

JOHN HAY,
Secretary of State.

HAWAIIAN CABLE CONCESSION

To all to whom these presents shall come, Greeting:

Know ye, that: Whereas, by an Indenture made the 2d day of July, in the year of our Lord one thousand eight hundred and ninety-eight between Sanford B. Dole, President of the Republic of Hawaii for and in behalf of the Hawaiian Government of the one part and the Pacific Cable Company, a corporation organized and existing under the laws of the State of New York of the United States of America, of the other part, there was granted, conceded, and confirmed unto the party of the second part and its successors and assigns the right and privilege to lay, construct, land, maintain and operate telegraphic and magnetic lines or cables from a point or points on the Pacific Coast of the United States to a suitable landing place or places to be selected by the party of the second part in the Hawaiian Islands with terminus at Honolulu, Island of Oahu, and from and beyond the Hawaiian Islands to Japan and any islands or places necessary for stations for such cables between the Hawaiian Islands and Japan that lie north of the tenth degree or parallel of north latitude in the North Pacific Ocean, as an exclusive right and privilege together with an exemption from duties, charges, and taxes for and during the term of twenty years from the date expressed in said Indenture, to wit, the 21st day of June, A. D. 1898,—said right, privilege, and exemption being subject to the terms and conditions set forth in said Indenture;

And whereas among said terms and conditions it is declared and agreed by said Indenture that the party of the second part within two years from the approval (within eighteen months from the date of said contract) of an act by the Congress of the United States authorizing the party of the second part to construct and operate a submarine cable line between the United States and the Hawaiian Islands shall construct, lay in proper working order, and establish a submarine telegraph cable from a point or points on the Pacific coast of the United States to a landing place or places in the Hawaiian Islands with terminus at Honolulu, Island of Oahu, according to the specifications of said Indenture, and further, within three years from the approval of such act by the Congress of the United States, shall in like manner construct, lay in proper working order, and establish a submarine telegraph cable from a point or points at or near said Honolulu to Japan;

And whereas it is provided by said Indenture that the contract therein made and set forth shall not take effect, if at any time within six months from the date thereof, to wit, the 2d day of July, A. D., 1898, "the United States State Department" shall express its disapproval thereof;

And whereas, pursuant to a Joint Resolution of the Senate and House of Representatives of the United States of America in Congress assembled, approved July 7, 1898, to provide for annexing the Hawaiian Islands to the United States, the sovereignty of the said Hawaiian Islands was yielded up to the United States on the 12th day of August, A. D., 1898, becoming thenceforth vested in the United States of America.

And whereas, in view of the provisions of said Joint Resolution for the determination by the Congress of the United States of all matters of municipal legislation concerning the Hawaiian Islands, and because the subject matter and provisions of said Indenture are deemed to be proper subjects for the consideration and determination of the Congress of the United States, it is deemed expedient and necessary that the Congress of the United States consider and adopt such legislation, especially in regard to grants and contractual obligations to be controlled by and rest upon the United States of America as vested with sovereignty over said Hawaiian Islands, without let or hindrance by reason of any action of the Government of the Republic of Hawaii in respect to such grants and contractual obligations initiated by the said Government of the Republic of Hawaii prior to and incomplete at the time of the yielding up of the sovereignty of the Hawaiian Islands to the United States;

Now, therefore, I, John Hay, Secretary of State of the United States, do hereby express on the part of "the United States State Department" its disapproval of the contract stipulated in the said Indenture to the end that the same shall not take effect.

Given under my hand and the seal of the Department of State of the United States, in the city of Washington, D. C., this thirty-

[SEAL.] first day of December in the year of our Lord one thousand eight hundred and ninety-eight.

JOHN HAY.

BY THE PRESIDENT OF THE UNITED STATES OF AMERICA.

A PROCLAMATION.

Whereas it is provided by section twenty-four of the act of Congress, approved March third, eighteen hundred and ninety-one, entitled, "An act to repeal timber-culture laws, and for other purposes," "That the President of the United States may, from time to time, set apart and reserve in any State or Territory having public land bearing forests, in any part of the public lands wholly or in part covered with timber or undergrowth, whether of commercial value or not, as public reservations, and the President shall, by public proclamation, declare the establishment of such reservations and the limits thereof;"

And whereas it is further provided by the act of Congress, approved June fourth, eighteen hundred and ninety-seven, entitled, "An act making appropriations for sundry civil expenses of the Government for the fiscal year ending June thirtieth, eighteen hundred and ninety-eight, and for other purposes," that "The President is hereby authorized at any time to modify any executive order that has been or may hereafter be made establishing any forest reserve, and by such modification may reduce the area or change the boundary lines of such reserve, or may vacate altogether any order creating such reserve;".

And whereas the public lands in the State of California, within the limits hereinafter described, are in part covered with timber, and it appears that the public good would be promoted by setting apart and reserving said lands as a public reservation;

Now, therefore, I, William McKinley, President of the United States, by virtue of the power in me vested by the aforesaid acts of Congress, do hereby make known and proclaim that the boundary lines of the Forest Reservation in the State of California, known as "The Trabuco Cañon Forest Reserve," created by proclamation of February twenty-fifth, eighteen hundred and ninety-three, are hereby so changed and enlarged as to include all those certain tracts, pieces or parcels of land lying and being situate in the State of California, and within the boundaries particularly described as follows, to wit:

Beginning at the northeast corner of Section thirteen (13), Township five (5) South, Range six (6) West, San Bernardino Base and Meridian, California; thence westerly along the section line to the southeast corner of Section nine (9), said township; thence northerly along the section line to the northeast corner of Section four (4), said township; thence westerly along the township line to the northwest corner of Section three (3), Township five (5) South, Range seven (7) West; thence southerly along the section line to the southwest corner of Section thirty-four (34), said township; thence easterly along the township line to the southeast corner of said township; thence southerly along the range line between Ranges six (6) and seven (7) West, to its intersection with the northern boundary of the Rancho Mission Viejo or La Paz; thence along the northern and eastern boundary of said rancho to its intersection with the northern boundary of the Rancho Santa Margarita y Las Flores; thence along the northern boundary of said rancho to its intersection with the range line between Ranges four (4) and five (5) West; thence northerly along said range line to its intersection with the southern boundary of the Rancho Santa Rosa; thence in a northwesterly and northeasterly direction along the southern and western boundary of said rancho to its intersection with the township line between Townships six (6) and seven (7) South; thence westerly along said township line to the southeast corner of Township six (6) South, Range six (6) West; thence northerly along the range line to the northeast corner of Section thirteen (13), Township five (5) South, Range six (6) West, the place of beginning.

Excepting from the force and effect of this proclamation all lands which may have been, prior to the date hereof, embraced in any legal entry or covered by any lawful filing duly of record in the proper United States Land Office, or upon which any valid settlement has been made pursuant to law, and the statutory period within which to make entry or filing of record has not expired; *Provided*, that this exception shall not continue to apply to any particular tract of land unless the entryman, settler, or claimant continues to comply with the law under which the entry, filing, or settlement was made.

Warning is hereby expressly given to all persons not to make settlement upon the tract of land reserved by this proclamation.

In witness whereof, I have hereunto set my hand and caused the seal of the United States to be affixed.

Done at the city of Washington, this 30th day of January, in the year of our Lord one thousand eight hundred and ninety-nine, [SEAL.] and of the Independence of the United States the one hundred and twenty-third.

WILLIAM McKINLEY.

By the President:
    JOHN HAY,
        Secretary of State.

BY THE PRESIDENT OF THE UNITED STATES OF AMERICA.

A PROCLAMATION.

Whereas satisfactory proof has been given to me by the Government of Mexico that no discriminating duties of tonnage or imposts are imposed or levied in the ports of Mexico upon vessels wholly belonging to citizens of the United States, or upon the produce, manufactures, or merchandise imported in the same from the United States, or from any foreign country:

Now, therefore, I, William McKinley, President of the United States of America, by virtue of the authority vested in me by section four thousand two hundred and twenty-eight of the Revised Statutes of the United States, do hereby declare and proclaim that, from and after the date of this, my proclamation, so long as vessels of the United States and their cargoes shall be exempt from discriminating duties as aforesaid, any such duties on Mexican vessels entering the ports of the United States, or on the produce, manufactures, or merchandise imported in such vessels, shall be suspended and discontinued, and no longer.

In testimony whereof I have hereunto set my hand and caused the seal of the United States to be affixed.

Done at the city of Washington, the 9th day of February, in the year of our Lord one thousand eight hundred and ninety-[SEAL.] nine, and of the Independence of the United States the one hundred and twenty-third.

WILLIAM McKINLEY.

By the President:

JOHN HAY,

Secretary of State.

BY THE PRESIDENT OF THE UNITED STATES OF AMERICA.

A PROCLAMATION.

Whereas it is provided by section twenty-four of the act of Congress, approved March third, eighteen hundred and ninety-one, entitled "An act to repeal timber-culture laws, and for other purposes," "That the President of the United States may, from time to time, set apart and reserve, in any State or Territory having public land bearing forests, in any part of the public lands wholly or in part covered with timber or undergrowth, whether of commercial value or not, as public reservations, and the President shall, by public proclamation, declare the establishment of such reservations and the limits thereof;"

And whereas the public lands in the State of Montana, within the limits hereinafter described, are in part covered with timber, and it appears that the public good would be promoted by setting apart and reserving said lands as public reservations;

Now, therefore, I, William McKinley, President of the United States, by virtue of the power in me vested by section twenty-four of the aforesaid act of Congress, do hereby make known and proclaim that there are hereby reserved from entry or settlement and set apart as Public Reservations all those certain tracts, pieces, or parcels of land lying and being situate in the State of Montana and particularly described as follows, to wit:

Sections fourteen (14), twenty-four (24), twenty-six (26), and thirty-six (36), Township three (3) South, Range five (5) East; Sections two (2), twelve (12), fourteen (14), twenty-four (24), twenty-six (26), and thirty-six (36), Township four (4) South, Range five (5) East; Sections two (2), twelve (12), fourteen (14), and twenty-four (24), Township five (5) South, Range five (5) East; Sections fourteen (14), sixteen (16), eighteen (18), twenty (20), twenty-two (22), twenty-four (24), twenty-six (26), twenty-eight (28), thirty (30), thirty-two (32), thirty-four (34), and thirty-six (36), Township three (3) South, Range six (6) East; Sections two (2), four (4), six (6), eight (8), ten (10), twelve (12), fourteen (14), sixteen (16), eighteen (18), twenty (20), twenty-two (22), twenty-four (24), twenty-six (26), twenty-eight (28), thirty (30), thirty-two (32), thirty-four (34), and thirty-six (36), Township four (4) South, Range six (6) East; Sections two (2), four (4), six (6), eight (8), ten (10), twelve (12), fourteen (14), sixteen (16), eighteen (18), twenty (20), twenty-two (22), and twenty-four (24), Township five (5) South, Range six (6) East; Sections eighteen (18), and thirty (30), Township three (3) South, Range seven (7) East; Sections six (6), eighteen (18), and thirty (30), Township four (4) South, Range seven (7) East; and Sections six (6) and eighteen (18), Township five (5) South, Range seven (7) East, Principal Meridian, Montana.

Excepting from the force and effect of this proclamation all lands which may have been, prior to the date hereof, embraced in any legal entry or covered by any lawful filing duly of record in the proper United States Land Office, or upon which any valid settlement has been made pursuant to law, and the statutory period within which to make entry or filing of record has not expired; *Provided*, that this exception shall not continue to apply to any particular tract of land unless the entryman, settler, or claimant continues to comply with the law under which the entry, filing, or settlement was made.

Warning is hereby expressly given to all persons not to make settlement upon the tracts of land reserved by this proclamation.

In witness whereof, I have hereunto set my hand and caused the seal of the United States to be affixed.

Done at the city of Washington, this 10th day of February, in the year of our Lord one thousand eight hundred and ninety-nine, and of the Independence of the United States the one hundred and twenty-third.

[SEAL.]

WILLIAM McKINLEY.

By the President:
JOHN HAY,
    Secretary of State.

BY THE PRESIDENT OF THE UNITED STATES OF AMERICA.

A PROCLAMATION.

Whereas it is provided by section twenty-four of the act of Congress, approved March third, eighteen hundred and ninety-one, entitled, "An act to repeal timber-culture laws, and for other purposes," "That the President of the United States may, from time to time, set apart and reserve, in any State or Territory having public land bearing forests, in any part of the public lands wholly or in part covered with timber or undergrowth, whether of commercial value or not, as public reservations, and the President shall, by public proclamation, declare the establishment of such reservations and the limits thereof;"

And whereas the public lands in the State of Utah, within the limits hereinafter described, are in part covered with timber, and it appears that the public good would be promoted by setting apart and reserving said lands as a public reservation;

Now, therefore, I, William McKinley, President of the United States, by virtue of the power in me vested by section twenty-four of the aforesaid act of Congress, do hereby make known and proclaim that there is hereby reserved from entry or settlement and set apart as a Public Reservation all those certain tracts, pieces or parcels of land lying and being situate in the State of Utah and within the boundaries particularly described as follows, to wit:

Beginning at the northeast corner of Section twenty-four (24), Township twenty-four (24) South, Range two (2) East, Salt Lake Base and Meridian, Utah; thence southerly along the range line to the northeast corner of Section thirteen (13), Township twenty-five (25) South, Range two (2) East; thence easterly along the section line to the northeast corner of Section eighteen (18), Township twenty-five (25) South, Range three (3) East; thence southerly along the section line to the Fifth (5th) Standard Parallel South; thence westerly along said parallel to the northeast corner of Township twenty-six (26) South, Range two (2) East; thence southerly along the range line to the southeast corner of said township; thence westerly along the township line to the southwest corner of Section thirty-five (35), Township twenty-six (26) South, Range one (1) East; thence northerly along the section line to the Fifth (5th) Standard Parallel South; thence easterly along said parallel to the southwest corner of Township twenty-five (25) South, Range two (2) East; thence northerly along the range line to the northwest corner of Section nineteen (19), Township twenty-four (24) South, Range two (2) East; thence easterly along the section line to the northeast corner of Section twenty-four (24), said township, the place of beginning.

Excepting from the force and effect of this proclamation all lands which may have been, prior to the date hereof, embraced in any legal entry or covered by any lawful filing duly of record in the proper United

States Land Office, or upon which any valid settlement has been made pursuant to law, and the statutory period within which to make entry or filing of record has not expired; *Provided*, that this exception shall not continue to apply to any particular tract of land unless the entry-man, settler or claimant continues to comply with the law under which the entry, filing, or settlement was made.

Warning is hereby expressly given to all persons not to make settlement upon the tract of land reserved by this proclamation.

In witness whereof, I have hereunto set my hand and caused the seal of the United States to be affixed.

Done at the city of Washington this 10th day of February, in the year of our Lord one thousand eight hundred and ninety-[SEAL.] nine, and of the Independence of the United States the one hundred and twenty-third.

WILLIAM McKINLEY.

By the President:
      JOHN HAY,
            Secretary of State.

BY THE PRESIDENT OF THE UNITED STATES OF AMERICA.

A PROCLAMATION.

Whereas, it is provided by section twenty-four of the act of Congress, approved March third, eighteen hundred and ninety-one, entitled, "An act to repeal timber-culture laws, and for other purposes," "That the President of the United States may, from time to time, set apart and reserve, in any State or Territory having public land bearing forests, in any part of the public lands wholly or in part covered with timber or undergrowth, whether of commercial value or not, as public reservations, and the President shall, by public proclamation, declare the establishment of such reservations and the limits thereof;"

And whereas, the public lands in the Territory of New Mexico, within the limits hereinafter described, are in part covered with timber, and it appears that the public good would be promoted by setting apart and reserving said lands as a public reservation;

Now, therefore, I, William McKinley, President of the United States, by virtue of the power in me vested by section twenty-four of the aforesaid act of Congress, do hereby make known and proclaim that there is hereby reserved from entry or settlement and set apart as a Public Reservation all those certain tracts, pieces or parcels of land lying and being situate in the Territory of New Mexico and within the boundaries particularly described as follows, to-wit:

Beginning at a point on the boundary line between New Mexico and Arizona where it is intersected by the north line of Township five (5)

South, Range twenty-one (21) West, New Mexico Principal Meridian, New Mexico; thence easterly along the township line to the northeast corner of Township five (5) South, Range sixteen (16) West; thence southerly along the range line between Ranges fifteen (15) and sixteen (16) West, to the southeast corner of Township eight (8) South, Range sixteen (16) West; thence easterly along the township line to the northeast corner of Township nine (9) South, Range fifteen (15) West; thence southerly along the range line to the southeast corner of said township; thence easterly along the township line to the northeast corner of Township ten (10) South, Range ten (10) West; thence south-erly along the First Guide Meridian West, between Ranges nine (9) and ten (10) West, to its intersection with the Third (3rd) Standard Parallel South, between Townships fifteen (15) and sixteen (16) South; thence westerly along the said Third (3rd) Standard Parallel South to the southwest corner of Township fifteen (15) South, Range sixteen (16) West; thence northerly along the range line to the northwest corner of said township; thence westerly along the township line to the northeast corner of Township fifteen (15) South, Range nineteen (19) West; thence southerly along the range line to its intersection with the Third (3rd) Standard Parallel South; thence westerly along the Third (3rd) Standard Parallel South to its intersection with the boundary line between New Mexico and Arizona; thence northerly along said boundary line to the point where it intersects the north line of Township five (5) South, Range twenty-one (21) West, the place of beginning.

Excepting from the force and effect of this proclamation all lands which may have been, prior to the date hereof, embraced in any legal entry or covered by any lawful filing duly of record in the proper United States Land Office, or upon which any valid settlement has been made pursuant to law, and the statutory period within which to make entry or filing of record has not expired; *Provided*, that this exception shall not continue to apply to any particular tract of land unless the entryman, settler or claimant continues to comply with the law under which the entry, filing or settlement was made.

Warning is hereby expressly given to all persons not to make settlement upon the tract of land reserved by this proclamation.

In witness whereof, I have hereunto set my hand and caused the seal of the United States to be affixed.

Done at the city of Washington this second day of March, in the year of our Lord one thousand eight hundred and ninety-nine, and [SEAL.] of the Independence of the United States the one hundred and twenty-third.

WILLIAM McKINLEY.

By the President:
JOHN HAY,
        Secretary of State.

By the President of the United States.

A PROCLAMATION.

Whereas by a proclamation of the President of the United States, dated the second day of December, eighteen hundred and ninety-one, upon proof then appearing satisfactory that no tonnage or light-house dues or other equivalent tax or taxes were imposed upon American vessels entering the ports of the Island of Tobago, one of the British West India Islands, and that vessels belonging to the United States of America and their cargoes were not required in the ports of the said Island of Tobago to pay any fee or due of any kind or nature, or any import due higher than was payable by vessels from ports or places in the said Island of Tobago, or their cargoes, in the United States, the President did therefore declare and proclaim, from and after the date of his said proclamation of December second, eighteen hundred and ninety-one, the suspension of the collection of the whole of the duty of three cents per ton, not to exceed fifteen cents per ton per annum, imposed upon vessels entered in the ports of the United States from any of the ports of the Island of Tobago by section 11 of the act of Congress approved June nineteenth, eighteen hundred and eighty-six, entitled "An act to abolish certain fees for official services to American vessels and to amend the laws relating to shipping commissioners, seamen, and owners of vessels and for other purposes."

And whereas the President did further declare and proclaim in his proclamation of December second, eighteen hundred and ninety-one, that the said suspension should continue so long as the reciprocal exemption of vessels belonging to citizens of the United States and their cargoes should be continued in the said ports of the Island of Tobago and no longer;

And whereas it now appears upon satisfactory proof that tonnage or light-house dues, or a tax or taxes equivalent thereto, are in fact imposed upon American vessels and their cargoes entered in ports of the Island of Tobago higher and other than those imposed upon vessels and their cargoes entered in ports of the Island of Tobago, or their cargoes, entered in ports of the United States, so that said proclamation of December second, eighteen hundred and ninety-one, in its operation and effect contravenes the meaning and intent of said section 11 of the act of Congress approved June nineteenth, eighteen hundred and eighty-six;

Now, therefore, I, William McKinley, President of the United States of America, by virtue of the aforesaid section 11 of the act aforesaid, as well as in pursuance of the terms of said proclamation itself, do hereby revoke the said proclamation of December second, eighteen hundred and ninety-one suspending the collection of the whole of the duty of three cents per ton, not to exceed fifteen cents per ton per annum (which is imposed by the aforesaid section of said act) upon vessels entered in the ports of the United States from any of the ports of the Island of Tobago; this revocation of said proclamation to take effect on and after the date of this my proclamation.

In witness whereof, I have hereunto set my hand and caused the seal of the United States to be affixed.

Done at the city of Washington, this 13th day of March, in the year of our Lord one thousand eight hundred and ninety-nine, [SEAL.] and of the Independence of the United States the one hundred and twenty-third.

WILLIAM McKINLEY.

By the President:
> JOHN HAY,
>> *Secretary of State.*

BY THE PRESIDENT OF THE UNITED STATES.

A PROCLAMATION.

Whereas by a proclamation of the President of the United States, dated April seventh, eighteen hundred and eighty-five upon proof then appearing satisfactory that upon vessels of the United States arriving at the Island of Trinidad, British West Indies, no due was imposed by the ton as tonnage or as light money and that no other equivalent tax on vessels of the United States was imposed at said island by the British Government, the President did declare and proclaim from and after the date of his said proclamation of April seventh, eighteen hundred and eighty-five, the suspension of the collection of the tonnage duties of three cents per ton, not to exceed fifteen cents per ton per annum, imposed upon vessels entered in ports of the United States from any of the ports of the Island of Trinidad by section 14 of the act of Congress approved June twenty-six, eighteen hundred and eighty-four, entitled "An act to remove certain burdens on the American merchant marine and encourage the American foreign carrying trade and for other purposes;"

And whereas it now appears upon satisfactory proof that tonnage or light-house dues, or a tax or taxes equivalent thereto, are in fact imposed upon American vessels and their cargoes entered in ports of the Island of Trinidad higher and other than those imposed upon vessels from ports in the Island of Trinidad or their cargoes entered in ports of the United States, so that said proclamation of April seventh, eighteen hundred and eighty-five, in its operation and effect contravenes the

THE CONTESTANTS IN THE BOER WAR

THE BOER WAR

War to-day is like a conflagration in a crowded district: it affects and endangers the interests of neighboring States as well as those of the contending parties. Our relations with Great Britain during the Boer War have been frequently mentioned by the Presidents. For the story of the war and for citations of presidential references to it, see the article "Boer War" in the index (volume eleven).

The upper illustration shows the British Army approaching a ford of the Tugela River. The lower photograph is a truthful and eloquent reproduction of the people who for three years held Great Britain at bay. The British sent 450,000 men into South Africa to overcome a force which authorities variously estimate as being from 60,000 to 90,000 men. On one side was this vast army, splendidly equipped, with all the enginery known to military science, its personnel the best that Britain could produce; on the other side were the Boers, outnumbered more than five to one, lacking the munitions of war; and yet, by their individual marksmanship and courage and the conformation of the country, they were enabled to protract the struggle for three years, during which period the British lost 21,944 soldiers by battle and disease, 1,072 of whom were officers, not to speak of the 1,851 officers and 20,978 men disabled by wounds.

The United States is devoted to peace; but war is always a possibility. Our army is absurdly small; the lack of shipping would be a vast obstacle to foreign operations; our coast defenses are an unknown quantity; and a modern war is finished before recruits can be trained into soldiers. We would do well to think of war and by preparation assure ourselves of at least a fighting chance. (See "Army" and "Navy" in the index.)

meaning and intent of section 14 of the act of Congress approved June twenty-six, eighteen hundred and eighty-four, as amended by section 11 of the act of Congress approved June nineteenth, eighteen hundred and eighty-six, entitled "An act to abolish certain fees for official services to American vessels and to amend the laws relating to shipping commissioners, seamen, and owners of vessels and for other purposes;"

Now, therefore, I, William McKinley, President of the United States of America, by virtue of the aforesaid section 14 of the act of Congress approved June twenty-six, eighteen hundred and eighty-four as amended by the aforesaid section 11 of the act approved June nineteenth, eighteen hundred and eighty-six, do hereby revoke the said proclamation of April seventh, eighteen hundred and eighty-five, suspending the collection of the whole of the duty of three cents per ton, not to exceed fifteen cents per ton per annum (which is imposed by the aforesaid sections of said acts), upon vessels entered in the ports of the United States from any of the ports of the Island of Trinidad; this revocation of said proclamation to take effect on and after the date of this my proclamation.

In witness whereof, I have hereunto set my hand and caused the seal of the United States to be affixed.

Done at the city of Washington, this 13th day of March, in the year of our Lord one thousand eight hundred and ninety-nine, [SEAL.] and of the Independence of the United States the one hundred and twenty-third.

WILLIAM McKINLEY.

By the President:
JOHN HAY,
Secretary of State.

BY THE PRESIDENT OF THE UNITED STATES.

A PROCLAMATION.

Whereas, it is deemed necessary in the public interests that certain lands lying to the eastward of the city of San Juan, in Puerto Rico, be immediately reserved for naval purposes;

Now, therefore, I, William McKinley, President of the United States, by virtue of the authority in me vested, do hereby, declare, proclaim, and make known that the following-described lands be and the same are hereby reserved for naval purposes until such time as the Congress of the United States shall otherwise direct, to wit:

1st. The public land, natural, reclaimed, partly reclaimed, or which may be reclaimed, lying south of the Caguas Road, shown on the U. S. Hydrographic Map No. 1745 of July, 1898, and for 250 feet north of said Caguas Road, to be bounded on the west by a true north and south line passing through the eastern corner of the railway station shown on said map, on the south by the shore of the harbor, and to extend east 2,400 feet, more or less, to include 80 acres.

2nd. The entire island lying to the southward of the above-described land, and described on the U. S. Hydrographic Map No. 1745, of July, 1898, as Isla Grande, or Manglar.

The Military Governor of the Island of Puerto Rico will make this transfer through the representative of the Navy, the Commandant of the United States Naval Station, San Juan, Puerto Rico, who will present this proclamation.

March 29, 1899.　　　　　　　　　　WILLIAM McKINLEY.
By the President:
　JOHN HAY,
　　　Secretary of State.

BY THE PRESIDENT OF THE UNITED STATES OF AMERICA.

A PROCLAMATION.

Whereas, it is provided by section twenty-four of the act of Congress, approved March third, eighteen hundred and ninety-one, entitled, "An act to repeal timber-culture laws, and for other purposes," "That the President of the United States may, from time to time, set apart and reserve, in any State or Territory having public land bearing forests, in any part of the public lands wholly or in part covered with timber or undergrowth, whether of commercial value or not, as public reservations, and the President shall, by public proclamation, declare the establishment of such reservations and the limits thereof;"

And whereas, the public lands in the State of California, within the limits hereinafter described, are in part covered with timber, and it appears that the public good would be promoted by setting apart and reserving said lands as a public reservation;

Now, therefore, I, William McKinley, President of the United States, by virtue of the power in me vested by section twenty-four of the aforesaid act of Congress, do hereby make known and proclaim that there is hereby reserved from entry or settlement and set apart as a Public Reservation all those certain tracts, pieces or parcels of land lying and being situate in the State of California and particularly described as follows, to wit:

Townships eleven (11), twelve (12) and thirteen (13) North, Range sixteen (16) East, Mount Diablo Base and Meridian, California; Townships eleven (11), twelve (12) and thirteen (13) North, Range seventeen (17) East; and so much of Township eleven (11) North, Range